PEOPLE
IN
BOOKS

PEOPLE

IN

BOOKS

A Selective Guide to Biographical
Literature Arranged by Vocations and
Other Fields of Reader Interest

By MARGARET E. NICHOLSEN

NEW YORK
The H. W. Wilson Company
1969

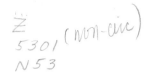
PREFACE

HISTORY

The idea for PEOPLE IN BOOKS grew out of a question raised by Jane Manthorne of the Boston Public Library at a 1963 meeting of the Board of Directors of the Young Adult Services Division of the American Library Association. Young adult librarians in public libraries and high school librarians presented the problem of locating books to answer high school requests for biographies of persons of a certain period or from a certain country or persons engaged in a certain vocation or profession. The librarians needed to be able to find biographies of chemists from Russia, or eighteenth century French poets, or life stories of victims of polio, or biographies of twentieth century Brazilians. No present reference tool provides this information on the scale needed. *Biography Index* gives some help but covers only material published since 1946, includes both magazines and books, and does not indicate whether the latter are recommended for libraries or their reading difficulty, although it does indicate juvenile titles. Hence it was felt that an index was needed which would include only books recommended for libraries and would indicate the interest level of the books.

The Young Adult Services Division Board investigated the question and after considering several alternatives recommended the plan and method used in PEOPLE IN BOOKS.

PURPOSE

The purpose of this reference tool is to identify by vocation or field of activity, by country, and by century, the subjects of biographies and other biographical writings which are recommended for libraries serving children, young adults, and adults. Originally the work was planned to locate books of interest to young adults, but the need to include both children's books and adult books in order to provide for the broad range of reading ability of young adults led to the decision to expand the coverage to biographical books for all age levels. This extends the usefulness of the index, as it can be used with elementary school children, high school students, and adults.

SCOPE

Materials indexed are the biographical books included in the major standard lists recommended for libraries. Seventeen annotated lists were selected as sources of the books to be indexed in PEOPLE IN BOOKS (see pages xvii-xviii for complete list). All the biographies and biographical writings in those lists have been included. Only lists with adequate annotations could be used, since the annotations provide the basis for establishing the categories under which the biographical books are listed. Unfortunately, some excellent selected lists could not be used because they were not annotated or because they have "not recommended" as well as "recommended" titles. *Choice* is an example of a selection aid which could not be used, as many of the listed titles are not recommended for library purchase. In addition to the annotations, Webster's *Biographical Dictionary*, Chambers's *Biographical Dictionary*, and *Biography Index* were used to define further the vocation or field of activity under which to list each individual. They also helped in determining forms of headings.

After the selected lists were chosen it became evident there is considerable variation in the way they define and classify biography. Some include fictionalized biography in this category, but others classify such works as fiction. How should biography be defined for the purposes of this list? Should fictionalized biography be used? Should memoirs be included? Letters? What of a book which covers only a part of a man's life, and if it is to be included, how much of his life must be covered? Five years? Five days? Since inclusion rather than exclusion would add to the usefulness of the index, it was decided to enlarge the scope and to include biographies, autobiographies, memoirs, personal accounts, letters, reminiscences, literary criticism unless of a single work of the author, biographical fiction, biographical plays and poems, and reference books such as biographical dictionaries in special fields. All fulfill the mission of biography as stated by P. M. Kendall in *The Art of Biography* (Norton 1965): "to perpetuate a man as he was in the days he lived."

PEOPLE IN BOOKS will serve librarians and teachers in working with children, young adults, and adults. Its primary use is as a reference tool but it may also be used at all levels in reading guidance. In addition, it serves as a guide to the biographical material available on individuals in hundreds of vocational fields.

PEOPLE IN BOOKS has a main section arranged by vocation or activity, a country-century appendix which indexes by country and by century the persons whose biographies are listed in the main section, a second appendix listing alphabetically by author books of an autobiographical nature, and an index listing all those persons about whom a book or part of a collective biography is included in the main section.

ARRANGEMENT

The main section entries are under the vocation or field of activity with which the biographee is associated. Under each vocation, activity, or characteristic the entries are arranged first by country and under that by century. For example:

BLIND

American—19th century

Laura Dewey Bridgman, 1829-1889

Hunter, Edith Fisher. Child of the Silent
　　Night. Houghton 1963
　　　Bkl C(3-5)—CC(3-5)—ESLC—IndJ(4-6)

American—20th century

Hector Chevigny, 1904-1965

Chevigny, Hector. My Eyes Have a Cold
　　Nose. Yale Univ. 1946
　　　BY—SCPL

Canadian—20th century

David Scott Blackhall, 1910-

Blackhall, David Scott. This House Had
　　Windows. Obolensky 1962
　　　Bkl A

French—19th century

Louis Braille, 1809-1852

DeGering, Etta. Seeing Fingers: The
　　Story of Louis Braille. McKay 1962
　　　Bkl C(5-7)—CC(5-7)—ESLC
Kugelmass, J. Alvin. Louis Braille: Windows for the Blind. Messner 1951
　　　BBJH—JH—SCHS

COLLECTIONS

Freedman, Russell. Teenagers Who Made
　　History. Holiday 1961
　　　BY—JH—SCHS—YR

In the sample only a few of the entries under BLIND are given. In explanation of the entries: Laura Bridgman is an American who lived in the nineteenth century. The book about her, *Child of the Silent Night* by Edith Fisher Hunter, was published in 1963 by Houghton Mifflin Company. This book was in four of the lists of recommended books as indicated by the symbols (the key to the symbols is on pages xvii-xviii). The Hunter book about Laura Bridgman was in the children's book section of *The Booklist* and its level of reading difficulty was indicated as grade three to five. In the *Children's Catalog* it was also graded three to five. *The Elementary School Library Collection* does not give definite grades for which the title is suitable. In the *Junior Booklist* of the National Association of Independent Schools it was graded four to six. Following blind individuals who were Americans of the twentieth century and Canadians of the twentieth century comes Louis Braille, a Frenchman of the nineteenth century. After the books about him there is a list of the collective biographies which contain material about him. An example of a collective biography entry is *Teenagers Who Made History* by Russell Freedman. It was published by Holiday in 1961 and was found in four of the lists—*Books for You, Junior High School Library Catalog, Standard Catalog for High School Libraries,* and *Your Reading.*

When grade levels are not indicated the nature of the list may indicate enough about the book for a user of PEOPLE IN BOOKS to know if it might meet his need. A title marked CA (*The College and Adult Reading List*) would obviously be inappropriate for an elementary school child. In the sample the book about and by Hector Chevigny under BLIND—American—20th century was listed in *Books for You* and *Standard Catalog for Public Libraries*—listings that indicate it is an adult book which is also of interest to high-school-age young people.

NAMES

The personal name forms used have been based chiefly on those in *Biography Index,* the *Standard Catalog* series, Webster's *Biographical Dictionary,* and *The Booklist.* For books which are accounts of families, one individual has usually been selected under whose name the book is listed and no entries for that book appear under the names of other members of the family. As examples, books on the Kennedy family are listed under John Fitzgerald Kennedy, and books on the Rockefellers under John Davison Rockefeller.

VOCATIONS

Most individuals are identified with one vocation, characteristic, or field of activity. Longfellow was known chiefly as a poet, Dickens as a novelist, Lincoln as a president. The majority are listed under only one vocation, but many are listed under two fields of activity or characteristics. Helen Keller, for example, is found under both BLIND and DEAF. Some individuals, equally outstanding in many fields, are listed under several headings. Benjamin Franklin is listed under AUTHORS, PHILOSOPHERS, PRINTERS, SCIENTISTS, and STATESMEN. Albert Schweitzer is listed under ORGANISTS, PHILOSOPHERS, PHYSICIANS, and RELIGIOUS LEADERS. The lists of titles under each of these vocations include the general books about the person but may not include the titles which deal with only one aspect of his life. All the titles about Robert E. Lee are listed under SOLDIERS—American—19th century, and only one title under EDUCATORS—American—19th century, as that one book deals with Lee's career as a college president after the war. When material about an individual is found in a collective biography, as a rule that title is listed under only one of an individual's vocations rather than under all.

Specific headings, such as novelists, chemists, and pianists, are used whenever possible, rather than general headings such as authors, scientists, or musicians. Cross references are included from general headings to the many specific ones. When an individual's work covers many different facets of the general heading, books about him are listed under the general term. For example, when a writer is known both as a poet and a novelist, he is listed as an author, rather than under the two specific headings.

The heading STATESMEN is used for all individuals in government or politics. The task of separating statesmen from politicians or demagogues was avoided by giving all the benefit of the doubt.

The feminine form of the word for certain vocations, such as Actress, has not been used. All those in the acting profession, male and female, are listed under ACTORS. However, women of royalty are listed as QUEENS, EMPRESSES, or PRINCESSES. The biographies of some women have been written because of the prominence of their husbands or other relatives; such women are listed as WIVES OF FAMOUS MEN or RELATIVES OF FAMOUS MEN. This is especially true of wives of the Presidents of the United States, who have been entered as WIVES OF FAMOUS MEN—American.

In assigning headings, usefulness has been considered of more importance than strict logic. *Circus Doctor* is entered under CIRCUS PERFORMERS although the author, J. Y. Henderson, was not a performer but a veterinarian with the circus. He is also entered under the heading VETERINARIANS. Billy Mitchell is entered with AVIATORS, although he was not famous as a flyer but was of great influence in the history of military aviation. INDIAN LEADERS—American is the heading used for all Indians, whether or not they were "leaders." This heading is also used for white individuals closely associated with American Indians.

Some of the general headings, such as CIVIL RIGHTS LEADERS, REFORMERS, and ABOLITIONISTS, do not include all the individuals who could reasonably be placed under them, but mainly those who do not fit easily into other categories. Rosa Lee Parks is entered under CIVIL RIGHTS LEADERS, but Martin Luther King, Jr., is found under RELIGIOUS LEADERS. Grant Pearson is listed under CONSERVATIONISTS, but William O. Douglas and many others who are interested in conservation—but who are even better known in other fields—are not.

COLLECTIVE BIOGRAPHIES

Collective biographies are included under appropriate headings and precede entries for individuals under those headings. When the annotation in one or more of the seventeen sources gives the names of ten or fewer persons included in one collection each such individual is listed in a contents note following the main entry. For example:

POETS

COLLECTIONS

Brenner, Rica. Poets of Our Time. Harcourt 1941
SCHS–SCPL
W. H. Auden; Stephen Vincent Benét; T. S. Eliot; Vachel Lindsay; Archibald MacLeish; Stephen Spender; Sara Teasdale; Elinor Wylie; William Butler Yeats

In addition, under the entry in the main section for each of those nine individuals the fact that information about him is available in this collective biography is noted. For example:

POETS

American—20th century

Teasdale, Sara, 1884-1933

Carpenter, Margaret Haley. Sara Teasdale: A Biography. Schulte 1960
Bkl A
COLLECTIONS
Brenner, Rica. Poets of Our Time. Harcourt 1941
SCHS–SCPL

The names of each of the individuals in a collective biography will also be found in the country-century list. Although no complete biographies of Stephen Spender are listed, he is included in the country-century list under POETS—English —20th century, because there is information about him in a collective biography.

Some collective biographies include individuals from many different countries. These are listed under appropriate headings, with the subhead COLLECTIONS. For example:

STATESMEN

COLLECTIONS

Larson, Egon. Men Who Fought for Freedom. Roy 1959
AB
Simón Bolívar; Mohandas Gandhi; Marquis
de Lafayette; William Penn; Sun Yat-sen;
and others

Other collective biographies include individuals from only one country and sometimes from only one century. These are listed under appropriate headings, with subheads for nationality and the additional subhead COLLECTIONS. No attempt has been made to list collective biographies by century. For example:

STATESMEN

American

COLLECTIONS

Sevareid, Eric, ed. Candidates 1960: Be-
hind the Headlines in the Presidential
Race. Basic Bks 1959
SCPL
Hubert Humphrey; Lyndon B. Johnson; John
F. Kennedy; Richard M. Nixon; Nelson
Rockefeller; Adlai Stevenson; Stuart Syming-
ton

Sometimes the annotations in the sources state that the individuals listed are "among those described." In such cases, after the list of the names of the biographees in the contents note, the phrase "and others" is added so that the user will realize that the list given is not the complete contents of that collective biography.

COUNTRY-CENTURY LIST

The first appendix, the country-century list, makes possible a country and century approach to the main section. It will also assist those who desire the names of individuals associated with a certain country or a certain century. Entries in this section refer to the main section in which the books about those individuals will be found.

The following sample shows how the country-century list entries from several parts of the alphabet lead back to the persons and books in the preceding main section sample:

Canada—20th century
Blackhall, David Scott   BLIND—Canadian;
POETS—Canadian

France—19th century
Braille, Louis   BLIND—French; EDUCA-
TORS—French; ORGANISTS—French

United States—19th century
Bridgman, Laura Dewey   BLIND—American; DEAF—American

United States—20th century
Chevigny, Hector   BLIND—American

Usually the country of birth is the country in which the individual accomplished his life work and under which he is listed. For many, however, the country in which their work was done was not their native land, and this was of greater interest in connection with their lives than the land of their birth. For example, Schweitzer is better known for his work in Africa than for being French; Dooley is known for his work in Laos and Livingstone for his work in Africa rather than for being American or Scottish. Such individuals have usually been entered under both their native lands and the countries in which they achieved their fame. In the country-century list this sometimes results in an apparent contradiction. Gordon Seagrave is listed under Burma with a reference to PHYSICIANS—American and it is under this heading that books about him will be found in the main section. Herman Mautner is listed under Bolivia with a reference to PHYSICIANS—Austrian, and Wilfred Grenfell under Labrador with a reference to RELIGIOUS LEADERS—English. It is under these headings that the books about them are listed. Felix Kersten, the physiotherapist who treated Nazi leaders during World War II is noted under Germany—20th century with the reference to PHYSIO-THERAPISTS—Finnish, under which the books about him appear.

In this appendix people from Hawaii and Alaska who achieved fame before Hawaii and Alaska became states have not been included under the United States. Hawaii and Alaska are in their alphabetical places in the country-century list. As an illustration of the problem, no one would look under United States for books about Kamehameha I, the Great, King of the Hawaiian Islands. His name appears under Hawaii and refers to KINGS—Hawaiian, under which the books about him are listed in the main section.

The national adjectives *English, Irish, Welsh,* and *Scottish* are used and *British* is not. This has created some difficulties. T. E. Lawrence was born in Wales, and the Duke of Wellington in Ireland, but both are known as English, so the heading used for both is SOLDIERS—English. Most British individuals are listed under the country of their birth, e.g., Dylan Thomas, POETS—Welsh, and Robert Burns, POETS—Scottish.

America—15th century, America—16th century, and America—17th century are the headings used for books about colonists and explorers. United States—18th century is used as a heading for individuals in that century.

Some individuals have been entered under two centuries since they distinguished themselves in both, as in the case of John D. Rockefeller. Many lived during two centuries, but since their chief accomplishments were in only one century they are listed under only one. In some cases books about the individuals are listed under only one century in the main section and a cross-reference is given under the other century. In some instances individuals are found in one century under a certain heading and in another century under a different heading. Thomas Jefferson was an important figure in eighteenth century America and is listed under United States—18th century with the heading STATESMEN—American. He is also found under United States—19th century with the heading PRESIDENTS—American. Books limited to the childhood and youth of an individual are frequently found under the century preceding that under which are found books describing his mature accomplishments.

AUTOBIOGRAPHIES, PERSONAL ACCOUNTS, AND LETTERS

The second appendix brings together in one place the autobiographical books which are included in the list. Ways to locate this type of material are few and inadequate and requests for it are numerous. As in the first appendix, reference is given to the headings under which the full information about the books is given in the main section. There are two autobiographies in the sample of the main section used on page vi. The reference to them in the second appendix is as follows:

> Blackhall, David Scott. This House Had
> Windows BLIND—Canadian—20th century
> Chevigny, Hector. My Eyes Have a Cold
> Nose BLIND—American—20th century

INDEX

The index includes all persons about whom biographical material is listed in PEOPLE IN BOOKS. Cross-references are given from variant name forms to those selected for use.

ACKNOWLEDGMENTS

The cooperation of the publishers of the seventeen lists indexed has been most valuable in preparing PEOPLE IN BOOKS. The following have generously supplied copies of the latest edition of the lists as well as supplements and new editions as they have appeared:

American Library Association
Bro-Dart Foundation
National Association of Independent Schools
National Council of Teachers of English
The H. W. Wilson Company

Credit is also due Mildred Batchelder, who was executive secretary of the Children's Services Division and the Young Adult Services Division of the American Library Association at the time this project started and who has continued to provide encouragement.

MARGARET E. NICHOLSEN

March 1969
Evanston, Illinois

CONTENTS

CONTENTS

EXPLANATION OF THE SYMBOLS

The book selection aids indexed in *People in Books* are listed below with the symbol which is used in the entries in the main section to identify the list or lists in which the book appeared. If the grade range is indicated in the list, it is given in parentheses following the symbol.

AB Adventuring with Books: A Reading List for the Elementary Grades; ed. by Muriel Crosby and Beatrice Davis Hurley. National Council of Teachers of English 1960
    Adventuring with Books: 1963 Supplement: Books from 1960 to 1963 for the Elementary Grades. National Council of Teachers of English 1963
    Adventuring with Books: A Book List for Elementary Schools; ed. by Elizabeth Guilfoile. New Am. Lib. 1966

BBEL A Basic Book Collection for Elementary Grades; comp. by Miriam Snow Mathes. 7th ed. A.L.A. 1960

BBHS A Basic Book Collection for High Schools; comp. by Eileen F. Noonan. 7th ed. A.L.A. 1963

BBJH A Basic Book Collection for Junior High Schools; ed. by Margaret V. Spengler. 3rd ed. A.L.A. 1960

    The Booklist and Subscription Books Bulletin; ed. by Edna Vanek. A.L.A. January 1960-December 1966
Bkl A The Booklist: Adult Books

Bkl C The Booklist: Children's Books

Bkl Y The Booklist: Books for Young Adults

BY Books for You: A Reading List for Senior High School Students; ed. by Richard S. Alm and Committee on the Senior High School Book List of the National Council of Teachers of English. Washington Square Press 1964

CA The College and Adult Reading List of Books in Literature and the Fine Arts; ed. by Edward Lueders and Committee on College and Adult Reading List of the National Council of Teachers of English. Washington Square Press 1962

CC Children's Catalog; ed. by Dorothy Herbert West and Rachel Shor. 10th ed. Wilson 1961
    Children's Catalog, 1962 supplement to the 10th edition, 1961; ed. by Estelle A. Fidell. Wilson 1962
    Children's Catalog, 1963 supplement to the 10th edition, 1961; ed. by Rachel Shor and Estelle A. Fidell. Wilson 1963
    Children's Catalog, 1964 supplement to the 10th edition, 1961; ed. by Rachel Shor and Estelle A. Fidell. Wilson [1964]
    Children's Catalog, 1965 supplement to the 10th edition, 1961; ed. by Rachel Shor. Wilson [1965]
    Children's Catalog; ed. by Rachel Shor and Estelle A. Fidell. 11th ed. Wilson 1966

ESLC The Elementary School Library Collection, Phases 1-2-3; ed. by Mary V. Gaver. 2nd ed. Bro-Dart Foundation 1966
    The Elementary School Library Collection; supplement to the Second Edition. Bro-Dart Foundation 1966

GR   Good Reading; ed. by J. Sherwood Weber and prepared by The Com-
          mittee on College Reading; sponsored by College English Associa-
          tion. New Am. Lib. 1960
          Good Reading: A Helpful Guide for Serious Readers; ed. by J. Sher-
          wood Weber and prepared by The Committee on College Reading;
          sponsored by College English Association. New Am. Lib. 1964

Ind J   Junior Booklist: Current Books. National Association of Independent
          Schools 1964
          Junior Booklist: Current Books. National Association of Independent
          Schools 1965
          Junior Booklist: Current Books. National Association of Independent
          Schools 1966

Ind S   Senior Booklist: Current Books including the Best Adult Books of 1963
          for the Pre-college Reader. National Association of Independent
          Schools 1964
          Senior Booklist: Current Books Including the Ten Best Adult Books of
          1964 for the Pre-college Reader. National Association of Indepen-
          dent Schools 1965
          Senior Booklist: Current Books Including the Ten Best Adult Books of
          1965 for the Pre-college Reader. National Association of Indepen-
          dent Schools 1966

JH   Junior High School Library Catalog; ed. by Rachel Shor and Estelle A.
          Fidell. 1st ed. Wilson 1965

SCHS   Standard Catalog for High School Libraries; ed. by Dorothy Herbert
          West, Estelle A. Fidell and Rachel Shor. 8th ed. Wilson 1962
          Standard Catalog for High School Libraries, 1963 supplement to the
          8th edition, 1962; ed. by Rachel Shor and Estelle A. Fidell. Wilson
          1963
          Standard Catalog for High School Libraries, 1964 supplement to the
          8th edition, 1962; ed. by Rachel Shor. Wilson 1964
          Standard Catalog for High School Libraries, 1965 supplement to the
          8th edition; ed. by Rachel Shor. Wilson 1965

SCPL   Standard Catalog for Public Libraries; ed. by Dorothy Herbert West
          and Estelle A. Fidell. 4th ed. Wilson 1958
          Standard Catalog for Public Libraries, 1959 supplement to the 4th
          edition, 1958; comp. by Dorothy Herbert West and Estelle A. Fidell.
          Wilson 1960
          Standard Catalog for Public Libraries, 1960 supplement to the 4th
          edition, 1958; ed. by Dorothy Herbert West and Estelle A. Fidell.
          Wilson 1961
          Standard Catalog for Public Libraries, 1961 supplement to the 4th
          edition, 1958; ed. by Dorothy Herbert West and Estelle A. Fidell.
          Wilson 1962
          Standard Catalog for Public Libraries, 1962 supplement to the 4th
          edition, 1958; ed. by Estelle A. Fidell and Rachel Shor. Wilson 1963
          Standard Catalog for Public Libraries, 1959-1963; ed. by Estelle A.
          Fidell and Rachel Shor. Wilson 1964
          Standard Catalog for Public Libraries, 1964 supplement; ed. by Estelle
          A. Fidell and Rachel Shor. Wilson 1965

3000   3000 Books for Secondary School Libraries: A Basic List; comp. by the
          Library Committee of the Independent Schools Education Board.
          Bowker 1961

YR   Your Reading: A Book List for Junior High Schools; ed. by Charles B.
          Willard. New Am. Lib. 1966

PEOPLE IN BOOKS

ABOLITIONISTS

American—18th century

John Woolman, 1720-1772

Woolman, John. Journal; ed. by Janet Whitney. Regnery 1950
  SCPL

American—19th century

Susan Brownell Anthony, 1820-1906

Bryan, Florence Horn. Susan B. Anthony: Champion of Women's Rights. Messner 1947
  BY
Lutz, Alma. Susan B. Anthony: Rebel, Crusader, Humanitarian. Beacon Press 1959
  SCPL

COLLECTIONS

Daugherty, Sonia. Ten Brave Women. Lippincott 1953
  BY–CC(7-9)–ESLC–JH–SCHS

Jehudi Ashmun, 1794-1828

Orrmont, Arthur. Fighter Against Slavery: Jehudi Ashmun. Messner 1966
  Bkl C(7-9)&Y–ESLC

John Brown, 1800-1859

Ansley, Delight. The Sword and the Spirit: A Life of John Brown. Crowell 1955
  SCHS
Benét, Stephen Vincent. John Brown's Body; ed. by Mabel A. Bessey. Holt 1954 (Poem)
  BBHS–SCHS–SCPL
Nolan, Jeannette (Covert). John Brown. Messner 1950
  JH–SCHS

Lydia Maria (Francis) Child, 1802-1880

Baer, Helene (Gilbert). The Heart Is Like Heaven: The Life of Lydia Maria Child. Univ. of Pa. 1964
  Bkl A
Meltzer, Milton. Tongue of Flame: The Life of Lydia Maria Child. Crowell 1965
  Bkl C&Y

Frederick Douglass, 1817-1895

Bontemps, Arna. Frederick Douglass: Slave–Fighter–Freeman. Knopf 1959
  CC(4-7)–ESLC–JH
Douglass, Frederick. Life and Times of Frederick Douglass; adapted by Barbara Ritchie. Crowell 1966
  Bkl Y&C–ESLC

Graham, Shirley. There Was Once a Slave: The Heroic Story of Frederick Douglass. Messner 1947
  SCHS–YR
Patterson, Lillie. Frederick Douglass. Garrard 1965
  AB(3-7)–ESLC

COLLECTIONS

Bontemps, Arna. 100 Years of Negro Freedom. Dodd 1961
  Bkl A–ESLC–SCPL

Charles Theodore Christian Follen, 1795-1840

COLLECTIONS

Cunz, Dieter. They Came from Germany: The Story of Famous German-Americans. Dodd 1966
  ESLC

William Lloyd Garrison, 1805-1879

Merrill, Walter McIntosh. Against Wind and Tide: A Biography of Wm. Lloyd Garrison. Harvard Univ. 1963
  Bkl A&Y
Thomas, John L. The Liberator: William Lloyd Garrison: A Biography. Little 1963
  Bkl A&Y–IndS(11-12)

Adam Gurowski, 1805-1866

Fischer, LeRoy H. Lincoln's Gadfly, Adam Gurowski. Univ. of Okla. 1964
  Bkl A

Thomas Wentworth Higginson, 1823-1911

Wells, Anna Mary. Dear Preceptor: The Life and Times of Thomas Wentworth Higginson. Houghton 1963
  Bkl A

Elijah Parish Lovejoy, 1802-1837

Dillon, Merton Lynn. Elijah P. Lovejoy, Abolitionist Editor. Univ. of Ill. 1961
  Bkl A
Simon, Paul. Lovejoy, Martyr to Freedom. Concordia 1964
  Bkl A

COLLECTIONS

McNeer, May Yonge and Ward, Lynd Kendall. Give Me Freedom. Abingdon 1964
  Bkl C(5-8)–CC(5-7)–ESLC–JH–YR

Lucretia (Coffin) Mott, 1793-1880

Sterling, Dorothy. Lucretia Mott: Gentle Warrior. Doubleday 1964
  Bkl C(7-9)&Y–CC–ESLC–JH

ABOLITIONISTS

American—19th century—*Continued*

Theodore Parker, 1810-1860

Commager, Henry Steele. Theodore Parker. Beacon Press 1947
SCPL

Wendell Phillips, 1811-1884

Bartlett, Irving H. Wendell Phillips: Brahmin Radical. Beacon Press 1961
BY

Lucy Stone, 1818-1893

Hays, Elinor (Rice). Morning Star: A Biography of Lucy Stone, 1818-1893. Harcourt 1961
Bkl A&Y—BY

Harriet Elizabeth (Beecher) Stowe, 1811-1896

Adams, John R. Harriet Beecher Stowe. Twayne 1964
Bkl A&Y
Furnas, Joseph Chamberlain. Goodbye to Uncle Tom. Sloane 1956
SCPL
Jackson, Phyllis Wynn. Victorian Cinderella: The Story of Harriet Beecher Stowe. Holiday 1947
BY—SCHS—YR
Johnston, Johanna. Runaway to Heaven: The Story of Harriet Beecher Stowe. Doubleday 1963
Bkl A&Y—SCPL
Wagenknecht, Edward Charles. Harriet Beecher Stowe: The Known and the Unknown. Oxford 1965
Bkl A&Y

COLLECTIONS

Vance, Marguerite. The Lamp Lighters: Women in the Hall of Fame. Dutton 1960
Bkl C(7-9)&Y—SCHS—YR

Charles Sumner, 1811-1874

Donald, David Herbert. Charles Sumner and the Coming of the Civil War. Knopf 1960
Bkl A—SCPL

Sojourner Truth, 1797?-1883?

Pauli, Hertha Ernestine. Her Name Was Sojourner Truth. Appleton 1962
Bkl A—BY

Harriet (Ross) Tubman, 1815?-1913

Parrish, Anne. A Clouded Star. Harper 1948 (Fiction)
BBHS
Petry, Ann. Harriet Tubman: Conductor on the Underground Railroad. Crowell 1955
AB(7-10)—BBEL(7-8)—BBJH—BBHS—CC(7-9)—JH—SCHS—YR

Sterling, Dorothy. Freedom Train: The Story of Harriet Tubman. Doubleday 1954
CC(7-9)—ESLC—JH—SCHS
Swift, Hildegarde Hoyt. The Railroad to Freedom: A Story of the Civil War. Harcourt 1932 (Fiction)
BBEL—CC(7-9)—JH—SCHS

COLLECTIONS

Buckmaster, Henrietta. Women Who Shaped History. Collier Bks 1966
Bkl C(7-10)&Y

ABORIGINES

Australian—19th century

Yagan, ?-1834

Durack, Mary. The Courteous Savage: Yagan of Swan River. Nelson 1964
ESLC

ACCOMPANISTS

See Pianists

ACTORS

See also Circus Performers; Playwrights; Scenic Designers; Theatrical Producers

COLLECTIONS

Allen, Steve. The Funny Men. Simon & Schuster 1956
SCPL
Davidson, William. The Real and the Unreal. Harper 1961
Bkl A
Fred Astaire; Ingrid Bergman; Dick Clark; Clark Gable; Joshua Logan; Kim Novak; Elizabeth Taylor
Funke, Lewis and Booth, John Erlanger, eds. Actors Talk About Acting: Fourteen Interviews with Stars of the Theatre. Random House 1961
Bkl A&Y
Marinacci, Barbara. Leading Ladies: A Gallery of Famous Actresses. Dodd 1961
Bkl A&Y
Ross, Lillian and Ross, Helen. The Player: A Profile of an Art. Simon & Schuster 1962
Bkl A&Y
Trease, Geoffrey. Seven Stages. Vanguard 1965
Bkl C&Y—IndS(9-10)
Henry Irving; Jenny Lind; Anna Pavlova; Sarah Siddons
Wagenknecht, Edward Charles. Seven Daughters of the Theater. Univ. of Okla. 1964
Bkl A
Sarah Bernhardt; Isadora Duncan; Mary Garden; Jenny Lind; Julia Marlowe; Marilyn Monroe; Dame Ellen Terry

ACTORS—*Continued*

Who's Who in the Theatre: A Biographical Record of the Contemporary Stage; ed. by John Parker. Pitman 1957
SCPL

American

COLLECTIONS

Cahn, William. Laugh Makers: A Pictorial History of American Comedians. Putnam 1957
SCPL

Harriman, Margaret (Case). Vicious Circle: The Story of the Algonquin Round Table. Rinehart 1951
SCPL

Martin, Thornton. Pete Martin Calls on . . . . Simon & Schuster 1962
Bkl A
Marlon Brando; Gary Cooper; Grace Patricia, Consort of Rainier III, Prince of Monaco; Helen Hayes; Nunnally Johnson; Danny Kaye; Marilyn Monroe; and others

Vance, Marguerite. Hear the Distant Applause! Dutton 1963
YR
Maude Adams; Charlotte Saunders Cushman; and others

Wagner, Frederick and Brady, Barbara. Famous American Actors and Actresses. Dodd 1961
YR
Maude Adams; Ethel Barrymore; John Barrymore; Lionel Barrymore; Edwin Thomas Booth; Edwin Forrest; Julie Harris; Helen Hayes; Joseph Jefferson; and others

Wilson, Garff B. A History of American Acting. Ind. Univ. 1966
Bkl A&Y

Zierold, Norman J. The Child Stars. Coward-McCann 1965
Bkl A
Freddie Bartholomew; Judy Garland; Mickey Rooney; and others

American—19th century

Edwin Thomas Booth, 1833-1893

Ruggles, Eleanor. Prince of Players: Edwin Booth. Norton 1953
BY—SCPL

COLLECTIONS

Wagner, Frederick and Brady, Barbara. Famous American Actors and Actresses. Dodd 1961
YR

John Wilkes Booth, 1838-1865

Stacton, David. The Judges of the Secret Court. Pantheon 1961 (Fiction)
Bkl A

Charlotte Saunders Cushman, 1816-1876

COLLECTIONS

Vance, Marguerite. Hear the Distant Applause! Dutton 1963
YR

Vance, Marguerite. The Lamp Lighters: Women in the Hall of Fame. Dutton 1960
Bkl C(7-9)&Y—SCHS—YR

Maxine Elliott, 1868-1940

Forbes-Robertson, Diana. My Aunt Maxine: The Story of Maxine Elliott. Viking 1964
Bkl A—IndS(12)

Minnie Maddern Fiske, 1865-1932

Binns, Archie. Mrs. Fiske and the American Theatre. Crown 1955
SCPL

Edwin Forrest, 1806-1872

Moody, Richard. Edwin Forrest, First Star of the American Stage. Knopf 1960
Bkl A

COLLECTIONS

Wagner, Frederick and Brady, Barbara. Famous American Actors and Actresses. Dodd 1961
YR

Joseph Jefferson, 1829-1905

Latham, Jean Lee. On Stage, Mr. Jefferson! Harper 1958
CC(7-9)—JH—YR

Malvern, Gladys. Good Troupers All. Macrae 1945
YR

COLLECTIONS

Wagner, Frederick and Brady, Barbara. Famous American Actors and Actresses. Dodd 1961
YR

Adah Isaacs Menken, 1835?-1868

Lewis, Paul. Queen of the Plaza: A Biography of Adah Isaacs Menken. Funk 1964
Bkl A

American—20th century

Maude Adams, 1872-1953

Robbins, Phyllis. Maude Adams: An Intimate Portrait. Putnam 1956
SCPL

COLLECTIONS

Vance, Marguerite. Hear the Distant Applause! Dutton 1963
YR

Wagner, Frederick and Brady, Barbara. Famous American Actors and Actresses. Dodd 1961
YR

ACTORS

American—20th century—*Continued*

Fred Allen, 1894-1956

Allen, Fred. Letters; ed. by Joe McCarthy. Doubleday 1965
Bkl A

Allen, Fred. Much Ado About Me. Little 1956
SCPL

Auerbach, Arnold M. Funny Men Don't Laugh. Doubleday 1965
Bkl A

Steve Allen, 1921-

Allen, Steve. Mark It and Strike It: An Autobiography. Holt 1960
Bkl A

Fred Astaire, 1899-

Astaire, Fred. Steps in Time. Harper 1959
SCHS—SCPL

COLLECTIONS

Davidson, William. The Real and the Unreal. Harper 1961
Bkl A

Ethel Barrymore, 1879-1959

Alpert, Hollis. The Barrymores. Dial 1964
Bkl A

Barrymore, Ethel. Memories: An Autobiography. Harper 1955
SCPL

COLLECTIONS

Wagner, Frederick and Brady, Barbara. Famous American Actors and Actresses. Dodd 1961
YR

John Barrymore, 1882-1942

Alpert, Hollis. The Barrymores. Dial 1964
Bkl A

COLLECTIONS

Wagner, Frederick and Brady, Barbara. Famous American Actors and Actresses. Dodd 1961
YR

Lionel Barrymore, 1878-1954

Alpert, Hollis. The Barrymores. Dial 1964
Bkl A

Barrymore, Lionel. We Barrymores. Appleton 1951
SCPL

COLLECTIONS

Wagner, Frederick and Brady, Barbara. Famous American Actors and Actresses. Dodd 1961
YR

Freddie Bartholomew, 1924-

COLLECTIONS

Zierold, Norman J. The Child Stars. Coward-McCann 1965
Bkl A

Eleanor (Robson) Belmont, 1879-

Belmont, Eleanor (Robson). Fabric of Memory. Farrar 1957
SCPL

Gertrude Berg, 1900-1966

Berg, Gertrude and Berg, Cherney. Molly and Me. McGraw 1961
Bkl A&Y

Humphrey Bogart, 1900-1957

Hyams, Joe. Bogie: The Biography of Humphrey Bogart. New Am. Lib. 1966
Bkl A

Marlon Brando, 1924-

COLLECTIONS

Martin, Thornton. Pete Martin Calls on . . . . Simon & Schuster 1962
Bkl A

Heywood Hale Broun, 1918-

Broun, Heywood Hale. A Studied Madness. Doubleday 1965
Bkl A

Jimmy Brown, 1936-

Brown, Jimmy and Cope, Myron. Off My Chest. Doubleday 1964
Bkl A&Y

Terzian, James P. and Benagh, Jim. The Jimmy Brown Story. Messner 1964
ESLC—IndJ(6-9)

Ilka Chase, 1905-

Chase, Ilka. The Carthaginian Rose. Doubleday 1961
Bkl A

Gary Cooper, 1901-1961

COLLECTIONS

Martin, Thornton. Pete Martin Calls on . . . . Simon & Schuster 1962
Bkl A

Katharine Cornell, 1898-

McClintic, Guthrie. Me and Kit. Little 1955
BY—SCHS—SCPL

Malvern, Gladys. Curtain Going Up! The Story of Katharine Cornell. Messner 1943
SCHS—SCPL—YR

COLLECTIONS

Forsee, Aylesa. American Women Who Scored Firsts. Macrae 1958
SCHS

Wallace Cox, 1924-

Cox, Wallace. My Life as a Small Boy. Simon & Schuster 1961
Bkl A

Bing Crosby, 1904-

Crosby, Bing. Call Me Lucky. Simon & Schuster 1953
SCPL

ACTORS

American—20th century—*Continued*

Sammy Davis, 1926-

Davis, Sammy. Yes I Can. Farrar 1965
Bkl A&Y

Jimmy Durante, 1893-

Fowler, Gene. Schnozzola: The Story of Jimmy Durante. Viking 1951
SCPL

Maxine Elliott, 1868-1940

Forbes-Robertson, Diana. My Aunt Maxine: The Story of Maxine Elliott. Viking 1964
Bkl A—IndS(12)

Lynn Fontanne, 1887-

Freedley, George. The Lunts: An Illustrated Study of Their Work. Macmillan 1958
SCPL

Zolotow, Maurice. Stagestruck: The Romance of Alfred Lunt and Lynn Fontanne. Harcourt 1965
Bkl A&Y

Clark Gable, 1901-1960

COLLECTIONS

Davidson, William. The Real and the Unreal. Harper 1961
Bkl A

Judy Garland, 1922-

COLLECTIONS

Zierold, Norman J. The Child Stars. Coward-McCann 1965
Bkl A

Grace Patricia, Consort of Rainier III, Prince of Monaco, 1929-

COLLECTIONS

Martin, Thornton. Pete Martin Calls on . . . . Simon & Schuster 1962
Bkl A

Dick Gregory, 1932-

Gregory, Dick and Lipsyte, Robert. Nigger: An Autobiography. Dutton 1964
Bkl A&Y—IndS(11-12)

Oliver Norvell Hardy, 1892-1957

McCabe, John. Mr. Laurel and Mr. Hardy. Doubleday 1961
Bkl A

Julie Harris, 1925-

COLLECTIONS

Wagner, Frederick and Brady, Barbara. Famous American Actors and Actresses. Dodd 1961
YR

Sterling Hayden, 1916-

Hayden, Sterling. Wanderer. Knopf 1963
Bkl A

Helen Hayes, 1900-

Hayes, Helen and Funke, Lewis. A Gift of Joy. Evans 1965
Bkl A&Y

COLLECTIONS

Martin, Thornton. Pete Martin Calls on . . . . Simon & Schuster 1962
Bkl A

Wagner, Frederick and Brady, Barbara. Famous American Actors and Actresses. Dodd 1961
YR

Al Jolson, 1888-1950

Sieben, Pearl. The Immortal Jolson: His Life and Times. Fell 1962
BY

Danny Kaye, 1913-

COLLECTIONS

Martin, Thornton. Pete Martin Calls on . . . . Simon & Schuster 1962
Bkl A

Buster Keaton, 1896-1966

Blesh, Rudi. Keaton. Macmillan 1966
Bkl A

Keaton, Buster and Samuels, Charles. My Wonderful World of Slapstick. Doubleday 1960
Bkl A

Stan Laurel, 1890-1965

McCabe, John. Mr. Laurel and Mr. Hardy. Doubleday 1961
Bkl A

Eva Le Gallienne, 1899-

Le Gallienne, Eva. At 33. Longmans 1934
SCPL

Le Gallienne, Eva. With a Quiet Heart: An Autobiography. Viking 1953
BY—SCHS—SCPL

Harold Clayton Lloyd, 1893-

Cahn, William. Harold Lloyd's World of Comedy. Duell 1964
Bkl A

Alfred Lunt, 1893-

Freedley, George. The Lunts: An Illustrated Study of Their Work. Macmillan 1958
SCPL

Zolotow, Maurice. Stagestruck: The Romance of Alfred Lunt and Lynn Fontanne. Harcourt 1965
Bkl A&Y

Julia Marlowe, 1866-1950

COLLECTIONS

Wagenknecht, Edward Charles. Seven Daughters of the Theater. Univ. of Okla. 1964
Bkl A

ACTORS

American—20th century—Continued

Harpo Marx, 1893-1964

Marx, Harpo and Barber, Rowland. Harpo Speaks! Geis 1961
Bkl A

Marilyn Monroe, 1926-1962

COLLECTIONS

Martin, Thornton. Pete Martin Calls on . . . . Simon & Schuster 1962
Bkl A

Wagenknecht, Edward Charles. Seven Daughters of the Theater. Univ. of Okla. 1964
Bkl A

Kim Novak, 1933-

COLLECTIONS

Davidson, William. The Real and the Unreal. Harper 1961
Bkl A

Elliott Nugent, 1899-

Nugent, Elliott. Events Leading Up to the Comedy: An Autobiography. Trident Press 1965
Bkl A

Jack Paar, 1918-

Paar, Jack and Reddy, John. I Kid You Not. Little 1960
Bkl A

Molly Picon, 1898-

Picon, Molly and Rosenberg, Eth Clifford. So Laugh a Little. Messner 1962
Bkl A&Y

Kathleen Eloisa Rockwell, 1876-1957

Lucia, Ellis. Klondike Kate: The Life & Legend of Kitty Rockwell, the Queen of the Yukon. Hastings House 1962
Bkl A

Mickey Rooney, 1920-

COLLECTIONS

Zierold, Norman J. The Child Stars. Coward-McCann 1965
Bkl A

Cornelia Otis Skinner, 1901-

Skinner, Cornelia Otis. Family Circle. Houghton 1948
BY—SCPL

Elizabeth Taylor, 1932-

COLLECTIONS

Davidson, William. The Real and the Unreal. Harper 1961
Bkl A

Laurette (Cooney) Taylor, 1884-1946

Courtney, M. T. Laurette. Rinehart 1955
SCPL

Ethel Waters, 1900-

Waters, Ethel. His Eye Is on the Sparrow: An Autobiography. Doubleday 1951
SCPL

Johnny Weissmuller, 1904-

COLLECTIONS

Gallico, Paul. The Golden People. Doubleday 1965
Bkl A&Y

Peggy Wood, 1892-

Wood, Peggy. Arts and Flowers. Morrow 1963
Bkl A—IndS(9-12)

Keenan Wynn, 1916-

Wynn, Keenan and Brough, James. Ed Wynn's Son. Doubleday 1959
Bkl A

Burmese—20th century

Po Sein, 1880?-1952

Sein, Kenneth and Withey, Joseph A. The Great Po Sein: A Chronicle of the Burmese Theater. Ind. Univ. 1966
Bkl A

English—16th century

John Heming, 1556?-1630

Chute, Marchette. The Wonderful Winter. Dutton 1954 (Fiction)
CC(7-9)—JH—SCHS

English—17th century

John Heming, 1556?-1630

Chute, Marchette. The Wonderful Winter. Dutton 1954 (Fiction)
CC(7-9)—JH—SCHS

English—18th century

Colley Cibber, 1671-1757

Ashley, Leonard R.N. Colley Cibber. Twayne 1965
Bkl A

Cibber, Colley. An Apology for the Life of Colley Cibber. 1740
CA

David Garrick, 1717-1779

Barton, Margaret. Garrick. Macmillan 1949
SCPL

Garrick, David. Letters; ed. by David M. Little and George M. Kahrl. 3v. Harvard Univ. 1963
Bkl A

Sarah Siddons, 1755-1831

De La Torre, Lillian. The Actress: The Story of Sarah Siddons. Nelson 1957
YR

ACTORS

English—18th century

Sarah Siddons—Continued

Haycraft, Molly C. First Lady of the Theater: Sarah Siddons. Messner 1958
YR

COLLECTIONS

Trease, Geoffrey. Seven Stages. Vanguard 1965
Bkl C&Y—IndS(9-10)

English—19th century

Mrs. Patrick Campbell, 1865-1940

Kilty, Jerome. Dear Liar: A Comedy of Letters Adapted from the Correspondence of Bernard Shaw and Mrs. Patrick Campbell. Dodd 1960
Bkl A

Shaw, George Bernard. Bernard Shaw and Mrs. Patrick Campbell: Their Correspondence. Knopf 1952
SCPL

Henry Irving, 1838-1905

Irving, Laurence Henry Forster. Henry Irving: The Actor and His World. Macmillan 1952
SCPL

COLLECTIONS

Trease, Geoffrey. Seven Stages. Vanguard 1965
Bkl C&Y—IndS(9-10)

Edmund Kean, 1787-1833

Berstl, Julius. Kean: The Imaginary Memoirs of an Actor. Orion 1962 (Fiction)
Bkl A

Sartre, Jean Paul. Kean. Knopf 1960
Bkl A

Frances Anne ("Fanny") Kemble, 1809-1893

Kerr, Laura. Footlights to Fame. Funk 1962
BY

Sarah Siddons, 1755-1831

De La Torre, Lillian. The Actress: The Story of Sarah Siddons. Nelson 1957
YR

Haycraft, Molly C. First Lady of the Theater: Sarah Siddons. Messner 1958
YR

COLLECTIONS

Trease, Geoffrey. Seven Stages. Vanguard 1965
Bkl C&Y—IndS(9-10)

Dame Ellen Terry, 1847-1928

Terry, Dame Ellen. Ellen Terry's Memoirs. Putnam 1932
SCPL

COLLECTIONS

Wagenknecht, Edward Charles. Seven Daughters of the Theater. Univ. of Okla. 1964
Bkl A

Beerbohm Tree, 1853-1917

Pearson, Hesketh. Beerbohm Tree: His Life and Laughter. Harper 1956
SCPL

English—20th century

Charles Chaplin, 1889-

Chaplin, Charles. My Autobiography. Simon & Schuster 1964
Bkl A

Chaplin, Charles and others. My Father, Charlie Chaplin. Random House 1960
Bkl A

Huff, Theodore. Charlie Chaplin. Abelard-Schuman 1951
SCPL

Diana (Manners) Cooper, Viscountess Norwich, 1892-

Cooper, Diana (Manners) Viscountess Norwich. Trumpets from the Steep. Houghton 1960
Bkl A

Noel Pierce Coward, 1899-

Coward, Noel Pierce. Future Indefinite. Doubleday 1954
SCPL

Judith Furse, 1912-1944

Whistler, Laurence. The Initials in the Heart. Houghton 1964
Bkl A

Margalo Gillmore, 1897-

Gillmore, Margalo. Four Flights Up. Houghton 1964
Bkl A&Y

Sir Cedric Hardwicke, 1893-1964

Hardwicke, Sir Cedric and Brough, James. A Victorian in Orbit: The Irreverent Memoirs of Sir Cedric Hardwicke. Doubleday 1961
Bkl A

Audrey Hepburn, 1929-

COLLECTIONS

Forsee, Aylesa. Women Who Reached for Tomorrow. Macrae 1960
Bkl C&Y

Leslie Howard, 1893-1943

Howard, L. R. A Quite Remarkable Father. Harcourt 1959
SCPL

Vivien Leigh, 1913-1967

Barker, Felix. The Oliviers: A Biography. Lippincott 1953
SCPL

ACTORS

English—20th century—*Continued*

Sir Laurence Kerr Olivier, 1907-

Barker, Felix. The Oliviers: A Biography. Lippincott 1953
SCPL

Dame Ellen Terry, 1847-1928

Terry, Dame Ellen. Ellen Terry's Memoirs. Putnam 1932
SCPL

COLLECTIONS

Wagenknecht, Edward Charles. Seven Daughters of the Theater. Univ. of Okla. 1964
Bkl A

Beerbohm Tree, 1853-1917

Pearson, Hesketh. Beerbohm Tree: His Life and Laughter. Harper 1956
SCPL

French—18th century

Claire Josèphe Hippolyte Legris de Latude Clairon, 1723-1803

COLLECTIONS

Herold, J. Christopher. Love in Five Temperaments. Atheneum 1961
Bkl A

French—19th century

Sarah Bernhardt, 1844-1923

Noble, Iris. Great Lady of the Theatre: Sarah Bernhardt. Messner 1960
Bkl C&Y—BY—JH—SCHS—YR

COLLECTIONS

Wagenknecht, Edward Charles. Seven Daughters of the Theater. Univ. of Okla. 1964
Bkl A

French—20th century

Sarah Bernhardt, 1844-1923

Noble, Iris. Great Lady of the Theatre: Sarah Bernhardt. Messner 1960
Bkl C&Y—BY—JH—SCHS—YR

COLLECTIONS

Wagenknecht, Edward Charles. Seven Daughters of the Theater. Univ. of Okla. 1964
Bkl A

Maurice Chevalier, 1888-

Chevalier, Maurice. With Love, As Told to Eileen and Robert Mason Pollock. Little 1960
Bkl A

Frédéric O'Brady, ?

O'Brady, Frédéric. All Told. Simon & Schuster 1964
Bkl A

Italian—19th century

Eleonora Duse, 1858-1924

Le Gallienne, Eva. The Mystic in the Theatre: Eleonora Duse. Farrar 1966
Bkl A&Y

Winwar, Frances. Wingless Victory: A Biography of Gabriele D'Annunzio and Eleonora Duse. Harper 1956
SCPL

Italian—20th century

Eleonora Duse, 1858-1924

Le Gallienne, Eva. The Mystic in the Theatre: Eleonora Duse. Farrar 1966
Bkl A&Y

Winwar, Frances. Wingless Victory: A Biography of Gabriele D'Annunzio and Eleonora Duse. Harper 1956
SCPL

Russian—20th century

Constantin Stanislavski, 1863-1938

Stanislavski, Constantin. My Life in Art. Theatre Arts 1948
SCPL

Tulane Drama Review. Stanislavski and America: An Anthology; ed. by Erika Munk. Hill & Wang 1966
Bkl A

Scottish—20th century

George Sanders, 1906-

Sanders, George. Memoirs of a Professional Cad. Putnam 1960
Bkl A

Swedish—20th century

Ingrid Bergman, 1916-

COLLECTIONS

Davidson, William. The Real and the Unreal. Harper 1961
Bkl A

Welsh—20th century

Emlyn Williams, 1905-

Williams, Emlyn. George: An Early Autobiography. Random House 1961
Bkl A—BY—SCPL

ACTRESSES

See Actors

ADMIRALS

See Naval Officers and Other Seafarers

ADVENTURERS

See Explorers; Frontiersmen

ADVERTISING EXECUTIVES

American—20th century

Albert D. Lasker, 1880-1952

Gunther, John. Taken at the Flood: The Story of Albert D. Lasker. Harper 1960
Bkl A—SCPL

ADVOCATES

See Lawyers

AERONAUTS

See Aviators

AERONAUTICAL ENGINEERS

See Engineers, Aeronautical

AGNOSTICS

American—19th century

Robert Green Ingersoll, 1833-1899

Larson, Orvin Prentiss. American Infidel: Robert G. Ingersoll—A Biography. Citadel 1962
Bkl A

AGRICULTURAL CHEMISTS

See Chemists

AGRICULTURALISTS

See Farmers; Horticulturists

AIR FORCE OFFICERS

See Aviators

AIR MARSHALS

See Aviators

AIR PILOTS

See Aviators

AIRCRAFT INDUSTRY WORKERS

See Aviators; Engineers, Aeronautical

AIRLINE STEWARDESSES

American—20th century

Sherry Waterman, ?

Waterman, Sherry. From Another Island. Chilton 1962
Bkl Y&A

AIRPLANE MANUFACTURERS

See Aviators

ALCHEMISTS

COLLECTIONS

Cummings, Richard. The Alchemists: Fathers of Practical Chemistry. McKay 1966
Bkl C&Y
Saint Albert the Great; Bolos Democritos; John Dee; Nicholas Flamel; Geber; Go-Hung; Philippus Aureolus Paracelsus; James Price; Alexander Seton

Chinese—3rd century

Go-Hung, 254-334

COLLECTIONS

Cummings, Richard. The Alchemists: Fathers of Practical Chemistry. McKay 1966
Bkl C&Y

English—16th century

John Dee, 1527-1608

COLLECTIONS

Cummings, Richard. The Alchemists: Fathers of Practical Chemistry. McKay 1966
Bkl C&Y

French—14th century

Nicholas Flamel, 1330?-1418

COLLECTIONS

Cummings, Richard. The Alchemists: Fathers of Practical Chemistry. McKay 1966
Bkl C&Y

Greek—3rd century B.C.

Bolos Democritos, fl. 200 B.C.

COLLECTIONS

Cummings, Richard. The Alchemists: Fathers of Practical Chemistry. McKay 1966
Bkl C&Y

Scottish—16th century

Alexander Seton, 1520-1604

COLLECTIONS

Cummings, Richard. The Alchemists: Fathers of Practical Chemistry. McKay 1966
Bkl C&Y

Swiss—16th century

Philippus Aureolus Paracelsus, 1493?-1541

Rosen, Sidney. Doctor Paracelsus. Little 1959
CC(7-9)—JH

ALCHEMISTS

Swiss—16th century

Philippus Aureolus Paracelsus—Continued

COLLECTIONS

Cummings, Richard. The Alchemists: Fathers of Practical Chemistry. McKay 1966
Bkl C&Y

ALPINISTS

See Mountaineers

AMBASSADORS

See Statesmen

ANARCHISTS

American—19th century

Emma Goldman, 1869-1940

Drinnon, Richard. Rebel in Paradise: A Biography of Emma Goldman. Univ. of Chicago 1961
Bkl A

American—20th century

Emma Goldman, 1869-1940

Drinnon, Richard. Rebel in Paradise: A Biography of Emma Goldman. Univ. of Chicago 1961
Bkl A

Nicola Sacco, 1891-1927

Felix, David. Protest: Sacco-Vanzetti and the Intellectuals. Ind. Univ. 1965
Bkl A
Russell, Francis. Tragedy in Dedham: The Story of the Sacco-Vanzetti Case. McGraw 1962
Bkl A—SCPL

Bartolomeo Vanzetti, 1888-1927

Felix, David. Protest: Sacco-Vanzetti and the Intellectuals. Ind. Univ. 1965
Bkl A
Russell, Francis. Tragedy in Dedham: The Story of the Sacco-Vanzetti Case. McGraw 1962
Bkl A—SCPL

ANATOMISTS

American—20th century

Florence Rena Sabin, 1871-1953

COLLECTIONS

Forsee, Aylesa. Women Who Reached for Tomorrow. Macrae 1960
Bkl C&Y

Belgian—16th century

Andreas Vesalius, 1514-1564

COLLECTIONS

Hume, Ruth Fox. Great Men of Medicine. Random House 1961
CC(7-9)—ESLC—JH—SCHS—YR

English—17th century

William Harvey, 1578-1657

Marcus, Rebecca B. William Harvey: Trail-Blazer of Scientific Medicine. Watts 1963
Bkl C(5-9)&Y—ESLC—JH

COLLECTIONS

Hume, Ruth Fox. Great Men of Medicine. Random House 1961
CC(7-9)—ESLC—JH—SCHS—YR
Sterne, Emma (Gelders). Blood Brothers: Four Men of Science. Knopf 1959
Bkl C(7-9)—JH

Italian—17th century

Marcello Malpighi, 1628-1694

COLLECTIONS

Sterne, Emma (Gelders). Blood Brothers: Four Men of Science. Knopf 1959
Bkl C(7-9)—JH

Scottish—18th century

John Hunter, 1728-1793

Kobler, John. The Reluctant Surgeon: A Biography of John Hunter. Doubleday 1960
Bkl A—SCPL

ANESTHETISTS

American—19th century

William Thomas Green Morton, 1819-1868

Baker, Rachel. Dr. Morton: Pioneer in the Use of Ether. Messner 1946
SCHS
Ludovici, Laurence James. The Discovery of Anaesthesia. Crowell 1962
Bkl A
Woodward, Grace Steele. The Man Who Conquered Pain: A Biography of William Thomas Green Morton. Beacon Press 1962
Bkl A&Y—BY

COLLECTIONS

Hume, Ruth Fox. Great Men of Medicine. Random House 1961
CC(7-9)—ESLC—JH—SCHS—YR

ANIMAL TRAINERS

See Horse Trainers

ANTHROPOLOGISTS

See also Ethnologists

American—20th century

Ruth (Fulton) Benedict, 1887-1948

Benedict, Ruth (Fulton). An Anthropologist at Work; ed. by Margaret Mead. Houghton 1959
SCPL

Margaret Mead, 1901-

COLLECTIONS

Nathan, Dorothy. Women of Courage. Random House 1964
CC(4-6)—ESLC—JH

Hortense Powdermaker, 1900-

Powdermaker, Hortense. Stranger and Friend: The Way of an Anthropologist. Norton 1966
Bkl A&Y

English—20th century

Verrier Elwin, 1902-1964

Elwin, Verrier. The Tribal World of Verrier Elwin. Oxford 1964
Bkl A

French—20th century

Pierre Teilhard de Chardin, 1881-1955

Corte, Nicolas. Pierre Teilhard de Chardin: His Life and Spirit; tr. by Martin Jarrett-Kerr. Macmillan 1960
Bkl A

Cuénot, Claude. Teilhard de Chardin: A Biographical Study; tr. by Vincent Colimore; ed. by René Hague. Helicon Press 1965
Bkl A

De Terra, Helmut. Memories of Teilhard de Chardin; tr. from the German by J. Maxwell Brownjohn. Harper 1965
Bkl A

Grenet, Paul. Teilhard de Chardin: The Man and His Theories; tr. from the French by R. A. Rudorff. Eriksson 1966
Bkl A

Lubac, Henri de. Teilhard de Chardin: The Man and His Meaning; tr. by René Hague. Hawthorn 1965
Bkl A

Rabut, Olivier A. Teilhard de Chardin: A Critical Study. Sheed 1961
Bkl A

Teilhard de Chardin, Pierre. The Making of a Mind: Letters from a Soldier-Priest, 1914-1919; tr. from the French by René Hague. Harper 1965
Bkl A

New Zealand—20th century

Thomas Robert Alexander Harries Davis, 1918?-

Davis, Thomas Robert Alexander Harries. Doctor to the Islands. Little 1954
BY—SCPL

APOSTLES

See Biblical Figures—New Testament

ARCHBISHOPS

See Religious Leaders

ARCHEOLOGISTS

COLLECTIONS

Daugherty, Charles Michael. The Great Archaeologists. Crowell 1962
Bkl C(6-9)—ESLC

American—20th century

James Henry Breasted, 1865-1935

Breasted, Charles. Pioneer to the Past: The Story of James Henry Breasted, Archaeologist. Scribner 1943
SCPL

English—19th century

Sir Arthur John Evans, 1851-1941

Cottrell, Leonard. The Bull of Minos. Holt 1958
SCHS—SCPL

Honour, Alan. Secrets of Minos: Sir Arthur Evans' Discoveries at Crete. McGraw 1961
Bkl C(6-9)

Selden, George. Sir Arthur Evans, Discoverer of Knossos. Macmillan 1964
ESLC—IndJ(4-6)

Sir Austen Henry Layard, 1817-1894

Kubie, Nora Benjamin. Road to Nineveh: The Adventures and Excavations of Sir Austen Henry Layard. Doubleday 1964
Bkl A&Y

Silverberg, Robert. The Man Who Found Nineveh: The Story of Austen Henry Layard. Holt 1964
Bkl C(7-10)&Y—ESLC—IndJ(6-9)

English—20th century

Sir Arthur John Evans, 1851-1941

Cottrell, Leonard. The Bull of Minos. Holt 1958
SCHS—SCPL

Honour, Alan. Secrets of Minos: Sir Arthur Evans' Discoveries at Crete. McGraw 1961
Bkl C(6-9)

ARCHEOLOGISTS

English—20th century

Sir Arthur John Evans—Continued

Selden, George. Sir Arthur Evans, Discoverer of Knossos. Macmillan 1964
ESLC—IndJ(4-6)

Thomas Edward Lawrence, 1888-1935

MacLean, Alistair. Lawrence of Arabia. Random House 1962
Bkl   C(6-9)—CC(5-7)—ESLC—JH—SCHS—YR

Rattigan, Terence. Ross: A Dramatic Portrait. Random House 1962 (Play)
Bkl A

Thomas, John. The True Story of Lawrence of Arabia. Childrens Press 1964
IndJ(4-6)

French—20th century

Henri Breuil, 1877-1961

Brodrick, Alan Houghton. Father of Prehistory: The Abbé Henri Breuil—His Life and Times. Morrow 1963
Bkl A

German—18th century

Johann Joachim Winckelmann, 1717-1768

COLLECTIONS

Pater, Walter Horatio. Renaissance Studies in Art and Poetry. Modern Lib.
SCPL

German—19th century

Heinrich Schliemann, 1822-1890

Braymer, Marjorie. The Walls of Windy Troy: A Biography of Heinrich Schliemann. Harcourt 1960
AB(6up)—Bkl C(7-9)&Y—CC(7-9)—ESLC—JH—SCHS

Cottrell, Leonard. The Bull of Minos. Holt 1958
SCHS—SCPL

Honour, Alan. The Unlikely Hero. McGraw 1960
Bkl C(7-9)

Payne, Robert. The Gold of Troy. Funk 1958
BY

Selden, George. Heinrich Schliemann: Discoverer of Buried Treasure. Macmillan 1964.
CC(3-6)

Italian—19th century

Giovanni Battista Belzoni, 1778-1823

Mayes, Stanley. The Great Belzoni, Archaeologist Extraordinary. Walker & Co. 1961
Bkl A

ARCHERS

Swiss—14th century

William Tell, ?

Buff, Mary (Marsh) and Buff, Conrad. Apple and the Arrow. Houghton 1951 (Fiction)
BBEL—CC(3-6)

ARCHITECTS

COLLECTIONS

Blake, Peter. The Master Builders. Knopf 1960
Bkl A—SCPL
Le Corbusier; Ludwig Mies van der Rohe; Frank Lloyd Wright

Forsee, Aylesa. Men of Modern Architecture: Giants in Glass, Steel, and Stone. Macrae 1966
Bkl C&Y
Walter Gropius; Eric Mendelsohn; Ludwig Mies van der Rohe; Richard Neutra; Eero Saarinen; Edward Durell Stone; Louis Henry Sullivan; Frank Lloyd Wright

Peter, John, ed. Masters of Modern Architecture. Braziller 1958
SCPL—3000

American

COLLECTIONS

McCallum, Ian Robert More. Architecture USA. Reinhold 1959
SCPL

American—19th century

Louis Henry Sullivan, 1856-1924

Bush-Brown, Albert. Louis Sullivan. Braziller 1960
Bkl A

Connely, Willard. Louis Sullivan as He Lived: A Biography. Horizon 1960
Bkl A

COLLECTIONS

Forsee, Aylesa. Men of Modern Architecture: Giants in Glass, Steel, and Stone. Macrae 1966
Bkl C&Y

American—20th century

Philip Cortelyou Johnson, 1906-

Jacobus, John M. Philip Johnson. Braziller 1962
Bkl A

Louis I. Kahn, 1901-

Scully, Vincent Joseph. Louis I. Kahn. Braziller 1962
Bkl A

Ludwig Mies van der Rohe, 1886-

Drexler, Arthur. Ludwig Mies van der Rohe. Braziller 1960
Bkl A

ARCHITECTS

American—20th century

Ludwig Mies van der Rohe—Continued

COLLECTIONS

Blake, Peter. The Master Builders. Knopf 1960
Bkl A—SCPL

Forsee, Aylesa. Men of Modern Architecture: Giants in Glass, Steel, and Stone. Macrae 1966
Bkl C&Y

Richard Joseph Neutra, 1892-

McCoy, Esther. Richard Neutra. Braziller 1960
Bkl A

Neutra, Richard Joseph. Life and Shape. Appleton 1962
Bkl A

COLLECTIONS

Forsee, Aylesa. Men of Modern Architecture: Giants in Glass, Steel, and Stone. Macrae 1966
Bkl C&Y

Eero Saarinen, 1910-1961

Saarinen, Eero. Eero Saarinen on His Work: A Selection of Buildings with Statements by the Architect; ed. by Aline B. Saarinen. Yale Univ. 1962
Bkl A

Temko, Allan. Eero Saarinen. Braziller 1962
Bkl A—SCPL

COLLECTIONS

Forsee, Aylesa. Men of Modern Architecture: Giants in Glass, Steel, and Stone. Macrae 1966
Bkl C&Y

Edward Durell Stone, 1902-

Stone, Edward Durell. The Evolution of an Architect. Horizon 1962
Bkl A

COLLECTIONS

Forsee, Aylesa. Men of Modern Architecture: Giants in Glass, Steel, and Stone. Macrae 1966
Bkl C&Y

Louis Henry Sullivan, 1856-1924

Bush-Brown, Albert. Louis Sullivan. Braziller 1960
Bkl A

Connely, Willard. Louis Sullivan as He Lived: A Biography. Horizon 1960
Bkl A

COLLECTIONS

Forsee, Aylesa. Men of Modern Architecture: Giants in Glass, Steel, and Stone. Macrae 1966
Bkl C&Y

Frank Lloyd Wright, 1869-1959

Barney, Maginel (Wright). The Valley of the God-Almighty Joneses. Appleton 1965
Bkl A

Farr, Finis. Frank Lloyd Wright: A Biography. Scribner 1961
Bkl A

Forsee, Aylesa. Frank Lloyd Wright: Rebel in Concrete. Macrae 1959
Bkl C&Y—JH—SCHS

Hitchcock, Henry Russell. In the Nature of Materials, 1887-1941: The Buildings of Frank Lloyd Wright. Duell 1942
SCPL

Jacobs, Herbert Austin. Frank Lloyd Wright: America's Greatest Architect. Harcourt 1965
Bkl C(7-10)&Y

Ransohoff, Doris. Living Architecture: Frank Lloyd Wright. Encyc. Britannica 1962
JH

Scully, Vincent Joseph. Frank Lloyd Wright. Braziller 1960
Bkl A—SCPL

Smith, Norris Kelly. Frank Lloyd Wright: A Study in Architectural Content. Prentice-Hall 1966
Bkl A

Wright, Frank Lloyd. Frank Lloyd Wright: An Autobiography. Duell 1943
SCPL

Wright, Frank Lloyd. A Testament. Horizon 1957
SCPL

COLLECTIONS

Blake, Peter. The Master Builders. Knopf 1960
Bkl A—SCPL

Forsee, Aylesa. Men of Modern Architecture: Giants in Glass, Steel, and Stone. Macrae 1966
Bkl C&Y

Brazilian—20th century

Oscar Niemeyer, 1907-

Papadaki, Stamo. Oscar Niemeyer. Braziller 1960
Bkl A

English—17th century

Sir Christopher Wren, 1632-1723

Sekler, E. F. Wren and His Place in European Architecture; tr. by Peter Murray. Macmillan 1956
SCPL

ARCHITECTS—*Continued*

English—19th century

William Morris, 1834-1896

Thompson, Edward Palmer. William Morris, Romantic to Revolutionary. Monthly Review 1961
Bkl A

Finnish—20th century

Alvar Aalto, 1898-

Gutheim, Frederick Albert. Alvar Aalto. Braziller 1960
Bkl A

German—20th century

Walter Gropius, 1883-

Fitch, James Marston. Walter Gropius. Braziller 1960
Bkl A

COLLECTIONS

Forsee, Aylesa. Men of Modern Architecture: Giants in Glass, Steel, and Stone. Macrae 1966
Bkl C&Y

Eric Mendelsohn, 1887-1953

Von Eckhardt, Wolf. Eric Mendelsohn. Braziller 1960
Bkl A

COLLECTIONS

Forsee, Aylesa. Men of Modern Architecture: Giants in Glass, Steel, and Stone. Macrae 1966
Bkl C&Y

Italian—16th century

Michelangelo Buonarroti, 1475-1564

Brandes, Georg Morris Cohen. Michelangelo; tr. by Heinz Norden. Ungar 1963
Bkl A
De Tolnay, Charles. The Art and Thought of Michelangelo. Pantheon 1964
Bkl A
Michelangelo Buonarroti. I, Michelangelo, Sculptor: An Autobiography Through Letters; ed. by Irving and Jean Stone; tr. by Charles Speroni. Doubleday 1962
Bkl A
Michelangelo Buonarroti. Michelangelo: Paintings, Sculptures, Architecture, by Ludwig Goldscheider. Phaidon 1962
SCPL
Morgan, Charles H. The Life of Michelangelo. Reynal 1960
Bkl A—BY—GR
Peck, Anne Merriman. Wings of an Eagle. Hawthorn 1963
IndS(9-11)

Ripley, Elizabeth. Michelangelo: A Biography. Walck 1953
CC(7-9)—ESLC—JH—SCHS
Schott, Rudolf. Michelangelo; tr. from the German by Constance McNab. Abrams 1965
Bkl A&Y
Stone, Irving. The Agony and the Ecstasy: A Novel of Michelangelo. Doubleday 1961 (Fiction)
Bkl A—SCHS
Stone, Irving. The Great Adventure of Michelangelo. Doubleday 1965 (Fiction)
JH
Symonds, J. A.   Life of Michelangelo. Modern Lib.
GR

Raphael, 1483-1520

Ripley, Elizabeth. Raphael: A Biography. Lippincott 1961
Bkl C(7-9)&Y—BY—CC—JH—SCHS

Italian—20th century

Pier Luigi Nervi, 1891-

Huxtable, Ada Louise. Pier Luigi Nervi. Braziller 1960
Bkl A—SCPL

Japanese—20th century

Kenzo Tange, 1913-

Boyd, Robin. Kenzo Tange. Braziller 1962
Bkl A

Spanish—20th century

Antonio Gaudí y Cornet, 1852-1926

Collins, George Roseborough. Antonio Gaudí. Braziller 1960
Bkl A—SCPL
Sweeney, James Johnson and Sert, José Luis. Antoni Gaudí. Praeger 1961
Bkl A

Swiss—20th century

Le Corbusier (Charles Édouard Jeanneret-Gris), 1887-1965

Choay, Françoise. Le Corbusier. Braziller 1960
Bkl A—SCPL
Papadaki, Stamo, ed. Le Corbusier: Architect, Painter, Writer. Macmillan 1948
SCPL

COLLECTIONS

Blake, Peter. The Master Builders. Knopf 1960
Bkl A—SCPL

ARCTIC EXPLORERS

See Explorers

ARMY COMMANDERS

See Soldiers

ARMY ENGINEERS

See Engineers, Military

ARMY OFFICERS

See Soldiers

ART COLLECTORS

COLLECTIONS

Cabanne, Pierre. The Great Collectors. Farrar 1963
Bkl A
Albert Coombs Barnes; Catherine II, Empress of Russia; Marguerite Guggenheim; Sir Richard Wallace; Georges Wildenstein; and others

American

COLLECTIONS

Saarinen, Aline B. The Proud Possessors: The Lives, Times, and Tastes of Some Adventurous American Art Collectors. Random House 1958
SCPL
Katherine Sophie Dreier; Isabella Stewart Gardner; Henry Osborne Havemeyer; John Pierpont Morgan; Potter Palmer; John Davison Rockefeller; Michael Stein; and others

American—19th century

Isabella Stewart Gardner, 1840-1924

Tharp, Louise (Hall). Mrs. Jack: A Biography of Isabella Stewart Gardner. Little 1965
Bkl A

COLLECTIONS

Saarinen, Aline B. The Proud Possessors: The Lives, Times, and Tastes of Some Adventurous American Art Collectors. Random House 1958
SCPL

Henry Osborne Havemeyer, 1847-1907

COLLECTIONS

Saarinen, Aline B. The Proud Possessors: The Lives, Times, and Tastes of Some Adventurous American Art Collectors. Random House 1958
SCPL

John Pierpont Morgan, 1837-1913

COLLECTIONS

Saarinen, Aline B. The Proud Possessors: The Lives, Times, and Tastes of Some Adventurous American Art Collectors. Random House 1958
SCPL

Potter Palmer, 1826-1902

COLLECTIONS

Saarinen, Aline B. The Proud Possessors: The Lives, Times, and Tastes of Some Adventurous American Art Collectors. Random House 1958
SCPL

Jacques Seligmann, 1858-1923

Seligman, Germain. Merchants of Art, 1880-1960: Eighty Years of Professional Collecting. Appleton 1962
Bkl A

American—20th century

Albert Coombs Barnes, 1872-1951

Hart, Henry. Dr. Barnes of Merion: An Appreciation. Farrar 1963
Bkl A–BY

Schack, William. Art and Argyrol: The Life and Career of Dr. Albert C. Barnes. Yoseloff 1960
Bkl A

COLLECTIONS

Cabanne, Pierre. The Great Collectors. Farrar 1963
Bkl A

Bernard Berenson, 1865-1959

Berenson, Bernard. The Selected Letters of [the author]; ed. by A. K. McComb. Houghton 1964
Bkl A

Etta Cone, 1870-1949

Pollack, Barbara. The Collectors: Dr. Claribel and Miss Etta Cone. Bobbs 1962
Bkl A

Katherine Sophie Dreier, 1877-1952

COLLECTIONS

Saarinen, Aline B. The Proud Possessors: The Lives, Times, and Tastes of Some Adventurous American Art Collectors. Random House 1958
SCPL

Marguerite Guggenheim, 1898-

COLLECTIONS

Cabanne, Pierre. The Great **Collectors**. Farrar 1963
Bkl A

ART COLLECTORS

American—20th century—*Continued*

Jacques Seligmann, 1858-1923

Seligman, Germain. Merchants of Art,
  1880-1960: Eighty Years of Professional
  Collecting. Appleton 1962
  Bkl A

Michael Stein, 1865-1938

COLLECTIONS

Saarinen, Aline B. The Proud Possessors:
  The Lives, Times, and Tastes of Some
  Adventurous American Art Collectors.
  Random House 1958
  SCPL

English—18th century

*Horace Walpole, 4th Earl of Orford,
1717-1797*

Walpole, Horace. Selected Letters of
  Horace Walpole. Dutton n.d.
  SCPL

English—19th century

Sir Richard Wallace, 1818-1890

COLLECTIONS

Cabanne, Pierre. The Great Collectors.
  Farrar 1963
  Bkl A

French—20th century

Georges Wildenstein, 1892-1963

COLLECTIONS

Cabanne, Pierre. The Great Collectors.
  Farrar 1963
  Bkl A

Russian—18th century

*Catherine II, Empress of Russia, 1729-
1796*

COLLECTIONS

Cabanne, Pierre. The Great Collectors.
  Farrar 1963
  Bkl A

ART CRITICS

See Critics

ART DEALERS

English—20th century

*Joseph Duveen, 1st Baron Duveen,
1869-1939*

Behrman, Samuel Nathaniel. Duveen.
  Random House 1952
  SCPL

ART TEACHERS

See Educators

ARTHRITIS VICTIMS

See Victims of Arthritis

ARTISTS

See also Architects; Art Collectors; Art
Dealers; Caricaturists; Cartoonists;
Dancers; Engravers; Etchers; Glass Paint-
ers and Stainers; Goldsmiths; Illustrators;
Industrial Designers; Painters; Photogra-
phers; Potters; Sculptors; Silversmiths

COLLECTIONS

Chase, Alice Elizabeth. Famous Artists of
  the Past. Platt 1964
  Bkl C(5-9)&Y—CC—ESLC—JH
Flanner, Janet. Men and Monuments.
  Harper 1957
  SCPL
  Georges Braque; André Malraux; Henri
  Matisse; Pablo Picasso
Mallett, Daniel Trowbridge. Mallett's In-
  dex of Artists, International-Biographi-
  cal: Including Painters, Sculptors, Illus-
  trators, Engravers and Etchers of the
  Past and the Present. Smith, P. 1948
  SCPL
Pater, Walter Horatio. Renaissance Stud-
  ies in Art and Poetry. Modern Lib.
  SCPL
  Joachim du Bellay; Sandro Botticelli; Michel-
  angelo Buonarroti; Count Giovanni Pico della
  Mirandola; Luca della Robbia; Leonardo da
  Vinci; Johann Joachim Winckelmann
Vasari, Giorgio. The Lives of the Painters,
  Sculptors and Architects; ed. by Wil-
  liam Gaunt. 4v. Dutton 1963
  SCPL

American

COLLECTIONS

Bailey, Carolyn Sherwin. Children of the
  Handcrafts. Viking 1935
  BBJH—CC(4-7)—ESLC
  John Chapman; Duncan Phyfe; Paul Revere;
  Henry David Thoreau
Kuh, Katharine. The Artist's Voice: Talks
  with Seventeen Artists. Harper 1962
  Bkl A&Y—SCPL
New-York Historical Society. New-York
  Historical Society's Dictionary of Artists
  in America, 1564-1860; comp. by
  George C. Groce and David H. Wal-
  lace. Yale Univ. 1957
  SCPL
Pearson, Ralph M. Modern Renaissance in
  American Art: Presenting the Work and
  Philosophy of 54 Distinguished Artists.
  Harper 1954
  SCPL

ARTISTS

American—*Continued*

Taft, Robert. Artists and Illustrators of the Old West, 1850-1900. Scribner 1953
SCPL

Who's Who in American Art. Am. Federation of Arts. First published 1935; triennial
SCPL

American—19th century

Samuel Finley Breese Morse, 1791-1872

Latham, Jean Lee. Samuel F. B. Morse, Artist-Inventor. Garrard 1961
AB(3-7)—ESLC

Mabee, F. C. American Leonardo: A Life of Samuel F. B. Morse. Knopf 1943
SCPL

Japanese

COLLECTIONS

Statler, Oliver. Modern Japanese Prints: An Art Reborn. Tuttle 1956
SCPL

Mexican

COLLECTIONS

Stewart, Virginia. 45 Contemporary Mexican Artists: A Twentieth-Century Renaissance. Stanford Univ. 1951
SCPL

ASSASSINS

See Criminals

ASTROBIOLOGISTS

See Biologists

ASTRONAUTS

See also Aviators; Engineers, Aeronautical

COLLECTIONS

Newlon, Clarke. Famous Pioneers in Space. Dodd 1963
Bkl C(7-9)&Y—IndS(9-12)

American

COLLECTIONS

Hoyt, Mary Finch. American Women of the Space Age. Atheneum 1966
Bkl C&Y

Poole, Lynn and Poole, Gray. Scientists Who Work with Astronauts. Dodd 1964
JH

Thomas, Shirley. Men of Space: Profiles of the Leaders in Space Research, Development, and Exploration. Chilton 1965
Bkl A&Y
Virgil Grissom; Andrew Haley; James Henry; Donald Putt; Edward Welsh

U.S. Congress. Senate. Committee on Aeronautical and Space Sciences. United States Astronauts. U.S. Govt. Printing Office 1963
ESLC

We Seven, by the Astronauts Themselves. Simon & Schuster 1962
Bkl A&Y—SCHS—SCPL
Malcolm Carpenter; Leroy Cooper; John Glenn; Virgil Grissom; Walter Marty Schirra; Alan Shepard; Donald Slayton

American—20th century

Malcolm Scott Carpenter, 1925-

COLLECTIONS

We Seven, by the Astronauts Themselves. Simon & Schuster 1962
Bkl A&Y—SCHS—SCPL

Leroy Gordon Cooper, 1927-

COLLECTIONS

We Seven, by the Astronauts Themselves. Simon & Schuster 1962
Bkl A&Y—SCHS—SCPL

John Herschel Glenn, 1921-

Pierce, Philip N. and Schuon, Karl. John H. Glenn, Astronaut. Watts 1962
Bkl A&Y&C

COLLECTIONS

We Seven, by the Astronauts Themselves. Simon & Schuster 1962
Bkl A&Y—SCHS—SCPL

Virgil Ivan Grissom, 1926-1967

COLLECTIONS

Thomas, Shirley. Men of Space: Profiles of the Leaders in Space Research, Development, and Exploration. Chilton 1965
Bkl A&Y

We Seven, by the Astronauts Themselves. Simon & Schuster 1962
Bkl A&Y—SCHS—SCPL

Walter Marty Schirra, 1923-

COLLECTIONS

We Seven, by the Astronauts Themselves. Simon & Schuster 1962
Bkl A&Y—SCHS—SCPL

Alan Bartlett Shepard, 1923-

COLLECTIONS

We Seven, by the Astronauts Themselves. Simon & Schuster 1962
Bkl A&Y—SCHS—SCPL

ASTRONAUTS

American—20th century—*Continued*

Donald Kent Slayton, 1924-

COLLECTIONS

We Seven, by the Astronauts Themselves. Simon & Schuster 1962
Bkl A&Y—SCHS—SCPL

Russian—20th century

German Stepanovich Titov, 1935-

Titov, German Stepanovich and Caidin, Martin. I Am Eagle! based on interviews with Wilfred Burchett and Anthony Purdy. Bobbs 1962
Bkl A&Y

ASTRONOMERS

COLLECTIONS

Ronan, Colin A. The Astronomers. Hill & Wang 1964
Bkl A&Y
Sullivan, Navin. Pioneer Astronomers. Atheneum 1964
AB(5up)—Bkl C(6-9)&Y—CC—ESLC

American—18th century

David Rittenhouse, 1732-1796

COLLECTIONS

Douty, Esther (Morris). Under the New Roof: Five Patriots of the Young Republic. Rand McNally 1965
Bkl C&Y

American—19th century

Nathaniel Bowditch, 1773-1838

Latham, Jean Lee. Carry On, Mr. Bowditch. Houghton 1955
BBEL(6-8)—BBJH—BY—CC(6-9)—ESLC—JH—SCHS

George Ellery Hale, 1868-1938

Woodbury, David O. The Glass Giant of Palomar. Dodd 1953
JH—SCHS
Wright, Helen. Explorer of the Universe: A Biography of George Ellery Hale. Dutton 1966
Bkl A&Y

Maria Mitchell, 1818-1889

Baker, Rachel (Mininberg) and Merlen, Joanna (Baker). America's First Woman Astronomer, Maria Mitchell. Messner 1960
Bkl C(5-8)
Wilkie, Katharine E. Maria Mitchell: Stargazer. Garrard 1966
ESLC

COLLECTIONS

Vance, Marguerite. The Lamp Lighters: Women in the Hall of Fame. Dutton 1960
Bkl C(7-9)&Y—SCHS—YR

American—20th century

Frank Donald Drake, 1930-

COLLECTIONS

Thomas, Shirley. Men of Space: v. 6, Profiles of Scientists Who Probe for Life in Space. Chilton 1963
Bkl A&Y

George Ellery Hale, 1868-1938

Woodbury, David O. The Glass Giant of Palomar. Dodd 1953
JH—SCHS
Wright, Helen. Explorer of the Universe: A Biography of George Ellery Hale. Dutton 1966
Bkl A&Y

German—17th century

Johann Kepler, 1571-1630

Knight, David C. Johannes Kepler & Planetary Motion. Watts 1963
Bkl C(7-9)&Y—ESLC
Koestler, Arthur. The Watershed: A Biography of Johannes Kepler. Doubleday 1960
BBHS—Bkl A&Y—3000
Land, Barbara. The Quest of Johannes Kepler, Astronomer. Doubleday 1963
AB(6up)—IndJ(6-9)
Rosen, Sidney. The Harmonious World of Johann Kepler. Little 1962
AB(7up)—Bkl C(7-9)&Y—CC(7-9)—JH—YR

Greek—6th century B.C.

Anaximander, 611-547 B.C.

COLLECTIONS

Jaspers, Karl. The Great Philosophers: v. 2, The Original Thinkers; ed. by Hannah Arendt; tr. by Ralph Manheim. Harcourt 1966
Bkl A

Italian—16th century

Galileo Galilei, 1564-1642

Brodrick, James. Galileo: The Man, His Work, His Misfortunes. Harper 1965
Bkl A&Y
Fermi, Laura and Bernardini, Gilberto. Galileo and the Scientific Revolution. Basic Bks 1961
BBHS—Bkl C&Y—JH

ASTRONOMERS

Italian—16th century

Galileo Galilei—Continued

Geymonat, Ludovico. Galileo Galilei: A
Biography and Inquiry into His Philosophy of Science; tr. from the Italian
by Stillman Drake. McGraw 1965
Bkl A

Gregor, Arthur S. Galileo. Scribner 1965
IndJ(4-6)

Horizon Magazine. The Universe of Galileo and Newton, by William Bixby
and Giorgio de Santillana. Am. Heritage 1964
AB(6-10)—Bkl C(7-9)—CC(5-9)—ESLC—
IndS(9-12)—JH—SCHS

Levinger, Elma Ehrlich. Galileo: First
Observer of Marvelous Things. Mess-
ner 1952
BBJH—BY—SCHS

Marcus, Rebecca B. Galileo and Experimental Science. Watts 1961
ESLC

Rosen, Sidney. Galileo and the Magic
Numbers. Little 1958
AB(7up)—BBEL(8)—BBJH—CC(7-9)—
ESLC—JH—SCHS

COLLECTIONS

Freedman, Russell. Teenagers Who Made
History. Holiday 1961
BY—JH—SCHS—YR

Thomas, Norman Mattoon. Great Dissenters. Norton 1961
Bkl A&Y

Italian—17th century

Galileo Galilei, 1564-1642

Brodrick, James. Galileo: The Man, His
Work, His Misfortunes. Harper 1965
Bkl A&Y

Fermi, Laura and Bernardini, Gilberto.
Galileo and the Scientific Revolution.
Basic Bks 1961
BBHS—Bkl C&Y—JH

Geymonat, Ludovico. Galileo Galilei: A
Biography and Inquiry into His Philosophy of Science; tr. from the Italian
by Stillman Drake. McGraw 1965
Bkl A

Gregor, Arthur S. Galileo. Scribner 1965
IndJ(4-6)

Horizon Magazine. The Universe of Galileo and Newton, by William Bixby and
Giorgio de Santillana. Am. Heritage
1964
AB(6-10)—BklC(7-9)—CC—ESLC—IndS(9-
12)—JH—SCHS

Levinger, Elma Ehrlich. Galileo: First
Observer of Marvelous Things. Mess-
ner 1952
BBJH—BY—SCHS

Marcus, Rebecca B. Galileo and Experimental Science. Watts 1961
ESLC

Rosen, Sidney. Galileo and the Magic
Numbers. Little 1958
AB(7up) — BBEL(8) — BBJH — CC(7-9) —
ESLC—JH—SCHS

COLLECTIONS

Thomas, Norman Mattoon. Great Dissenters. Norton 1961
Bkl A&Y

Polish—16th century

Nicolaus Copernicus, 1473-1543

Armitage, Angus. The World of Copernicus. New Am. Lib. 1947
GR

Kesten, Hermann. Copernicus and His
World. Roy 1945
SCPL

Knight, David C. Copernicus: Titan of
Modern Astronomy. Watts 1965
Bkl C&Y

Thomas, Henry. Copernicus. Messner
1960
Bkl C(7-10)&Y—ESLC—JH

ATHLETES

See also Archers; Baseball Players; Basketball Players; Boxers; Football Players;
Gladiators; Golfers; Mountaineers; Skaters; Skiers; Swimmers; Tennis Players;
Track Athletes and Field Athletes

COLLECTIONS

Gelman, Steve. Young Olympic Champions. Norton 1964
Bkl C(6-9)&Y—ESLC—JH
Cassius Clay; Sonja Henie; Johnny Weissmuller; and others

Heyn, Ernest Victor, ed. Twelve More
Sport Immortals. Putnam 1951
BBEL(6-8)—BBJH

American

COLLECTIONS

Bontemps, Arna. Famous Negro Athletes.
Dodd 1964
Bkl C&Y—ESLC—JH
Jimmy Brown; Wilton Norman Chamberlain;
Althea Gibson; Joe Louis; Willie Mays; Jesse
Owens; LeRoy Paige; John Roosevelt Robin-
son; Ray Robinson

Boynick, David King. Champions by Set-
back: Athletes Who Overcame Physi-
cal Handicaps. Crowell 1954
SCHS
William Bonthron; Charles Albert Boswell;
James J. Braddock; Glenn Cunningham; John
Hackett; Martin Whiteford Marion; Frank
Holten Norris; Hamilton Farrar Richardson;
Archie San Romani; George Monroe Woolf

ATHLETES

American—*Continued*

Durant, John. The Sports of Our Presidents. Hastings House 1964
ESLC

Famous American Athletes of Today: 13th-14th series. 2v. Page 1953-1956
SCPL

Gallico, Paul. The Golden People. Doubleday 1965
Bkl A&Y
Jack Dempsey; Knute Kenneth Rockne; George Herman Ruth; Johnny Weissmuller; Mildred (Didrikson) Zaharias; and others

Heuman, William. Famous American Athletes. Dodd 1963
Bkl C(7-12)&Y

Jacobs, Helen Hull. Famous American Women Athletes. Dodd 1964
ESLC—YR

Lindop, Edmund and Jares, Joseph. White House Sportsmen. Houghton 1965
ESLC

Pratt, John Lowell, ed. Sport, Sport, Sport: True Stories of Great Athletes and Great Human Beings. Watts 1960
AB(6up)—SCHS

Young, Andrew Sturgeon Nash. Negro Firsts in Sports. Johnson Pub. 1963
Bkl A&Y
John Arthur Johnson; Joe Louis; Jesse Owens; John Roosevelt Robinson; and others

American—20th century

Grantland Rice, 1880-1954

Rice, Grantland. The Tumult and the Shouting: My Life in the Sport. Barnes 1954
SCHS

James Francis Thorpe, 1888-1953

Heuman, William. The Indians of Carlisle. Putnam 1965
ESLC

Schoor, Gene. The Jim Thorpe Story: America's Greatest Athlete. Messner 1951
BBEL(7-8)—BBJH—BY—ESLC—JH—SCHS

Mildred (Didrikson) Zaharias, 1913-1956

De Grummond, Lena Young and Delaune, Lynne (de Grummond). Babe Didrikson. Bobbs 1963
AB(4-7)

Zaharias, Mildred (Didrikson) and Paxton, Harry T. This Life I've Led: My Autobiography. Barnes 1955
BY—SCPL

COLLECTIONS

Freedman, Russell. Teenagers Who Made History. Holiday 1961
BY—JH—SCHS—YR

Gallico, Paul. The Golden People. Doubleday 1965
Bkl A&Y

Higdon, Hal. Heroes of the Olympics. Prentice-Hall 1965
ESLC

ATTORNEYS

See Lawyers

AUCTIONEERS

American—20th century

Emma Bailey, ?

Bailey, Emma. Sold to the Lady in the Green Hat. Dodd 1962
Bkl A

AUNTS OF FAMOUS MEN

See Relatives of Famous Men

AUTHORS

See also Critics; Essayists; Folklorists; Historians; Humorists; Journalists; Lexicographers; Novelists; Philosophers; Playwrights; Poets; Satirists; Sportswriters

COLLECTIONS

Breit, Harvey. The Writer Observed. World 1956
SCPL

Brooks, Cleanth. The Hidden God: Studies in Hemingway, Faulkner, Yeats, Eliot, and Warren. Yale Univ. 1963
Bkl A
Thomas Stearns Eliot; William Faulkner; Ernest Hemingway; Robert Penn Warren; William Butler Yeats

Coffman, Ramon Peyton and Goodman, Nathan. Famous Authors for Young People. Dodd 1943
BBJH—JH—SCHS

Contemporary Authors: The International Bio-bibliographical Guide to Current Authors and Their Works. Quarterly, first published 1962. Gale Res.
SCPL

Dunaway, Philip and Evans, Mel, eds. Treasury of the World's Great Diaries. Doubleday 1957
SCPL

Fuller, Muriel, ed. More Junior Authors. Wilson 1963
Bkl C&Y—CC—ESLC—JH—SCHS—SCPL

Hoehn, Matthew, ed. Catholic Authors· Contemporary Biographical Sketches, 1930-1947. St. Mary's Abbey 1957
SCPL

AUTHORS—*Continued*

Hoff, Rhoda. Why They Wrote. Walck 1961
Bkl C(7-10)&Y—SCHS
Samuel Langhorne Clemens; Charles Dickens; Gustave Flaubert; Robert Louis Stevenson; Henry David Thoreau

Kunitz, Stanley Jasspon and Haycraft, Howard, eds. The Junior Book of Authors. Wilson 1951
BBEL—BBJH—CC—ESLC—JH—SCHS—SCPL

Kunitz, Stanley Jasspon and Haycraft, Howard, eds. Twentieth Century Authors: A Biographical Dictionary of Modern Literature. Wilson 1942
BBHS—BBJH—JH—SCHS—SCPL

Kunitz, Stanley Jasspon and Colby, Vineta, eds. Twentieth Century Authors: First Supplement: A Biographical Dictionary of Modern Literature. Wilson 1955
BBHS—JH—SCHS—SCPL

Ludovici, L. J., ed. Nobel Prize Winners. Associated Booksellers 1957
SCHS

Magill, Frank Northen, ed. Cyclopedia of World Authors. 4v. Harper 1958-1962
BBHS—SCPL

Montgomery, Elizabeth Rider. The Story Behind Great Books. Dodd 1946
BBEL(5-8)—BBJH—ESLC—SCHS

Montgomery, Elizabeth Rider. The Story Behind Great Stories. Dodd 1947
BBEL(5-8)—BBJH—SCHS

Montgomery, Elizabeth Rider. The Story Behind Modern Books. Dodd 1949
BBEL(5-8)—BBJH—SCHS

Paris Review. Writers at Work: The Paris Review Interviews; ed. by Malcolm Cowley. Viking 1958
SCPL

Paris Review. Writers at Work: The Paris Review Interviews; 2d series. Viking 1963
Bkl A—IndS(12)—SCHS—SCPL

Saturday Review. The Saturday Review Gallery; comp. by Jerome Beatty. Simon & Schuster 1959
SCPL

Stirling, Nora B. Who Wrote the Classics? Day 1965
Bkl A&C&Y
Jane Austen; Charlotte Brontë; Samuel Langhorne Clemens; Charles Dickens; Nathaniel Hawthorne; Rudyard Kipling; Edgar Allan Poe; William Shakespeare; Robert Louis Stevenson; Jules Verne

Ward, Martha E. and Marquardt, Dorothy A. Authors of Books for Young People. Scarecrow 1964
ESLC

Wilson, Edmund. Axel's Castle: A Study in the Imaginative Literature of 1870-1930. Scribner 1931
SCPL
Thomas Stearns Eliot; James Joyce; Marcel Proust; Jean Nicolas Arthur Rimbaud; Gertrude Stein; Paul Ambroise Valéry; William Butler Yeats

Woolf, Virginia (Stephen). Contemporary Writers. Harcourt 1966
Bkl A

American

COLLECTIONS

Arvin, Newton. American Pantheon; ed. by Daniel Aaron and Sylvan Schendler. Delacorte 1966
Bkl A&Y
George Washington Cable; Ralph Waldo Emerson; Hamlin Garland; Nathaniel Hawthorne; William Dean Howells; Herman Melville; James Whitcomb Riley; Henry David Thoreau; Walt Whitman; and others

Bolton, Sarah (Knowles). Famous American Authors; rev. by William Fahey. Crowell 1954
BBJH—CC(7-9)—JH—SCHS—SCPL—YR

Burke, William Jeremiah and Howe, Will D. American Authors and Books: 1640 to the Present Day; rev. by Irving R. Weiss. Crown 1962
Bkl A&Y—SCPL

Canby, Henry Seidel. Classic Americans: A Study of Eminent American Writers from Irving to Whitman. Russell & Russell 1959
SCPL
James Fenimore Cooper; Ralph Waldo Emerson; Nathaniel Hawthorne; Washington Irving; Herman Melville; Edgar Allan Poe; Henry David Thoreau; Walt Whitman

Cantwell, Robert. Famous American Men of Letters. Dodd 1956
BBHS—BBJH—JH—SCHS—YR

Harriman, Margaret (Case). Vicious Circle: The Story of the Algonquin Round Table. Rinehart 1951
SCPL

Helmstadter, Frances. Picture Book of American Authors. Sterling 1962
AB(6up)

Kunitz, Stanley Jasspon and Haycraft, Howard, eds. American Authors, 1600-1900: A Biographical Dictionary of American Literature. Wilson 1938
BBHS—JH—SCHS—SCPL

Levin, Harry. Power of Blackness: Hawthorne, Poe, Melville. Knopf 1958
SCPL

Littlejohn, David. Black on White: A Critical Survey of Writing by American Negroes. Grossman 1966
Bkl A

AUTHORS

American—*Continued*

Morgan, Howard Wayne. Writers in Transition: Seven Americans. Hill & Wang 1963
Bkl A
Sherwood Anderson; Willa Cather; Hart Crane; Stephen Crane; Ellen Glasgow; Edith Wharton; Thomas Wolfe

Muir, Jane. Famous Modern American Women Writers. Dodd 1959
SCHS—YR

Scherman, David Edward and Redlich, Rosemarie. America: The Land and Its Writers. Dodd 1956
BBJH

American—18th century

Benjamin Franklin, 1706-1790

Amacher, Richard E. Benjamin Franklin. Twayne 1962
Bkl A&Y

Franklin, Benjamin. Autobiographical Writings; ed. by Carl Van Doren. Viking 1945
SCPL

Franklin, Benjamin. Autobiography. Univ. of Calif.; Modern Lib.; Houghton; Harper; Dutton; etc.
BY—CA—CC(7-9)—GR—SCHS—SCPL—3000

Franklin, Benjamin. The Autobiography, and Other Writings of Benjamin Franklin. Dodd 1963
SCHS

Franklin, Benjamin. The Autobiography of Benjamin Franklin; ed. by Leonard W. Labaree and others. Yale Univ. 1964
JH—SCPL

Franklin, Benjamin. The Benjamin Franklin Papers; ed. by Frank Donovan. Dodd 1962
Bkl A&Y—SCHS

Thomas Paine, 1737-1809

Aldridge, Alfred Owen. Man of Reason: The Life of Thomas Paine. Lippincott 1959
SCPL

Brett, Grace Neff. The Picture Story and Biography of Tom Paine. Follett 1965
ESLC

Gurko, Leo. Tom Paine, Freedom's Apostle. Crowell 1957
AB(7-10)—BBHS—BBJH—CC(7-9)—JH—SCHS—YR

McKown, Robin. Thomas Paine. Putnam 1962
AB(6-9)—Bkl C(6-9)

Woodward, William E. Tom Paine: America's Godfather, 1737-1809. Dutton 1945
SCPL

COLLECTIONS

McNeer, May Yonge and Ward, Lynd Kendall. Give Me Freedom. Abingdon 1964
Bkl C(5-8)—CC(5-7)—ESLC—JH—YR

American—19th century

Louisa May Alcott, 1832-1888

Meigs, Cornelia Lynde. Invincible Louisa. Little 1933
AB(5-9)—BBEL(7-8)—BBHS—BBJH—CC—ESLC—JH—SCHS—SCPL—YR

Papashvily, Helen (Waite). Louisa May Alcott. Houghton 1965
Bkl C(4-7)—CC(4-7)—ESLC—IndJ(4-6)

Peare, Catherine Owens. Louisa May Alcott: Her Life. Holt 1954
BBEL—CC(4-6)

Stern, Madeleine Bettina. Louisa May Alcott. Univ. of Okla. 1950
SCPL

Thomas Bailey Aldrich, 1836-1907

Samuels, Charles E. Thomas Bailey Aldrich. Twayne 1966
Bkl A

Horatio Alger, 1832-1899

Gardner, Ralph D. Horatio Alger: Or, The American Hero Era. Wayside 1964
Bkl A

Tebbel, John William. From Rags to Riches: Horatio Alger, Jr. and the American Dream. Macmillan 1964
Bkl A

James Lane Allen, 1849-1925

Bottorff, William K. James Lane Allen. Twayne 1964
Bkl A

Delia Salter Bacon, 1811-1859

Hopkins, Vivian Constance. Prodigal Puritan: A Life of Delia Bacon. Harvard Univ. 1959
Bkl A

COLLECTIONS

Bacon, Martha Sherman. Puritan Promenade. Houghton 1964
Bkl A&Y—IndS(9-12)

Edward Bellamy, 1850-1898

Bowman, Sylvia E. and others. Edward Bellamy Abroad: An American Prophet's Influence. Twayne 1962
Bkl A

Morgan, Arthur Ernest. Edward Bellamy. Columbia Univ. 1944
SCPL

Ambrose Bierce, 1842-1914?

Woodruff, Stuart C. The Short Stories of Ambrose Bierce: A Study in Polarity. Univ. of Pittsburgh 1965
Bkl A

AUTHORS

American—19th century—Continued

John Ross Browne, 1821-1875

Dillon, Richard H. J. Ross Browne, Confidential Agent in Old California. Univ. of Okla. 1965
Bkl A

Frances Hodgson Burnett, 1849-1924

Burnett, Constance (Buel). Happily Ever After: A Portrait of Frances Hodgson Burnett. Vanguard 1965
Bkl C(6-8)—ESLC

John Burroughs, 1837-1921

Swift, Hildegarde (Hoyt). The Edge of April: A Biography of John Burroughs. Morrow 1957
AB(7-10)—BBEL(7-8)—BBJH—CC(7-9)—ESLC—JH—SCHS

Stephen Crane, 1871-1900

Berryman, John. Stephen Crane. Sloane 1950
SCPL

Cady, Edwin Harrison. Stephen Crane. Twayne 1962
SCHS

Franchere, Ruth. Stephen Crane: The Story of an American Writer. Crowell 1961
Bkl Y&C—SCHS—YR

Hoffman, Daniel Gerard. Poetry of Stephen Crane. Columbia Univ. 1957
SCPL

Zara, Louis. Dark Rider: A Novel Based on the Life of Stephen Crane. World 1961 (Fiction)
Bkl A

COLLECTIONS

Geismar, Maxwell David. Rebels and Ancestors: The American Novel, 1890-1915. Houghton 1953
SCPL

Morgan, Howard Wayne. Writers in Transition: Seven Americans. Hill & Wang 1963
Bkl A

Schneider, Robert W. Five Novelists of the Progressive Era. Columbia Univ. 1965
Bkl A

Richard Henry Dana, 1815-1882

Dana, Richard Henry. Two Years before the Mast. Dodd; Macmillan; Modern Lib.; World; etc.
BBHS—BY—GR—SCHS—SCPL

Frederick Douglass, 1817-1895

Bontemps, Arna. Frederick Douglass: Slave—Fighter—Freeman. Knopf 1959
CC(4-7)—ESLC—JH

Douglass, Frederick. Life and Times of Frederick Douglass; adapted by Barbara Ritchie. Crowell 1966
Bkl Y&C—ESLC

Graham, Shirley. There Was Once a Slave: The Heroic Story of Frederick Douglass. Messner 1947
SCHS—YR

Patterson, Lillie. Frederick Douglass. Garrard 1965
AB(3-7)—ESLC

COLLECTIONS

Bontemps, Arna. 100 Years of Negro Freedom. Dodd 1961
Bkl A—ESLC—SCPL

Ralph Waldo Emerson, 1803-1882

Emerson, Ralph Waldo and Carlyle, Thomas. The Correspondence of [the authors]; ed. by Joseph Slater. Columbia Univ. 1964
Bkl A

Emerson, Ralph Waldo. Heart of Emerson's Journals; ed. by Bliss Perry. Houghton 1926
SCPL

Rusk, Ralph Leslie. Life of Ralph Waldo Emerson. Columbia Univ. 1957
3000

Wood, James Playsted. Trust Thyself: A Life of Ralph Waldo Emerson for the Young Reader. Pantheon 1964
Bkl C(7-9)&Y

COLLECTIONS

Arvin, Newton. American Pantheon; ed. by Daniel Aaron and Sylvan Schendler. Delacorte 1966
Bkl A&Y

Canby, Henry Seidel. Classic Americans: A Study of Eminent American Writers from Irving to Whitman. Russell & Russell 1959
SCPL

Van Wesep, H. B. Seven Sages: The Story of American Philosophy. Longmans 1960
SCPL

James Thomas Fields, 1816-1881

Tryon, Warren Stenson. Parnassus Corner: A Life of James T. Fields, Publisher to the Victorians. Houghton 1963
Bkl A—IndS(12)

Hamlin Garland, 1860-1940

Garland, Hamlin. A Son of the Middle Border. Macmillan 1917
BBHS—GR—SCHS

AUTHORS

American—19th century

Hamlin Garland—Continued

COLLECTIONS

Arvin, Newton. American Pantheon; ed. by Daniel Aaron and Sylvan Schendler. Delacorte 1966
Bkl A&Y

Morgan, Howard Wayne. American Writers in Rebellion, from Mark Twain to Dreiser. Hill & Wang 1965
Bkl A&Y

Sarah Josepha (Buell) Hale, 1788-1879

Burt, Olive. First Woman Editor: Sarah J. Hale. Messner 1960
Bkl C(7-10)&Y—SCHS—YR

Bret Harte, 1836-1902

Harlowe, Alvin F. Bret Harte of the Old West. Messner 1943
YR

O'Connor, Richard. Bret Harte: A Biography. Little 1966
Bkl A&Y

Lafcadio Hearn, 1850-1904

Stevenson, Elizabeth. Lafcadio Hearn. Macmillan 1961
Bkl A

Thomas Wentworth Higginson, 1823-1911

Wells, Anna Mary. Dear Preceptor: The Life and Times of Thomas Wentworth Higginson. Houghton 1963
Bkl A

Oliver Wendell Holmes, 1809-1894

Tilton, Eleanor Marguerite. Amiable Autocrat: A Biography of Dr. Oliver Wendell Holmes. Schuman 1947
SCPL

Julia Ward Howe, 1819-1910

Tharp, Louise (Hall). Three Saints and a Sinner: Julia Ward Howe, Louisa, Annie, and Sam Ward. Little 1956
SCHS—SCPL

COLLECTIONS

Daugherty, Sonia. Ten Brave Women. Lippincott 1953
BY—CC(7-9)—ESLC—JH—SCHS

Mark Antony De Wolfe Howe, 1864-1960

Howe, Helen Huntington. The Gentle Americans, 1864-1960. Harper 1965
Bkl A

William Dean Howells, 1837-1920

Brooks, Van Wyck. Howells: His Life and World. Dutton 1959
SCPL

Howells, William Dean. Mark Twain-Howells Letters: The Correspondence, 1872-1910; ed. by Henry Nash Smith and others. 2v. Harvard Univ. 1960
Bkl A

Kirk, Clara (Marburg). W. D. Howells and Art in His Time. Rutgers Univ. 1965
Bkl A

COLLECTIONS

Arvin, Newton. American Pantheon; ed. by Daniel Aaron and Sylvan Schendler. Delacorte 1966
Bkl A&Y

Morgan, Howard Wayne. American Writers in Rebellion, from Mark Twain to Dreiser. Hill & Wang 1965
Bkl A&Y

Schneider, Robert W. Five Novelists of the Progressive Era. Columbia Univ. 1965
Bkl A

Washington Irving, 1783-1859

Benét, Laura. Washington Irving, Explorer of American Legend. Dodd 1944
CC(7-9)—JH—SCHS—YR

Peare, Catherine Owens. Washington Irving: His Life. Holt 1957
CC(4-6)

Seton, Anya. Washington Irving. Houghton 1960
Bkl Y&C(7-9)—JH

Wagenknecht, Edward Charles. Washington Irving. Oxford 1962
BY

COLLECTIONS

Canby, Henry Seidel. Classic Americans: A Study of Eminent American Writers from Irving to Whitman. Russell & Russell 1959
SCPL

Sarah Orne Jewett, 1849-1909

Cary, Richard. Sarah Orne Jewett. Twayne 1962
Bkl A

COLLECTIONS

Auchincloss, Louis. Pioneers and Caretakers: A Study of Nine American Women Novelists. Univ. of Minn. 1965
Bkl A&Y

Edgar Allan Poe, 1809-1849

Allen, Hervey. Israfel: The Life and Times of Edgar Allan Poe. Rinehart 1949
SCPL

AUTHORS

American—19th century

Edgar Allan Poe—Continued

Benét, Laura. Young Edgar Allan Poe. Dodd 1941
CC(8-9)—JH—SCHS—SCPL

Bittner, William Robert. Poe: A Biography. Little 1962
Bkl A&Y

Buranelli, Vincent. Edgar Allan Poe. Twayne 1961
Bkl A&Y

Davidson, E. H. Poe: A Critical Study. Harvard Univ. 1957
SCPL

Miller, Perry Gilbert Eddy. Raven and the Whale: The War of Words and Wits in the Era of Poe and Melville. Harcourt 1956
SCPL

Porges, Irwin. Edgar Allan Poe. Chilton 1963
Bkl Y&C

Quinn, Arthur Hobson. Edgar Allan Poe: A Critical Biography. Appleton 1941
3000

Wagenknecht, Edward. Edgar Allan Poe: The Man behind the Legend. Oxford 1963
Bkl A—SCHS—SCPL

Winwar, Frances. Haunted Palace: A Life of Edgar Allan Poe. Harper 1959
BBHS—SCHS—SCPL

COLLECTIONS

Canby, Henry Seidel. Classic Americans: A Study of Eminent American Writers from Irving to Whitman. Russell & Russell 1959
SCPL

Stirling, Nora B. Who Wrote the Classics? Day 1965
Bkl Y&A&C

William Sydney Porter, 1862-1910

Arnett, Ethel Stephens. O. Henry from Polecat Creek: A Memorial Edition for William Sydney Porter, Published on the Occasion of His Hundredth Birthday. Piedmont Press 1962
Bkl A

Current-García, Eugene. O. Henry (William Sidney Porter). Twayne 1965
Bkl A&Y

Nolan, Jeannette Covert. O. Henry: The Story of William Sydney Porter. Messner 1943
SCHS—YR

Ernest Thompson Seton, 1860-1946

Garst, Doris Shannon and Garst, Warren. Ernest Thompson Seton, Naturalist. Messner 1959
JH—YR

Lydia Howard (Huntley) Sigourney, 1791-1865

COLLECTIONS

Bacon, Martha Sherman. Puritan Promenade. Houghton 1964
Bkl A&Y—IndS(9-12)

Henry David Thoreau, 1817-1862

Derleth, August. Concord Rebel: A Life of Henry D. Thoreau. Chilton 1962
Bkl A&Y—BY—SCHS

Harding, Walter Roy. The Days of Henry Thoreau. Knopf 1965
Bkl A&Y—IndS(12)

Krutch, Joseph Wood. Henry David Thoreau. Sloane 1948
SCPL

Longstreth, T. Morris. Henry Thoreau, American Rebel. Dodd 1963
AB(6-11)

Meltzer, Milton and Harding, Walter Roy, eds. A Thoreau Profile. Crowell 1962
Bkl A&Y—IndS(11-12)

Norman, Charles. To a Different Drum: The Story of Henry David Thoreau. Harper 1954
SCHS

North, Sterling. Thoreau of Walden Pond. Houghton 1959
CC(6-7)

Thoreau, Henry David. Consciousness in Concord: The Text of Thoreau's Hitherto "Lost Journal" (1840-1841); ed. by Perry Miller. Houghton 1958
SCPL

Van Doren, Mark. Henry David Thoreau: A Critical Study. Russell & Russell 1961
SCPL

Wood, James Playsted. A Hound, a Bay Horse, and a Turtle-Dove: A Life of Thoreau for the Young Reader. Pantheon 1963
Bkl Y&C

COLLECTIONS

Arvin, Newton. American Pantheon; ed. by Daniel Aaron and Sylvan Schendler. Delacorte 1966
Bkl A&Y

Canby, Henry Seidel. Classic Americans: A Study of Eminent American Writers from Irving to Whitman. Russell & Russell 1959
SCPL

Hoff, Rhoda. Why They Wrote. Walck 1961
Bkl C(7-10)&Y—SCHS

Schechter, Betty. The Peaceable Revolution. Houghton 1963
CC(8-9)—ESLC—JH

AUTHORS

American—19th century—*Continued*

Kate Douglas (Smith) Wiggin, 1856-1923

Mason, Miriam E. Kate Douglas Wiggin. Bobbs 1958
AB(4-7)

Mason, Miriam E. Yours with Love, Kate. Houghton 1952
CC(7-9)–JH

Constance Fenimore Woolson, 1840-1894

Moore, Rayburn S. Constance Fenimore Woolson. Twayne 1963
Bkl A

American—20th century

James Agee, 1909-1955

Agee, James. Letters of James Agee to Father Flye. Braziller 1962
Bkl A–SCPL

Sherwood Anderson, 1876-1941

White, Ray Lewis, ed. The Achievement of Sherwood Anderson: Essays in Criticism. Univ. of N.C. 1966
Bkl A

COLLECTIONS

Geismar, Maxwell David. Last of the Provincials: The American Novel, 1915-1925. Houghton 1947
SCPL

Morgan, Howard Wayne. Writers in Transition: Seven Americans. Hill & Wang 1963
Bkl A

Mary Antin, 1881-1949

Antin, Mary. Promised Land. Houghton 1912
SCPL

Mary (Hunter) Austin, 1868-1934

Pearce, Thomas Matthews. Mary Hunter Austin. Twayne 1966
Bkl A

Stephen Vincent Benét, 1898-1943

Fenton, Charles A. Stephen Vincent Benét: The Life and Times of an American Man of Letters, 1898-1943. Yale Univ. 1958
SCPL

Stroud, Parry. Stephen Vincent Benét. Twayne 1963
SCHS

COLLECTIONS

Brenner, Rica. Poets of Our Time. Harcourt 1941
SCHS–SCPL

Bernard Berenson, 1865-1959

Berenson, Bernard. The Bernard Berenson Treasury; ed. by Hanna Kiel. Simon & Schuster 1962
Bkl A

Berenson, Bernard. Conversations with Berenson, by Umberto Morra; tr. from the Italian by Florence Hammond. Houghton 1965
Bkl A–IndS(12)

Berenson, Bernard. One Year's Reading for Fun. Knopf 1960
SCPL

Berenson, Bernard. The Passionate Sightseer: From the Diaries, 1947 to 1956. Simon & Schuster 1960
Bkl A

Berenson, Bernard. Rumor and Reflection. Simon & Schuster 1952
SCPL

Berenson, Bernard. The Selected Letters of [the author]; ed. by A. K. McComb. Houghton 1964
Bkl A

Berenson, Bernard. Sunset and Twilight: From the Diaries of 1947-1958; ed. by Nicky Mariano. Harcourt 1963
Bkl A–SCPL

Sprigge, Sylvia (Saunders). Berenson: A Biography. Houghton 1960
Bkl A–SCPL

Thyra (Ferré) Bjorn, 1905-

Bjorn, Thyra (Ferré). This Is My Life. Holt 1966
Bkl A

Catherine (Drinker) Bowen, 1897-

Bowen, Catherine (Drinker). Adventures of a Biographer. Little 1959
BBHS–SCPL

Claude Gernade Bowers, 1878-1958

Bowers, Claude Gernade. My Life: The Memoirs of Claude Bowers. Simon & Schuster 1962
Bkl A

Elizabeth Bowne, ?

Bowne, Elizabeth. Gift from the African Heart. Dodd 1961
Bkl A

Gladys Rice (Billings) Brooks, ?

Brooks, Gladys Rice (Billings). Boston and Return. Atheneum 1962
Bkl A–BY

Van Wyck Brooks, 1886-1963

Brooks, Van Wyck. An Autobiography. Dutton 1965
Bkl A

AUTHORS

American—20th century

Van Wyck Brooks—Continued

Brooks, Van Wyck. Days of the Phoenix: The Nineteen-Twenties I Remember. Dutton 1957
SCPL

Brooks, Van Wyck. From the Shadow of the Mountain: My Post-Meridian Years. Dutton 1961
Bkl A

Brooks, Van Wyck. Scenes and Portraits: Memories of Childhood and Youth. Dutton 1954
SCPL

Thornton Waldo Burgess, 1874-1965

Burgess, Thorton Waldo. Now I Remember: The Autobiography of an Amateur Naturalist. Little 1960
Bkl A—BY

James Branch Cabell, 1879-1958

Cabell, James Branch. Between Friends: Letters; ed. by Padraic Colum and Margaret Freeman Cabell. Harcourt 1962
Bkl A

Erskine Caldwell, 1903-

COLLECTIONS

Beach, Joseph Warren. American Fiction, 1920-1940. Russell & Russell 1960
SCPL

Fay G. Calkins, 1921-

Calkins, Fay G. My Samoan Chief. Doubleday 1962
Bkl A&Y—BY

Whittaker Chambers, 1901-1961

Chambers, Whittaker. Cold Friday; ed. by Duncan Norton-Taylor. Random House 1964
Bkl A

Chambers, Whittaker. Witness. Random House 1952
SCPL

Cooke, Alistair. Generation on Trial: U.S.A. v. Alger Hiss. Knopf 1952
SCPL

Zeligs, Meyer A. Friendship and Fratricide: An Analysis of Whittaker Chambers and Alger Hiss. Viking 1966
Bkl A

John Jay Chapman, 1862-1933

Bernstein, Melvin Herbert. John Jay Chapman. Twayne 1964
Bkl A

Hovey, Richard Bennett. John Jay Chapman: An American Mind. Columbia Univ. 1959
Bkl A

Olive (Ewing) Clapper, 1896-

Clapper, Olive (Ewing). One Lucky Woman. Doubleday 1961
Bkl A

Edward Estlin Cummings, 1894-1962

Friedman, Norman. E. E. Cummings: The Growth of a Writer. Southern Ill. Univ. 1964
Bkl A

Norman, Charles. E. E. Cummings: The Magic-Maker. Duell 1964
IndS(11-12)

Borghild Margarethe Dahl, 1890-

Dahl, Borghild Margarethe. Finding My Way. Dutton 1962
Bkl Y—YR

Dahl, Borghild Margarethe. I Wanted to See. Macmillan 1944
SCHS

Edward Dahlberg, 1900-

Dahlberg, Edward. Because I Was Flesh: The Autobiography. New Directions 1964
Bkl A

Paul Henry De Kruif, 1890-

De Kruif, Paul Henry. Life Among the Doctors. Harcourt 1949
SCPL

De Kruif, Paul Henry. The Sweeping Wind: A Memoir. Harcourt 1962
Bkl A

August William Derleth, 1909-

Derleth, August William. Countryman's Journal. Duell 1963
Bkl A

Derleth, August William. Walden West. Duell 1961
Bkl A

Bernard Augustine De Voto, 1897-1955

Four Portraits and One Subject: Bernard De Voto. Houghton 1963
Bkl A

Hildegarde Dolson, ?

Dolson, Hildegarde. We Shook the Family Tree. Random House 1941
BY

Thomas Anthony Dooley, 1927-1961

Dooley, Agnes (Wise). Promises to Keep: The Life of Dr. Thomas A. Dooley. Farrar 1962
Bkl A&Y—BY—SCHS—SCPL

Dooley, Thomas Anthony. Deliver Us from Evil: The Story of Viet Nam's Flight to Freedom. Farrar 1956
SCHS

AUTHORS

American—20th century

Thomas Anthony Dooley—Continued

Dooley, Thomas Anthony. Dr. Tom Dooley: My Story. Ariel Bks 1962
CC(6-7)—ESLC—JH—SCHS

Dooley, Thomas Anthony. Dr. Tom Dooley's Three Great Books: Deliver Us from Evil, The Edge of Tomorrow, The Night They Burned the Mountain. Farrar 1960
BBHS—SCHS—SCPL

Dooley, Thomas Anthony. Edge of Tomorrow. Farrar 1958
SCHS—SCPL

Dooley, Thomas Anthony. The Night They Burned the Mountain. Farrar 1960
Bkl A&Y—SCHS—SCPL

Gallagher, Teresa. Give Joy to My Youth: A Memoir of Dr. Tom Dooley. Farrar 1965
Bkl A&Y

Monahan, James, ed. Before I Sleep . . . The Last Days of Dr. Tom Dooley. Farrar 1961
Bkl A&Y—BY—SCHS—SCPL

Morris, Terry. Doctor America: The Story of Tom Dooley. Hawthorn 1963
IndJ(6-9)

John Roderigo Dos Passos, 1896-

COLLECTIONS

Beach, Joseph Warren. American Fiction, 1920-1940. Russell & Russell 1960
SCPL

Geismar, Maxwell David. Writers in Crisis: The American Novel between Two Wars. Houghton 1942
SCPL

Frank Dufresne, 1896-1966

Dufresne, Frank. My Way Was North: An Alaskan Autobiography. Holt 1966
Bkl A&Y

John Erskine, 1879-1951

Erskine, John. My Life in Music. Morrow 1950
SCPL

Negley Farson, 1890-1960

Farson, Negley. Mirror for Narcissus. Doubleday 1957
SCPL

Howard Melvin Fast, 1914-

Fast, Howard Melvin. Naked God: The Writer and the Communist Party. Praeger 1957
SCPL

Hamlin Garland, 1860-1940

Garland, Hamlin. A Son of the Middle Border. Macmillan 1917
BBHS—GR—SCHS

COLLECTIONS

Arvin, Newton. American Pantheon; ed. by Daniel Aaron and Sylvan Schendler. Delacorte 1966
Bkl A&Y

Morgan, Howard Wayne. American Writers in Rebellion, from Mark Twain to Dreiser. Hill & Wang 1965
Bkl A&Y

Ferris Greenslet, 1875-1959

Greenslet, Ferris. Under the Bridge: An Autobiography. Houghton 1943
SCPL

Alfred Bertram Guthrie, 1901-

Guthrie, Alfred Bertram. The Blue Hen's Chick. McGraw 1965
Bkl A—IndS(11-12)

Hermann Hagedorn, 1882-1964

Hagedorn, Hermann. The Hyphenated Family: An American Saga. Macmillan 1960
Bkl A&Y—SCPL

James Norman Hall, 1887-1951

Briand, Paul L. In Search of Paradise: The Nordhoff-Hall Story. Duell 1966
Bkl A&Y

Hall, James Norman. My Island Home: An Autobiography. Little 1952
SCPL

Richard Halliburton, 1900-1939

Root, Jonathan. Halliburton, the Magnificent Myth: A Biography. Coward-McCann 1965
Bkl A

Mark Harris, 1922-

Harris, Mark. Twentyone Twice: A Journal. Little 1966
Bkl A

Ben Hecht, 1893-1964

Hecht, Ben. Child of the Century. Simon & Schuster 1954
GR—SCPL

Hecht, Ben. Letters from Bohemia. Doubleday 1964
Bkl A

Granville Hicks, 1901-

Hicks, Granville. Part of the Truth. Harcourt 1965
Bkl A

Abigail (Adams) Homans, 1879?-

Homans, Abigail (Adams). Education by Uncles. Houghton 1966
Bkl A&Y

AUTHORS

American—20th century—*Continued*

Mark Antony De Wolfe Howe, 1864-1960

Howe, Helen Huntington. The Gentle Americans, 1864-1960. Harper 1965
Bkl A

William Dean Howells, 1837-1920

Brooks, Van Wyck. Howells: His Life and World. Dutton 1959
SCPL

Howells, William Dean. Mark Twain-Howells Letters: The Correspondence, 1872-1910; ed. by Henry Nash Smith and others. 2v. Harvard Univ. 1960
Bkl A

Kirk, Clara (Marburg). W. D. Howells and Art in His Time. Rutgers Univ. 1965
Bkl A

COLLECTIONS

Arvin, Newton. American Pantheon; ed. by Daniel Aaron and Sylvan Schendler. Delacorte 1966
Bkl A&Y

Morgan, Howard Wayne. American Writers in Rebellion, from Mark Twain to Dreiser. Hill & Wang 1965
Bkl A&Y

Schneider, Robert W. Five Novelists of the Progressive Era. Columbia Univ. 1965
Bkl A

Langston Hughes, 1902-1967

Hughes, Langston. I Wonder as I Wander: An Autobiographical Journey. Rinehart 1956
SCPL

Will James, 1892-1942

James, Will. Lone Cowboy: My Life Story. Scribner 1930
BY—JH—SCHS—SCPL—YR

James Weldon Johnson, 1871-1938

COLLECTIONS

Sterling, Dorothy and Quarles, Benjamin. Lift Every Voice. Doubleday 1965
Bkl C(6-9)&Y—ESLC

Nunnally Johnson, 1897-

COLLECTIONS

Martin, Thornton. Pete Martin Calls on . . . . Simon & Schuster 1962
Bkl A

Paul Jordan-Smith, 1885-

Jordan-Smith, Paul. The Road I Came: Some Recollections and Reflections Concerning Changes in American Life and Manners since 1890. Caxton 1960
Bkl A

Matthew Josephson, 1899-

Josephson, Matthew. Life among the Surrealists: A Memoir. Holt 1962
Bkl A

Helen Adams Keller, 1880-1968

Brooks, Van Wyck. Helen Keller: Sketch for a Portrait. Dutton 1956
BY—SCPL

Gibson, William. The Miracle Worker: A Play for Television. Knopf 1957 (Play)
SCHS

Graff, Stewart and Graff, Polly Anne. Helen Keller: Toward the Light. Garrard 1965
ESLC

Harrity, Richard and Martin, Ralph G. The Three Lives of Helen Keller. Doubleday 1962
Bkl A&Y

Hickok, Lorena A. The Story of Helen Keller. Grosset 1948
CC(4-6)

Keller, Helen Adams. Story of My Life. Doubleday or Houghton
BBHS—BBJH—BY—CA—CC(7-9)—JH—SCHS—SCPL—3000

Peare, Catherine Owens. The Helen Keller Story. Crowell 1959
CC(6-9)—ESLC—JH—SCHS

Waite, Helen E. Valiant Companions: Helen Keller and Anne Sullivan Macy. Macrae 1959
JH—SCHS

Jack Kerouac, 1922-

Kerouac, Jack. Lonesome Traveler. McGraw 1960
Bkl A

Emily Kimbrough, 1899-

Kimbrough, Emily. Innocents from Indiana. Harper 1950
SCPL

Joseph Wood Krutch, 1893-

Krutch, Joseph Wood. More Lives Than One. Sloane 1962
Bkl A—BY

Anita Loos, 1893-

Loos, Anita. A Girl Like I. Viking 1966
Bkl A

Edmund G. Love, 1912-

Love, Edmund G. The Situation in Flushing. Harper 1965
Bkl A&Y—IndS(11-12)

Carson (Smith) McCullers, 1917-1967

Evans, Oliver Wendell. The Ballad of Carson McCullers: **A Biography.** Coward-McCann 1966
Bkl A

AUTHORS

American—20th century

Carson (Smith) McCullers—Continued

COLLECTIONS

Auchincloss, Louis. Pioneers and Caretakers: A Study of Nine American Women Novelists. Univ. of Minn. 1965
Bkl A&Y

Betty (Bard) MacDonald, 1908-1958

MacDonald, Betty (Bard). The Egg and I. Lippincott 1946
SCPL

Phyllis McGinley, 1905-

McGinley, Phyllis. Sixpence in Her Shoe. Macmillan 1964
SCPL

Robert Neal Manry, 1918-

Manry, Robert Neal. Tinkerbelle. Harper 1966
Bkl A&Y

Earl Schenck Miers, 1910-

Miers, Earl Schenck. The Trouble Bush. Rand McNally 1966
Bkl A

Ralph Moody, 1898-

Moody, Ralph. The Dry Divide. Norton 1963
Bkl A&Y
Moody, Ralph. Shaking the Nickel Bush. Norton 1962
Bkl A&Y—YR

William Vaughn Moody, 1869-1910

Halpern, Martin. William Vaughn Moody. Twayne 1964
Bkl A

Charles Bernard Nordhoff, 1887-1947

Briand, Paul L. In Search of Paradise: The Nordhoff-Hall Story. Duell 1966
Bkl A&Y

Fulton Oursler, 1893-1952

Oursler, Fulton. Behold This Dreamer! An Autobiography; ed. by Fulton Oursler, Jr. Little 1964
Bkl A

Gilbert Patten, 1866-1945

Patten, Gilbert. Frank Merriwell's "Father": An Autobiography by "Burt L. Standish"; ed. by Harriet Hinsdale and Tony London. Univ. of Okla. 1964
Bkl A

William Alexander Percy, 1885-1942

Percy, William Alexander. Lanterns on the Levee: Recollections of a Planter's Son. Knopf 1941
SCPL

Katherine Anne Porter, 1890-

Hendrick, George. Katherine Anne Porter. Twayne 1965
Bkl A&Y
Nance, William L. Katherine Anne Porter and the Art of Rejection. Univ. of N.C. 1964
Bkl A

COLLECTIONS

Aldridge, John W. Time to Murder and Create: The Contemporary Novel in Crisis. McKay 1966
Bkl A
Auchincloss, Louis. Pioneers and Caretakers: A Study of Nine American Women Novelists. Univ. of Minn. 1965
Bkl A&Y
Wescott, Glenway. Images of Truth: Remembrances and Criticism. Harper 1962
Bkl A

William Sydney Porter, 1862-1910

Arnett, Ethel Stephens. O. Henry from Polecat Creek: A Memorial Edition for William Sydney Porter, Published on the Occasion of His Hundredth Birthday. Piedmont Press 1962
Bkl A
Current-García, Eugene. O. Henry (William Sydney Porter). Twayne 1965
Bkl A&Y
Nolan, Jeannette Covert. O. Henry: The Story of William Sydney Porter. Messner 1943
SCHS—YR

Emily Post, 1873-1960

Post, Edwin. Truly Emily Post. Funk 1961
Bkl A—SCPL

Russell Potter Reeder, 1902-

Reeder, Russell Potter. Born at Reveille, by Red Reeder. Duell 1966
Bkl A&Y

Conrad Richter, 1890-1968

Gaston, Edwin W. Conrad Richter. Twayne 1965
Bkl A&Y

Eleanor (Roosevelt) Roosevelt, 1884-1962

Douglas, Helen (Gahagan). The Eleanor Roosevelt We Remember. Hill & Wang 1963
Bkl A&Y—SCPL
Eaton, Jeanette. The Story of Eleanor Roosevelt. Morrow 1956
BBJH—CC(6-8)—JH—SCHS
Hickok, Lorena A. Reluctant First Lady. Dodd 1962
Bkl A&Y—SCPL

AUTHORS

American—20th century

Eleanor (Roosevelt) Roosevelt—Continued

Lash, Joseph P. Eleanor Roosevelt: A Friend's Memoir. Doubleday 1964
Bkl A

McKown, Robin. Eleanor Roosevelt's World. Grosset 1964
ESLC—JH

MacLeish, Archibald. The Eleanor Roosevelt Story. Houghton 1965
Bkl A

Roosevelt, Eleanor (Roosevelt). The Autobiography of Eleanor Roosevelt. Harper 1961
Bkl A&Y—BY—JH—SCHS—SCPL

Roosevelt, Eleanor (Roosevelt). On My Own. Harper 1958
BBHS—SCHS—SCPL—3000

Roosevelt, Eleanor (Roosevelt). This I Remember. Harper 1949
BBHS—BY—GR—SCHS—SCPL

Roosevelt, Eleanor (Roosevelt). This Is My Story. Harper 1937
BBHS—SCPL

Roosevelt, Eleanor (Roosevelt) and Ferris, Helen Josephine. Your Teens and Mine. Doubleday 1961
Bkl C&Y—CC—JH—SCHS

Steinberg, Alfred. Eleanor Roosevelt. Putnam 1959
CC(5-7)

Steinberg, Alfred. Mrs. R: The Life of Eleanor Roosevelt. Putnam 1958
BY—SCPL

COLLECTIONS

Bowie, Walter Russell. Women of Light. Harper 1964
Bkl A&Y

Daugherty, Sonia. Ten Brave Women. Lippincott 1953
BY—CC(7-9)—ESLC—JH—SCHS

Douglas, Emily (Taft). Remember the Ladies: The Story of Great Women Who Helped Shape America. Putnam 1966
Bkl A&Y

Forsee, Aylesa. American Women Who Scored Firsts. Macrae 1958
SCHS

Robert Chester Ruark, 1915-1965

Ruark, Robert Chester. Old Man and the Boy. Holt 1957
BY—SCHS—SCPL

Ruark, Robert. The Old Man's Boy Grows Older. Holt 1961
Bkl A&Y—SCPL

Damon Runyon, 1880-1946

Hoyt, Edwin Palmer. A Gentleman of Broadway. Little 1964
Bkl A—IndS(10-12)

Maurice Samuel, 1895-

Samuel, Maurice. Little Did I Know. Knopf 1963
Bkl A

Carl Sandburg, 1878-1967

Corwin, Norman, ed. The World of Carl Sandburg: A Stage Presentation. Harcourt 1961
Bkl A—SCPL

Crowder, Richard. Carl Sandburg. Twayne 1964
SCHS

Golden, Harry Lewis. Carl Sandburg. World 1961
BBHS—Bkl A&Y—BY—SCPL

Sandburg, Carl. Always the Young Strangers. Harcourt 1953
SCHS—SCPL

Sandburg, Carl. Prairie-Town Boy: Taken from "Always the Young Strangers." Harcourt 1955
BBJH—BY—CC(7-9)—ESLC—JH—SCHS—YR

Sandburg, Helga. Sweet Music: A Book of Family Reminiscence and Song. Dial 1963
Bkl A&Y

Steichen, Edward, ed. Sandburg: Photographers View Carl Sandburg. Harcourt 1966
Bkl A

William Saroyan, 1908-

Saroyan, William. Here Comes, There Goes, You Know Who. Simon & Schuster 1961
Bkl A

Saroyan, William. Not Dying. Harcourt 1963
Bkl A

May Sarton, 1912-

Sarton, May. I Knew a Phoenix: Sketches for an Autobiography. Rinehart 1959
SCPL

Ruth Sawyer, 1880-

Haviland, Virginia. Ruth Sawyer. Walck 1965
ESLC

Ernest Thompson Seton, 1860-1946

Garst, Doris Shannon and Garst, Warren. Ernest Thompson Seton, Naturalist. Messner 1959
JH—YR

AUTHORS

American—20th century—Continued

Lillian Eugenia Smith, 1897-1966

Smith, Lillian Eugenia. The Journey. World 1954
SCPL

Smith, Lillian Eugenia. Memory of a Large Christmas. Norton 1962
Bkl A

Vincent Starrett, 1886-

Starrett, Vincent. Born in a Bookshop: Chapters from the Chicago Renascence. Univ. of Okla. 1965
Bkl A

Gertrude Stein, 1874-1946

Spriggs, Elizabeth. Gertrude Stein: Her Life and Work. Harper 1957
SCPL

Toklas, Alice B. What Is Remembered. Holt 1963
Bkl A

COLLECTIONS

Wilson, Edmund. Axel's Castle: A Study in the Imaginative Literature of 1870-1930. Scribner 1931
SCPL

Jesse Stuart, 1907-

Stuart, Jesse. Thread That Runs So True. Scribner 1958
BBHS—BY—SCHS—SCPL

K'tut Tantri, ?

Tantri, K'tut. Revolt in Paradise. Harper 1960
Bkl A&Y—BY

Ida Minerva Tarbell, 1857-1944

COLLECTIONS

Daugherty, Sonia. Ten Brave Women. Lippincott 1953
BY—CC(7-9)—ESLC—JH—SCHS

Lowell Jackson Thomas, 1892-

Comfort, Mildred Houghton. Lowell Thomas, Adventurer. Denison 1965
JH

Jim Thorne, 1921-

Thorne, Jim. Occupation: Adventure. Doubleday 1961
Bkl A&Y

Elizabeth (Borton) Treviño, 1904-

Treviño, Elizabeth (Borton). My Heart Lies South: The Story of My Mexican Marriage. Crowell 1953
BY—SCHS

Treviño, Elizabeth (Borton). Where the Heart Is. Doubleday 1962
Bkl A&Y—BY—SCHS

John Roberts Tunis, 1889-

Tunis, John Roberts. A Measure of Independence. Atheneum 1964
Bkl A&Y

John Updike, 1932-

COLLECTIONS

Galloway, David D. The Absurd Hero in American Fiction. Univ. of Tex. 1966
Bkl A&Y

Levin, Martin, ed. Five Boyhoods. Doubleday 1962
Bkl A&Y

Dorothy (Graffe) Van Doren, 1896-

Van Doren, Dorothy (Graffe). The Professor and I. Appleton 1959
SCPL

Mark Van Doren, 1894-

Van Doren, Mark. Autobiography of Mark Van Doren. Harcourt 1958
SCPL

Robert Penn Warren, 1905-

Bohner, Charles H. Robert Penn Warren. Twayne 1965
Bkl A

Longley, John Lewis, ed. Robert Penn Warren: A Collection of Critical Essays. N.Y. Univ. 1965
Bkl A

COLLECTIONS

Brooks, Cleanth. The Hidden God: Studies in Hemingway, Faulkner, Yeats, Eliot, and Warren. Yale Univ. 1963
Bkl A

Eudora Welty, 1909-

Vande Kieft, Ruth Marguerite. Eudora Welty. Twayne 1962
Bkl A

Glenway Wescott, 1901-

Rueckert, William Howe. Glenway Wescott. Twayne 1965
Bkl A

Jessamyn West, 1907-

West, Jessamyn. To See the Dream. Harper 1957
SCPL

Walter White, 1893-1955

Cannon, Poppy. Gentle Knight: My Husband, Walter White. Rinehart 1956
SCPL

William Allen White, 1868-1944

Hinshaw, David. Man from Kansas: The Story of William Allen White. Putnam 1945
SCPL

White, William Allen. Autobiography. Macmillan 1946
SCHS—SCPL

AUTHORS

American—20th century—*Continued*

Margaret Widdemer, 1889-

Widdemer, Margaret. Golden Friends I Had. Doubleday 1964
Bkl A

Kate Douglas (Smith) Wiggin, 1856-1923

Mason, Miriam E. Kate Douglas Wiggin. Bobbs 1958
AB(4-7)

Mason, Miriam E. Yours with Love, Kate. Houghton 1952
CC(7-9)—JH

Laura Ingalls Wilder, 1867-1957

Wilder, Laura Ingalls. On the Way Home: The Diary of a Trip from South Dakota to Mansfield, Missouri, in 1894. Harper 1962
CC(6-9)—ESLC—JH—YR

Thornton Niven Wilder, 1897-

Burbank, Rex. Thornton Wilder. Twayne 1961
Bkl A&Y—SCPL

Goldstein, Malcolm. The Art of Thornton Wilder. Univ. of Neb. 1965
Bkl A

COLLECTIONS

Wescott, Glenway. Images of Truth: Remembrances and Criticism. Harper 1962
Bkl A

William Carlos Williams, 1883-1963

Williams, William Carlos. Autobiography. Random House 1951
SCPL

Elinor Morton (Hoyt) Wylie, 1885-1928

COLLECTIONS

Brenner, Rica. Poets of Our Time. Harcourt 1941
SCHS—SCPL

Australian—20th century

Alan John Villiers, 1903-

Villiers, Alan John. Set of the Sails: The Story of a Cape Horn Seaman. Scribner 1949
SCPL

Austrian—20th century

Stefan Zweig, 1881-1942

Zweig, Stefan. World of Yesterday: An Autobiography. Viking 1943
SCPL

Brazilian—19th century

Alice (Dayrell) Brant, 1880?-

Brant, Alice (Dayrell). Diary of "Helena Morley"; tr. from the Portuguese by Elizabeth Bishop. Farrar 1957
SCPL

Canadian—20th century

Harry J. Boyle, 1915?-

Boyle, Harry J. Homebrew and Patches. Dutton 1964
IndS(9-11)

Boyle, Harry J. With a Pinch of Sin. Doubleday 1966
Bkl A&Y

Morley Callaghan, 1903-

Callaghan, Morley. That Summer in Paris: Memories of Tangled Friendships with Hemingway, Fitzgerald, and Some Others. Coward-McCann 1963
Bkl A

Lovat Dickson, 1902-

Dickson, Lovat. The Ante-room. Atheneum 1960
Bkl A

Dickson, Lovat. The House of Words. Atheneum 1963
Bkl A

Chinese—20th century

Han Suyin, 1917-

Han, Suyin. Many-Splendored Thing. Little 1952
SCPL

Han, Suyin. A Mortal Flower—China: Autobiography, History. Putnam 1966
Bkl A

Danish—19th century

Hans Christian Andersen, 1805-1875

Böök, Fredrik. Hans Christian Andersen: A Biography; tr. from the Swedish by George C. Schoolfield. Univ. of Okla. 1962
Bkl A

Collin, Hedvig. Young Hans Christian Andersen. Viking 1955
AB(5-9)—CC(5-7)—ESLC

Garst, Shannon. Hans Christian Andersen: Fairy Tale Author. Houghton 1965
CC(4-6)

Godden, Rumer. Hans Christian Andersen: A Great Life in Brief. Knopf 1955
BY—ESLC—SCHS—SCPL

Spink, Reginald. The Young Hans Andersen. Roy 1963
IndJ(6-9)

Stirling, Monica. The Wild Swan: The Life and Times of Hans Christian Andersen. Harcourt 1965
Bkl A&Y—IndS(9-12)

AUTHORS—*Continued*

Danish—20th century

Karen (Dinesen) Blixen, Baronesse, 1885-1962

Svendsen, Clara, ed. Isak Dinesen: A Memorial. Random House 1965
Bkl A

COLLECTIONS

Wescott, Glenway. Images of Truth: Remembrances and Criticism. Harper 1962
Bkl A

English

COLLECTIONS

Allsop, Kenneth. The Angry Decade: A Survey of the Cultural Revolt of the Nineteen-fifties. British Bk Centre 1958
SCPL

Drew, Elizabeth A. The Literature of Gossip: Nine English Letterwriters. Norton 1964
Bkl A&Y
Lord Byron; Jane Baillie (Welsh) Carlyle; William Cowper; Edward FitzGerald; Charles Lamb; Lady Mary Wortley Montagu; Jonathan Swift; Dorothy (Osborne) Temple; Horace Walpole

Green, Roger Lancelyn. Authors & Places: A Literary Pilgrimage. Putnam 1963
ESLC
Charles Lutwidge Dodgson; Rudyard Kipling; Robert Louis Stevenson; and others

Green, Roger Lancelyn. Tellers of Tales: British Authors of Children's Books from 1800 to 1964. Watts 1965
ESLC
Charles Lutwidge Dodgson; Rudyard Kipling; George Macdonald; and others

Heppenstall, Rayner. Four Absentees. Dufour 1963
Bkl A
Eric Gill; John Middleton Murry; George Orwell; Dylan Thomas

Kunitz, Stanley Jasspon and Haycraft, Howard, eds. British Authors before 1800: A Biographical Dictionary. Wilson 1952
BBHS—JH—SCHS—SCPL

Kunitz, Stanley Jasspon and Haycraft, Howard, eds. British Authors of the Nineteenth Century. Wilson 1936
BBHS—JH—SCHS—SCPL

Pearson, Hesketh. Lives of the Wits. Harper 1962
Bkl A—BY

Swinnerton, Frank Arthur. A Galaxy of Fathers. Doubleday 1966
Bkl A
Fanny Burney; Maria Edgeworth; Mary Russell Mitford; Anna Seward

English—16th century

Sir Thomas More, Saint, 1478-1535

Basset, Bernard. Born for Friendship: The Spirit of Sir Thomas More. Sheed 1965
Bkl A&Y

Bolt, Robert. A Man for All Seasons: A Play in Two Acts. Random House 1962 (Play)
Bkl A—SCHS—SCPL

Maynard, Theodore. Humanist as Hero: The Life of Sir Thomas More. Macmillan 1947
SCPL

Newell, Virginia. His Own Good Daughter. McKay 1961
YR

Reynolds, Ernest Edwin. The Trial of St. Thomas More. Kenedy 1964
Bkl A

Stanley-Wrench, Margaret. The Conscience of a King. Hawthorn 1962
AB(5-9)

English—17th century

Francis Bacon, Viscount St. Albans, 1561-1626

Anderson, Fulton H. Francis Bacon: His Career and His Thought. Univ. of Southern Calif. 1962
Bkl A

Bowen, Catherine (Drinker). Francis Bacon: The Temper of a Man. Little 1963
Bkl A&Y—IndS(11-12)—SCHS—SCPL

Eiseley, Loren C. Francis Bacon and the Modern Dilemma. Univ. of Neb. 1963
Bkl A

John Bunyan, 1628-1688

Barr, Gladys (Hutchison). The Pilgrim Prince: A Novel Based on the Life of John Bunyan. Holt 1963 (Fiction)
Bkl A—IndS(9-12)

Brittain, Vera Mary. In the Steps of John Bunyan: An Excursion into Puritan England (reprint of Valiant Pilgrim: The Story of John Bunyan and Puritan England). Macmillan 1951
SCPL

Smith, David Edwin. John Bunyan in America. Ind. Univ. 1966
Bkl A

Winslow, Ola Elizabeth. John Bunyan. Macmillan 1961
Bkl A

John Evelyn, 1620-1706

Evelyn, John. Diary of John Evelyn. 2v. Dutton 1930
SCPL

AUTHORS

English—17th century—*Continued*

Ben Jonson, 1573?-1637

Barish, Jonas A., ed. Ben Jonson: A Collection of Critical Essays. Prentice-Hall 1963
Bkl A

Chute, Marchette Gaylord. Ben Jonson of Westminster. Dutton 1953
BBHS—GR—SCHS—SCPL

Thayer, Calvin Graham. Ben Jonson: Studies in the Plays. Univ. of Okla. 1963
Bkl A

Samuel Pepys, 1633-1703

Pepys, Samuel. Diary. Random House, Modern Lib., etc.
GR—SCPL

Pepys, Samuel. Everybody's Pepys: The Diary of Samuel Pepys, 1660-1669, abridged from the complete copyright text and ed. by O. F. Morshead. Harcourt 1926
SCHS—3000

Pepys, Samuel. Passages from the Diary of Samuel Pepys; ed. by Richard Le Gallienne. Modern Lib. 1921
BBHS—SCPL

Varble, Rachel (McBrayer). Three Against London. Doubleday 1962 (Fiction)
Bkl C(7-9)&Y

Dorothy (Osborne) Temple, 1627-1694

COLLECTIONS

Drew, Elizabeth A. The Literature of Gossip: Nine English Letterwriters. Norton 1964
Bkl A&Y

Izaak Walton, 1593-1683

Walton, Izaak. Compleat Angler. Modern Lib. 1939
SCPL

English—18th century

Philip Dormer Stanhope, 4th Earl of Chesterfield, 1694-1773

Shellabarger, Samuel. Lord Chesterfield and His World. Little 1951
SCPL

Lady Mary Wortley Montagu, 1689-1762

Halsband, Robert. Life of Lady Mary Wortley Montagu. Oxford 1957
SCPL

COLLECTIONS

Drew, Elizabeth A. The Literature of Gossip: Nine English Letterwriters. Norton 1964
Bkl A&Y

Sir Richard Steele, 1672-1729

Winton, Calhoun. Captain Steele: v. 1, The Early Career of Richard Steele. Johns Hopkins 1964
Bkl A

Horace Walpole, 4th Earl of Orford, 1717-1797

Walpole, Horace. Selected Letters of Horace Walpole. Dutton n.d.
SCPL

COLLECTIONS

Drew, Elizabeth A. The Literature of Gossip: Nine English Letterwriters. Norton 1964
Bkl A&Y

English—19th century

George Henry Borrow, 1803-1881

Borrow, George Henry. Romany Rye. Dutton 1907
SCPL

Branwell Brontë, 1817-1848

Du Maurier, Daphne. The Infernal World of Branwell Brontë. Doubleday 1961
Bkl A

Sir Richard Francis Burton, 1821-1890

Farwell, Byron. Burton: A Biography of Sir Richard Francis Burton. Holt 1964
Bkl A

Thomas De Quincey, 1785-1859

De Quincey, Thomas. Confessions of an English Opium Eater. Dutton, Oxford, etc.
GR

Charles Lutwidge Dodgson, 1832-1898

Green, Roger Lancelyn. The Story of Lewis Carroll. Abelard-Schuman 1951 or Walck 1962
YR

Hudson, Derek. Lewis Carroll. Constable 1954
SCPL

Wood, James Playsted. The Snark Was a Boojam: A Life of Lewis Carroll. Pantheon 1966
Bkl C(7-9)&Y

COLLECTIONS

Green, Roger Lancelyn. Authors & Places: A Literary Pilgrimage. Putnam 1963
ESLC

AUTHORS

English—19th century

Charles Lutwidge Dodgson—Continued

Green, Roger Lancelyn. Tellers of Tales: British Authors of Children's Books from 1800 to 1964. Watts 1965
ESLC

Edward FitzGerald, 1809-1883

COLLECTIONS

Drew, Elizabeth A. The Literature of Gossip: Nine English Letterwriters. Norton 1964
Bkl A&Y

Charles Cavendish Fulke Greville, 1794-1865

Greville, Charles Cavendish Fulke. The Great World: Portraits and Scenes from Greville's Memoirs, 1814-1860; ed. by Louis Kronenberger. Doubleday 1963
Bkl A

Thomas Hardy, 1840-1928

Carpenter, Richard C. Thomas Hardy. Twayne 1964
Bkl A

Hardy, Emma Lavinia (Gifford). Some Recollections; ed. by Evelyn Hardy and Robert Gittings. Oxford 1961
Bkl A

Hardy, Thomas. "Dearest Emmie," [the author's] Letters to His First Wife; ed. by Carl J. Weber. St Martins 1963
Bkl A

William Henry Hudson, 1841-1922

Hudson, William Henry. Far Away and Long Ago: A History of My Early Life. Dutton 1931
BY—SCHS—SCPL

Rudyard Kipling, 1865-1936

Carrington, Charles Edmund. Life of Rudyard Kipling. Doubleday 1955
SCPL

Gilbert, Elliot L., ed. Kipling and the Critics. N. Y. Univ. 1965
Bkl A

Manley, Seon. Rudyard Kipling, Creative Adventurer. Vanguard 1965
Bkl Y&C—IndS(9-10)—JH

Rutherford, Andrew, ed. Kipling's Mind and Art: Selected Critical Essays. Stanford Univ. 1964
Bkl A

Stewart, John Innes Mackintosh. Rudyard Kipling. Dodd 1966
Bkl A

COLLECTIONS

Green, Roger Lancelyn. Authors & Places: A Literary Pilgrimage. Putnam 1963
ESLC

Green, Roger Lancelyn. Tellers of Tales: British Authors of Children's Books from 1800 to 1964. Watts 1965
ESLC

Stirling, Nora B. Who Wrote the Classics? Day 1965
Bkl Y&A&C

Ada Leverson, 1865-1936

Wyndham, Violet. The Sphinx and Her Circle: A Biographical Sketch of Ada Leverson, 1862-1933. Vanguard 1964
Bkl A

Harriet Martineau, 1802-1876

Webb, Robert Kiefer. Harriet Martineau: A Radical Victorian. Columbia Univ. 1960
Bkl A

Mary Russell Mitford, 1787-1855

COLLECTIONS

Swinnerton, Frank Arthur. A Galaxy of Fathers. Doubleday 1966
Bkl A

Lady Ottoline Violet Anne (Cavendish-Bentinck) Morrell, 1873-1938

Morrell, Lady Ottoline Violet Anne (Cavendish-Bentinck). Memoirs: A Study in Friendship, 1873-1915; ed. by Robert Gathorne-Hardy. Knopf 1964
Bkl A

John Addington Symonds, 1840-1893

Grosskurth, Phyllis. The Woeful Victorian: A Biography of John Addington Symonds. Holt 1965
Bkl A

English—20th century

Sir Max Beerbohm, 1872-1956

Beerbohm, Sir Max. Max Beerbohm's Letters to Reggie Turner; ed. by Rupert Hart-Davis. Lippincott 1965
Bkl A

Behrman, S. N. Portrait of Max: An Intimate Memoir of Sir Max Beerbohm. Random House 1960
Bkl A—SCPL

Cecil, Lord David. Max: A Biography. Houghton 1965
Bkl A—IndS(12)

Hilaire Belloc, 1870-1953

Speaight, Robert. Life of Hilaire Belloc. Farrar 1957
SCPL

AUTHORS

English—20th century—*Continued*

Edith (Nesbit) Bland, 1858-1924

Bell, Anthea. E. Nesbit. Walck 1960
ESLC

Bland, Edith (Nesbit). Long Ago When I Was Young. Watts 1966
Bkl A&C—ESLC

Gerald Brenan, 1894-

Brenan, Gerald. A Life of One's Own: Childhood and Youth. Farrar 1963
Bkl A

Vera Mary Brittain, 1893?-

Brittain, Vera Mary. Testament of Experience: An Autobiographical Story of the Years 1925-50. Macmillan 1957
SCPL

Winifred Bryher, 1894-

Bryher, Winifred. The Heart to Artemis. Harcourt 1962
Bkl A

Joyce Cary, 1888-1957

Hoffmann, Charles G. Joyce Cary: The Comedy of Freedom. Univ. of Pittsburgh 1965
Bkl A

Mahood, Molly Maureen. Joyce Cary's Africa. Houghton 1965
Bkl A

COLLECTIONS

Hall, James. The Tragic Comedians: Seven Modern British Novelists. Ind. Univ. 1963
Bkl A

Gilbert Keith Chesterton, 1874-1936

Chesterton, Gilbert Keith. Autobiography. Sheed 1936
SCPL

Ward, Maisie. Gilbert Keith Chesterton. Sheed 1943
SCPL

Richard Church, 1893-

Church, Richard. Golden Sovereign: A Conclusion to Over the Bridge. Dutton 1957
SCPL

Nan Fairbrother, 1913-

Fairbrother, Nan. The House in the Country. Knopf 1965
Bkl A

Eleanor Farjeon, 1881-1965

A Book for Eleanor Farjeon: A Tribute to Her Life and Work, 1881-1965. Walck 1966
Bkl C(3-6)—ESLC

Ford Madox Ford, 1873-1939

Ford, Ford Madox. Letters; ed. by Richard M. Ludwig. Princeton Univ. 1965
Bkl A

Lid, Richard Wald. Ford Madox Ford: The Essence of His Art. Univ. of Calif. 1964
Bkl A

Wiley, Paul L. Novelist of Three Worlds: Ford Madox Ford. Syracuse Univ. 1962
Bkl A

Rumer Godden, 1907-

Godden, Rumer and Godden, Jon. Two Under the Indian Sun. Knopf 1966
Bkl A

William Gerald Golding, 1911-

Baker, James R. William Golding: A Critical Study. St. Martins 1965
Bkl A

COLLECTIONS

Shapiro, Charles, ed. Contemporary British Novelists. Southern Ill. Univ. 1965
Bkl A

Graham Greene, 1904-

De Vitis, A. A. Graham Greene. Twayne 1964
Bkl A

Evans, Robert Owen, ed. Graham Greene: Some Critical Considerations. Univ. of Ky. 1963
Bkl A

COLLECTIONS

O'Faoláin, Seán. Vanishing Hero: Studies in Novelists of the Twenties. Little 1957
SCPL

Ralph Hammond-Innes, 1913-

Hammond-Innes, Ralph. Harvest of Journeys. Knopf 1960
Bkl A

Thomas Hardy, 1840-1928

Carpenter, Richard C. Thomas Hardy. Twayne 1964
Bkl A

Hardy, Emma Lavinia (Gifford). Some Recollections; ed. by Evelyn Hardy and Robert Gittings. Oxford 1961
Bkl A

Hardy, Thomas. "Dearest Emmie," [the author's] Letters to His First Wife; ed. by Carl J. Weber. St. Martins 1963
Bkl A

COLLECTIONS

Daiches, David. Poetry and the Modern World: A Study of Poetry in England Between 1900 and 1939. Univ. of Chicago 1940
SCPL

AUTHORS

English—20th century—*Continued*

Frances Caryll Houselander, 1901-1954

Ward, Maisie. Caryll Houselander, That Divine Eccentric. Sheed 1962
Bkl A

William Henry Hudson, 1841-1922

Hudson, William Henry. Far Away and Long Ago: A History of My Early Life. Dutton 1931
BY—SCHS—SCPL

Aldous Leonard Huxley, 1894-1963

Atkins, John Alfred. Aldous Huxley: A Literary Study. Roy 1956
SCPL
Huxley, Sir Julian Sorell, ed. Aldous Huxley, 1894-1963: A Memorial Volume. Harper 1966
Bkl A

COLLECTIONS

Hall, James. The Tragic Comedians: Seven Modern British Novelists. Ind. Univ. 1963
Bkl A
O'Faoláin, Seán. Vanishing Hero: Studies in Novelists of the Twenties. Little 1957
SCPL

Elspeth Josceline (Grant) Huxley, 1907-

Huxley, Elspeth Josceline (Grant). Flame Trees of Thika: Memories of an African Childhood. Morrow 1959
SCPL
Huxley, Elspeth Josceline (Grant). On the Edge of the Rift. Morrow 1962
Bkl A

Rudyard Kipling, 1865-1936

Carrington, Charles Edmund. Life of Rudyard Kipling. Doubleday 1955
SCPL
Gilbert, Elliot L., ed. Kipling and the Critics. N. Y. Univ. 1965
Bkl A
Manley, Seon. Rudyard Kipling, Creative Adventurer. Vanguard 1965
Bkl Y&C—ESLC—IndS(9-10)—JH
Rutherford, Andrew, ed. Kipling's Mind and Art: Selected Critical Essays. Stanford Univ. 1964
Bkl A
Stewart, John Innes Mackintosh. Rudyard Kipling. Dodd 1966
Bkl A

COLLECTIONS

Green, Roger Lancelyn. Authors & Places: A Literary Pilgrimage. Putnam 1963
ESLC
Green, Roger Lancelyn. Tellers of Tales: British Authors of Children's Books from 1800 to 1964. Watts 1965
ESLC
Stirling, Nora B. Who Wrote the Classics? Day 1965
Bkl Y&A&C

James Laver, 1899-

Laver, James. Museum Piece: Or, The Education of an Iconographer. Houghton 1964
Bkl A

Doris May Lessing, 1919-

Brewster, Dorothy. Doris Lessing. Twayne 1965
Bkl A

COLLECTIONS

Shapiro, Charles, ed. Contemporary British Novelists. Southern Ill. Univ. 1965
Bkl A

Ada Leverson, 1865-1936

Wyndham, Violet. The Sphinx and Her Circle: A Biographical Sketch of Ada Leverson, 1862-1933. Vanguard 1964
Bkl A

Clive Staples Lewis, 1898-1963

Gibb, Jocelyn, ed. Light on C. S. Lewis, by Owen Barfield and others. Harcourt 1966
Bkl A
Lewis, Clive Staples. Surprised by Joy: The Shape of My Early Life. Harcourt 1955
SCPL

Wyndham Lewis, 1884-1957

Lewis, Wyndham. Letters; ed. by W. K. Rose. New Directions 1964
Bkl A

John Masefield, 1878-1967

Masefield, John. So Long to Learn. Macmillan 1952
SCPL

William Somerset Maugham, 1874-1965

Cordell, Richard Albert. Somerset Maugham: A Biographical and Critical Study. Ind. Univ. 1961
Bkl A
Jonas, K. W., ed. World of Somerset Maugham: An Anthology. British Bk Centre 1959
SCPL

AUTHORS

English—20th century

William Somerset Maugham—Continued

Kanin, Garson. Remembering Mr. Maugham. Atheneum 1966
Bkl A

Maugham, Robin. Somerset and All the Maughams. New Am. Lib. 1966
Bkl A

Maugham, William Somerset. The Summing Up. Doubleday 1938
GR—SCPL

Menard, Wilmon. The Two Worlds of Somerset Maugham. Sherbourne Press 1965
Bkl A

Gavin Maxwell, 1914-

Maxwell, Gavin. The House of Elrig. Dutton 1965
Bkl A

Jessica Mitford, 1917-

Mitford, Jessica. Daughters and Rebels: The Autobiography of Jessica Mitford. Houghton 1960
Bkl A

Lady Ottoline Violet Anne (Cavendish-Bentinck) Morrell, 1873-1938

Morrell, Lady Ottoline Violet Anne (Cavendish-Bentinck). Memoirs: A Study in Friendship, 1873-1915; ed. by Robert Gathorne-Hardy. Knopf 1964
Bkl A

John Middleton Murry, 1889-1957

COLLECTIONS

Heppenstall, Rayner. Four Absentees. Dufour 1963
Bkl A

George Orwell, 1903-1950

Rees, Sir Richard. George Orwell: Fugitive from the Camp of Victory. Southern Ill. Univ. 1962
Bkl A

Woodcock, George. The Crystal Spirit: A Study of George Orwell. Little 1966
Bkl A

COLLECTIONS

Heppenstall, Rayner. Four Absentees. Dufour 1963
Bkl A

Hesketh Pearson, 1889-1964

Pearson, Hesketh. Hesketh Pearson, by Himself. Harper 1966
Bkl A

Beatrix Potter, 1866-1943

Lane, Margaret. Tale of Beatrix Potter: A Biography. Warne 1946
ESLC—SCPL

Potter, Beatrix. Art of Beatrix Potter. Warne 1964
CC—ESLC—SCPL

Potter, Beatrix. The Journal of Beatrix Potter from 1881 to 1897; transcribed from her Code Writing by Leslie Linder. Warne 1966
Bkl A

Peter Quennell, 1905-

Quennell, Peter. The Sign of the Fish. Viking 1960
Bkl A

Chaim Raphael, 1908-

Raphael, Chaim. Memoirs of a Special Case. Little 1962
Bkl A

Nevil Shute, 1899-1960

Shute, Nevil. Slide Rule: The Autobiography of an Engineer. Morrow 1954
SCPL

Sir Osbert Sitwell, Bart., 1892-1969

Sitwell, Sir Osbert. Great Morning! Little 1947
SCPL

Sitwell, Sir Osbert. Laughter in the Next Room. Little 1948
SCPL

Sitwell, Sir Osbert. Left Hand, Right Hand! Little 1944
SCPL

Sitwell, Sir Osbert. Noble Essences: A Book of Characters. Little 1950
SCPL

Sitwell, Sir Osbert. Tales My Father Taught Me: An Evocation of Extravagant Episodes. Little 1962
Bkl A—SCPL

COLLECTIONS

Daiches, David. Poetry and the Modern World: A Study of Poetry in England Between 1900 and 1939. Univ. of Chicago 1940
SCPL

Freya Madeline Stark, 1893-

Stark, Freya Madeline. Dust in the Lion's Paw: Autobiography, 1939-1946. Harcourt 1962
Bkl A—SCPL

Marie Charlotte Carmichael Stopes, 1880-1958

Briant, Keith. Passionate Paradox: The Life of Marie Stopes. Norton 1962
Bkl A

AUTHORS

English—20th century—*Continued*

Lytton Strachey, 1880-1932

Sanders, C. R. Lytton Strachey: His Mind and Art. Yale Univ. 1957
SCPL

Noel Streatfeild, ?

Streatfeild, Noel. A Vicarage Family: An Autobiographical Story. Watts 1963
Bkl A

Frank Arthur Swinnerton, 1884-

Swinnerton, Frank Arthur. Figures in the Foreground: Literary Reminiscences, 1917-1940. Doubleday 1964
Bkl A

Reginald Turner, 1869?-1938

Beerbohm, Sir Max. Max Beerbohm's Letters to Reggie Turner; ed. by Rupert Hart-Davis. Lippincott 1965
Bkl A

Weintraub, Stanley. Reggie: A Portrait of Reginald Turner. Braziller 1965
Bkl A

Maisie Ward, 1889-

Ward, Maisie. Unfinished Business. Sheed 1964
Bkl A

Alec Waugh, 1898-

Waugh, Alec. The Early Years of Alec Waugh. Farrar 1963
Bkl A

Evelyn Waugh, 1903-1966

Waugh, Evelyn. A Little Learning: An Autobiography. v. 1, The Early Years. Little 1964
Bkl A

COLLECTIONS

Hall, James. The Tragic Comedians: Seven Modern British Novelists. Ind. Univ. 1963
Bkl A

O'Faoláin, Seán. Vanishing Hero: Studies in Novelists of the Twenties. Little 1957
SCPL

Leonard Sidney Woolf, 1880-

Woolf, Leonard Sidney. Beginning Again: An Autobiography of the Years 1911 to 1918. Harcourt 1964
Bkl A

Woolf, Leonard Sidney. Sowing: An Autobiography of the Years 1880 to 1904. Harcourt 1960
Bkl A

Virginia (Stephen) Woolf, 1882-1941

Guiguet, Jean. Virginia Woolf and Her Works; tr. by Jean Stewart. Harcourt 1966
Bkl A

French—17th century

Marie (de Rabutin Chantal), Marquise de Sévigné, 1626-1696

Sévigné, Marie (de Rabutin Chantal), Marquise de. Letters of Madame de Sévigné to Her Daughter and Her Friends; comp. by Richard Aldington. 2v. Dutton n.d.
GR—SCPL

French—18th century

Charlotte Élisabeth Aïssé, 1694?-1733

COLLECTIONS

Herold, J. Christopher. Love in Five Temperaments. Atheneum 1961
Bkl A

Julie Jeanne Éléonore de Lespinasse, 1732-1776

Bouissounouse, Janine. Julie—The Life of Mademoiselle de Lespinasse: Her Salon, Her Friends, Her Loves; tr. by Pierre de Fontnouvelle. Appleton 1962
BY

COLLECTIONS

Herold, J. Christopher. Love in Five Temperaments. Atheneum 1961
Bkl A

Jean Jacques Rousseau, 1712-1778

Endore, S. Guy. Voltaire! Voltaire! A Novel. Simon & Schuster 1961 (Fiction)
Bkl A

Guéhenno, Jean. Jean-Jacques Rousseau. v. 1, 1712-1758; v.2, 1758-1778; tr. from the French by John and Doreen Weightman. 2v. Columbia Univ. 1966
Bkl A

Rousseau, Jean Jacques. Confessions. Modern Lib., Dutton, etc.
CA—GR—SCPL

Winwar, Frances. Jean-Jacques Rousseau: Conscience of an Era. Random House 1961
Bkl A

Louis de Rouvroy, Duc de Saint-Simon, 1675-1755

Saint-Simon, Louis de Rouvroy, Duc de. The Age of Magnificence: The Memoirs of Saint-Simon; ed. and tr. by Sanche de Gramont. Putnam 1963
Bkl A

AUTHORS

French—18th century—*Continued*

Marguerite Jeanne (Cordier) Baronne de Staal de Launay, 1684-1750

COLLECTIONS

Herold, J. Christopher. Love in Five Temperaments. Atheneum 1961
Bkl A

Anne Louise Germaine (Necker), Baronne de Staël-Holstein, 1766-1817

Andrews, Wayne. Germaine: A Portrait of Madame de Staël. Atheneum 1963
Bkl A

Herold, Jean Christopher. Mistress to an Age: A Life of Madame de Staël. Bobbs 1958
SCPL

Claudine Alexandrine Guérin de Tencin, 1685-1749

COLLECTIONS

Herold, J. Christopher. Love in Five Temperaments. Atheneum 1961
Bkl A

François Marie Arouet de Voltaire, 1694-1778

Endore, S. Guy. Voltaire! Voltaire! A Novel. Simon & Schuster 1961 (Fiction)
Bkl A

Mitford, Nancy. Voltaire in Love. Harper 1957.
SCPL

Nixon, Edna. Voltaire and the Calas Case. Vanguard 1963
IndS(11-12)

COLLECTIONS

Hill, Frank Ernest. Famous Historians. Dodd 1966
Bkl Y&C

French—19th century

Marie Henri Beyle, 1783-1842

Caraccio, Armand. Stendhal; tr. by Dolores Bagley. N. Y. Univ. 1965
Bkl A

Dutourd, Jean. The Man of Sensibility; tr. from the French by Robin Chancellor. Simon & Schuster 1961
Bkl A

COLLECTIONS

Levin, Harry. The Gates of Horn: A Study of Five French Realists. Oxford 1963
Bkl A

Maugham, William Somerset. Art of Fiction: An Introduction to Ten Novels and Their Authors. Doubleday 1955
SCPL

Turnell, Martin. The Art of French Fiction. New Directions 1959
SCPL

André Paul Guillaume Gide, 1869-1951

Delay, Jean Paul Louis. The Youth of André Gide; abr. and tr. by June Guicharnaud. Univ. of Chicago 1963
Bkl A

Fowlie, Wallace. André Gide: His Life and Art. Macmillan 1965
Bkl A—IndS(12)

Gide, André Paul Guillaume. Journals of André Gide; tr. by Justin O'Brien. 4v. Knopf 1947-51
SCPL

Gide, André Paul Guillaume and Valéry, Paul. Self-portraits: The Gide/Valéry Letters, 1890-1942; ed. by Robert Mallet; abr. and tr. by June Guicharnaud. Univ. of Chicago 1966
Bkl A

Guerard, Albert Joseph. André Gide. Harvard Univ. 1951
SCPL

Mauriac, Claude. Conversations with André Gide; tr. from the French by Michael Lebeck. Braziller 1965
Bkl A

COLLECTIONS

Brennan, Joseph Gerard. Three Philosophical Novelists. Macmillan 1964
Bkl A

Turnell, Martin. The Art of French Fiction. New Directions 1959
SCPL

Victor Marie Hugo, 1802-1885

Maurois, Andre. Olympio: The Life of Victor Hugo; tr. by Gerard Hopkins. Harper 1956
SCPL

Guy de Maupassant, 1850-1893

COLLECTIONS

Turnell, Martin. The Art of French Fiction. New Directions 1959
SCPL

Charles Pierre Péguy, 1873-1914

Villiers, Marjorie (Howard). Charles Péguy: A Study in Integrity. Harper 1966
Bkl A

Jules Renard, 1864-1910

Renard, Jules. Journal; ed. and tr. by Louise Bogan and Elizabeth Roget. Braziller 1964
Bkl A

AUTHORS

French—19th century—*Continued*

Anne Louise Germain (Necker), Baronne de Staël-Holstein, 1766-1817

Andrews, Wayne. Germaine: A Portrait of Madame de Staël. Atheneum 1963
  Bkl A
Herold, Jean Christopher. Mistress to an Age: A Life of Madame de Staël. Bobbs 1958
  SCPL

Alexis Charles Henri Maurice Clérel de Tocqueville, 1805-1859

Drescher, Seymour. Tocqueville and England. Harvard Univ. 1964
  Bkl A

French—20th century

Simone de Beauvoir, 1908-

Beauvoir, Simone de. Force of Circumstance; tr. from the French by Richard Howard. Putnam 1965
  Bkl A
Beauvoir, Simone de. The Prime of Life; tr. by Peter Green. World 1962
  Bkl A—SCPL

Albert Camus, 1913-1960

Brée, Germaine. Camus. Rutgers Univ. 1961
  SCPL
Brée, Germaine, ed. Camus: A Collection of Critical Essays. Prentice-Hall 1962
  SCPL
Maquet, Albert. Albert Camus: The Invincible Summer; tr. from the French by Herma Briffault. Braziller 1958
  SCPL
Thody, Philip. Albert Camus, 1913-1960. Macmillan 1961
  SCPL
Thody, Philip. Albert Camus: A Study of His Work. Hamilton 1957
  SCPL

Sidonie Gabrielle Colette, 1873-1954

Colette, Sidonie Gabrielle. The Blue Lantern; tr. by Roger Senhouse. Farrar 1963
  Bkl A
Colette, Sidonie Gabrielle. Earthly Paradise: An Autobiography, Drawn from Her Lifetime Writings by Robert Phelps; tr. by Herma Briffault and Derek Coltman. Farrar 1966
  Bkl A
Goudeket, Maurice. Close to Colette: An Intimate Portrait of a Woman of Genius. Farrar 1957
  SCPL

Goudeket, Maurice. The Delights of Growing Old; tr. from the French by Patrick O'Brian. Farrar 1966
  Bkl A
Marks, Elaine. Colette. Rutgers Univ. 1960
  Bkl A

COLLECTIONS

Wescott, Glenway. Images of Truth: Remembrances and Criticism. Harper 1962
  Bkl A

Romain Gary, 1914-

Gary, Romain. Promise at Dawn; tr. from the French by John M. Beach. Harper 1961
  Bkl A—BY—SCPL

André Paul Guillaume Gide, 1869-1951

Fowlie, Wallace. André Gide: His Life and Art. Macmillan 1965
  Bkl A—IndS(12)
Gide, André Paul Guillaume. Journals of André Gide; tr. by Justin O'Brien. 4v. Knopf 1947-51
  SCPL
Gide, André Paul Guillaume and Valéry, Paul. Self-portraits: The Gide/Valéry Letters, 1890-1942; ed. by Robert Mallet; abr. and tr. by June Guicharnaud. Univ. of Chicago 1966
  Bkl A
Mauriac, Claude. Conversations with André Gide; tr. from the French by Michael Lebeck. Braziller 1965
  Bkl A
Guerard, Albert Joseph. André Gide. Harvard Univ. 1951
  SCPL

COLLECTIONS

Brennan, Joseph Gerard. Three Philosophical Novelists. Macmillan 1964
  Bkl A
Turnell, Martin. The Art of French Fiction. New Directions 1959
  SCPL

Madeleine (Gal) Henrey, 1906-

Henrey, Madeleine (Gal). Madeleine Grown Up: The Autobiography of a French Girl. Dutton 1953
  SCPL
Henrey, Madeleine (Gal). Madeleine, Young Wife: The Autobiography of a French Girl. Dutton 1954
  SCPL

AUTHORS

French—20th century—*Continued*

François Mauriac, 1885-

COLLECTIONS

Turnell, Martin. The Art of French Fiction. New Directions 1959
SCPL

Charles Pierre Péguy, 1873-1914

Villiers, Marjorie (Howard). Charles Péguy: A Study in Integrity. Harper 1966
Bkl A

Jules Renard, 1864-1910

Renard, Jules. Journal; ed. and tr. by Louise Bogan and Elizabeth Roget. Braziller 1964
Bkl A

Antoine de Saint-Exupéry, 1900-1944

Migeo, Marcel. Saint-Exupéry; tr. from the French by Herma Briffault. McGraw 1960
Bkl A—SCPL

Rumbold, Richard and Stewart, Lady Margaret. Winged Life: A Portrait of Antoine de Saint-Exupéry, Poet and Airman. McKay 1955
SCPL

Saint-Exupéry, Antoine de. Airman's Odyssey. Harcourt 1943
SCPL

Jean Paul Sartre, 1905-

Sartre, Jean Paul. The Words; tr. from the French by Bernard Frechtman. Braziller 1964
Bkl A

Paul Ambroise Valéry, 1871-1945

COLLECTIONS

Wilson, Edmund. Axel's Castle: A Study in the Imaginative Literature of 1870-1930. Scribner 1931
SCPL

German—20th century

Erich Kästner, 1899-

Kästner, Erich. When I Was a Boy; tr. from the German by Isabel and Florence McHugh. Watts 1961
Bkl A

Thomas Mann, 1875-1955

Mann, Monika. Past & Present; tr. from the German by Frances F. Reid and Ruth Hein. St Martins 1960
Bkl A

Mann, Thomas. A Sketch of My Life; tr. from the German by H. T. Lowe-Porter. Knopf 1960
Bkl A—SCPL

Mann, Thomas. The Story of a Novel: The Genesis of Doctor Faustus; tr. from the German by Richard and Clara Winston. Knopf 1961
Bkl A—SCPL

Neider, Charles, ed. Stature of Thomas Mann. New Directions 1947
SCPL

Thirwall, John Connop. In Another Language: A Record of the Thirty-Year Relationship Between Thomas Mann and His English Translator, Helen Tracy Lowe-Porter. Knopf 1966
Bkl A

COLLECTIONS

Brennan, Joseph Gerard. Three Philosophical Novelists. Macmillan 1964
Bkl A

Wescott, Glenway. Images of Truth: Remembrances and Criticism. Harper 1962
Bkl A

Gustav Regler, 1898-1963

Regler, Gustav. The Owl of Minerva: The Autobiography of Gustav Regler; tr. from the German by Norman Denny. Farrar 1960
Bkl A

Greek—1st century

Plutarch, 46?-120?

COLLECTIONS

Hill, Frank Ernest. Famous Historians. Dodd 1966
Bkl Y&C

Greek—20th century

Nikos Kazantzakēs, 1885-1957

Kazantzakēs, Nikos. Report to Greco; tr. from the Greek by P. A. Bien. Simon & Schuster 1965
Bkl A

Hungarian—20th century

Arthur Koestler, 1905-

Koestler, Arthur. Arrow in the Blue: An Autobiography. Macmillan 1952
SCPL

Koestler, Arthur. Invisible Writing . . . An Autobiography. Macmillan 1954
SCPL

Indian—20th century

Ved Parkash Mehta, 1934-

Mehta, Ved Parkash. Face to Face: An Autobiography. Little 1957
BBHS—SCHS—SCPL

AUTHORS

Indian—20th century—*Continued*

Dhan Gopal Mukerji, 1890-1936

Mukerji, Dhan Gopal. Caste and Outcast.
Dutton 1923
SCPL

Santha Rama Rau, 1923-

Rama Rau, Santha. Gifts of Passage.
Harper 1961
BBHS—Bkl A&Y—BY—SCHS—SCPL

Irish

COLLECTIONS

Howarth, Herbert. The Irish Writers,
1880-1940. Hill & Wang 1959
Bkl A
Lady Augusta (Persse) Gregory; James
Joyce; George Moore; George William Russell (Æ); John Millington Synge; William
Butler Yeats

Irish—19th century

Oscar Wilde, 1854-1900

Hyde, Harford Montgomery. Oscar
Wilde: The Aftermath. Farrar 1963
Bkl A
Pearson, Hesketh. Oscar Wilde. Grosset
1946
GR
Wilde, Oscar. The Letters of Oscar
Wilde; ed. by Rupert Hart-Davis. Harcourt 1962
Bkl A—SCPL
Winwar, Frances. Oscar Wilde and the
Yellow Nineties. Harper 1958
SCPL

Irish—20th century

Oliver St. John Gogarty, 1878-1957

O'Connor, Ulick. The Times I've Seen:
Oliver St. John Gogarty, a Biography.
Obolensky 1964
Bkl A

James Joyce, 1882-1941

Burgess, Anthony. Re Joyce. Norton 1965
Bkl A
Colum, Mary (Maguire) and Colum,
Padraic. Our Friend James Joyce. Doubleday 1958
SCPL
Ellman, Richard. James Joyce. Oxford
1959
CA—GR—SCPL
Freund, Gisèle and Carleton, Verna B.
James Joyce in Paris: His Final Years.
Harcourt 1965
Bkl A
Gorman, Herbert Sherman. James Joyce.
Rinehart 1948
SCPL

Joyce, James. Letters of James Joyce; ed.
by Stuart Gilbert. Viking 1957
SCPL
Joyce, Stanislaus. My Brother's Keeper:
James Joyce's Early Years; ed. by
Richard Ellmann. Viking 1958
SCPL
Magalaner, Marvin and Kain, Richard
M. Joyce: The Man, the Work, the
Reputation. N. Y. Univ. 1956
SCPL
Scholes, Robert E. and Kain, Richard
Morgan, eds. The Workshop of Daedalus: James Joyce and the Raw Materials for A Portrait of the Artist As
a Young Man. Northwestern Univ.
1965
Bkl A

COLLECTIONS

Brennan, Joseph Gerard. Three Philosophical Novelists. Macmillan 1964
Bkl A
Howarth, Herbert. The Irish Writers,
1880-1940. Hill & Wang 1959
Bkl A
O'Faoláin, Seán. Vanishing Hero: Studies in Novelists of the Twenties. Little
1957
SCPL
Wilson, Edmund. Axel's Castle: A Study
in the Imaginative Literature of 1870-
1930. Scribner 1931
SCPL

John O'Donoghue, 1900-

O'Donoghue, John. In a Quiet Land.
Coward-McCann 1958
SCPL
O'Donoghue, John. In Kerry Long Ago.
Norton 1960
Bkl A

Seán O'Faoláin, 1900-

O'Faoláin, Seán. Vive Moi! Little 1964
Bkl A—IndS(11-12)

George William Russell (Æ), 1867-1935

COLLECTIONS

Howarth, Herbert. The Irish Writers,
1880-1940. Hill & Wang 1959
Bkl A

William Butler Yeats, 1865-1939

Gibbon, Monk. The Masterpiece and the
Man: Yeats As I Knew Him. Macmillan 1959
Bkl A
Jeffares, Alexander Norman and Cross,
K. G. W., eds. In Excited Reverie: A
Centenary Tribute to William Butler
Yeats, 1865-1939. Macmillan 1965
Bkl A—IndS(10-12)

AUTHORS

Irish—20th century

William Butler Yeats—Continued

Skelton, Robin and Saddlemyer, Ann, eds. The World of W. B. Yeats: Essays in Perspective. Univ. of Wash. 1965
Bkl A

Yeats, William Butler. Autobiography, Consisting of Reveries over Childhood and Youth, The Trembling of the Veil, and Dramatis Personae. Macmillan 1953
SCPL

Zwerdling, Alex. Yeats and the Heroic Ideal. N. Y. Univ. 1965
Bkl A

COLLECTIONS

Brenner, Rica. Poets of Our Time. Harcourt 1941
SCHS—SCPL

Brooks, Cleanth. The Hidden God: Studies in Hemingway, Faulkner, Yeats, Eliot, and Warren. Yale Univ. 1963
Bkl A

Daiches, David. Poetry and the Modern World: A Study of Poetry in England between 1900 and 1939. Univ. of Chicago 1940
SCPL

Howarth, Herbert. The Irish Writers, 1880-1940. Hill & Wang 1959
Bkl A

Wilson, Edmund. Axel's Castle: A Study in the Imaginative Literature of 1870-1930. Scribner 1931
SCPL

Italian—15th century

Count Giovanni Pico della Mirandola, 1463-1494

COLLECTIONS

Pater, Walter Horatio. Renaissance Studies in Art and Poetry. Modern Lib.
SCPL

Italian—19th century

Gabriele D'Annunzio, 1863-1938

Winwar, Frances. Wingless Victory: A Biography of Gabriele D'Annunzio and Eleonora Duse. Harper 1956
SCPL

Italian—20th century

Gabriele D'Annunzio, 1863-1938

Winwar, Frances. Wingless Victory: A Biography of Gabriele D'Annunzio and Eleonora Duse. Harper 1956
SCPL

Danilo Dolci, 1924-

McNeish, James. Fire Under the Ashes: The Life of Danilo Dolci. Beacon Press 1966
Bkl A

Japanese—20th century

Toyohiko Kagawa, 1888-1960

Simon, Charlie May. A Seed Shall Serve: The Story of Toyohiko Kagawa, Spiritual Leader of Modern Japan. Dutton 1958
BY—SCHS—YR

New Zealand—20th century

Katherine Mansfield, 1888-1923

Alpers, Antony. Katherine Mansfield: A Biography. Knopf 1953
SCPL

Ngaio Marsh, 1899-

Marsh, Ngaio. Black Beech and Honeydew: An Autobiography. Little 1965
Bkl A&Y

Russian

COLLECTIONS

Carlisle, Olga (Andreyev). Voices in the Snow: Encounters with Russian Writers. Random House 1963
Bkl A
Il'ia Grigor'evich Ehrenburg; Eugeniĭ Aleksandrovich Evtushenko; Boris Leonidovich Pasternak; Mikhail Aleksandrovich Sholokhov; and others

Muchnic, Helen. From Gorky to Pasternak: Six Writers in Soviet Russia. Random House 1961
Bkl A
Aleksandr Aleksandrovich Blok; Maxim Gorky; Leonid Maksimovich Leonov; Vladimir Vladimirovich Mayakovski; Boris Leonidovich Pasternak; Mikhail Aleksandrovich Sholokhov

Slonim, Mark L'vovĭch. Modern Russian Literature: From Chekhov to the Present. Oxford 1953
SCPL

Russian—19th century

Anton Pavlovich Chekhov, 1860-1904

Magarshack, David. Chekhov: A Life. Grove 1952
SCPL

Saunders, Beatrice. Tchekhov, the Man. Dufour 1961
Bkl A

Simmons, Ernest Joseph. Chekhov: A Biography. Little 1962
Bkl A—SCPL

AUTHORS

Russian—19th century—*Continued*

Nikolaĭ Vasil'evich Gogol, 1809-1852

Magarshack, David. Gogol: A Life. Grove 1957
SCPL

Setschkareff, Vsevolod. Gogol: His Life and Works; tr. by Robert Kramer. N. Y. Univ. 1965
Bkl A

Russian—20th century

Isaak Emmanuilovich Babel', 1894-1938

Babel', Isaak Emmanuilovich. Isaak Babel: The Lonely Years, 1925-1939: Unpublished Stories and Private Correspondence; tr. from the Russian by Andrew R. MacAndrew and Max Hayward; ed. by Nathalie Babel. Farrar 1964
Bkl A—IndS(12)

IUlii Markovich Daniel, 1925?-

Siniavskiĭ, Andreĭ Donat'evich and Daniel, IUlii Markovich. On Trial: The Soviet State versus "Abram Tertz" and "Nikolai Arzhak"; tr. by Max Hayward. Harper 1966
Bkl A

Il'ia Grigor'evich Ehrenburg, 1891-1967

Ehrenburg, Il'ia Grigor'evich. Memoirs: 1921-1941; tr. by Tatania Shebunina and Yvonne Kapp. World 1964
Bkl A

Ehrenburg, Il'ia Grigor'evich. People and Life, 1891-1921; tr. from the Russian by Anna Bostock and Yvonne Kapp. Knopf 1962
Bkl A

COLLECTIONS

Carlisle, Olga (Andreyev). Voices in the Snow: Encounters with Russian Writers. Random House 1963
Bkl A

Maxim Gorky, 1868-1936

Levin, Dan. Stormy Petrel: The Life and Work of Maxim Gorky. Appleton 1965
Bkl A

COLLECTIONS

Muchnic, Helen. From Gorky to Pasternak: Six Writers in Soviet Russia. Random House 1961
Bkl A

Samuil IAkovlevich Marshak, 1887-1964

Marshak, Samuil IAkovlevich. At Life's Beginning: Some Pages of Reminiscence; tr. by Katherine Hunter Blair. Dutton 1964
Bkl A—IndS(11-12)

Boris Leonidovich Pasternak, 1890-1960

Conquest, Robert. The Pasternak Affair: Courage of Genius. Lippincott 1962
Bkl A

Pasternak, Boris Leonidovich. I Remember: Sketch for an Autobiography. Pantheon 1959
SCPL

Pasternak, Boris Leonidovich. Safe Conduct. New Directions 1949
GR

Payne, Pierre Stephen Robert. The Three Worlds of Boris Pasternak. Coward-McCann 1961
Bkl A—SCPL

COLLECTIONS

Carlisle, Olga (Andreyev). Voices in the Snow: Encounters with Russian Writers. Random House 1963
Bkl A

Muchnic, Helen. From Gorky to Pasternak: Six Writers in Soviet Russia. Random House 1961
Bkl A

Mikhail Aleksandrovich Sholokhov, 1905-

COLLECTIONS

Carlisle, Olga (Andreyev). Voices in the Snow: Encounters with Russian Writers. Random House 1963
Bkl A

Muchnic, Helen. From Gorky to Pasternak: Six Writers in Soviet Russia. Random House 1961
Bkl A

Andreĭ Donat'evich Siniavskiĭ, 1925-

Siniavskiĭ, Andreĭ Donat'evich and Daniel, IUlii Markovich. On Trial: The Soviet State versus "Abram Tertz" and "Nikolai Arzhak"; tr. by Max Hayward. Harper 1966
Bkl A

Scottish—18th century

James Boswell, 1740-1795

Boswell, James. Boswell for the Defence, 1769-1774; ed. by William K. Wimsatt, Jr. and Frederick A. Pottle. McGraw 1959
Bkl A

AUTHORS
Scottish—18th century
James Boswell—Continued

Boswell, James. Boswell in Holland, 1763-1764. McGraw 1952
SCPL

Boswell, James. Boswell in Search of a Wife, 1766-1769. McGraw 1956
SCPL

Boswell, James. Boswell on the Grand Tour: Germany and Switzerland, 1764. McGraw 1953
SCPL

Boswell, James. Boswell on the Grand Tour: Italy, Corsica, and France, 1765-1766. McGraw 1955
SCPL

Boswell, James. Boswell: The Ominous Years, 1774-1776; ed. by Charles Ryskamp and Frederick A. Pottle. McGraw 1963
Bkl A—SCPL

Boswell, James. Boswell's London Journal, 1762-1763. McGraw 1950
GR—SCPL

Boswell, James. Journal of a Tour to the Hebrides with Samuel Johnson, LL.D., 1773; ed. by Frederick A. Pottle and Charles H. Bennett. McGraw 1962
Bkl A

Pottle, Frederick Albert. James Boswell: The Earlier Years, 1740-1769. McGraw 1966
Bkl A

Scottish—19th century
Jane Baillie (Welsh) Carlyle, 1801-1866

COLLECTIONS

Drew, Elizabeth A. The Literature of Gossip: Nine English Letterwriters. Norton 1964
Bkl A&Y

Kenneth Grahame, 1859-1932

Green, Peter. Kenneth Grahame: A Biography. World 1959
SCPL

George Macdonald, 1824-1905

COLLECTIONS

Green, Roger Lancelyn. Tellers of Tales: British Authors of Children's Books from 1800 to 1964. Watts 1965
ESLC

Sir Walter Scott, 1771-1832

Gray, Elizabeth Janet. Young Walter Scott. Viking 1935
BBJH—CC(7-9)—JH—SCHS

Pearson, Hesketh. Sir Walter Scott: His Life and Personality. Harper 1954
BBHS—SCHS—SCPL

Keith, Christina. The Author of Waverley: A Study in the Personality of Sir Walter Scott. Roy 1966
Bkl A

Robert Louis Stevenson, 1850-1894

Bailey, Alice Cooper. To Remember Robert Louis Stevenson. McKay 1966
Bkl Y&C—ESLC

Caldwell, Elsie (Noble). Last Witness for Robert Louis Stevenson. Univ. of Okla. 1960
Bkl A

Daiches, David. Robert Louis Stevenson. New Directions 1947
SCPL

Furnas, Joseph Chamberlain. Voyage to Windward: The Life of Robert Louis Stevenson. Sloane 1951
SCPL

Kiely, Robert. Robert Louis Stevenson and the Fiction of Adventure. Harvard Univ. 1964
Bkl A&Y

Peare, Catherine Owens. Robert Louis Stevenson: His Life. Holt 1955
CC(4-7)—ESLC

Proudfit, Isabel. The Treasure Hunter: The Story of Robert Louis Stevenson. Messner 1939
CC(7-9)—ESLC—JH—SCHS—YR

Stevenson, Fanny (Van de Grift) Osbourne and Stevenson, Robert Louis. Our Samoan Adventure; ed. by Charles Neider. Harper 1955
SCPL

Wood, James Playsted. The Lantern Bearer: A Life of Robert Louis Stevenson. Pantheon 1965
Bkl C(7-10)&Y—IndJ(6-9)

COLLECTIONS

Green, Roger Lancelyn. Authors & Places: A Literary Pilgrimage. Putnam 1963
ESLC

Hoff, Rhoda. Why They Wrote. Walck 1961
Bkl C(7-10)&Y—SCHS

Stirling, Nora B. Who Wrote the Classics? Day 1965
Bkl Y&A&C

Scottish—20th century
Kenneth Grahame, 1859-1932

Green, Peter. Kenneth Grahame: A Biography. World 1959
SCPL

AUTHORS—*Continued*

Spanish—20th century

Antonio Machado y Ruiz, 1875-1939

COLLECTIONS

Young, Howard Thomas. The Victorious Expression: A Study of Four Contemporary Spanish Poets. Univ. of Wis. 1964
   Bkl A

Miguel de Unamuno y Jugo, 1864-1936

COLLECTIONS

Young, Howard Thomas. The Victorious Expression: A Study of Four Contemporary Spanish Poets. Univ. of Wis. 1964
   Bkl A

Swedish—19th century

August Strindberg, 1849-1912

Klaf, Franklin S. Strindberg: The Origin of Psychology in Modern Drama. Citadel 1963
   Bkl A
Lucas, Frank Laurence. The Drama of Ibsen and Strindberg. Macmillan 1962
   Bkl A
Sprigge, Elizabeth. Strange Life of August Strindberg. Macmillan 1949
   SCPL

AUTOMOBILE INDUSTRY WORKERS

American—20th century

Henry Ford, 1863-1947

Burlingame, Roger. Henry Ford: A Great Life in Brief. Knopf 1955
   BBHS—BY—SCHS—SCPL—3000
Nevins, Allan and Hill, Frank Ernest. Ford: v. 1, The Times, the Man, the Company. Scribner 1954
   BY—SCPL
Nevins, Allan and Hill, Frank Ernest. Ford: v. 2, Expansion and Challenge, 1915-1933. Scribner 1957
   SCPL
Nevins, Allan and Hill, Frank Ernest. Ford: v. 3, Decline and Rebirth, 1933-1962. Scribner 1963
   Bkl A—SCPL
Neyhart, Louise Albright. Henry Ford, Engineer. Houghton 1950
   BBJH—JH

COLLECTIONS

American Heritage. Captains of Industry, by Bernard A. Weisberger. Harper 1966
   Bkl C(7-10)&Y—ESLC

Clifton, Paul. The Fastest Men on Earth. Day 1966
   Bkl A&Y

Charles Franklin Kettering, 1876-1958

Lavine, Sigmund A. Kettering: Master Inventor. Dodd 1960
   SCHS—YR
Young, Rosamond McPherson. Boss Ket. McKay 1961
   YR

Alfred Pritchard Sloan, 1875-1966

Sloan, Alfred Pritchard. My Years with General Motors; ed. by John McDonald and Catharine Stevens. Doubleday 1964
   Bkl A—SCPL

English—20th century

Charles Stewart Rolls, 1877-1910

COLLECTIONS

Clifton, Paul. The Fastest Men on Earth. Day 1966
   Bkl A&Y

German—20th century

Emil Jellinek-Mercédès, 1863-1918

Jellinek-Mercédès, Guy. My Father, Mr. Mercédès; tr. by Ruth Hassell. Chilton 1966
   Bkl A

AUTOMOBILE RACERS

COLLECTIONS

Clifton, Paul. The Fastest Men on Earth. Day 1966
   Bkl A&Y
   Art Arfons; Donald Campbell; Sir Malcolm Campbell; John Cobb; Henry Ford; Barney Oldfield; C. S. Rolls; Mickey Thompson; and others
MacPherson, Tom. Great Racing Drivers. Putnam 1962
   Bkl Y&C
Miller, Peter. The Fast Ones. Sportshelf 1963
   Bkl A&Y
Miller, Peter. Men at the Wheel. Arco 1965
   Bkl A&Y
Nolan, William F. Men of Thunder: Fabled Daredevils of Motor Sport. Putnam 1964
   Bkl A&Y

American—20th century

Art Arfons, 1925?-

COLLECTIONS

Clifton, Paul. The Fastest Men on Earth. Day 1966
   Bkl A&Y

AUTOMOBILE RACERS

American—20th century—Continued

John Fitch, 1917-

Fitch, John and Nolan, William F. Adventure on Wheels: The Autobiography of a Road Racing Champion. Putnam 1959
Bkl A&Y

Barney Oldfield, 1878-1946

Nolan, William F. Barney Oldfield. Putnam 1961
Bkl A

COLLECTIONS

Clifton, Paul. The Fastest Men on Earth. Day 1966
Bkl A&Y

Wilbur Shaw, 1902-1954

Shaw, Wilbur. Gentlemen, Start Your Engines. Coward-McCann 1955
SCHS

Carroll Hall Shelby, ?

Shelby, Carroll Hall and Bentley, John. The Cobra Story. Trident Press 1965
Bkl A&Y

Mickey Thompson, 1928-

Thompson, Mickey and Borgeson, Griffith. Challenger: Mickey Thompson's Own Story of His Life of Speed. Prentice-Hall 1964
Bkl A&Y

COLLECTIONS

Clifton, Paul. The Fastest Men on Earth. Day 1966
Bkl A&Y

English—20th century

Donald Campbell, 1921-1967

Pearson, John George. The Last Hero: The Gallant Story of Donald Campbell and the Land Speed Record, 1964. McKay 1966
Bkl A&Y

COLLECTIONS

Clifton, Paul. The Fastest Men on Earth. Day 1966
Bkl A&Y

Sir Malcolm Campbell, 1885-1948

COLLECTIONS

Clifton, Paul. The Fastest Men on Earth. Day 1966
Bkl A&Y

John Cobb, 1899-1952

COLLECTIONS

Clifton, Paul. The Fastest Men on Earth Day 1966
Bkl A&Y

Stirling Moss, 1929-

Moss, Stirling and Purdy, Ken W. All But My Life. Dutton 1963
Bkl A&Y

German—20th century

Rudolf Caracciola, 1901-1959

Caracciola, Rudolf. A Racing Car Driver's World. Farrar 1961
Bkl A&Y—BY

Scottish—20th century

James Clark, 1936-1968

Clark, James. Jim Clark at the Wheel: The World Motor Racing Champion's Own Story. Coward-McCann 1965
Bkl A&Y

AVIATORS

See also Airline Stewardesses; Astronauts; Engineers, Aeronautical

COLLECTIONS

Army Times. Famous Fighters of World War I. Dodd 1964
Bkl C&Y—YR

Glines, C. V. Polar Aviation. Watts 1964
ESLC
Salomon August Andrée; Richard Evelyn Byrd; Robert Lee Scott; and others

Gurney, Gene. Flying Aces of World War I. Random House 1965
ESLC

Newlon, Clarke. Famous Pioneers in Space. Dodd 1963
Bkl C(7-9)&Y—IndS(9-12)

Oughton, Frederick. The Aces. Putnam 1960
Bkl A&Y
Max Immelmann; Edward Mannock; Charles Nungesser; Baron Manfred von Richthofen; Eddie Rickenbacker; and others

Shippen, Katherine Binney. A Bridle for Pegasus. Viking 1951
BBEL(7-8)—BBHS—BBJH—CC(7-9)—ESLC—JH

Sunderman, James F., ed. Early Air Pioneers, 1862-1935. Watts 1961
Bkl Y&C—JH

American

COLLECTIONS

Anders, Curtis. Fighting Airmen. Putnam 1966
Bkl A&Y
Henry Harley Arnold; Claire Lee Chennault; James Harold Doolittle; George Churchill Kenney; Curtis Emerson LeMay; William Mitchell; Eddie Rickenbacker

Feeny, William D. In Their Honor: True Stories of Fliers for Whom United States Air Force Bases Are Named. Duell 1963
Bkl A&Y

AVIATORS

American—*Continued*

Hoyt, Mary Finch. American Women of the Space Age. Atheneum 1966
Bkl C&Y

Loomis, Robert D. Great American Fighter Pilots of World War II. Random House 1961
Bkl C(5-8)&Y—SCHS—YR
Richard Ira Bong; Gregory Boyington; Don Gentile; Robert Lee Scott; and others

Sims, Edward H. Greatest Fighter Missions of the Top Navy and Marine Aces of World War II. Harper 1962
Bkl A&Y

American—19th century

Thaddeus Sobieski Coulincourt Lowe, 1832-1913

Block, Eugene B. Above the Civil War: The Story of Thaddeus Lowe, Balloonist, Inventor, Railway Builder. Howell-North 1966
Bkl A&Y

Sims, Lydel. Thaddeus Lowe: Uncle Sam's First Airman. Putnam 1964
Bkl C(7-9)&Y—ESLC—JH

American—20th century

Henry Harley Arnold, 1886-1950

COLLECTIONS

Anders, Curtis. Fighting Airmen. Putnam 1966
Bkl A&Y

Bernt Balchen, 1899-

Balchen, Bernt. Come North with Me: An Autobiography. Dutton 1958
BBHS—BY—SCHS—SCPL

Richard Ira Bong, 1920-1945

Kenney, George Churchill. Dick Bong, Ace of Aces. Duell 1960
Bkl A&Y

COLLECTIONS

Loomis, Robert D. Great American Fighter Pilots of World War II. Random House 1961
Bkl C(5-8)&Y—SCHS—YR

Gregory Boyington, 1912-

Boyington, Gregory. Baa Baa Black Sheep. Putnam 1958
SCPL

COLLECTIONS

Loomis, Robert D. Great American Fighter Pilots of World War II. Random House 1961
Bkl C(5-8)&Y—SCHS—YR

William Barton Bridgeman, 1917?-1968

Bridgeman, William Barton and Hazard, Jacqueline. The Lonely Sky. Holt 1955
BY—SCHS—SCPL

Richard Evelyn Byrd, 1888-1957

Byrd, Richard Evelyn. Alone. Putnam 1938
BY—SCHS—SCPL

Byrd, Richard Evelyn. Little America. Putnam 1930
SCPL—YR

Byrd, Richard Evelyn. Skyward. Putnam 1928
SCPL

De Leeuw, Adele. Richard E. Byrd: Adventurer to the Poles. Garrard 1963
AB(2-6)—ESLC

Gladych, Michael. Admiral Byrd of Antarctica. Messner 1960
Bkl C(5-8)—ESLC

Rink, Paul. Conquering Antarctica: Richard E. Byrd. Encyc. Britannica 1961
JH

COLLECTIONS

Glines, C. V. Polar Aviation. Watts 1964
ESLC

Claire Lee Chennault, 1890-1958

Archibald, Joseph. Commander of the Flying Tigers: Claire Lee Chennault. Messner 1966
Bkl C(7-10)&Y

Chennault, Anna C. Chennault and the Flying Tigers. Eriksson 1963
Bkl A&Y—SCHS

Chennault, Anna C. A Thousand Springs: The Biography of a Marriage. Eriksson 1962
Bkl A&Y—BY—SCPL

COLLECTIONS

Anders, Curtis. Fighting Airmen. Putnam 1966
Bkl A&Y

Jacqueline Cochran, 1910?-

Cochran, Jacqueline. Stars at Noon. Little 1954
SCHS—SCPL

Alfred Scott Crossfield, 1921-

Crossfield, Alfred Scott and Blair, Clay. Always Another Dawn. World 1960
Bkl A&Y

Glenn Curtiss, 1878-1930

Hatch, Alden. Glenn Curtiss, Pioneer in Naval Aviation. Messner 1942
YR

AVIATORS

American—20th century—*Continued*

Alexander Procofieff De Seversky, 1894-

COLLECTIONS

Gelfand, Revina and Patterson, Leitha. They Wouldn't Quit. Lerner Publications 1962
AB(5-9)

James Harold Doolittle, 1896-

COLLECTIONS

Anders, Curtis. Fighting Airmen. Putnam 1966
Bkl A&Y

Amelia Earhart, 1898-1937

Briand, Paul L. Daughter of the Sky: The Story of Amelia Earhart. Duell 1960
Bkl A&Y—BY—SCPL
Garst, Shannon. Amelia Earhart, Heroine of the Skies. Messner 1947
BY—CC(6-9)—JH
Goerner, Fred G. The Search for Amelia Earhart. Doubleday 1966
Bkl A&Y
Parlin, John. Amelia Earhart. Garrard 1962
AB(3-7)
Seibert, Jerry. Amelia Earhart: First Lady of the Air. Houghton 1960
CC(3-5)

COLLECTIONS

Boynick, David. Pioneers in Petticoats. Crowell 1959
YR
Forsee, Aylesa. American Women Who Scored Firsts. Macrae 1958
SCHS
Nathan, Dorothy. Women of Courage. Random House 1964
CC(4-6)—ESLC—JH

Frank K. Everest, 1920-

Everest, Frank K. and Guenther, John. The Fastest Man Alive: A Test Pilot Tells His Story. Dutton 1958
BY—SCHS

Don Gentile, 1920?-1951

COLLECTIONS

Loomis, Robert D. Great American Fighter Pilots of World War II. Random House 1961
Bkl C(5-8)&Y—SCHS—YR

Howard Robard Hughes, 1905-

Keats, John. Howard Hughes. Random House 1966
Bkl A

George Churchill Kenney, 1889-

COLLECTIONS

Anders, Curtis. Fighting Airmen. Putnam 1966
Bkl A&Y

Iven Carl Kincheloe, 1928-1958

Haggerty, James J. First of the Spacemen, Iven C. Kincheloe, Jr. Duell 1960
Bkl A&Y

Joseph W. Kittinger, ?

Kittinger, Joseph W. and Caidin, Martin. The Long, Lonely Leap. Dutton 1961
Bkl A&Y—YR

Curtis Emerson LeMay, 1906-

LeMay, Curtis Emerson and Kantor, MacKinlay. Mission with LeMay: My Story. Doubleday 1965
Bkl A&Y

COLLECTIONS

Anders, Fighting Airmen. Putnam 1966
Bkl A&Y

Anthony William Le Vier, 1913-

Le Vier, Anthony William. Pilot; ed. by John Guenther. Harper 1954
BY—SCHS

Charles Augustus Lindbergh, 1902-

Dalgliesh, Alice, ed. Ride on the Wind. Scribner 1956
BBEL—CC(3-5)—ESLC
Davis, Kenneth S. The Hero: Charles A. Lindbergh and the American Dream. Doubleday 1959
Bkl A&Y—SCPL
Lindbergh, Charles Augustus. Spirit of St. Louis. Scribner 1956
SCHS—SCPL—3000—YR
Lindbergh, Charles Augustus. "We." Putnam 1927
SCPL
Waller, George. Kidnap: The Story of the Lindbergh Case. Dial 1961
Bkl A—SCPL

Glenn Luther Martin, 1886-1955

Still, Henry. To Ride the Wind: A Biography of Glenn L. Martin. Messner 1964
Bkl A&Y

William Mitchell, 1879-1936

Hurley, Alfred F. Billy Mitchell: Crusader for Air Power. Watts 1964
Bkl A&Y
Levine, Isaac Don. Mitchell, Pioneer of Air Power. Duell 1958
SCPL
Whitehouse, Arthur George Joseph. Billy Mitchell: America's Eagle of Air Power. Putnam 1962
Bkl C(7-10)&Y—JH

AVIATORS

American—20th century

William Mitchell—Continued

COLLECTIONS

Anders, Curtis. Fighting Airmen. Putnam 1966
Bkl A&Y

Francis Gary Powers, 1929-

COLLECTIONS

Army Times. Modern American Secret Agents. Dodd 1966
Bkl C(7-9)&Y

William H. Rankin, 1920-

Rankin, William H. The Man Who Rode the Thunder. Prentice-Hall 1960
Bkl A&Y—BY—SCHS

Eddie Rickenbacker, 1890-

COLLECTIONS

Anders, Curtis. Fighting Airmen. Putnam 1966
Bkl A&Y

Oughton, Frederick. The Aces. Putnam 1960
Bkl A&Y

Robert Lee Scott, 1908-

Scott, Robert Lee. Boring a Hole in the Sky: Six Million Miles with a Fighter Pilot. Random House 1961
Bkl A&Y

COLLECTIONS

Glines, C. V. Polar Aviation. Watts 1964
ESLC

Loomis, Robert D. Great American Fighter Pilots of World War II. Random House 1961
Bkl C(5-8)&Y—SCHS—YR

Dean C. Smith, ?

Smith, Dean C. By the Seat of My Pants. Little 1961
Bkl A&Y

Frank Kingston Smith, 1919-

Smith, Frank Kingston. Flights of Fancy. Random House 1960
Bkl A

Gustave Whitehead, 1874-1927

Randolph, Stella. Before the Wrights Flew: The Story of Gustave Whitehead. Putnam 1966
Bkl C(7-10)&Y

Wilbur Wright, 1867-1912

Gardner, Jeanne McMonnier. Sky Pioneers. Harcourt 1963
AB(4-7)—ESLC

Haines, Madge and Morrill, Leslie. The Wright Brothers, First to Fly. Abingdon 1955
AB(4-7)—ESLC

Kaufman, Mervyn D. The Wright Brothers. Garrard 1964
AB(3-6)

Reynolds, Quentin James. The Wright Brothers: Pioneers of American Aviation. Random House 1950
BBEL(5-7)—BBJH—CC(4-6)—ESLC—JH—SCHS

Sobol, Donald J. The Wright Brothers at Kitty Hawk. Nelson 1961
AB(5-9)

Thomas, Henry. The Wright Brothers. Putnam 1960
Bkl C(5-7)—CC(4-7)

Wright, Orville. How We Invented the Airplane; ed. by Fred C. Kelly. McKay 1953
SCPL

Wright, Wilbur and Wright, Orville. Miracle at Kitty Hawk: The Letters of Wilbur and Orville Wright; ed. by F. C. Kelly. Farrar 1951
SCPL

COLLECTIONS

Bixby, William. Great Experimenters. McKay 1964
Bkl C(7-8)&Y—ESLC

Australian—20th century

Sir Patrick Gordon Taylor, 1896-

Taylor, Sir Patrick Gordon. The Sky Beyond. Houghton 1963
Bkl A&Y

Sir George Hubert Wilkins, 1888-1958

Thomas, Lowell Jackson. Sir Hubert Wilkins—His World of Adventure: A Biography. McGraw 1961
Bkl A&Y

Brazilian—20th century

Alberto Santos-Dumont, 1873-1932

Wykeham, Peter. Santos-Dumont: A Study in Obsession. Harcourt 1963
Bkl A—IndS(9-12)

Canadian—20th century

William Avery Bishop, 1894-1956

Bishop, William Arthur. The Courage of the Early Morning: A Frank Biography of Billy Bishop, the Great Ace of World War I. McKay 1966
Bkl A&Y

AVIATORS—*Continued*

English—19th century

Sir George Cayley, 1773-1857

Pritchard, John Laurence. Sir George Cayley, the Inventor of the Aeroplane. Horizon 1962
Bkl A

English—20th century

Douglas Bader, 1910-

Brickhill, Paul. Reach for the Sky: The Story of Douglas Bader, Legless Ace of the Battle of Britain. Norton 1954
BBHS—BY—SCHS—SCPL

Sir Francis Charles Chichester, 1901?-

Chichester, Sir Francis Charles. The Lonely Sea and the Sky. Coward-McCann 1964
Bkl A

Christopher Draper, 1892-

Draper, Christopher. The Mad Major. Aero 1962
Bkl A

Edward Mannock, ?-1918

COLLECTIONS

Oughton, Frederick. The Aces. Putnam 1960
Bkl A&Y

Charles Stewart Rolls, 1877-1910

COLLECTIONS

Clifton, Paul. The Fastest Men on Earth. Day 1966
Bkl A&Y

Hugh Montague Trenchard, Baron Trenchard, 1873-1956

Boyle, Andrew. Trenchard. Norton 1962
Bkl A

Arthur George Joseph Whitehouse, 1895-

Whitehouse, Arthur George Joseph. The Fledgling: An Autobiography. Duell 1964
Bkl A&Y

French—20th century

Charles Nungesser, 1892-1927

COLLECTIONS

Oughton, Frederick. The Aces. Putnam 1960
Bkl A&Y

Antoine de Saint-Exupéry, 1900-1944

Migeo, Marcel. Saint-Exupéry; tr. from the French by Herma Briffault. McGraw 1960
Bkl A—SCPL

Rumbold, Richard and Stewart, Lady Margaret. Winged Life: A Portrait of Antoine de Saint-Exupéry, Poet and Airman. McKay 1955?
SCPL

Saint-Exupéry, Antoine de. Airman's Odyssey. Harcourt 1943
SCPL

German—20th century

Hermann Göring, 1893-1946

Bewley, Charles Henry. Hermann Göring and the Third Reich. Devin-Adair 1962
Bkl A

Manvell, Roger and Fraenkel, Heinrich. Goering. Simon & Schuster 1962
Bkl A

Max Immelmann, 1890-1916

COLLECTIONS

Oughton, Frederick. The Aces. Putnam 1960
Bkl A&Y

Baron Manfred von Richthofen, 1892-1918

COLLECTIONS

Oughton, Frederick. The Aces. Putnam 1960
Bkl A&Y

Swedish—19th century

Salomon August Andrée, 1854-1897

COLLECTIONS

Glines, C. V. Polar Aviation. Watts 1964
ESLC

Swiss—20th century

Auguste Piccard, 1884-1962

Honour, Alan. Ten Miles High, Two Miles Deep: The Adventures of the Piccards. McGraw 1957
AB(5-9)—JH—SCHS

BACTERIOLOGISTS

COLLECTIONS

De Kruif, Paul Henry. Microbe Hunters. Harcourt 1926, Pocket Bks 1959
BBHS—SCHS—SCPL—3000

Sullivan, Navin. Pioneer Germ Fighters. Atheneum 1962
AB(4up)—CC(5-7)—ESLC
Ernest William Goodpasture; Edward Jenner; Robert Koch; Louis Pasteur; and others

American—19th century

Walter Reed, 1851-1902

Dolan, Edward F. Vanquishing Yellow Fever: Walter Reed. Encyc. Britannica 1962
JH

BACTERIOLOGISTS

American—19th century

Walter Reed—Continued

Hill, Ralph Nading. The Doctors Who
Conquered Yellow Fever. Random
House 1957
SCHS

Wood, Laura Newbold. Walter Reed,
Doctor in Uniform. Messner 1943
BBEL(7-8)—BBHS—CC(7-9)—ESLC—JH—
SCHS

American—20th century

Paul Henry De Kruif, 1890-

De Kruif, Paul Henry. Life Among the
Doctors. Harcourt 1949
SCPL

De Kruif, Paul Henry. The Sweeping
Wind: A Memoir. Harcourt 1962
Bkl A

Edward Francis, 1872-1957

COLLECTIONS

De Kruif, Paul Henry. Hunger Fighters.
Harcourt 1928
BBHS—SCHS—SCPL—3000

Selman Abraham Waksman, 1888-

COLLECTIONS

Life International. Nine Who Chose
America. Dutton 1959
Bkl Y&C—SCHS

Hans Zinsser, 1878-1940

Zinsser, Hans. As I Remember Him: The
Biography of R. S. Little 1940
SCPL

Australian—20th century

Sir David Bruce, 1855-1931

COLLECTIONS

McGrady, Mike. Jungle Doctors. Lippincott 1962
Bkl C(6-9)&Y

French—19th century

Louis Pasteur, 1822-1895

Burton, Mary June. Louis Pasteur:
Founder of Microbiology. Watts 1963
JH

Cuny, Hilaire. Louis Pasteur: The Man
and His Theories; tr. by Patrick Evans.
Eriksson 1966
Bkl A&Y

Dolan, Edward E. Pasteur and the Invisible Giants. Dodd 1958
SCHS

Dubos, René Jules. Louis Pasteur: Free
Lance of Science. Little 1950
SCPL

Dubos, René Jules. Pasteur and Modern
Science. Doubleday 1960
Bkl A&Y—3000

Grant, Madeleine P. Louis Pasteur:
Fighting Hero of Science. McGraw
1959
AB(4up)—CC

Lauber, Patricia. The Quest of Louis
Pasteur. Garden City 1960
ESLC

Mann, John Harvey. Louis Pasteur:
Founder of Bacteriology. Scribner 1964
Bkl C(6-9)&Y

Nicolle, Jacques. Louis Pasteur: The
Story of His Major Discoveries. Basic
Bks 1961
Bkl Y

Vallery-Radot, René. The Life of Pasteur;
tr. by R. L. Devonshire. Dover 1960
SCPL

Vallery-Radot, René. Louis Pasteur: A
Great Life in Brief. Knopf 1958
BBHS—SCHS—SCPL

Wood, Laura N. Louis Pasteur. Messner
1948
BBJH—CC(7-9)—ESLC—JH—SCHS

COLLECTIONS

Riedman, Sarah Regal. Shots Without
Guns: The Story of Vaccination. Rand
McNally 1960
BBHS—Bkl Y&C—CC(7-9)—ESLC—JH—
SCHS—YR

Sullivan, Navin. Pioneer Germ Fighters.
Atheneum 1962
CC(5-7)—ESLC

Williams, Greer. Virus Hunters. Knopf
1959
Bkl A&Y—3000

German—19th century

Paul Ehrlich, 1854-1915

COLLECTIONS

Riedman, Sarah Regal. Shots Without
Guns: The Story of Vaccination. Rand
McNally 1960
BBHS—Bkl Y&C—CC(7-9)—ESLC—JH—
SCHS—YR

Robert Koch, 1843-1910

Dolan, Edward F. Adventure with a Mi-
croscope: A Story of Robert Koch.
Dodd 1964
Bkl C(6-9)&Y—ESLC—JH

Knight, David C. Robert Koch, Father
of Bacteriology. Watts 1961
Bkl C(6-9)—JH

COLLECTIONS

Riedman, Sarah Regal. Shots Without
Guns: The Story of Vaccination. Rand
McNally 1960
BBHS—Bkl Y&C—CC(7-9)—ESLC—JH—
SCHS

BACTERIOLOGISTS

German—19th century

Robert Koch—Continued

Sullivan, Navin. Pioneer Germ Fighters. Atheneum 1962
CC(5-7)—ESLC

German—20th century

Paul Ehrlich, 1854-1915

COLLECTIONS

Riedman, Sarah Regal. Shots Without Guns: The Story of Vaccination. Rand McNally 1960
BBHS—Bkl Y&C—CC(7-9)—ESLC—JH—SCHS—YR

Scottish—20th century

Sir Alexander Fleming, 1881-1955

Maurois, André. Life of Sir Alexander Fleming: Discoverer of Penicillin; tr. by Gerard Hopkins. Dutton 1959
BBHS—SCPL

Rowland, John. The Penicillin Man: The Story of Alexander Fleming. Roy 1957
AB(5-9)—JH

BALLET DANCERS

See Dancers

BALLOONISTS

See Aviators

BAND LEADERS

See Bandmasters; Conductors

BANDITS

See Criminals

BANDMASTERS

See also Conductors

American

COLLECTIONS

Schwartz, Harry Wayne. Bands of America. Doubleday 1957
BBHS—SCPL
Giuseppe Creatore; Patrick Sarsfield Gilmore; Louis Antoine Jullien; Bohumir Kryl; John Philip Sousa; and others

American—19th century

Patrick Sarsfield Gilmore, 1829-1892

COLLECTIONS

Schwartz, Harry Wayne. Bands of America. Doubleday 1957
BBHS—SCPL

John Philip Sousa, 1854-1932

Lingg, Ann M. John Philip Sousa. Holt 1954
SCHS

Sousa, John Philip. Marching Along: Recollections of Men, Women and Music. Hale 1928
SCPL

COLLECTIONS

Schwartz, Harry Wayne. Bands of America. Doubleday 1957
BBHS—SCPL

Bohumir Kryl, 1898?-1935?

COLLECTIONS

Schwartz, Harry Wayne. Bands of America. Doubleday 1957
BBHS—SCPL

American—20th century

John Philip Sousa, 1854-1932

Lingg, Ann M. John Philip Sousa. Holt 1954
SCHS

Sousa, John Philip. Marching Along: Recollections of Men, Women and Music. Hale 1928
SCPL

COLLECTIONS

Schwartz, Harry Wayne. Bands of America. Doubleday 1957
BBHS—SCPL

Italian—20th century

Giuseppe Creatore, 1870?-1952

COLLECTIONS

Schwartz, Harry Wayne. Bands of America. Doubleday 1957
BBHS—SCPL

BANKERS

See Financiers

BARRISTERS

See Lawyers

BASEBALL EXECUTIVES

See Baseball Managers

BASEBALL MANAGERS

American

COLLECTIONS

Pope, Edwin. Baseball's Greatest Managers. Doubleday 1960
Bkl A&Y

BASEBALL MANAGERS—*Continued*

American—20th century

Walter Emmons ("Smokey") Alston, 1911-

Alston, Walter Emmons ("Smokey") and Burick, Si. Alston and the Dodgers. Doubleday 1966
Bkl A&Y

Joe Cronin, 1906-

Hirshberg, Albert. From Sandlots to League President: The Story of Joe Cronin. Messner 1962
Bkl C(7-12)—BY

Leo Ernest Durocher, 1906-

Schoor, Gene. The Leo Durocher Story. Messner 1955
SCHS

Gene Williams Mauch, 1925-

Richter, Ed. View from the Dugout: A Season with Baseball's Amazing Gene Mauch. Chilton 1964
Bkl A&Y

Wesley Branch Rickey, 1881-1965

Lipman, David. Mr. Baseball: The Story of Branch Rickey. Putnam 1966
Bkl C(7-10)&Y—ESLC

Charles Dillon ("Casey") Stengel, 1891-

Allen, Maury. Now Wait a Minute, Casey! Doubleday 1965
Bkl A&Y

Felker, Clay. Casey Stengel's Secret. Walker & Co. 1961
Bkl A&Y

Stengel, Charles Dillon ("Casey") and Paxton, Harry T. Casey at the Bat: The Story of My Life in Baseball. Random House 1962
Bkl A&Y—BY

William Veeck, 1914-

Veeck, William and Linn, Ed. Veeck— As in Wreck: The Autobiography of Bill Veeck. Putnam 1962
Bkl A&Y—SCPL

BASEBALL PLAYERS

American

COLLECTIONS

Allen, Lee and Meany, Thomas. Kings of the Diamond: The Immortals in Baseball's Hall of Fame. Putnam 1965
Bkl A&Y

Brosnan, Jim. Great Baseball Pitchers. Random House 1965
CC—ESLC
Jerome Herman Dean; Robert Feller; Edward Charles Ford; Carl Hubbell; Walter Johnson; Sanford Koufax; Salvatore Maglie; Christopher Mathewson; LeRoy Paige; Warren Spahn

Daley, Arthur. Kings of the Home Run. Putnam 1962
Bkl A&Y—BY

Epstein, Sam and Epstein, Beryl. Stories of Champions. Garrard 1965
AB(3-7)—ESLC—JH
Tyrus Cobb; Walter Johnson; Christopher Mathewson; George Herman Ruth; John Peter Wagner

Gelman, Steve. Young Baseball Champions. Norton 1966
Bkl C(5-9)
Henry Louis Aaron; Tyrus Cobb; Joseph Di Maggio; Donald Drysdale; Robert Feller; Mickey Mantle; Willie Mays; Melvin Thomas Ott; George Herman Ruth; Theodore Williams

Hirshberg, Albert. Baseball's Greatest Catchers. Putnam 1966
Bkl C&Y

Meany, Thomas and Holmes, Tommy. Baseball's Best: The All-Time Major League Baseball Team. Watts 1964
Bkl A&Y

Meany, Tom. Baseball's Greatest Pitchers. Barnes 1951
SCHS

Meany, Tom. Baseball's Greatest Players. Grosset 1953
BBEL(6-8)—SCHS

Newcombe, Jack. The Fireballers: Baseball's Fastest Pitchers. Putnam 1964
Bkl C(5-9)&Y—ESLC

Reeder, Red. On the Mound: Three Great Pitchers. Garrard 1966
ESLC
Howard Ehmke; Robert Feller; Carl Hubbell

Ritter, Lawrence S. The Glory of Their Times: The Story of the Early Days of Baseball Told by the Men Who Played It. Macmillan 1966
Bkl A&Y

Robinson, John Roosevelt. Baseball Has Done It; ed. by Charles Dexter. Lippincott 1964
Bkl A&Y
Henry Aaron; Ernest Banks; Elston Howard; Frank Robinson

Robinson, Ray. Speed Kings of the Base Paths: Baseball's Greatest Runners. Putnam 1964
Bkl C(5-8)—IndJ(6-9)
Luis Aparicio; Max Carey; Tyrus Cobb; Edward Collins; John ("Pepper") Martin; Willie Mays; Harold ("Pete") Reiser; John Robinson; Maurice Wills

Shapiro, Milton J. The Year They Won the Most Valuable Player Award. Messner 1966
Bkl Y&C

Silverman, Al. Heroes of the World Series. Putnam 1964
Bkl C(6-9)&Y—ESLC—JH

Smith, Ken. Baseball's Hall of Fame. Barnes 1952
SCPL

BASEBALL PLAYERS—*Continued*

American—20th century

Henry Louis Aaron, 1934-

Shapiro, Milton J. The Hank Aaron Story. Messner 1961
JH

COLLECTIONS

Gelman, Steve. Young Baseball Champions. Norton 1966
Bkl C(5-9)

Robinson, John Roosevelt. Baseball Has Done It; ed. by Charles Dexter. Lippincott 1964
Bkl A&Y

Luis Ernesto Aparicio, 1934-

COLLECTIONS

Robinson, Ray. Speed Kings of the Base Paths: Baseball's Greatest Runners. Putnam 1964
Bkl C(5-8)—IndJ(6-9)

Ernest Banks, 1931-

COLLECTIONS

Robinson, John Roosevelt. Baseball Has Done It; ed. by Charles Dexter. Lippincott 1964
Bkl A&Y

Yogi Berra, 1925-

Berra, Yogi and Fitzgerald, Edward E. Yogi: The Autobiography of a Professional Baseball Player. Doubleday 1961
Bkl A&Y—BY

Roswell, Gene. The Yogi Berra Story. Messner 1958
CC(5-7)

James Paul David Bunning, 1931-

Bunning, James Paul David and Bernstein, Ralph. The Story of Jim Bunning. Lippincott 1965
Bkl A&Y

Roy Campanella, 1921-

Campanella, Roy. It's Good to Be Alive. Little 1959
BBHS—SCHS—YR

Schoor, Gene. Roy Campanella: Man of Courage. Putnam 1959
CC—ESLC

Shapiro, Milton J. The Roy Campanella Story. Messner 1958
CC—JH—YR

Max George Carey, 1890-

COLLECTIONS

Robinson, Ray. Speed Kings of the Base Paths: Baseball's Greatest Runners. Putnam 1964
Bkl C(5-8)—IndJ(6-9)

Tyrus Raymond Cobb, 1886-1961

Cobb, Tyrus Raymond and Stump, Al. My Life in Baseball: The True Record. Doubleday 1961
Bkl A&Y—SCPL

Schoor, Gene and Gilfond, Henry. The Story of Ty Cobb, Baseball's Greatest Player. Messner 1952
BBEL(7-8)—ESLC—SCHS

COLLECTIONS

Epstein, Sam and Epstein, Beryl. Stories of Champions. Garrard 1965
AB(3-7)—ESLC—JH

Gelman, Steve. Young Baseball Champions. Norton 1966
Bkl C(5-9)

Robinson, Ray. Speed Kings of the Base Paths: Baseball's Greatest Runners. Putnam 1964
Bkl C(5-8)—IndJ(6-9)

Edward Trowbridge Collins, 1887-1951

COLLECTIONS

Robinson, Ray. Speed Kings of the Base Paths: Baseball's Greatest Runners. Putnam 1964
Bkl C(5-8)—IndJ(6-9)

Jerome Herman ("Dizzy") Dean, 1911-

Shapiro, Milton J. The Dizzy Dean Story. Messner 1963
Bkl C(7-10)&Y

COLLECTIONS

Brosnan, Jim. Great Baseball Pitchers. Random House 1965
CC—ESLC

Joseph Paul Di Maggio, 1914-

Di Maggio, Joseph Paul. Lucky to Be a Yankee. Grosset 1946
SCHS

Schoor, Gene. Joe Di Maggio, the Yankee Clipper. Messner 1956
SCHS

COLLECTIONS

Gelman, Steve. Young Baseball Champions. Norton 1966
Bkl C(5-9)

Donald Scott Drysdale, 1936-

Shapiro, Milton J. The Don Drysdale Story. Messner 1964
JH

COLLECTIONS

Gelman, Steve. Young Baseball Champions. Norton 1966
Bkl C(5-9)

BASEBALL PLAYERS

American—20th century—*Continued*

Howard John Ehmke, 1894-1959

COLLECTIONS

Reeder, Red. On the Mound: Three Great Pitchers. Garrard 1966
ESLC

Robert William Andrew Feller, 1918-

Schoor, Gene. Bob Feller, Hall of Fame Strikeout Star. Doubleday 1962
Bkl C(7-9)&Y

COLLECTIONS

Brosnan, Jim. Great Baseball Pitchers. Random House 1965
CC—ESLC

Gelman, Steve. Young Baseball Champions. Norton 1966
Bkl C(5-9)

Reeder, Red. On the Mound: Three Great Pitchers. Garrard 1966
ESLC

Edward Charles Ford, 1928-

Shapiro, Milton J. The Whitey Ford Story. Messner 1962
Bkl Y&C—ESLC

COLLECTIONS

Brosnan, Jim. Great Baseball Pitchers. Random House 1965
CC—ESLC

Lou Gehrig, 1903-1941

Graham, Frank. Lou Gehrig: A Quiet Hero. Putnam 1942
BBEL(6-8)—BBJH—BY—CC(6-9)—JH—SCHS—SCPL

Hubler, Richard. Lou Gehrig: The Iron Horse of Baseball. Houghton 1941
BY

Gilbert Ray Hodges, 1924-

Shapiro, Milton J. The Gil Hodges Story. Messner 1960
Bkl Y&C—JH

Elston Gene Howard, 1930-

COLLECTIONS

Robinson, John Roosevelt. Baseball Has Done It; ed. by Charles Dexter. Lippincott 1964
Bkl A&Y

Carl Owen Hubbell, 1903-

COLLECTIONS

Brosnan, Jim. Great Baseball Pitchers. Random House 1965
CC—ESLC

Reeder, Red. On the Mound: Three Great Pitchers. Garrard 1966
ESLC

Walter Perry Johnson, 1887-1946

COLLECTIONS

Brosnan, Jim. Great Baseball Pitchers. Random House 1965
CC—ESLC

Epstein, Sam and Epstein, Beryl. Stories of Champions. Garrard 1965
AB(3-7)—ESLC—JH

Albert William Kaline, 1934-

Hirshberg, Albert. The Al Kaline Story. Messner 1964
Bkl C(7-9)&Y

Sanford Koufax, 1935-

Hano, Arnold. Sandy Koufax: Strikeout King. Putnam 1964
Bkl C(7-9)&Y—ESLC—JH

Koufax, Sanford and Linn, Ed. Koufax. Viking 1966
Bkl A&Y

COLLECTIONS

Brosnan, Jim. Great Baseball Pitchers. Random House 1965
CC—ESLC

Salvatore Anthony Maglie, 1917-

COLLECTIONS

Brosnan, Jim. Great Baseball Pitchers. Random House 1965
CC—ESLC

Mickey Charles Mantle, 1931-

Schoor, Gene. Mickey Mantle of the Yankees. Putnam 1958
BBJH—JH—SCHS

Shapiro, Milton J. Mickey Mantle, Yankee Slugger. Messner 1962
AB(7-9)—Bkl Y&C—BY—JH—SCHS

Silverman, Al. Mickey Mantle, Mister Yankee. Putnam 1963
Bkl C(7-9)&Y—ESLC

COLLECTIONS

Gelman, Steve. Young Baseball Champions. Norton 1966
Bkl C(5-9)

Martin Whiteford Marion, 1917-

COLLECTIONS

Boynick, David King. Champions by Setback: Athletes Who Overcame Physical Handicaps. Crowell 1954
SCHS

Roger Eugene Maris, 1934-

Maris, Roger and Ogle, Jim. Roger Maris at Bat. Duell 1962
Bkl A&Y—BY

BASEBALL PLAYERS

American—20th century—*Continued*

John Leonard ("Pepper") Martin, 1904-1965

COLLECTIONS

Robinson, Ray. Speed Kings of the Base Paths: Baseball's Greatest Runners. Putnam 1964
Bkl C(5-8)—IndJ(6-9)

Christopher Mathewson, 1880-1925

Schoor, Gene. Christy Mathewson. Messner n.d.
BBEL(7-8)

COLLECTIONS

Brosnan, Jim. Great Baseball Pitchers. Random House 1965
CC—ESLC

Epstein, Sam and Epstein, Beryl. Stories of Champions. Garrard 1965
AB(3-7)—ESLC—JH

Willie Howard Mays, 1931-

Einstein, Charles. Willie Mays: Coast to Coast Giant. Putnam 1963
ESLC

Mays, Willie Howard and Einstein, Charles. Born to Play Ball: Willie Mays' Own Story. Putnam 1955
BY—SCHS

Mays, Willie Howard and Einstein, Charles. Willie Mays: My Life in and out of Baseball. Dutton 1966
Bkl A&Y

Shapiro, Milton J. The Willie Mays Story. Messner 1960
Bkl Y&C—BY—JH—SCHS

COLLECTIONS

Bontemps, Arna. Famous Negro Athletes. Dodd 1964
Bkl C&Y—ESLC—JH

Gelman, Steve. Young Baseball Champions. Norton 1966
Bkl C(5-9)

Robinson, Ray. Speed Kings of the Base Paths: Baseball's Greatest Runners. Putnam 1964
Bkl C(5-8)—IndJ(6-9)

Stanley Frank Musial, 1920-

Musial, Stanley Frank and Broeg, Robert M. Stan Musial: "The Man's" Own Story. Doubleday 1964
Bkl A&Y

Robinson, Ray. Stan Musial: Baseball's Durable "Man." Putnam 1963
Bkl C(7-9)&Y—ESLC

Melvin Thomas Ott, 1909-1958

Shapiro, Milton J. The Mel Ott Story. Messner 1959
Bkl Y&C

COLLECTIONS

Gelman, Steve. Young Baseball Champions. Norton 1966
Bkl C(5-9)

LeRoy ("Satchel") Paige, 1906-

Paige, LeRoy and Lipman, David. Maybe I'll Pitch Forever. Doubleday 1962
Bkl A—BY—YR

COLLECTIONS

Bontemps, Arna. Famous Negro Athletes. Dodd 1964
Bkl C&Y—ESLC—JH

Brosnan, Jim. Great Baseball Pitchers. Random House 1965
CC—ESLC

James Anthony Piersall, 1929-

Piersall, James Anthony and Hirshberg, Al. Fear Strikes Out: The Jim Piersall Story. Little 1955
BBHS—BY—SCHS

Harold Patrick ("Pete") Reiser, 1920-

COLLECTIONS

Robinson, Ray. Speed Kings of the Base Paths: Baseball's Greatest Runners. Putnam 1964
Bkl C(5-8)—IndJ(6-9)

Frank Robinson, 1935-

COLLECTIONS

Robinson, John Roosevelt. Baseball Has Done It; ed. by Charles Dexter. Lippincott 1964
Bkl A&Y

John Roosevelt Robinson, 1919-

Mann, Arthur William. The Jackie Robinson Story. Grosset 1956
SCHS

Robinson, John Roosevelt and Duckett, Alfred. Breakthrough to the Big League: The Story of Jackie Robinson. Harper 1965
Bkl C(6-9)&Y—CC(5-7)—ESLC—IndJ(4-6)

Rowan, Carl Thomas and Robinson, John Roosevelt. Wait till Next Year. Random House 1960
Bkl A&Y—BY

Shapiro, Milton J. Jackie Robinson of the Brooklyn Dodgers. Messner 1957
BY

COLLECTIONS

Bontemps, Arna. Famous Negro Athletes. Dodd 1964
Bkl C&Y—ESLC—JH

Robinson, Ray. Speed Kings of the Base Paths: Baseball's Greatest Runners. Putnam 1964
Bkl C(5-8)—IndJ(6-9)

Young, Andrew Sturgeon Nash. Negro Firsts in Sports. Johnson Pub. 1963
Bkl A&Y

BASEBALL PLAYERS

American—20th century—*Continued*

George Herman ("Babe") Ruth, 1895-1948

Meany, Tom. Babe Ruth: The Big Moments of the Big Fellow. Grosset 1951
CC

Ruth, George Herman. Babe Ruth Story. Dutton 1948
SCHS—SCPL

COLLECTIONS

Epstein, Sam and Epstein, Beryl. Stories of Champions. Garrard 1965
AB(3-7)—ESLC—JH

Gallico, Paul. The Golden People. Doubleday 1965
Bkl A&Y

Gelman, Steve. Young Baseball Champions. Norton 1966
Bkl C(5-9)

Edwin Donald Snider, 1926-

Winehouse, Irwin. The Duke Snider Story. Messner 1964
ESLC—JH

Warren Edward Spahn, 1921-

COLLECTIONS

Brosnan, Jim. Great Baseball Pitchers. Random House 1965
CC—ESLC

John Peter Wagner, 1874-1955

COLLECTIONS

Epstein, Sam and Epstein, Beryl. Stories of Champions. Garrard 1965
AB(3-7)—ESLC—JH

Theodore Samuel Williams, 1918-

Robinson, Ray. Ted Williams. Putnam 1962
AB(5-11)—Bkl Y&C—BY

Schoor, Gene and Gilfond, Henry. The Ted Williams Story. Messner 1954
CC(5-7)

COLLECTIONS

Gelman, Steve. Young Baseball Champions. Norton 1966
Bkl C(5-9)

Maurice Morning Wills, 1932-

COLLECTIONS

Robinson, Ray. Speed Kings of the Base Paths: Baseball's Greatest Runners. Putnam 1964
Bkl C(5-8)—IndJ(6-9)

BASKETBALL PLAYERS

American

COLLECTIONS

Hirshberg, Albert. Basketball's Greatest Stars. Putnam 1963
Bkl Y&C—CC—ESLC—JH

American—20th century

William Warren Bradley, 1943-

McPhee, John A. A Sense of Where You Are: A Profile of William Warren Bradley. Farrar 1965
Bkl A&Y—IndS(9-12)

Wilton Norman Chamberlain, 1936-

COLLECTIONS

Bontemps, Arna. Famous Negro Athletes. Dodd 1964
Bkl C&Y—ESLC—JH

Robert Cousy, 1928-

Cousy, Robert and Hirshberg, Al. Basketball Is My Life. Prentice-Hall 1958
BY

Cousy, Robert and Linn, Ed. The Last Loud Roar. Prentice-Hall 1964
Bkl A&Y

Devaney, John. Bob Cousy. Putnam 1965
ESLC

Robert Pettit, 1932-

Pettit, Robert and Wolff, Bob. Bob Pettit: The Drive Within Me. Prentice-Hall 1966
Bkl A&Y

William Felton Russell, 1934-

Hirshberg, Albert. Bill Russell of the Boston Celtics. Messner 1963
Bkl C(7-10)&Y

Russell, William Felton and McSweeny, William Francis. Go Up for Glory. Coward-McCann 1966
Bkl A&Y

BEAUTICIANS

See Cosmeticians

BIBLICAL FIGURES

COLLECTIONS

Bowie, Walter Russell. Great Men of the Bible. Harper 1937
SCPL

Deen, Edith. All of the Women of the Bible. Harper 1955
SCHS—SCPL

Macartney, Clarence Edward Noble. Greatest Men of the Bible. Abingdon 1941
SCPL

BIBLICAL FIGURES—*Continued*

Morton, Henry Canova Vollam. Women of the Bible. Dodd 1956
SCPL

Yates, Elizabeth. Children of the Bible. Dutton 1950
CC(2-5)—ESLC

BIBLICAL FIGURES—NEW TESTAMENT

Jesus Christ

Anderson, Hugh. Jesus and Christian Origins: A Commentary on Modern Viewpoints. Oxford 1964
Bkl A

Asch, Sholem. The Nazarene; tr. by Maurice Samuel. Putnam 1939 (Fiction)
BBHS—SCHS

Barclay, William. Jesus as They Saw Him: New Testament Interpretations of Jesus. Harper 1963
Bkl A

Barclay, William. The Mind of Jesus. Harper 1961
Bkl A—SCPL

Bauman, Edward W. The Life and Teaching of Jesus. Westminster 1960
3000

Bible. New Testament. The Gospel Story, Based on the Translation of the Four Gospels, by Ronald Knox. Sheed 1958
SCPL

Bible. New Testament. Jesus' Story: A Little New Testament; Bible Text Selected from King James Version. Macmillan 1942
CC(3-6)

Bible. New Testament. Life of Christ in Masterpieces of Art and the Words of the New Testament; comp. by Marvin Ross. Harper 1957
SCPL

Bible. New Testament. Story of Jesus: A Little New Testament; Bible Text Selected from the Confraternity of Christian Doctrine Edition. Macmillan 1944
CC(3-7)

Bishop, James Alonzo. The Day Christ Died. Harper 1957
SCHS—SCPL

Bishop, James Alonzo. The Day Christ Was Born: A Reverential Reconstruction. Harper 1960
Bkl A—SCPL

Bornkamm, Gunther. Jesus of Nazareth; tr. by Irene and Fraser McLuskey. Harper 1961
Bkl A

Bowie, Walter Russell. The Bible Story for Boys and Girls: New Testament. Abingdon 1951
ESLC

Bowie, Walter Russell. Story of Jesus for Young People. Scribner 1937
SCPL

Branley, Franklyn Mansfield. The Christmas Sky. Crowell 1966
Bkl C(3-6)—ESLC

Bruckberger, Raymond Léopold; tr. from the French by Denver Lindley. The History of Jesus Christ. Viking 1965
Bkl A

Carmichael, Joel. The Death of Jesus. Macmillan 1963
IndS(10-12)

Chute, Marchette Gaylord. Jesus of Israel. Dutton 1961
Bkl Y&C—SCHS

Clark, Thomas Curtis and Clark, Hazel Davis, eds. Christ in Poetry: An Anthology. Assn. Press 1952 (Poem)
SCPL

Daniel-Rops, Henry. Daily Life in the Time of Jesus; tr. by Patrick O'Brian. Hawthorn 1962
SCPL

Daniel-Rops, Henry. Jesus and His Times; tr. by Ruby Millar. Dutton 1956
SCPL

Douglas, Lloyd C. The Robe. Houghton 1942 (Fiction)
JH—SCHS

Fast, Howard Melvin. The Hill: An Original Screenplay. Doubleday 1964 (Play)
Bkl A

Fitch, Florence Mary. The Child Jesus. Lothrop 1955
BBEL—CC(K-3)—ESLC

Fosdick, Harry Emerson. Jesus of Nazareth. Random House 1959
JH—SCHS

Gaer, Joseph. Lore of the New Testament. Little 1952
SCPL

Goodspeed, Edgar Johnson. Life of Jesus. Harper 1950
SCHS—SCPL—3000

Graham, Aelred. Christ of Catholicism: A Meditative Study. Longmans 1947
SCPL

Guardini, Romano. The Lord. Regnery 1954
SCPL

Hamilton, Edith. Witness to the Truth: Christ and His Interpreters. Norton 1957
SCPL

Johnson, Sherman Elbridge. Jesus in His Homeland. Scribner 1957
SCPL

Kazantzakēs, Nikos. The Last Temptation of Christ; tr. from the Greek by P. A. Bien. Simon & Schuster 1960 (Fiction)
Bkl A

BIBLICAL FIGURES—NEW TESTAMENT

Jesus Christ—Continued

Klausner, Joseph. Jesus of Nazareth: His Life, Times and Teaching; tr. by Herbert Danby. Macmillan 1925
SCPL

Komroff, Manuel, ed. Jesus Through the Centuries: His Figure and Teachings as Reflected in the Minds of Many Men. Sloane 1953
SCPL

Lynch, John W. The Deed of God. Sheed 1961 (Poem)
Bkl A

Malvern, Gladys. Tamar. Longmans 1952 (Fiction)
JH

Mauriac, François. The Son of Man; tr. by Bernard Murchland. World 1960
Bkl A

Maus, Cynthia Pearl. Christ and the Fine Arts: An Anthology of Pictures, Poetry, Music, and Stories Centering in the Life of Christ. Harper 1959
SCHS—SCPL

Nussbaumer, Mares and Nussbaumer, Paul. Away in a Manger: A Story of the Nativity. Harcourt 1965
ESLC

Oursler, Fulton. Greatest Story Ever Told: A Tale of the Greatest Life Ever Lived. Doubleday 1949
SCHS—SCPL

Paul, Leslie Allen. Son of Man: The Life of Christ. Dutton 1961
Bkl A

Payne, Robert. The Lord Jesus. Abelard-Schuman 1964 (Fiction)
IndS(11-12)

Petersham, Maud and Petersham, Miska. The Christ Child: As Told by Matthew and Luke. Doubleday 1931
CC(K-3)—ESLC

Quadflieg, Josef. The Book of the Twelve Apostles; tr. from the German by Isabel and Florence McHugh. Pantheon 1961
Bkl C(5-8)

Renan, Ernest. The Life of Jesus. Dutton; Modern Lib.; etc.
CA—GR—SCPL

Ricciotti, Guiseppe. The Life of Christ. Bruce 1947
CA—SCPL

Schonfield, Hugh Joseph. The Passover Plot: New Light on the History of Jesus. Geis 1966
Bkl A

Schweitzer, Albert. Quest of the Historical Jesus: A Critical Study of Its Progress from Reimarus to Wrede. Macmillan 1948
SCPL

Sheed, Francis Joseph. To Know Christ Jesus. Sheed 1962
Bkl A

Sheen, Fulton John, Bishop. Life of Christ. McGraw 1958
SCPL

Slaughter, Frank Gill. The Crown and the Cross: The Life of Christ. World 1959
SCPL

Speare, Elizabeth George. The Bronze Bow. Houghton 1961 (Fiction)
AB(6-9)—Bkl C(6-10)&Y—CC(6-9)—ESLC—JH—SCHS

Steinmann, Jean. The Life of Jesus; tr. from the French by Peter Green. Little 1963
Bkl A

Trueblood, David Elton. The Humor of Christ. Harper 1964
Bkl A

Vaart Smit, H. W. van der. Born in Bethlehem: Christmas as It Really Was; tr. from the German by Thomas R. Milligan. Helicon Press 1963
Bkl A

Waltari, Miki Toimi. The Secret of the Kingdom; tr. by Naomi Walford. Putnam 1961 (Fiction)
Bkl A

COLLECTIONS

Jaspers, Karl. The Great Philosophers: v. 1, The Foundations; ed. by Hannah Arendt; tr. by Ralph Manheim. Harcourt 1962
Bkl A—SCPL

Kagan, Henry Enoch. Six Who Changed the World. Yoseloff 1963
Bkl A

Saint Joseph

COLLECTIONS

Haughton, Rosemary. Six Saints for Parents. Sheed 1963
Bkl A

Joseph of Arimathea

Steedman, Marguerite. Refuge in Avalon: A Novel. Doubleday 1962 (Fiction)
Bkl A

Saint Luke

Caldwell, Taylor. Dear and Glorious Physician. Doubleday 1959 (Fiction)
SCHS

Saint Mark

Chinn, Laurene. Marcus. Morrow 1965 (Fiction)
IndS(11-12)

Virgin Mary

Lofts, Norah (Robinson). How Far to Bethlehem? A Novel. Doubleday 1965 (Fiction)
Bkl A&Y

BIBLICAL FIGURES—NEW TESTAMENT—*Continued*

Saint Paul, Apostle

Asch, Sholem. The Apostle; tr. by Maurice Samuel. Putnam 1943 (Fiction)
SCHS

Buckmaster, Henrietta. Paul: A Man Who Changed the World. McGraw 1965
Bkl A

Cannon, William Ragsdale. Journeys after St. Paul: An Excursion into History. Macmillan 1963
Bkl A

Fosdick, Harry Emerson. The Life of Saint Paul. Random House 1962
AB(5up)—Bkl C(5-9)—CC(6-9)—ESLC—JH

Kepler, Thomas Samuel, comp. Contemporary Thinking about Paul: An Anthology. Abingdon 1950
SCPL

Rall, Harris Franklin. According to Paul. Scribner 1944
SCPL

Schweitzer, Albert. Mysticism of Paul the Apostle; tr. by William Montgomery. Macmillan 1955
SCPL

Thompson, Blanche Jennings. Peter and Paul: The Rock and the Sword. Farrar 1964
ESLC

COLLECTIONS

Cluny, Roland. Holiness in Action; tr. from the French by D. A. Askew. Hawthorn 1963
Bkl A

Kagan, Henry Enoch. Six Who Changed the World. Yoseloff 1963
Bkl A

Saint Peter, Apostle

Cullman, Oscar. Peter—Disciple, Apostle, Martyr: A Historical and Theological Study; tr. by F. V. Filson. Westminster 1953
SCPL

Douglas, Lloyd C. The Big Fisherman. Houghton 1948 (Fiction)
SCHS

Slaughter, Frank Gill. Upon This Rock: A Novel of Simon Peter, Prince of the Apostles. Coward-McCann 1963 (Fiction)
Bkl A

Thompson, Blanche Jennings. Peter and Paul: The Rock and the Sword. Farrar 1964
ESLC

COLLECTIONS

Walsh, William Thomas. Saints in Action. Hanover House 1961
Bkl A

Pontius Pilate

Blythe, LeGette. Hear Me, Pilate! Holt 1961 (Fiction)
Bkl A

Caillois, Roger. Pontius Pilate; tr. by Charles Lam Markmann. Macmillan 1963 (Fiction)
Bkl A

BIBLICAL FIGURES—OLD TESTAMENT

COLLECTIONS

Bible. Old Testament. Daniel. Shadrach, Meshach and Abednego: From The Book of Daniel. McGraw 1965
ESLC

Chase, Mary Ellen. The Prophets for the Common Reader. Norton 1963
Bkl A—SCPL
Amos; Hosea; Isaiah; Jeremiah; Micah

DeJong, Meindert. The Mighty Ones (Great Men and Women of Early Bible Days). Harper n.d.
ESLC

Fichtner, Joseph. Forerunners of Christ: Studies of Old Testament Characters. Bruce 1965
Bkl A

Hamilton, Edith. Spokesmen for God: The Great Teachers of the Old Testament. Norton 1949
SCPL

James, Fleming. Personalities of the Old Testament. Scribner 1939
SCPL
David, King of Israel; Joshua, Son of Nun; Moses; Samuel, Judge of Israel; Solomon, King of Israel; and others

Lofts, Norah (Robinson). Women in the Old Testament: Twenty Psychological Portraits. Macmillan 1949
SCPL

Paterson, John. Goodly Fellowship of the Prophets: Studies, Historical, Religious, and Expository in the Hebrew Prophets. Scribner 1948
SCPL

Samuel, Maurice. Certain People of the Book. Knopf 1955
SCPL
Balaam; David, King of Israel; Jezebel, Wife of Ahab; Joseph, the Patriarch; Naomi; Rebekah; Xerxes I, King of Persia; and others

Staack, Hagen. Living Personalities of the Old Testament. Harper 1964
Bkl A

Williams, Walter George. The Prophets: Pioneers to Christianity. Abingdon 1956
SCPL
Amos; Ezekiel; Hosea; Isaiah; Jeremiah

BIBLICAL FIGURES—OLD TESTAMENT—*Continued*

Abednego

COLLECTIONS

Bible. Old Testament. Daniel. Shadrach, Meshach and Abednego: From the Book of Daniel. McGraw 1965
ESLC

Amos, Prophet

COLLECTIONS

Chase, Mary Ellen. The Prophets for the Common Reader. Norton 1963
Bkl A—SCPL

Williams, Walter George. The Prophets: Pioneers to Christianity. Abingdon 1956
SCPL

Balaam

COLLECTIONS

Samuel, Maurice. Certain People of the Book. Knopf 1955
SCPL

David, King of Israel

DeRegniers, Beatrice Schenk. David and Goliath. Viking 1965
Bkl C(1-3)—ESLC—IndJ(2-4)

De Wohl, Louis. David of Jerusalem; tr. from the German by Elisabeth Abbott. Lippincott 1963 (Fiction)
Bkl A—IndS(9-12)

Jenkins, Gwyn. King David. Doubleday 1961 (Fiction)
Bkl A

McClintock, Mike. David and the Giant. Harper 1960
CC(K-3)

Parmiter, Geoffrey de Clinton. King David. Nelson 1961
Bkl A

Petersham, Maud and Petersham, Miska. David: From the Story Told in the First Book of Samuel and the First Book of Kings. Macmillan 1958
CC(3-5)—ESLC

Slaughter, Frank Gill. David, Warrior and King: A Biblical Biography. World 1962
Bkl A

COLLECTIONS

James, Fleming. Personalities of the Old Testament. Scribner 1939
SCPL

Samuel, Maurice. Certain People of the Book. Knopf 1955
SCPL

Deborah

Jenkins, Sara Lucile. Song of Deborah: A Novel. Day 1963 (Fiction)
JH

Elijah, Prophet

Zador, Henry Bela. Hear the Word: A Novel about Elijah and Elisha; tr. by Robert W. Fenn. McGraw 1962 (Fiction)
Bkl A

Elisha, Prophet

Zador, Henry Bela. Hear the Word: A Novel about Elijah and Elisha; tr. by Robert W. Fenn. McGraw 1962 (Fiction)
Bkl A

Esther, Queen of Persia

Malvern, Gladys. Behold Your Queen! Longmans 1951 (Fiction)
BBEL—BBJH—CC(7-9)—JH—SCHS

Ezekiel, Prophet

COLLECTIONS

Williams, Walter George. The Prophets: Pioneers to Christianity. Abingdon 1956
SCPL

Hosea, Prophet

COLLECTIONS

Chase, Mary Ellen. The Prophets for the Common Reader. Norton 1963
Bkl A—SCPL

Williams, Walter George. The Prophets: Pioneers to Christianity. Abingdon 1956
SCPL

Isaiah, Prophet

COLLECTIONS

Chase, Mary Ellen. The Prophets for the Common Reader. Norton 1963
Bkl A—SCPL

Williams, Walter George. The Prophets: Pioneers to Christianity. Abingdon 1956
SCPL

Jeremiah, Prophet

COLLECTIONS

Chase, Mary Ellen. The Prophets for the Common Reader. Norton 1963
Bkl A—SCPL

Williams, Walter George. The Prophets: Pioneers to Christianity. Abingdon 1956
SCPL

Jezebel, Wife of Ahab, King of Israel

COLLECTIONS

Samuel, Maurice. Certain People of the Book. Knopf 1955
SCPL

**BIBLICAL FIGURES—OLD TESTA-
MENT—***Continued*

Joseph, the Patriarch

Petersham, Maud and Petersham, Miska.
Joseph and His Brothers: From the
Story Told in the Book of Genesis. Mac-
millan 1958
CC(3-5)—ESLC

COLLECTIONS

Samuel, Maurice. Certain People of the
Book. Knopf 1955
SCPL

Joshua, Son of Nun

COLLECTIONS

James, Fleming. Personalities of the Old
Testament. Scribner 1939
SCPL

Meshach

COLLECTIONS

Bible. Old Testament. Daniel. Shadrach,
Meshach and Abednego: From the
Book of Daniel. McGraw 1965
ESLC

Micah, Prophet

COLLECTIONS

Chase, Mary Ellen. The Prophets for the
Common Reader. Norton 1963
Bkl A—SCPL

Moses

Petersham, Maud and Petersham, Miska.
Moses: From the Story Told in the Old
Testament. Macmillan 1958
CC(3-5)—ESLC

Saporta, Raphael. A Basket in the Reeds.
Lerner Publications 1964
CC(1-4)—ESLC

Shippen, Katherine B. Moses. Harper
1949
BY—CC(6-9)—ESLC—JH—SCHS

Wheeler, Opal. Moses. Dutton 1962
AB(2-6)—Bkl C(3-5)

COLLECTIONS

James, Fleming. Personalities of the Old
Testament. Scribner 1939
SCPL

Kagan, Henry Enoch. Six Who Changed
the World. Yoseloff 1963
Bkl A

Naomi

COLLECTIONS

Samuel, Maurice. Certain People of the
Book. Knopf 1955
SCPL

Rebekah

COLLECTIONS

Samuel, Maurice. Certain People of the
Book. Knopf 1955
SCPL

Ruth

Malvern, Gladys. The Foreigner: The
Story of a Girl Named Ruth. Longmans
1954 (Fiction)
BBEL—BBJH—JH—SCHS

Petersham, Maud and Petersham, Miska.
Ruth: From the Story Told in the Book
of Ruth. Macmillan 1958
CC(3-5)—ESLC

Samuel, Judge of Israel

COLLECTIONS

James, Fleming. Personalities of the Old
Testament. Scribner 1939
SCPL

Shadrach

COLLECTIONS

Bible. Old Testament. Daniel. Shadrach,
Meshach and Abednego: From the
Book of Daniel. McGraw 1965
ESLC

Solomon, King of Israel

COLLECTIONS

James, Fleming. Personalities of the Old
Testament. Scribner 1939
SCPL

Xerxes I, King of Persia

COLLECTIONS

Samuel, Maurice. Certain People of the
Book. Knopf 1955
SCPL

BIBLIOGRAPHERS

See Librarians

BIBLIOPHILES

See Book Collectors

BIOCHEMISTS

See Biologists

BIOGRAPHERS

See Authors

BIOLOGISTS
See also Naturalists

American—20th century

Sidney Walter Fox, 1912-

COLLECTIONS

Thomas, Shirley. Men of Space: v. 6, Profiles of Scientists Who Probe for Life in Space. Chilton 1963
Bkl A&Y

John Cunningham Lilly, 1915-

COLLECTIONS

Thomas, Shirley. Men of Space: v. 6, Profiles of Scientists Who Probe for Life in Space. Chilton 1963
Bkl A&Y

Olaus Johan Murie, 1889-1963

Murie, Olaus Johan and Murie, Margaret E. Wapiti Wilderness. Knopf 1966
Bkl A&Y

Carl Sagan, 1934-

COLLECTIONS

Thomas, Shirley. Men of Space: v. 6, Profiles of Scientists Who Probe for Life in Space. Chilton 1963
Bkl A&Y

Harry Steenbock, 1886-1967

COLLECTIONS

De Kruif, Paul Henry. Hunger Fighters. Harcourt 1928
BBHS—SCHS—SCPL—3000

Wolf Vishniac, 1922-

COLLECTIONS

Thomas, Shirley. Men of Space: v. 6, Profiles of Scientists Who Probe for Life in Space. Chilton 1963
Bkl A&Y

English—19th century

Thomas Henry Huxley, 1825-1895

Irvine, William. Apes, Angels, and Victorians: The Story of Darwin, Huxley and Evolution. McGraw 1955
SCPL

English—20th century

W. N. P. Barbellion, 1889-1919

Barbellion, W. N. P. The Journal of a Disappointed Man. Penguin 1919
GR

BIOPHYSICISTS
See Biologists

BISHOPS
See Religious Leaders

BLIND

American—19th century

Laura Dewey Bridgman, 1829-1889

Hunter, Edith Fisher. Child of the Silent Night. Houghton 1963
Bkl C(3-5)—CC(3-5)—ESLC—IndJ(4-6)

Samuel Gridley Howe, 1801-1876

Meltzer, Milton. A Light in the Dark: The Life of Samuel Gridley Howe. Crowell 1964
Bkl C(6-9)&Y—CC—ESLC

American—20th century

Charles Albert Boswell, 1916-

COLLECTIONS

Boynick, David King. Champions by Setback: Athletes Who Overcame Physical Handicaps. Crowell 1954
SCHS

Genevieve Caulfield, 1888-

Caulfield, Genevieve. The Kingdom Within; ed. by Ed Fitzgerald. Harper 1960
Bkl A&Y—BY
Rau, Margaret. Dawn from the West: The Story of Genevieve Caulfield. Hawthorn 1964
ESLC

Hector Chevigny, 1904-1965

Chevigny, Hector. My Eyes Have a Cold Nose. Yale Univ. 1946
BY—SCPL

Bernice Clifton, ?

Clifton, Bernice. None So Blind. Rand McNally 1963
Bkl A&Y

Borghild Margarethe Dahl, 1890-

Dahl, Borghild Margarethe. Finding My Way. Dutton 1962
Bkl Y—YR
Dahl, Borghild Margarethe. I Wanted to See. Macmillan 1944
SCHS

Morris S. Frank, 1908?-

Frank, Morris S. and Clark, Blake. First Lady of the Seeing Eye. Holt 1957
SCHS—SCPL

Helen Adams Keller, 1880-1968

Brooks, Van Wyck. Helen Keller: Sketch for a Portrait. Dutton 1956
BY—SCPL
Gibson, William. The Miracle Worker: A Play for Television. Knopf 1957 (Play)
SCHS

BLIND

American—20th century

Helen Keller—Continued

Graff, Stewart and Graff, Polly Anne. Helen Keller: Toward the Light. Garrard 1965
ESLC

Harrity, Richard and Martin, Ralph G. The Three Lives of Helen Keller. Doubleday 1962
Bkl A&Y

Hickok, Lorena A. The Story of Helen Keller. Grosset 1948
CC(4-6)

Keller, Helen Adams. Story of My Life. Doubleday; Houghton
BBHS—BBJH—BY—CA—CC(7-9)—JH—SCHS—SCPL—3000

Peare, Catherine Owens. The Helen Keller Story. Crowell 1959
CC(6-9)—ESLC—JH—SCHS

Waite, Helen E. Valiant Companions: Helen Keller and Anne Sullivan Macy. Macrae 1959
JH—SCHS

Marie (Bell) McCoy, ?

McCoy, Marie (Bell). Journey out of Darkness. McKay 1963
Bkl A

Anne (Sullivan) Macy, 1866-1936

Brown, Marion Marsh and Crone, Ruth. The Silent Storm. Abingdon 1963
Bkl C(5-8)—CC(5-7)—ESLC

Davidson, Mickie. Helen Keller's Teacher. Four Winds Press 1965
ESLC

Gibson, William. The Miracle Worker: A Play for Television. Knopf 1957 (Play)
SCHS

Hickok, Lorena A. The Touch of Magic: The Story of Helen Keller's Great Teacher, Anne Sullivan Macy. Dodd 1961
Bkl A&Y—BY—JH—SCPL—YR

Keller, Helen Adams. Teacher: Anne Sullivan Macy—A Tribute by the Foster-Child of Her Mind. Doubleday 1955
SCHS—SCPL

Robert Rex Moore, 1915-

Moore, Virginia Blanck. Seeing Eye Wife. Chilton 1960
Bkl A&Y

Peter Putnam, 1920-

Putnam, Peter. "Keep Your Head Up, Mr. Putnam!" Harper 1952
SCPL

Robert Russell, 1924-

Russell, Robert. To Catch an Angel: Adventures in the World I Cannot See. Vanguard 1962
Bkl A&Y—BY

Canadian—20th century

David Scott Blackhall, 1910-

Blackhall, David Scott. This House Had Windows. Obolensky 1962
Bkl A

French—19th century

Louis Braille, 1809-1852

DeGering, Etta. Seeing Fingers: The Story of Louis Braille. McKay 1962
Bkl C(5-7)—CC(5-7)—ESLC

Kugelmass, J. Alvin. Louis Braille: Windows for the Blind. Messner 1951
BBJH—JH—SCHS

Webster, Gary. Journey into Light: The Story of Louis Braille. Hawthorn 1964
AB(7up)

COLLECTIONS

Freedman, Russell. Teenagers Who Made History. Holiday 1961
BY—JH—SCHS—YR

French—20th century

Jacques Lusseyran, ?

Lusseyran, Jacques. And There Was Light; tr. from the French by Elizabeth R. Cameron. Little 1963
Bkl A&Y—IndS(11-12)

Indian—20th century

Ved Parkash Mehta, 1934-

Mehta, Ved Parkash. Face to Face: An Autobiography. Little 1957
BBHS—SCHS—SCPL

BOOK COLLECTORS

American—20th century

Stuart Brent, ?

Brent, Stuart. The Seven Stairs. Houghton 1962
Bkl A

Abraham Simon Wolf Rosenbach, 1876-1952

Wolf, Edwin and Fleming, John F. Rosenbach: A Biography. World 1960
Bkl A—SCPL

Vincent Starrett, 1886-

Starrett, Vincent. Born in a Bookshop: Chapters from the Chicago Renascence. Univ. of Okla. 1965
Bkl A

Frances Steloff, 1887-

Rogers, William Garland. Wise Men Fish Here: The Story of Frances Steloff and the Gotham Book Mart. Harcourt 1965
Bkl A

BOOK ILLUSTRATORS

See Illustrators

BOOK REVIEWERS

See Critics

BOOKSELLERS

See Businessmen; Book Collectors

BOTANISTS

See also Plant Pathologists

COLLECTIONS

Eifert, Virginia Louise (Snider). Tall Trees and Far Horizons: Adventures and Discoveries of Early Botanists in America. Dodd 1965
Bkl A&Y
Jane Colden; David Douglas; André Michaux; John Muir; Thomas Nuttall

American—18th century

John Bartram, 1699-1777

Herbst, Josephine. New Green World. Hastings House 1954
SCPL
Sutton, Ann and Sutton, Myron. Exploring with the Bartrams. Rand McNally 1963
IndJ(6-9)—YR

COLLECTIONS

Blassingame, Wyatt. Naturalist-Explorers. Watts 1964
ESLC

Jane Colden, 1724-1766

COLLECTIONS

Eifert, Virginia Louise (Snider). Tall Trees and Far Horizons: Adventures and Discoveries of Early Botanists in America. Dodd 1965
Bkl A&Y

American—19th century

Thomas Nuttall, 1786-1859

COLLECTIONS

Eifert, Virginia Louise (Snider). Tall Trees and Far Horizons: Adventures and Discoveries of Early Botanists in America. Dodd 1965
Bkl A&Y

Edward Palmer, 1831-1911

Beaty, Janice J. Plants in His Pack. Pantheon 1964
Bkl C(6-9)&Y

American—20th century

Constantine John Alexopoulos, 1907-

COLLECTIONS

Poole, Lynn and Poole, Gray. Scientists Who Work with Cameras. Dodd 1965
Bkl C(7-12)&Y—IndS(11-12)

George Washington Carver, 1864-1943

Aliki. A Weed Is a Flower: The Life of George Washington Carver. Prentice-Hall 1965
ESLC
Bontemps, Arna. The Story of George Washington Carver. Grosset 1954
CC(4-6)—SCHS
Epstein, Samuel and Epstein, Beryl. George Washington Carver: Negro Scientist. Garrard 1960
ESLC
Graham, Shirley and Lipscomb, George Dewey. Dr. George Washington Carver, Scientist. Messner 1944
BBEL(6-8)—BBJH—BY—CC—ESLC—JH—SCHS—SCPL
Holt, Rackham. George Washington Carver: An American Biography. Doubleday 1963
BBHS—Bkl A&Y—BY—SCHS—SCPL
Means, Florence Crannell. Carvers' George: A Biography of George Washington Carver. Houghton 1952
AB(4-8)—CC(5-7)
White, Anne Terry. George Washington Carver: The Story of a Great American. Random House 1953
AB(5-10)—CC(6-9)—ESLC—JH

COLLECTIONS

McNeer, May Yonge and Ward, Lynd Kendall. Armed with Courage. Abingdon 1957
AB(5-8)—BBEL(5-8)—CC(5-7)—ESLC—JH—YR

David Grandison Fairchild, 1869-1954

Fairchild, David Grandison. World Was My Garden: Travels of a Plant Explorer. Scribner 1938
SCPL
Williams, Beryl and Epstein, Samuel. Plant Explorer. Messner 1961
AB(5-9)—Bkl C(6-9)&Y—ESLC

Donald Culross Peattie, 1898-1964

Peattie, Donald Culross. Road of a Naturalist. Houghton 1941
SCPL

George Harrison Shull, 1874-1954

COLLECTIONS

De Kruif, Paul Henry. Hunger Fighters. Harcourt 1928
BBHS—SCHS—SCPL—3000

BOTANISTS—*Continued*

Austrian—19th century

Gregor Johann Mendel, 1822-1884

Sootin, Harry. Gregor Mendel: Father of the Science of Genetics. Vanguard 1959
JH—SCHS

Webb, Robert N. Gregor Mendel and Heredity. Watts 1963
Bkl C(7-10)&Y

Webster, Gary. The Man Who Found Out Why: The Story of Gregor Mendel. Hawthorn 1963
ESLC

English—18th century

Erasmus Darwin, 1731-1802

COLLECTIONS

Crowther, James Gerald. Scientists of the Industrial Revolution. Dufour 1963
Bkl A

French—18th century

André Michaux, 1746-1802

COLLECTIONS

Eifert, Virginia Louise (Snider). Tall Trees and Far Horizons: Adventures and Discoveries of Early Botanists in America. Dodd 1965
Bkl A&Y

Scottish—19th century

David Douglas, 1798-1834

Stoutenburg, Adrien and Baker, Laura Nelson. Wild Treasure: The Story of David Douglas. Scribner 1958
BBJH

COLLECTIONS

Eifert, Virginia Louise (Snider). Tall Trees and Far Horizons: Adventures and Discoveries of Early Botanists in America. Dodd 1965
Bkl A&Y

Swedish—18th century

Carl von Linné, 1707-1778

Stoutenburg, Adrien and Baker, Laura Nelson. Beloved Botanist: The Story of Carl Linnaeus. Scribner 1961
Bkl C(7-9)&Y—JH—YR

COLLECTIONS

Blassingame, Wyatt. Naturalist-Explorers. Watts 1964
ESLC

BOXERS

COLLECTIONS

Bromberg, Lester. Boxing's Unforgettable Fights. Ronald 1962
Bkl A

American—20th century

James J. Braddock, 1905-

COLLECTIONS

Boynick, David King. Champions by Setback: Athletes Who Overcame Physical Handicaps. Crowell 1954
SCHS

Cassius Clay, 1942-

COLLECTIONS

Gelman, Steve. Young Olympic Champions. Norton 1964
Bkl C(6-9)&Y—ESLC—JH

Jack Dempsey, 1895-

Dempsey, Jack and others. Dempsey, by the Man Himself. Simon & Schuster 1960
Bkl A

Schoor, Gene. Jack Dempsey Story. Messner 1954
ESLC—SCHS

COLLECTIONS

Gallico, Paul. The Golden People. Doubleday 1965
Bkl A&Y

John Arthur Johnson, 1878-1946

Farr, Finis. Black Champion: The Life and Times of Jack Johnson. Scribner 1964
Bkl A

COLLECTIONS

Young, Andrew Sturgeon Nash. Negro Firsts in Sports. Johnson Pub. 1963
Bkl A&Y

Joe Louis, 1914-

COLLECTIONS

Bontemps, Arna. Famous Negro Athletes. Dodd 1964
Bkl C&Y—ESLC—JH

Young, Andrew Sturgeon Nash. Negro Firsts in Sports. Johnson Pub. 1963
Bkl A&Y

Archie Moore, 1913-

Moore, Archie. The Archie Moore Story. McGraw 1960
Bkl A

Floyd Patterson, 1935-

Patterson, Floyd and Gross, Milton. Victory over Myself. Geis 1962
Bkl A&Y—BY—JH

BOXERS

American—20th century—*Continued*

Ray Robinson, 1921-

COLLECTIONS

Bontemps, Arna. Famous Negro Athletes. Dodd 1964
Bkl C&Y—ESLC—JH

BOY SCOUT WORKERS

American—20th century

Daniel Carter Beard, 1850-1941

Seibert, Jerry. Dan Beard: Boy Scout Pioneer. Houghton 1963
AB(5-9)—ESLC

English—20th century

Robert Stephenson Smyth Baden-Powell, Baron Baden-Powell, 1857-1941

Hillcourt, William and Baden-Powell, Olave. Baden-Powell: The Two Lives of a Hero. Putnam 1964
Bkl A

BOYS

See Youths

BRIDGE BUILDERS

See Engineers, Civil

BRIGANDS

See Criminals

BUCCANEERS

See Criminals

BUDDHIST LEADERS

See Religious Leaders

BULLFIGHTERS

American—20th century

Harper Baylor Lee, 1884-1941

Hail, Marshall. Knight in the Sun: Harper B. Lee, First Yankee Matador. Little 1962
Bkl A

BURGLARS

See Criminals

BUSINESS EXECUTIVES

See Businessmen

BUSINESSMEN

See also Advertising Executives; Financiers; Hotel Owners and Managers; Industrial Designers; Industrialists; Restaurateurs; Shipping Executives

COLLECTIONS

Mahoney, Tom. Great Merchants: The Stories of Twenty Famous Retail Operations and the People Who Made Them Great. Harper 1955
SCPL

World Who's Who in Commerce and Industry: The International Business Who's Who. Annual; first published 1936. Marquis
SCPL

American

COLLECTIONS

Fanning, Leonard M. Titans of Business. Lippincott 1964
Bkl C(7-9)&Y—JH—SCHS
Henry Ford; Samuel Gompers; Alexander Hamilton; John Llewellyn Lewis; John Pierpont Morgan; John Davison Rockefeller; Alfred Pritchard Sloan

Lavine, Sigmund A. Famous Merchants. Dodd 1965
Bkl Y(7-10)&C—ESLC

McCall, Edith. Pioneer Traders. Childrens Press 1964
AB(4-7)

Rachlis, Eugene and Marqusee, John E. The Land Lords. Random House 1963
Bkl A

American—18th century

Timothy Dexter, 1747-1806

Marquand, John Phillips. Timothy Dexter Revisited. Little 1960
Bkl A

Aaron Lopez, 1731-1782

Alexander, Lloyd. The Flagship Hope: Aaron Lopez. Farrar 1960
Bkl C(6-9)&Y

American—19th century

Harriet (Hubbard) Ayer, 1854-1903

Ayer, Margaret Hubbard. Three Lives of Harriet Hubbard Ayer. Lippincott 1957
SCPL

Milton Bradley, 1836-1911

Shea, James J. and Mercer, Charles. It's All in the Game. Putnam 1960
Bkl A

Peter Cooper, 1791-1883

Gurko, Miriam. The Lives and Times of Peter Cooper. Crowell 1959
Bkl Y&C(7-10)—BY—CC(7-9)—ESLC

BUSINESSMEN

American—19th century—*Continued*

Potter Palmer, 1826-1902

COLLECTIONS

Saarinen, Aline B. The Proud Possessors: The Lives, Times, and Tastes of Some Adventurous American Art Collectors. Random House 1958
SCPL

Samuel ("Uncle Sam") Wilson, 1766-1854

Gerson, Thomas I. and Hood, Flora M. Uncle Sam. Bobbs 1963
AB(3-7)

Ketchum, Alton. Uncle Sam: The Man and the Legend. Hill & Wang 1959
Bkl A&Y

Frank Winfield Woolworth, 1852-1919

Baker, Nina Brown. Nickels and Dimes: The Story of F. W. Woolworth. Harcourt 1954
CC(5-7)

American—20th century

Bernard Mannes Baruch, 1870-1965

Baruch, Bernard Mannes. Baruch: My Own Story. Holt 1957
BY—SCHS—SCPL—3000

Baruch, Bernard Mannes. Baruch: The Public Years. Holt 1960
Bkl A&Y—SCHS—SCPL

Coit, Margaret Louise. Mr. Baruch. Houghton 1957
SCPL

White, W. L. Bernard Baruch: Portrait of a Citizen. Harcourt 1950
SCPL

Stuart Brent, ?

Brent, Stuart. The Seven Stairs. Houghton 1962
Bkl A

Jacqueline Cochran, 1910?-

Cochran, Jacqueline. Stars at Noon. Little 1954
SCHS—SCPL

Marshall Field III, 1893-1956

Becker, Stephen D. Marshall Field III: A Biography. Simon & Schuster 1964
Bkl A

Alfred Carl Fuller, 1885-

Fuller, Alfred Carl and Spence, Hartzell. A Foot in the Door: The Life Appraisal of the Original Fuller Brush Man. McGraw 1960
Bkl A

Ira Arthur Hirschmann, 1901-

Hirschmann, Ira Arthur. Caution to the Winds. McKay 1962
Bkl A

David Eli Lilienthal, 1899-

Lilienthal, David. The Journals of David E. Lilienthal: v. 1, The TVA Years, 1939-1945. Harper 1964
Bkl A—SCPL

Lilienthal, David. The Journals of David E. Lilienthal: v. 2, The Atomic Energy Years, 1945-1950. Harper 1964
Bkl A—SCPL

William Loeb, 1866-1937

COLLECTIONS

Koenig, Louis William. The Invisible Presidency. Rinehart 1960
Bkl A

James Cash Penney, 1875-

Penney, James Cash. View from the Ninth Decade: Jottings from a Merchant's Daybook. Nelson 1960
Bkl A

Clarence Belden Randall, 1891-1967

Randall, Clarence Belden. Adventures in Friendship. Little 1965
Bkl A

Randall, Clarence Belden. Sixty-five Plus: The Joy and Challenge of the Years of Retirement. Little 1963
Bkl A

John William Rockefeller, ?

Rockefeller, John William. The Poor Rockefellers. Vanguard 1962
Bkl A

Helena Rubinstein, 1870?-1965

Rubinstein, Helena. My Life for Beauty. Simon & Schuster 1966
Bkl A

Frances Steloff, 1887-

Rogers, William Garland. Wise Men Fish Here: The Story of Frances Steloff and the Gotham Book Mart. Harcourt 1965
Bkl A

Edith Warner, 1891?-1951

Church, Peggy Pond. The House at Otowi Bridge: The Story of Edith Warner and Los Alamos. Univ. of N. Mex. 1960
Bkl A

Frank Winfield Woolworth, 1852-1919

Baker, Nina Brown. Nickels and Dimes: The Story of F. W. Woolworth. Harcourt 1954
CC(5-7)

BUSINESSMEN—*Continued*
English—20th century

Oliver Lyttelton, 1st Viscount Chandos, 1893-

Chandos, Oliver Lyttelton, 1st Viscount. Memoirs: An Unexpected View from the Summit. New Am. Lib. 1963
Bkl A

French—15th century

Jacques Cœur, 1395?-1456

Costain, Thomas Bertram. The Moneyman. Doubleday 1947 (Fiction)
SCHS

BUSINESSWOMEN

See Auctioneers; Businessmen; Cosmeticians

CABINET MEMBERS

See Statesmen

CABINETMAKERS
American—19th century

Duncan Phyfe, 1768-1854

COLLECTIONS

Bailey, Carolyn Sherwin. Children of the Handcrafts. Viking 1935
BBJH–CC(4-7)–ESLC

CAPITALISTS

See Financiers

CAPTAINS, SEA

See Naval Officers and Other Seafarers

CARDINALS

See Religious Leaders

CARICATURISTS

See also Cartoonists

French—19th century

Honoré Victorin Daumier, 1808-1879

Larkin, Oliver W. Daumier, Man of His Time. McGraw 1966
Bkl A

CARTOONISTS

See also Caricaturists; Illustrators

American—19th century

Thomas Nast, 1840-1902

Veglahn, Nancy. The Tiger's Tail: A Story of America's Great Political Cartoonist Thomas Nast. Harper 1964
Bkl Y&C–ESLC

COLLECTIONS

Cunz, Dieter. They Came from Germany: The Story of Famous German-Americans. Dodd 1966
ESLC

American—20th century

Al Capp, 1909-

COLLECTIONS

Gelfand, Ravina and Patterson, Letha. They Wouldn't Quit. Lerner Publications 1962
AB(5-9)

Walt Kelly, 1913-

COLLECTIONS

Levin, Martin, ed. Five Boyhoods. Doubleday 1962
Bkl A&Y

Robert Le Roy Ripley, 1893-1949

Considine, Robert Bernard. Ripley, the Modern Marco Polo. Doubleday 1961
Bkl A

CATTLEMEN

See Cowboys

CELLISTS
American—20th century

Leonard Rose, 1918-

COLLECTIONS

Ewen, David. Famous Instrumentalists. Dodd 1965
Bkl Y&C

Russian—20th century

Gregor Piatigorsky, 1903-

Piatigorsky, Gregor. Cellist. Doubleday 1965
Bkl A&Y

Spanish—20th century

Pablo Casals, 1876-

Forsee, Aylesa. Pablo Casals: Cellist for Freedom. Crowell 1965
Bkl Y&C(7-9)–ESLC

Taper, Bernard. Cellist in Exile: A Portrait of Pablo Casals. McGraw 1962
Bkl A

CEREBRAL PALSY VICTIMS

See Victims of Cerebral Palsy

CHANCELLORS

See Statesmen

CHAPLAINS

See Religious Leaders

CHEMISTS

See also Alchemists

COLLECTIONS

Irwin, Keith Gordon. The Romance of Chemistry from Ancient Alchemy to Nuclear Fission. Viking 1959
JH
Robert Boyle; Marie (Sklodowska) Curie; John Dalton; Joseph Louis Gay-Lussac; Antoine Laurent Lavoisier; Dimitri Ivanovich Mendeleyev; Henry Gwyn-Jeffreys Moseley; Joseph Priestley; and others

Jaffe, Bernard. Crucibles: The Story of Chemistry, from Ancient Alchemy to Nuclear Fission. Simon & Schuster 1948
SCPL

Kendall, James. Great Discoveries by Young Chemists. Crowell 1954
JH

American—19th century

Stephen Moulton Babcock, 1843-1931

COLLECTIONS

De Kruif, Paul Henry. Hunger Fighters. Harcourt 1928
BBHS—SCHS—SCPL—3000

Ellen Henrietta (Swallow) Richards, 1842-1911

Douty, Esther (Morris). America's First Woman Chemist, Ellen Richards. Messner 1961
Bkl C(7-9)&Y—CC—JH—YR

Benjamin Silliman, 1779-1864

COLLECTIONS

Burlingame, Roger. Scientists Behind the Inventors. Harcourt 1960
AB(7up)—Bkl C(7-9)&Y—CC(6-9)—ESLC—JH—SCHS

James Smithson, 1765-1829

Carmichael, Leonard and Long, John Cuthbert. James Smithson and the Smithsonian Story. Putnam 1965
Bkl A&Y

American—20th century

Melvin Calvin, 1911-

COLLECTIONS

Thomas, Shirley. Men of Space: v. 6, Profiles of Scientists Who Probe for Life in Space. Chilton 1963
Bkl A&Y

Marion Dorset, 1872-1935

COLLECTIONS

De Kruif, Paul Henry. Hunger Fighters. Harcourt 1928
BBHS—SCHS—SCPL—3000

Stanley Lloyd Miller, 1930-

COLLECTIONS

Thomas, Shirley. Men of Space: v. 6, Profiles of Scientists Who Probe for Life in Space. Chilton 1963
Bkl A&Y

Ellen Henrietta (Swallow) Richards, 1842-1911

Douty, Esther (Morris). America's First Woman Chemist, Ellen Richards. Messner 1961
Bkl C(7-9)&Y—CC—JH—YR

Harold Clayton Urey, 1893-

COLLECTIONS

Thomas, Shirley. Men of Space: v. 6, Profiles of Scientists Who Probe for Life in Space. Chilton 1963
Bkl A&Y

Arabian—8th century

Geber, 721?-776?

COLLECTIONS

Cummings, Richard. The Alchemists, Fathers of Practical Chemistry. McKay 1966
Bkl C&Y

English—17th century

Robert Boyle, 1627-1691

Sootin, Harry. Robert Boyle, Founder of Modern Chemistry. Watts 1962
Bkl C(5-8)—ESLC

COLLECTIONS

Irwin, Keith Gordon. The Romance of Chemistry from Ancient Alchemy to Nuclear Fission. Viking 1959
JH

English—18th century

Henry Cavendish, 1731-1810

COLLECTIONS

Crowther, James Gerald. Scientists of the Industrial Revolution. Dufour 1963
Bkl A

CHEMISTS

English—18th century—*Continued*

John Dalton, 1766-1844

COLLECTIONS

Irwin, Keith Gordon. The Romance of Chemistry from Ancient Alchemy to Nuclear Fission. Viking 1959
JH

James Price, 1752-1783

COLLECTIONS

Cummings, Richard. The Alchemists, Fathers of Practical Chemistry. McKay 1966
Bkl C&Y

Joseph Priestley, 1733-1804

Crane, William Dwight. The Discoverer of Oxygen: Joseph Priestley. Messner 1962
Bkl C(7-12)&Y

Davis, Kenneth Sydney. The Cautionary Scientists: Priestley, Lavoisier, and the Founding of Modern Chemistry. Putnam 1966
Bkl A&Y

Marcus, Rebecca B. Joseph Priestley, Pioneer Chemist. Watts 1961
Bkl C(5-8)—CC—ESLC

COLLECTIONS

Crowther, James Gerald. Scientists of the Industrial Revolution. Dufour 1963
Bkl A

Irwin, Keith Gordon. The Romance of Chemistry from Ancient Alchemy to Nuclear Fission. Viking 1959
JH

English—19th century

John Dalton, 1766-1844

COLLECTIONS

Irwin, Keith Gordon. The Romance of Chemistry from Ancient Alchemy to Nuclear Fission. Viking 1959
JH

Michael Faraday, 1791-1867

Harvey, Tad. The Quest of Michael Faraday. Doubleday 1961
AB(5-11)—ESLC

May, Charles Paul. Michael Faraday and the Electric Dynamo. Watts 1961
Bkl C(5-8)

Sootin, Harry. Michael Faraday: From Errand Boy to Master Physicist. Messner 1954
JH—SCHS—YR

Williams, Leslie Pearce. Michael Faraday: A Biography. Basic Bks 1965
Bkl A&Y

COLLECTIONS

Bixby, William. Great Experimenters. McKay 1964
Bkl C(7-8)&Y—ESLC

MacDonald, David Keith Chalmers. Faraday, Maxwell, and Kelvin. Doubleday 1964
Bkl A&Y

French—18th century

Antoine Laurent Lavoisier, 1743-1794

Davis, Kenneth Sydney. The Cautionary Scientists: Priestley, Lavoisier, and the Founding of Modern Chemistry. Putnam 1966
Bkl A&Y

Marcus, Rebecca B. Antoine Lavoisier and the Revolution in Chemistry. Watts 1964
Bkl C(7-10)&Y—JH

Riedman, Sarah R. Antoine Lavoisier, Scientist and Citizen. Nelson 1957
ESLC

COLLECTIONS

Irwin, Keith Gordon. The Romance of Chemistry from Ancient Alchemy to Nuclear Fission. Viking 1959
JH

French—19th century

Joseph Louis Gay-Lussac, 1778-1850

COLLECTIONS

Irwin, Keith Gordon. The Romance of Chemistry from Ancient Alchemy to Nuclear Fission. Viking 1959
JH

Louis Pasteur, 1822-1895

Burton, Mary June. Louis Pasteur: Founder of Microbiology. Watts 1963
JH

Cuny, Hilaire. Louis Pasteur: The Man and His Theories; tr. by Patrick Evans. Eriksson 1966
Bkl A&Y

Dolan, Edward E. Pasteur and the Invisible Giants. Dodd 1958
SCHS

Dubos, René Jules. Louis Pasteur: Free Lance of Science. Little 1950
SCPL

Dubos, René Jules. Pasteur and Modern Science. Doubleday 1960
Bkl A&Y—3000

Grant, Madeleine P. Louis Pasteur: Fighting Hero of Science. McGraw 1959
AB(4up)—CC

Lauber, Patricia. The Quest of Louis Pasteur. Garden City 1960
ESLC

CHEMISTS

French—19th century

Louis Pasteur—Continued

Mann, John Harvey. Louis Pasteur: Founder of Bacteriology. Scribner 1964
Bkl C(6-9)&Y

Nicolle, Jacques. Louis Pasteur: The Story of His Major Discoveries. Basic Bks 1961
Bkl Y

Vallery-Radot, René. The Life of Pasteur; tr. by R. L. Devonshire. Dover 1960
BBHS—SCPL

Vallery-Radot, René. Louis Pasteur: A Great Life in Brief. Knopf 1958
SCHS—SCPL

Wood, Laura N. Louis Pasteur. Messner 1948
BBJH—CC(7-9)—ESLC—JH—SCHS

COLLECTIONS

Burlingame, Roger. Scientists Behind the Inventors. Harcourt 1960
AB(7up)—Bkl C(7-9)&Y—CC(6-9)—ESLC—JH—SCHS

German—13th century

Saint Albert the Great, 1206-1280

COLLECTIONS

Cummings, Richard. The Alchemists, Fathers of Practical Chemistry. McKay 1966
Bkl C&Y

Israeli—20th century

Chaim Weizmann, 1874-1952

Baker, Rachel. Chaim Weizmann: Builder of a Nation. Messner 1950
BY—SCHS—YR

Chaim Weizmann: A Biography by Several Hands; ed. by Meyer W. Weisgal and Joel Carmichael. Atheneum 1963
Bkl A

Weizmann, Chaim. Trial and Error: The Autobiography of Chaim Weizmann; ed. by B. Horovitz. Harper 1950
GR—SCPL

Polish—20th century

Marie (Sklodowska) Curie, 1867-1934

Bigland, Eileen. Madame Curie. Criterion Bks 1957
AB(6-9)—BBJH—CC(6-9)—YR

Curie, Eve. Madame Curie: A Biography; tr. by Vincent Sheean. Doubleday 1949
BBHS—BY—ESLC—GR—JH—SCHS—SCPL—3000

Doorly, Eleanor. The Radium Woman: A Life of Marie Curie. Roy 1955
CC(5-7)—ESLC

Henry, Joanne Landers. Marie Curie, Discoverer of Radium. Macmillan 1966
ESLC

McKown, Robin. Marie Curie. Putnam 1959
AB(4up)

Rubin, Elizabeth. The Curies and Radium. Watts 1961
JH

COLLECTIONS

Burlingame, Roger. Scientists Behind the Inventors. Harcourt 1960
AB(7up)—Bkl C(7-9)&Y—CC(6-9)—ESLC—JH—SCHS

Hume, Ruth Fox. Great Women of Medicine. Random House 1964
CC—JH

Irwin, Keith Gordon. The Romance of Chemistry from Ancient Alchemy to Nuclear Fission. Viking 1959
JH

Russian—19th century

Dimitri Ivanovich Mendeleyev, 1834-1907

McKown, Robin. Mendeleyev and His Periodic Table. Messner 1965
IndS(11-12)

COLLECTIONS

Irwin, Keith Gordon. The Romance of Chemistry from Ancient Alchemy to Nuclear Fission. Viking 1959
JH

Scottish—18th century

Joseph Black, 1728-1799

COLLECTIONS

Burlingame, Roger. Scientists Behind the Inventors. Harcourt 1960
AB(7up)—Bkl C(7-9)&Y—CC(6-9)—ESLC—JH—SCHS

Crowther, James Gerald. Scientists of the Industrial Revolution. Dufour 1963
Bkl A

Swedish—19th century

Alfred Bernhard Nobel, 1833-1896

Bergengren, Erik. Alfred Nobel: The Man and His Work. Nelson 1962
BY

Meyer, Edith Patterson. Dynamite and Peace. Little 1958
AB(5up)—BBJH—CC(7-9)—JH—SCHS

CHESS PLAYERS

American—19th century

Paul Charles Morphy, 1837-1884

Keyes, Frances Parkinson (Wheeler). The Chess Players. Farrar 1960 (Fiction)
Bkl A

CHESS PLAYERS—*Continued*

American—20th century

Robert Fischer, 1943-

Brady, Frank. Profile of a Prodigy: The Life and Games of Bobby Fischer McKay 1965
Bkl A&Y—IndS(9-12)

CHIEF JUSTICES

See Lawyers

CHIEFS, INDIAN

See Indian Leaders, American

CHIEFS OF STATE

See Czars; Emperors; Empresses; Kings; Presidents; Princes; Queens; Stadholders; Sultans

CHILDREN

See Youths

CHOREOGRAPHERS

See Dancers

CHRISTIAN SCIENCE LEADERS

See Religious Leaders

CHRONICLERS

See Historians

CIRCUS MANAGERS

American—19th century

Phineas Taylor Barnum, 1810-1891

Wallace, Irving. The Fabulous Showman: The Life and Times of P. T. Barnum. Knopf 1959
SCPL
Wells, Helen. Barnum, Showman of America. McKay 1957
YR

John Ringling, 1866-1936

Harlow, Alvin Fay. The Ringlings: Wizards of the Circus. Messner 1951
SCHS
North, Henry Ringling and Hatch, Alden. The Circus Kings: Our Ringling Family Story. Doubleday 1960
Bkl A

American—20th century

John Ringling, 1866-1936

Harlow, Alvin Fay. The Ringlings: Wizards of the Circus. Messner 1951
SCHS

North, Henry Ringling and Hatch, Alden. The Circus Kings: Our Ringling Family Story. Doubleday 1960
Bkl A

CIRCUS PERFORMERS

See also Circus Managers; Marksmen

COLLECTIONS

Murray, Marion. Children of the Big Top. Little 1958
AB(4-7)

American—19th century

Charles Sherwood Stratton, 1838-1883

Hunt, Mabel Leigh. "Have You Seen Tom Thumb?" Lippincott 1942
CC(6-9)—ESLC

American—20th century

J. Y. Henderson, ?

Henderson, J. Y. and Taplinger, Richard. Circus Doctor. Little 1951
BY—SCHS—SCPL

Emmett Kelly, 1898?-

Kelly, Emmett. Clown. Prentice-Hall 1954
SCPL

Italian—20th century

Cristiani Family

Hubler, Richard Gibson. The Cristianis. Little 1966
Bkl A&Y

CIVIL ENGINEERS

See Engineers, Civil

CIVIL RIGHTS LEADERS

See also Religious Leaders

American—20th century

James Farmer, 1920-

COLLECTIONS

Sterne, Emma (Gelders). I Have a Dream. Knopf 1965
Bkl Y&C

Russell Wesley Jelliffe, 1891-

Selby, John. Beyond Civil Rights. World 1966
Bkl A

John Lewis, 1940?-

COLLECTIONS

Sterne, Emma (Gelders). I Have a Dream. Knopf 1965
Bkl Y&C

CIVIL RIGHTS LEADERS

American—20th century—*Continued*

Rosa Lee Parks, 1913-

COLLECTIONS

Sterne, Emma (Gelders). I Have a Dream. Knopf 1965
Bkl Y&C

Fred Shuttlesworth, 1922?-

COLLECTIONS

Sterne, Emma (Gelders). I Have a Dream. Knopf 1965
Bkl Y&C

CLAIRVOYANTS

American—20th century

Edgar Cayce, 1877-1945

Cayce, Hugh Lynn. Venture Inward. Harper 1964
Bkl A

CLARINETISTS

American—20th century

Sidney Bechet, 1897-1959

Bechet, Sidney. Treat It Gentle. Hill & Wang 1960
Bkl A

CLERGYMEN

See Religious Leaders

CLOWNS

See Circus Performers

COLLECTORS

See Art Collectors; Book Collectors

COLLEGE PRESIDENTS

See Educators

COLLEGE PROFESSORS

See Educators

COLONISTS

American

COLLECTIONS

Carse, Robert. The Young Colonials: A History. Norton 1963
ESLC

American—17th century

William Bradford, 1590-1657

Gerson, Noel Bertram. The Land Is Bright. Doubleday 1961 (Fiction)
Bkl A&Y

Smith, Bradford. Bradford of Plymouth. Lippincott 1951
SCPL

Smith, E. Brooks and Meredith, Robert, eds. Pilgrim Courage: From a First-hand Account by William Bradford, Governor of Plymouth Colony. Little 1962
CC(5-7)

COLLECTIONS

Daugherty, Sonia. Ten Brave Men: Makers of the American Way. Lippincott 1951
SCHS

William Penn, 1644-1718

Aliki. The Story of William Penn. Prentice-Hall 1964
ESLC—IndJ(2-4)

Buranelli, Vincent. The King & the Quaker: A Study of William Penn and James II. Univ. of Pa. 1962
Bkl A

Dolson, Hildegarde. William Penn, Quaker Hero. Random House 1961
AB(5-9)—Bkl C(5-8)—ESLC

Gray, Elizabeth Janet. Penn. Viking 1938
BBEL—BBJH—CC(7-9)—ESLC—JH—SCHS

Haviland, Virginia. William Penn: Founder and Friend. Abingdon 1952
AB(4-7)—BBEL—CC(4-6)—ESLC

Illick, Joseph E. William Penn, the Politician: His Relations with the English Government. Cornell Univ. 1965
Bkl A

Peare, Catherine Owens. William Penn: A Biography. Holt 1958
BBHS—BBJH—CC(7-9)—JH—SCHS

Syme, Ronald. William Penn, Founder of Pennsylvania. Morrow 1966
Bkl C(4-6)

Wallace, Willard M. Friend William. Nelson 1958
YR

COLLECTIONS

Larson, Egon. Men Who Fought for Freedom. Roy 1959
AB

Sir William Phips, 1651-1695

Alderman, Clifford Lindsey. The Silver Keys. Putnam 1960
Bkl A

Samuel Sewall, 1652-1730

Winslow, Ola Elizabeth. Samuel Sewall of Boston. Macmillan 1964
Bkl A&Y

COLONISTS

American—17th century—*Continued*

John Smith, 1580-1631

Barbour, Philip L. The Three Worlds of Captain John Smith. Houghton 1964
Bkl A&Y—SCPL

Gerson, Noel Bertram. The Great Rogue: A Biography of Captain John Smith. McKay 1966
Bkl A&Y

Graves, Charles P. A World Explorer: John Smith. Garrard 1965
ESLC

Latham, Jean Lee. This Dear-Bought Land. Harper 1957 (Fiction)
BBEL—BBJH—CC(7-9)—JH—SCHS

Lawson, Marie A. Pocahontas and Captain John Smith: The Story of the Virginia Colony. Random House 1950
CC(6-9)—ESLC—JH—SCHS

Leighton, Margaret. The Sword and the Compass: The Far-Flung Adventures of Captain John Smith. Houghton 1951
SCHS

Smith, Bradford. Captain John Smith: His Life & Legend. Lippincott 1956
SCPL

Syme, Ronald. John Smith of Virginia. Morrow 1954
CC(5-7)—ESLC—JH

Peter Stuyvesant, 1592-1672

Crouse, Anna and Crouse, Russel. Peter Stuyvesant of Old New York. Random House 1954
JH—SCHS

Roger Williams, 1603-1683

Covey, Cyclone. The Gentle Radical: A Biography of Roger Williams. Macmillan 1966
Bkl A&Y

Eaton, Jeanette. Lone Journey: The Life of Roger Williams. Harcourt 1944
BBJH—CC(7-9)—JH—SCHS—YR

Winslow, O. E. Master Roger Williams: A Biography. Macmillan 1957
SCPL

COLLECTIONS

Daugherty, Sonia. Ten Brave Men: Makers of the American Way. Lippincott 1951
SCHS

John Winthrop, 1588-1649

Morgan, Edmund Sears. Puritan Dilemma: The Story of John Winthrop; ed. by Oscar Handlin. Little 1958
SCPL

American—18th century

William Byrd, 1674-1744

Byrd, William. The Secret Diary of William Byrd of Westover, 1709-12. Dietz 1941
CA

Samuel Sewall, 1652-1730

Winslow, Ola Elizabeth. Samuel Sewall of Boston. Macmillan 1964
Bkl A&Y

COLUMNISTS

See Journalists

COMEDIANS

See Actors

COMMUNISTS

Yugoslav—20th century

Milovan Djilas, 1911-

Djilas, Milovan. Land Without Justice. Harcourt 1958
BBHS—SCPL

COMPOSERS

COLLECTIONS

Austin, William W. Music in the 20th Century: From Debussy Through Stravinsky. Norton 1966
Bkl A&Y
Béla Bartók; Claude Debussy; Arnold Schoenberg; Igor Fedorovich Stravinsky; and others

Bakeless, Katherine (Little). Story-Lives of Great Composers. Lippincott 1953
BBEL(6-8)—BBJH—CC(7-9)—ESLC—JH—SCHS

Berkowitz, Freda Pastor. Unfinished Symphony and Other Stories of Men and Music. Atheneum 1963
Bkl C(6-9)

Biancolli, Louis Leopold and Peyser, Herbert F., eds. Masters of the Orchestra, from Bach to Prokofieff. Putnam 1954
SCPL

Brockway, Wallace and Weinstock, Herbert. Men of Music: Their Lives, Times, and Achievements. Simon & Schuster 1958
SCPL

Burch, Gladys and Wolcott, John. Famous Composers for Young People. Dodd 1945
CC(5-9)—ESLC—JH

Burch, Gladys. Modern Composers for Young People. Dodd 1941
BBJH—CC(5-9)—ESLC—JH—SCHS

COMPOSERS—*Continued*

Copland, Aaron. Our New Music: Leading Composers in Europe and America. McGraw 1941
SCPL
Béla Bartók; Carlos Chavez; Claude Debussy; Modest Petrovich Mussorgsky; Maurice Joseph Ravel; Arnold Schoenberg; Igor Fedorovich Stravinsky; and others

Cross, Milton and Ewen, David. Encyclopedia of the Great Composers and Their Music. 2v. Doubleday 1962
SCHS—SCPL

Ewen, David, ed. Book of Modern Composers. Knopf 1950
SCPL

Ewen, David, ed. Composers of Yesterday: A Biographical and Critical Guide to the Most Important Composers of the Past. Wilson 1937
SCPL

Ewen, David, ed. European Composers Today: A Biographical and Critical Guide. Wilson 1954
JH—SCHS—SCPL

Ewen, David, ed. From Bach to Stravinsky: The History of Music by Its Foremost Critics. Norton 1933
SCPL
Johann Sebastian Bach; Ludwig van Beethoven; Johannes Brahms; Claude Debussy; Georg Friedrich Handel; Maurice Joseph Ravel; Robert Alexander Schumann; Igor Fedorovich Stravinsky; Peter Ilyich Tchaikovsky; and others

Ewen, David, ed. Great Composers, 1300-1900: A Biographical and Critical Guide. Wilson 1966
Bkl A&Y

Ewen, David, ed. The New Book of Modern Composers. Knopf 1961
SCHS

Ewen, David, ed. The World of Great Composers. Prentice-Hall 1962
Bkl A&Y—SCHS—SCPL

Gal, Hans, ed. The Musician's World: Great Composers in Their Letters. Arco 1966
Bkl A

Gough, Catherine. Boyhoods of Great Composers, Book One. Walck 1960
CC(2-5)—ESLC

Gough, Catherine. Boyhoods of Great Composers, Book Two. Walck 1965
CC(2-5)—ESLC—IndJ(4-6)
Frédéric François Chopin; Giuseppe Verdi; and others

Hoover, Kathleen O'Donnell. Makers of Opera. Beechhurst Press 1955
SCPL

Kaufmann, Helen L. History's 100 Greatest Composers. Grosset 1957
YR

Montgomery, Elizabeth Rider. The Story Behind Popular Songs. Dodd 1958
BBJH—JH—SCHS—YR

Paris, Leonard Allen. Men and Melodies. Crowell 1954
BBJH

Shippen, Katherine B. and Seidlova, Anca. The Heritage of Music. Viking 1963
ESLC

Wicker, Ireene. Young Music Makers: Boyhoods of Famous Composers. Bobbs 1961
AB(3-9)—ESLC

American

COLLECTIONS

Bakeless, Katherine (Little). Story-Lives of American Composers. Lippincott 1962
BBEL(6-8)—BBJH—CC(7-9)—ESLC—JH—SCHS

Burton, Jack. Blue Book of Tin Pan Alley: A Human Interest Anthology of American Popular Music. Century House 1951
SCPL

Ewen, David, ed. American Composers Today: A Biographical and Critical Guide. Wilson 1949
JH—SCHS—SCPL

Ewen, David, ed. Popular American Composers, from Revolutionary Times to the Present: A Biographical and Critical Guide. Wilson 1962
Bkl A&Y—JH—SCHS—SCPL

Green, Stanley. The World of Musical Comedy: The Story of the American Musical Stage as Told Through the Careers of Its Foremost Composers and Lyricists. Ziff-Davis 1960
SCPL

Howard, John Tasker. Our American Music: Three Hundred Years of It. Crowell 1954
SCPL

Machlis, Joseph. American Composers of Our Time. Crowell 1963
Bkl Y&C—CC(6-9)—ESLC—JH—YR

Posell, Elsa Z. American Composers. Houghton 1963
Bkl C(5-8)—CC—ESLC—IndJ(4-6)—JH

Reis, Claire (Raphael). Composers in America: Biographical Sketches of Contemporary Composers with a Record of Their Works. Macmillan 1947
SCPL

American—19th century

Stephen Collins Foster, 1826-1864

Howard, John Tasker. Stephen Foster, America's Troubador. Crowell 1954
CA

COMPOSERS

American—19th century

Stephen Collins Foster—Continued

Purdy, Claire Lee. He Heard America Sing: The Story of Stephen Foster. Messner 1940
BBEL(6-8)—BBJH—BY—CC(6-9)—ESLC—JH—SCHS

Wheeler, Opal. Stephen Foster and His Little Dog Tray. Dutton 1941
BBEL—CC(4-6)

Victor Herbert, 1859-1924

Purdy, Claire Lee. Victor Herbert: American Music-Master. Messner 1944
SCHS

Waters, Edward Neighbor. Victor Herbert: A Life in Music. Macmillan 1955
SCPL

Edward Alexander MacDowell, 1861-1908

Wheeler, Opal and Deucher, Sybil. Edward MacDowell and His Cabin in the Pines. Dutton 1940
CC(4-6)

John Philip Sousa, 1854-1932

Lingg, Ann M. John Philip Sousa. Holt 1954
SCHS

Sousa, John Philip. Marching Along: Recollections of Men, Women and Music. Hale 1928
SCPL

American—20th century

Harold Arlen, 1905-

Jablonski, Edward. Harold Arlen: Happy with the Blues. Doubleday 1961
Bkl A

Irving Berlin, 1888-

Ewen, David. Story of Irving Berlin. Holt 1950
SCHS—SCPL—YR

COLLECTIONS

Life International. Nine Who Chose America. Dutton 1959
Bkl Y&C—SCHS

Leonard Bernstein, 1918-

Bernstein, Shirley. Making Music: Leonard Bernstein. Encyc. Britannica 1963
Bkl C(7-9)

Briggs, John. Leonard Bernstein: The Man, His Work, and His World. World 1961
Bkl A&Y—SCHS—SCPL

Ewen, David. Leonard Bernstein: A Biography for Young People. Chilton 1960
Bkl Y&C—BY—ESLC—JH—SCHS

Hoagy Carmichael, 1899-

Carmichael, Hoagy and Longstreet, Stephen. Sometimes I Wonder: The Story of Hoagy Carmichael. Farrar 1965
Bkl A

Aaron Copland, 1900-

Berger, Arthur Victor. Aaron Copland. Oxford 1953
SCPL

Smith, Julia Frances. Aaron Copland: His Work and Contribution to American Music. Dutton 1955
SCPL

George Gershwin, 1898-1937

Ewen, David. Journey to Greatness: The Life and Music of George Gershwin. Holt 1956
CA—SCPL

Ewen, David. The Story of George Gershwin. Holt 1943
BBJH—CC(7-9)—JH—SCHS

Jablonski, Edward. George Gershwin. Putnam 1962
Bkl C(7-9)

Jablonski, Edward and Stewart, L. D. Gershwin Years. Doubleday 1958
SCPL

William Christopher Handy, 1873-1958

Handy, William Christopher. Father of the Blues: An Autobiography; ed. by Arna Bontemps. Macmillan 1941
SCPL

Victor Herbert, 1859-1924

Purdy, Claire Lee. Victor Herbert: American Music-Master. Messner 1944
SCHS

Waters, Edward Neighbor. Victor Herbert: A Life in Music. Macmillan 1955
SCPL

Jerome David Kern, 1885-1945

Ewen, David. Story of Jerome Kern. Holt 1953
SCPL

Ewen, David. The World of Jerome Kern: A Biography. Holt 1960
SCHS

Edward Alexander MacDowell, 1861-1908

Wheeler, Opal and Deucher, Sybil. Edward MacDowell and His Cabin in the Pines. Dutton 1940
CC(4-6)

Cole Porter, 1893-1964

Ewen, David. The Cole Porter Story. Holt 1965
Bkl Y&C—IndS(9-12)

COMPOSERS

American—20th century

Cole Porter—Continued

Porter, Cole and Hubler, Richard Gibson. The Cole Porter Story. World 1965
Bkl A

Claire (Raphael) Reis, ?

Reis, Claire (Raphael). Composers, Conductors and Critics. Oxford 1955
SCPL

Richard Rodgers, 1902-

Ewen, David. Richard Rodgers. Holt 1957
SCPL

Ewen, David. With a Song in His Heart: The Story of Richard Rodgers. Holt 1963
Bkl Y&C—CC(7-9)—ESLC—JH—SCHS

Green, Stanley. The Rodgers and Hammerstein Story. Day 1963
Bkl A&Y

COLLECTIONS

Chotzinoff, Samuel. A Little Nightmusic. Harper 1964
Bkl A&Y—IndS(12)

John Philip Sousa, 1854-1932

Lingg, Ann M. John Philip Sousa. Holt 1954
SCHS

Sousa, John Philip. Marching Along: Recollections of Men, Women and Music. Hale 1928
SCPL

Virgil Thomson, 1896-

Thomson, Virgil. Virgil Thomson. Knopf 1966
Bkl A

Austrian—18th century

Franz Joseph Haydn, 1732-1809

Geiringer, Karl. Haydn: A Creative Life in Music. Norton 1946
SCPL

Mirsky, Reba Paeff. Haydn. Follett 1963
AB(5up)—Bkl C(5-7)—CC(4-6)—ESLC—IndJ(4-6)—JH

Wheeler, Opal and Deucher, Sybil. Joseph Haydn, the Merry Little Peasant. Dutton 1936
CC(4-6)

Johann Chrysostom Wolfgang Amadeus Mozart, 1756-1791

Davenport, Marcia (Gluck). Mozart. Scribner 1956; Watts, large type ed. 1965
SCPL

Einstein, Alfred. Mozart: His Character, His Work; tr. by Arthur Mendel and Nathan Broder. Oxford 1945
SCPL

Haldane, Charlotte (Franken). Mozart. Oxford 1960
Bkl A

Kaufmann, Helen L. The Story of Mozart. Grosset 1955
YR

Komroff, Manuel. Mozart. Knopf 1956
BBEL(6-8)—BBJH—CC(6-9)—ESLC—JH—SCHS

Mirsky, Reba Paeff. Mozart. Follett 1960
Bkl C(4-6)—CC(4-6)—ESLC

Seroff, Victor Ilyitch. Wolfgang Amadeus Mozart. Macmillan 1965
Bkl Y&C(7-9)—ESLC—IndJ(6-9)

Turner, W. J. Mozart: The Man and His Works. Knopf 1938
CA

Valentin, Erich. Mozart: A Pictorial Biography; tr. by Margaret Shenfield. Studio 1960
Bkl A&Y

Wheeler, Opal and Deucher, Sybil. Mozart, the Wonder Boy. Dutton 1941
AB(4-6)—BBEL—CC(4-6)

Austrian—19th century

Gustav Mahler, 1860-1911

Mahler, Alma Maria (Schindler). Gustav Mahler: Memories and Letters; tr. by Basil Creighton. Viking 1946
SCPL

Walter, Bruno. Gustav Mahler; tr. by L. W. Lindt. Knopf 1958
SCPL

Franz Peter Schubert, 1797-1828

Brown, M. J. E. Schubert: A Critical Biography. St Martins 1958
CA—SCPL

Deutsch, Otto Erich, ed. Schubert: Memoirs by His Friends; tr. by Rosamond Ley and John Nowell. Macmillan 1958
SCPL

Deutsch, Otto Erich. Schubert Reader: A Life of Franz Schubert in Letters and Documents; tr. by Eric Blom. Norton 1947
SCPL

Einstein, Alfred. Schubert: A Musical Portrait. Oxford 1951
SCPL

Schauffler, R. H. Franz Schubert: The Ariel of Music. Putnam 1949
SCPL

Wheeler, Opal and Deucher, Sybil. Franz Schubert and His Merry Friends. Dutton 1939
CC(4-6)—ESLC

COMPOSERS

Austrian—19th century—*Continued*

Johann Strauss, 1825-1899

Ewen, David. Tales from the Vienna Woods: The Story of Johann Strauss. Holt 1944
CC(7-9)—JH—SCHS—SCPL

Pahlen, Kurt. The Waltz King: Johann Strauss, Jr.; tr. from the German by Theodore McClintock. Rand McNally 1965
ESLC—IndJ(6-9)—JH

Austrian—20th century

Alban Berg, 1885-1935

Reich, Willi. Alban Berg; tr. by Cornelius Cardew. Harcourt 1965
Bkl A

Gustav Mahler, 1860-1911

Mahler, Alma Maria (Schindler). Gustav Mahler: Memories and Letters; tr. by Basil Creighton. Viking 1946
SCPL

Walter, Bruno. Gustav Mahler; tr. by L. W. Lindt. Knopf 1958
SCPL

Arnold Schoenberg, 1874-1951

Schoenberg, Arnold. Letters; ed. by Erwin Stein; tr. from the German by Eithne Wilkins and Ernst Kaiser. St Martins 1965
Bkl A

COLLECTIONS

Austin, William W. Music in the 20th Century: From Debussy Through Stravinsky. Norton 1966
Bkl A&Y

Copland, Aaron. Our New Music: Leading Composers in Europe and America. McGraw 1941
SCPL

Bohemian—19th century

Antonín Dvořák, 1841-1904

Purdy, Claire Lee. Antonín Dvořák, Composer from Bohemia. Messner 1950
CC(7-9)—JH—SCHS

Czech—20th century

Leoš Janáček, 1854-1938

Hollander, Hans. Leoš Janáček: His Life and Work; tr. by Paul Hamburger. St Martins 1963
Bkl A

English—17th century

Henry Purcell, 1659-1695

Holst, Imogen, ed. Henry Purcell, 1658?-1695: Essays on His Music. Oxford 1959
SCPL

English—18th century

Georg Friedrich Handel, 1685-1759

Deutsch, Otto Erich. Handel: A Documentary Biography. Norton 1955
SCPL

Flower, Sir Newman. George Frideric Handel: His Personality and His Times. Scribner 1948
SCPL

Lang, Paul Henry. George Frideric Handel. Norton 1966
Bkl A&Y

Weinstock, Herbert. Handel. Knopf 1959
SCPL

Wheeler, Opal. Händel at the Court of Kings. Dutton 1943
CC(4-6)

COLLECTIONS

Ewen, David, ed. From Bach to Stravinsky: The History of Music by Its Foremost Critics. Norton 1933
SCPL

English—19th century

Frederick Delius, 1862-1934

Beecham, Sir Thomas. Frederick Delius. Knopf 1960
Bkl A—SCPL

Sir Arthur Seymour Sullivan, 1842-1900

Baily, Leslie. Gilbert & Sullivan Book. Coward-McCann 1957
SCPL

Purdy, Claire Lee. Gilbert and Sullivan: Masters of Mirth and Melody. Messner 1946
SCHS

Wymer, Norman. Gilbert and Sullivan. Dutton 1963
Bkl C(7-10)&Y—YR

English—20th century

Benjamin Britten, 1913-

Holst, Imogen. Britten. Crowell 1966
Bkl Y&C

Frederick Delius, 1862-1934

Beecham, Sir Thomas. Frederick Delius. Knopf 1960
Bkl A—SCPL

COMPOSERS

English—20th century—*Continued*

Ralph Vaughan Williams, 1872-1958

Vaughan Williams, Ursula. R. V. W.: A Biography of Ralph Vaughan Williams. Oxford 1964
Bkl A

Finnish—20th century

Jean Sibelius, 1865-1957

Abraham, Gerald Ernest Heal, ed. Music of Sibelius. Norton 1947
SCPL

Ringbom, Nils Eric. Jean Sibelius: A Master and His Work; tr. by G. I. C. de Courcy. Univ. of Okla. 1954
SCPL

French—19th century

Louis Hector Berlioz, 1803-1869

Barzun, Jacques. Berlioz and the Romantic Century. 2v. Little 1950
CA

Georges Bizet, 1838-1875

Curtiss, Mina K. Bizet and His World. Knopf 1959
SCPL

Claude Debussy, 1862-1918

La Mure, Pierre. Clair de Lune. Random House 1962 (Fiction)
Bkl A

Lockspeiser, Edward. Debussy. Pellegrini & Cudahy 1952
SCPL

Lockspeiser, Edward. Debussy—His Life and Mind: v. 1, 1862-1902. Macmillan 1962
Bkl A—SCPL

Lockspeiser, Edward. Debussy—His Life and Mind: v. 2, 1902-1918. Macmillan 1965
Bkl A

Seroff, Victor Ilyitch. Debussy: Musician of France. Putnam 1956
CA—SCPL

COLLECTIONS

Austin, William W. Music in the 20th Century: From Debussy Through Stravinsky. Norton 1966
Bkl A&Y

Copland, Aaron. Our New Music: Leading Composers in Europe and America. McGraw 1941
SCPL

Ewen, David, ed. From Bach to Stravinsky: The History of Music by Its Foremost Critics. Norton 1933
SCPL

César Auguste Franck, 1822-1890

Demuth, Norman. César Franck. Philosophical Lib. 1949
SCPL

French—20th century

Claude Debussy, 1862-1918

La Mure, Pierre. Clair de Lune. Random House 1962 (Fiction)
Bkl A

Lockspeiser, Edward. Debussy. Pellegrini & Cudahy 1952
SCPL

Lockspeiser, Edward. Debussy—His Life and Mind: v. 1, 1862-1902. Macmillan 1962
Bkl A—SCPL

Lockspeiser, Edward. Debussy—His Life and Mind: v. 2, 1902-1918. Macmillan 1965
Bkl A

Seroff, Victor Ilyitch. Debussy: Musician of France. Putnam 1956
CA—SCPL

COLLECTIONS

Austin, William W. Music in the 20th Century: From Debussy Through Stravinsky. Norton 1966
Bkl A&Y

Copland, Aaron. Our New Music: Leading Composers in Europe and America. McGraw 1941
SCPL

Ewen, David, ed. From Bach to Stravinsky: The History of Music by Its Foremost Critics. Norton 1933
SCPL

Arthur Honegger, 1892-1955

Honegger, Arthur. I Am a Composer; tr. from the French by Wilson O. Clough and Allan Arthur Willman. St Martins 1966
Bkl A

Darius Milhaud, 1892-

Milhaud, Darius. Notes Without Music; tr. by Donald Evans. Knopf 1953
SCPL

Maurice Joseph Ravel, 1875-1937

COLLECTIONS

Copland, Aaron. Our New Music: Leading Composers in Europe and America. McGraw 1941
SCPL

Ewen, David, ed. From Bach to Stravinsky: The History of Music by Its Foremost Critics. Norton 1933
SCPL

COMPOSERS—*Continued*

German—18th century

Johann Sebastian Bach, 1685-1750

David, Hans Theodore, ed. Bach Reader: A Life of Johann Sebastian Bach; ed. by H. T. David and Arthur Mendel. Norton 1945
SCPL

Geiringer, Karl. Bach Family: Seven Generations of Creative Genius. Oxford 1954
SCPL

Goss, Madeleine. Deep-Flowing Brook: The Story of Johann Sebastian Bach. Holt 1938
CC(6-9)—JH—SCHS

Holst, Imogen. Bach. Crowell 1965
Bkl C(7-9)&Y—ESLC—IndJ(4-6)

Manton, Jo. A Portrait of Bach. Abelard-Schuman 1957
BBEL(7-8)—BBJH—CC(7-9)—ESLC—JH—YR

Mirsky, Reba Paeff. Johann Sebastian Bach. Follett 1965
Bkl C(5-8)

Neumann, Werner. Bach: A Pictorial Biography; tr. by Stefan de Haan. Studio 1961
Bkl A&Y

Schweitzer, Albert. J. S. Bach; tr. by Ernest Newman. 2v. Black 1923
SCPL

Spitta, Philipp. Johann Sebastian Bach: His Work and Influence on the Music of Germany, 1685-1750; tr. by Clara Bell and J. A. Fuller-Maitland. 3v. in 2. Dover 1951
SCPL

Terry, Charles Sanford. Bach: A Biography. Oxford 1933
CA—SCPL

Wheeler, Opal and Deucher, Sybil. Sebastian Bach, the Boy from Thuringia. Dutton 1937
BBEL—CC(4-6)—ESLC

COLLECTIONS

Ewen, David, ed. From Bach to Stravinsky: The History of Music by Its Foremost Critics. Norton 1933
SCPL

German—19th century

Ludwig van Beethoven, 1770-1827

Beethoven, Ludwig van. The Letters of Beethoven; ed. by Emily Anderson. 3v. St Martins 1961
SCPL

Burk, John Naglee. Life and Works of Beethoven. Modern Lib. 1946
CA—SCPL

Goss, Madeleine. Beethoven, Master Musician. Holt 1946
BBJH—CC(6-9)—ESLC—JH—SCHS—YR

Kaufmann, Helen L. The Story of Beethoven. Grosset 1957
YR

Komroff, Manuel. Beethoven and the World of Music. Dodd 1961
JH—SCHS

Mirsky, Reba Paeff. Beethoven. Follett 1957
AB(5-9)—CC(5-7)

Rodman, Selden. The Heart of Beethoven. Shorewood Pubs 1962
Bkl A

Schindler, Anton Felix. Beethoven as I Knew Him: A Biography; ed. by Donald W. MacArdle; tr. by Constance S. Jolly. Univ. of N. C. 1966
Bkl A

Steichen, Dana. Beethoven's Beloved. Doubleday 1959
Bkl A

Sullivan, John William Navin. Beethoven: His Spiritual Development. Knopf 1927
SCPL

Thayer, Alexander Wheelock. The Life of Ludwig van Beethoven. 3v. Southern Ill. Univ. 1960
SCPL

Wheeler, Opal. Ludwig Beethoven and the Chiming Tower Bells. Dutton 1942
CC(4-6)—ESLC

COLLECTIONS

Ewen, David, ed. From Bach to Stravinsky: The History of Music by Its Foremost Critics. Norton 1933
SCPL

Johannes Brahms, 1833-1897

Deucher, Sybil. The Young Brahms. Dutton 1949
BBJH—CC(4-6)—ESLC—JH

Gál, Hans. Johannes Brahms: His Work and Personality; tr. from the German by Joseph Stein. Knopf 1963
Bkl A

Geiringer, Karl. Brahms: His Life and Work; tr. by H. B. Weiner and Bernard Miall. Oxford 1947
CA—SCPL

COLLECTIONS

Ewen, David, ed. From Bach to Stravinsky: The History of Music by Its Foremost Critics. Norton 1933
SCPL

Franz Xaver Gruber, 1787-1863

Moore, John Travers. The Story of Silent Night. Concordia 1965
CC

COMPOSERS

German—19th century

Franz Xaver Gruber—Continued

Pauli, Hertha. Silent Night: The Story
of a Song. Knopf 1943
CC(4-7)—ESLC

*Felix Mendelssohn-Bartholdy, 1809-
1847*

Erskine, John. Song Without Words.
Messner 1941
YR

Jacob, Heinrich Eduard. Felix Mendelssohn and His Times; tr. from the German by Richard and Clara Winston.
Prentice-Hall 1963
Bkl A

Mendelssohn-Bartholdy, Felix. Letters;
ed. by G. Selden-Goth. Pantheon 1945
CA

Werner, Eric. Mendelssohn: A New
Image of the Composer and His Age;
tr. from the German by Dika Newlin.
Free Press 1963
Bkl A—SCPL

*Robert Alexander Schumann, 1810-
1856*

Wheeler, Opal. Robert Schumann and
Mascot Ziff. Dutton 1947
CC(4-6)

COLLECTIONS

Ewen, David, ed. From Bach to Stravinsky: The History of Music by Its Foremost Critics. Norton 1933
SCPL

Richard Wagner, 1813-1883

Bulla, Clyde Robert. The Ring and the
Fire. Crowell 1962
YR

Newman, Ernest. Life of Richard Wagner. 4v. Knopf 1933-46
CA—SCPL

Panofsky, Walter. Wagner: A Pictorial
Biography; tr. from the German by
Richard Rickett. Studio 1964
Bkl A—IndS(10-12)

Wheeler, Opal. Adventures of Richard
Wagner. Dutton 1960
CC(3-5)

German—20th century

Richard Strauss, 1864-1949

Strauss, Richard and Hofmannsthal, Hugo
Hofmann, Edler von. A Working
Friendship: The Correspondence Be-
tween [the authors]; tr. by Hanns
Hammelmann and Ewald Osers. Ran-
dom House 1962
Bkl A

Hungarian—19th century

Franz Liszt, 1811-1886

Beckett, Walter. Liszt. Farrar 1956
SCPL

Rousselot, Jean. Hungarian Rhapsody:
The Life of Franz Liszt; tr. by Moura
Budberg. Putnam 1961 (Fiction)
Bkl A

Sitwell, Sacheverell. Liszt. Cassell 1955
CA

Hungarian—20th century

Béla Bartók, 1881-1945

Fassett, Agatha. Béla Bartók's American
Years: The Naked Face of Genius.
Houghton 1958
SCPL

Stevens, Halsey. Life and Music of Béla
Bartók. Oxford 1953
CA—SCPL

COLLECTIONS

Austin, William W. Music in the 20th
Century: From Debussy Through Stra-
vinsky. Norton 1966
Bkl A&Y

Copland, Aaron. Our New Music: Leading Composers in Europe and America. McGraw 1941
SCPL

Italian—17th century

Arcangelo Corelli, 1653-1713

Pincherle, Marc. Corelli: His Life, His
Work; tr. by H. E. M. Russell. Norton
1956
SCPL

Claudio Monteverdi, 1567-1643

Schrade, Leo. Monteverdi, Creator of
Modern Music. Norton 1950
CA

Alessandro Scarlatti, 1659-1725

Dent, Edward J. Alessandro Scarlatti:
His Life and Works. Arnold 1960
SCPL

Italian—18th century

Alessandro Scarlatti, 1659-1725

Dent, Edward J. Alessandro Scarlatti:
His Life and Works. Arnold 1960
SCPL

Domenico Scarlatti, 1685-1757

Kirkpatrick, Ralph. Domenico Scarlatti.
Princeton Univ. 1953
SCPL

Antonio Vivaldi, 1675?-1741

Pincherle, Marc. Vivaldi, Genius of the
Baroque; tr. by Christopher Hatch.
Norton 1957
SCPL

COMPOSERS—*Continued*

Italian—19th century

Gaetano Donizetti, 1797-1848

Weinstock, Herbert. Donizetti and the World of Opera in Italy, Paris and Vienna in the First Half of the Nineteenth Century. Pantheon 1963
Bkl A

Giuseppe Verdi, 1813-1901

Gatti, Carlo. Verdi: The Man and His Music; tr. by Elisabeth Abbott. Putnam 1955
SCPL

Malvern, Gladys. On Golden Wings: The Story of Giuseppe Verdi. Macrae 1960
Bkl C(6-9)&Y—YR

Martin, George Whitney. Verdi: His Music, Life and Times. Dodd 1963
Bkl A—SCPL

Sheean, Vincent. Orpheus at Eighty. Random House 1958
SCPL

Toye, Francis. Giuseppe Verdi: His Life and Works. Knopf 1931
CA

Walker, Frank. The Man Verdi. Knopf 1962
Bkl A—SCPL

COLLECTIONS

Gough, Catherine. Boyhoods of Great Composers, Book Two. Walck 1965
IndJ(4-6)

Trease, Geoffrey. Seven Stages. Vanguard 1965
Bkl Y&C—IndS(9-10)

Italian—20th century

Gian-Carlo Menotti, 1911-

COLLECTIONS

Chotzinoff, Samuel. A Little Nightmusic. Harper 1964
Bkl A&Y—IndS(12)

Life International. Nine Who Chose America. Dutton 1959
Bkl Y&C—SCHS

Mexican—20th century

Carlos Chávez, 1899-

COLLECTIONS

Copland, Aaron. Our New Music: Leading Composers in Europe and America. McGraw 1941
SCPL

Norwegian—19th century

Edvard Hagerup Grieg, 1843-1907

Deucher, Sybil. Edvard Grieg, Boy of the Northland. Dutton 1946
CC(4-6)

Purdy, Claire Lee. Song of the North: The Story of Edvard Grieg. Messner 1941
BBJH—CC(7-9)—JH—SCHS

Polish—19th century

Frédéric François Chopin, 1810-1849

Boucourechliev, André. Chopin: A Pictorial Biography; tr. from the French by Edward Hyams. Viking 1963
Bkl A&Y

Chissell, Joan. Chopin. Crowell 1965
Bkl C(7-9)&Y—IndJ(4-6)

Seroff, Victor. Frederic Chopin. Macmillan 1964
CC—ESLC—IndS(9-10)—JH

Weinstock, Herbert. Chopin: The Man and His Music. Knopf 1949
SCPL

Wheeler, Opal. Frederic Chopin, Son of Poland: Early Years. Dutton 1948
CC(4-6)

Wheeler, Opal. Frederic Chopin, Son of Poland: Later Years. Dutton 1949
CC(4-6)

Wierzynski, Kazimierz. Life and Death of Chopin; tr. by Norbert Guteman. Simon & Schuster 1949
SCPL

COLLECTIONS

Gough, Catherine. Boyhoods of Great Composers, Book Two. Walck 1965
IndJ(4-6)

Russian—19th century

Modest Petrovich Mussorgsky, 1839-1881

Calvocoressi, Michel Dimitri. Modest Mussorgsky: His Life and Works. Essential Bks 1956
SCPL

Leyda, Jay, ed. Musorgsky Reader: A Life of Modeste Petrovich Musorgsky in Letters and Documents. Norton 1947
SCPL

COLLECTIONS

Copland, Aaron. Our New Music: Leading Composers in Europe and America. McGraw 1941
SCPL

Anton Rubinstein, 1829-1894

Bowen, Catherine (Drinker). Free Artist: The Story of Anton and Nicholas Rubinstein. Little 1961
Bkl A

COMPOSERS

Russian—19th century—*Continued*

Peter Ilyich Tchaikovsky, 1840-1893

Bowen, Catherine (Drinker) and Meck, Barbara von. "Beloved Friend": The Story of Tchaikowsky and Nadejda von Meck. Little 1961
Bkl A—SCPL

Hanson, Lawrence and Hanson, Elisabeth M. Tchaikovsky: The Man Behind the Music. Dodd 1966
Bkl A

Purdy, Claire Lee. Stormy Victory: The Story of Tchaikovsky. Messner 1942
CC(7-9)—JH—SCHS

Weinstock, Herbert. Tchaikovsky. Knopf 1943
SCPL

Wheeler, Opal. Peter Tschaikowsky and the Nutcracker Ballet. Dutton 1959
CC(4-6)—ESLC

COLLECTIONS

Ewen, David, ed. From Bach to Stravinsky: The History of Music by Its Foremost Critics. Norton 1933
SCPL

Russian—20th century

Sergei Sergeevich Prokofiev, 1891-1953

Hanson, Lawrence and Hanson, Elisabeth M. Prokofiev: A Biography in Three Movements. Random House 1964
Bkl A

Sergei Rachmaninoff, 1873-1943

Culshaw, John. Rachmaninov: The Man and His Music. Oxford 1950
SCPL

Igor Fedorovich Stravinsky, 1882-

Stravinsky, Igor Fedorovich. An Autobiography. Simon & Schuster 1936
CA

Stravinsky, Igor Fedorovich and Craft, Robert. Dialogues and a Diary. Doubleday 1963
Bkl A

Stravinsky, Igor Fedorovich and Craft, Robert. Expositions and Developments. Doubleday 1962
Bkl A

Stravinsky, Igor Fedorovich and Craft, Robert. Memories and Commentaries. Doubleday 1960
Bkl A—SCPL

Stravinsky, Igor Fedorovich and Craft, Robert. Themes and Episodes. Knopf 1966
Bkl A

Tansman, Alexandre. Igor Stravinsky: The Man and His Music; tr. by Therese and Charles Bleefield. Putnam 1949
SCPL

Vlad, Roman. Stravinsky; tr. by Frederick and Ann Fuller. Oxford 1960
Bkl A

White, Eric Walter. Stravinsky: A Critical Survey. Philosophical Lib. 1948
SCPL

COLLECTIONS

Austin, William W. Music in the 20th Century: From Debussy Through Stravinsky. Norton 1966
Bkl A&Y

Copland, Aaron. Our New Music: Leading Composers in Europe and America. McGraw 1941
SCPL

Ewen, David, ed. From Bach to Stravinsky: The History of Music by Its Foremost Critics. Norton 1933
SCPL

CONDUCTORS

See also Bandmasters

COLLECTIONS

Blaukopf, Kurt. Great Conductors; tr. from the German by Miriam Blaukopf. Arco 1955
SCPL

Ewen, David. Dictators of the Baton. Ziff-Davis 1948
SCPL

Ewen, David. Famous Conductors. Dodd 1966
Bkl Y&C—ESLC
Sir Thomas Beecham; Wilhelm Furtwaengler; Serge Koussevitzky; Dimitri Mitropoulos; Pierre Monteux; Fritz Reiner; Arturo Toscanini; Bruno Walter

Stoddard, Hope. Symphony Conductors of the U.S.A. Crowell 1957
SCPL—YR

American—19th century

Frank Heino Damrosch, 1859-1937

Stebbins, Lucy (Poate) and Poate, Richard. Frank Damrosch: Let the People Sing. Duke Univ. 1945
SCPL

American—20th century

Leonard Bernstein, 1918-

Bernstein, Shirley. Making Music: Leonard Bernstein. Encyc. Britannica 1963
Bkl C(7-9)

Briggs, John. Leonard Bernstein: The Man, His Work, and His World. World 1961
Bkl A&Y—SCHS—SCPL

CONDUCTORS

American—20th century

Leonard Bernstein—Continued

Ewen, David. Leonard Bernstein: A Biography for Young People. Chilton 1960
Bkl Y&C—BY—ESLC—JH—SCHS

Frank Heino Damrosch, 1859-1937

Stebbins, Lucy (Poate) and Poate, Richard. Frank Damrosch: Let the People Sing. Duke Univ. 1945
SCPL

Walter Damrosch, 1862-1950

Finletter, G. B. D. From the Top of the Stairs. Little 1946
SCPL

English—20th century

Sir Thomas Beecham, 1879-1961

Reid, Charles. Thomas Beecham: An Independent Biography. Dutton 1962
Bkl A

COLLECTIONS

Ewen, David. Famous Conductors. Dodd 1966
Bkl Y&C—ESLC

French—19th century

Louis Antoine Jullien, 1812-1860

COLLECTIONS

Schwartz, Harry Wayne. Bands of America. Doubleday 1957
BBHS—SCPL

French—20th century

Pierre Monteux, 1875-1964

Monteux, Doris Gerald (Hodgkins). It's All in the Music. Farrar 1965
Bkl A

Monteux, Fifi. Everyone Is Someone. Farrar 1962
BY

COLLECTIONS

Ewen, David. Famous Conductors. Dodd 1966
Bkl Y&C—ESLC

Charles Munch, 1891-1968

Munch, Charles. I Am a Conductor; tr. by Leonard Burkat. Oxford 1955
SCPL

German—20th century

Wilhelm Furtwaengler, 1886-1954

COLLECTIONS

Ewen, David. Famous Conductors. Dodd 1966
Bkl Y&C—ESLC

Bruno Walter, 1876-1962

Walter, Bruno. Of Music and Musicmaking; tr. by Paul Hamburger. Norton 1961
Bkl A

Walter, Bruno. Theme and Variations: An Autobiography; tr. by J. A. Galston. Knopf 1946
SCPL

COLLECTIONS

Ewen, David. Famous Conductors. Dodd 1966
Bkl Y&C—ESLC

Greek—20th century

Dimitri Mitropoulos, 1896-1960

COLLECTIONS

Ewen, David. Famous Conductors. Dodd 1966
Bkl Y&C—ESLC

Hungarian—20th century

Fritz Reiner, 1888-1963

COLLECTIONS

Ewen, David. Famous Conductors. Dodd 1966
Bkl Y&C—ESLC

Italian—20th century

Arturo Toscanini, 1867-1957

Ewen, David. Story of Arturo Toscanini. Holt 1960
BBHS—CC(7-9)—JH—SCHS—SCPL

Sacchi, Filippo. Magic Baton: Toscanini's Life for Music. Putnam 1957
SCPL

COLLECTIONS

Ewen, David. Famous Conductors. Dodd 1966
Bkl Y&C—ESLC

Freedman, Russell. Teenagers Who Made History. Holiday 1961
BY—JH—SCHS—YR

Russian—20th century

Serge Koussevitzky, 1874-1951

COLLECTIONS

Ewen, David. Famous Conductors. Dodd 1966
Bkl Y&C—ESLC

Nikolai Andreevich Mal'ko, 1883-1961

Mal'ko, Nikolai Andreevich. A Certain Art. Morrow 1966
Bkl A

CONGRESSMEN

See Statesmen

CONQUERORS

See Soldiers

CONSERVATIONISTS

American—20th century

Grant H. Pearson, ?

Pearson, Grant H. and Newill, Philip. My Life of High Adventure. Prentice-Hall 1962
Bkl A&Y

CORNETISTS

See Trumpeters

CORONERS

American—20th century

George Petit LeBrun, 1862-1966

LeBrun, George Petit and Radin, Edward D. It's Time to Tell. Morrow 1962
Bkl A

COSMETICIANS

American—19th century

Harriet (Hubbard) Ayer, 1854-1903

Ayer, Margaret Hubbard. Three Lives of Harriet Hubbard Ayer. Lippincott 1957
SCPL

American—20th century

Jacqueline Cochran, 1910?-

Cochran, Jacqueline. Stars at Noon. Little 1954
SCHS–SCPL

Helena Rubinstein, 1870?-1965

Rubinstein, Helena. My Life for Beauty. Simon & Schuster 1966
Bkl A

COLLECTIONS

Life International. Nine Who Chose America. Dutton 1959
Bkl Y&C–SCHS

COSMONAUTS

See Astronauts

COSTUME DESIGNERS

American—20th century

Bettina (Hill) Ballard, 1905?-1961

Ballard, Bettina (Hill). In My Fashion. McKay 1960
Bkl A

Edith Head, ?

COLLECTIONS

Forsee, Aylesa. Women Who Reached for Tomorrow. Macrae 1960
Bkl Y&C

English—20th century

Mary Quant, 1934-

Quant, Mary. Quant by Quant. Putnam 1966
Bkl A

French—20th century

Pierre Balmain, 1914-

Balmain, Pierre. My Years and Seasons; tr. by Edward Lanchberry and Gordon Young. Doubleday 1965
Bkl A

Ginette Spanier, ?

Spanier, Ginette. It Isn't All Mink. Random House 1960
Bkl A

COUSINS OF FAMOUS MEN

See Relatives of Famous Men

COWBOYS

American—19th century

Andy Adams, 1859-1935

Adams, Andy. Trail Drive: A True Narrative of Cowboy Life from Andy Adams' Log of a Cowboy; ed. by Glen Rounds. Holiday 1965
IndS(9-12)

Nelson Story, 1838-1926

Wagner, Paul Iselin. The Greatest Cattle Drive. Houghton 1964
Bkl C(5-9)–ESLC

American—20th century

Ed ("Fat") Alford, 1901-

Gipson, Fred. Cowhand: The Story of a Working Cowboy. Harper 1953
BY

Frank Collinson, ?-1943

Collinson, Frank. Life in the Saddle; ed. by Mary Whatley Clarke. Univ. of Okla. 1963
Bkl A

Will James, 1892-1942

James, Will. Lone Cowboy: My Life Story. Scribner 1930
BY–JH–SCHS–SCPL–YR

COWBOYS

American—20th century—*Continued*

Bob Kennon, 1876-

Kennon, Bob and Adams, Ramon Frederick. From the Pecos to the Powder: A Cowboy's Autobiography. Univ. of Okla. 1965
Bkl A

CRIMINALS

See also Prisoners; Traitors

COLLECTIONS

Boyd, Mildred. Black Flags and Pieces of Eight. Criterion Bks 1965
ESLC
Snow, Edward Rowe. True Tales of Pirates and Their Gold. Dodd 1953
SCHS
Yolen, Jane H. Pirates in Petticoats. McKay 1963
YR

American

COLLECTIONS

Drago, Harry Sinclair. Outlaws on Horseback. Dodd 1964
Bkl A
Wellman, Paul Iselin. A Dynasty of Western Outlaws. Doubleday 1961
Bkl A
Wellman, Paul Iselin. Spawn of Evil: The Invisible Empire of Soulless Men Which for a Generation Held the Nation in a Spell of Terror. Doubleday 1964
Bkl A

American—19th century

William Harrison ("Billy the Kid") Bonney, 1859-1881

Adams, Ramon Frederick. A Fitting Death for Billy the Kid. Univ. of Okla. 1960
Bkl A
Garrett, Patrick Floyd. Authentic Life of Billy, the Kid, the Noted Desperado of the Southwest. Univ. of Okla. 1954
SCPL

COLLECTIONS

Steckmesser, Kent Ladd. The Western Hero in History and Legend. Univ. of Okla. 1965
Bkl A

John Wilkes Booth, 1838-1865

Stacton, David. The Judges of the Secret Court. Pantheon 1961 (Fiction)
Bkl A

Lizzie Andrew Borden, 1860-1927

Radin, Edward D. Lizzie Borden: The Untold Story. Simon & Schuster 1961
Bkl A

Jesse Woodson James, 1847-1882

Croy, Homer. Jesse James Was My Neighbor. Duell 1949
BY—SCPL

Jean Lafitte, 1780-1826

Sperry, Armstrong. Black Falcon: A Story of Piracy and Old New Orleans. Winston 1949 (Fiction)
CC(7-9)—JH—SCHS
Tallant, Robert. Pirate Lafitte and the Battle of New Orleans. Random House 1951
CC(5-7)—ESLC—JH—SCHS

William D'Alton Mann, 1839-1920

Logan, Andy. The Man Who Robbed Robber Barons. Norton 1965
Bkl A

John Harrison Surratt, 1844-1916

Campbell, Helen Jones. Confederate Courier. St Martins 1964
Bkl A&Y

William Marcy Tweed, 1823-1878

Bales, William Alan. Tiger in the Streets. Dodd 1962
Bkl A

American—20th century

Arthur Barry, 1896-

Hickey, Neil. The Gentleman Was a Thief. Holt 1961
Bkl A

Caryl Chessman, 1921-1960

Machlin, Milton and Woodfield, William Read. Ninth Life. Putnam 1961
Bkl A

Anthony De Angelis, 1915-

Miller, Norman C. The Great Salad Oil Swindle. Coward-McCann 1965
Bkl A

John Dillinger, 1902-1934

Cromie, Robert Allen and Pinkston, Joseph. Dillinger: A Short and Violent Life. McGraw 1962
Bkl A
Toland, John. The Dillinger Days. Random House 1963
Bkl A

Samuel Insull, 1859-1938

McDonald, Forrest. Insull. Univ. of Chicago 1962
Bkl A

CRIMINALS

American—20th century—*Continued*

Nathan Freudenthal Leopold, 1904-

Leopold, Nathan Freudenthal. Life Plus 99 Years. Doubleday 1958
SCPL

Victor Lustig, ?

Johnson, James Francis and Miller, Floyd. The Man Who Sold the Eiffel Tower. Doubleday 1961
Bkl A

William D'Alton Mann, 1839-1920

Logan, Andy. The Man Who Robbed the Robber Barons. Norton 1965
Bkl A

Philip Musica, 1884-1938

Keats, Charles. Magnificent Masquerade: The Strange Case of Dr. Coster and Mr. Musica. Funk 1964
Bkl A

Lee Harvey Oswald, 1939-1963

Ford, Gerald R. and Stiles, John R. Portrait of the Assassin. Simon & Schuster 1965
Bkl A

Hartogs, Renatus and Freeman, Lucy. The Two Assassins. Crowell 1965
Bkl A

Sauvage, Léo. The Oswald Affair: An Examination of the Contradictions and Omissions of the Warren Report; tr. from the French by Charles Gaulkin. World 1966
Bkl A

Jack Ruby, 1911-1967

Hartogs, Renatus and Freeman, Lucy. The Two Assassins. Crowell 1965
Bkl A

Kaplan, John and Waltz, Jon R. The Trial of Jack Ruby. Macmillan 1965
Bkl A

Nicola Sacco, 1891-1927

Felix, David. Protest: Sacco-Vanzetti and the Intellectuals. Ind. Univ. 1965
Bkl A

Russell, Francis. Tragedy in Dedham: The Story of the Sacco-Vanzetti Case. McGraw 1962
Bkl A–SCPL

Bartolomeo Vanzetti, 1888-1927

Felix, David. Protest: Sacco-Vanzetti and the Intellectuals. Ind. Univ. 1965
Bkl A

Russell, Francis. Tragedy in Dedham: The Story of the Sacco-Vanzetti Case. McGraw 1962
Bkl A–SCPL

Australian—19th century

Edward Kelly, 1854-1880

Melville, Robert. The Legend of Ned Kelly, Australia's Outlaw Hero. Studio 1964
Bkl A

English

COLLECTIONS

Whipple, Addison Beecher Colvin. Famous Pirates of the New World. Random House 1958
CC
Dixey Bull; James Flood; Edward ("Blackbeard") Teach; and others

English—17th century

Dixey Bull, fl.1632-1633

COLLECTIONS

Whipple, Addison Beecher Colvin. Famous Pirates of the New World. Random House 1958
CC

James Flood, ?

COLLECTIONS

Whipple, Addison Beecher Colvin. Famous Pirates of the New World. Random House 1958
CC

Sir Henry Morgan, 1635?-1688

Syme, Ronald. Sir Henry Morgan, Buccaneer. Morrow 1965
AB(4-7)–ESLC

English—18th century

William Henry Ireland, 1777-1835

Grebanier, Bernard D. N. The Great Shakespeare Forgery. Norton 1965
Bkl A&Y

Edward ("Blackbeard") Teach, ?-1718

COLLECTIONS

Whipple, Addison Beecher Colvin. Famous Pirates of the New World. Random House 1958
CC

English—19th century

Charles Frederick Peace, 1832-1879

Ward, George David Allen. The Shortest Route to Paradise: The Story of the Master Criminal Charles Peace. Horizon 1964
Bkl A

CRIMINALS—*Continued*

English—20th century

John Reginald Halliday Christie, 1899?-1953

Kennedy, Ludovic Henry Coverley. Ten Rillington Place. Simon & Schuster 1961
Bkl A

Timothy John Evans, 1924-1950

Kennedy, Ludovic Henry Coverley. Ten Rillington Place. Simon & Schuster 1961
Bkl A

French—20th century

Henri Désiré Landru, 1869-1922

Masson, René. Landru; tr. from the French by Gillian Tindall. Doubleday 1965 (Fiction)
Bkl A

German—20th century

Adolf Eichmann, 1906-1962

Arendt, Hannah. Eichmann in Jerusalem: A Report on the Banality of Evil. Viking 1963
Bkl A

Friedman, Tuviah. The Hunter; tr. by David C. Gross. Doubleday 1961
Bkl A

Glock, Charles Y. The Apathetic Majority: A Study Based on Public Responses to the Eichmann Trial. Harper 1966
Bkl A

Hausner, Gideon. Justice in Jerusalem. Harper 1966
Bkl A

Pearlman, Maurice. The Capture and Trial of Adolf Eichmann. Simon & Schuster 1963
Bkl A

Robinson, Jacob. And the Crooked Shall Be Made Straight: The Eichmann Trial, the Jewish Catastrophe, and Hannah Arendt's Narrative. Macmillan 1965
Bkl A

Bruno Richard Hauptmann, 1899-1936

Waller, George. Kidnap: The Story of the Lindbergh Case. Dial 1961
Bkl A—SCPL

Heinrich Himmler, 1900-1945

Manvell, Roger and Fraenkel, Heinrich. Himmler. Putnam 1965
IndS(11-12)

Italian—20th century

Alessandro Serenelli, ?

Di Donato, Pietro. The Penitent. Hawthorn 1962
Bkl A

Scottish—17th century

William Kidd, 1645?-1701

Lawson, Robert. Captain Kidd's Cat. Little 1956 (Fiction)
CC(6-9)—ESLC—JH

CRIMINOLOGISTS

English—20th century

Sir Sydney Alfred Smith, 1883-

Smith, Sir Sydney Alfred. Mostly Murder. McKay 1960
Bkl A

CRIPPLES

See Physically Handicapped

CRITICS

American—20th century

Brooks Atkinson, 1894-

COLLECTIONS

Lewis, Mildred and Lewis, Milton. Famous Modern Newspaper Writers. Dodd 1962
Bkl Y&C

Bernard Berenson, 1865-1959

Berenson, Bernard. The Bernard Berenson Treasury; ed. by Hanna Kiel. Simon & Schuster 1962
Bkl A

Berenson, Bernard. Conversations with Berenson by Umberto Morra; tr. from the Italian by Florence Hammond. Houghton 1965
Bkl A—IndS(12)

Berenson, Bernard. One Year's Reading for Fun. Knopf 1960
SCPL

Berenson, Bernard. The Passionate Sightseer: From the Diaries, 1947 to 1956. Simon & Schuster 1960
Bkl A

Berenson, Bernard. Rumor and Reflection. Simon & Schuster 1952
SCPL

Berenson, Bernard. The Selected Letters of [the author]; ed. by A. K. McComb. Houghton 1964
Bkl A

Berenson, Bernard. Sunset and Twilight: From the Diaries of 1947-1958; ed. by Nicky Mariano. Harcourt 1963
Bkl A—SCPL

Sprigge, Sylvia (Saunders). Berenson: A Biography. Houghton 1960
Bkl A—SCPL

CRITICS
American—20th century—*Continued*

Van Wyck Brooks, 1886-1963

Brooks, Van Wyck. An Autobiography. Dutton 1965
Bkl A

Brooks, Van Wyck. Days of the Phoenix: The Nineteen-Twenties I Remember. Dutton 1957
SCPL

Brooks, Van Wyck. From the Shadow of the Mountain: My Post-Meridian Years. Dutton 1961
Bkl A

Brooks, Van Wyck. Scenes and Portraits: Memories of Childhood and Youth. Dutton 1954
SCPL

Alfred Kazin, 1915-

Kazin, Alfred. Starting Out in the Thirties. Little 1965
Bkl A

Joseph Wood Krutch, 1893-

Krutch, Joseph Wood. More Lives Than One. Sloane 1962
Bkl A—BY

Orville Prescott, 1906-

Prescott, Orville. Five-Dollar Gold Piece: The Development of a Point of View. Random House 1956
SCPL

Virgil Thomson, 1896-

Thomson, Virgil. Virgil Thomson. Knopf 1966
Bkl A

English—18th century

Samuel Johnson, 1709-1784

Boswell, James. Life of Samuel Johnson. Modern Lib.; Oxford; etc.
BY—CA—GR—SCHS—SCPL—3000

Brown, Ivor John Carnegie. Dr. Johnson and His World. Walck 1966
Bkl Y&C

Clifford, James Lowry. Young Sam Johnson. McGraw 1955
SCPL

Greene, Donald Johnson, ed. Samuel Johnson: A Collection of Critical Essays. Prentice-Hall 1965
Bkl A

Hodgart, Matthew John Caldwell. Samuel Johnson and His Times. Arco 1963
Bkl A&Y

Johnson, Samuel. Dr. Johnson: His Life in Letters; ed. by David Littlejohn. Prentice-Hall 1965
Bkl A

English—19th century

Walter Horatio Pater, 1839-1894

COLLECTIONS

Knoepflmacher, U. C. Religious Humanism and the Victorian Novel. Princeton Univ. 1965
Bkl A

English—20th century

Victor Gollancz, 1893-1967

Gollancz, Victor. Journey Towards Music: A Memoir. Dutton 1965
Bkl A

James Laver, 1899-

Laver, James. Museum Piece: Or, The Education of an Iconographer. Houghton 1964
Bkl A

Ernest Newman, 1868-1959

Newman, Vera. Ernest Newman: A Memoir by His Wife. Knopf 1964
Bkl A

Sir John Knewstub Maurice Rothenstein, 1901-

Rothenstein, Sir John Knewstub Maurice. Summer's Lease: Autobiography, 1901-1938. Holt 1966
Bkl A

French—19th century

Charles Augustin Sainte-Beuve, 1804-1869

Nicolson, Sir H. G. Sainte-Beuve. Doubleday 1957
SCPL

Irish—19th century

George Bernard Shaw, 1856-1950

See also under Critics—Irish—20th century

Rosset, B. C. Shaw of Dublin: The Formative Years. Pa. State Univ. 1964
Bkl A

Shaw, George Bernard. Collected Letters. v. 1: 1874-1897; ed. By Dan H. Laurence. Dodd 1965
Bkl A

Smith, Joseph Percy. The Unrepentant Pilgrim: A Study of the Development of Bernard Shaw. Houghton 1965
Bkl A

Irish—20th century

George Bernard Shaw, 1856-1950

See also under Critics—Irish—19th century

Chappelow, Allan, ed. Shaw the Villager and Human Being: A Biographical Symposium. Macmillan 1962
Bkl A

CRITICS

Irish—20th century

George Bernard Shaw—Continued

Du Cann, Charles Garfield Lott. The Loves of George Bernard Shaw. Funk 1963
Bkl A

Ervine, St. John Greer. Bernard Shaw: His Life, Work and Friends. Morrow 1956
SCPL

Henderson, Archibald. George Bernard Shaw: Man of the Century. Appleton 1956
SCPL

Kilty, Jerome. Dear Liar: A Comedy of Letters Adapted from the Correspondence of Bernard Shaw and Mrs. Patrick Campbell. Dodd 1960 (Play)
Bkl A

Langner, Lawrence. G. B. S. and the Lunatic: Reminiscences of the Long, Lively, and Affectionate Friendship between George Bernard Shaw and the Author. Atheneum 1963
Bkl A

Meisel, Martin. Shaw and the Nineteenth-Century Theater. Princeton Univ. 1963
Bkl A

Pearson, Hesketh. G. B. S.: A Full Length Portrait, and a Postscript. Harper 1952
BBHS—SCHS—SCPL—3000

Shaw, George Bernard. Bernard Shaw and Mrs. Patrick Campbell: Their Correspondence. Knopf 1952
SCPL

Shaw, George Bernard. Sixteen Self Sketches. Dodd 1949
SCPL

Shenfield, Margaret. Bernard Shaw: A Pictorial Biography. Viking 1962
Bkl A&Y

Weintraub, Stanley. Private Shaw and Public Shaw: A Dual Portrait of Lawrence of Arabia and G. B. S. Braziller 1963
Bkl A

Woodbridge, Homer E. George Bernard Shaw, Creative Artist. Southern Ill. Univ. 1963
Bkl A&Y

CUSTOMS OFFICIALS

American—20th century

Alvin Freidheim Scharff, 1891?-

Roark, Garland. The Coin of Contraband Doubleday 1964
Bkl A

CZARS

See also Emperors

Russian—16th century

Ivan IV, the Terrible, Czar of Russia, 1530-1584

Grey, Ian. Ivan the Terrible. Lippincott 1964
Bkl A—IndS(9-12)

Koslow, Jules. Ivan the Terrible. Hill & Wang 1962
Bkl A

Lamb, Harold. March of Muscovy: Ivan the Terrible and the Growth of the Russian Empire, 1400-1648. Doubleday 1948
SCPL

DAME OF SARK

English—20th century

Sibyl (Collings) Hathaway, 1881?-

Hathaway, Sibyl (Collings). Dame of Sark: An Autobiography. Coward-McCann 1961
Bkl A&Y

DANCERS

COLLECTIONS

Atkinson, Margaret F. and Hillman, May. Dancers of the Ballet: Biographies. Knopf 1955
BBJH—CC(6-9)—ESLC—JH—YR

McConnell, Jane T. Famous Ballet Dancers. Crowell 1955
JH—SCHS

American

COLLECTIONS

Maynard, Olga. American Modern Dancers: The Pioneers. Little 1965
Bkl Y&A&C—IndS(10-12)
Isadora Duncan; Martha Graham; Ruth St. Denis; Ted Shawn; and others

American—20th century

Fred Astaire, 1899-

Astaire, Fred. Steps in Time. Harper 1959
SCHS—SCPL

George Balanchine, 1904-

Taper, Bernard. Balanchine. Harper 1963
Bkl A&Y—IndS(12)—SCPL

Agnes George De Mille, 1908-

De Mille, Agnes George. And Promenade Home. Little 1958
BY—SCHS—SCPL

DANCERS

American—20th century

Agnes George De Mille—Continued

De Mille, Agnes George. Dance to the Piper. Little 1962
BBHS—BY—SCHS—SCPL

COLLECTIONS

Forsee, Aylesa. American Women Who Scored Firsts. Macrae 1958
SCHS

Isadora Duncan, 1878-1927

Duncan, Irma. Duncan Dancer: An Autobiography. Wesleyan Univ. 1966
Bkl A&Y

Macdougall, Allan Ross. Isadora: A Revolutionary in Art and Love. Nelson 1960
Bkl A

Terry, Walter. Isadora Duncan: Her Life, Her Art, Her Legacy. Dodd 1964
Bkl A—IndS(10-12)

COLLECTIONS

Maynard, Olga. American Modern Dancers: The Pioneers. Little 1965
Bkl Y&A&C—IndS(10-12)

Wagenknecht, Edward Charles. Seven Daughters of the Theater. Univ. of Okla. 1964
Bkl A

Martha Graham, 1893-

Leatherman, Le Roy. Martha Graham: Portrait of the Lady as an Artist. Knopf 1966
Bkl A&Y

COLLECTIONS

Maynard, Olga. American Modern Dancers: The Pioneers. Little 1965
Bkl Y&A&C—IndS(10-12)

Ruth St. Denis, 1878-1968

COLLECTIONS

Maynard, Olga. American Modern Dancers: The Pioneers. Little 1965
Bkl Y&A&C—IndS(10-12)

Ted Shawn, 1891-

Shawn, Ted and Poole, Gray. One Thousand and One Night Stands. Doubleday 1960
Bkl A&Y

COLLECTIONS

Maynard, Olga. American Modern Dancers: The Pioneers. Little 1965
Bkl Y&A&C—IndS(10-12)

Maria Tallchief, 1925-

Maynard, Olga. Bird of Fire. Dodd 1961
Bkl A&Y—YR

Regina Llewellyn (Jones) Woody, 1894-

Woody, Regina Llewellyn (Jones). Dancing for Joy. Dutton 1959
Bkl Y&C

English—20th century

Dame Ninette De Valois, 1898-

De Valois, Dame Ninette. Come Dance with Me: A Memoir 1898-1956. World 1957
SCPL

Beryl Grey, 1927-

Grey, Beryl. Through the Bamboo Curtain. Reynal 1966
Bkl A

Russian—19th century

Matil'da Feliksovna Kshesinskaîa, 1872-

Kshesinskaîa, Matil'da Feliksovna. Dancing in Petersburg: The Memoirs of Kschessinska, H.S.H. the Princess Romanovsky-Krassinsky; tr. by Arnold Haskell. Doubleday 1961
Bkl A

Russian—20th century

Tamara Karsavina, 1885-

Karsavina, Tamara. Theatre Street: The Reminiscences of Tamara Karsavina. Dutton 1950
BY—SCPL

Matil'da Feliksovna Kshesinskaîa, 1872-

Kshesinskaîa, Matil'da Feliksovna. Dancing in Petersburg: The Memoirs of Kschessinska, H.S.H. the Princess Romanovsky-Krassinsky; tr. by Arnold Haskell. Doubleday 1961
Bkl A

Anna Pavlova, 1885-1931

Franks, A. H. Pavlova. Macmillan 1956
YR

Malvern, Gladys. Dancing Star: The Story of Anna Pavlova. Messner 1942
BBJH—BY—CC(7-9)—JH—SCHS

Olivéroff, André and Gill, John. Flight of the Swan: A Memory of Anna Pavlova. Dutton 1932
SCPL

COLLECTIONS

Trease, Geoffrey. Seven Stages. Vanguard 1965
Bkl Y&C—IndS(9-10)

Galina Sergeevna Ulanova, 1910-

Kahn, Albert Eugene. Days with Ulanova. Simon & Schuster 1962
Bkl A&Y

DAUGHTERS OF FAMOUS MEN

American—18th century

Jemima (Boone) Callaway, ?

Sutton, Margaret. Jemima, Daughter of
Daniel Boone. Scribner 1942 (Fiction)
SCHS

*Martha (Jefferson) Randolph, 1772-
1836*

Vance, Marguerite. Patsy Jefferson of
Monticello. Dutton 1948
CC(7-9)—JH—SCHS

American—19th century

Theodosia (Burr) Alston, 1783-1813

Colver, Anne. Theodosia: Daughter of
Aaron Burr. Holt 1962
AB(5-7)

Jessie (Benton) Frémont, 1824-1902

Higgins, Marguerite. Jessie Benton Frémont. Houghton 1962
ESLC

Randall, Ruth (Painter). I Jessie: A Biog-
raphy of the Girl Who Married John
Charles Frémont, Famous Explorer of
the West. Little 1963
AB(4-7)—Bkl C(7-10)&Y—IndS(9-12)—
SCHS—YR

Stone, Irving. Immortal Wife: The Biographical Novel of Jessie Benton Fremont. Doubleday 1944 (Fiction)
BBHS—SCHS

*Mary (Garfield) Stanley-Brown, 1867-
1947*

Feis, Ruth (Stanley-Brown). Mollie Gar-
field in the White House. Rand Mc-
Nally n.d.
AB(4-7)

*Martha (Jefferson) Randolph, 1772-
1836*

Vance, Marguerite. Patsy Jefferson of
Monticello. Dutton 1948
CC(7-9)—JH—SCHS

*Catherine Jane (Chase) Sprague, 1840-
1899*

Ross, Ishbel. Proud Kate: Portrait of an
Ambitious Woman. Harper 1953
SCPL

American—20th century

Janice Wylie, 1942-1963

Wylie, Max. The Gift of Janice. Doubleday 1964
Bkl A

Patricia Ziegfeld, 1916-

Ziegfeld, Patricia. The Ziegfelds' Girl:
Confessions of an Abnormally Happy
Childhood. Little 1964
Bkl A—IndS(9-12)

English—19th century

*Sarah Thompson, Countess Rumford,
1774-1852*

Cost, March. The Countess. Vanguard
1963 (Fiction)
Bkl A

Roman—1st century B.C.

*Julia, Daughter of the Emperor Au-
gustus, 39 B.C.-14 A.D.*

Dored, Elisabeth. I Loved Tiberius; tr.
from the Norwegian by Naomi Walford. Pantheon 1963 (Fiction)
Bkl A

Russian—20th century

*Anastasîa, Grand Duchess of Russia,
1901-1918?*

Anastasîa, Grand Duchess of Russia. Anastasia: The Autobiography of H.I.H.
the Grand Duchess Anastasia Nicholaevna of Russia. v. 1. Speller 1963
Bkl A

DAUGHTERS OF FAMOUS WOMEN

Indian—20th century

Nayantara (Pandit) Sahgal, 1927-

Sahgal, Nayantara (Pandit). From Fear
Set Free. Norton 1963
Bkl A&Y—IndS(10-12)—SCHS

DEAF

American—19th century

Laura Dewey Bridgman, 1829-1889

Hunter, Edith Fisher. Child of the Silent
Night. Houghton 1963
Bkl C(3-5)—CC(3-5)—ESLC—IndJ(4-6)

Thomas Hopkins Gallaudet, 1787-1851

DeGering, Etta. Gallaudet, Friend of the
Deaf. McKay 1964
CC—ESLC—IndJ(4-6)

American—20th century

Helen Adams Keller, 1880-1968

Brooks, Van Wyck. Helen Keller: Sketch
for a Portrait. Dutton 1956
BY—SCPL

Gibson, William. The Miracle Worker: A
Play for Television. Knopf 1957 (Play)
SCHS

DEAF

American—20th century

Helen Adams Keller—Continued

Graff, Stewart and Graff, Polly Anne. Helen Keller: Toward the Light. Garrard 1965
ESLC

Harrity, Richard and Martin, Ralph G. The Three Lives of Helen Keller. Doubleday 1962
Bkl A&Y

Hickok, Lorena A. The Story of Helen Keller. Grosset 1948
CC(4-6)

Keller, Helen Adams. Story of My Life. Doubleday; Houghton
BBHS—BBJH—BY—CA—CC(7-9)—JH—SCHS—SCPL—3000

Peare, Catherine Owens. The Helen Keller Story. Crowell 1959
CC(6-9)—ESLC—JH—SCHS

Waite, Helen E. Valiant Companions: Helen Keller and Anne Sullivan Macy. Macrae 1959
JH—SCHS

DEEP SEA DIVERS

See Divers

DEMAGOGUES

See Statesmen

DENTISTS

American—19th century

William Thomas Green Morton, 1819-1868

Baker, Rachel. Dr. Morton, Pioneer in the Use of Ether. Messner 1946
SCHS

Ludovici, Laurence James. The Discovery of Anaesthesia. Crowell 1962
Bkl A

Woodward, Grace Steele. The Man Who Conquered Pain: A Biography of William Thomas Green Morton. Beacon Press 1962
Bkl A&Y—BY

COLLECTIONS

Hume, Ruth Fox. Great Men of Medicine. Random House 1961
CC(7-9)—ESLC—JH—SCHS—YR

DESIGNERS, INDUSTRIAL

See Industrial Designers

DESPERADOES

See Criminals

DETECTIVES

American—19th century

Allan Pinkerton, 1819-1884

Lavine, Sigmund A. Allan Pinkerton: America's First Private Eye. Dodd 1963
Bkl Y&C

Ormont, Arthur. Master Detective: Allan Pinkerton. Messner 1965
Bkl C(6-9)—IndJ(6-9)—JH

Wise, William. Detective Pinkerton and Mr. Lincoln. Dutton 1964
AB(5-9)—IndJ(4-6)

American—20th century

Urbanus Edmund Baughman, 1905-

Baughman, Urbanus Edmund and Robinson, Leonard Wallace. Secret Service Chief. Harper 1962
Bkl A&Y

Louis Cochran, 1899-

Cochran, Louis. FBI Man: A Personal History. Duell 1966
Bkl A&Y

Frank John Wilson, 1888-

Wilson, Frank John and Day, Beth (Feagles). Special Agent: A Quarter Century with the Treasury Department and the Secret Service. Holt 1965
Bkl A&Y—IndS(10-12)

DIARISTS

See Authors

DICTATORS

See Statesmen

DIPLOMATS

See Statesmen

DIVERS

French—20th century

Jacques Yves Cousteau, 1910-

Dugan, James. Undersea Explorer: The Story of Captain Cousteau. Harper 1957
BBHS—BBJH—CC(7-9)—ESLC—JH—SCHS

DOCTORS

See Neurologists; Physicians; Surgeons

DRAMA CRITICS

See Critics

DRAMATISTS

See Playwrights

DWARFS

See Circus Performers

ECCLESIASTICS

See Religious Leaders

ECONOMISTS

COLLECTIONS

Heilbroner, Robert Louis. Worldly Philosophers: The Lives, Times and Ideas of the Great Economic Thinkers. Simon & Schuster 1953
SCPL
John Maynard Keynes; Thomas Robert Malthus; Karl Marx; David Ricardo; Adam Smith; Thorstein Bunde Veblen

Schumpeter, Joseph Alois. Ten Great Economists, from Marx to Keynes. Oxford 1951
SCPL
Eugen Böhm von Bawerk; Irving Fisher; John Maynard Keynes; Alfred Marshall; Karl Marx; Karl Menger; Wesley Clair Mitchell; Vilfredo Pareto; Frank William Taussig; Léon Walras

American—19th century

Henry George, 1839-1897

COLLECTIONS

Holbrook, Stewart Hall. Dreamers of the American Dream. Doubleday 1957
SCPL

Frank William Taussig, 1859-1940

COLLECTIONS

Schumpeter, Joseph Alois. Ten Great Economists, from Marx to Keynes. Oxford 1951
SCPL

American—20th century

Emily Greene Balch, 1867-1961

Randall, Mercedes (Moritz). Improper Bostonian: Emily Greene Balch: Nobel Peace Laureate, 1946. Twayne 1964
Bkl A&Y

Irving Fisher, 1867-1947

COLLECTIONS

Schumpeter, Joseph Alois. Ten Great Economists, from Marx to Keynes. Oxford 1951
SCPL

Alvin Saunders Johnson, 1874-

Johnson, Alvin Saunders. Pioneer's Progress: An Autobiography. Viking 1952
SCPL

Wesley Clair Mitchell, 1874-1948

COLLECTIONS

Schumpeter, Joseph Alois. Ten Great Economists, from Marx to Keynes. Oxford 1951
SCPL

Frank William Taussig, 1859-1940

COLLECTIONS

Schumpeter, Joseph Alois. Ten Great Economists, from Marx to Keynes. Oxford 1951
SCPL

Rexford Guy Tugwell, 1891-

Sternsher, Bernard. Rexford Tugwell and the New Deal. Rutgers Univ. 1964
Bkl A

Tugwell, Rexford Guy. The Light of Other Days. Doubleday 1962
Bkl A

Thorstein Bunde Veblen, 1857-1929

COLLECTIONS

Heilbroner, Robert Louis. Worldly Philosophers: The Lives, Times and Ideas of the Great Economic Thinkers. Simon & Schuster 1953
SCPL

Edward Cristy Welsh, 1909-

COLLECTIONS

Thomas, Shirley. Men of Space: v. 7, Profiles of the Leaders in Space Research, Development, and Exploration. Chilton 1965
Bkl A&Y

Wladimir Savelievich Woytinsky, 1885-1960

Woytinsky, Emma (Shadkhan), ed. So Much Alive: The Life and Work of Wladimir S. Woytinsky. Vanguard 1962
Bkl A

Woytinsky, Emma (Shadkhan). Two Lives in One. Praeger 1965
Bkl A

Woytinsky, Wladimir Savelievich. Stormy Passage: A Personal History Through Two Russian Revolutions to Democracy and Freedom, 1905-1960. Vanguard 1961
Bkl A

Austrian—19th century

Eugen Böhm von Bawerk, 1851-1914

COLLECTIONS

Schumpeter, Joseph Alois. Ten Great Economists, from Marx to Keynes. Oxford 1951
SCPL

ECONOMISTS

Austrian—19th century—*Continued*

Karl Menger, 1840-1921

COLLECTIONS

Schumpeter, Joseph Alois. Ten Great Economists, from Marx to Keynes. Oxford 1951
SCPL

English—19th century

Thomas Robert Malthus, 1766-1834

COLLECTIONS

Heilbroner, Robert Louis. Wordly Philosophers: The Lives, Times and Ideas of the Great Economic Thinkers. Simon & Schuster 1953
SCPL

Alfred Marshall, 1842-1924

COLLECTIONS

Schumpeter, Joseph Alois. Ten Great Economists, from Marx to Keynes. Oxford 1951
SCPL

John Stuart Mill, 1806-1873

Mill, John Stuart. Autobiography. Columbia Univ.; Univ. of Ill.; etc.
GR—SCPL

David Ricardo, 1772-1823

COLLECTIONS

Heilbroner, Robert Louis. Worldly Philosophers: The Lives, Times and Ideas of the Great Economic Thinkers. Simon & Schuster 1953
SCPL

English—20th century

John Maynard Keynes, 1883-1946

Lekachman, Robert. The Age of Keynes. Random House 1966
Bkl A

COLLECTIONS

Heilbroner, Robert Louis. Worldly Philosophers: The Lives, Times and Ideas of the Great Economic Thinkers. Simon & Schuster 1953
SCPL

Schumpeter, Joseph Alois. Ten Great Economists, from Marx to Keynes. Oxford 1951
SCPL

Alfred Marshall, 1842-1924

COLLECTIONS

Schumpeter, Joseph Alois. Ten Great Economists, from Marx to Keynes. Oxford 1951
SCPL

French—19th century

Léon Walras, 1834-1910

COLLECTIONS

Schumpeter, Joseph Alois. Ten Great Economists, from Marx to Keynes. Oxford 1951
SCPL

German 19th century

Karl Marx, 1818-1883

COLLECTIONS

Heilbroner, Robert Louis. Worldly Philosophers: The Lives, Times and Ideas of the Great Economic Thinkers. Simon & Schuster 1953
SCPL

Schumpeter, Joseph Alois. Ten Great Economists, from Marx to Keynes. Oxford 1951
SCPL

Italian—20th century

Vilfredo Pareto, 1848-1923

COLLECTIONS

Schumpeter, Joseph Alois. Ten Great Economists, from Marx to Keynes. Oxford 1951
SCPL

Scottish—18th century

Adam Smith, 1723-1790

COLLECTIONS

Crowther, James Gerald. Scientists of the Industrial Revolution. Dufour 1963
Bkl A

Heilbroner, Robert Louis. Worldly Philosophers: The Lives, Times and Ideas of the Great Economic Thinkers. Simon & Schuster 1953
SCPL

EDITORS

See Journalists; Publishers

EDUCATORS

See also Librarians

American

COLLECTIONS

Fleming, Alice (Mulcahey). Great Women Teachers. Lippincott 1965
Bkl C(6-9)&Y—ESLC—JH
Martha Berry; Mary Jane (McLeod) Bethune; Florence Dunlop; Virginia Gildersleeve; Mary Lyon; Alice Nash; Alice Freeman Palmer; Elizabeth Palmer Peabody; Emma Willard; Ella Flagg Young

EDUCATORS

American—*Continued*

Leaders in Education: A Biographical Directory; ed. by Jaques Cattell and E. E. Ross. Science Press 1948
SCPL

Who's Who in American Education: An Illustrated Biographical Directory of Eminent Living Educators of the United States and Canada. Who's Who in Am. Educ. Biennial, first published 1928
SCPL

American—19th century

Catharine Esther Beecher, 1800-1878

COLLECTIONS

Bacon, Martha Sherman. Puritan Promenade. Houghton 1964
Bkl A&Y—IndS(9-12)

Prudence Crandall, 1803-1889

Yates, Elizabeth. Prudence Crandall: Woman of Courage. Dutton 1955
CC(7-9)—ESLC—JH

COLLECTIONS

Buckmaster, Henrietta. Women Who Shaped History. Collier Bks 1966
Bkl C(7-10)&Y

Douglas, Emily (Taft). Remember the Ladies: The Story of Great Women Who Helped Shape America. Putnam 1966
Bkl A&Y

John Dewey, 1859-1952

Schilpp, Paul Arthur, ed. Philosophy of John Dewey. Tudor 1951
SCPL

Thomas Eakins, 1844-1916

Porter, Fairfield. Thomas Eakins. Braziller 1959
SCPL

Thomas Hopkins Gallaudet, 1787-1851

DeGering, Etta. Gallaudet, Friend of the Deaf. McKay 1964
CC—ESLC—IndJ(4-6)

Samuel Gridley Howe, 1801-1876

Meltzer, Milton. A Light in the Dark: The Life of Samuel Gridley Howe. Crowell 1964
Bkl C(6-9)&Y—CC—ESLC

Robert Edward Lee, 1807-1870

Fishwick, Marshall William. Lee after the War. Dodd 1963
Bkl A&Y

Mary Lyon, 1797-1849

Banning, Evelyn I. Mary Lyon of Putnam's Hill. Vanguard 1965
IndS(9-11)

COLLECTIONS

Daugherty, Sonia. Ten Brave Women. Lippincott 1953
BY—CC(7-9)—ESLC—JH—SCHS

Fleming, Alice (Mulcahey). Great Women Teachers. Lippincott 1965
Bkl C(6-9)&Y—ESLC—JH

Vance, Marguerite. The Lamp Lighters: Women in the Hall of Fame. Dutton 1960
Bkl C(7-9)&Y—SCHS—YR

Horace Mann, 1796-1859

Tharp, Louise (Hall). Until Victory: Horace Mann and Mary Peabody. Little 1953
BY—SCPL

Alice Freeman Palmer, 1855-1902

COLLECTIONS

Fleming, Alice (Mulcahey). Great Women Teachers. Lippincott 1965
Bkl C(6-9)&Y—ESLC—JH

Vance, Marguerite. The Lamp Lighters: Women in the Hall of Fame. Dutton 1960
Bkl C(7-9)&Y—SCHS—YR

Elizabeth Palmer Peabody, 1804-1894

Tharp, Louise (Hall). The Peabody Sisters of Salem. Little 1950
BBHS—BY—SCHS—SCPL

COLLECTIONS

Fleming, Alice (Mulcahey). Great Women Teachers. Lippincott 1965
Bkl C(6-9)&Y—ESLC—JH

Elizabeth Ann Seton, 1774-1821

Dirvin, Joseph I. Mrs. Seton, Foundress of the American Sisters of Charity. Farrar 1962
Bkl A

Melville, Annabelle (McConnell). Elizabeth Bayley Seton, 1774-1821. Scribner 1951
SCPL

Booker Taliaferro Washington, 1856-1915

Graham, Shirley. Booker T. Washington: Educator of Hand, Head, and Heart. Messner 1955
BBEL(6-8)—BBJH—BY—CC(6-9)—ESLC—JH—SCHS

Patterson, Lillie G. Booker T. Washington. Garrard 1962
AB(3-7)

EDUCATORS

American—19th century

Booker Taliaferro Washington—Continued

Washington, Booker Taliaferro. Up from Slavery: An Autobiography. Doubleday 1963; Dodd 1965
BBEL—BBHS—BBJH—CC(6-9)—GR—SCHS—SCPL

COLLECTIONS

Bontemps, Arna Wendell. 100 Years of Negro Freedom. Dodd 1961
Bkl A—ESLC—SCPL
Sterling, Dorothy and Quarles, Benjamin. Lift Every Voice. Doubleday 1965
Bkl C(6-9)&Y—ESLC

Emma (Hart) Willard, 1787-1870

COLLECTIONS

Fleming, Alice (Mulcahey). Great Women Teachers. Lippincott 1965
Bkl C(6-9)&Y—ESLC—JH
Vance, Marguerite. The Lamp Lighters: Women in the Hall of Fame. Dutton 1960
Bkl C(7-9)&Y—SCHS—YR

Frances Elizabeth Caroline Willard, 1839-1898

COLLECTIONS

Holbrook, Stewart Hall. Dreamers of the American Dream. Doubleday 1957
SCPL
Vance, Marguerite. The Lamp Lighters: Women in the Hall of Fame. Dutton 1960
Bkl C(7-9)&Y—SCHS—YR

Ella (Flagg) Young, 1845-1918

COLLECTIONS

Fleming, Alice (Mulcahey). Great Women Teachers. Lippincott 1965
Bkl C(6-9)&Y—ESLC—JH

American—20th century

Daisy Lee (Gatson) Bates, 1920-

Bates, Daisy Lee (Gatson). The Long Shadow of Little Rock: A Memoir. McKay 1962
Bkl A&Y

COLLECTIONS

Sterne, Emma (Gelders). I Have a Dream. Knopf 1965
Bkl Y&C

Charles Austin Beard, 1874-1948

COLLECTIONS

Hill, Frank Ernest. Famous Historians. Dodd 1966
Bkl Y&C

Martha McChesney Berry, 1866-1942

Kane, Harnett Thomas and Henry, Inez. Miracle in the Mountains. Doubleday 1956
BY—SCHS—SCPL

COLLECTIONS

Fleming, Alice (Mulcahey). Great Women Teachers. Lippincott 1965
Bkl C(6-9)&Y—ESLC—JH
Forsee, Aylesa. Women Who Reached for Tomorrow. Macrae 1960
Bkl Y&C

Hazel Dunaway Berto, ?

Berto, Hazel Dunaway. North to Alaska's Shining River. Bobbs 1959
Bkl A

Mary Jane (McLeod) Bethune, 1875-1955

Carruth, Ella Kaiser. She Wanted to Read: The Story of Mary McLeod Bethune. Abingdon 1966
Bkl C(3-5)—ESLC
Holt, Rackham. Mary McLeod Bethune: A Biography. Doubleday 1964
Bkl A&Y—SCPL
Peare, Catherine Owens. Mary McLeod Bethune. Vanguard 1951
CC(7-9)—JH—SCHS
Sterne, Emma (Gelders). Mary McLeod Bethune. Knopf 1957
BBEL(7-8)—BBJH—BY—CC(7-9)—ESLC—JH—SCHS

COLLECTIONS

Fleming, Alice (Mulcahey). Great Women Teachers. Lippincott 1965
Bkl C(6-9)&Y—ESLC—JH
Nathan, Dorothy. Women of Courage. Random House 1964
CC(4-6)—ESLC—JH

Gerald F. Carlson, 1925-

Carlson, Gerald F. Two on the Rocks. McKay 1966
Bkl A&Y

Mary Ellen Chase, 1887-

Chase, Mary Ellen. Goodly Fellowship. Macmillan 1939
SCPL
Chase, Mary Ellen. A Goodly Heritage. Holt 1932
BY
Chase, Mary Ellen. White Gate: Adventures in the Imagination of a Child. Norton 1954
SCPL

Septima (Poinsette) Clark, 1898-

Clark, Septima (Poinsette) and Blythe, LeGette. Echo in My Soul. Dutton 1962
Bkl A&Y

EDUCATORS

American—20th century—*Continued*

Morris Raphael Cohen, 1880-1947

Rosenfield, Leonora Davidson (Cohen). Portrait of a Philosopher: Morris R. Cohen. Harcourt 1962
Bkl A

Charles Townsend Copeland, 1860-1952

Adams, James Donald. Copey of Harvard: A Biography of Charles Townsend Copeland. Houghton 1960
Bkl A

Wilbur Lucius Cross, 1862-1948

Cross, Wilbur Lucius. Connecticut Yankee: An Autobiography. Yale Univ. 1943
SCPL

John Dewey, 1859-1952

Schilpp, Paul Arthur, ed. Philosophy of John Dewey. Tudor 1951
SCPL

Samuel Smith Drury, 1878-1938

Drury, Roger W. Drury and St. Paul's: The Scars of a Schoolmaster. Little 1964
IndS(10-12)

William Edward Burghardt Du Bois, 1868-1963

COLLECTIONS

Bontemps, Arna Wendell. 100 Years of Negro Freedom. Dodd 1961
Bkl A—ESLC—SCPL

Sterling, Dorothy and Quarles, Benjamin. Lift Every Voice. Doubleday 1965
Bkl C(6-9)&Y—ESLC

Thomas Eakins, 1844-1916

Porter, Fairfield. Thomas Eakins. Braziller 1959
SCPL

John Erskine, 1879-1951

Erskine, John. My Life in Music. Morrow 1950
SCPL

Abraham Flexner, 1866-1959

Flexner, Abraham. Abraham Flexner: An Autobiography. (A revision, brought up to date, of the author's I Remember, published in 1940) Simon & Schuster 1960
Bkl A

Virginia Crocheron Gildersleeve, 1877-1965

COLLECTIONS

Fleming, Alice (Mulcahey). Great Women Teachers. Lippincott 1965
Bkl C(6-9)&Y—ESLC—JH

Rufus Matthew Jones, 1863-1948

Vining, E. G. Friend of Life: The Biography of Rufus M. Jones. Lippincott 1958
SCPL

Frank Charles Laubach, 1884-

Laubach, Frank Charles. Thirty Years with the Silent Billion: Adventuring in Literacy. Revell 1960
Bkl A

Medary, Marjorie. Each One Teach One: Frank Laubach, Friend to Millions. Longmans 1954
SCHS—SCPL

Mabel (Barbee) Lee, 1886-

Lee, Mabel (Barbee). And Suddenly It's Evening: A Fragment of Life. Doubleday 1963
Bkl A

Lee, Mabel (Barbee). The Rainbow Years: A Happy Interlude. Doubleday 1966
Bkl A&Y

Anne (Sullivan) Macy, 1866-1936

Brown, Marion Marsh and Crone, Ruth. The Silent Storm. Abingdon 1963
Bkl C(5-8)—CC(5-7)—ESLC

Davidson, Mickie. Helen Keller's Teacher. Four Winds Press 1965
ESLC

Gibson, William. The Miracle Worker: A Play for Television. Knopf 1957 (Play)
SCHS

Hickok, Lorena A. The Touch of Magic: The Story of Helen Keller's Great Teacher, Anne Sullivan Macy. Dodd 1961
Bkl A&Y—BY—JH—SCPL—YR

Keller, Helen Adams. Teacher: Anne Sullivan Macy—A Tribute by the Foster-Child of Her Mind. Doubleday 1955
SCHS—SCPL

White, Helen E. Valiant Companions: Helen Keller and Anne Sullivan Macy. Macrae 1959
JH—SCHS

Joseph Edgar Maddy, 1891-1966

Browning, Norma Lee. Joe Maddy of Interlochen. Regnery 1963
Bkl A&Y

EDUCATORS

American—20th century—*Continued*

Alice (Morrison) Nash, 1879?-1966

COLLECTIONS

Fleming, Alice (Mulcahey). Great Women Teachers. Lippincott 1965
Bkl C(6-9)&Y—ESLC—JH

Arthur Meier Schlesinger, 1888-1965

Schlesinger, Arthur Meier. In Retrospect: The History of a Historian. Harcourt 1963
Bkl A

Ethel (Reed) Strainchamps, ?

Strainchamps, Ethel (Reed). Don't Never Say Cain't. Doubleday 1965
Bkl A&Y

Ellen Tarry, 1906-

Tarry, Ellen. The Third Door: The Autobiography of an American Negro Woman. McKay 1955
BY

Rexford Guy Tugwell, 1891-

Tugwell, Rexford Guy. The Light of Other Days. Doubleday 1962
Bkl A

Booker Taliaferro Washington, 1856-1915

Graham, Shirley. Booker T. Washington: Educator of Hand, Head, and Heart. Messner 1955
BBEL(6-8)—BBJH—BY—CC(6-9)—ESLC—JH—SCHS

Patterson, Lillie G. Booker T. Washington. Garrard 1962
AB(3-7)

Washington, Booker Taliaferro. Up from Slavery: An Autobiography. Doubleday 1963; Dodd 1965
BBEL — BBHS — BBJH — CC(6-9) — GR — SCHS—SCPL

COLLECTIONS

Bontemps, Arna Wendell. 100 Years of Negro Freedom. Dodd 1961
Bkl A—ESLC—SCPL

Sterling, Dorothy and Quarles, Benjamin. Lift Every Voice. Doubleday 1965
Bkl C(6-9)&Y—ESLC

Woodrow Wilson, 1856-1924

Craig, Hardin. Woodrow Wilson at Princeton. Univ. of Okla. 1960
Bkl A

Dodd, William Edward. Woodrow Wilson and His Work. Smith, P. 1932
SCPL

Garraty, John Arthur. Woodrow Wilson: A Great Life in Brief. Knopf 1956
SCPL—3000

Grayson, Cary Travers. Woodrow Wilson: An Intimate Memoir. Holt 1960
Bkl A

Hatch, Alden. Woodrow Wilson: A Biography for Young People. Holt 1947
SCHS

Hoover, Herbert Clark. Ordeal of Woodrow Wilson. McGraw 1958
BBHS—SCPL

Link, Arthur Stanley. Wilson: The New Freedom. Princeton Univ. 1956
SCPL

Link, Arthur Stanley. Woodrow Wilson: A Brief Biography. World 1963
Bkl A&Y—SCPL

Peare, Catherine Owens. The Woodrow Wilson Story: An Idealist in Politics. Crowell 1963
Bkl C(7up)&Y—CC(6-9)—ESLC—IndJ(6-9)—JH—SCHS—YR

Steinberg, Alfred. Woodrow Wilson. Putnam 1961
Bkl C(7-9)&Y

Walworth, Arthur Clarence. Woodrow Wilson. 2v. Longmans 1958
SCPL

Wilson, Woodrow. A Day of Dedication: The Essential Writings and Speeches of Woodrow Wilson; ed. by Albert Fried. Macmillan 1965
Bkl A&Y

Wilson, Woodrow. The Priceless Gift: The Love Letters of Woodrow Wilson and Ellen Louise Axson Wilson; ed. by Eleanor Wilson McAdoo. McGraw 1962
Bkl A

Ella (Flagg) Young, 1845-1918

COLLECTIONS

Fleming, Alice (Mulcahey). Great Women Teachers. Lippincott 1965
Bkl C(6-9)&Y—ESLC—JH

Canadian—20th century

Florence Dunlop, 1896-1963

COLLECTIONS

Fleming, Alice (Mulcahey). Great Women Teachers. Lippincott 1965
Bkl C(6-9)&Y—ESLC—JH

Dutch—16th century

Desiderius Erasmus, 1466?-1536

Trease, Geoffrey. Shadow of the Hawk. Harcourt 1949 (Fiction)
SCHS

French—19th century

Louis Braille, 1809-1852

DeGering, Etta. Seeing Fingers: The Story of Louis Braille. McKay 1962
Bkl C(5-7)—CC(5-7)—ESLC

EDUCATORS

French—19th century

Louis Braille—Continued

Kugelmass, J. Alvin. Louis Braille: Windows for the Blind. Messner 1951
BBJH–JH–SCHS

Webster, Gary. Journey into Light: The Story of Louis Braille. Hawthorn 1964
AB(7up)

Greek—5th century B.C.

Socrates, 470?-399 B.C.

Anderson, Maxwell. Barefoot in Athens. Sloane 1951 (Play)
SCPL

Brun, Jean. Socrates; tr. by Douglas Scott. Walker & Co. 1963
Bkl A&Y

Mason, Cora. Socrates: The Man Who Dared to Ask. Beacon Press 1953
BY–SCHS

Silverberg, Robert. Socrates. Putnam 1965
Bkl Y(7-10)&C–IndS(9-11)–JH

Guyanian—20th century

Eustace Ricardo Braithwaite, 1922?-

Braithwaite, Eustace Ricardo. To Sir, with Love. Prentice-Hall 1959
Bkl A–BY–SCPL

Korean—20th century

Induk Pak, ?

Pak, Induk. The Hour of the Tiger. Harper 1965
Bkl A

Russian—20th century

Julian Brodetsky, ?-1962

Wibberley, Leonard Patrick O'Connor. Ah, Julian! A Memoir of Julian Brodetsky. Washburn 1963
Bkl A

Georges Ivanovitch Gurdjieff, 1872-1949

Peters, Arthur Anderson. Boyhood with Gurdjieff. Dutton 1964
Bkl A

F. Vigdorova, ?

Vigdorova, F. Diary of a Russian Schoolteacher; tr. from the Russian by Rose Prokofieva. Grove 1960
Bkl A&Y

Welsh—19th century

Anna Harriette (Crawford) Leonowens, 1834-1914

Landon, Margaret Dorothea (Mortenson). Anna and the King. Day 1947
BBJH–JH

Landon, Margaret Dorothea (Mortenson). Anna and the King of Siam. Day 1944
SCHS–SCPL

ELECTRICAL ENGINEERS

See Engineers, Electrical

EMBEZZLERS

See Criminals

EMPERORS

See also Czars; Kings

Ethiopian—20th century

Haile Selassie I, Emperor of Ethiopia, 1891-

Gorham, Charles Orson. The Lion of Judah: A Life of Haile Selassie I, Emperor of Ethiopia. Ariel Bks 1966
Bkl C(6-9)&Y–ESLC

COLLECTIONS

Kaula, Edna Mason. Leaders of the New Africa. World 1966
Bkl C(6-10)–ESLC

Melady, Thomas P. Profiles of African Leaders. Macmillan 1961
Bkl A&Y–SCPL

French—19th century

Napoleon I, Emperor of the French, 1769-1821

Aronson, Theo. The Golden Bees: The Story of the Bonapartes. N. Y. Graphic 1964
Bkl A–SCPL

Brett-James, Antony, ed. The Hundred Days: Napoleon's Last Campaign from Eyewitness Accounts. St Martins 1964
Bkl A

Brookes, Dame Mabel (Emmerton). St. Helena Story. Dodd 1961
Bkl A

Butterfield, Herbert. Napoleon. Macmillan 1956
SCPL

Cammiade, Audrey. Napoleon. Roy 1963
IndJ(6-9)

Costain, Thomas B. The Last Love. Doubleday 1963 (Fiction)
SCHS

Delderfield, Ronald Frederick. The Golden Millstones: Napoleon's Brothers and Sisters. Harper 1965
Bkl A

Delderfield, Ronald Frederick. Napoleon in Love. Little 1960
Bkl A

EMPERORS

French—19th century

Napoleon I—Continued

Delderfield, Ronald Frederick. Napoleon's Marshals. Chilton 1966
Bkl A&Y

Goodspeed, Donald James. Napoleon's Eighty Days. Houghton 1965
Bkl A—IndS(10-12)

Guerard, Albert Leon. Napoleon I: A Great Life in Brief. Knopf 1956
SCPL

Hales, Edward Elton Young. The Emperor and the Pope. Doubleday 1961
Bkl A

Herold, J. Christopher. Bonaparte in Egypt. Harper 1963
Bkl A—SCPL

Horizon Magazine. The Horizon Book of the Age of Napoleon, by J. Christopher Herold. Am. Heritage 1963
Bkl A—SCHS—SCPL

Komroff, Manuel. Napoleon. Messner 1954
BBHS—BBJH—BY—CC(7-9)—ESLC—JH—SCHS

Ludwig, Emil. Napoleon; tr. by Eden and Cedar Paul. Modern Lib., etc.
BBHS—CA—SCHS—SCPL

Maurois, André. Napoleon: A Pictorial Biography; tr. from the French by D. J. S. Thomson. Studio 1964
Bkl A&Y—IndS(9-12)

Mossiker, Frances. Napoleon and Josephine: The Biography of a Marriage. Simon & Schuster 1964
Bkl A

Robbins, Ruth. The Emperor and the Drummer Boy. Parnassus Press 1962 (Fiction)
AB(4-7)—Bkl C(4-6)—CC(3-6)—ESLC

Saunders, Edith. The Hundred Days. Norton 1964
Bkl A

Stacton, David. The Bonapartes. Simon & Schuster 1966
Bkl A

Thompson, James Matthew. Napoleon Bonaparte: His Rise and Fall. Oxford 1952
3000

Tolstoi, Lev Nikolaevich. War and Peace. Modern Lib.; Oxford; Grosset; etc. (Fiction)
SCHS

Weiner, Margery. The Parvenue Princesses: The Lives and Loves of Napoleon's Sisters. Morrow 1964
Bkl A—IndS(11-12)

Napoleon III, Emperor of the French, 1808-1873

Guerard, Albert Leon. Napoleon III: A Great Life in Brief. Knopf 1955
SCPL

German—20th century

William II, Emperor of Germany, 1859-1941

Balfour, Michael Leonard Graham. The Kaiser and His Times. Houghton 1964
Bkl A&Y

Cowles, Virginia Spencer. The Kaiser. Harper 1963
Bkl A&Y—IndS(11-12)—SCPL

Wilson, Lawrence Patrick Roy. The Incredible Kaiser: A Portrait of William II. Barnes 1965
Bkl A

Hindustani—16th century

Akbar, Emperor of Hindustan, 1542-1605

Bothwell, Jean. The Promise of the Rose. Harcourt 1958 (Fiction)
JH

Babar, Emperor of Hindustan, 1483-1530

Lamb, Harold. Babur, the Tiger: First of the Great Moguls. Doubleday 1961
Bkl A

Indian—17th century

Shāhjāhan, Emperor of India, 1592?-1666

Prokosch, Frederic. The Dark Dancer. Farrar 1964 (Fiction)
Bkl A

Japanese—20th century

Hirohito, Emperor of Japan, 1901-

COLLECTIONS

Bliven, Bruce. The World Changers. Day 1965
Bkl A&Y—IndS(10-12)

Mexican—15th century

Montezuma I, Emperor of Mexico, 1398-1468

Gillmor, Frances. The King Danced in the Marketplace. Univ. of Ariz. 1964
Bkl A

Mexican—19th century

Maximilian, Emperor of Mexico, 1832-1867

Harding, Bertita. Phantom Crown: The Story of Maximilian & Carlota of Mexico. Heinman 1960
SCPL

EMPERORS

Mexican—19th century

Maximilian—Continued

Vance, Marguerite. Ashes of Empire: Carlota and Maximilian of Mexico. Dutton 1959
BY—CC(7-9)

Roman—1st century B.C.

Augustus, Emperor of Rome, 63 B.C.-14 A.D.

Buchan, John. Augustus. Houghton 1937
SCPL

Roman—1st century

Caligula, Emperor of Rome, 12-41

Camus, Albert. Caligula and Three Other Plays; tr. from the French by Stuart Gilbert. Knopf 1958 (Play)
SCPL

Claudius I, Emperor of Rome, 10 B.C.-54 A.D.

Graves, Robert. I, Claudius: From the Autobiography of Tiberius Claudius, Born B.C. 10, Murdered and Deified A.D. 54. Modern Lib. 1937 (Fiction)
SCHS

Nero, Emperor of Rome, 37-68

Bishop, John H. Nero, the Man and the Legend. Barnes 1965
Bkl A

Sheean, Vincent. Beware of Caesar. Random House 1965 (Fiction)
Bkl A

Roman—2nd century

Marcus Aurelius Antoninus, Emperor of Rome, 121-180

Gibbs, Willa. A Fig in Winter: A Novel. Morrow 1963 (Fiction)
Bkl A

White, Edward Lucas. The Unwilling Vestal: A Tale of Rome under the Caesars. Dutton 1918 (Fiction)
SCHS

Hadrian, Emperor of Rome, 76-138

Perowne, Stewart. Hadrian. Norton 1962
Bkl A

Trease, Geoffrey. Message to Hadrian. Vanguard 1956 (Fiction)
BBJH—JH

Roman—3rd century

Aurelian, Emperor of Rome, 212?-275

Dulin, Ralph. The Unconquered Sun. Macmillan 1963 (Fiction)
Bkl A

Heliogabalus, Emperor of Rome, 204-222

Duggan, Alfred Leo. Family Favorites. Pantheon 1961 (Fiction)
Bkl A

Roman—4th century

Julian, Emperor of Rome, 331-363

Vidal, Gore. Julian: A Novel. Little 1964 (Fiction)
Bkl A—IndS(10-12)

Roman—8th century

Charlemagne, 742-814

Bullough, Donald A. The Age of Charlemagne. Putnam 1966
Bkl A&Y

Komroff, Manuel. Charlemagne. Messner 1964
Bkl C(7-9)&Y—ESLC—JH

Lamb, Harold Albert. Charlemagne: The Legend and the Man. Doubleday 1954
SCHS—SCPL-3000

Russian—15th century

Ivan III, the Great, Emperor of Russia, 1440-1505

Fennell, John Lister Illingworth. Ivan the Great of Moscow. St Martins 1961
Bkl A

Russian—18th century

Peter I, the Great, Emperor of Russia, 1672-1725

Baker, Nina Brown. Peter the Great. Vanguard 1943
CC(7-9)—SCHS

Grey, Ian. Peter the Great, Emperor of All Russia. Lippincott 1960
Bkl A—BY

Klyuchevsky, Vasili. Peter the Great. St Martins 1958
3000

Lamb, Harold. City and the Tsar: Peter the Great and the Move to the West, 1648-1762. Doubleday 1948
SCPL

Russian—20th century

Nicholas II, Emperor of Russia, 1868-1918

Frankland, Noble. Imperial Tragedy: Nicholas II, Last of the Tsars. Coward-McCann 1961
Bkl A

EMPRESSES

Austrian—19th century

Elizabeth, Consort of Francis Joseph I, Emperor of Austria, 1837-1898

Haslip, Joan. The Lonely Empress: A Biography of Elizabeth of Austria. World 1965
Bkl A

French—19th century

Eugénie, Consort of Napoleon III, Emperor of the French, 1826-1920

Chapman, Hester W. Eugénie: A Novel. Little 1961 (Fiction)
Bkl A&Y
Kurtz, Harold. The Empress Eugenie, 1826-1920. Houghton 1964
Bkl A—IndS(12)

Joséphine, Consort of Napoleon I, 1763-1814

Cole, Hubert. Joséphine. Viking 1963
Bkl A—IndS(10-12)
Knapton, Ernest John. Empress Josephine. Harvard Univ. 1963
Bkl A
Malvern, Gladys. Stephanie. Macrae 1956 (Fiction)
SCHS
Vance, Marguerite. The Empress Josephine: From Martinique to Malmaison. Dutton 1956
SCHS

Russian—18th century

Catherine II, Empress of Russia, 1729-1796

Almedingen, Martha Edith. Catherine, Empress of Russia. Dodd 1961
Bkl A—SCPL
Grey, Ian. Catherine the Great: Autocrat and Empress of All Russia. Lippincott 1962
Bkl A—BY
Oldenbourg, Zoé. Catherine the Great; tr. from the French by Anne Carter. Pantheon 1965
Bkl A—IndS(10-12)

COLLECTIONS

Cabanne, Pierre. The Great Collectors. Farrar 1963
Bkl A

Russian—19th century

Maria Fedorovna, Empress of Russia, 1847-1928

Tisdall, Evelyn Ernest Percy. Marie Fedorovna: Empress of Russia. Day 1958
SCPL

ENGINEERS

See also Engineers, Aeronautical; Engineers, Civil; Engineers, Efficiency; Engineers, Electrical; Engineers, Mechanical; Engineers, Military; Engineers, Mining; Engineers, Radio and Television; Engineers, Traffic

COLLECTIONS

Evans, Idrisyn Oliver. Engineers of the World. Warne 1963
Bkl C(6-9)&Y

American

COLLECTIONS

Yost, Edna. Modern American Engineers. Lippincott 1958
ESLC—SCHS—YR

ENGINEERS, AERONAUTICAL

See also Aviators

COLLECTIONS

Poole, Lynn and Poole, Gray. Scientists Who Work with Astronauts. Dodd 1964
Bkl C(6-9)&Y
Stewart, Oliver. Aviation: The Creative Ideas. Praeger 1966
Bkl A

American

COLLECTIONS

Thomas, Shirley. Men of Space: v. 7, Profiles of the Leaders in Space Research, Development, and Exploration. Chilton 1965
Bkl A&Y
Joseph Vincent Charyk; Robert F. Freitag; Herbert Friedman; Harry Joseph Goett; Robert J. Parks

American—20th century

Joseph Vincent Charyk, 1920-

COLLECTIONS

Thomas, Shirley. Men of Space: v. 7, Profiles of the Leaders in Space Research, Development, and Exploration. Chilton 1965
Bkl A&Y

Alfred Scott Crossfield, 1921-

Crossfield, Alfred Scott and Blair, Clay. Always Another Dawn. World 1960
Bkl A&Y

Alexander Procofieff De Seversky, 1894-

COLLECTIONS

Gelfand, Ravina and Patterson, Letha. They Wouldn't Quit. Lerner Publications 1962
AB(5-9)

ENGINEERS, AERONAUTICAL

American—20th century—*Continued*

Robert F. Freitag, 1920-

COLLECTIONS

Thomas, Shirley. Men of Space: v. 7, Profiles of the Leaders in Space Research, Development, and Exploration. Chilton 1965
Bkl A&Y

Robert Hutchings Goddard, 1882-1945

Dewey, Anne Perkins. Robert Goddard, Space Pioneer. Little 1962
Bkl C(6-9)&Y—CC(6-9)—ESLC—JH—YR

Lehman, Milton. This High Man: The Life of Robert H. Goddard. Farrar 1963
Bkl A&Y

Verral, Charles Spain. Robert Goddard: Father of the Space Age. Prentice-Hall 1963
ESLC—IndJ(4-6)

Harry Joseph Goett, 1910-

COLLECTIONS

Thomas, Shirley. Men of Space: v. 7, Profiles of the Leaders in Space Research, Development, and Exploration. Chilton 1965
Bkl A&Y

Glenn Luther Martin, 1886-1955

Still, Henry. To Ride the Wind: A Biography of Glenn L. Martin. Messner 1964
Bkl A&Y

Robert J. Parks, 1922-

COLLECTIONS

Thomas, Shirley. Men of Space: v. 7, Profiles of the Leaders in Space Research, Development, and Exploration. Chilton 1965
Bkl A&Y

Igor Ivan Sikorsky, 1889-

COLLECTIONS

Life International. Nine Who Chose America. Dutton 1959
Bkl Y&C—SCHS

Manchester, Harland Frank. Trail Blazers of Technology: The Story of Nine Inventors. Scribner 1962
Bkl Y&C—JH—YR

Wernher Von Braun, 1912-

Bergaust, Erik. Reaching for the Stars. Doubleday 1960
Bkl A—BY

Walters, Helen B. Wernher von Braun: Rocket Engineer. Macmillan 1964
Bkl C(7-9)&Y—ESLC—JH

COLLECTIONS

Cunz, Dieter. They Came from Germany: The Story of Famous German-Americans. Dodd 1966
ESLC

Freedman, Russell. Teenagers Who Made History. Holiday 1961
BY—JH—SCHS—YR

English—20th century

Nevil Shute, 1899-1960

Shute, Nevil. Slide Rule: The Autobiography of an Engineer. Morrow 1954
SCPL

German—20th century

Hermann Oberth, 1894-

Walters, Helen B. Hermann Oberth: Father of Space Travel. Macmillan 1962
Bkl C(6-9)&Y

Hungarian—20th century

Theodor von Kármán, 1881-1963

Halacy, Daniel Stephen. Father of Supersonic Flight, Theodor von Kármán. Messner 1965
Bkl C(7-10)&Y

ENGINEERS, CIVIL

American—19th century

John Roebling, 1806-1869

Steinman, D. B. Builders of the Bridge: The Story of John Roebling and His Son. Harcourt 1950
SCPL

American—20th century

Joseph Baermann Strauss, 1870-1938

Chester, Michael. Joseph Strauss: Builder of the Golden Gate Bridge. Putnam 1965
ESLC

French—19th century

Ferdinand Marie, Vicomte de Lesseps, 1805-1894

Horizon Magazine. Building the Suez Canal, by S. C. Burchell. Am. Heritage 1966
Bkl C(7-9)&Y

Long, Laura. De Lesseps: Builder of Suez. Longmans 1958
JH—SCHS—YR

ENGINEERS, EFFICIENCY

American—20th century

Frank Bunker Gilbreth, 1868-1924

Gilbreth, Frank Bunker, Jr. and Carey, Ernestine (Gilbreth). Cheaper by the Dozen. Crowell 1948; 1963
Bkl A—BBHS—BY—JH—SCHS—SCPL

Lillian Evelyn (Moller) Gilbreth, 1878-

Gilbreth, Frank Bunker, Jr. and Carey, Ernestine (Gilbreth). Belles on Their Toes. Crowell 1950
BBHS—BY—SCHS—SCPL

COLLECTIONS

Boynick, David. Pioneers in Petticoats. Crowell 1959
YR

ENGINEERS, ELECTRICAL

American—20th century

Harold Eugene Edgerton, 1903-

COLLECTIONS

Poole, Lynn and Poole, Gray. Scientists Who Work with Cameras. Dodd 1965
Bkl C(7-12)&Y—IndS(11-12)

Charles Franklin Kettering, 1876-1958

Lavine, Sigmund A. Kettering: Master Inventor. Dodd 1960
SCHS—YR
Young, Rosamond McPherson. Boss Ket. McKay 1961
YR

Charles Proteus Steinmetz, 1865-1923

Berry, Erick. Charles Proteus Steinmetz: Wizard of Electricity. Macmillan 1966
ESLC
Lavine, Sigmund A. Steinmetz: Maker of Lightning. Dodd 1955
BBHS—BBJH—BY—JH—SCHS
Miller, Floyd. The Electrical Genius of Liberty Hall: Charles Proteus Steinmetz. McGraw 1962
Bkl C(7-9)—ESLC—JH—YR
Thomas, Henry. Charles Steinmetz. Putnam 1960
AB(5-9)—Bkl C(6-8)

Nikola Tesla, 1857-1943

Beckhard, Arthur J. Electrical Genius Nikola Tesla. Messner 1959
Bkl Y&C
Hunt, Inez and Draper, Wanetta W. Lightning in His Hand: The Life Story of Nikola Tesla. Sage 1964
Bkl A&Y
Walters, Helen B. Nikola Tesla: Giant of Electricity. Crowell 1961
JH—YR

COLLECTIONS

Manchester, Harland Frank. Trail Blazers of Technology: The Story of Nine Inventors. Scribner 1962
Bkl Y&C—JH—YR

Italian—18th century

Alessandro Giuseppe Antonio Anastasio, Conte Volta, 1745-1827

Dibner, Bern. Alessandro Volta and the Electric Battery. Watts 1964
Bkl C(7-10)&Y

Italian—19th century

Alessandro Giuseppe Antonio Anastasio, Conte Volta, 1745-1827

Dibner, Bern. Alessandro Volta and the Electric Battery. Watts 1964
Bkl C(7-10)&Y

ENGINEERS, MECHANICAL

American—18th century

Robert Fulton, 1765-1815

Hill, Ralph Nading. Robert Fulton and the Steamboat. Random House 1954
CC(4-6)—JH—SCHS
Judson, Clara (Ingram). Boat Builder: The Story of Robert Fulton. Scribner 1940
BBJH—CC(4-6)—ESLC—JH—SCHS

American—19th century

John Ericsson, 1803-1889

Burnett, Constance (Buel). Captain John Ericsson: Father of the Monitor. Vanguard 1961
Bkl C(6-10)&Y
Latham, Jean Lee. Man of the Monitor: The Story of John Ericsson. Harper 1962
Bkl C(5-7)—CC(5-7)—ESLC—JH—YR
Pratt, Fletcher. The Monitor and the Merrimac. Random House 1951
BBJH—ESLC—JH

George Washington Gale Ferris, 1859-1896

Lawson, Robert. The Great Wheel. Viking 1957 (Fiction)
CC(7-9)—SCHS—YR

Robert Fulton, 1765-1815

Hill, Ralph Nading. Robert Fulton and the Steamboat. Random House 1954
CC(4-6)—JH—SCHS
Judson, Clara (Ingram). Boat Builder: The Story of Robert Fulton. Scribner 1940
BBJH—CC(4-6)—ESLC—JH—SCHS

ENGINEERS, MECHANICAL—*Continued*

American—20th century

Richard Buckminster Fuller, 1895-

McHale, John. R. Buckminster Fuller. Braziller 1962
   Bkl A

Simon Lake, 1866-1945

COLLECTIONS

Manchester, Harland Frank. Trail Blazers of Technology: The Story of Nine Inventors. Scribner 1962
   Bkl Y&C—JH—YR

Scottish—18th century

James Watt, 1736-1819

Crane, William Dwight. The Man Who Transformed the World: James Watt. Messner 1963
   Bkl C(7-10)&Y—YR

ENGINEERS, MILITARY

American—19th century

George Washington Goethals, 1858-1928

Fast, Howard M. Goethals and the Panama Canal. Messner 1942
   CC(6-9)—JH—SCHS
Latham, Jean Lee. George W. Goethals: Panama Canal Engineer. Garrard 1965
   ESLC

American—20th century

George Washington Goethals, 1858-1928

Fast, Howard M. Goethals and the Panama Canal. Messner 1942
   CC(6-9)—JH—SCHS
Latham, Jean Lee. George W. Goethals: Panama Canal Engineer. Garrard 1965
   ESLC

ENGINEERS, MINING

American—19th century

Adolph Heinrich Joseph Sutro, 1830-1898

Stewart, Robert Ernest and Stewart, Mary Frances. Adolph Sutro: A Biography. Howell-North 1962
   Bkl A

American—20th century

Herbert Clark Hoover, 1874-1964

Lyons, Eugene. Herbert Hoover: A Biography. Doubleday 1964
   Bkl A—SCPL

McGee, Dorothy Horton. Herbert Hoover: Engineer, Humanitarian, Statesman. Dodd 1965
   BBHS—Bkl C(7-10)&Y—SCHS
Peare, Catherine Owens. The Herbert Hoover Story. Crowell 1965
   Bkl C(7-9)&Y—ESLC

English—20th century

Doreen Stanford, 1896-

Stanford, Doreen. Siberian Odyssey. Dutton 1964
   Bkl A&Y—IndJ(6-9)

ENGINEERS, RADIO AND TELEVISION

American—20th century

Lee De Forest, 1873-1961

Levine, Irving Englander. Electronics Pioneer: Lee De Forest. Messner 1964
   Bkl C(6-9)&Y—JH—YR

COLLECTIONS

Manchester, Harland Frank. Trail Blazers of Technology: The Story of Nine Inventors. Scribner 1962
   Bkl Y&C—JH—YR

David Sarnoff, 1891-

Lyons, Eugene. David Sarnoff: A Biography. Harper 1966
   Bkl A&Y

Italian—20th century

Guglielmo Marconi, Marchese, 1874-1937

Coe, Douglas. Marconi: Pioneer of Radio. Messner 1943
   CC(7-9)—JH—SCHS
Marconi, Degna. My Father, Marconi. McGraw 1962
   Bkl A—SCPL

ENGINEERS, TRAFFIC

American—20th century

Henry A. Barnes, 1906-1968

Barnes, Henry A. The Man with the Red and Green Eyes: The Autobiography of the Traffic Commissioner, New York City. Dutton 1965
   Bkl A&Y

ENGRAVERS

COLLECTIONS

Bryan, Michael. Dictionary of Painters and Engravers; rev. and enl. by George C. Williamson. 5v. Kennikat 1964
   SCPL

ENGRAVERS—*Continued*

Longstreet, Stephen, ed. A Treasury of the World's Great Prints. Simon & Schuster 1961
SCPL

English—18th century

William Blake, 1757-1827

Bronowski, Jacob. William Blake and the Age of Revolution. Harper 1965
Bkl A

Daugherty, James Henry. William Blake. Viking 1960
BBHS—Bkl Y—BY—SCHS—YR

William Hogarth, 1697-1764

Antal, Frederick. Hogarth and His Place in European Art. Basic Bks 1962
Bkl A

Berry, Erick. The Four Londons of William Hogarth. McKay 1964
Bkl Y—IndJ(6-9)

Quennell, Peter. Hogarth's Progress. Viking 1955
SCPL

English—19th century

William Blake, 1757-1827

Bronowski, Jacob. William Blake and the Age of Revolution. Harper 1965
Bkl A

Daugherty, James. William Blake. Viking 1960
BBHS—Bkl Y—BY—SCHS—YR

English—20th century

Eric Gill, 1882-1940

Speaight, Robert. The Life of Eric Gill. Kenedy 1966
Bkl A

COLLECTIONS

Heppenstall, Rayner. Four Absentees. Dufour 1963
Bkl A

German—16th century

Albrecht Dürer, 1471-1528

Grote, Ludwig. Dürer: Biographical and Critical Study; tr. from the German by Helga Harrison. Skira 1965
Bkl A

Levey, Michael. Dürer. Norton 1964
Bkl A&Y

Ripley, Elizabeth. Dürer: A Biography. Lippincott 1958
BBJH—CC(7-9)—YR

Steck, Max. Dürer and His World; tr. from the German by J. Maxwell Brownjohn. Studio 1964
Bkl A&Y—IndS(12)

Waetzoldt, Wilhelm. Dürer and His Times; tr. by R. H. Boothroyd. Phaidon 1955
SCPL

ENTERTAINERS

See Actors; Circus Performers; Dancers; Magicians; Radio and Television Performers; Singers

ESSAYISTS

COLLECTIONS

Benét, Laura. Famous English and American Essayists. Dodd 1966
Bkl Y(7-10)

English—18th century

Charles Lamb, 1775-1834

Lamb, Charles. Letters. 2v. Dutton 1930
SCPL

Lamb, Charles. Selected Letters; ed. by T. S. Matthews. Farrar 1956
SCPL

COLLECTIONS

Drew, Elizabeth A. The Literature of Gossip: Nine English Letterwriters. Norton 1964
Bkl A&Y

English—19th century

Charles Lamb, 1775-1834

Lamb, Charles. Letters. 2v. Dutton 1930
SCPL

Lamb, Charles. Selected Letters; ed. by T. S. Matthews. Farrar 1956
SCPL

COLLECTIONS

Drew, Elizabeth A. The Literature of Gossip: Nine English Letterwriters. Norton 1964
Bkl A&Y

Walter Horatio Pater, 1839-1894

COLLECTIONS

Knoepflmacher, U. C. Religious Humanism and the Victorian Novel. Princeton Univ. 1965
Bkl A

French—16th century

Michel Eyquem de Montaigne, 1533-1592

Frame, Donald Murdoch. Montaigne: A Biography. Harcourt 1965
Bkl A

ESSAYISTS—*Continued*

Scottish—19th century

Thomas Carlyle, 1795-1881

Emerson, Ralph Waldo and Carlyle, Thomas. The Correspondence of [the authors]; ed. by Joseph Slater. Columbia Univ. 1964
Bkl A

ETCHERS

American—19th century

James Abbott McNeill Whistler, 1834-1903

Pearson, Hesketh. The Man Whistler. Harper. 1952
SCPL

Sutton, Denys. Nocturne: The Art of James McNeill Whistler. Lippincott 1964
Bkl A

ETHNOLOGISTS

See also Anthropologists

American—19th century

George Catlin, 1796-1872

Plate, Robert. Palette and Tomahawk: The Story of George Catlin, July 27, 1796-December 23, 1872. McKay 1962
Bkl A&Y—YR

EVANGELISTS

See Religious Leaders

EXPLORERS

See also Colonists—American; Frontiersmen; Scouts

COLLECTIONS

American Heritage. Discoverers of the New World, by Josef Berger. Am. Heritage 1960
CC(5-7)—ESLC—YR

Bailey, Bernadine (Freeman). Famous Modern Explorers. Dodd 1963
Bkl C(5-8)

Bakeless, Katherine L. and Bakeless, John Edwin. They Saw America First: Our First Explorers and What They Saw. Lippincott 1957
CC(7-9)—ESLC—SCPL
Jacques Cartier; Samuel de Champlain; Francisco Vásquez Coronado; Robert Cavelier, Sieur de La Salle; Pierre Gaultier de Varennes, Sieur de La Verendrye; Pierre Esprit Radisson; Hernando de Soto

Clark, William R. Explorers of the World. Natural Hist. Press 1964
CC—ESLC
Alexander the Great; James Cook; Vasco da Gama; David Livingstone; Ferdinand Magellan; Sir William Edward Parry; Robert Edwin Peary; Marco Polo; Sir Henry Morton Stanley

Coffman, Ramon Peyton and Goodman, Nathan G. Famous Explorers for Young People. Dodd 1945
BBJH—SCHS

Duvoisin, Roger. They Put Out to Sea: The Story of the Map. Knopf 1943
CC(5-7)—ESLC
Alexander the Great; Darius I, King of Persia; Genghis Khan; Ferdinand Magellan; Marco Polo; and others

Hayward, Arthur L. Explorers and Their Discoveries. Abelard-Schuman 1955
SCHS

Hoff, Rhoda and De Terra, Helmut. They Explored! Walck 1959
AB(5)
John Charles Frémont; Sven Anders Hedin; Maurice Herzog; Alexander Humboldt; David Livingstone; Robert Falcon Scott

Horizon Magazine. Heroes of Polar Exploration, by Ralph K. Andrist. Am. Heritage 1962
ESLC—JH—SCHS

Lucas, Mary Seymour. Vast Horizons. Viking 1943
SCHS
Genghis Khan; Henry the Navigator; Marco Polo; Tamerlane; and others

Protter, Eric. Explorers and Explorations. Grosset 1962
ESLC

Rich, Louise Dickinson. The First Book of New World Explorers. Watts 1960
CC(4-6)—ESLC
Bjarni; Christopher Columbus; Robert Cavelier, Sieur de La Salle; Ferdinand Magellan; Francisco Pizarro; and others

Rittenhouse, Mignon. Seven Women Explorers. Lippincott 1964
CC

Sutton, Felix. Discoverers of America: Primitive Man to Spanish Conquerors. Grosset 1965
ESLC
John Cabot; Christopher Columbus; and others

Villiers, Alan. The Ocean: Man's Conquest of the Sea. Dutton 1963
YR

Wright, Helen and Rapport, Samuel. The Great Explorers. Harper 1957
SCHS

EXPLORERS—*Continued*

American

COLLECTIONS

Andrews, Roy Chapman. Beyond Adventure: The Lives of Three Explorers. Duell 1954
BY—SCPL—YR
Carl Ethan Akeley; Roy Chapman Andrews; Robert Edwin Peary

Buehr, Walter. Westward: With American Explorers. Putnam 1963
ESLC
Daniel Boone; John Charles Frémont; and others

American—19th century

James Bridger, 1804-1881

Allen, Merritt Parmelee. Western Star: A Story of Jim Bridger. Longmans 1941 (Fiction)
SCHS

Caesar, Gene. King of the Mountain Men: The Life of Jim Bridger. Dutton 1961
Bkl A

Garst, Shannon. Jim Bridger, Greatest of the Mountain Men. Houghton 1952
CC(6-9)—ESLC—JH—SCHS

Luce, Willard and Luce, Celia. Jim Bridger: Man of the Mountains. Garrard 1966
ESLC

Vestal, Stanley. Jim Bridger, Mountain Man: A Biography. Morrow 1946
SCPL

COLLECTIONS

Reinfeld, Fred. Trappers of the West. Crowell 1957
BBEL(7-8)

William Clark, 1770-1838

Bakeless, John Edwin. Lewis & Clark: Partners in Discovery. Morrow 1947
SCPL

Daugherty, James. Of Courage Undaunted: Across the Continent with Lewis and Clark. Viking 1951
BBEL—CC(7-9)—ESLC—JH

Davis, Julia. No Other White Men. Dutton 1937
CC(7-9)—JH

Neuberger, Richard L. The Lewis and Clark Expedition. Random House 1951
BBEL—CC(4-7)—ESLC

Peattie, Donald Culross. Forward the Nation. Putnam 1942
SCPL

COLLECTIONS

Blassingame, Wyatt and Glendinning, Richard. Frontier Doctors. Watts 1963
Bkl C(6-9)

Frederick Albert Cook, 1865-1940

Freeman, Andrew A. The Case for Doctor Cook. Coward-McCann 1961
Bkl A

Weems, John Edward. Race for the Pole. Holt 1960
Bkl A&Y

John Charles Frémont, 1813-1890

Burt, Olive. John Charles Frémont: Trail Marker of the Old West. Messner 1955
BBJH—JH—SCHS

Frazee, Steve. Year of the Big Snow: John Charles Frémont's Fourth Expedition. Holt 1962
ESLC

Frémont, John Charles. Narratives of Exploration and Adventure; ed. by Allan Nevins. Longmans 1956
SCPL

Nevins, Allan. Frémont, Pathmaker of the West. Longmans 1955
SCPL

Smith, Fredrika Shumway. Frémont: Soldier, Explorer, Statesman. Rand McNally 1966
ESLC

COLLECTIONS

American Heritage. Trappers and Mountain Men, by Evan Jones. Am. Heritage 1961
AB—CC(6-9)—ESLC—YR

Buehr, Walter. Westward: With American Explorers. Putnam 1963
ESLC

Hoff, Rhoda and De Terra, Helmut. They Explored! Walck 1959
AB(5)

Charles Francis Hall, 1821-1871

Steelman, Robert. Call of the Arctic. Coward-McCann 1960 (Fiction)
Bkl A

Matthew Alexander Henson, 1866-1955

Angell, Pauline Knickerbocker. To the Top of the World: The Story of Peary and Henson. Rand McNally 1964
Bkl C&Y

Miller, Floyd. Ahdoolo! The Biography of Matthew A. Henson. Dutton 1963
AB(5up)—Bkl A&Y—YR

Ripley, Sheldon N. Matthew Henson: Arctic Hero. Houghton 1966
ESLC

Elisha Kent Kane, 1820-1857

Kendall, Lace. Elisha Kent Kane: Arctic Challenger. Macrae 1963
IndJ(6-9)

EXPLORERS
American—19th century

Elisha Kent Kane—Continued

Villarejo, Oscar Milton. Dr. Kane's Voyage to the Polar Lands. Univ. of Pa. 1965
Bkl A

Meriwether Lewis, 1774-1809

Bakeless, John Edwin. The Adventures of Lewis and Clark. Houghton 1962
Bkl C(5-8)

Bakeless, John Edwin. Lewis & Clark: Partners in Discovery. Morrow 1947
SCPL

Daugherty, James. Of Courage Undaunted: Across the Continent with Lewis and Clark. Viking 1951
BBEL—CC(7-9)—ESLC—JH

Davis, Julia. No Other White Men. Dutton 1937
CC(7-9)—JH

Dillon, Richard H. Meriwether Lewis: A Biography. Coward-McCann 1965
Bkl A&Y—IndS(11-12)

Lewis, Meriwether. The Journals of Lewis and Clark; ed. by Bernard De Voto. Houghton 1953
SCHS—SCPL

Neuberger, Richard L. The Lewis and Clark Expedition. Random House 1951
BBEL—CC(4-7)—ESLC

Peattie, Donald Culross. Forward the Nation. Putnam 1942
SCPL

COLLECTIONS

Blassingame, Wyatt and Glendinning, Richard. Frontier Doctors. Watts 1963
Bkl C(6-9)

Robert Edwin Peary, 1856-1920

Angell, Pauline Knickerbocker. To the Top of the World: The Story of Peary and Henson. Rand McNally 1964
AB(5up)—Bkl C&Y

Berry, Erick. Robert E. Peary: North Pole Conqueror. Garrard 1963
AB (3-5)—ESLC

Lord, Walter. Peary to the Pole. Harper 1963
Bkl C(5-9)&Y—ESLC

Owen, Russell. The Conquest of the North and South Poles: Adventures of the Peary and Byrd Expeditions. Random House 1952
CC(5-9)—ESLC—JH

Stafford, Marie Peary. Discoverer of the North Pole: The Story of Robert E. Peary. Morrow 1959
CC(6-9)—JH

Weems, John Edward. Race for the Pole. Holt 1960
Bkl A&Y

COLLECTIONS

Andrews, Roy Chapman. Beyond Adventure: The Lives of Three Explorers. Duell 1954
BY—SCPL—YR

Clark, William R. Explorers of the World. Natural Hist. Press 1964
CC—ESLC

Zebulon Montgomery Pike, 1779-1813

Baker, Nina Brown. Pike of Pike's Peak. Harcourt 1953
CC(5-7)

Keating, Bern. Zebulon Pike: Young America's Frontier Scout. Putnam 1965
ESLC

Wibberley, Leonard. Zebulon Pike: Soldier and Explorer. Funk 1961
Bkl C(7-9)—BY—YR

George Shannon, 1786?-1836

Eifert, Virginia Louise (Snider). George Shannon: Young Explorer with Lewis and Clark. Dodd 1963
Bkl C(7-9)

American—20th century
Carl Ethan Akeley, 1864-1926

Sutton, Felix. Big Game Hunter: Carl Akeley. Messner 1960
Bkl C(5-9)&Y

COLLECTIONS

Andrews, Roy Chapman. Beyond Adventure: The Lives of Three Explorers. Duell 1954
BY—SCPL—YR

Roy Chapman Andrews, 1884-1960

COLLECTIONS

Andrews, Roy Chapman. Beyond Adventure: The Lives of Three Explorers. Duell 1954
BY—SCPL—YR

Howard Blackburn, 1859-1932

Garland, Joseph E. Lone Voyager. Little 1963
Bkl A

Richard Evelyn Byrd, 1888-1957

Byrd, Richard Evelyn. Alone. Putnam 1938
BY—SCHS—SCPL

Byrd, Richard Evelyn. Little America. Putnam 1930
SCPL—YR

Byrd, Richard Evelyn. Skyward. Putnam 1928
SCPL

De Leeuw, Adele. Richard E. Byrd: Adventurer to the Poles. Garrard 1963
AB(2-6)—ESLC

EXPLORERS

American—20th century

Richard Evelyn Byrd—Continued

Gladych, Michael. Admiral Byrd of Antarctica. Messner 1960
Bkl C(5-8)—ESLC

Owen, Russell. The Conquest of the North and South Poles: Adventures of the Peary and Byrd Expeditions. Random House 1952
CC(5-9)—ESLC—JH

Rink, Paul. Conquering Antarctica: Richard E. Byrd. Encyc. Britannica 1961
JH

Frederick Albert Cook, 1865-1940

Freeman, Andrew A. The Case for Doctor Cook. Coward-McCann 1961
Bkl A

Weems, John Edward. Race for the Pole. Holt 1960
Bkl A&Y

Richard Halliburton, 1900-1939

Root, Jonathan. Halliburton—The Magnificent Myth: A Biography. Coward-McCann 1965
Bkl A

Matthew Alexander Henson, 1866-1955

Angell, Pauline Knickerbocker. To the Top of the World: The Story of Peary and Henson. Rand McNally 1964
Bkl C&Y

Miller, Floyd. Ahdoolo! The Biography of Matthew A. Henson. Dutton 1963
AB(5up)—Bkl A&Y—YR

Ripley, Sheldon N. Matthew Henson: Arctic Hero. Houghton 1966
ESLC

Donald Baxter MacMillan, 1874-

Allen, Everett S. Arctic Odyssey. Dodd 1962
Bkl A&Y

MacMillan, Miriam (Look). Green Seas and White Ice. Dodd 1948
SCPL

Robert Neal Manry, 1918-

Manry, Robert Neal. Tinkerbelle. Harper 1966
Bkl A&Y

Robert Edwin Peary, 1856-1920

Angell, Pauline Knickerbocker. To the Top of the World: The Story of Peary and Henson. Rand McNally 1964
AB(5up)—Bkl C&Y

Berry, Erick. Robert E. Peary: North Pole Conqueror. Garrard 1963
AB(3-5)—ESLC

Lord, Walter. Peary to the Pole. Harper 1963
Bkl C(5-9)&Y—ESLC

Owen, Russell. The Conquest of the North and South Poles: Adventures of the Peary and Byrd Expeditions. Random House 1952
CC(5-9)—ESLC—JH

Stafford, Marie Peary. Discoverer of the North Pole: The Story of Robert E. Peary. Morrow 1959
CC(6-9)—JH

Weems, John Edward. Race for the Pole. Holt 1960
Bkl A&Y

COLLECTIONS

Andrews, Roy Chapman. Beyond Adventure: The Lives of Three Explorers. Duell 1954
BY—SCPL—YR

Clark, William R. Explorers of the World. Natural Hist. Press 1964
CC—ESLC

Wayne Short, 1926-

Short, Wayne. The Cheechakoes. Random House 1964 (Fiction)
Bkl A&Y—IndS(10-12)

Australian—20th century

Sir George Hubert Wilkins, 1888-1958

Thomas, Lowell Jackson. Sir Hubert Wilkins—His World of Adventure: A Biography. McGraw 1961
Bkl A&Y

Canadian—17th century

Louis Joliet, 1645-1700

Eifert, Virginia Louise (Snider). Louis Jolliet: Explorer of Rivers. Dodd 1961
Bkl A&Y

Canadian—18th century

Pierre Gaultier de Varennes, Sieur de La Vérendrye, 1685-1749

COLLECTIONS

American Heritage. Trappers and Mountain Men, by Evan Jones. Am. Heritage 1961
AB—CC(6-9)—ESLC—YR

Bakeless, Katherine L. and Bakeless, John Edwin. They Saw America First: Our First Explorers and What They Saw. Lippincott 1957
CC(7-9)—ESLC—SCPL

Canadian—19th century

John Palliser, 1807-1887

Spry, Irene Mary (Biss). The Palliser Expedition. St Martins 1964
Bkl A

EXPLORERS—*Continued*

Canadian—20th century

Vilhjálmur Stefánsson, 1879-1962

Stefánsson, Vilhjálmur. Discovery: The Autobiography of Vilhjálmur Stefánsson. McGraw 1964
Bkl A&Y—IndS(12)—SCPL

Stefánsson, Vilhjálmur. Friendly Arctic: The Story of Five Years in Polar Regions. Macmillan 1943
SCPL

Danish—18th century

Vitus Jonassen Bering, 1680-1741

Murphy, Robert William. The Haunted Journey. Doubleday 1961
Bkl A&Y

Danish—20th century

Peter Freuchen, 1886-1957

Freuchen, Peter. Vagrant Viking: My Life and Adventures. Messner 1953
SCPL

Knud Johan Victor Rasmussen, 1879-1933

Freuchen, Peter. I Sailed with Rasmussen. Messner 1958
SCPL

Dutch—16th century

Jan Huyghen van Linschoten, 1563?-1611

Parr, Charles McKew. Jan van Linschoten: The Dutch Marco Polo. Crowell 1964
Bkl A

English—16th century

Sir Francis Drake, 1540-1596

Bradford, Ernle Dusgate Selby. The Wind Commands Me: A Life of Sir Francis Drake. Harcourt 1965
Bkl A&Y—IndS(11-12)

Foltz, Mary Jane. Awani. Morrow 1964 (Fiction)
ESLC

Knight, Frank. The Young Drake. Roy 1963
IndJ(6-9)

Latham, Jean Lee. Drake: The Man They Called a Pirate. Harper 1960
CC(5-7)—ESLC

Syme, Donald. Francis Drake: Sailor of Unknown Seas. Morrow 1961
Bkl C(4-6)

Wood, William. Elizabethan Sea-Dogs: A Chronicle of Drake and His Companions. Yale Univ. 1918
SCHS

Sir Walter Raleigh, 1552?-1618

Baker, Nina Brown. Sir Walter Raleigh. Harcourt 1950
CC(7-9)—JH—SCHS

Buckmaster, Henrietta. Walter Raleigh: Man of Two Worlds. Random House 1964
Bkl C(5-8)—ESLC—JH

De Leeuw, Adele. Sir Walter Raleigh. Garrard 1964
AB(3-7)—CC(3-6)

Irwin, Margaret. That Great Lucifer: A Portrait of Sir Walter Raleigh. Harcourt 1960
Bkl A&Y—SCPL

Rowse, Alfred Leslie. Sir Walter Ralegh: His Family and Private Life. Harper 1962
Bkl A—SCPL

Syme, Ronald. Walter Raleigh. Morrow 1962
Bkl C(4-6)—CC(3-6)—ESLC

Trease, Geoffrey. Sir Walter Raleigh, Captain & Adventurer. Vanguard 1950
BBJH—CC(7-9)—ESLC—JH

English—17th century

Henry Hudson, ?-1611

Baker, Nina Brown. Henry Hudson. Knopf 1958
CC(4-6)

Carmer, Carl. Henry Hudson: Captain of Ice-Bound Seas. Garrard 1960
ESLC

Lambert, Richard S. Mutiny in the Bay. St Martins 1963
IndJ(6-9)

Rachlis, Eugene. The Voyages of Henry Hudson. Random House 1962
Bkl C(5-8)—CC(5-7)

Scott, James Maurice. Hudson of Hudson's Bay. Schuman 1951
SCHS

Syme, Ronald. Henry Hudson. Morrow 1955
BBEL(5-8)—BBJH—CC(5-7)—ESLC—JH—SCHS

Vail, Philip. The Magnificent Adventures of Henry Hudson. Dodd 1965
IndJ(6-9)

Sir Walter Raleigh, 1552?-1618

Baker, Nina Brown. Sir Walter Raleigh. Harcourt 1950
CC(7-9)—JH—SCHS

Buckmaster, Henrietta. Walter Raleigh: Man of Two Worlds. Random House 1964
Bkl C(5-8)—ESLC—JH

De Leeuw, Adele. Sir Walter Raleigh. Garrard 1964
AB(3-7)—CC(3-6)

EXPLORERS

English—17th century

Sir Walter Raleigh—Continued

Irwin, Margaret. That Great Lucifer: A Portrait of Sir Walter Raleigh. Harcourt 1960
Bkl A&Y—SCPL

Rowse, Alfred Leslie. Sir Walter Ralegh: His Family and Private Life. Harper 1962
Bkl A—SCPL

Syme, Ronald. Walter Raleigh. Morrow 1962
Bkl C(4-6)—CC(3-6)—ESLC

Trease, Geoffrey. Sir Walter Raleigh: Captain & Adventurer. Vanguard 1950
BBJH—CC(7-9)—ESLC—JH

English—18th century

James Cook, 1728-1779

Cameron, Roderick William. The Golden Haze: With Captain Cook in the South Pacific. World 1964
Bkl A

Gwyther, John Michael. Captain Cook and the South Pacific: The Voyage of the "Endeavour" 1768-1771. Houghton 1955
SCPL

Horizon Magazine. Captain Cook and the South Pacific, by Oliver Warner. Am. Heritage 1963
Bkl C(6-9)—CC—ESLC—JH—YR

Moorehead, Alan. The Fatal Impact: An Account of the Invasion of the South Pacific, 1767-1840. Harper 1966
Bkl A&Y

Selsam, Millicent (Ellis). The Quest of Captain Cook. Doubleday 1962
Bkl C(5-7)—CC(5-7)—ESLC

Sperry, Armstrong. Captain Cook Explores the South Seas. Random House 1955
BBJH—ESLC—JH—SCHS

Swenson, Eric. The South Sea Shilling: Voyages of Captain Cook, R. N. Viking 1952
JH—SCHS

Syme, Ronald. Captain Cook: Pacific Explorer. Morrow 1960
AB(3-7)—Bkl C(4-6)—CC(4-6)—ESLC

Vandercook, John Womack. Great Sailor: A Life of the Discoverer Captain James Cook. Dial 1951
SCPL

COLLECTIONS

Clark, William R. Explorers of the World. Natural Hist. Press 1964
CC—ESLC

Samuel Hearne, 1745-1792

Syme, Ronald. On Foot to the Arctic: The Story of Samuel Hearne. Morrow 1959
Bkl C(6-9)

English—19th century

Sir Richard Francis Burton, 1821-1890

Farwell, Byron. Burton: A Biography of Sir Richard Francis Burton. Holt 1964
Bkl A

Sir John Franklin, 1786-1847

Sutton, Ann and Sutton, Myron. Journey into Ice: John Franklin and the Northwest Passage. Rand McNally 1965
Bkl Y&C—IndJ(6-9)

Mary Henrietta Kingsley, 1862-1900

Syme, Ronald. African Traveler: The Story of Mary Kingsley. Morrow 1962
Bkl C(5-7)—BY—CC(5-7)—ESLC

Sir William Edward Parry, 1790-1855

COLLECTIONS

Clark, William R. Explorers of the World. Natural Hist. Press 1964
CC—ESLC

James Richardson, 1806-1851

Seufert, Karl Rolf. Caravan in Peril; tr. from the German by Stella Humphries. Pantheon 1963 (Fiction)
Bkl C&Y

English—20th century

Jim Corbett, 1875-1955

Corbett, Jim. Jungle Lore. Oxford 1953
BY—SCHS

Robert Falcon Scott, 1868-1912

Scott, Robert Falcon. Scott's Last Expedition: From the Personal Journals of [the author]. Dodd 1965
Bkl A&Y&C

COLLECTIONS

Hoff, Rhoda and De Terra, Helmut. They Explored! Walck 1959
AB(5)

French—16th century

Jacques Cartier, 1491-1557

Averill, Esther Holden. Cartier Sails the St. Lawrence. Harper 1956
AB(4-7)—BBEL(5-7)—CC(4-7)—ESLC

Syme, Ronald. Cartier: Finder of the St. Lawrence. Morrow 1958
BBEL—CC(4-6)—ESLC

EXPLORERS

French—16th century

Jacques Cartier—Continued

COLLECTIONS

Bakeless, Katherine L. and Bakeless, John Edwin. They Saw America First: Our First Explorers and What They Saw. Lippincott 1957
CC(7-9)—ESLC—SCPL

French—17th century

Samuel de Champlain, 1567-1635

Kent, Louise (Andrews). He Went with Champlain. Houghton 1959 (Fiction)
BBJH—SCHS

Syme, Ronald. Champlain of the St. Lawrence. Morrow 1952
CC(6-9)—ESLC—JH

Tharp, Louise Hall. Champlain: Northwest Voyager. Little 1957
SCHS

COLLECTIONS

Bakeless, Katherine L. and Bakeless, John Edwin. They Saw America First: Our First Explorers and What They Saw. Lippincott 1957
CC(7-9)—ESLC—SCPL

Médart Chouart, Sieur de Groseilliers, 1625?-1697?

COLLECTIONS

American Heritage. Trappers and Mountain Men, by Evan Jones. Am Heritage 1961
AB—CC(6-9)—ESLC—YR

Robert Cavelier, Sieur de La Salle, 1643-1687

Allen, Merritt Parmelee. Wilderness Way. Longmans 1954 (Fiction)
JH—SCHS

Graham, Alberta (Powell). La Salle: River Explorer. Abingdon 1954
BBEL(4-6)—ESLC

Nolan, Jeannette Covert. La Salle and the Grand Enterprise. Messner 1951
SCHS

Parkman, Francis. Discovery of the Great West: La Salle; ed. by William R. Taylor. Rinehart 1956
SCPL

Parkman, Francis. La Salle and the Discovery of the Great West. Signet 1963
IndS(10-12)

Syme, Ronald. La Salle of the Mississippi. Morrow 1953
BBEL—CC(6-9)—ESLC—JH—SCHS

COLLECTIONS

Bakeless, Katherine L. and Bakeless, John Edwin. They Saw America First: Our First Explorers and What They Saw. Lippincott 1957
CC(7-9)—ESLC—SCPL

Rich, Louise Dickinson. The First Book of New World Explorers. Watts 1960
CC(4-6)—ESLC

Jacques Marquette, 1637-1675

Kjelgaard, Jim. Explorations of Père Marquette. Random House 1951
CC(6-8)—ESLC—JH—SCHS

Pierre Esprit Radisson, 1632-1710

Ridle, Julia Brown. Mohawk Gamble. Harper 1963
BY

Syme, Ronald. Bay of the North: The Story of Pierre Radisson. Morrow 1950
CC

COLLECTIONS

American Heritage. Trappers and Mountain Men, by Evan Jones. Am. Heritage 1961
AB—CC(6-9)—ESLC—YR

Bakeless, Katherine L. and Bakeless, John Edwin. They Saw America First: Our First Explorers and What They Saw. Lippincott 1957
CC(7-9)—ESLC—SCPL

French—19th century

Pierre Paul François Camille Savorgnan de Brazza, 1852-1905

Carbonnier, Jeanne. Congo Explorer: Pierre Savorgnan de Brazza, 1852-1905. Scribner 1960
Bkl C(5-8)

French—20th century

Jacques Yves Cousteau, 1910-

Dugan, James. Undersea Explorer: The Story of Captain Cousteau. Harper 1957
BBHS—BBJH—CC(7-9)—ESLC—JH—SCHS

Maurice Herzog, 1919-

COLLECTIONS

Hoff, Rhoda and De Terra, Helmut. They Explored! Walck 1959
AB(5)

German—19th century

Heinrich Barth, 1821-1865

Seufert, Karl Rolf. Caravan in Peril; tr. from the German by Stella Humphries. Pantheon 1963
Bkl C&Y

EXPLORERS

German—19th century—*Continued*

Alexander, Freiherr von Humboldt, 1769-1859

COLLECTIONS

Hoff, Rhoda and De Terra, Helmut. They Explored! Walck 1959
AB(5)

Irish—20th century

Sir Ernest Henry Shackleton, 1874-1922

Bixby, William. The Impossible Journey of Sir Ernest Shackleton. Little 1960
Bkl C(5-8)—CC(5-8)—ESLC—SCHS
Fisher, Margery (Turner) and Fisher, James. Shackleton and the Antarctic. Houghton 1958
SCPL
Lansing, Alfred. Endurance: Shackleton's Incredible Voyage. McGraw 1959
BBHS—SCHS—SCPL
Lansing, Alfred. Shackleton's Valiant Voyage. McGraw 1960
Bkl C(6-9)—JH—SCHS

Italian—13th century

Marco Polo, 1254?-1324?

Buehr, Walter. The World of Marco Polo. Putnam 1961
Bkl C(4-6)
Graves, Charles P. Marco Polo. Garrard 1963
AB(3-7)—ESLC
Hart, H. H. Venetian Adventurer: Being an Account of the Life and Times and of the Book of Messer Marco Polo. Stanford Univ. 1947
SCPL
Horizon Magazine. Marco Polo's Adventures in China, by Milton Rugoff. Am. Heritage 1964
Bkl C(5-9)&Y—CC—ESLC—JH—SCHS—YR
Kent, Louise (Andrews). He Went with Marco Polo: A Story of Venice and Cathay. Houghton 1935 (Fiction)
BBEL—BBJH—CC(7-9)—ESLC—JH—SCHS—YR
Komroff, Manuel. Marco Polo. Messner 1952
BBJH—BY—CC—JH—SCHS
Polo, Marco. The Travels of Marco Polo. Liveright, Modern Lib., Crown, etc.
CA—GR—SCHS—SCPL
Shor, Jean (Bowie). After You, Marco Polo. McGraw 1955
BBHS—SCHS—SCPL
Walsh, Richard J. Adventures and Discoveries of Marco Polo. Random House 1953
CC(5-7)—ESLC

COLLECTIONS

Clark, William R. Explorers of the World. Natural Hist. Press 1964
CC—ESLC
Duvoisin, Roger. They Put Out to Sea: The Story of the Map. Knopf 1943
CC(5-7)—ESLC
Lucas, Mary Seymour. Vast Horizons. Viking 1943
SCHS

Italian—15th century

John Cabot, 1450-1498

COLLECTIONS

Sutton, Felix. Discoverers of America: Primitive Man to Spanish Conquerors. Grosset 1965
ESLC

Christopher Columbus, 1451?-1506

Aulaire, Ingri d' and Aulaire, Edgar Parin d'. Columbus. Doubleday 1955
BBEL—CC(3-5)—ESLC
Belfrage, Cedric. My Master, Columbus. Doubleday 1961 (Fiction)
Bkl A
Colón, Fernando. The Quest of Columbus; ed. by Robert Meredith and E. Brooks Smith. Little 1966
Bkl C(6-9)&Y—ESLC
Dalgliesh, Alice. The Columbus Story. Scribner 1955
AB(1-4)—BBEL(1-4)—CC(3-5)—ESLC
Hodges, C. Walter. Columbus Sails. Coward-McCann 1950
BY—CC(7-9)—SCHS
Judson, Clara (Ingram). Christopher Columbus. Follett 1960
CC(2-4)
Kent, Louise (Andrews). He Went with Christopher Columbus. Houghton 1940 (Fiction)
BBJH—CC(7-9)—JH—SCHS
Lawson, Robert. I Discover Columbus. Little 1941 (Fiction)
BBJH
McGovern, Ann. The Story of Christopher Columbus. Random House 1963
IndJ(2-4)
Madariaga, Salvador de. Christopher Columbus: Being the Life of the Very Magnificent Lord, Don Cristobal Colón. Macmillan 1949
SCPL
Marx, Robert F. Following Columbus: The Voyage of the Niña II. World 1964
CC(5-7)—ESLC—IndS(9-10)
Morison, Samuel Eliot. Admiral of the Ocean Sea: A Life of Christopher Columbus. 2v. Little 1942
BY—CA—GR—SCPL

EXPLORERS

Italian—15th century

Christopher Columbus—Continued

Morison, Samuel Eliot and Obregón, Mauricio. The Caribbean as Columbus Saw It. Little 1964
Bkl A

Morison, Samuel Eliot. Christopher Columbus, Mariner. Little 1955
BBHS—BY—SCHS—SCPL—3000

Showers, Paul. Columbus Day. Crowell 1965
ESLC

Smith, Bradley. Columbus in the New World. Doubleday 1962
Bkl A

Sperry, Armstrong. The Voyages of Christopher Columbus. Random House 1950
BBEL(6-8)—BBJH—CC(5-7)—ESLC—JH—SCHS

Syme, Ronald. Columbus, Finder of the New World. Morrow 1952
BBEL(4-6)—CC(4-6)—ESLC

COLLECTIONS

Rich, Louise Dickinson. The First Book of New World Explorers. Watts 1960
CC(4-6)—ESLC

Sutton, Felix. Discoverers of America: Primitive Man to Spanish Conquerors. Grosset 1965
ESLC

Amerigo Vespucci, 1451-1512

Arciniegas, Germán. Amerigo and the New World: The Life & Times of Amerigo Vespucci; tr. by Harriet De Onís. Knopf 1955
CA—SCPL

Baker, Nina (Brown). Amerigo Vespucci. Knopf 1956
BBEL(5-8)—CC(5-8)—ESLC—JH

Italian—16th century

Amerigo Vespucci, 1451-1512

Arciniegas, Germán. Amerigo and the New World: The Life & Times of Amerigo Vespucci; tr. by Harriet De Onís. Knopf 1955
CA—SCPL

Baker, Nina (Brown). Amerigo Vespucci. Knopf 1956
BBEL(5-8)—CC(5-8)—ESLC—JH

Norwegian—10th century

Bjarni, ?

COLLECTIONS

Rich, Louise Dickinson. The First Book of New World Explorers. Watts 1960
CC(4-6)—ESLC

Norwegian—11th century

Leif Ericson, fl. 1000

Aulaire, Ingri d' and Aulaire, Edgar Parin d'. Leif the Lucky. Doubleday 1951
BBEL—CC(3-5)—ESLC

Berry, Erik. Leif the Lucky. Garrard 1961
AB(4-6)—ESLC

Janeway, Elizabeth. The Vikings. Random House 1951
CC(5-7)—JH—SCHS

Johansen, Margaret Alison. Voyagers West. Washburn 1959
ESLC

Marshall, Edison. West with the Vikings. Doubleday 1961 (Fiction)
Bkl A

Shippen, Katherine Binney. Leif Eriksson: First Voyager to America. Harper 1951
BBEL(6-8)—BBJH—BY—CC(6-9)—ESLC—JH—SCHS

Weir, Ruth Cromer. Leif Ericsson, Explorer. Abingdon 1951
CC(3-5)

Norwegian—19th century

Fridtjof Nansen, 1861-1930

Hall, Anna Gertrude. Nansen. Viking 1940
CC(7-9)—JH—SCHS

Noel-Baker, Francis. Fridtjof Nansen, Arctic Explorer. Putnam 1958
AB(4up)

Reynolds, Ernest E. Nansen. Penguin 1932
GR

Norwegian—20th century

Roald Engelbregt Gravning Amundsen, 1872-1928

Kugelmass, J. Alvin. Roald Amundsen: A Saga of the Polar Seas. Messner 1955
SCHS

Vaeth, J. Gordon. To the Ends of the Earth. Harper 1962
Bkl C(7-9)—BY—ESLC

Fridtjof Nansen, 1861-1930

Hall, Anna Gertrude. Nansen. Viking 1940
CC(7-9)—JH—SCHS

Noel-Baker, Francis. Fridtjof Nansen, Arctic Explorer. Putnam 1958
AB(4up)

Reynolds, Ernest E. Nansen. Penguin 1932
GR

EXPLORERS—*Continued*

Portuguese

COLLECTIONS

Buehr, Walter. The Portuguese Explorers. Putnam 1966
  Bkl C(4-6)

Portuguese—15th century

Vasco da Gama, 1469?-1525

Hewes, Agnes Danforth. Spice and the Devil's Cave. Knopf 1930 (Fiction)
  CC(7-9)—JH
Kent, Louise (Andrews). He Went with Vasco da Gama. Houghton 1938 (Fiction)
  CC(7-9)—ESLC—JH—SCHS
Sanderlin, George William. Eastward to India: Vasco da Gama's Voyage. Harper 1965
  Bkl C(6-9)&Y—ESLC
Syme, Ronald. Vasco da Gama: Sailor Toward the Sunrise. Morrow 1959
  CC(4-7)—ESLC

COLLECTIONS

Clark, William R. Explorers of the World. Natural Hist. Press 1964
  CC—ESLC

Portuguese—16th century

Vasco da Gama, 1469?-1525

Hewes, Agnes Danforth. Spice and the Devil's Cave. Knopf 1930 (Fiction)
  CC(7-9)—JH
Kent, Louise (Andrews). He Went with Vasco da Gama. Houghton 1938 (Fiction)
  CC(7-9)—ESLC—JH—SCHS
Syme, Ronald. Vasco da Gama: Sailor Toward the Sunrise. Morrow 1959
  CC(4-7)—ESLC

COLLECTIONS

Clark, William R. Explorers of the World. Natural Hist. Press 1964
  CC—ESLC

Ferdinand Magellan, 1480?-1521

Daniel, Hawthorne. Ferdinand Magellan. Doubleday 1964
  Bkl A&Y
Engle, Eloise. Sea Challenge—The Epic Voyage of Magellan: A Novel. Hammond 1962 (Fiction)
  Bkl C(6-8)
Finger, Charles. Courageous Companions. Longmans 1929 (Fiction)
  SCHS
Kent, Louise (Andrews). He Went with Magellan. Houghton 1943 (Fiction)
  ESLC—JH—SCHS

Lomask, Milton. Ship's Boy with Magellan. Doubleday 1960 (Fiction)
  AB(4-7)
Parr, Charles McKew. So Noble a Captain: The Life and Times of Ferdinand Magellan. Crowell 1953
  SCPL
Pond, S. G. Ferdinand Magellan, Master Mariner. Random House 1957
  BBEL—ESLC
Sanderlin, George. First Around the World: A Journal of Magellan's Voyage. Harper 1964
  Bkl C(7-9)&Y—ESLC
Syme, Ronald. Magellan: First Around the World. Morrow 1953
  BBEL(4-6)—CC(4-6)—ESLC
Welch, Ronald. Ferdinand Magellan. Criterion Bks 1956
  JH—YR
Wilkie, Katherine. Ferdinand Magellan: Noble Captain. Houghton 1963
  AB(5-9)—IndJ(4-6)

COLLECTIONS

Blacker, Irwin R. The Bold Conquistadores. Bobbs 1961
  Bkl C(7-9)&Y
Clark, William R. Explorers of the World. Natural Hist. Press 1964
  CC—ESLC
Duvoisin, Roger. They Put Out to Sea: The Story of the Map. Knopf 1943
  CC(5-7)—ESLC
Rich, Louise Dickinson. The First Book of New World Explorers. Watts 1960
  CC(4-6)—ESLC

Scottish—18th century

Alexander Mackenzie, 1763-1820

Syme, Ronald. Alexander Mackenzie, Canadian Explorer. Morrow 1964
  AB(5-9)—Bkl C(4-6)—CC(3-6)—ESLC
Vail, Philip. The Magnificent Adventures of Alexander Mackenzie. Dodd 1964
  Bkl A&Y—IndS(9-11)

Scottish—19th century

David Livingstone, 1813-1873

Eaton, Jeanette. David Livingstone, Foe of Darkness. Morrow 1947
  BBJH—CC(7-9)—ESLC—JH—SCHS
Seaver, George. David Livingstone: His Life and Letters. Harper 1957
  SCPL

COLLECTIONS

Clark, William R. Explorers of the World. Natural Hist. Press 1964
  CC—ESLC
Hoff, Rhoda and De Terra, Helmut. They Explored! Walck 1959
  AB(5)

EXPLORERS—*Continued*

Spanish

COLLECTIONS

Blacker, Irwin R. The Bold Conquistadores. Bobbs 1961
Bkl C(7-9)&Y
Vasco Núñez de Balboa; Álvar Núñez Cabeza de Vaca; Francisco Vásquez de Coronado; Hernando Cortés; Ferdinand Magellan; Francisco Pizarro; Hernando de Soto

Buehr, Walter. The Spanish Conquistadores in North America. Putnam 1962
CC(4-6)—ESLC
Hernando Cortés and others

Spanish—16th century

Vasco Núñez de Balboa, 1475-1517

Mirsky, Jeannette. Balboa: Discoverer of the Pacific; ed. by Walter Lord. Harper 1964
Bkl C(5-8)—ESLC

Riesenberg, Felix. Balboa: Swordsman and Conquistador. Random House 1956
JH—SCHS

Sterne, Emma (Gelders). Vasco Nunez de Balboa. Knopf 1961
Bkl C(5-7)—ESLC

Syme, Ronald. Balboa: Finder of the Pacific. Morrow 1956
BBEL(5-7)—CC(4-6)—ESLC

COLLECTIONS

Blacker, Irwin R. The Bold Conquistadores. Bobbs 1961
Bkl C(7-9)&Y

Álvar Núñez Cabeza de Vaca, 1490?-1557?

Baker, Betty. Walk the World's Rim. Harper 1965 (Fiction)
CC(5-7)—ESLC

Cabeza de Vaca, Álvar Núñez. The Journey of [the author]; tr. from His Own Narrative by Fanny Bandelier. Rio Grande 1964
Bkl A

Syme, Ronald. First Man to Cross America: The Story of Cabeza de Vaca. Morrow 1961
Bkl C(5-8)

Terrell, John Upton. Journey into Darkness. Morrow 1962
Bkl A

Wojciechowska, Maia. Odyssey of Courage: The Story of Álvar Núñez Cabeza de Vaca. Atheneum 1965
AB(5-9)—Bkl C(7-9)&Y—ESLC—IndJ(6-9)

COLLECTIONS

Blacker, Irwin R. The Bold Conquistadores. Bobbs 1961
Bkl C(7-9)&Y

Francisco Vásquez de Coronado, 1510-1554

Campbell, Camilla. Coronado and His Captains. Follett 1958
BBJH

Meredith, Robert K. and Smith, Edric Brooks, eds. Riding with Coronado: From Pedro de Casteñeda's Eyewitness Account of the Exploration of the Southwest. Little 1964
Bkl C(6-9)—ESLC

Syme, Ronald. Francisco Coronado and the Seven Cities of Gold. Morrow 1965
ESLC—IndJ(4-6)

Winship, George Parker, ed. The Coronado Expedition, 1540-1542. Rio Grande 1964
Bkl A

COLLECTIONS

Bakeless, Katherine L. and Bakeless, John Edwin. They Saw America First: Our First Explorers and What They Saw. Lippincott 1957
CC(7-9)—ESLC—SCPL

Blacker, Irwin R. The Bold Conquistadores. Bobbs 1961
Bkl C(7-9)&Y

Hernando Cortés, 1485-1547

Gómara, Francisco López de. Cortés: The Life of the Conqueror by His Secretary; tr. and ed. by Lesley Byrd Simpson. Univ. of Calif. 1964
Bkl A

Haller, Adolf. He Served Two Masters: The Story of the Conquest of Mexico; tr. from the German by Clara and Richard Winston. Pantheon 1962
Bkl C(7-9)&Y

Horizon Magazine. Cortés and the Aztec Conquest, by Irwin R. Blacker. Am. Heritage 1965
Bkl C(6-9)&Y—ESLC—JH

Johnson, William. Captain Cortés Conquers Mexico. Random House 1960
JH—SCHS

Madariaga, Salvador de. Hernan Cortés: Conqueror of Mexico. Regnery 1955
SCPL

Nevins, Albert J. The Young Conquistador. Dodd 1960 (Fiction)
SCHS

Syme, Ronald. Cortés of Mexico. Morrow 1951
CC(6-9)—ESLC—SCHS

COLLECTIONS

Blacker, Irwin R. The Bold Conquistadores. Bobbs 1961
Bkl C(7-9)&Y

Buehr, Walter. The Spanish Conquistadores in North America. Putnam 1962
CC(4-6)—ESLC

EXPLORERS

Spanish—16th century—*Continued*

Martín López, 1487?-1577
Norman, James. The Navy That Crossed Mountains. Putnam 1963
ESLC

Francisco de Orellana, 1500-1549
Syme, Ronald. Man Who Discovered the Amazon. Morrow 1958
BBJH

Francisco, Marqués Pizarro, 1478?-1541
Duvoisin, Roger A. The Four Corners of the World. Knopf 1948
CC(4-6)
Shaffer, Peter. The Royal Hunt of the Sun: A Play Concerning the Conquest of Peru. Stein & Day 1965 (Play)
Bkl A
Syme, Ronald. Francisco Pizarro: Finder of Peru. Morrow 1963
AB(4-7)—Bkl C(5-7)—CC(4-7)—ESLC
COLLECTIONS
Blacker, Irwin R. The Bold Conquistadores. Bobbs 1961
Bkl C(7-9)&Y
Rich, Louise Dickinson. The First Book of New World Explorers. Watts 1960
CC(4-6)—ESLC

Juan Ponce de León, 1460?-1521
Baker, Nina (Brown). Juan Ponce de León. Knopf 1957
BBEL(5-8)—CC(5-7)—ESLC
Blassingame, Wyatt. Ponce de León. Garrard 1965
ESLC

Hernando de Soto, 1500?-1542
Montgomery, Elizabeth Rider. Hernando De Soto. Garrard 1964
ESLC
Syme, Ronald. De Soto, Finder of the Mississippi. Morrow 1957
BBEL(4-6)—CC(3-5)—ESLC
COLLECTIONS
Bakeless, Katherine L. and Bakeless, John Edwin. They Saw America First: Our First Explorers and What They Saw. Lippincott 1957
CC(7-9)—ESLC—SCPL
Blacker, Irwin R. The Bold Conquistadores. Bobbs 1961
Bkl C(7-9)&Y

Swedish—19th century

Sven Anders Hedin, 1865-1952
COLLECTIONS
Hoff, Rhoda and De Terra, Helmut. They Explored! Walck 1959
AB(5)

Swedish—20th century

Sven Anders Hedin, 1865-1952
COLLECTIONS
Hoff, Rhoda and De Terra, Helmut. They Explored! Walck 1959
AB(5)

Welsh—19th century

Sir Henry Morton Stanley, 1841-1904
Anstruther, Ian. Dr. Livingstone, I Presume? Dutton 1957
SCPL
Benét, Laura. Stanley, Invincible Explorer. Dodd 1955
BY—SCHS
Busoni, Rafaello. Stanley's Africa. Viking 1944
BBJH—CC(7-9)—SCHS
Farwell, Byron. Man Who Presumed: A Biography of Henry M. Stanley. Holt 1957
SCPL
Hall-Quest, Olga (Wilbourne). With Stanley in Africa. Dutton 1961
Bkl C(6-9)—CC—ESLC—JH—SCHS
Stanley, Sir Henry Morton. The Exploration Diaries; ed. by Richard Stanley and Alan Neame. Vanguard 1962
Bkl A
Sterling, Thomas L. Stanley's Way: A Sentimental Journey Through Central Africa. Atheneum 1960
Bkl A
COLLECTIONS
Clark, William R. Explorers of the World. Natural Hist. Press 1964
CC—ESLC

FBI AGENTS
See Detectives

FARMERS
See also Soil Scientists

American—20th century

Betty (Bard) MacDonald, 1908-1958
MacDonald, Betty (Bard). The Egg and I. Lippincott 1946
SCPL

William A. Owens, 1905-
Owens, William A. This Stubborn Soil. Scribner 1966
Bkl A&Y

FARMERS—*Continued*

Canadian—19th century

Angus MacKay, 1841-1931

COLLECTIONS

De Kruif, Paul Henry. Hunger Fighters.
    Harcourt 1928
    BBHS–SCHS–SCPL–3000

Canadian—20th century

Angus MacKay, 1841-1931

COLLECTIONS

De Kruif, Paul Henry. Hunger Fighters.
    Harcourt 1928
    BBHS–SCHS–SCPL–3000

French—20th century

Dominique Laxalt, ?

Laxalt, Robert. Sweet Promised Land.
    Harper 1957
    SCHS–SCPL

FASHION DESIGNERS

See Costume Designers

FEMINISTS

American—19th century

Susan Brownell Anthony, 1820-1906

Bryan, Florence Horn. Susan B. Anthony:
    Champion of Women's Rights. Messner
    1947
    BY

Lutz, Alma. Susan B. Anthony: Rebel,
    Crusader, Humanitarian. Beacon Press
    1959
    SCPL

COLLECTIONS

Daugherty, Sonia. Ten Brave Women.
    Lippincott 1953
    BY–CC(7-9)–ESLC–JH–SCHS

Nathan, Dorothy. Women of Courage.
    Random House 1964
    CC(4-6)–ESLC–JH

Vance, Marguerite. The Lamp Lighters:
    Women in the Hall of Fame. Dutton
    1960
    Bkl C(7-9)&Y–SCHS–YR

Abigail Jane (Scott) Duniway, 1834-1915

COLLECTIONS

Ross, Nancy Wilson. Heroines of the
    Early West. Random House 1960
    Bkl C(5-9)–BY–CC(5-7)–ESLC–JH

Belva Ann (Bennett) Lockwood, 1830-1917

COLLECTIONS

Boynick, David. Pioneers in Petticoats.
    Crowell 1959
    YR

Lucretia (Coffin) Mott, 1793-1880

Sterling, Dorothy. Lucretia Mott: Gentle
    Warrior. Doubleday 1964
    Bkl C(7-9)&Y–CC–ESLC–JH

Elizabeth (Cady) Stanton, 1815-1902

COLLECTIONS

Buckmaster, Henrietta. Women Who
    Shaped History. Collier Bks 1966
    Bkl C(7-10)&Y

McNeer, May Yonge and Ward, Lynd
    Kendall. Give Me Freedom. Abingdon
    1964
    Bkl C(5-8)–CC(5-7)–ESLC–JH–YR

Lucy Stone, 1818-1893

Hays, Elinor (Rice). Morning Star: A
    Biography of Lucy Stone, 1818-1893.
    Harcourt 1961
    Bkl A&Y–BY

American—20th century

Mary (Church) Terrell, 1863-1954

COLLECTIONS

Sterling, Dorothy and Quarles, Benjamin.
    Lift Every Voice. Doubleday 1965
    Bkl C(6-9)&Y–ESLC

FICTION WRITERS

See Novelists

FIELD MARSHALS

See Soldiers

FINANCIERS

COLLECTIONS

Wechsberg, Joseph. The Merchant Bank-
    ers. Little 1966
    Bkl A

American

COLLECTIONS

Holbrook, Stewart Hall. Age of the Mo-
    guls. Doubleday 1953
    BBHS–SCHS–SCPL

Josephson, Matthew. Robber Barons: The
    Great American Capitalists, 1861-1901.
    Harcourt 1934
    SCPL
    Andrew Carnegie; Henry Clay Frick; Jay
    Gould; Edward Henry Harriman; James
    Jerome Hill; Collis Potter Huntington; John
    Pierpont Morgan; John Davison Rockefeller;
    Cornelius Vanderbilt; and others

FINANCIERS

American—*Continued*

Myers, Gustavus. History of the Great American Fortunes. Modern Lib. 1936
SCPL
John Jacob Astor; Jay Gould; John Pierpont Morgan; Andrew William Mellon; John Davison Rockefeller; Russell Sage; Cornelius Vanderbilt; and others

Tebbel, John William. The Inheritors: A Study of America's Great Fortunes and What Happened to Them. Putnam 1962
Bkl A

American—18th century

Haym Salomon, 1740?-1785

Fast, Howard. Haym Salomon, Son of Liberty. Messner 1941
BBHS—CC(7-9)—JH—SCHS

American—19th century

John Jacob Astor, 1763-1848

Daugherty, James. Trappers and Traders of the Far West. Random House 1952
CC(6-9)—JH—SCHS

Kavaler, Lucy. The Astors: A Family Chronicle of Pomp and Power. Dodd 1966
Bkl A

Terrell, John Upton. Furs by Astor. Morrow 1963
Bk A&Y

COLLECTIONS

Cunz, Dieter. They Came from Germany: The Story of Famous German-Americans. Dodd 1966
ESLC

Myers, Gustavus. History of the Great American Fortunes. Modern Lib. 1936
SCPL

William Andrews Clark, 1839-1925

COLLECTIONS

Place, Marian T. The Copper Kings of Montana. Random House 1961
ESLC—JH—SCHS—YR

Cyrus West Field, 1819-1892

Latham, Jean Lee. Young Man in a Hurry: The Story of Cyrus W. Field. Harper 1958
AB(4-7)—BBEL(6-8)—CC(6-9)—ESLC—JH —YR

Nathan, Adele Gutman. The First Transatlantic Cable. Random House 1959
ESLC—JH

Albert Gallatin, 1761-1849

Walters, Raymond. Albert Gallatin: Jeffersonian Financier and Diplomat. Macmillan 1957
SCPL

Jay Gould, 1836-1892

O'Connor, Richard. Gould's Millions. Doubleday 1962
Bkl A

COLLECTIONS

Josephson, Matthew. Robber Barons: The Great American Capitalists, 1861-1901. Harcourt 1934
SCPL

Myers, Gustavus. History of the Great American Fortunes. Modern Lib. 1936
SCPL

Hetty Howland (Robinson) Green, 1834-1916

Lewis, Arthur H. The Day They Shook the Plum Tree. Harcourt 1963
Bkl A—SCPL

Daniel Guggenheim, 1856-1930

Lomask, Milton. Seed Money: The Guggenheim Story. Farrar 1964
Bkl A

Meyer Guggenheim, 1828-1905

COLLECTIONS

American Heritage. Captains of Industry, by Bernard A. Weisberger. Harper 1966
Bkl C(7-10)&Y—ESLC

Edward Henry Harriman, 1848-1909

COLLECTIONS

Josephson Matthew. Robber Barons: The Great American Capitalists, 1861-1901. Harcourt 1934
SCPL

James Jerome Hill, 1838-1916

COLLECTIONS

Josephson Matthew. Robber Barons: The Great American Capitalists, 1861-1901. Harcourt 1934
SCPL

Collis Potter Huntington, 1821-1900

COLLECTIONS

Josephson Matthew. Robber Barons: The Great American Capitalists, 1861-1901. Harcourt 1934
SCPL

John Pierpont Morgan, 1837-1913

COLLECTIONS

Fanning, Leonard M. Titans of Business. Lippincott 1964
Bkl C(7-9)&Y—JH—SCHS

Josephson, Matthew. Robber Barons: The Great American Capitalists, 1861-1901. Harcourt 1934
SCPL

FINANCIERS

American—19th century

John Pierpont Morgan—Continued

Myers, Gustavus. History of the Great American Fortunes. Modern Lib. 1936
SCPL

Saarinen, Aline B. The Proud Possessors: The Lives, Times, and Tastes of Some Adventurous American Art Collectors. Random House 1958
SCPL

Russell Sage, 1816-1906

COLLECTIONS

Myers, Gustavus. History of the Great American Fortunes. Modern Lib. 1936
SCPL

Cornelius Vanderbilt, 1794-1877

Hoyt, Edwin Palmer. The Vanderbilts and Their Fortunes. Doubleday 1962
Bkl A

COLLECTIONS

American Heritage. Captains of Industry, by Bernard A. Weisberger. Harper 1966
Bkl C(7-10)&Y—ESLC

Josephson, Matthew. Robber Barons: The Great American Capitalists, 1861-1901. Harcourt 1934
SCPL

Myers, Gustavus. History of the Great American Fortunes. Modern Lib. 1936
SCPL

American—20th century

William Andrews Clark, 1839-1925

COLLECTIONS

Place, Marian T. The Copper Kings of Montana. Random House 1961
ESLC—JH—SCHS—YR

Anthony De Angelis, 1915-

Miller, Norman C. The Great Salad Oil Swindle. Coward-McCann 1965
Bkl A

Cyrus Stephen Eaton, 1883-

Gleisser, Marcus. The World of Cyrus Eaton. Barnes 1965
Bkl A

Hetty Howland (Robinson) Green, 1834-1916

Lewis, Arthur H. The Day They Shook the Plum Tree. Harcourt 1963
Bkl A—SCPL

Daniel Guggenheim, 1856-1930

Lomask, Milton. Seed Money: The Guggenheim Story. Farrar 1964
Bkl A

Samuel Insull, 1859-1938

McDonald, Forrest. Insull. Univ. of Chicago 1962
Bkl A

Jesse Holman Jones, 1874-1956

Jones, Jesse Holman and Angly, Edward. Fifty Billion Dollars: My Thirteen Years with RFC (1932-1945). Macmillan 1951
SCPL

Otto Hermann Kahn, 1867-1934

Matz, Mary Jane. The Many Lives of Otto Kahn. Macmillan 1964
Bkl A—IndS(11-12)

Herbert Henry Lehman, 1878-1963

Nevins, Allan. Herbert H. Lehman and His Era. Scribner 1963
Bkl A—IndS(10-12)

Andrew William Mellon, 1855-1937

COLLECTIONS

Myers, Gustavus. History of the Great American Fortunes. Modern Lib. 1936
SCPL

James Paul Warburg, 1896-

Warburg, James Paul. The Long Road Home: The Autobiography of a Maverick. Doubleday 1964
Bkl A

English—19th century

Marcus Samuel, 1st Viscount Bearsted, 1853-1927

Henriques, Robert David Quixano. Bearsted: A Biography of Marcus Samuel, First Viscount Bearsted, and Founder of "Shell" Transport and Trading Company. Viking 1960
Bkl A

Cecil John Rhodes, 1853-1902

Gibbs, Peter. The True Story of Cecil Rhodes in Africa. Childrens Press 1964
ESLC

Lockhart, John Gilbert and Woodhouse, Christopher Montague. Cecil Rhodes: The Colossus of Southern Africa. Macmillan 1963
Bkl A—SCPL

Maurois, André. Cecil Rhodes. Collins 1953
SCPL

FINANCIERS—*Continued*

English—20th century

Marcus Samuel, 1st Viscount Bearsted, 1853-1927

Henriques, Robert David Quixano. Bearsted: A Biography of Marcus Samuel, First Viscount Bearsted, and Founder of "Shell" Transport and Trading Company. Viking 1960
Bkl A

German—19th century

Meyer Amschel Rothschild, 1743-1812

Morton, Frederic. The Rothschilds: A Family Portrait. Atheneum 1962
Bkl A—BY—GR—SCHS—SCPL

Iranian—20th century

Nubar Sarkis Gulbenkian, 1896-

Gulbenkian, Nubar Sarkis. Portrait in Oil: The Autobiography of Nubar Gulbenkian. Simon & Schuster 1965
Bkl A

Swedish—20th century

Ivar Kreuger, 1880-1932

Shaplen, Robert. Kreuger: Genius and Swindler. Knopf 1960
Bkl A

FOLKLORISTS

American—19th century

Joel Chandler Harris, 1848-1908

Brookes, Stella (Brewer). Joel Chandler Harris, Folklorist. Univ. of Ga. 1950
SCPL
Harlow, Alvin F. Joel Chandler Harris (Uncle Remus) Plantation Storyteller. Messner 1941
SCHS—YR

American—20th century

John Avery Lomax, 1867-1948

Lomax, John Avery. Adventures of a Ballad Hunter. Macmillan 1947
SCPL

Jean Ritchie, 1922-

Ritchie, Jean. Singing Family of the Cumberlands. Oxford 1955
SCPL

FOOTBALL COACHES

See Football Players

FOOTBALL PLAYERS

American

COLLECTIONS

Anderson, Dave. Great Quarterbacks of the NFL. Random House 1965
Bkl C(5-9)&Y
Samuel Adrian Baugh; Otto Everett Graham; Charles Johnson; Sidney Luckman; Frank Beall Ryan; Bart Starr; Francis Asbury Tarkenton; Yelberton Abraham Tittle; John Unitas; Norman Mack Van Brocklin
Daley, Arthur. Pro Football's Hall of Fame: The Official Book. Quadrangle 1963
Bkl A&Y
Hand, Jack J. Heroes of the NFL. Random House 1965
Bkl C(5-9)&Y
Raymond Berry; Frank Gifford; Louis Groza; Elroy Hirsch; Edward Wayne Le Baron; Thomas McDonald; Leonard Moore; Allie Sherman; Emlen Tunnell; William Barry Wood
Riper, Guernsey Van. Yea, Coach! Three Great Football Coaches. Garrard 1966
ESLC
John William Heisman; Knute Kenneth Rockne; Glenn Scobey ("Pop") Warner
Weyand, Alexander M. Football Immortals. Macmillan 1962
Bkl A&Y

American—20th century

Samuel Adrian Baugh, 1914-

COLLECTIONS

Anderson, Dave. Great Quarterbacks of the NFL. Random House 1965
Bkl C(5-9)&Y

Raymond Berry, 1933-

COLLECTIONS

Hand, Jack J. Heroes of the NFL. Random House 1965
Bkl C(5-9)&Y

Jimmy Brown, 1936-

Brown, Jimmy and Cope, Myron. Off My Chest. Doubleday 1964
Bkl A&Y

Terzian, James P. and Benagh, Jim. The Jimmy Brown Story. Messner 1964
ESLC—IndJ(6-9)

COLLECTIONS

Bontemps, Arna. Famous Negro Athletes. Dodd 1964
Bkl C&Y—ESLC—JH

Frank Gifford, 1930-

COLLECTIONS

Hand, Jack J. Heroes of the NFL. Random House 1965
Bkl C(5-9)&Y

FOOTBALL PLAYERS

American—20th century

Otto Everett Graham, 1921-

COLLECTIONS

Anderson, Dave. Great Quarterbacks of the NFL. Random House 1965
Bkl C(5-9)&Y

Louis Groza, 1924?-

COLLECTIONS

Hand, Jack J. Heroes of the NFL. Random House 1965
Bkl C(5-9)&Y

John Hackett, 1930-

COLLECTIONS

Boynick, David King. Champions by Setback: Athletes Who Overcame Physical Handicaps. Crowell 1954
SCHS

John William Heisman, 1869-1936

COLLECTIONS

Riper, Guernsey Van. Yea, Coach! Three Great Football Coaches. Garrard 1966
ESLC

Elroy Hirsch, 1924?-

COLLECTIONS

Hand, Jack J. Heroes of the NFL. Random House 1965
Bkl C(5-9)&Y

Charles Johnson, 1938-

COLLECTIONS

Anderson, Dave. Great Quarterbacks of the NFL. Random House 1965
Bkl C(5-9)&Y

Edward Wayne LeBaron, 1930?-

COLLECTIONS

Hand, Jack J. Heroes of the NFL. Random House 1965
Bkl C(5-9)&Y

Sidney Luckman, 1916-

COLLECTIONS

Anderson, Dave. Great Quarterbacks of the NFL. Random House 1965
Bkl C(5-9)&Y

Thomas McDonald, ?

COLLECTIONS

Hand, Jack J. Heroes of the NFL. Random House 1965
Bkl C(5-9)&Y

Leonard Moore, ?

COLLECTIONS

Hand, Jack J. Heroes of the NFL. Random House 1965
Bkl C(5-9)&Y

Knute Kenneth Rockne, 1888-1931

Lovelace, Delos W. Rockne of Notre Dame. Putnam 1931
BBJH—JH—SCHS

Riper, Guernsey Van. Knute Rockne: Young Athlete. Bobbs 1947
BBEL(4-6)

COLLECTIONS

Gallico, Paul. The Golden People. Doubleday 1965
Bkl A&Y

Riper, Guernsey Van. Yea, Coach! Three Great Football Coaches. Garrard 1966
ESLC

Frank Beall Ryan, 1936?-

COLLECTIONS

Anderson, Dave. Great Quarterbacks of the NFL. Random House 1965
Bkl C(5-9)&Y

Allie Sherman, 1923?-

COLLECTIONS

Hand, Jack J. Heroes of the NFL. Random House 1965
Bkl C(5-9)&Y

Bart Starr, 1934-

COLLECTIONS

Anderson, Dave. Great Quarterbacks of the NFL. Random House 1965
Bkl C(5-9)&Y

Harry Augustus Stuhldreher, 1901-1965

Stuhldreher, Mary A. Many a Saturday Afternoon. McKay 1964
Bkl A&Y

Francis Asbury Tarkenton, 1940-

COLLECTIONS

Anderson, Dave. Great Quarterbacks of the NFL. Random House 1965
Bkl C(5-9)&Y

Yelberton Abraham Tittle, 1926-

Tittle, Yelberton Abraham. I Pass: My Story as Told to Don Smith. Watts 1964
Bkl A&Y—JH

COLLECTIONS

Anderson, Dave. Great Quarterbacks of the NFL. Random House 1965
Bkl C(5-9)&Y

Emlen Tunnell, 1926?-

Tunnell, Emlen and Gleason, William. Footsteps of a Giant. Doubleday 1966
Bkl A&Y

COLLECTIONS

Hand, Jack J. Heroes of the NFL. Random House 1965
Bkl C(5-9)&Y

FOOTBALL PLAYERS

American—20th century

John Unitas, 1933-

Greene, Lee. The Johnny Unitas Story. Putnam 1962
Bkl Y&C—ESLC

Unitas, John and Fitzgerald, Edward E. Pro Quarterback: My Own Story. Simon & Schuster 1965
Bkl A&Y

COLLECTIONS

Anderson, Dave. Great Quarterbacks of the NFL. Random House 1965
Bkl C(5-9)&Y

Norman Mack Van Brocklin, 1926-

COLLECTIONS

Anderson, Dave. Great Quarterbacks of the NFL. Random House 1965
Bkl C(5-9)&Y

Glenn Scobey ("Pop") Warner, 1871-1954

COLLECTIONS

Riper, Guernsey Van. Yea, Coach! Three Great Football Coaches. Garrard 1966
ESLC

William Barry Wood, 1910-

COLLECTIONS

Hand, Jack J. Heroes of the NFL. Random House 1965
Bkl C(5-9)&Y

FOREST RANGERS

See Conservationists

FREETHINKERS

See Agnostics

FRIARS

See Religious Leaders

FRONTIERSMEN

See also Explorers; Scouts

American

COLLECTIONS

American Heritage. Trappers and Mountain Men, by Evan Jones. Am. Heritage 1961
AB—CC(6-9)—ESLC—YR
Christopher Carson; John Charles Frémont; Médart Chouart, Sieur de Groseilliers; Wilson Price Hunt; Pierre Gaultier de Varennes, Sieur de La Vérendrye; Manuel Lisa; Pierre Esprit Radisson

Folsom, Franklin. Famous Pioneers. Harvey 1963
ESLC—IndJ(6-9)—YR

Heiderstadt, Dorothy. Frontier Leaders and Pioneers. McKay 1962
AB(5up)—Bkl C(5-8)—ESLC

Johnson, Dorothy M. Some Went West. Dodd 1965
Bkl C(7-9)&Y
Bethenia Angelina (Owens) Adair; Elizabeth (Bacon) Custer; Asa Shinn Mercer; and others

Johnson, Jalmar. Builders of the Northwest. Dodd 1963
Bkl A&Y—IndS(9-12)

Johnston, Charles Haven Ladd. Famous Frontiersmen and Heroes of the Border: Their Adventurous Lives and Stirring Experiences in Pioneer Days. Page 1913
SCPL

McSpadden, J. Walker. Pioneer Heroes. Crowell 1954
SCHS

Reinfeld, Fred. Trappers of the West. Crowell 1957
BBEL(7-8)
James Bridger; Christopher Carson; John Colter; Jedediah Strong Smith; William Sherley Williams

Ross, Nancy Wilson. Heroines of the Early West. Random House 1960
Bkl C(5-9)—BY—CC(5-7)—ESLC—JH
Mary Baldwin; Abigail Jane (Scott) Duniway; Sacagawea; Sister Mary Loyola Vath; Narcissa (Prentiss) Whitman

Schaefer, Jack Warner. Heroes Without Glory: Some Goodmen of the Old West. Houghton 1965
Bkl A&Y
John Capen Adams; Elfego Baca; Valentine Trant O'Connell McGillycuddy; Washakie, Shoshone Chief; and others

Steckmesser, Kent Ladd. The Western Hero in History and Legend. Univ. of Okla. 1965
Bkl A
William Harrison ("Billy the Kid") Bonney; Christopher Carson; George Armstrong Custer; James Butler ("Wild Bill") Hickok

Steele, William O. Westward Adventure: The True Stories of Six Pioneers. Harcourt 1962
AB(4-9)—Bkl C(7-9)&Y—CC—ESLC—JH
James Adair; Richard Henderson; Mary Ingles; Martin Schneider; James Smith; Eleazar Wiggan

American—18th century

James Adair, 1709?-1783?

COLLECTIONS

Steele, William O. Westward Adventure: The True Stories of Six Pioneers. Harcourt 1962
AB(4-9)—Bkl C(7-9)&Y—CC—ESLC—JH

FRONTIERSMEN

American—18th century—*Continued*

Daniel Boone, 1734-1820

Averill, Esther. Daniel Boone. Harper 1945
CC(3-6)—ESLC

Bakeless, John Edwin. Fighting Frontiersman: The Life of Daniel Boone; based on Daniel Boone, Master of the Wilderness. Morrow 1948
CC(7-9)—JH—SCHS

Bakeless, John Edwin. Master of the Wilderness: Daniel Boone. Morrow 1939
SCPL

Brown, John Mason. Daniel Boone: The Opening of the Wilderness. Random House 1952
CC(6-9)—ESLC—JH

Daugherty, James. Daniel Boone. Viking 1939
AB(6-10)—BBEL(6-8)—BBJH—BY—CC (5-7)—ESLC—JH—SCHS

Martin, Patricia Miles. Daniel Boone. Putnam 1965
ESLC

Meadowcroft, Enid La Monte. Holding the Fort with Daniel Boone. Crowell 1958
AB(3-6)—CC(3-5)

Meadowcroft, Enid La Monte. On Indian Trails with Daniel Boone. Crowell 1947
BBEL—CC(3-5)—ESLC

Seifert, Shirley. Never No More: A Novel. Lippincott 1964 (Fiction)
Bkl A&Y—IndS(9-11)

Steele, William O. Daniel Boone's Echo. Harcourt 1957 (Fiction)
CC(4-6)

White, Stewart Edward. Daniel Boone, Wilderness Scout: The Life Story and True Adventures of the Great Hunter, Long Knife, Who First Blazed the Wilderness Trail Through the Indian's Country to Kentucky. Doubleday 1946
BY—CC(7-9)—JH—SCHS

Wilkie, Katharine E. Daniel Boone: Taming the Wilds. Garrard 1960
ESLC

COLLECTIONS

Buehr, Walter. Westward: With American Explorers. Putnam 1963
ESLC

George Rogers Clark, 1752-1818

Bakeless, John Edwin. Background to Glory: The Life of George Rogers Clark. Lippincott 1957
SCHS—SCPL

Grant, Bruce. Northwest Campaign: The George Rogers Clark Expedition. Putnam 1963
ESLC

Lancaster, Bruce. The Big Knives. Little 1964 (Fiction)
Bkl A&Y—IndS(9-10)—SCHS

Nolan, Jeannette (Covert). George Rogers Clark, Soldier and Hero (November 19, 1752 - February 13, 1818). Messner 1954
AB(5-7)—BBEL(6-8)—BBJH—CC(6-9)—JH—SCHS

Richard Henderson, 1735-1785

COLLECTIONS

Steele, William O. Westward Adventure: The True Stories of Six Pioneers. Harcourt 1962
AB(4-9)—Bkl C(7-9)&Y—CC—ESLC—JH

Mary Ingles, ?

COLLECTIONS

Steele, William O. Westward Adventure: The True Stories of Six Pioneers. Harcourt 1962
AB(4-9)—Bkl C(7-9)&Y—CC—ESLC—JH

Simon Kenton, 1755-1836

Garst, Doris Shannon. Frontier Hero: Simon Kenton. Messner 1963
AB(5-9)—Bkl C(7-9)—ESLC

Manuel Lisa, 1772-1820

Oglesby, Richard Edward. Manuel Lisa and the Opening of the Missouri Fur Trade. Univ. of Okla. 1963
Bkl A

COLLECTIONS

American Heritage. Trappers and Mountain Men, by Evan Jones. Am. Heritage 1961
AB—CC(6-9)—ESLC—YR

Martin Schneider, ?

COLLECTIONS

Steele, William O. Westward Adventure: The True Stories of Six Pioneers. Harcourt 1962
AB(4-9)—Bkl C(7-9)&Y—CC—ESLC—JH

James Smith, ?

COLLECTIONS

Steele, William O. Westward Adventure: The True Stories of Six Pioneers. Harcourt 1962
AB(4-9)—Bkl C(7-9)&Y—CC—ESLC—JH

Eleazar Wiggan, ?

COLLECTIONS

Steele, William O. Westward Adventure: The True Stories of Six Pioneers. Harcourt 1962
AB(4-9)—Bkl C(7-9)&Y—CC—ESLC—JH

FRONTIERSMEN—*Continued*

American—19th century

John Capen Adams, 1812-1860

Dillon, Richard H. The Legend of Grizzly Adams, California's Greatest Mountain Man. Coward-McCann 1966
Bkl A&Y

James, Harry C. Grizzly Adams. Childrens Press 1963
AB(3-7)

COLLECTIONS

Schaefer, Jack Warner. Heroes Without Glory: Some Goodmen of the Old West. Houghton 1965
Bkl A&Y

Bethenia Angelina (Owens) Adair, 1840-1926

COLLECTIONS

Johnson, Dorothy M. Some Went West. Dodd 1965
Bkl C(7-9)&Y

John Jacob Astor, 1763-1848

Daugherty, James. Trappers and Traders of the Far West. Random House 1952
CC(6-9)—JH—SCHS

Kavaler, Lucy. The Astors: A Family Chronicle of Pomp and Power. Dodd 1966
Bkl A

Terrell, John Upton. Furs by Astor. Morrow 1963
Bkl A&Y

COLLECTIONS

Cunz, Dieter. They Came from Germany: The Story of Famous German-Americans. Dodd 1966
ESLC

Elfego Baca, 1865-1945

COLLECTIONS

Schaefer, Jack Warner. Heroes Without Glory: Some Goodmen of the Old West. Houghton 1965
Bkl A&Y

Mary Baldwin, ?

COLLECTIONS

Ross, Nancy Wilson. Heroines of the Early West. Random House 1960
Bkl C(5-9)—BY—CC(5-7)—ESLC—JH

James Pierson Beckwourth, 1798-1866

Felton, Harold W. Jim Beckwourth, Negro Mountain Man. Dodd 1966
ESLC

John Bidwell, 1819-1900

Beals, Frank Lee. The Rush for Gold. Row 1962
ESLC

William Harrison ("Billy the Kid") Bonney, 1859-1881

COLLECTIONS

Steckmesser, Kent Ladd. The Western Hero in History and Legend. Univ. of Okla. 1965
Bkl A

James Bowie, 1796-1836

Baugh, Virgil E. Rendezvous at the Alamo: Highlights in the Lives of Bowie, Crockett, and Travis. Pageant 1961
Bkl A

Garst, Doris Shannon. James Bowie and His Famous Knife. Messner 1955
CC(7-9)—ESLC—JH—SCHS

Tabitha (Moffatt) Brown, 1780-1858

Lampman, Evelyn Sibley. Wheels West: The Story of Tabitha Brown. Doubleday 1965
ESLC

John Chapman, 1775-1847

Atkinson, Eleanor. Johnny Appleseed: The Romance of the Sower. Harper 1943 (Fiction)
SCHS

Douglas, Emily Taft. Appleseed Farm. Abingdon 1948 (Fiction)
CC(3-5)—ESLC

Hunt, Mabel Leigh. Better Known as Johnny Appleseed. Lippincott 1950
BBEL(7-8)—BBJH—CC(7-9)—JH—SCHS—YR

Le Sueur, Meridel. Little Brother of the Wilderness: The Story of Johnny Appleseed. Knopf 1947
AB(4-7)—BBEL—CC(3-5)—ESLC

COLLECTIONS

Bailey, Carolyn Sherwin. Children of the Handcrafts. Viking 1935
BBJH—CC(4-7)—ESLC

John Colter, 1775?-1813

COLLECTIONS

Reinfeld, Fred. Trappers of the West. Crowell 1957
BBEL(7-8)

David Crockett, 1786-1836

Baugh, Virgil E. Rendezvous at the Alamo: Hightlights in the Lives of Bowie, Crockett, and Travis. Pageant 1961
Bkl A

Beals, Frank L. Davy Crockett. Harper 1960
ESLC

Blair, Walter. Davy Crockett, Frontier Hero: The Truth as He Told It, the Legend as Friends Built It. Coward-McCann 1955
CC(5-7)

FRONTIERSMEN

American—19th century

David Crockett—Continued

Crockett, David. Autobiography. New Am. Lib.
GR

Holbrook, Stewart. Davy Crockett. Random House 1955
JH—SCHS

Le Sueur, Meridel. Chanticleer of Wilderness Road: A Story of Davy Crockett. Knopf 1951
CC(5-7)—ESLC

Rourke, Constance Mayfield. Davy Crockett. Harcourt 1934
BBEL(7-8)—BBJH—BY—CC(7-9)—ESLC—JH—SCHS—SCPL

Shackford, James Atkins. David Crockett: The Man and the Legend. Univ. of N.C. 1956
SCPL

Shapiro, Irwin. Yankee Thunder: The Legendary Life of Davy Crockett. Messner 1944
BBEL—CC(6-9)—ESLC—JH

Steele, William O. Davy Crockett's Earthquake. Harcourt 1956 (Fiction)
CC(4-6)

George Armstrong Custer, 1839-1876

COLLECTIONS

Steckmesser, Kent Ladd. The Western Hero in History and Legend. Univ. of Okla. 1965
Bkl A

Abigail Jane (Scott) Duniway, 1834-1915

COLLECTIONS

Ross, Nancy Wilson. Heroines of the Early West. Random House 1960
Bkl C(5-9)—BY—CC(5-7)—ESLC—JH

Wilson Price Hunt, 1782?-1842

COLLECTIONS

American Heritage. Trappers and Mountain Men, by Evan Jones. Am. Heritage 1961
AB—CC(6-9)—ESLC—YR

Solomon Laurent Juneau, 1793-1856

Lawson, Marion. Solomon Juneau, Voyageur. Crowell 1960
ESLC

Manuel Lisa, 1772-1820

Oglesby, Richard Edward. Manuel Lisa and the Opening of the Missouri Fur Trade. Univ. of Okla. 1963
Bkl A

COLLECTIONS

American Heritage. Trappers and Mountain Men, by Evan Jones. Am. Heritage 1961
AB—CC(6-9)—ESLC—YR

Valentine Trant O'Connell McGillycuddy, 1849-1939

COLLECTIONS

Schaefer, Jack Warner. Heroes Without Glory: Some Goodmen of the Old West. Houghton 1965
Bkl A&Y

Joseph Lafayette Meek, 1810-1875

Garst, Doris Shannon. Joe Meek, Man of the West. Messner 1954
SCHS

Asa Shinn Mercer, 1839-1917

COLLECTIONS

Johnson, Dorothy M. Some Went West. Dodd 1965
Bkl C(7-9)&Y

Jedediah Strong Smith, 1798-1831

Burt, Olive. Jedediah Smith, Fur Trapper of the Old West. Messner 1951
SCHS

Smith, Alson Jesse. Men Against the Mountains: Jedediah Smith and the South West Expedition of 1826-1829. Day 1965
Bkl A&Y—IndS(9-12)

COLLECTIONS

Reinfeld, Fred. Trappers of the West. Crowell 1957
BBEL(7-8)

John Augustus Sutter, 1803-1880

Booth, Edwin. John Sutter, Californian. Bobbs 1964
IndJ(6-9)

Lauritzen, Jonreed. Captain Sutter's Gold. Doubleday 1964 (Fiction)
Bkl A

Lewis, Oscar. Sutter's Fort: Gateway to the Gold Fields. Prentice-Hall 1966
Bkl A&Y

Sister Mary Loyola Vath, ?

COLLECTIONS

Ross, Nancy Wilson. Heroines of the Early West. Random House 1960
Bkl C(5-9)—BY—CC(5-7)—ESLC—JH

Marcus Whitman, 1802-1847

Allen, T. D. Doctor in Buckskin. Harper 1951 (Fiction)
SCHS

Daugherty, James. Marcus and Narcissa Whitman, Pioneers of Oregon. Viking 1953
BBEL—BY—CC(7-9)—ESLC—JH—SCHS

FRONTIERSMEN

American—19th century

Marcus Whitman—Continued

Jones, Nard. The Great Command: The Story of Marcus and Narcissa Whitman and the Oregon Country Pioneers. Little 1959
Bkl A

COLLECTIONS

Blassingame, Wyatt and Glendinning, Richard. Frontier Doctors. Watts 1963
Bkl C(6-9)

William Sherley Williams, 1787-1849

COLLECTIONS

Reinfeld, Fred. Trappers of the West. Crowell 1957
BBEL(7-8)

Scottish—19th century

Sir William George Drummond Stewart, Bart., 1796-1871

Porter, Mae Reed and Davenport, Odessa. Scotsman in Buckskin: Sir William Drummond Stewart and the Rocky Mountain Fur Trade. Hastings 1963
Bkl A&Y

FUR TRADERS

See Frontiersmen

GAMBLERS

American—19th century

Luke Short, 1854-1893

Cox, William Robert. Luke Short and His Era. Doubleday 1961
Bkl A

GENERALS

See Soldiers

GENETICISTS

Austrian—19th century

Gregor Johann Mendel, 1822-1884

Sootin, Harry. Gregor Mendel: Father of the Science of Genetics. Vanguard 1959
JH—SCHS
Webb, Robert N. Gregor Mendel and Heredity. Watts 1963
Bkl C(7-10)&Y
Webster, Gary. The Man Who Found Out Why: The Story of Gregor Mendel. Hawthorn 1963
ESLC

GEOLOGISTS

See also Oceanographers; Paleontologists

COLLECTIONS

Fenton, Carroll Lane and Fenton, Mildred Adams. Giants of Geology. Doubleday 1952
SCHS—SCPL

American—19th century

John Wesley Powell, 1834-1902

Frazee, Steve. First Through the Grand Canyon. Winston 1960
Bkl C(7-9)&Y
Place, Marian F. John Wesley Powell: Canyon's Conqueror. Houghton 1963
AB(5-9)—IndJ(4-6)
Stegner, Wallace Earle. Beyond the Hundredth Meridian: John Wesley Powell and the Second Opening of The West. Houghton 1954
SCPL
White, Dale. John Wesley Powell: Geologist-Explorer. Messner 1958
YR

French—20th century

Pierre Teilhard de Chardin, 1881-1955

Corte, Nicolas. Pierre Teilhard de Chardin: His Life and Spirit; tr. by Martin Jarrett-Kerr. Macmillan 1960
Bkl A
Cuénot, Claude. Teilhard de Chardin: A Biographical Study; tr. by Vincent Colimore; ed. by René Hague. Helicon Press 1965
Bkl A
De Terra, Helmut. Memories of Teilhard de Chardin; tr. from the German by J. Maxwell Brownjohn. Harper 1965
Bkl A
Grenet, Paul. Teilhard de Chardin: The Man and His Theories; tr. from the French by R. A. Rudorff. Eriksson 1966
Bkl A
Lubac, Henri de. Teilhard de Chardin: The Man and His Meaning; tr. by René Hague. Hawthorn 1965
Bkl A
Rabut, Olivier A. Teilhard de Chardin: A Critical Study. Sheed 1961
Bkl A
Teilhard de Chardin, Pierre. The Making of a Mind: Letters from a Soldier-Priest, 1914-1919; tr. from the French by René Hague. Harper 1965
Bkl A

Scottish—19th century

Sir Charles Lyell, Bart., 1797-1875

Bailey, Sir Edward Battersby. Charles Lyell. Doubleday 1963
Bkl A

GIRL SCOUT WORKERS

American—20th century

Juliette (Gordon) Low, 1860-1927

Pace, Mildred Mastin. Juliette Low. Scribner 1947
BY—CC(6-8)—JH

Radford, Ruby L. Juliette Low: Girl Scout Founder. Garrard 1965
ESLC

Shultz, Gladys (Denny). Lady from Savannah: The Life of Juliette Low. Lippincott 1958
SCPL

COLLECTIONS

Forsee, Aylesa. American Women Who Scored Firsts. Macrae 1958
SCHS

GLADIATORS

Roman—1st century B.C.

Spartacus, ?-71 B.C.

Houghton, Eric. They Marched with Spartacus. McGraw 1963
Bkl C(5-7)

GLASS PAINTERS

American—20th century

Louis Comfort Tiffany, 1848-1933

Koch, Robert. Louis C. Tiffany, Rebel in Glass. Crown 1964
Bkl A—IndS(11-12)

GOLDSMITHS

Italian—16th century

Benvenuto Cellini, 1500-1571

Cellini, Benvenuto. Autobiography; tr. by John Addington Symonds. Modern Lib; Oxford; Dodd; etc.
Bkl A—CA—GR—SCPL—3000

GOLFERS

American—20th century

Charles Albert Boswell, 1916-

COLLECTIONS

Boynick, David King. Champions by Setback: Athletes Who Overcame Physical Handicaps. Crowell 1954
SCHS

Robert Tyre Jones, 1902-

Jones, Robert Tyre. Golf Is My Game. Doubleday 1960
Bkl A

Samuel Jackson Snead, 1912-

Snead, Samuel Jackson and Stump, Al. The Education of a Golfer. Simon & Schuster 1962
Bkl A&Y

Mildred (Didrikson) Zaharias, 1913-1956

De Grummond, Lena Young and Delaune, Lynne (de Grummond). Babe Didrikson. Bobbs 1963
AB(4-7)

Zaharias, Mildred (Didrikson) and Paxton, Harry T. This Life I've Led: My Autobiography. Barnes 1955
BY—SCPL

GOVERNMENT OFFICIALS

See Statesmen

GOVERNORS

See Statesmen

GUITARISTS

English—20th century

Julian Bream, 1933?-

COLLECTIONS

Ewen, David. Famous Instrumentalists. Dodd 1965
Bkl Y&C

Spanish—20th century

Andrés Segovia, 1894-

COLLECTIONS

Chotzinoff, Samuel. A Little Nightmusic. Harper 1964
Bkl A&Y—IndS(12)

GUNMAKERS

American—19th century

John Moses Browning, 1855-1926

Browning, John and Gentry, Curt. John M. Browning, American Gunmaker: An Illustrated Biography of the Man and His Guns. Doubleday 1964
Bkl A&Y

Winders, Gertrude (Hecker). Browning: World's Greatest Gunmaker. Day 1961
Bkl C(5-8)—YR

American—20th century

John Moses Browning, 1855-1926

Browning, John and Gentry, Curt. John M. Browning, American Gunmaker: An Illustrated Biography of the Man and His Guns. Doubleday 1964
Bkl A&Y

GUNMAKERS
American—19th century

John Moses Browning—Continued

Winders, Gertrude (Hecker). Browning: World's Greatest Gunmaker. Day 1961
Bkl C(5-8)—YR

HANDICAPPED

See Blind; Deaf; Physically Handicapped; Poverty-Stricken; Recluses; Siamese Twins; Victims of Arthritis; Victims of Cerebral Palsy; Victims of Leprosy; Victims of Polio

HARPSICHORDISTS

See Pianists

HERPETOLOGISTS
American—20th century

Ross Allen, 1908-

Hylander, Clarence John. Adventures with Reptiles: The Story of Ross Allen. Messner 1951
SCHS

William E. Haast, 1911-

Kursh, Harry. Cobras in His Garden. Harvey 1965
Bkl A&Y

English—20th century

Constantine John Philip Ionides, 1901-

Ionides, Constantine John Philip. Mambas and Man-Eaters: A Hunter's Story. Holt 1966
Bkl A&Y

Lane, Margaret. Life with Ionides. Viking 1963
Bkl A

Wykes, Alan. Snake Man. Simon & Schuster 1961
Bkl A

HISTORIANS
COLLECTIONS

Hill, Frank Ernest. Famous Historians. Dodd 1966
Bkl Y&C
Henry Adams; Charles Austin Beard; Sir Winston Leonard Spencer Churchill; Jean Froissart; Edward Gibbon; Samuel Eliot Morison; Allan Nevins; Francis Parkman; Plutarch; Thucydides; Arnold Joseph Toynbee; François Marie Arouet de Voltaire

American
COLLECTIONS

Homans, Abigail (Adams). Education by Uncles. Houghton 1966
Bkl A&Y
Brooks Adams; Charles Francis Adams; Henry Adams

American—19th century

Brooks Adams, 1848-1927

Donovan, Timothy Paul. Henry Adams and Brooks Adams: The Education of Two American Historians. Univ. of Okla. 1961
Bkl A

COLLECTIONS

Homans, Abigail (Adams). Education by Uncles. Houghton 1966
Bkl A&Y

Charles Francis Adams, 1835-1915
COLLECTIONS

Homans, Abigail (Adams). Education by Uncles. Houghton 1966
Bkl A&Y

Henry Brooks Adams, 1838-1918

Adams, Henry Brooks. Education of Henry Adams: An Autobiography. Houghton, Modern Lib., etc.
CA—GR—SCPL—3000

Donovan, Timothy Paul. Henry Adams and Brooks Adams: The Education of Two American Historians. Univ. of Okla. 1961
Bkl A

Hochfield, George. Henry Adams: An Introduction and Interpretation. Barnes & Noble 1962
Bkl A

Levenson, Jacob Claver. The Mind and Art of Henry Adams. Houghton 1957
SCPL

Samuels, Ernest. Henry Adams: The Major Phase. Harvard Univ. 1964
Bkl A

Samuels, Ernest. Henry Adams: The Middle Years. Harvard Univ. 1958
SCPL

Samuels, Ernest. Young Henry Adams. Harvard Univ. 1948
SCPL

Sayre, Robert F. The Examined Self: Benjamin Franklin, Henry Adams, Henry James. Princeton Univ. 1964
Bkl A

Stevenson, Elizabeth. Henry Adams: A Biography. Macmillan 1955
SCPL

HISTORIANS

American—19th century

Henry Brooks Adams—Continued

COLLECTIONS

Hill, Frank Ernest. Famous Historians.
Dodd 1966
Bkl Y&C

Homans, Abigail (Adams). Education by
Uncles. Houghton 1966
Bkl A&Y

Francis Parkman, 1823-1893

Doughty, Howard. Francis Parkman.
Macmillan 1962
Bkl A

COLLECTIONS

Hill, Frank Ernest. Famous Historians.
Dodd 1966
Bkl Y&C

American—20th century

Brooks Adams, 1848-1927

Donovan, Timothy Paul. Henry Adams
and Brooks Adams: The Education of
Two American Historians. Univ. of
Okla. 1961
Bkl A

COLLECTIONS

Homans, Abigail (Adams). Education by
Uncles. Houghton 1966
Bkl A&Y

Charles Austin Beard, 1874-1948

COLLECTIONS

Hill, Frank Ernest. Famous Historians.
Dodd 1966
Bkl Y&C

James Henry Breasted, 1865-1935

Breasted, Charles. Pioneer to the Past:
The Story of James Henry Breasted,
Archaeologist. Scribner 1943
SCPL

Otto Eisenschiml, 1880-1963

Eisenschiml, Otto. O. E.: Historian Without an Armchair. Bobbs 1963
Bkl A&Y

Samuel Eliot Morison, 1887-

Morison, Samuel Eliot. One Boy's Boston,
1887-1901. Houghton 1962
Bkl A

COLLECTIONS

Hill, Frank Ernest. Famous Historians.
Dodd 1966
Bkl Y&C

Allan Nevins, 1890-

COLLECTIONS

Hill, Frank Ernest. Famous Historians.
Dodd 1966
Bkl Y&C

Arthur Meier Schlesinger, 1888-1965

Schlesinger, Arthur Meier. In Retrospect:
The History of a Historian. Harcourt
1963
Bkl A

Canadian—20th century

James Thomson Shotwell, 1874-1965

Shotwell, James Thomson. Autobiography. Bobbs 1961
Bkl A

English—18th century

Edward Gibbon, 1737-1794

Gibbon, Edward. Autobiography; ed. by
Lord Sheffield. Oxford 1907
SCPL

COLLECTIONS

Hill, Frank Ernest. Famous Historians.
Dodd 1966
Bkl Y&C

English—20th century

*Sir Winston Leonard Spencer Church-
ill, 1874-1965*

COLLECTIONS

Hill, Frank Ernest. Famous Historians.
Dodd 1966
Bkl Y&C

Basil Henry Liddell Hart, 1895-

Liddell Hart, Basil Henry. The Liddell
Hart Memoirs: v. 1, 1895-1938. Put-
nam 1966
Bkl A

Liddell Hart, Basil Henry. The Liddell
Hart Memoirs: v. 2, The Later Years.
Putnam 1966
Bkl A

Arnold Joseph Toynbee, 1889-

COLLECTIONS

Hill, Frank Ernest. Famous Historians.
Dodd 1966
Bkl Y&C

French—14th century

Jean Froissart, 1333?-1400?

COLLECTIONS

Hill, Frank Ernest. Famous Historians.
Dodd 1966
Bkl Y&C

HISTORIANS—*Continued*

French—18th century

François Marie Arouet de Voltaire, 1694-1778

COLLECTIONS

Hill, Frank Ernest. Famous Historians. Dodd 1966
Bkl Y&C

French—19th century

Antoine Frédéric Ozanam, 1813-1853

Derum, James Patrick. Apostle in a Top Hat: The Life of Frédéric Ozanam. Hanover House 1960
Bkl A

Greek—5th century B.C.

Thucydides, 471?-400? B.C.

COLLECTIONS

Hill, Frank Ernest. Famous Historians. Dodd 1966
Bkl Y&C

Greek—4th century B.C.

Xenophon, 434?-355? B.C.

Household, Geoffrey. The Exploits of Xenophon. Random House 1955
ESLC

Greek—1st century

Plutarch, 46?-120?

COLLECTIONS

Hill, Frank Ernest. Famous Historians. Dodd 1966
Bkl Y&C

Italian—16th century

Giorgio Vasari, 1512-1574

Rud, Einar. Vasari's Life and Lives: The First Art Historian. Van Nostrand 1963
SCPL

Palestinian—1st century

Flavius Josephus, 37?-100

Williamson, Geoffrey Arthur. The World of Josephus. Little 1965
Bkl A

Scottish—19th century

Thomas Carlyle, 1795-1881

Emerson, Ralph Waldo and Carlyle, Thomas. The Correspondence of [the authors]; ed. by Joseph Slater. Columbia Univ. 1964
Bkl A

Spanish—16th century

Bernal Díaz del Castillo, 1492-1581

Cerwin, Herbert. Bernal Díaz, Historian of the Conquest. Univ. of Okla. 1963
Bkl A

HORSE TRAINERS

American—20th century

James E. Fitzsimmons, 1874-1966

Breslin, Jimmy. Sunny Jim: The Life of America's Most Beloved Horseman, James Fitzsimmons. Doubleday 1962
Bkl A&Y

Austrian—20th century

Alois Podhajsky, 1898-

Podhajsky, Alois. My Dancing White Horses; tr. by Frances Hogarth-Gaute. Holt 1965
Bkl A—IndS(12)

HORTICULTURISTS

American—19th century

Luther Burbank, 1849-1926

Beaty, John Y. Luther Burbank, Plant Magician. Messner 1943
CC(7-9)—ESLC—JH—SCHS

Bragdon, Lillian J. Luther Burbank, Nature's Helper. Abingdon 1959
AB(3up)—CC(4-6)

American—20th century

Luther Burbank, 1849-1926

Beaty, John Y. Luther Burbank, Plant Magician. Messner 1943
CC(7-9)—ESLC—JH—SCHS

Bragdon, Lillian J. Luther Burbank, Nature's Helper. Abingdon 1959
AB(3up)—CC(4-6)

HOTEL OWNERS AND MANAGERS

American—20th century

Conrad Nicholson Hilton, 1887-

Hilton, Conrad Nicholson. Be My Guest. Prentice-Hall 1957
SCPL

English—20th century

Rosa (Ovendon) Lewis, 1867?-1952

Fielding, Daphne (Vivian). The Duchess of Jermyn Street: The Life and Good Times of Rosa Lewis of the Cavendish Hotel. Little 1964
Bkl A

HOTEL OWNERS AND MANAGERS—
Continued

Russian—20th century

Boris Lissanevitch, P

Peissel, Michel. Tiger for Breakfast: The Story of Boris of Kathmandu. Dutton 1966
Bkl A&Y

HUMANITARIANS

See Philanthropists; Red Cross Workers; Social Workers

HUMORISTS

See also Cartoonists

American

COLLECTIONS

Benét, Laura. Famous American Humorists. Dodd 1959
BBJH—BY—JH—SCHS—YR

American—19th century

Charles Farrar Browne, 1834-1867

Austin, James C. Artemus Ward. Twayne 1964
Bkl A

Samuel Langhorne Clemens, 1835-1910

Allen, Jerry. Adventures of Mark Twain. Little 1954
SCPL

Brooks, Van Wyck. The Ordeal of Mark Twain. Meridian 1920
GR

Budd, Louis J. Mark Twain: Social Philosopher. Ind. Univ. 1962
Bkl A

Clemens, Samuel Langhorne. Autobiography of Mark Twain; ed. by Charles Neider. Harper 1959
BBHS—SCHS—SCPL—3000

Clemens, Samuel Langhorne. Letters from the Earth, by Mark Twain; ed. by Bernard DeVoto. Harper 1962
Bkl A

Clemens, Samuel Langhorne. Letters to Mary; ed. by Lewis Leary. Columbia Univ. 1961
Bkl A

Clemens, Samuel Langhorne. Mark Twain-Howells Letters: The Correspondence, 1872-1910; ed. by Henry Nash Smith and others. 2v. Harvard Univ. 1960
Bkl A

Clemens, Samuel Langhorne. Mark Twain's Letters from Hawaii; ed. by A. Grove Day. Appleton 1966
Bkl A

De Voto, Bernard Augustine. Mark Twain's America. Houghton 1951
CA—SCPL

Eaton, Jeanette. America's Own Mark Twain. Morrow 1958
BBEL—BBJH—CC(6-9)—ESLC—JH—SCHS—YR

Fatout, Paul. Mark Twain in Virginia City. Ind. Univ. 1964
Bkl A

Fatout, Paul. Mark Twain on the Lecture Circuit. Ind. Univ. 1960
Bkl A—SCPL

Holbrook, Hal. Mark Twain Tonight! An Actor's Portrait. Washburn 1959
Bkl A&Y—SCPL

Kaplan, Justin. Mr. Clemens and Mark Twain: A Biography. Simon & Schuster 1966
Bkl A

Lynn, Kenneth Schuyler. Mark Twain and Southwestern Humor. Little 1960
Bkl A

McNeer, May Yonge. America's Mark Twain. Houghton 1962
Bkl C(5-8)—CC(5-8)—ESLC—JH—SCHS—YR

Meltzer, Milton. Mark Twain Himself: A Pictorial Biography. Crowell 1960
Bkl A

Miers, Earl Schenck. Mark Twain on the Mississippi. World 1957 (Fiction)
BBJH—JH—SCHS—YR

North, Sterling. Mark Twain and the River. Houghton 1961
Bkl C(5-8)—CC(5-7)—JH

Paine, Albert Bigelow. The Boys' Life of Mark Twain: The Story of a Man Who Made the World Laugh and Love Him. Harper 1916
BBJH—CC(8-9)—JH—SCHS

Peare, Catherine Owens. Mark Twain: His Life. Holt 1954
AB(5-7)—CC(4-6)

Proudfit, Isabel (Boyd). River-Boy: The Story of Mark Twain. Messner 1940
BBEL(6-8)—CC(7-9)—ESLC—JH—SCHS—YR

Quick, Dorothy. Enchantment: A Little Girl's Friendship with Mark Twain. Univ. of Okla. 1961
Bkl A

Salsbury, Edith Colgate. Susy and Mark Twain: Family Dialogues. Harper 1965
Bkl A&Y—IndS(12)

Smith, Henry Nash. Mark Twain: The Development of a Writer. Harvard Univ. 1962
Bkl A

Wagenknecht, Edward. Mark Twain: The Man and His Work. Univ. of Okla. 1961
Bkl A—SCPL

HUMORISTS

American—19th century

Samuel Langhorne Clemens—Continued

Wecter, Dixon. Sam Clemens of Hannibal. Houghton 1952
SCPL

COLLECTIONS

Hoff, Rhoda. Why They Wrote. Walck 1961
Bkl C(7-10)&Y—SCHS

Morgan, Howard Wayne. American Writers in Rebellion: From Mark Twain to Dreiser. Hill & Wang 1965
Bkl A&Y

Stirling, Nora B. Who Wrote the Classics? Day 1965
Bkl Y&A&C

Finley Peter Dunne, 1867-1936

Dunne, Finley Peter. Mr. Dooley Remembers; ed. by Philip Dunne. Little 1963
Bkl A—IndS(10-12)

American—20th century

Robert Charles Benchley, 1889-1945

Benchley, Nathaniel. Robert Benchley: A Biography McGraw 1955
SCPL

Finley Peter Dunne, 1867-1936

Dunne, Finley Peter. Mr. Dooley Remembers; ed. by Philip Dunne. Little 1963
Bkl A—IndS(10-12)

Ring Wilmer Lardner, 1885-1933

Elder, Donald. Ring Lardner: A Biography. Doubleday 1956
SCPL

Patrick, Walton R. Ring Lardner. Twayne 1963
Bkl A&Y—SCPL

COLLECTIONS

Geismar, Maxwell David. Writers in Crisis: The American Novel Between Two Wars. Houghton 1942
SCPL

Samuel Levenson, 1911-

Levenson, Samuel. Everything but Money. Simon & Schuster 1966
Bkl A

Don Marquis, 1878-1937

Anthony, Edward. O Rare Don Marquis: A Biography. Doubleday 1962
Bkl A—SCPL

Will Rogers, 1879-1935

Day, Donald and Day, Beth. Will Rogers, the Boy Roper. Houghton 1950
CC(4-7)

Day, Donald. Will Rogers: A Biography. McKay 1962
Bkl A—SCHS

Garst, Doris Shannon. Will Rogers, Immortal Cowboy. Messner 1950
BY—SCHS

Keith, Harold. Boys' Life of Will Rogers. Crowell 1953
SCHS

Rogers, Will. Autobiography; ed. by Donald Day. Houghton 1949
SCHS—SCPL

Harry Allen Smith, 1907-

Smith, Harry Allen. To Hell in a Handbasket. Doubleday 1962
Bkl A

English

COLLECTIONS

Hazlitt, William. Lectures on the English Comic Writers. Oxford 1951
SCPL

Thackeray, William Makepeace. English Humourists. Dutton (first published 1853)
SCPL

English—20th century

Pelham Grenville Wodehouse, 1881-

Wodehouse, Pelham Grenville. Author! Author! Simon & Schuster 1962
Bkl A

COLLECTIONS

Aldridge, John W. Time to Murder and Create: The Contemporary Novel in Crisis. McKay 1966
Bkl A

ICHTHYOLOGISTS

American—20th century

Eugenie Clark, 1922-

Clark, Eugenie. Lady with a Spear. Harper 1953
BY—SCHS—SCPL

Robert P. L. Straughan, ?

Straughan, Robert P. L. Sharks, Morays, and Treasure. Barnes 1965
Bkl A&Y

ILLUSTRATORS

See also Cartoonists

COLLECTIONS

Guitar, Mary Ann. 22 Famous Painters and Illustrators Tell How They Work. McKay 1964
IndS(10-12)

Mahony, Bertha E.; Latimer, Louise Payson; and Folmsbee, Beulah, comps. Illustrators of Children's Books, 1744-1945. Horn Bk 1947
Bkl A&C—CC—SCHS

Mahony, Bertha E.; Viguers, Ruth Hill; and Dalphin, Marcia, comps. Illustrators of Children's Books, 1946-1956. Horn Bk 1958
CC—SCPL

New York Museum of Modern Art. Modern Painters and Sculptors as Illustrators, by Monroe Wheeler. Mus. of Modern Art 1947
SCPL

American

COLLECTIONS

Taft, Robert. Artists and Illustrators of the Old West, 1850-1900. Scribner 1953
SCPL

American—19th century

Ernest Thompson Seton, 1860-1946

Seton, Ernest Thompson. Trail of an Artist-Naturalist: The Autobiography of Ernest Thompson Seton. Scribner 1940
SCPL

American—20th century

Will James, 1892-1942

James, Will. Lone Cowboy: My Life Story. Scribner 1930
BY—JH—SCHS—SCPL—YR

Norman Rockwell, 1894-

Guptill, Arthur Leighton. Norman Rockwell, Illustrator. Watson-Guptill 1946
SCPL

Rockwell, Norman and Rockwell, Thomas. Norman Rockwell. Doubleday 1959
Bkl A&Y

Ernest Thompson Seton, 1860-1946

Seton, Ernest Thompson. Trail of an Artist-Naturalist: The Autobiography of Ernest Thompson Seton. Scribner 1940
SCPL

Chinese—20th century

Chiang Yee, 1903-

Chiang, Yee. Chinese Childhood. Day 1952
SCPL

English—20th century

Beatrix Potter, 1866-1943

Lane, Margaret. Tale of Beatrix Potter: A Biography. Warne 1946
ESLC—SCPL

Potter, Beatrix. Art of Beatrix Potter. Warne 1964
CC—ESLC—SCPL

Potter, Beatrix. The Journal of Beatrix Potter from 1881 to 1897; transcribed from her code writing by Leslie Linder. Warne 1966
Bkl A

Arthur Rackham, 1867-1939

Hudson, Derek. Arthur Rackham: His Life and Work. Scribner 1960
Bkl A&C—BY

Gwendolen Mary (Darwin) Raverat, 1885-

Raverat, Gwendolen Mary (Darwin). Period Piece. Norton 1952
SCPL

Ernest Howard Shepard, 1879-

Shepard, Ernest Howard. Drawn from Life. Dutton 1962
Bkl A

IMMIGRANTS TO CANADA

20th century

Otto Jelinek, ?

Jelinek, Henry and Pinchot, Ann. On Thin Ice. Prentice-Hall 1965
Bkl A&Y—IndS(9-12)

IMMIGRANTS TO UNITED STATES

COLLECTIONS

Beard, Annie E. S. Our Foreign-Born Citizens: What They Have Done for America; rev. by William A. Fahey. Crowell 1955
BBEL(7-8)—BBJH—CC(7-9)—ESLC—JH—SCHS—SCPL

Cunz, Dieter. They Came from Germany: The Story of Famous German-Americans. Dodd 1966
ESLC
John Jacob Astor; Charles Follen; Ottmar Mergenthaler; Thomas Nast; John Augustus Roebling; Carl Schurz; Friedrich Wilhelm von Steuben; Wernher Von Braun; John Peter Zenger

Life International. Nine Who Chose America. Dutton 1959
Bkl Y&C—SCHS
Irving Berlin; David Dubinsky; Felix Frankfurter; Gian-Carlo Menotti; Helena Rubinstein; Dalip Saund; Igor Ivan Sikorsky; Spyros Panagiotes Skouras; Selman Abraham Waksman

IMMIGRANTS TO UNITED STATES—
Continued

18th century

Friedrich Wilhelm von Steuben, 1730-1794

COLLECTIONS

Cunz, Dieter. They Came from Germany: The Story of Famous German-Americans. Dodd 1966
ESLC

John Peter Zenger, 1697-1746

COLLECTIONS

Cunz, Dieter. They Came from Germany: The Story of Famous German-Americans. Dodd 1966
ESLC

19th century

John Peter Altgeld, 1847-1902

COLLECTIONS

Kunstler, William Moses. The Case for Courage. Morrow 1962
Bkl A&Y

John Jacob Astor, 1763-1848

COLLECTIONS

Cunz, Dieter. They Came from Germany: The Story of Famous German-Americans. Dodd 1966
ESLC

Alexander Graham Bell, 1847-1922

Burlingame, Roger. Out of Silence into Sound: The Life of Alexander Graham Bell. Macmillan 1964
Bkl C(6-8)—YR

Costain, Thomas Bertram. The Chord of Steel: The Story of the Invention of the Telephone. Doubleday 1960
Bkl A&Y—SCHS—SCPL

Montgomery, Elizabeth Rider. Alexander Graham Bell. Garrard 1963
AB(4-7)

Shippen, Katherine Binney. Mr. Bell Invents the Telephone. Random House 1952
BBEL(5-8)—BBJH—CC(4-7)—ESLC—JH—SCHS

Stevenson, Orlando John. The Talking Wire: The Story of Alexander Graham Bell. Messner 1947
SCHS—YR

Waite, Helen Elmira. Make a Joyful Sound—The Romance of Mabel Hubbard and Alexander Graham Bell: An Authorized Biography. Macrae 1961
Bkl A&Y

Irving Berlin, 1888-

Ewen, David. Story of Irving Berlin. Holt 1950
SCHS—SCPL—YR

COLLECTIONS

Life International. Nine Who Chose America. Dutton 1959
Bkl Y&C—SCHS

Frances Xavier Cabrini, Saint, 1850-1917

Di Donato, Pietro. Immigrant Saint: The Life of Mother Cabrini. McGraw 1960
Bkl A

Morris Raphael Cohen, 1880-1947

Rosenfield, Leonora Davidson (Cohen). Portrait of a Philosopher: Morris R. Cohen. Harcourt 1962
Bkl A

Marcus Daly, 1841-1900

COLLECTIONS

Place, Marian T. The Copper Kings of Montana. Random House 1961
ESLC—JH—SCHS—YR

Walter Damrosch, 1862-1950

Finletter, G. B. D. From the Top of the Stairs. Little 1946
SCPL

John Ericsson, 1803-1889

Burnett, Constance (Buel). Captain John Ericsson: Father of the Monitor. Vanguard 1961
Bkl C(6-10)&Y

Latham, Jean Lee. Man of the Monitor: The Story of John Ericsson. Harper 1962
Bkl C(5-7)—CC(5-7)—ESLC—JH—YR

Pratt, Fletcher. The Monitor and the Merrimac. Random House 1951
BBJH—ESLC—JH

Charles Theodore Christian Follen, 1795-1840

COLLECTIONS

Cunz, Dieter. They Came from Germany: The Story of Famous German-Americans. Dodd 1966
ESLC

Felix Frankfurter, 1882-1965

Frankfurter, Felix. Felix Frankfurter Reminisces; recorded in talks with Harlan B. Phillips. Reynal 1960
Bkl A

Mendelson, Wallace, ed. Felix Frankfurter: A Tribute. Reynal 1964
Bkl A

Mendelson, Wallace, ed. Felix Frankfurter, the Judge. Reynal 1964
Bkl A

IMMIGRANTS TO UNITED STATES

19th century

Felix Frankfurter—Continued

COLLECTIONS

Life International. Nine Who Chose America. Dutton 1959
Bkl Y&C—SCHS

Emma Goldman, 1869-1940

Drinnon, Richard. Rebel in Paradise: A Biography of Emma Goldman. Univ. of Chicago 1961
Bkl A

Victor Herbert, 1859-1924

Purdy, Claire Lee. Victor Herbert: American Music-Master. Messner 1944
SCHS

Waters, Edward Neighbor. Victor Herbert: A Life in Music. Macmillan 1955
SCPL

Alexander Herrmann, 1844-1896

COLLECTIONS

Gibson, Walter Brown. The Master Magicians: Their Lives and Most Famous Tricks. Doubleday 1966
Bkl Y&A&C

Kendall, Lace. Masters of Magic. Macrae 1966
Bkl C(6-9)&Y

Samuel Insull, 1859-1938

McDonald, Forrest. Insull. Univ. of Chicago 1962
Bkl A

Al Jolson, 1888-1950

Sieben, Pearl. The Immortal Jolson: His Life and Times. Fell 1962
BY

Otto Hermann Kahn, 1867-1934

Matz, Mary Jane. The Many Lives of Otto Kahn. Macmillan 1964
Bkl A—IndS(11-12)

Ivar Kreuger, 1880-1932

Shaplen, Robert. Kreuger, Genius and Swindler. Knopf 1960
Bkl A

Samuel Sidney McClure, 1857-1949

Lyon, Peter. Success Story: The Life and Times of S. S. McClure. Scribner 1963
Bkl A

Ottmar Mergenthaler, 1854-1899

Levine, Israel E. Miracle Man of Printing: Ottmar Mergenthaler. Messner 1963
Bkl Y&C

COLLECTIONS

Cunz, Dieter. They Came from Germany: The Story of Famous German-Americans. Dodd 1966
ESLC

John Muir, 1838-1914

Douglas, William Orville. Muir of the Mountains. Houghton 1961
Bkl C(6-9)—BY—ESLC—JH—YR

Grossman, Adrienne and Beardwood, Valerie. Trails of His Own: The Story of John Muir and His Fight to Save Our National Parks. McKay 1961
JH—YR

Haines, Madge and Morrill, Leslie. John Muir, Protector of the Wilds. Abingdon 1957
AB(3-7)

Muir, John. Story of My Boyhood and Youth. Houghton 1913
SCPL

Norman, Charles. John Muir: Father of Our National Parks. Messner 1957
BBJH—JH—SCHS

Swift, Hildegarde Hoyt. From the Eagle's Wing: A Biography of John Muir. Morrow 1962
Bkl Y&C—CC(6-9)—ESLC—JH—YR

Wolfe, Linnie (Marsh). Son of the Wilderness: The Life of John Muir. Knopf 1945
SCPL

Thomas Nast, 1840-1902

COLLECTIONS

Cunz, Dieter. They Came from Germany: The Story of Famous German-Americans. Dodd 1966
ESLC

Allan Pinkerton, 1819-1884

Lavine, Sigmund A. Allan Pinkerton: America's First Private Eye. Dodd 1963
Bkl Y&C

Orrmont, Arthur. Master Detective: Allan Pinkerton. Messner 1965
Bkl C(6-9)—IndJ(6-9)—JH

Wise, William. Detective Pinkerton and Mr. Lincoln. Dutton 1964
AB(5-9)—IndJ(4-6)

Joseph Pulitzer, 1847-1911

Granberg, W. J. The World of Joseph Pulitzer. Abelard-Schuman 1965
ESLC

Noble, Iris. Joseph Pulitzer: Front Page Pioneer. Messner 1957
BBJH—JH—SCHS—YR

IMMIGRANTS TO UNITED STATES

19th century—*Continued*

Michael Idvorsky Pupin, 1858-1935

Markey, Dorothy. Explorer of Sound: Michael Pupin. Messner 1964
YR

Pupin, Michael Idvorsky. From Immigrant to Inventor. Scribner 1923
BBHS—SCPL

Jacob August Riis, 1849-1914

Riis, Jacob August. Making of an American. Macmillan 1929
GR—SCPL

Knute Kenneth Rockne, 1888-1931

Lovelace, Delos W. Rockne of Notre Dame. Putnam 1931
BBJH—JH—SCHS

Riper, Guernsey Van. Knute Rockne, Young Athlete. Bobbs 1947
BBEL(4-6)

John Augustus Roebling, 1806-1869

COLLECTIONS

Cunz, Dieter. They Came from Germany: The Story of Famous German-Americans. Dodd 1966
ESLC
BBEL(4-6)

Carl Schurz, 1829-1906

Schurz, Carl. Autobiography; an abridgment in one volume by Wayne Andrews. Scribner 1961
Bkl A

Terzian, James P. Defender of Human Rights, Carl Schurz. Messner 1965
Bkl C(7-10)&Y

COLLECTIONS

Cunz, Dieter. They Came from Germany: The Story of Famous German-Americans. Dodd 1966
ESLC

Charles Proteus Steinmetz, 1865-1923

Berry, Erick. Charles Proteus Steinmetz: Wizard of Electricity. Macmillan 1966
ESLC

Lavine, Sigmund A. Steinmetz: Maker of Lightning. Dodd 1955
BBHS—BBJH—BY—JH—SCHS

Miller, Floyd. The Electrical Genius of Liberty Hall: Charles Proteus Steinmetz. McGraw 1962
Bkl C(7-9)—ESLC—JH—YR

Thomas, Henry. Charles Steinmetz. Putnam 1960
AB(5-9)—Bkl C(6-8)

Maurice Sterne, 1878-1957

Sterne, Maurice. Shadow and Light: The Life, Friends and Opinions of Maurice Sterne; ed. by Charlotte Leon Mayerson. Harcourt 1965
Bkl A

Hudson Stuck, 1863-1920

Herron, Edward A. Conqueror of Mount McKinley. Messner 1964
YR

20th century

Mary Antin, 1881-1949

Antin, Mary. Promised Land. Houghton 1912
SCPL

Bernt Balchen, 1899-

Balchen, Bernt. Come North with Me: An Autobiography. Dutton 1958
BBHS—BY—SCHS—SCPL

Vicki Baum, 1888-1960

Baum, Vicki. It Was All Quite Different: The Memoirs of [the author]. Funk 1964
Bkl A

Richard Berczeller, 1902-

Berczeller, Richard. Displaced Doctor. Odyssey 1964
Bkl A

Thyra (Ferré) Bjorn, 1905-

Bjorn, Thyra (Ferré). This Is My Life. Holt 1966
Bkl A

Alexander Procofieff De Seversky, 1894-

COLLECTIONS

Gelfand, Ravina and Paterson, Letha. They Wouldn't Quit. Lerner Publications 1962
AB(5-9)

David Dubinsky, 1892-

Danish, Max D. The World of David Dubinsky. World 1957
BY—SCPL

COLLECTIONS

Life International. Nine Who Chose America. Dutton 1959
Bkl Y&C—SCHS

Albert Einstein, 1879-1955

Beckhard, Arthur. Albert Einstein. Putnam 1959
AB—CC(5-7)—ESLC—SCHS

Forsee, Aylesa. Albert Einstein: Theoretical Physicist. Macmillan 1963
Bkl C&Y—YR

IMMIGRANTS TO UNITED STATES

20th century

Albert Einstein—Continued

Frank, Philipp. Einstein: His Life and Times. Knopf 1953
3000

Freeman, Mae Blacker. The Story of Albert Einstein: The Scientist Who Searched Out the Secrets of the Universe. Random House 1958
AB(3-7)—JH

Infeld, Leopold. Albert Einstein: His Work and Its Influence on Our World. Scribner 1950
SCPL

Levinger, Elma (Ehrlich). Albert Einstein. Messner 1949
BBEL(7-8)—BBJH—BY—CC(7-9)—ESLC—JH—SCHS

Michelmore, Peter. Einstein: Profile of the Man. Dodd 1962
Bkl A&Y

Hermann Hagedorn, 1882-1964

Hagedorn, Hermann. The Hyphenated Family: An American Saga. Macmillan 1960
Bkl A&Y—SCPL

Hans Isbrandtsen, 1891-1953

Dugan, James. American Viking. Harper 1963
Bkl A—BY

Theodor von Kármán, 1881-1963

Halacy, Daniel Stephen. Father of Supersonic Flight, Theodor von Kármán. Messner 1965
Bkl C(7-10)&Y

Taiwon (Kim) Koh, 1926-

Koh, Taiwon (Kim). The Bitter Fruit of Kom-Pawi. Holt 1959
BBHS—BY

Fritz Kreisler, 1875-1962

Lochner, Louis Paul. Fritz Kreisler. Macmillan 1950
SCPL

Dominique Laxalt, ?

Laxalt, Robert. Sweet Promised Land. Harper 1957
SCHS—SCPL

Raymond Fernand Loewy, 1893-

Loewy, Raymond Fernand. Never Leave Well Enough Alone. Simon & Schuster 1951
GR

John McCormack, 1884-1945

McCormack, Lily (Foley). I Hear You Calling Me. Bruce 1949
SCPL

Thomas Mann, 1875-1955

Mann, Monika. Past & Present; tr. from the German by Frances F. Reid and Ruth Hein. St Martins 1960
Bkl A

Mann, Thomas. A Sketch of My Life; tr. by H. T. Lowe-Porter. Knopf 1960
Bkl A—SCPL

Mann, Thomas. The Story of a Novel: The Genesis of Doctor Faustus; tr. from the German by Richard and Clara Winston. Knopf 1961
Bkl A—SCPL

Neider, Charles, ed. Stature of Thomas Mann. New Directions 1947
SCPL

Thirwall, John Connop. In Another Language: A Record of the Thirty-Year Relationship Between Thomas Mann and His English Translator, Helen Tracy Lowe-Porter. Knopf 1966
Bkl A

George Magar Mardikian, 1902-

Mardikian, George Magar. Song of America. McGraw 1956
BY—SCPL

Louis Burt Mayer, 1885-1957

Crowther, Bosley. Hollywood Rajah: The Life and Times of Louis B. Mayer. Holt 1960
Bkl A

Gian-Carlo Menotti, 1911-

COLLECTIONS

Life International. Nine Who Chose America. Dutton 1959
Bkl Y&C—SCHS

Hugh Nathaniel Mulzac, 1886-

Mulzac, Hugh Nathaniel. A Star to Steer By. Int. Pubs 1963
Bkl A

Richard Joseph Neutra, 1892-

McCoy, Esther. Richard Neutra. Braziller 1960
Bkl A

Neutra, Richard Joseph. Life and Shape. Appleton 1962
Bkl A

George Papashvily, 1898-

Papashvily, George and Papashvily, Helen Waite. Anything Can Happen. Harper 1945
BBHS—BY—SCHS—SCPL

IMMIGRANTS TO UNITED STATES

20th century—*Continued*

Salom Rizk, 1909-

Rizk, Salom. Syrian Yankee. Doubleday
1943
BY—SCHS

Helena Rubinstein, 1870?-1965

Rubinstein, Helena. My Life for Beauty.
Simon & Schuster 1966
Bkl A

COLLECTIONS

Life International. Nine Who Chose
America. Dutton 1959
Bkl Y&C—SCHS

Eero Saarinen, 1910-1961

Saarinen, Eero. Eero Saarinen on His
Work: A Selection of Buildings with
Statements by the Architect; ed. by
Aline B. Saarinen. Yale Univ. 1962
Bkl A

Temko, Allan. Eero Saarinen. Braziller
1962
Bkl A—SCPL

Nicola Sacco, 1891-1927

Felix, David. Protest: Sacco-Vanzetti and
the Intellectuals. Ind. Univ. 1965
Bkl A

Russell, Francis. Tragedy in Dedham:
The Story of the Sacco-Vanzetti Case.
McGraw 1962
Bkl A—SCPL

Maurice Samuel, 1895-

Samuel, Maurice. Little Did I Know.
Knopf 1963
Bkl A

David Sarnoff, 1891-

Lyons, Eugene. David Sarnoff: A Biography. Harper 1966
Bkl A&Y

Dalip Singh Saund, 1899-

Saund, Dalip Singh. Congressman from
India. Dutton 1960
Bkl A

COLLECTIONS

Life International. Nine Who Chose
America. Dutton 1959
Bkl Y&C—SCHS

Dore Schary, 1905-

Schary, Dore. For Special Occasions.
Random House 1962
Bkl A—BY

Béla Schick, 1877-1967

Noble, Iris. Physician to the Children:
Bela Schick. Messner 1963
IndJ(6-9)—YR

Lore Segal, ?

Segal, Lore. Other People's Houses. Harcourt 1964
Bkl A&Y—IndS(10-12)

Igor Ivan Sikorsky, 1889-

COLLECTIONS

Life International. Nine Who Chose
America. Dutton 1959
Bkl Y&C—SCHS

Spyros Panagiotes Skouras, 1893-

COLLECTIONS

Life International. Nine Who Chose
America. Dutton 1959
Bkl Y&C—SCHS

Robert Strausz-Hupé, 1903-

Strausz-Hupé, Robert. In My Time. Norton 1965
Bkl A

Igor Fedorovich Stravinsky, 1882-

Stravinsky, Igor Fedorovich. An Autobiography. Simon & Schuster 1936
CA

Stravinsky, Igor Fedorovich and Craft,
Robert. Dialogues and a Diary. Dou-
bleday 1963
Bkl A

Stravinsky, Igor Fedorovich and Craft,
Robert. Expositions and Developments.
Doubleday 1962
Bkl A

Stravinsky, Igor Fedorovich and Craft,
Robert. Memories and Commentaries.
Doubleday 1960
Bkl A—SCPL

Stravinsky, Igor Fedorovich and Craft,
Robert. Themes and Episodes. Knopf
1966
Bkl A

Tansman, Alexandre. Igor Stravinsky:
The Man and His Music; tr. by
Therese and Charles Bleefield. Putnam
1949
SCPL

Vlad, Roman. Stravinsky; tr. by Frederick and Ann Fuller. Oxford 1960
Bkl A

White, Eric Walter. Stravinsky: A Critical Survey. Philosophical Lib. 1948
SCPL

Nikola Tesla, 1857-1943

Beckhard, Arthur J. Electrical Genius Nikola Tesla. Messner 1959
Bkl Y&C

Hunt, Inez and Draper, Wanetta W.
Lightning in His Hand: The Life Story
of Nikola Tesla. Sage 1964
Bkl A&Y

Walters, Helen B. Nikola Tesla, Giant
of Electricity. Crowell 1961
JH—YR

IMMIGRANTS TO UNITED STATES

20th century—*Continued*

Maria Augusta Trapp, 1905-

Rodgers, Richard and Hammerstein II, Oscar. The Sound of Music: A New Musical Play. Random House 1960 (Play)
Bkl A

Trapp, Maria Augusta and Murdock, Ruth T. A Family on Wheels: Further Adventures of the Trapp Family Singers. Lippincott 1959
BY—SCPL

Trapp, Maria Augusta. Story of the Trapp Family Singers. Lippincott 1949
BY—SCHS—SCPL

Bartolomeo Vanzetti, 1888-1927

Felix, David. Protest: Sacco-Vanzetti and the Intellectuals. Ind. Univ. 1965
Bkl A

Russell, Francis. Tragedy in Dedham: The Story of the Sacco-Vanzetti Case. McGraw 1962
Bkl A—SCPL

Wernher Von Braun, 1912-

Bergaust, Erik. Reaching for the Stars. Doubleday 1960
Bkl A—BY

Walters, Helen B. Wernher von Braun: Rocket Engineer. Macmillan 1964
Bkl C(7-9)&Y—ESLC—JH

COLLECTIONS

Cunz, Dieter. They Came from Germany: The Story of Famous German-Americans. Dodd 1966
ESLC

Selman Abraham Waksman, 1888-

COLLECTIONS

Life International. Nine Who Chose America. Dutton 1959
Bkl Y&C—SCHS

James Paul Warburg, 1896-

Warburg, James Paul. The Long Road Home: The Autobiography of a Maverick. Doubleday 1964
Bkl A

Wladimir Savelievich Woytinsky, 1885-1960

Woytinsky, Emma (Shadkhan), ed. So Much Alive: The Life and Work of Wladimir S. Woytinsky. Vanguard 1962
Bkl A

Woytinsky, Emma (Shadkhan). Two Lives in One. Praeger 1965
Bkl A

Woytinsky, Wladimir Savelievich. Stormy Passage: A Personal History Through Two Russian Revolutions to Democracy and Freedom, 1905-1960. Vanguard 1961
Bkl A

IMPRESARIOS

See Opera Managers

INDIAN FIGHTERS

See Frontiersmen

INDIAN LEADERS

American

COLLECTIONS

Cooke, David C. Fighting Indians of the West. Dodd 1954
BBJH—SCHS

Heiderstadt, Dorothy. Indian Friends and Foes. McKay 1958
AB(4-7)

Heiderstadt, Dorothy. More Indian Friends and Foes. McKay 1963
AB(5-9)

Josephy, Alvin M. The Patriot Chiefs: A Chronicle of American Indian Leadership. Viking 1961
Bkl A&Y
Black Hawk, Sauk Chief; Crazy Horse, Sioux Chief; Hiawatha, Iroquois Chief; Joseph, Nez Percé Chief; Osceola, Seminole Chief; Philip, King (Metacomet), Sachem of the Wampanoag; Pontiac, Ottawa Chief; Popé; Tecumseh, Shawnee Chief

Porter, C. Fayne. Our Indian Heritage: Profiles of 12 Great Leaders. Chilton 1964
Bkl A&Y

American—16th century

Hiawatha, Iroquois Chief, fl. 1570

COLLECTIONS

Josephy, Alvin M. The Patriot Chiefs: A Chronicle of American Indian Leadership. Viking 1961
Bkl A&Y

American—17th century

Philip, King (Metacomet), Sachem of the Wampanoag, ?-1676

Averill, Esther. King Philip, the Indian Chief. Harper 1950
SCHS

COLLECTIONS

Josephy, Alvin M. The Patriot Chiefs: A Chronicle of American Indian Leadership. Viking 1961
Bkl A&Y

INDIAN LEADERS

American—17th century—*Continued*

Pocahontas, 1595?-1617

Aulaire, Ingri d' and Aulaire, Edgar Parin d'. Pocahontas. Doubleday 1946
CC(3-5)—ESLC

Carpenter, Frances. Pocahontas and Her World. Knopf 1957
BBJH

Lawson, Marie A. Pocahontas and Captain John Smith: The Story of the Virginia Colony. Random House 1950
CC(6-9)—ESLC—JH—SCHS

Martin, Patricia Miles. Pocahontas. Putnam 1964
ESLC

Popé, fl. 1675-1688

COLLECTIONS

Josephy, Alvin M. The Patriot Chiefs: A Chronicle of American Indian Leadership. Viking 1961
Bkl A&Y

Squanto, Wampanoag Indian, ?-1622

Bulla, Clyde Robert. John Billington, Friend of Squanto. Crowell 1956 (Fiction)
CC(3-5)

Bulla, Clyde Robert. Squanto, Friend of the White Men. Crowell 1954
BBEL(3-4)—CC(2-4)—ESLC

Graff, Stewart and Graff, Polly Anne. Squanto, Indian Adventurer. Garrard 1965
AB(3-5)

Stevenson, Augusta. Squanto, Young Indian Hunter. Bobbs 1962
AB(3-6)

Ziner, Feenie. Dark Pilgrim: The Story of Squanto. Chilton 1965
ESLC

Uncas, 1588?-1683

Voight, Virginia Frances. Uncas, Sachem of the Wolf People. Funk 1963
IndJ(6-9)—YR

American—18th century

William Augustus Bowles, 1763-1805

Millard, Joseph. The Incredible William Bowles. Chilton 1966 (Fiction)
Bkl Y

Mary Jemison, 1743-1833

Lenski, Lois. Indian Captive: The Story of Mary Jemison. Lippincott 1941
BBEL(6-8)—CC(6-9)—ESLC—JH

Pontiac, Ottawa Chief, ?-1769

Hays, Wilma Pitchford. Pontiac: Lion in the Forest. Houghton 1965
ESLC

COLLECTIONS

Josephy, Alvin M. The Patriot Chiefs: A Chronicle of American Indian Leadership. Viking 1961
Bkl A&Y

Sequoya, Cherokee Indian, 1770?-1843

Marriott, Alice Lee. Sequoyah: Leader of the Cherokees. Random House 1956
BBEL(5-8)—CC(5-7)—JH—SCHS

American—19th century

Black Hawk, Sauk Chief, 1767-1838

Fuller, Iola. The Shining Trail. Duell 1951 (Fiction)
SCHS

COLLECTIONS

Josephy, Alvin M. The Patriot Chiefs: A Chronicle of American Indian Leadership. Viking 1961
Bkl A&Y

Cochise, Apache Chief, 1815?-1874

Arnold, Elliott. Blood Brother. Duell 1950 (Fiction)
SCHS

Arnold, Elliott. Broken Arrow. Duell 1954 (Fiction)
BBJH—JH

Wyatt, Edgar. Cochise, Apache Warrior and Statesman. McGraw 1953
BBEL(6-8)—BBJH—CC(6-8)—ESLC—JH—SCHS

Crazy Horse, Sioux Chief, 1849-1877

Garst, Doris Shannon. Crazy Horse, Great Warrior of the Sioux. Houghton 1950
BBEL(5-8)—BY—CC(7-9)—ESLC—JH—SCHS

Meadowcroft, Enid La Monte. Crazy Horse, Sioux Warrior. Garrard 1965
AB(3-7)

COLLECTIONS

Josephy, Alvin M. The Patriot Chiefs: A Chronicle of American Indian Leadership. Viking 1961
Bkl A&Y

Geronimo, Apache Chief, 1829-1909

Betzinez, Jason and Nye, Wilbur Sturtevant. I Fought with Geronimo. Stackpole 1959
Bkl A

Wyatt, Edgar. Geronimo, the Last Apache War Chief. McGraw 1952
BBEL—CC(4-7)—ESLC—JH

INDIAN LEADERS

American—19th century—*Continued*

Joseph, Nez Percé Chief, 1840-1904

Davis, Russell G. and Ashabranner, Brent K. Chief Joseph: War Chief of the Nez Percé. McGraw 1962
AB(6-9)—Bkl C(5-8)—CC(5-7)—ESLC—YR

Garst, Doris Shannon. Chief Joseph of the Nez Percés. Messner 1953
BBEL(5-8)

COLLECTIONS

Josephy, Alvin M. The Patriot Chiefs: A Chronicle of American Indian Leadership. Viking 1961
Bkl A&Y

Hosteen Klah, ?

Newcomb, Franc (Johnson). Hosteen Klah, Navaho Medicine Man and Sand Painter. Univ. of Okla. 1964
Bkl A

Mangas Colorados, Apache Chief, 1793?-1863

Cooke, David Coxe. Apache Warrior. Norton 1963
Bkl C(5-9)&Y—IndJ(6-9)—YR

Moses, Sinkiuse-Columbia Chief, 1829?-1899

Ruby, Robert H. and Brown, John Arthur. Half-Sun on the Columbia: A Biography of Chief Moses. Univ. of Okla. 1965
Bkl A

Osceola, Seminole Chief, 1800-1838

Bleeker, Sonia. The Seminole Indians. Morrow 1954
CC(4-7)

Hall, Gordon Langley. Osceola. Holt 1964
IndJ(6-9)

McNeer, May Yonge. War Chief of the Seminoles. Random House 1954
BBEL(5-8)—CC(5-9)—ESLC—JH—SCHS

COLLECTIONS

Josephy, Alvin M. The Patriot Chiefs: A Chronicle of American Indian Leadership. Viking 1961
Bkl A&Y

Red Eagle, Choctaw Indian, ?

O'Moran, M. Red Eagle, Buffalo Bill's Adopted Son. Lippincott 1948
CC(6-9)

Sacagawea, Shoshone Indian, 1787-1812

Blassingame, Wyatt. Sacagawea, Indian Guide. Garrard 1965
ESLC

Farnsworth, Frances Joyce. Winged Moccasins: The Story of Sacajawea. Messner 1954
CC(7-9)—JH—SCHS

Peattie, Donald Culross. Forward the Nation. Putnam 1942
SCPL

COLLECTIONS

Ross, Nancy Wilson. Heroines of the Early West. Random House 1960
Bkl C(5-9)—BY—CC(5-7)—ESLC—JH

Seattle, Dwamish Chief, 1786-1866

Montgomery, Elizabeth Rider. Chief Seattle: Great Statesman. Garrard 1966
ESLC

Seqouya, Cherokee Indian, 1770?-1843

Marriott, Alice Lee. Sequoyah: Leader of the Cherokees. Random House 1956
BBEL(5-8)—CC(5-7)—JH—SCHS

Sitting Bull, Dakota Chief, 1834-1890

Garst, Doris Shannon. Sitting Bull, Champion of His People. Messner 1946
BBEL—CC(6-9)—JH—SCHS

John Tanner, 1780?-1847

Arnold, Elliott. White Falcon. Knopf 1955 (Fiction)
CC(7-9)—JH—SCHS

O'Meara, Walter. The Last Portage. Houghton 1962
Bkl A&Y—YR

Tecumseh, Shawnee Chief, 1768-1813

Cooke, David C. Tecumseh: Destiny's Warrior. Messner 1959
JH—SCHS

Creighton, Luella Bruce. Tecumseh: The Story of the Shawnee Chief. St Martins 1965
CC—IndJ(4-6)

Tucker, Glenn. Tecumseh: Vision of Glory. Bobbs 1956
SCPL

COLLECTIONS

Josephy, Alvin M. The Patriot Chiefs: A Chronicle of American Indian Leadership. Viking 1961
Bkl A&Y

Washakie, Shoshone Chief, 1804?-1900

COLLECTIONS

Schaefer, Jack Warner. Heroes Without Glory: Some Goodmen of the Old West. Houghton 1965
Bkl A&Y

American—20th century

Harriet M. Bedell, 1875-

Hartley, William B. and Hartley, Ellen. A Woman Set Apart. Dodd 1963
Bkl A—IndS(11-12)

INDIAN LEADERS

American—20th century—*Continued*

Ishi, 1861?-1916

Kroeber, Theodora. Ishi: Last of His Tribe. Parnassus Press 1964
AB(3-7)—Bkl C(5-8)—CC—ESLC

Kroeber, Theodora. Ishi in Two Worlds: A Biography of the Last Wild Indian in North America. Univ. of Calif. 1961
Bkl A—BY—SCHS

Hosteen Klah, ?

Newcomb, Franc (Johnson). Hosteen Klah, Navaho Medicine Man and Sand Painter. Univ. of Okla. 1964
Bkl A

Mountain Wolf Woman, 1884-1960

Mountain Wolf Woman. Mountain Wolf Woman, Sister of Crashing Thunder: The Autobiography of a Winnebago Indian; ed. by Nancy Oestreich Lurie. Univ. of Mich. 1961
Bkl A

Carl Sweezy, 1881-1953

Sweezy, Carl. The Arapaho Way: A Memoir of an Indian Boyhood, by Althea Bass. Potter 1966
Bkl A&Y

James Francis Thorpe, 1888-1953

Schoor, Gene. The Jim Thorpe Story: America's Greatest Athlete. Messner 1951
BBEL(7-8)—BBJH—BY—ESLC—JH—SCHS

INDUSTRIAL DESIGNERS

American—20th century

Raymond Loewy, 1893-

Loewy, Raymond. Never Leave Well Enough Alone. Simon & Schuster 1951
GR

INDUSTRIALISTS

See also Businessmen; Railroad Officials

American

COLLECTIONS

American Heritage. Captains of Industry, by Bernard A. Weisberger. Harper 1966
Bkl C(7-10)&Y—ESLC
Philip Danforth Armour; Andrew Carnegie; James Buchanan Duke; Henry Ford; Meyer Guggenheim; Cyrus Hall McCormick; John Davison Rockefeller; Cornelius Vanderbilt

Famous Leaders of Industry, sixth series; ed. by William H. Clark and J. H. S. Moynahan. Page 1955
SCPL

Lavine, Sigmund A. Famous Industrialists. Dodd 1961
Bkl Y&C—CC—ESLC—JH—YR

Place, Marian T. The Copper Kings of Montana. Random House 1961
ESLC—JH—SCHS—YR
William Andrews Clark; Marcus Daly; Frederick Augustus Heinze

American—19th century

Philip Danforth Armour, 1832-1901

COLLECTIONS

American Heritage. Captains of Industry, by Bernard A. Weisberger. Harper 1966
Bkl C(7-10)&Y—ESLC

Andrew Carnegie, 1835-1919

Carnegie, Andrew. Autobiography. Houghton 1920
SCPL

Harlow, Alvin Fay. Andrew Carnegie. Messner 1953
SCHS

Judson, Clara (Ingram). Andrew Carnegie. Follett 1964
CC(5-7)—JH

Shippen, Katherine B. Andrew Carnegie and the Age of Steel. Random House 1958
CC(5-7)—ESLC

COLLECTIONS

American Heritage. Captains of Industry, by Bernard A. Weisberger. Harper 1966
Bkl C(7-10)&Y—ESLC

Josephson, Matthew. Robber Barons: The Great American Capitalists, 1861-1901. Harcourt 1934
SCPL

Marcus Daly, 1841-1900

COLLECTIONS

Place, Marian T. The Copper Kings of Montana. Random House 1961
ESLC—JH—SCHS—YR

James Buchanan Duke, 1856-1925

COLLECTIONS

American Heritage. Captains of Industry, by Bernard A. Weisberger. Harper 1966
Bkl C(7-10)&Y—ESLC

Éleuthère Irénée Du Pont, 1771-1834

Carr, William H. A. The du Ponts of Delaware. Dodd 1964
Bkl A&Y

INDUSTRIALISTS

American—19th century

Éleuthère Irénée Du Pont—Continued

Dorian, Max. The du Ponts: From Gunpowder to Nylon; tr. by Edward B. Garside. Little 1962
Bkl A

Henry Clay Frick, 1849-1919

COLLECTIONS

Josephson, Matthew. Robber Barons: The Great American Capitalists, 1861-1901. Harcourt 1934
SCPL

Meyer Guggenheim, 1828-1905

COLLECTIONS

American Heritage. Captains of Industry, by Bernard A. Weisberger. Harper 1966
Bkl C(7-10)&Y—ESLC

Henry Osborne Havemeyer, 1847-1907

COLLECTIONS

Saarinen, Aline B. The Proud Possessors: The Lives, Times, and Tastes of Some Adventurous American Art Collectors. Random House 1958
SCPL

Frederick Augustus Heinze, 1869-1914

COLLECTIONS

Place, Marian T. The Copper Kings of Montana. Random House 1961
ESLC—JH—SCHS—YR

Cyrus Hall McCormick, 1809-1884

COLLECTIONS

American Heritage. Captains of Industry, by Bernard A. Weisberger. Harper 1966
Bkl C(7-10)&Y—ESLC

James O'Hara, 1752-1819

Turnbull, Agnes (Sligh). The King's Orchard. Houghton 1963 (Fiction)
Bkl A&Y

John Davison Rockefeller, 1839-1937

Abels, Jules. The Rockefeller Billions: The Story of the World's Most Stupendous Fortune. Macmillan 1965
Bkl A—IndS(11-12)

Carr, Albert H. Z. John D. Rockefeller's Secret Weapon. McGraw 1962
Bkl A

Manchester, William R. A Rockefeller Family Portrait: From John D. to Nelson. Little 1959
BY—SCPL

Nevins, Allan. John D. Rockefeller; a one-volume abridgement by William Greenleaf of Study in Power. Scribner 1959
SCPL—3000

Pyle, Tom and Day, Beth (Feagles). Pocantico: Fifty Years on the Rockefeller Domain. Duell 1964
Bkl A

COLLECTIONS

American Heritage. Captains of Industry, by Bernard A. Weisberger. Harper 1966
Bkl C(7-10)&Y—ESLC

Fanning, Leonard M. Titans of Business. Lippincott 1964
Bkl C(7-9)&Y—JH—SCHS

Josephson, Matthew. Robber Barons: The Great American Capitalists, 1861-1901. Harcourt 1934
SCPL

Myers, Gustavus. History of the Great American Fortunes. Modern Lib. 1936
SCPL

Saarinen, Aline B. The Proud Possessors: The Lives, Times, and Tastes of Some Adventurous American Art Collectors. Random House 1958
SCPL

John Augustus Roebling, 1806-1869

Steinman, D. B. Builders of the Bridge: The Story of John Roebling and His Son. Harcourt 1950
SCPL

COLLECTIONS

Cunz, Dieter. They Came from Germany: The Story of Famous German-Americans. Dodd 1966
ESLC

George Westinghouse, 1846-1914

Levine, Israel E. Inventive Wizard: George Westinghouse. Messner 1962
AB(7up)—Bkl Y&C—JH—YR

Thomas, Henry. George Westinghouse. Putnam 1960
Bkl C(5-8)—ESLC

American—20th century

Walter Percy Chrysler, 1875-1940

Chrysler, Walter Percy. Life of an American Workman. Dodd 1950
SCPL

James Buchanan Duke, 1856-1925

COLLECTIONS

American Heritage. Captains of Industry, by Bernard A. Weisberger. Harper 1966
Bkl C(7-10)&Y—ESLC

INDUSTRIALISTS

American—20th century—*Continued*

Irénée Du Pont, 1876-1963

Carr, William H. A. The du Ponts of Delaware. Dodd 1964
Bkl A&Y

Dorian, Max. The du Ponts: From Gunpowder to Nylon; tr. by Edward B. Garside. Little 1962
Bkl A

Henry Ford, 1863-1947

Burlingame, Roger. Henry Ford: A Great Life in Brief. Knopf 1955
BBHS—BY—SCHS—SCPL—3000

Nevins, Allan and Hill, Frank Ernest. Ford: v. 1, The Times, the Man, the Company. Scribner 1954
BY—SCPL

Nevins, Allan and Hill, Frank Ernest. Ford: v. 2, Expansion and Challenge, 1915-1933. Scribner 1957
SCPL

Nevins, Allan and Hill, Frank Ernest. Ford: v. 3, Decline and Rebirth, 1933-1962. Scribner 1963
Bkl A—SCPL

Neyhart, Louise Albright. Henry Ford, Engineer. Houghton 1950
BBJH—JH

COLLECTIONS

American Heritage. Captains of Industry, by Bernard A. Weisberger. Harper 1966
Bkl C(7-10)&Y—ESLC

Fanning, Leonard M. Titans of Business. Lippincott 1964
Bkl C(7-9)&Y—JH—SCHS

Jean Paul Getty, 1892-

Getty, Jean Paul. My Life and Fortunes. Duell 1963
Bkl A

Howard Robard Hughes, 1905-

Keats, John. Howard Hughes. Random House 1966
Bkl A

Charles Franklin Kettering, 1876-1958

Lavine, Sigmund A. Kettering: Master Inventor. Dodd 1960
SCHS—YR

Young, Rosamond McPherson. Boss Ket. McKay 1961
YR

Edward Lamb, 1902-

Lamb, Edward. No Lamb for Slaughter: An Autobiography. Harcourt 1963
Bkl A

Charles Stewart Mott, 1875-

Young, Clarence H. and Quinn, William A. Foundation for Living: The Story of Charles Stewart Mott and Flint. McGraw 1963
Bkl A

John Davison Rockefeller, 1839-1937

See entries under Industrialists—American—19th century

David Sarnoff, 1891-

Lyons, Eugene. David Sarnoff: A Biography. Harper 1966
Bkl A&Y

Alfred Pritchard Sloan, 1875-1966

Sloan, Alfred Pritchard. My Years with General Motors; ed. by John McDonald and Catharine Stevens. Doubleday 1964
Bkl A—SCPL

COLLECTIONS

Fanning, Leonard M. Titans of Business. Lippincott 1964
Bkl C(7-9)&Y—JH—SCHS

Thomas John Watson, 1874-1956

Belden, Thomas Graham and Belden, Marva Robins. The Lengthening Shadow: The Life of Thomas J. Watson. Little 1962
Bkl A

Swedish—20th century

Ivar Kreuger, 1880-1932

Shaplen, Robert. Kreuger, Genius and Swindler. Knopf 1960
Bkl A

INTELLIGENCE AGENTS

See also Spies

American

COLLECTIONS

Army Times. Modern American Secret Agents. Dodd 1966
Bkl C(7-9)&Y
William ("Wild Bill") Donovan; Allen Dulles; Francis Gary Powers; and others

American—20th century

William Joseph ("Wild Bill") Donovan, 1883-1959

COLLECTIONS

Army Times. Modern American Secret Agents. Dodd 1966
Bkl C(7-9)&Y

INTELLIGENCE AGENTS

American—20th century—*Continued*

Allen Welsh Dulles, 1893-1969

COLLECTIONS

Army Times. Modern American Secret Agents. Dodd 1966
Bkl C(7-9)&Y

Francis Gary Powers, 1929-

COLLECTIONS

Army Times. Modern American Secret Agents. Dodd 1966
Bkl C(7-9)&Y

INVALIDS

See Physically Handicapped

INVENTORS

COLLECTIONS

Bachman, Frank P. Great Inventors and Their Inventions. Am. Bk 1946
CC(6-8)—JH—SCHS

Evans, Idrisyn Oliver. Inventors of the World. Warne 1962
Bkl Y&C(6-9)—ESLC—JH

Fanning, Leonard M. Fathers of Industries. Lippincott 1962
Bkl C(6-9)&Y—ESLC—JH

Larsen, Egon. Men Who Changed the World: Stories of Invention and Discovery. Roy 1952
SCHS

Manchester, Harland Frank. Trail Blazers of Technology: The Story of Nine Inventors. Scribner 1962
Bkl Y&C—JH—YR
Thomas Davenport; Lee De Forest; Rudolf Diesel; Charles Goodyear; Simon Lake; Sir Hiram Stevens Maxim; Alfred Nobel; Igor Sikorsky; Nikola Tesla

Pratt, Fletcher. All About Famous Inventors and Their Inventions. Random House 1955
AB(6-9)—BBEL—CC(5-8)—JH—SCHS

Wagner, Frederick. Famous Underwater Adventurers. Dodd 1962
Bkl C(7up)&Y—ESLC—JH

American

COLLECTIONS

American Heritage. Men of Science and Invention, by Michael Blow and Robert P. Multhauf. Am. Heritage 1960
Bkl C(5-8)—CC(5-8)—ESLC—JH—SCHS—YR

Burlingame, Roger. Inventors Behind the Inventor. Harcourt 1947
JH—SCHS

De Camp, Lyon Sprague. The Heroic Age of American Invention. Doubleday 1961
Bkl A&Y

Hylander, Clarence John. American Inventors. Macmillan 1934
BBEL(6-8)—SCHS—SCPL

American—18th century

David Bushnell, 1742?-1824

Wagner, Frederick. Submarine Fighter of the American Revolution. Dodd 1963
Bkl Y&C—IndS(11-12)

Robert Fulton, 1765-1815

Hill, Ralph Nading. Robert Fulton and the Steamboat. Random House 1954
CC(4-6)—JH—SCHS

Judson, Clara (Ingram). Boat Builder: The Story of Robert Fulton. Scribner 1940
BBJH—CC(4-6)—ESLC—JH—SCHS

Eli Whitney, 1765-1825

Hays, Wilma Pitchford. Eli Whitney and the Machine Age. Watts 1959
Bkl C(4-5)

Latham, Jean Lee. Eli Whitney: Great Inventor. Garrard 1963
ESLC

Mirsky, Jeanette and Nevins, Allan. World of Eli Whitney. Macmillan 1952
SCPL

American—19th century

Alexander Graham Bell, 1847-1922

Burlingame, Roger. Out of Silence into Sound: The Life of Alexander Graham Bell. Macmillan 1964
Bkl C(6-8)—YR

Costain, Thomas Bertram. The Chord of Steel: The Story of the Invention of the Telephone. Doubleday 1960
Bkl A&Y—SCHS—SCPL

Montgomery, Elizabeth Rider. Alexander Graham Bell. Garrard 1963
AB(4-7)

Shippen, Katherine Binney. Mr. Bell Invents the Telephone. Random House 1952
BBEL(5-8)—BBJH—CC(4-7)—ESLC—JH—SCHS

Stevenson, Orlando John. The Talking Wire: The Story of Alexander Graham Bell. Messner 1947
SCHS—YR

Waite, Helen Elmira. Make a Joyful Sound: The Romance of Mabel Hubbard and Alexander Graham Bell; an authorized biography. Macrae 1961
Bkl A&Y

INVENTORS

American—19th century—*Continued*

John Moses Browning, 1855-1926

Browning, John and Gentry, Curt. John M. Browning, American Gunmaker: An Illustrated Biography of the Man and His Guns. Doubleday 1964
Bkl A&Y

Winders, Gertrude (Hecker). Browning: World's Greatest Gunmaker. Day 1961
Bkl C(5-8)—YR

Samuel Colt, 1814-1862

COLLECTIONS

Freedman, Russell. Teenagers Who Made History. Holiday 1961
BY—JH—SCHS—YR

Thomas Davenport, 1802-1851

COLLECTIONS

Manchester, Harland Frank. Trail Blazers of Technology: The Story of Nine Inventors. Scribner 1962
Bkl Y&C—JH—YR

John Ericsson, 1803-1889

Burnett, Constance (Buel). Captain John Ericsson: Father of the Monitor. Vanguard 1961
Bkl C(6-10)&Y

Latham, Jean Lee. Man of the Monitor: The Story of John Ericsson. Harper 1962
Bkl C(5-7)—CC(5-7)—ESLC—JH—YR

Pratt, Fletcher. The Monitor and the Merrimac. Random House 1951
BBJH—ESLC—JH

Robert Fulton, 1765-1815

Hill, Ralph Nading. Robert Fulton and the Steamboat. Random House 1954
CC(4-6)—JH—SCHS

Judson, Clara (Ingram). Boat Builder: The Story of Robert Fulton. Scribner 1940
BBJH—CC(4-6)—ESLC—JH—SCHS

Charles Goodyear, 1800-1860

COLLECTIONS

Manchester, Harland Frank. Trail Blazers of Technology: The Story of Nine Inventors. Scribner 1962
Bkl Y&C—JH—YR

Thaddeus Sobieski Coulincourt Lowe, 1832-1913

Block, Eugene B. Above the Civil War: The Story of Thaddeus Lowe, Balloonist, Inventor, Railway Builder. Howell-North 1966
Bkl A&Y

Sims, Lydel. Thaddeus Lowe: Uncle Sam's First Airman. Putnam 1964
Bkl C(7-9)&Y—ESLC—JH

Cyrus Hall McCormick, 1809-1884

COLLECTIONS

American Heritage. Captains of Industry, by Bernard A. Weisberger. Harper 1966
Bkl C(7-10)&Y—ESLC

Ottmar Mergenthaler, 1854-1899

Levine, Israel E. Miracle Man of Printing: Ottmar Mergenthaler. Messner 1963
Bkl Y&C

COLLECTIONS

Cunz, Dieter. They Came from Germany: The Story of Famous German-Americans. Dodd 1966
ESLC

Samuel Finley Breese Morse, 1791-1872

Hays, Wilma Pitchford. Samuel Morse and the Electronic Age. Watts 1966
Bkl C(4-7)

Hays, Wilma Pitchford. Samuel Morse and the Telegraph. Watts 1960
Bkl C(4-6)

Latham, Jean Lee. Samuel F. B. Morse, Artist-Inventor. Garrard 1961
AB(3-7)—ESLC

Mabee, F. C. American Leonardo: A Life of Samuel F. B. Morse. Knopf 1943
SCPL

Nicholas J. Roosevelt, 1767-1854

North, Sterling. The First Steamboat on the Mississippi. Houghton 1962
YR

George Westinghouse, 1846-1914

Levine, Israel E. Inventive Wizard: George Westinghouse. Messner 1962
AB(7up)—Bkl Y&C—JH—YR

Thomas, Henry. George Westinghouse. Putnam 1960
Bkl C(5-8)—ESLC

Eli Whitney, 1765-1825

Hays, Wilma Pitchford. Eli Whitney and the Machine Age. Watts 1959
Bkl C(4-5)

Latham, Jean Lee. Eli Whitney: Great Inventor. Garrard 1963
ESLC

Mirsky, Jeanette and Nevins, Allan. World of Eli Whitney. Macmillan 1952
SCPL

INVENTORS—*Continued*

American—20th century

Alexander Graham Bell, 1847-1922

Burlingame, Roger. Out of Silence into Sound: The Life of Alexander Graham Bell. Macmillan 1964
Bkl C(6-8)—YR

Costain, Thomas Bertram. The Chord of Steel: The Story of the Invention of the Telephone. Doubleday 1960
Bkl A&Y—SCHS—SCPL

Montgomery, Elizabeth Rider. Alexander Graham Bell. Garrard 1963
AB(4-7)

Shippen, Katherine Binney. Mr. Bell Invents the Telephone. Random House 1952
BBEL(5-8)—BBJH—CC(4-7)—ESLC—JH SCHS

Stevenson, Orlando John. The Talking Wire: The Story of Alexander Graham Bell. Messner 1947
SCHS—YR

Waite, Helen Elmira. Make a Joyful Sound: The Romance of Mabel Hubbard and Alexander Graham Bell; an authorized biography. Macrae 1961
Bkl A&Y

John Moses Browning, 1855-1926

Browning, John and Gentry, Curt. John M. Browning, American Gunmaker: An Illustrated Biography of the Man and His Guns. Doubleday 1964
Bkl Y&A

Winders, Gertrude (Hecker). Browning: World's Greatest Gunmaker. Day 1961
Bkl C(5-8)—YR

Lee De Forest, 1873-1961

Levine, Irving Englander. Electronics Pioneer: Lee De Forest. Messner 1964
Bkl C(6-9)&Y—JH—YR

COLLECTIONS

Manchester, Harland Frank. Trail Blazers of Technology: The Story of Nine Inventors. Scribner 1962
Bkl Y&C—JH—YR

Thomas Alva Edison, 1847-1931

Compere, Mickie. The Wizard of Menlo Park: The Story of Thomas Alva Edison, Inventor. Scholastic 1964
ESLC

Cousins, Margaret. The Story of Thomas Alva Edison. Random House 1965
Bkl C(4-6)—ESLC

Edison, Thomas Alva. Diary and Sundry Observations; ed. by D. D. Runes. Philosophical Lib. 1948
SCPL

Josephson, Matthew. Edison: A Biography. McGraw 1959
BBHS—BY—SCPL—3000

Lewis, Floyd A. The Incandescent Light: A Review of Its Invention and Application; ed. by Henry H. Urrows. Shorewood Pubs 1961
ESLC

Meadowcroft, W. H. The Boy's Life of Edison, with Autobiographical Notes by Mr. Edison. Harper 1929
CC(6-7)—JH

North, Sterling. Young Thomas Edison. Houghton 1958
AB(5-9)—BBJH—CC(5-7)—ESLC—JH—SCHS

Shapp, Martha and Shapp, Charles. Let's Find Out about Thomas Alva Edison. Watts 1966
ESLC

Thomas, Henry. Thomas Alva Edison. Putnam 1958
BBEL(5-8)—ESLC

Van de Water, Marjorie. Edison Experiments You Can Do: Based on the Original Notebooks of Thomas Alva Edison. Harper 1960
CC(5-7)—ESLC

Weir, Ruth C. Thomas Alva Edison, Inventor. Abingdon 1953
AB(3-7)

COLLECTIONS

Bixby, William. Great Experimenters. McKay 1964
Bkl C(7-8)&Y—ESLC

Charles Franklin Kettering, 1876-1958

Lavine, Sigmund A. Kettering: Master Inventor. Dodd 1960
SCHS—YR

Young, Rosamond McPherson. Boss Ket. McKay 1961
YR

Michael Idvorsky Pupin, 1858-1935

Markey, Dorothy. Explorer of Sound: Michael Pupin. Messner 1964
YR

Pupin, Michael Idvorsky. From Immigrant to Inventor. Scribner 1923
BBHS—SCPL

Nikola Tesla, 1857-1943

Beckhard, Arthur J. Electrical Genius Nikola Tesla. Messner 1959
Bkl Y&C

Hunt, Inez and Draper, Wanetta W. Lightning in His Hand: The Life Story of Nikola Tesla. Sage 1964
Bkl A&Y

Walters, Helen B. Nikola Tesla, Giant of Electricity. Crowell 1961
JH—YR

INVENTORS

American—20th century

Nikola Tesla—Continued

COLLECTIONS

Manchester, Harland Frank. Trail Blazers of Technology: The Story of Nine Inventors. Scribner 1962
Bkl Y&C—JH—YR

English—19th century

Sir George Cayley, Bart., 1773-1857

Pritchard, John Laurence. Sir George Cayley, the Inventor of the Aeroplane. Horizon 1962
Bkl A

Sir Hiram Stevens Maxim, 1840-1916

COLLECTIONS

Manchester, Harland Frank. Trail Blazers of Technology: The Story of Nine Inventors. Scribner 1962
Bkl Y&C—JH—YR

German—19th century

Rudolf Diesel, 1858-1913

Wilson, Charles Morrow. Diesel: His Engine Changed the World. Van Nostrand 1966
ESLC

COLLECTIONS

Manchester, Harland Frank. Trail Blazers of Technology: The Story of Nine Inventors. Scribner 1962
Bkl Y&C—JH—YR

Greek—3rd century B.C.

Archimedes, 287?-212 B.C.

Bendick, Jeanne. Archimedes and the Door of Science. Watts 1962
Bkl C(6-9)—ESLC—JH
Jonas, Arthur. Archimedes and His Wonderful Discoveries. Prentice-Hall 1963
CC(3-6)—ESLC—IndJ(4-6)

Italian—15th century

Leonardo da Vinci, 1452-1519

Cooper, Margaret. The Inventions of Leonardo da Vinci. Macmillan 1965
Bkl Y&C
McLanathan, Richard B. K. Images of the Universe: Leonardo da Vinci, the Artist as Scientist. Doubleday 1966
Bkl Y&A

Italian—16th century

Leonardo da Vinci, 1452-1519

Cooper, Margaret. The Inventions of Leonardo da Vinci. Macmillan 1965
Bkl Y&C

McLanathan, Richard B. K. Images of the Universe: Leonardo da Vinci, the Artist as Scientist. Doubleday 1966
Bkl Y&A

Italian—20th century

Guglielmo Marconi, Marchese, 1874-1937

Coe, Douglas. Marconi, Pioneer of Radio. Messner 1943
CC(7-9)—JH—SCHS
Marconi, Degna. My Father, Marconi. McGraw 1962
Bkl A—SCPL

Scottish—18th century

James Watt, 1736-1819

Crane, William Dwight. The Man Who Transformed the World: James Watt. Messner 1963
Bkl C(7-10)&Y—YR

COLLECTIONS

Bixby, William. Great Experimenters. McKay 1964
Bkl C(7-8)&Y—ESLC
Burlingame, Roger. Scientists Behind the Inventors. Harcourt 1960
AB(7up)—Bkl C(7-9)&Y—CC(6-9)—ESLC—JH—SCHS
Crowther, James Gerald. Scientists of the Industrial Revolution. Dufour 1963
Bkl A

Swedish—19th century

Alfred Bernhard Nobel, 1833-1896

Bergengren, Erik. Alfred Nobel: The Man and His Work. Nelson 1962
BY
Meyer, Edith Patterson. Dynamite and Peace. Little 1958
AB(5up)—BBJH—CC(7-9)—JH—SCHS

COLLECTIONS

Manchester, Harland Frank. Trail Blazers of Technology: The Story of Nine Inventors. Scribner 1962
Bkl Y&C—JH—YR

JAZZ MUSICIANS

See Musicians—American—Collections; also names of instrumentalists, e.g., Clarinetists; Trumpeters

JEWS

COLLECTIONS

Kagan, Henry Enoch. Six Who Changed the World. Yoseloff 1963
Bkl A
Albert Einstein; Sigmund Freud; Jesus Christ; Karl Marx; Moses; Saint Paul

JOCKEYS

American—20th century

George Monroe Woolf, 1910-1946

COLLECTIONS

Boynick, David King. Champions by Setback: Athletes Who Overcame Physical Handicaps. Crowell 1954
SCHS

JOURNALISTS

See also Printers; Sportswriters

American

COLLECTIONS

Chalmers, David Mark. The Social and Political Ideas of the Muckrakers. Citadel 1964
Bkl A

Lewis, Mildred and Lewis, Milton. Famous Modern Newspaper Writers. Dodd 1962
Bkl Y&C
Brooks Atkinson; Meyer Berger; Heywood Campbell Broun; Art Buchwald; Abel Green; Sylvia (Field) Porter; Ernest Taylor Pyle; James Barrett Reston; Walter Wellesley ("Red") Smith

American—18th century

John Peter Zenger, 1697-1746

Galt, Thomas Franklin. Peter Zenger, Fighter for Freedom. Crowell 1951
AB(5-9)—BBEL(7-8)—BY—CC(7-9)—ESLC—JH—SCHS

COLLECTIONS

Cunz, Dieter. They Came from Germany: The Story of Famous German-Americans. Dodd 1966
ESLC

American—19th century

James Gordon Bennett, 1841-1918

O'Connor, Richard. The Scandalous Mr. Bennett. Doubleday 1962
Bkl A

Josephus Daniels, 1862-1948

Daniels, Josephus. Shirt-Sleeve Diplomat. Univ. of N. C. 1947
SCPL

Daniels, Josephus. Tar Heel Editor. Univ. of N. C. 1939
SCPL

Richard Harding Davis, 1864-1916

Langford, Gerald. The Richard Harding Davis Years: A Biography of a Mother and Son. Holt 1961
Bkl A

Miner, Lewis S. Front Lines and Headlines: Richard Harding Davis. Messner 1959
YR

Horace Greeley, 1811-1872

Faber, Doris. Horace Greeley: The People's Editor. Prentice-Hall 1964
ESLC

Winders, Gertrude Hecker. Horace Greeley: Newspaperman. Day 1962
AB(5-9)

Sarah Josepha (Buell) Hale, 1788-1879

Burt, Olive. First Woman Editor: Sarah J. Hale. Messner 1960
Bkl C(7-10)&Y—SCHS—YR

Henry Hotze, 1834-1887

COLLECTIONS

Dufour, Charles L. Nine Men in Gray. Doubleday 1963
Bkl A&Y

William D'Alton Mann, 1839-1920

Logan, Andy. The Man Who Robbed the Robber Barons. Norton 1965
Bkl A

Joseph Pulitzer, 1847-1911

Granberg, W. J. The World of Joseph Pulitzer. Abelard-Schuman 1965
ESLC

Noble, Iris. Joseph Pulitzer: Front Page Pioneer. Messner 1957
BBJH—JH—SCHS—YR

Henry Jarvis Raymond, 1820-1869

Brown, E. Francis. Raymond of the Times. Norton 1951
SCPL

Jacob August Riis, 1849-1914

Riis, Jacob August. Making of an American. Macmillan 1929
GR—SCPL

Edmund Gibson Ross, 1826-1907

Erdman, Loula Grace. Many a Voyage. Dodd 1960 (Fiction)
Bkl A&Y

Carl Schurz, 1829-1906

Schurz, Carl. Autobiography; an abridgement in one volume by Wayne Andrews. Scribner 1961
Bkl A

COLLECTIONS

Cunz, Dieter. They Came from Germany: The Story of Famous German-Americans. Dodd 1966
ESLC

JOURNALISTS

American—19th century—*Continued*

Elizabeth (Cochrane) Seaman, 1867-1922

Baker, Nina Brown. Nellie Bly. Holt 1956
BBJH—SCHS—YR

Lincoln Steffens, 1866-1936

Steffens, Lincoln. The Autobiography of Lincoln Steffens. Harcourt 1931
BBHS—BY—CA—GR—SCHS—SCPL—3000

Steffens, Lincoln. Boy on Horseback; reprinted from The Autobiography of Lincoln Steffens. Harcourt 1935
AB(6-10)—BY—CC(6-9)—JH—SCHS

Oswald Garrison Villard, 1872-1949

Wreszin, Michael. Oswald Garrison Villard, Pacifist at War. Ind. Univ. 1965
Bkl A

American—20th century

Hamilton Fish Armstrong, 1893-

Armstrong, Hamilton Fish. Those Days. Harper 1963
Bkl A

Bettina (Hill) Ballard, 1905?-1961

Ballard, Bettina (Hill). In My Fashion. McKay 1960
Bkl A

Meyer Berger, 1898-1959

COLLECTIONS

Lewis, Mildred and Lewis, Milton. Famous Modern Newspaper Writers. Dodd 1962
Bkl Y&C

Claude Gernade Bowers, 1878-1958

Bowers, Claude Gernade. My Life: The Memoirs of Claude Bowers. Simon & Schuster 1962
Bkl A

Heywood Campbell Broun, 1888-1939

COLLECTIONS

Lewis, Mildred and Lewis, Milton. Famous Modern Newspaper Writers. Dodd 1962
Bkl Y&C

Art Buchwald, 1925-

COLLECTIONS

Lewis, Mildred and Lewis, Milton. Famous Modern Newspaper Writers. Dodd 1962
Bkl Y&C

Hodding Carter, 1907-

Carter, Hodding. First Person Rural. Doubleday 1963
Bkl A

Dickey Chapelle, 1918-1965

Chapelle, Dickey. What's a Woman Doing Here? A Reporter's Report on Herself. Morrow 1962
Bkl A&Y—BY

Ilka Chase, 1905-

Chase, Ilka. The Carthaginian Rose. Doubleday 1961
Bkl A

Bill Corum, 1894-1958

Corum, Bill. Off and Running; ed. by Arthur Mann. Holt 1959
Bkl A

Josephus Daniels, 1862-1948

Daniels, Josephus. Shirt-Sleeve Diplomat. Univ. of N. C. 1947
SCPL

Daniels, Josephus. Tar Heel Editor. Univ. of N. C. 1939
SCPL

Elmer Davis, 1890-1958

Burlingame, Roger. Don't Let Them Scare You: The Life and Times of Elmer Davis. Lippincott 1961
Bkl A—BY

Richard Harding Davis, 1864-1916

Langford, Gerald. The Richard Harding Davis Years: A Biography of a Mother and Son. Holt 1961
Bkl A

Miner, Lewis S. Front Lines and Headlines: Richard Harding Davis. Messner 1959
YR

Ralph De Toledano, 1916-

De Toledano, Ralph. Lament for a Generation. Farrar 1960
Bkl A

George Dixon, 1900?-

Dixon, George. Leaning on a Column. Lippincott 1961
Bkl A

Robert Luther Duffus, 1888-

Duffus, Robert Luther. The Tower of Jewels: Memories of San Francisco. Norton 1960
Bkl A

P. D. East, 1922-

East, P. D. The Magnolia Jungle: The Life, Times, and Education of a Southern Editor. Simon & Schuster 1960
Bkl A

JOURNALISTS

American—20th century—_Continued_

Max Eastman, 1883-1969

Eastman, Max. Love and Revolution: My Journey Through an Epoch. Random House 1965
Bkl A

Marshall Field III, 1893-1956

Becker, Stephen D. Marshall Field III: A Biography. Simon & Schuster 1964
Bkl A

Gene Fowler, 1890-1960

Fowler, Gene. Skyline: A Reporter's Reminiscence of the 1920's. Viking 1961
Bkl A—SCPL
Fowler, Will. The Young Man from Denver. Doubleday 1962
Bkl A

Harry Lewis Golden, 1902-

COLLECTIONS

Levin, Martin, ed. Five Boyhoods. Doubleday 1962
Bkl A&Y

Abel Green, 1900-

COLLECTIONS

Lewis, Mildred and Lewis, Milton. Famous Modern Newspaper Writers. Dodd 1962
Bkl Y&C

John Gunther, 1901-

Gunther, John. A Fragment of Autobiography. Harper 1962
Bkl A&Y—BY

William Randolph Hearst, 1863-1951

Swanberg, W. A. Citizen Hearst: A Biography of William Randolph Hearst. Scribner 1961
Bkl A&Y—BY—GR—SCPL
Tebbel, John William. Life and Good Times of William Randolph Hearst. Dutton 1952
SCPL

Ernest Hemingway, 1898-1961

Baker, Carlos Heard. Hemingway: The Writer as Artist. Princeton Univ. 1956
SCPL
Baker, Carlos Heard, ed. Hemingway and His Critics: An International Anthology. Hill & Wang 1961
SCPL
Hemingway, Ernest. A Moveable Feast. Scribner 1964
Bkl A—IndS(11-12)—SCHS—SCPL
Hemingway, Leicester. My Brother, Ernest Hemingway. World 1962
Bkl A

Hotchner, A. E. Papa Hemingway: A Personal Memoir. Random House 1966
Bkl A
Lania, Leo. Hemingway: A Pictorial Biography. Viking 1961
Bkl A&Y
McCaffery, John Kerwin Michael. Ernest Hemingway: The Man and His Work. World 1950
SCPL
Ross, Lillian. Portrait of Hemingway. Simon & Schuster 1961
Bkl A
Rovit, Earl H. Ernest Hemingway. Twayne 1963
Bkl A—SCHS—SCPL
Sanford, Marcelline (Hemingway). At the Hemingways: A Family Portrait. Little 1962
Bkl A&Y—BY—SCHS

Marguerite Higgins, 1920-1966

COLLECTIONS

Forsee, Aylesa. American Women Who Scored Firsts. Macrae 1958
SCHS

Ralph McAllister Ingersoll, 1900-

Ingersoll, Ralph McAllister. Point of Departure: An Adventure in Autobiography. Harcourt 1961
Bkl A

Paul Jacobs, 1918-

Jacobs, Paul. Is Curly Jewish? A Political Self-Portrait Illuminating Three Turbulent Decades of Social Revolt, 1935-1965. Atheneum 1965
Bkl A

Weimar Jones, ?

Jones, Weimar. My Affair with a Weekly. Blair 1960
Bkl A

Hans von Kaltenborn, 1878-1965

Kaltenborn, Hans von. Fifty Fabulous Years, 1900-1950: A Personal Review. Putnam 1950
SCPL

John Kieran, 1892-

Kieran, John. Not under Oath: Recollections and Reflections. Houghton 1964
Bkl A&Y

Walter Lippmann, 1889-

Childs, Marquis and Reston, James, eds. Walter Lippmann and His Times. Harcourt 1959
SCPL

Samuel Sidney McClure, 1857-1949

Lyon, Peter. Success Story: The Life and Times of S. S. McClure. Scribner 1963
Bkl A

JOURNALISTS

American—20th century—_Continued_

Robert Rutherford McCormick, 1880-1955

Waldrop, Frank C. McCormick of Chicago: An Unconventional Portrait of a Controversial Figure. Prentice-Hall 1966
Bkl A

William D'Alton Mann, 1839-1920

Logan, Andy. The Man Who Robbed the Robber Barons. Norton 1965
Bkl A

Thomas Stanley Matthews, 1901-

Matthews, Thomas Stanley. Name and Address: An Autobiography. Simon & Schuster 1960
Bkl A

Henry Louis Mencken, 1880-1956

Angoff, Charles. H. L. Mencken: A Portrait from Memory. Yoseloff 1956
SCPL
Mencken, Henry Louis. Days of H. L. Mencken. 3v. Knopf 1940-43
GR
Mencken, Henry Louis. Heathen Days, 1890-1936. Knopf 1943
SCPL
Mencken, Henry Louis. Letters; selected and annotated by Guy J. Forgue. Knopf 1961
Bkl A

COLLECTIONS

Geismar, Maxwell David. Last of the Provincials: The American Novel, 1915-1925. Houghton 1947
SCPL

Charles W. Morton, 1899-

Morton, Charles W. It Has Its Charms. Lippincott 1966
Bkl A

Frank Luther Mott, 1886-1964

Mott, Frank Luther. Time Enough: Essays in Autobiography. Univ. of N. C. 1962
Bkl A

Carl M. Mydans, 1907-

Mydans, Carl M. More than Meets the Eye. Harper 1959
SCPL

Adolph S. Ochs, 1858-1935

Faber, Doris. Printer's Devil to Publisher: Adolph S. Ochs of The New York Times. Messner 1963
Bkl C(7-10)&Y—BY—ESLC—YR

Louella (Oettinger) Parsons, 1893-

Parsons, Louella (Oettinger). Tell It to Louella. Putnam 1961
Bkl A

Eleanor Medill Patterson, 1884-1948

Healy, Paul F. Cissy: The Biography of Eleanor M. "Cissy" Patterson. Doubleday 1966
Bkl A
Hoge, Alice Albright. Cissy Patterson. Random House 1966
Bkl A

Maxwell Evarts Perkins, 1884-1947

Perkins, Maxwell Evarts. Editor to Author: The Letters of Maxwell E. Perkins; ed. by J. H. Wheelock. Scribner 1950
SCPL

Virgilia Peterson, 1904-1966

Peterson, Virgilia. A Matter of Life and Death. Atheneum 1961
Bkl A

Sylvia (Field) Porter, 1913-

COLLECTIONS

Lewis, Mildred and Lewis, Milton. Famous Modern Newspaper Writers. Dodd 1962
Bkl Y&C

Ernest Taylor Pyle, 1900-1945

COLLECTIONS

Lewis, Mildred and Lewis, Milton. Famous Modern Newspaper Writers. Dodd 1962
Bkl Y&C

James Barrett Reston, 1909-

COLLECTIONS

Lewis, Mildred and Lewis, Milton. Famous Modern Newspaper Writers. Dodd 1962
Bkl Y&C

Quentin James Reynolds, 1902-1965

Reynolds, Quentin James. By Quentin Reynolds. McGraw 1963
Bkl A&Y—IndS(9-12)

Grantland Rice, 1880-1954

Rice, Grantland. The Tumult and the Shouting: My Life in the Sport. Barnes 1954
SCHS

Jacob August Riis, 1849-1914

Riis, Jacob August. Making of an American. Macmillan 1929
GR—SCPL

JOURNALISTS

American—20th century—Continued

Harold Wallace Ross, 1892-1951

Thurber, James. Years with Ross. Little
    1959
    SCPL

Damon Runyon, 1880-1946

Hoyt, Edwin Palmer. A Gentleman of
    Broadway. Little 1964
    Bkl A—IndS(10-12)

Robert St. John, 1902-

St. John, Robert. Foreign Correspondent.
    Doubleday 1957
    SCPL
St. John, Robert. This Was My World.
    Doubleday 1953
    SCPL

Ralph Schoenstein, 1933-

Schoenstein, Ralph. The Block. Random
    House 1960
    Bkl A

*Elizabeth (Cochrane) Seaman, 1867-
1922*

Baker, Nina Brown. Nellie Bly. Holt
    1956
    BBJH—SCHS—YR

Ellery Sedgwick, 1872-1960

Sedgwick, Ellery. Happy Profession. Lit-
    tle 1946
    SCPL

Arnold Eric Sevareid, 1912-

Sevareid, Arnold Eric. Not So Wild a
    Dream. Knopf 1946
    BY—SCPL

Paul Clifford Smith, 1908-

Smith, Paul Clifford. Personal File. Ap-
    pleton 1964
    Bkl A

Carmel (White) Snow, 1890-1961

Snow, Carmel (White) and Aswell, Mary
    Louise (White). The World of Carmel
    Snow. McGraw 1962
    Bkl A

Edgar Snow, 1905-

Snow, Edgar. Journey to the Beginning.
    Random House 1958
    SCPL

Lincoln Steffens, 1866-1936

Steffens, Lincoln. The Autobiography of
    Lincoln Steffens. Harcourt 1931
    BBHS—BY—CA—GR—SCHS—SCPL—3000

Julius David Stern, 1886-

Stern, Julius David. Memoirs of a Mav-
    erick Publisher. Simon & Schuster 1962
    Bkl A

Michael Stern, ?

Stern, Michael. An American in Rome.
    Geis 1964
    Bkl A

Raymond Swing, 1887-1968

Swing, Raymond. "Good Evening!" Har-
    court 1964
    Bkl A

Herbert Bayard Swope, 1882-1958

Kahn, Ely Jacques. The World of Swope.
    Simon & Schuster 1965
    Bkl A

Lowell Jackson Thomas, 1892-

Comfort, Mildred Houghton. Lowell
    Thomas, Adventurer. Denison 1965
    JH

Dorothy Thompson, 1894-1961

Sheean, Vincent. Dorothy and Red.
    Houghton 1963
    Bkl A—SCPL

Oswald Garrison Villard, 1872-1949

Wreszin, Michael. Oswald Garrison Vil-
    lard, Pacifist at War. Ind. Univ. 1965
    Bkl A

William Allen White, 1868-1944

Hinshaw, David. Man from Kansas: The
    Story of William Allen White. Putnam
    1945
    SCPL
White, William Allen. Autobiography.
    Macmillan 1946
    SCHS—SCPL

Ella Winter, 1898-

Winter, Ella. And Not to Yield: An Au-
    tobiography. Harcourt 1963
    Bkl A

William Knowlton Zinsser, 1922-

COLLECTIONS

Levin, Martin, ed. Five Boyhoods. Dou-
    bleday 1962
    Bkl A&Y

English—20th century

Gerald Brenan, 1894-

Brenan, Gerald. A Life of One's Own:
    Childhood and Youth. Farrar 1963
    Bkl A

Patrick Skene Catling, ?

Catling, Patrick Skene. Better Than
    Working. Macmillan 1960
    Bkl A

JOURNALISTS

English—20th century—*Continued*

Gilbert Keith Chesterton, 1874-1936

Chesterton, Gilbert Keith. Autobiography. Sheed 1936
SCPL

Ward, Maisie. Gilbert Keith Chesterton. Sheed 1943
SCPL

Arthur Christiansen, 1904-1963

Christiansen, Arthur. Headlines All My Life. Harper 1962
Bkl A

Randolph Frederick Edward Spencer Churchill, 1911-1968

Churchill, Randolph Frederick Edward Spencer. Twenty-one Years. Houghton 1965
Bkl A

Claud Cockburn, 1904-

Cockburn, Claud. Crossing the Line, Being the Second Volume of Autobiography. Monthly Review 1960
Bkl A

Cockburn, Claud. View from the West, Being the Third Volume of Autobiography. Monthly Review 1962
Bkl A

Richard Collier, 1924-

Collier, Richard. A House Called Memory. Dutton 1961
BY

James Wedgwood Drawbell, 1899-

Drawbell, James Wedgwood. James Drawbell: An Autobiography. Pantheon 1964
Bkl A

Willi Frischauer, 1906-

Frischauer, Willi. European Commuter. Macmillan 1964
Bkl A

Sheilah Graham, ?

Graham, Sheilah. Beloved Infidel: The Education of a Woman. Holt 1958
SCPL

Graham, Sheilah. The Rest of the Story. Coward-McCann 1964
Bkl A

Eric Hawkins, 1888-

Hawkins, Eric and Sturdevant, Robert N. Hawkins of the Paris Herald. Simon & Schuster 1963
Bkl A

Lina (Duff-Gordon) Waterfield, 1874-

Waterfield, Lina (Duff-Gordon). Castle in Italy: An Autobiography. Crowell 1962
Bkl A

Desmond Young, 1892?-1966

Young, Desmond. All the Best Years. Harper 1961
Bkl A&Y—BY

German—20th century

Richard Sorge, 1895-1944

Johnson, Chalmers A. An Instance of Treason: Ozaki Hotsumi and the Sorge Spy Ring. Stanford Univ. 1964
Bkl A

South African—20th century

Noni Jabavu, 1919?-

Jabavu, Noni. The Ochre People: Scenes from a South African Life. St Martins 1963
IndS(11-12)

Bloke Modisane, ?

Modisane, Bloke. Blame Me on History. Dutton 1963
Bkl A

Welsh—19th century

Sir Henry Morton Stanley, 1841-1904

Anstruther, Ian. Dr. Livingstone, I Presume? Dutton 1957
SCPL

Benét, Laura. Stanley, Invincible Explorer. Dodd 1955
BY—SCHS

Busoni, Rafaello. Stanley's Africa. Viking 1944
BBJH—CC(7-9)—SCHS

Farwell, Byron. Man Who Presumed: A Biography of Henry M. Stanley. Holt 1957
SCPL

Hall-Quest, Olga (Wilbourne). With Stanley in Africa. Dutton 1961
Bkl C(6-9)—CC—ESLC—JH—SCHS

Stanley, Sir Henry Morton. The Exploration Diaries; ed. by Richard Stanley and Alan Neame. Vanguard 1962
Bkl A

Sterling, Thomas L. Stanley's Way: A Sentimental Journey through Central Africa. Atheneum 1960
Bkl A

JUDGES

See Lawyers

JURISTS

See Lawyers

JUSTICES OF THE SUPREME COURT

See Lawyers

KINGS

See also Czars; Emperors, Sultans

COLLECTIONS

Coen, Rena Neumann. Kings and Queens in Art. Lerner Publications 1965
ESLC

Coffman, Ramon Peyton. Famous Kings and Queens for Young People. Dodd 1947
BBJH–JH

Dobler, Lavinia and Brown, William A. Great Rulers of the African Past. Doubleday 1965
ESLC

Farjeon, Eleanor and Mayne, William, eds. A Cavalcade of Kings. Walck 1964
ESLC

Herodotus. Stories from Herodotus: A Panorama of Events and Peoples of the Ancient World; tr. by Glanville Downey. Dutton 1965
ESLC
Croesus, King of Lydia; Darius I, King of Persia; Xerxes I, King of Persia

Bafutan—20th century

Achirimbi II, Fon of Bafut, 1884-

Ritzenthaler, Pat. The Fon of Bafut. Crowell 1966
Bkl A

Belgian—19th century

Leopold II, King of Belgium, 1835-1909

Ascherson, Neal. The King Incorporated: Leopold II in the Age of Trusts. Doubleday 1964
Bkl A

Belgian—20th century

Leopold II, King of Belgium, 1835-1909

Ascherson, Neal. The King Incorporated: Leopold II in the Age of Trusts. Doubleday 1964
Bkl A

Egyptian—15th century B.C.

Amenhetep II, King of Egypt, fl. 1447-1420 B.C.

Meadowcroft, Enid La Monte. Scarab for Luck: A Story of Ancient Egypt. Crowell 1964 (Fiction)
CC(4-6)–ESLC

Egyptian—14th century B.C.

Amenhetep IV, King of Egypt, 1388-1358 B.C.

Bratton, Fred Gladstone. The First Heretic: The Life and Times of Ikhnaton the King. Beacon Press 1962
Bkl A

Silverberg, Robert. Akhnaten, the Rebel Pharaoh. Chilton 1964
Bkl A

Velikovsky, Immanuel. Oedipus and Akhnaton: Myth and History. Doubleday 1960
Bkl A

Tutankhamen, King of Egypt, fl. 1350 B.C.

Bruckner, Karl. The Golden Pharaoh; tr. by Frances Lobb. Pantheon 1959 (Fiction)
Bkl A&Y

Cottrell, Leonard. Land of the Pharaohs. World 1960
Bkl C(6-8)–CC

Cottrell, Leonard. The Secrets of Tutankhamen's Tomb. N. Y. Graphic 1964
Bkl C(7-9)&Y–ESLC–JH

Desroches-Noblecourt, Christiane. Tutankhamen: Life and Death of a Pharaoh. N. Y. Graphic 1963
Bkl A&Y–SCPL

Morrison, Lucile. The Lost Queen of Egypt. Lippincott 1937 (Fiction)
CC(7-9)–ESLC–JH–SCHS

Wise, William. The Two Reigns of Tutankhamen. Putnam 1964
JH

English

COLLECTIONS

Berton, Pierre. Royal Family: The Story of the British Monarchy from Victoria to Elizabeth. Knopf 1954
SCPL

Costain, Thomas Bertram. The Three Edwards. Doubleday 1962
SCPL
Edward I, King of England; Edward II, King of England; Edward III, King of England

Farjeon, Eleanor and Farjeon, Herbert. Kings and Queens. Lippincott 1953 (Poems)
ESLC–SCHS

Trease, Geoffrey. Seven Kings of England. Vanguard 1955
JH–SCHS
Alfred the Great, King of England; Charles I, King of Great Britain; Charles II, King of Great Britain; George VI, King of Great Britain; Richard I, King of England; William I, the Conqueror, King of England; William III, King of Great Britain

KINGS—*Continued*

English—6th century

Arthur, King of the Britons, ?

Bulla, Clyde Robert. The Sword in the Tree. Crowell 1956 (Fiction)
CC(3-5)—ESLC

Fadiman, Clifton. The Story of Young King Arthur. Random House 1961
AB(4-7)

Jewett, Eleanore M. The Hidden Treasure of Glaston. Viking 1946 (Fiction)
CC(7-9)—JH

Lerner, Alan Jay and Loewe, Frederick. Camelot: A New Musical. Random House 1961 (Play)
Bkl A&Y—SCHS—SCPL

MacLeod, Mary. The Book of King Arthur and His Noble Knights. World; Dodd; Lippincott; etc.
BBJH—CC(5-8)—JH—SCHS—SCPL

MacLeod, Mary. King Arthur: Stories from Sir Thomas Malory's Morte d'Arthur. Macmillan 1963
CC(5-8)—ESLC—SCHS

Malory, Sir Thomas. The Boy's King Arthur: Sir Thomas Malory's History of King Arthur and His Knights of the Round Table; ed. by Sidney Lanier. Scribner 1917; Grosset 1950
BBJH—ESLC—JH—SCHS

Picard, Barbara Leonie. Stories of King Arthur and His Knights; retold. Walck 1955
BBJH—CC(5-7)—JH

Pyle, Howard. The Story of King Arthur and His Knights. Scribner 1933
BBJH—CC(6-9)—ESLC—JH—SCHS

Pyle, Howard. The Story of the Champions of the Round Table. Scribner 1933
BBJH—CC(6-9)—JH—SCHS

Pyle, Howard. Story of the Grail and the Passing of Arthur. Scribner 1910
BBJH—CC(6-9)—JH

Schiller, Barbara. The Kitchen Knight. Holt 1965
ESLC

Sutcliff, Rosemary. Sword at Sunset. Coward-McCann 1963 (Fiction)
Bkl A&Y—SCHS

Tennyson, Alfred, Lord. Idylls of the King. Macmillan; St Martins; etc. (Poem)
SCHS

Twain, Mark. A Connecticut Yankee in King Arthur's Court. Dodd; Harper; etc. (Fiction)
CC(7-9)—JH—SCHS

White, T. H. The Once and Future King. Putnam 1958 (Fiction)
SCHS

White, T. H. The Sword in the Stone. Putnam 1939 (Fiction)
ESLC—JH—SCHS

COLLECTIONS

Sutcliff, Rosemary. Heroes and History. Putnam 1966
Bkl C(7-10)&Y

English—9th century

Alfred the Great, King of England, 849-901

Duckett. Eleanor Shipley. Alfred the Great: The King and His England. Univ. of Chicago 1956
SCPL—3000

Duggan, Alfred Leo. The Right Line of Cerdic. Pantheon 1961 (Fiction)
Bkl A

Helm, Peter J. Alfred the Great. Crowell 1965
Bkl A&Y

Hodges, Cyril Walter. The Namesake. Coward-McCann 1964 (Fiction)
Bkl C(7-9)—CC—ESLC

Leighton, Margaret (Carver). Journey for a Princess. Farrar 1960 (Fiction)
Bkl C(7-9)&Y—JH

Leighton, Margaret (Carver). Voyage to Coromandel. Ariel Bks 1965 (Fiction)
ESLC

Trease, Geoffrey. Escape to King Alfred. Vanguard 1959 (Fiction)
BBJH—JH—SCHS

COLLECTIONS

Sutcliff, Rosemary. Heroes and History. Putnam 1966
Bkl C(7-10)&Y

Trease, Geoffrey. Seven Kings of England. Vanguard 1955
JH—SCHS

English—11th century

Edward, the Confessor, King of England, Saint, 1002?-1066

Duggan, Alfred Leo. The Cunning of the Dove. Pantheon 1960 (Fiction)
Bkl A

Harold II, King of England, 1022-1066

Muntz, Hope. The Golden Warrior: The Story of Harold and William. Scribner 1949 (Fiction)
BBHS—SCHS

William I, the Conqueror, King of England, 1027-1087

Costain, Thomas Bertram. William the Conqueror. Random House 1959
Bkl C(6-8)—JH—SCHS

Douglas, David Charles. William the Conqueror: The Norman Impact upon England. Univ. of Calif. 1964
Bkl A

KINGS

English—11th century

William I—Continued

Lloyd, Alan. The Making of the King. Holt 1966
    Bkl A&Y

Luckock, Elizabeth. William the Conqueror. Putnam 1966
    Bkl C(6-9)&Y

Muntz, Hope. The Golden Warrior: The Story of Harold and William. Scribner 1949 (Fiction)
    BBHS—SCHS

Slocombe, George Edward. William, the Conqueror. Putnam 1961
    Bkl A&Y

COLLECTIONS

Trease, Geoffrey. Seven Kings of England. Vanguard 1955
    JH—SCHS

English—12th century

Henry II, King of England, 1133-1189

Anouilh, Jean. Becket: Or, The Honor of God; tr. by Lucienne Hill. Coward-McCann 1960 (Play)
    Bkl A—SCPL

Appleby, John Tate. Henry II, the Vanquished King. Macmillan 1962
    Bkl A

Eliot, Thomas Stearns. Murder in the Cathedral. Harcourt 1935 (Play)
    SCHS

Fry, Christopher. Curtmantle: A Play. Oxford 1961 (Play)
    Bkl A

Richard I, King of England, 1157-1199

Scott, Sir Walter. Ivanhoe. Dodd; Doubleday; Dutton; Houghton; Prentice-Hall; etc. (Fiction)
    BBHS—BBJH—CC(7-9)—JH—SCHS

Scott, Sir Walter. The Talisman. Dodd; Dutton; Nelson (Fiction)
    SCHS

COLLECTIONS

Trease, Geoffrey. Seven Kings of England. Vanguard 1955
    JH—SCHS

English—13th century

Edward I, King of England, 1239-1307

COLLECTIONS

Costain, Thomas Bertram. The Three Edwards. Doubleday 1962
    SCPL

Henry III, King of England, 1207-1272

Costain, Thomas Bertram. The Magnificent Century. Doubleday 1951
    SCHS

John, King of England, 1167?-1216

Warren, Wilfred Lewis. King John. Norton 1961
    Bkl A

English—14th century

Edward II, King of England, 1284-1327

COLLECTIONS

Costain, Thomas Bertram. The Three Edwards. Doubleday 1962
    SCPL

Edward III, King of England, 1312-1377

Druon, Maurice. The Lily and the Lion: A Novel; tr. from the French by Humphrey Hare. Scribner 1962 (Fiction)
    Bkl A

COLLECTIONS

Costain, Thomas Bertram. The Three Edwards. Doubleday 1962
    SCPL

Richard II, King of England, 1367-1400

Hutchison, Harold F. The Hollow Crown: A Life of Richard II. Day 1961
    Bkl A—SCPL

Lewis, Hilda Winifred. The Gentle Falcon. Criterion Bks 1957 (Fiction)
    BBJH—CC(7-9)—JH—SCHS

Shakespeare, William. Richard II. Scott, etc. (Play)
    SCPL

English—15th century

Edward IV, King of England, 1442-1483

Simons, Eric N. The Reign of Edward IV. Barnes & Noble 1966
    Bkl A

Henry IV, King of England, 1367-1413

Pyle, Howard. Men of Iron. Harper 1891 (Fiction)
    BBJH—ESLC—JH

Henry V, King of England, 1387-1422

Maughan, A. M. Harry of Monmouth. Sloane 1956 (Fiction)
    SCHS

KINGS

English—15th century—*Continued*

Henry VI, King of England, 1421-1471

Lewis, Hilda Winifred. Here Comes Harry. Criterion Bks 1960 (Fiction)
Bkl C(6-9)

Richard III, King of England, 1452-1485

Barnes, Margaret Campbell. The King's Bed. Macrae 1962 (Fiction)
Bkl A&Y

Eckerson, Olive. The Golden Yoke: A Novel of the War of the Roses. Coward-McCann 1961 (Fiction)
Bkl A&Y

Kendall, Paul Murray. Richard the Third. Norton 1956
BBHS—SCPL

Shakespeare, William. Richard III. Scott, etc. (Play)
SCPL

Stevenson, Robert Louis. The Black Arrow. Scribner; Dodd; etc. (Fiction)
CC(7-9)—ESLC—JH—SCHS

Vance, Marguerite. Song for a Lute. Dutton 1958 (Fiction)
SCHS

English—16th century

Edward VI, King of England, 1537-1553

Twain, Mark. The Prince and the Pauper. World; Harper; etc. (Fiction)
BBJH—CC(6-9)—ESLC—JH—SCHS—YR

Henry VIII, King of England, 1491-1547

Barnes, Margaret Campbell. King's Fool. Macrae 1959 (Fiction)
SCHS

Bowle, John. Henry VIII: A Biography. Little 1965
Bkl A&Y

Hackett, Francis. Henry the Eighth. Liveright or Modern Lib.
GR—SCPL—3000

Morrison, Nancy Brysson. The Private Life of Henry VIII. Vanguard 1964
Bkl A&Y—IndS(11-12)

English—17th century

Charles I, King of Great Britain, 1600-1649

Anthony, Evelyn. Charles, the King. Doubleday 1961 (Fiction)
Bkl A

Wedgwood, Cicely Veronica. A Coffin for King Charles: The Trial and Execution of Charles I. Macmillan 1964
Bkl A&Y

COLLECTIONS

Trease, Geoffrey. Seven Kings of England. Vanguard 1955
JH—SCHS

Charles II, King of Great Britain, 1630-1685

Chapman, Hester W. The Tragedy of Charles II in the Years 1630-1660. Little 1964
Bkl A—IndS(12)

Pearson, Hesketh. Merry Monarch: The Life and Likeness of Charles II. Harper 1960
Bkl A—SCPL

COLLECTIONS

Trease, Geoffrey. Seven Kings of England. Vanguard 1955
JH—SCHS

James II, King of Great Britain, 1633-1701

Buranelli, Vincent. The King & the Quaker: A Study of William Penn and James II. Univ. of Pa. 1962
Bkl A

James II, King of Great Britain. The Memoirs of James II: His Campaigns as Duke of York, 1652-1660; tr. by A. Lytton Sells. Ind. Univ. 1962
Bkl A

William III, King of Great Britain, 1650-1702

Baxter, Stephen Bartow. William III and the Defense of European Liberty, 1650-1702. Harcourt 1966
Bkl A

Edwards, Samuel. The Queen's Husband. McGraw 1960 (Fiction)
Bkl A

Robb, Nesca Adeline. William of Orange—A Personal Portrait: v. 1, 1650-1673. St Martins 1963
Bkl A

Robb, Nesca Adeline. William of Orange—A Personal Portrait: v. 2, 1674-1702. St Martins 1966
Bkl A

COLLECTIONS

Trease, Geoffrey. Seven Kings of England. Vanguard 1955
JH—SCHS

English—18th century

George III, King of Great Britain, 1738-1820

Chenevix-Trench, Charles Pocklington. The Royal Malady. Harcourt 1965
Bkl A

Long, John Cuthbert. George III: The Story of a Complex Man. Little 1961
Bkl A

KINGS—*Continued*

English—19th century

George III, King of Great Britain, 1738-1820

Chenevix-Trench, Charles Pocklington. The Royal Malady. Harcourt 1965
Bkl A

Long, John Cuthbert. George III: The Story of a Complex Man. Little 1961
Bkl A

English—20th century

Edward VII, King of Great Britain, 1841-1910

Cowles, Virginia Spencer. Gay Monarch: The Life and Pleasures of Edward VII. Harper 1956
SCPL

Magnus, Sir Philip Montefiore. King Edward the Seventh. Dutton 1964
Bkl A—SCPL

Edward VIII, King of Great Britain, 1894-

Beaverbrook, William Maxwell Aitken, Baron. The Abdication of King Edward VIII; ed. by A. J. P. Taylor. Atheneum 1966
Bkl A

Edward VIII, King of Great Britain. A King's Story: The Memoirs of the Duke of Windsor. Putnam 1951
SCPL

Edward VIII, King of Great Britain. Windsor Revisited, by H. R. H. the Duke of Windsor. Houghton 1960
Bkl A

Inglis, Brian. Abdication. Macmillan 1966
Bkl A

George VI, King of Great Britain, 1895-1952

Wheeler-Bennett, John Wheeler. King George VI: His Life and Reign. St Martins 1958
SCPL

COLLECTIONS

Trease, Geoffrey. Seven Kings of England. Vanguard 1955
JH—SCHS

Ethiopian—8th century B.C.

Piankhi, King of Ethiopia, fl. 741-721 B.C.

Johnson, E. Harper. Piankhy the Great. Nelson 1962
AB(6up)—Bkl C(4-6)—ESLC

French—8th century

Charlemagne, 742-814

Bullough, Donald A. The Age of Charlemagne. Putnam 1966
Bkl A&Y

Komroff, Manuel. Charlemagne. Messner 1964
Bkl C(7-9)&Y—ESLC—JH

Lamb, Harold Albert. Charlemagne: The Legend and the Man. Doubleday 1954
SCHS—SCPL—3000

French—16th century

Francis I, King of France, 1494-1547

Shellabarger, Samuel. The King's Cavalier. Little 1950 (Fiction)
SCHS

Henry IV, King of France, 1553-1610

Pearson, Hesketh. Henry of Navarre: The King Who Dared. Harper 1964
Bkl A—SCPL

Wilkinson, Burke. The Helmet of Navarre. Macmillan 1965
ESLC

French—17th century

Henry IV, King of France, 1553-1610

Pearson, Hesketh. Henry of Navarre: The King Who Dared. Harper 1964
Bkl A—SCPL

Wilkinson, Burke. The Helmet of Navarre. Macmillan 1965
ESLC

Louis XIV, King of France, 1638-1715

Apsler, Alfred. The Sun King: Louis XIV of France. Messner 1965
Bkl C(7-10)&Y

Buranelli, Vincent. Louis XIV. Twayne 1966
Bkl A&Y

Cronin, Vincent. Louis XIV. Houghton 1965
Bkl A&Y—IndS(10-12)

Sanders, Joan. The Marquis. Houghton 1963 (Fiction)
IndS(11-12)

French—18th century

Louis XIV, King of France, 1638-1715

Apsler, Alfred. The Sun King: Louis XIV of France. Messner 1965
Bkl C(7-10)&Y

Buranelli, Vincent. Louis XIV. Twayne 1966
Bkl A&Y

Cronin, Vincent. Louis XIV. Houghton 1965
Bkl A&Y—IndS(10-12)

KINGS

French—18th century—*Continued*

Louis XVII, King of France, 1785-1795

Wallower, Lucille. The Lost Prince Louis XVII of France. McKay 1963
AB(6-9)

German—5th century

Attila, King of the Huns, 406?-453

Costain, Thomas Bertram. The Darkness and the Dawn: A Novel. Doubleday 1959 (Fiction)
SCHS

Webb, Robert N. Attila, King of the Huns. Watts 1965
Bkl C(7-9)&Y

German—18th century

Frederick II, the Great, King of Prussia, 1712-1786

Simon, Edith. The Making of Frederick the Great. Little 1963
Bkl A—IndS(12)

Wright, Constance. A Royal Affinity: The Story of Frederick the Great and His Sister, Wilhelmina of Bayreuth. Scribner 1965
Bkl A

Haitian—19th century

Henri Christophe, King of Haiti, 1767-1820

Newcomb, Covelle. Black Fire: A Story of Henri Christophe. Longmans 1940
CC(7-9)—JH—YR

Hawaiian—18th century

Kamehameha I, the Great, King of the Hawaiian Islands, 1737?-1819

Miner, Lewis S. King of the Hawaiian Islands: Kamahameha I. Messner 1963
IndJ(6-9)

Pole, James T. Hawaii's First King. Bobbs 1959
Bkl A

Hawaiian—19th century

Kamehameha I, the Great, King of the Hawaiian Islands, 1737?-1819

Miner, Lewis S. King of the Hawaiian Islands: Kamehameha I. Messner 1963
IndJ(6-9)

Pole, James T. Hawaii's First King. Bobbs 1959
Bkl A

Jordanian—20th century

Hussein, King of Jordan, 1935-

Hussein, King of Jordan. Uneasy Lies the Head: The Autobiography of His Majesty King Hussein I of the Hashemite Kingdom of Jordan. Geis 1962
Bkl A&Y

Lydian—6th century B.C.

Croesus, King of Lydia, ?-546 B.C.

COLLECTIONS

Herodotus. Stories from Herodotus: A Panorama of Events and Peoples of the Ancient World; tr. by Glanville Downey. Dutton 1965
ESLC

Macedonian—4th century B.C.

Alexander the Great, 356-323 B.C.

Andrews, Mary (Evans). Hostage to Alexander. Longmans 1961 (Fiction)
Bkl C(7-9)&Y—JH

Burn, Andrew Robert. Alexander the Great and the Hellenistic Empire. Macmillan 1951
3000

Druon, Maurice. Alexander, the God: A Novel; tr. from the French by Humphrey Hare. Scribner 1961 (Fiction)
Bkl A

Gunther, John. Alexander the Great. Random House 1953
BBJH—BY—CC(5-7)—ESLC—JH—SCHS

Horizon Magazine. Alexander the Great, by Charles E. Mercer. Am. Heritage 1962
Bkl C(5-9)&Y—BY—CC(7-9)—JH—SCHS—YR

Lamb, Harold Albert. Alexander of Macedon: The Journey to World's End. Doubleday 1946
BY—SCHS—SCPL

Marshall, Edison. The Conqueror. Doubleday 1962 (Fiction)
Bkl A

Robinson, Charles Alexander. Alexander the Great, Conqueror and Creator of a New World. Watts 1963
Bkl C(7-10)&Y—ESLC

Robinson, Charles Alexander. Alexander the Great: The Meeting of East and West in World Government and Brotherhood. Dutton 1947
SCPL

Stark, Freya Madeline. Alexander's Path: From Caria to Cilicia. Harcourt 1958
SCPL

Stark, Freya Madeline. Lycian Shore. Harcourt 1956
SCPL

KINGS

Macedonian—4th century B.C.

Alexander the Great—Continued

COLLECTIONS

Clark, William R. Explorers of the World. Natural Hist. Press 1964
CC—ESLC

Duvoisin, Roger. They Put Out to Sea: The Story of the Map. Knopf 1943
CC(5-7)—ESLC

Plutarch. Ten Famous Lives; the Dryden translation rev. by Arthur Hugh Clough; ed. for young readers by Charles Robinson, Jr. Dutton 1962
Bkl C(7-10)&Y—BY—CC(7-9)—JH—SCHS—YR

Macedonian—3rd century B.C.

Demetrius Poliorcetes, King of Macedonia, 337-283 B.C.

Duggan, Alfred Leo. Besieger of Cities. Pantheon 1963 (Fiction)
Bkl A

Persian—6th century B.C.

Cyrus the Great, King of Persia, 600?-529 B.C.

Lamb, Harold Albert. Cyrus the Great. Doubleday 1960
Bkl A—SCPL

Darius I, King of Persia, 558?-486 B.C.

COLLECTIONS

Duvoisin, Roger. They Put Out to Sea: The Story of the Map. Knopf 1943
CC(5-7)—ESLC

Herodotus. Stories from Herodotus: A Panorama of Events and Peoples of the Ancient World; tr. by Glanville Downey. Dutton 1965
ESLC

Persian—5th century B.C.

Xerxes I, King of Persia, 519-465? B.C.

De Camp, Lyon Sprague. The Dragon of the Ishtar Gate. Doubleday 1961 (Fiction)
Bkl A

COLLECTIONS

Herodotus. Stories from Herodotus: A Panorama of Events and Peoples of the Ancient World; tr. by Glanville Downey. Dutton 1965
ESLC

Samuel, Maurice. Certain People of the Book. Knopf 1955
SCPL

Roman—6th century B.C.

Lucius Tarquinius Superbus, King of Rome, 534-510 B.C.

Franzero, Charles Marie. The Life and Times of Tarquin the Etruscan. Day 1961
Bkl A

Roman—19th century

Napoléon II, King of Rome, 1811-1832

Castelot, André. King of Rome: A Biography of Napoleon's Tragic Son; tr. from the French by Robert Baldick. Harper 1960
Bkl A

Scottish—11th century

Malcolm III, King of Scotland, ?-1093

Polland, Madeleine. The Queen's Blessing. Holt 1964 (Fiction)
CC—ESLC

Scottish—13th century

Alexander III, King of Scotland, 1241-1285

Oliver, Jane. Alexander the Glorious. Putnam 1965 (Fiction)
Bkl A&Y—IndS(11-12)

Scottish—14th century

Robert Bruce, King of Scotland, 1274-1329

Baker, Nina Brown. Robert Bruce: King of Scots. Vanguard 1948
BY

Porter, Jane. Scottish Chiefs; ed. by Kate Douglas Wiggin and Nora C. Wyeth. Scribner (Fiction)
CC(7-9)—JH—SCHS

Stephens, Peter John. Outlaw King: The Story of Robert the Bruce. Atheneum 1964 (Fiction)
ESLC—IndJ(6-9)

COLLECTIONS

Sutcliff, Rosemary. Heroes and History. Putnam 1966
Bkl C(7-10)&Y

Scottish—15th century

James IV, King of Scotland, 1473-1513

Oliver, Jane. Sunset at Noon. Putnam 1963 (Fiction)
Bkl A&Y

Scottish—16th century

James IV, King of Scotland, 1473-1513

Oliver, Jane. Sunset at Noon. Putnam 1963 (Fiction)
Bkl A&Y

KINGS—*Continued*

Siamese—19th century

Mongkut, King of Siam, 1804-1868

Landon, Margaret Dorothea (Mortenson). Anna and the King. Day 1947
BBJH—JH

Landon, Margaret Dorothea (Mortenson). Anna and the King of Siam. Day 1944
BBHS—SCPL

Spanish—16th century

Philip II, King of Spain, 1527-1598

Petrie, Sir Charles Alexander. Philip II of Spain. Norton 1963
Bkl A—IndS(12)

LABOR LEADERS

American—19th century

Eugene Victor Debs, 1855-1926

Morgan, Howard Wayne. Eugene V. Debs: Socialist for President. Syracuse Univ. 1962
Bkl A

Selvin, David F. Eugene Debs—Rebel Labor Leader, Prophet: A Biography. Lothrop 1966
Bkl Y(7-10)&C

Samuel Gompers, 1850-1924

Gompers, Samuel. Seventy Years of Life and Labor: An Autobiography; ed. by Philip Taft. Dutton 1957
SCPL

Mandel, Bernard. Samuel Gompers: A Biography. Antioch Press 1963
Bkl A

Selvin, David F. Sam Gompers: Labor's Pioneer. Abelard-Schuman 1964
ESLC—JH

Taft, Philip. A. F. of L. in the Time of Gompers. Harper 1957
SCPL

COLLECTIONS

Fanning, Leonard M. Titans of Business. Lippincott 1964
Bkl C(7-9)&Y—JH—SCHS

American—20th century

Eugene Victor Debs, 1855-1926

Morgan, Howard Wayne. Eugene V. Debs: Socialist for President. Syracuse Univ. 1962
Bkl A

Selvin, David F. Eugene Debs—Rebel Labor Leader, Prophet: A Biography. Lothrop 1966
Bkl Y(7-10)&C

David Dubinsky, 1892-

Danish, Max D. The World of David Dubinsky. World 1957
BY—SCPL

COLLECTIONS

Life International. Nine Who Chose America. Dutton 1959
Bkl Y&C—SCHS

Samuel Gompers, 1850-1924

Gompers, Samuel. Seventy Years of Life and Labor: An Autobiography; ed. by Philip Taft. Dutton 1957
SCPL

Mandel, Bernard. Samuel Gompers: A Biography. Antioch Press 1963
Bkl A

Selvin, David F. Sam Gompers: Labor's Pioneer. Abelard-Schuman 1964
ESLC—JH

Taft, Philip. A. F. of L. in the Time of Gompers. Harper 1957
SCPL

COLLECTIONS

Fanning, Leonard M. Titans of Business. Lippincott 1964
Bkl C(7-9)&Y—JH—SCHS

John Llewellyn Lewis, 1880-

COLLECTIONS

Fanning, Leonard M. Titans of Business. Lippincott 1964
Bkl C(7-9)&Y—JH—SCHS

Asa Philip Randolph, 1889-

COLLECTIONS

Sterne, Emma (Gelders). I Have a Dream. Knopf 1965
Bkl Y&C

English—20th century

Clement Richard Attlee, 1st Earl Attlee, 1883-1967

Attlee, Sir Clement Richard. As It Happened. Viking 1954
SCPL

Williams, Francis. Twilight of Empire: Memoirs of Prime Minister Clement Attlee. Barnes 1962
Bkl A

Irish—20th century

James Larkin, 1876-1947

Larkin, Emmet J. James Larkin: Irish Labour Leader, 1876-1947. Mass. Inst. of Technology 1965
Bkl A

LAWYERS

COLLECTIONS

Seagle, William. Men of Law: From Hammurabi to Holmes. Macmillan 1947
SCPL

American

COLLECTIONS

Frank, John Paul. The Warren Court. Macmillan 1964
Bkl A

Kunstler, William Moses. The Case for Courage. Morrow 1962
Bkl A&Y
John Adams; John Peter Altgeld; Homer Stillé Cummings; Clarence Seward Darrow; Andrew Hamilton; Reverdy Johnson; Harold Raymond Medina; William Henry Seward; William Goodrich Thompson; Joseph Nye Welch

American—17th century

Samuel Sewall, 1652-1730

Winslow, Ola Elizabeth. Samuel Sewall of Boston. Macmillan 1964
Bkl A&Y

American—18th century

John Adams, 1735-1826

COLLECTIONS

Kunstler, William Moses. The Case for Courage. Morrow 1962
Bkl A&Y

Andrew Hamilton, 1676?-1741

COLLECTIONS

Kunstler, William Moses. The Case for Courage. Morrow 1962
Bkl A&Y

Samuel Sewall, 1652-1730

Winslow, Ola Elizabeth. Samuel Sewall of Boston. Macmillan 1964
Bkl A&Y

American—19th century

Charles Francis Adams, 1835-1915

COLLECTIONS

Homans, Abigail (Adams). Education by Uncles. Houghton 1966
Bkl A&Y

John Peter Altgeld, 1847-1902

COLLECTIONS

Kunstler, William Moses. The Case for Courage. Morrow 1962
Bkl A&Y

Elfego Baca, 1865-1945

COLLECTIONS

Schaefer, Jack Warner. Heroes Without Glory: Some Goodmen of the Old West. Houghton 1965
Bkl A&Y

Judah Philip Benjamin, 1811-1884

COLLECTIONS

Mapp, Alf Johnson. Frock Coats and Epaulets. Yoseloff 1963
Bkl A&Y

William Jennings Bryan, 1860-1925

Glad, Paul W. McKinley, Bryan, and the People. Lippincott 1964
Bkl A&Y

John Caldwell Calhoun, 1782-1850

Coit, Margaret Louise. John C. Calhoun: American Portrait. Houghton 1950
SCPL

Salmon Portland Chase, 1808-1873

Belden, T. G. and Belden, M. R. So Fell the Angels. Little 1956
SCPL

William Henry Herndon, 1818-1891

Donald, David Herbert. Lincoln's Herndon. Knopf 1948
SCPL

Oliver Wendell Holmes, 1841-1935

Biddle, Francis Beverley. Justice Holmes, Natural Law, and the Supreme Court. Macmillan 1961
Bkl A

Bowen, Catherine (Drinker). Yankee from Olympus: Justice Holmes and His Family. Little 1944
BBHS—BY—GR—SCHS—SCPL—3000

Bowen, Catherine (Drinker). Yankee from Olympus: Justice Holmes and His Family. School ed. Houghton 1962
SCHS

Howe, Mark De Wolfe. Justice Oliver Wendell Holmes: v. 1, The Shaping Years, 1841-1870. Harvard Univ. 1957
SCPL

Howe, Mark De Wolfe. Justice Oliver Wendell Holmes: v. 2, The Proving Years, 1870-1882. Harvard Univ. 1963
Bkl A—SCPL

Judson, Clara (Ingram). Mr. Justice Holmes. Follett 1956
BBEL(7-8)—BBJH—CC(7-9)—ESLC—JH—SCHS

Lavery, Emmet Godfrey. Magnificent Yankee: A Play in Three Acts. French 1946 (Play)
SCPL

LAWYERS

American—19th century—*Continued*

Robert Green Ingersoll, 1833-1899

Larson, Orvin Prentiss. American Infidel —Robert G. Ingersoll: A Biography. Citadel 1962
Bkl A

Reverdy Johnson, 1796-1876

COLLECTIONS

Kunstler, William Moses. The Case for Courage. Morrow 1962
Bkl A&Y

Francis Scott Key, 1779-1843

Patterson, Lillie. Francis Scott Key: Poet and Patriot. Garrard 1963
AB(4-7)

Abraham Lincoln, 1809-1865

Frank, John Paul. Lincoln as a Lawyer. Univ. of Ill. 1961
Bkl A

Belva Ann (Bennett) Lockwood, 1830-1917

COLLECTIONS

Boynick, David. Pioneers in Petticoats. Crowell 1959
YR

John Marshall, 1755-1835

Beveridge, Albert Jeremiah. Life of John Marshall. Houghton 1929
SCPL—3000
Konefsky, Samuel Joseph. John Marshall and Alexander Hamilton: Architects of the American Constitution. Macmillan 1964
Bkl A
Steinberg, Alfred. John Marshall. Putnam 1962
Bkl Y&C(7-9)
Tucker, Caroline. John Marshall: The Great Chief Justice. Farrar 1962
Bkl C(5-8)—BY—ESLC

COLLECTIONS

Dos Passos, John Roderigo. Men Who Made the Nation. Doubleday 1957
SCPL

Albert Pike, 1809-1891

Duncan, Robert Lipscomb. Reluctant General: The Life and Times of Albert Pike. Dutton 1961
Bkl A

William Henry Seward, 1801-1872

COLLECTIONS

Kunstler, William Moses. The Case for Courage. Morrow 1962
Bkl A&Y

Edwin McMasters Stanton, 1814-1869

Pratt, Fletcher. Stanton, Lincoln's Secretary of War. Norton 1953
SCPL
Thomas, Benjamin Platt and Hyman, Harold Melvin. Stanton: The Life and Times of Lincoln's Secretary of War. Knopf 1962
Bkl A

William Howard Taft, 1857-1930

Ross, Ishbel. An American Family: The Tafts, 1678 to 1964. World 1964
Bkl A&Y

Roger Brooke Taney, 1777-1864

Lewis, Walker. Without Fear or Favor: A Biography of Chief Justice Roger Brooke Taney. Houghton 1965
Bkl A
Schumacher, Alvin J. Thunder on Capitol Hill: The Life of Chief Justice Roger B. Taney. Bruce 1964
ESLC

Daniel Webster, 1782-1852

Benét, Stephen Vincent. The Devil and Daniel Webster. Farrar 1937 (Fiction)
JH—SCHS
Benét, Stephen Vincent and Moore, Douglas. Devil and Daniel Webster: An Opera in One Act. Rinehart 1939 (Play)
SCPL

American—20th century

Florence Ellinwood Allen, 1884-1966

COLLECTIONS

Forsee, Aylesa. American Women Who Scored Firsts. Macrae 1958
SCHS

Thurman Wesley Arnold, 1891-

Arnold, Thurman Wesley. Fair Fights and Foul: A Dissenting Lawyer's Life. Harcourt 1965
Bkl A—IndS(11-12)

Francis Beverley Biddle, 1886-1968

Biddle, Francis Beverley. A Casual Past. Doubleday 1961
Bkl A
Biddle, Francis Beverley. In Brief Authority. Doubleday 1962
Bkl A

Louis Dembitz Brandeis, 1856-1941

Mason, Alpheus Thomas. Brandeis: A Free Man's Life. Viking 1956
SCPL
Todd, Alden. Justice on Trial: The Case of Louis D. Brandeis. McGraw 1964
Bkl A

LAWYERS

American—20th century—*Continued*

William Jennings Bryan, 1860-1925

Levine, Lawrence W. Defender of the Faith—William Jennings Bryan: The Last Decade, 1915-1925. Oxford 1965
Bkl A

Litta Belle (Hibben) Campbell, 1886-

Campbell, Litta Belle (Hibben). Here I Raise Mine Ebenezer. Simon & Schuster 1963
Bkl A—IndS(10-12)

Thomas Gardiner Corcoran, 1900-

COLLECTIONS

Koenig, Louis William. The Invisible Presidency. Rinehart 1960
Bkl A

Joseph Force Crater, 1889-?

Crater, Stella (Wheeler) and Fraley, Oscar. The Empty Robe. Doubleday 1961
Bkl A

Homer Stillé Cummings, 1870-1956

COLLECTIONS

Kunstler, William Moses. The Case for Courage. Morrow 1962
Bkl A&Y

Clarence Seward Darrow, 1857-1938

Gurko, Miriam. Clarence Darrow. Crowell 1965
Bkl Y&C—IndS(9-11)
Noble, Iris. Clarence Darrow, Defense Attorney. Messner 1958
BBJH—BY—JH—SCHS—SCPL
Stone, Irving. Clarence Darrow for the Defense: A Biography. Doubleday 1949
SCPL

COLLECTIONS

Kunstler, William Moses. The Case for Courage. Morrow 1962
Bkl A&Y

Thomas Edmund Dewey, 1902-

COLLECTIONS

Roper, Elmo Burns. You and Your Leaders: Their Actions and Your Reactions, 1936-1956. Morrow 1957
SCPL

William Joseph ("Wild Bill") Donovan, 1883-1959

COLLECTIONS

Army Times. Modern American Secret Agents. Dodd 1966
Bkl C(7-9)&Y

William Orville Douglas, 1898-

Douglas, William Orville. Of Men and Mountains. Harper 1950
BY—SCHS—SCPL

Allen Welsh Dulles, 1893-1969

COLLECTIONS

Army Times. Modern American Secret Agents. Dodd 1966
Bkl C(7-9)&Y

John Foster Dulles, 1888-1959

Beal, John Robinson. John Foster Dulles: 1888-1959. Harper 1959
Bkl A—SCPL
Beal, John Robinson. John Foster Dulles: A Biography. Harper 1957
SCPL
Goold-Adams, Richard John Morton. John Foster Dulles: A Reappraisal. Appleton 1962
Bkl A
Heller, Deane and Heller, David. John Foster Dulles, Soldier for Peace. Holt 1960
Bkl A—SCPL

Jacob W. Ehrlich, 1900-

Ehrlich, Jacob W. A Life in My Hands. Putnam 1965
Bkl A
Ehrlich, Jacob W. A Reasonable Doubt. World 1964
Bkl A

Morris Leopold Ernst, 1888-

Ernst, Morris Leopold. Untitled: The Diary of My 72nd Year. Luce 1962
Bkl A

Raymond B. Fosdick, 1883-

Fosdick, Raymond B. Chronicle of a Generation: An Autobiography. Harper 1958
SCPL

Felix Frankfurter, 1882-1965

Frankfurter, Felix. Felix Frankfurter Reminisces; recorded in talks with Harlan B. Phillips. Reynal 1960
Bkl A
Mendelson, Wallace, ed. Felix Frankfurter: A Tribute. Reynal 1964
Bkl A
Mendelson, Wallace, ed. Felix Frankfurter, the Judge. Reynal 1964
Bkl A

COLLECTIONS

Life International. Nine Who Chose America. Dutton 1959
Bkl Y&C—SCHS

LAWYERS

American—20th century—*Continued*

Elmer Gertz, 1906-

Gertz, Elmer. A Handful of Clients. Follett 1965
Bkl A

Harold Lee ("Jerry") Giesler, 1890-1962

Giesler, Harold Lee and Martin, Thornton. The Jerry Giesler Story. Simon & Schuster 1960
Bkl A

Andrew Gallagher Haley, 1904-1966

COLLECTIONS

Thomas, Shirley. Men of Space: v. 7, Profiles of the Leaders in Space Research, Development, and Exploration. Chilton 1965
Bkl A&Y

Vincent Hallinan, 1896-

Hallinan, Vincent. A Lion in Court. Putnam 1963
Bkl A

Alger Hiss, 1904-

Cooke, Alistair. Generation on Trial: U. S. A. v. Alger Hiss. Knopf 1952
SCPL

Hiss, Alger. In the Court of Public Opinion. Knopf 1957
SCPL

Zeligs, Meyer A. Friendship and Fratricide: An Analysis of Whittaker Chambers and Alger Hiss. Viking 1966
Bkl A

Oliver Wendell Holmes, 1841-1935

Biddle, Francis Beverley. Justice Holmes, Natural Law, and the Supreme Court. Macmillan 1961
Bkl A

Bowen, Catherine (Drinker). Yankee from Olympus: Justice Holmes and His Family. Little 1944
BBHS--BY–GR–SCHS–SCPL–3000

Bowen, Catherine (Drinker). Yankee from Olympus: Justice Holmes and His Family. School ed. Houghton 1962
SCHS

Holmes, Oliver Wendell and Einstein, Lewis. The Holmes-Einstein Letters: Correspondence, 1903-1935; ed. by James Bishop Peabody. St Martins 1964
Bkl A

Holmes, Oliver Wendell. Holmes-Laski Letters: The Correspondence of Mr. Justice Holmes and Harold J. Laski, 1916-1935; ed. by M. D. Howe. 2v. Harvard Univ. 1953
SCPL

Judson, Clara (Ingram). Mr. Justice Holmes. Follett 1956
BBEL(7-8)–BBJH–CC(7-9)–ESLC–JH–SCHS

Lavery, Emmet Godfrey. Magnificent Yankee: A Play in Three Acts. French 1946 (Play)
SCPL

Charles Evans Hughes, 1862-1948

Perkins, Dexter. Charles Evans Hughes and American Democratic Statesmanship; ed. by Oscar Handlin. Little 1956
SCPL

Pusey, Merlo John. Charles Evans Hughes. 2v. Macmillan 1951
SCPL

William Travers Jerome, 1859-1934

O'Connor, Richard. Courtroom Warrior: The Combative Career of William Travers Jerome. Little 1963
Bkl A

William Moses Kunstler, 1919-

Kunstler, William Moses. Deep in My Heart. Morrow 1966
Bkl A&Y

Edward Lamb, 1902-

Lamb, Edward. No Lamb for Slaughter: An Autobiography. Harcourt 1963
Bkl A

Thurgood Marshall, 1908-

COLLECTIONS

Sterne, Emma (Gelders). I Have a Dream. Knopf 1965
Bkl Y&C

Harold Raymond Medina, 1888-

Daniel, Hawthorne. Judge Medina: A Biography. Funk 1952
SCPL

COLLECTIONS

Kunstler, William Moses. The Case for Courage. Morrow 1962
Bkl A&Y

Louis Nizer, 1902-

Nizer, Louis. My Life in Court. Doubleday 1961
Bkl A–BY–SCHS–SCPL

Earl Andrus Rogers, 1870-1922

St. Johns, Adela (Rogers). Final Verdict. Doubleday 1962
Bkl A–SCPL

Samuel Seabury, 1873-1958

Mitgang, Herbert. The Man Who Rode the Tiger: The Life and Times of Judge Samuel Seabury. Lippincott 1963
Bkl A–IndS(11-12)

LAWYERS

American—20th century—_Continued_

Adlai Ewing Stevenson, 1900-1965

Brown, Stuart Gerry. Conscience in Politics: Adlai E. Stevenson in the 1950's. Syracuse Univ. 1961
Bkl A

Busch, Noel Fairchild. Adlai E. Stevenson of Illinois: A Portrait. Farrar 1952
SCPL

Davis, Kenneth Sydney. Prophet in His Own Country: The Triumphs and Defeats of Adlai E. Stevenson. Doubleday 1957
SCPL

Doyle, Edward P., ed. As We Knew Adlai: The Stevenson Story by Twenty-two Friends. Harper 1966
Bkl A&Y

Ross, Lillian. Adlai Stevenson. Lippincott 1966
Bkl A

Severn, William. Adlai Stevenson, Citizen of the World. McKay 1966
Bkl C(7-10)&Y—ESLC

Harlan Fiske Stone, 1872-1946

Mason, Alpheus Thomas. Harlan Fiske Stone: Pillar of the Law. Viking 1956
SCPL

Robert Alphonso Taft, 1889-1953

White, William Smith. The Taft Story. Harper 1954
SCPL

William Howard Taft, 1857-1930

Ross, Ishbel. An American Family: The Tafts, 1678 to 1964. World 1964
Bkl A&Y

William Goodrich Thompson, 1864-1935

COLLECTIONS

Kunstler, William Moses. The Case for Courage. Morrow 1962
Bkl A&Y

Joe Tumulty, 1879-1954

Blum, J. M. Joe Tumulty and the Wilson Era. Houghton 1951
SCPL

Earl Warren, 1891-

Huston, Luther A. Pathway to Judgment: A Study of Earl Warren. Chilton 1966
Bkl A&Y

COLLECTIONS

Frank, John Paul. The Warren Court. Macmillan 1964
Bkl A

Joseph Nye Welch, 1890-1960

COLLECTIONS

Kunstler, William Moses. The Case for Courage. Morrow 1962
Bkl A&Y

Wendell Lewis Willkie, 1892-1944

COLLECTIONS

Roper, Elmo Burns. You and Your Leaders: Their Actions and Your Reactions, 1936-1956. Morrow 1957
SCPL

James Horace Wood, ?

Wood, James Horace and Ross, John M. Nothing but the Truth. Doubleday 1960
Bkl A

English—17th century

Sir Edward Coke, 1552-1634

Bowen, Catherine (Drinker). The Lion and the Throne: The Life and Times of Sir Edward Coke, 1552-1634. Little 1957
SCPL

English—18th century

Jeremy Bentham, 1748-1832

Mack, Mary Peter. Jeremy Bentham: An Odyssey of Ideas. Columbia Univ. 1963
Bkl A

English—19th century

Jeremy Bentham, 1748-1832

Mack, Mary Peter. Jeremy Bentham: An Odyssey of Ideas. Columbia Univ. 1963
Bkl A

English—20th century

Norman Birkett, Baron Birkett, 1883-1962

Hyde, Harford Montgomery. Lord Justice: The Life and Times of Lord Birkett of Ulverston. Random House 1965
Bkl A

Bill Mortlock, ?

Mortlock, Bill. Lawyer, Heal Thyself! Macmillan 1960
Bkl A

German—20th century

Max Isidor Bodenheimer, 1865-1940

Bodenheimer, Max Isidor. Prelude to Israel: The Memoirs of [the author]; tr. by Israel Cohen; ed. by Henriette Hannah Bodenheimer. Yoseloff 1963
Bkl A

LAWYERS—*Continued*

Indian—20th century

Mohammed Ali Jinnah, 1876-1948

Bolitho, Hector. Jinnah: Creator of Pakistan. Macmillan 1955
BY

LEPERS

See Victims of Leprosy

LETTER WRITERS

See Authors

LEXICOGRAPHERS

American—18th century

Noah Webster, 1758-1843

Proudfit, Isabel. Noah Webster, Father of the Dictionary. Messner 1942
CC(7-9)—JH—SCHS—YR

American—19th century

Noah Webster, 1758-1843

Proudfit, Isabel. Noah Webster, Father of the Dictionary. Messner 1942
CC(7-9)—JH—SCHS—YR

English—18th century

Samuel Johnson, 1709-1784

Boswell, James. Life of Samuel Johnson. Modern Lib.; Oxford; etc.
BY—CA—GR—SCHS—SCPL—3000
Brown, Ivor John Carnegie. Dr. Johnson and His World. Walck 1966
Bkl Y&C
Clifford, James Lowry. Young Sam Johnson. McGraw 1955
SCPL
Greene, Donald Johnson, ed. Samuel Johnson: A Collection of Critical Essays. Prentice-Hall 1965
Bkl A
Hodgart, Matthew John Caldwell. Samuel Johnson and His Times. Arco 1963
Bkl A&Y
Johnson, Samuel. Dr. Johnson: His Life in Letters; ed. by David Littlejohn. Prentice-Hall 1965
Bkl A

LIBRARIANS

COLLECTIONS

Who's Who in Library Service: A Biographical Directory of Professional Librarians in the United States and Canada; ed. by Lee Ash. Shoe String 1966
Bkl A—SCPL

American—19th century

John Cotton Dana, 1856-1929

Hadley, Chalmers. John Cotton Dana: A Sketch. A.L.A. 1943
SCPL

Melvil Dewey, 1851-1931

Rider, Fremont. Melvil Dewey. A. L. A. 1944
SCPL

Charles Evans, 1850-1935

Holley, Edward G. Charles Evans: American Bibliographer. Univ. of Ill. 1963
Bkl A

William Frederick Poole, 1821-1894

Williamson, William Landram. William Frederick Poole and the Modern Library Movement. Columbia Univ. 1963
Bkl A

American—20th century

John Cotton Dana, 1856-1929

Hadley, Chalmers. John Cotton Dana: A Sketch. A. L. A. 1943
SCPL

Melvil Dewey, 1851-1931

Rider, Fremont. Melvil Dewey. A.L.A. 1944
SCPL

Charles Evans, 1850-1935

Holley, Edward G. Charles Evans: American Bibliographer. Univ. of Ill. 1963
Bkl A

Anne Carroll Moore, 1871-1961

COLLECTIONS

Forsee, Aylesa. Women Who Reached for Tomorrow. Macrae 1960
Bkl Y&C

LIBRETTISTS

See Playwrights

LITERARY CRITICS

See Critics

LOBBYISTS

American—19th century

Samuel Ward, 1814-1884

Thomas, Lately. Sam Ward: King of the Lobby. Houghton 1965
Bkl A

LUMBERMEN

American—20th century

Samuel J. Churchill, 1870?-1941

Churchill, Samuel. Big Sam. Doubleday 1965
Bkl A&Y

MAGICIANS

COLLECTIONS

Gibson, Walter Brown. The Master Magicians: Their Lives and Most Famous Tricks. Doubleday 1966
Bkl Y&A&C
John Henry Anderson; Alexander Herrmann; Harry Houdini; Harry Kellar; Jean Eugène Robert-Houdin; William Ellsworth Robinson; Raymond ("Raymond the Great") Saunders; Howard Thurston

Kendall, Lace. Masters of Magic. Macrae 1966
Bkl C(6-9)&Y
Harry Blackstone; Alexander Herrmann; Harry Houdini; Harry Kellar; John Nevil Maskelyne; Jean Eugène Robert-Houdin; Howard Thurston; and others

Severn, William. Magic and Magicians. McKay 1958
BBJH—JH

American—19th century

Alexander Herrmann, 1844-1896

COLLECTIONS

Gibson, Walter Brown. The Master Magicians: Their Lives and Most Famous Tricks. Doubleday 1966
Bkl Y&A&C

Kendall, Lace. Masters of Magic. Macrae 1966
Bkl C(6-9)&Y

William Ellsworth Robinson, 1861-1918

COLLECTIONS

Gibson, Walter Brown. The Master Magicians: Their Lives and Most Famous Tricks. Doubleday 1966
Bkl Y&A&C

American—20th century

Harry Blackstone, 1885-1965

COLLECTIONS

Kendall, Lace. Masters of Magic. Macrae 1966
Bkl C(6-9)&Y

Harry Houdini, 1874-1926

Gibson, Walter Brown and Young, Morris N. Houdini's Fabulous Magic. Chilton 1961
Bkl A&Y

Gresham, William Lindsay. Houdini: The Man Who Walked Through Walls. Holt 1959
SCHS—SCPL

Kendall, Lace. Houdini: Master of Escape. Macrae 1960
Bkl C(6-9)&Y—SCHS

Williams, Beryl and Epstein, Samuel. The Great Houdini: Magician Extraordinary. Messner 1950
BY—JH—SCHS

COLLECTIONS

Gibson, Walter Brown. The Master Magicians: Their Lives and Most Famous Tricks. Doubleday 1966
Bkl Y&A&C

Kendall, Lace. Masters of Magic. Macrae 1966
Bkl C(6-9)&Y

Harry Kellar, 1849-1922

COLLECTIONS

Gibson, Walter Brown. The Master Magicians: Their Lives and Most Famous Tricks. Doubleday 1966
Bkl Y&A&C

Kendall, Lace. Masters of Magic. Macrae 1966
Bkl C(6-9)&Y

William Ellsworth Robinson, 1861-1918

COLLECTIONS

Gibson, Walter Brown. The Master Magicians: Their Lives and Most Famous Tricks. Doubleday 1966
Bkl Y&A&C

Raymond ("Raymond the Great") Saunders, 1877-1948

COLLECTIONS

Gibson, Walter Brown. The Master Magicians: Their Lives and Most Famous Tricks. Doubleday 1966
Bkl Y&A&C

John Scarne, 1903-

Scarne, John. The Odds Against Me: An Autobiography. Simon & Schuster 1966
Bkl A&Y

Howard Thurston, 1869-1936

COLLECTIONS

Gibson, Walter Brown. The Master Magicians: Their Lives and Most Famous Tricks. Doubleday 1966
Bkl Y&A&C

Kendall, Lace. Masters of Magic. Macrae 1966
Bkl C(6-9)&Y

MAGICIANS—*Continued*

English—19th century

John Nevil Maskelyne, 1839-1917

COLLECTIONS

Kendall, Lace. Masters of Magic. Macrae 1966
Bkl C(6-9)&Y

French—19th century

Jean Eugène Robert-Houdin, 1805-1871

COLLECTIONS

Gibson, Walter Brown. The Master Magicians: Their Lives and Most Famous Tricks. Doubleday 1966
Bkl Y&A&C

Kendall, Lace. Masters of Magic. Macrae 1966
Bkl C(6-9)&Y

Scottish—19th century

John Henry Anderson, 1814-1874

COLLECTIONS

Gibson, Walter Brown. The Master Magicians: Their Lives and Most Famous Tricks. Doubleday 1966
Bkl Y&A&C

MANUFACTURERS

See Businessmen; Industrialists

MARINES

See Soldiers

MARINE ENGINEERS

See Engineers, Mechanical

MARKSMEN

American—19th century

Annie Oakley, 1860-1926

Havighurst, Walter. Annie Oakley of the Wild West. Macmillan 1954
SCPL

American—20th century

Annie Oakley, 1860-1926

Havighurst, Walter. Annie Oakley of the Wild West. Macmillan 1954
SCPL

MARSHALS

See Sheriffs

MARTYRS

English—16th century

Anne Askew, 1521-1546

MacLeod, Alison. The Heretic: A Novel. Houghton 1966 (Fiction)
Bkl A

MATHEMATICIANS

COLLECTIONS

Bell, Eric Temple. Men of Mathematics. Simon & Schuster 1937
BBHS—JH—SCHS—SCPL—3000

Muir, Jane. Of Men and Numbers: The Story of the Great Mathematicians. Dodd 1961
Bkl A&Y—JH—YR

Stonaker, Frances Benson. Famous Mathematicians. Lippincott 1966
ESLC

Turnbull, Herbert Westren. The Great Mathematicians. N. Y. Univ. 1961
SCPL

American—18th century

Benjamin Banneker, 1731-1806

Graham, Shirley. Your Most Humble Servant: The Story of Benjamin Banneker. Messner 1949
BY

American—19th century

Nathaniel Bowditch, 1773-1838

Latham, Jean Lee. Carry On, Mr. Bowditch. Houghton 1955
BBEL(6-8)—BBJH—BY—CC(6-9)—ESLC—JH—SCHS

Charles Sanders Peirce, 1839-1914

COLLECTIONS

Van Wesep, H. B. Seven Sages: The Story of American Philosophy. Longmans 1960
SCPL

English—16th century

John Dee, 1527-1608

COLLECTIONS

Cummings, Richard. The Alchemists: Fathers of Practical Chemistry. McKay 1966
Bkl C&Y

English—17th century

Sir Isaac Newton, 1642-1727

Andrade, Edward Neville da Costa. Sir Isaac Newton. Doubleday 1965
Bkl A&Y

MATHEMATICIANS

English—17th century

Sir Isaac Newton—Continued

Horizon Magazine. The Universe of Galileo and Newton, by William Bixby and Giorgio de Santillana. Harper 1964
AB(6-10)—Bkl C(7-9)—CC(5-9)—ESLC—IndS(9-12)—JH—SCHS

Land, Barbara and Land, Myrick. The Quest of Isaac Newton. Garden City 1960
ESLC

Moore, Patrick. Isaac Newton. Putnam 1958
AB(5-9)—BBJH—SCHS

Sootin, Harry. Isaac Newton. Messner **1955**
BY—JH—SCHS

Tannenbaum, Beulah and Stillman, Myra. Isaac Newton, Pioneer of Space Mathematics. McGraw 1959
AB(6-9)—Bkl Y&C(7-9)—JH

English—18th century

Sir Isaac Newton, 1642-1727

Andrade, Edward Neville da Costa. Sir Isaac Newton. Doubleday 1965
Bkl A&Y

Horizon Magazine. The Universe of Galileo and Newton, by William Bixby and Giorgio de Santillana. Harper 1964
AB(6-10)—Bkl C(7-9)—CC(5-9)—ESLC—IndS(9-12)—JH—SCHS

Land, Barbara and Land, Myrick. The Quest of Isaac Newton. Garden City 1960
ESLC

Moore, Patrick. Isaac Newton. Putnam 1958
AB(5-9)—BBJH—ESLC—SCHS

Sootin, Harry. Isaac Newton. Messner 1955
BY—CC—JH—SCHS

Tannenbaum, Beulah and Stillman, Myra. Isaac Newton, Pioneer of Space Mathematics. McGraw 1959
AB(6-9)—Bkl Y&C(7-9)—JH

English—19th century

Charles Lutwidge Dodgson, 1832-1898

Green, Roger Lancelyn. The Story of Lewis Carroll. Walck 1962
YR

Hudson, Derek. Lewis Carroll. Constable 1954
SCPL

Wood, James Playsted. The Snark Was a Boojum: A Life of Lewis Carroll. Pantheon 1966
Bkl C(7-9)&Y

English—20th century

Bertrand Arthur William Russell, 3rd Earl Russell, 1872-

Wood, Alan. Bertrand Russell—The Passionate Skeptic: A Biography. Simon & Schuster 1958
SCPL

French—17th century

René Descartes, 1596-1650

Jaspers, Karl. Three Essays: Leonardo, Descartes, Max Weber; tr. by Ralph Manheim. Harcourt 1964
Bkl A

Blaise Pascal, 1623-1662

Steinmann, Jean. Pascal; tr. by Martin Turnell. Harcourt 1966
Bkl A

German—19th century

Carl Friedrich Gauss, 1777-1855

Schaaf, William Leonard. Carl Friedrich Gauss, Prince of Mathematicians. Watts 1964
Bkl Y

Greek—3rd century B.C.

Archimedes, 287?-212 B.C.

Bendick, Jeanne. Archimedes and the Door of Science. Watts 1962
Bkl C(6-9)—ESLC—JH

Jonas, Arthur. Archimedes and His Wonderful Discoveries. Prentice-Hall 1963
CC(3-6)—ESLC—IndJ(4-6)

COLLECTIONS

Mann, A. L. and Vivian, A. C. Famous Physicists. Day 1963
ESLC—JH

Irish—19th century

William Thomson, Baron Kelvin, 1824-1907

MacDonald, David Keith Chalmers. Faraday, Maxwell, and Kelvin. Doubleday 1964
Bkl A&Y

MAYORS

See Statesmen

MECHANICAL ENGINEERS

See Engineers, Mechanical

MEDICAL MISSIONARIES

See Physicians; Religious Leaders

MEN OF LETTERS

See Authors

MENTAL HYGIENISTS

American—20th century

Clifford Whittingham Beers, 1876-1943

Beers, Clifford Whittingham. Mind That Found Itself: An Autobiography. Doubleday 1953
SCPL

COLLECTIONS

McKown, Robin. Pioneers in Mental Health. Dodd 1961
Bkl A&Y

MERCHANTS

See Businessmen

MICROBIOLOGISTS

Dutch—17th century

Anthony van Leeuwenhoek, 1632-1723

Schierbeek, Abraham. Measuring the Invisible World: The Life and Works of Antoni van Leeuwenhoek. Abelard-Schuman 1960
Bkl A

Dutch—18th century

Anthony van Leeuwenhoek, 1632-1723

Schierbeek, Abraham. Measuring the Invisible World: The Life and Works of Antoni van Leeuwenhoek. Abelard-Schuman 1960
Bkl A

MIDGETS

See Circus Performers

MILITARY ENGINEERS

See Engineers, Military

MINING ENGINEERS

See Engineers, Mining

MINISTERS

See Religious Leaders

MISSIONARIES

See Religious Leaders

MISTRESSES OF FAMOUS MEN

COLLECTIONS

Kelen, Betty. The Mistresses: Domestic Scandals of Nineteenth-Century Monarchs. Random House 1966
Bkl A

French—16th century

Gabrielle d'Estrées, 1573-1599

Lewis, Paul. Lady of France. Funk 1963
Bkl A

French—17th century

Françoise Athénaïs (de Rochechouart) de Pardaillan de Gondrin, Marquise de Montespan, 1641-1707

Sanders, Joan. The Marquis: A Novel. Houghton 1963 (Fiction)
Bkl A

French—18th century

Marie Jeanne Bécu, Comtesse du Barry, 1743-1793

Loomis, Stanley. Du Barry: A Biography. Lippincott 1959
SCPL

Jeanne Antoinette (Poisson), Marquise de Pompadour, 1721-1764

Levron, Jacques. Pompadour; tr. by Claire Eliane Engel. St Martins 1963
Bkl A

Smythe, D. M. Madame de Pompadour: Mistress of France. Funk 1953
SCPL

German—19th century

Marie Esther (Lee) Grafin von Waldersee, 1837?-1914

Smith, Alson Jesse. A View of the Spree. Day 1962
Bkl A

German—20th century

Marie Esther (Lee) Grafin von Waldersee, 1837?-1914

Smith, Alson Jesse. A View of the Spree. Day 1962
Bkl A

Roman—1st century A.D.

Berenice, 28?-81?

Fast, Howard Melvin. Agrippa's Daughter. Doubleday 1964 (Fiction)
Bkl A

MONKS

See Religious Leaders

MORMON LEADERS

See Religious Leaders

MOTHERS OF FAMOUS MEN

American—18th century

Abigail (Smith) Adams, 1744-1818

Criss, Mildred. Abigail Adams: Leading
Lady. Dodd 1953
BY
Whitney, Janet (Payne). Abigail Adams.
Little 1947
SCPL

Mary (Ball) Washington, 1708-1789

Desmond, Alice (Curtis). George Washington's Mother. Dodd 1961
Bkl C(7-10)&Y—YR

American—19th century

Jane (Lampton) Clemens, 1803-1890

Varble, Rachel (McGrayer). Jane Clem-
ens: The Story of Mark Twain's
Mother. Doubleday 1964
Bkl A&Y

American—20th century

Marguerite (Claverie) Oswald, 1907-

Stafford, Jean. A Mother in History. Farrar 1966
Bkl A

Corsican—18th century

*Maria Letizia (Ramolino) Bonaparte,
1750-1836*

Stirling, Monica. Madame Letizia: A
Portrait of Napoleon's Mother. Harper
1962
Bkl A—BY

MOTION PICTURE ACTORS

See Actors

MOTION PICTURE DIRECTORS

See Motion Picture Producers

MOTION PICTURE PRODUCERS

COLLECTIONS

Taylor, John Russell. Cinema Eye, Cine-
ma Ear: Some Key Film-Makers of the
Sixties. Hill & Wang 1964
Bkl A
Michelangelo Antonioni; Ingmar Bergman;
Robert Bresson; Luis Bunuel; Federico Fel-
lini; Alfred Joseph Hitchcock; and others

American—20th century

Robert Joseph Flaherty, 1884-1951

Calder-Marshall, Arthur. The Innocent
Eye: The Life of Robert J. Flaherty.
Harcourt 1966
Bkl A
Flaherty, Frances (Hubbard). The Odys-
sey of a Film-Maker: Robert Flaherty's
Story. Univ. of Ill. 1960
Bkl A&Y

Louis Burt Mayer, 1885-1957

Crowther, Bosley. Hollywood Rajah: The
Life and Times of Louis B. Mayer.
Holt 1960
Bkl A

Dore Schary, 1905-

Schary, Dore. For Special Occasions.
Random House 1962
Bkl A—BY

Spyros Panagiotes Skouras, 1893-

COLLECTIONS

Life International. Nine Who Chose
America. Dutton 1959
Bkl Y&C—SCHS

Jack Leonard Warner, 1892-

Warner, Jack Leonard and Jennings,
Dean Southern. My First Hundred
Years in Hollywood. Random House
1965
Bkl A

Austrian—20th century

Josef Von Sternberg, 1894?-

Von Sternberg, Josef. Fun in a Chinese
Laundry. Macmillan 1965
Bkl A

English—20th century

Alfred Joseph Hitchcock, 1899-

COLLECTIONS

Taylor, John Russell. Cinema Eye, Cine-
ma Ear: Some Key Film-Makers of the
Sixties. Hill & Wang 1964
Bkl A

Sir Alexander Korda, 1893-1956

Tabori, Paul. Alexander Korda. Living
Books 1966
Bkl A

French—20th century

Robert Bresson, 1907-

COLLECTIONS

Taylor, John Russell. Cinema Eye, Cine-
ma Ear: Some Key Film-Makers of the
Sixties. Hill & Wang 1964
Bkl A

MOTION PICTURE PRODUCERS—
Continued

Italian—20th century

Michelangelo Antonioni, 1912-

COLLECTIONS

Taylor, John Russell. Cinema Eye, Cinema Ear: Some Key Film-Makers of the Sixties. Hill & Wang 1964
Bkl A

Federico Fellini, 1920-

COLLECTIONS

Taylor, John Russell. Cinema Eye, Cinema Ear: Some Key Film-Makers of the Sixties. Hill & Wang 1964
Bkl A

Mexican—20th century

Luis Buñuel, 1900-

COLLECTIONS

Taylor, John Russell. Cinema Eye, Cinema Ear: Some Key Film-Makers of the Sixties. Hill & Wang 1964
Bkl A

Swedish—20th century

Ingmar Bergman, 1918-

COLLECTIONS

Taylor, John Russell. Cinema Eye, Cinema Ear: Some Key Film-Makers of the Sixties. Hill & Wang 1964
Bkl A

MOUNTAIN MEN

See Frontiersmen

MOUNTAINEERS

American—20th century

Grant H. Pearson, ?

Pearson, Grant H. and Newill, Philip. My Life of High Adventure. Prentice-Hall 1962
Bkl A&Y

Hudson Stuck, 1863-1920

Herron, Edward A. Conqueror of Mount McKinley. Messner 1964
YR

Austrian—20th century

Heinrich Harrer, 1912-

Harrer, Heinrich. I Come from the Stone Age; tr. from the German by Edward Fitzgerald. Dutton 1965
Bkl A&Y—IndS(10-12)

English—20th century

Sir Edmund Hillary, 1919-

Hillary, Sir Edmund. High Adventure. Dutton 1955
SCPL—YR

Hillary, Sir Edmund and Doig, Desmond. High in the Thin Cold Air. Doubleday 1962
Bkl A&Y—SCHS

Sir John Hunt, 1910-

Hunt, Sir John. The Conquest of Everest. Dutton 1954
BBHS—SCHS—SCPL

Gwen Moffat, ?

Moffat, Gwen. Space Below My Feet. Houghton 1961
Bkl A

French—20th century

Maurice Herzog, 1919-

COLLECTIONS

Hoff, Rhoda and De Terra, Helmut. They Explored! Walck 1959
AB(5)

Lionel Terray, 1921?-1965

Terray, Lionel. The Borders of the Impossible: From the Alps to Annapurna; tr. by Geoffrey Sutton. Doubleday 1964
Bkl A&Y

Nepalese—20th century

Norgay Tenzing, 1914-

Tenzing, Norgay. Tiger of the Snows: The Autobiography of Tenzing of Everest. Putnam 1955
BBHS—BY—SCHS—SCPL

Pakistani—20th century

Mohammad Ata-ullah, 1903-

Ata-ullah, Mohammad. Citizen of Two Worlds. Harper 1960
Bkl A&Y—BY

MURDERERS

See Criminals; Victims of Murderers

MUSEUM DIRECTORS

English—19th century

Sydney Carlyle Cockerell, 1867-1962

Blunt, Wilfrid. Cockerell: Sydney Carlyle Cockerell, Friend of Ruskin and William Morris and Director of the Fitzwilliam Museum, Cambridge. Knopf 1965
Bkl A

MUSEUM DIRECTORS—*Continued*

English—20th century

Sydney Carlyle Cockerell, 1867-1962

Blunt, Wilfrid. Cockerell: Sydney Carlyle Cockerell, Friend of Ruskin and William Morris and Director of the Fitzwilliam Museum, Cambridge. Knopf 1965
Bkl A

Sir John Knewstub Maurice Rothenstein, 1901-

Rothenstein, Sir John Knewstub Maurice. Summer's Lease: Autobiography, 1901-1938. Holt 1966
Bkl A

MUSIC CRITICS

See Critics

MUSIC TEACHERS

See Educators

MUSICIANS

See also Bandmasters; Cellists; Clarinetists; Composers; Conductors; Critics; Educators; Guitarists; Organists; Pianists; Singers; Trumpeters; Violinists

COLLECTIONS

Baker, Theodore. Biographical Dictionary of Musicians. 5th ed. rev. by Nicolas Slonimsky. Schirmer 1958
SCPL

Chotzinoff, Samuel. A Little Nightmusic. Harper 1964
Bkl A&Y—IndS(12)
Jascha Heifetz; Vladimir Horowitz; Gian-Carlo Menotti; Leontyne Price; Richard Rodgers; Artur Rubinstein; Andrés Segovia

Ewen, David. Famous Instrumentalists. Dodd 1965
Bkl Y&C
Julian Bream; Van Cliburn; Emil Grigor'-evich Gilels; Leonard Rose; Isaac Stern; and others

Ewen, David, ed. Living Musicians. Wilson 1940
JH—SCHS—SCPL

Ewen, David, ed. Living Musicians: First Supplement. Wilson 1957
JH—SCHS—SCPL

Ewen, David. Men and Women Who Make Music. Merlin 1949
SCPL

Gelatt, Roland. Music Makers: Some Outstanding Musical Performers of Our Day. Knopf 1953
SCPL

Pincherle, Marc. The World of the Virtuoso; tr. from the French by Lucille H. Brockway. Norton 1963
Bkl A
Wanda Landowska; Yehudi Menuhin; Nicolò Paganini; and others

American

COLLECTIONS

Feather, Leonard G. Encyclopedia of Jazz. Horizon 1955
SCPL

Gitler, Ira. Jazz Masters of the Forties. Macmillan 1966
Bkl A&Y

Goldberg, Joe. Jazz Masters of the Fifties. Macmillan 1965
Bkl A&Y

Hadlock, Richard. Jazz Masters of the Twenties. Macmillan 1965
Bkl A&Y
Louis Armstrong; Leon Bismarck ("Bix") Beiderbecke; Bessie Smith; and others

Hare, Maud (Cuney). Negro Musicians and Their Music. Associated Pubs 1936
SCPL

Hughes, Langston. Famous Negro Music Makers. Dodd 1955
CC—SCHS—SCPL

Shapiro, Nat and Hentoff, Nat, eds. Jazz Makers. Rinehart 1957
SCPL

Terkel, Studs. Giants of Jazz. Crowell 1957
BBJH—BY—JH—SCHS—YR

MYCOLOGISTS

See Botanists

MYSTICS

See Religious Leaders

NATURALISTS

See also Biologists; Botanists; Geologists; Herpetologists; Ornithologists; Paleontologists; Zoologists

COLLECTIONS

Blassingame, Wyatt. Naturalist-Explorers. Watts 1964
ESLC
Sir Joseph Banks; John Bartram; Charles Robert Darwin; Alexander von Humboldt; Carl von Linné; John Muir; Alfred Russel Wallace

Shippen, Katherine Binney. Men, Microscopes, and Living Things. Viking 1955
BBEL(7-8)—BBJH—CC(7-9)—ESLC—JH—SCHS—SCPL

NATURALISTS—*Continued*

Terres, John K., ed. Discovery: Great Moments in the Lives of Outstanding Naturalists. Lippincott 1961
Bkl A&Y

American—19th century

John Burroughs, 1837-1921

Swift, Hildegarde (Hoyt). The Edge of April: A Biography of John Burroughs. Morrow 1957
AB(7-10)—BBEL(7-8)—BBJH—CC(7-9)—ESLC—JH—SCHS

John Muir, 1838-1914

Douglas, William Orville. Muir of the Mountains. Houghton 1961
Bkl C(6-9)—BY—ESLC—JH—YR
Grossman, Adrienne and Beardwood, Valerie. Trails of His Own: The Story of John Muir and His Fight to Save Our National Parks. McKay 1961
JH—YR
Haines, Madge and Morrill, Leslie. John Muir: Protector of the Wilds. Abingdon 1957
AB(3-7)
Muir, John. Story of My Boyhood and Youth. Houghton 1913
SCPL
Norman, Charles. John Muir: Father of Our National Parks. Messner 1957
BBJH—JH—SCHS
Swift, Hildegarde (Hoyt). From the Eagle's Wing: A Biography of John Muir. Morrow 1962
Bkl Y&C—CC(6-9)—ESLC—JH—YR
Wolfe, Linnie (Marsh). Son of the Wilderness: The Life of John Muir. Knopf 1945
SCPL

COLLECTIONS

Blassingame, Wyatt. Naturalist-Explorers. Watts 1964
ESLC
Eifert, Virginia Louise (Snider). Tall Trees and Far Horizons: Adventures and Discoveries of Early Botanists in America. Dodd 1965
Bkl A&Y

Ernest Thompson Seton, 1860-1946

Garst, Doris Shannon and Garst, Warren. Ernest Thompson Seton, Naturalist. Messner 1959
JH—YR
Seton, Ernest Thompson. Trail of an Artist-Naturalist: The Autobiography of Ernest Thompson Seton. Scribner 1940
SCPL

Henry David Thoreau, 1817-1862

Derleth, August. Concord Rebel: A Life of Henry D. Thoreau. Chilton 1962
Bkl A&Y—BY—SCHS
Harding, Walter Roy. The Days of Henry Thoreau. Knopf 1965
Bkl A&Y—IndS(12)
Krutch, Joseph Wood. Henry David Thoreau. Sloane 1948
SCPL
Longstreth, T. Morris. Henry Thoreau, American Rebel. Dodd 1963
AB(6-11)
Meltzer, Milton and Harding, Walter Roy, eds. A Thoreau Profile. Crowell 1962
Bkl A&Y—IndS(11-12)
Norman, Charles. To a Different Drum: The Story of Henry David Thoreau. Harper 1954
SCHS
North, Sterling. Thoreau of Walden Pond. Houghton 1959
CC(6-7)
Thoreau, Henry David. Consciousness in Concord: The Text of Thoreau's Hitherto "Lost Journal," (1840-1841); ed. by Perry Miller. Houghton 1958
SCPL
Van Doren, Mark. Henry David Thoreau: A Critical Study. Russell & Russell 1961
SCPL
Wood, James Playsted. A Hound, a Bay Horse, and a Turtle-Dove: A Life of Thoreau for the Young Reader. Pantheon 1963
Bkl Y&C

COLLECTIONS

Bailey, Carolyn Sherwin. Children of the Handcrafts. Viking 1935
BBJH—CC(4-7)—ESLC
Schechter, Betty. The Peaceable Revolution. Houghton 1963
CC(8-9)—ESLC—IndJ(6-9)—JH

American—20th century

Carl Ethan Akeley, 1864-1926

Sutton, Felix. Big Game Hunter: Carl Akeley. Messner 1960
Bkl C(5-9)&Y

COLLECTIONS

Andrews, Roy Chapman. Beyond Adventure: The Lives of Three Explorers. Duell 1954
BY—SCPL—YR

Roy Chapman Andrews, 1884-1960

COLLECTIONS

Andrews, Roy Chapman. Beyond Adventure: The Lives of Three Explorers. Duell 1954
BY—SCPL—YR

NATURALISTS

American—20th century—*Continued*

Thornton Waldo Burgess, 1874-1965

Burgess, Thornton Waldo. Now I Remember: The Autobiography of an Amateur Naturalist. Little 1960
Bkl A—BY

Raymond Lee Ditmars, 1876-1942

Wood, L. N. Raymond L. Ditmars: His Exciting Career with Reptiles, Animals, and Insects. Messner 1944
CC(7-9)—JH—SCHS

William Orville Douglas, 1898-

Douglas, William Orville. Of Men and Mountains. Harper 1950
BY—SCHS—SCPL

Haydn Sanborn Pearson, 1901-1967

Pearson, Haydn Sanborn. New England Flavor: Memories of a Country Boyhood. Norton 1961
Bkl A

Pearson, Haydn Sanborn. The New England Year. Norton 1966
Bkl A

Ernest Thompson Seton, 1860-1946

Garst, Doris Shannon and Garst, Warren. Ernest Thompson Seton, Naturalist. Messner 1959
JH—YR

Seton, Ernest Thompson. Trail of an Artist-Naturalist: The Autobiography of Ernest Thompson Seton. Scribner 1940
SCPL

Edwin Way Teale, 1899-

Dodd, Edward Howard. Of Nature, Time, and Teale: A Biographical Sketch of Edwin Way Teale. Dodd 1960
Bkl A

Teale, Edwin Way. Dune Boy: The Early Years of a Naturalist. Dodd 1957
SCHS—SCPL

Dutch—17th century

Anthony van Leeuwenhoek, 1632-1723

Schierbeek, Abraham. Measuring the Invisible World: The Life and Works of Antoni van Leeuwenhoek. Abelard-Schuman 1960
Bkl A

Dutch—18th century

Anthony van Leeuwenhoek, 1632-1723

Schierbeek, Abraham. Measuring the Invisible World: The Life and Works of Antoni van Leeuwenhoek. Abelard-Schuman 1960
Bkl A

English—18th century

Sir Joseph Banks, 1743-1820

COLLECTIONS

Blassingame, Wyatt. Naturalist-Explorers. Watts 1964
ESLC

English—19th century

Charles Robert Darwin, 1809-1882

Darwin, Charles Robert. Autobiography of Charles Darwin; ed. by Nora Barlow. Harcourt 1959
BBHS—CA—SCPL

Darwin, Charles Robert. The Voyage of the Beagle. Bantam; Everyman; Anchor; etc.
GR—SCPL

Darwin, Charles Robert. The Voyage of the Beagle; abr. and ed. by Millicent E. Selsam. Harper 1959
BBHS—Bkl Y&C—CC—ESLC—JH—SCHS—SCPL

De Beer, Sir Gavin Rylands. Charles Darwin: Evolution by Natural Selection. Doubleday 1964
Bkl A&Y—SCPL

Dickinson, Alice. Charles Darwin & Natural Selection. Watts 1964
Bkl Y&C

Huxley, Sir Julian Sorell and Kettlewell, N. B. D. Charles Darwin and His World. Studio 1965
Bkl A&Y—IndS(10-12)

Irvine, William. Apes, Angels, and Victorians: The Story of Darwin, Huxley, and Evolution. McGraw 1955
SCPL

Life (Periodical). The Wonders of Life on Earth. Golden Press 1960
CC(6-9)—ESLC—JH—SCHS—SCPL

Moore, Ruth E. Charles Darwin: A Great Life in Brief. Knopf 1955
SCHS—SCPL

Selsam, Millicent E. Around the World with Darwin. Harper 1960
CC(3-6)—ESLC

COLLECTIONS

Blassingame, Wyatt. Naturalist-Explorers. Watts 1964
ESLC

NATURALISTS

English—19th century—*Continued*

William Henry Hudson, 1841-1922

Hudson, William Henry. Far Away and Long Ago: A History of My Early Life. Dutton 1931
BY—SCHS—SCPL

Alfred Russel Wallace, 1823-1913

George, Wilma B. Biologist Philosopher: A Study of the Life and Writings of Alfred Russel Wallace. Abelard-Schuman 1964
Bkl A

COLLECTIONS

Blassingame, Wyatt. Naturalist-Explorers. Watts 1964
ESLC

English—20th century

William Henry Hudson, 1841-1922

Hudson, William Henry. Far Away and Long Ago: A History of My Early Life. Dutton 1931
BY—SCHS—SCPL

German—18th century

George Wilhelm Steller, 1709-1746

Bell, Margaret Elizabeth. Touched with Fire: Alaska's George William Steller. Morrow 1960
Bkl C(7-9)&Y
Ford, Corey. Where the Sea Breaks Its Back: The Epic Story of a Pioneer Naturalist and the Discovery of Alaska. Little 1966
Bkl A&Y
Sutton, Ann and Sutton, Myron. Steller of the North. Rand McNally 1961
YR

German—19th century

Alexander, Freiherr von Humboldt, 1769-1859

Dolan, Edward F. Green Universe. Dodd 1959
Bkl A&Y
Gendron, Val. The Dragon Tree: A Life of Alexander, Baron von Humboldt. Longmans 1961
Bkl Y&C
Thomas, M. Z. Alexander von Humboldt, Scientist, Explorer, Adventurer. Pantheon 1960
Bkl C(6-9)—BY—YR

COLLECTIONS

Blassingame, Wyatt. Naturalist-Explorers. Watts 1964
ESLC

Hoff, Rhoda and De Terra, Helmut. They Explored! Walck 1959
AB(5)

Swiss—19th century

Louis Agassiz, 1807-1873

Forsee, Aylesa. Louis Agassiz: Pied Piper of Science. Viking 1958
CC(6-9)—YR
Peare, Catherine O. A Scientist of Two Worlds: Louis Agassiz. Lippincott 1958
BBJH—CC—ESLC—JH—SCHS
Tharp, Louise Hall. Adventurous Alliance: The Story of the Agassiz Family of Boston. Little 1959
BBHS—CC—SCHS—SCPL
Tharp, Louise Hall. Louis Agassiz, Adventurous Scientist. Little 1961
Bkl C(5-8)—CC(5-7)—ESLC

NAVAL HEROES

See Naval Officers and Other Seafarers

NAVAL OFFICERS AND OTHER SEAFARERS

See also Explorers

COLLECTIONS

Army Times. Famous Fighters of World War I. Dodd 1964
Bkl C&Y—YR

American

COLLECTIONS

Braun, Saul M. Seven Heroes: Medal of Honor Stories of the War in the Pacific. Putnam 1965
Bkl C(6-9)&Y
Navy Times. Great American Naval Heroes. Dodd 1965
Bkl C(6-9)&Y—ESLC

American—18th century

John Paul Jones, 1747-1792

Ellsberg, Edward. "I Have Just Begun to Fight": The Story of John Paul Jones. Dodd 1942 (Fiction)
BBJH—CC(7-9)—JH—SCHS
Graff, Stewart. John Paul Jones: Sailor Hero. Garrard 1961
ESLC
Kent, Louise (Andrews). He Went with John Paul Jones. Houghton 1958 (Fiction)
BBJH—CC(7-9)—JH—SCHS
Lorenz, Lincoln. John Paul Jones: Fighter for Freedom and Glory. U.S. Naval Inst. 1943
SCPL
Morison, Samuel Eliot. John Paul Jones: A Sailor's Biography. Little 1959
BBHS—SCHS—SCPL—3000

NAVAL OFFICERS AND OTHER SEA-FARERS

American—18th century

John Paul Jones—Continued

Sperry, Armstrong. John Paul Jones, Fighting Sailor. Random House 1953
BBEL(5-8)—BBJH—CC(5-7)—ESLC—JH

COLLECTIONS

Daugherty, Sonia. Ten Brave Men: Makers of the American Way. Lippincott 1951
SCHS

American—19th century

William Bainbridge, 1774-1833

Vail, Philip. The Sea Panther: A Novel about the Commander of the U.S.S. Constitution. Dodd 1962 (Fiction)
Bkl A

Franklin Buchanan, 1800-1874

Eliot, George Fielding. Daring Sea Warrior: Franklin Buchanan. Messner 1962
Bkl Y&C

John Mansfield Cavarly, 1832-1895

Hulme, Kathryn. Annie's Captain. Little 1961
Bkl A&Y—BY—SCHS

Richard Henry Dana, 1815-1882

Dana, Richard Henry. Two Years Before the Mast. Modern Lib.; Bantam; Dodd; Macmillan; World; etc.
BBHS—BY—GR—SCHS—SCPL

Stephen Decatur, 1779-1820

Blassingame, Wyatt. Stephen Decatur: Fighting Sailor. Garrard 1964
AB(4-7)

George Dewey, 1837-1917

Smith, Fredrika Shumway. George Dewey, Admiral of the Navy. Rand McNally 1963
AB(6-9)

David Glasgow Farragut, 1801-1870

Mudra, Marie. David Farragut, Sea Fighter. Messner 1953
BBJH—JH—SCHS

Uriah Phillips Levy, 1792-1862

Fitzpatrick, Donovan and Saphire, Saul. Navy Maverick: Uriah Phillips Levy. Doubleday 1963
Bkl A&Y

Thomas MacDonough, 1783-1825

Muller, Charles G. The Proudest Day: Macdonough on Lake Champlain. Day 1960
Bkl A

Matthew Fontaine Maury, 1806-1873

Latham, Jean Lee. Trail Blazer of the Seas. Houghton 1956 (Fiction)
BY—CC(7-9)—JH

Williams, Frances Leigh. Matthew Fontaine Maury, Scientist of the Sea. Rutgers Univ. 1963
Bkl A

Williams, Frances Leigh. Ocean Pathfinder: A Biography of Matthew Fontaine Maury. Harcourt 1966
Bkl C(7-9)&Y—ESLC

John O'Brien, 1851-1931

Herron, Edward A. Dynamite Johnny O'Brien: Alaska's Sea Captain. Messner 1962
AB(7up)

James William Pattillo, 1806-1887

Garland, Joseph E. That Great Pattillo. Little 1966
Bkl A

Robert Edwin Peary, 1856-1920

Angell, Pauline Knickerbocker. To the Top of the World: The Story of Peary and Henson. Rand McNally 1964
AB(5up)—Bkl C&Y

Berry, Erick. Robert E. Peary: North Pole Conqueror. Garrard 1963
AB(3-5)—ESLC

Lord, Walter. Peary to the Pole. Harper 1963
Bkl C(5-9)&Y—ESLC

Owen, Russell. The Conquest of the North and South Poles: Adventures of the Peary and Byrd Expeditions. Random House 1952
CC(5-9)—ESLC—JH

Stafford, Marie Peary. Discoverer of the North Pole: The Story of Robert E. Peary. Morrow 1959
CC(6-9)—JH

Weems, John Edward. Race for the Pole. Holt 1960
Bkl A&Y

Matthew Calbraith Perry, 1794-1858

American Heritage. Commodore Perry in Japan, by Robert Lincoln Reynolds. Am. Heritage 1963
Bkl C(6-9)&Y—CC(7-9)—ESLC—IndJ(6-9)—JH—SCHS—YR

Kuhn, Ferdinand. Commodore Perry and the Opening of Japan. Random House 1955
BBEL—JH—SCHS

Orrmont, Arthur. The Indestructible Commodore Matthew Perry. Messner 1962
AB(7up)—Bkl C(6-9)

NAVAL OFFICERS AND OTHER SEA-FARERS

American—19th century—*Continued*

Oliver Hazard Perry, 1785-1819

Mason, Francis Van Wyck. The Battle of Lake Erie. Houghton 1960
Bkl C(5-8)—ESLC

Charles William Read, 1840-1890

COLLECTIONS

Dufour, Charles L. Nine Men in Gray. Doubleday 1963
Bkl A&Y

Raphael Semmes, 1809-1877

Foster, John. Rebel Sea Raider: The Story of Raphael Semmes. Morrow 1965
ESLC

Joshua Slocum, 1844-1910

Teller, Walter Magnes. Search for Captain Slocum: A Biography. Scribner 1956
SCPL

Edgar Wakeman, 1813-1875

Newell, Gordon R. Paddlewheel Pirate: The Life and Adventures of Captain Ned Wakeman. Dutton 1959
Bkl A

Ellsworth Luce West, 1864-1949

West, Ellsworth Luce and Mayhew, Eleanor Ransom. Captain's Papers: A Log of Whaling and Other Sea Experiences. Barre 1965
Bkl A

American—20th century

Edward Latimer Beach, 1918-

Beach, Edward Latimer. Around the World Submerged. Holt 1962
Bkl A&Y

Richard Evelyn Byrd, 1888-1957

Byrd, Richard Evelyn. Alone. Putnam 1938
SCHS—SCPL
Byrd, Richard Evelyn. Little America. Putnam 1930
SCPL—YR
Byrd, Richard Evelyn. Skyward. Putnam 1928
SCPL
Gladych, Michael. Admiral Byrd of Antarctica. Messner 1960
Bkl C(5-8)
Owen, Russell. The Conquest of the North and South Poles: Adventures of the Peary and Byrd Expeditions. Random House 1952
CC(5-9)—ESLC—JH

Rink, Paul. Conquering Antarctica: Richard E. Byrd. Encyc. Britannica 1961
JH

George Dewey, 1837-1917

Smith, Fredrika Shumway. George Dewey, Admiral of the Navy. Rand McNally 1963
AB(6-9)

Daniel Vincent Gallery, 1901-

Gallery, Daniel Vincent. Eight Bells, and All's Well. Norton 1965
Bkl A&Y

William Frederick Halsey, 1882-1959

Keating, Lawrence A. Fleet Admiral: The Story of William F. Halsey. Westminster 1965
ESLC

John Fitzgerald Kennedy, 1917-1963

Donovan, Robert J. PT 109: John F. Kennedy in World War II. McGraw 1961
Bkl A&Y—CC—SCHS
Shepard, Tazewell Taylor. John F. Kennedy, Man of the Sea. Morrow 1965
Bkl A
Tregaskis, Richard. John F. Kennedy and PT-109. Random House 1962
Bkl C(6-9)—CC(5-7)—ESLC—JH—SCHS

Husband Edward Kimmel, 1882-1968

Kimmel, Husband Edward. Admiral Kimmel's Story. Regnery 1955
SCPL

Hugh Nathaniel Mulzac, 1886-

Mulzac, Hugh Nathaniel. A Star to Steer By. Int. Pubs 1963
Bkl A

COLLECTIONS

Sterne, Emma (Gelders). I Have a Dream. Knopf 1965
Bkl Y&C

John O'Brien, 1851-1931

Herron, Edward A. Dynamite Johnny O'Brien: Alaska's Sea Captain. Messner 1962
AB(7up)

Robert Edwin Peary, 1856-1920

Angell, Pauline Knickerbocker. To the Top of the World: The Story of Peary and Henson. Rand McNally 1964
AB(5up)—Bkl C&Y
Berry, Erick. Robert E. Peary: North Pole Conqueror. Garrard 1963
AB(3-5)—ESLC
Lord, Walter. Peary to the Pole. Harper 1963
Bkl C(5-9)&Y—ESLC

NAVAL OFFICERS AND OTHER SEA-FARERS

American—20th century

Robert Edwin Peary—Continued

Owen, Russell. The Conquest of the North and South Poles: Adventures of the Peary and Byrd Expeditions. Random House 1952
CC(5-9)—ESLC—JH

Stafford, Marie Peary. Discoverer of the North Pole: The Story of Robert E. Peary. Morrow 1959
CC(6-9)—JH

Weems, John Edward. Race for the Pole. Holt 1960
Bkl A&Y

Ellsworth Luce West, 1864-1949

West, Ellsworth Luce and Mayhew, Eleanor Ransom. Captain's Papers: A Log of Whaling and Other Sea Experiences. Barre 1965
Bkl A

English

COLLECTIONS

Jameson, Sir William. The Fleet That Jack Built: Nine Men Who Made a Modern Navy. Harcourt 1962
Bkl A
John Arbuthnot Fisher and others

English—16th century

Sir Francis Drake, 1540-1596

Bradford, Ernle Dusgate Selby. The Wind Commands Me: A Life of Sir Francis Drake. Harcourt 1965
Bkl A&Y—IndS(11-12)

Knight, Frank. The Young Drake. Roy 1963
IndJ(6-9)

Latham, Jean Lee. Drake: The Man They Called a Pirate. Harper 1960
CC(5-7)—ESLC

Syme, Donald. Francis Drake, Sailor of Unknown Seas. Morrow 1961
Bkl C(4-6)

Wood, William. Elizabethan Sea-Dogs: A Chronicle of Drake and His Companions. Yale Univ. 1918
SCHS

English—17th century

William Adams, 1564-1620

Lund, Robert. Daishi-san: A Novel. Day 1961 (Fiction)
Bkl A

Christopher Jones, 1570?-1622

DeGering, Etta. Christopher Jones, Captain of the Mayflower. McKay 1965
Bkl C(4-6)—ESLC

English—18th century

George Anson, Baron Anson, 1697-1762

Mason, Francis Van Wyck. Manila Galleon. Little 1961 (Fiction)
Bkl A

William Bligh, 1754-1817

Nordhoff, Charles and Hall, James Norman. Mutiny on the Bounty. Little 1932 (Fiction)
JH—SCHS

Horatio Nelson, Viscount Nelson, 1758-1805

Gimpel, Herbert J. Lord Nelson. Watts 1966
Bkl Y&C

Horizon Magazine. Nelson and the Age of Fighting Sail, by Oliver Warner. Harper 1963
Bkl C(7up)—BY—CC(7-9)—JH—SCHS

Southey, Robert. Life of Horatio, Lord Nelson. Dutton 1929
GR—SCPL

Stacton, David. Sir William, or, A Lesson in Love: A Novel. Putnam 1963 (Fiction)
Bkl A

Warner, Oliver. Victory: The Life of Lord Nelson. Little 1958
SCPL

Whipple, Addison Beecher Colvin. Hero of Trafalgar. Random House 1963
Bkl C(7-9)

George Brydges Rodney, Baron Rodney, 1719-1792

Macintyre, Donald G. F. W. Admiral Rodney. Norton 1963
Bkl A

English—19th century

John Arbuthnot Fisher, 1841-1920

COLLECTIONS

Jameson, Sir William. The Fleet That Jack Built: Nine Men Who Made a Modern Navy. Harcourt 1962
Bkl A

Horatio Nelson, Viscount Nelson, 1758-1805

Gimpel, Herbert J. Lord Nelson. Watts 1966
Bkl Y&C

Horizon Magazine. Nelson and the Age of Fighting Sail, by Oliver Warner. Harper 1963
Bkl C(7up)—BY—CC(7-9)—ESLC—JH—SCHS

Southey, Robert. Life of Horatio, Lord Nelson. Dutton 1929
GR—SCPL

NAVAL OFFICERS AND OTHER SEA-FARERS

English—19th century

Horatio Nelson—Continued

Stacton, David. Sir William, or, A Lesson in Love: A Novel. Putnam 1963 (Fiction)
Bkl A

Warner, Oliver. Victory: The Life of Lord Nelson. Little 1958
SCPL

Whipple, Addison Beecher Colvin. Hero of Trafalgar: The Story of Lord Nelson. Random House 1963
Bkl C(7-9)—ESLC

English—20th century

Sir Francis Charles Chichester, 1901-

Chichester, Sir Francis Charles. The Lonely Sea and the Sky. Coward-McCann 1964
Bkl A

Lionel Philip Kenneth Crabb, 1910-1956

Hutton, J. Bernard. Frogman Spy: The Incredible Cast of Commander Crabb. Obolensky 1960
Bkl A

John Arbuthnot Fisher, 1841-1920

COLLECTIONS

Jameson, Sir William. The Fleet That Jack Built: Nine Men Who Made a Modern Navy. Harcourt 1962
Bkl A

Harry Grattidge, 1890-

Grattidge, Harry. Captain of the Queens: The Autobiography of Captain Harry Grattidge, Former Commodore of the Cunard Line. Dutton 1956
SCPL

John Rushworth Jellicoe, 1st Earl Jellicoe, 1859-1935

COLLECTIONS

Barnett, Correlli. The Swordbearers: Supreme Command in the First World War. Morrow 1964
Bkl A

French—20th century

Raoul de Beaudéan, 1903-

Beaudéan, Raoul de. Captain of the Ile; tr. from the French by Salvator Attanasio. McGraw 1960
Bkl A

Jacques Yves Cousteau, 1910-

Dugan, James. Undersea Explorer: The Story of Captain Cousteau. Harper 1957
BBHS—BBJH—CC(7-9)—ESLC—JH—SCHS

François Darlan, 1881-1942

Tompkins, Peter. The Murder of Admiral Darlan: A Study in Conspiracy. Simon & Schuster 1965
Bkl A

Japanese—19th century

Heihachiro Togo, 1847-1934

Blond, Georges. Admiral Togo; tr. by Edward Hyams. Macmillan 1960
Bkl A

Japanese—20th century

Heihachiro Togo, 1847-1934

Blond, Georges. Admiral Togo; tr. by Edward Hyams. Macmillan 1960
Bkl A

Isoroku Yamamoto, 1884-1943

Potter, John Deane. Yamamoto: The Man Who Menaced America. Viking 1965
IndS(11-12)

NAVIGATORS, OCEAN

See Explorers

NAZI LEADERS

See Statesmen, German

NEGROES

American

COLLECTIONS

Bontemps, Arna Wendell. Famous Negro Athletes. Dodd 1964
Bkl C&Y—ESLC—JH
James Nathaniel Brown; Wilton Norman Chamberlain; Althea Gibson; Joe Louis; Willie Mays; Jesse Owens; LeRoy ("Satchel") Paige; John Roosevelt Robinson; Ray Robinson

Bontemps, Arna Wendell. 100 Years of Negro Freedom. Dodd 1961
Bkl A—ESLC—SCPL
Frederick Douglass; William Edward Burghardt Du Bois; Booker Taliaferro Washington; and others

Bontemps, Arna Wendell. We Have Tomorrow. Houghton 1945
BY—SCHS

Dobler, Lavinia and Toppin, Edgar A. Pioneers and Patriots: The Lives of Six Negroes of the Revolutionary Era. Doubleday 1965
ESLC

NEGROES

American—*Continued*

Gloster, Hugh Morris. Negro Voices in American Fiction. Univ. of N. C. 1948
SCPL

Hare, Maud (Cuney). Negro Musicians and Their Music. Associated Pubs 1936
SCPL

Hughes, Langston. Famous American Negroes. Dodd 1954
BBEL(7-8)—BBJH—CC(7-9)—ESLC—JH—SCHS

Hughes, Langston. Famous Negro Heroes of America. Dodd 1958
BBEL(7-8)—ESLC—JH—YR

Hughes, Langston. Famous Negro Music Makers. Dodd 1955
CC—SCHS—SCPL

Littlejohn, David. Black on White: A Critical Survey of Writing by American Negroes. Grossman 1966
Bkl A

Redding, Jay Saunders. Lonesome Road: The Story of the Negro's Part in America. Doubleday 1958
SCPL

Richardson, Ben Albert. Great American Negroes; rev. by William A. Fahey. Crowell 1956
BBHS—CC(7-9)—ESLC—JH—SCHS—SCPL

Robinson, John Roosevelt. Baseball Has Done It; ed. by Charles Dexter. Lippincott 1964
Bkl A&Y
Henry Louis Aaron; Ernest Banks; Elston Gene Howard; Frank Robinson

Rollins, Charlemae Hill. Famous American Negro Poets. Dodd 1965
Bkl C(6-9)&Y—ESLC

Rollins, Charlemae Hill. They Showed the Way: Forty American Negro Leaders. Crowell 1964
Bkl C(5-8)—CC(5-7)—ESLC—IndJ(6-9)

Starkey, Marion L. Striving to Make It My Home. Norton 1964
IndS(11-12)

Sterling, Dorothy and Quarles, Benjamin. Lift Every Voice: The Lives of Booker T. Washington, W. E. B. Du Bois, Mary Church Terrell, and James Weldon Johnson. Doubleday 1965
Bkl C(6-9)&Y—ESLC
William Edward Burghardt Du Bois; James Weldon Johnson; Mary (Church) Terrell; Booker Taliaferro Washington

Sterne, Emma (Gelders). I Have a Dream. Knopf 1965
Bkl Y&C
Marian Anderson; Daisy Bates; James Farmer; John Lewis; Thurgood Marshall; Hugh Mulzac; Rosa Lee Parks; Asa Philip Randolph; Fred Shuttlesworth

Stratton, Madeline Robinson. Negroes Who Helped Build America. Ginn 1965
Bkl C(6-9)&Y—ESLC

Young, Andrew Sturgeon Nash. Negro Firsts in Sports. Johnson Pub. 1963
Bkl A&Y
John Arthur Johnson; Joe Louis; Jesse Owens; John Roosevelt Robinson; and others

NEUROLOGISTS

Austrian—20th century

Sigmund Freud, 1856-1939

Baker, Rachel. Sigmund Freud. Messner 1952
BY

Costigan, Giovanni. Sigmund Freud: A Short Biography. Macmillan 1965
Bkl A&Y

Denker, Henry. A Far Country: A New Play. Random House 1961 (Play)
Bkl A

Freud, Sigmund. Letters; selected and ed. by Ernst L. Freud; tr. by Tania and James Stern. Basic Bks 1960
Bkl A

Fromm, Erich. Sigmund Freud's Mission: An Analysis of His Personality. Harper 1959
SCPL

Jones, Ernest. Life and Work of Sigmund Freud. 3v. Basic Bks 1957
GR—SCPL

Jones, Ernest. The Life and Work of Sigmund Freud; ed. and abr. by Lionel Trilling and Steven Marens. Basic Bks 1961
SCPL

Ruitenbeek, Hendrik Marinus. Freud and America. Macmillan 1966
Bkl A

Sachs, Hanns. Freud, Master and Friend. Harvard Univ. 1944
SCPL

Stoutenburg, Adrien and Baker, Laura Nelson. Explorer of the Unconscious: Sigmund Freud. Scribner 1965
Bkl Y

COLLECTIONS

Kagan, Henry Enoch. Six Who Changed the World. Yoseloff 1963
Bkl A

McKown, Robin. Pioneers in Mental Health. Dodd 1961
Bkl A&Y

French—19th century

Jean Martin Charcot, 1825-1893

COLLECTIONS

McKown, Robin. Pioneers in Mental Health. Dodd 1961
Bkl A&Y

NEWS COMMENTATORS
See Journalists

NEWSMEN
See Journalists

NEWSPAPER EDITORS
See Journalists

NEWSPAPER PUBLISHERS
See Journalists

NEWSPAPER REPORTERS
See Journalists

NIECES OF FAMOUS MEN
See Relatives of Famous Men

NOVELISTS
COLLECTIONS

Aldridge, John W. Time to Murder and Create: The Contemporary Novel in Crisis. McKay 1966
Bkl A
Saul Bellow; Francis Scott Key Fitzgerald; Mary Therese McCarthy; Norman Mailer; John O'Hara; Katherine Anne Porter; Pelham Grenville Wodehouse; and others

Brennan, Joseph Gerard. Three Philosophical Novelists. Macmillan 1964
Bkl A
André Paul Guillaume Gide; James Joyce; Thomas Mann

Maugham, William Somerset. Art of Fiction: An Introduction to Ten Novels and Their Authors. Doubleday 1955
SCPL
Jane Austen; Honoré de Balzac; Marie Henri Beyle; Emily Brontë; Charles Dickens; Fedor Mikhailovich Dostoevsky; Henry Fielding; Gustave Flaubert; Herman Melville; Lev Nikolaevich Tolstoi

O'Faoláin, Seán. Vanishing Hero: Studies in Novelists of the Twenties. Little 1957
SCPL
Elizabeth Bowen; William Faulkner; Graham Greene; Ernest Hemingway; Aldous Leonard Huxley; James Joyce; Evelyn Waugh; Thomas Wolfe

Wescott, Glenway. Images of Truth: Remembrances and Criticism. Harper 1962
Bkl A
Karen Blixen; Sidonie Gabrielle Colette; Thomas Mann; William Somerset Maugham; Katherine Anne Porter; Thornton Niven Wilder

American

COLLECTIONS

Auchincloss, Louis. Pioneers and Caretakers: A Study of Nine American Women Novelists. Univ. of Minn. 1965
Bkl A&Y
Willa Sibert Cather; Ellen Anderson Gholson Glasgow; Sarah Orne Jewett; Mary Therese McCarthy; Carson (Smith) McCullers; Katherine Anne Porter; Elizabeth Madox Roberts; Jean Stafford; Edith Newbold (Jones) Wharton

Beach, Joseph Warren. American Fiction, 1920-1940. Russell & Russell 1960
SCPL
Erskine Caldwell; John Roderigo Dos Passos; James Thomas Farrell; William Faulkner; Ernest Hemingway; John Phillips Marquand; John Steinbeck; Thomas Wolfe

Cournos, John and Norton, Sybil. Famous Modern American Novelists. Dodd 1952
SCHS

Galloway, David D. The Absurd Hero in American Fiction: Updike, Styron, Bellow, Salinger. Univ. of Tex. 1966
Bkl A&Y
Saul Bellow; Jerome David Salinger; William Styron; John Updike

Geismar, Maxwell David. Last of the Provincials: The American Novel, 1915-1925. Houghton 1947
SCPL
Sherwood Anderson; Willa Sibert Cather; Francis Scott Key Fitzgerald; Sinclair Lewis; Henry Louis Mencken

Geismar, Maxwell David. Rebels and Ancestors: The American Novel, 1890-1915. Houghton 1953
SCPL
Stephen Crane; Theodore Dreiser; Ellen Anderson Gholson Glasgow; Jack London; Frank Norris

Geismar, Maxwell David. Writers in Crisis: The American Novel Between Two Wars. Houghton 1942
SCPL
John Roderigo Dos Passos; William Faulkner; Ernest Hemingway; Ring Wilmer Lardner; John Steinbeck; Thomas Wolfe

Gloster, Hugh Morris. Negro Voices in American Fiction. Univ. of N.C. 1948
SCPL

Moore, Harry Thorton, ed. Contemporary American Novelists. Southern Ill. Univ. 1964
Bkl A

Morgan, Howard Wayne. American Writers in Rebellion, from Mark Twain to Dreiser. Hill & Wang 1965
Bkl A&Y
Samuel Langhorne Clemens; Theodore Dreiser; Hamlin Garland; William Dean Howells; Frank Norris

NOVELISTS

American—*Continued*

O'Connor, William Van, ed. Seven Modern American Novelists: An Introduction. Univ. of Minn. 1964
Bkl A&Y—SCHS
William Faulkner; Francis Scott Key Fitzgerald; Ernest Hemingway; Sinclair Lewis; Nathanael West; Edith Newbold (Jones) Wharton; Thomas Wolfe

Papashvily, Helen (Waite). All the Happy Endings. Harper 1956
SCPL
Augusta Jane Evans; Mary Jane (Hawes) Holmes; Laura Jean Libbey; Emma Dorothy Eliza (Nevitte) Southworth; Harriet Elizabeth (Beecher) Stowe; Susan Bogert Warner; and others

Schneider, Robert W. Five Novelists of the Progressive Era. Columbia Univ. 1965
Bkl A
Winston Churchill; Stephen Crane; Theodore Dreiser; William Dean Howells; Frank Norris

Van Doren, Carl Clinton. American Novel, 1789-1939. Macmillan 1940
SCPL

Wagenknecht, Edward Charles. Cavalcade of the American Novel: From the Birth of the Nation to the Middle of the Twentieth Century. Holt 1952
SCPL

Warfel, Harry Redcay. American Novelists of Today. Am. Bk 1951
SCPL

American—18th century

Susanna (Haswell) Rowson, 1762-1824

COLLECTIONS

Douty, Esther (Morris). Under the New Roof: Five Patriots of the Young Republic. Rand McNally 1965
Bkl Y&C

American—19th century

George Washington Cable, 1844-1925

Butcher, Charles Philip. George W. Cable. Twayne 1962
Bkl A

COLLECTIONS

Arvin, Newton. American Pantheon; ed. by Daniel Aaron and Sylvan Schendler. Delacorte 1966
Bkl A&Y

James Fenimore Cooper, 1789-1851

Grossman, James Mortimer. James Fenimore Cooper. Sloane 1949
SCPL

Proudfit, Isabel. James Fenimore Cooper. Messner 1946
SCHS—YR

Ringe, Donald A. James Fenimore Cooper. Twayne 1962
Bkl A&Y

Walker, Warren S. James Fenimore Cooper: An Introduction and Interpretation. Barnes & Noble 1962
Bkl A

COLLECTIONS

Canby, Henry Seidel. Classic Americans: A Study of Eminent American Writers from Irving to Whitman. Russell & Russell 1959
SCPL

Augusta Jane Evans, 1835-1909

COLLECTIONS

Papashvily, Helen (Waite). All the Happy Endings. Harper 1956
SCPL

Nathaniel Hawthorne, 1804-1864

Fairbanks, Henry George. The Lasting Loneliness of Nathaniel Hawthorne: A Study of the Sources of Alienation in Modern Man. Magi Books 1965
Bkl A

Hawthorne, Hildegarde. Romantic Rebel: The Story of Nathaniel Hawthorne. Appleton 1932
BBHS—CC(8-9)—JH—SCHS

Hoeltje, Hubert H. Inward Sky: The Mind and Heart of Nathaniel Hawthorne. Duke Univ. 1962
Bkl A

Kaul, A. N., ed. Hawthorne: A Collection of Critical Essays. Prentice-Hall 1966
Bkl A&Y

Martin, Terence. Nathaniel Hawthorne. Twayne 1965
Bkl A&Y

Pearce, Roy Harvey, ed. Hawthorne Centenary Essays. Ohio State Univ. 1964
Bkl A

Van Doren, Mark. Nathaniel Hawthorne. Sloane 1949
SCPL

Wagenknecht, Edward Charles. Nathaniel Hawthorne: Man and Writer. Oxford 1961
Bkl A&Y—BY—SCPL

COLLECTIONS

Arvin, Newton. American Pantheon; ed. by Daniel Aaron and Sylvan Schendler. Delacorte 1966
Bkl A&Y

Canby, Henry Seidel. Classic Americans: A Study of Eminent American Writers from Irving to Whitman. Russell & Russell 1959
SCPL

Stirling, Nora B. Who Wrote the Classics? Day 1965
Bkl Y&A&C

NOVELISTS

American—19th century—*Continued*

Mary Jane (Hawes) Holmes, 1825-1907

COLLECTIONS

Papashvily, Helen (Waite). All the Happy Endings. Harper 1956
SCPL

Henry James, 1843-1916

Bell, Millicent. Edith Wharton & Henry James: The Story of Their Friendship. Braziller 1965
Bkl A

Dupee, Frederick Wilcox. Henry James. Sloane 1951
SCPL

Edel, Leon, ed. Henry James: A Collection of Critical Essays. Prentice-Hall 1963
SCPL

Edel, Leon. Henry James: v. 1, The Untried Years, 1843-1870. Lippincott 1953
GR—SCPL

Edel, Leon. Henry James: v. 2, The Conquest of London, 1870-1881. Lippincott 1962
Bkl A—GR—SCPL

Edel, Leon. Henry James: v. 3, The Middle Years, 1882-1895. Lippincott 1962
Bkl A—GR—SCPL

Geismar, Maxwell David. Henry James and the Jacobites. Houghton 1963
Bkl A

James, Henry. Henry James: Autobiography; ed. by F. W. Dupee. Criterion Bks 1956
SCPL

Sayre, Robert F. The Examined Self: Benjamin Franklin, Henry Adams, Henry James. Princeton Univ. 1964
Bkl A

Laura Jean Libbey, 1862-1924

COLLECTIONS

Papashvily, Helen (Waite). All the Happy Endings. Harper 1956
SCPL

Herman Melville, 1819-1891

Arvin, Newton. Herman Melville. Sloane 1950
CA—GR—SCPL—3000

Berthoff, Warner. The Example of Melville. Princeton Univ. 1962
Bkl A

Gould, Jean. Young Mariner Melville. Dodd 1956
SCHS

Hillway, Tyrus. Herman Melville. Twayne 1963
Bkl A&Y—SCPL

Hough, Henry Beetle. Melville in the South Pacific. Houghton 1960
BY

Howard, Leon. Herman Melville: A Biography. Univ. of Calif. 1921
SCPL

Miller, James Edwin. A Reader's Guide to Herman Melville. Farrar 1962
Bkl A&Y

Miller, Perry Gilbert Eddy. Raven and the Whale: The War of Words and Wits in the Era of Poe and Melville. Harcourt 1956
SCPL

COLLECTIONS

Arvin, Newton. American Pantheon; ed. by Daniel Aaron and Sylvan Schendler. Delacorte 1966
Bkl A&Y

Canby, Henry Seidel. Classic Americans: A Study of Eminent American Writers from Irving to Whitman. Russell & Russell 1959
SCPL

Donoghue, Denis. Connoisseurs of Chaos. Macmillan 1965
IndS(10-12)

Maugham, William Somerset. Art of Fiction: An Introduction to Ten Novels and Their Authors. Doubleday 1955
SCPL

Emma Dorothy Eliza (Nevitte) Southworth, 1819-1899

COLLECTIONS

Papashvily, Helen (Waite). All the Happy Endings. Harper 1956
SCPL

Harriet Elizabeth (Beecher) Stowe, 1811-1896

Adams, John R. Harriet Beecher Stowe. Twayne 1964
Bkl A&Y

Furnas, Joseph Chamberlain. Goodbye to Uncle Tom. Sloane 1956
SCPL

Jackson, Phyllis Wynn. Victorian Cinderella: The Story of Harriet Beecher Stowe. Holiday 1947
BY—SCHS—YR

Johnston, Johanna. Runaway to Heaven: The Story of Harriet Beecher Stowe. Doubleday 1963
Bkl A&Y—SCPL

Wagenknecht, Edward Charles. Harriet Beecher Stowe: The Known and the Unknown. Oxford 1965
Bkl A&Y

COLLECTIONS

Papashvily, Helen (Waite). All the Happy Endings. Harper 1956
SCPL

NOVELISTS

American—19th century

Harriet Elizabeth (Beecher) Stowe—Continued

Vance, Marguerite. The Lamp Lighters: Women in the Hall of Fame. Dutton 1960
Bkl C(7-9)&Y—SCHS—YR

Susan Bogert Warner, 1819-1885

COLLECTIONS

Papashvily, Helen (Waite). All the Happy Endings. Harper 1956
SCPL

American—20th century

Nelson Algren, 1909-

Algren, Nelson and Donohue, H. E. F. Conversations with Nelson Algren. Hill & Wang 1964
Bkl A

Saul Bellow, 1915-

COLLECTIONS

Aldridge, John W. Time to Murder and Create: The Contemporary Novel in Crisis. McKay 1966
Bkl A
Galloway, David D. The Absurd Hero in American Fiction. Univ. of Tex. 1966
Bkl A&Y

Louis Bromfield, 1896-1956

Anderson, David D. Louis Bromfield. Twayne 1964
Bkl A
Geld, Ellen (Bromfield). The Heritage: A Daughter's Memories of Louis Bromfield. Harper 1962
Bkl A

Pearl (Sydenstricker) Buck, 1892-

Buck, Pearl (Sydenstricker). A Bridge for Passing. Day 1962
Bkl A—BY—SCPL
Buck, Pearl (Sydenstricker). My Several Worlds: A Personal Record. Day 1954
BY—SCHS—SCPL—YR
Buck, Pearl (Sydenstricker). My Several Worlds; abridged for younger readers. Day 1957
SCPL

George Washington Cable, 1844-1925

Butcher, Charles Philip. George W. Cable. Twayne 1962
Bkl A

COLLECTIONS

Arvin, Newton. American Pantheon; ed. by Daniel Aaron and Sylvan Schendler. Delacorte 1966
Bkl A&Y

Gladys (Hasty) Carroll, 1904-

Carroll, Gladys (Hasty). Only Fifty Years Ago. Little 1962
Bkl A&Y
Carroll, Gladys (Hasty). To Remember Forever: The Journal of a College Girl, 1922-1923. Little 1963
Bkl A&Y—IndS(10-12)

Willa Sibert Cather, 1873-1947

Brown, Edward Killoran. Willa Cather: A Critical Biography; completed by Leon Edel. Knopf 1953
SCPL
Daiches, David. Willa Cather: A Critical Introduction. Cornell Univ. 1951
SCPL
Franchere, Ruth. Willa. Crowell 1958 (Fiction)
CC(5-7)—JH

COLLECTIONS

Auchincloss, Louis. Pioneers and Caretakers: A Study of Nine American Women Novelists. Univ. of Minn. 1965
Bkl A&Y
Geismar, Maxwell David. Last of the Provincials: The American Novel, 1915-1925. Houghton 1947
SCPL
Morgan, Howard Wayne. Writers in Transition: Seven Americans. Hill & Wang 1963
Bkl A

Mary Ellen Chase, 1887-

Chase, Mary Ellen. Goodly Fellowship. Macmillan 1939
SCPL
Chase, Mary Ellen. A Goodly Heritage. Holt 1932
BY
Chase, Mary Ellen. White Gate: Adventures in the Imagination of a Child. Norton 1954
SCPL

Winston Churchill, 1871-1947

COLLECTIONS

Schneider, Robert W. Five Novelists of the Progressive Era. Columbia Univ. 1965
Bkl A

Lloyd Cassel Douglas, 1877-1951

Douglas, Lloyd Cassel. Time to Remember. Houghton 1951
SCPL

Theodore Dreiser, 1871-1945

Elias, Robert Henry. Theodore Dreiser: Apostle of Nature. Knopf 1949
SCPL

NOVELISTS

American—20th century

Theodore Dreiser—Continued

Matthiessen, Francis Otto. Theodore Dreiser. Sloane 1951
SCPL

Shapiro, Charles. Theodore Dreiser: Our Bitter Patriot. Southern Ill. Univ. 1962
Bkl A

Swanberg, W. A. Dreiser. Scribner 1965
Bkl A

Tjader, Marguerite. Theodore Dreiser: A New Dimension. Silvermine Publishers 1965
Bkl A

COLLECTIONS

Geismar, Maxwell David. Rebels and Ancestors: The American Novel, 1890-1915. Houghton 1953
SCPL

Morgan, Howard Wayne. American Writers in Rebellion, from Mark Twain to Dreiser. Hill & Wang 1965
Bkl A&Y

Schneider, Robert W. Five Novelists of the Progressive Era. Columbia Univ. 1965
Bkl A

James Thomas Farrell, 1904-

COLLECTIONS

Beach, Joseph Warren. American Fiction, 1920-1940. Russell & Russell 1960
SCPL

William Faulkner, 1897-1962

Brooks, Cleanth. William Faulkner: The Yoknapatawpha Country. Yale Univ. 1963
Bkl A—SCPL

Coughlan, Robert. Private World of William Faulkner. Harper 1954
SCPL

Cowley, Malcolm. The Faulkner-Cowley File: Letters and Memories, 1944-1962. Viking 1966
Bkl A

Cullen, John B. and Watkins, Floyd C. Old Times in the Faulkner Country. Univ. of N.C. 1961
Bkl A

Dain, Martin J. Faulkner's Country: Yoknapatawpha. Random House 1964
Bkl A

Fant, Joseph L., ed. Faulkner at West Point. Random House 1964
Bkl A—IndS(10-12)

Faulkner, John. My Brother Bill: An Affectionate Reminiscence. Trident Press 1963
Bkl A&Y

Hoffman, Frederick John. William Faulkner. Twayne 1961
Bkl A&Y

Hunt, John Wesley. William Faulkner: Art in Theological Tension. Syracuse Univ. 1965
Bkl A

Longley, John Lewis. The Tragic Mask: A Study of Faulkner's Heroes. Univ. of N.C. 1963
Bkl A

Malin, Irving. William Faulkner: An Interpretation. Stanford Univ. 1957
SCPL

Swiggart, Peter. The Art of Faulkner's Novels. Univ. of Tex. 1962
Bkl A

Thompson, Lawrance Roger. William Faulkner: An Introduction and Interpretation. Barnes & Noble 1963
Bkl A

Tuck, Dorothy. Crowell's Handbook of Faulkner. Crowell 1964
Bkl A&Y

Vickery, Olga W. The Novels of William Faulkner: A Critical Interpretation. La. State Univ. 1959
SCPL

Webb, James W. and Green, Adwin Wigfall, eds. William Faulkner of Oxford. La. State Univ. 1965
Bkl A

COLLECTIONS

Beach, Joseph Warren. American Fiction, 1920-1940. Russell & Russell 1960
SCPL

Brooks, Cleanth. The Hidden God: Studies in Hemingway, Faulkner, Yeats, Eliot, and Warren. Yale Univ. 1963
Bkl A

Geismar, Maxwell David. Writers in Crisis: The American Novel Between Two Wars. Houghton 1942
SCPL

O'Connor, William Van, ed. Seven Modern American Novelists: An Introduction. Univ. of Minn. 1964
Bkl A&Y—SCHS

O'Faoláin, Seán. Vanishing Hero: Studies in Novelists of the Twenties. Little 1957
SCPL

Edna Ferber, 1887-1968

Ferber, Edna. A Kind of Magic. Doubleday 1963
Bkl A—SCPL

Ferber, Edna. A Peculiar Treasure. Doubleday 1960
SCHS—SCPL

NOVELISTS

American—20th century—*Continued*

Dorothea Frances (Canfield) Fisher, 1879-1958

Yates, Elizabeth. Pebble in a Pool. Dutton 1958
SCHS

Francis Scott Key Fitzgerald, 1896-1940

Eble, Kenneth Eugene. F. Scott Fitzgerald. Twayne 1963
Bkl A

Fitzgerald, Francis Scott Key. The Letters of F. Scott Fitzgerald; ed. by Andrew Turnbull. Scribner 1963
Bkl A—IndS(11-12)—SCPL

Fitzgerald, Francis Scott Key. Scott Fitzgerald: Letters to His Daughter; ed. by Andrew Turnbull. Scribner 1965
Bkl A—IndS(9-12)

Goldhurst, William. F. Scott Fitzgerald and His Contemporaries. World 1963
Bkl A

Mizener, Arthur Moore. The Far Side of Paradise: A Biography of F. Scott Fitzgerald. Houghton 1951
CA—GR—SCPL—3000

Turnbull, Andrew. Scott Fitzgerald. Scribner 1962
Bkl A—BY—SCPL

COLLECTIONS

Aldridge, John W. Time to Murder and Create: The Contemporary Novel in Crisis. McKay 1966
Bkl A

Geismar, Maxwell David. Last of the Provincials: The American Novel, 1915-1925. Houghton 1947
SCPL

O'Connor, William Van, ed. Seven Modern American Novelists: An Introduction. Univ. of Minn. 1964
Bkl A&Y—SCHS

Rose Franken, 1898-

Franken, Rose. When All Is Said and Done: An Autobiography. Doubleday 1963
Bkl A

Ellen Anderson Gholson Glasgow, 1873-1945

Glasgow, Ellen Anderson Gholson. The Woman Within. Harcourt 1954
SCPL

COLLECTIONS

Auchincloss, Louis. Pioneers and Caretakers: A Study of Nine American Women Novelists. Univ. of Minn. 1965
Bkl A&Y

Geismar, Maxwell David. Rebels and Ancestors: The American Novel, 1890-1915. Houghton 1953
SCPL

Morgan, Howard Wayne. Writers in Transition: Seven Americans. Hill & Wang 1963
Bkl A

Ernest Hemingway, 1898-1961

Baker, Carlos Heard. Hemingway: The Writer as Artist. Princeton Univ. 1956
SCPL

Baker, Carlos Heard, ed. Hemingway and His Critics: An International Anthology. Hill & Wang 1961
SCPL

Hemingway, Ernest. A Moveable Feast. Scribner 1964
Bkl A—IndS(11-12)—SCHS—SCPL

Hemingway, Leicester. My Brother, Ernest Hemingway. World 1962
Bkl A

Hotchner, A. E. Papa Hemingway: A Personal Memoir. Random House 1966
Bkl A

Lania, Leo. Hemingway: A Pictorial Biography. Viking 1961
Bkl A&Y

McCaffery, John Kerwin Michael. Ernest Hemingway: The Man and His Work. World 1950
SCPL

Ross, Lillian. Portrait of Hemingway. Simon & Schuster 1961
Bkl A

Rovit, Earl H. Ernest Hemingway. Twayne 1963
Bkl A—SCHS—SCPL

Sanford, Marcelline (Hemingway). At the Hemingways: A Family Portrait. Little 1962
Bkl A&Y—BY—SCHS

COLLECTIONS

Beach, Joseph Warren. American Fiction, 1920-1940. Russell & Russell 1960
SCPL

Brooks, Cleanth. The Hidden God: Studies in Hemingway, Faulkner, Yeats, Eliot, and Warren. Yale Univ. 1963
Bkl A

Geismar, Maxwell David. Writers in Crisis: The American Novel Between Two Wars. Houghton 1942
SCPL

O'Connor, William Van, ed. Seven Modern American Novelists: An Introduction. Univ. of Minn. 1964
Bkl A&Y—SCHS

O'Faoláin, Seán. Vanishing Hero: Studies in Novelists of the Twenties. Little 1957
SCPL

NOVELISTS

American—20th century—*Continued*

Alice Tisdale Hobart, 1882-1967

Hobart, Alice Tisdale. Gusty's Child.
Longmans 1959
BBHS—SCPL

Fannie Hurst, 1889-1968

Hurst, Fannie. Anatomy of Me: A
Wonderer in Search of Herself. Dou-
bleday 1958
SCPL

Henry James, 1843-1916

Bell, Millicent. Edith Wharton & Henry
James: The Story of Their Friendship.
Braziller 1965
Bkl A
Dupee, Frederick Wilcox. Henry James.
Sloane 1951
SCPL
Edel, Leon, ed. Henry James: A Collec-
tion of Critical Essays. Prentice-Hall
1963
SCPL
Edel, Leon. Henry James: v. 1, The Un-
tried Years, 1843-1870. Lippincott
1953
GR—SCPL
Edel, Leon. Henry James: v. 2, The Con-
quest of London, 1870-1881. Lippin-
cott 1962
Bkl A—GR—SCPL
Edel, Leon. Henry James: v. 3, The Mid-
dle Years, 1882-1895. Lippincott 1962
Bkl A—GR—SCPL
Geismar, Maxwell David. Henry James
and the Jacobites. Houghton 1963
Bkl A
James, Henry. Henry James: Autobiog-
raphy; ed. by F. W. Dupee. Criterion
Bks 1956
SCPL
Sayre, Robert F. The Examined Self:
Benjamin Franklin, Henry Adams,
Henry James. Princeton Univ. 1964
Bkl A

*Frances Parkinson (Wheeler) Keyes,
1885-*

Keyes, Frances Parkinson (Wheeler).
Roses in December. Doubleday 1960
Bkl A

Sinclair Lewis, 1885-1951

Grebstein, Sheldon Norman. Sinclair
Lewis. Twayne 1962
Bkl A&Y
Lewis, G. L. H. With Love from
"Gracie": Sinclair Lewis, 1912-1925.
Harcourt 1956
SCPL

Schorer, Mark, ed. Sinclair Lewis: A Col-
lection of Critical Essays. Prentice-Hall
1962
SCPL
Schorer, Mark. Sinclair Lewis: An Amer-
ican Life. McGraw 1961
Bkl A—SCPL
Sheean, Vincent. Dorothy and Red.
Houghton 1963
Bkl A—SCPL

COLLECTIONS

Geismar, Maxwell David. Last of the
Provincials: The American Novel,
1915-1925. Houghton 1947
SCPL
O'Connor, William Van, ed. Seven Mod-
ern American Novelists: An Introduc-
tion. Univ. of Minn. 1964
Bkl A&Y—SCHS

Jack London, 1876-1916

Calder-Marshall, Arthur. Lone Wolf.
Duell 1962
BY
Franchere, Ruth. Jack London: The Pur-
suit of a Dream. Crowell 1962
Bkl Y&C—BY—SCHS—YR
Garst, Doris Shannon. Jack London,
Magnet for Adventure. Messner 1944
SCHS—YR
London, Jack. Cruise of the Snark. Mac-
millan 1911
SCPL
London, Jack. Letters from Jack London,
Containing an Unpublished Corres-
pondence Between London and Sin-
clair Lewis; ed. by King Hendricks
and Irving Shepard. Odyssey 1965
Bkl A
O'Connor, Richard. Jack London: A Bi-
ography. Little 1964
Bkl A&Y
Stone, Irving. Jack London—Sailor on
Horseback: A Biographical Novel.
Doubleday 1947
SCPL

COLLECTIONS

Geismar, Maxwell David. Rebels and Ancestors: The American Novel, 1890-
1915. Houghton 1953
SCPL

Mary Therese McCarthy, 1912-

COLLECTIONS

Aldridge, John W. Time to Murder and
Create: The Contemporary Novel in
Crisis. McKay 1966
Bkl A
Auchincloss, Louis. Pioneers and Care-
takers: A Study of Nine American
Women Novelists. Univ. of Minn. 1965
Bkl A&Y

NOVELISTS

American—20th century—*Continued*

Norman Mailer, 1923-

COLLECTIONS

Aldridge, John W. Time to Murder and Create: The Contemporary Novel in Crisis. McKay 1966
Bkl A

John Phillips Marquand, 1893-1960

COLLECTIONS

Beach, Joseph Warren. American Fiction, 1920-1940. Russell & Russell 1960
SCPL

James Albert Michener, 1907-

Day, Arthur Grove. James A. Michener. Twayne 1964
Bkl A&Y

Henry Miller, 1891-

Miller, Henry. Lawrence Durrell [and] Henry Miller: A Private Correspondence; ed. by George Wickes. Dutton 1963
Bkl A—SCPL
Widmer, Kingsley. Henry Miller. Twayne 1963
SCPL

Margaret Mitchell, 1900-1949

Farr, Finis. Margaret Mitchell of Atlanta: The Author of Gone with the Wind. Morrow 1965
Bkl A

Frank Norris, 1870-1902

COLLECTIONS

Geismar, Maxwell David. Rebels and Ancestors: The American Novel, 1890-1915. Houghton 1953
SCPL
Morgan, Howard Wayne. American Writers in Rebellion, from Mark Twain to Dreiser. Hill & Wang 1965
Bkl A&Y
Schneider, Robert W. Five Novelists of the Progressive Era. Columbia Univ. 1965
Bkl A

John Henry O'Hara, 1905-

COLLECTIONS

Aldridge, John W. Time to Murder and Create: The Contemporary Novel in Crisis. McKay 1966
Bkl A

Mary O'Hara, 1885-

O'Hara, Mary. A Musical in the Making. Taplinger 1966
Bkl A

Olive (Higgins) Prouty, 1882-

Prouty, Olive (Higgins). Pencil Shavings: Memoirs. Riverside Press 1962
Bkl A

Ayn Rand, 1905?-

Branden, Nathaniel. Who Is Ayn Rand? An Analysis of the Novels of Ayn Rand. Random House 1962
Bkl A

Marjorie (Kinnan) Rawlings, 1896-1953

Rawlings, Marjorie (Kinnan). Cross Creek. Scribner 1942
SCPL

Mary (Roberts) Rinehart, 1876-1958

Rinehart, Mary (Roberts). My Story. Rinehart 1948
SCPL

Elizabeth Madox Roberts, 1886-1941

McDowell, Frederick P. W. Elizabeth Madox Roberts. Twayne 1963
Bkl A

COLLECTIONS

Auchincloss, Louis. Pioneers and Caretakers: A Study of Nine American Women Novelists. Univ. of Minn. 1965
Bkl A&Y

Kenneth Lewis Roberts, 1885-1957

Roberts, Kenneth Lewis. I Wanted to Write. Doubleday 1949
SCPL

Jerome David Salinger, 1919-

French, Warren. J. D. Salinger. Twayne 1963
Bkl A
Grunwald, Henry A., ed. Salinger: A Critical Portrait. Harper 1962
BY

COLLECTIONS

Galloway, David D. The Absurd Hero in American Fiction. Univ. of Tex. 1966
Bkl A&Y

Upton Beall Sinclair, 1878-1968

Sinclair, Upton Beall. Autobiography. Harcourt 1962
Bkl A

Jean Stafford, 1915-

COLLECTIONS

Auchincloss, Louis. Pioneers and Caretakers: A Study of Nine American Women Novelists. Univ. of Minn. 1965
Bkl A&Y

NOVELISTS

American—20th century—*Continued*

John Steinbeck, 1902-1968

Fontenrose, Joseph Eddy. John Steinbeck: An Introduction and Interpretation. Barnes & Noble 1964
Bkl A

French, Warren. John Steinbeck. Twayne 1961
Bkl A&Y

Lisca, Peter. Wide World of John Steinbeck. Rutgers Univ. 1958
SCPL

COLLECTIONS

Beach, Joseph Warren. American Fiction, 1920-1940. Russell & Russell 1960
SCPL

Geismar, Maxwell David. Writers in Crisis: The American Novel Between Two Wars. Houghton 1942
SCPL

William Styron, 1925-

COLLECTIONS

Galloway, David D. The Absurd Hero in American Fiction. Univ. of Tex. 1966
Bkl A&Y

Nathanael West, 1904-1940

COLLECTIONS

O'Connor, William Van, ed. Seven Modern American Novelists: An Introduction. Univ. of Minn. 1964
Bkl A&Y—SCHS

Edith Newbold (Jones) Wharton, 1862-1937

Bell, Millicent. Edith Wharton & Henry James: The Story of Their Friendship. Braziller 1965
Bkl A

Coolidge, Olivia E. Edith Wharton, 1862-1937. Scribner 1964
AB(6-11)—Bkl Y—IndS(10-12)—SCHS

Griffith, Grace (Kellogg). The Two Lives of Edith Wharton: The Woman and Her Work. Appleton 1965
Bkl A

Lyde, Marilyn Jones. Edith Wharton: Convention and Morality in the Work of a Novelist. Univ. of Okla. 1959
Bkl A

COLLECTIONS

Auchincloss, Louis. Pioneers and Caretakers: A Study of Nine American Women Novelists. Univ. of Minn. 1965
Bkl A&Y

Morgan, Howard Wayne. Writers in Transition: Seven Americans. Hill & Wang 1963
Bkl A

O'Connor, William Van, ed. Seven Modern American Novelists: An Introduction. Univ. of Minn. 1964
Bkl A&Y—SCHS

Owen Wister, 1860-1938

Wister, Owen. Owen Wister Out West: His Journals and Letters; ed. by F. K. Wister. Univ. of Chicago 1958
BBHS—SCPL

Thomas Wolfe, 1900-1938

Kennedy, Richard S. The Window of Memory: The Literary Career of Thomas Wolfe. Univ. of N. C. 1962
Bkl A

McElderry, Bruce Robert. Thomas Wolfe. Twayne 1964
Bkl A&Y

Muller, Herbert Joseph. Thomas Wolfe. New Directions 1947
SCPL

Nowell, Elizabeth. Thomas Wolfe: A Biography. Doubleday 1960
Bkl A—SCPL

Wheaton, Mabel Wolfe and Blythe, Le Gette. Thomas Wolfe and His Family. Doubleday 1961
Bkl A

Wolfe, Thomas. Letters of Thomas Wolfe; ed. by Elizabeth Nowell. Scribner 1956
SCPL

Wolfe, Thomas. Thomas Wolfe's Letters to His Mother Julia Elizabeth Wolfe; ed. by J. S. Terry. Scribner 1943
SCPL

COLLECTIONS

Beach, Joseph Warren. American Fiction, 1920-1940. Russell & Russell 1960
SCPL

Geismar, Maxwell David. Writers in Crisis: The American Novel Between Two Wars. Houghton 1942
SCPL

Morgan, Howard Wayne. Writers in Transition: Seven Americans. Hill & Wang 1963
Bkl A

O'Connor, William Van, ed. Seven Modern American Novelists: An Introduction. Univ. of Minn. 1964
Bkl A&Y—SCHS

O'Faoláin, Seán. Vanishing Hero: Studies in Novelists of the Twenties. Little 1957
SCPL

Richard Wright, 1908-1960

Wright, Richard. Black Boy: A Record of Childhood and Youth. World 1950
GR—SCPL

NOVELISTS—*Continued*

Austrian—20th century

Vicki Baum, 1888-1960

Baum, Vicki. It Was All Quite Different: The Memoirs of [the author]. Funk 1964
Bkl A

Canadian—20th century

Mazo de la Roche, 1879-1961

De la Roche, Mazo. Ringing the Changes: An Autobiography. Little 1957
SCPL

Czech—20th century

Franz Kafka, 1883-1924

Kafka, Franz. Diaries, 1910-1923; ed. by Max Brod. 2v. Schocken 1948-49
SCPL

Spilka, Mark. Dickens and Kafka: A Mutual Interpretation. Ind. Univ. 1963
Bkl A

English

COLLECTIONS

Cecil, Lord David. Victorian Novelists: Essays in Revaluation. Univ. of Chicago 1958
SCPL
Charlotte Brontë; Emily Brontë; Charles Dickens; George Eliot; Elizabeth Cleghorn (Stevenson) Gaskell; William Makepeace Thackeray; Anthony Trollope

Cournos, John and Norton, Sybil. Famous British Novelists. Dodd 1952
SCHS

Hall, James. The Tragic Comedians: Seven Modern British Novelists. Ind. Univ. 1963
Bkl A
Joyce Cary; Edward Morgan Forster; Henry Green; Leslie Poles Hartley; Aldous Leonard Huxley; Anthony Powell; Evelyn Waugh

Knoepflmacher, U. C. Religious Humanism and the Victorian Novel. Princeton Univ. 1965
Bkl A
Samuel Butler; George Eliot; Walter Horatio Pater

McCullough, Bruce Walker. Representative English Novelists: Defoe to Conrad. Harper 1946
BBHS–SCPL

Quiller-Couch, Sir Arthur Thomas. Charles Dickens and Other Victorians. Cambridge 1925
SCPL
Charles Dickens; Benjamin Disraeli; Elizabeth Cleghorn (Stevenson) Gaskell; William Makepeace Thackeray; Anthony Trollope

Shapiro, Charles, ed. Contemporary British Novelists. Southern Ill. Univ. 1965
Bkl A
Kingsley Amis; Lawrence George Durrell; William Gerald Golding; Doris May Lessing; Iris Murdoch; Anthony Powell; Alan Sillitoe; Charles Percy Snow, Baron Snow of Leicester; Muriel Spark; Angus Wilson

Wagenknecht, Edward Charles. Cavalcade of the English Novel. Holt 1954
SCPL

English—18th century

Fanny Burney, 1752-1840

Burney, Fanny. Diary of Fanny Burney. Dutton 1940
SCPL

Gérin, Winifred. The Young Fanny Burney. Nelson 1961
Bkl C(7-9)&Y

Hemlow, Joyce. History of Fanny Burney. Oxford 1958
SCPL

COLLECTIONS

Swinnerton, Frank Arthur. A Galaxy of Fathers. Doubleday 1966
Bkl A

Henry Fielding, 1707-1754

COLLECTIONS

Maugham, William Somerset. Art of Fiction: An Introduction to Ten Novels and Their Authors. Doubleday 1955
SCPL

English—19th century

Jane Austen, 1775-1817

Austen, Jane. Jane Austen's Letters to Her Sister Cassandra and Others. Oxford 1952
SCPL

Becker, May (Lamberton). Presenting Miss Jane Austen. Dodd 1952
BBHS–JH–SCHS–SCPL–YR

Jenkins, Elizabeth. Jane Austen. Farrar 1959
SCPL–3000

Litz, A. Walton. Jane Austen: A Study of Her Artistic Development. Oxford 1965
Bkl A

COLLECTIONS

Maugham, William Somerset. Art of Fiction: An Introduction to Ten Novels and Their Authors. Doubleday 1955
SCPL

Stirling, Nora B. Who Wrote the Classics? Day 1965
Bkl Y&A&C

NOVELISTS

English—19th century—Continued

Charlotte Brontë, 1816-1855

Bentley, Phyllis Eleanor. The Young Brontës. Roy 1961
Bkl C(6-8)—JH

Gaskell, Elizabeth Cleghorn (Stevenson). Life of Charlotte Brontë. Oxford 1919
BBHS—CA—SCPL—3000

Jarden, Mary Louise. The Young Brontës: Charlotte and Emily, Branwell and Anne. Viking 1938
SCHS

Kyle, Elisabeth. Girl with a Pen: Charlotte Brontë. Holt 1964
Bkl C&Y—CC—IndJ(6-9)—JH—SCHS

Martin, Robert Bernard. The Accents of Persuasion: Charlotte Brontë's Novels. Norton 1966
Bkl A&Y

Vipont, Elfrida. Weaver of Dreams: The Girlhood of Charlotte Brontë. Walck 1966
Bkl C(5-8)—ESLC

White, Hilda. Wild Decembers: A Biographical Portrait of the Brontës. Dutton 1957
SCHS—YR

COLLECTIONS

Cecil, Lord David. Victorian Novelists: Essays in Revaluation. Univ. of Chicago 1958
SCPL

Stirling, Nora B. Who Wrote the Classics? Day 1965
Bkl Y&A&C

Emily Brontë, 1818-1848

Bentley, Phyllis Eleanor. The Young Brontës. Roy 1961
Bkl C(6-8)—JH

Jarden, Mary Louise. The Young Brontës: Charlotte and Emily, Branwell and Anne. Viking 1938
SCHS

White, Hilda. Wild Decembers: A Biographical Portrait of the Brontës. Dutton 1957
SCHS—YR

COLLECTIONS

Cecil, Lord David. Victorian Novelists: Essays in Revaluation. Univ. of Chicago 1958
SCPL

Maugham, William Somerset. Art of Fiction: An Introduction to Ten Novels and Their Authors. Doubleday 1955
SCPL

Fanny Burney, 1752-1840

Burney, Fanny. Diary of Fanny Burney. Dutton 1940
SCPL

Gérin, Winifred. The Young Fanny Burney. Nelson 1961
Bkl C(7-9)&Y

Hemlow, Joyce. History of Fanny Burney. Oxford 1958
SCPL

COLLECTIONS

Swinnerton, Frank Arthur. A Galaxy of Fathers. Doubleday 1966
Bkl A

Samuel Butler, 1835-1902

COLLECTIONS

Knoepflmacher, U. C. Religious Humanism and the Victorian Novel. Princeton Univ. 1965
Bkl A

Wilkie Collins, 1824-1889

Robinson, Kenneth. Wilkie Collins: A Biography. Macmillan 1952
SCPL

Marie Louise De la Ramée, 1839-1908

Stirling, Monica. The Fine and the Wicked: The Life and Times of Ouida. Coward-McCann 1958
SCPL

Charles Dickens, 1812-1870

Becker, May (Lamberton). Introducing Charles Dickens. Dodd 1940
BBJH—CC(8-9)—JH—SCHS—SCPL

Brown, Ivor John Carnegie. Dickens in His Time. Nelson 1964
Bkl A

Chesterton, Gilbert Keith. Charles Dickens: A Critical Study. Dodd 1906
SCPL

Collins, Philip Arthur William. Dickens and Crime. St Martins 1962
Bkl A

Collins, Philip Arthur William. Dickens and Education. St Martins 1963
Bkl A

Dickens, Charles. Selected Letters; ed. by F. W. Dupee. Farrar 1960
Bkl A

Forster, John. Life of Charles Dickens. 2v. Dutton 1927
SCPL—3000

Graham, Eleanor. The Story of Charles Dickens. Abelard-Schuman 1954
JH—SCHS—YR

Johnson, Edgar. Charles Dickens: His Tragedy and Triumph. 2v. Simon & Schuster 1952
GR—SCPL

Lincoln, Victoria. Charles: A Novel. Little 1962 (Fiction)
Bkl A&Y

NOVELISTS

English—19th century

Charles Dickens—Continued

Miller, J. Hillis. Charles Dickens: The World of His Novels. Harvard Univ. 1958
SCPL

Peare, Catherine Owens. Charles Dickens: His Life. Holt 1959
SCHS

Priestley, John Boynton. Charles Dickens: A Pictorial Biography. Viking 1962
Bkl A&Y—BY—SCHS

Spilka, Mark. Dickens and Kafka: A Mutual Interpretation. Ind. Univ. 1963
Bkl A

Wagenknecht, Edward Charles. Dickens and the Scandalmongers: Essays in Criticism. Univ. of Okla. 1965
Bkl A

COLLECTIONS

Cecil, Lord David. Victorian Novelists: Essays in Revaluation. Univ. of Chicago 1958
SCPL

Hoff, Rhoda. Why They Wrote. Walck 1961
Bkl C(7-10)&Y—SCHS

Maugham, William Somerset. Art of Fiction: An Introduction to Ten Novels and Their Authors. Doubleday 1955
SCPL

Quiller-Couch, Sir Arthur Thomas. Charles Dickens and Other Victorians. Cambridge 1925
SCPL

Stirling, Nora B. Who Wrote the Classics? Day 1965
Bkl Y&A&C

Benjamin Disraeli, 1804-1881

COLLECTIONS

Quiller-Couch, Sir Arthur Thomas. Charles Dickens and Other Victorians. Cambridge 1925
SCPL

Sir Arthur Conan Doyle, 1859-1930

Carr, John Dickson. Life of Sir Arthur Conan Doyle. Harper 1949
SCHS—SCPL

Hardwick, John Michael Drinkrow and Hardwick, Mollie. The Man Who Was Sherlock Holmes. Doubleday 1964
Bkl A&Y

Hoehling, Mary (Duprey). The Real Sherlock Holmes: Arthur Conan Doyle. Messner 1965
Bkl C(7-9)&Y

Starrett, Vincent. The Private Life of Sherlock Holmes. Univ. of Chicago 1960
Bkl A

Wood, James Playsted. The Man Who Hated Sherlock Holmes: A Life of Sir Arthur Conan Doyle. Pantheon 1965
Bkl C(7-10)&Y—ESLC—IndJ(6-9)

Maria Edgeworth, 1767-1849

COLLECTIONS

Swinnerton, Frank Arthur. A Galaxy of Fathers. Doubleday 1966
Bkl A

George Eliot, 1819-1880

Allen, Walter Ernest. George Eliot. Macmillan 1964
Bkl A&Y

COLLECTIONS

Cecil, Lord David. Victorian Novelists: Essays in Revaluation. Univ. of Chicago 1958
SCPL

Knoepflmacher, U. C. Religious Humanism and the Victorian Novel. Princeton Univ. 1965
Bkl A

Elizabeth Cleghorn (Stevenson) Gaskell, 1810-1865

Pollard, Arthur. Mrs. Gaskell: Novelist and Biographer. Harvard Univ. 1966
Bkl A

COLLECTIONS

Cecil, Lord David. Victorian Novelists: Essays in Revaluation. Univ. of Chicago 1958
SCPL

Quiller-Couch, Sir Arthur Thomas. Charles Dickens and Other Victorians. Cambridge 1925
SCPL

George Robert Gissing, 1857-1903

Gissing, George Robert and Wells, Herbert George. George Gissing and H. G. Wells: Their Friendship and Correspondence; ed. by Royal A. Gettmann. Univ. of Ill. 1961
Bkl A

Sir Henry Rider Haggard, 1856-1925

Cohen, Morton Norton. Rider Haggard: His Life and Works. Walker & Co. 1961
Bkl A

Walter Horatio Pater, 1839-1894

COLLECTIONS

Knoepflmacher, U. C. Religious Humanism and the Victorian Novel. Princeton Univ. 1965
Bkl A

NOVELISTS

English—19th century—*Continued*

Mary Wollstonecraft (Godwin) Shelley, 1797-1851

Bolton, Guy Reginald. The Olympians. World 1961 (Fiction)
Bkl A

Shelley, Mary Wollstonecraft (Godwin). Letters; ed. by F. L. Jones. 2v. Univ. of Okla. 1944
SCPL

Shelley, Mary Wollstonecraft (Godwin). Mary Shelley's Journal; ed. by F. L. Jones. Univ. of Okla. 1947
SCPL

William Makepeace Thackeray, 1811-1863

Ray, Gordon Norton. Thackeray: The Age of Wisdom, 1847-1863. McGraw 1958
SCPL

COLLECTIONS

Cecil, Lord David. Victorian Novelists: Essays in Revaluation. Univ. of Chicago 1958
SCPL

Quiller-Couch, Sir Arthur Thomas. Charles Dickens and Other Victorians. Cambridge 1925
SCPL

Anthony Trollope, 1815-1882

Trollope, Anthony. An Autobiography. Univ. of Calif. 1947
CA—SCPL

COLLECTIONS

Cecil, Lord David. Victorian Novelists: Essays in Revaluation. Univ. of Chicago 1958
SCPL

Quiller-Couch, Sir Arthur Thomas. Charles Dickens and Other Victorians. Cambridge 1925
SCPL

Herbert George Wells, 1866-1946

Vallentin, Antonina. H. G. Wells, Prophet of Our Day; tr. by Daphne Woodward. Day 1950
SCPL

Wells, Herbert George and Gissing, George Robert. George Gissing and H. G. Wells: Their Friendship and Correspondence; ed. by Royal A. Gettmann. Univ. of Ill. 1961
Bkl A

Israel Zangwill, 1864-1926

Wohlgelernter, Maurice. Israel Zangwill: A Study. Columbia Univ. 1964
Bkl A

English—20th century

Kingsley Amis, 1922-

COLLECTIONS

Shapiro, Charles, ed. Contemporary British Novelists. Southern Ill. Univ. 1965
Bkl A

Arnold Bennett, 1867-1931

Bennett, Arnold. The Truth About an Author. 1911
CA

Phyllis Eleanor Bentley, 1894-

Bentley, Phyllis Eleanor. "O Dreams, O Destinations": An Autobiography. Macmillan 1962
Bkl A

Phyllis Bottome, 1884-1963

Bottome, Phyllis. The Goal. Vanguard 1963
Bkl A

Ivy Compton-Burnett, 1892-

Valdanza, Frank. Ivy Compton-Burnett. Twayne 1964
Bkl A

Joseph Conrad, 1857-1924

Allen, Jerry. The Sea Years of Joseph Conrad. Doubleday 1965
Bkl A

Baines, Jocelyn. Joseph Conrad: A Critical Biography. McGraw 1960
Bkl A

Guérard, A. J. Conrad the Novelist. Harvard Univ. 1958
SCPL

Gurko, Leo. Joseph Conrad, Giant in Exile. Macmillan 1962
Bkl A

Gurko, Leo. The Two Lives of Joseph Conrad. Crowell 1965
Bkl Y&C

Jean-Aubry, Gérard. The Sea Dreamer: A Definitive Biography of Joseph Conrad; tr. by Helen Sebba. Doubleday 1957
SCPL—3000

Sherry, Norman. Conrad's Eastern World. Cambridge 1966
Bkl A

Lawrence George Durrell, 1912-

Durrell, Lawrence George. Lawrence Durrell [and] Henry Miller: A Private Correspondence; ed. by George Wickes. Dutton 1963
Bkl A—SCPL

Moore, Harry Thornton, ed. The World of Lawrence Durrell. Southern Ill. Univ. 1962
Bkl A

NOVELISTS

English—20th century

Lawrence George Durrell—Continued

COLLECTIONS

Shapiro, Charles, ed. Contemporary British Novelists. Southern Ill. Univ. 1965
Bkl A

Edward Morgan Forster, 1879-

Beer, John B. The Achievement of E. M. Forster. Barnes & Noble 1963
Bkl A

Forster, Edward Morgan. Hill of Devi. Harcourt 1953
SCPL

McConkey, James. Novels of E. M. Forster. Cornell Univ. 1957
SCPL

Natwar-Singh, K., ed. E. M. Forster: A Tribute. Harcourt 1964
Bkl A—IndS(12)

Stone, Wilfred Healey. The Cave and the Mountain: A Study of E. M. Forster. Stanford Univ. 1966
Bkl A

Wilde, Alan. Art and Order: A Study of E. M. Forster. N. Y. Univ. 1964
Bkl A

COLLECTIONS

Hall, James. The Tragic Comedians: Seven Modern British Novelists. Ind. Univ. 1963
Bkl A

Pamela Frankau, 1908-1967

Frankau, Pamela. Pen to Paper: A Novelist's Notebook. Doubleday 1962
Bkl A

David Garnett, 1892-

Garnett, David. The Golden Echo: v. 3, The Familiar Faces. Harcourt 1963
Bkl A

Henry Green, 1905-

COLLECTIONS

Hall, James. The Tragic Comedians: Seven Modern British Novelists. Ind. Univ. 1963
Bkl A

Sir Henry Rider Haggard, 1856-1925

Cohen, Morton Norton. Rider Haggard: His Life and Works. Walker & Co. 1961
Bkl A

Leslie Poles Hartley, 1895-

COLLECTIONS

Hall, James. The Tragic Comedians: Seven Modern British Novelists. Ind. Univ. 1963
Bkl A

David Herbert Lawrence, 1885-1930

Lawrence, David Herbert. Collected Letters; ed. by Harry T. Moore. 2v. Viking 1962
Bkl A

Lawrence, David Herbert. Selected Letters; ed. by Diana Trilling. Farrar 1958
SCPL

Lawrence, Frieda (von Richthofen). Frieda Lawrence: The Memoirs and Correspondence; ed. by E. W. Tedlock, Jr. Knopf 1964
Bkl A

Moore, Harry Thornton. Intelligent Heart: The Story of D. H. Lawrence. Farrar 1954
SCPL

Moore, Harry Thornton. Life and Works of D. H. Lawrence. Twayne 1951
SCPL

Moynahan, Julian. The Deed of Life: The Novels and Tales of D. H. Lawrence. Princeton Univ. 1963
Bkl A

Sagar, Keith. The Art of D. H. Lawrence. Cambridge 1966
Bkl A

Tedlock, E. W. D. H. Lawrence, Artist & Rebel. Univ. of N. Mex. 1963
Bkl A

Malcolm Lowry, 1909-1957

Lowry, Malcolm. Selected Letters; ed. by Harvey Breit and Margerie Bonner Lowry. Lippincott 1965
Bkl A

Dame Rose Macaulay, 1889?-1958

Macaulay, Dame Rose. Last Letters to a Friend, 1952-1958; ed. by Constance Babington-Smith. Atheneum 1963
Bkl A

Macaulay, Dame Rose. Letters to a Friend, 1950-1952; ed. by Constance Babington-Smith. Atheneum 1962
Bkl A

Macaulay, Dame Rose. Letters to a Sister; ed. by Constance Babington-Smith. Atheneum 1964
Bkl A

William Somerset Maugham, 1874-1965

COLLECTIONS

Wescott, Glenway. Images of Truth: Remembrances and Criticism. Harper 1962
Bkl A

NOVELISTS

English—20th century—*Continued*

Anthony Powell, 1905-

COLLECTIONS

Hall, James. The Tragic Comedians: Seven Modern British Novelists. Ind. Univ. 1963
Bkl A

Shapiro, Charles, ed. Contemporary British Novelists. Southern Ill. Univ. 1965
Bkl A

John Boynton Priestley, 1894-

Priestley, John Boynton. Margin Released: A Writer's Reminiscences and Reflections. Harper 1963
Bkl A

Priestley, John Boynton. Midnight on the Desert: Being an Excursion into Autobiography During a Winter in America, 1935-36. Harper 1937
SCPL

Alan Sillitoe, 1928-

COLLECTIONS

Shapiro, Charles, ed. Contemporary British Novelists. Southern Ill. Univ. 1965
Bkl A

Charles Percy Snow, Baron Snow of Leicester, 1905-

Karl, Frederick Robert. C. P. Snow: The Politics of Conscience. Southern Ill. Univ. 1963
Bkl A

Thale, Jerome. C. P. Snow. Scribner 1965
Bkl A

COLLECTIONS

Shapiro, Charles, ed. Contemporary British Novelists. Southern Ill. Univ. 1965
Bkl A

John Wain, 1925-

Wain, John. Sprightly Running: Part of an Autobiography. St Martins 1963
Bkl A

Hugh Walpole, 1884-1941

Hart-Davis, Rupert. Hugh Walpole: A Biography. Macmillan 1952
SCPL

Herbert George Wells, 1866-1946

Vallentin, Antonina. H. G. Wells, Prophet of Our Day; tr. by Daphne Woodward. Day 1950
SCPL

Angus Wilson, 1913-

COLLECTIONS

Shapiro, Charles, ed. Contemporary British Novelists. Southern Ill. Univ. 1965
Bkl A

Virginia (Stephen) Woolf, 1882-1941

Pippett, Aileen. Moth and the Star: A Biography of Virginia Woolf. Little 1955
SCPL

Woolf, Virginia (Stephen). Writer's Diary, Being Extracts from the Diary of Virginia Woolf; ed. by Leonard Woolf. Harcourt 1954
SCPL

Israel Zangwill, 1864-1926

Wohlgelernter, Maurice. Israel Zangwill: A Study. Columbia Univ. 1964
Bkl A

French

COLLECTIONS

Levin, Harry. The Gates of Horn: A Study of Five French Realists. Oxford 1963
Bkl A
Honoré de Balzac; Marie Henri Beyle; Gustave Flaubert; Marcel Proust; Émile Zola

Turnell, Martin. The Art of French Fiction. New Directions 1959
SCPL
Marie Henri Beyle; André Paul Guillaume Gide; Guy de Maupassant; François Mauriac; Antoine François Prévost d'Exiles; Marcel Proust; Émile Zola

French—18th century

Antoine François Prévost d'Exiles, 1697-1763

COLLECTIONS

Turnell, Martin. The Art of French Fiction. New Directions 1959
SCPL

French—19th century

Honoré de Balzac, 1799-1850

Maurois, André. Prometheus: The Life of Balzac; tr. by Norman Denny. Harper 1966
Bkl A

Zweig, Stephan. Balzac. Viking 1946
CA

COLLECTIONS

Levin, Harry. The Gates of Horn: A Study of Five French Realists. Oxford 1963
Bkl A

Maugham, William Somerset. Art of Fiction: An Introduction to Ten Novels and Their Authors. Doubleday 1955
SCPL

NOVELISTS

French—19th century—*Continued*

Alexandre Dumas, Père, 1802-1870

Maurois, André. Alexandre Dumas: A Great Life in Brief; tr. from the French by Jack Palmer White. Knopf 1955
SCHS—SCPL

Maurois, André. The Titans: A Three-Generation Biography of the Dumas; tr. by Gerard Hopkins. Harper 1957
SCPL

Gustave Flaubert, 1821-1880

Giraud, Raymond Dorner, ed. Flaubert: A Collection of Critical Essays. Prentice-Hall 1964
Bkl A

Steegmuller, Francis. Flaubert and Madame Bovary: A Double Portrait. Farrar 1950
GR—SCPL

COLLECTIONS

Hoff, Rhoda. Why They Wrote. Walck 1961
Bkl C(7-10)&Y—SCHS

Levin, Harry. The Gates of Horn: A Study of Five French Realists. Oxford 1963
Bkl A

Maugham, William Somerset. Art of Fiction: An Introduction to Ten Novels and Their Authors. Doubleday 1955
SCPL

Edmond Louis Antoine Huot de Goncourt, 1822-1896

Goncourt, Edmond Louis Antoine Huot de and Goncourt, Jules Alfred Huot de. Pages from the Goncourt Journal; ed. and tr. by Robert Baldick. Oxford 1962
Bkl A

George Sand, 1804-1876

Maurois, André. Lélia: The Life of George Sand; tr. by Gerard Hopkins. Harper 1953
SCPL

Jules Verne, 1828-1905

Born, Franz. Jules Verne: The Man Who Invented the Future; tr. from the German by Juliana Biro. Prentice-Hall 1964
Bkl C(6-10)&Y—CC—ESLC—JH

Freedman, Russell. Jules Verne: Portrait of a Prophet. Holiday 1965
Bkl C(7-10)&Y

Peare, Catherine Owens. Jules Verne: His Life. Holt 1956
CC(4-6)

COLLECTIONS

Stirling, Nora B. Who Wrote the Classics? Day 1965
Bkl Y&A&C

Émile Zola, 1840-1902

COLLECTIONS

Levin, Harry. The Gates of Horn: A Study of Five French Realists. Oxford 1963
Bkl A

Turnell, Martin. The Art of French Fiction. New Directions 1959
SCPL

French—20th century

Julian Green, 1900-

Green, Julian. Diary 1928-1957. Harcourt 1964
Bkl A

Joseph Kessel, 1898-

Kessel, Joseph. They Weren't All Angels; tr. by Humphrey Hare. McKay 1965
Bkl A

André Malraux, 1901-

COLLECTIONS

Flanner, Janet. Men and Monuments. Harper 1957
SCPL

Marcel Proust, 1871-1922

March, Harold. Two Worlds of Marcel Proust. Univ. of Pa. 1948
SCPL

Moss, Howard. The Magic Lantern of Marcel Proust. Macmillan 1962
Bkl A

Painter, George Duncan. Proust: v. 1, The Early Years. Little 1959
Bkl A

Painter, George Duncan. Proust: v. 2, The Later Years. Little 1965
Bkl A

COLLECTIONS

Levin, Harry. The Gates of Horn: A Study of Five French Realists. Oxford 1963
Bkl A

Turnell, Martin. The Art of French Fiction. New Directions 1959
SCPL

Wilson, Edmund. Axel's Castle: A Study in the Imaginative Literature of 1870-1930. Scribner 1931
SCPL

Irish—19th century

George Moore, 1852-1933

Moore, George. Hail and Farewell. 3v. 1911-14
CA

NOVELISTS

Irish—19th century

George Moore—Continued

COLLECTIONS

Howarth, Herbert. The Irish Writers, 1880-1940. Hill & Wang 1959
Bkl A

Irish—20th century

Elizabeth Bowen, 1899-

Bowen, Elizabeth. Seven Winters: Memories of a Dublin Childhood; &, Afterthoughts: Pieces on Writing. Knopf 1962
Bkl A

COLLECTIONS

O'Faoláin, Seán. Vanishing Hero: Studies in Novelists of the Twenties. Little 1957
SCPL

George Moore, 1852-1933

Moore, George. Hail and Farewell. 3v. 1911-14
CA

COLLECTIONS

Howarth, Herbert. The Irish Writers, 1880-1940. Hill & Wang 1959
Bkl A

Iris Murdoch, 1919-

COLLECTIONS

Shapiro, Charles, ed. Contemporary British Novelists. Southern Ill. Univ. 1965
Bkl A

New Zealand—20th century

Katherine Mansfield, 1888-1923

Daly, Saralyn R. Katherine Mansfield. Twayne 1965
Bkl A

Russian—19th century

Fedor Mikhaĭlovich Dostoevsky, 1821-1881

Coulson, Jessie. Dostoevsky: A Self-Portrait. Oxford 1962
Bkl A
Fülöp-Miller, René. Fyodor Dostoevsky: Insight, Faith, and Prophecy. Scribner 1950
SCPL
Magarshack, David. Dostoevsky. Harcourt 1963
Bkl A
Payne, Pierre Stephen Robert. Dostoyevsky: A Human Portrait. Knopf 1961
Bkl A—BY

Sajković, Miriam Taylor. F. M. Dostoevsky: His Image of Man. Univ. of Pa. 1962
Bkl A

COLLECTIONS

Maugham, William Somerset. Art of Fiction: An Introduction to Ten Novels and Their Authors. Doubleday 1955
SCPL

Lev Nikolaevich Tolstoi, 1828-1910

Tolstaĭa, Aleksandra L'vovna, Grafinĭa. Tolstoy: A Life of My Father; tr. by E. R. Hapgood. Harper 1953
CA—SCPL
Tolstoi, Sergei L'vovich. Tolstoy Remembered by His Son; tr. from the Russian by Moura Budberg. Atheneum 1962
Bkl A

COLLECTIONS

Maugham, William Somerset. Art of Fiction: An Introduction to Ten Novels and Their Authors. Doubleday 1955
SCPL

Ivan Sergeevich Turgenev, 1818-1883

Yarmolinsky, Avrahm. Turgenev: The Man, His Art and His Age. Orion 1959
SCPL

Russian—20th century

Leonid Maksimovich Leonov, 1899-

COLLECTIONS

Muchnic, Helen. From Gorky to Pasternak: Six Writers in Soviet Russia. Random House 1961
Bkl A

Scottish—18th century

Tobias George Smollett, 1721-1771

Bruce, Donald James Williams. Radical Doctor Smollett. Houghton 1965
Bkl A

Scottish—20th century

John Buchan, 1st Baron Tweedsmuir, 1875-1940

Buchan, John, 1st Baron Tweedsmuir. Pilgrim's Way: An Essay in Recollection. Houghton 1940
SCPL
Smith, Janet Adam. John Buchan: A Biography. Little 1966
Bkl A

Archibald Joseph Cronin, 1896-

Cronin, Archibald Joseph. Adventures in Two Worlds. Little 1957
BY—SCPL

NOVELISTS

Scottish—20th century—*Continued*

Muriel Spark, 1918-

COLLECTIONS

Shapiro, Charles, ed. Contemporary British Novelists. Southern Ill. Univ. 1965
Bkl A

Spanish—16th century

Miguel de Cervantes Saavedra, 1547-1616

Bell, Aubrey Fitzgerald. Cervantes. Univ. of Okla. 1947
SCPL

Busoni, Rafaello. The Man Who Was Don Quixote: The Story of Miguel Cervantes. Prentice-Hall 1958
BBJH—BY—CC(7-9)—JH—SCHS—YR

NUNS

See Religious Leaders

NURSES

See also Red Cross Workers

COLLECTIONS

Wright, Helen and Rapport, Samuel Berder, eds. Great Adventures in Nursing. Harper 1960
BBHS—Bkl Y&C

American

COLLECTIONS

Yost, Edna. American Women of Nursing. Lippincott 1965
Bkl Y&C—SCHS—SCPL
Florence G. Blake; Theodora A. Floyd; Annie Warburton Goodrich; Sister Mary Olivia Gowan; Mary Adelaide Nutting; Estelle (Massey) Osborne; Lucile Petry; Anne Prochazka; Isabel Maitland Stewart; Lillian Wald

American—19th century

Clara Harlowe Barton, 1821-1912

Boylston, Helen Dore. Clara Barton, Founder of the American Red Cross. Random House 1955
BBJH—CC(4-7)—ESLC—JH—SCHS

Epler, P. H. Life of Clara Barton. Macmillan 1915
SCPL

Graham, Alberta P. Clara Barton, Red Cross Pioneer. Abingdon 1956
CC(3-5)

Nolan, Jeannette (Covert). The Story of Clara Barton of the Red Cross. Messner 1941
CC(7-9)—JH—SCHS

Pace, Mildred Mastin. Clara Barton. Scribner 1941
BBEL—CC(4-7)—YR

Rose, Mary Catherine. Clara Barton: Soldier of Mercy. Garrard 1960
ESLC

Ross, Ishbel. Angel of the Battlefield: The Life of Clara Barton. Harper 1956
BY—SCHS—SCPL

Dorothea Lynde Dix, 1802-1887

Baker, Rachel. Angel of Mercy: The Story of Dorothea Lynde Dix. Messner 1955
BY—SCHS—YR

COLLECTIONS

Buckmaster, Henrietta. Women Who Shaped History. Collier Bks 1966
Bkl C(7-10)&Y

Daugherty, Sonia. Ten Brave Women. Lippincott 1953
BY—CC(7-9)—ESLC—JH—SCHS

McKown, Robin. Pioneers in Mental Health. Dodd 1961
Bkl A&Y

Linda Ann Judson Richards, 1841-1930

Baker, Rachel. America's First Trained Nurse, Linda Richards—Born: July 27, 1841; Died: April 16, 1930. Messner 1959
CC(7-9)—JH—SCHS

American—20th century

Florence G. Blake, 1907-

COLLECTIONS

Yost, Edna. American Women of Nursing. Lippincott 1965
Bkl Y&C—SCHS—SCPL

Alice Louise Florence Fitzgerald, 1874-1962

Noble, Iris. Nurse Around the World: Alice Fitzgerald. Messner 1964
Bkl C(7-9)&Y—ESLC—JH

Theodora A. Floyd, 1896-

COLLECTIONS

Yost, Edna. American Women of Nursing. Lippincott 1965
Bkl Y&C—SCHS—SCPL

Annie Warburton Goodrich, 1866-1954

COLLECTIONS

Yost, Edna. American Women of Nursing. Lippincott 1965
Bkl Y&C—SCHS—SCPL

NURSES

American—20th century—*Continued*

Sister Mary Olivia Gowan, 1888-

COLLECTIONS

Yost, Edna. American Women of Nursing. Lippincott 1965
Bkl Y&C—SCHS—SCPL

Mary Adelaide Nutting, 1858-1948

COLLECTIONS

Yost, Edna. American Women of Nursing. Lippincott 1965
Bkl Y&C—SCHS—SCPL

Estelle (Massey) Osborne, 1903-

COLLECTIONS

Yost, Edna. American Women of Nursing. Lippincott 1965
Bkl Y&C—SCHS—SCPL

Lucile Petry, 1903-

COLLECTIONS

Yost, Edna. American Women of Nursing. Lippincott 1965
Bkl Y&C—SCHS—SCPL

Anne Prochazka, 1897-

COLLECTIONS

Yost, Edna. American Women of Nursing. Lippincott 1965
Bkl Y&C—SCHS—SCPL

Linda Ann Judson Richards, 1841-1930

Baker, Rachel. America's First Trained Nurse, Linda Richards—Born: July 27, 1841; Died: April 16, 1930. Messner 1959
CC(7-9)—JH—SCHS

Isabel Maitland Stewart, 1878-1963

COLLECTIONS

Yost, Edna. American Women of Nursing. Lippincott 1965
Bkl Y&C—SCHS—SCPL

Lillian Wald, 1867-1940

COLLECTIONS

Yost, Edna. American Women of Nursing. Lippincott 1965
Bkl Y&C—SCHS—SCPL

Australian—20th century

Elizabeth Kenny, 1886-1952

Kenny, Elizabeth. And They Shall Walk: The Life Story of Sister Elizabeth Kenny. Dodd 1943
SCHS—SCPL

English—19th century

Florence Nightingale, 1820-1910

Garnett, Emmeline. Florence Nightingale's Nuns. Farrar 1961
Bkl C(5-9)

Hume, Ruth (Fox). Florence Nightingale. Random House 1960
Bkl C(5-8)

Nolan, Jeannette (Covert). Florence Nightingale. Messner 1946
BBEL(6-8)—CC(7-9)—ESLC—JH—SCHS

Woodham Smith, Cecil Blanche (Fitz-Gerald). Florence Nightingale, 1820-1910. McGraw 1951
SCPL

Woodham Smith, Cecil Blanche (Fitz-Gerald). Lonely Crusader: The Life of Florence Nightingale 1820-1910. McGraw 1951
BBEL—BBHS—BBJH—CC(7-9)—JH—SCHS—SCPL

COLLECTIONS

Bowie, Walter Russell. Women of Light. Harper 1964
Bkl A&Y

Hume, Ruth Fox. Great Women of Medicine. Random House 1964
CC—JH

McNeer, May Yonge and Ward, Lynd Kendall. Armed with Courage. Abingdon 1957
AB(5-8)—BBEL(5-8)—CC(5-7)—ESLC—JH—YR

Strachey, Giles Lytton. Eminent Victorians. Modern Lib. 1933
BY—SCPL

English—20th century

Mary Ball, 1894?-1952

Earl, Lawrence. She Loved a Wicked City: The Story of Mary Ball, Missionary. Dutton 1962
Bkl A&Y—BY

Edith Louisa Cavell, 1865-1915

Elkon, Juliette. Edith Cavell, Heroic Nurse. Messner 1956
SCHS

Grey, Elizabeth. Friend Within the Gates. Houghton 1961
Bkl Y&C—JH—SCHS

COLLECTIONS

Bowie, Walter Russell. Women of Light. Harper 1964
Bkl A&Y

Teresa Lightwood, 1906-

Lightwood, Teresa. My Three Lives. Dutton 1960
Bkl A—BY

OBSTETRICIANS

See Physicians

OCCUPATIONAL THERAPISTS

American—20th century

Ora Ruggles, 1894-

Carlova, John and Ruggles, Ora. The Healing Heart. Messner 1961
Bkl A&Y

OCEANOGRAPHERS

COLLECTIONS

Wagner, Frederick. Famous Underwater Adventurers. Dodd 1962
Bkl C(7up)&Y—ESLC—JH

American—19th century

Alexander Agassiz, 1835-1910

Epstein, Beryl (Williams) and Epstein, Samuel. Pioneer Oceanographer: Alexander Agassiz. Messner 1963
Bkl C(7-10)&Y—YR

Matthew Fontaine Maury, 1806-1873

Latham, Jean Lee. Trail Blazer of the Seas. Houghton 1956 (Fiction)
BY—CC(7-9)—JH
Williams, Frances Leigh. Matthew Fontaine Maury, Scientist of the Sea. Rutgers Univ. 1963
Bkl A
Williams, Frances Leigh. Ocean Pathfinder: A Biography of Matthew Fontaine Maury. Harcourt 1966
Bkl C(7-9)&Y

OIL INDUSTRY WORKERS

See Industrialists; Petroleum Industry Workers

OLD TESTAMENT FIGURES

See Biblical Figures—Old Testament

OPERA MANAGERS

American—20th century

Oscar Hammerstein, 1847-1919

Sheean, Vincent. Oscar Hammerstein I: The Life and Exploits of an Impresario. Simon & Schuster 1956
SCPL

OPERA SINGERS

See Singers

ORCHESTRA CONDUCTORS

See Conductors

ORGANISTS

French—19th century

Louis Braille, 1809-1852

DeGering, Etta. Seeing Fingers: The Story of Louis Braille. McKay 1962
Bkl C(5-7)—CC(5-7)—ESLC
Kugelmass, J. Alvin. Louis Braille: Windows for the Blind. Messner 1951
BBJH—JH—SCHS
Webster, Gary. Journey into Light: The Story of Louis Braille. Hawthorn 1964
AB(7up)

French—20th century

Albert Schweitzer, 1875-1965

Anderson, Erica. Albert Schweitzer's Gift of Friendship. Harper 1964
Bkl A&Y
Anderson, Erica and Exman, Eugene. The World of Albert Schweitzer: A Book of Photographs. Harper 1955
BY—SCHS—SCPL
Daniel, Anita. The Story of Albert Schweitzer. Random House 1957
CC—ESLC—JH—SCHS
Hagedorn, Hermann. Prophet in the Wilderness: The Story of Albert Schweitzer. Macmillan 1954
SCPL
McKnight, Gerald. Verdict on Schweitzer: The Man Behind the Legend of Lambaréné. Day 1964
Bkl A
Manton, Jo. The Story of Albert Schweitzer. Abelard-Schuman 1955
AB(7up)—BBEL(6)—CC—JH
Merrett, John. The True Story of Albert Schweitzer. Childrens Press 1964
IndJ(4-6)
Payne, Pierre Stephen Robert. Three Worlds of Albert Schweitzer. Nelson 1957
SCHS—SCPL
Picht, Werner Robert Valentin. The Life and Thought of Albert Schweitzer; tr. from the German by Edward Fitzgerald. Harper 1964
Bkl A
Schweitzer, Albert. Memoirs of Childhood and Youth. Macmillan 1949
SCPL
Schweitzer, Albert. Out of My Life and Thought: An Autobiography; tr. by C. T. Campion. Holt 1949
BBHS—GR—SCPL—3000
Seaver, George. Albert Schweitzer: The Man and His Mind. Harper 1955
SCPL
Simon, Charlie May. All Men Are Brothers: A Portrait of Albert Schweitzer. Dutton 1956
AB(7-10)—BBJH—JH

ORNITHOLOGISTS

American—19th century

John James Audubon, 1785-1851

Adams, Alexander B. John James Audubon: A Biography. Putnam 1966
Bkl A&Y

Audubon, John James. Audubon in the West; ed. by John Francis McDermott. Univ. of Okla. 1966
Bkl A

Ayars, James Sterling. John James Audubon: Bird Artist. Garrard 1966
ESLC

Hogeboom, Amy. Audubon and His Sons. Lothrop 1956
AB(6-9)—YR

Kieran, Margaret and Kieran, John. John James Audubon. Random House 1954
AB(5-10)—CC(5-7)—ESLC—JH—SCHS

Peattie, Donald Culross. Singing in the Wilderness: A Salute to John James Audubon. Putnam 1935
SCPL

Rourke, Constance Mayfield. Audubon. Harcourt 1936
BBJH—CC(7-9)—SCPL

Alexander Wilson, 1766-1813

Cantwell, Robert. Alexander Wilson, Naturalist and Pioneer. Lippincott 1961
BY

English—20th century

Peter Markham Scott, 1909-

Scott, Peter Markham. The Eye of the Wind. Houghton 1961
Bkl A

OUTLAWS

See Criminals

PACIFISTS

American—19th century

Jane Addams, 1860-1935

Addams, Jane. Twenty Years at Hull-House; with autobiographical notes. Macmillan 1910
SCHS—SCPL

Gilbert, Miriam. Jane Addams, World Neighbor. Abingdon 1960
Bkl C(4-6)

Judson, Clara Ingram. City Neighbor: The Story of Jane Addams. Scribner 1951
CC(5-7)—ESLC—JH—SCHS—YR

Tims, Margaret. Jane Addams of Hull House, 1860-1935: A Centenary Study. Macmillan 1961
SCPL

Wagoner, Jean Brown. Jane Addams: Little Lame Girl. Bobbs 1962
CC(3-6)

Wise, Winifred E. Jane Addams of Hull-House: A Biography. Harcourt 1935
SCHS

COLLECTIONS

McNeer, May Yonge and Ward, Lynd Kendall. Armed with Courage. Abingdon 1957
AB(5-8)—BBEL(5-8)—CC(5-7)—ESLC—JH—YR

Oswald Garrison Villard, 1872-1949

Wreszin, Michael. Oswald Garrison Villard, Pacifist at War. Ind. Univ. 1965
Bkl A

American—20th century

Jane Addams, 1860-1935

Addams, Jane. Twenty Years at Hull-House; with autobiographical notes. Macmillan 1910
SCHS—SCPL

Gilbert, Miriam. Jane Addams, World Neighbor. Abingdon 1960
Bkl C(4-6)

Judson, Clara Ingram. City Neighbor: The Story of Jane Addams. Scribner 1951
CC(5-7)—ESLC—JH—SCHS—YR

Tims, Margaret. Jane Addams of Hull House, 1860-1935: A Centenary Study. Macmillan 1961
SCPL

Wagoner, Jean Brown. Jane Addams: Little Lame Girl. Bobbs 1962
CC(3-6)

Wise, Winifred E. Jane Addams of Hull-House: A Biography. Harcourt 1935
SCHS

COLLECTIONS

McNeer, May Yonge and Ward, Lynd Kendall. Armed with Courage. Abingdon 1957
AB(5-8)—BBEL(5-8)—CC(5-7)—ESLC—JH—YR

Emily Greene Balch, 1867-1961

Randall, Mercedes (Moritz). Improper Bostonian: Emily Greene Balch, Nobel Peace Laureate, 1946. Twayne 1964
Bkl A&Y

Oswald Garrison Villard, 1872-1949

Wreszin, Michael. Oswald Garrison Villard, Pacifist at War. Ind. Univ. 1965
Bkl A

PACIFISTS—*Continued*

Austrian—20th century

Franz Jägerstätter, 1907-1943

Zahn, Gordon Charles. In Solitary Witness: The Life and Death of Franz Jägerstätter. Holt 1965
Bkl A

English—20th century

Julian Bell, 1908-1937

Stansky, Peter and Abrahams, William Miller. Journey to the Frontier: Two Roads to the Spanish Civil War. Little 1966
Bkl A

Russian—20th century

Maxim Gorky, 1868-1936

Levin, Dan. Stormy Petrel: The Life and Work of Maxim Gorky. Appleton 1965
Bkl A

PAINTERS

See also Glass Painters

COLLECTIONS

Bryan, Michael. Dictionary of Painters and Engravers; rev. and enl. by George C. Williamson. 5v. Kennikat 1964
SCPL

Chandler, Anna Curtis. Story-Lives of Master Artists. Lippincott 1953
CC(6-9)—ESLC—JH—YR

Craven, Thomas. Men of Art. Simon & Schuster 1931
SCPL

Fernau, Joachim. Praeger Encyclopedia of Old Masters; tr. from the German by James Cleugh and Monica Brooksbank. Praeger 1959
SCPL

Kielty, Bernardine. Masters of Painting: Their Works/Their Lives/Their Times. Doubleday 1964
ESLC—IndS(10-12)—JH

Liberman, Alexander. The Artist in His Studio. Studio 1960
Bkl A

Rosenberg, Jakob. Great Draughtsmen from Pisanello to Picasso. Harvard Univ. 1959
SCPL
Hilaire Germain Edgar Degas; Albrecht Dürer; Pablo Picasso; Antonio Pisano, known as Pisanello; Raphael; Rembrandt Harmenszoon van Rijn; Leonardo da Vinci; Jean Antoine Watteau

Venturi, Lionello. Four Steps Toward Modern Art. Columbia Univ. 1956
SCPL
Michelangelo Merisi da Caravaggio; Paul Cézanne; Giorgione da Castelfranco (Giorgio Barbarelli); Édouard Manet

Venturi, Lionello. Modern Painters. Scribner 1947
SCPL
John Constable; Jean Baptiste Camille Corot; Gustave Courbet; Honoré Victorin Daumier; Jacques Louis David; Eugène Delacroix; José de Goya y Lucientes; Jean Auguste Dominique Ingres

American

COLLECTIONS

Baur, John Ireland Howe, ed. New Art in America: Fifty Painters of the 20th Century. N. Y. Graphic 1957
SCPL

Freedgood, Lillian. Great Artists of America. Crowell 1963
Bkl C&Y—CC(6-9)—ESLC—YR

Guitar, Mary Ann. 22: Famous Painters and Illustrators Tell How They Work. McKay 1964
IndS(10-12)

Hollmann, Clide. Five Artists of the Old West. Hastings House 1965
ESLC
Karl Bodmer; George Catlin; Alfred Jacob Miller; Frederic Remington; Charles Marion Russell

Nordness, Lee, ed. Art: USA: Now. 2v. Viking 1963
Bkl A&Y

Simon, Charlie May. Art in the New Land: Stories of Some American Artists and Their Work. Dutton 1945
BBJH—CC(7-9)—JH—SCHS—YR

American—18th century

John Singleton Copley, 1738-1815

Prown, Jules David. John Singleton Copley. 2v. Nat. Gallery of Art 1966
Bkl A

Charles Willson Peale, 1741-1827

Peare, Catherine Owens. Painter of Patriots: Charles Willson Peale. Holt 1964
ESLC

Gilbert Stuart, 1755-1828

Flexner, James Thomas. Gilbert Stuart: A Great Life in Brief. Knopf 1955
SCPL

Mount, Charles Merrill. Gilbert Stuart: A Biography. Norton 1964
Bkl A

Benjamin West, 1738-1820

Henry, Marguerite. Benjamin West and His Cat Grimalkin. Bobbs 1947
CC(4-6)—ESLC—YR

American—19th century

John James Audubon, 1785-1851

Adams, Alexander B. John James Audubon: A Biography. Putnam 1966
Bkl A&Y

PAINTERS

American—19th century

John James Audubon—Continued

Audubon, John James. Audubon in the West; ed. by John Francis McDermott. Univ. of Okla. 1966
Bkl A

Ayars, James Sterling. John James Audubon: Bird Artist. Garrard 1966
ESLC

Hogeboom, Amy. Audubon and His Songs. Lothrop 1956
AB(6-9)—YR

Kieran, Margaret and Kieran, John. John James Audubon. Random House 1954
AB(5-10)—CC(5-7)—ESLC—JH—SCHS

Peattie, Donald Culross. Singing in the Wilderness: A Salute to John James Audubon. Putnam 1935
SCPL

Rourke, Constance Mayfield. Audubon. Harcourt 1936
BBJH—CC(7-9)—SCPL

John Banvard, 1815-1891

Agle, Nan Hayden and Bacon, Frances Elizabeth Atchinson. The Ingenious John Banvard. Seabury 1966
Bkl C(4-7)—ESLC

George Caleb Bingham, 1811-1879

McDermott, John Francis. George Caleb Bingham, River Portraitist. Univ. of Okla. 1959
Bkl A

Mary Cassatt, 1845-1926

Sweet, Frederick Arnold. Miss Mary Cassatt, Impressionist from Pennsylvania. Univ. of Okla. 1966
Bkl A

George Catlin, 1796-1872

Plate, Robert. Palette and Tomahawk: The Story of George Catlin, July 27, 1796—December 23, 1872. McKay 1962
Bkl A&Y—YR

COLLECTIONS

Hollmann, Clide. Five Artists of the Old West. Hastings House 1965
ESLC

Thomas Eakins, 1884-1916

Porter, Fairfield. Thomas Eakins. Braziller 1959
SCPL

Winslow Homer, 1836-1910

Beam, Philip C. Winslow Homer at Prout's Neck. Little 1966
Bkl A

Gardner, Albert Ten Eyck. Winslow Homer, American Artist: His World and His Work. Potter 1961
SCPL

Goodrich, Lloyd. Winslow Homer. Macmillan 1944
SCPL

Goodrich, Lloyd. Winslow Homer. Braziller 1959
SCPL

Gould, Jean. Winslow Homer: A Portrait. Dodd 1962
Bkl A&Y

Ripley, Elizabeth. Winslow Homer: A Biography. Lippincott 1963
Bkl Y&C(7-9)—CC(7-9)—ESLC—YR

Alfred Jacob Miller, 1810-1874

COLLECTIONS

Hollmann, Clide. Five Artists of the Old West. Hastings House 1965
ESLC

Thomas Moran, 1837-1926

Wilkins, Thurman. Thomas Moran, Artist of the Mountains. Univ. of Okla. 1966
Bkl A

Frederic Remington, 1861-1909

McCracken, Harold. Frederic Remington, Artist of the Old West. Lippincott 1947
SCPL

McKown, Robin. Painter of the Wild West. Messner 1959
YR

COLLECTIONS

Hollmann, Clide. Five Artists of the Old West. Hastings House 1965
ESLC

Charles Marion Russell, 1864-1926

Renner, Frederic G. Charles M. Russell: Paintings, Drawings, and Sculpture in the Amon G. Carter Collection: A Descriptive Catalogue. Univ. of Tex. 1966
Bkl A

COLLECTIONS

Hollmann, Clide. Five Artists of the Old West. Hastings House 1965
ESLC

Gilbert Stuart, 1755-1828

Flexner, James Thomas. Gilbert Stuart: A Great Life in Brief. Knopf 1955
SCPL

Mount, Charles Merrill. Gilbert Stuart: A Biography. Norton 1964
Bkl A

Louis Comfort Tiffany, 1848-1933

Koch, Robert. Louis C. Tiffany, Rebel in Glass. Crown 1964
Bkl A—IndS(11-12)

PAINTERS

American—19th century—*Continued*

James Abbott McNeill Whistler, 1834-1903

Pearson, Hesketh. The Man Whistler. Harper 1952
SCPL

Sutton, Denys. Nocturne: The Art of James McNeill Whistler. Lippincott 1964
Bkl A

American—20th century

George Wesley Bellows, 1882-1925

Morgan, Charles Hill. George Bellows, Painter of America. Reynal 1965
Bkl A

Nugent, Frances R. George Bellows, American Painter. Rand McNally 1964
AB(6up)—IndJ(4-6)—YR

Charles Burchfield, 1893-1967

Baur, John Ireland Howe. Charles Burchfield. Macmillan 1956
SCPL

Mary Cassatt, 1845-1926

Sweet, Frederick Arnold. Miss Mary Cassatt, Impressionist from Pennsylvania. Univ. of Okla. 1966
Bkl A

Katherine Sophie Dreier, 1877-1952

COLLECTIONS

Saarinen, Aline B. The Proud Possessors: The Lives, Times, and Tastes of Some Adventurous American Art Collectors. Random House 1958
SCPL

Thomas Eakins, 1844-1916

Porter, Fairfield. Thomas Eakins. Braziller 1959
SCPL

Lyonel Charles Adrian Feininger, 1871-1956

Hess, Hans. Lyonel Feininger. Abrams 1961
Bkl A

Scheyer, Ernst. Lyonel Feininger: Caricature & Fantasy. Wayne State Univ. 1964
Bkl A

William Glackens, 1870-1938

Glackens, Ira. William Glackens and the Ashcan Group: The Emergence of Realism in American Art. Crown 1957
SCPL

Harold Osman Kelly, 1884-1955

Johnson, William Weber. Kelly Blue. Doubleday 1960
Bkl A

Thomas Moran, 1837-1926

Wilkins, Thurman. Thomas Moran, Artist of the Mountains. Univ. of Okla. 1966
Bkl A

Anna Mary (Robertson) Moses, 1860-1961

Moses, Anna Mary (Robertson). Grandma Moses: My Life's History. Harper 1952
SCHS—SCPL

Norman Rockwell, 1894-

Guptill, Arthur Leighton. Norman Rockwell, Illustrator. Watson-Guptill 1946
SCPL

Rockwell, Norman and Rockwell, Thomas. Norman Rockwell. Doubleday 1959
Bkl A&Y

Charles Marion Russell, 1864-1926

Garst, Doris Shannon. Cowboy-Artist, Charles M. Russell. Messner 1960
YR

McCracken, Harold. The Charles M. Russell Book: The Life and Work of the Cowboy Artist. Doubleday 1957
SCPL

Renner, Frederic G. Charles M. Russell: Paintings, Drawings, and Sculpture in the Amon G. Carter Collection: A Descriptive Catalogue. Univ. of Tex. 1966
Bkl A

Shelton, Lola. Charles Marion Russell: Cowboy, Artist, Friend. Dodd 1962
YR

COLLECTIONS

Hollmann, Clide. Five Artists of the Old West. Hastings House 1965
ESLC

John Sloan, 1871-1925

Brooks, Van Wyck. John Sloan: A Painter's Life. Dutton 1955
SCPL

Sloan, John. New York Scene: From Diaries, Notes and Correspondence, 1906-1913; ed. by Bruce St. John. Harper 1965
Bkl A

Joseph Lindon Smith, 1863-1950

Smith, Corinna Haven (Putnam). Interesting People: Eighty Years with the Great and Near-Great. Univ. of Okla. 1962
Bkl A

PAINTERS

American—20th century—Continued

Joseph Solman, 1909-
Chanin, A. L. Joseph Solman. Crown 1966
Bkl A

Maurice Sterne, 1878-1957
Sterne, Maurice. Shadow and Light: The Life, Friends and Opinions of Maurice Sterne; ed. by Charlotte Leon Mayerson. Harcourt 1965
Bkl A

William Thon, 1906-
Gruskin, Alan D. The Painter and His Techniques: William Thon. Viking 1964
IndS(10-12)

Grant Wood, 1892-1942
Garwood, Darrell. Artist in Iowa: A Life of Grant Wood. Norton 1944
SCPL

Austrian—20th century

Oskar Kokoschka, 1886-
Bosman, Anthony. Kokoschka. Barnes 1964
IndS(9-12)

Dutch—15th century

Hieronymus Bosch, 1450?-1516
Delevoy, Robert L. Bosch: Biographical and Critical Study; tr. by Stuart Gilbert. Skira 1960
Bkl A—SCPL

Dutch—17th century

Rembrandt Harmenszoon van Rijn, 1606-1669
Benesch, Otto. Rembrandt: Biographical and Critical Study; tr. by James Emmons. Skira 1957
SCPL
Ripley, Elizabeth. Rembrandt: A Biography. Walck 1955
CC(7-9)—ESLC—JH—SCHS
Rosenberg, Jakob. Rembrandt. 2v. Harvard Univ. 1948
SCPL
Schmitt, Gladys. Rembrandt: A Novel. Random House 1961 (Fiction)
Bkl A
White, Christopher. Rembrandt and His World. Studio 1964
Bkl A—IndS(12)

COLLECTIONS
Rosenberg, Jakob. Great Draughtsmen from Pisanello to Picasso. Harvard Univ. 1959
SCPL

Johannes Vermeer, 1632-1675
Brion, Marcel. Vermeer; tr. from the French by Sally Marks. Abrams 1963
Bkl A

Dutch—19th century

Vincent van Gogh, 1853-1890
Estienne, Charles. Van Gogh; tr. by S. J. C. Harrison. Skira 1953
SCPL
Gogh, Vincent van. Complete Letters, with Reproductions of All the Drawings in the Correspondence. 3v. N. Y. Graphic 1958
SCPL
Gogh, Vincent van. Dear Theo: The Autobiography; ed. by Irving Stone. Doubleday 1957
SCPL
Gogh, Vincent van. Van Gogh: A Self-Portrait: Letters Revealing His Life as a Painter; selected by W. H. Auden. N. Y. Graphic 1961
Bkl A
Hanson, Lawrence and Hanson, Elisabeth M. The Seekers: Gauguin, Van Gogh, Cézanne. Random House 1963
Bkl A
Poldermans, Joost. Vincent: A Novel Based on the Life of Van Gogh. Holt 1962 (Fiction)
Bkl A
Ripley, Elizabeth. Vincent van Gogh: A Biography. Walck 1954
CC(7-9)—ESLC—JH—SCHS
Stone, Irving. Lust for Life. Modern Lib. 1944 (Fiction)
GR—SCHS
Tralbaut, Mark Edo. Van Gogh: A Pictorial Biography; tr. by Margaret Shenfield. Studio 1959
Bkl A
Uhde, Wilhelm. Vincent Van Gogh. Phaidon 1951
SCPL

English—18th century

William Blake, 1757-1827
Bronowski, Jacob. William Blake and the Age of Revolution. Harper 1965
Bkl A
Daugherty, James Henry. William Blake. Viking 1960
BBHS—Bkl Y—BY—SCHS—YR

Thomas Gainsborough, 1727-1788
Ripley, Elizabeth. Gainsborough: A Biography. Lippincott 1964
Bkl C(7-9)&Y—ESLC—JH

William Hogarth, 1697-1764
Antal, Frederick. Hogarth and His Place in European Art. Basic Bks 1962
Bkl A

PAINTERS

English—18th century

William Hogarth—Continued

Berry, Erick. The Four Londons of William Hogarth. McKay 1964
  Bkl Y—IndJ(6-9)
Quennell, Peter. Hogarth's Progress. Viking 1955
  SCPL

English—19th century

William Blake, 1757-1827

Bronowski, Jacob. William Blake and the Age of Revolution. Harper 1965
  Bkl A
Daugherty, James Henry. William Blake. Viking 1960
  BBHS—Bkl Y—BY—SCHS—YR

John Constable, 1776-1837

COLLECTIONS

Venturi, Lionello. Modern Painters. Scribner 1947
  SCPL

Joseph Mallord William Turner, 1775-1851

Lindsay, Jack. J. M. W. Turner: His Life and Work: A Critical Biography. N. Y. Graphic 1966
  Bkl A

English—20th century

John Spencer Churchill, 1909-

Churchill, John Spencer. A Churchill Canvas. Little 1962
  Bkl A

Wyndham Lewis, 1844-1957

Lewis, Wyndham. Letters; ed. by W. K. Rose. New Directions 1964
  Bkl A

Peter Markham Scott, 1909-

Scott, Peter Markham. The Eye of the Wind. Houghton 1961
  Bkl A

Flemish—15th century

Jan van Eyck, 1370?-1440?

Nugent, Frances Roberts. Jan Van Eyck: Master Painter. Rand McNally 1962
  AB(5-9)—YR

Flemish—16th century

Peeter Brueghel, the Elder, 1520?-1569

Delevoy, Robert L. Bruegel: Historical and Critical Study; tr. by Stuart Gilbert. Skira 1959
  Bkl A—SCPL

Flemish—17th century

Sir Peter Paul Rubens, 1577-1640

Ripley, Elizabeth. Rubens: A Biography. Walck 1957
  CC(7-9)—JH—SCHS

French

COLLECTIONS

Dorival, Bernard. Twentieth Century Painters. 2v. Univ. Bks 1958
  SCPL
Wilenski, Reginald Howard. Modern French Painters. Harcourt 1949
  SCPL
  Paul Cézanne; Hilaire Germain Edgar Degas; Paul Gauguin; Auguste Renoir; Henri Julien Félix Rousseau; Georges Pierre Seurat; Henri Marie Raymond de Toulouse-Lautrec

French—18th century

Jean Baptiste Siméon Chardin, 1699-1779

Rosenberg, Pierre. Chardin; tr. from the French by Helga Harrison. Skira 1963
  Bkl A

Jacques Louis David, 1748-1825

COLLECTIONS

Venturi, Lionello. Modern Painters. Scribner 1947
  SCPL

Marie Louise Élisabeth (Vigée) Lebrun, 1755-1842

Kyle, Elisabeth. Portrait of Lisette. Nelson 1963 (Fiction)
  Bkl Y&C—YR

Jean Antoine Watteau, 1684-1721

COLLECTIONS

Rosenberg, Jakob. Great Draughtsmen from Pisanello to Picasso. Harvard Univ. 1959
  SCPL

French—19th century

Paul Cézanne, 1839-1906

Beucken, Jean de. Cézanne: A Pictorial Biography; tr. and adapted by Lothian Small. Studio 1962
  Bkl A
Fry, Roger Eliot. Cézanne: A Study of His Development. Macmillan 1952
  SCPL
Hanson, Lawrence. Mortal Victory: A Biography of Paul Cézanne. Holt 1960
  Bkl A
Hanson, Lawrence and Hanson, Elisabeth M. The Seekers: Gauguin, Van Gogh, Cézanne. Random House 1963
  Bkl A

PAINTERS
French—19th century
Paul Cézanne—Continued

Huyghe, René. Cézanne; tr. from the French by Kenneth Martin Leake. Abrams 1963
Bkl A

Perruchot, Henri. Cézanne; tr. by Humphrey Hare. World 1962
Bkl A

Reynal, Maurice. Cézanne: Biographical and Critical Studies; tr. by James Emmons. Skira 1954
SCPL

COLLECTIONS

Venturi, Lionello. Four Steps Toward Modern Art. Columbia Univ. 1956
SCPL

Wilenski, Reginald Howard. Modern French Painters. Harcourt 1949
SCPL

Jean Baptiste Camille Corot, 1796-1875

COLLECTIONS

Venturi, Lionello. Modern Painters. Scribner 1947
SCPL

Gustave Courbet, 1819-1877

Mack, Gerstle. Gustave Courbet. Knopf 1951
SCPL

COLLECTIONS

Venturi, Lionello. Modern Painters. Scribner 1947
SCPL

Honoré Victorin Daumier, 1808-1879

Larkin, Oliver W. Daumier, Man of His Time. McGraw 1966
Bkl A

COLLECTIONS

Venturi, Lionello. Modern Painters. Scribner 1947
SCPL

Jacques Louis David, 1748-1825

COLLECTIONS

Venturi, Lionello. Modern Painters. Scribner 1947
SCPL

Hilaire Germain Edgar Degas, 1834-1917

Foska, François. Degas: Biographical and Critical Studies; tr. by James Emmons. Skira 1954
SCPL

Halévy, Daniel. My Friend Degas; tr. and ed. by Mina Curtiss. Wesleyan Univ. 1964
Bkl A

COLLECTIONS

Rosenberg, Jakob. Great Draughtsmen from Pisanello to Picasso. Harvard Univ. 1959
SCPL

Wilenski, Reginald Howard. Modern French Painters. Harcourt 1949
SCPL

Eugène Delacroix, 1798-1863

Deslandres, Yvonne. Delacroix: A Pictorial Biography; tr. from the French by Jonathan Griffin. Viking 1963
Bkl A

Huyghe, René. Delacroix; tr. from the French by Jonathan Griffin. Abrams 1964
Bkl A

COLLECTIONS

Venturi, Lionello. Modern Painters. Scribner 1947
SCPL

Paul Gauguin, 1848-1903

Estienne, Charles. Gauguin: Biographical and Critical Studies; tr. by James Emmons. Skira 1953
SCPL

Hanson, Lawrence and Hanson, Elisabeth M. Noble Savage: The Life of Paul Gauguin. Random House 1954
SCPL

Hanson, Lawrence and Hanson, Elisabeth M. The Seekers: Gauguin, Van Gogh, Cézanne. Random House 1963
Bkl A

Huyghe, René. Gauguin; tr. by Helen C. Slonim. Crown 1959
Bkl A

Perruchot, Henri. Gauguin; tr. by Humphrey Hare; ed. by Jean Ellsmoor. World 1964
Bkl A

Rewald, John. Gauguin. Hyperion 1949
SCPL

COLLECTIONS

Wilenski, Reginald Howard. Modern French Painters. Harcourt 1949
SCPL

Jean Auguste Dominique Ingres, 1780-1867

COLLECTIONS

Venturi, Lionello. Modern Painters. Scribner 1947
SCPL

PAINTERS

French—19th century—*Continued*

Édouard Manet, 1832-1883

Bataille, Georges. Manet: Biographical and Critical Study. Skira 1955
SCPL

Manet, Édouard. Portrait of Manet, by Himself and His Contemporaries; ed. by Pierre Courthion and Pierre Cailler; tr. by Michael Ross. Roy 1962
Bkl A

Perruchot, Henri. Manet; tr. by Humphrey Hare; ed. by Jean Ellsmoor. World 1963
Bkl A

COLLECTIONS

Venturi, Lionello. Four Steps Toward Modern Art. Columbia Univ. 1956
SCPL

Claude Monet, 1840-1926

Rouart, Denis. Claude Monet; tr. by James Emmons. Skira 1958
SCPL

Taillandier, Yvon. Monet; tr. from the French by A. P. H. Hamilton. Crown 1963
Bkl A

Weekes, C. P. The Invincible Monet. Appleton 1960
Bkl A

Camille Pissarro, 1831-1903

Rewald, John. Camille Pissarro. Abrams 1963
Bkl A

Odilon Redon, 1840-1916

Berger, Klaus. Odilon Redon: Fantasy and Colour; tr. by Michael Bullock. McGraw 1965
Bkl A

Auguste Renoir, 1841-1919

Fosca, François. Renoir: His Life and Work; tr. from the French by Mary I. Martin. Prentice-Hall 1962
Bkl A

Renoir, Jean. Renoir, My Father; tr. by Randolph and Dorothy Weaver. Little 1962
Bkl A—SCHS—SCPL

Rouart, Denis. Renoir: Biographical and Critical Studies; tr. by James Emmons. Skira 1954
SCPL

COLLECTIONS

Wilenski, Reginald Howard. Modern French Painters. Harcourt 1949
SCPL

Henri Julien Félix Rousseau, 1844-1910

Salmon, André. Rousseau; tr. from the French by Paul Colacicchi. Abrams 1963
Bkl A

Vallier, Dora. Henri Rousseau. Abrams 1964
Bkl A

COLLECTIONS

Wilenski, Reginald Howard. Modern French Painters. Harcourt 1949
SCPL

Georges Pierre Seurat, 1859-1891

Fry, Roger. Seurat; ed. by Anthony Blunt. N. Y. Graphic 1965
IndS(10-12)

Russell, John. Seurat. Praeger 1965
Bkl A

COLLECTIONS

Wilenski, Reginald Howard. Modern French Painters. Harcourt 1949
SCPL

Henri Marie Raymond de Toulouse-Lautrec, 1864-1901

Hanson, Lawrence and Hanson, Elisabeth M. Tragic Life of Toulouse-Lautrec. Random House 1956
SCPL

Huisman, P. and Dortu, M. G. Lautrec by Lautrec. Viking 1964
IndS(11-12)

Julien, Edouard. Lautrec; tr. by Helen C. Slonim. Crown 1959
Bkl A

Lassaigne, Jacques. Lautrec: Biographical and Critical Studies; tr. by Stuart Gilbert. Skira 1953
SCPL

Perruchot, Henri. T-Lautrec; tr. by Humphrey Hare. World 1961
Bkl A

COLLECTIONS

Wilenski, Reginald Howard. Modern French Painters. Harcourt 1949
SCPL

French—20th century

Pierre Bonnard, 1867-1947

Soby, James Thrall. Bonnard and His Environment. Mus. of Modern Art 1964
Bkl A

Terrasse, Antoine. Bonnard: Biographical and Critical Study; tr. from the French by Stuart Gilbert. Skira 1965
Bkl A

PAINTERS

French—20th century

Pierre Bonnard—Continued

Vaillant, Annette. Bonnard; tr. from the French by David Britt. N. Y. Graphic 1966
Bkl A

Georges Braque, 1882-1963

Brion, Marcel. Braque; tr. from the French by A. H. N. Molesworth. Abrams 1962
Bkl A

Leymarie, Jean. Braque; tr. by James Emmons. Skira 1961
Bkl A—SCPL

Russell, John. G. Braque. Doubleday 1960
Bkl A

COLLECTIONS

Flanner, Janet. Men and Monuments. Harper 1957
SCPL

Hilaire Germain Edgar Degas, 1834-1917

Foska, François. Degas: Biographical and Critical Studies; tr. by James Emmons. Skira 1954
SCPL

Halévy, Daniel. My Friend Degas; tr. and ed. by Mina Curtiss. Wesleyan Univ. 1964
Bkl A

COLLECTIONS

Rosenberg, Jakob. Great Draughtsmen from Pisanello to Picasso. Harvard Univ. 1959
SCPL

Wilenski, Reginald Howard. Modern French Painters. Harcourt 1949
SCPL

André Derain, 1880-1954

Diehl, Gaston. Derain; tr. from the French by A. P. H. Hamilton. Crown 1964
Bkl A

Raoul Dufy, 1877-1953

Lassaigne, Jacques. Dufy: Biographical and Critical Studies; tr. by James Emmons. Skira 1954
SCPL

Fernand Léger, 1881-1955

Delevoy, Robert L. Léger; tr. from the French by Stuart Gilbert. Skira 1962
Bkl A

Henri Matisse, 1869-1954

Escholier, Raymond. Matisse: A Portrait of the Artist and the Man; tr. by Geraldine and H. M. Colvile. Praeger 1960
Bkl A

Lassaigne, Jacques. Matisse: Biographical and Critical Study; tr. by Stuart Gilbert. Skira 1959
Bkl A—SCPL

Selz, Jean. Matisse; tr. from the French by A. P. H. Hamilton. Crown 1964
Bkl A—IndS(9-12)

COLLECTIONS

Flanner, Janet. Men and Monuments. Harper 1957
SCPL

Claude Monet, 1840-1926

Rouart, Denis. Claude Monet; tr. by James Emmons. Skira 1958
SCPL

Taillandier, Yvon. Monet; tr. from the French by A. P. H. Hamilton. Crown 1963
Bkl A

Weekes, C. P. The Invincible Monet. Appleton 1960
Bkl A

Georges Rouault, 1871-1958

Courthion, Pierre. Georges Rouault. Abrams 1962
Bkl A

Venturi, Lionello. Rouault: Biographical and Critical Study; tr. by James Emmons. Skira 1959
SCPL

Maurice de Vlaminck, 1876-1958

Selz, Jean. Vlaminck; tr. from the French by Graham Snell. Crown 1963
Bkl A

German—16th century

Lucas Cranach, 1472-1553

Ruhmer, E. Cranach; tr. from the German by Joan Spencer. Phaidon 1963
Bkl A

Albrecht Dürer, 1471-1528

Grote, Ludwig. Dürer: Biographical and Critical Study; tr. from the German by Helga Harrison. Skira 1965
Bkl A

Levey, Michael. Dürer. Norton 1964
Bkl A&Y

Ripley, Elizabeth. Dürer: A Biography. Lippincott 1958
BBJH—CC(7-9)—YR

Steck, Max. Dürer and His World; tr. from the German by J. Maxwell Brownjohn. Studio 1964
Bkl A&Y—IndS(12)

PAINTERS

German—16th century

Albrecht Dürer—Continued

Waetzoldt, Wilhelm. Dürer and His Times; tr. by R. H. Boothroyd. Phaidon 1955
SCPL

COLLECTIONS

Rosenberg, Jakob. Great Draughtsmen from Pisanello to Picasso. Harvard Univ. 1959
SCPL

German—20th century

Max Beckmann, 1884-1950

Selz, Peter and others. Max Beckmann. Doubleday 1964
Bkl A

Italian

COLLECTIONS

Berenson, Bernard. Italian Pictures of the Renaissance: A List of the Principal Artists and Their Works, with an Index of Places. 2v. Phaidon 1963
SCPL

Italian—14th century

Giotto di Bondone, 1276?-1337?

Battisti, Eugenio. Giotto: Biographical and Critical Study; tr. by James Emmons. Skira 1960
Bkl A—SCPL
Semenzato, Camillo. Giotto. Barnes 1964
IndS(9-12)

Italian—15th century

Sandro Botticelli, 1447?-1510

Argan, Giulio Carlo. Botticelli: Biographical and Critical Study; tr. by James Emmons. Skira 1957
SCPL
Ripley, Elizabeth. Botticelli: A Biography. Lippincott 1960
Bkl C(6-9)—CC(6-9)—JH—YR

COLLECTIONS

Pater, Walter Horatio. Renaissance Studies in Art and Poetry. Modern Lib.
SCPL

Giovanni da Fiesole, 1387-1455

Argan, Giulio Carlo. Fra Angelico: Biographical and Critical Study; tr. by James Emmons. Skira 1955
SCPL

Piero della Francesca, 1416?-1492

Venturi, Lionello. Piero della Francesca: Biographical and Critical Studies; tr. by James Emmons. Skira 1954
SCPL

Antonio Pisano, known as Pisanello, 1395-1455

Sindona, Enio. Pisanello; tr. from the Italian by John Ross. Abrams 1964
Bkl A

COLLECTIONS

Rosenberg, Jakob. Great Draughtsmen from Pisanello to Picasso. Harvard Univ. 1959
SCPL

Leonardo da Vinci, 1452-1519

Almedingen, E. M. The Young Leonardo da Vinci. Roy 1963
ESLC
Clark, Sir Kenneth McKenzie. Leonardo da Vinci: An Account of His Development as an Artist. Cambridge 1952
GR—SCPL
Friedenthal, Richard. Leonardo da Vinci: A Pictorial Biography; tr. by Margaret Shenfield. Studio 1960
Bkl A&Y
Gillette, Henry S. Leonardo da Vinci, Pathfinder of Science. Watts 1962
Bkl C(6-9)
Hahn, Emily. Leonardo da Vinci. Random House 1956
ESLC—JH—SCHS
Hart, Ivor Blashka. The World of Leonardo da Vinci, Man of Science, Engineer and Dreamer of Flight. Viking 1962
Bkl A&Y
Heydenreich, Ludwig Heinrich. Leonardo da Vinci. Macmillan 1954
SCPL
Horizon Magazine. Leonardo da Vinci, by Jay Williams. Am. Heritage 1965
Bkl Y&C—ESLC—IndS(10-12)
Jaspers, Karl. Three Essays: Leonardo, Descartes, Max Weber; tr. by Ralph Manheim. Harcourt 1964
Bkl A
Newcomb, Covelle. Leonardo da Vinci, Prince of Painters. Dodd 1965
Bkl Y(7-10)
Noble, Iris. Leonardo da Vinci: The Universal Genius. Norton 1965
ESLC—IndJ(6-9)—JH
Ripley, Elizabeth. Leonardo da Vinci: A Biography. Walck 1952
BBJH—BY—CC(7-9)—ESLC—JH—SCHS
Thomas, John. Leonardo da Vinci. Criterion Bks 1957
YR
Vallentin, Antonina. Leonardo da Vinci: The Tragic Pursuit of Perfection; tr. by E. W. Dickes. Viking 1952
SCPL

PAINTERS

Italian—15th century

Leonardo da Vinci—Continued

Vinci, Leonardo da. Leonardo da Vinci: Life and Work, Paintings and Drawings, with the Leonardo Biography by Vasari. Doubleday 1959
SCPL

COLLECTIONS

Pater, Walter Horatio. Renaissance Studies in Art and Poetry. Modern Lib.
SCPL

Rosenberg, Jakob. Great Draughtsmen from Pisanello to Picasso. Harvard Univ. 1959
SCPL

Italian—16th century

Michelangelo Merisi da Caravaggio, 1569?-1609

Berenson, Bernard. Caravaggio: His Incongruity and His Fame. Macmillan 1954
SCPL

COLLECTIONS

Venturi, Lionello. Four Steps Toward Modern Art. Columbia Univ. 1956
SCPL

Giorgione da Castelfranco (Giorgio Barbarelli) 1478-1510

Baldass, Ludwig von. Giorgione; tr. from the German by J. Maxwell Brownjohn. Abrams 1965
Bkl A

COLLECTIONS

Venturi, Lionello. Four Steps Toward Modern Art. Columbia Univ. 1956
SCPL

Lorenzo Lotto, 1480?-1556?

Berenson, Bernard. Lorenzo Lotto. Phaidon 1956
SCPL

Michelangelo Buonarroti, 1475-1564

Brandes, Georg Morris Cohen. Michelangelo; tr. by Heinz Norden. Ungar 1963
Bkl A

De Tolnay, Charles. The Art and Thought of Michelangelo. Pantheon 1964
Bkl A

Michelangelo Buonarroti. I, Michelangelo, Sculptor: An Autobiography through Letters; ed. by Irving and Jean Stone; tr. by Charles Speroni. Doubleday 1962
Bkl A

Michelangelo Buonarroti. Michelangelo: Paintings, Sculptures, Architecture, by Ludwig Goldscheider. Phaidon 1962
SCPL

Morgan, Charles H. The Life of Michelangelo. Reynal 1960
Bkl A—BY—GR

Peck, Anne Merriman. Wings of an Eagle. Hawthorn 1963
IndS(9-11)

Ripley, Elizabeth. Michelangelo: A Biography. Walck 1953
CC(7-9)—ESLC—JH—SCHS

Schott, Rudolf. Michelangelo; tr. from the German by Constance McNab. Abrams 1965
Bkl A&Y

Stone, Irving. The Agony and the Ecstasy: A Novel of Michelangelo. Doubleday 1961 (Fiction)
Bkl A—SCHS

Stone, Irving. The Great Adventure of Michelangelo. Doubleday 1965 (Fiction)
JH

Symonds, J. A. Life of Michelangelo. Modern Lib.
GR

COLLECTIONS

Pater, Walter Horatio. Renaissance Studies in Art and Poetry. Modern Lib.
SCPL

Raphael, 1483-1520

Ripley, Elizabeth. Raphael: A Biography. Lippincott 1961
Bkl C(7-9)&Y—BY—CC—JH—SCHS

COLLECTIONS

Rosenberg, Jakob. Great Draughtsmen from Pisanello to Picasso. Harvard Univ. 1959
SCPL

Tintoretto, 1518-1594

Tietze, Hans. Tintoretto: The Paintings and Drawings. Phaidon 1948
SCPL

Titian, 1477-1576

Ripley, Elizabeth. Titian: A Biography. Lippincott 1962
Bkl C(6-9)&Y—CC(7-9)—JH

Giorgio Vasari, 1512-1574

Rud, Einar. Vasari's Life and Lives: The First Art Historian. Van Nostrand 1963
SCPL

Leonardo da Vinci, 1452-1519

Almedingen, E. M. The Young Leonardo da Vinci. Roy 1963
ESLC

PAINTERS

Italian—16th century

Leonardo da Vinci—Continued

Clark, Sir Kenneth McKenzie. Leonardo da Vinci: An Account of His Development as an Artist. Cambridge 1952
GR—SCPL

Friedenthal, Richard. Leonardo da Vinci: A Pictorial Biography; tr. by Margaret Shenfield. Studio 1960
Bkl A&Y

Hahn, Emily. Leonardo da Vinci. Random House 1956
ESLC—JH—SCHS

Heydenreich, Ludwig Heinrich. Leonardo da Vinci. Macmillan 1954
SCPL

Horizon Magazine. Leonardo da Vinci, by Jay Williams. Am. Heritage 1965
Bkl Y&C—ESLC—IndS(10-12)

Jaspers, Karl. Three Essays: Leonardo, Descartes, Max Weber; tr. by Ralph Manheim. Harcourt 1964
Bkl A

Newcomb, Covelle. Leonardo da Vinci, Prince of Painters. Dodd 1965
Bkl Y(7-10)

Noble, Iris. Leonardo da Vinci: The Universal Genius. Norton 1965
ESLC—IndJ(6-9)—JH

Ripley, Elizabeth. Leonardo da Vinci: A Biography. Walck 1952
BBJH—BY—CC(7-9)—ESLC—JH—SCHS

Thomas, John. Leonardo da Vinci. Criterion Bks 1957
YR

Vallentin, Antonina. Leonardo da Vinci: The Tragic Pursuit of Perfection; tr. by E. W. Dickes. Viking 1952
king 1952
SCPL

Vinci, Leonardo da. Leonardo da Vinci: Life and Work, Paintings and Drawings, with the Leonardo Biography by Vasari. Doubleday 1959
SCPL

COLLECTIONS

Pater, Walter Horatio. Renaissance Studies in Art and Poetry. Modern Lib.
SCPL

Rosenberg, Jakob. Great Draughtsmen from Pisanello to Picasso. Harvard Univ. 1959
SCPL

Italian—17th century

Michelangelo Merisi da Caravaggio, 1569-1609

Berenson, Bernard. Caravaggio: His Incongruity and His Fame. Macmillan 1954
SCPL

COLLECTIONS

Venturi, Lionello. Four Steps Toward Modern Art. Columbia Univ. 1956
SCPL

Italian—20th century

Amedeo Modigliani, 1884-1920

Roy, Claude. Modigliani; tr. by James Emmons and Stuart Gilbert. Skira 1958
SCPL

Salmon, André. Modigliani: A Memoir; tr. by Dorothy and Randolph Weaver. Putnam 1961
Bkl A

Mexican—20th century

José Clemente Orozco, 1883-1949

Orozco, José Clemente. An Autobiography; tr. by Robert C. Stephenson. Univ. of Tex. 1962
Bkl A

Reed, Alma. Orozco. Oxford 1956
SCPL

Diego Rivera, 1886-1957

Wolfe, Bertram David. The Fabulous Life of Diego Rivera. Stein & Day 1963
Bkl A

Norwegian—20th century

Edvard Munch, 1863-1944

Langaard, Johan Henrik and Revold, Reidar. Edvard Munch: Masterpieces from the Artist's Collection in the Munch Museum in Oslo; tr. from the German by Michael Bullock. McGraw 1964
Bkl A

Russian—20th century

Marc Chagall, 1887-

Brion, Marcel. Chagall; tr. from the French by A. H. N. Molesworth. Abrams 1962
Bkl A

Cassou, Jean. Chagall; tr. from the French by Alisa Jaffa. Praeger 1966
Bkl A

Cogniat, Raymond. Chagall; tr. from the French by Anne Ross. Crown 1965
Bkl A

Erben, Walter. Marc Chagall; tr. by Michael Bullock. Praeger 1957
SCPL

Freund, Miriam Kottler. Jewels for a Crown: The Story of the Chagall Windows. McGraw 1963
Bkl C(6-9)&A&Y—CC—ESLC—YR

Meyer, Franz. Marc Chagall; tr. from the German by Robert Allen. Abrams 1964
Bkl A

PAINTERS

Russian—20th century

Marc Chagall—Continued

Venturi, Lionello. Chagall: Biographical and Critical Study; tr. by S. J. C. Harrison and James Emmons. Skira 1956
SCPL

Wassily Kandinsky, 1866-1944

Brion, Marcel. Kandinsky. Abrams 1962
Bkl A

Dollman, Cornelius. Kandinsky. Barnes 1964
IndS(9-12)

Lassaigne, Jacques. Kandinsky: Biographical and Critical Study; tr. from the French by H. S. B. Harrison. Skira 1964
Bkl A

Spanish—16th century

El Greco, 1548?-1614?

Guinard, Paul. El Greco: Biographical and Critical Study; tr. by James Emmons. Skira 1956
SCPL

Spanish—17th century

Juan de Pareja, 1606-1670

Treviño, Elizabeth (Borton). I, Juan de Pareja. Farrar 1965 (Fiction)
Bkl C(6-10)&Y—ESLC

Diego Rodríguez de Silva y Velázquez, 1599-1660

Lafuente Ferrari, Enrique. Velázquez: Biographical and Critical Study; tr. by James Emmons. Skira 1960
Bkl A—SCPL

Ripley, Elizabeth. Velásquez: A Biography. Lippincott 1965
Bkl C(6-9)&Y—ESLC

Treviño, Elizabeth (Borton). I, Juan de Pareja. Farrar 1965 (Fiction)
Bkl C(6-10)&Y—ESLC

Spanish—18th century

Francisco José de Goya y Lucientes, 1746-1828

Gassier, Pierre. Goya: Biographical and Critical Study; tr. by James Emmons. Skira 1955
SCPL

Gudiol, José. Goya; tr. by Priscilla Muller. Abrams 1965
Bkl A

Lassaigne, Jacques. Goya; tr. by Rosamund Frost. Macmillan 1948
SCPL

Ripley, Elizabeth. Goya: A Biography. Walck 1956
AB—CC(6-9)—ESLC—JH—SCHS

COLLECTIONS

Venturi, Lionello. Modern Painters. Scribner 1947
SCPL

Spanish—20th century

Salvador Dalí, 1904-

Cowles, Fleur. The Case of Salvador Dalí. Little 1960
Bkl A

Dalí, Salvador. Diary of a Genius; tr. from the French by Richard Howard. Doubleday 1965
Bkl A

Joan Miró, 1893-

Dupin, Jacques. Miró; tr. from the French by Norbert Guterman. Abrams 1962
Bkl A

Lassaigne, Jacques. Miró: Biographical and Critical Study; tr. by Stuart Gilbert. Skira 1963
Bkl A

Pablo Picasso, 1881-

Buchheim, Lothar-Günther. Picasso: A Pictorial Biography. Studio 1959
Bkl A

Duncan, David Douglas. Picasso's Picassos. Harper 1961
Bkl A—SCPL

Duncan, David Douglas. Private World of Pablo Picasso. Harper 1958
SCPL

Elgar, Frank. Picasso: A Study of His Work, by Frank Elgar: A Biographical Study, by Robert Maillard. Praeger 1956
SCPL

Gilot, Françoise and Lake, Carlton. Life with Picasso. McGraw 1964
Bkl A

Jaffé, Hans Ludwig. Pablo Picasso; tr. by Norbert Guterman. Abrams 1964
Bkl A

Kay, Helen. Henri's Hands for Pablo Picasso. Abelard-Schuman 1965 (Fiction)
ESLC

New York Museum of Modern Art. Picasso: Fifty Years of His Art, by A. H. Barr, Jr. Mus. of Modern Art 1946
SCPL

Raynal, Maurice. Picasso: Biographical and Critical Studies; tr. by James Emmons. Skira 1953
SCPL

Ripley, Elizabeth. Picasso: A Biography. Lippincott 1959
CC(7-9)—ESLC—JH—SCHS

PAINTERS

Spanish—20th century

Pablo Picasso—Continued

Vallentin, Antonina. Picasso. Doubleday 1963
Bkl A

COLLECTIONS

Flanner, Janet. Men and Monuments. Harper 1957
SCPL

Rosenberg, Jakob. Great Draughtsmen from Pisanello to Picasso. Harvard Univ. 1959
SCPL

Swiss—19th century

Karl Bodmer, 1809-1893

COLLECTIONS

Hollmann, Clide. Five Artists of the Old West. Hastings House 1965
ESLC

Swiss—20th century

Paul Klee, 1879-1940

Grohmann, Will. Paul Klee. Abrams 1954
SCPL

Klee, Paul. The Diaries of Paul Klee; ed. by Felix Klee. Univ. of Calif. 1964
Bkl A—IndS(11-12)

Ponente, Nello. Klee: Biographical and Critical Study; tr. by James Emmons. Skira 1960
Bkl A—SCPL

San Lazzaro, Gualtiere di. Klee: A Study of His Life and Work; tr. by Stuart Hood. Praeger 1957
SCPL

PALEONTOLOGISTS

American—19th century

Edward Drinker Cope, 1840-1897

Plate, Robert. The Dinosaur Hunters: Othniel C. Marsh and Edward D. Cope. McKay 1964
ESLC—IndS(9-12)

Othniel Charles Marsh, 1831-1899

Plate, Robert. The Dinosaur Hunters: Othniel C. Marsh and Edward D. Cope. McKay 1964
ESLC—IndS(9-12)

English—20th century

Marie Charlotte Carmichael Stopes, 1880-1958

Briant, Keith. Passionate Paradox: The Life of Marie Stopes. Norton 1962
Bkl A

French—20th century

Pierre Teilhard de Chardin, 1881-1955

Corte, Nicolas. Pierre Teilhard de Chardin: His Life and Spirit; tr. by Martin Jarrett-Kerr. Macmillan 1960
Bkl A

Cuénot, Claude. Teilhard de Chardin: A Biographical Study; tr. by Vincent Colimore; ed. by René Hague. Helicon Press 1965
Bkl A

De Terra, Helmut. Memories of Teilhard de Chardin; tr. from the German by J. Maxwell Brownjohn. Harper 1965
Bkl A

Grenet, Paul. Teilhard de Chardin: The Man and His Theories; tr. from the French by R. A. Rudorff. Ericksson 1966
Bkl A

Lubac, Henri de. Teilhard de Chardin: The Man and His Meaning; tr. by René Hague. Hawthorn 1965
Bkl A

Rabut, Olivier A. Teilhard de Chardin: A Critical Study. Sheed 1961
Bkl A

Teilhard de Chardin, Pierre. The Making of a Mind: Letters from a Soldier-Priest, 1914-1919; tr. from the French by René Hague. Harper 1965
Bkl A

PATHOLOGISTS

American—20th century

Karl Landsteiner, 1868-1943

COLLECTIONS

Sterne, Emma (Gelders). Blood Brothers: Four Men of Science. Knopf 1959
Bkl C(7-9)—JH

John Robbins Mohler, 1875-1952

COLLECTIONS

De Kruif, Paul Henry. Hunger Fighters. Harcourt 1928
BBHS—SCHS—SCPL—3000

English—20th century

Sir Bernard Spilsbury, 1877-1947

Browne, D. G. Scalpel of Scotland Yard: The Life of Sir Bernard Spilsbury. Dutton 1952
SCPL

PATRIOTS

See Statesmen

PEDIATRICIANS

See Physicians

PENOLOGISTS

American—20th century

Miriam Van Waters, 1887-

Rowles, Burton J. The Lady at Box 99: The Story of Miriam Van Waters. Seabury 1962
Bkl A

PETROLEUM INDUSTRY WORKERS

American—19th century

Edwin Laurentine Drake, 1819-1880

Wolfe, Louis. Drake Drills for Oil. Putnam 1965
ESLC

American—20th century

Jean Paul Getty, 1892-

Getty, Jean Paul. My Life and Fortunes. Duell 1963
Bkl A

Iranian—20th century

Nubar Sarkis Gulbenkian, 1896-

Gulbenkian, Nubar Sarkis. Portrait in Oil: The Autobiography of Nubar Gulbenkian. Simon & Schuster 1965
Bkl A

PHILANTHROPISTS

American—19th century

Andrew Carnegie, 1835-1919

Carnegie, Andrew. Autobiography. Houghton 1920
SCPL

Harlow, Alvin Fay. Andrew Carnegie. Messner 1953
SCHS

Judson, Clara Ingram. Andrew Carnegie. Follett 1964
CC(5-7)—JH

Shippen, Katherine B. Andrew Carnegie and the Age of Steel. Random House 1958
CC(5-7)—ESLC

Peter Cooper, 1791-1883

Gurko, Miriam. The Lives and Times of Peter Cooper. Crowell 1959
Bkl Y&C(7-10)—BY—CC(7-9)—ESLC

Dorothea Lynde Dix, 1802-1887

Baker, Rachel. Angel of Mercy: The Story of Dorothea Lynde Dix. Messner 1955
BY—SCHS—YR

Samuel Gridley Howe, 1801-1876

Meltzer, Milton. A Light in the Dark: The Life of Samuel Gridley Howe. Crowell 1964
Bkl C(6-9)&Y—CC—ESLC

John Davison Rockefeller, 1839-1937

Abels, Jules. The Rockefeller Billions: The Story of the World's Most Stupendous Fortune. Macmillan 1965
Bkl A—IndS(11-12)

Nevins, Allan. John D. Rockefeller; a one-volume abridgement by William Greenleaf of Study in Power. Scribner 1959
SCPL—3000

Pyle, Tom and Day, Beth (Feagles). Pocantico: Fifty Years on the Rockefeller Domain. Duell 1964
Bkl A

American—20th century

Minnie (Schafer) Guggenheimer, 1881-1966

Untermeyer, Sophie (Guggenheimer) and Williamson, Alix. Mother Is Minnie. Doubleday 1960
Bkl A

Charles Stewart Mott, 1875-

Young, Clarence H. and Quinn, William A. Foundation for Living: The Story of Charles Stewart Mott and Flint. McGraw 1963
Bkl A

John Davison Rockefeller, 1839-1937

Abels, Jules. The Rockefeller Billions: The Story of the World's Most Stupendous Fortune. Macmillan 1965
Bkl A—IndS(11-12)

Carr, Albert H. Z. John D. Rockefeller's Secret Weapon. McGraw 1962
Bkl A

Manchester, William R. A Rockefeller Family Portrait: From John D. to Nelson. Little 1959
BY—SCPL

Nevins, Allan. John D. Rockefeller; a one-volume abridgement by William Greenleaf of Study in Power. Scribner 1959
SCPL—3000

Pyle, Tom and Day, Beth (Feagles). Pocantico: Fifty Years on the Rockefeller Domain. Duell 1964
Bkl A

John D. Rockefeller, Jr., 1874-1960

Fosdick, Raymond Blaine. John D. Rockefeller, Jr.: A Portrait. Harper 1956
SCPL

PHILANTHROPISTS

American—20th century—*Continued*

Nelson Aldrich Rockefeller, 1908-

Morris, Joe Alex. Those Rockefeller Brothers: An Informal Biography of Five Extraordinary Young Men. Harper 1953
SCPL

Swedish—19th century

Alfred Bernhard Nobel, 1833-1896

Bergengren, Erik. Alfred Nobel: The Man and His Work. Nelson 1962
BY

Meyer, Edith Patterson. Dynamite and Peace. Little 1958
AB(5up)—BBJH—CC(7-9)—JH—SCHS

PHILOSOPHERS

See also Religious Leaders

COLLECTIONS

Jaspers, Karl. The Great Philosophers: v. 1, The Foundations; ed. by Hannah Arendt; tr. by Ralph Manheim. Harcourt 1962
Bkl A—SCPL
Saint Augustine; Buddha; Confucius; Jesus Christ; Immanuel Kant; Plato; Socrates

Jaspers, Karl. The Great Philosophers: v. 2, The Original Thinkers; ed. by Hannah Arendt; tr. by Ralph Manheim. Harcourt 1966
Bkl A
Anaximander; Saint Anselm; Heraclitus; Lao-tzu; Nagarjuna; Nicholas of Cusa; Parmenides; Plotinus; Benedict Spinoza

Minkin, Jacob Samuel. The Shaping of the Modern Mind: The Life and Thought of the Great Jewish Philosophers. Yoseloff 1963
Bkl A

Neill, Thomas Patrick. Makers of the Modern Mind. Bruce 1949
SCPL

Thomas, Henry and Thomas, Dana Lee. Living Adventures in Philosophy. Hanover House 1954
SCPL

Thomas, Henry and Thomas, Dana Lee. Living Biographies of Great Philosophers. Garden City 1959
SCPL

Tomlin, Eric Walter Frederick. Great Philosophers: The Western World. Wyn 1952
SCPL

American

COLLECTIONS

Van Wesep, H. B. Seven Sages: The Story of American Philosophy. Longmans 1960
SCPL
John Dewey; Ralph Waldo Emerson; Benjamin Franklin; William James; Charles Sanders Peirce; George Santayana; Alfred North Whitehead

American—18th century

Benjamin Franklin, 1706-1790

Aldridge, Alfred Owen. Benjamin Franklin: Philosopher & Man. Lippincott 1965
Bkl A&Y

American Heritage. The Many Worlds of Benjamin Franklin, by Frank R. Donovan. Am. Heritage 1963
Bkl C(6-9)&Y—CC(6-9)—ESLC—IndJ(6-9)—JH—SCHS—YR

Cohen, I. B. Benjamin Franklin: His Contribution to the American Tradition. Bobbs 1953
SCPL

Cousins, Margaret. Ben Franklin of Old Philadelphia. Random House 1952
CC(4-7)—SCHS

Daugherty, James. Poor Richard. Viking 1941
BBEL—BBJH—CC(7-9)—JH—SCHS

Eaton, Jeanette. That Lively Man, Ben Franklin. Morrow 1948
BBJH—CC(5-7)—JH—SCHS

Franklin, Benjamin. Autobiographical Writings; ed. by Carl Van Doren. Viking 1945
SCPL

Franklin, Benjamin. Autobiography. Univ. of Calif.; Modern Lib.; Houghton; Harper; Dutton; etc.
BY—CA—CC(7-9)—GR—SCHS—SCPL—3000

Franklin, Benjamin. The Autobiography, and Other Writings of Benjamin Franklin. Dodd 1963
SCHS

Franklin, Benjamin. The Autobiography of Benjamin Franklin; ed. by Leonard W. Labaree and others. Yale Univ. 1964
JH—SCPL

Franklin, Benjamin. The Benjamin Franklin Papers; ed. by Frank Donovan. Dodd 1962
Bkl A&Y—SCHS

Judson, Clara (Ingram). Benjamin Franklin. Follett 1957
AB(5-7)—BBEL(6-8)—BBJH—CC(5-7)—ESLC—JH

McKown, Robin. Benjamin Franklin. Putnam 1963
Bkl C(7-9)&Y

PHILOSOPHERS

American—18th century

Benjamin Franklin—Continued

Sayre, Robert F. The Examined Self: Benjamin Franklin, Henry Adams, Henry James. Princeton Univ. 1964
Bkl A

Van Doren, Carl Clinton. Benjamin Franklin. Viking 1956
BBHS—SCHS—SCPL—3000

COLLECTIONS

Van Wesep, H. B. Seven Sages: The Story of American Philosophy. Longmans 1960
SCPL

American—19th century

John Dewey, 1859-1952

COLLECTIONS

Van Wesep, H. B. Seven Sages: The Story of American Philosophy. Longmans 1960
SCPL

Ralph Waldo Emerson, 1803-1882

COLLECTIONS

Van Wesep, H. B. Seven Sages: The Story of American Philosophy. Longmans 1960
SCPL

William James, 1842-1910

James, William. Selected Letters; ed. by Elizabeth Hardwick. Farrar 1961
Bkl A

Matthiessen, Francis Otto. The James Family: Including Selections from the Writing of Henry James, Senior, William, Henry, & Alice James. Knopf 1947
GR—SCPL

COLLECTIONS

Van Wesep, H. B. Seven Sages: The Story of American Philosophy. Longmans 1960
SCPL

Charles Sanders Peirce, 1839-1914

COLLECTIONS

Van Wesep, H. B. Seven Sages: The Story of American Philosophy. Longmans 1960
SCPL

Josiah Royce, 1855-1916

Buranelli, Vincent. Josiah Royce. Twayne 1963
Bkl A

American—20th century

Morris Raphael Cohen, 1880-1947

Rosenfield, Leonora Davidson (Cohen). Portrait of a Philosopher: Morris R. Cohen. Harcourt 1962
Bkl A

John Dewey, 1859-1952

COLLECTIONS

Van Wesep, H. B. Seven Sages: The Story of American Philosophy. Longmans 1960
SCPL

Josiah Royce, 1855-1916

Buranelli, Vincent. Josiah Royce. Twayne 1963
Bkl A

George Santayana, 1863-1952

Cory, Daniel. Santayana: The Later Years: A Portrait with Letters. Braziller 1963
Bkl A—SCPL

Santayana, George. Persons and Places. 3v. Scribner 1944-1953 or 3v. in 1 Scribner 1963
IndS(12)—SCPL

Schilpp, Paul Arthur, ed. Philosophy of George Santayana. Tudor 1951
SCPL

COLLECTIONS

Van Wesep, H. B. Seven Sages: The Story of American Philosophy. Longmans 1960
SCPL

Alfred North Whitehead, 1861-1947

Schilpp, Paul Arthur, ed. Philosophy of Alfred North Whitehead. Tudor 1951
SCPL

COLLECTIONS

Van Wesep, H. B. Seven Sages: The Story of American Philosophy. Longmans 1960
SCPL

Chinese—6th century B.C.

Lao-tzu, 604-531 B.C.

COLLECTIONS

Jaspers, Karl. The Great Philosophers: v. 2, The Original Thinkers; ed. by Hannah Arendt; tr. by Ralph Manheim. Harcourt 1966
Bkl A

Chinese—5th century B.C.

Confucius, 551-478 B.C.

Creel, Herrlee Glessner. Confucius: The Man and the Myth. Day 1949
SCPL

PHILOSOPHERS

Chinese—5th century B.C.

Confucius—Continued

COLLECTIONS

Jaspers, Karl. The Great Philosophers: v. 1, The Foundations; ed. by Hannah Arendt; tr. by Ralph Manheim. Harcourt 1962
Bkl A—SCPL

Danish—19th century

Søren Aabye Kierkegaard, 1813-1855

Kierkegaard, Søren Aabye. The Last Years: Journals, 1853-1855; ed. and tr. by Ronald Gregor Smith. Harper 1965
Bkl A

Dutch—17th century

Benedict Spinoza, 1632-1677

COLLECTIONS

Jaspers, Karl. The Great Philosophers: v. 2, The Original Thinkers; ed. by Hannah Arendt; tr. by Ralph Manheim. Harcourt 1966
Bkl A

English—11th century

Saint Anselm, 1033-1109

COLLECTIONS

Jaspers, Karl. The Great Philosophers: v. 2, The Original Thinkers; ed. by Hannah Arendt; tr. by Ralph Manheim. Harcourt 1966
Bkl A

English—17th century

Francis Bacon, Viscount St. Albans, 1561-1626

Anderson, Fulton H. Francis Bacon: His Career and His Thought. Univ. of Southern Calif. 1962
Bkl A

Bowen, Catherine (Drinker). Francis Bacon: The Temper of a Man. Little 1963
Bkl A&Y—IndS(11-12)—SCHS—SCPL

Eiseley, Loren C. Francis Bacon and the Modern Dilemma. Univ. of Neb. 1963
Bkl A

Edward Herbert, 1583-1648

Herbert, Edward. Autobiography of Edward, Lord Herbert of Cherbury.
CA

John Locke, 1632-1704

COLLECTIONS

Bainton, Roland Herbert. Travail of Religious Liberty: Nine Biographical Studies. Westminster 1951
SCPL

English—18th century

Jeremy Bentham, 1748-1832

Mack, Mary Peter. Jeremy Bentham: An Odyssey of Ideas. Columbia Univ. 1963
Bkl A

English—19th century

Jeremy Bentham, 1748-1832

Mack, Mary Peter. Jeremy Bentham: An Odyssey of Ideas. Columbia Univ. 1963
Bkl A

Thomas Hill Green, 1836-1882

Richter, Melvin. The Politics of Conscience: T. H. Green and His Age Harvard Univ. 1964
Bkl A

John Stuart Mill, 1806-1873

Mill, John Stuart. Autobiography. Columbia Univ.; Univ. of Ill.; etc.
GR—SCPL

English—20th century

Bertrand Arthur William Russell, 3rd Earl Russell, 1872-

Wood, Alan. Bertrand Russell—The Passionate Skeptic: A Biography. Simon & Schuster 1958
SCPL

Lancelot Law Whyte, 1896-

Whyte, Lancelot Law. Focus and Diversions. Braziller 1964
Bkl A

French—17th century

René Descartes, 1596-1650

Jaspers, Karl. Three Essays: Leonardo, Descartes, Max Weber; tr. by Ralph Manheim. Harcourt 1964
Bkl A

Blaise Pascal, 1623-1662

Steinmann, Jean. Pascal; tr. by Martin Turnell. Harcourt 1966
Bkl A

PHILOSOPHERS—*Continued*

French—18th century

Jean Jacques Rousseau, 1712-1778

Endore, S. Guy. Voltaire! Voltaire! A Novel. Simon & Schuster 1961 (Fiction)
Bkl A

Guéhenno, Jean. Jean-Jacques Rousseau: v. 1, 1712-1758; v. 2, 1758-1778; tr. from the French by John and Doreen Weightman. 2v. Columbia Univ. 1966
Bkl A

Rousseau, Jean Jacques. Confessions. Modern Lib.; Dutton; etc.
CA—GR—SCPL

Winwar, Frances. Jean-Jacques Rousseau: Conscience of an Era. Random House 1961
Bkl A

François Marie Arouet de Voltaire, 1694-1778

Endore, S. Guy. Voltaire! Voltaire! A Novel. Simon & Schuster 1961 (Fiction)
Bkl A

Mitford, Nancy. Voltaire in Love. Harper 1957
SCPL

Nixon, Edna. Voltaire and the Calas Case. Vanguard 1963
IndS(11-12)

French—20th century

Étienne Henry Gilson, 1884-

Gilson, Étienne Henry. The Philosopher and Theology; tr. from the French by Cécile Gilson. Random House 1962
Bkl A

Jacques Maritain, 1882-

Evans, Joseph William, ed. Jacques Maritain: The Man and His Achievement. Sheed 1963
Bkl A

Jean Paul Sartre, 1905-

Sartre, Jean Paul. The Words; tr. from the French by Bernard Frechtman. Braziller 1964
Bkl A

Albert Schweitzer, 1875-1965

Anderson, Erica. Albert Schweitzer's Gift of Friendship. Harper 1964
Bkl A&Y

Anderson, Erica. The Schweitzer Album: A Portrait in Words and Pictures. Harper 1965
Bkl A&Y

Anderson, Erica and Exman, Eugene. The World of Albert Schweitzer: A Book of Photographs. Harper 1955
BY—SCHS—SCPL

Berrill, Jacquelyn. Albert Schweitzer, Man of Mercy. Dodd 1956
BBJH—BY—JH

Cousins, Norman. Dr. Schweitzer of Lambaréné. Harper 1960
Bkl Y—SCHS—SCPL

Cousins, Norman. Lambaréné: Doctor Schweitzer and His People. Harper 1960
Bkl A&Y

Daniel, Anita. The Story of Albert Schweitzer. Random House 1957
CC—ESLC—JH—SCHS

Franck, Frederick. Days with Albert Schweitzer: A Lambaréné Landscape. Holt 1959
SCPL

Gollomb, Joseph. Albert Schweitzer: Genius in the Jungle. Vanguard 1949
BBEL(7-8)—BY—CC(7-9)—ESLC—JH—SCHS

Hagedorn, Hermann. Prophet in the Wilderness: The Story of Albert Schweitzer. Macmillan 1954
SCPL

Joy, Charles R. and Arnold, Melvin. The Africa of Albert Schweitzer. Harper 1958
SCPL

McKnight, Gerald. Verdict on Schweitzer: The Man behind the Legend of Lambaréné. Day 1964
Bkl A

Manton, Jo. The Story of Albert Schweitzer. Abelard-Schuman 1955
AB(7up)—BBEL(6)—CC—JH

Merrett, John. The True Story of Albert Schweitzer. Childrens Press 1964
IndJ(4-6)

Ostergaard Christensen, Lavrids. At Work with Albert Schweitzer; tr. from the Danish by F. H. Lyon. Beacon Press 1962
Bkl A

Payne, Pierre Stephen Robert. Three Worlds of Albert Schweitzer. Nelson 1957
SCHS—SCPL

Picht, Werner Robert Valentin. The Life and Thought of Albert Schweitzer; tr. from the German by Edward Fitzgerald. Harper 1964
Bkl A

Schweitzer, Albert. Memoirs of Childhood and Youth. Macmillan 1949
SCPL

Schweitzer, Albert. Out of My Life and Thought: An Autobiography; tr. by C. T. Campion. Holt 1949
BBHS—GR—SCPL—3000

PHILOSOPHERS

French—20th century

Albert Schweitzer—Continued

Seaver, George. Albert Schweitzer: Christian Revolutionary. Harper 1956
SCPL

Seaver, George. Albert Schweitzer: The Man and His Mind. Harper 1955
SCPL

Simon, Charlie May. All Men Are Brothers: A Portrait of Albert Schweitzer. Dutton 1956
AB(7-10)—BBJH—JH

Simone Weil, 1909-1943

Caboud, Jacques. Simone Weil: A Fellowship in Love. Channel 1965
Bkl A

Rees, Richard. Simone Weil: A Sketch for a Portrait. Southern Ill. Univ. 1966
Bkl A

German—15th century

Nicholas of Cusa, 1401-1464

COLLECTIONS

Jaspers, Karl. The Great Philosophers: v. 2, The Original Thinkers; ed. by Hannah Arendt; tr. by Ralph Manheim. Harcourt 1966
Bkl A

German—18th century

Immanuel Kant, 1724-1804

COLLECTIONS

Jaspers, Karl. The Great Philosophers: v. 1, The Foundations; ed. by Hannah Arendt; tr. by Ralph Manheim. Harcourt 1962
Bkl A—SCPL

German—19th century

Georg Wilhelm Friedrich Hegel, 1770-1831

Kaufmann, Walter Arnold. Hegel: Reinterpretation, Texts, and Commentary. Doubleday 1965
Bkl A

Friedrich Wilhelm Nietzsche, 1844-1900

Brinton, Clarence Crane. Nietzsche. Harvard Univ. 1941
SCPL

Greek—6th century B.C.

Anaximander, 611-547 B.C.

COLLECTIONS

Jaspers, Karl. The Great Philosophers: v. 2, The Original Thinkers; ed. by Hannah Arendt; tr. by Ralph Manheim. Harcourt 1966
Bkl A

Greek—5th century B.C.

Heraclitus, fl. 5th century B.C.

COLLECTIONS

Jaspers, Karl. The Great Philosophers: v. 2, The Original Thinkers; ed. by Hannah Arendt; tr. by Ralph Manheim. Harcourt 1966
Bkl A

Parmenides, fl. 5th century B.C.

COLLECTIONS

Jaspers, Karl. The Great Philosophers: v. 2, The Original Thinkers; ed. by Hannah Arendt; tr. by Ralph Manheim. Harcourt 1966
Bkl A

Socrates, 470?-399 B.C.

Anderson, Maxwell. Barefoot in Athens. Sloane 1951 (Play)
SCPL

Brun, Jean. Socrates; tr. by Douglas Scott. Walker & Co. 1963
Bkl A&Y

Mason, Cora. Socrates: The Man Who Dared to Ask. Beacon Press 1953
BY—SCHS

Silverberg, Robert. Socrates. Putnam 1965
Bkl Y(7-10)&C—IndS(9-11)—JH

COLLECTIONS

Jaspers, Karl. The Great Philosophers: v. 1, The Foundations; ed. by Hannah Arendt; tr. by Ralph Manheim. Harcourt 1962
Bkl A—SCPL

Thomas, Norman Mattoon. Great Dissenters. Norton 1961
Bkl A&Y

Greek—4th century B.C.

Aristotle, 384-322 B.C.

Downey, Glanville. Aristotle, Dean of Early Science. Watts 1962
Bkl Y&C—JH

Grene, Marjorie (Glicksman). A Portrait of Aristotle. Univ. of Chicago 1963
Bkl A

Plato, ?-347 B.C.

Shorey, Paul. What Plato Said. Univ. of Chicago 1957
SCPL

Taylor, Alfred Edward. Plato: the Man and His Work. Methuen 1949
SCPL

COLLECTIONS

Jaspers, Karl. The Great Philosophers: v. 1, The Foundations; ed. by Hannah Arendt; tr. by Ralph Manheim. Harcourt 1962
Bkl A—SCPL

PHILOSOPHERS—*Continued*

Italian—13th century

Saint Thomas Aquinas, 1225?-1274

Chesterton, Gilbert Keith. St. Thomas Aquinas. Sheed 1933
SCPL

D'Arcy, Martin Cyril. St. Thomas Aquinas. Clonmore 1953
SCPL

Mexican—20th century

José Vasconcelos, 1882-1959

Vasconcelos, José. A Mexican Ulysses: An Autobiography; tr. and abr. by W. Rex Crawford. Ind. Univ. 1963
Bkl

Roman—3rd century

Plotinus, 205?-270

COLLECTIONS

Jaspers, Karl. The Great Philosophers: v. 2, The Original Thinkers; ed. by Hannah Arendt; tr. by Ralph Manheim. Harcourt 1966
Bkl A

Russian—20th century

Nikolai Aleksandrovich Berdiaev, 1874-1948

Lowrie, Donald Alexander. Rebellious Prophet: A Life of Nicolai Berdyaev. Harper 1960
Bkl A

PHOTOGRAPHERS

COLLECTIONS

Newhall, Beaumont and Newhall, Nancy, ed. Masters of Photography. Braziller 1958
SCPL

Poole, Lynn and Poole, Gray. Scientists Who Work with Cameras. Dodd 1965
Bkl C(7-12)&Y—IndS(11-12)
Constantine John Alexopoulos; Harold Eugene Edgerton; Russell Hedley Morgan; and others

American

COLLECTIONS

Andrews, Ralph Warren. Picture Gallery Pioneers, 1850-1875. Superior Pub. 1964
Bkl A

American—19th century

Mathew B. Brady, 1823?-1896

Horan, James David. Mathew Brady: Historian with a Camera. Crown 1955
SCPL

Komroff, Manuel. Photographing History: Mathew Brady. Encyc. Britannica 1962
ESLC

William Henry Jackson, 1843-1942

Forsee, Aylesa. William Henry Jackson: Pioneer Photographer of the West. Viking 1964
ESLC

Miller, Helen Markley. Lens on the West: The Story of William Henry Jackson. Doubleday 1966
ESLC

Alfred Stieglitz, 1864-1946

Norman, Dorothy. Alfred Stieglitz: Introduction to an American Seer. Duell 1960
Bkl A

American—20th century

Ansel Easton Adams, 1902-

Newhall, Nancy (Wynne). Ansel Adams: v. 1, The Eloquent Light. Sierra Club 1964
Bkl A

Margaret Bourke-White, 1905-

Bourke-White, Margaret. Portrait of Myself. Simon & Schuster 1963
Bkl A&Y—IndS(10-12)—SCHS—SCPL

Dickey Chapelle, 1918-1965

Chapelle, Dickey. What's a Woman Doing Here? A Reporter's Report on Herself. Morrow 1962
Bkl A&Y—BY

David Douglas Duncan, 1916-

Duncan, David Douglas. Yankee Nomad: A Photographic Odyssey. Holt 1966
Bkl A

Martin Elmer Johnson, 1884-1937

Johnson, Osa Helen (Leighty). I Married Adventure: The Lives and Adventures of Martin and Osa Johnson. Lippincott 1940
BBHS—BY—SCHS—SCPL

Johnson, Osa Helen (Leighty). Last Adventure: The Martin Johnsons in Borneo; ed. by Pascal James Imperato. Morrow 1966
Bkl A&Y

Carl M. Mydans, 1907-

Mydans, Carl M. More than Meets the Eye. Harper 1959
SCPL

Gordon Parks, 1912-

Parks, Gordon. A Choice of Weapons. Harper 1966
Bkl A&Y

PHOTOGRAPHERS

American—20th century—*Continued*

Edward Steichen, 1879-

New York Museum of Modern Art. Steichen the Photographer. Mus. of Modern Art 1961
Bkl A

Steichen, Edward. A Life in Photography. Doubleday 1963
Bkl A—SCPL

Alfred Stieglitz, 1864-1946

Norman, Dorothy. Alfred Stieglitz: Introduction to an American Seer. Duell 1960
Bkl A

Belgian—20th century

Armand Denis, 1896-

Denis, Armand. On Safari. Dutton 1963
Bkl A&Y—IndS(10-12)—YR

English—20th century

Ronald Austing, 1932?-

Austing, Ronald. I Went to the Woods: The Autobiography of a Bird Photographer. Coward-McCann 1964
Bkl A&Y

PHYSICALLY HANDICAPPED

See also Blind; Deaf; Siamese Twins; Victims of Arthritis; Victims of Cerebral Palsy; Victims of Leprosy; Victims of Polio

COLLECTIONS

Gelfand, Ravina and Patterson, Letha. They Wouldn't Quit. Lerner Publications 1962
AB(5-9)
Al Capp; Alexander Procofieff de Seversky; and others

American

COLLECTIONS

Boynick, David King. Champions by Setback: Athletes Who Overcame Physical Handicaps. Crowell 1954
SCHS
William Bonthron; Charles Albert Boswell; James J. Braddock; Glenn Cunningham; John Hackett; Martin Whiteford Marion; Frank Holten Norris; Hamilton Farrar Richardson; Archie San Romani; George Monroe Woolf

American—20th century

Louise (Maxwell) Baker, 1909-

Baker, Louise (Maxwell). Out on a Limb. McGraw 1946
BBHS—BY—SCHS—SCPL

John Gunther, 1929-1947

Gunther, John. Death Be Not Proud: A Memoir. Harper 1949
BBHS—BY—SCHS—SCPL

Katharine (Butler) Hathaway, 1890-1942

Hathaway, Katharine (Butler). Little Locksmith. Coward-McCann 1943
SCPL

Jill Kinmont, 1936?-

Valens, Evans G. A Long Way Up: The Story of Jill Kinmont. Harper 1966
Bkl A&Y

Cole Porter, 1893-1964

Ewen, David. The Cole Porter Story. Holt 1965
Bkl Y&C—IndS(9-12)

Edward Sheldon, 1886-1946

Barnes, Eric Wollencott. The Man Who Lived Twice: The Biography of Edward Sheldon. Scribner 1956
BY—SCPL

Australian—20th century

Alan John ("Jock") Marshall, 1911-1967

Marshall, Alan. I Can Jump Puddles. World 1957
BY—YR

Austrian—20th century

Edeltraud Fulda, 1916-

Fulda, Edeltraud. And I Shall Be Healed: The Autobiography of a Woman Miraculously Cured at Lourdes; tr. by John Coombs. Simon & Schuster 1961
Bkl A

English—20th century

Douglas Bader, 1910-

Brickhill, Paul. Reach for the Sky: The Story of Douglas Bader, Legless Ace of the Battle of Britain. Norton 1954
BBHS—BY—SCHS—SCPL

W. N. P. Barbellion, 1889-1919

Barbellion, W. N. P. The Journal of a Disappointed Man. Penguin 1919
GR

Indian—20th century

Mary Verghese, 1925-

Wilson, Dorothy Clarke. Take My Hands: The Remarkable Story of Dr. Mary Verghese. McGraw 1963
Bkl A&Y

PHYSICIANS

See also Anatomists; Anesthetists; Coroners; Dentists; Neurologists; Occupational Therapists; Pathologists; Physiologists; Physiotherapists; Psychiatrists; Radiologists; Surgeons; Veterinarians; Virologists

COLLECTIONS

Chandler, Caroline Augusta. Famous Men of Medicine. Dodd 1950
BBJH—CC(6-9)—JH—SCHS

Chandler, Caroline Augusta. Famous Modern Men of Medicine. Dodd 1965
Bkl C(6-9)&Y
Anna Freud; William James Mayo; Charles Frederick Menninger; Benjamin McLane Spock; Paul Dudley White; and others

Farr, Muriel. Children in Medicine. Prentice-Hall 1964
ESLC

Hume, Ruth Fox. Great Men of Medicine. Random House 1961
CC(7-9)—ESLC—JH—SCHS—YR
William Harvey; Edward Jenner; Robert Koch; René Théophile Hyacinthe Laennec; Joseph Lister; William Thomas Green Morton; Ambroise Paré; Ignaz Philipp Semmelweiss; Andreas Vesalius

Hume, Ruth Fox. Great Women of Medicine. Random House 1964
CC—JH
Elizabeth Garrett Anderson; Elizabeth Blackwell; Marie (Sklodowska) Curie; Mary (Putnam) Jacobi; Sophia Louisa Jex-Blake; Florence Nightingale

McGrady, Mike. Jungle Doctors. Lippincott 1962
Bkl C(6-9)&Y
Theodor Binder; Sir David Bruce; Thomas Anthony Dooley; William Larimer Mellon; Walter Reed; Albert Schweitzer; and others

Mardus, Elaine and Lang, Miriam. Doctors to the Great. Dial 1962
BY—YR

Montgomery, Elizabeth Rider. The Story Behind Great Medical Discoveries. Dodd 1945
SCHS

Poole, Lynn and Poole, Gray. Doctors Who Saved Lives. Dodd 1966
Bkl Y(7-9)&C

Riedman, Sarah Regal and Gustafson, Elton T. Portraits of Nobel Laureates in Medicine and Physiology. Abelard-Schuman 1964
Bkl Y&C

Riedman, Sarah Regal. Shots Without Guns: The Story of Vaccination. Rand McNally 1960
BBHS—Bkl Y&C—CC(7-9)—ESLC—JH—SCHS—YR
George Frederick Dick; Gladys Rowena (Henry) Dick; Paul Ehrlich; Edward Jenner; Robert Koch; Louis Pasteur; Jonas Edward Salk; Bela Schick

Shippen, Katherine Binney. Men of Medicine. Viking 1957
AB(6-10)—BBEL—CC(7-9)—ESLC—JH—SCHS

Silverberg, Robert. The Great Doctors. Putnam 1964
Bkl C(7-9)&Y—ESLC

Sterne, Emma (Gelders). Blood Brothers: Four Men of Science. Knopf 1959
Bkl C(7-9)—JH
Charles Richard Drew; William Harvey; Karl Landsteiner; Marcello Malpighi

Williams, Greer. Virus Hunters. Knopf 1959
Bkl A&Y—3000
Ernest William Goodpasture; Edward Jenner; Louis Pasteur; Jonas Edward Salk; and others

American

COLLECTIONS

American Medical Directory. Am. Medical Assn. Biennial; first published 1906
SCPL

Blassingame, Wyatt and Glendinning, Richard. Frontier Doctors. Watts 1963
Bkl C(6-9)
Bethenia Angelina (Owens) Adair; William Beaumont; William Clark; Samuel Jay Crumbine; Meriwether Lewis; Crawford Williamson Long; Ephraim McDowell; Marcus Whitman

Dunlop, Richard. Doctors of the American Frontier. Doubleday 1965
Bkl A&Y
William Beaumont; Ephraim McDowell; and others

Fleming, Alice (Mulcahey). Doctors in Petticoats. Lippincott 1964
Bkl C(6-9)—CC—JH
Emily (Dunning) Barringer; Leona Baumgartner; Connie Myers Guion; Alice Hamilton; Karen (Danielson) Horney; Mary (Putnam) Jacobi; Sara (Murray) Jordan; Louise Pearce; Clara A. Swain; Marie Elizabeth Zakrzewska

American—18th century

Benjamin Rush, 1745?-1813

Douty, Esther M. Patriot Doctor: The Story of Benjamin Rush. Messner 1959
ESLC

Riedman, Sarah Regal and Green, Clarence Corleon. Benjamin Rush: Physician, Patriot, Founding Father. Abelard-Schuman 1964
Bkl Y(7-10)&C—JH

COLLECTIONS

McKown, Robin. Pioneers in Mental Health. Dodd 1961
Bkl A&Y

PHYSICIANS—*Continued*

American—19th century

Bethenia Angelina (Owens) Adair, 1840-1926

Miller, Helen Markley. Woman Doctor of the West, Bethenia Owens-Adair. Messner 1960
Bkl C(7-10)&Y

COLLECTIONS

Blassingame, Wyatt and Glendinning, Richard. Frontier Doctors. Watts 1963
Bkl C(6-9)

Johnson, Dorothy M. Some Went West. Dodd 1965
Bkl C(7-9)&Y

Elizabeth Blackwell, 1821-1910

Baker, Rachel. The First Woman Doctor: The Story of Elizabeth Blackwell, M.D. Messner 1944
BBJH—CC(7-9)—JH—SCHS—YR

Chambers, Peggy. A Doctor Alone: Biography of Elizabeth Blackwell, First Woman Doctor. Abelard-Schuman 1958
BY

COLLECTIONS

Buckmaster, Henrietta. Women Who Shaped History. Collier Bks 1966
Bkl C(7-10)&Y

Hume, Ruth Fox. Great Women of Medicine. Random House 1964
CC—JH

Samuel Pellman Boyer, ?

Boyer, Samuel Pellman. Naval Surgeon: v. 1, Blockading the South, 1862-1866. Ind. Univ. 1963
Bkl A

Boyer, Samuel Pellman. Naval Surgeon: v. 2, Revolt in Japan, 1868-1869. Ind. Univ. 1963
Bkl A

Frederick Albert Cook, 1865-1940

Freeman, Andrew A. The Case for Doctor Cook. Coward-McCann 1961
Bkl A

Weems, John Edward. Race for the Pole. Holt 1960
Bkl A&Y

Edward S. Gifford, 1868-

Gifford, Edward S. Father Against the Devil. Doubleday 1966
Bkl A

Mary (Putnam) Jacobi, 1842-1906

COLLECTIONS

Fleming, Alice (Mulcahey). Doctors in Petticoats. Lippincott 1964
Bkl C(6-9)—CC—JH

Hume, Ruth Fox. Great Women of Medicine. Random House 1964
CC—JH

William James Mayo, 1861-1939

Clapesattle, Helen Bernice. The Mayo Brothers. Houghton 1962
Bkl C(5-8)—CC(6-8)—ESLC—JH—YR

Clapesattle, Helen Bernice. Doctors Mayo; 2d ed. condensed. Univ. of Minn. 1954
SCHS—SCPL

Regli, Adolph. The Mayos, Pioneers in Medicine. Messner 1942
SCHS

COLLECTIONS

Chandler, Caroline Augusta. Famous Modern Men of Medicine. Dodd 1965
Bkl C(6-9)&Y

Samuel Alexander Mudd, 1833-1883

Higdon, Hal. The Union vs. Dr. Mudd. Follett 1964
Bkl A&Y

Walter Reed, 1851-1902

Dolan, Edward F. Vanquishing Yellow Fever: Walter Reed. Encyc. Britannica 1962
JH

Hill, Ralph Nading. The Doctors Who Conquered Yellow Fever. Random House 1957
SCHS

Wood, Laura Newbold. Walter Reed, Doctor in Uniform. Messner 1943
BBEL(7-8)—BBHS—CC(7-9)—ESLC—JH—SCHS

COLLECTIONS

McGrady, Mike. Jungle Doctors. Lippincott 1962
Bkl C(6-9)&Y

Clara A. Swain, 1834-1910

COLLECTIONS

Fleming, Alice (Mulcahey). Doctors in Petticoats. Lippincott 1964
Bkl C(6-9)—CC-JH

Edward Livingston Trudeau, 1848-1915

Harrod, Kathryn E. Man of Courage. Messner 1959
Bkl Y&C

William Henry Welch, 1850-1934

Crane, William Dwight. Prophet with Honor: Dr. William Henry Welch. Messner 1966
Bkl C(7-10)&Y

PHYSICIANS

American—19th century—*Continued*

Marie Elizabeth Zakrzewska, 1829-1902

COLLECTIONS

Fleming, Alice (Mulcahey). Doctors in Petticoats. Lippincott 1964
Bkl C(6-9)—CC—JH

American—20th century

Bethenia Angelina (Owens) Adair, 1840-1926

Miller, Helen Markley. Woman Doctor of the West, Bethenia Owens-Adair. Messner 1960
Bkl C(7-10)&Y

COLLECTIONS

Blassingame, Wyatt and Glendinning, Richard. Frontier Doctors. Watts 1963
Bkl C(6-9)

Albert Coombs Barnes, 1872-1951

Hart, Henry. Dr. Barnes of Merion: An Appreciation. Farrar 1963
Bkl A—BY

Schack, William. Art and Argyrol: The Life and Career of Dr. Albert C. Barnes. Yoseloff 1960
Bkl A

Leona Baumgartner, 1902-

COLLECTIONS

Fleming, Alice (Mulcahey). Doctors in Petticoats. Lippincott 1964
Bkl C(6-9)—CC—JH

John Romulus Brinkley, 1885-1942

Carson, Gerald. The Roguish World of Doctor Brinkley. Rinehart 1960
Bkl A

James Gordon Bryson, 1884-

Bryson, James Gordon. One Hundred Dollars & a Horse: The Reminiscences of a Country Doctor. Morrow 1965
Bkl A

Grafton Burke, 1884-1938

Burke, Clara (Heintz) and Comandini, Adele. Doctor Hap. Coward-McCann 1961
Bkl A&Y—BY

Edward Gaine Cannon, 1900-

Blythe, LeGette. Mountain Doctor. Morrow 1964
Bkl A&Y

Paul Earle Carlson, 1928-1964

Carlson, Lois. Monganga Paul: The Congo Ministry and Martyrdom of Paul Carlson, M. D. Harper 1966
Bkl A&Y

Frederick Albert Cook, 1865-1940

Freeman, Andrew A. The Case for Doctor Cook. Coward-McCann 1961
Bkl A

Weems, John Edward. Race for the Pole. Holt 1960
Bkl A&Y

Samuel Jay Crumbine, 1862-1954

COLLECTIONS

Blassingame, Wyatt and Glendinning, Richard. Frontier Doctors. Watts 1963
Bkl C(6-9)

George Frederick Dick, 1881-

COLLECTIONS

Riedman, Sarah Regal. Shots Without Guns: The Story of Vaccination. Rand McNally 1960
BBHS—Bkl Y&C—CC(7-9)—ESLC—JH—SCHS—YR

Gladys Rowena (Henry) Dick, 1881-1963

COLLECTIONS

Riedman, Sarah Regal. Shots Without Guns: The Story of Vaccination. Rand McNally 1960
BBHS—Bkl Y&C—CC(7-9)—ESLC—JH—SCHS—YR

Thomas Anthony Dooley, 1927-1961

Dooley, Agnes (Wise). Promises to Keep: The Life of Dr. Thomas A. Dooley. Farrar 1962
Bkl A&Y—BY—SCHS—SCPL

Dooley, Thomas Anthony. Deliver Us from Evil: The Story of Viet Nam's Flight to Freedom. Farrar 1956
SCHS

Dooley, Thomas Anthony. Dr. Tom Dooley: My Story. Ariel Bks 1962
CC—ESLC—JH—SCHS

Dooley, Thomas Anthony. Dr. Tom Dooley's Three Great Books: Deliver Us from Evil, The Edge of Tomorrow, The Night They Burned the Mountain. Farrar 1960
BBHS—SCHS—SCPL

Dooley, Thomas Anthony. Edge of Tomorrow. Farrar 1958
SCHS—SCPL

Dooley, Thomas Anthony. The Night They Burned the Mountain. Farrar 1960
Bkl A&Y—SCHS—SCPL

Gallagher, Teresa. Give Joy to My Youth: A Memoir of Dr. Tom Dooley. Farrar 1965
Bkl A&Y

Monahan, James, ed. Before I Sleep . . . The Last Days of Dr. Tom Dooley. Farrar 1961
Bkl A&Y—BY—SCHS—SCPL

PHYSICIANS

American—20th century

Thomas Anthony Dooley—Continued

Morris, Terry. Doctor America: The Story of Tom Dooley. Hawthorn 1963
IndJ(6-9)

COLLECTIONS

Kittler, Glenn D. The Wings of Eagles. Doubleday 1966
Bkl A&Y

McGrady, Mike. Jungle Doctors. Lippincott 1962
Bkl C(6-9)&Y

John Thacker Ferguson, 1908-1968

De Kruif, Paul Henry. Man Against Insanity. Harcourt 1957
SCPL

Edward S. Gifford, 1868-

Gifford, Edward S. Father Against the Devil. Doubleday 1966
Bkl A

Joseph Goldberger, 1874-1929

COLLECTIONS

De Kruif, Paul Henry. Hunger Fighters. Harcourt 1928
BBHS—SCHS—SCPL—3000

Ernest William Goodpasture, 1886-1960

COLLECTIONS

Sullivan, Navin. Pioneer Germ Fighters. Atheneum 1962
CC(5-7)—ESLC

Williams, Greer. Virus Hunters. Knopf 1959
Bkl A&Y—3000

William Crawford Gorgas, 1854-1920

Judson, Clara (Ingram). Soldier Doctor: The Story of William Gorgas. Scribner 1942
BBEL(5-7)—BBJH—CC(5-7)—JH—SCHS

Williams, Beryl and Epstein, Samuel. William Crawford Gorgas: Tropic Fever Fighter. Messner 1953
BY

Connie Myers Guion, 1882-

Campion, Nardi (Reeder) and Stanton, Rosamond Wilfley. Look to This Day! The Lively Education of a Great Woman Doctor. Little 1965
Bkl C&Y—IndS(9-10)

COLLECTIONS

Fleming, Alice (Mulcahey). Doctors in Petticoats. Lippincott 1964
Bkl C(6-9)—CC—JH

Alice Hamilton, 1869-

COLLECTIONS

Boynick, David. Pioneers in Petticoats. Crowell 1959
YR

Fleming, Alice (Mulcahey). Doctors in Petticoats. Lippincott 1964
Bkl C(6-9)—CC—JH

Victor George Heiser, 1873-

Heiser, Victor George. An American Doctor's Odyssey: Adventures in Forty-five Countries. Norton 1936
BY—SCHS—SCPL

Albert Haley Henderson, 1866-1937

Read, Katherine L. (Henderson) and Ballou, Robert O. Bamboo Hospital: The Story of a Missionary Family in Burma. Lippincott 1961
Bkl A&Y

James Paget Henry, 1914-

COLLECTIONS

Thomas, Shirley. Men of Space: v. 7, Profiles of the Leaders in Space Research, Development, and Exploration. Chilton 1965
Bkl A&Y

Sara (Murray) Jordan, 1884-1959

COLLECTIONS

Fleming, Alice (Mulcahey). Doctors in Petticoats. Lippincott 1964
Bkl C(6-9)—CC—JH

William James Mayo, 1861-1939

Clapesattle, Helen Bernice. The Mayo Brothers. Houghton 1962
Bkl C(5-8)—CC(6-8)—ESLC—JH—YR

Clapesattle, Helen Bernice. Doctors Mayo; 2d ed. condensed. Univ. of Minn. 1954
SCHS—SCPL

Regli, Adolph. The Mayos, Pioneers in Medicine. Messner 1942
SCHS

COLLECTIONS

Chandler, Caroline Augusta. Famous Modern Men of Medicine. Dodd 1965
Bkl C(6-9)&Y

William Larimer Mellon, 1910-

Michelmore, Peter. Dr. Mellon of Haiti. Dodd 1964
Bkl A&Y

COLLECTIONS

McGrady, Mike. Jungle Doctors. Lippincott 1962
Bkl C(6-9)&Y

PHYSICIANS

American—20th century—*Continued*

Kate Pelham Newcomb, 1885-1956

Comandini, Adele. Doctor Kate, Angel on Snowshoes: The Story of Kate Pelham Newcomb. Rinehart 1956
SCHS—SCPL

Louise Pearce, 1885-1959

COLLECTIONS

Fleming, Alice (Mulcahey). Doctors in Petticoats. Lippincott 1964
Bkl C(6-9)—CC—JH

Albert Bruce Sabin, 1906-

COLLECTIONS

Berland, Theodore. The Scientific Life. Coward-McCann 1962
Bkl A&Y

Clarence Grant Salsbury, 1886-

Means, Florence Crannell. Sagebrush Surgeon. Friendship Press 1956
BY

Béla Schick, 1877-1967

Noble, Iris. Physician to the Children: Bela Schick. Messner 1963
IndJ(6-9)—YR

COLLECTIONS

Reidman, Sarah Regal. Shots Without Guns: The Story of Vaccination. Rand McNally 1960
BBHS—Bkl Y&C—CC(7-9)—ESLC—JH—SCHS—YR

Ida Scudder, 1870-1960

Wilson, Dorothy Clarke. Dr. Ida: The Story of Dr. Ida Scudder of Vellore. McGraw 1959
Bkl A&Y—SCPL

Gordon Stifler Seagrave, 1897-1965

Seagrave, Gordon Stifler. The Life of a Burma Surgeon. Norton 1961
Bkl A

Seagrave, Gordon Stifler. My Hospital in the Hills. Norton 1955
BY—SCPL

Mary T. (Martin) Sloop, 1873-1962

Sloop, Mary T. (Martin). Miracle in the Hills. McGraw 1953
SCPL

Benjamin McLane Spock, 1903-

COLLECTIONS

Chandler, Caroline Augusta. Famous Modern Men of Medicine. Dodd 1965
Bkl C(6-9)&Y

William Henry Welch, 1850-1934

Crane, William Dwight. Prophet with Honor: Dr. William Henry Welch. Messner 1966
Bkl C(7-10)&Y

Paul Dudley White, 1886-

COLLECTIONS

Chandler, Caroline Augusta. Famous Modern Men of Medicine. Dodd 1965
Bkl C(6-9)&Y

William Carlos Williams, 1883-1963

Williams, William Carlos. Autobiography. Random House 1951
SCPL

Australian—20th century

Sir David Bruce, 1855-1931

COLLECTIONS

McGrady, Mike. Jungle Doctors. Lippincott 1962
Bkl C(6-9)&Y

Austrian—18th century

Friedrich Anton Mesmer, 1734-1815

COLLECTIONS

McKown, Robin. Pioneers in Mental Health. Dodd 1961
Bkl A&Y

Austrian—20th century

Richard Berczeller, 1902-

Berczeller, Richard. Displaced Doctor. Odyssey 1964
Bkl A

Herman Eric Mautner, 1911-

Mautner, Herman Eric. Doctor in Bolivia. Chilton 1960
Bkl A

Canadian—19th century

Sir William Osler, Bart., 1849-1919

Cushing, Harvey Williams. Life of Sir William Osler. 2v. Oxford 1956
SCPL

Noble, Iris. The Doctor Who Dared: William Osler. Messner 1959
CC(7-9)—JH—SCHS

Reid, Edith (Gittings). Great Physician: A Short Life of Sir William Osler. Oxford 1931
SCPL

Canadian—20th century

Sir Frederick Grant Banting, 1891-1941

Levine, Israel E. The Discoverer of Insulin: Dr. Frederick G. Banting. Messner 1959
BBHS—CC(7-9)—JH—SCHS

PHYSICIANS

Canadian—20th century—*Continued*

Marion Hilliard, 1902-1958

Robinson, Marion O. Give My Heart:
The Dr. Marion Hilliard Story. Dou-
bleday 1964
Bkl A&Y

Joseph Palmer Moody, 1919-

Moody, Joseph Palmer and Van Emb-
den, W. de Groot. Arctic Doctor. Dodd
1955
BY—SCPL

Sir William Osler, Bart., 1849-1919

Cushing, Harvey Williams. Life of Sir
William Osler. 2v. Oxford 1956
SCPL

Noble, Iris. The Doctor Who Dared:
William Osler. Messner 1959
CC(7-9)—JH—SCHS

Reid, Edith (Gittings). Great Physician:
A Short Life of Sir William Osler. Ox-
ford 1931
SCPL

Paul Léon Rivard, ?

Trent, Bill. Northwoods Doctor. Lippincott 1962
Bkl A

English—17th century

William Harvey, 1578-1657

Marcus, Rebecca B. William Harvey,
Trail-Blazer of Scientific Medicine.
Watts 1963
Bkl C(5-9)&Y—ESLC—JH

COLLECTIONS

Hume, Ruth Fox. Great Men of Medicine. Random House 1961
CC(7-9)—ESLC—JH—SCHS—YR

Sterne, Emma (Gelders). Blood Brothers: Four Men of Science. Knopf 1959
Bkl C(7-9)—JH

English—18th century

Erasmus Darwin, 1731-1802

COLLECTIONS

Crowther, James Gerald. Scientists of the
Industrial Revolution. Dufour 1963
Bkl A

Edward Jenner, 1749-1823

Eberle, Irmengarde. Edward Jenner and
Smallpox Vaccination. Watts 1962
ESLC—JH

Gibbs, Willa. The Dedicated. Morrow
1960 (Fiction)
BBHS—Bkl A&Y

Levine, Israel E. Conqueror of Smallpox:
Dr. Edward Jenner. Messner 1960
Bkl Y&C

COLLECTIONS

Hume, Ruth Fox. Great Men of Medicine. Random House 1961
CC(7-9)—ESLC—JH—SCHS—YR

Riedman, Sarah Regal. Shots Without
Guns: The Story of Vaccination. Rand
McNally 1960
BBHS—Bkl Y&C—CC(7-9)—ESLC—JH—
SCHS—YR

Sullivan, Navin. Pioneer Germ Fighters.
Atheneum 1962
CC(5-7)—ESLC

Williams, Greer. Virus Hunters. Knopf
1959
Bkl A&Y—3000

English—19th century

Elizabeth Garrett Anderson, 1836-1917

Manton, Jo. Elizabeth Garrett, M.D.
Abelard-Schuman 1960
Bkl Y&C(6-9)

COLLECTIONS

Hume, Ruth Fox. Great Women of Medicine. Random House 1964
CC—JH

*Sir Wilfred Thomason Grenfell, 1865-
1940*

Grenfell, Sir Wilfred Thomason. Adrift
on an Ice-Pan. Houghton 1939
SCPL

Grenfell, Sir Wilfred Thomason. Forty
Years for Labrador. Houghton 1932
SCPL

Kerr, James Lennox. Wilfred Grenfell:
His Life and Work. Dodd 1959
Bkl A&Y

Pumphrey, George H. Grenfell of Labrador. Dodd 1959
AB(7-10)—JH

Sophia Louisa Jex-Blake, 1840-1912

COLLECTIONS

Hume, Ruth Fox. Great Women of Medicine. Random House 1964
CC—JH

English—20th century

Elizabeth Garrett Anderson, 1836-1917

Manton, Jo. Elizabeth Garrett, M.D.
Abelard-Schuman 1960
Bkl Y&C(6-9)

COLLECTIONS

Hume, Ruth Fox. Great Women of Medicine. Random House 1964
CC—JH

Hubert Bagster, 1902-

Bagster, Hubert. Doctor's Weekend.
Simon & Schuster 1960
Bkl A

PHYSICIANS

English—20th century—*Continued*

Sir Wilfred Thomason Grenfell, 1865-1940

Grenfell, Sir Wilfred Thomason. Adrift on an Ice-Pan. Houghton 1939
SCPL

Grenfell, Sir Wilfred Thomason. Forty Years for Labrador. Houghton 1932
SCPL

Kerr, James Lennox. Wilfred Grenfell: His Life and Work. Dodd 1959
Bkl A&Y

Pumphrey, George H. Grenfell of Labrador. Dodd 1959
AB(7-10)—JH

Sir Ronald Ross, 1857-1932

Kamm, Josephine. Malaria Ross. Criterion Bks 1964
Bkl C(7-9)—ESLC

Rowland, John. The Mosquito Man. Roy 1963
IndJ(6-9)

Sir Sydney Alfred Smith, 1883-

Smith, Sir Sydney Alfred. Mostly Murder. McKay 1960
Bkl A

Jonathan Whitby, ?

Whitby, Jonathan. Bundu Doctor. Roy 1962
Bkl A

French—19th century

René Théophile Hyacinthe Laennec, 1781-1826

Carbonnier, Jeanne. Above All a Physician: René Théophile Laennec, 1781-1826. Scribner 1961
Bkl C(7-9)—JH—YR

COLLECTIONS

Hume, Ruth Fox. Great Men of Medicine. Random House 1961
CC(7-9)—ESLC—JH—SCHS—YR

French—20th century

Albert Schweitzer, 1875-1965

Anderson, Erica. Albert Schweitzer's Gift of Friendship. Harper 1964
Bkl A&Y

Anderson, Erica. The Schweitzer Album: A Portrait in Words and Pictures. Harper 1965
Bkl A&Y

Anderson, Erica and Exman, Eugene. The World of Albert Schweitzer: A Book of Photographs. Harper 1955
BY—SCHS—SCPL

Berrill, Jacquelyn. Albert Schweitzer, Man of Mercy. Dodd 1956
BBJH—BY—JH

Cousins, Norman. Dr. Schweitzer of Lambaréné. Harper 1960
Bkl Y—SCHS—SCPL

Cousins, Norman. Lambaréné: Doctor Schweitzer and His People. Harper 1960
Bkl A&Y

Daniel, Anita. The Story of Albert Schweitzer. Random House 1957
CC—ESLC—JH—SCHS

Franck, Frederick. Days with Albert Schweitzer: A Lambaréné Landscape. Holt 1959
SCPL

Franck, Frederick. My Friend in Africa. Bobbs 1960 (Fiction)
ESLC

Gollomb, Joseph. Albert Schweitzer: Genius in the Jungle. Vanguard 1949
BBEL(7-8)—BY—CC(7-9)—ESLC—JH—SCHS

Hagedorn, Hermann. Prophet in the Wilderness: The Story of Albert Schweitzer. Macmillan 1954
SCPL

Joy, Charles R. and Arnold, Melvin. The Africa of Albert Schweitzer. Harper 1958
SCPL

McKnight, Gerald. Verdict on Schweitzer: The Man behind the Legend of Lambaréné. Day 1964
Bkl A

Manton, Jo. The Story of Albert Schweitzer. Abelard-Schuman 1955
AB(7up)—BBEL(6)—CC—JH

Merrett, John. The True Story of Albert Schweitzer. Childrens Press 1964
IndJ(4-6)

Ostergaard Christensen, Lavrids. At Work with Albert Schweitzer; tr. from the Danish by F. H. Lyon. Beacon Press 1962
Bkl A

Payne, Pierre Stephen Robert. Three Worlds of Albert Schweitzer. Nelson 1957
SCHS—SCPL

Picht, Werner Robert Valentin. The Life and Thought of Albert Schweitzer; tr. from the German by Edward Fitzgerald. Harper 1964
Bkl A

Schweitzer, Albert. Memoirs of Childhood and Youth. Macmillan 1949
SCPL

Schweitzer, Albert. On the Edge of the Primeval Forest & More from the Primeval Forest: Experiences and Observations of a Doctor in Equatorial Africa. Macmillan 1948
SCPL

PHYSICIANS

French—20th century

Albert Schweitzer—Continued

Schweitzer, Albert. Out of My Life and
    Thought: An Autobiography; tr. by
    C. T. Campion. Holt 1949
    BBHS—GR—SCPL—3000
Seaver, George. Albert Schweitzer:
    Christian Revolutionary. Harper 1956
    SCPL
Seaver, George. Albert Schweitzer: The
    Man and His Mind. Harper 1955
    SCPL
Simon, Charlie May. All Men Are Broth-
    ers: A Portrait of Albert Schweitzer.
    Dutton 1956
    AB(7-10)—BBJH—JH

COLLECTIONS

McGrady, Mike. Jungle Doctors. Lippin-
    cott 1962
    Bkl C(6-9)&Y

German—19th century

Robert Koch, 1843-1910

Dolan, Edward F. Adventure with a
    Microscope: A Story of Robert Koch.
    Dodd 1964
    Bkl C(6-9)&Y—ESLC—JH
Knight, David C. Robert Koch, Father
    of Bacteriology. Watts 1961
    Bkl C(6-9)—JH

COLLECTIONS

Hume, Ruth Fox. Great Men of Medi-
    cine. Random House 1961
    CC(7-9)—ESLC—JH—SCHS—YR
Riedman, Sarah Regal. Shots Without
    Guns: The Story of Vaccination. Rand
    McNally 1960
    BBHS—Bkl Y&C—CC(7-9)—ESLC—JH—
    SCHS—YR
Sullivan, Navin. Pioneer Germ Fighters.
    Atheneum 1962
    CC(5-7)—ESLC

German—20th century

Theodor Binder, 1919-

Mendelsohn, Jack. The Forest Calls
    Back. Little 1965
    IndS(10-12)

COLLECTIONS

McGrady, Mike. Jungle Doctors. Lippin-
    cott 1962
    Bkl C(6-9)&Y

Herbert Ludwig Schrader, 1919-

Schrader, Herbert Ludwig. No Other
    Way: The Story of a Doctor from East
    Germany; tr. from German by E.
    Osers. McKay 1964
    Bkl A

Greek—5th century B.C.

Hippocrates, 460?-377? B.C.

Goldberg, Herbert S. Hippocrates:
    Father of Medicine. Watts 1963
    AB(7up)—ESLC—JH
Penfield, Wilder. The Torch. Little 1960
    (Fiction)
    Bkl A

Hungarian—19th century

Ignaz Philipp Semmelweiss, 1818-
1865

COLLECTIONS

Hume, Ruth Fox. Great Men of Medi-
    cine. Random House 1961
    CC(7-9)—ESLC—JH—SCHS—YR

Hungarian—20th century

Edith Bone, 1889-

Bone, Edith. 7 Years' Solitary. Harcourt
    1957
    SCPL

Indian—20th century

Mary Verghese, 1925-

Wilson, Dorothy Clarke. Take My
    Hands: The Remarkable Story of Dr.
    Mary Verghese. McGraw 1963
    Bkl A&Y

Irish—20th century

Oliver St. John Gogarty, 1878-1957

O'Connor, Ulick. The Times I've Seen—
    Oliver St. John Gogarty: A Biography.
    Obolensky 1964
    Bkl A

Italian—20th century

Sir Aldo Castellani, 1875-

Castellani, Sir Aldo. A Doctor in Many
    Lands: The Autobiography. Double-
    day 1960
    Bkl A

New Zealand—20th century

Thomas Robert Alexander Harries
Davis, 1918?-

Davis, Thomas Robert Alexander Har-
    ries. Doctor to the Islands. Little 1954
    BY—SCPL

Pakistani—20th century

Mohammad Ata-ullah, 1903-

Ata-ullah, Mohammad. Citizen of Two
    Worlds. Harper 1960
    Bkl A&Y—BY

PHYSICIANS—*Continued*

Scottish—20th century

Archibald Joseph Cronin, 1896-

Cronin, Archibald Joseph. Adventures in Two Worlds. Little 1957
BY—SCPL

Spanish—12th century

Maimonides, 1135-1204

Morrison, Lester M. and Hubler, Richard Gibson. Trial & Triumph: A Novel about Maimonides. Crown 1965 (Fiction)
Bkl A

Spanish—20th century

Eduardo Martínez Alonso, ?

Martínez Alonso, Eduardo. Memoirs of a Medico. Doubleday 1961
Bkl A

Swedish—20th century

Axel Martin Fredrik Munthe, 1857-1949

Munthe, Axel Martin Fredrik. Story of San Michele. Dutton 1953
SCPL

Swiss—16th century

Philippus Aureolus Paracelsus, 1493?-1541

Rosen, Sidney. Doctor Paracelsus. Little 1959
CC(7-9)—ESLC—JH

PHYSICISTS

COLLECTIONS

Cline, Barbara Lovett. The Questioners: Physicists and the Quantum Theory. Crowell 1965
Bkl Y&C—IndS(11-12)
Niels Henrik David Bohr; Albert Einstein; Max Karl Ernst Ludwig Planck; Ernest Rutherford; and others

Mann, A. L. and Vivian, A. C. Famous Physicists. Day 1963
ESLC—JH
Archimedes; Roger Bacon; Michael Faraday; Benjamin Franklin; Galileo Galilei; Luigi Galvani; Otto von Guericke; Sir Isaac Newton; Alessandro Giuseppe Antonio Anastasio Volta

Shippen, Katherine Binney. Bright Design. Viking 1949
BBHS—BBJH—ESLC—JH
John Dalton; Albert Einstein; Lise Meitner; Wilhelm Roentgen; and others

American—19th century

Joseph Henry, 1797-1878

Riedman, Sarah Regal. Trailblazer of American Science: The Life of Joseph Henry. Rand McNally 1961
Bkl Y&C—JH

COLLECTIONS

Burlingame, Roger. Scientists Behind the Inventors. Harcourt 1960
AB(7up)—Bkl C(7-9)&Y—CC(6-9)—ESLC—JH—SCHS

Albert Abraham Michelson, 1852-1931

Jaffe, Bernard. Michelson and the Speed of Light. Doubleday 1960
Bkl A&Y—SCHS—3000

Wilson, John H. Albert A. Michelson: America's First Nobel Prize Physicist. Messner 1958
SCHS

Charles Sanders Peirce, 1839-1914

COLLECTIONS

Van Wesep, H. B. Seven Sages: The Story of American Philosophy. Longmans 1960
SCPL

American—20th century

Philip Hauge Abelson, 1913-

COLLECTIONS

Thomas, Shirley. Men of Space: v. 6, Profiles of Scientists Who Probe for Life in Space. Chilton 1963
Bkl A&Y

Albert Einstein, 1879-1955

Beckhard, Arthur. Albert Einstein. Putnam 1959
AB—CC(5-7)—ESLC—SCHS

Forsee, Aylesa. Albert Einstein: Theoretical Physicist. Macmillan 1963
Bkl C&Y—YR

Frank, Philipp. Einstein: His Life and Times. Knopf 1953
3000

Freeman, Mae Blacker. The Story of Albert Einstein: The Scientist Who Searched Out the Secrets of the Universe. Random House 1958
AB(3-7)—JH

Infeld, Leopold. Einstein: His Work and Its Influence on Our World. Scribner 1950
SCPL

Levinger, Elma (Ehrlich). Albert Einstein. Messner 1949
BBEL(7-8)—BBJH—BY—CC(7-9)—ESLC—JH—SCHS

Michelmore, Peter. Einstein: Profile of the Man. Dodd 1962
Bkl A&Y

COLLECTIONS

Burlingame, Roger. Scientists Behind the Inventors. Harcourt 1960
AB(7up)—Bkl C(7-9)&Y—CC(6-9)—ESLC—JH—SCHS

PHYSICISTS

American—20th century

Albert Einstein—Continued

Cline, Barbara Lovett. The Questioners: Physicists and the Quantum Theory. Crowell 1965
Bkl Y&C—IndS(11-12)

Kagan, Henry Enoch. Six Who Changed the World. Yoseloff 1963
Bkl A

McNeer, May Yonge and Ward, Lynd Kendall. Give Me Freedom. Abingdon 1964
Bkl C(5-8)—CC(5-7)—ESLC—JH—YR

Shippen, Katherine Binney. Bright Design. Viking 1949
BBHS—BBJH—ESLC—JH

Herbert Friedman, 1916-

COLLECTIONS

Thomas, Shirley. Men of Space: v. 7, Profiles of the Leaders in Space Research, Development, and Exploration. Chilton 1965
Bkl A&Y

Robert Hutchings Goddard, 1882-1945

Dewey, Anne Perkins. Robert Goddard, Space Pioneer. Little 1962
Bkl C(6-9)&Y—CC(6-9)—ESLC—JH—YR

Lehman, Milton. This High Man: The Life of Robert H. Goddard. Farrar 1963
Bkl A&Y

Verral, Charles Spain. Robert Goddard: Father of the Space Age. Prentice-Hall 1963
ESLC—IndJ(4-6)

Albert Abraham Michelson, 1852-1931

Jaffe, Bernard. Michelson and the Speed of Light. Doubleday 1960
Bkl A&Y—SCHS—3000

Wilson, John H. Albert A. Michelson: America's First Nobel Prize Physicist. Messner 1958
SCHS

J. Robert Oppenheimer, 1904-1967

Chevalier, Haakon Maurice. Oppenheimer: The Story of a Friendship. Braziller 1965
Bkl A

Kuglemass, J. Alvin. J. Robert Oppenheimer and the Atomic Story. Messner 1953
AB(5-9)—SCHS

Rouzé, Michel. Robert Oppenheimer: The Man and His Theories; tr. by Patrick Evans. Ericksson 1965
Bkl A

Michael Idvorsky Pupin, 1858-1935

Markey, Dorothy. Explorer of Sound: Michael Pupin. Messner 1964
YR

Pupin, Michael Idvorsky. From Immigrant to Inventor. Scribner 1923
BBHS—SCPL

COLLECTIONS

Burlingame, Roger. Scientists Behind the Inventors. Harcourt 1960
AB(7up)—Bkl C(7-9)&Y—CC(6-9)—ESLC—JH—SCHS

James Alfred Van Allen, 1914-

COLLECTIONS

Berland, Theodore. The Scientific Life. Coward-McCann 1962
Bkl A&Y

Austrian—20th century

Lise Meitner, 1878-1968

COLLECTIONS

Shippen, Katherine Binney. Bright Design. Viking 1949
BBHS—BBJH—ESLC—JH

Danish—20th century

Niels Henrik David Bohr, 1885-1962

Silverberg, Robert. Niels Bohr: The Man Who Mapped the Atom. Macrae 1965
Bkl C(7-10)&Y—IndS(9-12)

COLLECTIONS

Cline, Barbara Lovett. The Questioners: Physicists and the Quantum Theory. Crowell 1965
Bkl Y&C—IndS(11-12)

English—17th century

Robert Boyle, 1627-1691

Sootin, Harry. Robert Boyle, Founder of Modern Chemistry. Watts 1962
Bkl C(5-8)—ESLC

Sir Isaac Newton, 1642-1727

Andrade, Edward Neville da Costa. Sir Isaac Newton. Doubleday 1965
Bkl A&Y

Horizon Magazine. The Universe of Galileo and Newton, by William Bixby and Giorgio de Santillana. Harper 1964
AB(6-10)—Bkl C(7-9)—CC—ESLC—IndS(9-12)—JH—SCHS

Land, Barbara and Land, Myrick. The Quest of Isaac Newton. Garden City 1960
ESLC

Moore, Patrick. Isaac Newton. Putnam 1958
AB(5-9)—BBJH—ESLC—SCHS

PHYSICISTS

English—17th century

Sir Isaac Newton—Continued

Sootin, Harry. Isaac Newton. Messner 1955
BY—CC—JH—SCHS

Tannenbaum, Beulah and Stillman, Myra. Isaac Newton, Pioneer of Space Mathematics. McGraw 1959
AB(6-9)—Bkl Y&C(7-9)—JH

COLLECTIONS

Bixby, William. Great Experimenters. McKay 1964
Bkl C(7-8)&Y—ESLC

Mann, A. L. and Vivian, A. C. Famous Physicists. Day 1963
ESLC—JH

English—18th century

Henry Cavendish, 1731-1810

COLLECTIONS

Crowther, James Gerald. Scientists of the Industrial Revolution. Dufour 1963
Bkl A

John Dalton, 1766-1844

COLLECTIONS

Irwin, Keith Gordon. The Romance of Chemistry from Ancient Alchemy to Nuclear Fission. Viking 1959
JH

Shippen, Katherine Binney. Bright Design. Viking 1949
BBHS—BBJH—ESLC—JH

Sir Isaac Newton, 1642-1727

Andrade, Edward Neville da Costa. Sir Isaac Newton. Doubleday 1965
Bkl A&Y

Horizon Magazine. The Universe of Galileo and Newton, by William Bixby and Giorgio de Santillana. Harper 1964
AB(6-10)—Bkl C(7-9)—CC—ESLC—IndS(9-12)—JH—SCHS

Land, Barbara and Land, Myrick. The Quest of Isaac Newton. Garden City 1960
ESLC

Moore, Patrick. Isaac Newton. Putnam 1958
AB(5-9)—BBJH—ESLC—SCHS

Sootin, Harry. Isaac Newton. Messner 1955
BY—CC—JH—SCHS

Tannenbaum, Beulah and Stillman, Myra. Isaac Newton, Pioneer of Space Mathematics. McGraw 1959
AB(6-9)—Bkl Y&C(7-9)—JH

COLLECTIONS

Bixby, William. Great Experimenters. McKay 1964
Bkl C(7-8)&Y—ESLC

Mann, A. L. and Vivian, A. C. Famous Physicists. Day 1963
ESLC—JH

Sir Benjamin Thompson, Count Rumford, 1753-1814

Brown, Sanborn Connor. Count Rumford, Physicist Extraordinary. Doubleday 1962
Bkl A&Y

English—19th century

John Dalton, 1766-1844

COLLECTIONS

Irwin, Keith Gordon. The Romance of Chemistry from Ancient Alchemy to Nuclear Fission. Viking 1959
JH

Shippen, Katherine Binney. Bright Design. Viking 1949
BBHS—BBJH—ESLC—JH

Michael Faraday, 1791-1867

MacDonald, David Keith Chalmers. Faraday, Maxwell, and Kelvin. Doubleday 1964
Bkl A&Y

COLLECTIONS

Bixby, William. Great Experimenters. McKay 1964
Bkl C(7-8)&Y—ESLC

Mann, A. L. and Vivian, A. C. Famous Physicists. Day 1963
ESLC—JH

Sir Joseph John Thomson, 1856-1940

Thomson, Sir George Paget. J. J. Thomson and the Cavendish Laboratory in His Day. Doubleday 1965
Bkl A

English—20th century

Frederick Alexander Lindemann, Viscount Cherwell, 1886-1957

Birkenhead, Frederick Winston Furneaux Smith, 2nd Earl of. The Professor and the Prime Minister: The Official Life of Professor F. A. Lindemann, Viscount Cherwell. Houghton 1962
Bkl A

Klaus Emil Julius Fuchs, 1911-

COLLECTIONS

Moorehead, Alan. The Traitors. Harper 1963
Bkl A

PHYSICISTS

English—20th century—*Continued*

Allan Nunn May, 1911-

COLLECTIONS

Moorehead, Alan. The Traitors. Harper 1963
Bkl A

Henry Gwyn-Jeffreys Moseley, 1887-1915

COLLECTIONS

Irwin, Keith Gordon. The Romance of Chemistry from Ancient Alchemy to Nuclear Fission. Viking 1959
JH

Bruno Pontecorvo, 1913-

COLLECTIONS

Moorehead, Alan. The Traitors. Harper 1963
Bkl A

Ernest Rutherford, Baron Rutherford, 1871-1937

Andrade, Edward Neville da Costa. Rutherford and the Nature of the Atom. Doubleday 1964
Bkl Y&A

McKown, Robin. Giant of the Atom: Ernest Rutherford. Messner 1962
Bkl Y&C—JH—YR

COLLECTIONS

Bixby, William. Great Experimenters. McKay 1964
Bkl C(7-8)&Y—ESLC

Cline, Barbara Lovett. The Questioners: Physicists and the Quantum Theory. Crowell 1965
Bkl Y&C—IndS(11-12)

Sir Joseph John Thomson, 1856-1940

Thomson, Sir George Paget. J. J. Thomson and the Cavendish Laboratory in His Day. Doubleday 1965
Bkl A

French—19th century

Joseph Louis Gay-Lussac, 1778-1850

COLLECTIONS

Irwin, Keith Gordon. The Romance of Chemistry from Ancient Alchemy to Nuclear Fission. Viking 1959
JH

French—20th century

Frédéric Joliot, 1900-1958

Biquard, Pierre. Frédéric Joliot-Curie: The Man and His Theories; tr. by Geoffrey Strachan. Eriksson 1966
Bkl A&Y

Irène Joliot-Curie, 1897-1956

McKown, Robin. She Lived for Science: Irène Joliot-Curie. Messner 1961
JH

German—17th century

Otto von Guericke, 1602-1686

COLLECTIONS

Mann, A. L. and Vivian, A. C. Famous Physicists. Day 1963
ESLC—JH

German—19th century

Wilhelm Conrad Roentgen, 1845-1923

COLLECTIONS

Shippen, Katherine Binney. Bright Design. Viking 1949
BBHS—BBJH—ESLC—JH

German—20th century

Hermann Oberth, 1894-

Walters, Helen B. Hermann Oberth: Father of Space Travel. Macmillan 1962
Bkl C(6-9)&Y

Max Karl Ernst Ludwig Planck, 1858-1947

COLLECTIONS

Cline, Barbara Lovett. The Questioners: Physicists and the Quantum Theory. Crowell 1965
Bkl Y&C—IndS(11-12)

Wilhelm Conrad Roentgen, 1845-1923

COLLECTIONS

Shippen, Katherine Binney. Bright Design. Viking 1949
BBHS—BBJH—ESLC—JH

Irish—19th century

William Thomson, Baron Kelvin, 1824-1907

MacDonald, David Keith Chalmers. Faraday, Maxwell, and Kelvin. Doubleday 1964
Bkl A&Y

Italian—16th century

Galileo Galilei, 1564-1642

Brodrick, James. Galileo: The Man, His Work, His Misfortunes. Harper 1965
Bkl A&Y

Fermi, Laura and Bernardini, Gilberto. Galileo and the Scientific Revolution. Basic Bks 1961
BBHS—Bkl Y&C—JH

PHYSICISTS

Italian—16th century

Galileo Galilei—Continued

Geymonat, Ludovico. Galileo Galilei: A Biography and Inquiry into His Philosophy of Science; tr. from the Italian by Stillman Drake. McGraw 1965
Bkl A

Gregor, Arthur S. Galileo. Scribner 1965
IndJ(4-6)

Horizon Magazine. The Universe of Galileo and Newton, by William Bixby and Giorgio de Santillana. Am. Heritage 1964
AB(6-10)—Bkl C(7-9)—CC—ESLC—IndS(9-12)—JH—SCHS

Levinger, Elma (Ehrlich). Galileo: First Observer of Marvelous Things. Messner 1952
BBJH—BY—SCHS

Marcus, Rebecca B. Galileo and Experimental Science. Watts 1961
ESLC

Rosen, Sidney. Galileo and the Magic Numbers. Little 1958
AB(7up)—BBEL(8)—BBJH—CC(7-9)—ESLC—JH—SCHS

COLLECTIONS

Mann, A. L. and Vivian, A. C. Famous Physicists. Day 1963
ESLC—JH

Italian—17th century

Galileo Galilei, 1564-1642

Brodrick, James. Galileo: The Man, His Work, His Misfortunes. Harper 1965
Bkl A&Y

Fermi, Laura and Bernardini, Gilberto. Galileo and the Scientific Revolution. Basic Bks 1961
BBHS—Bkl Y&C—JH

Geymonat, Ludovico. Galileo Galilei: A Biography and Inquiry into His Philosophy of Science; tr. from the Italian by Stillman Drake. McGraw 1965
Bkl A

Gregor, Arthur S. Galileo. Scribner 1965
IndJ(4-6)

Horizon Magazine. The Universe of Galileo and Newton, by William Bixby and Giorgio de Santillana. Am. Heritage 1964
AB(6-10)—Bkl C(7-9)—ESLC—IndS(9-12)—JH—SCHS

Levinger, Elma (Ehrlich). Galileo: First Observer of Marvelous Things. Messner 1952
BBJH—BY—SCHS

Marcus, Rebecca B. **Galileo and Experimental Science.** Watts 1961
ESLC

Rosen, Sidney. Galileo and the Magic Numbers. Little 1958
AB(7up)—BBEL(8)—BBJH—CC(7-9)—ESLC—JH—SCHS

COLLECTIONS

Mann, A. L. and Vivian, A. C. Famous Physicists. Day 1963
ESLC—JH

Italian—18th century

Luigi Galvani, 1737-1798

COLLECTIONS

Mann, A. L. and Vivian, A. C. Famous Physicists. Day 1963
ESLC—JH

Alessandro Giuseppe Antonio Anastasio, Conte Volta, 1745-1827

Dibner, Bern. Alessandro Volta and the Electric Battery. Watts 1964
Bkl C(7-10)&Y

COLLECTIONS

Mann, A. L. and Vivian, A. C. Famous Physicists. Day 1963
ESLC—JH

Italian—19th century

Alessandro Giuseppe Antonio Anastasio, Conte Volta, 1745-1827

Dibner, Bern. Alessandro Volta and the Electric Battery. Watts 1964
Bkl C(7-10)&Y

COLLECTIONS

Mann, A. L. and Vivian, A. C. Famous Physicists. Day 1963
ESLC—JH

Italian—20th century

Enrico Fermi, 1901-1954

Fermi, Laura (Capon). Atoms in the Family: My Life with Enrico Fermi. Univ. of Chicago 1954
BBHS—BY—SCHS—SCPL

Latil, Pierre de. Enrico Fermi: The Man and His Theories; tr. from the French by Len Ortzen. Eriksson 1966
Bkl A&Y

COLLECTIONS

Bixby, William. Great Experimenters. McKay 1964
Bkl C(7-8)&Y—ESLC

Russian—20th century

Lev Davidovich Landau, 1908-1968

Dorozynski, Alexander. The Man They Wouldn't Let Die. Macmillan 1965
Bkl A&Y—IndS(9-12)

PHYSICISTS—*Continued*

Scottish—19th century

James Clerk Maxwell, 1831-1879

MacDonald, David Keith Chalmers. Faraday, Maxwell, and Kelvin. Doubleday 1964
Bkl A&Y

May, Charles Paul. James Clerk Maxwell and Electromagnetism. Watts 1962
Bkl C(5-9)

Swiss—20th century

Auguste Piccard, 1884-1962

Honour, Alan. Ten Miles High, Two Miles Deep: The Adventures of the Piccards. McGraw 1957
AB(5-9)—JH—SCHS

PHYSIOLOGISTS

American—20th century

Orr Esrey Reynolds, 1920-

COLLECTIONS

Thomas, Shirley. Men of Space: v. 6, Profiles of Scientists Who Probe for Life in Space. Chilton 1963
Bkl A&Y

PHYSIOTHERAPISTS

Finnish—20th century

Felix Kersten, 1898-1960

Kessel, Joseph. The Man with the Miraculous Hands; tr. from the French by Helen Weaver and Leo Raditsa. Farrar 1961
BY

PIANISTS

COLLECTIONS

Chasins, Abram. Speaking of Pianists. Knopf 1961
Bkl A—SCPL

Schonberg, Harold C. The Great Pianists. Simon & Schuster 1963
SCPL

American—19th century

Louis Moreau Gottschalk, 1829-1869

Gottschalk, Louis Moreau. Notes of a Pianist. Knopf 1964
IndS(12)

Loggins, Vernon. Where the Word Ends: The Life of Louis Moreau Gottschalk. La. State Univ. 1958
SCPL

Edward Alexander MacDowell, 1861-1908

Wheeler, Opal and Deucher, Sybil. Edward MacDowell and His Cabin in the Pines. Dutton 1940
CC(4-6)

American—20th century

Lloyd Alexander, 1924-

Alexander, Lloyd. My Love Affair with Music. Crowell 1960
BBHS—Bkl A&Y

Samuel Chotzinoff, 1889-1964

Chotzinoff, Samuel. Day's at the Morn. Harper 1964
Bkl A&Y—IndS(11-12)

Van Cliburn, 1934-

Chasins, Abram and Stiles, Villa. Van Cliburn Legend. Doubleday 1959
SCPL

COLLECTIONS

Ewen, David. Famous Instrumentalists. Dodd 1965
Bkl Y&C

Vladimir Horowitz, 1904-

COLLECTIONS

Chotzinoff, Samuel. A Little Nightmusic. Harper 1964
Bkl A&Y—IndS(12)

Oscar Levant, 1906-

Levant, Oscar. The Memoirs of an Amnesiac. Putnam 1965
Bkl A

Edward Alexander MacDowell, 1861-1908

Wheeler, Opal and Deucher, Sybil. Edward MacDowell and His Cabin in the Pines. Dutton 1940
CC(4-6)

Artur Rubinstein, 1889-

COLLECTIONS

Chotzinoff, Samuel. A Little Nightmusic. Harper 1964
Bkl A&Y—IndS(12)

Willie Smith, 1897-

Smith, Willie and Hoefer, George. Music on My Mind: The Memoirs of an American Pianist. Doubleday 1964
Bkl A

Austrian—20th century

Artur Schnabel, 1882-1951

Schnabel, Artur. My Life and Music. St Martins 1963
Bkl A&Y

PIANISTS

Austrian—20th century

Artur Schnabel—Continued

Saerchinger, César. Artur Schnabel: A
Biography. Dodd 1957
SCPL

English—20th century

Gerald Moore, 1899-

Moore, Gerald. Am I Too Loud? A Musical Autobiography. Macmillan 1962
Bkl A

German—19th century

*Clara Josephine (Wieck) Schumann,
1819-1896*

Harding, Bertita (Leonarz). Concerto:
The Glowing Story of Clara Schumann.
Bobbs 1961
Bkl A&Y

White, Hilda. Song Without End: The
Love Story of Clara and Robert Schu-
mann. Dutton 1959 (Fiction)
BBHS—Bkl Y—SCHS

Hungarian—19th century

Franz Liszt, 1811-1886

Beckett, Walter. Liszt. Farrar 1956
SCPL

Rousselot, Jean. Hungarian Rhapsody:
The Life of Franz Liszt; tr. by Moura
Budberg. Putnam 1961 (Fiction)
Bkl A

Sitwell, Sacheverell. Liszt. Cassell 1955
CA

Polish—19th century

Ignacy Jan Paderewski, 1860-1941

Hume, Ruth and Hume, Paul. The Lion
of Poland: The Story of Paderewski.
Hawthorn 1962
JH

Kellogg, Charlotte. Paderewski. Viking
1956
AB(7-10)—BBJH—SCHS—YR

Polish—20th century

Wanda Landowska, 1877-1959

COLLECTIONS

Forsee, Aylesa. Women Who Reached
for Tomorrow. Macrae 1960
Bkl Y&C

Pincherle, Marc. The World of the Vir-
tuoso; tr. from the French by Lucille
H. Brockway. Norton 1963
Bkl A

Ignacy Jan Paderewski, 1860-1941

Hume, Ruth and Hume, Paul. The Lion
of Poland: The Story of Paderewski.
Hawthorn 1962
JH

Kellogg, Charlotte. Paderewski. Viking
1956
AB(7-10)—BBJH—SCHS—YR

Russian—19th century

Anton Rubinstein, 1829-1894

Bowen, Catherine (Drinker). Free Art-
ist: The Story of Anton and Nicholas
Rubinstein. Little 1961
Bkl A

Russian—20th century

Emil Grigor'evich Gilels, 1916-

COLLECTIONS

Ewen, David. Famous Instrumentalists.
Dodd 1965
Bkl Y&C

PILGRIM FATHERS

See Colonists—American

PILOTS

See Aviators

PIONEERS

See Frontiersmen; Scouts

PIRATES

See Criminals

PLANT PATHOLOGISTS

American—20th century

Mark Alfred Carleton, 1866-1925

COLLECTIONS

De Kruif, Paul Henry. Hunger Fighters.
Harcourt 1928
BBHS—SCHS—SCPL—3000

PLAYWRIGHTS

COLLECTIONS

Gassner, John. Masters of the Drama.
Dover 1954
SCPL

Trease, Geoffrey. Seven Stages. Van-
guard 1965
Bkl Y&C—IndS(9-10)
Christopher Marlowe; Jean Baptiste Poquelin
Molière; Giuseppe Verdi

PLAYWRIGHTS—*Continued*

American

COLLECTIONS

Gould, Jean. Modern American Playwrights. Dodd 1966
Bkl A&Y

American—20th century

George Abbott, 1889-

Abbott, George. "Mister Abbott." Random House 1963
Bkl A

Philip Barry, 1896-1949

Roppolo, Joseph Patrick. Philip Barry. Twayne 1965
Bkl A

Samuel Nathaniel Behrman, 1893-

Behrman, Samuel Nathaniel. Worcester Account. Random House 1954
SCPL

Arthur Cavanaugh, ?

Cavanaugh, Arthur. My Own Back Yard. Doubleday 1962
Bkl A

Oscar Hammerstein, 1895-1960

Green, Stanley. The Rodgers and Hammerstein Story. Day 1963
Bkl A&Y

Moss Hart, 1904-1961

Hart, Moss. Act One: An Autobiography. Random House 1959
BBHS—BY—GR—SCHS—SCPL

Howard Lindsay, 1889-1968

COLLECTIONS

Levin, Martin, ed. Five Boyhoods. Doubleday 1962
Bkl A&Y

Charles MacArthur, 1895-1956

Hecht, Ben. Charlie: The Improbable Life and Times of Charles MacArthur. Harper 1957
SCPL

Arthur Miller, 1915-

Huftel, Sheila. Arthur Miller: The Burning Glass. Citadel 1965
Bkl A

Clifford Odets, 1906-1963

Shuman, Robert Baird. Clifford Odets. Twayne 1962
Bkl A

Eugene Gladstone O'Neill, 1888-1953

Alexander, Doris. The Tempering of Eugene O'Neill. Harcourt 1962
Bkl A—SCPL

Bowen, Croswell. Curse of the Misbegotten: A Tale of the House of O'Neill. McGraw 1959
SCPL

Cargill, Oscar and others, eds. O'Neill and His Plays: Four Decades of Criticism. N.Y. Univ. 1961
SCPL

Clark, Barrett Harper. Eugene O'Neill: The Man and His Plays. Dover 1947
SCPL—3000

Gelb, Arthur and Gelb, Barbara. O'Neill. Harper 1962
Bkl A—SCPL

Raleigh, John Henry. The Plays of Eugene O'Neill. Southern Ill. Univ. 1965
Bkl A

Elmer L. Rice, 1892-1967

Rice, Elmer L. Minority Report: An Autobiography. Simon & Schuster 1963
Bkl A

Edward Sheldon, 1886-1946

Barnes, Eric Wollencott. The Man Who Lived Twice: The Biography of Edward Sheldon. Scribner 1956
BY—SCPL

Robert Emmet Sherwood, 1896-1955

Brown, John Mason. The Worlds of Robert E. Sherwood: Mirror to His Times, 1896-1939. Harper 1965
Bkl A

Shuman, Robert Baird. Robert E. Sherwood. Twayne 1964
Bkl A&Y

Tennessee Williams, 1914-

Falk, Signi Lenea. Tennessee Williams. Twayne 1962
Bkl A—SCPL

Jackson, Esther Merle. The Broken World of Tennessee Williams. Univ. of Wis. 1965
Bkl A

Nelson, Benjamin. Tennessee Williams: The Man and His Work. Obolensky 1961
Bkl A

Tischler, Nancy Marie (Patterson). Tennessee Williams: Rebellious Puritan. Citadel 1961
Bkl A

Williams, Edwina Dakin and Freeman, Lucy. Remember Me to Tom. Putnam 1963
Bkl A

PLAYWRIGHTS—*Continued*

English—16th century

Christopher Marlowe, 1564-1593

Rowse, Alfred Leslie. Christopher Marlowe: His Life and Work. Harper 1965
Bkl A

Wraight, A. D. In Search of Christopher Marlowe: A Pictorial Biography. Vanguard 1965
Bkl A&Y

COLLECTIONS

Trease, Geoffrey. Seven Stages. Vanguard 1965
Bkl Y&C—IndS(9-10)

William Shakespeare, 1564-1616

Adams, Joseph Quincy. Life of William Shakespeare. Houghton 1923
GR—SCPL—3000

Brown, Ivor John Carnegie. How Shakespeare Spent the Day. Hill & Wang 1964
Bkl A

Brown, Ivor John Carnegie. Shakespeare and His World. Walck 1964
Bkl Y&C—ESLC—JH—SCHS

Brown, Ivor John Carnegie. Shakespeare in His Time. Nelson 1960
Bkl A&Y—SCHS—YR

Buckmaster, Henrietta. All the Living. Random House 1962 (Fiction)
Bkl A

Burgess, Anthony. Nothing Like the Sun: A Story of Shakespeare's Lovelife. Norton 1964 (Fiction)
Bkl A

Chambers, Sir Edmund Kerchever. Short Life of Shakespeare. Oxford 1933
SCPL

Chute, Marchette Gaylord. Introduction to Shakespeare. Dutton 1951
CC(7-9)—JH—SCPL

Chute, Marchette Gaylord. Shakespeare of London. Dutton 1949
BBHS—GR—SCHS—SCPL—3000

Drinkwater, John. Shakespeare. Macmillan 1956
SCPL

Fisher, Edward. The Best House in Stratford. Abelard-Schuman 1965 (Fiction)
Bkl A

Fisher, Edward. Love's Labour's Won: A Novel about Shakespeare's Lost Years. Abelard-Schuman 1963 (Fiction)
Bkl A

Fisher, Edward. Shakespeare & Son: A Novel. Abelard-Schuman 1962 (Fiction)
Bkl A

Granville-Barker, Harley Granville, and Harrison, G. B., eds. Companion to Shakespeare Studies. Macmillan 1934
SCPL

Gray, Elizabeth Janet. I Will Adventure. Viking 1962 (Fiction)
AB(7-9)—CC(5-7)—YR

Halliday, Frank Ernest. Shakespeare. Yoseloff 1961
Bkl A&Y

Halliday, Frank Ernest. Shakespeare: A Pictorial Biography. Studio 1956
SCHS

Halliday, Frank Ernest. Shakespeare in His Age. Yoseloff 1964
Bkl A&Y—SCHS

Harbage, Alfred. Conceptions of Shakespeare. Harvard Univ. 1966
Bkl A

Horizon Magazine. Shakespeare's England, by Louis B. Wright. Am. Heritage 1964
Bkl C&Y—CC—ESLC—IndJ(6-9)—SCHS—SCPL

Jowett, Margaret. A Cry of Players. Roy 1961 (Fiction)
ESLC

Kirsch, James. Shakespeare's Royal Self. Putnam 1966
Bkl A

Marder, Louis. His Exits and His Entrances: The Story of Shakespeare's Reputation. Lippincott 1963
Bkl A

Neilson, William Allan and Thorndike, Ashley Horace. Facts about Shakespeare. Macmillan 1931
SCPL

Nicoll, Allardyce. Shakespeare. Essential Bks 1952
SCPL

Noble, Iris. William Shakespeare. Messner 1961
Bkl C(7-9)&Y

Norman, Charles. The Playmaker of Avon. McKay 1949
SCHS

Ogburn, Dorothy and Ogburn, Charlton. Shake-speare: The Man behind the Name. Morrow 1962
Bkl A

Parrott, Thomas Marc. William Shakespeare: A Handbook. Scribner 1955
SCPL

Quennell, Peter. Shakespeare: A Biography. World 1963
Bkl A&Y—IndS(11-12)—SCPL

Reese, Max Meredith. William Shakespeare. St Martins 1964
Bkl C(6-9)&Y—ESLC—IndS(9-11)

Rowse, A. L. William Shakespeare: A Biography. Harper 1963
Bkl A&Y—SCHS—SCPL

PLAYWRIGHTS

English—16th century

William Shakespeare—Continued

Sutherland, James Runcieman and Hurstfield, Joel, eds. Shakespeare's World. St Martins 1964
Bkl A

White, Anne Terry. Will Shakespeare and the Globe Theater. Random House 1955
JH—SCHS

COLLECTIONS

Stirling, Nora B. Who Wrote the Classics? Day 1965
Bkl Y&A&C

Nicholas Udall, 1505-1556

Edgerton, William L. Nicholas Udall. Twayne 1966
Bkl A

English—17th century

William Congreve, 1670-1729

Congreve, William. Letters & Documents; ed. by John C. Hodges. Harcourt 1964
Bkl A

William Shakespeare, 1564-1616
See entries under Playwrights—English—16th century

English—18th century

Colley Cibber, 1671-1757

Ashley, Leonard R. N. Colley Cibber. Twayne 1965
Bkl A

Cibber, Colley. An Apology for the Life of Colley Cibber. Written 1740
CA

English—19th century

Sir William Schwenck Gilbert, 1836-1911

Baily, Leslie. Gilbert & Sullivan Book. Coward-McCann 1957
SCPL

Pearson, Hesketh. Gilbert: His Life and Strife. Harper 1957
SCPL

Purdy, Claire Lee. Gilbert and Sullivan: Masters of Mirth and Melody. Messner 1946
SCHS

Wymer, Norman. Gilbert and Sullivan. Dutton 1963
Bkl C(7-10)&Y—YR

Israel Zangwill, 1864-1926

Wohlgelernter, Maurice. Israel Zangwill: A Study. Columbia Univ. 1964
Bkl A

English—20th century

Noel Pierce Coward, 1899-

Coward, Noel Pierce. Future Indefinite. Doubleday 1954
SCPL

Bernard Kops, 1926-

Kops, Bernard. The World Is a Wedding. Coward-McCann 1963
Bkl A

Israel Zangwill, 1864-1926

Wohlgelernter, Maurice. Israel Zangwill: A Study. Columbia Univ. 1964
Bkl A

French—17th century

Jean Baptiste Poquelin Molière, 1622-1673

Gossman, Lionel. Men and Masks: A Study of Molière. Johns Hopkins 1963
Bkl A

Guicharnaud, Jacques. Molière: A Collection of Critical Essays. Prentice-Hall 1964
Bkl A

Lewis, Dominic Bevan Wyndham. Molière: The Comic Mask. Coward-McCann 1959
Bkl A

COLLECTIONS

Trease, Geoffrey. Seven Stages. Vanguard 1965
Bkl Y&C—IndS(9-10)

French—18th century

Pierre Augustin Caron de Beaumarchais, 1732-1799

Cox, Cynthia. The Real Figaro: The Extraordinary Career of Caron de Beaumarchais. Coward-McCann 1963
Bkl A

Ruskin, Ariane. Spy for Liberty: The Adventurous Life of Beaumarchais, Playwright and Secret Agent for the American Revolution. Pantheon 1965
Bkl Y(7-10)&C

French—20th century

Jean Anouilh, 1910-

Harvey, John E. Anouilh: A Study in Theatrics. Yale Univ. 1964
Bkl A

Jean Genet, 1909-

Sartre, Jean Paul. Saint Genet, Actor and Martyr; tr. from the French by Bernard Frechtman. Braziller 1963
Bkl A

PLAYWRIGHTS

French—20th century—*Continued*

Marcel Pagnol, 1895-

Pagnol, Marcel. The Days Were Too Short; tr. from the French by Rita Barisse. Doubelday 1960
Bkl A

Pagnol, Marcel. The Time of Secrets; tr. from the French by Rita Barisse. Doubleday 1962
Bkl A

Greek—5th century B.C.

Aeschylus, 525-456 B.C.

Murray, Gilbert. Aeschylus: The Creator of Tragedy. Oxford 1940
SCPL

Aristophanes, 448?-380? B.C.

Murray, Gilbert. Aristophanes: A Study. Oxford 1933
SCPL

Euripides, 480?-406 B.C.

Murray, Gilbert. Euripides and His Age. Oxford 1946
SCPL

Irish—18th century

Richard Brinsley Sheridan, 1751-1816

Gibbs, Lewis. Sheridan: His Life and His Theatre. Morrow 1948
SCPL

Irish—19th century

Lady Augusta (Persse) Gregory, 1859?-1932

Coxhead, Elizabeth. Lady Gregory: A Literary Portrait. Harcourt 1961
Bkl A

COLLECTIONS

Howarth, Herbert. The Irish Writers, 1880-1940. Hill & Wang 1959
Bkl A

George Bernard Shaw, 1856-1950

See also *under* Playwrights—Irish—20th century

Meisel, Martin. Shaw and the Nineteenth-Century Theater. Princeton Univ. 1963
Bkl A

Rosset, B. C. Shaw of Dublin: The Formative Years. Pa. State Univ. 1964
Bkl A

Shaw, George Bernard. Collected Letters: v. 1, 1874-1897; ed. by Dan H. Laurence. Dodd 1965
Bkl A

Irish—20th century

Lady Augusta (Persse) Gregory, 1859?-1932

Coxhead, Elizabeth. Lady Gregory: A Literary Portrait. Harcourt 1961
Bkl A

COLLECTIONS

Howarth, Herbert. The Irish Writers, 1880-1940. Hill & Wang 1959
Bkl A

Sean O'Casey, 1884-1964

Cowasjee, Saros. Sean O'Casey: The Man Behind the Plays. St Martins 1964
Bkl A

Fallon, Gabriel. Sean O'Casey: The Man I Knew. Little 1965
Bkl A

Krause, David. Sean O'Casey: The Man and His Work. Macmillan 1960
SCPL

O'Casey, Sean. Drums Under the Windows. Macmillan 1946
SCPL

O'Casey, Sean. I Knock at the Door: Swift Glances Back at Things That Made Me. Macmillan 1949
SCPL

O'Casey, Sean. Inishfallen, Fare Thee Well. Macmillan 1949
SCPL

O'Casey, Sean. Mirror in My House: The Autobiographies of Sean O'Casey. 2v. Macmillan 1956
SCPL

O'Casey, Sean. Pictures in the Hallway. Macmillan 1942
SCPL

O'Casey, Sean. Rose and Crown. Macmillan 1952
SCPL

O'Casey, Sean. Sunset and Evening Star. Macmillan 1954
SCPL

George Bernard Shaw, 1856-1950

See also *under* Playwrights—Irish—19th century

Chappelow, Allan, ed. Shaw the Villager and Human Being: A Biographical Symposium. Macmillan 1962
Bkl A

Du Cann, Charles Garfield Lott. The Loves of George Bernard Shaw. Funk 1963
Bkl A

Ervine, St. John Greer. Bernard Shaw: His Life, Work and Friends. Morrow 1956
SCPL

PLAYWRIGHTS
Irish—20th century

George Bernard Shaw—Continued

Henderson, Archibald. George Bernard Shaw: Man of the Century. Appleton 1956
SCPL

Kilty, Jerome. Dear Liar: A Comedy of Letters Adapted from the Correspondence of Bernard Shaw and Mrs. Patrick Campbell. Dodd 1960 (Play)
Bkl A

Langner, Lawrence. G. B. S. and the Lunatic: Reminiscences of the Long, Lively, and Affectionate Friendship between George Bernard Shaw and the Author. Atheneum 1963
Bkl A

Pearson, Hesketh. G. B. S.: A Full Length Portrait and a Postscript. Harper 1952
BBHS–SCHS–SCPL–3000

Shaw, George Bernard. Bernard Shaw and Mrs. Patrick Campbell: Their Correspondence. Knopf 1952
SCPL

Shaw, George Bernard. Sixteen Self Sketches. Dodd 1949
SCPL

Shenfield, Margaret. Bernard Shaw: A Pictorial Biography. Viking 1962
Bkl A&Y

Smith, Joseph Percy. The Unrepentant Pilgrim: A Study of the Development of Bernard Shaw. Houghton 1965
Bkl A

Weintraub, Stanley. Private Shaw and Public Shaw: A Dual Portrait of Lawrence of Arabia and G. B. S. Braziller 1963
Bkl A

Woodbridge, Homer E. George Bernard Shaw: Creative Artist. Southern Ill. Univ. 1963
Bkl A&Y

John Millington Synge, 1871-1909

Gerstenberger, Donna Lorine. John Millington Synge. Twayne 1965
Bkl A

Greene, David H. and Stephens, E. M. J. M. Synge, 1871-1909. Macmillan 1959
SCPL

COLLECTIONS

Howarth, Herbert. The Irish Writers, 1880-1940. Hill & Wang 1959
Bkl A

Norwegian—19th century

Henrik Ibsen, 1828-1906

Bradbrook, Muriel Clara. Ibsen the Norwegian: A Revaluation. Macmillan 1948
SCPL

Ibsen, Henrik. Letters and Speeches; ed. by Evert Sprinchorn. Hill & Wang 1964
Bkl A

Lucas, Frank Laurence. The Drama of Ibsen and Strindberg. Macmillan 1962
Bkl A

Roman—3rd century B.C.

Titus Maccius Plautus, 254?-184 B.C.

COLLECTIONS

Sellar, William Young. Roman Poets of the Republic. Oxford 1889
SCPL

Roman—2nd century B.C.

Terence, 185-159 B.C.

COLLECTIONS

Sellar, William Young. Roman Poets of the Republic. Oxford 1889
SCPL

Scottish—20th century

Osborne Henry Mavor, 1888-1951

Luyben, Helen L. James Bridie: Clown and Philosopher. Univ. of Pa. 1965
Bkl A

Spanish—20th century

Federico García Lorca, 1899-1936

Lima, Robert. The Theatre of García Lorca. Las Américas Pub. 1963
Bkl A

COLLECTIONS

Young, Howard Thomas. The Victorious Expression: A Study of Four Contemporary Spanish Poets. Univ. of Wis. 1964
Bkl A

Welsh—20th century

Emlyn Williams, 1905-

Williams, Emlyn. George: An Early Autobiography. Random House 1961
Bkl A–BY–SCPL

POETS

COLLECTIONS

Benét, Laura. Famous Poets for Young People. Dodd 1964
Bkl C(6-9)–CC–ESLC–JH

POETS—*Continued*

Brenner, Rica. Poets of Our Time. Harcourt 1941
SCHS—SCPL
Wystan Hugh Auden; Stephen Vincent Benét; Thomas Stearns Eliot; Vachel Lindsay; Archibald MacLeish; Stephen Spender; Sara Teasdale; Elinor Morton (Hoyt) Wylie; William Butler Yeats

Spender, Stephen and Hall, Donald, eds. The Concise Encyclopedia of English and American Poets and Poetry. Hawthorn 1963
SCHS—SCPL

Untermeyer, Louis. Lives of the Poets: The Story of One Thousand Years of English and American Poetry. Simon & Schuster 1959
BBHS—SCHS—SCPL—3000

American

COLLECTIONS

Benét, Laura. Famous American Poets. Dodd 1950
BBJH—CC(6-8)—JH—SCHS

Donoghue, Denis. Connoisseurs of Chaos. Macmillan 1965
IndS(10-12)
Emily Dickinson; Robert Frost; James Russell Lowell; Herman Melville; Wallace Stevens; Walt Whitman; and others

Rollins, Charlemae Hill. Famous American Negro Poets. Dodd 1965
Bkl C(6-9)&Y—ESLC

Simon, Charlie May (Hogue). Lays of the New Land: Stories of Some American Poets and Their Work. Dutton 1943
BBJH—JH

Stepanchev, Stephen. American Poetry Since 1945: A Critical Survey. Harper 1965
Bkl A&Y

American—17th century

Edward Taylor, 1642-1729

Grabo, Norman S. Edward Taylor. Twayne 1961
Bkl A

American—18th century

Phillis Wheatley, 1753?-1784

Graham, Shirley. The Story of Phillis Wheatley. Messner 1949
BY—CC(7-9)—JH—SCHS

COLLECTIONS

Bacon, Martha Sherman. Puritan Promenade. Houghton 1964
Bkl A&Y—IndS(9-12)

American—19th century

William Cullen Bryant, 1794-1878

McLean, Albert F. William Cullen Bryant. Twayne 1964
Bkl A&Y

Emily Dickinson, 1830-1886

Blake, Caesar Robert and Wells, Carlton Frank, eds. The Recognition of Emily Dickinson: Selected Criticism Since 1890. Univ. of Mich. 1964
Bkl A

Chase, Richard. Emily Dickinson. Sloane 1951
SCPL

Dickinson, Emily. Letters; ed. by T. H. Johnson. Harvard Univ. 1958
SCPL

Fisher, Aileen and Rabe, Olive. We Dickinsons. Atheneum 1965
ESLC—IndJ(6-9)

Gelpi, Albert J. Emily Dickinson: The Mind of the Poet. Harvard Univ. 1965
Bkl A

Griffith, Clark. The Long Shadow: Emily Dickinson's Tragic Poetry. Princeton Univ. 1964
Bkl A

Johnson, Thomas Herbert, ed. Emily Dickinson: An Interpretative Biography. Harvard Univ. 1955
3000

Longsworth, Polly. Emily Dickinson: Her Letter to the World. Crowell 1965
Bkl Y&C

Sewall, Richard Benson, ed. Emily Dickinson: A Collection of Critical Essays. Prentice-Hall 1963
Bkl A&Y

Ward, Theodora (Van Wagenen). The Capsule of the Mind: Chapters in the Life of Emily Dickinson. Harvard Univ. 1961
Bkl A

Wells, Henry Willis. Introduction to Emily Dickinson. Hendricks House 1947
SCPL

COLLECTIONS

Donoghue, Denis. Connoisseurs of Chaos. Macmillan 1965
IndS(10-12)

Paul Laurence Dunbar, 1872-1906

Cunningham, Virginia. Paul Laurence Dunbar and His Song. Dodd 1947
BBHS—SCHS

Gould, Jean. That Dunbar Boy: The Story of America's Famous Negro Poet. Dodd 1958
CC(5-7)—JH—YR

POETS

American—19th century—*Continued*

Eugene Field, 1850-1895

Nolan, Jeannette (Covert). The Gay Poet: The Story of Eugene Field. Messner 1940
CC(7-9)—JH—SCHS—YR

Francis Scott Key, 1779-1843

Miller, Natalie. The Story of the Star-Spangled Banner. Childrens Press 1965
ESLC

Patterson, Lillie. Francis Scott Key: Poet and Patriot. Garrard 1963
AB(4-7)

Emma Lazarus, 1849-1887

Merriam, Eve. The Voice of Liberty: The Story of Emma Lazarus. Farrar 1959
AB(7-10)

Henry Wadsworth Longfellow, 1807-1882

Arvin, Newton. Longfellow: His Life and Work. Little 1963
Bkl A&Y—IndS(11-12)—SCPL

Holberg, Ruth (Langland). An American Bard: The Story of Henry Wadsworth Longfellow. Crowell 1963
Bkl C(5-7)—ESLC—IndJ(4-6)—JH—SCHS—YR

Peare, Catherine Owens. Henry Wadsworth Longfellow: His Life. Holt 1953
BBEL(4-7)—CC(4-7)—ESLC

Wagenknecht, Edward Charles. Longfellow: A Full-Length Portrait. Longmans 1955
SCPL

James Russell Lowell, 1819-1891

Browning, Robert. Browning to His American Friends: Letters Between the Brownings, the Storys and James Russell Lowell, 1841-1890; ed. by Gertrude Reese Hudson. Barnes & Noble 1965
Bkl A

COLLECTIONS

Donoghue, Denis. Connoisseurs of Chaos. Macmillan 1965
IndS(10-12)

James Whitcomb Riley, 1849-1916

COLLECTIONS

Arvin, Newton. American Pantheon; ed. by Daniel Aaron and Sylvan Schendler. Delacorte 1966
Bkl A&Y

Walt Whitman, 1819-1892

Allen, Gay Wilson. Solitary Singer: A Critical Biography of Walt Whitman. Macmillan 1955
BBHS—GR—SCPL—3000

Canby, Henry Seidel. Walt Whitman, an American: A Study in Biography. Houghton 1943
SCPL

Deutsch, Babette. Walt Whitman: Builder for America. Messner 1941
BBHS—JH—SCHS

Miller, James Edwin. Walt Whitman. Twayne 1962
Bkl A&Y

COLLECTIONS

Arvin, Newton. American Pantheon; ed. by Daniel Aaron and Sylvan Schendler. Delacorte 1966
Bkl A&Y

Canby, Henry Seidel. Classic Americans: A Study of Eminent American Writers from Irving to Whitman. Russell & Russell 1959
SCPL

Donoghue, Denis. Connoisseurs of Chaos. Macmillan 1965
IndS(10-12)

John Greenleaf Whittier, 1807-1892

Holberg, Ruth Langland. John Greenleaf Whittier, Fighting Quaker. Crowell 1958
CC(6-9)—JH—YR

American—20th century

Conrad Potter Aiken, 1889-

Hoffman, Frederick John. Conrad Aiken. Twayne 1962
Bkl A

Martin, Jay. Conrad Aiken: A Life of His Art. Princeton Univ. 1962
Bkl A

Helen (Smith) Bevington, 1906-

Bevington, Helen (Smith). Charley Smith's Girl: A Memoir. Simon & Schuster 1965
Bkl A

Robert Peter Tristram Coffin, 1892-1955

Coffin, Robert Peter Tristram. Lost Paradise: A Boyhood on a Maine Coast Farm. Macmillan 1934
SCPL

Hart Crane, 1899-1932

Hazo, Samuel John. Hart Crane: An Introduction and Interpretation. Barnes & Noble 1963
Bkl A

POETS

American—20th century

Hart Crane—Continued

Quinn, Vincent. Hart Crane. Twayne 1963
SCPL

COLLECTIONS

Morgan, Howard Wayne. Writers in Transition: Seven Americans. Hill & Wang 1963
Bkl A

Hilda Doolittle, 1886-1961

Swann, Thomas Burnett. The Classical World of H. D. Univ. of Neb. 1962
Bkl A

Paul Laurence Dunbar, 1872-1906

Cunningham, Virginia. Paul Laurence Dunbar and His Song. Dodd 1947
BBHS—SCHS
Gould, Jean. That Dunbar Boy: The Story of America's Famous Negro Poet. Dodd 1958
CC(5-7)—JH—YR

Robert Frost, 1874-1963

Anderson, Margaret (Bartlett). Robert Frost and John Bartlett: The Record of a Friendship. Holt 1963
Bkl A
Cox, Sidney Hayes. Swinger of Birches: A Portrait of Robert Frost. N.Y. Univ. 1957
SCPL
Faber, Doris. Robert Frost: America's Poet. Prentice-Hall 1964
ESLC
Frost, Robert. Interviews with Robert Frost; ed. by Edward Connery Lathem. Holt 1966
Bkl A
Frost, Robert. The Letters of Robert Frost to Louis Untermeyer. Holt 1963
Bkl A—SCHS—SCPL
Frost, Robert. Selected Letters; ed. by Lawrence Thompson. Holt 1964
Bkl A
Gould, Jean. Robert Frost: The Aim Was Song. Dodd 1964
Bkl A—SCHS—SCPL
Reed, Meredith. Our Year Began in April. Lothrop 1963 (Fiction)
JH
Reeve, Franklin D. Robert Frost in Russia. Little 1964
Bkl A—IndS(10-12)
Sergeant, Elizabeth Shepley. Robert Frost: The Trial by Existence. Holt 1960
Bkl A&Y—BY—SCHS—SCPL—3000

Squires, Radcliffe. The Major Themes of Robert Frost. Univ. of Mich. 1963
Bkl A&Y—SCPL

COLLECTIONS

Donoghue, Denis. Connoisseurs of Chaos. Macmillan 1965
IndS(10-12)

Sadakichi Hartmann, 1867-1944

Fowler, Gene. Minutes of the Last Meeting. Viking 1954
SCPL

Robinson Jeffers, 1887-1962

Carpenter, Frederic Ives. Robinson Jeffers. Twayne 1962
Bkl A

Vachel Lindsay, 1879-1931

COLLECTIONS

Brenner, Rica. Poets of Our Time. Harcourt 1941
SCHS—SCPL

Archibald MacLeish, 1892-

Falk, Signi Lenea. Archibald MacLeish. Twayne 1966
Bkl A&Y

COLLECTIONS

Brenner, Rica. Poets of Our Time. Harcourt 1941
SCHS—SCPL

Edwin Markham, 1852-1940

COLLECTIONS

McNeer, May Yonge and Ward, Lynd Kendall. Give Me Freedom. Abingdon 1964
Bkl C(5-8)—CC(5-7)—ESLC—JH—YR

Edna St. Vincent Millay, 1892-1950

Gurko, Miriam. Restless Spirit: The Life of Edna St. Vincent Millay. Crowell 1962
BBHS—Bkl A&Y—BY—CC—JH—SCHS
Millay, Edna St. Vincent. Letters; ed. by A. R. Macdougall. Harper 1952
SCPL
Shafter, Toby. Edna St. Vincent Millay. Messner 1957
YR
Sheean, Vincent. Indigo Bunting: A Memoir of Edna St. Vincent Millay. Harper 1951
SCPL

Marianne Moore, 1887-

Engel, Bernard F. Marianne Moore. Twayne 1964
Bkl A

POETS

American—20th century

Marianne Moore—Continued

Tambimuttu, Thurairaiah, ed. Festschrift for Marianne Moore's Seventy-seventh Birthday, by Various Hands. Tambimuttu & Mass 1964
Bkl A

Ezra Loomis Pound, 1885-

Davie, Donald. Ezra Pound: Poet as Sculptor. Oxford 1964
Bkl A
Hutchins, Patricia. Ezra Pound's Kensington: An Exploration, 1885-1913. Regnery 1965
Bkl A
Norman, Charles. Ezra Pound. Macmillan 1960
Bkl A
Pound, Ezra Loomis. Letters of Ezra Pound, 1907-1941; ed. by D. D. Paige. Harcourt 1950
SCPL

Kenneth Rexroth, 1905-

Rexroth, Kenneth. An Autobiographical Novel. Doubleday 1966
Bkl A

James Whitcomb Riley, 1849-1916

COLLECTIONS

Arvin, Newton. American Pantheon; ed. by Daniel Aaron and Sylvan Schendler. Delacorte 1966
Bkl A&Y

Edwin Arlington Robinson, 1869-1935

Neff, Emery Edward. Edwin Arlington Robinson. Sloane 1948
SCPL
Smith, Chard Powers. Where the Light Falls: A Portrait of Edwin Arlington Robinson. Macmillan 1965
Bkl A—IndS(11-12)

George Santayana, 1863-1952

Cory, Daniel. Santayana: The Later Years, a Portrait with Letters. Brazionler 1963
Bkl A—SCPL
Santayana, George. Persons and Places. 3v. Scribner 1944-1953 or 3v. in 1. Scribner 1963
IndS(12)—SCPL

Wallace Stevens, 1879-1955

Brown, Ashley and Haller, Robert S., eds. The Achievement of Wallace Stevens. Lippincott 1962
Bkl A

Enck, John Jacob. Wallace Stevens: Images and Judgments. Southern Ill. Univ. 1964
Bkl A
Fuchs, Daniel. The Comic Spirit of Wallace Stevens. Duke Univ. 1963
Bkl A
Wells, Henry Willis. Introduction to Wallace Stevens. Ind. Univ. 1964.
Bkl A

COLLECTIONS

Donoghue, Denis. Connoisseurs of Chaos. Macmillan 1965
IndS(10-12)

Sara Teasdale, 1884-1933

Carpenter, Margaret Haley. Sara Teasdale: A Biography. Schulte 1960
Bkl A

COLLECTIONS

Brenner, Rica. Poets of Our Time. Harcourt 1941
SCHS—SCPL

Jean (Starr) Untermeyer, 1886-

Untermeyer, Jean (Starr). Private Collection. Knopf 1965
Bkl A

Louis Untermeyer, 1885-

Frost, Robert. The Letters of Robert Frost to Louis Untermeyer. Holt 1963
Bkl A—SCHS—SCPL
Untermeyer, Louis. Bygones: The Recollections of Louis Untermeyer. Harcourt 1965
Bkl A

Canadian—20th century

David Scott Blackhall, 1910-

Blackhall, David Scott. This House Had Windows. Obolensky 1962
Bkl A

Chilean—20th century

Lucila Godoy Alcayaga, 1889-1957

Arce de Vazquez, Margot. Gabriela Mistral: The Poet and Her Work; tr. by Helene Masslo Anderson. N.Y. Univ. 1964
Bkl A

Chinese—12th century

Li Ch'ing-chao, 1081- 1141?

Hu, P'in-ch'ing. Li Ch'ing-chao. Twayne 1966
Bkl A

POETS—*Continued*

English

COLLECTIONS

Bennett, Joan (Frankau). Four Metaphysical Poets. Cambridge 1953
SCPL
Richard Crashaw; John Donne; George Herbert; Henry Vaughan

Daiches, David. Poetry and the Modern World: A Study of Poetry in England Between 1900 and 1939. Univ. of Chicago 1940
SCPL
Wystan Hugh Auden; Cecil Day-Lewis; Thomas Stearns Eliot; Thomas Hardy; Gerard Manley Hopkins; Alfred Edward Housman; Thomas Ernest Hulme; Dame Edith Sitwell; Sir Osbert Sitwell; Stephen Spender; William Butler Yeats

Hazlitt, William. Lectures on the English Poets. Oxford 1924
SCPL

Norton, Sybil and Cournos, John. Famous British Poets. Dodd 1952
SCHS

English—14th century

Geoffrey Chaucer, 1340?-1400

Bowden, Muriel Amanda. A Reader's Guide to Geoffrey Chaucer. Farrar 1964
Bkl A

Brewer, Derek. Chaucer in His Time. Nelson 1963
SCPL

Chute, Marchette Gaylord. Geoffrey Chaucer of England. Dutton 1946
BBHS—GR—SCHS—SCPL—3000

Faulkner, Nancy. The Yellow Hat. Doubleday 1958 (Fiction)
BBJH—JH

Howard, Edwin Johnston. Geoffrey Chaucer. Twayne 1964
Bkl A&Y

Kittredge, George Lyman. Chaucer and His Poetry. Harvard Univ. 1915
SCPL

Loomis, Roger Sherman. A Mirror of Chaucer's World. Princeton Univ. 1965
Bkl A

English—16th century

Henry Howard, Earl of Surrey, 1517-1547

Chapman, Hester W. Two Tudor Portraits: Henry Howard, Earl of Surrey, and Lady Katherine Grey. Little 1963
Bkl A—IndS(11-12)

William Shakespeare, 1564-1616

See entries under Playwrights—English—16th century

English—17th century

Richard Crashaw, 1613?-1649

COLLECTIONS

Bennett, Joan (Frankau). Four Metaphysical Poets. Cambridge 1953
SCPL

John Donne, 1573-1631

Le Comte, Edward Semple. Grace to a Witty Sinner: A Life of Donne. Walker & Co. 1965
Bkl A

Vining, Elizabeth (Gray). Take Heed of Loving Me. Lippincott 1964 (Fiction)
Bkl A—IndS(10-12)

COLLECTIONS

Bennett, Joan (Frankau). Four Metaphysical Poets. Cambridge 1953
SCPL

John Dryden, 1631-1700

Wasserman, George Russell. John Dryden. Twayne 1964
Bkl A

George Herbert, 1593-1633

Chute, Marchette Gaylord. Two Gentle Men: The Lives of George Herbert and Robert Herrick. Dutton 1959
GR—SCPL

COLLECTIONS

Bennett, Joan (Frankau). Four Metaphysical Poets. Cambridge 1953
SCPL

Robert Herrick, 1591-1674

Chute, Marchette Gaylord. Two Gentle Men: The Lives of George Herbert and Robert Herrick. Dutton 1959
GR—SCPL

John Milton, 1608-1674

Bush, Douglas. John Milton: A Sketch of His Life and Writings. Macmillan 1964
Bkl A

Hanford, James Holly. Milton Handbook. Appleton 1946
SCPL

Saillens, Emile. John Milton: Man, Poet, Polemist. Barnes & Noble 1964
Bkl A

COLLECTIONS

Bainton, Roland Herbert. Travail of Religious Liberty: Nine Biographical Studies. Westminster 1951
SCPL

POETS—*Continued*

English—18th century

William Blake, 1757-1827

Bronowski, Jacob. William Blake and the Age of Revolution. Harper 1965
Bkl A

Daugherty, James Henry. William Blake. Viking 1960
BBHS—Bkl Y—BY—SCHS—YR

William Cowper, 1731-1800

COLLECTIONS

Drew, Elizabeth A. The Literature of Gossip: Nine English Letterwriters. Norton 1964
Bkl A&Y

Alexander Pope, 1688-1744

Sitwell, Dame Edith. Alexander Pope. Penguin 1930
GR

Anna Seward, 1742-1809

COLLECTIONS

Swinnerton, Frank Arthur. A Galaxy of Fathers. Doubleday 1966
Bkl A

English—19th century

Matthew Arnold, 1822-1888

Duffin, Henry Charles. Arnold, the Poet. Barnes & Noble 1963
Bkl A

William Blake, 1757-1827

Bronowski, Jacob. William Blake and the Age of Revolution. Harper 1965
Bkl A

Daugherty, James Henry. William Blake. Viking 1960
BBHS—Bkl Y—BY—SCHS—YR

Elizabeth (Barrett) Browning, 1806-1861

Besier, Rudolf. The Barretts of Wimpole Street: A Comedy in Five Acts. Little 1930 (Play)
SCHS—SCPL

Hayter, Alethea. Mrs. Browning: A Poet's Work and Its Setting. Barnes & Noble 1963
Bkl A

Taplin, Gardner B. Life of Elizabeth Barrett Browning. Yale Univ. 1957
3000

Waite, Helen Elmira. How Do I Love Thee? The Story of Elizabeth Barrett Browning. Macrae 1953
BY—CC(8-9)—JH—SCHS

Winwar, Frances. Elizabeth: The Romantic Story of Elizabeth Barrett Browning. World 1957
BBJH—SCHS—YR

Winwar, Frances. Immortal Lovers: Elizabeth Barrett and Robert Browning: A Biography. Harper 1950
BBHS—SCHS—SCPL

Woolf, Virginia (Stephen). Flush: A Biography. Harcourt 1933
BY—SCHS—SCPL

Robert Browning, 1812-1889

Browning, Robert. Browning to His American Friends: Letters Between the Brownings, the Storys and James Russell Lowell, 1841-1890; ed. by Gertrude Reese Hudson. Barnes & Noble 1965
Bkl A

Chesterton, Gilbert Keith. Robert Browning. St Martins n.d.
3000

Miller, Betty Bergson (Spiro). Robert Browning: A Portrait. Scribner 1953
SCPL

Sprague, Rosemary. Forever in Joy: The Life of Robert Browning. Chilton 1965
Bkl Y&C

George Gordon Noël Byron, 6th Baron Byron, 1788-1824

Marchand, Leslie Alexis. Byron: A Biography. 3v. Knopf 1957
SCPL

Maurois, André. Byron. Ungar 1964
SCPL

Moore, Doris (Langley-Levy). The Late Lord Byron: Posthumous Dramas. Lippincott 1961
Bkl A

Whipple, Addison Beecher Colvin. The Fatal Gift of Beauty: The Final Years of Byron and Shelley. Harper 1964
Bkl A

COLLECTIONS

Drew, Elizabeth A. The Literature of Gossip: Nine English Letterwriters. Norton 1964
Bkl A&Y

Ernest Christopher Dowson, 1867-1900

Swann, Thomas Burnett. Ernest Dowson. Twayne 1965
Bkl A

Lord Alfred Bruce Douglas, 1870-1945

Croft-Cooke, Rupert. Bosie: Lord Alfred Douglas—His Friends and Enemies. Bobbs 1964
Bkl A

POETS

English—19th century—*Continued*

Gerard Manley Hopkins, 1844-1889

Hartman, Geoffrey H., ed. Hopkins: A Collection of Critical Essays. Prentice-Hall 1966
Bkl A

COLLECTIONS

Daiches, David. Poetry and the Modern World: A Study of Poetry in England Between 1900 and 1939. Univ. of Chicago 1940
SCPL

Alfred Edward Housman, 1859-1936

Gow, Andrew Sydenham Farrar. A. E. Housman: A Sketch, Together with a List of His Writings and Indexes to His Classical Papers. Cambridge 1936
SCPL
Hawkins, M. M. A. E. Housman: Man Behind the Mask. Regnery 1958
SCPL

Leigh Hunt, 1784-1859

Hunt, Leigh. Autobiography. Orig. pub. 1850
CA

John Keats, 1795-1821

Bate, Walter Jackson. John Keats. Harvard Univ. 1963
Bkl A—SCPL
Bate, Walter Jackson, ed. Keats: A Collection of Critical Essays. Prentice-Hall 1964
Bkl A
Bush, Douglas. John Keats: His Life and Writings. Macmillan 1966
Bkl A&Y
Gittings, Robert and Manton, Jo. The Story of John Keats. Dutton 1963
Bkl Y&C—YR
Ward, Aileen. John Keats: The Making of a Poet. Viking 1963
Bkl A&Y—IndS(11-12)—SCHS—SCPL

William Morris, 1834-1896

Thompson, Edward Palmer. William Morris: Romantic to Revolutionary. Monthly Review 1961
Bkl A

Christina Georgina Rossetti, 1830-1894

Packer, Lona Mosk. Christina Rossetti. Univ. of Calif. 1963
Bkl A

Percy Bysshe Shelley, 1792-1822

Benét, Laura. The Boy Shelley. Dodd 1937
SCHS

Bolton, Guy Reginald. The Olympians. World 1961 (Fiction)
Bkl A
Maurois, André. Ariel: The Life of Shelley. Ungar 1952
SCPL
Whipple, Addison Beecher Colvin. The Fatal Gift of Beauty: The Final Years of Byron and Shelley. Harper 1964
Bkl A
White, Newman Ivey. Portrait of Shelley. Knopf 1945
SCPL

Alfred Tennyson, Baron Tennyson, 1809-1892

Smith, Elton Edward. The Two Voices: A Tennyson Study. Univ. of Neb. 1964
Bkl A

William Wordsworth, 1770-1850

Rountree, Thomas J. This Mighty Sum of Things: Wordsworth's Theme of Benevolent Necessity. Univ. of Ala. 1965
Bkl A

English—20th century

Wystan Hugh Auden, 1907-

COLLECTIONS

Brenner, Rica. Poets of Our Time. Harcourt 1941
SCHS—SCPL
Daiches, David. Poetry and the Modern World: A Study of Poetry in England Between 1900 and 1939. Univ. of Chicago 1940
SCPL

Julian Bell, 1908-1937

Stansky, Peter and Abrahams, William Miller. Journey to the Frontier: Two Roads to the Spanish Civil War. Little 1966
Bkl A

Rupert Brooke, 1887-1915

Hassall, Christopher Vernon. Rupert Brooke: A Biography. Harcourt 1964
Bkl A—SCPL

John Cornford, 1908-1936

Stansky, Peter and Abrahams, William Miller. Journey to the Frontier: Two Roads to the Spanish Civil War. Little 1966
Bkl A

William Henry Davies, 1871-1940

Stonesifer, Richard James. W. H. Davies: A Critical Biography. Wesleyan Univ. 1965
Bkl A

POETS

English—20th century—*Continued*

Cecil Day-Lewis, 1904-

Day-Lewis, Cecil. The Buried Day.
Harper 1960
Bkl A

COLLECTIONS

Daiches, David. Poetry and the Modern
World: A Study of Poetry in England
Between 1900 and 1939. Univ. of
Chicago 1940
SCPL

*Lord Alfred Bruce Douglas, 1870-
1945*

Croft-Cooke, Rupert. Bosie: Lord Alfred
Douglas—His Friends and Enemies.
Bobbs 1964
Bkl A

Thomas Stearns Eliot, 1888-1965

Headings, Philip Ray. T. S. Eliot.
Twayne 1964
Bkl A&Y

Howarth, Herbert. Notes on Some Figures Behind T. S. Eliot. Houghton
1964
Bkl A

Unger, Leonard, ed. T. S. Eliot: A Selected Critique. Rinehart 1948
SCPL

COLLECTIONS

Brenner, Rica. Poets of Our Time. Harcourt 1941
SCHS—SCPL

Brooks, Cleanth. The Hidden God: Stud-
ies in Hemingway, Faulkner, Yeats,
Eliot, and Warren. Yale Univ. 1963
Bkl A

Daiches, David. Poetry and the Modern
World: A Study of Poetry in England
Between 1900 and 1939. Univ. of
Chicago 1940
SCPL

Wilson, Edmund. Axel's Castle: A Study
in the Imaginative Literature of 1870-
1930. Scribner 1931
SCPL

Robert Graves, 1895-

Day, Douglas. Swifter than Reason: The
Poetry and Criticism of Robert
Graves. Univ. of N.C. 1963
Bkl A

Alfred Edward Housman, 1859-1936

Gow, Andrew Sydenham Farrar. A. E.
Housman: A Sketch, Together with a
List of His Writings and Indexes to
His Classical Papers. Cambridge 1936
SCPL

Hawkins, M. M. A. E. Housman: Man
Behind the Mask. Regnery 1958
SCPL

COLLECTIONS

Daiches, David. Poetry and the Modern
World: A Study of Poetry in England
Between 1900 and 1939. Univ. of
Chicago 1940
SCPL

Thomas Ernest Hulme, 1883-1917

COLLECTIONS

Daiches, David. Poetry and the Modern
World: A Study of Poetry in England
Between 1900 and 1939. Univ. of
Chicago 1940
SCPL

Laurie Lee, 1914-

Lee, Laurie. The Edge of Day: A Boyhood in the West of England. Morrow
1960
Bkl A—BY—SCPL

Alfred Noyes, 1880-1958

Noyes, Alfred. Two Worlds for Memory.
Lippincott 1953
SCPL

Dame Edith Sitwell, 1887-1964

Sitwell, Dame Edith. Taken Care Of:
The Autobiography of Edith Sitwell.
Atheneum 1965
Bkl A

COLLECTIONS

Daiches, David. Poetry and the Modern
World: A Study of Poetry in England
Between 1900 and 1939. Univ. of
Chicago 1940
SCPL

Stephen Spender, 1909-

COLLECTIONS

Brenner, Rica. Poets of Our Time. Harcourt 1941
SCHS—SCPL

Daiches, David. Poetry and the Modern
World: A Study of Poetry in England
Between 1900 and 1939. Univ. of
Chicago 1940
SCPL

French—15th century

François Villon, 1431-1463?

Leslie, Doris. Vagabond's Way: The
Story of François Villon. Doubleday
1962 (Fiction)
Bkl A

POETS—*Continued*

French—16th century

Joachim du Bellay, 1522-1560

COLLECTIONS

Pater, Walter Horatio. Renaissance Studies in Art and Poetry. Modern Lib n.d.
SCPL

French—19th century

Charles Pierre Baudelaire, 1821-1867

Ruff, Marcel A. Baudelaire; tr. and abr. by Agnes Kertesz. N.Y. Univ. 1966
Bkl A

Starkie, Enid. Baudelaire. New Directions 1958
SCPL

Jean Nicolas Arthur Rimbaud, 1854-1891

Hanson, Elisabeth M. My Poor Arthur: A Biography of Arthur Rimbaud. Holt 1960
Bkl A

Starkie, Enid. Arthur Rimbaud. New Directions 1961
SCPL

COLLECTIONS

Wilson, Edmund. Axel's Castle: A Study in the Imaginative Literature of 1870-1930. Scribner 1931
SCPL

French—20th century

Guillaume Apollinaire, 1880-1918

Davies, Margaret (Brown). Apollinaire. St Martins 1965
Bkl A

Steegmuller, Francis. Apollinaire, Poet Among the Painters. Farrar 1963
Bkl A

German—18th century

Johann Wolfgang von Goethe, 1749-1832

Friedenthal, Richard. Goethe: His Life and Times. World 1965
Bkl A

Goethe, Johann Wolfgang von. Autobiography: Poetry and Truth from My Own Life; tr. by R. O. Moon. Public Affairs Press 1949
CA–SCPL

Goethe, Johann Wolfgang von. Goethe: The Story of a Man, Being the Life of Goethe, as Told in His Own Words; ed. by Ludwig Lewisohn. 2v. Farrar 1949
SCPL

Schweitzer, Albert. Goethe: Four Studies; tr. by Charles R. Joy. Beacon Press 1949
SCPL

German—19th century

Johann Wolfgang von Goethe, 1749-1832

Friedenthal, Richard. Goethe: His Life and Times. World 1965
Bkl A

Goethe, Johann Wolfgang von. Autobiography: Poetry and Truth from My Own Life; tr. by R. O. Moon. Public Affairs Press 1949
CA–SCPL

Goethe, Johann Wolfgang von. Goethe: The Story of a Man, Being the Life of Goethe, as Told in His Own Words; ed. by Ludwig Lewisohn. 2v. Farrar 1949
SCPL

Schweitzer, Albert. Goethe: Four Studies; tr. by Charles R. Joy. Beacon Press 1949
SCPL

Greek—9th century B.C.

Homer, 9th century B.C.

Michalopoulos, André. Homer. Twayne 1966
Bkl A&Y

Indian—17th century

Begam Jahānārā, Daughter of Shāhjāhan, 1614-1680

Bothwell, Jean. Omen for a Princess: The Story of Jahanara, Royal Poet of the Seventeenth Century. Abelard-Schuman 1963 (Fiction)
Bkl C(7-9)

Indian—20th century

Rabindranath Tagore, 1861-1941

Kripalani, Krishna. Rabindranath Tagore: A Biography. Grove 1962
Bkl A

Italian—14th century

Dante Alighieri, 1265-1321

Bergin, Thomas Goddard. Dante. Orion 1965
Bkl A

Dante Alighieri. New Life (La Vita Nuova). Written c. 1320
CA

Fergusson, Francis. Dante. Macmillan 1966
Bkl A

POETS

Italian—14th century

Dante Alighieri—Continued

Freccero, John, ed. Dante: A Collection of Critical Essays. Prentice-Hall 1965
Bkl A

Francesco Petrarch, 1304-1374

Bishop, Morris. Petrarch and His World. Ind. Univ. 1963
Bkl A

Roman

COLLECTIONS

Highet, Gilbert Arthur. Poets in a Landscape. Knopf 1957
BBHS—SCPL
Gaius Valerius Catullus; Horace; Decimus Junius Juvenal; Ovid; Sextus Propertius; Albius Tibullus; Virgil

Sellar, William Young. Roman Poets of the Republic. Oxford 1889
SCPL
Gaius Valerius Catullus; Quintus Ennius; Lucretius; Titus Maccius Plautus; Terence

Roman—2nd century B.C.

Quintus Ennius, 239-169? B.C.

COLLECTIONS

Sellar, William Young, Roman Poets of the Republic. Oxford 1889
SCPL

Roman—1st century B.C.

Gaius Valerius Catullus, 84?-54 B.C.

COLLECTIONS

Highet, Gilbert Arthur. Poets in a Landscape. Knopf 1957
BBHS—SCPL

Sellar, William Young. Roman Poets of the Republic. Oxford 1889
SCPL

Horace (Quintus Horatius Flaccus), 65-8 B.C.

Perret, Jacques. Horace; tr. by Bertha Humez. N.Y. Univ. 1964
Bkl A

COLLECTIONS

Highet, Gilbert Arthur. Poets in a Landscape. Knopf 1957
BBHS—SCPL

Titus Lucretius Carus, 96?-55 B.C.

COLLECTIONS

Sellar, William Young, Roman Poets of the Republic. Oxford 1889
SCPL

Ovid, 43 B.C.-18 A.D.

Horia, Vintila. God Was Born in Exile: A Novel; tr. from the French by A. Lytton Sells. St Martins 1961 (Fiction)
Bkl A

COLLECTIONS

Highet, Gilbert Arthur. Poets in a Landscape. Knopf 1957
BBHS—SCPL

Sextus Propertius, 50?-15? B.C.

COLLECTIONS

Highet, Gilbert Arthur. Poets in a Landscape. Knopf 1957
BBHS—SCPL

Albius Tibullus, 54?-18? B.C.

COLLECTIONS

Highet, Gilbert Arthur. Poets in a Landscape. Knopf 1957
BBHS—SCPL

Virgil, 70-19 B.C.

COLLECTIONS

Highet, Gilbert Arthur. Poets in a Landscape. Knopf 1957
BBHS—SCPL

Russian—20th century

Aleksandr Aleksandrovich Blok, 1880-1921

COLLECTIONS

Muchnic, Helen. From Gorky to Pasternak: Six Writers in Soviet Russia. Random House 1961
Bkl A

Eugenii Aleksandrovich Evtushenko, 1933-

Evtushenko, Eugenii Aleksandrovich. A Precocious Autobiography; tr. from the Russian by Andrew R. MacAndrew. Dutton 1963
Bkl A—IndS(9-12)—SCPL

COLLECTIONS

Carlisle, Olga (Andreyev). Voices in the Snow: Encounters with Russian Writers. Random House 1963
Bkl A

Vladimir Vladimirovich Mayakovski, 1893-1930

COLLECTIONS

Muchnic, Helen. From Gorky to Pasternak: Six Writers in Soviet Russia. Random House 1961
Bkl A

POETS—*Continued*

Scottish—17th century

Lady Grizel (Hume) Baillie, 1665-1746

Kyle, Elisabeth. The Story of Grizel. Nelson 1961 (Fiction)
Bkl C(7-9)&Y

Scottish—18th century

Robert Burns, 1759-1796

Burns, Robert. Letters; ed. from the original manuscripts by J. De Lancey Ferguson. Oxford 1931
SCPL

South African—20th century

Peter Abrahams, 1919-

Abrahams, Peter. Tell Freedom: Memories of Africa. Knopf 1954
SCPL

Spanish

COLLECTIONS

Young, Howard Thomas. The Victorious Expression: A Study of Four Contemporary Spanish Poets. Univ. of Wis. 1964
Bkl A
Federico García Lorca; Juan Ramón Jiménez; Antonio Machado y Ruiz; Miguel de Unamuno y Jugo

Spanish—20th century

Federico García Lorca, 1899-1936

COLLECTIONS

Young, Howard Thomas. The Victorious Expression: A Study of Four Contemporary Spanish Poets. Univ. of Wis. 1964
Bkl A

Juan Ramón Jiménez, 1881-1958

COLLECTIONS

Young, Howard Thomas. The Victorious Expression: A Study of Four Contemporary Spanish Poets. Univ. of Wis. 1964
Bkl A

Welsh—17th century

Henry Vaughan, 1622-1695

COLLECTIONS

Bennett, Joan (Frankau). Four Metaphysical Poets. Cambridge 1953
SCPL

Welsh—20th century

Dylan Thomas, 1914-1953

Ackerman, John. Dylan Thomas: His Life and Work. Oxford 1964
Bkl A
Brinnin, John Malcolm, ed. A Casebook on Dylan Thomas. Crowell 1961
Bkl A
Cox, C. B., ed. Dylan Thomas: A Collection of Critical Essays. Prentice-Hall 1966
Bkl A
Firmage, George James, ed. A Garland for Dylan Thomas. Clarke & Way 1963
Bkl A
FitzGibbon, Constantine. The Life of Dylan Thomas. Little 1965
Bkl A—IndS(11-12)
Korg, Jacob. Dylan Thomas. Twayne 1965
Bkl A
Michaels, Sidney. Dylan. Random 1964 (Play)
Bkl A—SCPL
Olson, Elder. Poetry of Dylan Thomas. Univ. of Chicago 1954
SCPL
Read, Bill. The Days of Dylan Thomas. McGraw 1964
Bkl A
Tindall, William York. A Reader's Guide to Dylan Thomas. Farrar 1962
Bkl A—SCPL

COLLECTIONS

Heppenstall, Rayner. Four Absentees. Dufour 1963
Bkl A

POLICE

See also Detectives; Sheriffs

American—19th century

William Alexander Anderson Wallace, 1817-1899

Garst, Doris Shannon. Big Foot Wallace of the Texas Rangers. Messner 1951
CC(5-7)

American—20th century

Francis D. J. Phillips, 1904?-

Reynolds, Quentin James. Headquarters. Harper 1955
SCPL

Canadian—20th century

Charles Rivett-Carnac, 1901?-

Rivett-Carnac, Charles. Pursuit in the Wilderness. Little 1965
Bkl A&Y—IndS(10-12)

POLIO VICTIMS

See Victims of Polio

POLITICAL LEADERS

See Presidents; Statesmen

POLITICAL PHILOSOPHERS

See Political Scientists

POLITICAL SCIENTISTS

American—18th century

Thomas Paine, 1737-1809

Aldridge, Alfred Owen. Man of Reason: The Life of Thomas Paine. Lippincott 1959
SCPL

Brett, Grace Neff. The Picture Story and Biography of Tom Paine. Follett 1965
ESLC

Gurko, Leo. Tom Paine, Freedom's Apostle. Crowell 1957
AB(7-10)—BBHS—BBJH—CC(7-9)—JH—SCHS—YR

McKown, Robin. Thomas Paine. Putnam 1962
AB(6-9)—Bkl C(6-9)

Woodward, William E. Tom Paine: America's Godfather, 1737-1809. Dutton 1945
SCPL

COLLECTIONS

McNeer, May Yonge and Ward, Lynd Kendall. Give Me Freedom. Abingdon 1964
Bkl C(5-8)—CC(5-7)—ESLC—JH—YR

Thomas, Norman Mattoon. Great Dissenters. Norton 1961
Bkl A&Y

Austrian—20th century

Robert Strausz-Hupé, 1903-

Strausz-Hupé, Robert. In My Time. Norton 1965
Bkl A

English—20th century

Cyril Northcote Parkinson, 1909-

Parkinson, Cyril Northcote. A Law unto Themselves: Twelve Portraits. Houghton 1966
Bkl A

German—19th century

Karl Marx, 1818-1883

Berlin, Isiah. Karl Marx: His Life and Environment. Oxford 1948
3000

COLLECTIONS

Coolidge, Olivia. Makers of the Red Revolution. Houghton 1963
CC(7-9)

Heilbroner, Robert Louis. Worldly Philosophers: The Lives, Times and Ideas of the Great Economic Thinkers. Simon & Schuster 1953
SCPL

Kagan, Henry Enoch. Six Who Changed the World. Yoseloff 1963
Bkl A

Schumpeter, Joseph Alois. Ten Great Economists, from Marx to Keynes. Oxford 1951
SCPL

Japanese—20th century

Ozaki Hatsumi, 1901-1944

Johnson, Chalmers A. An Instance of Treason: Ozaki Hatsumi and the Sorge Spy Ring. Stanford Univ. 1964
Bkl A

Russian—19th century

Georgi Valentinovich Plekhanov, 1857-1918

Baron, Samuel Haskell. Plekhanov: The Father of Russian Marxism. Stanford Univ. 1963
Bkl A

Russian—20th century

Georgi Valentinovich Plekhanov, 1857-1918

Baron, Samuel Haskell. Plekhanov: The Father of Russian Marxism. Stanford Univ. 1963
Bkl A

POLITICIANS

See Statesmen

POPES

See Religious Leaders—Italian

POSTAL OFFICIALS

American—19th century

John Butterfield, 1801-1869

Pinkerton, Robert. The First Overland Mail. Random House 1953
CC—SCHS

POSTAL OFFICIALS—*Continued*

American—20th century

James Edward Day, 1914-

Day, James Edward. My Appointed Round: 929 Days as Postmaster General. Holt 1965
Bkl A

POTTERS

American—20th century

Jade Snow Wong, 1922-

Wong, Jade Snow. Fifth Chinese Daughter. Harper 1950
BBHS—BY—SCHS—SCPL—YR

English—18th century

Josiah Wedgwood, 1730-1795

COLLECTIONS

Crowther, James Gerald. Scientists of the Industrial Revolution. Dufour 1963
Bkl A

POVERTY-STRICKEN

American—20th century

Ethel Waters, 1900-

Waters, Ethel. His Eye Is on the Sparrow: An Autobiography. Doubleday 1951
SCPL

Brazilian—20th century

Carolina Maria de Jesus, 1921?-

Jesus, Carolina Maria de. Child of the Dark: The Diary of [the author]; tr. from the Portuguese by David St. Clair. Dutton 1962
Bkl A

PREACHERS

See Religious Leaders

PRELATES

See Religious Leaders

PREMIERS

See Statesmen

PRESIDENTS

American

COLLECTIONS

Armbruster, Maxim Ethan. The Presidents of the United States: A New Appraisal. Horizon 1960
Bkl A

Bailey, Thomas Andrew. Presidential Greatness: The Image and the Man from George Washington to the Present. Appleton 1966
Bkl A

Bassett, Margaret. Profiles & Portraits of American Presidents. Bond Wheelwright 1964
Bkl A&Y&C—JH

Beard, Charles A. The Presidents in American History; brought forward since 1948 by William Beard. Messner 1965
BBHS—BBJH—Bkl C(7-9)&Y—CC(7-9)—ESLC—JH—SCHS—SCPL

Bergere, Thea. Homes of the Presidents. Dodd 1962
Bkl C(5-8)

Cary, Sturges F. Arrow Book of Presidents. Scholastic 1965
ESLC

Cavanah, Frances and Crandall, Elizabeth L. Meet the Presidents. Macrae 1965
AB(6up)—JH

Cooke, Donald E. Atlas of the Presidents. Hammond 1964
CC

Cormier, Frank. Presidents Are People Too. Public Affairs Press 1966
Bkl A

Coy, Harold. The First Book of Presidents. Watts 1964
CC(3-6)—ESLC

Durant, John and Durant, Alice. Pictorial History of American Presidents. Barnes 1965
CC—JH—SCHS—SCPL

Durant, John. The Sports of Our Presidents. Hastings House 1964
ESLC

Fields, Alonzo. My 21 Years in the White House. Coward-McCann 1961
Bkl A
Dwight David Eisenhower; Herbert Clark Hoover; John Fitzgerald Kennedy; Franklin Delano Roosevelt; Harry S. Truman

Hurd, Charles. The White House Story. Hawthorn 1966
Bkl A&Y

Jeffries, Ona Griffin. In and Out of the White House, from Washington to the Eisenhowers: An Intimate Glimpse into the Social and Domestic Aspects of the Presidential Life. Funk 1960
Bkl A

Jensen, Amy (La Follette). The White House and Its Thirty-four Families. McGraw 1965
Bkl A&Y—SCPL

PRESIDENTS

American—*Continued*

Johnson, Walter. 1600 Pennsylvania Avenue: Presidents and the People, 1929-1959. Little 1960
Bkl A
Dwight David Eisenhower; Herbert Clark Hoover; Franklin Delano Roosevelt; Harry S. Truman

Jones, Cranston. Homes of the American Presidents. McGraw 1962
Bkl A&Y

Kane, Joseph Nathan. Facts About the Presidents: A Compilation of Biographical and Historical Data. Wilson 1959
Bkl A&C&Y—CC—ESLC—SCHS—3000

Lawson, Don. Young People in the White House. Abelard-Schuman 1961
ESLC

Lengyel, Cornel Adam. Presidents of the United States. Golden Press 1964
CC—ESLC

Lindop, Edmund and Jares, Joseph. White House Sportsmen. Houghton 1964
ESLC

Lomask, Milton. "I Do Solemnly Swear . . .": The Story of the Presidential Inauguration. Ariel Bks 1966
ESLC
Thomas Jefferson; John Fitzgerald Kennedy; Abraham Lincoln; Franklin Delano Roosevelt; Theodore Roosevelt; George Washington; Woodrow Wilson

McConnell, Jane (Tompkins) and McConnell, Burt Morton. Presidents of the United States. Crowell 1951
BBEL—BBJH

Marx, Rudolph. The Health of the Presidents. Putnam 1961
Bkl A&Y

Miers, Earl Schenck. America and Its Presidents. Grosset 1964
AB(5up)—ESLC—JH

Miers, Earl Schenck. The White House and the Presidency. Grosset 1965
CC(3-7)—ESLC

Morgan, James. Our Presidents: Brief Biographies of Our Chief Magistrates from Washington to Eisenhower, 1789-1958. Macmillan 1958
BBHS—CC(7-9)—JH—SCHS—SCPL

Parks, Lillian (Rogers) and Leighton, Frances Spatz. My Thirty Years Backstairs at the White House. Fleet 1961
Bkl A&Y
Dwight David Eisenhower; Herbert Clark Hoover; Franklin Delano Roosevelt; Harry S. Truman

Petersham, Maud and Petersham, Miska. Story of the Presidents of the United States of America. Macmillan 1966
AB(3-6)—BBEL(4-7)—CC(4-7)—ESLC

American—18th century

John Adams, 1735-1826

Adams, John. The Adams-Jefferson Letters; ed. by Lester J. Cappon. 2v. Univ. of N.C. 1959
Bkl A

Adams, John. Diary and Autobiography; ed. by L. H. Butterfield. 4v. Harvard Univ. 1961
SCPL

Adams, John. The John Adams Papers; ed. by Frank Donovan. Dodd 1965
Bkl A&Y

Bowen, Catherine (Drinker). John Adams and the American Revolution. Little 1950
BBHS—BY—GR—SCHS—SCPL

Bragdon, Lillian J. Meet the Remarkable Adams Family. Atheneum 1964
AB(6-9)—YR

Kelly, Regina Z. The Picture Story and Biography of John Adams. Follett 1965
ESLC

Smith, Page. John Adams: v. 1, 1735-1784; v. 2, 1784-1826. Doubleday 1962
Bkl A—SCPL

COLLECTIONS

Dos Passos, John Roderigo. Men Who Made the Nation. Doubleday 1957
SCPL

Kunstler, William Moses. The Case for Courage. Morrow 1962
Bkl A&Y

Lawson, Don. Famous American Political Families. Abelard-Schuman 1965
Bkl C(7-12)&Y

George Washington, 1732-1799

American Heritage. George Washington and the Making of a Nation, by Marcus Cunliffe. Am. Heritage 1966
ESLC

Aulaire, Ingri d' and Aulaire, Edgar Parin d'. George Washington. Doubleday 1936
BBEL(2-5)—CC(2-4)—ESLC

Boller, Paul F. George Washington & Religion. Southern Methodist Univ. 1963
Bkl A

Boyce, Burke. Man from Mt. Vernon. Harper 1961 (Fiction)
Bkl A&Y

Boyce, Burke. Morning of a Hero: A Novel. Harper 1963 (Fiction)
Bkl A—IndS(9-10)

Cunliffe, Marcus. George Washington: Man and Monument. Little 1958
BBHS—GR—SCPL—3000

PRESIDENTS

American—18th century

George Washington—Continued

Desmond, Alice (Curtis). Sword and Pen for George Washington. Dodd 1964
Bkl Y

Eaton, Jeanette. Leader by Destiny: George Washington, Man and Patriot. Harcourt 1938
BBHS—BBJH—CC(7-9)—JH—SCHS

Eaton, Jeanette. Washington, the Nation's First Hero. Morrow 1951
AB(3-6)—CC(4-6)

Flexner, James Thomas. George Washington: The Forge of Experience, 1732-1775. Little 1965
Bkl A&Y—IndS(11-12)

Ford, Paul Leicester. Janice Meredith: A Story of the American Revolution. Dodd 1899 (Fiction)
SCHS

Foster, Genevieve. George Washington: An Initial Biography. Scribner 1949
AB(4-6)—BBEL—CC(3-5)—ESLC

Freeman, Douglas Southall. George Washington: A Biography. 7v. Scribner. 1948-1957
SCPL

Freidel, Frank and Aikman, Lonnelle. G. Washington: Man and Monument. Grosset 1965
Bkl A&Y&C—ESLC

Hays, Wilma Pitchford. George Washington's Birthdays. Coward-McCann 1963
IndJ(2-4)

Judson, Clara (Ingram). George Washington, Leader of the People. Follett 1951
BBEL(5-8)—BBJH—CC(4-7)—ESLC—JH—SCHS

Lindop, Edmund. George Washington and the First Balloon Flight. Whitman 1964 (Fiction)
ESLC

Miller, Natalie. The Story of Mount Vernon. Childrens Press 1965
ESLC

North, Sterling. George Washington, Frontier Colonel. Random House 1957
CC(5-7)—JH—SCHS

Thane, Elswyth. Potomac Squire. Duell 1963
Bkl A&Y

Washington, George. The George Washington Papers; ed. by Frank Donovan. Dodd 1964
Bkl A&Y

Woodward, William E. George Washington: The Image and the Man. Liveright 1946
SCPL

COLLECTIONS

Daugherty, Sonia. Ten Brave Men: Makers of the American Way. Lippincott 1951
SCHS

Dos Passos, John Roderigo. Men Who Made the Nation. Doubleday 1957
SCPL

Lomask, Milton. "I Do Solemnly Swear . . .": The Story of the Presidential Inauguration. Ariel Bks 1966
ESLC

Parlin, John. Patriots' Days. Garrard 1964
ESLC

American—19th century

John Quincy Adams, 1767-1848

Adams, John Quincy. Diary of John Quincy Adams, 1794-1845. Scribner 1951
CA—SCPL

Bemis, Samuel Flagg. John Quincy Adams and the Foundations of American Foreign Policy. Knopf 1949
SCPL—3000

Bemis, Samuel Flagg. John Quincy Adams and the Union. Knopf 1956
SCPL—3000

Clarke, Fred G. John Quincy Adams. Collier Bks 1966
Bkl C(7-10)&Y

East, Robert Abraham. John Quincy Adams: The Critical Years, 1785-1794. Bookman Associates 1962
Bkl A&Y

Hoehling, Mary. Yankee in the White House: John Quincy Adams. Messner 1963
YR

Hoyt, Edwin Palmer. John Quincy Adams: A Biography of the Sixth President of the United States. Reilly & Lee 1963
Bkl Y&C

Lomask, Milton. John Quincy Adams, Son of the American Revolution. Farrar 1965
Bkl C(7-9)&Y—ESLC—JH

James Buchanan, 1791-1868

Klein, Philip Shriver. President James Buchanan: A Biography. Pa. State Univ. 1962
Bkl A

Grover Cleveland, 1837-1908

Hoyt, Edwin Palmer. Grover Cleveland. Reilly & Lee 1962
Bkl C(7-12)&Y—BY

Nevins, Allan. Grover Cleveland: A Study in Courage. Dodd 1932
SCPL—3000

PRESIDENTS

American—19th century—*Continued*

James Abram Garfield, 1831-1881

Garfield, James Abram. The Wild Life of the Army: Civil War Letters; ed. by Frederick D. Williams. Mich. State Univ. 1964
Bkl A

Severn, Bill. Teacher, Soldier, President: The Life of James A. Garfield. Washburn 1964
ESLC—IndJ(6-9)

Ulysses Simpson Grant, 1822-1885

Catton, Bruce. Grant Moves South. Little 1960
Bkl A&Y—BY—SCHS—SCPL

Catton, Bruce. U. S. Grant and the American Military Tradition. Little 1954
SCPL—3000

Kantor, MacKinlay. Lee and Grant at Appomattox. Random House 1950
CC(6-9)—ESLC—JH—SCHS—YR

Lewis, Lloyd. Captain Sam Grant. Little 1950
SCPL

Meyer, Howard N. Let Us Have Peace: The Story of Ulysses S. Grant. Collier Bks 1966
Bkl Y(7-10)&C

Reeder, Red. Ulysses S. Grant: Horseman and Fighter. Garrard 1964
AB(4-7)

Thomas, Henry. Ulysses S. Grant. Putnam 1961
Bkl C(6-9)—YR

Woodward, W. E. Meet General Grant. Liveright 1928
SCPL

Benjamin Harrison, 1833-1901

COLLECTIONS

Lawson, Don. Famous American Political Families. Abelard-Schuman 1965
Bkl C(7-12)&Y

Rutherford Birchard Hayes, 1822-1893

Hayes, Rutherford Birchard. Hayes: The Diary of a President 1875-1881; ed. by T. Harry Williams. McKay 1964
Bkl A

Williams, Thomas Harry. Hayes of the Twenty-third: The Civil War Volunteer Officer. Knopf 1965
Bkl A

Andrew Jackson, 1767-1845

American Heritage. Andrew Jackson, Soldier and Statesman, by Ralph K. Andrist. Am. Heritage 1963
CC(6-9)—JH—SCHS—YR

Coit, Margaret L. Andrew Jackson. Houghton 1965
Bkl C(7-10)&Y—ESLC—IndJ(4-6)

Foster, Genevieve. Andrew Jackson: An Initial Biography. Scribner 1951
CC(4-6)—ESLC

Gerson, Noel Bertram. Old Hickory. Doubleday 1964 (Fiction)
Bkl A&Y

James, Marquis. Andrew Jackson: Portrait of a President. Bobbs 1937
BBHS—SCPL

Judson, Clara (Ingram). Andrew Jackson, Frontier Statesman. Follett 1954
BBEL(5-8)—BBJH—CC(5-7)—ESLC—JH—SCHS

Martin, Patricia Miles. Andrew Jackson. Putnam 1966
ESLC

Nolan, Jeannette (Covert). Andrew Jackson. Messner 1949
CC(7-9)—JH—SCHS

Ogg, Frederic Austin. The Reign of Andrew Jackson: A Chronicle of the Frontier in Politics. Yale Univ. 1919
SCHS

Palmer, Bruce and Giles, John Clifford. Horseshoe Bend. Simon & Schuster 1962 (Fiction)
Bkl A

Parlin, John. Andrew Jackson. Garrard 1962
AB(3-7)

Remini, Robert Vincent. Andrew Jackson. Twayne 1966
Bkl A&Y

Schlesinger, Arthur Meier. Age of Jackson. Little 1945
SCPL

Stone, Irving. The President's Lady. Doubleday 1951 (Fiction)
BBHS—SCHS

Syrett, Harold C. Andrew Jackson: His Contribution to the American Tradition. Bobbs 1953
BBHS—3000

Vance, Marguerite. The Jacksons of Tennessee. Dutton 1953
BBEL—BBJH—CC(7-9)—ESLC—JH—SCHS

Wellman, Paul Iselin. Magnificent Destiny: A Novel About the Great Secret Adventure of Andrew Jackson and Sam Houston. Doubleday 1962 (Fiction)
Bkl A

Wright, Frances. Andrew Jackson. Abingdon 1958
AB(4-7)

COLLECTIONS

Coit, Margaret L. The Fight for Union. Houghton 1961
CC(6-7)—ESLC

PRESIDENTS

American—19th century

Andrew Jackson—Continued

Daugherty, Sonia. Ten Brave Men: Makers of the American Way. Lippincott 1951
SCHS

Hofstadter, Richard. American Political Tradition and the Men Who Made It. Knopf 1948
SCPL

Thomas Jefferson, 1743-1826

American Heritage. Thomas Jefferson and His World, by Henry Moscow and Dumas Malone. Am. Heritage 1960
Bkl C(6-9)—BY—CC—JH—SCHS—YR

Bowers, Claude Gernade. Jefferson and Hamilton: The Struggle for Democracy in America. Houghton 1925
SCHS—SCPL

Bowers, Claude Gernade. Jefferson in Power: The Death Struggle of the Federalists. Houghton 1936
SCPL

Chinard, Gilbert. Thomas Jefferson, the Apostle of Americanism. Univ. of Mich. 1957
3000

Conant, James Bryant. Thomas Jefferson and the Development of American Public Education. Univ. of Calif. 1962
Bkl A—SCPL

Dos Passos, John Roderigo. Thomas Jefferson: The Making of a President. Houghton 1964
ESLC

Eichner, James A. Thomas Jefferson: The Complete Man. Watts 1966
Bkl Y(7-10)&C

Gurney, Gene and Gurney, Clare. Monticello. Watts 1966
Bkl C(5-9)&Y—ESLC

Hall, Gordon Langley. Mr. Jefferson's Ladies. Beacon Press 1966
Bkl A&Y

Jefferson, Thomas. The Adams-Jefferson Letters; ed. by Lester J. Cappon. 2v. Univ. of N.C. 1959
Bkl A

Jefferson, Thomas. The Thomas Jefferson Papers; ed. by Frank Donovan. Dodd 1963
Bkl A&Y—IndS(10-12)

Jefferson, Thomas. To the Girls and Boys, Being the Delightful, Little-Known Letters of Thomas Jefferson to and from His Children and Grandchildren; comp. by Edward Boykin. Funk 1964
Bkl A

Johnston, Johanna. Thomas Jefferson: His Many Talents. Dodd 1961
AB(3-6)—Bkl C(6-9)—YR

Judson, Clara (Ingram). Thomas Jefferson, Champion of the People. Follett 1952
BBEL(6-8)—BBJH—CC—ESLC—JH—SCHS

Komroff, Manuel. Thomas Jefferson. Messner 1961
Bkl C(6-9)—SCHS

Levy, Leonard William. Jefferson & Civil Liberties: The Darker Side. Harvard Univ. 1963
Bkl A

Lisitzky, Gene. Thomas Jefferson. Viking 1933
BBHS—BBJH—CC(7-9)—SCHS

Malone, Dumas. Jefferson and His Time: v. 3, Jefferson and the Ordeal of Liberty. Little 1962
Bkl A—SCPL

Rosenberger, F. C., ed. Jefferson Reader: A Treasury of Writings about Thomas Jefferson. Dutton 1953
SCPL

Schachner, Nathan. Thomas Jefferson: A Biography. Yoseloff 1957
SCPL

Sheean, Vincent. Thomas Jefferson, Father of Democracy. Random House 1953
BBJH—CC—JH—SCHS

Van der Linden, Frank. The Turning Point: Jefferson's Battle for the Presidency. Luce 1962
Bkl A

Van Loon, Hendrik Willem. Fighters for Freedom: Jefferson and Bolivar. Dodd 1962
Bkl C(7-12)&Y

Wibberley, Leonard. Time of the Harvest: Thomas Jefferson—The Years 1801-1826. Farrar 1966
ESLC

COLLECTIONS

Coit, Margaret L. The Fight for Union. Houghton 1961
CC(6-7)—ESLC

Daugherty, Sonia. Ten Brave Men: Makers of the American Way. Lippincott 1951
SCHS

Dos Passos, John Roderigo. Men Who Made the Nation. Doubleday 1957
SCPL

Hofstadter, Richard. American Political Tradition and the Men Who Made It. Knopf 1948
SCPL

Lomask, Milton. "I Do Solemnly Swear . . .": The Story of the Presidential Inauguration. Ariel Bks 1966
ESLC

PRESIDENTS

American—19th century

Thomas Jefferson—Continued

Parlin, John. Patriots' Days. Garrard 1964
ESLC

Andrew Johnson, 1808-1875

Green, Margaret. Defender of the Constitution: Andrew Johnson. Messner 1962
AB(4-9)—Bkl C(6-9)&Y—BY—YR

Lomask, Milton. Andy Johnson: The Tailor Who Became President. Farrar 1962
Bkl C(6-9)&Y

Severn, William. In Lincoln's Footsteps: The Life of Andrew Johnson. Washburn 1966
Bkl C(7-9)&Y—ESLC

Abraham Lincoln, 1809-1865

American Heritage. Abraham Lincoln in Peace and War, by Earl Schenck Miers. Am. Heritage 1964
Bkl C(6-9)&Y—CC—ESLC—IndJ(6-9)—JH

Andrews, Mary Raymond Shipman. The Perfect Tribute. Scribner 1956 (Fiction)
SCHS

Aulaire, Ingri d' and Aulaire, Edgar Parin d'. Abraham Lincoln. Doubleday 1939
BBEL(2-5)—CC(3-5)—ESLC

Betts, William Wilson, ed. Lincoln and the Poets: An Anthology. Univ. of Pittsburgh 1965 (Poem)
Bkl A&Y

Bishop, James Alonzo. The Day Lincoln Was Shot. Harper 1955
BY—SCHS—SCPL

Borreson, Ralph. When Lincoln Died. Appleton 1965
Bkl A

Bulla, Clyde Robert. Lincoln's Birthday. Crowell 1965
ESLC

Candy, Courtlandt, ed. Lincoln and the Civil War. Braziller 1960
BY

Catton, Bruce. Mr. Lincoln's Army. Doubleday 1951
SCPL

Catton, William Bruce and Catton, Bruce. Two Roads to Sumter. McGraw 1963
Bkl A

Colver, Anne. Abraham Lincoln for the People. Garrard 1960
ESLC

Commager, Henry Steele. The Great Proclamation: A Book for Young Americans. Bobbs 1960
ESLC

Current, Richard Nelson. Lincoln and the First Shot. Lippincott 1963
Bkl A

Daugherty, James. Abraham Lincoln. Viking 1943
BBEL—BBJH—CC(7-9)—JH—SCHS

De Regniers, Beatrice Schenk. The Abraham Lincoln Joke Book. Random House 1965
Bkl C(4-7)—ESLC

Douglas, William Orville. Mr. Lincoln & the Negroes: The Long Road to Equality. Atheneum 1963
Bkl A&Y—SCHS

Drinkwater, John. Abraham Lincoln: A Play. Houghton 1927 (Play)
SCHS—SCPL

Eifert, Virginia Louise (Snider). Buffalo Trace. Dodd 1955 (Fiction)
BBJH—JH—SCHS

Eifert, Virginia Louise (Snider). New Birth of Freedom. Dodd n.d. (Fiction)
BBJH

Eifert, Virginia Louise (Snider). Out of the Wilderness. Dodd 1956 (Fiction)
BBJH—SCHS

Eifert, Virginia Louise (Snider). Three Rivers South. Dodd n.d. (Fiction)
BBJH

Eifert, Virginia Louise (Snider). With a Task Before Me: Abraham Lincoln Leaves Springfield. Dodd 1966 (Fiction)
BBJH—Bkl C(7-9)&Y

Fehrenbacher, Don Edward. Prelude to Greatness: Lincoln in the 1850's. Stanford Univ. 1962
Bkl A

Fisher, Aileen Lucia. My Cousin Abe. Nelson 1962
Bkl C(6-9)&Y—CC(7-9)—ESLC—YR

Foster, Genevieve. Abraham Lincoln: An Initial Biography. Scribner 1950
CC(4-6)—ESLC—JH—SCHS

Frank, John Paul. Lincoln as a Lawyer. Univ. of Ill. 1961
Bkl A

Frazier, Carl and Frazier, Rosalie. The Lincoln Country in Pictures. Hastings House 1963
ESLC

Freeman, Andrew A. Abraham Lincoln Goes to New York. Coward-McCann 1960
Bkl A&Y

Hamilton, Charles and Ostendorf, Lloyd. Lincoln in Photographs: An Album of Every Known Pose. Univ. of Okla. 1963
Bkl A

PRESIDENTS

American—19th century

Abraham Lincoln—Continued

Hesseltine, William Best. Lincoln and the War Governors. Knopf 1948
SCPL

Horgan, Paul. Citizen of New Salem. Farrar 1961
Bkl A&Y—BY—JH—SCHS

Horgan, Paul. Songs after Lincoln. Farrar 1965 (Poem)
Bkl A&Y

Judson, Clara (Ingram). Abraham Lincoln. Follett 1961
CC(3-5)

Judson, Clara (Ingram). Abraham Lincoln, Friend of the People. Follett 1950
BBEL(5-8)—CC(6-9)—ESLC—JH—SCHS

Kelly, Regina Z. Lincoln and Douglas: The Years of Decision. Random House 1954
JH—SCHS

Kunhardt, Dorothy (Meserve) and Kunhardt, Philip B. Twenty Days: A Narrative in Text and Pictures of the Assassination of Abraham Lincoln and the Twenty Days and Nights That Followed. Harper 1965
Bkl A—IndS(11-12)

Le Sueur, Meridel. The River Road: A Story of Abraham Lincoln. Knopf 1954 (Fiction)
CC(5-7)—JH

Lincoln, Abraham. Conversations with Lincoln; comp. by Charles M. Segal. Putnam 1961
Bkl A

Lincoln, Abraham. The First Book Edition of the Gettysburg Address and the Second Inaugural. Watts 1963
Bkl C(7-9)—CC

Lorant, Stefan. The Life of Abraham Lincoln. New Am. Lib. 1941
GR

Lorant, Stefan. Lincoln: A Picture Story of His Life. Harper 1957
SCPL

Luthin, Reinhard Henry. The Real Abraham Lincoln: A Complete One-Volume History of His Life and Times. Prentice-Hall 1960
Bkl A&Y—BY

McGovern, Ann. If You Grew Up with Abraham Lincoln. Four Winds Press 1966
ESLC

McNeer, May. America's Abraham Lincoln. Houghton 1957
BBEL(5-8)—CC(5-7)—ESLC

McNicol, Jacqueline Morrell. Elizabeth for Lincoln. McKay 1960 (Fiction)
AB(4-7)

Meadowcroft, Enid La Monte. Abraham Lincoln. Crowell 1942
CC(6-9)

Mearns, David Chambers. Largely Lincoln. St Martins 1961
Bkl A

Mearns, David Chambers. Lincoln Papers. 2v. Doubleday 1948
SCPL

Miers, Earl Schenck. With Lincoln in the White House. Grosset 1963
IndJ(4-6)

Morrow, Honore Willsie. Forever Free. Morrow 1927 (Fiction)
SCHS

Morrow, Honore Willsie. With Malice Toward None. Morrow 1928 (Fiction)
SCHS

Nevins, Allan and Stone, Irving, eds. Lincoln: A Contemporary Portrait. Doubleday 1962
Bkl A

Nevins, Allan, ed. Lincoln and the Gettysburg Address: Commemorative Papers. Univ. of Ill. 1964
Bkl A

Newman, Ralph G., ed. Lincoln for the Ages. Doubleday 1960
Bkl A

Neyhart, Louise A. Henry's Lincoln. Holiday 1958 (Fiction)
CC(4-6)—ESLC

North, Sterling. Abe Lincoln: Log Cabin to White House. Random House 1956
CC(6-9)—JH—SCHS

Phelan, Mary Kay. Mr. Lincoln Speaks at Gettysburg. Norton 1966
Bkl C(4-7)—ESLC

Potter, John Mason. Thirteen Desperate Days. Obolensky 1964
Bkl A&Y

Quarles, Benjamin. Lincoln and the Negro. Oxford 1962
Bkl A

Randall, James Garfield. Lincoln, the President. 4v. Dodd 1945-1955
SCPL

Randall, James Garfield. Mr. Lincoln; ed. by R. N. Current. Dodd 1957
SCPL

Randall, Ruth Elaine (Painter). Courtship of Mr. Lincoln. Little 1957
SCPL

Randall, Ruth Elaine (Painter). Lincoln's Sons. Little 1955
SCHS—SCPL

Sandburg, Carl. Abe Lincoln Grows Up. Harcourt 1928
AB(6-10)—BBJH—BY—CC(7-9)—ESLC—JH—SCHS

Sandburg, Carl. Abraham Lincoln. 6v. Harcourt 1926-1939
CA—GR—SCPL

PRESIDENTS

American—19th century

Abraham Lincoln—Continued

Sandburg, Carl. Abraham Lincoln: The Prairie Years. 2v. Harcourt 1926
BBJH—BY—GR—SCHS

Sandburg, Carl. Abraham Lincoln: The War Years. 4v. Harcourt 1939
BY—SCPL

Sandburg, Carl. Abraham Lincoln: The Prairie Years and The War Years. One volume edition. Harcourt 1954
BBHS—SCHS—SCPL—3000

Searcher, Victor. Lincoln's Journey to Greatness: A Factual Account of the Twelve-Day Inaugural Trip. Winston 1960
Bkl A

Shapp, Martha and Shapp, Charles. Let's Find Out About Abraham Lincoln. Watts 1965
ESLC

Sherwood, Robert Emmet. Abe Lincoln in Illinois: A Play in Twelve Scenes. Scribner 1939 (Play)
SCHS—SCPL

Simon, Paul. Lincoln's Preparation for Greatness: The Illinois Legislative Years. Univ. of Okla. 1966
Bkl A

Stone, Irving. Love Is Eternal. Doubleday 1954 (Fiction)
BBHS—JH—SCHS

Thomas, Benjamin Platt. Abraham Lincoln: A Biography. Knopf 1952
GR—SCHS—SCPL—3000

Tyrner-Tyrnauer, A. R. Lincoln and the Emperors. Harcourt 1962
Bkl A

Van Doren, Mark. Last Days of Lincoln: A Play in Six Scenes. Hill & Wang 1959 (Play)
SCPL

Warren, Louis Austin. Lincoln's Youth: Indiana Years, Seven to Twenty-one, 1816-1830. Appleton 1959
Bkl A

Weaver, John Downing. Tad Lincoln, Mischief-Maker in the White House. Dodd 1963
Bkl C(5-8)—ESLC—IndJ(6-9)

Williams, Thomas Harry. Lincoln and His Generals. Knopf 1952
SCPL

Wise, William. Detective Pinkerton and Mr. Lincoln. Dutton 1964
AB(5-9)—IndJ(4-6)

Wolf, William J. The Almost Chosen People: A Study of the Religion of Abraham Lincoln. Doubleday 1959
Bkl A

COLLECTIONS

Daugherty, Sonia. Ten Brave Men: Makers of the American Way. Lippincott 1951
SCHS

Hofstadter, Richard. American Political Tradition and the Men Who Made It. Knopf 1948
SCPL

Lomask, Milton. "I Do Solemnly Swear . . .": The Story of the Presidential Inauguration. Ariel Bks 1966
ESLC

Parlin, John. Patriots' Days. Garrard 1964
ESLC

William McKinley, 1843-1901

Glad, Paul W. McKinley, Bryan, and the People. Lippincott 1964
Bkl A&Y

Leech, Margaret. In the Days of McKinley. Harper 1959
BBHS—SCPL

Morgan, Howard Wayne. William McKinley and His America. Syracuse Univ. 1963
Bkl A&Y

James Madison, 1751-1836

Brant, Irving. James Madison. 6v. Bobbs 1941-1961
Bkl A—SCPL

Koch, Adrienne. Madison's "Advice to My Country." Princeton Univ. 1966
Bkl A

Madison, James. The Papers of James Madison; ed. by W. T. Hutchinson and W. M. E. Rachal. 2v. Univ. of Chicago 1962
SCPL

Steinberg, Alfred. James Madison. Putnam 1965
Bkl C(7-9)&Y—IndJ(6-9)

Wilkie, Katharine E. and Moseley, Elizabeth R. Father of the Constitution: James Madison. Messner 1963
AB(7up)

COLLECTIONS

Dos Passos, John Roderigo. Men Who Made the Nation. Doubleday 1957
SCPL

James Monroe, 1758-1831

COLLECTIONS

Dos Passos, John Roderigo. Men Who Made the Nation. Doubleday 1957
SCPL

PRESIDENTS

American—19th century—*Continued*

James Knox Polk, 1795-1849

Gerson, Noel Bertram. The Slender Reed: A Biographical Novel of James Knox Polk, Eleventh President of the United States. Doubleday 1965 (Fiction)
Bkl A&Y

Hoyt, Edwin Palmer. James Knox Polk. Reilly & Lee 1965
Bkl C(7-9)&Y—ESLC

Zachary Taylor, 1784-1850

Hoyt, Edwin Palmer. Zachary Taylor. Reilly & Lee 1966
Bkl C(7-9)&Y

Nichols, Edward Jay. Zach Taylor's Little Army. Doubleday 1963
Bkl A&Y

John Tyler, 1790-1862

Seager, Robert. And Tyler Too: A Biography of John & Julia Gardiner Tyler. McGraw 1963
Bkl A

Martin Van Buren, 1782-1862

COLLECTIONS

Koenig, Louis William. The Invisible Presidency. Rinehart 1960
Bkl A

American—20th century

Calvin Coolidge, 1872-1933

Lathem, Edward Connery, ed. Meet Calvin Coolidge: The Man Behind the Myth. Stephen Greene 1960
Bkl A

Dwight David Eisenhower, 1890-1969

Albertson, Dean, ed. Eisenhower as President. Hill & Wang 1963
Bkl A

Army Times. The Challenge and the Triumph: The Story of General Dwight D. Eisenhower. Putnam 1966
Bkl A&Y

Childs, Marquis William. Eisenhower, Captive Hero: A Critical Study of the General and the President. Harcourt 1958
BBHS—SCPL

Davis, Kenneth Sydney. Soldier of Democracy: A Biography of Dwight Eisenhower. Doubleday 1952
SCPL

Donovan, Robert John. Eisenhower: The Inside Story. Harper 1956
SCPL

Eisenhower, Dwight David. The White House Years: v. 1, Mandate for Change, 1953-1956. Doubleday 1963
Bkl A&Y—SCPL

Eisenhower, Dwight David. The White House Years: v. 2, Waging Peace, 1956-1961. Doubleday 1965
Bkl A

Gunther, John. Eisenhower: The Man and the Symbol. Harper 1952
SCHS—SCPL

Kornitzer, Bela. Great American Heritage: The Story of the Five Eisenhower Brothers. Farrar 1955
SCPL

Lovelace, Delos W. "Ike" Eisenhower, Statesman and Soldier of Peace. Crowell 1961
BBJH—CC(6-9)—ESLC—JH—SCHS

Moos, Malcolm. Dwight D. Eisenhower. Random House 1964
CC(5-7)—ESLC—JH

Smith, A. Merriman. A President's Odyssey. Harper 1961
Bkl A&Y

COLLECTIONS

Brown, John Mason. Through These Men: Some Aspects of Our Passing History. Harper 1956
SCPL

Fields, Alonzo. My 21 Years in the White House. Coward-McCann 1961
Bkl A

Johnson, Walter. 1600 Pennsylvania Avenue: Presidents and the People, 1929-1959. Little 1960
Bkl A

Parks, Lillian (Rogers) and Leighton, Frances Spatz. My Thirty Years Backstairs at the White House. Fleet 1961
Bkl A&Y

Roper, Elmo Burns. You and Your Leaders: Their Actions and Your Reactions, 1936-1956. Morrow 1957
SCPL

Warren Gamaliel Harding, 1865-1923

Sinclair, Andrew. The Available Man: The Life Behind the Masks of Warren Gamaliel Harding. Macmillan 1965
Bkl A&Y—IndS(10-12)

Herbert Clark Hoover, 1874-1964

Hoover, Herbert Clark. Memoirs. 3v. Macmillan 1951-52
SCPL

Lyons, Eugene. Herbert Hoover: A Biography. Doubleday 1964
Bkl A—SCPL

PRESIDENTS

American—20th century

Herbert Clark Hoover—Continued

McGee, Dorothy Horton. Herbert Hoover: Engineer, Humanitarian, Statesman. Dodd 1965
BBHS—Bkl C(7-10)&Y—SCHS

Peare, Catherine Owens. The Herbert Hoover Story. Crowell 1965
Bkl C(7-9)&Y—ESLC

Warren, Harris G. Herbert Hoover and the Great Depression. Oxford 1959
BBHS—SCPL

COLLECTIONS

Fields, Alonzo. My 21 Years in the White House. Coward-McCann 1961
Bkl A

Hofstadter, Richard. American Political Tradition and the Men Who Made It. Knopf 1948
SCPL

Johnson, Walter. 1600 Pennsylvania Avenue: Presidents and the People, 1929-1959. Little 1960
Bkl A

Parks, Lillian (Rogers) and Leighton, Frances Spatz. My Thirty Years Backstairs at the White House. Fleet 1961
Bkl A&Y

Lyndon Baines Johnson, 1908-

Amrine, Michael. This Awesome Challenge: The Hundred Days of Lyndon Johnson. Putnam 1964
Bkl A

Baker, Leonard. The Johnson Eclipse: A President's Vice Presidency. Macmillan 1966
Bkl A

Bell, Jack. The Johnson Treatment: How Lyndon B. Johnson Took Over the Presidency and Made It His Own. Harper 1965
Bkl A&Y

Caidin, Martin and Hymoff, Edward. The Mission. Lippincott 1964
Bkl A&Y—IndS(9-12)

Davie, Michael. LBJ: A Foreign Observer's Viewpoint. Duell 1966
Bkl A

Evans, Rowland and Novak, Robert D. Lyndon B. Johnson—The Exercise of Power: A Political Biography. New Am. Lib. 1966
Bkl A&Y

Geyelin, Philip L. Lyndon B. Johnson and the World. Praeger 1966
Bkl A

Mooney, Booth. The Lyndon Johnson Story. Farrar 1964
Bkl A&Y

Newlon, Clarke. L. B. J., the Man from Johnson City. Dodd 1964
Bkl A&Y

Provence, Harry. Lyndon B. Johnson: A Biography. Fleet 1964
Bkl A

White, William S. The Professional: Lyndon B. Johnson. Houghton 1964
SCPL

COLLECTIONS

Sevareid, Eric, ed. Candidates 1960: Behind the Headlines in the Presidential Race. Basic Bks 1959
SCPL

John Fitzgerald Kennedy, 1917-1963

Adler, Bill, comp. and ed. John F. Kennedy and the Young People of America. McKay 1965
ESLC

Bishop, James Alonzo. A Day in the Life of President Kennedy. Random House 1964
Bkl A&Y—IndJ(6-9)—SCPL

Burns, James MacGregor. John Kennedy: A Political Profile. Harcourt 1960
BBHS—Bkl A&Y—SCHS—SCPL—3000

Dinneen, Joseph Francis. The Kennedy Family. Little 1960
Bkl A

Donovan, Robert J. PT 109: John F. Kennedy in World War II. McGraw 1961
Bkl A&Y—CC—SCHS

Epstein, Edward Jay. Inquest: The Warren Commission and the Establishment of Truth. Viking 1966
Bkl A

Fay, Paul Burgess. The Pleasure of His Company. Harper 1966
Bkl A&Y

Golden, Harry Lewis. Mr. Kennedy and the Negroes. World 1964
Bkl A&Y—IndS(9-12)—SCHS

Kazan, Molly. Kennedy. Stein & Day 1964 (Poem)
Bkl A

Kennedy, John Fitzgerald. The First Book Edition of John F. Kennedy's Inaugural Address. Watts 1964
Bkl C(4up)—CC—IndJ(4-6)

Kennedy, John Fitzgerald. Kennedy and the Press: The News Conferences; ed. by Harold W. Chase and Allen H. Lerman. Crowell 1965
Bkl A

Lasky, Victor. J. F. K.: The Man and the Myth. Macmillan 1963
Bkl A

Lee, Bruce. Boys' Life of John F. Kennedy. Sterling 1961
CC(5-7)—YR

PRESIDENTS

American—20th century

John Fitzgerald Kennedy—Continued

Levine, I. E. Young Man in the White House: John Fitzgerald Kennedy. Messner 1964
ESLC–JH

Lieberson, Goddard, ed. John Fitzgerald Kennedy as We Remember Him. Atheneum 1965
Bkl A&Y

Lincoln, Evelyn. My Twelve Years with John F. Kennedy. McKay 1965
Bkl A&Y–IndS(10-12)

McCarthy, Joe. The Remarkable Kennedys. Dial 1960
Bkl A

Manchester, William Raymond. Portrait of a President: John F. Kennedy in Profile. Little 1962
Bkl A&Y–SCHS

Markmann, Charles Lam and Sherwin, Mark. John F. Kennedy: A Sense of Purpose. St Martins 1961
Bkl A&Y

Martin, Patricia Miles. John Fitzgerald Kennedy. Putnam 1964
ESLC

Miers, Earl Schenck. The Story of John F. Kennedy; ed. by Paul E. Blackwood. Grosset 1964
JH

New York Times. The Kennedy Years. Viking 1964
Bkl A&Y–IndS(9-12)

Salinger, Pierre and Vanocur, Sander, eds. A Tribute to John F. Kennedy. Encyc. Britannica 1964
Bkl A&Y–SCHS

Salinger, Pierre. With Kennedy. Doubleday 1966
Bkl A&Y

Saunders, Doris E., ed. The Kennedy Years and the Negro: A Photographic Record. Johnson Pub. 1964
Bkl A

Sauvage, Léo. The Oswald Affair: An Examination of the Contradictions and Omissions of the Warren Report; tr. from the French by Charles Gaulkin. World 1966
Bkl A

Schlesinger, Arthur Meier. A Thousand Days: John F. Kennedy in the White House. Houghton 1965
Bkl A&Y–IndS(9-12)

Schoor, Gene. Young John Kennedy. Harcourt 1963
AB(5-10)–CC–YR

Shaw, Mark. The John F. Kennedys: A Family Album. Farrar 1964
Bkl A

Shaw, Maud. White House Nannie: My Years with Caroline and John Kennedy, Jr. New Am. Lib. 1966
Bkl A

Shepard, Tazewell Taylor. John F. Kennedy, Man of the Sea. Morrow 1965
Bkl A

Sidey, Hugh. John F. Kennedy, President. Atheneum 1964
Bkl A&Y–SCHS–SCPL

Sorensen, Theodore C. Kennedy. Harper 1965
Bkl A&Y

Spina, Tony. This Was the President. Barnes 1964
Bkl A

The Torch Is Passed: The Associated Press Story of the Death of a President. Associated Press 1964
CC–SCHS

Tregaskis, Richard. John F. Kennedy and PT-109. Random House 1962
Bkl C(6-9)–CC(5-7)–ESLC–JH–SCHS

United Press International and American Heritage Magazine. Four Days: The Historical Record of the Death of President Kennedy. Am. Heritage 1964
Bkl A&Y&C–CC–SCHS–SCPL

United States. President's Commission on the Assassination of President Kennedy. The Official Warren Commission Report on the Assassination of President John F. Kennedy. Doubleday 1964
Bkl A

United States. President's Commission on the Assassination of President Kennedy. The Witnesses; ed. from the Warren Commission's Hearings by the New York Times. McGraw 1965
Bkl A

Webb, Robert N. The Living JFK. Grosset 1964
IndJ(6-9)

White, Nancy Bean. Meet John F. Kennedy. Random House 1965
ESLC

Wicker, Tom. Kennedy Without Tears: The Man Beneath the Myth. Morrow 1964
Bkl A&Y

Wood, James Playsted. The Life and Words of John F. Kennedy. Doubleday 1964
ESLC

COLLECTIONS

Fields, Alonzo. My 21 Years in the White House. Coward-McCann 1961
Bkl A

Kittler, Glenn D. The Wings of Eagles. Doubleday 1966
Bkl A&Y

PRESIDENTS

American—20th century

John Fitzgerald Kennedy—Continued

Lawson, Don. Famous American Political Families. Abelard-Schuman 1965
Bkl C(7-12)&Y

Lomask, Milton. "I Do Solemnly Swear . . .": The Story of the Presidential Inauguration. Ariel Bks 1966
ESLC

Parlin, John. Patriots' Days. Garrard 1964
ESLC

Sevareid, Eric, ed. Candidates 1960: Behind the Headlines in the Presidential Race. Basic Bks 1959
SCPL

Franklin Delano Roosevelt, 1882-1945

Asbell, Bernard. When F. D. R. Died. Holt 1961
Bkl A

Brogan, Denis William. Era of Franklin D. Roosevelt: A Chronicle of the New Deal and Global War. Yale Univ. 1950
SCPL

Burns, James MacGregor. Roosevelt: The Lion and the Fox. Harcourt 1956
BBHS—SCPL—3000

Butterfield, Roger. FDR (Television Program by Robert D. Graff and Robert Emmett Ginna). Harper 1963
Bkl A&Y

Cavanah, Frances. Triumphant Adventure: The Story of Franklin Delano Roosevelt. Rand McNally 1964
JH

Churchill, Allen. The Roosevelts: American Aristocrats. Harper 1965
Bkl A&Y

Gould, Jean. A Good Fight: The Story of F. D. R.'s Conquest of Polio. Dodd 1960
Bkl A&Y

Gunther, John. Roosevelt in Retrospect: A Profile in History. Harper 1950
SCHS—SCPL

Halasz, Nicholas. Roosevelt Through Foreign Eyes. Van Nostrand 1961
Bkl A

Harrity, Richard and Martin, Ralph G. The Human Side of F. D. R. Duell 1960
Bkl A&Y

Hassett, William D. Off the Record with F. D. R. 1942-1945. Rutgers Univ. 1958
SCPL

Hickok, Lorena A. The Road to the White House. Chilton 1962
BY

Hickok, Lorena A. The Story of Franklin D. Roosevelt. Grosset 1956
CC(4-6)—ESLC

Leuchtenburg, William E. Franklin D. Roosevelt and the New Deal, 1932-1940. Harper 1963
Bkl A&Y—SCHS—SCPL

Peare, Catherine Owens. The FDR Story. Crowell 1962
Bkl C(7-9)&Y—BY—CC—ESLC—JH—SCHS—YR

Perkins, Dexter. New Age of Franklin Roosevelt, 1932-1945. Univ. of Chicago 1957
SCPL

Perkins, Frances. The Roosevelt I Knew. Viking 1946
SCPL

Rollins, Alfred Brooks. Roosevelt and Howe. Knopf 1962
Bkl A

Roosevelt, Franklin Delano. F. D. R.: His Personal Letters; ed. by Elliott Roosevelt. 4v. Duell 1947-50
SCPL

Roosevelt, James and Shalett, Sidney. Affectionately, F. D. R.: A Son's Story of a Lonely Man. Harcourt 1959
SCPL

Schary, Doré. Sunrise at Campobello: A Play in Three Acts. Random House 1958 (Play)
SCHS—SCPL

Schlesinger, Arthur Meier. Crisis of the Old Order, 1919-1933. Houghton 1957
SCPL

Sherwood, Robert Emmet. Roosevelt and Hopkins: An Intimate History. Harper 1950
GR—SCHS—SCPL

Thomas, Henry. Franklin Delano Roosevelt. Putnam 1962
Bkl C(7-9)&Y

Tugwell, Rexford Guy. Democratic Roosevelt: A Biography of Franklin D. Roosevelt. Doubleday 1957
SCPL

Viorst, Milton. Hostile Allies: FDR and Charles de Gaulle. Macmillan 1965
Bkl A

Weingast, David Elliott. Franklin D. Roosevelt, Man of Destiny. Messner 1952
BBJH—JH

COLLECTIONS

Bliven, Bruce. The World Changers. Day 1965
Bkl A&Y—IndS(10-12)

Fields, Alonzo. My 21 Years in the White House. Coward-McCann 1961
Bkl A

PRESIDENTS

American—20th century

Franklin Delano Roosevelt—Continued

Hofstadter, Richard. American Political Tradition and the Men Who Made It. Knopf 1948
SCPL

Johnson, Walter. 1600 Pennsylvania Avenue: Presidents and the People, 1929-1959. Little 1960
Bkl A

Lawson, Don. Famous American Political Families. Abelard-Schuman 1965
Bkl C(7-12)&Y

Lomask, Milton. "I Do Solemnly Swear . . .": The Story of the Presidential Inauguration. Ariel Bks 1966
ESLC

Parks, Lillian (Rogers) and Leighton, Frances Spatz. My Thirty Years Backstairs at the White House. Fleet 1961
Bkl A&Y

Parlin, John. Patriots' Days. Garrard 1964
ESLC

Roper, Elmo Burns. You and Your Leaders: Their Actions and Your Reactions, 1936-1956. Morrow 1957
SCPL

Theodore Roosevelt, 1858-1919

Busch, Noel Fairchild. T. R.: The Story of Theodore Roosevelt and His Influence on Our Times. Reynal 1963
Bkl A&Y

Cavanah, Frances. Adventures in Courage: The Story of Theodore Roosevelt. Rand McNally 1961
AB(5-7)

Cook, Fred J. Theodore Roosevelt: Rallying a Free People. Lippincott 1961
BY

Foster, Genevieve. Theodore Roosevelt: An Initial Biography. Scribner 1954
BBEL—CC(4-6)

Hagedorn, Hermann. The Boys' Life of Theodore Roosevelt. Harper 1950
SCHS

Hagedorn, Hermann. Roosevelt Family of Sagamore Hill. Macmillan 1954
BBHS—BY—SCHS—SCPL

Harbaugh, William Henry. Power and Responsibility: The Life and Times of Theodore Roosevelt. Farrar 1961
Bkl A—BY—SCPL

Howland, Harold. Theodore Roosevelt and His Times: A Chronicle of the Progressive Movement. Yale Univ. 1921
SCHS

Judson, Clara (Ingram). Theodore Roosevelt, Fighting Patriot. Follett 1953
BBEL(5-8)—BBJH—CC(5-7)—ESLC—JH

Lorant, Stefan. The Life and Times of Theodore Roosevelt. Doubleday 1959
Bkl A—SCPL

Pringle, Henry Fowles. Theodore Roosevelt: A Biography. Harcourt 1956
SCPL—3000

Putnam, Carleton. Theodore Roosevelt: v. 1, The Formative Years, 1858-1886: A Biography. Scribner 1958
SCPL

Rixey, Lilian. Bamie: Theodore Roosevelt's Remarkable Sister. McKay 1963
Bkl A&Y—IndS(10-12)

Roosevelt, Kermit. A Sentimental Safari. Knopf 1963
Bkl A

Roosevelt, Theodore. Autobiography of Theodore Roosevelt; condensed from the original edition; ed. by Wayne Andrews. Scribner 1958
SCPL

Roosevelt, Theodore. Theodore Roosevelt Treasury: A Self-Portrait from His Writings; comp. by Hermann Hagedorn. Putnam 1957
SCPL

Roosevelt, Theodore. Theodore Roosevelt's Letters to His Children; ed. by J. B. Bishop. Scribner 1919
SCPL

Wagenknecht, Edward Charles. Seven Worlds of Theodore Roosevelt. Longmans 1958
SCPL

COLLECTIONS

Hofstadter, Richard. American Political Tradition and the Men Who Made It. Knopf 1948
SCPL

Lomask, Milton. "I Do Solemnly Swear . . .": The Story of the Presidential Inauguration. Ariel Bks 1966
ESLC

William Howard Taft, 1857-1930

Ross, Ishbel. An American Family: The Tafts, 1678 to 1964. World 1964
Bkl A&Y

COLLECTIONS

Lawson, Don. Famous American Political Families. Abelard-Schuman 1965
Bkl C(7-12)&Y

Harry S. Truman, 1884-

Bernstein, Barton J. and Matusow, Allen J., eds. The Truman Administration: A Documentary History. Harper 1966
Bkl A

PRESIDENTS

American—20th century

Harry S. Truman—Continued

Daniels, Jonathan. Man of Independence. Lippincott 1950
SCPL

Martin, Ralph G. President from Missouri: Harry S. Truman. Messner 1964
IndJ(6-9)—JH

Steinberg, Alfred. Harry S. Truman. Putnam 1963
Bkl C(6up)&Y—IndJ(6-9)—JH

Steinberg, Alfred. The Man from Missouri: The Life and Times of Harry S. Truman. Putnam 1962
Bkl A&Y—SCPL

Truman, Harry S. Memoirs: v. 1, Year of Decisions. Doubleday 1955
GR—SCHS—SCPL

Truman, Harry S. Memoirs: v. 2, Years of Trial and Hope. Doubleday 1956
GR—SCHS—SCPL

Truman, Harry S. Mr. Citizen. Random House 1960
Bkl A—SCPL

COLLECTIONS

Brown, John Mason. Through These Men: Some Aspects of Our Passing History. Harper 1956
SCPL

Fields, Alonzo. My 21 Years in the White House. Coward-McCann 1961
Bkl A

Johnson, Walter. 1600 Pennsylvania Avenue: Presidents and the People, 1929-1959. Little 1960
Bkl A

Parks, Lillian (Rogers) and Leighton, Frances Spatz. My Thirty Years Backstairs at the White House. Fleet 1961
Bkl A&Y

Roper, Elmo Burns. You and Your Leaders: Their Actions and Your Reactions, 1936-1956. Morrow 1957
SCPL

Woodrow Wilson, 1856-1924

Bailey, Thomas Andrew. Wilson and the Peacemakers. Macmillan 1947
SCPL

Daniels, Josephus. Wilson Era: Years of Peace—1910-1917. Univ. of N. C. 1944
SCPL

Dodd, William Edward. Woodrow Wilson and His Work. Smith, P. 1932
SCPL

Garraty, John Arthur. Woodrow Wilson: A Great Life in Brief. Knopf 1956
SCPL—3000

Grayson, Cary Travers. Woodrow Wilson: An Intimate Memoir. Holt 1960
Bkl A

Hatch, Alden. Woodrow Wilson: A Biography for Young People. Holt 1947
SCHS

Hoover, Herbert Clark. Ordeal of Woodrow Wilson. McGraw 1958
BBHS—SCPL

Link, Arthur Stanley. Wilson: Campaigns for Progressivism and Peace, 1916-1917. Princeton Univ. 1965
Bkl A

Link, Arthur Stanley. Wilson: Confusions and Crises, 1915-1916. Princeton Univ. 1964
Bkl A

Link, Arthur Stanley. Wilson: The New Freedom. Princeton Univ. 1956
SCPL

Link, Arthur Stanley. Wilson: The Road to the White House. Princeton Univ. 1947
SCPL

Link, Arthur Stanley. Wilson: The Struggle for Neutrality, 1914-1915. Princeton Univ. 1960
Bkl A

Link, Arthur Stanley. Woodrow Wilson: A Brief Biography. World 1963
Bkl A&Y—SCPL

Peare, Catherine Owens. The Woodrow Wilson Story: An Idealist in Politics. Crowell 1963
Bkl C(7up)&Y—CC(6-9)—ESLC—IndJ(6-9)—JH—SCHS—YR

Smith, Gene. When the Cheering Stopped: The Last Years of Woodrow Wilson. Morrow 1964
Bkl A—IndS(10-12)—SCPL

Steinberg, Alfred. Woodrow Wilson. Putnam 1961
Bkl C(7-9)&Y

Walworth, Arthur Clarence. Woodrow Wilson. 2v. Longmans 1958
SCPL

Wilson, Woodrow. A Day of Dedication: The Essential Writings & Speeches of Woodrow Wilson; ed. by Albert Fried. Macmillan 1965
Bkl A&Y

Wilson, Woodrow and Wilson, Ellen Louise (Axson). The Priceless Gift: The Love Letters of [the authors]; ed. by Eleanor Wilson McAdoo. McGraw 1962
Bkl A

COLLECTIONS

Hofstadter, Richard. American Political Tradition and the Men Who Made It. Knopf 1948
SCPL

PRESIDENTS

American—20th century

Woodrow Wilson—Continued

Lomask, Milton. "I Do Solemnly Swear . . .": The Story of the Presidential Inauguration. Ariel Bks 1966
ESLC

American Confederate—19th century

Jefferson Davis, 1808-1889

Catton, William Bruce and Catton, Bruce. Two Roads to Sumter. McGraw 1963
Bkl A

Green, Margaret. President of the Confederacy: Jefferson Davis. Messner 1963
Bkl C(7-9)—YR

Strode, Hudson. Jefferson Davis: American Patriot. Harcourt 1955
SCPL

Strode, Hudson. Jefferson Davis: Confederate President. Harcourt 1959
SCPL

Strode, Hudson. Jefferson Davis: Tragic Hero. Harcourt 1964
IndS(11-12)

COLLECTIONS

Mapp, Alf Johnson. Frock Coats and Epaulets. Yoseloff 1963
Bkl A&Y

Argentinian—20th century

Juan Domingo Perón, 1895-

Alexander, Robert Jackson. Perón Era. Columbia Univ. 1951
SCPL

COLLECTIONS

Szulc, Tad. Twilight of the Tyrants. Holt 1959
Bkl A

Bolivian—19th century

Antonio José de Sucre, 1795-1830

COLLECTIONS

Bailey, Bernadine (Freeman). Famous Latin-American Liberators. Dodd 1960
Bkl C(6-9)&Y—ESLC—SCHS

Brazilian—20th century

Getulio Vargas, 1882-1954

COLLECTIONS

Szulc, Tad. Twilight of the Tyrants. Holt 1959
Bkl A

Colombian—20th century

Gustavo Rojas Pinilla, 1900-

COLLECTIONS

Szulc, Tad. Twilight of the Tyrants. Holt 1959
Bkl A

Dominican Republican—20th century

Rafael Leónidas Trujillo Molina, 1891-1961

Crassweller, Robert D. Trujillo: The Life and Times of a Caribbean Dictator. Macmillan 1966
Bkl A

Egyptian—20th century

Gamal Abdel Nasser, 1918-

St. John, Robert. The Boss: The Story of Gamal Abdel Nasser. McGraw 1960
Bkl A&Y—SCPL

French—20th century

Charles de Gaulle, 1890-

Aron, Robert. An Explanation of de Gaulle; tr. from the French by Marianne Sinclair. Harper 1966
Bkl A

Clark, Stanley. The Man Who Is France: The Story of General de Gaulle. Dodd 1963
Bkl A&Y—SCHS—SCPL

Furniss, Edgar Stephenson. De Gaulle and the French Army: A Crisis in Civil-Military Relations. Twentieth Cent. Fund 1964
Bkl A

Gaulle, Charles de. War Memoirs: v. 1, The Call to Honour, 1940-1942; tr. by J. Griffin. Simon & Schuster 1955
SCPL

Gaulle, Charles de. War Memoirs: v. 2, Unity, 1942-1944; tr. from the French by Richard Howard. Simon & Schuster 1959
SCPL

Gaulle, Charles de. War Memoirs: v. 3, Salvation, 1944-1946; tr. from the French by Richard Howard. Simon & Schuster 1960
Bkl A

Harrity, Richard and Martin, Ralph G. Man of Destiny: De Gaulle of France. Duell 1961
Bkl A&Y

Hatch, Alden. The de Gaulle Nobody Knows: An Intimate Biography of Charles de Gaulle. Hawthorn 1960
Bkl A&Y

PRESIDENTS

French—20th century

Charles de Gaulle—Continued

Lacouture, Jean. De Gaulle; tr. by Francis K. Price. New Am. Lib. 1966
Bkl A

Mauriac, François. De Gaulle; tr. from the French by Richard Howard. Doubleday 1966
Bkl A

Schoenbrun, David. The Three Lives of Charles de Gaulle. Atheneum 1966
Bkl A&Y

Sulzberger, Cyrus Leo. The Test: De Gaulle and Algeria. Harcourt 1962
Bkl A

Tournoux, Jean Raymond. Sons of France: Pétain and de Gaulle; tr. by Oliver Coburn. Viking 1966
Bkl A

Viansson-Ponté, Pierre. The King and His Court; tr. by Elaine P. Halperin. Houghton 1965
Bkl A

Viorst, Milton. Hostile Allies: FDR and Charles de Gaulle. Macmillan 1965
Bkl A

Werth, Alexander. De Gaulle: A Political Biography. Simon & Schuster 1966
Bkl A

Ghanaian—20th century

Kwame Nkrumah, 1909-

Ames, Sophia Ripley. Nkrumah of Ghana. Rand McNally 1961
Bkl Y&C—ESLC

Nkrumah, Kwame. Ghana: The Autobiography of Kwame Nkrumah. Nelson 1957
SCPL

Phillips, John Frederick Vicars. Kwame Nkrumah and the Future of Africa. Praeger 1961
Bkl A

COLLECTIONS

Lengyel, Emil. From Prison to Power. Follett 1964
Bkl A&Y

Melady, Thomas P. Profiles of African Leaders. Macmillan 1961
Bkl A&Y—SCPL

Guinean—20th century

Sékou Touré, 1922-

COLLECTIONS

Melady, Thomas P. Profiles of African Leaders. Macmillan 1961
Bkl A&Y—SCPL

Indonesian—20th century

Sukarno, 1901-

COLLECTIONS

Lengyel, Emil. From Prison to Power. Follett 1964
Bkl A&Y

Irish—20th century

Arthur Griffith, 1872-1922

Colum, Padraic. Ourselves Alone! The Story of Arthur Griffith and the Origin of the Irish Free State. Crown 1960
Bkl A

Israeli—20th century

Chaim Weizmann, 1874-1952

Baker, Rachel. Chaim Weizmann: Builder of a Nation. Messner 1950
BY—SCHS—YR

Chaim Weizmann: A Biography by Several Hands; ed. by Meyer W. Weisgal and Joel Carmichael. Atheneum 1963
Bkl A

Crossman, Richard Howard Stafford. A Nation Reborn: A Personal Report on the Roles Played by Weizmann, Bevin, and Ben-Gurion in the Story of Israel. Atheneum 1960
Bkl A

Weizmann, Chaim. Trial and Error: The Autobiography of Chaim Weizmann; ed. by B. Horovitz. Harper 1950
GR—SCPL

Liberian—20th century

William Vacanarat Shadrach Tubman, 1895-

COLLECTIONS

Melady, Thomas P. Profiles of African Leaders. Macmillan 1961
Bkl A&Y—SCPL

Mexican—19th century

Benito Pablo Juárez, 1806-1872

Baker, Nina Brown. Juárez, Hero of Mexico; adapted by William Kottmeyer. Vanguard 1942
BBHS—BY—CC(7-9)—JH—SCHS

Roeder, Ralph. Juárez and His Mexico: A Biographical History. 2v. Viking 1957
SCPL

Smart, Charles Allen. Viva Juárez! A Biography. Lippincott 1963
Bkl A—IndS(10-12)

COLLECTIONS

Bailey, Bernardine (Freeman). Famous Latin-American Liberators. Dodd 1960
Bkl C(6-9)&Y—ESLC—SCHS

PRESIDENTS—*Continued*

Nicaraguan—19th century

William Walker, 1824-1860

Carr, Albert H. Z. The World and William Walker. Harper 1963
Bkl A

Peruvian—20th century

Manuel Arturo Odría, 1897-

COLLECTIONS

Szulc, Tad. Twilight of the Tyrants. Holt 1959
Bkl A

Philippine—20th century

Diosdado Macapagal, 1910-

Reynolds, Quentin James and Bocca, Geoffrey. Macapagal, the Incorruptible. McKay 1965
Bkl A

Ramón R. Magsaysay, 1907-1957

Romulo, Carlos Pena. The Magsaysay Story. Day 1956
SCPL

Senegalese—20th century

Léopold Sédar Senghor, 1906-

COLLECTIONS

Melady, Thomas P. Profiles of African Leaders. Macmillan 1961
Bkl A&Y—SCPL

Spanish—20th century

Manuel Azaña, 1880-1940

Sedwick, Frank. The Tragedy of Manuel Azaña and the Fate of the Spanish Republic. Ohio State Univ. 1964
Bkl A

Tanganyikan—20th century

Julius Kambarage Nyerere, 1921-

COLLECTIONS

Melady, Thomas P. Profiles of African Leaders. Macmillan 1961
Bkl A&Y—SCPL

Tunisian—20th century

Habib ben Ali Bourguiba, 1904-

COLLECTIONS

Lengyel, Emil. From Prison to Power. Follett 1964
Bkl A&Y

Turkish—20th century

Kamâl Atatürk, 1881-1938

Balfour, Patrick, Baron Kinross. Ataturk: A Biography of Mustafa Kemal, Father of Modern Turkey, by Lord Kinross. Morrow 1964
Bkl A—IndS(12)
Lengyel, Emil. They Called Him Ataturk. Day 1962
AB(7-11)—Bkl C(6-9)&Y—BY

Venezuelan—20th century

Marcos Pérez Jiménez, 1914-

COLLECTIONS

Szulc, Tad. Twilight of the Tyrants. Holt 1959
Bkl A

Vietnamese—20th century

Ngo-dinh Diem, 1901-1963

COLLECTIONS

Hanna, Willard Anderson. Eight Nation Makers: Southeast Asia's Charismatic Statesmen. St Martins 1964
Bkl A&Y

Yugoslav—20th century

Josip Broz Tito, 1892-

Maclean, Fitzroy. Heretic: The Life and Times of Josip Broz Tito. Harper 1957
SCPL

COLLECTIONS

Coolidge, Olivia. Makers of the Red Revolution. Houghton 1963
CC(7-9)
Lengyel, Emil. From Prison to Power. Follett 1964
Bkl A&Y

PRIESTS

See Religious Leaders

PRIME MINISTERS

See Statesmen

PRINCES

English

COLLECTIONS

Joelson, Annette. England's Princes of Wales. Chilton 1966
Bkl A

English—18th century

Charles Edward, The Young Pretender, 1720-1788

Linklater, Eric. The Prince in the Heather. Harcourt 1966
Bkl A&Y

PRINCES—*Continued*

English—20th century

Philip, Consort of Elizabeth II, 1921-

Aleksandra, Consort of Peter II, King of Yugoslavia. Prince Philip: A Family Portrait. Bobbs 1960
Bkl A

Hatch, Alden. The Mountbattens: The Last Royal Success Story. Random House 1965
Bkl A

Japanese—20th century

Akihito, Crown Prince of Japan, 1933-

Simon, Charlie May. The Sun and the Birch: The Story of Crown Prince Akihito and Crown Princess Michiko. Dutton 1960
Bkl Y&C—BY—SCHS

Vining, Elizabeth Gray. Return to Japan. Lippincott 1960
BBHS—SCPL

Vining, Elizabeth Gray. Windows for the Crown Prince. Lippincott 1952
BBHS—BY—JH—SCHS—SCPL—YR

Persian—5th century B.C.

Cyrus the Younger, 424?-401 B.C.

Household, Geoffrey. The Exploits of Xenophon. Random House 1955
ESLC

Portuguese—15th century

Henry the Navigator, Prince of Portugal, 1394-1460

Bradford, Ernle Dusgate Selby. A Wind from the North: The Life of Henry the Navigator. Harcourt 1960
Bkl A&Y—BY

COLLECTIONS

Lucas, Mary Seymour. Vast Horizons. Viking 1943
SCHS

Welsh—13th century

Llewelyn ab Gruffydd, ?-1282

COLLECTIONS

Sutcliff, Rosemary. Heroes and History. Putnam 1966
Bkl C(7-10)&Y

Welsh—14th century

Owen Glendower, 1359?-1416?

COLLECTIONS

Sutcliff, Rosemary. Heroes and History. Putnam 1966
Bkl C(7-10)&Y

PRINCESSES

English—12th century

Matilda, Princess of England, Consort of Geoffrey, Count of Anjou, 1102-1167

COLLECTIONS

Trease, Geoffrey. Seven Queens of England. Vanguard 1953
JH—SCHS

English—14th century

Isabel, Princess of England, ?

Haycraft, Molly (Costain). The Lady Royal. Lippincott 1964 (Fiction)
Bkl A&Y—IndS(9-11)

English—19th century

Sophia, Princess of Great Britain, 1777-1848

Iremonger, Lucille. Love and the Princesses. Crowell 1960
Bkl A

French—9th century

Judith, Countess of Flanders, b. 844

Leighton, Margaret. Judith of France. Houghton 1948 (Fiction)
JH

Hawaiian—19th century

Kaiulani, Princess of Hawaii, 1875-1899

Webb, Nancy and Webb, Jean Francis. Kaiulani: Crown Princess of Hawaii. Viking 1962
Bkl Y&C—BY—YR

PRINTERS

See also Journalists

American—18th century

Benjamin Franklin, 1706-1790

See also under Statesmen—American—18th century

Weir, Ruth Cromer. Benjamin Franklin, Printer and Patriot. Abingdon 1955
ESLC

English—15th century

William Caxton, 1422?-1491

Harnett, Cynthia. Caxton's Challenge. World 1960 (Fiction)
Bkl C(7-9)—CC(7-9)—ESLC—JH—SCHS

PRISONERS

See also Criminals

American—20th century

J. Jerry Cacopardo, ?

Cacopardo, J. Jerry and Weldon, Don. Show Me a Miracle: The True Story of a Man Who Went from Prison to Pulpit. Dutton 1961
Bkl A

Clarence Earl Gideon, 1910-

Lewis, Anthony. Gideon's Trumpet. Random House 1964
Bkl A&Y—SCHS—SCPL

Samuel H. Sheppard, 1923?-

Holmes, Paul Allen. The Sheppard Murder Case. McKay 1961
Bkl A
Sheppard, Stephen A. and Holmes, Paul Allen. My Brother's Keeper. McKay 1964

Isidore Zimmerman, 1917?-

Zimmerman, Isidore and Bond, Francis. Punishment Without Crime: The True Story of a Man Who Spent Twenty-four Years in Prison for a Crime He Did Not Commit. Potter 1964
Bkl A

French—20th century

Marie (Davillaud) Besnard, 1896-

Besnard, Marie (Davillaud). The Trial of Marie Besnard; tr. from the French by Denise Folliot. Farrar 1963
Bkl A

PROHIBITIONISTS

See Temperance Workers

PROPHETS

See Religious Leaders

PSYCHIATRISTS

See also Mental Hygienists; Psychologists

COLLECTIONS

McKown, Robin. Pioneers in Mental Health. Dodd 1961
Bkl A&Y
Clifford Whittingham Beers; Jean Martin Charcot; Dorothea Lynde Dix; Sigmund Freud; Friedrich Anton Mesmer; Benjamin Rush; and others

American—20th century

Karen (Danielson) Horney, 1885-1952

COLLECTIONS

Fleming, Alice (Mulcahey). Doctors in Petticoats. Lippincott 1964
Bkl C(6-9)—CC—JH

Charles Frederick Menninger, 1862-1953

Winslow, Walker. Menninger Story. Doubleday 1956
SCPL

COLLECTIONS

Chandler, Caroline Augusta. Famous Modern Men of Medicine. Dodd 1965
Bkl C(6-9)&Y

Austrian—20th century

Alfred Adler, 1870-1937

Bottome, Phyllis. Alfred Adler: A Portrait from Life. Vanguard 1957
SCPL

Anna Freud, 1895-

COLLECTIONS

Chandler, Caroline Augusta. Famous Modern Men of Medicine. Dodd 1965
Bkl C(6-9)&Y

Sigmund Freud, 1856-1939

Baker, Rachel. Sigmund Freud. Messner 1952
BY
Costigan, Giovanni. Sigmund Freud: A Short Biography. Macmillan 1965
Bkl A&Y
Denker, Henry. A Far Country; a new play. Random House 1961 (Play)
Bkl A
Freud, Sigmund. Letters; selected and ed. by Ernst L. Freud; tr. by Tania and James Stern. Basic Bks 1960
Bkl A
Fromm, Erich. Sigmund Freud's Mission: An Analysis of His Personality. Harper 1959
SCPL
Jones, Ernest. Life and Work of Sigmund Freud. 3v. Basic Bks 1957
GR—SCPL
Jones, Ernest. The Life and Work of Sigmund Freud; ed. and abridged by Lionel Trilling and Steven Marcus. Basic Bks 1961
SCPL
Ruitenbeek, Hendrik Marinus. Freud and America. Macmillan 1966
Bkl A
Sachs, Hanns. Freud, Master and Friend. Harvard Univ. 1944
SCPL
Stoutenburg, Adrien and Baker, Laura Nelson. Explorer of the Unconscious: Sigmund Freud. Scribner 1965
Bkl Y

COLLECTIONS

Kagan, Henry Enoch. Six Who Changed the World. Yoseloff 1963
Bkl A

PSYCHIATRISTS

Austrian—20th century

Sigmund Freud—Continued

McKown, Robin. Pioneers in Mental Health. Dodd 1961
Bkl A&Y

German—19th century

Georg Walther Groddeck, 1866-1934

Grossman, Carl M. and Grossman, Sylva. The Wild Analyst: The Life and Work of Georg Groddeck. Braziller 1965
Bkl A

German—20th century

Georg Walther Groddeck, 1866-1934

Grossman, Carl M. and Grossman, Sylva. The Wild Analyst: The Life and Work of Georg Groddeck. Braziller 1965
Bkl A

Russian—19th century

Lou Andreas-Salomé, 1861-1937

Peters, Heinz Frederick. My Sister, My Spouse: A Biography of Lou Andreas-Salomé. Norton 1962
Bkl A

Swiss—20th century

Carl Gustav Jung, 1875-1961

Jung, Carl Gustav. Memories, Dreams, Reflections; recorded and ed. by Aniela Jaffé; tr. by Richard and Clara Winston. Pantheon 1963
Bkl A—SCPL

PSYCHOANALYSTS

See Psychiatrists

PSYCHOLOGISTS

See also Clairvoyants; Mental Hygienists; Psychiatrists

American—19th century

William James, 1842-1910

James, William. Selected Letters; ed. by Elizabeth Hardwick. Farrar 1961
Bkl A
Matthiessen, Francis Otto. The James Family: Including Selections from the Writing of Henry James, Senior, William, Henry, & Alice James. Knopf 1947
GR—SCPL

American—20th century

Evelyn West Ayrault, 1922-

Ayrault, Evelyn West. Take One Step. Doubleday 1963
Bkl A&Y

Austrian—20th century

Alfred Adler, 1870-1937

Bottome, Phyllis. Alfred Adler: A Portrait from Life. Vanguard 1957
SCPL

PUBLIC RELATIONS COUNSELS

American—20th century

Edward L. Bernays, 1891-

Bernays, Edward L. Biography of an Idea: Memoirs of Public Relations Counsel Edward L. Bernays. Simon & Schuster 1965
Bkl A

PUBLISHERS

American—19th century

James Thomas Fields, 1816-1881

Tryon, Warren Stenson. Parnassus Corner: A Life of James T. Fields, Publisher to the Victorians. Houghton 1963
Bkl A—IndS(12)

Miriam Florence (Folline) Squier Leslie, 1836-1914

Stern, Madeleine Bettina. Queen of Publishers' Row: Mrs. Frank Leslie. Messner 1965
Bkl C(7-9)&Y

American—20th century

Edward Anthony, 1895-

Anthony, Edward. This Is Where I Came In: The Impromptu Confessions of Edward Anthony. Doubleday 1960
Bkl A

Harold Strong Latham, 1887-

Latham, Harold Strong. My Life in Publishing. Dutton 1965
Bkl A

Maxwell Evarts Perkins, 1884-1947

Perkins, Maxwell Evarts. Editor to Author: The Letters of Maxwell E. Perkins; ed. by J. H. Wheelock. Scribner 1950
SCPL

PUBLISHERS—*Continued*

Canadian—20th century

Lovat Dickson, 1902-

Dickson, Lovat. The Ante-Room. Atheneum 1960
Bkl A

Dickson, Lovat. The House of Words. Atheneum 1963
Bkl A

English—18th century

John Newbery, 1713-1767

Blackstock, Josephine. Songs for Sixpence: A Story About John Newbery. Follett 1955
ESLC

English—20th century

Victor Gollancz, 1893-1967

Gollancz, Victor. Journey Towards Music: A Memoir. Dutton 1965
Bkl A

Sir Stanley Unwin, 1884-1968

Unwin, Sir Stanley. The Truth About a Publisher: An Autobiographical Record. Macmillan 1960
Bkl A

Maisie Ward, 1889-

Ward, Maisie. Unfinished Business. Sheed 1964
Bkl A

PUBLISHERS, NEWSPAPER

See Journalists

QUAKER LEADERS

See Religious Leaders

QUEENS

See also Empresses

COLLECTIONS

Coen, Rena Neumann. Kings and Queens in Art. Lerner Publications 1965
ESLC

Coffman, Ramon Peyton. Famous Kings and Queens for Young People. Dodd 1947
BBJH–JH

Farjeon, Eleanor and Mayne, William, eds. A Cavalcade of Queens. Walck 1965
ESLC

Farmer, Lydia (Hoyt). A Book of Famous Queens; rev. by Willard A. Heaps. Crowell 1964
Bkl C(5-9)–ESLC

Dutch—19th century

Hortense, Consort of Louis, King of Holland, 1783-1837

Wright, Constance. Daughter to Napoleon: A Biography of Hortense, Queen of Holland. Holt 1961
Bkl A&Y

Dutch—20th century

Wilhelmina, Queen of the Netherlands, 1880-1962

Wilhelmina, Queen of the Netherlands. Lonely but Not Alone; tr. from the Dutch by John Peereboom. McGraw 1960
Bkl A

Egyptian—14th century B.C.

Nefertiti, Queen of Egypt, ?

Chubb, Mary. Nefertiti Lived Here. Crowell 1955
SCHS

Vidal, Nicole. The Goddess Queen: A Novel Based on the Life of Nefertiti; tr. from the French by Johanna Harwood. McKay 1965 (Fiction)
Bkl A

Wells, Evelyn. Nefertiti. Doubleday 1964
Bkl A&Y–SCHS

Egyptian—1st century B.C.

Cleopatra, Queen of Egypt, 69-30 B.C.

Hornblow, Leonora. Cleopatra of Egypt. Random House 1961
CC(5-7)–JH–SCHS–YR

Ludwig, Emil. Cleopatra. Bantam 1937
GR

Noble, Iris. Egypt's Queen Cleopatra. Messner 1963
Bkl C(7-9)&Y–JH

English

COLLECTIONS

Berton, Pierre. Royal Family: The Story of the British Monarchy from Victoria to Elizabeth. Knopf 1954
SCPL

Farjeon, Eleanor and Farjeon, Herbert. Kings and Queens. Lippincott 1953 (Poem)
ESLC–SCHS

Trease, Geoffrey. Seven Queens of England. Vanguard 1953
JH–SCHS
Anne; Elizabeth I; Elizabeth II; Mary I; Mary II; Matilda; Victoria

Sitwell, Dame Edith. The Queens and the Hive. Little 1962
Bkl A
Elizabeth I; Mary I; Mary Stuart, Queen of the Scots

QUEENS—*Continued*

English—12th century

Eleanor of Aquitaine, 1122?-1204

Kelly, Amy Ruth. Eleanor of Aquitaine and the Four Kings. Harvard Univ. 1950
BY—SCPL—3000

English—15th century

Catherine of Valois, Consort of Henry V, King of England, 1401-1437

Ridge, Antonia. The Royal Pawn. Appleton 1963 (Fiction)
Bkl A&Y

Elizabeth, Consort of Henry VII, King of England, 1465-1503

Barnes, Margaret Campbell. The Tudor Rose. Macrae 1953 (Fiction)
SCHS

English—16th century

Anne Boleyn, Consort of Henry VIII, King of England, 1507-1536

Lofts, Norah (Robinson). The Concubine: A Novel Based upon the Life of Anne Boleyn. Doubleday 1963 (Fiction)
Bkl A

Catherine Howard, Consort of Henry VIII, King of England, 1520?-1542

Ford, Ford Madox. The Fifth Queen. Vanguard 1963 (Fiction)
IndS(11-12)

Smith, Lacey Baldwin. A Tudor Tragedy: The Life and Times of Catherine Howard. Pantheon 1961
Bkl A

Catherine Parr, Consort of Henry VIII, King of England, 1512-1548

Westcott, Jan (Vlachos). The Queen's Grace. Crown 1959 (Fiction)
Bkl A

Elizabeth I, Queen of England, 1533-1603

Anderson, Maxwell. Elizabeth the Queen. Harcourt 1940 (Play)
SCHS—SCPL

Anthony, Evelyn. All the Queen's Men. Crowell 1960 (Fiction)
Bkl A

Chidsey, Donald Barr. Elizabeth I: A Great Life in Brief. Knopf 1955
SCPL

Irwin, Margaret. Elizabeth: Captive Princess. Harcourt 1948 (Fiction)
BBHS—SCHS

Irwin, Margaret. Young Bess. Harcourt 1945 (Fiction)
BBHS—SCHS

Jenkins, Elizabeth. Elizabeth and Leicester. Coward-McCann 1962
Bkl A—SCPL

Jenkins, Elizabeth. Elizabeth the Great. Coward-McCann 1959
BBHS—BY—SCHS—SCPL—3000

Plaidy, Jean. The Young Elizabeth. Roy 1961
ESLC

Read, Conyers. Lord Burghley and Queen Elizabeth. Knopf 1960
Bkl A—SCPL

Strachey, Giles Lytton. Elizabeth and Essex: A Tragic History. Harcourt 1928
BBHS—SCPL

Thane, Elswyth. Tudor Wench. Duell 1948
SCPL

Vance, Marguerite. Elizabeth Tudor, Sovereign Lady. Dutton 1954
BBEL(7-8)—BBJH—JH—SCHS

Winwar, Frances. Queen Elizabeth and the Spanish Armada. Random House 1954
JH—SCHS

COLLECTIONS

Sitwell, Dame Edith. The Queens and the Hive. Little 1962
Bkl A

Trease, Geoffrey. Seven Queens of England. Vanguard 1953
JH—SCHS

Lady Jane Grey, 1537-1554

Chapman, Hester W. Lady Jane Grey, October 1537-February 1554. Little 1963
Bkl A&Y

Malvern, Gladys. The World of Lady Jane Grey. Vanguard 1964
Bkl C(7-9)&Y—IndS(9-11)—JH

Vance, Marguerite. Lady Jane Grey, Reluctant Queen. Dutton 1952
CC(7-9)—SCHS

Mary I, Queen of England, 1516-1558

Prescott, Hilda Frances Margaret. Mary Tudor. Macmillan 1953
SCPL

Simons, Eric N. The Queen and the Rebel: Mary Tudor and Wyatt the Younger. Sportshelf 1964
Bkl A

COLLECTIONS

Sitwell, Dame Edith. The Queens and the Hive. Little 1962
Bkl A

Trease, Geoffrey. Seven Queens of England. Vanguard 1953
JH—SCHS

QUEENS—*Continued*

English—17th century

Catherine of Braganza, Consort of Charles II, King of England, 1638-1705

Lewis, Hilda Winifred. Catherine. Putnam 1966 (Fiction)
Bkl A

Mary II, Queen of Great Britain, 1662-1694

Dunlop, Agnes Mary Robertson. Princess of Orange, by Elisabeth Kyle. Holt 1966
Bkl C(7-9)&Y

COLLECTIONS

Trease, Geoffrey. Seven Queens of England. Vanguard 1953
JH—SCHS

English—18th century

Anne, Queen of Great Britain, 1665-1714

COLLECTIONS

Trease, Geoffrey. Seven Queens of England. Vanguard 1953
JH—SCHS

English—19th century

Victoria, Queen of Great Britain, 1819-1901

Booth, Arthur H. True Story of Queen Victoria. Childrens Press 1964
AB(5-9)

Haycraft, Molly Costain. Queen Victoria, May 24, 1819-January 22, 1901. Messner 1956
JH

Longford, Elizabeth (Harman) Pakenham, Countess of. Queen Victoria: Born to Succeed. Harper 1965
Bkl A&Y

Strachey, Giles Lytton. Queen Victoria. Harcourt 1921
BBHS—GR—SCHS—SCPL—3000

Streatfeild, Noel. Queen Victoria. Random House 1958
BBEL(7-8)—BBJH—CC(6-9)—JH—SCHS

Victoria, Queen of Great Britain. Dearest Child: Letters Between Queen Victoria and the Princess Royal, 1858-1861; ed. by Roger Fulford. Holt 1965
Bkl A

Victoria, Queen of Great Britain. Leaves from a Journal. Farrar 1961
Bkl A

COLLECTIONS

Trease, Geoffrey. Seven Queens of England. Vanguard 1953
JH—SCHS

English—20th century

Elizabeth II, Queen of Great Britain, 1926-

Cathcart, Helen. Her Majesty the Queen: The Story of Elizabeth II. Dodd 1962
Bkl A&Y

Crawford, Marion. Elizabeth the Queen: The Story of Britain's New Sovereign. Prentice-Hall 1952
SCPL

Crawford, Marion. Little Princesses. Harcourt 1950
SCPL

Parker, Elinor M. Most Gracious Majesty: The Story of Queen Elizabeth II. Crowell 1953
BBJH—JH

COLLECTIONS

Trease, Geoffrey. Seven Queens of England. Vanguard 1953
JH—SCHS

Elizabeth, Consort of George VI, King of Great Britain, 1900-

Cathcart, Helen. The Queen Mother: The Story of Elizabeth, the Commoner Who Became Queen. Dodd 1966
Bkl A&Y

Mary, Consort of George V, King of Great Britain, 1867-1953

Crawford, Marion. Mother and Queen: The Story of Queen Mary. Prentice-Hall 1951
SCPL

Pope-Hennessy, James. Queen Mary, 1867-1953. Knopf 1960
Bkl A—SCPL

French—12th century

Eleanor of Aquitaine, 1122?-1204

Kelly, Amy Ruth. Eleanor of Aquitaine and the Four Kings. Harvard Univ. 1950
BY—SCPL—3000

French—16th century

Catherine de Médici, Consort of Henry II, King of France, 1519-1589

Héritier, Jean. Catherine de Medici; tr. by Charlotte Haldane. St Martins 1963
Bkl A

Vance, Marguerite. Dark Eminence: Catherine de Medici and Her Children. Dutton 1961
Bkl C(7-9)&Y—JH

QUEENS

French—16th century—*Continued*

Mary, Consort of Louis XII, King of France, 1496-1533

Haycraft, Molly Costain. The Reluctant Queen. Lippincott 1962 (Fiction)
Bkl A&Y—JH

French—18th century

Marie Antoinette, Consort of Louis XVI, King of France, 1755-1793

Castelot, Andre. Queen of France: A Biography of Marie Antoinette. Harper 1957
CA—SCHS—SCPL

Kielty, Bernardine. Marie Antoinette. Random House 1955
JH—SCHS

Mossiker, Frances. The Queen's Necklace. Simon & Schuster 1961
Bkl A

Vance, Marguerite. Marie Antoinette, Daughter of an Empress. Dutton 1950
BY—CC(7-9)—JH—SCHS

Hawaiian—19th century

Kaahumanu, Consort of Kamehameha I, the Great, King of the Hawaiian Islands, 1772-1832

Mellen, Kathleen D. Magnificent Matriarch. Hastings House 1952
BY

Liliuokalani, Queen of the Hawaiian Islands, 1838-1917

Wilson, Hazel. Last Queen of Hawaii: Liliuokalani. Knopf 1963
ESLC

Polish—14th century

Jadwiga, Consort of Vladislaus II Jagiello, King of Poland, 1370-1399

Mills, Lois. So Young a Queen. Lothrop 1961
Bkl C(6-9)&Y

Scottish—16th century

Mary Stuart, Queen of the Scots, 1542-1587

Anderson, Maxwell. Mary of Scotland. Harcourt 1940 (Play)
SCHS

Davison, M. H. Armstrong. The Casket Letters: A Solution to the Mystery of Mary Queen of Scots and the Murder of Lord Darnley. Univ. Press of Washington 1965
Bkl A

King, Marian. Young Mary Stuart, Queen of Scots. Lippincott 1954
BBJH—CC(6-9)—JH—SCHS

Morrison, Nancy Brysson. Mary, Queen of Scots. Vanguard 1960
Bkl A&Y—SCPL

Plaidy, Jean. The Young Mary, Queen of Scots. Roy n.d.
ESLC

Uttley, Alison. A Traveler in Time. Viking 1964 (Fiction)
JH

Vance, Marguerite. Scotland's Queen: The Story of Mary Stuart. Dutton 1962
Bkl C(7-9)&Y—ESLC—JH—SCHS—YR

COLLECTIONS

Sitwell, Dame Edith. The Queens and the Hive. Little 1962
Bkl A

Spanish—15th century

Isabel I, Queen of Spain, 1451-1504

Criss, Mildred. Isabella, Young Queen of Spain. Dodd 1957
SCHS

Swedish—17th century

Christina, Queen of Sweden, 1626-1689

Lewis, Paul. Queen of Caprice: A Biography of Kristina of Sweden. Holt 1962
Bkl A

Stephan, Ruth Walgreen. My Crown, My Love. Knopf 1960 (Fiction)
Bkl A

Stolpe, Sven. Christina of Sweden; tr. by Sir Alec Randall. Macmillan 1966
Bkl A

Swedish—19th century

Bernardine Eugénie Désirée, Consort of Charles XIV John, King of Sweden and Norway, 1777-1860

Selinko, Annemarie. Désirée. Morrow 1953 (Fiction)
SCHS

QUINTUPLETS

Canadian—20th century

Dionne Quintuplets, 1934-

Brough, James. "We Were Five": The Dionne Quintuplets' Story from Birth Through Girlhood to Womanhood. Simon & Schuster 1965
Bkl A&Y

RABBIS

See Religious Leaders

RACERS

See Automobile Racers

RADIO AND TELEVISION ENGINEERS

See Engineers, Radio, and Television

RADIO AND TELEVISION NEWSCASTERS

See Journalists

RADIO AND TELEVISION PERFORMERS

See also Actors; Journalists; Singers

American—20th century

Dick Clark, 1929-

COLLECTIONS

Davidson, William. The Real and the Unreal. Harper 1961
  Bkl A

Arthur Godfrey, 1903-

Godfrey, Jean and Godfrey, Kathy. Genius in the Family. Putnam 1962
  Bkl A

Curtis Gowdy, 1919-

Gowdy, Curtis and Hirshberg, Albert. Cowboy at the Mike. Doubleday 1966
  Bkl A&Y

Mary Margaret McBride, 1899-

McBride, Mary Margaret. Out of the Air. Doubleday 1960
  Bkl A

RADIOLOGISTS

American—20th century

Russell Hedley Morgan, 1911-

COLLECTIONS

Poole, Lynn and Poole, Gray. Scientists Who Work with Cameras. Dodd 1965
  Bkl C(7-12)&Y–IndS(11-12)

RAILROAD OFFICIALS

American

COLLECTIONS

Lewis, Oscar. The Big Four. Knopf 1938
  SCPL
  Charles Crocker; Mark Hopkins; Collis Potter Huntington; Leland Stanford

American—19th century

Charles Crocker, 1822-1888

COLLECTIONS

Lewis, Oscar. The Big Four. Knopf 1938
  SCPL

Edward Henry Harriman, 1848-1909

COLLECTIONS

Josephson, Matthew. Robber Barons: The Great American Capitalists, 1861-1901. Harcourt 1934
  SCPL

James Jerome Hill, 1838-1916

COLLECTIONS

Josephson, Matthew. Robber Barons: The Great American Capitalists, 1861-1901. Harcourt 1934
  SCPL

Mark Hopkins, 1813-1878

COLLECTIONS

Lewis, Oscar. The Big Four. Knopf 1938
  SCPL

Collis Potter Huntington, 1821-1900

COLLECTIONS

Josephson, Matthew. Robber Barons: The Great American Capitalists, 1861-1901. Harcourt 1934
  SCPL
Lewis, Oscar. The Big Four. Knopf 1938
  SCPL

Leland Stanford, 1824-1893

COLLECTIONS

Lewis, Oscar. The Big Four. Knopf 1938
  SCPL

American—20th century

James Jerome Hill, 1838-1916

COLLECTIONS

Josephson, Matthew. Robber Barons: The Great American Capitalists, 1861-1901. Harcourt 1934
  SCPL

RANGERS, FOREST

See Conservationists

RANGERS, TEXAS

See Police

RECLUSES

American—19th century

Ida Ellen (Walsh) Wood, 1838?-1932

Cox, Joseph A. The Recluse of Herald Square: The Mystery of Ida E. Wood. Macmillan 1964
  Bkl A

RECLUSES—*Continued*

American—20th century

Ida Ellen (Walsh) Wood, 1838?-1932

Cox, Joseph A. The Recluse of Herald Square: The Mystery of Ida E. Wood. Macmillan 1964
Bkl A

RED CROSS WORKERS

American—19th century

Clara Harlowe Barton, 1821-1912

Boylston, Helen Dore. Clara Barton, Founder of the American Red Cross. Random House 1955
BBJH—CC(4-7)—ESLC—JH—SCHS

Epler, Percy Harold. Life of Clara Barton. Macmillan 1915
SCPL

Graham, Alberta P. Clara Barton, Red Cross Pioneer. Abingdon 1956
CC(3-5)

Nolan, Jeannette (Covert). The Story of Clara Barton of the Red Cross. Messner 1941
CC(7-9)—JH—SCHS

Pace, Mildred Mastin. Clara Barton. Scribner 1941
BBEL(6-8)—CC(4-7)—YR

Rose, Mary Catherine. Clara Barton: Soldier of Mercy. Garrard 1960
ESLC

Ross, Ishbel. Angel of the Battlefield: The Life of Clara Barton. Harper 1956
BY—SCHS—SCPL

REFORMERS

See also Abolitionists; Pacifists; Philanthropists; Religious Leaders; Temperance Workers

COLLECTIONS

Harcourt, Melville. Portraits of Destiny. Sheed 1966
Bkl A
Danilo Dolci; Albert Luthuli; Kaj Munk; and others

Heroes of Our Time, by Lord Shackleton and others. Dutton 1962
Bkl Y&C

McNeer, May Yonge and Ward, Lynd Kendall. Armed with Courage. Abingdon 1957
AB(5-8)—BBEL(5-8)—CC(5-7)—ESLC—JH—YR
Jane Addams; George Washington Carver; Joseph Damien de Veuster; Mohandas Karamchand Gandhi; Sir Wilfred Thomason Grenfell; Florence Nightingale; Albert Schweitzer

Schechter, Betty. The Peaceable Revolution. Houghton 1963
IndJ(6-9)
Mohandas Karamchand Gandhi; Martin Luther King; Henry David Thoreau

Thomas, Norman Mattoon. Great Dissenters. Norton 1961
Bkl A&Y
Galileo; Mohandas Karamchand Gandhi; Thomas Paine; Wendell Phillips; Socrates

American

COLLECTIONS

Holbrook, Stewart Hall. Dreamers of the American Dream. Doubleday 1957
SCPL
Ethan Allen; Henry George; John Humphrey Noyes; Frances Willard; and others

McNeer, May Yonge and Ward, Lynd Kendall. Give Me Freedom. Abingdon 1964
Bkl C(5-8)—CC(5-7)—ESLC—JH—YR
Marian Anderson; Albert Einstein; Elijah Parish Lovejoy; Edwin Markham; Thomas Paine; William Penn; Elizabeth Stanton

American—19th century

Henry George, 1839-1897

COLLECTIONS

Holbrook, Stewart Hall. Dreamers of the American Dream. Doubleday 1957
SCPL

John Humphrey Noyes, 1811-1886

COLLECTIONS

Holbrook, Stewart Hall. Dreamers of the American Dream. Doubleday 1957
SCPL

Wendell Phillips, 1811-1884

Bartlett, Irving H. Wendell Phillips: Brahmin Radical. Beacon Press 1961
BY

COLLECTIONS

Hofstadter, Richard. American Political Tradition and the Men Who Made It. Knopf 1948
SCPL

Thomas, Norman Mattoon. Great Dissenters. Norton 1961
Bkl A&Y

Frances Elizabeth Caroline Willard, 1839-1898

COLLECTIONS

Holbrook, Stewart Hall. Dreamers of the American Dream. Doubleday 1957
SCPL

REFORMERS—*Continued*

English—19th century

Anthony Ashley Cooper, 7th Earl of Shaftesbury, 1801-1885

Best, Geoffrey Francis Andrew. Shaftesbury. Arco 1964
Bkl A

South African—20th century

Albert Luthuli, 1899-1967

COLLECTIONS

Harcourt, Melville. Portraits of Destiny. Sheed 1966
Bkl A

REGENTS

Dutch—16th century

Margaretha of Austria, Regent of the Netherlands, 1480-1530

Lewis, Paul. The Gentle Fury. Holt 1961 (Fiction)
Bkl A

RELATIVES OF FAMOUS MEN

See also Daughters of Famous Men; Daughters of Famous Women; Mothers of Famous Men; Relatives of Famous Women; Wives of Famous Men

American—18th century

Jane (Franklin) Mecom, 1712-1794

Van Doren, Carl Clinton. Jane Mecom. Viking 1950
SCPL

American—19th century

Anna (Roosevelt) Cowles, 1855-1931

Rixey, Lilian. Bamie: Theodore Roosevelt's Remarkable Sister. McKay 1963
Bkl A&Y—IndS(10-12)

American—20th century

Anna (Roosevelt) Cowles, 1855-1931

Rixey, Lilian. Bamie: Theodore Roosevelt's Remarkable Sister. McKay 1963
Bkl A&Y—IndS(10-12)

Gemma (La Guardia) Gluck, 1881-1962

Gluck, Gemma (La Guardia). My Story; ed. by S. L. Shneiderman. McKay 1961
Bkl A

English—16th century

Lady Arbella Stuart, 1575-1615

Haycraft, Molly Costain. Too Near the Throne: A Novel Based on the Life of Lady Arbella Stuart. Lippincott 1959 (Fiction)
JH

English—17th century

Lady Arbella Stuart, 1575-1615

Haycraft, Molly Costain. Too Near the Throne: A Novel Based on the Life of Lady Arbella Stuart. Lippincott 1959 (Fiction)
JH

English—19th century

Marianne Thornton, 1797-1887

Forster, E. M. Marianne Thornton: A Domestic Biography, 1797-1887. Harcourt 1956
SCPL

Dorothy Wordsworth, 1771-1855

Wordsworth, Dorothy. Journals; ed. by E. de Selincourt. 2v. St Martins 1941
SCPL

French

COLLECTIONS

Weiner, Margery. The Parvenu Princesses: The Lives and Loves of Napoleon's Sisters. Morrow 1964
Bkl A—IndS(11-12)
Caroline Bonaparte, Countess of Lipona; Elisa Bonaparte, Grand Duchess of Tuscany; Pauline Bonaparte, Duchess of Guastalla

French—19th century

Caroline Bonaparte, Countess of Lipona, 1782-1839

COLLECTIONS

Weiner, Margery. The Parvenu Princesses: The Lives and Loves of Napoleon's Sisters. Morrow 1964
Bkl A—IndS(11-12)

Elisa Bonaparte, Grand Duchess of Tuscany, 1777-1820

COLLECTIONS

Weiner, Margery. The Parvenu Princesses: The Lives and Loves of Napoleon's Sisters. Morrow 1964
Bkl A—IndS(11-12)

Pauline Bonaparte, Duchess of Guastalla, 1780-1825

Dixon, Sir Pierson. Pauline, Napoleon's Favourite Sister. McKay 1965
Bkl A

RELATIVES OF FAMOUS MEN

French—19th century

Pauline Bonaparte—Continued

COLLECTIONS

Weiner, Margery. The Parvenu Princesses: The Rives and Loves of Napoleon's Sisters. Morrow 1964
Bkl A—IndS(11-12)

Dorothée (von Biron) Duchesse de Talleyrand-Périgord, 1793-1862

Ziegler, Philip. The Duchess of Dino. Day 1963
Bkl A

Indian—20th century

Vijaya Lakshmi (Nehru) Pandit, 1900-

Guthrie, Anne. Madame Ambassador: The Life of Vijaya Lakshmi Pandit. Harcourt 1962
AB(6-9)—Bkl Y&C—BY—JH—SCHS—SCPL

Russian—20th century

Olga Alexandrovna, 1882-1960

Vorres, Ian. The Last Grand Duchess, Her Imperial Highness Grand Duchess Olga Alexandrovna, 1 June 1882-24 November 1960. Scribner 1965
Bkl A&Y

RELATIVES OF FAMOUS WOMEN

English—16th century

Lady Catherine Grey, ?

Chapman, Hester W. Two Tudor Portraits: Henry Howard, Earl of Surrey and Lady Katherine Grey. Little 1963
Bkl A—IndS(11-12)

RELIEF WORKERS

See Social Workers

RELIGIOUS LEADERS

See also Agnostics; Biblical Figures; Philosophers

COLLECTIONS

Attwater, Donald, comp. A Dictionary of Saints, Based on Butler's Lives of the Saints. Kenedy 1958
SCPL

Bainton, Roland Herbert. Travail of Religious Liberty: Nine Biographical Studies. Westminster 1951
SCPL
John Calvin; Sébastien Chateillon; David Joris; John Locke; John Milton; Bernardino Ochino; Michael Servetus; Tomás de Torquemada; Roger Williams

The Book of Saints: A Dictionary of Persons Canonized or Beatified by the Catholic Church; comp. by the Benedictine Monks of St. Augustine's Abbey, Ramsgate. Crowell 1966
Bkl A—SCPL

Butler, Alban. Lives of the Saints; ed. & rev. by Herbert Thurston and Donald Attwater. 4v. Kenedy 1956
SCPL

Cheney, Sheldon Warren. Men Who Have Walked with God: Being the Story of Mysticism Through the Ages Told in the Biographies of Representative Seers and Saints. Knopf 1945
SCPL

Cluny, Roland. Holiness in Action; tr. from the French by D. A. Askew. Hawthorn 1963
Bkl A
Saint Augustine; Saint Bernard of Clairvaux; Saint Francis of Assisi; Saint Ignatius Loyola; Saint Paul

Deen, Edith. Great Women of the Christian Faith. Harper 1959
SCPL

Eddy, George Sherwood. Pathfinders of the World Missionary Crusade. Abingdon 1945
SCPL

Elgin, Kathleen. Nun: A Gallery of Sisters. Random House 1964
IndS(9-12)

Farjeon, Eleanor. Ten Saints. Walck 1936
CC(6-9)—ESLC
Saint Bridget; Saint Christopher; Saint Dorothea; Saint Francis of Assisi; Saint Giles; Saint Hubert; Saint Martin; Saint Nicholas, Bishop of Myra; Saint Patrick; Saint Simeon Stylites

Goodspeed, Edgar Johnson. The Twelve: The Story of Christ's Apostles. Winston 1957
SCPL

Graef, Hilda C. Mystics of Our Times. Hanover House 1962
Bkl A
Augustin Marie du Très Saint Sacrement; Charles Eugène, Vicomte de Foucauld; Maximilian Kolbe; Francis Mary Paul Libermann; Edel Mary Quinn; Pierre Teilhard de Chardin

Harcourt, Melville, ed. Thirteen for Christ. Sheed 1963
Bkl A

Haughton, Rosemary. Six Saints for Parents. Sheed 1963
Bkl A
Saint Augustine; Saint Joseph; Saint Rose of Lima; Saint Thomas Aquinas; and others

RELIGIOUS LEADERS—*Continued*

Kittler, Glen D. The Wings of Eagles. Doubleday 1966
Bkl A&Y
Thomas Anthony Dooley; Mother Katharine Drexel; John XXIII, Pope; John Fitzgerald Kennedy; John La Farge; Pierre Teilhard de Chardin

Knowles, David. Saints and Scholars: Twenty-five Medieval Portraits. Cambridge 1962
Bkl A

Luce, Clare (Boothe), ed. Saints for Now. Sheed 1952
SCPL

O'Neill, Mary. Saints: Adventures in Courage. Doubleday 1963
AB(3-9)—ESLC

Quadflieg, Joseph. The Saints and Your Name; tr. from the German by Margaret Goldsmith. Pantheon 1957
ESLC

Staudacher, Rosemarian V. Chaplains in Action. Farrar 1962
AB(5up)

Turnbull, E. Lucia. Legends of the Saints. Lippincott 1959
Bkl C(3-6)

Walsh, William Thomas. Saints in Action. Hanover House 1961
Bkl A
Saint Athanasius; Saint Benedict; Saint Cyprian; Saint Gregory I, the Great, Pope; Saint Ignatius Theophorus; Saint Justin; Saint Patrick; Saint Peter, Apostle

Walton, Izaak. Lives. Oxford
GR
John Donne; George Herbert; and others

African—5th century

Saint Augustine, 354-430

Augustine, Saint. Confessions; tr. by Edward B. Pusey. Modern Lib.; Regnery; etc.
CA—GR—SCPL—3000

Chabannes, Jacques. St. Augustine; tr. by Julie Kernan. Doubleday 1962
Bkl A

Meer, Frederik van der. Augustine the Bishop: The Life and Work of a Father of the Church; tr. by Brian Battershaw and G. R. Lamb. Sheed 1962
Bkl A

COLLECTIONS

Cluny, Roland. Holiness in Action; tr. from the French by D. A. Askew. Hawthorn 1963
Bkl A

Haughton, Rosemary. Six Saints for Parents. Sheed 1963
Bkl A

Jaspers, Karl. The Great Philosophers: v. 1, The Foundations; ed. by Hannah Arendt; tr. by Ralph Manheim. Harcourt 1962
Bkl A—SCPL

American—17th century

John Cotton, 1584-1652

Emerson, Everett H. John Cotton. Twayne 1965
Bkl A

Anne (Marbury) Hutchinson, 1591-1643

Battis, Emery John. Saints and Sectaries. Univ. of N. C. 1962
Bkl A

COLLECTIONS

Daugherty, Sonia. Ten Brave Women. Lippincott 1953
BY—CC(7-9)—ESLC—JH—SCHS

Douglas, Emily (Taft). Remember the Ladies: The Story of Great Women Who Helped Shape America. Putnam 1966
Bkl A&Y

Increase Mather, 1639-1723

Murdock, Kenneth Ballard. Increase Mather, the Foremost American Puritan. Harvard Univ. 1925
SCPL

William Penn, 1644-1718

Aliki. The Story of William Penn. Prentice-Hall 1964
ESLC—IndJ(2-4)

Buranelli, Vincent. The King & the Quaker: A Study of William Penn and James II. Univ. of Pa. 1962
Bkl A

Dolson, Hildegarde. William Penn, Quaker Hero. Random House 1961
AB(5-9)—Bkl C(5-8)—ESLC

Gray, Elizabeth Janet. Penn. Viking 1938
BBEL(6-8)—BBJH—CC(7-9)—ESLC—JH—SCHS

Haviland, Virginia. William Penn, Founder and Friend. Abingdon 1952
AB(4-7)—BBEL—CC(4-6)—ESLC

Illick, Joseph E. William Penn, the Politician: His Relations with the English Government. Cornell Univ. 1965
Bkl A

Peare, Catherine Owens. William Penn: A Biography. Holt 1958
BBJH—CC(7-9)—JH—SCHS

Peare, Catherine Owens. William Penn: A Biography. Lippincott 1956
BBHS—SCPL

RELIGIOUS LEADERS

American—17th century

William Penn—Continued

Syme, Ronald. William Penn, Founder of Pennsylvania. Morrow 1966
Bkl C(4-6)

Wallace, Willard M. Friend William. Nelson 1958
YR

COLLECTIONS

McNeer, May Yonge and Ward, Lynd Kendall. Give Me Freedom. Abingdon 1964
Bkl C(5-8)—CC(5-7)—ESLC—JH—YR

Roger Williams, 1603-1683

Covey, Cyclone. The Gentle Radical: A Biography of Roger Williams. Macmillan 1966
Bkl A&Y

Eaton, Jeanette. Lone Journey: The Life of Roger Williams. Harcourt 1944
BBJH—CC(7-9)—ESLC—JH—SCHS—YR

Winslow, Ola Elizabeth. Master Roger Williams: A Biography. Macmillan 1957
SCPL

COLLECTIONS

Bainton, Roland Herbert. Travail of Religious Liberty: Nine Biographical Studies. Westminster 1951
SCPL

American—18th century

Richard Allen, 1760-1831

COLLECTIONS

Douty, Esther (Morris). Under the New Roof: Five Patriots of the Young Republic. Rand McNally 1965
Bkl Y&C

John Carroll, 1735-1815

Melville, Annabelle (McConnell). John Carroll of Baltimore, Founder of the American Catholic Hierarchy. Scribner 1955
SCPL

George Washington, 1732-1799

Boller, Paul F. George Washington & Religion. Southern Methodist Univ. 1963
Bkl A

John Woolman, 1720-1772

Woolman, John. Journal; ed. by Janet Whitney. Regnery 1950
SCPL

American—19th century

Richard Allen, 1760-1831

COLLECTIONS

Douty, Esther (Morris). Under the New Roof: Five Patriots of the Young Republic. Rand McNally 1965
Bkl Y&C

Lyman Beecher, 1775-1863

Beecher, Lyman. Autobiography; ed. by Barbara M. Cross. 2v. Harvard Univ. 1961
Bkl A

Antoinette Louisa (Brown) Blackwell, 1825-1921

COLLECTIONS

Douglas, Emily (Taft). Remember the Ladies: The Story of Great Women Who Helped Shape America. Putnam 1966
Bkl A&Y

Phillips Brooks, 1835-1893

Albright, Raymond Wolf. Focus on Infinity: A Life of Phillips Brooks. Macmillan 1961
Bkl A

Saint Frances Xavier Cabrini, 1850-1917

Di Donato, Pietro. Immigrant Saint: The Life of Mother Cabrini. McGraw 1960
Bkl A

Maynard, Theodore. Too Small a World: The Life of Francesca Cabrini. Bruce 1945
SCPL

Mary (Baker) Eddy, 1821-1910

Beasley, Norman. The Cross and the Crown: The History of Christian Science. Duell 1952
SCPL

Beasley, Norman. Mary Baker Eddy. Duell 1963
Bkl A

Peel, Robert. Mary Baker Eddy: The Years of Discovery. Holt 1966
Bkl A

Powell, Lyman Pierson. Mary Baker Eddy: A Life Size Portrait. Christian Science Pub. 1950
SCPL

Wilbur, Sibyl. Life of Mary Baker Eddy. Christian Science Pub. 1938
SCPL

COLLECTIONS

Buckmaster, Henrietta. Women Who Shaped History. Collier Bks 1966
Bkl C(7-10)&Y

RELIGIOUS LEADERS

American—19th century—*Continued*

James Cardinal Gibbons, 1834-1921

Ellis, John Tracy. Life of James Cardinal Gibbons, Archbishop of Baltimore, 1834-1921. 2v. Bruce 1952
SCPL

Ellis, John Tracy. Life of James Cardinal Gibbons, Archbishop of Baltimore, 1834-1921; ed. by Francis L. Broderick. Bruce 1963
IndS(10-12)

Tehan, Arline (Boucher) and Tehan, John. Prince of Democracy, James Cardinal Gibbons. Hanover House 1962
Bkl A

Sheldon Jackson, 1834-1909

Lazell, J. Arthur. Alaskan Apostle: The Life Story of Sheldon Jackson. Harper 1960
Bkl A

Rose (Hawthorne) Lathrop, 1851-1926

Burton, Katherine (Kurz). Sorrow Built a Bridge: A Daughter of Hawthorne. Longmans 1937
SCPL

Theodore Parker, 1810-1860

Commager, Henry Steele. Theodore Parker. Beacon Press 1947
SCPL

Elizabeth Ann Seton, 1774-1821

Dirvin, Joseph I. Mrs. Seton, Foundress of the American Sisters of Charity. Farrar 1962
Bkl A

Melville, Annabelle (McConnell). Elizabeth Bayley Seton, 1774-1821. Scribner 1951
SCPL

Joseph Smith, 1805-1844

Brodie, Fawn (McKay). No Man Knows My History: The Life of Joseph Smith, the Mormon Prophet. Knopf 1945
SCPL

West, Ray Benedict. Kingdom of the Saints: The Story of Brigham Young and the Mormons. Viking 1957
SCPL

John Smith ("Raccoon" John Smith) 1784-1868

Cochran, Louis. Raccoon John Smith: A Novel Based on the Life of the Famous Pioneer Kentucky Preacher. Duell 1963 (Fiction)
Bkl A

Marcus Whitman, 1802-1847

Allen, T. D. Doctor in Buckskin. Harper 1951 (Fiction)
SCHS

Daugherty, James. Marcus and Narcissa Whitman, Pioneers of Oregon. Viking 1953
BBEL—BY—CC(7-9)—ESLC—JH—SCHS

Jones, Nard. The Great Command: The Story of Marcus and Narcissa Whitman and the Oregon Country Pioneers. Little 1959
Bkl A

Narcissa (Prentiss) Whitman, 1808-1847

Cranston, Paul. To Heaven on Horseback: The Romantic Story of Narcissa Whitman. Messner 1952 (Fiction)
SCHS

Eaton, Jeanette. Narcissa Whitman, Pioneer of Oregon. Harcourt 1941
BBEL(7-8)—BY—CC(7-9)—ESLC—JH—SCHS—YR

COLLECTIONS

Daugherty, Sonia. Ten Brave Women. Lippincott 1953
BY—CC(7-9)—ESLC—JH—SCHS

Brigham Young, 1801-1877

Burt, Olive. Brigham Young. Messner 1956
SCHS

West, Ray Benedict. Kingdom of the Saints: The Story of Brigham Young and the Mormons. Viking 1957
SCPL

American—20th century

Leila W. Anderson, 1898-

Anderson, Leila W. and Dexter, Harriet Harmon. Pilgrim Circuit Rider. Harper 1960
Bkl A

Harriet M. Bedell, 1875-

Hartley, William B. and Hartley, Ellen. A Woman Set Apart. Dodd 1963
Bkl A—IndS(11-12)

Saint Frances Xavier Cabrini, 1850-1917

Di Donato, Pietro. Immigrant Saint: The Life of Mother Cabrini. McGraw 1960
Bkl A

Maynard, Theodore. Too Small a World: The Life of Francesca Cabrini. Bruce 1945
SCPL

RELIGIOUS LEADERS
American—20th century—*Continued*

J. Jerry Cacopardo, ?

Cacopardo, J. Jerry and Weldon Don. Show Me a Miracle: The True Story of a Man Who Went from Prison to Pulpit. Dutton 1961
Bkl A

Paul Earle Carlson, 1928-1964

Carlson, Lois. Monganga Paul: The Congo Ministry and Martyrdom of Paul Carlson, M.D. Harper 1966
Bkl A&Y

Walter J. Ciszek, 1904-

Ciszek, Walter J. and Flaherty, Daniel L. With God in Russia. McGraw 1964
Bkl A

Joseph Calvitt Clarke, 1888-

Janss, Edmund W. Yankee Si: The Story of Dr. J. Calvitt Clarke and His 36,000 Children. Morrow 1961
Bkl A&Y

Charles Edward Coughlin, 1891-

Tull, Charles J. Father Coughlin and the New Deal. Syracuse Univ. 1965
Bkl A

James F. Cunningham, 1901-

Cunningham, James F. American Pastor in Rome. Doubleday 1966
Bkl A

Richard James Cardinal Cushing, 1895-

Dever, Joseph. Cushing of Boston: A Candid Portrait. Bruce Humphries 1965
Bkl A
Fenton, John H. Salt of the Earth: An Informal Profile of Richard Cardinal Cushing. Coward-McCann 1965
Bkl A

Lillian Dickson, 1901-

Wilson, Kenneth L. Angel at Her Shoulder: Lillian Dickson and Her Taiwan Mission. Harper 1964
Bkl A&Y

Lloyd Cassel Douglas, 1877-1951

Douglas, Lloyd Cassel. Time to Remember. Houghton 1951
SCPL

Mother Katharine Drexel, 1858-1955
COLLECTIONS

Kittler, Glenn D. The Wings of Eagles. Doubleday 1966
Bkl A&Y

Daniel Francis Egan, 1915-

Harris, John D. The Junkie Priest, Father Daniel Egan, S.A. Coward-McCann 1964
Bkl A

Welthy (Honsinger) Fisher, 1880-

Fisher, Welthy (Honsinger). To Light a Candle. McGraw 1962
Bkl A—BY

Edward Joseph Flanagan, 1886-1948

Oursler, Fulton. Father Flanagan of Boys Town. Doubleday 1949
BY—SCHS—SCPL

Harry Emerson Fosdick, 1878-

Fosdick, Harry Emerson. Living of These Days: An Autobiography. Harper 1956
SCPL

James Cardinal Gibbons, 1834-1921

Ellis, John Tracy. Life of James Cardinal Gibbons, Archbishop of Baltimore, 1834-1921. 2v. Bruce 1952
SCPL
Ellis, John Tracy. Life of James Cardinal Gibbons, Archbishop of Baltimore, 1834-1921; ed. by Francis L. Broderick. Bruce 1963
IndS(10-12)
Tehan, Arline (Boucher) and Tehan, John. Prince of Democracy, James Cardinal Gibbons. Hanover House 1962
Bkl A

James Alfred Gusweller, 1923-

Ehle, John. Shepherd of the Streets: The Story of the Reverend James A. Gusweller and His Crusade on the New York West Side. Sloane 1960
Bkl A

Donald Hayne, 1908-

Hayne, Donald. Batter My Heart. Knopf 1963
Bkl A

Albert Haley Henderson, 1866-1937

Read, Katherine L. (Henderson) and Ballou, Robert O. Bamboo Hospital: The Story of a Missionary Family in Burma. Lippincott 1961
Bkl A&Y

Margaret (Kimball) Henrichsen, 1900-

Henrichsen, Margaret (Kimball). Seven Steeples. Houghton 1953
SCPL

RELIGIOUS LEADERS

American—20th century—*Continued*

Arthur Wentworth Hewitt, 1883-

Hewitt, Arthur Wentworth. The Old Brick Manse. Harper 1966
Bkl A

John Haynes Holmes, 1879-1964

Voss, Carl Hermann. Rabbi and Minister: The Friendship of Stephen S. Wise and John Haynes Holmes. World 1964
Bkl A

Rufus Matthew Jones, 1863-1948

Vining, Elizabeth Gray. Friend of Life: The Biography of Rufus M. Jones. Lippincott 1958
SCPL

Martin Luther King, 1929-1968

Bennett, Lerone. What Manner of Man: A Biography of Martin Luther King. Johnson Pub. 1964
Bkl A&Y

Clayton, Ed. Martin Luther King: The Peaceful Warrior. Prentice-Hall 1964
CC(5-7)—ESLC—IndJ(4-6)

Reddick, Lawrence Dunbar. Crusader Without Violence: A Biography of Martin Luther King, Jr. Harper 1959
SCPL

COLLECTIONS

Schechter, Betty. The Peaceable Revolution. Houghton 1963
IndJ(6-9)

John La Farge, 1880-1963

La Farge, John. The Manner Is Ordinary. Harcourt 1954
SCPL

COLLECTIONS

Kittler, Glenn D. The Wings of Eagles. Doubleday 1966
Bkl A&Y

Rose (Hawthorne) Lathrop, 1851-1926

Burton, Katherine (Kurz). Sorrow Built a Bridge: A Daughter of Hawthorne. Longmans 1937
SCPL

Burleigh A. Law, ?-1964

Law, Virginia W. Appointment Congo. Rand McNally 1966
Bkl A&Y

William A. Leising, ?

Leising, William A. Arctic Wings. Doubleday 1959
Bkl A

Malcolm Little ("Malcolm X"), 1925-1965

Little, Malcolm and Haley, Alex. The Autobiography of Malcolm X. Grove 1965
Bkl A

Little, Malcolm. Malcolm X Speaks: Selected Speeches and Statements; ed. by George Breitman. Merit Publishers 1965
Bkl A

Peter Marshall, 1902-1949

Marshall, Catherine (Wood). Man Called Peter: The Story of Peter Marshall. McGraw 1951
BY—SCHS—SCPL

Sister Maryanna, ?

Maryanna, Sister. With Love and Laughter: Reflections of a Dominican Nun. Hanover House 1960
Bkl A

Thomas Merton, 1915-1968

Merton, Thomas. Seven Storey Mountain. Harcourt 1948
CA—GR—SCPL

Merton, Thomas. Sign of Jonas. Harcourt 1953
SCPL

Merton, Thomas. Waters of Siloe. Harcourt 1949
SCPL

Robert Herbert Mize, 1907-

Neal, Emily Gardiner. Father Bob and His Boys. Bobbs 1963
Bkl A

Abraham John Muste, 1885-1967

Hentoff, Nat. Peace Agitator: The Story of A. J. Muste. Macmillan 1963
Bkl A

Reinhold Niebuhr, 1892-

Bingham, June. Courage to Change: An Introduction to the Life and Thought of Reinhold Niebuhr. Scribner 1961
Bkl A—SCPL

Harland, Gordon. The Thought of Reinhold Niebuhr. Oxford 1960
SCPL

James Joseph Reeb, 1927-1965

Howlett, Duncan. No Greater Love: The James Reeb Story. Harper 1966
Bkl A

Mary Joseph Rogers, 1882-1955

Lyons, Jeanne Marie. Maryknoll's First Lady. Dodd 1964
Bkl A&Y—IndS(9-12)

RELIGIOUS LEADERS

American—20th century—*Continued*

John Augustine Ryan, 1869-1945

Broderick, Francis L. Right Reverend New Dealer, John A. Ryan. Macmillan 1963
Bkl A

Albert Edward Saunders, 1892-1964

MacNair, John Van. Chaplain on the Waterfront: The Story of Father Saunders. Seabury 1963
Bkl A

Myra Scovel, ?

Scovel, Myra and Bell, Nelle Keys. The Chinese Ginger Jars. Harper 1962
Bkl A&Y

Ida Scudder, 1870-1960

Wilson, Dorothy Clarke. Dr. Ida: The Story of Dr. Ida Scudder of Vellore. McGraw 1959
Bkl A&Y—SCPL

Henry Knox Sherrill, 1890-

Sherrill, Henry Knox. Among Friends. Little 1962
Bkl A

Francis Joseph Cardinal Spellman, 1889-1967

Gannon, Robert Ignatius. The Cardinal Spellman Story. Doubleday 1962
Bkl A—SCPL

William H. Spence, 1875-1936

Spence, Hartzell. One Foot in Heaven: The Life of a Practical Parson. McGraw 1940
BY—SCHS

Hudson Stuck, 1863-1920

Herron, Edward A. Conqueror of Mount McKinley. Messner 1964
YR

Howard Thurman, 1899-

Yates, Elizabeth. Howard Thurman: Portrait of a Practical Dreamer. Day 1964
Bkl A&Y

James Edward Walsh, 1891-

Kerrison, Raymond. Bishop Walsh of Maryknoll: A Biography. Putnam 1962
Bkl A

Devorah Wigoder, ?

Wigoder, Devorah. Hope Is My House. Prentice-Hall 1966
Bkl A

Arthur Wilson, 1888-

Wilson, Arthur. Thy Will Be Done: The Autobiography of an Episcopal Minister. Dial 1960
Bkl A

Stephen Samuel Wise, 1874-1949

Voss, Carl Hermann. Rabbi and Minister: The Friendship of Stephen S. Wise and John Haynes Holmes. World 1964
Bkl A

Wise, Stephen Samuel. Challenging Years: The Autobiography of Stephen Wise. Putnam 1949
SCPL

Belgian—19th century

Joseph Damien de Veuster, 1840-1889

Farrow, John. Damien, the Leper. Sheed 1937
BY—SCPL

Roos, Ann. Man of Molokai: The Life of Father Damien. Lippincott 1943
CC(7-9)—JH—SCHS

COLLECTIONS

McNeer, May Yonge and Ward, Lynd Kendall. Armed with Courage. Abingdon 1957
AB(5-8)—BBEL(5-8)—CC(5-7)—ESLC—JH—YR

Pierre-Jean de Smet, 1801-1873

Terrell, John Upton. Black Robe: The Life of Pierre-Jean de Smet, Missionary, Explorer & Pioneer. Doubleday 1964
Bkl A&Y

Belgian—20th century

Dominique Pire, 1910-1969

Pire, Dominique and Vehenne, Hugues. The Story of Father Dominique Pire, Winner of the Nobel Peace Prize; tr. from the French by John L. Skeffington. Dutton 1961
BY

Canadian—17th century

Mère Marie (Guyard) Martin, 1599-1672

Repplier, Agnes. Mère Marie of the Ursulines: A Study in Adventure. Sheed 1951
BY—SCPL

Canadian—18th century

Esther Wheelright, 1696-1780

Vance, Marguerite. Esther Wheelright, Indian Captive. Dutton 1964
AB(3-6)—Bkl C(4-6)—ESLC

RELIGIOUS LEADERS—*Continued*

Carthaginian—3rd century

Saint Cyprian, 200?-258

COLLECTIONS

Walsh, William Thomas. Saints in Action. Hanover House 1961
Bkl A

Chinese—5th century B.C.

Confucius, 551-478 B.C.

Creel, Herrlee Glessner. Confucius, the Man and the Myth. Day 1949
SCPL

COLLECTIONS

Jaspers, Karl. The Great Philosophers: v. 1, The Foundations; ed. by Hannah Arendt; tr. by Ralph Manheim. Harcourt 1962
Bkl A—SCPL

Cypriote—20th century

Archbishop Makarios III, 1913-

COLLECTIONS

Lengyel, Emil. From Prison to Power. Follett 1964
Bkl A&Y

Danish—20th century

Kaj Munk, 1898-1944

COLLECTIONS

Harcourt, Melville. Portraits of Destiny. Sheed 1966
Bkl A

Dutch—16th century

David Joris, 1501?-1556

COLLECTIONS

Bainton, Roland Herbert. Travail of Religious Liberty: Nine Biographical Studies. Westminster 1951
SCPL

English—11th century

Saint Anselm, 1033-1109

COLLECTIONS

Jaspers, Karl. The Great Philosophers: v. 2, The Original Thinkers; ed. by Hannah Arendt; tr. by Ralph Manheim. Harcourt 1966
Bkl A

English—12th century

Saint Thomas à Becket, Archbishop of Canterbury, 1118-1170

Anouilh, Jean. Becket; or, The Honor of God; tr. by Lucienne Hill. Coward-McCann 1960 (Play)
Bkl A—SCPL

Duggan, Alfred Leo. My Life for My Sheep. Coward-McCann 1955
SCPL—3000

Eliot, Thomas Stearns. Murder in the Cathedral. Harcourt 1935 (Play)
SCHS—SCPL

Fry, Christopher. Curtmantle: A Play. Oxford 1961 (Play)
Bkl A

Mydans, Shelley Smith. Thomas: A Novel of the Life, Passion, and Miracles of Becket. Doubleday 1965 (Fiction)
Bkl A&Y

English—16th century

Sir Thomas More, Saint, 1478-1535

Basset, Bernard. Born for Friendship: The Spirit of Sir Thomas More. Sheed 1965
Bkl A&Y

Bolt, Robert. A Man for All Seasons: A Play in Two Acts. Random House 1962 (Play)
Bkl A—SCHS—SCPL

Maynard, Theodore. Humanist as Hero: The Life of Sir Thomas More. Macmillan 1947
SCPL

Newell, Virginia. His Own Good Daughter. McKay 1961
YR

Reynolds, Ernest Edwin. The Trial of St. Thomas More. Kenedy 1964
Bkl A

Stanley-Wrench, Margaret. The Conscience of a King. Hawthorn 1962
AB(5-9)

William Tyndale, 1492?-1536

Oliver, Jane. Flame of Fire. Putnam 1961 (Fiction)
Bkl A&Y

Oliver, Jane. Watch for the Morning. St. Martins 1964 (Fiction)
Bkl C(6-9)—ESLC

Thomas Cardinal Wolsey, 1475?-1530

Ferguson, Charles Wright. Naked to Mine Enemies: The Life of Cardinal Wolsey. Little 1958
SCPL—3000

English—17th century

John Bunyan, 1628-1688

Barr, Gladys (Hutchison). The Pilgrim Prince: A Novel Based on the Life of John Bunyan. Holt 1963 (Fiction)
Bkl A—IndS(9-12)

Brittain, Vera Mary. In the Steps of John Bunyan: An Excursion into Puritan England. Macmillan 1951
SCPL

RELIGIOUS LEADERS

English—17th century

John Bunyan—Continued

Winslow, Ola Elizabeth. John Bunyan. Macmillan 1961
  Bkl A

John Donne, 1573-1631

COLLECTIONS

Walton, Izaak. Lives. Oxford
  GR

George Fox, 1624-1691

Fox, George. Journal. Cambridge 1952
  SCPL
Wildes, Harry Emerson. Voice of the Lord: A Biography of George Fox. Univ. of Pa. 1965
  Bkl A

George Herbert, 1593-1633

COLLECTIONS

Walton, Izaak. Lives. Oxford
  GR

English—18th century

Joseph Priestley, 1733-1804

Crane, William Dwight. The Discoverer of Oxygen: Joseph Priestley. Messner 1962
  Bkl C(7-12)&Y—BY
Marcus, Rebecca B. Joseph Priestley, Pioneer Chemist. Watts 1961
  Bkl C(5-8)—CC—ESLC

John Wesley, 1703-1791

Grailsford, Mabel Richmond. Tale of Two Brothers: John and Charles Wesley. Oxford 1954
  SCPL
Green, Vivian Hubert Howard. The Young Mr. Wesley: A Study of John Wesley and Oxford. St Martins 1961
  Bkl A
McNeer, May Yonge and Ward, Lynd Kendall. John Wesley. Abingdon 1951
  BBEL(6-8)—CC(6-9)—JH

English—19th century

William Booth, 1829-1912

Collier, Richard. The General Next to God: The Story of William Booth and the Salvation Army. Dutton 1965
  Bkl A

Sir Wilfred Thomason Grenfell, 1865-1940

Grenfell, Sir Wilfred Thomason. Adrift on an Ice-Pan. Houghton 1939
  SCPL

Grenfell, Sir Wilfred Thomason. Forty Years for Labrador. Houghton 1932
  SCPL
Kerr, James Lennox. Wilfred Grenfell: His Life and Work. Dodd 1959
  Bkl A&Y
Pumphrey, George H. Grenfell of Labrador. Dodd 1959
  AB(7-10)—JH

COLLECTIONS

McNeer, May Yonge and Ward, Lynd Kendall. Armed with Courage. Abingdon 1957
  AB(5-8)—BBEL(5-8)—CC(5-7)—ESLC—JH—YR

John Henry Cardinal Newman, 1801-1890

Blehl, Vincent Ferrer and Connolly, Francis X., eds. Newman's Apologia: A Classic Reconsidered. Harcourt 1964
  Bkl A
Newman, John Henry, Cardinal. Apologia pro Vita Sua. Dutton; Modern Lib.; etc.
  GR
O'Faolain, Sean. Newman's Way: The Odyssey of John Henry Newman. Devin-Adair 1952
  SCPL
Trevor, Meriol. Newman: Light in Winter. Doubleday 1963
  Bkl A
Trevor, Meriol. Newman: The Pillar of the Cloud. Doubleday 1962
  Bkl A
Trevor, Meriol. Shadows and Images: A Novel. McKay 1962 (Fiction)
  Bkl A

James Hudson Taylor, 1832-1905

Pollock, John Charles. Hudson Taylor and Maria: Pioneers in China. McGraw 1962
  Bkl A

Nicholas Patrick Stephen Cardinal Wiseman, 1802-1865

Fothergill, Brian. Nicholas Wiseman. Doubleday 1963
  Bkl A

English—20th century

Gladys Aylward, 1903?-

Burgess, Alan. Small Woman. Dutton 1957
  BBHS—BY—SCHS—SCPL

Mary Ball, 1894?-1952

Earl, Lawrence. She Loved a Wicked City: The Story of Mary Ball, Missionary. Dutton 1962
  Bkl A&Y—BY

RELIGIOUS LEADERS

English—20th century—*Continued*

Sir Wilfred Thomason Grenfell, 1865-1940

Grenfell, Sir Wilfred Thomason. Adrift on an Ice-Pan. Houghton 1939
SCPL

Grenfell, Sir Wilfred Thomason. Forty Years for Labrador. Houghton 1932
SCPL

Kerr, James Lennox. Wilfred Grenfell: His Life and Work. Dodd 1959
Bkl A&Y

Pumphrey, George H. Grenfell of Labrador. Dodd 1959
AB(7-10)—JH

COLLECTIONS

McNeer, May Yonge and Ward, Lynd Kendall. Armed with Courage. Abingdon 1957
AB(5-8)—BBEL(5-8)—CC(5-7)—ESLC—JH—YR

Ronald Arbuthnott Knox, 1888-1957

Corbishley, Thomas and Speaight, Robert. Ronald Knox: The Priest and the Writer. Sheed 1965
Bkl A

Waugh, Evelyn. Monsignor Ronald Knox, Fellow of Trinity College, Oxford, and Protonotary Apostolic to His Holiness Pope Pius XII. Little 1959
Bkl A—SCPL

Teresa Lightwood, 1906-

Lightwood, Teresa. My Three Lives. Dutton 1960
Bkl A—BY

Edel Mary Quinn, 1907-1944

COLLECTIONS

Graef, Hilda C. Mystics of Our Times. Hanover House 1962
Bkl A

Arthur Michael Ramsey, Archbishop of Canterbury, 1904-

Simpson, James Beasley. The Hundredth Archbishop of Canterbury. Harper 1962
Bkl A

French—4th century

Saint Martin of Tours, 316?-400?

COLLECTIONS

Farjeon, Eleanor. Ten Saints. Walck 1936
CC(6-9)—ESLC

French—7th century

Saint Hubert, 656?-727

COLLECTIONS

Farjeon, Eleanor. Ten Saints. Walck 1936
CC(6-9)—ESLC

French—12th century

Saint Bernard of Clairvaux, 1090-1153

Daniel-Rops, Henry. Bernard of Clairvaux; tr. from the French by Elisabeth Abbott. Hawthorn 1964
Bkl A

COLLECTIONS

Cluny, Roland. Holiness in Action; tr. from the French by D. A. Askew. Hawthorn 1963
Bkl A

French—16th century

John Calvin, 1509-1564

Barr, Gladys H. The Master of Geneva: A Novel Based on the Life of John Calvin. Holt 1961 (Fiction)
Bkl A

Wendel, François. Calvin: The Origins and Development of His Religious Thought; tr. by Philip Mairet. Harper 1963
Bkl A

COLLECTIONS

Bainton, Roland Herbert. Travail of Religious Liberty: Nine Biographical Studies. Westminster 1951
SCPL

Sébastien Chateillon, 1515-1563

COLLECTIONS

Bainton, Roland Herbert. Travail of Religious Liberty: Nine Biographical Studies. Westminster 1951
SCPL

Antoine Cardinal Duprat, 1463-1535

Schoonover, Lawrence L. The Chancellor. Little 1961 (Fiction)
Bkl A

French—17th century

Jacques Bénigne Bossuet, Bishop of Meaux, 1627-1704

Reynolds, Ernest Edwin. Bossuet. Doubleday 1963
Bkl A

RELIGIOUS LEADERS

French—17th century—*Continued*

François de Salignac de La Mothe-Fénelon, Archbishop, 1651-1715

Fénelon, François de Salignac de La Mothe-, Archbishop. Letters of Love and Counsel; tr. by John McEwen. Harcourt 1964
Bkl A

Saint Isaac Jogues, 1607-1646

Kittler, Glenn D. Saint in the Wilderness: The Story of St. Isaac Jogues and the Jesuit Adventure in the New World. Doubleday 1964
Bkl A&Y

Father Joseph, 1577-1638

Huxley, Aldous Leonard. Grey Eminence: A Study in Religion and Politics. Harper 1941
SCPL

Jacques Marquette, 1637-1675

Kjelgaard, Jim. Explorations of Père Marquette. Random House 1951
CC(6-8)—JH—SCHS

Armand Jean du Plessis, Cardinal, Duc de Richelieu, 1585-1642

Belloc, Hilaire. Richelieu: A Study. Lippincott 1950
SCPL

Saint Vincent de Paul, 1581?-1660

Daniel-Rops, Henry. Monsieur Vincent: The Story of St. Vincent de Paul; tr. from the French by Julie Kernan. Hawthorn 1961
Bkl A
Purcell, Mary. The World of Monsieur Vincent. Scribner 1963
Bkl A

French—18th century

François de Salignac de La Mothe-Fénelon, Archbishop, 1651-1715

Fénelon, François de Salignac de La Mothe-, Archbishop. Letters of Love and Counsel; tr. by John McEwen. Harcourt 1964
Bkl A

French—19th century

Charles Eugène, Vicomte de Foucauld, 1858-1916

Garnett, Emmeline. Charles de Foucauld. Farrar 1962
BY

Six, Jean François. Witness in the Desert: The Life of Charles de Foucauld; tr. by Lucie Noel. Macmillan 1965
Bkl A

COLLECTIONS

Graef, Hilda C. Mystics of Our Times. Hanover House 1962
Bkl A

Francis Mary Paul Libermann, 1804-1852

COLLECTIONS

Graef, Hilda C. Mystics of Our Times. Hanover House 1962
Bkl A

Antoine Frédéric Ozanam, 1813-1853

Derum, James Patrick. Apostle in a Top Hat: The Life of Frédéric Ozanam. Hanover House 1960
Bkl A

Saint Thérèse, 1873-1897

Keyes, Frances Parkinson (Wheeler). Therese: Saint of a Little Way. Messner 1950
SCPL
Ulanov, Barry. The Making of a Modern Saint: A Biographical Study of Thérèse of Lisieux. Doubleday 1966
Bkl A

Saint Jean Baptiste Marie Vianney, 1786-1859

Saint-Pierre, Michel de. The Remarkable Curé of Ars: The Life and Achievements of St. John Mary Vianney; tr. by M. Angeline Bouchard. Doubleday 1963
Bkl A

French—20th century

Raymond Léopold Bruckberger, 1907-

Bruckberger, Raymond Léopold. One Sky to Share: The French and American Journals; tr. by Dorothy Carr Howell. Kenedy 1952
SCPL

Father Jacques, 1900-1945

Carrouges, Michel. Père Jacques; tr. by Salvator Attanasio. Macmillan 1961
Bkl A

Henri Perrin, 1914-1954

Perrin, Henri. Priest and Worker: The Autobiography; tr. by Bernard Wall. Holt 1964
Bkl A

RELIGIOUS LEADERS

French—20th century—*Continued*

Albert Schweitzer, 1875-1965

Anderson, Erica and Exman, Eugene. The World of Albert Schweitzer: A Book of Photographs. Harper 1955
BY—SCHS—SCPL

Berrill, Jacquelyn. Albert Schweitzer, Man of Mercy. Dodd 1956
BBJH—BY—JH

Cousins, Norman. Dr. Schweitzer of Lambaréné. Harper 1960
Bkl Y—SCHS—SCPL

Cousins, Norman. Lambaréné: Doctor Schweitzer and His People. Harper 1960
Bkl A&Y

Daniel, Anita. The Story of Albert Schweitzer. Random House 1957
JH—SCHS

Franck, Frederick. Days with Albert Schweitzer: A Lambaréné Landscape. Holt 1959
SCPL

Gollomb, Joseph. Albert Schweitzer: Genius in the Jungle. Vanguard 1949
BBEL(7-8)—BY—CC(7-9)—JH—SCHS

Hagedorn, Hermann. Prophet in the Wilderness: The Story of Albert Schweitzer. Macmillan 1954
SCPL

Manton, Jo. The Story of Albert Schweitzer. Abelard-Schuman 1955
AB(7up)—BBEL(6)—JH

Merrett, John. The True Story of Albert Schweitzer. Childrens Press 1964
IndJ(4-6)

Payne, Pierre Stephen Robert. Three Worlds of Albert Schweitzer. Nelson 1957
SCHS—SCPL

Picht, Werner Robert Valentin. The Life and Thought of Albert Schweitzer; tr. from the German by Edward Fitzgerald. Harper 1964
Bkl A

Schweitzer, Albert. Out of My Life and Thought: An Autobiography; tr. by C. T. Campion. Holt 1949
BBHS—GR—SCPL—3000

Seaver, George. Albert Schweitzer: Christian Revolutionary. Harper 1956
SCPL

Seaver, George. Albert Schweitzer: The Man and His Mind. Harper 1955
SCPL

Simon, Charlie May. All Men Are Brothers: A Portrait of Albert Schweitzer. Dutton 1956
AB(7-10)—BBJH—JH

COLLECTIONS

McNeer, May Yonge and Ward, Lynd Kendall. Armed with Courage. Abingdon 1957
AB(5-8)—BBEL(5-8)—CC(5-7)—ESLC—JH—YR

Pierre Teilhard de Chardin, 1881-1955

Corte, Nicolas. Pierre Teilhard de Chardin: His Life and Spirit; tr. by Martin Jarrett Kerr. Macmillan 1960
Bkl A

Cuénot, Claude. Teilhard de Chardin: A Biographical Study; ed. by René Hague; tr. by Vincent Colimore. Helicon Press 1965
Bkl A

De Terra, Helmut. Memories of Teilhard de Chardin; tr. from the German by J. Maxwell Brownjohn. Harper 1965
Bkl A

Grenet, Paul. Teilhard de Chardin: The Man and His Theories; tr. from the French by R. A. Rudorff. Eriksson 1966
Bkl A

Lubac, Henri de. Teilhard de Chardin: The Man and His Meaning; tr. by René Hague. Hawthorn 1965
Bkl A

Rabut, Olivier A. Teilhard de Chardin: A Critical Study. Sheed 1961
Bkl A

Teilhard de Chardin, Pierre. The Making of a Mind: Letters from a Soldier-Priest, 1914-1919; tr. from the French by René Hague. Harper 1965
Bkl A

COLLECTIONS

Graef, Hilda C. Mystics of Our Times. Hanover House 1962
Bkl A

Kittler, Glenn D. The Wings of Eagles. Doubleday 1966
Bkl A&Y

German—15th century

Nicholas of Cusa, 1401-1464

COLLECTIONS

Jaspers, Karl. The Great Philosophers: v. 2, The Original Thinkers; ed. by Hannah Arendt; tr. by Ralph Manheim. Harcourt 1966
Bkl A

German—16th century

Martin Luther, 1483-1546

Bainton, Roland Herbert. Here I Stand: A Life of Martin Luther. Abingdon 1950
SCPL—3000

RELIGIOUS LEADERS

German—16th century

Martin Luther—Continued

Fosdick, Harry Emerson. Martin Luther. Random House 1956
JH—SCHS

Green, Vivian Hubert Howard. Luther and the Reformation. Putnam 1964
Bkl A

McNeer, May Yonge and Ward, Lynd Kendall. Martin Luther. Abingdon 1953
BBEL(6-8)—CC(6-9)—ESLC—JH

Osborne, John. Luther: A Play. Criterion 1962 (Play)
Bkl A—IndS(11-12)

Ritter, Gerhard. Luther: His Life and Work; tr. from the German by John Riches. Harper 1964
Bkl A

Thulin, Oskar, ed. A Life of Luther, Told in Pictures and Narrative by the Reformer and His Contemporaries; tr. by Martin O. Dietrich. Fortress Press 1966
Bkl A

German—17th century

John Adam Schall, 1591-1666

Attwater, Rachel. Adam Schall: A Jesuit at the Court of China, 1592-1666; adapted from the French of Joseph Duhr. Bruce 1963
Bkl A

German—19th century

Father Augustin Marie du Très Saint Sacrement, 1820-1871

COLLECTIONS

Graef, Hilda C. Mystics of Our Times. Hanover House 1962
Bkl A

German—20th century

Martin Niemöller, 1892-

Schmidt, Dietmar. Pastor Niemöller; tr. from the German by Lawrence Wilson. Doubleday 1959
Bkl A

Paul Johannes Tillich, 1886-1965

Thomas, John Heywood. Paul Tillich: An Appraisal. Westminster 1963
Bkl A

Greek—3rd century

Saint Christopher, ?

COLLECTIONS

Farjeon, Eleanor. Ten Saints. Walck 1936
CC(6-9)—ESLC

Greek—4th century

Saint Athanasius, 293?-373

COLLECTIONS

Walsh, William Thomas. Saints in Action. Hanover House 1961
Bkl A

Greek—7th century

Saint Giles, ?

COLLECTIONS

Farjeon, Eleanor. Ten Saints. Walck 1936
CC(6-9)—ESLC

Hungarian—20th century

Joseph Cardinal Mindszenty, 1892-

Swift, Stephen K. Cardinal's Story: The Life and Work of Joseph, Cardinal Mindszenty, Archbishop of Esztergom, Primate of Hungary. Macmillan 1949
SCPL

Indian—6th century B.C.

Buddha, 563?-483? B.C.

Serage, Nancy. The Prince Who Gave Up a Throne: A Story of the Buddha. Crowell 1966
Bkl C(3-6)

COLLECTIONS

Jaspers, Karl. The Great Philosophers: v. 1, The Foundations; ed. by Hannah Arendt; tr. by Ralph Manheim. Harcourt 1962
Bkl A—SCPL

Indian—2nd century

Nagarjuna, ?

COLLECTIONS

Jaspers, Karl. The Great Philosophers: v. 2, The Original Thinkers; ed. by Hannah Arendt; tr. by Ralph Manheim. Harcourt 1966
Bkl A

Indian—19th century

Ramakrishna, 1836-1886

Isherwood, Christopher. Ramakrishna and His Disciples. Simon & Schuster 1965
Bkl A

Indian—20th century

Mohandas Karamchand Gandhi, 1869-1948

Eaton, Jeanette. Gandhi, Fighter Without a Sword. Morrow 1950
BBEL(7-8)—BBHS—BBJH—BY—CC(7-9)—ESLC—JH—SCHS—YR

RELIGIOUS LEADERS

Indian—20th century

Mohandas Karamchand Gandhi—Continued

Fischer, Louis. Gandhi: His Life and Message for the World. New Am. Lib. 1955
GR

Fischer, Louis. Life of Mahatma Gandhi. Harper 1950
SCPL—3000

Gandhi, Mohandas Karamchand. All Men Are Brothers. Columbia Univ. 1959
BBHS

Gandhi, Mohandas Karamchand. The Essential Gandhi: An Anthology; ed. by Louis Fischer. Random House 1962
Bkl A

Gandhi, Mohandas Karamchand. Gandhi's Autobiography: The Story of My Experiments with Truth; tr. by Mahadev Desai. Public Affairs Press 1954
GR—SCPL

Masani, Shakuntala. Gandhi's Story. Walck 1950
AB(4-7)

Reynolds, Reginald. The True Story of Gandhi. Childrens Press 1964
IndJ(4-6)

Shahani, Ranjee Gurdarsing. Mr. Gandhi. Macmillan 1961
Bkl A

Sheean, Vincent. Lead, Kindly Light. Random House 1949
SCPL

Sheean, Vincent. Mahatma Gandhi: A Great Life in Brief. Knopf 1955
SCHS—SCPL

Slade, Madeleine. The Spirit's Pilgrimage. Coward-McCann 1960
Bkl A&Y

Wolpert, Stanley. Nine Hours to Rama. Random House 1962 (Fiction)
Bkl A

COLLECTIONS

McNeer, May Yonge and Ward, Lynd Kendall. Armed with Courage. Abingdon 1957
AB(5-8)—BBEL(5-8)—CC(5-7)—ESLC—JH—YR

Schechter, Betty. The Peaceable Revolution. Houghton 1963
CC(8-9)—ESLC—IndJ(6-9)—JH

Thomas, Norman Mattoon. Great Dissenters. Norton 1961
Bkl A&Y

Irish—5th century

Saint Bridget, 453-524

COLLECTIONS

Farjeon, Eleanor. Ten Saints. Walck 1936
CC(6-9)—ESLC

Saint Patrick, 373?-463?

Gallico, Paul William. Steadfast Man: A Biography of St. Patrick. Doubleday 1958
SCPL

COLLECTIONS

Farjeon, Eleanor. Ten Saints. Walck 1936
CC(6-9)—ESLC

Walsh, William Thomas. Saints in Action. Hanover House 1961
Bkl A

Irish—6th century

Saint Columba, 521-597

Oliver, Jane. Isle of Glory. Putnam 1964 (Fiction)
Bkl A

Saint Columban, 543-615

MacManus, Francis. Saint Columban. Sheed 1962
Bkl A

Polland, Madeleine A. Fingal's Quest. Doubleday 1961 (Fiction)
Bkl C(7-9)

Irish—7th century

Saint Columban, 543-615

MacManus, Francis. Saint Columban. Sheed 1962
Bkl A

Polland, Madeleine A. Fingal's Quest. Doubleday 1961 (Fiction)
Bkl C(7-9)

Italian

See also Religious Leaders—Roman

COLLECTIONS

Farrow, John. Pageant of the Popes. Sheed 1950
SCPL

John, Eric, ed. The Popes: A Concise Biographical History. Hawthorn 1964
Bkl A

Keyes, Frances Parkinson (Wheeler). Three Ways of Love. Hawthorn 1963
Bkl A
Saint Agnes; Saint Catherine of Siena; Saint Frances of Rome

Sugrue, Francis. Popes in the Modern World. Crowell 1961
Bkl A
Benedict XV; John XXIII; Leo XIII; Pius X; Pius XI; Pius XII

RELIGIOUS LEADERS—*Continued*

Italian—4th century

Saint Agnes, 292-305

COLLECTIONS

Keyes, Frances Parkinson (Wheeler). Three Ways of Love. Hawthorn 1963
Bkl A

Italian—6th century

Saint Gregory I, the Great, Pope, 540?-604

COLLECTIONS

Walsh, William Thomas. Saints in Action. Hanover House 1961
Bkl A

Italian—13th century

Saint Francis of Assisi, 1182-1226

Chesterton, Gilbert Keith. St. Francis of Assisi. Doubleday 1924
SCPL
De La Bedoyère, Michael. Francis: A Biography of the Saint of Assisi. Harper 1962
Bkl A
Goudge, Elizabeth. My God and My All: The Life of St Francis of Assisi. Coward-McCann 1959
SCPL
Jewett, Eleanore M. Big John's Secret. Viking 1962 (Fiction)
AB(7up)
Jewett, Sophie. God's Troubadour: The Story of Saint Francis of Assisi. Crowell 1957
CC(6-9)—ESLC—JH—SCHS
Kazantzakēs, Nikos. Saint Francis: A Novel; tr. from the Greek by P. A. Bien. Simon & Schuster 1962 (Fiction)
Bkl A
Maynard, Theodore. Richest of the Poor: The Life of Saint Francis of Assisi. Doubleday 1948
SCPL
Politi, Leo. Saint Francis and the Animals. Scribner 1959
CC(1-3)—ESLC
Raymond, Ernest. In the Steps of St. Francis. Kinsey 1939
SCPL
St. Francis of Assisi: His Holy Life and Love of Poverty. Franciscan Herald 1964
Bkl A
Sticco, Maria. The Peace of St. Francis; tr. from the Italian by Salvator Attanasio. Hawthorn 1962
Bkl A

COLLECTIONS

Cluny, Roland. Holiness in Action; tr. from the French by D. A. Askew. Hawthorn 1963
Bkl A
Farjeon, Eleanor. Ten Saints. Walck 1936
CC(6-9)—ESLC

Saint Thomas Aquinas, 1225?-1274

Chesterton, Gilbert Keith. St. Thomas Aquinas. Sheed 1933
SCPL
D'Arcy, Martin Cyril. St. Thomas Aquinas. Clonmore 1953
SCPL

COLLECTIONS

Haughton, Rosemary. Six Saints for Parents. Sheed 1963
Bkl A

Italian—14th century

Saint Catherine of Siena, 1347-1380

De Wohl, Louis. Lay Siege to Heaven: A Novel of Saint Catherine of Siena. Lippincott 1961 (Fiction)
Bkl A
Jorgensen, Johannes. Saint Catherine of Siena; tr. from the Danish by Ingeborg Lund. Longmans 1938
SCPL
Raymond of Capua. The Life of St. Catherine of Siena; tr. by George Lamb. Kenedy 1960
Bkl A

COLLECTIONS

Keyes, Frances Parkinson (Wheeler). Three Ways of Love. Hawthorn 1963
Bkl A

Saint Rita of Cascia, 1381-1457

Spens, Willy de. Saint Rita; tr. by Julie Kernan. Hanover House 1962
Bkl A

Italian—15th century

Saint Frances of Rome, 1384-1440

COLLECTIONS

Keyes, Frances Parkinson (Wheeler). Three Ways of Love. Hawthorn 1963
Bkl A

Pius II, Pope, 1405-1464

Mitchell, Rosamond Joscelyne. The Laurels and the Tiara: Pope Pius II, 1458-1464. Doubleday 1963
Bkl A

Saint Rita of Cascia, 1381-1457

Spens, Willy de. Saint Rita; tr. by Julie Kernan. Hanover House 1962
Bkl A

RELIGIOUS LEADERS

Italian—15th century—*Continued*

Girolamo Savonarola, 1452-1498

De La Bedoyère, Michael. Meddlesome Friar and the Wayward Pope: The Story of the Conflict Between Savonarola and Alexander VI. Hanover House 1958
SCPL

Italian—16th century

Bernardino Ochino, 1487-1564

COLLECTIONS

Bainton, Roland Herbert. Travail of Religious Liberty: Nine Biographical Studies. Westminster 1951
SCPL

Italian—19th century

Clotilde de Savoie, Consort of Prince Napoleon Joseph Charles Paul Bonaparte, 1843-1911

Mary Estelle, Sister. Nuptials Without Love: The Life of Princess Clotilde of Savoy, 1843-1911. Kenedy 1963
Bkl A

Leo XIII, Pope, 1810-1903

Burton, Katherine (Kurz). Leo the Thirteenth, the First Modern Pope. McKay 1962
Bkl A&Y

COLLECTIONS

Sugrue, Francis. Popes in the Modern World. Crowell 1961
Bkl A

Pius VII, Pope, 1742-1823

Hales, Edward Elton Young. The Emperor and the Pope. Doubleday 1961
Bkl A

Italian—20th century

Benedict XV, Pope, 1854-1922

COLLECTIONS

Sugrue, Francis. Popes in the Modern World. Crowell 1961
Bkl A

John XXIII, Pope, 1881-1963

Aradi, Zsolt and Tucek, J. I. Pope John XXIII: An Authoritative Biography. Farrar 1959
SCPL

Balducci, Ernesto. John, "the Transitional Pope"; tr. by Dorothy White. McGraw 1965
Bkl A

Capovilla, Loris. The Heart and Mind of John XXIII: His Secretary's Intimate Recollection; tr. by Patrick Riley. Hawthorn 1964
Bkl A

Falconi, Carl. Pope John and the Ecumenical Council: A Diary of the Second Vatican Council, September-December 1962; tr. from the Italian by Muriel Grindrod. World 1964
Bkl A

Groppi, Ugo and Lombardi, J. S. Above All a Shepherd: Pope John XXIII. Kenedy 1959
SCPL

Hales, Edward Elton Young. Pope John and His Revolution. Doubleday 1965
Bkl A

Hatch, Alden. A Man Named John: The Life of Pope John XXIII. Hawthorn 1963
SCPL

John XXIII, Pope. Wit and Wisdom of Good Pope John; comp. by Henri Fesquet; tr. by Salvator Attanasio. Kenedy 1964
Bkl A

McGurn, Barrett. A Reporter Looks at the Vatican. Coward-McCann 1962
Bkl A

MacGregor-Hastie, Roy. Pope John XXIII. Criterion Bks 1962
Bkl C(7up)&Y—BY—ESLC

COLLECTIONS

Kittler, Glenn D. The Wings of Eagles. Doubleday 1966
Bkl A&Y

Sugrue, Francis. Popes in the Modern World. Crowell 1961
Bkl A

Paul VI, Pope, 1897-

Barrett, William Edmund. Shepherd of Mankind: A Biography of Pope Paul VI. Doubleday 1964
Bkl A

Clancy, John G. Apostle for Our Time, Pope Paul VI. Kenedy 1963
Bkl A&Y

McGregor-Hastie, Roy. Pope Paul VI. Criterion Bks 1965
Bkl Y&C—ESLC

Serafian, Michael. The Pilgrim. Farrar 1964
Bkl A

Pius X, Pope, 1835-1914

Giordani, Igino. Pius X: A Country Priest; tr. by T. J. Tobin. Bruce 1954
SCPL

RELIGIOUS LEADERS

Italian—20th century

Pius X, Pope—Continued

COLLECTIONS

Sugrue, Francis. Popes in the Modern World. Crowell 1961
Bkl A

Pius XI, Pope, 1857-1939

Aradi, Zsolt. Pius XI, the Pope and the Man. Hanover House 1958
SCPL

COLLECTIONS

Sugrue, Francis. Popes in the Modern World. Crowell 1961
Bkl A

Pius XII, Pope, 1876-1958

Friedländer, Saul. Pius XII and the Third Reich: A Documentation; tr. from the French and German by Charles Fullman. Knopf 1966
Bkl A

Halecki, Oskar and Murray, J. F. Pius XII: Eugenio Pacelli, Pope of Peace. Farrar 1954
SCPL

Hatch, Alden. Apostle of Peace. Hawthorn 1965
IndJ(6-9)

Hatch, Alden and Walshe, Seamus. Crown of Glory: The Life of Pope Pius XII. Hawthorn 1958
SCPL

Hochhuth, Rolf. The Deputy; tr. by Richard and Clara Winston. Grove 1964 (Play)
Bkl A—SCPL

Lavelle, Elise. The Man Who Was Chosen. McGraw 1957
AB(3-7)

McGurn, Barrett. A Reporter Looks at the Vatican. Coward-McCann 1962
Bkl A

COLLECTIONS

Sugrue, Francis. Popes in the Modern World. Crowell 1961
Bkl A

Japanese—20th century

Toyohiko Kagawa, 1888-1960

Simon, Charlie May. A Seed Shall Serve: The Story of Toyohiko Kagawa, Spiritual Leader of Modern Japan. Dutton 1958
BY—SCHS—YR

Kiyoshi Watanabe, 1890?-

Nolan, Liam. Small Man of Nanataki: The True Story of a Japanese Who Risked His Life to Provide Comfort for His Enemies. Dutton 1966
Bkl A&Y

Palestinian—1st century

Akiba Ben Joseph, 50?-132

Hubler, Richard Gibson. The Soldier and the Sage: A Novel about Akiba. Crown 1966 (Fiction)
Bkl A

Palestinian—4th century

Saint Dorothea, ?-311

COLLECTIONS

Farjeon, Eleanor. Ten Saints. Walck 1936
CC(6-9)—ESLC

Peruvian—16th century

Saint Martin de Porres, 1579-1639

Bishop, Claire Huchet. Martin de Porres, Hero. Houghton 1954
CC(6-9)—ESLC

Cavallini, Giuliana. St. Martin de Porres, Apostle of Charity; tr. by Caroline Holland. Herder 1963
Bkl A

Peruvian—17th century

Saint Rose of Lima, 1586-1617

COLLECTIONS

Haughton, Rosemary. Six Saints for Parents. Sheed 1963
Bkl A

Peruvian—20th century

Tariri, ?

Tariri and Wallis, Ethel Emily. My Story: From Jungle Killer to Christian Missionary. Harper 1965
Bkl A

Polish—20th century

Maximilian Kolbe, 1894-1941

COLLECTIONS

Graef, Hilda C. Mystics of Our Times. Hanover House 1962
Bkl A

Roman—2nd century

Saint Ignatius Theophorus, ?-107?

COLLECTIONS

Walsh, William Thomas. Saints in Action. Hanover House 1961
Bkl A

RELIGIOUS LEADERS

Roman—2nd century—*Continued*

Saint Justin, 100?-165?

COLLECTIONS

Walsh, William Thomas. Saints in Action. Hanover House 1961
Bkl A

Roman—6th century

Saint Benedict, 480-547

COLLECTIONS

Walsh, William Thomas. Saints in Action. Hanover House 1961
Bkl A

Russian—4th century

Saint Nicholas, Bishop of Myra,?

Bryson, Bernarda. The Twenty Miracles of Saint Nicolas. Little 1960
Bkl C(5-8)

Luckhardt, Mildred Madeleine (Corell). The Story of Saint Nicholas. Abingdon 1960
Bkl C(3-6)—ESLC

COLLECTIONS

Farjeon, Eleanor. Ten Saints. Walck 1936
CC(6-9)—ESLC

Russian—20th century

Leonid Ivanovich Feodorov, 1879-1935

Mailleux, Paul. Exarch Leonid Feodorov, Bridgebuilder Between Rome and Moscow. Kenedy 1964
Bkl A

Grigorii Efimovich Rasputin, 1871-1916

Wilson, Colin. Rasputin and the Fall of the Romanovs. Farrar 1964
IndS(11-12)

Scottish—19th century

David Livingstone, 1813-1873

Eaton, Jeanette. David Livingstone, Foe of Darkness. Morrow 1947
BBJH—CC(7-9)—ESLC—JH—SCHS

Seaver, George. David Livingstone: His Life and Letters. Harper 1957
SCPL

Mary Mitchell Slessor, 1848-1915

Syme, Ronald. Nigerian Pioneer. Morrow 1964
AB(5-9)—CC(5-7)—ESLC—IndJ(4-6)

Spanish—12th century

Maimonides, 1135-1204

Morrison, Lester M. and Hubler, Richard Gibson. Trial & Triumph: A Novel about Maimonides. Crown 1965 (Fiction)
Bkl A

Spanish—15th century

Tomás de Torquemada, 1420-1498

COLLECTIONS

Bainton, Roland Herbert. Travail of Religious Liberty: Nine Biographical Studies. Westminster 1951
SCPL

Spanish—16th century

Saint John of the Cross, 1542-1591

Cristiani, Léon. St. John of the Cross, Prince of Mystical Theology; tr. from the French. Doubleday 1962
Bkl A

Saint Ignatius Loyola, 1491-1556

Brodrick, James. Saint Ignatius Loyola: The Pilgrim Years, 1491-1538. Farrar 1956
SCPL

COLLECTIONS

Cluny, Roland. Holiness in Action; tr. from the French by D. A. Askew. Hawthorn 1963
Bkl A

Michael Servetus, 1511-1553

COLLECTIONS

Bainton, Roland Herbert. Travail of Religious Liberty: Nine Biographical Studies. Westminster 1951
SCPL

Saint Teresa, 1515-1582

Beevers, John. St. Teresa of Avila. Hanover House 1961
Bkl A

Hamilton, Elizabeth. Saint Teresa: A Journey to Spain. Scribner 1959
Bkl A

Teresa, Saint. Life.
CA

Spanish—18th century

Junípero Serra, 1713-1784

Lauritzen, Jonreed. The Cross and the Sword. Doubleday 1965 (Fiction)
Bkl A&Y

Politi, Leo. The Mission Bell. Scribner 1953
CC(2-5)—ESLC

RELIGIOUS LEADERS

Spanish—18th century

Junípero Serra—Continued

Repplier, Agnes. Junípero Serra: Pioneer Colonist of California. Doubleday 1933
SCPL

Swiss—20th century

Karl Barth, 1886-1968

Casalis, Georges. Portrait of Karl Barth; tr. by Robert McAfee Brown. Doubleday 1963
Bkl A

Syrian—5th century

Saint Simeon Stylites, 390?-459

COLLECTIONS

Farjeon, Eleanor. Ten Saints. Walck 1936
CC(6-9)—ESLC

Tibetan—20th century

Dalai Lama XIV, 1935-

Dalai Lama XIV. My Land and My People. McGraw 1962
Bkl A&Y—BY—SCPL

Thubten Jigme Norbu, 1922-

Thubten Jigme Norbu and Harrer, Heinrich. Tibet Is My Country; tr. from the German by Edward Fitzgerald. Dutton 1961
Bkl A&Y—BY

REPORTERS

See Journalists

RESTAURATEURS

American—20th century

George Magar Mardikian, 1902-

Mardikian, George Magar. Song of America. McGraw 1956
BY—SCPL

Patricia Murphy, 1911?-

Murphy, Patricia. Glow of Candlelight: The Story of Patricia Murphy. Prentice-Hall 1961
Bkl A

REVIEWERS

See Critics

REVOLUTIONISTS

See Statesmen

ROBBERS

See Criminals

ROCKET ENGINEERS

See Engineers, Aeronautical

RULERS

See Czars; Emperors; Empresses; Kings; Presidents; Princes; Queens; Regents; Stadholders; Sultans

RUNNERS

See Track and Field Athletes

SAILORS

See Naval Officers and other Seafarers

SAINTS

See Religious Leaders

SATIRISTS

English—18th century

Jonathan Swift, 1667-1745

Dennis, Nigel Forbes. Jonathan Swift: A Short Character. Macmillan 1964
Bkl A

COLLECTIONS

Drew, Elizabeth A. The Literature of Gossip: Nine English Letterwriters. Norton 1964
Bkl A&Y

English—19th century

Samuel Butler, 1835-1902

Butler, Samuel. The Family Letters of Samuel Butler, 1841-1886; ed. by Arnold Silver. Stanford Univ. 1962
Bkl A

COLLECTIONS

Knoepflmacher, U. C. Religious Humanism and the Victorian Novel. Princeton Univ. 1965
Bkl A

Roman—1st century

Decimus Junius Juvenal, 60?-140?

COLLECTIONS

Highet, Gilbert Arthur. Poets in a Landscape. Knopf 1957
BBHS—SCPL

SATIRISTS—*Continued*

Roman—2nd century

Decimus Junius Juvenal, 60?-140?

COLLECTIONS

Highet, Gilbert Arthur. Poets in a Landscape. Knopf 1957
BBHS—SCPL

SCENIC DESIGNERS

American—20th century

Norman Bel Geddes, 1893-1958

Geddes, Norman Bel. Miracle in the
Evening. Doubleday 1960
Bkl A

SCIENTISTS

See also Anatomists; Anthropologists;
Archeologists; Astronomers; Bacteriologists; Biologists; Botanists; Chemists;
Ethnologists; Explorers; Geneticists; Geologists; Herpetologists; Horticulturists;
Ichthyologists; Inventors; Mathematicians; Microbiologists; Naturalists; Neurologists; Oceanographers; Ornithologists; Paleontologists; Pathologists; Physicians; Physicists; Physiologists; Plant
Pathologists; Psychiatrists; Radiologists;
Soil Scientists; Virologists; Zoologists

COLLECTIONS

Asimov, Isaac. Breakthroughs in Science.
Houghton 1960
Bkl C(5-8)—CC(5-7)—ESLC—JH—SCHS
Bixby, William. Great Experimenters.
McKay 1964
Bkl C(7-8)&Y—ESLC
Thomas Edison; Michael Faraday; Enrico
Fermi; Joseph Lister; Sir Isaac Newton; Er-
nest Rutherford; James Watt; Wilbur Wright
Bolton, Sarah (Knowles). Famous Men
of Science; rev. by Barbara Lovett
Cline. Crowell 1960
BBJH—Bkl C(7-9)—CC(7-9)—ESLC—JH
—SCHS—SCPL—3000
Burlingame, Roger. Scientists Behind the
Inventors. Harcourt 1960
AB(7up)—Bkl C(7-9)&Y—CC(6-9)—ESLC
—JH—SCHS
Joseph Black; Marie Curie; Albert Einstein;
Joseph Henry; Louis Pasteur; Michael Pu-
pin; Benjamin Silliman; James Watt
Cane, Philip. Giants of Science. Grosset
1959
JH
Crowther, James. Six Great Scientists.
British Bk Centre n.d.
3000

De Kruif, Paul Henry. Hunger Fighters.
Harcourt 1928
BBHS—SCHS—SCPL—3000
Stephen Babcock; Mark Alfred Carleton;
Marion Dorset; Edward Francis; Joseph
Goldberger; George Hoffer; Angus MacKay;
John Mohler; George Shull; Harry Steenbock
De Kruif, Paul Henry. Men Against
Death. Harcourt 1932
BBHS—SCHS—SCPL
De Kruif, Paul Henry. Microbe Hunters.
Harcourt 1926
BBHS—SCHS—SCPL—3000
Gourlay, Walter E. Picture Book of To-
day's Scientists. Sterling 1962
Bkl Y
Howard, Arthur Vyvyan. Chambers's
Dictionary of Scientists. Dutton 1951
SCPL
Ireland, Norma Olin. Index to Scientists
of the World, from Ancient to Modern
Times: Biographies and Portraits.
Faxon 1962
SCPL
Lapage, Geoffrey. Man Against Disease.
Abelard-Schuman 1964
JH
Ludovici, L. J. ed. Nobel Prize Win-
ners. Associated Booksellers 1957
SCHS
Poole, Lynn and Poole, Gray. Scientists
Who Changed the World. Dodd 1960
Bkl Y&C—CC—JH—SCHS
Poole, Lynn and Poole, Gray. Scientists
Who Work Outdoors. Dodd 1963
IndS(9-12)
Poole, Lynn and Poole, Gray. Scientists
Who Work with Astronauts. Dodd
1964
Bkl C(6-9)&Y
Poole, Lynn and Poole, Gray. Scientists
Who Work with Cameras. Dodd 1965
Bkl C(7-12)&Y—IndS(11-12)
Constantine Alexopoulos; Harold Edgerton;
Russell Morgan; and others
Riedman, Sarah Regal. Men and Women
Behind the Atom. Abelard-Schuman
1958
BBJH—JH—SCHS
Scientific American. Lives in Science.
Simon & Schuster 1957
3000
Sootin, Harry. 12 Pioneers of Science.
Vanguard 1960
JH
Wagner, Frederick. Famous Underwater
Adventurers. Dodd 1962
Bkl C(7up)&Y—ESLC—JH—YR
Yost, Edna. Women of Modern Science.
Dodd 1959
SCHS—SCPL

SCIENTISTS—*Continued*

American

COLLECTIONS

American Heritage. Men of Science and Invention, by Michael Blow and Robert P. Multhauf. Am. Heritage 1960
Bkl C(5-8)—CC(5-8)—ESLC—JH—SCHS—YR

American Men of Science: A Biographical Directory; first published 1906. Cattell 1960-62
SCPL

Berland, Theodore. The Scientific Life. Coward-McCann 1962
Bkl A&Y
Albert Sabin; James Van Allen; and others

Fortune (Periodical). Great American Scientists: America's Rise to the Forefront of World Science. Prentice-Hall 1961
Bkl A&Y—ESLC—JH—SCHS—SCPL

Hylander, Clarence John. American Scientists. Macmillan 1935
BBEL(6-8)—ESLC—JH—SCPL

Jaffe, Bernard. Men of Science in America: The Story of American Science Told Through the Lives and Achievements of Twenty Outstanding Men from Earliest Colonial Times to the Present Day. Simon & Schuster 1958
BBHS—SCHS—SCPL

Leaders in American Science. Who's Who in Am. Educ.; biennial; first published 1953
SCPL

Thomas, Shirley. Men of Space: Profiles of the Leaders in Space Research, Development, and Exploration. 5v. Chilton 1960-62
Bkl A&Y—BY—SCPL

Thomas, Shirley. Men of Space: v. 6, Profiles of Scientists Who Probe for Life in Space. Chilton 1963
Bkl A&Y
Philip Abelson; Melvin Calvin; Frank Drake; Sidney Fox; John Lilly; Stanley Miller; Orr Reynolds; Carl Sagan; Harold Urey; Wolf Vishniac

Waltz, George H. What Makes a Scientist? Doubleday 1959
JH

Yost, Edna. American Women of Science. Lippincott 1955
SCHS—SCPL

Yost, Edna. Modern Americans in Science and Technology. Dodd 1962
Bkl C

American—18th century

Benjamin Franklin, 1706-1790

Aldridge, Alfred Owen. Benjamin Franklin, Philosopher & Man. Lippincott 1965
Bkl A&Y

American Heritage. The Many Worlds of Benjamin Franklin, by Frank R. Donovan. Am. Heritage 1963
Bkl C(6-9)&Y—CC(6-9)—ESLC—IndJ(6-9)—JH—SCHS—YR

Aulaire, Ingri d' and Aulaire, Edgar Parin d'. Benjamin Franklin. Doubleday 1950
BBEL—CC(3-5)—ESLC

Cohen, I. B. Benjamin Franklin: His Contribution to the American Tradition. Bobbs 1953
SCPL

Cousins, Margaret. Ben Franklin of Old Philadelphia. Random House 1952
CC(4-7)—SCHS

Eaton, Jeanette. That Lively Man, Ben Franklin. Morrow 1948
BBJH—CC(5-7)—JH—SCHS

Daugherty, James. Poor Richard. Viking 1941
BBEL—BBJH—CC(7-9)—JH—SCHS

Franklin, Benjamin. Autobiography. Dutton; Harper; Houghton; Modern Lib.; etc.
BY—CA—CC(7-9)—GR—SCHS—SCPL—3000

Franklin, Benjamin. The Autobiography, and Other Writings of Benjamin Franklin. Dodd 1963
SCHS

Franklin, Benjamin. The Autobiography of Benjamin Franklin; ed. by Leonard W. Labaree and others. Yale Univ. 1964
JH—SCPL

Franklin, Benjamin. Autobiographical Writings; ed. by Carl Van Doren. Viking 1945
SCPL

Franklin, Benjamin. The Benjamin Franklin Papers; ed. by Frank Donovan. Dodd 1962
Bkl A&Y—SCHS

Graves, Charles P. Benjamin Franklin. Garrard 1960
AB(3-6)

Judson, Clara (Ingram). Benjamin Franklin. Follett 1957
AB(5-7)—BBEL(6-8)—BBJH—CC(5-7)—ESLC—JH

Lawson, Robert. Ben and Me: A New and Astonishing Life of Benjamin Franklin as Written by His Good Mouse Amos. Little 1939 (Fiction)
BBEL—BBJH—CC(5-9)—ESLC—JH—SCHS

SCIENTISTS

American—18th century

Benjamin Franklin—Continued

McKown, Robin. Benjamin Franklin. Putnam 1963
Bkl C(7-9)&Y

Sandrich, Mark. Ben Franklin in Paris; lyrics by Sidney Michaels. Random House 1965 (Play)
Bkl A

Sayre, Robert F. The Examined Self: Benjamin Franklin, Henry Adams, Henry James. Princeton Univ. 1964
Bkl A

Van Doren, Carl Clinton. Benjamin Franklin. Viking 1956
BBHS–SCHS–SCPL–3000

Weir, Ruth Cromer. Benjamin Franklin, Printer and Patriot. Abingdon 1955
ESLC

COLLECTIONS

Mann, A. L. and Vivian, A. C. Famous Physicists. Day 1963
ESLC–JH

American—20th century

Wernher Von Braun, 1912-

Bergaust, Erik. Reaching for the Stars. Doubleday 1960
Bkl A–BY

Walters, Helen B. Wernher Von Braun: Rocket Engineer. Macmillan 1964
Bkl C(7-9)&Y–ESLC–JH

Czech—20th century

Rudolf Vrba, 1924-

Vrba, Rudolf and Bestic, Alan. I Cannot Forgive. Grove 1964
Bkl A

English

COLLECTIONS

Crowther, James Gerald. Scientists of the Industrial Revolution. Dufour 1963
Bkl A
Joseph Black; Henry Cavendish; Erasmus Darwin; Joseph Priestley; Adam Smith; James Watt; Josiah Wedgwood; and others

English—13th century

Roger Bacon, 1214?-1294

COLLECTIONS

Mann, A. L. and Vivian, A. C. Famous Physicists. Day 1963
ESLC–JH

English—20th century

Havelock Ellis, 1859-1939

Calder-Marshall, Arthur. The Sage of Sex: A Life of Havelock Ellis. Putnam 1960
Bkl A

French—20th century

Pierre Lecomte du Nouy, 1883-1947

Lecomte du Nouy, Mary Bishop Harriman. The Road to "Human Destiny": A Life of Pierre Lecomte du Nouy. Longmans 1955
SCPL

German—20th century

Dieter K. Huzel, ?

Huzel, Dieter K. Peenemünde to Canaveral. Prentice-Hall 1962
Bkl A&Y

Greek—4th century B.C.

Aristotle, 384-322 B.C.

Downey, Glanville. Aristotle, Dean of Early Science. Watts 1962
Bkl Y&C–JH

Grene, Marjorie (Glicksman). A Portrait of Aristotle. Univ. of Chicago 1963
Bkl A

Italian—15th century

Leonardo da Vinci, 1452-1519

See entries for Leonardo da Vinci under Scientists—Italian—16th century

Italian—16th century

Leonardo da Vinci, 1452-1519

Friedenthal, Richard. Leonardo da Vinci: A Pictorial Biography; tr. by Margaret Shenfield. Studio 1960
Bkl A&Y

Gillette, Henry S. Leonardo da Vinci, Pathfinder of Science. Watts 1962
Bkl C(6-9)

Hahn, Emily. Leonardo da Vinci. Random House 1956
ESLC–JH–SCHS

Hart, Ivor Blashka. The World of Leonardo da Vinci: Man of Science, Engineer and Dreamer of Flight. Viking 1962
Bkl A&Y

Heydenreich, Ludwig Heinrich. Leonardo da Vinci. Macmillan 1954
SCPL

McLanathan, Richard B. K. Images of the Universe: Leonardo da Vinci, the Artist as Scientist. Doubleday 1966
Bkl Y&A

SCIENTISTS
Italian—16th century
Leonardo da Vinci—Continued

Noble, Iris. Leonardo da Vinci: The Universal Genius. Norton 1965
ESLC—IndJ(6-9)—JH

Ripley, Elizabeth. Leonardo da Vinci: A Biography. Walck 1952
BBJH—BY—CC(7-9)—ESLC—JH—SCHS

Thomas, John. Leonardo da Vinci. Criterion Bks 1957
YR

Vallentin, Antonina. Leonardo da Vinci: The Tragic Pursuit of Perfection. Viking 1952
SCPL

SCOUTS

See also Boy Scout Workers; Explorers; Frontiersmen

American—19th century
James Bridger, 1804-1881

Allen, Merritt Parmelee. Western Star: A Story of Jim Bridger. Longmans 1941 (Fiction)
SCHS

Caesar, Gene. King of the Mountain Men: The Life of Jim Bridger. Dutton 1961
Bkl A

Garst, Doris Shannon. Jim Bridger, Greatest of the Mountain Men. Houghton 1952
CC(6-9)—ESLC—JH—SCHS

Luce, Willard and Luce, Celia. Jim Bridger: Man of the Mountains. Garrard 1966
ESLC

Vestal, Stanley. Jim Bridger, Mountain Man: A Biography. Morrow 1946
SCPL

COLLECTIONS

Reinfeld, Fred. Trappers of the West. Crowell 1957
BBEL(7-8)

Christopher ("Kit") Carson, 1809-1868

Allen, Merritt Parmelee. The Silver Wolf. Longmans 1951 (Fiction)
SCHS

Bell, Margaret E. Kit Carson, Mountain Man. Morrow 1952
BBEL—CC(5-7)—ESLC

Blackwelder, Bernice. Great Westerner: The Story of Kit Carson. Caxton 1962
Bkl A

Campion, Nardi Reeder. Kit Carson. Garrard 1963
AB(3-5)

Garst, Doris Shannon. Kit Carson: Trail Blazer and Scout. Messner 1942
BBEL(6-8)—BBJH—CC(6-9)—ESLC—JH—SCHS

Gerson, Noel Bertram. Kit Carson: Folk Hero and Man. Doubleday 1964
Bkl A&Y

Moody, Ralph. Kit Carson and the Wild Frontier. Random House 1955
CC—JH—SCHS

Vestal, Stanley. Kit Carson, the Happy Warrior of the Old West: A Biography. Houghton 1928
SCHS—SCPL

COLLECTIONS

American Heritage. Trappers and Mountain Men, by Evan Jones. Am. Heritage 1961
AB—CC(6-9)—ESLC—YR

Reinfeld, Fred. Trappers of the West. Crowell 1957
BBEL(7-8)

Steckmesser, Kent Ladd. The Western Hero in History and Legend. Univ. of Okla. 1965
Bkl A

William Frederick ("Buffalo Bill") Cody, 1846-1917

Aulaire, Ingri d' and Aulaire, Edgar Parin d'. Buffalo Bill. Doubleday 1952
BBEL—CC(3-5)—ESLC

Cody, William Frederick. Autobiography of Buffalo Bill (Colonel W. F. Cody). Rinehart 1947
SCPL

Cody, William Frederick. Buffalo Bill's Life Story (Colonel W. F. Cody). Rinehart n.d.
SCHS—SCPL

Garst, Doris Shannon. Buffalo Bill. Messner 1948
BBEL(6-8)—BBJH—CC(6-9)—JH—SCHS

Russell, Donald Bert. The Lives and Legends of Buffalo Bill. Univ. of Okla. 1960
Bkl A—SCPL

Sell, Henry B. and Weybright, Victor. Buffalo Bill and the Wild West. Doubleday 1955
GR

James Butler ("Wild Bill") Hickok, 1837-1876

Garst, Doris Shannon and Garst, Warren. Wild Bill Hickok. Messner 1952
BY—CC(7-9)—JH—SCHS

Holbrook, Stewart. Wild Bill Hickok Tames the West. Random House 1952
CC(5-7)—ESLC—JH—SCHS

SCOUTS

American—19th century

James Butler ("Wild Bill") Hickok—Continued

Rosa, Joseph G. They Called Him Wild Bill: The Life and Adventures of James Butler Hickok. Univ. of Okla. 1964
Bkl A

COLLECTIONS

Steckmesser, Kent Ladd. The Western Hero in History and Legend. Univ. of Okla. 1965
Bkl A

Albert Sieber, 1844-1907

Thrapp, Dan L. Al Sieber, Chief of Scouts. Univ. of Okla. 1964
Bkl A

SCULPTORS

COLLECTIONS

Dictionary of Modern Sculpture; ed. by Robert Maillard. Tudor 1962
Bkl A&Y—SCPL
Seuphor, Michel. The Sculpture of This Century. Braziller 1960
SCPL

American—20th century

Gutzon Borglum, 1871-1941

Price, Willadene. Gutzon Borglum: Artist and Patriot. Rand McNally 1961
YR

Malvina Hoffman, 1887-1966

Hoffman, Malvina. Yesterday Is Tomorrow: A Personal History. Crown 1965
Bkl A&Y

English—20th century

Sir Jacob Epstein, 1880-1959

Buckle, Richard. Jacob Epstein, Sculptor. World 1963
Bkl A
Epstein, Sir Jacob. Epstein: An Autobiography. Dutton 1955
SCPL

Eric Gill, 1882-1940

Speaight, Robert. The Life of Eric Gill. Kenedy 1966
Bkl A

COLLECTIONS

Heppenstall, Rayner. Four Absentees. Dufour 1963
Bkl A

Henry Spencer Moore, 1898-

Hall, Donald. Henry Moore: The Life and Work of a Great Sculptor. Harper 1966
Bkl A&Y
Read, Sir Herbert Edward. Henry Moore: A Study of His Life and Work. Praeger 1966
Bkl A

French—19th century

Frédéric Auguste Bartholdi, 1834-1904

Price, Willadene. Bartholdi and the Statue of Liberty. Rand McNally 1959
Bkl C(7-9)&Y—YR

Auguste Rodin, 1840-1917

Elsen, Albert Edward. Auguste Rodin: Readings on His Life and Work. Prentice-Hall 1965
Bkl A
Elsen, Albert Edward. Rodin. Mus. of Modern Art 1963
Bkl A
Ripley, Elizabeth. Rodin: A Biography. Lippincott 1966
Bkl C(7-9)&Y—ESLC
Rodin, Auguste. Rodin; text by Somerville Story. Phaidon 1956
SCPL
Weiss, David. Naked Came I: A Novel of Rodin. Morrow 1963 (Fiction)
Bkl A

Jacques Lipchitz, 1891-

Patai, Irene. Encounters: The Life of Jacques Lipchitz. Funk 1961
Bkl A

Italian—15th century

Luca della Robbia, 1400?-1482

COLLECTIONS

Pater, Walter Horatio. Renaissance Studies in Art and Poetry. Modern Lib. n.d.
SCPL

Leonardo da Vinci, 1452-1519

See entries for Leonardo da Vinci under Sculptors—Italian—16th century

Italian—16th century

Benvenuto Cellini, 1500-1571

Cellini, Benvenuto. Autobiography; tr. by John Addington Symonds. Modern Lib., Dodd, Oxford, etc.
Bkl A—CA—GR—SCPL—3000

SCULPTORS

Italian—16th century—*Continued*

Michelangelo Buonarroti, 1475-1564

Brandes, Georg Morris Cohen. Michelangelo; tr. by Heinz Norden. Ungar 1963
Bkl A

De Tolnay, Charles. The Art and Thought of Michelangelo. Pantheon 1964
Bkl A

Michelangelo Buonarroti. I, Michelangelo, Sculptor: An Autobiography Through Letters; ed. by Irving and Jean Stone; tr. by Charles Speroni. Doubleday 1962
Bkl A

Michelangelo Buonarroti. Michelangelo: Paintings, Sculptures, Architecture, by Ludwig Goldscheider. Phaidon 1962
SCPL

Morgan, Charles H. The Life of Michelangelo. Reynal 1960
Bkl A—BY—GR

Peck, Anne Merriman. Wings of an Eagle. Hawthorn 1963
IndS(9-11)

Ripley, Elizabeth. Michelangelo: A Biography. Walck 1953
CC(7-9)—ESLC—JH—SCHS

Schott, Rudolf. Michelangelo; tr. from the German by Constance McNab. Abrams 1965
Bkl A&Y

Stone, Irving. The Agony and the Ecstasy: A Novel of Michelangelo. Doubleday 1961 (Fiction)
Bkl A—SCHS

Stone, Irving. The Great Adventure of Michelangelo. Doubleday 1965 (Fiction)
JH

Symonds, J. A. Life of Michelangelo. Modern Lib. n.d.
GR

COLLECTIONS

Pater, Walter Horatio. Renaissance Studies in Art and Poetry. Modern Lib. n.d.
SCPL

Leonardo da Vinci, 1452-1519

Clark, Sir Kenneth McKenzie. Leonardo da Vinci: An Account of His Development as an Artist. Cambridge 1952
GR—SCPL

Friedenthal, Richard. Leonardo da Vinci: A Pictorial Biography; tr. by Margaret Shenfield. Studio 1960
Bkl A&Y

Gillette, Henry S. Leonardo da Vinci, Pathfinder of Science. Watts 1962
Bkl C(6-9)

Hahn, Emily. Leonardo da Vinci. Random House 1956
ESLC—JH—SCHS

Hart, Ivor Blashka. The World of Leonardo da Vinci: Man of Science, Engineer and Dreamer of Flight. Viking 1962
Bkl A&Y

Heydenreich, Ludwig Heinrich. Leonardo da Vinci. Macmillan 1954
SCPL

Horizon Magazine. Leonardo da Vinci, by Jay Williams. Am. Heritage 1965
Bkl Y&C—ESLC—IndS(10-12)

Jaspers, Karl. Three Essays: Leonardo, Descartes, Max Weber; tr. by Ralph Manheim. Harcourt 1964
Bkl A

Noble, Iris. Leonardo da Vinci: The Universal Genius. Norton 1965
ESLC—IndJ(6-9)—JH

Ripley, Elizabeth. Leonardo da Vinci: A Biography. Walck 1952
BBJH—BY—CC(7-9)—ESLC—JH—SCHS

Thomas, John. Leonardo da Vinci. Criterion Bks 1957
YR

Vallentin, Antonina. Leonardo da Vinci: The Tragic Pursuit of Perfection. Viking 1952
SCPL

Vinci, Leonardo da. Leonardo da Vinci: Life and Work, Paintings and Drawings; with the Leonardo Biography by Vasari. Doubleday 1959
SCPL

Italian—17th century

Giovanni Lorenzo Bernini, 1598-1680

Witkower, Rudolf. Gian Lorenzo Bernini: The Sculptor of the Roman Baroque. Phaidon 1955
SCPL

Italian—20th century

Medardo Rosso, 1858-1928

Barr, Margaret Scolari. Medardo Rosso. Mus. of Modern Art 1963
Bkl A

SEA CAPTAINS

See Naval Officers and Other Seafarers

SEAMEN

See Naval Officers and Other Seafarers

SECRET AGENTS

See Detectives; Intelligence Agents; Spies

SECRET SERVICE AGENTS

See Detectives

SHERIFFS

American—19th century

Elfego Baca, 1865-1945

COLLECTIONS

Schaefer, Jack Warner. Heroes Without Glory: Some Goodmen of the Old West. Houghton 1965
Bkl A&Y

Wyatt Berry Stapp Earp, 1848-1929

Holbrook, Stewart. Wyatt Earp, U.S. Marshal. Random House 1956
BBEL—CC(4-7)—ESLC—JH—SCHS
Lake, Stuart N. The Life and Times of Wyatt Earp. Houghton 1956
BBEL(8)—BBJH
Lake, Stuart N. Wyatt Earp, Frontier Marshal. Houghton 1931
BY

Henry Andrew Thomas, 1850-1912

Shirley, Glenn. Heck Thomas, Frontier Marshal: The Story of a Real Gunfighter. Chilton 1962
Bkl A

American—20th century

Wyatt Berry Stapp Earp, 1848-1929

Holbrook, Stewart. Wyatt Earp, U.S. Marshal. Random House 1956
BBEL—CC(4-7)—ESLC—JH—SCHS
Lake, Stuart N. The Life and Times of Wyatt Earp. Houghton 1956
BBEL(8)—BBJH
Lake, Stuart N. Wyatt Earp, Frontier Marshal. Houghton 1931
BY

SHIPPING EXECUTIVES

American—20th century

Hans Isbrandtsen, 1891-1953

Dugan, James. American Viking. Harper 1963
Bkl A—BY

SHORT STORY WRITERS

See Authors; Novelists

SHOWMEN

See Circus Managers

SIAMESE TWINS

Siamese—19th century

Chang and Eng Bunker, 1811-1874

Hunter, Kay. Duet for a Lifetime: The Story of the Original Siamese Twins. Coward-McCann 1964
Bkl A&Y

SILVERSMITHS

American—18th century

Paul Revere, 1735-1818

Fisher, Dorothy Canfield. Paul Revere and the Minute Men. Random House 1950
BBEL—CC(6-8)—ESLC—JH—SCHS
Forbes, Esther. America's Paul Revere. Houghton 1946
AB(5-9)—BBEL(5-8)—BBJH—CC(5-9)—ESLC—JH—SCHS—YR
Forbes, Esther. Paul Revere and the World He Lived In. Houghton 1942
BBHS—BY—SCHS—SCPL
Graves, Charles P. Paul Revere. Garrard 1964
AB(4-7)
Kelly, Regina (Zimmerman). Paul Revere: Colonial Craftsman. Houghton 1963
AB(5-9)—Bkl C(4-6)—IndJ(4-6)

COLLECTIONS

Bailey, Carolyn Sherwin. Children of the Handcrafts. Viking 1935
BBJH—CC(4-7)—ESLC

SINGERS

American

COLLECTIONS

Lawless, Ray M. Folksingers and Folksongs in America: A Handbook of Biography, Bibliography, and Discography. Duell 1960
SCPL

American—19th century

Lillian Nordica, 1859-1914

Glackens, Ira. Yankee Diva: Lillian Nordica and the Golden Days of Opera. Coleridge Press 1963
Bkl A

American—20th century

Marian Anderson, 1902-

Anderson, Marian. My Lord, What a Morning: An Autobiography. Viking 1956
BBHS—BY—SCHS—SCPL

SINGERS

American—20th century

Marian Anderson—Continued

Newman, Shirlee Petkin. Marian Anderson: Lady from Philadelphia. Westminster 1966
Bkl C(7-9)&Y

Stevenson, Janet. Singing for the World: Marian Anderson. Encyc. Britannica 1963
YR

COLLECTIONS

Forsee, Aylesa. American Women Who Scored Firsts. Macrae 1958
SCHS

McNeer, May Yonge and Ward, Lynd Kendall. Give Me Freedom. Abingdon 1964
Bkl C(5-8)—CC(5-7)—ESLC—JH—YR

Sterne, Emma (Gelders). I Have a Dream. Knopf 1965
Bkl Y&C

Harold Belafonte, 1927-

Shaw, Arnold. Belafonte: An Unauthorized Biography. Chilton 1960
Bkl A

Maria Callas, 1923-

Callas, Evangelia and Blochman, Lawrence Goldtree. My Daughter Maria Callas. Fleet 1960
Bkl A

Jellinek, George. Callas: Portrait of a Prima Donna. Ziff-Davis 1960
Bkl A

Bing Crosby, 1904-

Crosby, Bing. Call Me Lucky. Simon & Schuster 1953
SCPL

Mary Garden, 1877-1967

COLLECTIONS

Wagenknecht, Edward Charles. Seven Daughters of the Theater. Univ. of Okla. 1964
Bkl A

Lena Horne, 1917-

Horne, Lena and Schickel, Richard. Lena. Doubleday 1965
Bkl A&Y

Lotte Lehmann, 1885-

Lehmann, Lotte. Five Operas and Richard Strauss; tr. from the German by Ernst Pawel. Macmillan 1964
Bkl A

John McCormack, 1884-1945

McCormack, Lily (Foley). I Hear You Calling Me. Bruce 1949
SCPL

Robert Merrill, 1919-

Merrill, Robert and Dody, Sandford. Once More from the Beginning. Macmillan 1965
Bkl A&Y

Lillian Nordica, 1859-1914

Glackens, Ira. Yankee Diva: Lillian Nordica and the Golden Days of Opera. Coleridge Press 1963
Bkl A

Leontyne Price, 1927-

COLLECTIONS

Chotzinoff, Samuel. A Little Nightmusic. Harper 1964
Bkl A&Y—IndS(12)

Jean Ritchie, 1922-

Ritchie, Jean. Singing Family of the Cumberlands. Oxford 1955
SCPL

Bessie Smith, 1894-1937

COLLECTIONS

Hadlock, Richard. Jazz Masters of the Twenties. Macmillan 1965
Bkl A&Y

Kate Smith, 1909-

Smith, Kate. Upon My Lips a Song. Funk 1960
Bkl A

COLLECTIONS

Forsee, Aylesa. American Women Who Scored Firsts. Macrae 1958
SCHS

Australian—19th century

Dame Nellie Melba, 1861-1931

Wechsberg, Joseph. Red Plush and Black Velvet: The Story of Melba and Her Times. Little 1961
Bkl A

Australian—20th century

Marjorie Lawrence, 1909-

Lawrence, Marjorie. Interrupted Melody: The Story of My Life. Appleton 1949
SCHS—SCPL

Dame Nellie Melba, 1861-1931

Wechsberg, Joseph. Red Plush and Black Velvet: The Story of Melba and Her Times. Little 1961
Bkl A

Joan Sutherland, 1926-

Braddon, Richard. Joan Sutherland. St Martins 1962
Bkl A&Y—BY

SINGERS—*Continued*

Austrian—20th century

Leo Slezak, 1873-1946

Slezak, Walter. What Time's the Next Swan? As Told to Smith-Corona Model 88E. Doubleday 1962
Bkl A

Maria Augusta Trapp, 1905-

Rodgers, Richard and Hammerstein, Oscar II. The Sound of Music: A New Musical Play. Random House 1960 (Play)
Bkl A

Trapp, Maria Augusta and Murdock, Ruth T. A Family on Wheels: Further Adventures of the Trapp Family Singers. Lippincott 1959
BY—SCPL

Trapp, Maria Augusta. Story of the Trapp Family Singers. Lippincott 1949
BY—SCHS—SCPL

English—20th century

Margaret Curtis, ?

Curtis, Margaret. Planter's Punch. Appleton 1962
Bkl A

Gracie Fields, 1898-

Fields, Gracie. Sing as We Go: The Autobiography of Gracie Fields. Doubleday 1961
Bkl A—BY

French—20th century

Maurice Chevalier, 1888-

Chevalier, Maurice. With Love, as Told to Eileen and Robert Mason Pollock. Little 1960
Bkl A

Italian—20th century

Enrico Caruso, 1873-1921

Caruso, Dorothy Park (Benjamin). Enrico Caruso: His Life and Death. Simon & Schuster 1945
SCPL

Robinson, Francis. Caruso: His Life in Pictures. Crowell 1957
SCPL

Renata Tebaldi, 1922-

Seroff, Victor Ilyitch. Renata Tebaldi: The Woman and the Diva. Appleton 1961
Bkl A&Y

Norwegian—20th century

Kirsten Flagstad, 1895-1962

Flagstad, Kirsten. The Flagstad Manuscript. Putnam 1952
SCPL

McArthur, Edwin. Flagstad: A Personal Memoir. Knopf 1965
Bkl A&Y

Spanish—19th century

Manuel del Pópolo Vicente García, 1775-1832

Malvern, Gladys. The Great Garcías. McKay 1958
YR

Swedish—19th century

Jenny Lind, 1820-1887

Benét, Laura. Enchanting Jenny Lind. Dodd 1939
BY—CC(8-9)—SCHS

Cavanah, Frances. Jenny Lind and Her Listening Cat. Vanguard 1961 (Fiction)
Bkl C(4-6)

Cavanah, Frances. Two Loves for Jenny Lind. Macrae 1956 (Fiction)
SCHS—YR

Kielty, Bernardine. Jenny Lind Sang Here. Houghton 1959
Bkl C(6-8)

Kyle, Elisabeth. The Swedish Nightingale: Jenny Lind. Holt 1965
Bkl C(6-9)&Y—IndJ(6-9)

Shultz, Gladys (Denny). Jenny Lind, the Swedish Nightingale. Lippincott 1962
Bkl A&Y—BY—SCHS

COLLECTIONS

Trease, Geoffrey. Seven Stages. Vanguard 1965
Bkl Y&C—IndS(9-10)

Wagenknecht, Edward Charles. Seven Daughters of the Theater. Univ. of Okla. 1964
Bkl A

SISTERS OF FAMOUS MEN

See Relatives of Famous Men

SKATERS

American—20th century

Sonja Henie, 1912-

COLLECTIONS

Gelman, Steve. Young Olympic Champions. Norton 1964
Bkl C(6-9)&Y—ESLC—JH

SKATERS—*Continued*

Czech—20th century

Otto Jelinek, ?

Jelinek, Henry and Pinchot, Ann. On Thin Ice. Prentice-Hall 1965
Bkl A&Y—IndS(9-12)

SKIERS

American—20th century

Jill Kinmont, 1936?-

Valens, Evans G. A Long Way Up: The Story of Jill Kinmont. Harper 1966
Bkl A&Y

SNAKE COLLECTORS

See Herpetologists

SOCIAL SCIENTISTS

See Economists; Historians; Sociologists

SOCIAL WORKERS

American—19th century

Jane Addams, 1860-1935

See entries under Social Workers—American—20th century

Lillian Wald, 1867-1940

See entries under Social Workers—American—20th century

American—20th century

Jane Addams, 1860-1935

Addams, Jane. Twenty Years at Hull-House; with Autobiographical Notes. Macmillan 1910
SCHS—SCPL
Gilbert, Miriam. Jane Addams, World Neighbor. Abingdon 1960
Bkl C(4-6)
Judson, Clara (Ingram). City Neighbor: The Story of Jane Addams. Scribner 1951
CC(5-7)—ESLC—JH—SCHS—YR
Tims, Margaret. Jane Addams of Hull House, 1860-1935: A Centenary Study. Macmillan 1961
SCPL
Wagoner, Jean Brown. Jane Addams: Little Lame Girl. Bobbs 1962
CC(3-6)
Wise, Winifred E. Jane Addams of Hull-House: A Biography. Harcourt 1935
SCHS

COLLECTIONS

Bowie, Walter Russell. Women of Light. Harper 1964
Bkl A&Y

Nathan, Dorothy. Women of Courage. Random House 1964
CC(4-6)—ESLC—JH

Noel Haviland Field, 1904-

Lewis, Flora. Red Pawn: The Story of Noel Field. Doubleday 1965
Bkl A

Bernice Offenberg, ?

Offenberg, Bernice. The Angel of Hell's Kitchen. Geis 1962
Bkl A

Miriam Van Waters, 1887-

Rowles, Burton J. The Lady at Box 99: The Story of Miriam Van Waters. Seabury 1962
Bkl A

Lillian Wald, 1867-1940

Williams, Beryl. Lillian Wald: Angel of Henry Street. Messner 1948
JH—SCPL

COLLECTIONS

Forsee, Aylesa. American Women Who Scored Firsts. Macrae 1958
SCHS
Yost, Edna. American Women of Nursing. Lippincott 1965
Bkl Y&C—SCHS—SCPL

Iranian—20th century

Najmeh Najafi, ?

Najafi, Najmeh. Persia Is My Heart. Harper 1953
SCHS—SCPL
Najafi, Najmeh and Hinckley, Helen. Reveille for a Persian Village. Harper 1958
BBHS—SCHS—YR

Italian—20th century

Danilo Dolci, 1924-

McNeish, James. Fire Under the Ashes: The Life of Danilo Dolci. Beacon Press 1966
Bkl A

COLLECTIONS

Harcourt, Melville. Portraits of Destiny. Sheed 1966
Bkl A

SOCIETY LEADERS

English—20th century

Consuelo (Vanderbilt) Balsan, 1877-1964

Balsan, Consuelo (Vanderbilt). Glitter and the Gold. Harper 1952
SCPL

SOCIETY LEADERS—*Continued*

French—18th century

Charlotte Élisabeth Aïssé, 1694?-1733

COLLECTIONS

Herold, J. Christopher. Love in Five Temperaments. Atheneum 1961
Bkl A

Claudine Alexandrine Guérin de Tencin, 1685-1749

COLLECTIONS

Herold, J. Christopher. Love in Five Temperaments. Atheneum 1961
Bkl A

SOCIOLOGISTS

See also Criminologists; Penologists; Political Scientists

American—20th century

Horace Roscoe Cayton, 1903-

Cayton, Horace Roscoe. Long Old Road. Trident Press 1965
Bkl A

English—19th century

Beatrice (Potter) Webb, 1858-1943

Webb, Beatrice (Potter). American Diary, 1898; ed. by David A. Shannon. Univ. of Wis. 1963
Bkl A

German—20th century

Max Weber, 1864-1964

Jaspers, Karl. Three Essays: Leonardo, Descartes, Max Weber; tr. by Ralph Manheim. Harcourt 1964
Bkl A

Italian—20th century

Vilfredo Pareto, 1848-1923

COLLECTIONS

Schumpeter, Joseph Alois. Ten Great Economists, from Marx to Keynes. Oxford 1951
SCPL

SOIL SCIENTISTS

American—20th century

George Nissley Hoffer, 1887-1963

COLLECTIONS

De Kruif, Paul Henry. Hunger Fighters. Harcourt 1928
BBHS—SCHS—SCPL—3000

SOLDIERS

COLLECTIONS

Army Times. Famous Fighters of World War I. Dodd 1964
Bkl C&Y—YR

Barnett, Correlli. The Swordbearers: Supreme Command in the First World War. Morrow 1964
Bkl A
John Jellicoe; Erich Ludendorff; Helmuth von Moltke; Henri Pétain

Earle, Edward Mead, ed. Makers of Modern Strategy: Military Thought from Machiavelli to Hitler. Princeton Univ. 1943
SCPL

American

COLLECTIONS

Anders, Curtis. Fighting Generals. Putnam 1965
Bkl A&Y

Army Times. Famous American Military Leaders of World War II. Dodd 1962
Bkl C(7-9)&Y—SCHS

Army Times. Great American Cavalrymen. Dodd 1964
AB(5up)—Bkl C(6-9)&Y—JH

Billias, George Athan, ed. George Washington's Generals. Morrow 1964
Bkl A&Y—IndS(11-12)

Braun, Saul M. Seven Heroes: Medal of Honor Stories of the War in the Pacific. Putnam 1965
Bkl C(6-9)&Y

Cooke, Donald Edwin. For Conspicuous Gallantry: Winners of the Medal of Honor. Hammond 1966
Bkl C(5-9)

Dufour, Charles L. Nine Men in Gray. Doubleday 1963
Bkl A&Y
Edward Alexander; Turner Ashby; Patrick Cleburne; Henry Hotze; William Mahone; Lucius Northrop; William Pegram; Charles Read; Richard Taylor

McGiffin, Lee. Swords, Stars and Bars. Dutton 1958
BBJH—JH
Matthew Butler; Nathan Forrest; Wade Hampton; John Hunt Morgan; John Singleton Mosby; Joseph Shelby; James Ewell Brown Stuart; Joseph Wheeler

Mapp, Alf Johnson. Frock Coats and Epaulets. Yoseloff 1963
Bkl A&Y
Judah Philip Benjamin; Jefferson Davis; Thomas Jackson; Joseph Johnston; Robert Edward Lee; James Ewell Brown Stuart

Parrott, Marc. Hazard: Marines on Mission. Doubleday 1962
Bkl A&Y

SOLDIERS

American—*Continued*

Pasley, Virginia (Schmitz). 21 Stayed: The Story of the American GI's Who Chose Communist China—Who They Were and Why They Stayed. Farrar 1955
SCPL

Reeder, Russell Potter. The Northern Generals. Duell 1964
JH

Reeder, Russell Potter. The Southern Generals. Duell 1965
Bkl C(7-9)&Y

Sobol, Donald J. Lock, Stock and Barrel. Westminster 1965
Bkl C&Y—ESLC

Warner, Ezra J. Generals in Gray: Lives of the Confederate Commanders. La. State Univ. 1959
SCPL—3000

American—18th century

Ethan Allen, 1738-1789

Brown, Slater. Ethan Allen and the Green Mountain Boys. Random House 1956
AB(5-7)—CC(5-7)—JH—SCHS

Holbrook, Stewart Hall. America's Ethan Allen. Houghton 1949
BBEL(6-8)—BBJH—CC(5-7)—ESLC—JH—SCHS

Meigs, Cornelia Lynde. The Covered Bridge. Macmillan 1936 (Fiction)
BBEL—CC(4-6)

Van de Water, Frederic F. Catch a Falling Star. Duell 1949 (Fiction)
SCHS

Van de Water, Frederic F. Reluctant Rebel. Duell 1948 (Fiction)
SCHS

COLLECTIONS

Holbrook, Stewart Hall. Dreamers of the American Dream. Doubleday 1957
SCPL

Benedict Arnold, 1741-1801

Flexner, James Thomas. The Traitor and the Spy: Benedict Arnold and John André. Harcourt 1953
SCPL

Nolan, Jeannette (Covert). Benedict Arnold: Traitor to His Country. Messner 1956
BBHS—BBJH—JH—SCHS

Nolan, Jeannette (Covert). Treason at the Point. Messner 1944 (Fiction)
SCHS

Roberts, Kenneth Lewis. Arundel. Doubleday 1933 (Fiction)
BBHS—SCHS

Vail, Philip. The Twisted Saber: A Biographical Novel of Benedict Arnold. Dodd 1963 (Fiction)
Bkl A&Y—IndS(9-12)

COLLECTIONS

Bakeless, John. Turncoats, Traitors, and Heroes. Lippincott 1959
SCHS

Crispus Attucks, 1723?-1770

Millender, Dharathula H. Crispus Attucks, Boy of Valor. Bobbs 1965
ESLC

George Rogers Clark, 1752-1818

Bakeless, John Edwin. Background to Glory: The Life of George Rogers Clark. Lippincott 1957
SCHS—SCPL

Grant, Bruce. Northwest Campaign: The George Rogers Clark Expedition. Putnam 1963
ESLC

Lancaster, Bruce. The Big Knives. Little 1964 (Fiction)
Bkl A&Y—IndS(9-10)—SCHS

Nolan, Jeannette (Covert). George Rogers Clark, Soldier and Hero (November 19, 1752-February 13, 1818). Messner 1954
AB(5-7)—BBEL(6-8)—BBJH—CC(6-9)—JH—SCHS

John Glover, 1732-1797

Billias, George Athan. General John Glover and His Marblehead Mariners. Holt 1960
Bkl A&Y

Nathanael Greene, 1742-1786

Thayer, Theodore George. Nathanael Greene: Strategist of the American Revolution. Twayne 1960
Bkl A

Nathan Hale, 1755-1776

Brown, Marion Marsh. Young Nathan. Westminster 1949
BBJH—JH—SCHS

COLLECTIONS

Bakeless, John. Turncoats, Traitors, and Heroes. Lippincott 1959
SCHS

Henry ("Light-Horse Harry") Lee, 1756-1818

Gerson, Noel Bertram. Light-Horse Harry: A Biography of Washington's Great Cavalryman, General Henry Lee. Doubleday 1966
Bkl A&Y

SOLDIERS

American—18th century

Henry ("Light-Horse Harry") Lee—Continued

COLLECTIONS

Bakeless, John. Turncoats, Traitors, and Heroes. Lippincott 1959
SCHS

Francis Marion, 1732-1795

Allen, Merritt Parmelee. Battle Lanterns. Longmans 1949 (Fiction)
CC(7-9)—JH—SCHS

Brown, Marion Marsh. The Swamp Fox. Westminster 1950
BBEL(6-8)—CC(5-9)—ESLC—JH—SCHS

Carmer, Elizabeth and Carmer, Carl. Francis Marion. Garrard 1962
AB(4up)

Holbrook, Stewart Hall. The Swamp Fox of the Revolution. Random House 1959
Bkl C(5-8)

Williams, Beryl and Epstein, Samuel. Francis Marion. Messner 1956
BBJH

Joseph Plumb Martin, 1761?-

Martin, Joseph Plumb. Yankee Doodle Boy; ed. by George F. Scheer. Scott 1964
ESLC

Daniel Morgan, 1736-1802

Callahan, North. Daniel Morgan, Ranger of the Revolution. Holt 1961
Bkl A&Y

James O'Hara, 1752-1819

Turnbull, Agnes (Sligh). The King's Orchard. Houghton 1963 (Fiction)
Bkl A&Y

Israel Putnam, 1718-1790

Dwight, Allan. Soldier and Patriot: The Life of General Israel Putnam. Washburn 1965
Bkl C(5-8)

Robert Rogers, 1731-1795

Roberts, Kenneth. Northwest Passage. Doubleday 1937 (Fiction)
JH—SCHS

Friedrich Wilhelm von Steuben, 1730-1794

COLLECTIONS

Cunz, Dieter. They Came from Germany: The Story of Famous German-Americans. Dodd 1966
ESLC

Thomas Sumter, 1734-1832

Bass, Robert Duncan. Gamecock: The Life and Campaigns of General Thomas Sumter. Holt 1961
Bkl A

George Washington, 1732-1799

American Heritage. George Washington and the Making of a Nation, by Marcus Cunliffe. Am. Heritage 1966
ESLC

Aulaire, Ingri d' and Aulaire, Edgar Parin d'. George Washington. Doubleday 1936
BBEL(2-5)—CC(2-4)—ESLC

Boller, Paul F. George Washington & Religion. Southern Methodist Univ. 1963
Bkl A

Boyce, Burke. Man from Mt. Vernon. Harper 1961 (Fiction)
Bkl A&Y

Boyce, Burke. Morning of a Hero: A Novel. Harper 1963 (Fiction)
Bkl A—IndS(9-10)

Cunliffe, Marcus. George Washington, Man and Monument. Little 1958
BBHS—GR—SCPL—3000

Desmond, Alice (Curtis). Sword and Pen for George Washington. Dodd 1964
Bkl Y

Eaton, Jeanette. Leader by Destiny: George Washington, Man and Patriot. Harcourt 1938
BBHS—BBJH—CC(7-9)—JH—SCHS

Eaton, Jeanette. Washington, the Nation's First Hero. Morrow 1951
AB(3-6)—CC(4-6)

Flexner, James Thomas. George Washington: The Forge of Experience, 1732-1775. Little 1965
Bkl A&Y—IndS(11-12)

Ford, Paul Leicester. Janice Meredith: A Story of the American Revolution. Dodd 1899 (Fiction)
SCHS

Foster, Genevieve. George Washington: An Initial Biography. Scribner 1949
AB(4-6)—BBEL—CC(3-5)—ESLC

Freeman, Douglas Southall. George Washington: A Biography. 7v. Scribner 1948-1957
SCPL

Freidel, Frank and Aikman, Lonnelle. G. Washington: Man and Monument. Grosset 1965
Bkl A&Y&C—ESLC

Hays, Wilma Pitchford. George Washington's Birthdays. Coward-McCann 1963
IndJ(2-4)

SOLDIERS

American—18th century

George Washington—Continued

Judson, Clara (Ingram). George Washington, Leader of the People. Follett 1951
BBEL(5-8)—BBJH—CC(4-7)—ESLC—JH—SCHS

Meadowcroft, Enid La Monte. Silver for General Washington: A Story of Valley Forge. Crowell 1957 (Fiction)
CC(6-9)—ESLC—JH

North, Sterling. George Washington, Frontier Colonel. Random House 1957
CC(5-7)—JH—SCHS

Woodward, William E. George Washington: the Image and the Man. Liveright 1946
SCPL

American—19th century

Edward Porter Alexander, 1835-1910

COLLECTIONS

Dufour, Charles L. Nine Men in Gray. Doubleday 1963
Bkl A&Y

Turner Ashby, 1828-1862

COLLECTIONS

Dufour, Charles L. Nine Men in Gray. Doubleday 1963
Bkl A&Y

Pierre Gustave Toutant Beauregard, 1818-1893

Keyes, Frances Parkinson (Wheeler). Madame Castel's Lodger. Farrar 1962 (Fiction)
Bkl A

James Bowie, 1796-1836

Baugh, Virgil E. Rendezvous at the Alamo: Highlights in the Lives of Bowie, Crockett, and Travis. Pageant 1961
Bkl A

Garst, Doris Shannon. James Bowie and His Famous Knife. Messner 1955
CC(7-9)—ESLC—JH—SCHS

Benjamin Franklin Butler, 1818-1893

West, Richard Sedgewick. Lincoln's Scapegoat General: A Life of Benjamin F. Butler, 1818-1893. Houghton 1965
Bkl A&Y

Matthew Calbraith Butler, 1836-1909

COLLECTIONS

McGiffin, Lee. Swords, Stars and Bars. Dutton 1958
BBJH—JH

John Milton Chivington, 1821-1894

Werstein, Irving. Massacre at Sand Creek. Scribner 1963
ESLC

Patrick Ronayne Cleburne, 1828-1864

COLLECTIONS

Dufour, Charles L. Nine Men in Gray. Doubleday 1963
Bkl A&Y

George Armstrong Custer, 1839-1876

Brown, Dee. Showdown at Little Big Horn. Putnam 1964
ESLC

Custer, Elizabeth (Bacon). "Boots and Saddles"; or, Life in Dakota with General Custer. Harper 1913
SCHS—SCPL

Frost, Lawrence A. The Custer Album: A Pictorial Biography of General George A. Custer. Superior Pub. 1964
Bkl A

Garst, Doris Shannon. Custer, Fighter of the Plains. Messner 1944
BBEL(5-8)—CC(6-9)—JH—SCHS

Reynolds, Quentin. Custer's Last Stand. Random House 1951
BBJH—CC(5-7)—ESLC—JH—SCHS

COLLECTIONS

Steckmesser, Kent Ladd. The Western Hero in History and Legend. Univ. of Okla. 1965
Bkl A

Sarah Emma Edmundson, 1841-1898

Dannett, Sylvia G. L. She Rode with the Generals. Nelson 1960
Bkl A

Ephraim Elmer Ellsworth, 1837-1861

Randall, Ruth (Painter). Colonel Elmer Ellsworth: A Biography of Lincoln's Friend and First Hero of the Civil War. Little 1960
Bkl A

Nathan Bedford Forrest, 1821-1877

COLLECTIONS

McGiffin, Lee. Swords, Stars and Bars. Dutton 1958
BBJH—JH

John Charles Frémont, 1813-1890

Burt, Olive. John Charles Fremont: Trail Marker of the Old West. Messner 1955
BBJH—JH—SCHS

Frazee, Steve. Year of the Big Snow: John Charles Frémont's Fourth Expedition. Holt 1962
ESLC

SOLDIERS

American—19th century

John Charles Frémont—Continued

Frémont, John Charles. Narratives of Exploration and Adventure; ed. by Allan Nevins. Longmans 1956
SCPL

Nevins, Allan. Fremont, Pathmaker of the West. Longmans 1955
SCPL

Smith, Fredrika Shumway. Frémont: Soldier, Explorer, Statesman. Rand McNally 1966
ESLC

Ulysses Simpson Grant, 1822-1885

Catton, Bruce. Grant Moves South. Little 1960
Bkl A&Y—BY—SCHS—SCPL

Catton, Bruce. U. S. Grant and the American Military Tradition. Little 1954
SCPL—3000

Kantor, MacKinlay. Lee and Grant at Appomattox. Random House 1950
CC(6-9)—ESLC—JH—SCHS—YR

Lewis, Lloyd. Captain Sam Grant. Little 1950
SCPL

Meyer, Howard N. Let Us Have Peace: The Story of Ulysses S. Grant. Collier Bks 1966
Bkl Y(7-10)&C

Miers, Earl Schenck. Web of Victory: Grant at Vicksburg. Knopf 1955
SCPL

Reeder, Russell Potter. Ulysses S. Grant: Horseman and Fighter. Garrard 1964
AB(4-7)

Thomas, Henry. Ulysses S. Grant. Putnam 1961
Bkl C(6-9)—YR

Woodward, W. E. Meet General Grant. Liveright 1928
SCPL

Wade Hampton, 1818-1902

COLLECTIONS

McGiffin, Lee. Swords, Stars and Bars. Dutton 1958
BBJH—JH

Winfield Scott Hancock, 1824-1886

Tucker, Glenn. Hancock the Superb. Bobbs 1960
Bkl A

Rutherford Birchard Hayes, 1822-1893

Williams, Thomas Harry. Hayes of the Twenty-third: The Civil War Volunteer Officer. Knopf 1965
Bkl A

Thomas Wentworth Higginson, 1823-1911

Wells, Anna Mary. Dear Preceptor: The Life and Times of Thomas Wentworth Higginson. Houghton 1963
Bkl A

Daniel Harvey Hill, 1821-1889

Bridges, Leonard Hal. Lee's Maverick General, Daniel Harvey Hill. McGraw 1961
Bkl A

Samuel Houston, 1793-1863

James, Bessie Rowland and James, Marquis. Six Feet Six: The Heroic Story of Sam Houston. Bobbs 1931
BBJH—CC(6-9)—JH—SCHS

James, Marquis. The Raven. Bobbs 1953
BY

Johnson, William. Sam Houston, the Tallest Texan. Random House 1953
AB(5-10)—BBEL(5-8)—CC(5-7)—ESLC—JH

Latham, Jean Lee. Retreat to Glory: The Story of Sam Houston. Harper 1965
Bkl C(7-9)

Latham, Jean Lee. Sam Houston, Hero of Texas. Garrard 1965
AB(3-7)—ESLC

Wellman, Paul Iselin. Magnificent Destiny: A Novel About the Great Secret Adventure of Andrew Jackson and Sam Houston. Doubleday 1962 (Fiction)
Bkl A

Wisehart, Marion Karl. Sam Houston, American Giant. Luce 1962
Bkl A

Andrew Jackson, 1767-1845

American Heritage. Andrew Jackson, Soldier and Statesman, by Ralph K. Andrist. Am. Heritage 1963
CC(6-9)—JH—SCHS—YR

Coit, Margaret L. Andrew Jackson. Houghton 1965
Bkl C(7-10)&Y—ESLC—IndJ(4-6)

Gerson, Noel Bertram. Old Hickory. Doubleday 1964 (Fiction)
Bkl A&Y

James, Marquis. Andrew Jackson, the Border Captain. Bobbs 1933
BBHS—SCPL

Judson, Clara (Ingram). Andrew Jackson, Frontier Statesman. Follett 1954
BBEL(5-8)—BBJH—CC(5-7)—ESLC—JH—SCHS

Martin, Patricia Miles. Andrew Jackson. Putnam 1966
ESLC

Mason, Francis Van Wyck. The Battles for New Orleans. Houghton 1962
Bkl C(6-8)—ESLC

SOLDIERS

American—19th century

Andrew Jackson—Continued

Nolan, Jeannette (Covert). Andrew Jackson. Messner 1949
CC(7-9)—JH—SCHS

Ogg, Frederic Austin. The Reign of Andrew Jackson: A Chronicle of the Frontier in Politics. Yale Univ. 1919
SCHS

Palmer, Bruce and Giles, John Clifford. Horseshoe Bend. Simon & Schuster 1962 (Fiction)
Bkl A

Parlin, John. Andrew Jackson. Garrard 1962
AB(3-7)

Stone, Irving. The President's Lady. Doubleday 1951 (Fiction)
BBHS—SCHS

Syrett, Harold C. Andrew Jackson: His Contribution to the American Tradition. Bobbs 1953
BBHS—3000

Vance, Marguerite. The Jacksons of Tennessee. Dutton 1953
BBEL—BBJH—CC(7-9)—ESLC—JH—SCHS

Wellman, Paul Iselin. Magnificent Destiny: A Novel About the Great Secret Adventure of Andrew Jackson and Sam Houston. Doubleday 1962 (Fiction)
Bkl A

Wright, Frances. Andrew Jackson. Abingdon 1958
AB(4-7)

Thomas Jonathan ("Stonewall") Jackson, 1824-1863

Chambers, Lenoir. Stonewall Jackson. 2v. Morrow 1959
SCPL

Daniels, Jonathan. Stonewall Jackson. Random House 1959
Bkl C(6-8)—CC(5-7)—ESLC—JH—SCHS

Davis, Burke. They Called Him Stonewall: A Life of Lt. General T. J. Jackson, C. S. A. Rinehart 1954
SCPL

Kane, Harnett T. The Gallant Mrs. Stonewall: A Novel Based on the Lives of General and Mrs. Stonewall Jackson. Doubleday 1957 (Fiction)
SCHS

Sutton, Felix. The Valiant Virginian— Stonewall Jackson. Messner 1961
AB(5-9)—YR

Vandiver, Frank Everson. Mighty Stonewall. McGraw 1957
SCPL

COLLECTIONS
Mapp, Alf Johnson. Frock Coats and Epaulets. Yoseloff 1963
Bkl A&Y

Joseph Eggleston Johnston, 1807-1891
COLLECTIONS
Mapp, Alf Johnson. Frock Coats and Epaulets. Yoseloff 1963
Bkl A&Y

Myles Walter Keogh, 1840-1876

Leighton, Margaret. Comanche of the Seventh. Ariel Bks 1957
JH

Robert Edward Lee, 1807-1870

Carter, Hodding. Robert E. Lee and the Road of Honor. Random House 1955
CC(5-7)—JH—SCHS

Commager, Henry Steele and Ward, Lynd Kendall. America's Robert E. Lee. Houghton 1951
BBEL(6-8)—BBJH—CC(6-9)—ESLC—JH—SCHS

Daniels, Jonathan. Robert E. Lee. Houghton 1960
Bkl C(5-8)—CC

Davis, Burke. Gray Fox: Robert E. Lee and the Civil War. Rinehart 1956
SCPL

Dowdey, Clifford. Lee. Little 1965
Bkl A&Y

Dowdey, Clifford. The Seven Days: The Emergence of Lee. Little 1964
IndS(11-12)

Fishwick, Marshall William. Lee After the War. Dodd 1963
Bkl A&Y

Freeman, Douglas Southall. Lee; an abridgment in one volume, by Richard Harwell, of the four-volume R. E. Lee. Scribner 1961
Bkl A&Y—SCPL

Freeman, Douglas Southall. Lee of Virginia. Scribner 1958
BBHS—BBJH—BY—CC(8-9)—SCHS—SCPL

Freeman, Douglas Southall. R. E. Lee: A Biography. 4v. Scribner 1934-35
CA—GR—SCPL—3000

Graves, Charles P. Robert E. Lee, Hero of the South. Garrard 1964
ESLC

Kane, Harnett T. The Lady of Arlington: A Novel Based on the Life of Mrs. Robert E. Lee. Doubleday 1953 (Fiction)
SCHS

Kantor, MacKinlay. Lee and Grant at Appomattox. Random House 1950
CC(6-9)—ESLC—JH—SCHS—YR

Miers, Earl Schenck. Robert E. Lee: A Great Life in Brief. Knopf 1956
SCHS—SCPL—3000

SOLDIERS

American—19th century

Robert Edward Lee—Continued

Stern, Philip Van Doren. Robert E. Lee: The Man and the Soldier. McGraw 1963
IndS(9-12)

Taylor, Walter Herron. Four Years with General Lee. Ind. Univ. 1962
Bkl A

Vance, Marguerite. The Lees of Arlington: The Story of Mary and Robert E. Lee. Dutton 1949
BBEL–BBJH–CC(6-9)–JH–SCHS

COLLECTIONS

Mapp, Alf Johnson. Frock Coats and Epaulets. Yoseloff 1963
Bkl A&Y

Parlin, John. Patriots' Days. Garrard 1964
ESLC

George Brinton McClellan, 1826-1885

Catton, Bruce. Mr. Lincoln's Army. Doubleday 1951
SCHS

William Mahone, 1826-1895

COLLECTIONS

Dufour, Charles L. Nine Men in Gray. Doubleday 1963
Bkl A&Y

Nelson Appleton Miles, 1839-1925

Bailey, Ralph Edgar. Indian Fighter: The Story of Nelson A. Miles. Morrow 1965
Bkl C(6-9)&Y–ESLC

Haines, William Wister. The Winter War: A Historical Novel. Little 1961 (Fiction)
Bkl A

Johnson, Virginia Weisel. The Unregimented General. Houghton 1962
Bkl A&Y

John Hunt Morgan, 1825-1864

COLLECTIONS

McGiffin, Lee. Swords, Stars and Bars. Dutton 1958
BBJH–JH

John Singleton Mosby, 1833-1916

Daniels, Jonathan. Mosby, Gray Ghost of the Confederacy. Lippincott 1959
Bkl C(7-9)&Y–SCHS

Guy, Anne Welsh. John Mosby, Rebel Raider of the Civil War. Abelard-Schuman 1965
ESLC

COLLECTIONS

McGiffin, Lee. Swords, Stars and Bars. Dutton 1958
BBJH–JH

Lucius Bellinger Northrop, 1811-1894

COLLECTIONS

Dufour, Charles L. Nine Men in Gray. Doubleday 1963
Bkl A&Y

John Timothy O'Keefe, 1853?-1895

Felton, Harold W. Sergeant O'Keefe and His Mule, Balaam. Dodd 1962 (Fiction)
Bkl C(5-9)

William Ransom Johnson Pegram, 1841-1865

COLLECTIONS

Dufour, Charles L. Nine Men in Gray. Doubleday 1963
Bkl A&Y

Albert Pike, 1809-1891

Duncan, Robert Lipscomb. Reluctant General: The Life and Times of Albert Pike. Dutton 1961
Bkl A

Zebulon Montgomery Pike, 1779-1813

Baker, Nina Brown. Pike of Pike's Peak. Harcourt 1953
CC(5-7)

Keating, Bern. Zebulon Pike: Young America's Frontier Scout. Putnam 1965
ESLC

Wibberley, Leonard. Zebulon Pike, Soldier and Explorer. Funk 1961
Bkl C(7-9)–BY–YR

Marcus Albert Reno, 1834-1889

Terrell, John Upton and Walton, George H. Faint the Trumpet Sounds: The Life and Trial of Major Reno. McKay 1966
Bkl A

Theodore Roosevelt, 1858-1919

Busch, Noel Fairchild. T. R.: The Story of Theodore Roosevelt and His Influence on Our Times. Reynal 1963
Bkl A&Y

Castor, Henry. Teddy Roosevelt and the Rough Riders. Random House 1954
ESLC–JH–SCHS

Cavanah, Frances. Adventure in Courage: The Story of Theodore Roosevelt. Rand McNally 1961
AB(5-7)

SOLDIERS

American—19th century

Theodore Roosevelt—Continued

Cook, Fred J. Theodore Roosevelt: Rallying a Free People. Lippincott 1961
BY

Foster, Genevieve. Theodore Roosevelt: An Initial Biography. Scribner 1954
BBEL—CC(4-6)

Hagedorn, Hermann. The Boys' Life of Theodore Roosevelt. Harper 1950
SCHS

Hagedorn, Hermann. Roosevelt Family of Sagamore Hill. Macmillan 1954
BBHS—BY—SCHS—SCPL

Harbaugh, William Henry. Power and Responsibility: The Life and Times of Theodore Roosevelt. Farrar 1961
Bkl A—BY—SCPL

Howland, Harold. Theodore Roosevelt and His Times: A Chronicle of the Progressive Movement. Yale Univ. 1921
SCHS

Judson, Clara (Ingram). Theodore Roosevelt, Fighting Patriot. Follett 1953
BBEL(5-8)—BBJH—CC(5-7)—ESLC—JH

Lorant, Stefan. The Life and Times of Theodore Roosevelt. Doubleday 1959
Bkl A—SCPL

Pringle, Henry Fowles. Theodore Roosevelt: A Biography. Harcourt 1956
SCPL—3000

Putnam, Carleton. Theodore Roosevelt: v. 1, The Formative Years, 1858-1886. Scribner 1958
SCPL

Roosevelt, Theodore. Autobiography of Theodore Roosevelt; condensed from the original edition; ed. by Wayne Andrews. Scribner 1958
SCPL

Roosevelt, Theodore. Theodore Roosevelt Treasury: A Self-Portrait from His Writings; comp. by Hermann Hagedorn. Putnam 1957
SCPL

Roosevelt, Theodore. Theodore Roosevelt's Letters to His Children; ed. by J. B. Bishop. Scribner 1919
SCPL

Wagenknecht, Edward Charles. Seven Worlds of Theodore Roosevelt. Longmans 1958
SCPL

Carl Schurz, 1829-1906

Schurz, Carl. Autobiography; an abridgment in one volume, by Wayne Andrews. Scribner 1961
Bkl A

Robert Gould Shaw, 1837-1863

Burchard, Peter. One Gallant Rush: Robert Gould Shaw and His Brave Black Regiment. St Martins 1965
Bkl A&Y

Joseph Orville Shelby, 1830-1897

Duncan, Harley. West of Appomattox. Appleton 1961 (Fiction)
Bkl A

COLLECTIONS

McGiffin, Lee. Swords, Stars and Bars. Dutton 1958
BBJH—JH

Philip Henry Sheridan, 1831-1888

Allen, Merritt Parmelee. Blow, Bugles, Blow. Longmans 1956 (Fiction)
SCHS

Lampman, Evelyn Sibley. Witch Doctor's Son. Doubleday 1954 (Fiction)
SCHS

Lancaster, Bruce. Roll Shenandoah. Little 1956 (Fiction)
SCHS

Reeder, Russell Potter. Sheridan: The General Who Wasn't Afraid to Take a Chance. Duell 1962
Bkl C(7-9)&Y—BY

William Tecumseh Sherman, 1820-1891

Lewis, Lloyd. Sherman, Fighting Prophet. Harcourt 1958
SCPL—3000

Sherman, William Tecumseh. Memoirs of General William T. Sherman, by Himself. Ind. Univ. 1957
SCPL

Daniel Edgar Sickles, 1825-1914

Swanberg, W. A. Sickles the Incredible. Scribner 1956
SCPL

James Ewell Brown Stuart, 1833-1864

Davis, Burke. Jeb Stuart, the Last Cavalier. Rinehart 1957
SCPL

De Grummond, Lena Young and Delaune, Lynn (de Grummond). Jeb Stuart. Lippincott 1962
Bkl C(7-9)

Thomason, John William. Jeb Stuart. Scribner 1934
SCPL

COLLECTIONS

McGiffin, Lee. Swords, Stars and Bars. Dutton 1958
BBJH—JH

Mapp, Alf Johnson. Frock Coats and Epaulets. Yoseloff 1963
Bkl A&Y

SOLDIERS

American—19th century—*Continued*

Richard Taylor, 1826-1879

COLLECTIONS

Dufour, Charles L. Nine Men in Gray. Doubleday 1963
Bkl A&Y

Zachary Taylor, 1784-1850

Nichols, Edward Jay. Zach Taylor's Little Army. Doubleday 1963
Bkl A&Y

Hoyt, Edwin Palmer. Zachary Taylor. Reilly & Lee 1966
Bkl C(7-9)&Y

William Walker, 1824-1860

Carr, Albert H. Z. The World and William Walker. Harper 1963
Bkl A

Joseph Wheeler, 1836-1906

COLLECTIONS

McGiffin, Lee. Swords, Stars and Bars. Dutton 1958
BBJH–JH

American—20th century

Henry Harley Arnold, 1886-1950

COLLECTIONS

Anders, Curtis. Fighting Airmen. Putnam 1966
Bkl A&Y

Omar Nelson Bradley, 1893-

Bradley, Omar Nelson. Soldier's Story. Holt 1951
SCPL

Lucius DuBignon Clay, 1897-

COLLECTIONS

Acheson, Dean Gooderham. Sketches from Life of Men I Have Known. Harper 1961
Bkl A&Y–SCPL

William Frische Dean, 1899-

Dean, William Frische and Worden, William L. General Dean's Story. Viking 1954
SCPL

Roger H. C. Donlon, 1934-

Donlon, Roger H. C. and Rogers, Warren. Outpost of Freedom. McGraw 1965
Bkl A&Y

William Joseph ("Wild Bill") Donovan, 1883-1959

COLLECTIONS

Army Times. Modern American Secret Agents. Dodd 1966
Bkl C(7-9)&Y

James Harold Doolittle, 1896-

COLLECTIONS

Anders, Curtis. Fighting Airmen. Putnam 1966
Bkl A&Y

Dwight David Eisenhower, 1890-1969

Army Times. The Challenge and the Triumph: The Story of General Dwight D. Eisenhower. Putnam 1966
Bkl A&Y

Childs, Marquis William. Eisenhower—Captive Hero: A Critical Study of the General and the President. Harcourt 1958
BBHS–SCPL

Davis, Kenneth Sydney. Soldier of Democracy: A Biography of Dwight Eisenhower. Doubleday 1952
SCPL

Gunther, John. Eisenhower: The Man and the Symbol. Harper 1952
SCHS–SCPL

Kornitzer, Bela. Great American Heritage: The Story of the Five Eisenhower Brothers. Farrar 1955
SCPL

Lovelace, Delos W. "Ike" Eisenhower, Statesman and Soldier of Peace. Crowell 1961
BBJH–CC(6-9)–ESLC–JH–SCHS

Moos, Malcolm. Dwight D. Eisenhower. Random House 1964
CC(5-7)–ESLC–JH

Henry Earl Giles, ?

Giles, Henry Earl. The G.I. Journal of Sergeant Giles; ed. by Janice Holt Giles. Houghton 1965
Bkl A&Y

George Churchill Kenney, 1889-

COLLECTIONS

Anders, Curtis. Fighting Airmen. Putnam 1966
Bkl A&Y

Curtis Emerson Le May, 1906-

COLLECTIONS

Anders, Curtis. Fighting Airmen. Putnam 1966
Bkl A&Y

SOLDIERS

American—20th century—*Continued*

Douglas MacArthur, 1880-1964

Archer, Jules. Front-Line General: Douglas MacArthur. Messner 1963
Bkl Y&C—JH—YR

Army Times. The Banners and the Glory: The Story of General Douglas MacArthur. Putnam 1965
Bkl A&Y

Gunther, John. The Riddle of MacArthur: Japan, Korea and the Far East. Harper 1951
SCHS—SCPL

MacArthur, Douglas. Courage Was the Rule: General Douglas MacArthur's Own Story. McGraw 1965
Bkl C(7-9)&Y—ESLC

MacArthur, Douglas. Duty, Honor, Country: A Pictorial Autobiography. McGraw 1965
Bkl A&Y

MacArthur, Douglas. Reminiscences. McGraw 1964
Bkl A&Y—IndS(12)—SCPL

Rovere, Richard Halworth and Schlesinger, Arthur Meier. The MacArthur Controversy and American Foreign Policy. Farrar 1965
Bkl A

Sebald, William Joseph and Brines, Russell. With MacArthur in Japan: A Personal History of the Occupation. Norton 1965
Bkl A

Steinberg, Alfred. Douglas MacArthur. Putnam 1961
Bkl C(6-9)&Y

COLLECTIONS

Roper, Elmo Burns. You and Your Leaders: Their Actions and Your Reactions, 1936-1956. Morrow 1957
SCPL

David Marcus, 1901-1948

Berkman, Ted. Cast a Giant Shadow: The Story of Mickey Marcus Who Died to Save Jerusalem. Doubleday 1962
Bkl A&Y—BY

George Catlett Marshall, 1880-1959

Faber, Harold. Soldier and Statesman: General George C. Marshall. Ariel Bks 1964
Bkl Y&C—CC—ESLC—IndJ(6-9)—JH

Pogue, Forrest C. George C. Marshall: v. 1, Education of a General, 1880-1939. Viking 1963
Bkl A&Y—IndS(10-12)—SCPL

William Mitchell, 1879-1936

Hurley, Alfred F. Billy Mitchell: Crusader for Air Power. Watts 1964
Bkl A&Y

Levine, Isaac Don. Mitchell: Pioneer of Air Power. Duell 1958
SCPL

Whitehouse, Arthur George Joseph. Billy Mitchell: America's Eagle of Air Power. Putnam 1962
Bkl C(7-10)&Y—JH

COLLECTIONS

Anders, Curtis. Fighting Airmen. Putnam 1966
Bkl A&Y

Geddes Mumford, 1925-1944

Mumford, Lewis. Green Memories: The Story of Geddes Mumford. Harcourt 1947
SCPL

George Smith Patton, 1885-1945

Ayer, Fred. Before the Colors Fade: Portrait of a Soldier, George S. Patton, Jr. Houghton 1964
SCPL

Farago, Ladislas. Patton: Ordeal and Triumph. Obolensky 1964
Bkl A—IndS(12)

Hatch, Alden. George Patton, General in Spurs. Messner 1950
BY—SCHS

Patton, George Smith. War As I Knew It; annotated by Paul D. Harkins. Houghton 1947
SCPL

John Joseph Pershing, 1860-1948

Army Times. The Yanks Are Coming: The Story of General John J. Pershing. Putnam 1960
Bkl A&Y

Castor, Henry. America's First World War: General Pershing and the Yanks. Random House 1957
BBJH—JH—SCHS

Lawson, Don. The United States in World War I: The Story of General John J. Pershing and the American Expeditionary Forces. Abelard-Schuman 1963
JH

O'Connor, Richard. Black Jack Pershing. Doubleday 1961
Bkl A—SCPL

Palmer, Frederick. John J. Pershing, General of the Armies: A Biography. Military Service 1948
SCPL

Pershing, John Joseph. My Experiences in the World War. 2v. Lippincott 1931
SCPL

SOLDIERS

American—20th century—*Continued*

Lewis Burwell Puller, 1898-

Davis, Burke. Marine! The Life of Lt. Gen. Lewis B. (Chesty) Puller, USMC (Ret.). Little 1962
Bkl A

Donald Leander Putt, 1905-

COLLECTIONS

Thomas, Shirley. Men of Space: v. 7, Profiles of the Leaders in Space Research, Development, and Exploration. Chilton 1965
Bkl A&Y

Russell Potter Reeder, 1902-

Reeder, Russell Potter. Born at Reveille, by Red Reeder. Duell 1966
Bkl A&Y

Matthew Bunker Ridgway, 1895-

Ridgway, Matthew Bunker and Martin, H. H. Soldier: The Memoirs of Matthew B. Ridgway. Harper 1956
SCPL

Alexander Archer Vandegrift, 1887-

Vandegrift, Alexander Archer and Asprey, Robert B. Once a Marine: The Memoirs of General A. A. Vandegrift, United States Marine Corps. Norton 1964
Bkl A

Carthaginian—2nd century B.C.

Hannibal, 247-183 B.C.

Baumann, Hans. I Marched with Hannibal; tr. by Katharine Potts. Walck 1962 (Fiction)
Bkl C(6-9)&Y—CC(7-9)—ESLC—JH—SCHS—YR
Cottrell, Leonard. Hannibal, Enemy of Rome. Holt 1961
Bkl A&Y—SCHS
De Beer, Sir Gavin Reynolds. Alps and Elephants: Hannibal's March. Dutton 1956
SCPL
Dolan, Mary. Hannibal of Carthage. Macmillan 1955
BBHS—SCHS
Houghton, Eric. The White Wall. McGraw 1961 (Fiction)
ESLC
Kent, Louise (Andrews). He Went with Hannibal. Houghton 1964 (Fiction)
Bkl C(7-9)—ESLC
Lamb, Harold. Hannibal: One Man Against Rome. Doubleday 1958
BBHS—SCHS—SCPL—3000

Powers, Alfred. Hannibal's Elephants. Longmans 1944 (Fiction)
CC(7-9)—JH—SCHS

Chilean—19th century

Bernardo O'Higgins, 1778-1842

COLLECTIONS

Bailey, Bernadine (Freeman). Famous Latin-American Liberators. Dodd 1960
Bkl C(6-9)&Y—ESLC—SCHS

Chinese—20th century

Feng Yü-hsiang, 1880-1948

Sheridan, James E. Chinese Warlord: The Career of Feng Yü-hsiang. Stanford Univ. 1966
Bkl A

English

COLLECTIONS

Barnett, Correlli. The Desert Generals. Viking 1961
Bkl A
Sir Claude Auchinleck; Sir Alan Cunningham; Bernard Law Montgomery; Sir Richard O'Connor; Sir Neil Ritchie

English—11th century

Hereward ("Hereward the Wake"), fl. 1070-1071

Treece, Henry. Man with a Sword. Pantheon 1962 (Fiction)
Bkl C(7-9)&Y—JH

COLLECTIONS

Sutcliff, Rosemary. Heroes and History. Putnam 1966
Bkl C(7-10)&Y

English—14th century

John of Gaunt, Duke of Lancaster, 1340-1399

Seton, Anya. Katherine. Houghton 1954 (Fiction)
SCHS

English—15th century

Richard Neville, Earl of Warwick, 1421-1471

Kendall, Paul Murray. Warwick the Kingmaker. Norton 1957
SCPL

English—16th century

Henry Howard, Earl of Surrey, 1517-1547

Chapman, Hester W. Two Tudor Portraits: Henry Howard, Earl of Surrey and Lady Katherine Grey. Little 1963
Bkl A—IndS(11-12)

SOLDIERS

English—16th century—*Continued*

Henry Wriothesley, 3rd Earl of Southampton, 1573-1624

Rowse, Alfred Leslie. Shakespeare's Southampton, Patron of Virginia. Harper 1966
Bkl A

English—17th century

Sir Richard Grenville, 1600-1658

Du Maurier, Daphne. The King's General. Doubleday 1946 (Fiction)
SCHS

John Churchill, 1st Duke of Marlborough, 1650-1722

Rowse, Alfred Leslie. Early Churchills: An English Family. Harper 1956
SCPL

Henry Wriothesley, 3rd Earl of Southampton, 1573-1624

Rowse, Alfred Leslie. Shakespeare's Southampton, Patron of Virginia. Harper 1966
Bkl A

English—18th century

John André, 1751-1780

Flexner, James Thomas. The Traitor and the Spy: Benedict Arnold and John André. Harcourt 1953
SCPL

COLLECTIONS

Bakeless, John. Turncoats, Traitors, and Heroes. Lippincott 1959
SCHS

Sir Henry Clinton, 1738?-1795

Willcox, William Bradford. Portrait of a General: Sir Henry Clinton in the War of Independence. Knopf 1964
Bkl A—IndS(11-12)

John Churchill, 1st Duke of Marlborough, 1650-1722

Rowse, Alfred Leslie. Early Churchills: An English Family. Harper 1956
SCPL

James Edward Oglethorpe, 1696-1785

Mason, Francis Van Wyck. Rascals' Heaven. Doubleday 1964 (Fiction)
Bkl A

Robert Stobo, 1727-1770

Alberts, Robert C. The Most Extraordinary Adventures of Major Robert Stobo. Houghton 1965
Bkl A—IndS(11-12)

James Wolfe, 1727-1759

Mason, Francis Van Wyck. The Battle for Quebec. Houghton 1965
ESLC

Schull, Joseph. Battle for the Rock: The Story of Wolfe and Montcalm. Macmillan 1960
ESLC

English—19th century

Edmund Henry Hynman Allenby, 1861-1936

Gardner, Brian. Allenby of Arabia, Lawrence's General. Coward-McCann 1966
Bkl A

Robert Stephenson Smyth Baden-Powell, Baron Baden-Powell, 1857-1941

Hillcourt, William and Baden-Powell, Olave. Baden-Powell: The Two Lives of a Hero. Putnam 1964
Bkl A

James Thomas Brudenell, 7th Earl of Cardigan, 1797-1868

Woodham Smith, Cecil Blanche (Fitzgerald). Reason Why. McGraw 1954
SCPL

George, 2nd Duke of Cambridge, 1819-1904

St. Aubyn, Giles. The Royal George, 1819-1904: The Life of H. R. H. Prince George, Duke of Cambridge. Knopf 1964
Bkl A

Charles George Gordon, 1833-1885

Gordon, Charles George. Khartoum Journal; ed. by Lord Elton. Vanguard 1963
Bkl A—IndS(10-12)

John Luard, 1790-1875

Lunt, James D. Scarlet Lancer. Harcourt 1964
Bkl A&Y

George Charles Bingham, 3rd Earl of Lucan, 1800-1888

Woodham Smith, Cecil Blanche (Fitzgerald). Reason Why. McGraw 1954
SCPL

Fitzroy James Henry Somerset, Baron Raglan, 1788-1855

Hibbert, Christopher. The Destruction of Lord Raglan: A Tragedy of the Crimean War, 1854-55. Little 1962
Bkl A

SOLDIERS

English—19th century—*Continued*

Arthur Wellesley, 1st Duke of Wellington, 1769-1852

Cooper, Leonard. The Age of Wellington: The Life and Times of the Duke of Wellington, 1769-1852. Dodd 1963
Bkl A—IndS(11-12)

Ward, Stephen George Peregrine. Wellington. Arco 1964
Bkl A

Garnet Joseph Wolseley, Viscount Wolseley, 1833-1913

Lehmann, Joseph H. The Model Major-General: A Biography of Field-Marshal Lord Wolseley. Houghton 1964
Bkl A

English—20th century

Harold Rupert Leofric George Alexander, 1st Earl Alexander, 1891-

Alexander, Harold Rupert Leofric George Alexander, 1st Earl. The Alexander Memoirs, 1940-1945; ed. by John North. McGraw 1963
Bkl A

Edmund Henry Hynman Allenby, 1861-1936

Gardner, Brian. Allenby of Arabia, Lawrence's General. Coward-McCann 1966
Bkl A

Sir Claude John Eyre Auchinleck, 1884-

COLLECTIONS

Barnett, Correlli. The Desert Generals. Viking 1961
Bkl A

Sir Alan Gordon Cunningham, 1887-

COLLECTIONS

Barnett, Correlli. The Desert Generals. Viking 1961
Bkl A

Douglas Haig, 1st Earl Haig, 1861-1928

Terraine, John. Ordeal of Victory. Lippincott 1963
Bkl A

Hastings Lionel Ismay, Baron Ismay, 1887-1965

Ismay, Hastings Lionel Ismay, Baron. Memoirs. Viking 1960
Bkl A

Thomas Edward Lawrence, 1888-1935

MacLean, Alistair. Lawrence of Arabia. Random House 1962
Bkl C(6-9)—CC(5-7)—ESLC—JH—SCHS—YR

Nutting, Anthony. Lawrence of Arabia: The Man and the Motive. Potter 1961
GR—SCPL

Ocampo, Victoria. 338171 T. E. (Lawrence of Arabia); tr. by David Garnett. Dutton 1963
Bkl A

Rattigan, Terence. Ross: A Dramatic Portrait. Random House 1962 (Play)
Bkl A

Thomas, John. The True Story of Lawrence of Arabia. Childrens Press 1964
IndJ(4-6)

Weintraub, Stanley. Private Shaw and Public Shaw: A Dual Portrait of Lawrence of Arabia and G. B. S. Braziller 1963
Bkl A

Bernard Law Montgomery, 1st Viscount Montgomery, 1887-

Montgomery, Bernard Law Montgomery, 1st Viscount. Memoirs of Field-Marshal the Viscount Montgomery of Alamein. World 1958
SCPL

COLLECTIONS

Barnett, Correlli. The Desert Generals. Viking 1961
Bkl A

Sir Richard Nugent O'Connor, 1889-

COLLECTIONS

Barnett, Correlli. The Desert Generals. Viking 1961
Bkl A

Sir Neil Methuen Ritchie, 1897-

COLLECTIONS

Barnett, Correlli. The Desert Generals. Viking 1961
Bkl A

Flora Sandes, ?

Burgess, Alan. The Lovely Sergeant. Dutton 1963
Bkl A&Y

Archibald Percival Wavell, 1st Earl Wavell, 1883-1950

Robertson, John Henry. Wavell, Scholar and Soldier. Harcourt 1965
Bkl A

James Howard Williams, 1897-1958

Williams, Susan Margaret (Rowland). The Footprints of Elephant Bill. McKay 1963
Bkl A&Y—IndS(9-12)

SOLDIERS

English—20th century—*Continued*

Orde Charles Wingate, 1903-1944

Sykes, Christopher. Orde Wingate: A Biography. World 1959
SCPL

French—15th century

Saint Joan of Arc, 1412-1431

Anouilh, Jean. The Lark; tr. by Christopher Fry. Oxford 1956 (Play)
SCHS—SCPL

Anouilh, Jean. The Lark; adapted by Lillian Hellman. Random House 1956 (Play)
SCPL

Clemens, Samuel Langhorne. Personal Recollections of Joan of Arc, by the Sieur Louis de Conte (Her Page and Secretary). Harper 1926 (Fiction)
SCHS

Fabre, Lucien. Joan of Arc; tr. by Gerard Hopkins. McGraw 1954
CA—SCPL

Horizon Magazine. Joan of Arc, by Jay Williams. Am. Heritage 1963
AB—Bkl C(6-10)&Y—CC(7-9)—ESLC—IndJ(6-9)—JH—SCHS—YR

Johnston, Johanna. Joan of Arc. Doubleday 1961
Bkl C(4-7)

Lightbody, Charles Wayland. The Judgements of Joan: Joan of Arc—A Study in Cultural History. Harvard Univ. 1961
Bkl A

Michelet, Jules. Joan of Arc; tr. by Albert Guerard. Univ. of Mich. 1957
3000

Paine, Albert Bigelow. The Girl in White Armor: The True Story of Joan of Arc. Macmillan 1927
BBJH—BY—CC(7-9)—JH—SCHS

Ross, Nancy Wilson. Joan of Arc. Random House 1953
AB(6-9)—JH

Shaw, George Bernard. Saint Joan; Major Barbara; Androcles and the Lion. Modern Lib. 1956 (Play)
SCHS—SCPL

COLLECTIONS

Bowie, Walter Russell. Women of Light. Harper 1964
Bkl A&Y

French—17th century

Louis de Buade, Comte de Frontenac, 1620-1698

Cather, Willa Sibert. Shadows on the Rock. Knopf 1931 (Fiction)
JH—SCHS

French—18th century

Marie Joseph Paul Yves Roch Gilbert du Motier, Marquis de Lafayette, 1757-1834

Carter, Hodding. The Marquis de Lafayette: Bright Sword for Freedom. Random House 1958
BBJH—JH

Graham, Alberta (Powell). Lafayette, Friend of America. Abingdon 1952
BBEL(5-6)—CC(3-5)—ESLC

COLLECTIONS

Freedman, Russell. Teenagers Who Made History. Holiday 1961
BY—JH—SCHS—YR

Larson, Egon. Men Who Fought for Freedom. Roy 1959
AB

Louis Joseph de Montcalm, Marquis de Saint Véran, 1712-1759

Hays, Wilma Pitchford. Drummer Boy for Montcalm. Viking 1959 (Fiction)
Bkl C(5-8)—CC(5-7)

Mason, Francis Van Wyck. The Battle for Quebec. Houghton 1965
ESLC

Schull, Joseph. Battle for the Rock: The Story of Wolfe and Montcalm. Macmillan 1960
ESLC

Philippe II, Duc d'Orléans, 1674-1723

Lewis, Warren Hamilton. The Scandalous Regent. Harcourt 1961
Bkl A

Jean Baptiste Donatien de Vimeur, Comte de Rochambeau, 1725-1807

Whitridge, Arnold. Rochambeau. Macmillan 1965
Bkl A&Y—IndS(11-12)

Maurice, Comte de Saxe, 1696-1750

White, Jon Ewbank Manchip. Marshal of France: The Life and Times of Maurice, Comte de Saxe, 1696-1750. Rand McNally 1962
Bkl A

French—19th century

Alfred Dreyfus, 1859-1935

Chapman, Guy. The Dreyfus Case: A Reassessment. Reynal 1956
SCPL

Halasz, Nicholas. Captain Dreyfus: The Story of a Mass Hysteria. Simon & Schuster 1955
SCPL

Schechter, Betty. The Dreyfus Affair: A National Scandal. Houghton 1965
Bkl C&Y—IndS(9-10)

SOLDIERS

French—19th century—*Continued*

Charles Eugène, Vicomte de Fou-cauld, 1858-1916

Garnett, Emmeline. Charles de Fou-cauld. Farrar 1962
BY

Six, Jean François. Witness in the Desert: The Life of Charles de Foucauld; tr. by Lucie Noel. Macmillan 1965
Bkl A

Antoine Charles Louis, Comte de La-salle, 1775-1809

Johnson, David. The Proud Canaries. Sloane 1959
Bkl A

Napoleon I, Emperor of the French, 1769-1821

Aronson, Theo. The Golden Bees: The Story of the Bonapartes. N. Y. Graphic 1964
Bkl A—SCPL

Brett-James, Antony, ed. The Hundred Days: Napoleon's Last Campaign from Eye-Witness Accounts. St Martins 1964
Bkl A

Brookes, Dame Mabel (Emmerton). St. Helena Story. Dodd 1961
Bkl A

Butterfield, Herbert. Napoleon. Macmillan 1956
SCPL

Cammiade, Audrey. Napoleon. Roy 1963
IndJ(6-9)

Costain, Thomas Bertram. The Last Love. Doubleday 1963 (Fiction)
SCHS

Delderfield, Ronald Frederick. The Golden Millstones: Napoleon's Brothers and Sisters. Harper 1965
Bkl A

Delderfield, Ronald Frederick. Napoleon in Love. Little 1960
Bkl A

Delderfield, Ronald Frederick. Napoleon's Marshals. Chilton 1966
Bkl A&Y

Goodspeed, Donald James. Napoleon's Eighty Days. Houghton 1965
Bkl A—IndS(10-12)

Guerard, Albert Leon. Napoleon I: A Great Life in Brief. Knopf 1956
SCPL

Hales, Edward Elton Young. The Emperor and the Pope. Doubleday 1961
Bkl A

Herold, J. Christopher. Bonaparte in Egypt. Harper 1963
Bkl A—SCPL

Horizon Magazine. The Horizon Book of the Age of Napoleon, by J. Christopher Herold. Am. Heritage 1963
Bkl A—SCHS—SCPL

Komroff, Manuel. Napoleon. Messner 1954
BBHS—BBJH—BY—CC(7-9)—ESLC—JH—SCHS

Ludwig, Emil. Napoleon; tr. by Eden and Cedar Paul. Modern Lib., etc.
BBHS—CA—SCHS—SCPL

Maurois, André. Napoleon: A Pictorial Biography; tr. from the French by D. J. S. Thomson. Studio 1964
Bkl A&Y—IndS(9-12)

Mossiker, Frances. Napoleon and Josephine: The Biography of a Marriage. Simon & Schuster 1964
Bkl A

Raymond, John. The Marvelous March of Jean François. Doubleday 1965 (Fiction)
ESLC

Robbins, Ruth. The Emperor and the Drummer Boy. Parnassus Press 1962 (Fiction)
AB(4-7)—Bkl C(4-6)—ESLC

Saunders, Edith. The Hundred Days. Norton 1964
Bkl A

Stacton, David. The Bonapartes. Simon & Schuster 1966
Bkl A

Sutherland, John Patrick. Men of Waterloo. Prentice-Hall 1966
Bkl A

Thompson, James Matthew. Napoleon Bonaparte: His Rise and Fall. Oxford 1952
3000

Tolstoy, Leo. War and Peace. Grosset; Modern Lib.; Oxford; etc. (Fiction)
SCHS

French—20th century

Charles de Gaulle, 1890-

Aron, Robert. An Explanation of de Gaulle; tr. from the French by Marianne Sinclair. Harper 1966
Bkl A

Clark, Stanley. The Man Who Is France: The Story of General Charles de Gaulle. Dodd 1963
Bkl A&Y—SCHS—SCPL

Furniss, Edgar Stephenson. De Gaulle and the French Army: A Crisis in Civil-Military Relations. Twentieth Cent. Fund 1964
Bkl A

Gaulle, Charles de. War Memoirs: v. 1, The Call to Honour, 1940-1942; tr. by J. Griffin. Simon & Schuster 1955
SCPL

SOLDIERS

French—20th century

Charles de Gaulle—Continued

Gaulle, Charles de. War Memoirs: v. 2, Unity, 1942-1944; tr. from the French by Richard Howard. Simon & Schuster 1959
SCPL

Gaulle, Charles de. War Memoirs: v. 3, Salvation, 1944-1946; tr. from the French by Richard Howard. Simon & Schuster 1960
Bkl A

Harrity, Richard and Martin, Ralph G. Man of Destiny: De Gaulle of France. Duell 1961
Bkl A&Y

Hatch, Alden. The de Gaulle Nobody Knows: An Intimate Biography of Charles de Gaulle. Hawthorn 1960
Bkl A&Y

Lacouture, Jean. De Gaulle; tr. by Francis K. Price. New Am. Lib. 1966
Bkl A

Mauriac, François. De Gaulle; tr. from the French by Richard Howard. Doubleday 1966
Bkl A

Schoenbrun, David. The Three Lives of Charles de Gaulle. Atheneum 1966
Bkl A&Y

Sulzberger, Cyrus Leo. The Test: De Gaulle and Algeria. Harcourt 1962
Bkl A

Tournoux, Jean Raymond. Sons of France: Pétain and de Gaulle; tr. by Oliver Coburn. Viking 1966
Bkl A

Viansson-Ponté, Pierre. The King and His Court; tr. by Elaine P. Halperin. Houghton 1965
Bkl A

Viorst, Milton. Hostile Allies: FDR and Charles de Gaulle. Macmillan 1965
Bkl A

Werth, Alexander. De Gaulle: A Political Biography. Simon & Schuster 1966
Bkl A

Henri Philippe Pétain, 1856-1951

Tournoux, Jean Raymond. Sons of France: Pétain and de Gaulle; tr. by Oliver Coburn. Viking 1966
Bkl A

COLLECTIONS

Barnett, Corelli. The Swordbearers: Supreme Command in the First World War. Morrow 1964
Bkl A

German

COLLECTIONS

Liddell Hart, Basil Henry. German Generals Talk. Morrow 1948
SCPL

German—5th century

Attila, 406?-453

Costain, Thomas Bertram. The Darkness and the Dawn: A Novel. Doubleday 1959 (Fiction)
SCHS

Webb, Robert N. Attila, King of the Huns. Watts 1965
Bkl C(7-9)&Y

German—18th century

Friedrich Adolf, Freiherr von Riedesel, 1738-1800

Tharp, Louise (Hall). The Baroness and the General. Little 1962
Bkl A&Y

German—20th century

Adolf Ernst Heusinger, 1897-

Allen, Charles R. Heusinger of the Fourth Reich. Marzani & Munsell 1963
Bkl A

Reinhard Heydrich, 1904-1942

Burgess, Alan. Seven Men at Daybreak. Dutton 1960
Bkl A&Y

Wilhelm Keitel, 1882-1946

Keitel, Wilhelm. The Memoirs of Field-Marshal Keitel; ed. by Walter Gorlitz; tr. by David Irving. Stein & Day 1966
Bkl A

Erich Friedrich Wilhelm Ludendorff, 1865-1937

Goodspeed, Donald James. Ludendorff: Genius of World War I. Houghton 1966
Bkl A

COLLECTIONS

Barnett, Corelli. The Swordbearers: Supreme Command in the First World War. Morrow 1964
Bkl A

Helmuth von Moltke, 1848-1916

COLLECTIONS

Barnett, Corelli. The Swordbearers: Supreme Command in the First World War. Morrow 1964
Bkl A

SOLDIERS

German—20th century—*Continued*

Erwin Rommel, 1891-1944

Young, Desmond. Rommel, the Desert Fox. Harper 1951
GR—SCHS—SCPL

Fridolin von Senger und Etterlin, 1891-

Senger und Etterlin, Fridolin von. Neither Fear nor Hope; tr. from the German by George Malcolm. Dutton 1964
Bkl A

Greek—5th century B.C.

Alcibiades, 450?-404 B.C.

Marlowe, Stephen. The Shining. Trident Press 1963 (Fiction)
Bkl A

COLLECTIONS

Plutarch. Ten Famous Lives; the Dryden translations revised by Arthur Hugh Clough; ed. for young readers by Charles Robinson, Jr. Dutton 1962
Bkl C(7-10)&Y—BY—CC(7-9)—JH—SCHS—YR

Indian—20th century

Brij Mohan Kaul, 1912-

COLLECTIONS

Hangen, Welles. After Nehru, Who? Harcourt 1963
Bkl A

Kodendera Subayya Thimayya, 1906-1965

Evans, Humphrey. Thimayya of India: A Soldier's Life. Harcourt 1960
Bkl A

Irish—16th century

Grace O'Malley, 1530?-1600

Meyer, Edith Patterson. Pirate Queen: The Story of Ireland's Grania O'Malley in the Days of Queen Elizabeth. Little 1961 (Fiction)
Bkl C(7-10)

Italian—16th century

Gianpaolo Baglioni, 1471-1520

Durbin, Charles. The Mercenary: The Fortunes of Gianpaolo Baglioni of Perugia. Houghton 1963 (Fiction)
Bkl A

Italian—19th century

Gabriele D'Annunzio, 1863-1938

Winwar, Frances. Wingless Victory: A Biography of Gabriele D'Annunzio and Eleonora Duse. Harper 1956
SCPL

Giuseppe Garibaldi, 1807-1882

Trevelyan, George Macaulay. Garibaldi and the Making of Italy, June-November 1860. Longmans 1948
SCPL

Italian—20th century

Gabriele D'Annunzio, 1863-1938

Winwar, Frances. Wingless Victory: A Biography of Gabriele D'Annunzio and Eleonora Duse. Harper 1956
SCPL

Macedonian—4th century B.C.

Alexander the Great, 356-323 B.C.

Andrews, Mary (Evans). Hostage to Alexander. Longmans 1961 (Fiction)
Bkl C(7-9)&Y—JH

Burn, Andrew Robert. Alexander the Great and the Hellenistic Empire. Macmillan 1951
3000

Druon, Maurice. Alexander, the God: A Novel; tr. from the French by Humphrey Hare. Scribner 1961 (Fiction)
Bkl A

Gunther, John. Alexander the Great. Random House 1953
BBJH—BY—CC(5-7)—ESLC—JH—SCHS

Horizon Magazine. Alexander the Great, by Charles E. Mercer. Am. Heritage 1962
Bkl C(5-9)&Y—BY—CC(7-9)—JH—SCHS—YR

Lamb, Harold. Alexander of Macedon: The Journey to World's End. Doubleday 1946
BY—SCHS—SCPL

Marshall, Edison. The Conqueror. Doubleday 1962 (Fiction)
Bkl A

Robinson, Charles Alexander. Alexander the Great: Conqueror and Creator of a New World. Watts 1963
Bkl C(7-10)&Y—ESLC

Robinson, Charles Alexander. Alexander the Great: The Meeting of East and West in World Government and Brotherhood. Dutton 1947
SCPL

Stark, Freya Madeline. Alexander's Path from Caria to Cilicia. Harcourt 1958
SCPL

Stark, Freya Madeline. Lycian Shore. Harcourt 1956
SCPL

SOLDIERS—*Continued*

Mongolian—13th century

Genghis Khan, 1162-1227

Alberts, Frances Jacobs. A Gift for Genghis Khan. McGraw 1961 (Fiction)
Bkl C(4-6)

Baumann, Hans. Sons of the Steppe: The Story of How the Conqueror Genghis Khan Was Overcome. Walck 1958 (Fiction)
CC(7-9)—JH—SCHS

Lamb, Harold. Genghis Khan and the Mongol Horde. Random House 1954
BY—JH—SCHS

Lamb, Harold. Genghis Khan, the Emperor of All Men. Doubleday 1952
BBHS—SCPL—3000

Ritchie, Rita. The Golden Hawks of Genghis Khan. Dutton 1958 (Fiction)
BBJH—CC(7-9)—JH—SCHS

Ritchie, Rita. Secret Beyond the Mountains. Dutton 1960 (Fiction)
Bkl C(7-9)&Y—SCHS

Ritchie, Rita. The Year of the Horse. Dutton 1957 (Fiction)
CC(7-9)

COLLECTIONS

Duvoisin, Roger. They Put Out to Sea: The Story of the Map. Knopf 1943
CC(5-7)—ESLC

Lucas, Mary Seymour. Vast Horizons. Viking 1943
SCHS

Kublai Khan, 1216-1294

Silverberg, Robert. Kublai Khan, Lord of Xanadu. Bobbs 1966
Bkl C(7-9)&Y

Mongolian—14th century

Tamerlane, 1336-1405

COLLECTIONS

Lucas, Mary Seymour. Vast Horizons. Viking 1943
SCHS

New Zealand—20th century

Charles Hazlitt Upham, 1908-

Sandford, Kenneth. Mark of the Lion: The Story of Capt. Charles Upham, V.C. and Bar. Washburn 1963
Bkl A—IndS(10-12)

Norwegian—20th century

Odd Nansen, 1901-

Nansen, Odd. From Day to Day; tr. by Katherine John. Putnam 1949
SCPL

Gunnar Fridtjof Thurmann Sønsteby, ?

Sønsteby, Gunnar Fridtjof Thurmann. Report from No. 24; ed. by Maurice Michael. Stuart 1966
Bkl A&Y

Roman—3rd century B.C.

Quintus Maximus Verrucosus Fabius, ?-203 B.C.

COLLECTIONS

Plutarch. Ten Famous Lives; the Dryden translation revised by Arthur Hugh Clough; ed. for young readers by Charles Robinson, Jr. Dutton 1962
Bkl C(7-10)&Y—BY—CC(7-9)—JH—SCHS—YR

Roman—1st century B.C.

Caius Julius Caesar, 100-44 B.C.

Anderson, Paul L. Swords in the North. Biblo & Tannen 1957 (Fiction)
SCHS

Coolidge, Olivia. Caesar's Gallic War. Houghton 1961
CC(7-9)—ESLC—JH—SCHS

Duggan, Alfred Leo. Julius Caesar: A Great Life in Brief. Knopf 1955
BBHS—SCPL—3000

Fuller, John Frederick Charles. Julius Caesar: Man, Soldier, and Tyrant. Rutgers Univ. 1965
Bkl A

Gunther, John. Julius Caesar. Random House 1959
Bkl C(5-9)&Y—CC(6-9)—ESLC—JH—SCHS

Horizon Magazine. Caesar, by Irwin Isenberg. Am Heritage 1964
Bkl C(6-9)&Y—CC—ESLC—IndS(9-10)—JH

Komroff, Manuel. Julius Caesar. Messner 1955
BBJH—BY—CC(7-9)—JH—SCHS

Shakespeare, William. Julius Caesar. (Play)
SCHS

Shaw, George Bernard. Caesar and Cleopatra. Dodd 1948 (Play)
SCHS

Warner, Rex. Imperial Caesar. Little 1960 (Fiction)
Bkl A

Warner, Rex. The Young Caesar. Little 1958 (Fiction)
SCHS

Roman—1st century

Agricola, 37-93 A.D.

Tacitus. The Life of Agricola.
CA

SOLDIERS—_Continued_

Roman—6th century

Belisarius, 505?-565

Downey, Glanville. Belisarius. Dutton 1960
YR

Russian—18th century

Aleksandr Vasilievich Suvorov, 1729-1800

Longworth, Philip. The Art of Victory: The Life and Achievements of Field-Marshal Suvorov, 1729-1800. Holt 1966
Bkl A

Russian—19th century

Boris Uxkull, 1793-1870

Uxkull, Boris. Arms and the Woman: The Intimate Journal of a Baltic Nobleman in the Napoleonic Wars; tr. by Joel Carmichael. Macmillan 1966
Bkl A

Russian—20th century

Aleksandr Vassil'evich Gorbatov, 1892-

Gorbatov, Aleksandr Vassil'evich. Years Off My Life: The Memoirs of General of the Soviet Army; tr. by Gordon Clough and Anthony Cash. Norton 1965
Bkl A

Scottish—13th century

Sir William Wallace, 1272?-1305

COLLECTIONS

Sutcliff, Rosemary. Heroes and History. Putnam 1966
Bkl C(7-10)&Y

Scottish—14th century

Robert Bruce, King of Scotland, 1274-1329

Baker, Nina Brown. Robert Bruce, King of Scots. Vanguard 1948
BY

Porter, Jane. Scottish Chiefs; ed. by Kate Douglas Wiggin and Nora C. Wyeth. Scribner 1921 (Fiction)
CC(7-9)—JH—SCHS

Stephens, Peter John. Outlaw King: The Story of Robert the Bruce. Atheneum 1964 (Fiction)
ESLC

Scottish—17th century

James Graham, 1st Marquis of Montrose, 1612-1650

COLLECTIONS

Sutcliff, Rosemary. Heroes and History. Putnam 1966
Bkl C(7-10)&Y

South American—19th century

Simón Bolívar, 1783-1830

Baker, Nina (Brown). He Wouldn't Be King: The Story of Simón Bolívar. Vanguard 1941
BY—CC(7-9)—JH—SCHS—YR

Frank, W. D. Birth of a World: Bolivar in Terms of His Peoples. Houghton 1951
SCPL

Van Loon, Hendrik Willem. Fighters for Freedom: Jefferson and Bolivar. Dodd 1962
Bkl C(7-12)&Y

Webb, Robert N. Simón Bolívar, the Liberator. Watts 1966
Bkl Y(7-10)&C—ESLC

Whitridge, Arnold. Simón Bolívar, the Great Liberator. Random House 1954
JH—SCHS

COLLECTIONS

Bailey, Bernadine (Freeman). Famous Latin-American Liberators. Dodd 1960
Bkl C(6-9)&Y—ESLC—SCHS

Larson, Egon. Men Who Fought for Freedom. Roy 1959
AB

José de San Martín, 1778-1850

COLLECTIONS

Bailey, Bernadine (Freeman). Famous Latin-American Liberators. Dodd 1960
Bkl C(6-9)&Y—ESLC—SCHS

Antonio José de Sucre, 1795-1830

COLLECTIONS

Bailey, Bernadine (Freeman). Famous Latin-American Liberators. Dodd 1960
Bkl C(6-9)&Y—ESLC—SCHS

Spanish—8th century

'Abd al-Rahmān I, Caliph of Cordova, 731-788

Fon Eisen, Anthony. The Prince of Omeya. World 1964 (Fiction)
Bkl Y&C—JH

Spanish—11th century

El Cid Campeador, 1040-1099

Goldston, Robert C. The Legend of the Cid. Bobbs 1963
Bkl C(5-8)—ESLC—JH

SOLDIERS

Spanish—11th century

El Cid Campeador—Continued

Sherwood, Merriam. The Tale of the Warrior Lord: El Cantar de Mio Cid. Longmans 1930
SCHS

Spanish—16th century

Bernal Díaz del Castillo, 1492-1581

Cerwin, Herbert. Bernal Díaz, Historian of the Conquest. Univ. of Okla. 1963
Bkl A

Turkish—20th century

Kamâl Atatürk, 1881-1938

Balfour, Patrick. Ataturk: A Biography of Mustafa Kemal, Father of Modern Turkey, by Lord Kinross. Morrow 1964
Bkl A—IndS(12)
Lengyel, Emil. They Called Him Ataturk. Day 1962
AB(7-11)—Bkl C(6-9)&Y—BY

Venezuelan—19th century

Francisco de Miranda, 1750?-1816

COLLECTIONS

Bailey, Bernadine (Freeman). Famous Latin-American Liberators. Dodd 1960
Bkl C(6-9)&Y—ESLC—SCHS

Venezuelan—20th century

Thomas Russell Ybarra, 1880-

Ybarra, Thomas Russell. Young Man of Caracas. Washburn 1941
SCPL

SONG WRITERS

See Composers

SPEEDBOAT RACERS

See Automobile Racers

SPIES

See also Intelligence Agents

COLLECTIONS

Wighton, Charles. The World's Greatest Spies. Taplinger 1966
Bkl A&Y
Rudolf Abel; Klaus Fuchs; Ruth Kuehn; Mata Hari; Richard Sorge; and others
Bakeless, Katherine and Bakeless, John. Spies of the Revolution. Lippincott 1962
ESLC

Bakeless, John. Turncoats, Traitors, and Heroes. Lippincott 1959
SCHS
John André; Benedict Arnold; Lydia Darragh; Nathan Hale; Henry Lee; Paul Revere; and others
Foley, Rae. Famous American Spies. Dodd 1962
Bkl C(6-9)—ESLC—JH
Kane, Harnett Thomas. Spies for the Blue and Gray. Hanover House 1954
SCPL

American—18th century

Lydia (Barrington) Darragh, 1728?-1789

COLLECTIONS

Bakeless, John. Turncoats, Traitors, and Heroes. Lippincott 1959
SCHS

Nathan Hale, 1755-1776

COLLECTIONS

Bakeless, John. Turncoats, Traitors, and Heroes. Lippincott 1959
SCHS

John Honeyman, ?

Wise, William. The Spy and General Washington. Dutton 1965
CC(4-6)—ESLC

American—19th century

Rose (O'Neal) Greenhow, 1817-1864

Nolan, Jeannette (Covert). Spy for the Confederacy: Rose O'Neal Greenhow. Messner 1960
AB(8up)—Bkl C(7-9)&Y
Ross, Ishbel. Rebel Rose: Life of Rose O'Neal Greenhow, Confederate Spy. Harper 1954
SCPL

Thomas Henry Hines, 1838-1898

Horan, James David. Confederate Agent: A Discovery in History. Crown 1954
SCPL

Dutch—20th century

Mata Hari, 1876-1917

COLLECTIONS

Wighton, Charles. The World's Greatest Spies. Taplinger 1966
Bkl A&Y

English—18th century

John André, 1751-1780

Flexner, James Thomas. The Traitor and the Spy: Benedict Arnold and John André. Harcourt 1953
SCPL

SPIES

English—18th century

John André—Continued

COLLECTIONS

Bakeless, John. Turncoats, Traitors, and Heroes. Lippincott 1959
SCHS

English—20th century

Klaus Emil Julius Fuchs, 1911-

COLLECTIONS

Moorehead, Alan. The Traitors. Harper 1963
Bkl A

Wighton, Charles. The World's Greatest Spies. Taplinger 1966
Bkl A&Y

French—20th century

Michel Hollard, ?

Martelli, George. The Man Who Saved London. Doubleday 1961
Bkl A&Y

German—20th century

Ruth Kuehn, ?

COLLECTIONS

Wighton, Charles. The World's Greatest Spies. Taplinger 1966
Bkl A&Y

Richard Sorge, 1895-1944

Johnson, Chalmers A. An Instance of Treason: Ozaki Hotsumi and the Sorge Spy Ring. Stanford Univ. 1964
Bkl A

COLLECTIONS

Wighton, Charles. The World's Greatest Spies. Taplinger 1966
Bkl A&Y

Hungarian—20th century

Edith Bone, 1889-

Bone, Edith. 7 Years' Solitary. Harcourt 1957
SCPL

Japanese—20th century

Ozaki Hatsumi, 1901-1944

Johnson, Chalmers A. An Instance of Treason: Ozaki Hatsumi and the Sorge Spy Ring. Stanford Univ. 1964
Bkl A

Polish—20th century

Pawel Monat, ?

Monat, Pawel and Dille, John. Spy in the U.S. Harper 1962
Bkl A&Y—BY

Russian—20th century

Rudolf Ivanovich Abel, 1902-

Donovan, James Britt. Strangers on a Bridge: The Case of Colonel Abel. Atheneum 1964
Bkl A&Y—IndS(10-12)

Swedish—20th century

Stig Wennerström, 1906-

Rönblom, Hans Krister. The Spy Without a Country; tr. from the Swedish by Joan Bulman. Coward-McCann 1965
Bkl A

Whiteside, Thomas. An Agent in Place. Viking 1966
Bkl A

SPORTS EDITORS

See Sportswriters

SPORTSMEN

English—20th century

Hugh Cecil Lowther, 5th Earl of Lonsdale, 1857-1944

Sutherland, Douglas. The Yellow Earl: The Life of Hugh Lowther, 5th Earl of Lonsdale, K.G., G.C.V.O., 1857-1944. Coward-McCann 1966
Bkl A

SPORTSWRITERS

American—20th century

Grantland Rice, 1880-1954

Rice, Grantland. The Tumult and the Shouting: My Life in Sport. Barnes 1954
SCHS

Walter Wellesley ("Red") Smith, 1905-

COLLECTIONS

Lewis, Mildred and Lewis, Milton. Famous Modern Newspaper Writers. Dodd 1962
Bkl Y&C

John Roberts Tunis, 1889-

Tunis, John Roberts. A Measure of Independence. Atheneum 1964
Bkl A&Y

Stanley Woodward, 1895-1965

Woodward, Stanley. Paper Tiger. Atheneum 1964
Bkl A

STADHOLDERS

Dutch—16th century

William I (William the Silent), 1533-1584

Wedgwood, Cicely Veronica. William the Silent: William of Nassau, Prince of Orange, 1533-1584. Yale Univ. 1944
SCPL

STAGE DESIGNERS

See Scenic Designers

STAINED GLASS PAINTERS

See Glass Painters

STATESMEN

See also Colonists; Czars; Emperors; Kings; Presidents; Princes; Queens; Sultans

COLLECTIONS

Acheson, Dean Gooderham. Sketches from Life of Men I Have Known. Harper 1961
Bkl A&Y—SCPL
Konrad Adenauer; Ernest Bevin; Sir Winston Churchill; Lucius Clay; Sir Anthony Eden; George Marshall; Antonio Salazar; Robert Schuman; Arthur Vandenburg; Andrei Vishinsky; and others

Bliven, Bruce. The World Changers. Day 1965
Bkl A&Y—IndS(10-12)
Chiang Kai-shek; Sir Winston Churchill; Mohandas Gandhi; Hirohito; Adolf Hitler; Benito Mussolini; Franklin Delano Roosevelt; Joseph Stalin

Carr, Albert. Men of Power: A Book of Dictators. Viking 1956
BBJH—BY—CC(7-9)—JH—SCHS

Dean, Vera (Micheles). Builders of Emerging Nations. Holt 1961
Bkl A&Y—SCHS—SCPL

Donovan, Frank. Famous Twentieth Century Leaders. Dodd 1964
Bkl C(7-9)&Y—ESLC

Farjeon, Eleanor. Mighty Men. Appleton 1926
CC(4-6)—ESLC

Gunther, John. Procession. Harper 1965
Bkl A&Y

Hanna, Willard Anderson. Eight Nation Makers: Southeast Asia's Charismatic Statesmen. St Martins 1964
Bkl A&Y
Ngo-dinh-Diem and others

Kenworthy, Leonard S. Leaders of New Nations. Doubleday 1959
Bkl A&Y&C—SCHS

Larson, Egon. Men Who Fought for Freedom. Roy 1959
AB
Simón Bolívar; Mohandas Gandhi; Marquis de Lafayette; William Penn; Sun Yat-sen; and others

Lengyel, Emil. From Prison to Power. Follett 1964
Bkl A&Y
Ahmed Ben Bella; Habib ben Ali Bourguiba; Wladyslaw Gomulka; János Kádár; Jomo Kenyatta; Archbishop Makarios III; Jawaharlal Nehru; Kwame Nkrumah; Sukarno; Josip Broz Tito

Olcott, Frances Jenkins, ed. Good Stories for Great Birthdays, Arranged for Storytelling and Reading Aloud and for the Children's Own Reading. Houghton 1922
CC

Plutarch. Everybody's Plutarch; ed. by Raymond T. Bond. Dodd 1962
Bkl A

Plutarch. Lives of the Noble Grecians and Romans; tr. by John Dryden and revised by Arthur Hugh Clough. Modern Lib., etc.
GR—SCHS—SCPL—3000

Plutarch. Ten Famous Lives; the Dryden translation revised by Arthur Hugh Clough; ed. for young readers by Charles Robinson, Jr. Dutton 1962
Bkl C(7-10)&Y—BY—CC(7-9)—JH—SCHS—YR
Alcibiades; Alexander the Great; Marcus Antonius; Caius Julius Caesar; Marcus Porcius Cato; Marcus Cicero; Demosthenes; Quintus Fabius; Pericles; Themistocles

Smith, Bradford. Men of Peace. Lippincott 1964
Bkl A&Y

Sterling Publishing Co. Picture Book of New World Leaders. Sterling 1962
AB(6up)

Stringer, William H. Summit Roundup: Profiles of 21 World Leaders. Longmans 1959
Bkl A

Webb, Robert N. Leaders of Our Time, Series 1. Watts 1964
ESLC—JH

Webb, Robert N. Leaders of Our Time, Series 2. Watts 1965
Bkl C(6-9)&Y—JH

African

COLLECTIONS

Italiaander, Rolf. The New Leaders of Africa; tr. from the German by James McGovern. Prentice-Hall 1961
Bkl A&Y—SCPL

Kaula, Edna Mason. Leaders of the New Africa. World 1966
Bkl C(6-10)—ESLC
Haile Selassie I; Jomo Kenyatta; Albert Luthuli; and others

STATESMEN

African—*Continued*

Lens, Sidney. Africa—Awakening Giant. Putnam 1962
CC(5-7)—ESLC

Melady, Thomas P. Profiles of African Leaders. Macmillan 1961
Bkl A&Y—SCPL
Sir Abubakar Balewa; Haile Selassie I; Félix Houphouet-Boigny; Thomas Joseph Mboya; Kwame Nkrumah; Julius Nyerere; Léopold Senghor; Sékou Touré; William Tubman

Algerian—20th century

Ahmed Ben Bella, 1916-

COLLECTIONS

Lengyel, Emil. From Prison to Power. Follett 1964
Bkl A&Y

American

COLLECTIONS

Barker, Shirley. Builders of New England. Dodd 1965
Bkl A&Y

Benét, Rosemary (Carr) and Benét, Stephen Vincent. A Book of Americans. Rinehart 1952 (Poem)
BBEL(6-8)—BBJH—CC(5-7)—ESLC—JH—SCPL

Bowen, Catherine (Drinker). Miracle at Philadelphia: The Story of the Constitutional Convention, May to September 1787. Little 1966
Bkl A&Y
Alexander Hamilton; James Madison; George Mason; Edmund Randolph; James Wilson; and others

Brown, John Mason. Through These Men: Some Aspects of Our Passing History. Harper 1956
SCPL
Dwight Eisenhower; Adlai Stevenson; Harry S. Truman; and others

Coit, Margaret Louise. The Fight for Union. Houghton 1961
CC(6-7)—ESLC
John Calhoun; Henry Clay; Samuel Houston; Andrew Jackson; Thomas Jefferson; Daniel Webster; and others

Daugherty, Sonia. Ten Brave Men: Makers of the American Way. Lippincott 1951
SCHS
Samuel Adams; William Bradford; Benjamin Franklin; Patrick Henry; Andrew Jackson; Thomas Jefferson; John Paul Jones; Abraham Lincoln; George Washington; Roger Williams

Dos Passos, John Roderigo. Men Who Made the Nation. Doubleday 1957
SCPL
John Adams; Benjamin Franklin; Alexander Hamilton; Thomas Jefferson; James Madison; John Marshall; James Monroe; Gouverneur Morris; George Washington; and others

Douty, Esther (Morris). Under the New Roof: Five Patriots of the Young Republic. Rand McNally 1965
Bkl Y&C
Richard Allen; Joel Barlow; Albert Gallatin; David Rittenhouse; Susanna (Haswell) Rowson

The Evening Star, Washington, D.C. The New Frontiersmen: Profiles of the Men Around Kennedy. Public Affairs Press 1961
Bkl A

Fisher, Dorothy Canfield. And Long Remember: Some Great Americans Who Have Helped Me. McGraw 1959
JH

Fishwick, Marshall William. Gentlemen of Virginia. Dodd 1961
Bkl A&Y

Foley, Rae. Famous Makers of America. Dodd 1963
ESLC

Hess, Stephen. America's Political Dynasties from Adams to Kennedy. Doubleday 1966
Bkl A&Y

Hofstadter, Richard. American Political Tradition and the Men Who Made It. Knopf 1948
SCPL
William Jennings Bryan; John Calhoun; Herbert Hoover; Andrew Jackson; Thomas Jefferson; Abraham Lincoln; Wendell Phillips; Franklin Delano Roosevelt; Theodore Roosevelt; Woodrow Wilson

Holbrook, Stewart Hall. Lost Men of American History. Macmillan 1946
BBHS—SCPL

Hoyt, Edwin P. Lost Statesmen. Reilly & Lee 1961
BY

Kennedy, John Fitzgerald. Profiles in Courage. Harper 1964
BBHS—Bkl A—BY—CC—GR—JH—SCHS—SCPL—3000

Kennedy, John Fitzgerald. Profiles in Courage; young readers edition abridged. Harper 1964
CC(5-7)—ESLC—JH—SCHS

Koenig, Louis William. The Invisible Presidency. Rinehart 1960
Bkl A
Sherman Adams; Thomas Corcoran; Alexander Hamilton; Harry Hopkins; Edward Mandell House; William Loeb; Martin Van Buren

STATESMEN

American—Continued

Lawson, Don. Famous American Political Families. Abelard-Schuman 1965
Bkl C(7-12)&Y
John Adams; Benjamin Harrison; John Fitzgerald Kennedy; Robert Marion LaFollette; Huey Long; Franklin Delano Roosevelt; William Howard Taft

McGee, Dorothy Horton. Famous Signers of the Declaration. Dodd 1955
SCHS

Mooney, Booth. Mr. Speaker: Four Men Who Shaped the United States House of Representatives. Follett 1964
Bkl A&Y
Joseph Cannon; Henry Clay; Sam Rayburn; Thomas Reed

Morris, Richard B. and Woodress, James, eds. Voices from America's Past. 3v. Dutton 1963
ESLC

Opotowsky, Stan. The Kennedy Government. Dutton 1961
Bkl A&Y

Padover, Saul K. The Genius of America: Men Whose Ideas Shaped Our Civilization. McGraw 1960
SCPL

Parlin, John. Patriots' Days. Garrard 1964
ESLC
Thomas Jefferson; John Fitzgerald Kennedy; Robert Edward Lee; Abraham Lincoln; Franklin Delano Roosevelt; George Washington

Roper, Elmo Burns. You and Your Leaders: Their Actions and Your Reactions, 1936-1956. Morrow 1957
SCPL
Thomas Dewey; Dwight Eisenhower; Douglas MacArthur; George Marshall; Franklin Delano Roosevelt; Adlai Stevenson; Robert Taft; Harry S. Truman; Wendell Willkie

Ross, George E. Know Your Declaration of Independence and the 56 Signers. Rand McNally 1963
CC(5-7)—ESLC

Salter, John Thomas. American Politician. Univ. of N. C. 1938
SCPL

Sevareid, Eric, ed. Candidates 1960: Behind the Headlines in the Presidential Race. Basic Bks 1959
SCPL
Hubert Humphrey; Lyndon Johnson; John Fitzgerald Kennedy; Richard Nixon; Nelson Rockefeller; Adlai Stevenson; Stuart Symington

Severn, Bill and Severn, Sue. The State Makers. Putnam 1963
ESLC

Stone, Irving. They Also Ran: The Story of the Men Who Were Defeated for the Presidency. Doubleday 1945
SCHS—SCPL

Tanzer, Lester, ed. The Kennedy Circle. Luce 1961
Bkl A

United States Civil Service Commission. Official Register of the United States. U.S. Govt Printing Office, annual since 1925
SCPL

United States Congress. Biographical Directory of the American Congress, 1774-1961. U.S. Govt Printing Office 1961
SCPL

United States Congress. Official Congressional Directory. U.S. Govt Printing Office, published once during each Congressional session
ESLC—SCPL

Whitney, David C. Founders of Freedom in America. Ferguson 1965
CC
Patrick Henry; James Otis; and others

American—17th century

William Penn, 1644-1718

COLLECTIONS

Larson, Egon. Men Who Fought for Freedom. Roy 1959
AB

American—18th century

John Quincy Adams, 1767-1848

Clarke, Fred G. John Quincy Adams. Collier Bks 1966
Bkl C(7-10)&Y

Samuel Adams, 1722-1803

Alderman, Clifford Lindsey. Samuel Adams, Son of Liberty. Holt 1961
Bkl C(6-9)&Y—CC(7-9)—ESLC—JH—YR

Beach, Stewart. Samuel Adams: The Fateful Years, 1764-1776. Dodd 1965
Bkl A&Y

Hall-Quest, Olga (Wilbourne). Guardians of Liberty: Sam Adams and John Hancock. Dutton 1963
AB(5up)—Bkl C(6-9)&Y—CC(6-9)—ESLC—JH—YR

COLLECTIONS

Daugherty, Sonia. Ten Brave Men: Makers of the American Way. Lippincott 1951
SCHS

Joel Barlow, 1754-1812

COLLECTIONS

Douty, Esther (Morris). Under the New Roof: Five Patriots of the Young Republic. Rand McNally 1965
Bkl Y&C

STATESMEN

American—18th century—*Continued*

Aaron Burr, 1756-1836

Crouse, Anna Erskine and Crouse, Russel. Alexander Hamilton and Aaron Burr: Their Lives, Their Times, Their Duel. Random House 1958
AB(7-9)—CC(6-9)—JH—SCHS

Benjamin Franklin, 1706-1790

Aldridge, Alfred Owen. Benjamin Franklin, Philosopher & Man. Lippincott 1965
Bkl A&Y

Amacher, Richard E. Benjamin Franklin. Twayne 1962
Bkl A&Y

American Heritage. The Many Worlds of Benjamin Franklin, by Frank R. Donovan. Am. Heritage 1963
Bkl C(6-9)&Y—CC(6-9)—ESLC—IndJ(6-9) —JH—SCHS—YR

Aulaire, Ingrid d' and Aulaire, Edgar Parin d'. Benjamin Franklin. Doubleday 1950
BBEL—CC(3-5)—ESLC

Cohen, I. B. Benjamin Franklin: His Contribution to the American Tradition. Bobbs 1953
SCPL

Conner, Paul W. Poor Richard's Politicks: Benjamin Franklin and His New American Order. Oxford 1965
Bkl A

Cousins, Margaret. Ben Franklin of Old Philadelphia. Random House 1952
CC(4-7)—SCHS

Daugherty, James. Poor Richard. Viking 1941
BBEL—BBJH—CC(7-9)—JH—SCHS

Eaton, Jeanette. That Lively Man, Ben Franklin. Morrow 1948
BBJH—CC(5-7)—JH—SCHS

Franklin, Benjamin. Autobiography. Dutton; Harper; Houghton; Modern Lib.; etc.
BY—CA—CC(7-9)—GR—SCHS—SCPL—3000

Franklin, Benjamin. The Autobiography, and Other Writings of Benjamin Franklin. Dodd 1963
SCHS

Franklin, Benjamin. The Autobiography of Benjamin Franklin; ed. by Leonard W. Labaree. Yale Univ. 1964
JH—SCPL

Franklin, Benjamin. Autobiographical Writings; ed. by Carl Van Doren. Viking 1945
SCPL

Franklin, Benjamin. The Benjamin Franklin Papers; ed. by Frank Donovan. Dodd 1962
Bkl A&Y—SCHS

Graves, Charles P. Benjamin Franklin. Garrard 1960
AB(3-6)

Judson, Clara (Ingram). Benjamin Franklin. Follett 1957
AB(5-7)—BBEL(6-8)—BBJH—CC(5-7)— ESLC—JH

Lawson, Robert. Ben and Me: A New and Astonishing Life of Benjamin Franklin as Written by His Good Mouse Amos. Little 1939 (Fiction)
BBEL—BBJH—CC(5-9)—ESLC—JH—SCHS

McKown, Robin. Benjamin Franklin. Putnam 1963
Bkl C(7-9)&Y

Sandrich, Mark. Ben Franklin in Paris; lyrics by Sidney Michaels. Random House 1965 (Play)
Bkl A

Sayre, Robert F. The Examined Self: Benjamin Franklin, Henry Adams, Henry James. Princeton Univ. 1964
Bkl A

Van Doren, Carl Clinton. Benjamin Franklin. Viking 1956
BBHS—SCHS—SCPL—3000

Weir, Ruth Cromer. Benjamin Franklin, Printer and Patriot. Abingdon 1955
ESLC

COLLECTIONS

Daugherty, Sonia. Ten Brave Men: Makers of the American Way. Lippincott 1951
SCHS

Dos Passos, John Roderigo. Men Who Made the Nation. Doubleday 1957
SCPL

Albert Gallatin, 1761-1849

Walters, Raymond. Albert Gallatin: Jeffersonian Financier and Diplomat. Macmillan 1957
SCPL

COLLECTIONS

Douty, Esther (Morris). Under the New Roof: Five Patriots of the Young Republic. Rand McNally 1965
Bkl Y&C

Alexander Hamilton, 1757-1804

Atherton, Gertrude. The Conqueror: A Dramatized Biography of Alexander Hamilton. Lippincott 1943 (Fiction)
SCHS

Bowers, Claude Gernade. Jefferson and Hamilton: The Struggle for Democracy in America. Houghton 1925
SCHS—SCPL

STATESMEN

American—18th century

Alexander Hamilton—Continued

Crouse, Anna Erskine and Crouse, Russel. Alexander Hamilton and Aaron Burr: Their Lives, Their Times, Their Duel. Random House 1958
AB(7-9)—CC(6-9)—ESLC—JH—SCHS

Hamilton, Alexander. Mind of Alexander Hamilton; ed. by S. K. Padover. Harper 1958
SCPL

Konefsky, Samuel Joseph. John Marshall and Alexander Hamilton, Architects of the American Constitution. Macmillan 1964
Bkl A

Miller, John C. Alexander Hamilton: Portrait in Paradox. Harper 1959
Bkl A—SCPL

Mitchell, Broadus. Alexander Hamilton: v. 1, Youth to Maturity, 1755-1788. Macmillan 1957
SCPL

Mitchell, Broadus. Alexander Hamilton: v. 2, The National Adventure, 1788-1804. Macmillan 1962
SCPL

Orrmont, Arthur. The Amazing Alexander Hamilton. Messner 1964
Bkl C(7-9)&Y—YR

Rossiter, Clinton Lawrence. Alexander Hamilton and the Constitution. Harcourt 1964
Bkl A—IndS(12)

Schachner, Nathan. Alexander Hamilton, Nation Builder. McGraw 1952
SCHS—SCPL—3000

Wise, William. Alexander Hamilton. Putnam 1963
Bkl C(7-10)&Y—ESLC

COLLECTIONS

Bowen, Catherine (Drinker). Miracle at Philadelphia: The Story of the Constitutional Convention, May to September 1787. Little 1966
Bkl A&Y

Dos Passos, John Roderigo. Men Who Made the Nation. Doubleday 1957
SCPL

Fanning, Leonard M. Titans of Business. Lippincott 1964
Bkl C(7-9)&Y—JH—SCHS

Koenig, Louis William. The Invisible Presidency. Rinehart 1960
Bkl A

John Hancock, 1737-1793

Gerson, Noel Bertram. Yankee Doodle Dandy: A Biographical Novel of John Hancock. Doubleday 1965 (Fiction)
Bkl A&Y

Hall-Quest, Olga (Wilbourne). Guardians of Liberty: Sam Adams and John Hancock. Dutton 1963
AB(5up)—Bkl C(6-9)&Y—CC(6-9)—ESLC —JH—YR

Nolan, Jeannette (Covert). John Hancock: Friend of Freedom. Houghton 1966
ESLC

Wagner, Frederick. Patriot's Choice: The Story of John Hancock. Dodd 1964
Bkl Y&C—ESLC—JH

Patrick Henry, 1736-1799

Campion, Nardi (Reeder). Patrick Henry: Firebrand of the Revolution. Little 1961
Bkl C(5-8)—CC(5-7)—ESLC—JH—YR

Carson, Julia M. Son of Thunder: Patrick Henry. Longmans 1945
CC(7-9)—JH—SCHS

Gerson, Noel Bertram. Give Me Liberty: A Novel of Patrick Henry. Doubleday 1966 (Fiction)
Bkl A&Y

Meade, Robert Douthat. Patrick Henry: Patriot in the Making. Lippincott 1957
SCPL

COLLECTIONS

Daugherty, Sonia. Ten Brave Men: Makers of the American Way. Lippincott 1951
SCHS

Whitney, David C. Founders of Freedom in America. Ferguson 1965
CC

Thomas Jefferson, 1743-1826

Bowers, Claude Gernade. Young Jefferson, 1743-1789. Houghton 1945
SCHS—SCPL

Malone, Dumas. Jefferson and His Time: v. 1, Jefferson the Virginian, 1743-1784. Little 1948
CA—SCPL

Malone, Dumas. Jefferson and His Time: v. 2, Jefferson and the Rights of Man, 1784-1792. Little 1951
CA—SCPL

Wibberley, Leonard Patrick O'Connor. The Gales of Spring: Thomas Jefferson—The Years 1789-1801. Ariel Bks 1965
Bkl C(7-9)&Y—ESLC

Wibberley, Leonard Patrick O'Connor. A Dawn in the Trees: Thomas Jefferson—The Years 1776-1789. Ariel Bks 1964
Bkl C(7-9)&Y—ESLC—IndJ(6-9)—JH

STATESMEN

American—18th century

Thomas Jefferson—Continued

Wibberley, Leonard Patrick O'Connor. Young Man from the Piedmont: The Youth of Thomas Jefferson. Farrar 1963
Bkl C(7-9)&Y—CC(6-9)—ESLC—IndJ(6-9) —JH—YR

Henry ("Light-Horse Harry") Lee, 1756-1818

Gerson, Noel Bertram. Light-Horse Harry: A Biography of Washington's Great Cavalryman, General Henry Lee. Doubleday 1966
Bkl A&Y

Lewis Littlepage, 1762-1802

Davis, Curtis Carroll. The King's Chevalier: A Biography of Lewis Littlepage. Bobbs 1961
Bkl A

James Madison, 1751-1836

Brant, Irving. James Madison. 6v. Bobbs 1941-1961
Bkl A—SCPL

Madison, James. The Papers of James Madison; ed. by W. T. Hutchinson and W. M. E. Rachel. 2v. Univ. of Chicago 1962
SCPL

Steinberg, Albert. James Madison. Putnam 1965
Bkl C(7-9)&Y—IndJ(6-9)

Wilkie, Katharine E. and Moseley, Elizabeth R. Father of the Constitution: James Madison. Messner 1963
AB(7up)

COLLECTIONS

Bowen, Catherine (Drinker). Miracle at Philadelphia: The Story of the Constitutional Convention, May to September 1787. Little 1966
Bkl A&Y

George Mason, 1725-1792

Rutland, Robert A. George Mason, Reluctant Statesman. Holt 1961
YR

COLLECTIONS

Bowen, Catherine (Drinker). Miracle at Philadelphia: The Story of the Constitutional Convention, May to September 1787. Little 1966
Bkl A&Y

James Monroe, 1758-1831

COLLECTIONS

Dos Passos, John Roderigo. Men Who Made the Nation. Doubleday 1957
SCPL

Gouverneur Morris, 1752-1816

COLLECTIONS

Dos Passos, John Roderigo. Men Who Made the Nation. Doubleday 1957
SCPL

James Otis, 1725-1783

COLLECTIONS

Whitney, David C. Founders of Freedom in America. Ferguson 1965
CC

Edmund Jennings Randolph, 1753-1813

COLLECTIONS

Bowen, Catherine (Drinker). Miracle at Philadelphia: The Story of the Constitutional Convention, May to September 1787. Little 1966
Bkl A&Y

Paul Revere, 1735-1818

Fisher, Dorothy Canfield. Paul Revere and the Minute Men. Random House 1950
BBEL—CC(6-8)—ESLC—JH—SCHS

Forbes, Esther. America's Paul Revere. Houghton 1946
AB(5-9)—BBEL(5-8)—BBJH—CC(5-9)— ESLC—JH—SCHS—YR

Forbes, Esther. Paul Revere and the World He Lived In. Houghton 1942
BBHS—BY—SCHS—SCPL

Graves, Charles P. Paul Revere. Garrard 1964
AB(4-7)

Kelly, Regina (Zimmerman). Paul Revere: Colonial Craftsman. Houghton 1963
AB(5-9)—Bkl C(4-6)—IndJ(4-6)

Lawson, Robert. Mr. Revere and I. Little 1953 (Fiction)
BBEL—BBJH—CC(6-8)—ESLC—JH—SCHS

Longfellow, Henry Wadsworth. Paul Revere's Ride. Crowell 1963 (Poem)
AB(4-7)—CC(3-6)—ESLC

COLLECTIONS

Bakeless, John. Turncoats, Traitors, and Heroes. Lippincott 1959
SCHS

David Rittenhouse, 1732-1796

COLLECTIONS

Douty, Esther (Morris). Under the New Roof: Five Patriots of the Young Republic. Rand McNally 1965
Bkl Y&C

Benjamin Rush, 1745?-1813

Douty, Esther M. Patriot Doctor: The Story of Benjamin Rush. Messner 1959
ESLC

STATESMEN

American—18th century

Benjamin Rush—Continued

Riedman, Sarah Regal and Green, Clarence Corleon. Benjamin Rush: Physician, Patriot, Founding Father. Abelard-Schuman 1964
Bkl Y(7-10)&C—JH

James Wilson, 1742-1798

COLLECTIONS

Bowen, Catherine (Drinker). Miracle at Philadelphia: The Story of the Constitutional Convention, May to September 1787. Little 1966
Bkl A&Y

American—19th century

Charles Francis Adams, 1807-1886

Duberman, Martin B. Charles Francis Adams, 1807-1886. Houghton 1961
Bkl A

John Peter Altgeld, 1847-1902

COLLECTIONS

Kunstler, William Moses. The Case for Courage. Morrow 1962
Bkl A&Y

Judah Philip Benjamin, 1811-1884

COLLECTIONS

Mapp, Alf Johnson. Frock Coats and Epaulets. Yoseloff 1963
Bkl A&Y

Thomas Hart Benton, 1782-1858

Chambers, William Hisbet. Old Bullion Benton—Senator from the New West: Thomas Hart Benton. Little 1956
SCPL
Smith, Elbert Benjamin. Magnificent Missourian: The Life of Thomas Hart Benton. Lippincott 1958
SCPL

William Jennings Bryan, 1860-1925

Glad, Paul W. McKinley, Bryan, and the People. Lippincott 1964
Bkl A&Y

COLLECTIONS

Hofstadter, Richard. American Political Tradition and the Men Who Made It. Knopf 1948
SCPL

Aaron Burr, 1756-1836

Crouse, Anna Erskine and Crouse, Russel. Alexander Hamilton and Aaron Burr: Their Lives, Their Times, Their Duel. Random House 1958
AB(7-9)—CC(6-9)—JH—SCHS

John Caldwell Calhoun, 1782-1850

Coit, Margaret Louise. John C. Calhoun: American Portrait. Houghton 1950
SCPL

COLLECTIONS

Coit, Margaret Louise. The Fight for Union. Houghton 1961
CC(6-7)—ESLC
Hofstadter, Richard. American Political Tradition and the Men Who Made It. Knopf 1948
SCPL

Joseph Gurney ("Uncle Joe") Cannon, 1836-1926

COLLECTIONS

Mooney, Booth. Mr. Speaker: Four Men Who Shaped the United States House of Representatives. Follett 1964
Bkl A&Y

Salmon Portland Chase, 1808-1873

Belden, T. G. and Belden, M. R. So Fell the Angels. Little 1956
SCPL

William Andrews Clark, 1839-1925

COLLECTIONS

Place, Marian T. The Copper Kings of Montana. Random House 1961
ESLC—JH—SCHS—YR

Henry Clay, 1777-1852

Peterson, Helen Stone. Henry Clay: Leader in Congress. Garrard 1964
AB(4-7)
Wilkie, Katharine Elliott. The Man Who Wouldn't Give Up: Henry Clay. Messner 1961
Bkl Y&C—YR

COLLECTIONS

Coit, Margaret Louise. The Fight for Union. Houghton 1961
CC(6-7)—ESLC
Mooney, Booth. Mr. Speaker: Four Men Who Shaped the United States House of Representatives. Follett 1964
Bkl A&Y

Nelson Dewey, 1813-1889

Derleth, August William. The Shadow in the Glass. Duell 1963 (Fiction)
Bkl A

Stephen Arnold Douglas, 1813-1861

Kelly, Regina (Zimmerman). Lincoln and Douglas: The Years of Decision. Random House 1954
JH—SCHS
Nolan, Jeannette (Covert). The Little Giant: Stephen A. Douglas. Messner 1964
Bkl C(7-9)&Y—JH

STATESMEN

American—19th century—Continued

John Francis Fitzgerald, 1863-1950

Cutler, John Henry. "Honey Fitz"—Three Steps to the White House: The Life and Times of John F. (Honey Fitz) Fitzgerald. Bobbs 1962
Bkl A

Albert Gallatin, 1761-1849

Walters, Raymond. Albert Gallatin: Jeffersonian Financier and Diplomat. Macmillan 1957
SCPL

COLLECTIONS

Douty, Esther (Morris). Under the New Roof: Five Patriots of the Young Republic. Rand McNally 1965
Bkl Y&C

Winfield Scott Hancock, 1824-1886

Tucker, Glenn. Hancock the Superb. Bobbs 1960
Bkl A

Townsend Harris, 1804-1878

Levine, Israel E. Behind the Silken Curtain: The Story of Townsend Harris. Messner 1961
Bkl C(6-9)&Y—YR

Samuel Houston, 1793-1863

James, Bessie Rowland and James, Marquis. Six Feet Six: The Heroic Story of Sam Houston. Bobbs 1931
BBJH—CC(6-9)—JH—SCHS
James, Marquis. The Raven. Bobbs 1953
BY
Johnson, William. Sam Houston, the Tallest Texan. Random House 1953
AB(5-10)—BBEL(5-8)—CC(5-7)—ESLC—JH
Latham, Jean Lee. Retreat to Glory: The Story of Sam Houston. Harper 1965
Bkl C(7-9)
Latham, Jean Lee. Sam Houston, Hero of Texas. Garrard 1965
AB(3-7)—ESLC
Wellman, Paul Iselin. Magnificent Destiny: A Novel about the Great Secret Adventure of Andrew Jackson and Sam Houston. Doubleday 1962 (Fiction)
Bkl A
Wisehart, Marion Karl. Sam Houston, American Giant. Luce 1962
Bkl A

COLLECTIONS

Coit, Margaret Louise. The Fight for Union. Houghton 1961
CC(6-7)—ESLC

Reverdy Johnson, 1796-1876

COLLECTIONS

Kunstler, William Moses. The Case for Courage. Morrow 1962
Bkl A&Y

Solomon Laurent Juneau, 1793-1856

Lawson, Marion. Solomon Juneau, Voyageur. Crowell 1960
ESLC

Gouverneur Morris, 1752-1816

COLLECTIONS

Dos Passos, John Roderigo. Men Who Made the Nation. Doubleday 1957
SCPL

Thomas Brackett Reed, 1839-1902

COLLECTIONS

Mooney, Booth. Mr. Speaker: Four Men Who Shaped the United States House of Representatives. Follett 1964
Bkl A&Y

Edmund Gibson Ross, 1826-1907

Erdman, Loula Grace. Many a Voyage. Dodd 1960 (Fiction)
Bkl A&Y

Carl Schurz, 1829-1906

Schurz, Carl. Autobiography; an abridgement in one volume, by Wayne Andrews. Scribner 1961
Bkl A
Terzian, James P. Defender of Human Rights, Carl Schurz. Messner 1965
Bkl C(7-10)&Y

William Henry Seward, 1801-1872

Conrad, Earl. The Governor and His Lady: The Story of William Henry Seward and His Wife Frances. Putnam 1960
Bkl A&Y

COLLECTIONS

Kunstler, William Moses. The Case for Courage. Morrow 1962
Bkl A&Y

Robert Smalls, 1839-1915

Sterling, Dorothy. Captain of the Planter: The Story of Robert Smalls. Doubleday 1958
JH

Edwin McMasters Stanton, 1814-1869

Pratt, Fletcher. Stanton, Lincoln's Secretary of War. Norton 1953
SCPL
Thomas, Benjamin Platt and Hyman, Harold Melvin. Stanton: The Life and Times of Lincoln's Secretary of War. Knopf 1962
Bkl A

STATESMEN

American—19th century—*Continued*

Charles Sumner, 1811-1874

Donald, David Herbert. Charles Sumner and the Coming of the Civil War. Knopf 1960
Bkl A—SCPL

Daniel Webster, 1782-1852

Benét, Stephen Vincent. The Devil and Daniel Webster. Farrar 1937 (Fiction)
JH—SCHS
Benét, Stephen Vincent and Moore, Douglas. The Devil and Daniel Webster: An Opera in One Act. Rinehart 1939 (Play)
SCPL

COLLECTIONS

Coit, Margaret Louise. The Fight for Union. Houghton 1961
CC(6-7)—ESLC

American—20th century

Dean Gooderham Acheson, 1893-

Acheson, Dean Gooderham. Morning and Noon. Houghton 1965
Bkl A

Sherman Adams, 1899-

COLLECTIONS

Koenig, Louis William. The Invisible Presidency. Rinehart 1960
Bkl A

Bernard Mannes Baruch, 1870-1965

Baruch, Bernard Mannes. Baruch: My Own Story. Holt 1957
BY—SCHS—SCPL—3000
Baruch, Bernard Mannes. Baruch: The Public Years. Holt 1960
Bkl A&Y—SCHS—SCPL
Coit, Margaret Louise. Mr. Baruch. Houghton 1957
SCPL
White, William Lindsay. Bernard Baruch: Portrait of a Citizen. Harcourt 1950
SCPL

William Edgar Borah, 1865-1940

McKenna, Marian C. Borah. Univ. of Mich. 1961
SCPL

Claude Gernade Bowers, 1878-1958

Bowers, Claude Gernade. My Life: The Memoirs of Claude Bowers. Simon & Schuster 1962
Bkl A

Ellis Ormsbee Briggs, 1899-

Briggs, Ellis Ormsbee. Farewell to Foggy Bottom: The Recollections of a Career Diplomat. McKay 1964
Bkl A

William Jennings Bryan, 1860-1925

Levine, Lawrence W. Defender of the Faith: William Jennings Bryan—The Last Decade, 1915-1925. Oxford 1965
Bkl A

COLLECTIONS

Hofstadter, Richard. American Political Tradition and the Men Who Made It. Knopf 1948
SCPL

Wiley Thomas Buchanan, 1914-

Buchanan, Wiley Thomas and Gordon, Arthur. Red Carpet at the White House: Four Years as Chief of Protocol in the Eisenhower Administration. Dutton 1964
Bkl A&Y

Ralph Johnson Bunche, 1904-

Kugelmass, J. Alvin. Ralph J. Bunche: Fighter for Peace. Messner 1962
AB(6-9)—BBHS—BY—CC—ESLC—JH—SCHS

Joseph Gurney ("Uncle Joe") Cannon, 1836-1926

COLLECTIONS

Mooney, Booth. Mr. Speaker: Four Men Who Shaped the United States House of Representatives. Follett 1964
Bkl A&Y

Wilbur Lucius Cross, 1862-1948

Cross, Wilbur Lucius. Connecticut Yankee: An Autobiography. Yale Univ. 1943
SCPL

Josephus Daniels, 1862-1948

Daniels, Josephus. Shirt-Sleeve Diplomat. Univ. of N. C. 1947
SCPL
Daniels, Josephus. Tar Heel Editor. Univ. of N. C. 1939
SCPL

Eugene Victor Debs, 1855-1926

Morgan, Howard Wayne. Eugene V. Debs: Socialist for President. Syracuse Univ. 1962
Bkl A

Thomas Edmund Dewey, 1902-

COLLECTIONS

Roper, Elmo Burns. You and Your Leaders: Their Actions and Your Reactions, 1936-1956. Morrow 1957
SCPL

STATESMEN

American—20th century—*Continued*

John Foster Dulles, 1888-1959

Beal, John Robinson. John Foster Dulles: A Biography. Harper 1957
SCPL

Beal, John Robinson. John Foster Dulles: 1888-1959. Harper 1959
Bkl A—SCPL

Drummond, Roscoe and Coblentz, Gaston. Duel at the Brink: John Foster Dulles' Command of American Power. Doubleday 1960
Bkl A&Y

Finer, Herman. Dulles over Suez: The Theory and Practice of His Diplomacy. Quadrangle 1964
Bkl A

Goold-Adams, Richard John Morton. John Foster Dulles: A Reappraisal. Appleton 1962
Bkl A

Heller, Deane and Heller, David. John Foster Dulles, Soldier for Peace. Holt 1960
Bkl A—SCPL

John Francis Fitzgerald, 1863-1950

Cutler, John Henry. "Honey Fitz"—Three Steps to the White House: The Life and Times of John F. (Honey Fitz) Fitzgerald. Bobbs 1962
Bkl A

Ralph Edward Flanders, 1880-

Flanders, Ralph Edward. Senator from Vermont. Little 1961
Bkl A

James Vincent Forrestal, 1892-1949

Albion, Robert Greenhalgh and Connery, Robert Howe. Forrestal and the Navy. Columbia Univ. 1962
Bkl A

Forrestal, James. Forrestal Diaries; ed. by Walter Millis. Viking 1951
SCPL

Rogow, Arnold A. James Forrestal: A Study of Personality, Politics, and Policy. Macmillan 1963
Bkl A—SCPL

Barry Morris Goldwater, 1909-

De Toledano, Ralph. The Winning Side: The Case for Goldwater Republicanism. Putman 1963
Bkl A&Y

McDowell, Edwin. Barry Goldwater: Portrait of an Arizonan. Regnery 1964
Bkl A

Rovere, Richard Halworth. The Goldwater Caper. Harcourt 1965
Bkl A

Shadegg, Stephen C. Barry Goldwater: Freedom Is His Flight Plan. Fleet 1962
Bkl A

Harry Lloyd Hopkins, 1890-1946

Charles, Searle F. Minister of Relief: Harry Hopkins and the Depression. Syracuse Univ. 1963
Bkl A

COLLECTIONS

Koenig, Louis William. The Invisible Presidency. Rinehart 1960
Bkl A

Edward Mandell ("Colonel") House, 1858-1938

COLLECTIONS

Koenig, Louis William. The Invisible Presidency. Rinehart 1960
Bkl A

Cordell Hull, 1871-1955

Hull, Cordell. Memoirs of Cordell Hull. 2v. Macmillan 1948
SCPL

Pratt, J. W. Cordell Hull. Cooper Sq. 1964
Bkl A—SCPL

Hubert Horatio Humphrey, 1911-

Amrine, Michael. This Is Humphrey: The Story of the Senator. Doubleday 1960
Bkl A

Griffith, Winthrop. Humphrey: A Candid Biography. Morrow 1965
Bkl A&Y

COLLECTIONS

Sevareid, Eric, ed. Candidates 1960: Behind the Headlines in the Presidential Race. Basic Bks 1959
SCPL

Harold Le Claire Ickes, 1874-1952

Ickes, Harold Le Claire. Secret Diary. 3v. Simon & Schuster 1953-54
SCPL

Frank Billings Kellogg, 1856-1937

Ferrell, R. H. Frank B. Kellogg & Henry L. Stimson. Cooper Sq. 1963
Bkl A—SCPL

Edward Moore Kennedy, 1932-

Levin, Murray Burton. Kennedy Campaigning: The System and the Style as Practiced by Senator Edward Kennedy. Beacon Press 1966
Bkl A

STATESMEN

American—20th century—*Continued*

Robert Francis Kennedy, 1925-1968

Thinmesch, Nick and Johnson, William O. Robert Kennedy at 40. Norton 1965
Bkl A

Robert Marion LaFollette, 1855-1925

COLLECTIONS

Lawson, Don. Famous American Political Families. Abelard-Schuman 1965
Bkl C(7-12)&Y

Fiorello Henry La Guardia, 1882-1947

Bock, Jerry. Fiorello: A New Musical; book by Jerome Weidman and George Abbott; lyrics by Sheldon Harnick. Random House 1960 (Play)
Bkl A

Garrett, Charles. The La Guardia Years: Machine and Reform Politics in New York City. Rutgers Univ. 1961
Bkl A

Mann, Arthur. La Guardia—A Fighter Against His Times: v. 1, 1882-1933. Lippincott 1959
Bkl A

Mann, Arthur. La Guardia—A Fighter Against His Times: v. 2, La Guardia Comes to Power, 1933. Lippincott 1965
IndS(12)

Rodman, Bella and Sterling, Philip. Fiorello La Guardia. Hill & Wang 1962
Bkl Y

Herbert Henry Lehman, 1878-1963

Nevins, Allan. Herbert H. Lehman and His Era. Scribner 1963
Bkl A—IndS(10-12)

Earl Kemp Long, 1895-1960

Liebling, Abbott Joseph. The Earl of Louisiana. Simon & Schuster 1961
Bkl A

Huey Pierce Long, 1893-1935

Martin, Thomas. Dynasty: The Longs of Louisiana. Putnam 1960
Bkl A

Opotowsky, Stan. The Longs of Louisiana. Dutton 1960
Bkl A

COLLECTIONS

Lawson, Don. Famous American Political Families. Abelard-Schuman 1965
Bkl C(7-12)&Y

Joseph Raymond McCarthy, 1908-1957

Potter, Charles E. Days of Shame. Coward-McCann 1965
Bkl A&Y—IndS(11-12)

Rovere, Richard Halworth. Senator Joe McCarthy. Harcourt 1959
SCPL

Robert Strange McNamara, 1916-

Kaufmann, William W. The McNamara Strategy. Harper 1964
Bkl A

George Catlett Marshall, 1880-1959

Faber, Harold. Soldier and Statesman: General George C. Marshall. Ariel Bks 1964
Bkl Y&C—CC—ESLC—IndJ(6-9)—JH

Pogue, Forrest C. George C. Marshall: v. 1, Education of a General, 1880-1939. Viking 1963
Bkl A&Y—IndS(10-12)—SCPL

COLLECTIONS

Acheson, Dean Gooderham. Sketches from Life of Men I Have Known. Harper 1961
Bkl A&Y—SCPL

Roper, Elmo Burns. You and Your Leaders: Their Actions and Your Reactions, 1936-1956. Morrow 1957
SCPL

Joseph William Martin, 1884-1968

Martin, Joseph William and Donovan, Robert J. My First Fifty Years in Politics. McGraw 1960
Bkl A

Perle (Skirvin) Mesta, 1891-

Mesta, Perle (Skirvin) and Cahn, Robert. Perle: My Story. McGraw 1960
Bkl A

Henry Morgenthau, 1891-1967

Blum, John Morton. From the Morgenthau Diaries: v. 2, Years of Urgency, 1938-1941. Houghton 1965
Bkl A—IndS(11-12)

Wayne Lyman Morse, 1900-

Smith, Arthur Robert. The Tiger in the Senate: The Biography of Wayne Morse. Doubleday 1962
Bkl A

Robert Daniel Murphy, 1894-

Murphy, Robert Daniel. Diplomat Among Warriors. Doubleday 1964
Bkl A—SCPL

STATESMEN

American—20th century—*Continued*

Richard Milhous Nixon, 1913-

Alsop, Stewart Johonnot Oliver. Nixon & Rockefeller: A Double Portrait. Doubleday 1960
Bkl A

Costello, William. The Facts About Nixon: An Unauthorized Biography. Viking 1960
Bkl A

Harris, Mark. Mark the Glove Boy; or, The Last Days of Richard Nixon. Macmillan 1964
Bkl A

Kornitzer, Bela. The Real Nixon: An Intimate Biography. Rand McNally 1960
Bkl A

Mazo, Earl. Richard Nixon: A Political and Personal Portrait. Harper 1959
SCPL

Nixon, Richard Milhous. Six Crises. Doubleday 1962
SCPL

COLLECTIONS

Sevareid, Eric, ed. Candidates 1960: Behind the Headlines in the Presidential Race. Basic Bks 1959
SCPL

George William Norris, 1861-1944

Lowitt, Richard. George W. Norris: The Making of a Progressive, 1861-1912. Syracuse Univ. 1963
Bkl A

Zucker, Norman L. George W. Norris: Gentle Knight of American Democracy. Univ. of Ill. 1966
Bkl A

Elizabeth (Eyre) Pellet, ?

Pellet, Elizabeth (Eyre) and Klein, Alexander. "That Pellet Woman!" Stein & Day 1965
Bkl A

Adam Clayton Powell, 1908-

Hickey, Neil and Edwin, Ed. Adam Clayton Powell and the Politics of Race. Fleet 1965
Bkl A

Ivy Maude (Baker) Priest, 1905-

COLLECTIONS

Forsee, Aylesa. Women Who Reached for Tomorrow. Macrae 1960
Bkl Y&C

William Proxmire, 1915-

Proxmire, Ellen. One Foot in Washington: The Perilous Life of a Senator's Wife. Luce 1964
Bkl A

Sam Taliaferro Rayburn, 1882-1961

Allen, Edward. Leading the Lawmakers: Sam Rayburn. Encyc. Britannica 1963
YR

Dorough, C. Dwight. Mr. Sam. Random House 1962
Bkl A

COLLECTIONS

Mooney, Booth. Mr. Speaker: Four Men Who Shaped the United States House of Representatives. Follett 1964
Bkl A&Y

Nelson Aldrich Rockefeller, 1908-

Alsop, Stewart Johonnot Oliver. Nixon & Rockefeller: A Double Portrait. Doubleday 1960
Bkl A

Desmond, James. Nelson Rockefeller: A Political Biography. Macmillan 1964
Bkl A

Gervasi, Frank Henry. The Real Rockefeller: The Story of the Rise, Decline and Resurgence of the Presidential Aspirations of Nelson Rockefeller. Atheneum 1964
Bkl A

Morris, Joe Alex. Nelson Rockefeller: A Biography. Harper 1960
Bkl A

Morris, Joe Alex. Those Rockefeller Brothers: An Informal Biography of Five Extraordinary Young Men. Harper 1953
SCPL

COLLECTIONS

Sevareid, Eric, ed. Candidates 1960: Behind the Headlines in the Presidential Race. Basic Bks 1959
SCPL

Abraham Ruef, 1864-1936

Thomas, Lately. A Debonair Scoundrel: An Episode in the Moral History of San Francisco. Holt 1962
Bkl A

Dalip Singh Saund, 1899-

Saund, Dalip Singh. Congressman from India. Dutton 1960
Bkl A

COLLECTIONS

Life International. Nine Who Chose America. Dutton 1959
Bkl Y&C–SCHS

STATESMEN

American—20th century—*Continued*

Robert Sargent Shriver, 1915-

Liston, Robert A. Sargent Shriver: A Candid Portrait. Farrar 1964
Bkl A&Y

Alfred Emanuel Smith, 1873-1944

Graham, Frank. Al Smith, American: An Informal Biography. Putnam 1945
SCPL

Handlin, Oscar. Al Smith and His America. Little 1958
SCPL

Moses, Robert. A Tribute to Governor Smith. Simon & Schuster 1962
Bkl A

Frank Ellis Smith, 1918-

Smith, Frank Ellis. Congressman from Mississippi. Pantheon 1964
Bkl A&Y—IndS(11-12)

Margaret (Chase) Smith, 1898-

Graham, Frank. Margaret Chase Smith, Woman of Courage. Day 1964
Bkl A

Adlai Ewing Stevenson, 1900-1965

Brown, Stuart Gerry. Conscience in Politics: Adlai E. Stevenson in the 1950's. Syracuse Univ. 1961
Bkl A

Busch, Noel Fairchild. Adlai E. Stevenson of Illinois: A Portrait. Farrar 1952
SCPL

Davis, Kenneth Sydney. Prophet in His Own Country: The Triumphs and Defeats of Adlai E. Stevenson. Doubleday 1957
SCPL

Doyle, Edward P., ed. As We Knew Adlai: The Stevenson Story by Twenty-two Friends. Harper 1966
Bkl A&Y

Ross, Lillian. Adlai Stevenson. Lippincott 1966
Bkl A

Severn, William. Adlai Stevenson, Citizen of the World. McKay 1966
Bkl C(7-10)&Y—ESLC

Whitman, Alden Rogers. Portrait—Adlai E. Stevenson: Politician, Diplomat, Friend. Harper 1965
Bkl A&Y

COLLECTIONS

Brown, John Mason. Through These Men: Some Aspects of Our Passing History. Harper 1956
SCPL

Roper, Elmo Burns. You and Your Leaders: Their Actions and Your Reactions, 1936-1956. Morrow 1957
SCPL

Sevareid, Eric, ed. Candidates 1960: Behind the Headlines in the Presidential Race. Basic Bks 1959
SCPL

Henry Lewis Stimson, 1867-1950

Ferrell, R. H. Frank B. Kellogg & Henry L. Stimson. Cooper Sq. 1963
Bkl A—SCPL

Morison, Elting E. Turmoil and Tradition: A Study of the Life and Times of Henry L. Stimson. Houghton 1960
SCPL

Stuart Symington, 1901-

COLLECTIONS

Sevareid, Eric, ed. Candidates 1960: Behind the Headlines in the Presidential Race. Basic Bks 1959
SCPL

Robert Alphonso Taft, 1889-1953

White, William Smith. The Taft Story. Harper 1954
SCPL

COLLECTIONS

Roper, Elmo Burns. You and Your Leaders: Their Actions and Your Reactions, 1936-1956. Morrow 1957
SCPL

Norman Mattoon Thomas, 1884-1968

Fleischman, Harry. Norman Thomas: A Biography. Norton 1964
Bkl A&Y

Seidler, Murray Benjamin. Norman Thomas: Respectable Rebel. Syracuse Univ. 1961
Bkl A

Arthur Hendrick Vandenberg, 1884-1951

COLLECTIONS

Acheson, Dean Gooderham. Sketches from Life of Men I Have Known. Harper 1961
Bkl A&Y—SCPL

Earl Warren, 1891-

Huston, Luther A. Pathway to Judgment: A Study of Earl Warren. Chilton 1966
Bkl A&Y

Burton Kendall Wheeler, 1882-

Wheeler, Burton Kendall and Healy, Paul F. Yankee from the West: The Candid, Turbulent Life Story of the Yankee-Born U.S. Senator from Montana. Doubleday 1962
Bkl A

STATESMEN

American—20th century—*Continued*

Wendell Lewis Willkie, 1892-1944

COLLECTIONS

Roper, Elmo Burns. You and Your Leaders: Their Actions and Your Reactions, 1936-1956. Morrow 1957
SCPL

John Gilbert Winant, 1889-1947

Winant, John Gilbert. Letter from Grosvenor Square: An Account of a Stewardship. Houghton 1947
SCPL

Burmese—20th century

Nu, 1907-

Butwell, Richard A. U Nu of Burma. Stanford Univ. 1963
Bkl A

Canadian

COLLECTIONS

Hutchison, Bruce. Mr. Prime Minister, 1867-1964. Harcourt 1965
Bkl A

Canadian—20th century

William Lyon Mackenzie King, 1874-1950

Hutchison, Bruce. Incredible Canadian: A Candid Portrait of Mackenzie King: His Works, His Times, and His Nation. Longmans 1953
SCPL

Vincent Massey, 1887-1967

Massey, Vincent. What's Past Is Prologue: The Memoirs of the Right Honourable Vincent Massey, C.H. St Martins 1964
Bkl A

Lester Bowles Pearson, 1897-

Beal, John Robinson. Pearson of Canada. Duell 1964
Bkl A

Chilean—19th century

Bernardo O'Higgins, 1778-1842

COLLECTIONS

Bailey, Bernadine (Freeman). Famous Latin-American Liberators. Dodd 1960
Bkl C(6-9)&Y—ESLC—SCHS

Chinese

COLLECTIONS

Spencer, Cornelia. China's Leaders in Ideas and Action. Macrae 1966
Bkl C(7-9)&Y

Chinese—20th century

Chiang Kai-shek, 1886-

COLLECTIONS

Bliven, Bruce. The World Changers. Day 1965
Bkl A&Y—IndS(10-12)

Mao Tsê-tung, 1893-

Ch'ên, Jerome. Mao and the Chinese Revolution. Oxford 1965
Bkl A

Floyd, David. Mao Against Khrushchev: A Short History of the Sino-Soviet Conflict. Praeger 1964
Bkl A

Hsiao, Yü. Mao Tse-tung and I Were Beggars. Syracuse Univ. 1959
Bkl A

MacGregor-Hastie, Roy. The Red Barbarians: The Life and Times of Mao Tse-tung. Chilton 1962
Bkl A

Pálóczi Horváth, György. Mao Tse-tung, Emperor of the Blue Ants. Doubleday 1963
Bkl A

Payne, Pierre Stephen Robert. Portrait of a Revolutionary: Mao Tse-tung. Abelard-Schuman 1962
Bkl A&Y

Schram, Stuart R. The Political Thought of Mao Tse-tung. Praeger 1963
Bkl A

COLLECTIONS

Coolidge, Olivia. Makers of the Red Revolution. Houghton 1963
CC(7-9)

Sun Yat-sen, 1866-1925

Baker, Nina Brown. Sun Yat-sen. Vanguard 1946
JH—SCHS

COLLECTIONS

Larson, Egon. Men Who Fought for Freedom. Roy 1959
AB

Cuban—19th century

José Julian Martí, 1853-1895

COLLECTIONS

Bailey, Bernadine (Freeman). Famous Latin-American Liberators. Dodd 1960
Bkl C(6-9)&Y—ESLC—SCHS

Cuban—20th century

Fidel Castro, 1926-

Dubois, Jules. Fidel Castro, Rebel—Liberator or Dictator? Bobbs 1959
SCPL

STATESMEN—*Continued*

Cypriote—20th century

Archbishop Makarios III, 1913-

COLLECTIONS

Lengyel, Emil. From Prison to Power. Follett 1964
Bkl A&Y

Danish—20th century

Paul Bang-Jensen, 1909-1959

Copp, DeWitt and Peck, Marshall. Betrayal at the UN: The Story of Paul Bang-Jensen. Devin-Adair 1961
Bkl A

Dutch—20th century

Dirk Uipko Stikker, 1897-

Stikker, Dirk Uipko. Men of Responsibility: A Memoir. Harper 1966
Bkl A

English

COLLECTIONS

Sutcliff, Rosemary. Heroes and History. Putnam 1966
Bkl C(7-10)&Y
Alfred the Great; King Arthur; Robert Bruce; Owen Glendower; Hereward; Llewelyn ab Gruffydd; James Graham Montrose; Sir William Wallace

English—16th century

William Cecil, 1st Baron Burghley, 1520-1598

Read, Conyers. Lord Burghley and Queen Elizabeth. Knopf 1960
Bkl A—SCPL

Thomas Howard, 4th Duke of Norfolk, 1536-1572

Williams, Neville. Thomas Howard, Fourth Duke of Norfolk. Dutton 1965
Bkl A

Sir Thomas More, Saint, 1478-1535

Basset, Bernard. Born for Friendship: The Spirit of Sir Thomas More. Sheed 1965
Bkl A&Y
Bolt, Robert. A Man for All Seasons: A Play in Two Acts. Random House 1962 (Play)
Bkl A—SCHS—SCPL
Maynard, Theodore. Humanist as Hero: The Life of Sir Thomas More. Macmillan 1947
SCPL
Newell, Virginia. His Own Good Daughter. McKay 1961
YR

Reynolds, Ernest Edwin. The Trial of St. Thomas More. Kenedy 1964
Bkl A
Stanley-Wrench, Margaret. The Conscience of a King. Hawthorn 1962
AB(5-9)

Thomas Cardinal Wolsey, 1475?-1530

Ferguson, Charles Wright. Naked to Mine Enemies: The Life of Cardinal Wolsey. Little 1958
SCPL—3000

English—17th century

Francis Bacon, Viscount St. Albans, 1561-1626

Anderson, Fulton H. Francis Bacon: His Career and His Thought. Univ. of Southern Calif. 1962
Bkl A
Bowen, Catherine (Drinker). Francis Bacon: The Temper of a Man. Little 1963
Bkl A&Y—IndS(11-12)—SCHS—SCPL
Eiseley, Loren C. Francis Bacon and the Modern Dilemma. Univ. of Neb. 1963
Bkl A

Oliver Cromwell, 1599-1658

Ashley, Maurice Percy. Greatness of Oliver Cromwell. Macmillan 1958
SCPL
Levine, Israel E. Oliver Cromwell. Messner 1966
Bkl Y

John Churchill, 1st Duke of Marlborough, 1650-1722

Rowse, Alfred Leslie. Early Churchills: An English Family. Harper 1956
SCPL

John Mordaunt, Viscount Mordaunt, 1627-1675

Scott, Virgil. I, John Mordaunt. Harcourt 1964 (Fiction)
Bkl A

Sir Henry Morgan, 1635?-1688

Syme, Ronald. Sir Henry Morgan, Buccaneer. Morrow 1965
AB(4-7)—ESLC

Thomas Wentworth, 1st Earl of Strafford, 1593-1641

Wedgwood, Cicely Veronica. Thomas Wentworth, First Earl of Strafford, 1593-1641: A Revaluation. Macmillan 1962
Bkl A

STATESMEN—*Continued*

English—18th century

Henry Addington, 1st Viscount of Sidmouth, 1757-1844

Ziegler, Philip. Addington: A Life of Henry Addington, First Viscount Sidmouth. Day 1966
Bkl A

Philip Dormer Stanhope, 4th Earl of Chesterfield, 1694-1773

Shellabarger, Samuel. Lord Chesterfield and His World. Little 1951
SCPL

Henry Hamilton, ?-1796

Havighurst, Walter. Proud Prisoner. Holt 1964
ESLC

John Churchill, 1st Duke of Marlborough, 1650-1722

Rowse, Alfred Leslie. Early Churchills: An English Family. Harper 1956
SCPL

William Pitt, the Younger, 1759-1806

Rosebery, Archibald Philip Primrose, 5th Earl of. Pitt. St Martins 1892
SCPL

Charles Radcliffe, 1693-1746

Seton, Anya. Devil Water. Houghton 1962 (Fiction)
Bkl A

English—19th century

Henry Addington, 1st Viscount of Sidmouth, 1757-1844

Ziegler, Philip. Addington: A Life of Henry Addington, First Viscount Sidmouth. Day 1966
Bkl A

Lord Randolph Henry Spencer Churchill, 1849-1895

James, Robert Rhodes. Lord Randolph Churchill: Winston Churchill's Father. Barnes 1960
Bkl A

George Nathaniel Curzon, 1st Marquis Curzon, 1859-1925

Mosley, Leonard Oswald. The Glorious Fault: The Life of Lord Curzon. Harcourt 1960
Bkl A

Benjamin Disraeli, 1804-1881

Komroff, Manuel. Disraeli. Messner 1963
AB(7up)—Bkl C(7-9)&Y—JH

Maurois, André. Disraeli: A Picture of the Victorian Age. Modern Lib. 1942
CA—SCHS—SCPL

Pearson, Hesketh. Dizzy: The Life and Personality of Benjamin Disraeli, Earl of Beaconsfield. Harper 1951
SCPL

Edward John Eyre, 1815-1901

Semmel, Bernard. Jamaican Blood and Victorian Conscience: The Governor Eyre Controversy. Houghton 1963
Bkl A

William Ewart Gladstone, 1809-1898

Birrell, Francis. Gladstone. Macmillan 1957
SCPL

William Lamb, 2nd Viscount Melbourne, 1779-1848

Cecil, Lord David. Melbourne. Bobbs 1954
SCPL

Sir John Pope-Hennessy, 1834-1891

Pope-Hennessy, James. Verandah: Some Episodes in the Crown Colonies, 1867-1889. Knopf 1964
Bkl A

Archibald Philip Primrose, 5th Earl of Rosebery, 1847-1929

James, Robert Rhodes. Rosebery: A Biography of Archibald Philip, Fifth Earl of Rosebery. Macmillan 1964
Bkl A

Anthony Ashley Cooper, 7th Earl of Shaftesbury, 1801-1885

Best, Geoffrey Francis Andrew. Shaftesbury. Arco 1964
Bkl A

Arthur Wellesley, 1st Duke of Wellington, 1769-1852

Cooper, Leonard. The Age of Wellington: The Life and Times of the Duke of Wellington, 1769-1852. Dodd 1963
Bkl A—IndS(11-12)

Ward, Stephen George Peregrine. Wellington. Arco 1964
Bkl A

English—20th century

Herbert Henry Asquith, 1st Earl of Oxford and Asquith, 1852-1928

Jenkins, Roy. Asquith: Portrait of a Man and An Era. Chilmark 1964
Bkl A

STATESMEN

English—20th century—*Continued*

Nancy Witcher (Langhorne), Viscountess Astor, 1879-1964

Collis, Maurice. Nancy Astor. Dutton 1960
Bkl A

Clement Richard Attlee, 1st Earl Attlee, 1883-1967

Attlee, Sir Clement Richard. As It Happened. Viking 1954
SCPL

Williams, Francis. Twilight of Empire: Memoirs of Prime Minister Clement Attlee. Barnes 1962
Bkl A

Ernest Bevin, 1884-1951

COLLECTIONS

Acheson, Dean Gooderham. Sketches from Life of Men I Have Known. Harper 1961
Bkl A&Y—SCPL

Crossman, Richard Howard Stafford. A Nation Reborn: A Personal Report on the Roles Played by Weizmann, Bevin, and Ben-Gurion in the Story of Israel. Atheneum 1960
Bkl A

Neville Chamberlain, 1869-1940

Macleod, Iain. Neville Chamberlain. Atheneum 1962
Bkl A

Oliver Lyttelton, 1st Viscount Chandos, 1893-

Chandos, Oliver Lyttelton, 1st Viscount. Memoirs: An Unexpected View from the Summit. New Am. Lib. 1963
Bkl A

Sir Winston Leonard Spencer Churchill, 1874-1965

American Heritage. Churchill: The Life Triumphant. Am. Heritage 1965
IndJ(6-9)

Bocca, Geoffrey. The Adventurous Life of Winston Churchill. Messner 1962
BY

Broad, Lewis. Winston Churchill: v. 2, The Years of Achievement. Hawthorn 1963
Bkl A

Broad, Lewis. Winston Churchill: The Years of Preparation: A Biography. Hawthorn 1958
SCPL

Carter, Violet Bonham. Winston Churchill: An Intimate Portrait. Harcourt 1965
Bkl A

Churchill, Randolph Spencer. Winston S. Churchill: v. 1, Youth, 1874-1900. Houghton 1966
Bkl A

Churchill, Sir Winston Leonard Spencer. Amid These Storms: Thoughts and Adventures. Scribner 1932
SCPL

Churchill, Sir Winston Leonard Spencer. Churchill Reader: The Wit and Wisdom of Sir Winston Churchill. Houghton 1954
SCPL

Churchill, Sir Winston Leonard Spencer. Great Destiny: Sixty Years of the Memorable Events in the Life of the Man of the Century Recounted in His Own Incomparable Words; ed. by F. W. Heath. Putnam 1965
Bkl A&Y—IndS(11-12)

Churchill, Sir Winston Leonard Spencer. A Roving Commission: My Early Life. Scribner 1939
SCPL

Churchill, Sir Winston Leonard Spencer. Winston S. Churchill's Maxims and Reflections; comp. by Cohn Coote and Denzel Batchelor. Houghton 1949
SCPL

Coolidge, Olivia. Winston Churchill and the Story of Two World Wars. Houghton 1960
Bkl Y&C—CC(7-9)—JH—SCHS

Cowles, Virginia Spencer. Winston Churchill: The Era and the Man. Grosset 1956
BY—SCPL—3000

De Mendelssohn, Peter. The Age of Churchill: Heritage and Adventure, 1874-1911. Knopf 1961
Bkl A

Farrell, Alan. Sir Winston Churchill. Putnam 1964
ESLC

Ferrier, Neil, ed. Churchill, the Man of the Century: A Pictorial Biography. Doubleday 1965
Bkl A

Graebner, Walter. My Dear Mr. Churchill. Houghton 1965
Bkl A&Y

Harrity, Richard and Martin, Ralph G. Man of the Century: Churchill. Duell 1962
Bkl A&Y

Le Vien, Jack and Lord, John. Winston Churchill: The Valiant Years. Geis 1962
Bkl A&Y

Miers, Earl Schenck. The Story of Winston Churchill. Grosset 1965
CC(5-7)

STATESMEN

English—20th century

Sir Winston Leonard Spencer Churchill—Continued

Miller, Harry Tatlock and Sainthill, Loudon, comp. Churchill: The Walk with Destiny. Macmillan 1959
Bkl A

Moorehead, Alan. Churchill: A Pictorial Biography. Studio 1960
Bkl A&Y

Morin, Relman. Churchill: Portrait of Greatness. Prentice-Hall 1965
Bkl A&Y

Nathan, Adele Gutman. Churchill's England. Grosset 1963
AB(6-9)—ESLC

Pawle, Gerald. The War and Colonel Warden; based on the recollections of C. R. Thompson. Knopf 1963
Bkl A

Reynolds, Quentin James. Winston Churchill. Random House 1963
Bkl C(6-9)—ESLC—IndJ(6-9)—JH

Rowse, Alfred Leslie. The Churchills: From the Death of Marlborough to the Present. Harper 1958
SCPL

The Times (London). The Churchill Years, 1874-1965. Studio 1965
Bkl A&Y

Wibberley, Leonard. The Life of Winston Churchill. Ariel Bks 1956
BBJH—SCHS

COLLECTIONS

Acheson, Dean Gooderham. Sketches from Life of Men I Have Known. Harper 1961
Bkl A&Y—SCPL

Bliven, Bruce. The World Changers. Day 1965
Bkl A&Y—IndS(10-12)

Hill, Frank Ernest. Famous Historians. Dodd 1966
Bkl Y&C

George Nathaniel Curzon, 1st Marquis Curzon, 1859-1925

Mosley, Leonard Oswald. The Glorious Fault: The Life of Lord Curzon. Harcourt 1960
Bkl A

Sir Anthony Eden, 1897-

Churchill, Randolph Spencer. The Rise and Fall of Sir Anthony Eden. Putnam 1959
Bkl A

Eden, Sir Anthony. Facing the Dictators: The Memoirs of Anthony Eden, Earl of Avon. Houghton 1962
Bkl A—SCPL

Eden, Sir Anthony. Full Circle. Houghton 1960
Bkl A&Y—SCPL

Eden, Sir Anthony. The Reckoning: The Memoirs of Anthony Eden, Earl of Avon. Houghton 1965
Bkl A

COLLECTIONS

Acheson, Dean Gooderham. Sketches from Life of Men I Have Known. Harper 1961
Bkl A&Y—SCPL

Edward Frederick Lindley Wood, 1st Earl of Halifax, 1881-1959

Halifax, Edward Frederick Lindley Wood, 1st Earl of. Fullness of Days. Dodd 1957
SCPL

Alexander Frederick Douglas-Home, 14th Earl of Home, 1903-

Dickie, John. The Uncommon Commoner: A Study of Sir Alec Douglas-Home. Praeger 1964
Bkl A

David Lloyd George, 1st Earl Lloyd George, 1863-1945

Beaverbrook, William Maxwell Aitken, Baron. The Decline and Fall of Lloyd George. Duell 1963
Bkl A

Lloyd George, Richard Lloyd George, 2nd Earl. My Father, Lloyd George. Crown 1961
Bkl A

McCormick, Donald. The Mask of Merlin: A Critical Biography of David Lloyd George. Holt 1964
Bkl A

Walter Edward Guinness, Baron Moyne, 1880-1944

Frank, Gerold. The Deed. Simon & Schuster 1963
Bkl A

Sir Harold George Nicolson, 1886-1968

Nicolson, Sir Harold George. Diaries and Letters: v. 1, 1930-1939; ed. by Nigel Nicolson. Atheneum 1966
Bkl A

Archibald Philip Primrose, 5th Earl of Rosebery, 1847-1929

James, Robert Rhodes. Rosebery: A Biography of Archibald Philip, Fifth Earl of Rosebery. Macmillan 1964
Bkl A

STATESMEN

English—20th century—*Continued*

Robert Gilbert Vansittart, Baron Vansittart, 1881-1957

Colvin, Ian Goodhope. None So Blind: A British Diplomatic View of the Origins of World War II. Harcourt 1965
Bkl A

Harold Wilson, 1916-

Howard, Anthony and West, Richard. The Road to Number 10. Macmillan 1965
Bkl A
Smith, Leslie. Harold Wilson: The Authentic Portrait. Scribner 1965
Bkl A

French—14th century

Philip II, the Bold, Duke of Burgundy, 1342-1404

Vaughan, Richard. Philip the Bold: The Formation of the Burgundian State. Harvard Univ. 1962
Bkl A

French—15th century

John the Fearless, 1371-1419

Vaughan, Richard. John the Fearless: The Growth of Burgundian Power. Barnes & Noble 1966
Bkl A

French—16th century

Antoine Cardinal Duprat, 1463-1535

Schoonover, Lawrence L. The Chancellor. Little 1961 (Fiction)
Bkl A

French—17th century

Louis de Buade, Comte de Frontenac, 1620-1698

Cather, Willa. Shadows on the Rock. Knopf 1931 (Fiction)
JH–SCHS

Father Joseph, 1577-1638

Huxley, Aldous Leonard. Grey Eminence: A Study in Religion and Politics. Harper 1941
SCPL

Armand Jean du Plessis, Cardinal, Duc de Richelieu, 1585-1642

Belloc, Hilaire. Richelieu: A Study. Lippincott 1950
SCPL

French—18th century

Jean Paul Marat, 1743-1793

Weiss, Peter. The Persecution and Assassination of Jean-Paul Marat as Performed by the Inmates of the Asylum of Charenton Under the Direction of the Marquis de Sade; ed. by Geoffrey Skelton and Adrian Mitchell. Atheneum 1966 (Play)
Bkl A

Louis François Armand de Vignerot du Plessis, Duc de Richelieu, 1696-1788

Cole, Hubert. First Gentleman of the Bedchamber: The Life of Louis-François-Armand, Maréchal Duc de Richelieu. Viking 1965
Bkl A

Maximilien Marie Isidore de Robespierre, 1758-1794

Bois, Helma de. The Incorruptible: A Tale of Revolution and Royalty. Crown 1965 (Fiction)
Bkl A
Williamson, Joanne S. Jacobin's Daughter. Knopf 1956 (Fiction)
JH

Charles Maurice de Talleyrand-Périgord, 1754-1838

Cooper, Alfred Duff, 1st Viscount Norwich. Talleyrand. Cape 1947
SCPL
Komroff, Manuel. Talleyrand. Messner 1965
Bkl C(7-9)&Y

French—19th century

François Auguste René, Vicomte de Chateaubriand, 1768-1848

Brady, Charles Andrew. Crown of Grass. Doubleday 1964 (Fiction)
Bkl A
Chateaubriand, François Auguste René, Vicomte de. Memoirs; selected and tr. by Robert Baldick. Knopf 1961
Bkl A

Ferdinand Marie, Vicomte de Lesseps, 1805-1894

Long, Laura. De Lesseps, Builder of Suez. Longmans 1958
SCHS–YR

Charles Maurice de Talleyrand-Périgord, 1754-1838

Cooper, Alfred Duff, 1st Viscount Norwich. Talleyrand. Cape 1947
SCPL

STATESMEN

French—19th century

Charles Maurice de Talleyrand-Périgord—Continued

Komroff, Manuel. Talleyrand. Messner 1965
Bkl C(7-9)&Y

French—20th century

Léon Blum, 1872-1950

Colton, Joel G. Léon Blum, Humanist in Politics. Knopf 1966
Bkl A

Pierre Mendès-France, 1907-

Werth, Alexander. Lost Statesman: The Strange Story of Pierre Mendès-France. Abelard-Schuman 1958
SCPL

Henri Philippe Pétain, 1856-1951

Tournoux, Jean Raymond. Sons of France: Pétain and de Gaulle; tr. by Oliver Coburn. Viking 1966
Bkl A

Robert Schuman, 1886-1963

COLLECTIONS

Acheson, Dean Gooderham. Sketches from Life of Men I Have Known. Harper 1961
Bkl A&Y—SCPL

German—19th century

Otto, Fürst von Bismarck, 1815-1898

Richter, Werner. Bismarck; tr. from the German by Brian Battershaw. Putnam 1965
Bkl A

German—20th century

Konrad Adenauer, 1876-1967

Adenauer, Konrad. Memoirs: v. 1, 1945-53; tr. by Beate Ruhm von Oppen. Regnery 1966
Bkl A

Alexander, Edgar. Adenauer and the New Germany: The Chancellor of the Vanquished. Farrar 1957
SCPL

Weymar, Paul. Adenauer: His Authorized Biography. Dutton 1957
SCPL

COLLECTIONS

Acheson, Dean Gooderham. Sketches from Life of Men I Have Known. Harper 1961
Bkl A&Y—SCPL

Willy Brandt, 1913-

Brandt, Willy. My Road to Berlin; as told to Leo Lania. Doubleday 1960
Bkl A—BY—SCPL

Joseph Goebbels, 1897-1945

Manvell, Roger and Fraenkel, Heinrich. Dr. Goebbels: His Life and Death. Simon & Schuster 1960
Bkl A

Hermann Göring, 1893-1946

Bewley, Charles Henry. Hermann Göring and the Third Reich. Devin-Adair 1962
Bkl A

Manvell, Roger and Fraenkel, Heinrich. Goering. Simon & Schuster 1962
Bkl A

Rudolf Hess, 1894-

Leasor, James. The Uninvited Envoy. McGraw 1962
Bkl A

Adolf Hitler, 1889-1945

Appel, Benjamin. Hitler: From Power to Ruin. Grosset 1964
IndJ(6-9)—JH

Bullock, Alan. Hitler: A Study in Tyranny. Harper 1964
BY—SCPL—3000

Deakin, Frederick William. The Brutal Friendship: Mussolini, Hitler, and the Fall of Italian Fascism. Harper 1963
Bkl A

Higgins, Trumbull. Hitler and Russia: The Third Reich in a Two-Front War, 1937-1943. Macmillan 1966
Bkl A

Hitler, Adolf. Mein Kampf; tr. by Ralph Manheim. Houghton 1943
CA—SCHS—SCPL—3000

Shirer, William Lawrence. The Rise and Fall of Adolf Hitler. Random House 1961
Bkl Y&C—CC(6-9)—ESLC—JH—SCHS—YR

Snyder, Louis Leo. Hitler and Nazism. Watts 1961
Bkl Y—JH—SCHS—YR

Trevor-Roper, Hugh Redwald. Last Days of Hitler. Macmillan 1947
SCPL

COLLECTIONS

Bliven, Bruce. The World Changers. Day 1965
Bkl A&Y—IndS(10-12)

Walter Ulbricht, 1893-

Stern, Carola. Ulbricht: A Political Biography; tr. and ed. by Abe Farbstein. Praeger 1965
Bkl A

STATESMEN—*Continued*

Greek—5th century B.C.

Alcibiades, 450?-404 B.C.

COLLECTIONS

Plutarch. Ten Famous Lives; the Dryden translation revised by Arthur Hugh Clough; ed. for young readers by Charles Robinson, Jr. Dutton 1962
Bkl C(7-10)&Y—BY—CC(7-9)—JH—SCHS—YR

Pericles, ?-429 B.C.

Warner, Rex. Pericles the Athenian. Little 1963 (Fiction)
Bkl A

COLLECTIONS

Plutarch. Ten Famous Lives; the Dryden translation rev. by Arthur Hugh Clough; ed for young readers by Charles Robinson, Jr. Dutton 1962
Bkl C(7-10)&Y—BY—CC(7-9)—JH—SCHS—YR

Themistocles, 527?-460? B.C.

COLLECTIONS

Plutarch. Ten Famous Lives; the Dryden translation rev. by Arthur Hugh Clough; ed for young readers by Charles Robinson, Jr. Dutton 1962
Bkl C(7-10)&Y—BY—CC(7-9)—JH—SCHS—YR

Greek—4th century B.C.

Demosthenes, 385?-322 B.C.

COLLECTIONS

Plutarch. Ten Famous Lives; the Dryden translation rev. by Arthur Hugh Clough; ed for young readers by Charles Robinson, Jr. Dutton 1962
Bkl C(7-10)&Y—BY—CC(7-9)—JH—SCHS—YR

Haitian—18th century

Pierre Dominique Toussaint Louverture, 1743-1803

Scherman, Katharine. The Slave Who Freed Haiti: The Story of Toussaint Louverture. Random House 1954
CC—JH—SCHS

COLLECTIONS

Bailey, Bernadine (Freeman). Famous Latin-American Liberators. Dodd 1960
Bkl C(6-9)&Y—ESLC—SCHS

Hungarian—20th century

János Kádár, 1912-

COLLECTIONS

Lengyel, Emil. From Prison to Power. Follett 1964
Bkl A&Y

Indian

COLLECTIONS

Hangen, Welles. After Nehru, Who? Harcourt 1963
Bkl A
Yashwantrao Balwantrao Chavan; Morarji Desai; Indira (Nehru) Gandhi; Brij Mohan Kaul; Vengalil Krishnan Krishna Menon; Jayaprakash Narayan; Sadashiv Kamoji Patil; Lal Bahadur Shastri

Indian—19th century

Gopal Krishna Gokhale, 1866-1915

Wolpert, Stanley A. Tilak and Gokhale: Revolution and Reform in the Making of Modern India. Univ. of Calif. 1962
Bkl A

Bal Gangadhar Tilak, 1856-1920

Wolpert, Stanley A. Tilak and Gokhale: Revolution and Reform in the Making of Modern India. Univ. of Calif. 1962
Bkl A

Indian—20th century

Yashwantrao Balwantrao Chavan, 1914-

COLLECTIONS

Hangen, Welles. After Nehru, Who? Harcourt 1963
Bkl A

Morarji Desai, 1896-

COLLECTIONS

Hangen, Welles. After Nehru, Who? Harcourt 1963
Bkl A

Indira (Nehru) Gandhi, 1917-

COLLECTIONS

Hangen, Welles. After Nehru, Who? Harcourt 1963
Bkl A

Mohandas Karamchand Gandhi, 1869-1948

Eaton, Jeanette. Gandhi, Fighter Without a Sword. Morrow 1950
BBEL(7-8)—BBHS—BBJH—BY—CC(7-9)—ESLC—JH—SCHS—YR

Fischer, Louis. Gandhi: His Life and Message for the World. New Am. Lib. 1955
GR

Fischer, Louis. Life of Mahatma Gandhi. Harper 1950
SCPL—3000

Gandhi, Mohandas Karamchand. All Men Are Brothers. Columbia Univ. 1959
BBHS

STATESMEN

Indian—20th century

Mohandas Karamchand Gandhi—Continued

Gandhi, Mohandas Karamchand. The Essential Gandhi: An Anthology; ed. by Louis Fischer. Random House 1962
Bkl A

Gandhi, Mohandas Karamchand. Gandhi's Autobiography: The Story of My Experiments with Truth; tr. by Mahadev Desai. Public Affairs Press 1954
GR—SCPL

Masani, Shakuntala. Gandhi's Story. Walck 1950
AB(4-7)

Reynolds, Reginald. The True Story of Gandhi. Childrens Press 1964
IndJ(4-6)

Shahani, Ranjee Gurdarsing. Mr. Gandhi. Macmillan 1961
Bkl A

Sheean, Vincent. Lead, Kindly Light. Random House 1949
SCPL

Sheean, Vincent. Mahatma Gandhi: A Great Life in Brief. Knopf 1955
SCHS—SCPL

Slade, Madeleine. The Spirit's Pilgrimage. Coward-McCann 1960
Bkl A&Y

Wolpert, Stanley. Nine Hours to Rama. Random House 1962 (Fiction)
Bkl A

COLLECTIONS

Bliven, Bruce. The World Changers. Day 1965
Bkl A&Y—IndS(10-12)

Larson, Egon. Men Who Fought for Freedom. Roy 1959
AB

Schechter, Betty. The Peaceable Revolution. Houghton 1963
CC(8-9)—ESLC—JH

Gopal Krishna Gokhale, 1866-1915

Wolpert, Stanley A. Tilak and Gokhale: Revolution and Reform in the Making of Modern India. Univ. of Calif. 1962
Bkl A

Vengalil Krishnan Krishna Menon, 1897-

COLLECTIONS

Hangen, Welles. After Nehru, Who? Harcourt 1963
Bkl A

Jayaprakash Narayan, 1900-

COLLECTIONS

Hangen, Welles. After Nehru, Who? Harcourt 1963
Bkl A

Jawaharlal Nehru, 1889-1964

Apsler, Alfred. Fighter for Independence: Jawaharlal Nehru. Messner 1963
CC(7-9)—ESLC—IndJ(6-9)—JH

Das, Manmath Nath. The Political Philosophy of Jawaharlal Nehru. Day 1961
Bkl A

Edwardes, Michael. Nehru: A Pictorial Biography. Viking 1963
Bkl A&Y

Moraes, Francis Robert. Jawaharlal Nehru: A Biography. Macmillan 1956
SCPL—3000

Nanda, Bal Ram. The Nehrus: Motilal and Jawaharlal. Day 1963
Bkl A—IndS(11-12)

Nehru, Jawaharlal. Toward Freedom. Day 1941
CA—GR

Sheean, Vincent. Nehru: The Years of Power. Random House 1960
Bkl A&Y—SCPL

COLLECTIONS

Lengyel, Emil. From Prison to Power. Follett 1964
Bkl A&Y

Motilal Nehru, 1861-1931

Nanda, Bal Ram. The Nehrus: Motilal and Jawaharlal. Day 1963
Bkl A—IndS(11-12)

Vijaya Lakshmi (Nehru) Pandit, 1900-

Guthrie, Anne. Madame Ambassador: The Life of Vijaya Lakshmi Pandit. Harcourt 1962
AB(6-9)—Bkl Y&C—BY—JH—SCHS—SCPL

Sadashiv Kamoji Patil, 1900-

COLLECTIONS

Hangen, Welles. After Nehru, Who? Harcourt 1963
Bkl A

Lal Bahadur Shastri, 1904-1966

COLLECTIONS

Hangen, Welles. After Nehru, Who? Harcourt 1963
Bkl A

Bal Gangadhar Tilak, 1856-1920

Wolpert, Stanley A. Tilak and Gokhale: Revolution and Reform in the Making of Modern India. Univ. of Calif. 1962
Bkl A

STATESMEN—*Continued*

Irish—19th century

Charles Stewart Parnell, 1846-1891

Abels, Jules. The Parnell Tragedy. Macmillan 1966
Bkl A

Irish—20th century

Sir Roger David Casement, 1864-1916

MacColl, Rene. Roger Casement: A New Judgment. Norton 1957
SCPL

Eamon de Valera, 1882-

Steffan, Jack. The Long Fellow: The Story of the Great Irish Patroit, Eamon de Valera. Macmillan 1966
Bkl C(8-10)&Y

Israeli

COLLECTIONS

Crossman, Richard Howard Stafford. A Nation Reborn: A Personal Report on the Roles Played by Weizmann, Bevin, and Ben-Gurion in the Story of Israel. Atheneum 1960
Bkl A
David Ben-Gurion; Ernest Bevin; Chaim Weizmann

Sachar, Howard Morley. Aliyah: The Peoples of Israel. World 1961
Bkl A

St. John, Robert. They Came from Everywhere: Twelve Who Helped Mold Modern Israel. Coward-McCann 1962
Bkl A&Y

Israeli—20th century

David Ben-Gurion, 1886-

Ben-Gurion, David and Pearlman, Moshe. Ben-Gurion Looks Back in Talks with Moshe Pearlman. Simon & Schuster 1965
Bkl A

Edelman, Maurice. David: The Story of Ben-Gurion. Putnam 1965
Bkl A&Y

St. John, Robert. Ben-Gurion: The Biography of an Extraordinary Man. Doubleday 1959
BY—GR—SCHS—SCPL

St. John, Robert. Builder of Israel: The Story of Ben-Gurion. Doubleday 1961
Bkl C(6-9)—JH

Samuels, Gertrude. B-G—Fighter of Goliaths: The Story of David Ben-Gurion. Crowell 1961
Bkl Y—BY—CC(6-9)—ESLC—SCHS—YR

COLLECTIONS

Crossman, Richard Howard Stafford. A Nation Reborn: A Personal Report on the Roles Played by Weizmann, Bevin, and Ben-Gurion in the Story of Israel. Atheneum 1960
Bkl A

Golda (Mabovitz) Meir, 1898-

Syrkin, Marie. Golda Meir: Woman with a Cause. Putnam 1963
Bkl A&Y

Italian—19th century

Giuseppe Garibaldi, 1807-1882

Baker, Nina Brown. Garibaldi. Vanguard 1944
BY—CC(7-9)—SCHS

Davenport, Marcia. Garibaldi, Father of Modern Italy. Random House 1957
JH—SCHS

Hibbert, Christopher. Garibaldi and His Enemies: The Clash of Arms and Personalities in the Making of Italy. Little 1966
Bkl A

Mack Smith, Denis. Garibaldi: A Great Life in Brief. Knopf 1956
SCPL

Trevelyan, George Macaulay. Garibaldi and the Making of Italy, June-November 1860. Longmans 1948
SCPL

Italian—20th century

Galeazzo, Conte Ciano, 1903-1944

Ciano, Galeazzo, Conte. Ciano's Hidden Diary, 1937-1938. Dutton 1953
SCPL

Benito Mussolini, 1883-1945

Archer, Jules. Twentieth Century Caesar: Benito Mussolini. Messner 1964
Bkl Y&C—IndJ(6-9)—JH

Deakin, Frederick William. The Brutal Friendship: Mussolini, Hitler, and the Fall of Italian Fascism. Harper 1963
Bkl A

Fermi, Laura. Mussolini. Univ. of Chicago 1961
BBHS—Bkl A—SCPL

Hibbert, Christopher. Il Duce: The Life of Benito Mussolini. Little 1962
Bkl A—SCPL

Kirkpatrick, Sir Ivone. Mussolini: A Study in Power. Hawthorn 1964
Bkl A

MacGregor-Hastie, Roy. The Day of the Lion. Coward-McCann 1964
Bkl A

STATESMEN

Italian—20th century

Benito Mussolini—Continued

COLLECTIONS

Bliven, Bruce. The World Changers.
Day 1965
Bkl A&Y—IndS(10-12)

Ivory Coast—20th century

Félix Houphouet-Boigny, 1905-

COLLECTIONS

Melady, Thomas P. Profiles of African
Leaders. Macmillan 1961
Bkl A&Y—SCPL

Jewish

COLLECTIONS

Kamm, Josephine. Leaders of the People.
Abelard-Schuman 1959
BBHS

Kenyan—20th century

Jomo Kenyatta, 1893?-

Delf, George. Jomo Kenyatta: Towards
Truth about "The Light of Kenya."
Doubleday 1961
Bkl A

COLLECTIONS

Kaula, Edna Mason. Leaders of the New
Africa. World 1966
Bkl C(6-10)—ESLC
Lengyel, Emil. From Prison to Power.
Follett 1964
Bkl A&Y

Thomas Joseph Mboya, 1930-

Rake, Alan. Tom Mboya: Young Man
of New Africa. Doubleday 1962
Bkl A

COLLECTIONS

Melady, Thomas P. Profiles of African
Leaders. Macmillan 1961
Bkl A&Y—SCPL

Latin American

COLLECTIONS

Alexander, Robert Jackson. Prophets of
the Revolution: Profiles of Latin
American Leaders. Macmillan 1962
Bkl A
Bailey, Bernadine (Freeman). Famous
Latin-American Liberators. Dodd 1960
Bkl C(6-9)&Y—ESLC—SCHS
Simón Bolívar; Benito Pablo Juárez; José
Julian Marti; Francisco de Miranda; José
María Teclo Morelos y Pavón; Bernardo
O'Higgins; José de San Martín; Antonio José
de Sucre; Pierre Dominique Toussaint Lou-
verture

Szulc, Tad. Twilight of the Tyrants. Holt
1959
Bkl A
Manuel Arturo Odría; Marcos Pérez Jimé-
nez; Juan Domingo Perón; Gustavo Rojas
Pinilla; Getulio Vargas
Worcester, Donald Emmet. Makers of
Latin America. Dutton 1966
Bkl Y&C

Mexican—19th century

Porfirio Díaz, 1830-1915

Cosío Villegas, Daniel. The United States
versus Porfirio Díaz; tr. by Nettie Lee
Benson. Univ. of Neb. 1964
Bkl A

*José María Teclo Morelos y Pavón,
1765-1815*

COLLECTIONS

Bailey, Bernadine (Freeman). Famous
Latin-American Liberators. Dodd 1960
Bkl C(6-9)&Y—ESLC—SCHS

Mexican—20th century

José Vasconcelos, 1882-1959

Vasconcelos, José. A Mexican Ulysses:
An Autobiography; tr. and abr. by W.
Rex Crawford. Ind. Univ. 1963
Bkl A

Nigerian—20th century

*Sir Abubakar Tafawa Balewa, 1912-
1966*

COLLECTIONS

Melady, Thomas P. Profiles of African
Leaders. Macmillan 1961
Bkl A&Y—SCPL

Norwegian—20th century

Fridtjof Nansen, 1861-1930

Hall, Anna Gertrude. Nansen. Viking
1940
CC(7-9)—JH—SCHS
Noel-Baker, Francis. Fridtjof Nansen,
Arctic Explorer. Putnam 1958
AB(4up)
Reynolds, Ernest E. Nansen. Penguin
1932
GR

Pakistani—20th century

Mohammed Ali Jinnah, 1876-1948

Bolitho, Hector. Jinnah: Creator of
Pakistan. Macmillan 1955
BY

STATESMEN—*Continued*

Palestinian—20th century

Husseini, Haj Amin, Grand Mufti of Palestine, 1895-

Schechtman, Joseph B. The Mufti and the Fuehrer: The Rise and Fall of Haj Amin el-Husseini. Yoseloff 1965
Bkl A

Philippine—20th century

Ferdinand Edralin Marcos, 1917-

Spence, Hartzell. For Every Tear a Victory: The Story of Ferdinand E. Marcos. McGraw 1964
Bkl A&Y

Carlos Pena Romulo, 1899-

Romulo, Carlos Pena. I Walked with Heroes. Holt 1961
Bkl A&Y—BY—SCHS—SCPL

Wells, Evelyn. Carlos P. Romulo: Voice of Freedom. Funk 1964
Bkl C(7-10)&Y

Polish—20th century

Wladyslaw Gomulka, 1905-

COLLECTIONS

Lengyel, Emil. From Prison to Power. Follett 1964
Bkl A&Y

Ignacy Jan Paderewski, 1860-1941

Hume, Ruth and Hume, Paul. The Lion of Poland: The Story of Paderewski. Hawthorn 1962
JH

Kellogg, Charlotte. Paderewski. Viking 1956
AB(7-10)—BBJH—SCHS—YR

Portuguese—20th century

Antonio de Oliveira Salazar, 1889-

COLLECTIONS

Acheson, Dean Gooderham. Sketches from Life of Men I Have Known. Harper 1961
Bkl A&Y—SCPL

Roman

COLLECTIONS

Coolidge, Olivia E. Lives of Famous Romans. Houghton 1965
Bkl Y&C—IndJ(6-9)

Suetonius Tranquillus, Caius. Lives of the Caesars: Lives of Illustrious Men. Harvard Univ. 1914
SCPL

Suetonius Tranquillus, Caius. Twelve Caesars; tr. by Robert Graves. Penguin 1957
SCPL

Roman—3rd century B.C.

Quintus Maximus Verrucosus Fabius, ?-203 B.C.

COLLECTIONS

Plutarch. Ten Famous Lives; the Dryden translation revised by Arthur Hugh Clough; ed. for young readers by Charles Robinson, Jr. Dutton 1962
Bkl C(7-10)&Y—BY—CC(7-9)—JH—SCHS—YR

Roman—2nd century B.C.

Marcus Porcius Cato, 234-149 B.C.

COLLECTIONS

Plutarch. Ten Famous Lives; the Dryden translation rev. by Arthur Hugh Clough; ed. for young readers by Charles Robinson, Jr. Dutton 1962
Bkl C(7-10)&Y—BY—CC(7-9)—JH—SCHS—YR

Roman—1st century B.C.

Marcus Antonius, 83?-30 B.C.

COLLECTIONS

Plutarch. Ten Famous Lives; the Dryden translation rev. by Arthur Hugh Clough; ed. for young readers by Charles Robinson, Jr. Dutton 1962
Bkl C(7-10)&Y—BY—CC(7-9)—JH—SCHS—YR

Caius Julius Caesar, 100-44 B.C.

Anderson, Paul L. Swords in the North. Biblo & Tannen 1957 (Fiction)
SCHS

Coolidge, Olivia. Caesar's Gallic War. Houghton 1961
CC(7-9)—JH—SCHS

Duggan, Alfred Leo. Julius Caesar: A Great Life in Brief. Knopf 1955
BBHS—SCPL—3000

Fuller, John Frederick Charles. Julius Caesar: Man, Soldier, and Tyrant. Rutgers Univ. 1965
Bkl A

Gunther, John. Julius Caesar. Random House 1959
Bkl C(5-9)&Y—CC(6-9)—ESLC—JH—SCHS

Horizon Magazine. Caesar, by Irwin Isenberg. Am. Heritage 1964
Bkl C(6-9)&Y—CC—ESLC—IndS(9-10)—JH

Komroff, Manuel. Julius Caesar. Messner 1955
BBJH—BY—CC(7-9)—JH—SCHS

Shakespeare, William. Julius Caesar (Play)
SCHS

STATESMEN

Roman—1st century B.C.

Caius Julius Caesar—Continued

Shaw, George Bernard. Caesar and Cleopatra. Dodd 1948 (Play)
SCHS

Warner, Rex. Imperial Caesar. Little 1960 (Fiction)
Bkl A

Warner, Rex. The Young Caesar. Little 1958 (Fiction)
SCHS

COLLECTIONS

Plutarch. Ten Famous Lives; the Dryden translation rev. by Arthur Hugh Clough; ed. for young readers by Charles Robinson, Jr. Dutton 1962
Bkl C(7-10)&Y—BY—CC(7-9)—JH—SCHS—YR

Marcus Tullius Cicero, 106-43 B.C.

Church, Alfred J. Roman Life in the Days of Cicero: Sketches Drawn from His Letters and Speeches. Biblo & Tannen 1959
SCHS

Wagner, John and Wagner, Esther. The Gift of Rome. Little 1961 (Fiction)
Bkl A

COLLECTIONS

Plutarch. Ten Famous Lives; the Dryden translation rev. by Arthur Hugh Clough; ed. for young readers by Charles Robinson, Jr. Dutton 1962
Bkl C(7-10)&Y—BY—CC(7-9)—JH—SCHS—YR

Russian

COLLECTIONS

Coolidge, Olivia. Makers of the Red Revolution. Houghton 1963
CC(7-9)
Nikita Sergeevich Khrushchev; Vladimir Il'ich Lenin; Mao Tsê-tung; Karl Marx; Joseph Stalin; Josip Broz Tito; Lev Trotsky

Hare, Richard. Portraits of Russian Personalities Between Reform and Revolution. Oxford 1959
3000

Wolfe, Bertram David. Three Who Made a Revolution: A Biographical History. Dial 1964
Bkl A—SCPL—3000
Vladimir Il'ich Lenin; Joseph Stalin; Lev Trotsky

Russian—18th century

Grigori Aleksandrovich Potemkin, 1739-1791

Soloveytchik, George. Potemkin: Soldier, Statesman, Lover and Consort of Catherine of Russia. Norton 1947
SCPL

Russian—20th century

Alexander Fedorovich Kerensky, 1881-

Kerensky, Alexander Fedorovich. Russia and History's Turning Point. Duell 1965
Bkl A—IndS(11-12)

Nikita Sergeevich Khrushchev, 1894-

Crankshaw, Edward. Khrushchev: A Career. Viking 1966
Bkl A&Y

Floyd, David. Mao Against Khrushchev: A Short History of the Sino-Soviet Conflict. Praeger 1964
Bkl A

Hearst, William Randolph and others. Ask Me Anything: Our Adventures with Khrushchev. McGraw 1960
Bkl A

Johnson, Priscilla. Khrushchev and the Arts: The Politics of Soviet Culture, 1962-1964; ed. by Leopold Labedz. Mass. Inst. of Technology 1965
Bkl A

Keleen, Konrad. Khrushchev: A Political Portrait. Praeger 1961
Bkl A&Y

MacGregor-Hastie, Roy. The Man from Nowhere. Coward-McCann 1961
Bkl A&Y—BY—SCHS

McNeal, Robert Hatch. The Bolshevik Tradition: Lenin, Stalin, Khrushchev. Prentice-Hall 1963
Bkl A

Pistrak, Lazar. The Grand Tactician: Khrushchev's Rise to Power. Praeger 1961
Bkl A

COLLECTIONS

Coolidge, Olivia. Makers of the Red Revolution. Houghton 1963
CC(7-9)

Vladimir Il'ich Lenin, 1870-1924

Baker, Nina Brown. Lenin. Vanguard 1945
BY

Balabanoff, Angelica. Impressions of Lenin; tr. by Isotta Cesari. Univ. of Mich. 1964
Bkl A

Fischer, Louis. The Life of Lenin. Harper 1964
Bkl A—SCPL

McNeal, Robert Hatch. The Bolshevik Tradition: Lenin, Stalin, Khrushchev. Prentice-Hall 1963
Bkl A

Payne, Robert. The Life and Death of Lenin. Simon & Schuster 1964
Bkl A&Y—SCPL

STATESMEN

Russian—20th century

Vladimir Il'ich Lenin—Continued

Possony, Stefan Thomas. Lenin: The Compulsive Revolutionary. Regnery 1964
Bkl A

COLLECTIONS

Coolidge, Olivia. Makers of the Red Revolution. Houghton 1963
CC(7-9)

Wolfe, Bertram David. Three Who Made a Revolution: A Biographical History. Dial 1964
Bkl A—SCPL—3000

Joseph Stalin, 1879-1953

Archer, Jules. Man of Steel: Joseph Stalin. Messner 1965
Bkl Y(7-10)&C—IndJ(6-9)

Deutscher, Isaac. Stalin: A Political Biography. Oxford 1949
SCPL—3000

Djilas, Milovan. Conversations with Stalin; tr. from the Serbo-Croat by Michael B. Petrovich. Harcourt 1962
Bkl A&Y

McNeal, Robert Hatch. The Bolshevik Tradition: Lenin, Stalin, Khrushchev. Prentice-Hall 1963
Bkl A

Trotsky, Lev. Stalin: An Appraisal of the Man and His Influence; tr. by Charles Malamuth. Harper 1941
SCPL

COLLECTIONS

Bliven, Bruce. The World Changers. Day 1965
Bkl A&Y—IndS(10-12)

Coolidge, Olivia. Makers of the Red Revolution. Houghton 1963
CC(7-9)

Wolfe, Bertram David. Three Who Made a Revolution: A Biographical History. Dial 1964
Bkl A—SCPL—3000

Lev Trotsky, 1879-1940

Deutscher, Isaac. The Prophet Armed: Trotsky, 1879-1921. Oxford 1954
SCPL

Deutscher, Isaac. The Prophet Outcast: Trotsky, 1929-1940. Oxford 1963
Bkl A—SCPL

Deutscher, Isaac. The Prophet Unarmed: Trotsky, 1921-1929. Oxford 1959
SCPL

COLLECTIONS

Coolidge, Olivia. Makers of the Red Revolution. Houghton 1963
CC(7-9)

Wolfe, Bertram David. Three Who Made a Revolution: A Biographical History. Dial 1964
Bkl A—SCPL—3000

Andrei Vishinsky, 1883-1954

COLLECTIONS

Acheson, Dean Gooderham. Sketches from Life of Men I Have Known. Harper 1961
Bkl A&Y—SCPL

Scottish—16th century

James Stewart, 1st Earl of Moray, 1531?-1570

Harwood, Alice. No Smoke Without Fire: The Tragedy of Mary Stuart's Brother James. Bobbs 1964 (Fiction)
Bkl A

Scottish—20th century

John Buchan, 1st Baron Tweedsmuir, 1875-1940

Smith, Janet Adam. John Buchan: A Biography. Little 1966
Bkl A

South African—20th century

Jan Hendrik Hofmeyr, 1894-1948

Paton, Alan. South African Tragedy: The Life and Times of Jan Hofmeyr; abr. by Dudley C. Lunt. Scribner 1965
Bkl A—IndS(11-12)

Albert Luthuli, 1899-1967

Luthuli, Albert. Let My People Go. McGraw 1962
Bkl A&Y—BY—SCHS—SCPL

COLLECTIONS

Harcourt, Melville. Portraits of Destiny. Sheed 1966
Bkl A

Kaula, Edna Mason. Leaders of the New Africa. World 1966
Bkl C(6-10)—ESLC

South American—19th century

Simón Bolívar, 1783-1830

Baker, Nina (Brown). He Wouldn't Be King: The Story of Simon Bolivar. Vanguard 1941
BY—CC(7-9)—JH—SCHS—YR

Frank, Waldo David. Birth of a World: Bolivar in Terms of His Peoples. Houghton 1951
SCPL

Van Loon, Hendrik Willem. Fighters for Freedom: Jefferson and Bolivar. Dodd 1962
Bkl C(7-12)&Y

STATESMEN

South American—19th century

Simón Bolívar—Continued

Webb, Robert N. Simón Bolívar, the
  Liberator. Watts 1966
    Bkl Y(7-10)&C—ESLC
Whitridge, Arnold. Simón Bolívar, the
  Great Liberator. Random House 1954
    JH—SCHS

COLLECTIONS

Bailey, Bernadine (Freeman). Famous
  Latin-American Liberators. Dodd 1960
    Bkl C(6-9)&Y—ESLC—SCHS
Larson, Egon. Men Who Fought for
  Freedom. Roy 1959
    AB

José de San Martín, 1778-1850

COLLECTIONS

Bailey, Bernadine (Freeman). Famous
  Latin-American Liberators. Dodd 1960
    Bkl C(6-9)&Y—ESLC—SCHS

Spanish—15th century

Álvaro de Luna, 1388?-1453

Edwards, Samuel. Master of Castile.
  Morrow 1962 (Fiction)
    Bkl A

Swedish—20th century

Dag Hammarskjöld, 1905-1961

Gavshon, Arthur L. The Mysterious
  Death of Dag Hammarskjöld. Walker
  & Co. 1962
    Bkl A
Hammarskjöld, Dag. Markings; tr. from
  the Swedish by Leif Sjöberg and W.
  H. Auden. Knopf 1964
    Bkl A—IndS(11-12)
Kelen, Emery. Hammarskjöld. Putnam
  1966
    Bkl A&Y
Lash, Joseph P. Dag Hammarskjöld:
  Custodian of the Brushfire Peace.
  Doubleday 1961
    Bkl A&Y—SCHS
Levine, Israel E. Champion of World
  Peace: Dag Hammarskjöld. Messner
  1962
    Bkl Y&C—BY—CC—JH—SCHS
Miller, Richard I. Dag Hammarskjöld
  and Crisis Diplomacy. Oceana 1961
    Bkl A
Söderberg, Sten Valdemar. Hammar-
  skjöld: A Pictorial Biography. Viking
  1962
    Bkl A&Y—SCHS
Stolpe, Sven. Dag Hammarskjöld: A
  Spiritual Portrait; tr. by Naomi Wal-
  ford. Scribner 1966
    Bkl A&Y

Swiss—14th century

William Tell, ?

Buff, Mary (Marsh) and Buff, Conrad.
  The Apple and the Arrow. Houghton
  1951 (Fiction)
    BBEL(3-6)—CC(3-6)—ESLC

Tibetan—20th century

Dalai Lama XIV, 1935-

Dalai Lama XIV. My Land and My
  People. McGraw 1962
    Bkl A&Y—BY—SCPL

Welsh—20th century

Aneurin Bevan, 1897-1960

Foot, Michael. Aneurin Bevan: A Biography: v. 1, 1897-1945. Atheneum
  1963
    Bkl A—IndS(11-12)
Krug, Mark M. Aneurin Bevan: Cautious
  Rebel. Yoseloff 1961
    Bkl A

STEWARDESSES, AIRLINE

See Airline Stewardesses

SUFFRAGISTS

See Feminists

SULTANS

Turkish—16th century

Sulaiman I, the Magnificent, 1494-1566

Faulkner, Nancy. Knights Besieged.
  Doubleday 1964 (Fiction)
    JH
Lamb, Harold. Suleiman the Magnificent,
  Sultan of the East. Doubleday 1951
    GR—SCPL

SUPREME COURT JUSTICES

See Lawyers

SURGEONS

See also Physicians

COLLECTIONS

Riedman, Sarah Regal. Masters of the
  Scalpel: The Story of Surgery. Rand
  McNally 1962
    BBHS—Bkl Y&C—CC(7-9)—JH—SCHS

SURGEONS—*Continued*

American—19th century

William Beaumont, 1785-1853

COLLECTIONS

Blassingame, Wyatt and Glendinning, Richard. Frontier Doctors. Watts 1963
Bkl C(6-9)

Dunlop, Richard. Doctors of the American Frontier. Doubleday 1965
Bkl A&Y

William Stewart Halsted, 1852-1922

Beckhard, Arthur J. and Crane, William D. Cancer, Cocaine and Courage: The Story of Dr. William Halsted. Messner 1960
Bkl Y&C—JH—SCHS

Crawford Williamson Long, 1815-1878

COLLECTIONS

Blassingame, Wyatt and Glendinning, Richard. Frontier Doctors. Watts 1963
Bkl C(6-9)

Ephraim McDowell, 1771-1830

COLLECTIONS

Blassingame, Wyatt and Glendinning, Richard. Frontier Doctors. Watts 1963
Bkl C(6-9)

Dunlop, Richard. Doctors of the American Frontier. Doubleday 1965
Bkl A&Y

American—20th century

Emily (Dunning) Barringer, 1876-1961

Noble, Iris. First Woman Ambulance Surgeon: Emily Barringer. Messner 1962
Bkl Y&C

COLLECTIONS

Fleming, Alice (Mulcahey). Doctors in Petticoats. Lippincott 1964
Bkl C(6-9)—CC—JH

Harvey Williams Cushing, 1869-1939

Thomson, Elizabeth Harriet. Harvey Cushing: Surgeon, Author, Artist. Schuman 1950
SCPL

Charles Richard Drew, 1904-1950

COLLECTIONS

Sterne, Emma (Gelders). Blood Brothers: Four Men of Science. Knopf 1959
Bkl C(7-9)—JH

William Stewart Halsted, 1852-1922

Beckhard, Arthur J. and Crane, William D. Cancer, Cocaine and Courage: The Story of Dr. William Halsted. Messner 1960
Bkl Y&C—JH—SCHS

Paul Budd Magnuson, 1884-

Magnuson, Paul Budd. Ring the Night Bell: The Autobiography of a Surgeon; ed. by Finley Peter Dunne, Jr. Little 1960
Bkl A&Y

Chinese—20th century

Li Shu-fan, 1887-1966

Li, Shu-fan. Hong Kong Surgeon. Dutton 1964
Bkl A

English—19th century

Joseph Lister, 1st Baron Lister of Lyme Regis, 1827-1912

Farmer, Laurence. Master Surgeon: A Biography of Joseph Lister. Harper 1962
Bkl C(6-9)&Y—BY—ESLC—JH—YR

Noble, Iris. The Courage of Dr. Lister. Messner 1960
BBHS—Bkl Y&C

COLLECTIONS

Bixby, William. Great Experimenters. McKay 1964
Bkl C(7-8)&Y—ESLC

Hume, Ruth Fox. Great Men of Medicine. Random House 1961
CC(7-9)—ESLC—JH—SCHS—YR

French—16th century

Ambroise Paré, 1517-1590

Carbonnier, Jeanne. A Barber-Surgeon: A Life of Ambroise Paré, Founder of Modern Surgery. Pantheon 1965
Bkl C(6-8)

COLLECTIONS

Hume, Ruth Fox. Great Men of Medicine. Random House 1961
CC(7-9)—ESLC—JH—SCHS—YR

German—20th century

Ferdinand Sauerbruch, 1875-1951

Thorwald, Jürgen. The Dismissal: The Last Days of Ferdinand Sauerbruch; tr. from the German by Richard and Clara Winston. Pantheon 1962
Bkl A

SURGEONS—*Continued*

New Zealand—20th century

Sir Archibald Hector McIndoe, 1900-1960

Mosley, Leonard Oswald. Faces from the Fire. Prentice-Hall 1963
Bkl A&Y

Scottish—18th century

John Hunter, 1728-1793

Kobler, John. The Reluctant Surgeon: A Biography of John Hunter. Doubleday 1960
Bkl A—SCPL

SWIMMERS

American—20th century

Frank Holten Norris, ?

COLLECTIONS

Boynick, David King. Champions by Setback: Athletes Who Overcame Physical Handicaps. Crowell 1954
SCHS

Johnny Weissmuller, 1904-

COLLECTIONS

Gallico, Paul. The Golden People. Doubleday 1965
Bkl A&Y
Gelman, Steve. Young Olympic Champions. Norton 1964
Bkl C(6-9)&Y—ESLC—JH

SWINDLERS

See Criminals

TAXIDERMISTS

American—20th century

Carl Ethan Akeley, 1864-1926

Sutton, Felix. Big Game Hunter: Carl Akeley. Messner 1960
Bkl C(5-9)&Y

TEACHERS

See Educators

TEACHERS OF THE BLIND

See Blind

TELEPHONE OPERATORS

American—20th century

Margaret (Knudsen) Burke, ?

Springer, John A. Innocent in Alaska. Coward-McCann 1963
Bkl A&Y

TELEVISION ENGINEERS

See Engineers, Radio and Television

TELEVISION PERFORMERS

See Actors; Radio and Television Performers

TEMPERANCE WORKERS

American—20th century

Carry Amelia (Moore) Nation, 1846-1911

Beals, Carleton. Cyclone Carry: The Story of Carry Nation. Chilton 1962
Bkl A

TENNIS PLAYERS

American—20th century

Althea Gibson, 1927-

Gibson, Althea. I Always Wanted to Be Somebody; ed. by Ed Fitzgerald. Harper 1958
BY—SCHS

COLLECTIONS

Bontemps, Arna. Famous Negro Athletes. Dodd 1964
Bkl C&Y—ESLC—JH
Forsee, Aylesa. Women Who Reached for Tomorrow. Macrae 1960
Bkl Y&C

Hamilton Farrar Richardson, 1933-

COLLECTIONS

Boynick, David King. Champions by Setback: Athletes Who Overcame Physical Handicaps. Crowell 1954
SCHS

TEST PILOTS

See Aviators

THEATRICAL PRODUCERS

See also Actors; Motion Picture Producers; Playwrights; Scenic Designers

American—19th century

Oscar Hammerstein, 1847-1919

Sheean, Vincent. Oscar Hammerstein I: The Life and Exploits of an Impresario. Simon & Schuster 1956
SCPL

American—20th century

George Abbott, 1889-

Abbott, George. "Mister Abbott." Random House 1963
Bkl A

THEATRICAL PRODUCERS

American—20th century—*Continued*

Marguerite (Wagner) Cullman, ?

Cullman, Marguerite (Wagner). Occupation: Angel. Norton 1963
Bkl A&Y

Max Gordon, 1892-

Gordon, Max and Funke, Lewis. Max Gordon Presents. Geis 1963
Bkl A&Y

Oscar Hammerstein, 1847-1919

Sheean, Vincent. Oscar Hammerstein I: The Life and Exploits of an Impresario. Simon & Schuster 1956
SCPL

Theresa Helburn, 1887-1959

Helburn, Theresa. A Wayward Quest: The Autobiography of Theresa Helburn. Little 1960
Bkl A—BY

Joshua Lockwood Logan, 1908-

COLLECTIONS

Davidson, William. The Real and the Unreal. Harper 1961
Bkl A

Guthrie McClintic, 1893-1961

McClintic, Guthrie. Me and Kit. Little 1955
BY—SCHS—SCPL

English—19th century

Beerbohm Tree, 1853-1917

Pearson, Hesketh. Beerbohm Tree: His Life and Laughter. Harper 1956
SCPL

English—20th century

Sir Tyrone Guthrie, 1900-

Guthrie, Sir Tyrone. A Life in the Theatre. McGraw 1959
BBHS—Bkl A

Beerbohm Tree, 1853-1917

Pearson, Hesketh. Beerbohm Tree: His Life and Laughter. Harper 1956
SCPL

Russian—20th century

Constantin Stanislavski, 1863-1938

Stanislavski, Constantin. My Life in Art. Theatre Arts 1948
SCPL

THEOLOGIANS

See Religious Leaders

TRACK AND FIELD ATHLETES

COLLECTIONS

Higdon, Hal. Heroes of the Olympics. Prentice-Hall 1965
ESLC
Harold Connolly; Spiridon Loues; Herbert McKenley; Robert Bruce Mathias; James Edward ("Ted") Meredith; Billy Mills; Paavo Nurmi; Jesse Owens; Wilma Rudolph; Mildred (Didrikson) Zaharias

American—20th century

William Bonthron, 1920?-

COLLECTIONS

Boynick, David King. Champions by Setback: Athletes Who Overcame Physical Handicaps. Crowell 1954
SCHS

Harold Connolly, 1931-

COLLECTIONS

Higdon, Hal. Heroes of the Olympics. Prentice-Hall 1965
ESLC

Glenn Cunningham, 1910-

COLLECTIONS

Boynick, David King. Champions by Setback: Athletes Who Overcame Physical Handicaps. Crowell 1954
SCHS

Robert Bruce Mathias, 1930-

Scott, Jim. Bob Mathias: Champion of Champions. Denison 1963
JH

COLLECTIONS

Higdon, Hal. Heroes of the Olympics. Prentice-Hall 1965
ESLC

James Edward ("Ted") Meredith, 1893?-1957

COLLECTIONS

Higdon, Hal. Heroes of the Olympics. Prentice-Hall 1965
ESLC

Billy Mills, ?

COLLECTIONS

Higdon, Hal. Heroes of the Olympics. Prentice-Hall 1965
ESLC

Jesse Owens, 1913-

COLLECTIONS

Bontemps, Arna. Famous Negro Athletes. Dodd 1964
Bkl C&Y—ESLC—JH

TRACK AND FIELD ATHLETES

American—20th century

Jesse Owens—Continued

Higdon, Hal. Heroes of the Olympics. Prentice-Hall 1965
ESLC

Young, Andrew Sturgeon Nash. Negro Firsts in Sports. Johnson Pub. 1963
Bkl A&Y

Wilma Rudolph, 1940-

COLLECTIONS

Higdon, Hal. Heroes of the Olympics. Prentice-Hall 1965
ESLC

Archie San Romani, 1912?-

COLLECTIONS

Boynick, David King. Champions by Setback: Athletes Who Overcame Physical Handicaps. Crowell 1954
SCHS

Mildred (Didrikson) Zaharias, 1913-1956

COLLECTIONS

Higdon, Hal. Heroes of the Olympics. Prentice-Hall 1965
ESLC

English—20th century

Roger Bannister, 1929-

Bannister, Roger. The Four Minute Mile. Dodd 1955
BY—SCHS

Finnish—20th century

Paavo Nurmi, 1897-

COLLECTIONS

Higdon, Hal. Heroes of the Olympics. Prentice-Hall 1965
ESLC

Greek—19th century

Spiridon Loues, ?

COLLECTIONS

Higdon, Hal. Heroes of the Olympics. Prentice-Hall 1965
ESLC

Jamaican—20th century

Herbert McKenley, 1922-

COLLECTIONS

Higdon, Hal. Heroes of the Olympics. Prentice-Hall 1965
ESLC

TRADE UNION LEADERS

See Labor Leaders

TRAFFIC ENGINEERS

See Engineers, Traffic

TRAITORS

See also Criminals

American—18th century

Benedict Arnold, 1741-1801

Flexner, James Thomas. The Traitor and the Spy: Benedict Arnold and John André. Harcourt 1953
SCPL

Nolan, Jeannette (Covert). Benedict Arnold: Traitor to His Country. Messner 1956
BBHS—BBJH—JH—SCHS

Nolan, Jeannette (Covert). Treason at the Point. Messner 1944 (Fiction)
SCHS

Roberts, Kenneth Lewis. Arundel. Doubleday 1933 (Fiction)
BBHS—SCHS

Vail, Philip. The Twisted Saber: A Biographical Novel of Benedict Arnold. Dodd 1963 (Fiction)
Bkl A&Y—IndS(9-12)

COLLECTIONS

Bakeless, John. Turncoats, Traitors, and Heroes. Lippincott 1959
SCHS

English

COLLECTIONS

Moorehead, Alan. The Traitors. Harper 1963
Bkl A
Klaus Fuchs; Allan Nunn May; Bruno Pontecorvo

English—20th century

Klaus Emil Julius Fuchs, 1911-

COLLECTIONS

Moorehead, Alan. The Traitors. Harper 1963
Bkl A

Wighton, Charles. The World's Greatest Spies. Taplinger 1966
Bkl A&Y

William ("Lord Haw-Haw") Joyce, 1906-1946

Cole, John Alfred. Lord Haw-Haw and William Joyce: The Full Story. Farrar 1965
Bkl A

Allan Nunn May, 1911-

COLLECTIONS

Moorehead, Alan. The Traitors. Harper 1963
Bkl A

TRAITORS

English—20th century—*Continued*

Bruno Pontecorvo, 1913-

COLLECTIONS

Moorehead, Alan. The Traitors. Harper 1963
Bkl A

TRAPPERS

See Frontiersmen

TRAVELERS

See Explorers

TRUMPETERS

American—20th century

Louis ("Satchmo") Armstrong, 1900-

Eaton, Jeanette. Trumpeter's Tale: The Story of Young Louis Armstrong. Morrow 1955
BBJH—BY—CC—JH—SCHS

COLLECTIONS

Hadlock, Richard. Jazz Masters of the Twenties. Macmillan 1965
Bkl A&Y

Leon Bismarck ("Bix") Beiderbecke, 1903-1931

COLLECTIONS

Hadlock, Richard. Jazz Masters of the Twenties. Macmillan 1965
Bkl A&Y

Max Kaminsky, 1908-

Kaminsky, Max and Hughes, V. E. My Life in Jazz. Harper 1963
Bkl A

UNITED NATIONS OFFICIALS

Burmese—20th century

Thant, 1909-

Bingham, June. U Thant: The Search for Peace. Knopf 1966
Bkl A&Y

Swedish—20th century

Dag Hammarskjöld, 1905-1961

Gavshon, Arthur L. The Mysterious Death of Dag Hammarskjöld. Walker & Co. 1962
Bkl A

Hammarskjöld, Dag. Markings; tr. from the Swedish by Leif Sjöberg and W. H. Auden. Knopf 1964
Bkl A—IndS(11-12)

Kelen, Emery. Hammarskjöld. Putnam 1966
Bkl A&Y

Lash, Joseph P. Dag Hammarskjöld: Custodian of the Brushfire Peace. Doubleday 1961
Bkl A&Y—SCHS

Levine, Israel E. Champion of World Peace: Dag Hammarskjöld. Messner 1962
Bkl Y&C—BY—CC—JH—SCHS

Miller, Richard I. Dag Hammarskjöld and Crisis Diplomacy. Oceana 1961
Bkl A

Söderberg, Sten Valdemar. Hammarskjöld: A Pictorial Biography. Viking 1962
Bkl A&Y—SCHS

Stolpe, Sven. Dag Hammarskjöld: A Spiritual Portrait; tr. by Naomi Walford. Scribner 1966
Bkl A

VAUDEVILLE PERFORMERS

See Actors

VETERINARIANS

American—20th century

Louis J. Camuti, ?

Camuti, Louis J. and Alexander, Lloyd. Park Avenue Vet. Holt 1962
Bkl A&Y

J. Y. Henderson, ?

Henderson, J. Y. and Taplinger, Richard. Circus Doctor. Little 1951
BY—SCHS—SCPL

Louis L. Vine, ?

Vine, Louis L. and Forbus, Ina. Dogs in My Life. Appleton 1961
Bkl A&Y

VICTIMS OF ARTHRITIS

American—20th century

Faith Perkins, ?

Perkins, Faith. My Fight with Arthritis. Random House 1964
Bkl A

French—20th century

Sidonie Gabrielle Colette, 1873-1954

Colette, Sidonie Gabrielle. The Blue Lantern; tr. by Roger Senhouse. Farrar 1963
Bkl A

VICTIMS OF CEREBRAL PALSY

American—20th century

Evelyn West Ayrault, 1922-

Ayrault, Evelyn West. Take One Step. Doubleday 1963
Bkl A&Y

Earl Schenck Miers, 1910-

Miers, Earl Schenck. The Trouble Bush. Rand McNally 1966
Bkl A

Debra Jean Segal, ?

Segal, Marilyn M. Run Away, Little Girl. Random House 1966
Bkl A&Y

Irish—20th century

Christy Brown, 1932-

Brown, Christy. My Left Foot. Simon & Schuster 1955
BY—SCHS

VICTIMS OF LEPROSY

American—20th century

Ned Langford, ?

Burgess, Perry. Who Walk Alone. Holt 1940
SCHS—SCPL

Betty Martin, 1908-

Martin, Betty. Miracle at Carville; ed. by Evelyn Wells. Doubleday 1950
SCHS—SCPL

VICTIMS OF MURDERERS

American—20th century

Edward Wheeler Hall, 1881-1922

Kunstler, William Moses. The Minister and the Choir Singer: The Hall-Mills Murder Case. Morrow 1964
Bkl A—IndS(11-12)

Eleanor (Reinhardt) Mills, 1887?-1922

Kunstler, William Moses. The Minister and the Choir Singer: The Hall-Mills Murder Case. Morrow 1964
Bkl A—IndS(11-12)

Janice Wylie, 1942-1963

Wylie, Max. The Gift of Janice. Doubleday 1964
Bkl A

English—16th century

Sir Thomas Overbury, 1581-1613

De Ford, Miriam Allen. The Overbury Affair: The Murder Trial That Rocked the Court of King James I. Chilton 1960
Bkl A

VICTIMS OF POLIO

American—20th century

Beatrice Ann (Posner) Wright, 1917-

Chappell, Eleanor. On the Shoulders of Giants: The Bea Wright Story. Chilton 1960
Bkl A&Y

Australian—20th century

Marjorie Lawrence, 1909-

Lawrence, Marjorie. Interrupted Melody: The Story of My Life. Appleton 1949
SCHS—SCPL

English—20th century

Peter Marshall, 1939-

Marshall, Peter. Two Lives. Stein & Day 1963
Bkl A

New Zealand—20th century

June Opie, ?

Opie, June. Over My Dead Body. Dutton 1957
SCHS—YR

VIOLINISTS

American—20th century

Jascha Heifetz, 1901-

COLLECTIONS

Chotzinoff, Samuel. A Little Nightmusic. Harper 1964
Bkl A&Y—IndS(12)

Fritz Kreisler, 1875-1962

Lochner, Louis Paul. Fritz Kreisler. Macmillan 1950
SCPL

Yehudi Menuhin, 1916-

Magidoff, Robert. Yehudi Menuhin: The Story of the Man and the Musician. Doubleday 1955
SCPL

COLLECTIONS

Pincherle, Marc. The World of the Virtuoso; tr. from the French by Lucille H. Brockway. Norton 1963
Bkl A

VIOLINISTS

American—20th century—_Continued_

Isaac Stern, 1920-

COLLECTIONS

Ewen, David. Famous Instrumentalists. Dodd 1965
Bkl Y&C

Hungarian—20th century

Joseph Szigeti, 1892-

Szigeti, Joseph. With Strings Attached: Reminiscences and Reflections. Knopf 1947
SCPL

Irish—20th century

Walter Fitzwilliam Starkie, 1894-

Starkie, Walter Fitzwilliam. Scholars and Gypsies: An Autobiography. Univ. of Calif. 1963
Bkl A

Italian—19th century

Nicolò Paganini, 1782-1840

De Courcy, G. I. C. Paganini, the Genoese. Univ. of Okla. 1957
SCPL

Maynor, Eleanor. The Golden Key: A Story Biography of Nicolò Paganini. Criterion Bks 1966
ESLC

Wheeler, Opal. Paganini, Master of Strings. Dutton 1950
CC(4-6)—SCHS

COLLECTIONS

Pincherle, Marc. The World of the Virtuoso; tr. from the French by Lucille H. Brockway. Norton 1963
Bkl A

Russian—20th century

Julian Brodetsky, ?-1962

Wibberley, Leonard Patrick O'Connor. Ah, Julian! A Memoir of Julian Brodetsky. Washburn 1963
Bkl A

VIOLONCELLISTS

See Cellists

VIROLOGISTS

American—20th century

Ernest William Goodpasture, 1886-1960

COLLECTIONS

Sullivan, Navin. Pioneer Germ Fighters. Atheneum 1962
AB(4up)—CC(5-7)—ESLC

Jonas Edward Salk, 1914-

Carter, Richard. Breakthrough: The Saga of Jonas Salk. Trident Press 1966
Bkl A&Y

Rowland, John. The Polio Man: The Story of Dr. Jonas Salk. Roy 1961
Bkl C(6-9)&Y

COLLECTIONS

Riedman, Sarah Regal. Shots Without Guns: The Story of Vaccination. Rand McNally 1960
BBHS—Bkl Y&C—CC(7-9)—ESLC—JH—SCHS—YR

Williams, Greer. Virus Hunters. Knopf 1959
Bkl A&Y—3000

VOCALISTS

See Singers

WIVES OF FAMOUS MEN

American—18th century

Abigail (Smith) Adams, 1744-1818

Criss, Mildred. Abigail Adams: Leading Lady. Dodd 1953
BY

Whitney, Janet (Payne). Abigail Adams. Little 1947
SCPL

COLLECTIONS

Daugherty, Sonia. Ten Brave Women. Lippincott 1953
BY—CC(7-9)—ESLC—JH—SCHS

Sarah (Livingston) Jay, 1757-1802

Hobart, Lois. Patriot's Lady: The Life of Sarah Livingston Jay. Funk 1960
Bkl Y&C—YR

Martha (Dandridge) Custis Washington, 1732-1802

Desmond, Alice Curtis. Martha Washington, Our First Lady. Dodd 1942
CC(7-9)—JH—SCHS

Thane, Elswyth. Washington's Lady. Dodd 1960
BBHS—Bkl A&Y—SCPL

Vance, Marguerite. Martha, Daughter of Virginia: The Story of Martha Washington. Dutton 1947
BBJH—CC(5-7)—ESLC—JH—SCHS

American—19th century

Louisa Catherine (Johnson) Adams, 1775-1852

Kerr, Laura. Louisa: The Life of Mrs. John Quincy Adams. Funk 1964
JH

WIVES OF FAMOUS MEN

American—19th century—*Continued*

Olivia (Langdon) Clemens, 1845?-1904

Stoutenburg, Adrien and Baker, Laura Nelson. Dear Dear Livy: The Story of Mark Twain's Wife. Scribner 1963
Bkl C&Y—IndJ(6-9)—YR

Cora Crane, 1868-1910

Gilkes, Lillian Barnard. Cora Crane: A Biography of Mrs. Stephen Crane. Ind. Univ. 1960
Bkl A

Elizabeth (Bacon) Custer, 1842-1933

Leighton, Margaret. Bride of Glory. Farrar 1962
BY—YR

Randall, Ruth (Painter). I, Elizabeth: A Biography of the Girl Who Married General George Armstrong Custer of "Custer's Last Stand." Little 1966
Bkl C(7-10)

COLLECTIONS

Johnson, Dorothy M. Some Went West. Dodd 1965
Bkl C(7-9)&Y

Varina (Howell) Davis, 1826-1906

Kane, Harnett T. Bride of Fortune: A Novel Based on the Life of Mrs. Jefferson Davis. Doubleday 1948 (Fiction)
SCHS

Randall, Ruth (Painter). I, Varina: A Biography of the Girl Who Married Jefferson Davis and Became the First Lady of the South. Little 1962
Bkl Y&C—YR

Ross, Ishbel. First Lady of the South: The Life of Mrs. Jefferson Davis. Harper 1958
SCPL

Jessie (Benton) Frémont, 1824-1902

Higgins, Marguerite. Jessie Benton Frémont. Houghton 1962
ESLC

Randall, Ruth (Painter). I, Jessie: A Biography of the Girl Who Married John Charles Frémont, Famous Explorer of the West. Little 1963
AB(4-7)—Bkl C(7-10)&Y—IndS(9-12)—SCHS—YR

Stone, Irving. Immortal Wife: The Biographical Novel of Jessie Benton Fremont. Doubleday 1944 (Fiction)
BBHS—SCHS

Julia (Dent) Grant, 1826-1902

Ross, Ishbel. The General's Wife: The Life of Mrs. Ulysses S. Grant. Dodd 1959
SCPL

Eliza (Bowen) Jumel, 1769-1865

Falkner, Leonard. Painted Lady—Eliza Jumel: Her Life and Times. Dutton 1962
Bkl A

Mary (Todd) Lincoln, 1818-1882

Croy, Homer. The Trial of Mrs. Abraham Lincoln. Duell 1962
BY

Randall, Ruth (Painter). I, Mary: A Biography of the Girl Who Married Abraham Lincoln. Little 1959
SCHS

Randall, Ruth (Painter). Mary Lincoln: Biography of a Marriage. Little 1953
BBHS—SCHS—SCPL

Sandburg, Carl. Mary Lincoln, Wife and Widow. Harcourt 1932
SCPL

Dorothy (Payne) Todd Madison, 1768-1849

Davidson, Mary R. Dolly Madison, Famous First Lady. Garrard 1966
ESLC

Desmond, Alice Curtis. Glamorous Dolly Madison. Dodd 1946
BY—SCHS

Nolan, Jeannette (Covert). Dolley Madison. Messner 1958
BBJH—JH

COLLECTIONS

Daugherty, Sonia. Ten Brave Women. Lippincott 1953
BY—CC(7-9)—ESLC—JH—SCHS

Bertha (Honoré) Palmer, 1849-1918

Ross, Ishbel. Silhouette in Diamonds: The Life of Mrs. Potter Palmer. Harper 1960
Bkl A

Narcissa (Prentiss) Whitman, 1808-1847

Cranston, Paul. To Heaven on Horseback: The Romantic Story of Narcissa Whitman. Messner 1952 (Fiction)
SCHS

Eaton, Jeanette. Narcissa Whitman, Pioneer of Oregon. Harcourt 1941
BBEL(7-8)—BY—CC(7-9)—ESLC—JH—SCHS—YR

COLLECTIONS

Ross, Nancy Wilson. Heroines of the Early West. Random House 1960
Bkl C(5-9)—BY—CC(5-7)—ESLC—JH

WIVES OF FAMOUS MEN

American—19th century—*Continued*

Ann Eliza (Webb) Young, 1844?-?

Wallace, Irving. The Twenty-seventh Wife. Simon & Schuster 1961
Bkl A

American—20th century

Gladys Rice (Billings) Brooks, ?

Brooks, Gladys Rice (Billings). Boston and Return. Atheneum 1962
Bkl A—BY

Maurine (Doran) Clark, 1892?-1966

Clark, Maurine (Doran). Captain's Bride, General's Lady. McGraw 1956
SCPL

Grace Anna (Goodhue) Coolidge, 1879-1957

Ross, Ishbel. Grace Coolidge and Her Era: The Story of a President's Wife. Dodd 1962
Bkl A&Y—SCPL

Mamie (Doud) Eisenhower, 1896-

Brandon, Dorothy (Barrett). Mamie Doud Eisenhower: A Portrait of a First Lady. Scribner 1954
SCPL

Claudia Alta ("Lady Bird") (Taylor) Johnson, 1912-

Montgomery, Ruth (Schick). Mrs. LBJ. Holt 1964
Bkl A&Y

Smith, Marie D. The President's Lady: An Intimate Biography of Mrs. Lyndon B. Johnson. Random House 1964
Bkl A

Catherine (Wood) Marshall, 1914-

Marshall, Catherine (Wood). To Live Again. McGraw 1957
SCPL

Jacqueline Lee (Bouvier) Kennedy Onassis, 1929-

Thayer, Mary Van Rensselaer. Jacqueline Bouvier Kennedy. Doubleday 1961
Bkl A&Y—SCHS

Bertha (Honoré) Palmer, 1849-1918

Ross, Ishbel. Silhouette in Diamonds: The Life of Mrs. Potter Palmer. Harper 1960
Bkl A

Abby (Aldrich) Rockefeller, 1874-1948

Chase, Mary Ellen. Abby Aldrich Rockefeller. Macmillan n.d.
SCPL

Eleanor Butler (Alexander) Roosevelt, 1888?-1960

Roosevelt, Eleanor Butler (Alexander). Day Before Yesterday: The Reminiscences of Mrs. Theodore Roosevelt, Jr. Doubleday 1959
SCPL

Eleanor (Roosevelt) Roosevelt, 1884-1962

Douglas, Helen (Gahagan). The Eleanor Roosevelt We Remember. Hill & Wang 1963
Bkl A&Y—SCPL

Eaton, Jeanette. The Story of Eleanor Roosevelt. Morrow 1956
BBJH—CC(6-8)—JH—SCHS

Hickok, Lorena A. Reluctant First Lady. Dodd 1962
Bkl A&Y—SCPL

Lash, Joseph P. Eleanor Roosevelt: A Friend's Memoir. Doubleday 1964
Bkl A

McKown, Robin. Eleanor Roosevelt's World. Grosset 1964
ESLC—JH

MacLeish, Archibald. The Eleanor Roosevelt Story. Houghton 1965
Bkl A

Roosevelt, Eleanor (Roosevelt). The Autobiography of Eleanor Roosevelt. Harper 1961
Bkl A&Y—BY—JH—SCHS—SCPL

Roosevelt, Eleanor (Roosevelt). On My Own. Harper 1958
BBHS—SCHS—SCPL—3000

Roosevelt, Eleanor (Roosevelt). This I Remember. Harper 1949
BBHS—BY—GR—SCHS—SCPL

Roosevelt, Eleanor (Roosevelt). This Is My Story. Harper 1937
BBHS—SCPL

Roosevelt, Eleanor (Roosevelt) and Ferris, Helen Josephine. Your Teens and Mine. Doubleday 1961
Bkl C&Y—CC—JH—SCHS

Steinberg, Alfred. Eleanor Roosevelt. Putnam 1959
CC(5-7)

Steinberg, Alfred. Mrs. R: The Life of Eleanor Roosevelt. Putnam 1958
BY—SCPL

COLLECTIONS

Douglas, Emily (Taft). Remember the Ladies: The Story of Great Women Who Helped Shape America. Putnam 1966
Bkl A&Y

WIVES OF FAMOUS MEN

American—20th century—Continued

Ellen (Maury) Slayden, 1860-1926

Slayden, Ellen (Maury). Washington Wife: Journal of Ellen Slayden from 1897-1919. Harper 1963
Bkl A&Y

Dorothy (Graffe) Van Doren, 1896-

Van Doren, Dorothy (Graffe). The Professor and I. Appleton 1959
SCPL

Edith (Bolling) Galt Wilson, 1872-1961

Hatch, Alden. Edith Bolling Wilson, First Lady Extraordinary. Dodd 1961
Bkl A

English—16th century

Katharine (Willoughby) Brandon, Duchess of Suffolk, 1519-1580

Read, Evelyn. My Lady Suffolk: A Portrait of Catherine Willoughby, Duchess of Suffolk. Knopf 1963
Bkl A&Y

English—17th century

Sara (Jennings) Churchill, Duchess of Marlborough, 1660-1744

Kronenberger, Louis. Marlborough's Duchess: A Study in Worldliness. Knopf 1958
SCPL

Dorothy (Osborne) Temple, 1627-1694

COLLECTIONS

Drew, Elizabeth A. The Literature of Gossip: Nine English Letterwriters. Norton 1964
Bkl A&Y

English—18th century

Elizabeth Chudleigh, Countess of Bristol (calling herself Duchess of Kingston), 1720-1788

Mavor, Elizabeth. The Virgin Mistress: A Study in Survival. Doubleday 1964
Bkl A

Elizabeth (Hervey) Cavendish, Duchess of Devonshire, 1758-1824

Foster, Elizabeth. Children of the Mist: A True and Informal Account of an Eighteenth-Century Scandal. Macmillan 1961 (Fiction)
Bkl A

Maria Anne (Smythe) Fitzherbert, 1756-1837

Leslie, Anita. Mrs. Fitzherbert. Scribner 1960
Bkl A

Sara (Jennings) Churchill, Duchess of Marlborough, 1660-1744

Kronenberger, Louis. Marlborough's Duchess: A Study in Worldliness. Knopf 1958
SCPL

English—19th century

Anne Isabella (Milbanke) Byron, 1792-1860

Elwin, Malcolm. Lord Byron's Wife. Harcourt 1963
Bkl A

Mary Anne (Evans) Disraeli, 1792-1872

Leslie, Doris. The Prime Minister's Wife. Doubleday 1961 (Fiction)
Bkl A

Maria Anne (Smythe) Fitzherbert, 1756-1837

Leslie, Anita. Mrs. Fitzherbert. Scribner 1960
Bkl A

Caroline Lane (Reynolds) Slemmer, Lady Jebb, 1840-1930

Jebb, Caroline Lane (Reynolds) Slemmer, Lady. With Dearest Love to All: The Life and Letters of Lady Jebb, by Mary Reed Bobbitt. Regnery 1960
Bkl A

Charlotte Frances Payne-Townshend Shaw, 1857-1943

Dunbar, Janet. Mrs. G. B. S.: A Portrait. Harper 1963
Bkl A–SCPL

Mary Wollstonecraft (Godwin) Shelley, 1797-1851

Bolton, Guy Reginald. The Olympians. World 1961 (Fiction)
Bkl A

Shelley, Mary Wollstonecraft (Godwin). Letters; ed. by F. L. Jones. 2v. Univ. of Okla. 1944
SCPL

Shelley, Mary Wollstonecraft (Godwin). Mary Shelley's Journal; ed. by F. L. Jones. Univ. of Okla. 1947
SCPL

WIVES OF FAMOUS MEN—*Continued*

English—20th century

Margot Asquith, Countess of Oxford and Asquith, 1865-1945

Asquith, Margot. Autobiography; ed. by Mark Bonham Carter. Houghton 1963
Bkl A—IndS(10-12)

Clementine Ogilvy (Hozier) Spencer, Lady Churchill, 1885-

Fishman, Jack. My Darling Clementine: The Story of Lady Churchill. McKay 1963
Bkl A—SCHS—SCPL

Caroline Lane (Reynolds) Slemmer, Lady Jebb, 1840-1930

Jebb, Caroline Lane (Reynolds) Slemmer, Lady. With Dearest Love to All: The Life and Letters of Lady Jebb, by Mary Reed Bobbitt. Regnery 1960
Bkl A

Charlotte Frances Payne-Townshend Shaw, 1857-1943

Dunbar, Janet. Mrs. G. B. S.: A Portrait. Harper 1963
Bkl A—SCPL

French—18th century

Marie Adrienne Françoise (de Noailles), Marquise de Lafayette, 1759-1807

Maurois, André. Adrienne: The Life of the Marquise de La Fayette; tr. by Gerard Hopkins. McGraw 1961
Bkl A—SCPL

Wilson, Hazel. The Little Marquise: Madame Lafayette. Knopf 1957
CC(7-9)—JH

Wright, Constance. Madame de Lafayette. Holt 1959
BY

French—19th century

Elizabeth (Patterson) Bonaparte, 1785-1879

Desmond, Alice Curtis. Bewitching Betsy Bonaparte. Dodd 1958
BY—SCHS

Kane, Harnett T. The Amazing Mrs. Bonaparte: A Novel Based on the Life of Betsy Patterson. Doubleday 1963 (Fiction)
Bkl A&Y—SCHS

French—20th century

Raïssa (Oumansoff) Maritain, 1883-1960

Maritain, Raïssa (Oumansoff). We Have Been Friends Together: Memoirs. Longmans 1942
SCPL

German—18th century

Friederike Charlotte Luise (von Massow), Freifrau van Riedesel, 1746-1808

Riedesel, Friederike Charlotte Luise (von Massow), Freifrau von. Baroness von Riedesel and the American Revolution; tr. by Marvin L. Brown, Jr. Univ. of N. C. 1965
Bkl A

German—19th century

Clara Josephine (Wieck) Schumann, 1819-1896

Harding, Bertita (Leonarz). Concerto: The Glowing Story of Clara Schumann. Bobbs 1961
Bkl A&Y

White, Hilda. Song Without End: The Love Story of Clara and Robert Schumann. Dutton 1959 (Fiction)
BBHS—Bkl Y—SCHS

Russian—19th century

Sofia Andreevna (Behrs) Tolstoi, 1844-1919

Asquith, Lady Cynthia Mary Evelyn (Charteris). Married to Tolstoy. Houghton 1961
Bkl A

Scottish—19th century

Jane Baillie (Welsh) Carlyle, 1801-1866

COLLECTIONS

Drew, Elizabeth A. The Literature of Gossip: Nine English Letterwriters. Norton 1964
Bkl A&Y

WOMEN

COLLECTIONS

Bolton, Sarah (Knowles). Lives of Girls Who Became Famous. Crowell 1949
CC(7-9)—JH—SCHS—SCPL

Borer, Mary Cathcart. Women Who Made History. Warne 1963
IndJ(6-9)

WOMEN—*Continued*

Bowie, Walter Russell. Women of Light. Harper 1964
Bkl A&Y
Jane Addams; Edith Cavell; Joan of Arc; Florence Nightingale; Eleanor Roosevelt; and others

Boynick, David. Pioneers in Petticoats. Crowell 1959
YR
Amelia Earhart; Lillian Gilbreth; Alice Hamilton; Belva Lockwood; and others

Deen, Edith. All of the Women of the Bible. Harper 1955
SCHS—SCPL

Deen, Edith. Great Women of the Christian Faith. Harper 1959
SCPL

Forsee, Aylesa. Women Who Reached for Tomorrow. Macrae 1960
Bkl Y&C
Martha Berry; Althea Gibson; Edith Head; Audrey Hepburn; Wanda Landowska; Anne Carroll Moore; Ivy Maude Priest; Florence Sabin

Hume, Ruth Fox. Great Women of Medicine. Random House 1964
CC—JH
Elizabeth Garrett Anderson; Elizabeth Blackwell; Marie Curie; Mary Jacobi; Sophia Jex-Blake; Florence Nightingale

Lofts, Norah (Robinson). Women in the Old Testament: Twenty Psychological Portraits. Macmillan 1949
SCPL

Middleton, Dorothy. Victorian Lady Travellers. Dutton 1965
Bkl A

Morton, Henry Canova Vollam. Women of the Bible. Dodd 1956
SCPL

Rittenhouse, Mignon. Seven Women Explorers. Lippincott 1964
CC

Wagenknecht, Edward Charles. Seven Daughters of the Theater. Univ. of Okla. 1964
Bkl A
Sarah Bernhardt; Isadora Duncan; Mary Garden; Jenny Lind; Julia Marlowe; Marilyn Monroe; Dame Ellen Terry

Yolen, Jane H. Pirates in Petticoats. McKay 1963
YR

Yost, Edna. Women of Modern Science. Dodd 1959
CC—SCHS—SCPL

American

COLLECTIONS

Auchincloss, Louis. Pioneers and Caretakers: A Study of Nine American Women Novelists. Univ. of Minn. 1965
Bkl A&Y
Willa Cather; Ellen Glasgow; Sarah Orne Jewett; Mary McCarthy; Carson McCullers; Katherine Anne Porter; Elizabeth Madox Roberts; Jean Stafford; Edith Wharton

Bacon, Martha Sherman. Puritan Promenade. Houghton 1964
Bkl A&Y—IndS(9-12)
Delia Salter Bacon; Catharine Beecher; Lydia Sigourney; Phillis Wheatley

Buckmaster, Henrietta. Women Who Shaped History. Collier Bks 1966
Bkl C(7-10)&Y
Elizabeth Blackwell; Prudence Crandall; Dorothea Lynde Dix; Mary (Baker) Eddy; Elizabeth Stanton; Harriet Tubman

Clymer, Eleanor and Erlich, Lillian. Modern American Career Women. Dodd 1959
SCHS

Daugherty, Sonia. Ten Brave Women. Lippincott 1953
BY—CC(7-9)—ESLC—JH—SCHS
Abigail Adams; Susan Brownell Anthony; Dorothea Lynde Dix; Julia Ward Howe; Anne Hutchinson; Mary Lyon; Dorothy Madison; Eleanor Roosevelt; Ida Tarbell; Narcissa Whitman

Douglas, Emily (Taft). Remember the Ladies: The Story of Great Women Who Helped Shape America. Putnam 1966
Bkl A&Y
Antoinette Louisa (Brown) Blackwell; Prudence Crandall; Anne Hutchinson; Eleanor Roosevelt; and others

Fleming, Alice (Mulcahey). Doctors in Petticoats. Lippincott 1964
Bkl C(6-9)—CC—JH
Emily Barringer; Leona Baumgartner; Connie Myers Guion; Alice Hamilton; Karen Horney; Mary Jacobi; Sara Jordan; Louise Pearce; Clara Swain; Marie Zakrzewska

Fleming, Alice (Mulcahey). Great Women Teachers. Lippincott 1965
Bkl C(6-9)&Y—ESLC—JH
Martha Berry; Mary McLeod Bethune; Florence Dunlop; Virginia Gildersleeve; Mary Lyon; Alice Nash; Alice Freeman Palmer; Elizabeth Peabody; Emma Willard; Ella (Flagg) Young

Forsee, Aylesa. American Women Who Scored Firsts. Macrae 1958
SCHS
Florence Ellinwood Allen; Marian Anderson; Katharine Cornell; Agnes De Mille; Amelia Earhart; Marguerite Higgins; Juliette Low; Eleanor Roosevelt; Kate Smith; Lillian Wald

Hoyt, Mary Finch. American Women of the Space Age. Atheneum 1966
Bkl C&Y

WOMEN

American—*Continued*

Jacobs, Helen Hull. Famous American Women Athletes. Dodd 1964
ESLC—YR

Johnson, Dorothy M. Some Went West. Dodd 1965
Bkl C(7-9)&Y
Bethenia Adair; Elizabeth Custer; Asa Shinn Mercer; and others

Jones, Katharine M. Heroines of Dixie: Confederate Women Tell Their Story of the War. Bobbs 1955
SCPL

McConnell, Jane (Tompkins) and McConnell, Burt. Our First Ladies, from Martha Washington to Mamie Eisenhower. Crowell 1957
SCPL

Means, Marianne. The Woman in the White House: The Lives, Times and Influence of Twelve Notable First Ladies. Random House 1963
Bkl A&Y—SCHS

Muir, Jane. Famous Modern American Women Writers. Dodd 1959
SCHS—YR

Nathan, Dorothy. Women of Courage. Random House 1964
CC(4-6)—ESLC—JH
Jane Addams; Susan Brownell Anthony; Mary McLeod Bethune; Amelia Earhart; Margaret Mead

Papashvily, Helen (Waite). All the Happy Endings. Harper 1956
SCPL
Augusta Evans; Mary Jane Holmes; Laura Libbey; Emma Southworth; Harriet Beecher Stowe; Susan Warner; and others

Pearson, Hesketh. The Marrying Americans. Coward-McCann 1961
Bkl A

Prindiville, Kathleen. First Ladies. Macmillan 1964
BBJH—JH—SCHS—SCPL

Ross, Ishbel. Charmers and Cranks. Harper 1965
Bkl A

Ross, Nancy Wilson. Heroines of the Early West. Random House 1960
Bkl C(5-9)—BY—CC(5-7)—ESLC—JH
Mary Baldwin; Abigail Duniway; Sacagawea; Sister Mary Loyola Vath; Narcissa Whitman

Sickels, Eleanor. In Calico and Crinoline: True Stories of American Women, 1608-1865. Viking 1935
CC(8-9)—JH—SCHS

Stern, Madeleine Bettina. We the Women: Career Firsts of Nineteenth-Century America. Schulte 1963
Bkl A

Stevens, William Oliver. Famous Women of America. Dodd 1950
BBJH—JH

Truett, Randle Bond. The First Ladies in Fashion. Hastings House 1965
Bkl A

Vance, Marguerite. Hear the Distant Applause! Dutton 1963
YR
Maude Adams; Charlotte Saunders Cushman; and others

Vance, Marguerite. The Lamp Lighters: Women in the Hall of Fame. Dutton 1960
Bkl C(7-9)&Y—SCHS—YR
Susan Brownell Anthony; Charlotte Saunders Cushman; Mary Lyon; Maria Mitchell; Alice Freeman Palmer; Harriet Beecher Stowe; Emma Willard; Frances Willard

Who's Who of American Women: A Biographical Dictionary of Notable Living American Women. Marquis biennial; first published 1958/59
SCPL

Woodward, Helen Beal. Bold Women. Farrar 1953
SCPL

Yost, Edna. American Women of Nursing. Lippincott 1965
Bkl Y&C—SCHS—SCPL
Florence Blake; Theodora Floyd; Annie Goodrich; Sister Mary Olivia Gowan; Mary Nutting; Estelle Osborne; Lucile Petry; Anne Prochazka; Isabel Stewart; Lillian Wald

Yost, Edna. American Women of Science. Lippincott 1955
SCHS—SCPL

Yost, Edna. Famous American Pioneering Women. Dodd 1961
Bkl C(6-9)&Y

English

COLLECTIONS

Sitwell, Dame Edith. The Queens and the Hive. Little 1962
Bkl A
Elizabeth I; Mary I; Mary Stuart, Queen of the Scots

Swinnerton, Frank Arthur. A Galaxy of Fathers. Doubleday 1966
Bkl A
Fanny Burney; Maria Edgeworth; Mary Russell Mitford; Anna Seward

Trease, Geoffrey. Seven Queens of England. Vanguard 1953
JH—SCHS
Anne; Elizabeth I; Elizabeth II; Mary I; Mary II; Matilda; Victoria

French

COLLECTIONS

Herold, J. Christopher. Love in Five Temperaments. Atheneum 1961
Bkl A
Charlotte Élisabeth Aïssé; Claire Josèphe Hippolyte Legris de Latude Clairon; Julie Jeanne Éléonore de Lespinasse; Marguerite Jeanne (Cordier) Staal de Launay; Claudine Alexandrine Guérin de Tencin

WOMEN—*Continued*

Italian

COLLECTIONS

Keyes, Frances Parkinson (Wheeler). Three Ways of Love. Hawthorn 1963
Bkl A
Saint Agnes; Saint Catherine of Siena; Saint Frances of Rome

WOMEN SUFFRAGISTS

See Feminists

WRITERS

See Authors

YOUTHS

COLLECTIONS

Bolton, Sarah (Knowles). Lives of Girls Who Became Famous. Crowell 1949
CC(7-9)—JH—SCHS—SCPL

Bolton, Sarah (Knowles). Lives of Poor Boys Who Became Famous. Crowell 1962
CC(7-9)—ESLC—JH—SCHS—SCPL

Farr, Muriel. Children in Medicine. Prentice-Hall 1964
ESLC

Freedman, Russell. Teenagers Who Made History. Holiday 1961
BY—JH—SCHS—YR
Louis Braille; Samuel Colt; Galileo Galilei; Marquis de Lafayette; Arturo Toscanini; Wernher Von Braun; Mildred (Didrikson) Zaharias

Gough, Catherine. Boyhoods of Great Composers, Book One. Walck 1960
CC(2-5)—ESLC

Gough, Catherine. Boyhoods of Great Composers, Book Two. Walck 1965
CC(2-5)—ESLC—IndJ(4-6)
Frédéric François Chopin; Giuseppe Verdi; and others

Murray, Marion. Children of the Big Top. Little 1958
AB(4-7)

Wicker, Ireene. Young Music Makers: Boyhoods of Famous Composers. Bobbs 1961
AB(3-9)—ESLC

Yates, Elizabeth. Children of the Bible. Dutton 1950
CC(2-5)—ESLC

African—20th century

Prince Modupe, 1901-

Modupe, Prince. I Was a Savage. Harcourt 1957
SCPL

American

COLLECTIONS

Carse, Robert. The Young Colonials: A History. Norton 1963
ESLC

Lawson, Don. Young People in the White House. Abelard-Schuman 1961
ESLC

Levin, Martin, ed. Five Boyhoods. Doubleday 1962
Bkl A&Y
Harry Golden; Walt Kelly; Howard Lindsay; John Updike; William Zinsser

American—18th century

Thomas Jefferson, 1743-1826

Bowers, Claude Gernade. Young Jefferson, 1743-1789. Houghton 1945
SCHS—SCPL

Wibberley, Leonard Patrick O'Connor. Young Man from the Piedmont: The Youth of Thomas Jefferson. Farrar 1963
Bkl C(7-9)&Y—CC(6-9)—ESLC—IndJ(6-9)—JH—YR

American—19th century

Willa Sibert Cather, 1873-1947

Franchere, Ruth. Willa. Crowell 1958 (Fiction)
CC(5-7)—JH

Mary Ellen Chase, 1887-

Chase, Mary Ellen. A Goodly Heritage. Holt 1932
BY

Chase, Mary Ellen. White Gate: Adventures in the Imagination of a Child. Norton 1954
SCPL

Samuel Langhorne Clemens, 1835-1910

Proudfit, Isabel (Boyd). River-Boy: The Story of Mark Twain. Messner 1940
BBEL(6-8)—CC(7-9)—ESLC—SCHS—YR

Samuel Colt, 1814-1862

COLLECTIONS

Freedman, Russell. Teenagers Who Made History. Holiday 1961
BY—JH—SCHS—YR

Ethel Nathalie (Smith) Dana, 1878-

Dana, Ethel Nathalie (Smith). Young in New York: A Memoir of a Victorian Girlhood. Doubleday 1963
Bkl A

Thomas Alva Edison, 1847-1931

North, Sterling. Young Thomas Edison. Houghton 1958
AB(5-9)—BBJH—CC(5-7)—ESLC—JH—SCHS

YOUTHS

American—19th century—*Continued*

Oliver Wendell Holmes, 1841-1935

Howe, Mark De Wolfe. Justice Oliver Wendell Holmes: v. 1, The Shaping Years, 1841-1870. Harvard Univ. 1957
SCPL

Washington Irving, 1783-1859

Benét, Laura. Washington Irving, Explorer of American Legend. Dodd 1944
CC(7-9)—JH—SCHS—YR

Frances Parkinson (Wheeler) Keyes, 1885-

Keyes, Frances Parkinson (Wheeler). Roses in December. Doubleday 1960
Bkl A

Abraham Lincoln, 1809-1865

Eifert, Virginia Louise (Snider). Out of the Wilderness. Dodd 1956 (Fiction)
BBJH—SCHS

Fisher, Aileen Lucia. My Cousin Abe. Nelson 1962
Bkl C(6-9)&Y—CC(7-9)—ESLC—YR

Sandburg, Carl. Abe Lincoln Grows Up. Harcourt 1928
AB(6-10)—BBJH—BY—CC(7-9)—ESLC—JH—SCHS

Warren, Louis Austin. Lincoln's Youth: Indiana Years, Seven to Twenty-one, 1816-1830. Appleton 1959
Bkl A

Weaver, John Downing. Tad Lincoln, Mischief-Maker in the White House. Dodd 1963
Bkl C(5-8)—ESLC—IndJ(6-9)

Samuel Eliot Morison, 1887-

Morison, Samuel Eliot. One Boy's Boston, 1887-1901. Houghton 1962
Bkl A

Edgar Allan Poe, 1809-1849

Benét, Laura. Young Edgar Allan Poe. Dodd 1941
CC(8-9)—JH—SCHS—SCPL

Lincoln Steffens, 1866-1936

Steffens, Lincoln. Boy on Horseback; reprinted from "The Autobiography of Lincoln Steffens." Harcourt 1935
AB(6-10)—BY—CC(6-9)—JH—SCHS

American—20th century

Brooke (Russell) Astor, ?

Astor, Brooke (Russell). Patchwork Child: Memoir of Mrs. Vincent Astor. Harper 1962
Bkl A—BY

Helen (Brandmeir) Beardsley, ?

Beardsley, Helen (Brandmeir). Who Gets the Drumstick? The Story of the Beardsley Family. Random House 1965
Bkl A&Y

Hal Glen Borland, 1900-

Borland, Hal Glen. High, Wide and Lonesome. Lippincott 1956
BBHS

Claude Brown, 1937-

Brown, Claude. Manchild in the Promised Land. Macmillan 1965
Bkl A

Wallace Cox, 1924-

Cox, Wallace. My Life as a Small Boy. Simon & Schuster 1961
Bkl A

Helen Doss, 1915-

Doss, Helen. The Family Nobody Wanted. Little 1954
BY—SCHS

Harry Lewis Golden, 1902-

COLLECTIONS

Levin, Martin, ed. Five Boyhoods. Doubleday 1962
Bkl A&Y

John Gunther, 1929-1947

Gunther, John. Death Be Not Proud: A Memoir. Harper 1949
BBHS—BY—SCHS—SCPL

Nancy Hale, 1908-

Hale, Nancy. New England Girlhood. Little 1958
SCPL

Walt Kelly, 1913-

COLLECTIONS

Levin, Martin, ed. Five Boyhoods. Doubleday 1962
Bkl A&Y

Howard Lindsay, 1889-1968

COLLECTIONS

Levin, Martin, ed. Five Boyhoods. Doubleday 1962
Bkl A&Y

Edmund G. Love, 1912-

Love, Edmund G. The Situation in Flushing. Harper 1965
Bkl A&Y—IndS(11-12)

Ralph Moody, 1898-

Moody, Ralph. The Fields of Home. Norton 1953
BBHS

YOUTHS

American—20th century

Ralph Moody—Continued

Moody, Ralph. The Home Ranch. Norton 1956
BBJH—SCHS

Moody, Ralph. Little Britches: Father and I Were Ranchers. Norton 1962
BBHS—BBJH—BY—CC(6-9)—JH—SCHS—SCPL

Moody, Ralph. Man of the Family. Norton 1951
BBHS—BBJH—BY—SCPL

Moody, Ralph. Mary Emma & Company. Norton 1961
Bkl A&Y—JH

Moody, Ralph. Shaking the Nickel Bush. Norton 1962
Bkl A&Y—YR

Geddes Mumford, 1925-1944

Mumford, Lewis. Green Memories: The Story of Geddes Mumford. Harcourt 1947
SCPL

Olaus Johan Murie, 1889-1963

Murie, Margaret E. Two in the Far North. Knopf 1962
Bkl A&Y—BY

William A. Owens, 1905-

Owens, William A. This Stubborn Soil. Scribner 1966
Bkl A&Y

Haydn Sanborn Pearson, 1901-1967

Pearson, Haydn Sanborn. New England Flavor: Memories of a Country Boyhood. Norton 1961
Bkl A

Pearson, Haydn Sanborn. The New England Year. Norton 1966
Bkl A

Knute Kenneth Rockne, 1888-1931

Van Riper, Guernsey. Knute Rockne, Young Athlete. Bobbs 1947
BBEL(4-6)

Anna Perrott Rose, 1890-1968

Rose, Anna Perrott. Room for One More. Houghton 1950
SCHS

Carl Sandburg, 1878-1967

Sandburg, Carl. Prairie-Town Boy; taken from "Always the Young Strangers." Harcourt 1955
BBJH—BY—CC(7-9)—ESLC—JH—SCHS—YR

Dore Schary, 1905-

Schary, Dore. For Special Occasions. Random House 1962
Bkl A—BY

Ralph Schoenstein, 1933-

Schoenstein, Ralph. The Block. Random House 1960
Bkl A

Lillian Eugenia Smith, 1897-1966

Smith, Lillian Eugenia. Memory of a Large Christmas. Norton 1962
Bkl A

Edwin Way Teale, 1899-

Teale, Edwin Way. Dune Boy: The Early Years of a Naturalist. Dodd 1957
SCHS—SCPL

Jane Trahey, 1923-

Trahey, Jane. Life with Mother Superior. Farrar 1962
Bkl A&Y—BY

John Updike, 1932-

COLLECTIONS

Levin, Martin, ed. Five Boyhoods. Doubleday 1962
Bkl A&Y

Richard Wright, 1908-1960

Wright, Richard. Black Boy: A Record of Childhood and Youth. World 1950
GR—SCPL

Mildred (Didrikson) Zaharias, 1913-1956

COLLECTIONS

Freedman, Russell. Teenagers Who Made History. Holiday 1961
BY—JH—SCHS—YR

Patricia Ziegfeld, 1916-

Ziegfeld, Patricia. The Ziegfelds' Girl: Confessions of an Abnormally Happy Childhood. Little 1964
Bkl A—IndS(9-12)

William Knowlton Zinsser, 1922-

COLLECTIONS

Levin, Martin, ed. Five Boyhoods. Doubleday 1962
Bkl A&Y

Australian—20th century

Alan Marshall, 1911-1967

Marshall, Alan. I Can Jump Puddles. World 1957
BY—YR

YOUTHS—*Continued*

Austrian—18th century

Johann Chrysostom Wolfgang Amadeus Mozart, 1756-1791

Wheeler, Opal and Deucher, Sybil. Mozart, the Wonder Boy. Dutton 1941
AB(4-6)—BBEL—CC(4-6)

Canadian—20th century

Cyril Harris, 1891-

Harris, Cyril. Northern Exposure: A Nova Scotia Boyhood. Norton 1963
Bkl A—IndS(9-10)

Chinese—20th century

Chiang Yee, 1903-

Chiang, Yee. Chinese Childhood. Day 1952
SCPL

Chow Chung-cheng, ?

Chow, Chung-cheng. The Lotus Pool. Appleton 1961
BY

Soo Chin-yee, 1945?-

Soo, Chin-yee and Lord, Bette. Eighth Moon: The True Story of a Young Girl's Life in Communist China. Harper 1964
Bkl A&Y—IndS(10-12)

Danish—19th century

Hans Christian Andersen, 1805-1875

Collin, Hedvig. Young Hans Christian Andersen. Viking 1955
AB(5-9)—CC(5-7)—ESLC
Spink, Reginald. The Young Hans Andersen. Roy 1963
IndJ(6-9)

Dutch—20th century

Anne Frank, 1929-1945

Frank, Anne. Diary of a Young Girl; tr. from the Dutch by B. M. Mooyaart-Doubleday. Doubleday 1952
BBHS—CC—GR—JH—SCHS—SCPL—3000—YR
Frank, Anne. The Works of Anne Frank. Doubleday 1959
SCHS
Goodrich, Frances and Hackett, Albert. The Diary of Anne Frank; dramatized and based upon the book "Anne Frank: Diary of a Young Girl." Random House 1956 (Play)
SCHS—SCPL
Schnabel, Ernst. Anne Frank: A Portrait in Courage; tr. by Richard and Clara Winston. Harcourt 1958
BY—SCHS—SCPL

English—16th century

Sir Francis Drake, 1540-1596

Knight, Frank. The Young Drake. Roy 1963
IndJ(6-9)

Elizabeth I, Queen of England, 1533-1603

Irwin, Margaret. Young Bess. Harcourt 1945 (Fiction)
BBHS—SCHS
Plaidy, Jean. The Young Elizabeth. Roy 1961
ESLC
Vance, Marguerite. Elizabeth Tudor, Sovereign Lady. Dutton 1954
BBEL(7-8)—BBJH—JH—SCHS

English—19th century

Charlotte Brontë, 1816-1855

Bentley, Phyllis Eleanor. The Young Brontës. Roy 1961
Bkl C(6-8)—JH
Jarden, Mary Louise. The Young Brontës: Charlotte and Emily, Branwell and Anne. Viking 1938
SCHS
Vipont, Elfrida. Weaver of Dreams: The Girlhood of Charlotte Brontë. Walck 1966
Bkl C(5-8)—ESLC

Sir Winston Leonard Spencer Churchill, 1874-1965

Churchill, Randolph Spencer. Winston S. Churchill: v. 1, Youth, 1874-1900. Houghton 1966
Bkl A

William Henry Hudson, 1841-1922

Hudson, William Henry. Far Away and Long Ago: A History of My Early Life. Dutton 1931
BY—SCHS—SCPL

Gwendolen Mary (Darwin) Raverat, 1885-1957

Raverat, Gwendolen Mary (Darwin). Period Piece. Norton 1952
SCPL

Percy Bysshe Shelley, 1792-1822

Benét, Laura. The Boy Shelley. Dodd 1937
SCHS

Emma Smith, ?

Smith, Emma. Cornish Waif's Story: An Autobiography. Dutton 1956
SCPL

YOUTHS

English—19th century

Leonard Sidney Woolf, 1880-

Woolf, Leonard Sidney. Sowing: An Autobiography of the Years 1880 to 1904. Harcourt 1960
Bkl A

English—20th century

Madeleine Bingham, ?

Bingham, Madeleine. Cheapest in the End. Dodd 1963
Bkl A—IndS(9-11)

Victor Alexander Spencer, 2nd Viscount Churchill, 1890-

Churchill, Victor Alexander Spencer, 2nd Viscount. Be All My Sins Remembered. Coward-McCann 1965
Bkl A

Richard Collier, 1924-

Collier, Richard. A House Called Memory. Dutton 1961
BY

Nigel Eldridge, ?

Eldridge, Nigel. The Colonel's Son. Holt 1964
Bkl A

Nan Fairbrother, 1913-

Fairbrother, Nan. The Cheerful Day. Knopf 1960
Bkl A—SCPL

Rumer Godden, 1907-

Godden, Rumer and Godden, Jon. Two Under the Indian Sun. Knopf 1966
Bkl A

Elspeth Josceline (Grant) Huxley, 1907-

Huxley, Elspeth Josceline (Grant). Flame Trees of Thika: Memories of an African Childhood. Morrow 1959
SCPL
Huxley, Elspeth Josceline (Grant). On the Edge of the Rift. Morrow 1962
Bkl A

Laurie Lee, 1914-

Lee, Laurie. The Edge of Day: A Boyhood in the West of England. Morrow 1960
Bkl A—BY—SCPL

Gavin Maxwell, 1914-

Maxwell, Gavin. The House of Elrig. Dutton 1965
Bkl A

Noel Streatfeild, ?

Streatfeild, Noel. A Vicarage Family: An Autobiographical Story. Watts 1963
Bkl A

French—18th century

Marie Joseph Paul Yves Roch Gilbert du Motier, Marquis de Lafayette, 1757-1834

COLLECTIONS

Freedman, Russell. Teenagers Who Made History. Holiday 1961
BY—JH—SCHS—YR

French—19th century

Louis Braille, 1809-1852

COLLECTIONS

Freedman, Russell. Teenagers Who Made History. Holiday 1961
BY—JH—SCHS—YR

Albert Schweitzer, 1875-1965

Schweitzer, Albert. Memoirs of Childhood and Youth. Macmillan 1949
SCPL

French—20th century

Simone de Beauvoir, 1908-

Beauvoir, Simone de. Memoirs of a Dutiful Daughter; tr. by James Kirkup. World 1959
Bkl A—SCPL

Madeleine (Gal) Henrey, 1906-

Henrey, Madeleine (Gal). Little Madeleine: The Autobiography of a Young Girl in Montmartre. Dutton 1953
SCPL

Marcel Pagnol, 1895-

Pagnol, Marcel. The Days Were Too Short; tr. from the French by Rita Barisse. Doubleday 1960
Bkl A
Pagnol, Marcel. The Time of Secrets; tr. from the French by Rita Barisse. Doubleday 1962
Bkl A

German—17th century

Johann Sebastian Bach, 1685-1750

Wheeler, Opal and Deucher, Sybil. Sebastian Bach, the Boy from Thuringia. Dutton 1937
BBEL—CC(4-6)—ESLC

YOUTHS—*Continued*

German—19th century

Johannes Brahms, 1833-1897

Deucher, Sybil. The Young Brahms. Dutton 1949
BBJH—CC(4-6)—ESLC—JH

German—20th century

Erich Kästner, 1899-

Kästner, Erich. When I Was a Boy; tr. from the German by Isabel and Florence McHugh. Watts 1961
Bkl A

Wernher Von Braun, 1912-

COLLECTIONS

Freedman, Russell. Teenagers Who Made History. Holiday 1961
BY—JH—SCHS—YR

Indian—20th century

Dhan Gopal Mukerji, 1890-1936

Mukerji, Dhan Gopal. Caste and Outcast. Dutton 1923
SCPL

Irish—20th century

Patricia Lynch, 1898-

Lynch, Patricia. A Storyteller's Childhood. Norton 1962
Bkl A—BY

Frank O'Connor, 1903-1966

O'Connor, Frank. An Only Child. Knopf 1961
Bkl A—BY—SCPL

Italian—15th century

Leonardo da Vinci, 1452-1519

Almedingen, E. M. The Young Leonardo da Vinci. Roy 1963
ESLC

Italian—16th century

Galileo Galilei, 1564-1642

COLLECTIONS

Freedman, Russell. Teenagers Who Made History. Holiday 1961
BY—JH—SCHS—YR

Italian—19th century

Arturo Toscanini, 1867-1957

COLLECTIONS

Freedman, Russell. Teenagers Who Made History. Holiday 1961
BY—JH—SCHS—YR

Giuseppe Verdi, 1813-1901

COLLECTIONS

Gough, Catherine. Boyhoods of Great Composers, Book Two. Walck 1965
IndJ(4-6)

Japanese—20th century

Isoko Hatano, 1905-

Hatano, Isoko and Hatano, Ichiro. Mother and Son: The Wartime Correspondence of [the authors]. Houghton 1962
Bkl A&Y—BY

Reiko Hatsumi, ?

Hatsumi, Reiko. Rain and the Feast of the Stars. Houghton 1959
BY

Yōko Matsuoka, 1916-

Matsuoka, Yōko. Daughter of the Pacific. Harper 1952
BY

Monica (Itoi) Sone, 1919-

Sone, Monica (Itoi). Nisei Daughter. Little 1953
BY—SCHS

Kenyan—20th century

Reuel Mugo Gatheru, 1925-

Gatheru, Reuel Mugo. Child of Two Worlds: A Kikuyu's Story. Praeger 1964
Bkl A&Y

Korean—20th century

Joseph Anthony, ?

Anthony, Joseph. The Rascal and the Pilgrim. Farrar 1960
Bkl A

Taiwon (Kim) Koh, 1926-

Koh, Taiwon (Kim). The Bitter Fruit of Kom-Pawi. Holt 1959
BBHS—BY

Jong Yong Pak, ?

Pak, Jong Yong and Carroll, Jock. Korean Boy. Lothrop 1955
BY—SCHS

Malawi—20th century

Legson Kayira, ?

Kayira, Legson. I Will Try. Doubleday 1965
Bkl A&Y

Polish—19th century

Frédéric François Chopin, 1810-1849

Wheeler, Opal. Frederic Chopin, Son of Poland: Early Years. Dutton 1948
CC(4-6)

YOUTHS

Polish—19th century

Frédéric François Chopin—Continued

COLLECTIONS

Gough, Catherine. Boyhoods of Great Composers, Book Two. Walck 1965
IndJ(4-6)

Polish—20th century

Janina David, 1930-

David, Janina. A Square of Sky: Recollection of My Childhood. Norton 1966
Bkl A&Y

Russian—19th century

Samuil IAkovlevich Marshak, 1887-1964

Marshak, Samuil IAkovlevich. At Life's Beginning: Some Pages of Reminiscence; tr. by Katherine Hunter Blair. Dutton 1964
Bkl A—IndS(11-12)

Scottish—16th century

Mary Stuart, Queen of the Scots, 1542-1587

King, Marian. Young Mary Stuart, Queen of Scots. Lippincott 1954
BBJH—CC(6-9)—JH—SCHS

Scottish—18th century

Sir Walter Scott, 1771-1832

Gray, Elizabeth Janet. Young Walter Scott. Viking 1935
BBJH—CC(7-9)—JH—SCHS

Scottish—20th century

David Daiches, 1912-

Daiches, David. Two Worlds: An Edinburgh Jewish Childhood. Harcourt 1956
SCPL

Swedish—19th century

Jenny Lind, 1820-1887

Cavanah, Frances. Jenny Lind and Her Listening Cat. Vanguard 1961 (Fiction)
Bkl C(4-6)

Venezuelan—19th century

Thomas Russell Ybarra, 1880-

Ybarra, Thomas Russell. Young Man of Caracas. Washburn 1941
SCPL

Welsh—20th century

Joyce James Varney, ?

Varney, Joyce James. A Welsh Story. Bobbs 1965
Bkl A&Y

Richard Vaughan, 1904-

Vaughan, Richard. There Is a River. Dutton 1961
Bkl A

Emlyn Williams, 1905-

Williams, Emlyn. George: An Early Autobiography. Random House 1961
Bkl A—BY—SCPL

ZIONIST LEADERS

American—20th century

Henrietta Szold, 1860-1945

Fineman, Irving. Woman of Valor: The Life of Henrietta Szold, 1860-1945. Simon & Schuster 1961
Bkl A&Y

ZOOLOGISTS

See also Anatomists; Herpetologists; Ichthyologists; Ornithologists; Taxidermists; Veterinarians

American—19th century

Alexander Agassiz, 1835-1910

Epstein, Beryl (Williams) and Epstein, Samuel. Pioneer Oceanographer: Alexander Agassiz. Messner 1963
Bkl C(7-10)&Y—YR

American—20th century

Olaus Johan Murie, 1889-1963

Murie, Margaret E. Two in the Far North. Knopf 1962
Bkl A&Y—BY

Murie, Olaus Johan and Murie, Margaret E. Wapiti Wilderness. Knopf 1966
Bkl A&Y

UNCLASSIFIED

American—19th century

Amos Fortune, 1709?-1801

Yates, Elizabeth. Amos Fortune, Free Man. Dutton 1950
BBEL(7-8)—BBJH—BY—CC(7-9)—ESLC—JH—SCHS—YR

American—20th century

Elsie De Wolfe (Lady Mendl), 1865-1950

Bemelmans, Ludwig. To the One I Love the Best. Viking 1955
SCPL

UNCLASSIFIED—*Continued*

Canadian—20th century

Maud (Maloney) Watt, ?

Anderson, William Ashley. Angel of Hudson Bay: The True Story of Maud Watt. Dutton 1961
Bkl A&Y—BY

Mexican—17th century

Catarina de San Juan, 1608?-1688

Stinetorf, Louise A. La China Poblana. Bobbs 1960
Bkl A

Russian—19th century

Ellen Sarah (Southee) Poltoratzky, 1819-1908

Almedingen, E. M. Very Far Country. Appleton 1958
SCPL

Scottish—18th century

Flora (MacDonald) MacDonald, 1722-1790

Vining, Elizabeth (Gray). Flora: A Biography. Lippincott 1966
Bkl A

COUNTRY-CENTURY LIST

BIOGRAPHEES ARRANGED BY COUNTRY AND CENTURY

To find the book or books about any individual, look in the main section under the subject heading or headings given in capitals for each person, where will be found the author, title, publisher, and date, as well as the symbols for the lists recommending each book.

Africa—5th century

Augustine, Saint RELIGIOUS LEADERS—African

Africa—19th century

Barth, Heinrich EXPLORERS—German
Brazza, Pierre Paul François Camille Savorgnan de EXPLORERS—French
Foucauld, Charles Eugène, Vicomte de RELIGIOUS LEADERS—French; SOLDIERS—French
Gordon, Charles George SOLDIERS—English
Kingsley, Mary Henrietta EXPLORERS—English
Livingstone, David EXPLORERS—Scottish; RELIGIOUS LEADERS—Scottish
Richardson, James EXPLORERS—English
Stanley, Sir Henry Morton EXPLORERS—Welsh; Journalists—Welsh

Africa—20th century

Akeley, Carl Ethan EXPLORERS—American; NATURALISTS—American; TAXIDERMISTS—American
Bowne, Elizabeth AUTHORS—American
Harris, Mark AUTHORS—American
Johnson, Martin Elmer PHOTOGRAPHERS—American
Modupe, Prince YOUTHS—African
Quinn, Edel Mary RELIGIOUS LEADERS—English
Roosevelt, Theodore PRESIDENTS—American
Schweitzer, Albert ORGANISTS—French; PHILOSOPHERS — French; PHYSICIANS — French; RELIGIOUS LEADERS—French

Africa—20th century

Whitby, Jonathan PHYSICIANS—English

Alaska—18th century

Steller, Georg Wilhelm NATURALISTS—German

Alaska—19th century

Jackson, Sheldon RELIGIOUS LEADERS—American
O'Brien, John NAVAL OFFICERS AND OTHER SEAFARERS—American

Alaska—20th century

Berto, Hazel Dunaway EDUCATORS—American
Burke, Grafton PHYSICIANS—American

Burke, Margaret (Knudsen) TELEPHONE OPERATORS—American
Carlson, Gerald F. EDUCATORS—American
Dufresne, Frank AUTHORS—American
Murie, Olaus Johan BIOLOGISTS—American; YOUTHS—American; ZOOLOGISTS—American
O'Brien, John NAVAL OFFICERS AND OTHER SEAFARERS—American
Pearson, Grant H. CONSERVATIONISTS—American; MOUNTAINEERS—American
Rockwell, Kathleen Eloisa ACTORS—American
Short, Wayne EXPLORERS—American
Stuck, Hudson MOUNTAINEERS—American; RELIGIOUS LEADERS—American

Algeria—20th century

Ben Bella, Ahmed STATESMEN—Algerian

America—15th century

Cabot, John EXPLORERS—Italian
Columbus, Christopher EXPLORERS—Italian

America—16th century

Balboa, Vasco Núñez de EXPLORERS—Spanish
Cabeza de Vaca, Álvar Núñez EXPLORERS—Spanish
Cartier, Jacques EXPLORERS—French
Coronado, Francisco Vásquez de EXPLORERS—Spanish
Hiawatha, Iroquois Chief INDIAN LEADERS—American
Ponce de León, Juan EXPLORERS—Spanish
Soto, Hernando de EXPLORERS—Spanish

America—17th century

Bradford, William COLONISTS—American
Cotton, John RELIGIOUS LEADERS—American
Hutchinson, Anne (Marbury) RELIGIOUS LEADERS—American
Jogues, Isaac, Saint RELIGIOUS LEADERS—French
Jones, Christopher NAVAL OFFICERS AND OTHER SEAFARERS—English
La Salle, Robert Cavelier, Sieur de EXPLORERS—French
Marquette, Jacques EXPLORERS—French; RELIGIOUS LEADERS—French
Mather, Increase RELIGIOUS LEADERS—American
Penn, William COLONISTS—American; RELIGIOUS LEADERS—American; STATESMEN—American

America—17th century—*Continued*

Philip, King (Metacomet) Sachem of the Wampanoag INDIAN LEADERS—American
Phips, Sir William COLONISTS—American
Pocahontas INDIAN LEADERS—American
Popé INDIAN LEADERS—American
Sewall, Samuel COLONISTS—American; LAWYERS—American
Smith, John COLONISTS—American
Squanto, Wampanoag Indian INDIAN LEADERS—American
Stuyvesant, Peter COLONISTS—American
Taylor, Edward POETS—American
Uncas INDIAN LEADERS—American
Williams, Roger COLONISTS—American; RELIGIOUS LEADERS—American
Winthrop, John COLONISTS—American

Antarctic—20th century

Amundsen, Roald Engelbregt Gravning EXPLORERS—Norwegian
Byrd, Richard Evelyn AVIATORS—American; EXPLORERS—American; NAVAL OFFICERS AND OTHER SEAFARERS—American
Scott, Robert Falcon EXPLORERS—English
Shackleton, Sir Ernest Henry EXPLORERS—Irish
Smith, Dean C. AVIATORS—American
Wilkins, Sir George Hubert AVIATORS—Australian; EXPLORERS—Australian

Arabia—8th century

Geber CHEMISTS—Arabian

Arabia—20th century

Lawrence, Thomas Edward ARCHEOLOGISTS—English; SOLDIERS—English
Stark, Freya Madeline AUTHORS—English

Arctic—19th century

Cook, Frederick Albert EXPLORERS—American; PHYSICIANS—American
Franklin, Sir John EXPLORERS—English
Hall, Charles Francis EXPLORERS—American
Henson, Matthew Alexander EXPLORERS—American
Kane, Elisha Kent EXPLORERS—American
Nansen, Fridtjof EXPLORERS—Norwegian
Parry, Sir William Edward EXPLORERS—English
Peary, Robert Edwin EXPLORERS—American; NAVAL OFFICERS AND OTHER SEAFARERS—American

Arctic—20th century

Amundsen, Roald Engelbregt Gravning EXPLORERS—Norwegian
Byrd, Richard Evelyn AVIATORS—American; EXPLORERS—American; NAVAL OFFICERS AND OTHER SEAFARERS—American
Cook, Frederick Albert EXPLORERS—American; PHYSICIANS—American
Henson, Matthew Alexander EXPLORERS—American

MacMillan, Donald Baxter EXPLORERS—American
Nansen, Fridtjof EXPLORERS—Norwegian; STATESMEN—Norwegian
Peary, Robert Edwin EXPLORERS—American; NAVAL OFFICERS AND OTHER SEAFARERS—American
Rasmussen, Knud Johan Victor EXPLORERS—Danish
Stefánsson, Vilhjálmur EXPLORERS—Canadian
Wilkins, Sir George Hubert AVIATORS—Australian; EXPLORERS—Australian

Argentina—19th century

Hudson, William Henry AUTHORS—English; NATURALISTS—English; YOUTHS—English
San Martín, José de SOLDIERS—South American; STATESMEN—South American

Argentina—20th century

Hudson, William Henry AUTHORS—English; NATURALISTS—English
Perón, Juan Domingo PRESIDENTS—Argentinian

Australia—18th century

Cook, James (Captain Cook) EXPLORERS—English

Australia—19th century

Kelly, Edward CRIMINALS—Australian
Melba, Dame Nellie SINGERS—Australian
Yagan ABORIGINES—Australian

Australia—20th century

Bruce, Sir David BACTERIOLOGISTS—Australian; PHYSICIANS—Australian
Kenny, Elizabeth NURSES—Australian
Lawrence, Marjorie SINGERS—Australian; VICTIMS OF POLIO—Australian
Marshall, Alan John ("Jock") PHYSICALLY HANDICAPPED — Australian; YOUTHS — Australian
Melba, Dame Nellie SINGERS—Australian
Sutherland, Joan SINGERS—Australian
Taylor, Sir Patrick Gordon AVIATORS—Australian
Villiers, Alan John AUTHORS—Australian
Wilkins, Sir George Hubert AVIATORS—Australian; EXPLORERS—Australian

Austria—18th century

Haydn, Franz Joseph COMPOSERS—Austrian
Mesmer, Friedrich Anton PHYSICIANS—Austrian
Mozart, Johann Chrysostom Wolfgang Amadeus COMPOSERS—Austrian; YOUTHS—Austrian

Austria—19th century

Böhm von Bawerk, Eugen ECONOMISTS—Austrian
Elizabeth, Consort of Francis Joseph I EMPRESSES—Austrian
Mahler, Gustav COMPOSERS—Austrian
Mendel, Gregor Johann BOTANISTS—Austrian; GENETICISTS—Austrian

Austria—19th century—*Continued*

Menger, Karl ECONOMISTS—Austrian
Napoleon II, King of Rome KINGS—Roman
Schubert, Franz Peter COMPOSERS—Austrian
Strauss, Johann COMPOSERS—Austrian

Austria—20th century

Adler, Alfred PSYCHIATRISTS — Austrian; PSYCHOLOGISTS—Austrian
Baum, Vicki IMMIGRANTS TO UNITED STATES; NOVELISTS—Austrian
Berczeller, Richard IMMIGRANTS TO UNITED STATES; PHYSICIANS—Austrian
Berg, Alban COMPOSERS—Austrian
Freud, Anna PSYCHIATRISTS—Austrian
Freud, Sigmund NEUROLOGISTS—Austrian; PSYCHIATRISTS—Austrian
Harrer, Heinrich MOUNTAINEERS—Austrian
Jägerstätter, Franz PACIFISTS—Austrian
Kokoschka, Oskar PAINTERS—Austrian
Kreisler, Fritz IMMIGRANTS TO UNITED STATES; VIOLINISTS—American
Landsteiner, Karl PATHOLOGISTS—American
Lustig, Victor CRIMINALS—American
Mahler, Gustav COMPOSERS—Austrian
Meitner, Lise PHYSICISTS—Austrian
Neutra, Richard Joseph ARCHITECTS—American; IMMIGRANTS TO UNITED STATES
Podhajsky, Alois HORSE TRAINERS—Austrian
Schnabel, Artur PIANISTS—Austrian
Schoenberg, Arnold COMPOSERS—Austrian
Segal, Lore IMMIGRANTS TO UNITED STATES
Slezak, Leo SINGERS—Austrian
Strausz-Hupé, Robert IMMIGRANTS TO UNITED STATES; POLITICAL SCIENTISTS—Austrian
Trapp, Maria Augusta IMMIGRANTS TO UNITED STATES; SINGERS—Austrian
Zweig, Stefan AUTHORS—Austrian

Bali—20th century

Tantri, K'tut AUTHORS—American

Belgium—15th century

Eyck, Jan van PAINTERS—Flemish

Belgium—16th century

Brueghel, Peeter, The Elder PAINTERS—Flemish
Vesalius, Andreas ANATOMISTS—Belgian

Belgium—17th century

Rubens, Sir Peter Paul PAINTERS—Flemish

Belgium—19th century

Franck, César Auguste COMPOSERS—French
Leopold II, King of Belgium KINGS—Belgian
Smet, Pierre-Jean de RELIGIOUS LEADERS—Belgian

Belgium—20th century

Denis, Armand PHOTOGRAPHERS—Belgian
Leopold II, King of Belgium KINGS—Belgian

Pire, Dominique Georges Henri RELIGIOUS LEADERS—Belgian
Sarton, May AUTHORS—American; IMMIGRANTS TO UNITED STATES

Biblical Figures—New Testament

Jesus Christ BIBLICAL FIGURES—New Testament
Joseph of Arimathea BIBLICAL FIGURES—New Testament
Joseph, Saint BIBLICAL FIGURES—New Testament
Luke, Saint BIBLICAL FIGURES—New Testament
Mark, Saint BIBLICAL FIGURES—New Testament
Mary, Virgin BIBLICAL FIGURES—New Testament
Paul, Saint, Apostle BIBLICAL FIGURES—New Testament
Peter, Saint, Apostle BIBLICAL FIGURES—New Testament
Pilate, Pontius BIBLICAL FIGURES—New Testament

Biblical Figures—Old Testament

Abednego BIBLICAL FIGURES—Old Testament
Amos, Prophet BIBLICAL FIGURES—Old Testament
Balaam BIBLICAL FIGURES—Old Testament
David, King of Israel BIBLICAL FIGURES—Old Testament
Deborah BIBLICAL FIGURES—Old Testament
Elijah, Prophet BIBLICAL FIGURES—Old Testament
Elisha, Prophet BIBLICAL FIGURES—Old Testament
Esther, Queen of Persia BIBLICAL FIGURES—Old Testament
Ezekiel, Prophet BIBLICAL FIGURES—Old Testament
Hosea, Prophet BIBLICAL FIGURES—Old Testament
Isaiah, Prophet BIBLICAL FIGURES—Old Testament
Jeremiah, Prophet BIBLICAL FIGURES—Old Testament
Jezebel, Wife of Ahab, King of Israel BIBLICAL FIGURES—Old Testament
Joseph, the Patriarch BIBLICAL FIGURES—Old Testament
Joshua, Son of Nun BIBLICAL FIGURES—Old Testament
Meshach BIBLICAL FIGURES—Old Testament
Micah, Prophet BIBLICAL FIGURES—Old Testament
Moses BIBLICAL FIGURES—Old Testament
Naomi BIBLICAL FIGURES—Old Testament
Rebekah BIBLICAL FIGURES—Old Testament
Ruth BIBLICAL FIGURES—Old Testament
Samuel, Judge of Israel BIBLICAL FIGURES—Old Testament

Biblical Figures—Old Testament—*Continued*

Shadrach BIBLICAL FIGURES—Old Testament

Solomon, King of Israel BIBLICAL FIGURES—Old Testament

Bohemia

See also Czechoslovakia

Bohemia—19th century

Dvořák, Antonín COMPOSERS—Bohemian

Bolivia—19th century

Sucre, Antonio José de PRESIDENTS—Bolivian; SOLDIERS—South American

Bolivia—20th century

Mautner, Herman Eric PHYSICIANS—Austrian

Borneo—20th century

Johnson, Martin Elmer PHOTOGRAPHERS—American

Brazil—16th century

Orellana, Francisco de EXPLORERS—Spanish

Brazil—19th century

Brant, Alice (Dayrell) AUTHORS—Brazilian

Brazil—20th century

Jesus, Carolina Maria de POVERTY-STRICKEN—Brazilian

Niemeyer, Oscar ARCHITECTS—Brazilian

Santos-Dumont, Alberto AVIATORS—Brazilian

Vargas, Getulio PRESIDENTS—Brazilian

Burma—20th century

Henderson, Albert Haley PHYSICIANS—American; RELIGIOUS LEADERS—American

Nu STATESMEN—Burmese

Po Sein ACTORS—Burmese

Seagrave, Gordon Stifler PHYSICIANS—American

Thant UNITED NATIONS OFFICIALS—Burmese

Williams, James Howard SOLDIERS—English

Cameroons—20th century

Achirimbi II, Fon of Bafut KINGS—Bafutan

Canada—17th century

Champlain, Samuel de EXPLORERS—French

Frontenac, Louis de Buade, Comte de SOLDIERS—French; STATESMEN—French

Groseilliers, Médart Chouart, Sieur de EXPLORERS—French

Joliet, Louis EXPLORERS—Canadian

Martin, Mère Marie (Guyard) RELIGIOUS LEADERS—Canadian

Radisson, Pierre Esprit EXPLORERS—French

Canada—18th century

Hearne, Samuel EXPLORERS—English

La Vérendrye, Pierre Gaultier de Varennes, Sieur de EXPLORERS—Canadian

Mackenzie, Alexander EXPLORERS—Scottish

Montcalm, Louis Joseph de, Marquis de Saint Véran SOLDIERS—French

Wheelwright, Esther RELIGIOUS LEADERS—Canadian

Wolfe, James SOLDIERS—English

Canada—19th century

MacKay, Angus FARMERS—Canadian

Osler, Sir William, Bart. PHYSICIANS—Canadian

Palliser, John EXPLORERS—Canadian

Seton, Ernest Thompson AUTHORS—American; ILLUSTRATORS—American; NATURALISTS—American

Canada—20th century

Banting, Sir Frederick Grant PHYSICIANS—Canadian

Bishop, William Avery AVIATORS—Canadian

Blackhall, David Scott BLIND—Canadian; POETS—Canadian

Boyle, Harry J. AUTHORS—Canadian

Callaghan, Morley AUTHORS—Canadian

De la Roche, Mazo NOVELISTS—Canadian

Dickson, Lovat AUTHORS—Canadian; PUBLISHERS—Canadian

Dionne Quintuplets QUINTUPLETS—Canadian

Dunlop, Florence EDUCATORS—Canadian

Harris, Cyril YOUTHS—Canadian

Hilliard, Marion PHYSICIANS—Canadian

King, William Lyon Mackenzie STATESMEN—Canadian

Leising, William A. RELIGIOUS LEADERS—American

MacKay, Angus FARMERS—Canadian

Massey, Vincent STATESMEN—Canadian

Moody, Joseph Palmer PHYSICIANS—Canadian

Nutting, Mary Adelaide NURSES—American

Osler, Sir William, Bart. PHYSICIANS—Canadian

Pearson, Lester Bowles STATESMEN—Canadian

Rivard, Paul Léon PHYSICIANS—Canadian

Rivett-Carnac, Charles POLICE—Canadian

Shotwell, James Thomson HISTORIANS—Canadian

Stefánsson, Vilhjálmur EXPLORERS—Canadian

Stewart, Isabel Maitland NURSES—American

Watt, Maud (Maloney) UNCLASSIFIED—Canadian

Carthage—2nd Century B.C.

Hannibal SOLDIERS—Carthaginian

Carthage—3rd century

Cyprian, Saint RELIGIOUS LEADERS—Carthaginian

Chile—19th century

O'Higgins, Bernardo SOLDIERS—Chilean; STATESMEN—Chilean

Chile—20th century
Godoy Alcayaga, Lucila POETS—Chilean

China—6th century B.C.
Lao-tzu PHILOSOPHERS—Chinese

China—5th century B.C.
Confucius PHILOSOPHERS—Chinese; RELIGIOUS LEADERS—Chinese

China—3rd century
Go-Hung ALCHEMISTS—Chinese

China—12th century
Li Ch'ing-chao POETS—Chinese

China—13th century
Kublai Khan SOLDIERS—Mongolian
Polo, Marco EXPLORERS—Italian

China—17th century
Schall, John Adam RELIGIOUS LEADERS—German

China—19th century
Taylor, James Hudson RELIGIOUS LEADERS—English

China—20th century
Aylward, Gladys RELIGIOUS LEADERS—English
Ball, Mary NURSES—English; RELIGIOUS LEADERS—English
Buck, Pearl (Sydenstricker) NOVELISTS—American
Chennault, Claire Lee AVIATORS—American
Chiang Yee ILLUSTRATORS — Chinese; YOUTHS—Chinese
Chiang Kai-shek STATESMEN—Chinese
Chow Chung-cheng YOUTHS—Chinese
Feng Yü-hsiang SOLDIERS—Chinese
Fisher, Welthy (Honsinger) RELIGIOUS LEADERS—American
Grey, Beryl DANCERS—English
Han Suyin AUTHORS—Chinese
Hobart, Alice Tisdale NOVELISTS—American
Li Shu-fan SURGEONS—Chinese
Mao Tsê-tung STATESMEN—Chinese
Scovel, Myra RELIGIOUS LEADERS—American
Snow, Edgar Parks JOURNALISTS—American
Soo Chin-yee YOUTHS—Chinese
Sun Yat-sen STATESMEN—Chinese
Walsh, James Edward, Bishop RELIGIOUS LEADERS—American

Colombia—20th century
Rojas Pinilla, Gustavo PRESIDENTS—Colombian

Congo—20th century
Carlson, Paul Earle PHYSICIANS—American; RELIGIOUS LEADERS—American

Law, Burleigh A. RELIGIOUS LEADERS—American

Corsica—18th century
Bonaparte, Maria Letizia (Ramolino) MOTHERS OF FAMOUS MEN—Corsican

Crete—19th century
Evans, Sir Arthur John ARCHEOLOGISTS—English

Crete—20th century
Evans, Sir Arthur John ARCHEOLOGISTS—English

Cuba—19th century
Martí, José Julian STATESMEN—Cuban

Cuba—20th century
Castro, Fidel STATESMEN—Cuban

Cyprus—20th century
Makarios III, Archbishop RELIGIOUS LEADERS—Cypriote; STATESMEN—Cypriote

Czechoslovakia
See also Bohemia

Czechoslovakia—20th century
Janáček, Leoš COMPOSERS—Czech
Jelinek, Otto IMMIGRANTS TO CANADA; SKATERS—Czech
Kafka, Franz NOVELISTS—Czech
Vrba, Rudolf SCIENTISTS—Czech

Denmark—18th century
Bering, Vitus Jonassen EXPLORERS—Danish

Denmark—19th century
Andersen, Hans Christian AUTHORS—Danish; YOUTHS—Danish
Kierkegaard, Søren Aabye PHILOSOPHERS—Danish
Riis, Jacob August IMMIGRANTS TO UNITED STATES; JOURNALISTS—American

Denmark—20th century
Bang-Jensen, Paul STATESMEN—Danish
Blixen, Karen (Dinesen) Baronesse AUTHORS—Danish
Bohr, Niels Henrik David PHYSICISTS—Danish
Freuchen, Peter EXPLORERS—Danish
Munk, Kaj RELIGIOUS LEADERS—Danish
Rasmussen, Knud Johan Victor EXPLORERS—Danish

Dominican Republic—20th century
Trujillo Molina, Rafael Leónidas PRESIDENTS—Dominican

Egypt—15th century B.C.
Amenhetep II, King of Egypt KINGS—Egyptian

Egypt—14th century B.C.

Amenhetep IV, King of Egypt KINGS—Egyptian

Nefertiti, Queen of Egypt QUEENS—Egyptian

Tutankhamen, King of Egypt KINGS—Egyptian

Egypt—8th century B.C.

Piankhi, King of Ethiopia KINGS—Ethiopian

Egypt—1st century B.C.

Cleopatra, Queen of Egypt QUEENS—Egyptian

Egypt—20th century

Nasser, Gamal Abdel PRESIDENTS—Egyptian

England—6th century

Arthur, King of the Britons KINGS—English

England—9th century

Alfred the Great, King of England KINGS—English

England—11th century

Anselm, Saint PHILOSOPHERS—English; RELIGIOUS LEADERS—English

Edward, The Confessor, King of England, Saint KINGS—English

Harold II, King of England KINGS—English

Hereward ("Hereward the Wake") SOLDIERS—English

William I, The Conqueror, King of England KINGS—English

England—12th century

Eleanor of Aquitaine QUEENS—English; QUEENS—French

Henry II, King of England KINGS—English

Matilda, Princess of England, Consort of Geoffrey, Count of Anjou PRINCESSES—English

Richard I, King of England KINGS—English

Thomas à Becket, Saint, Archbishop of Canterbury RELIGIOUS LEADERS—English

England—13th century

Bacon, Roger SCIENTISTS—English

Edward I, King of England KINGS—English

Henry III, King of England KINGS—English

John, King of England KINGS—English

England—14th century

Chaucer, Geoffrey POETS—English

Edward II, King of England KINGS—English

Edward III, King of England KINGS—English

Isabel, Princess of England PRINCESSES—English

John of Gaunt, Duke of Lancaster SOLDIERS—English

Richard II, King of England KINGS—English

England—15th century

Catherine of Valois, Consort of Henry V, King of England QUEENS—English

Caxton, William PRINTERS—English

Edward IV, King of England KINGS—English

Elizabeth, Consort of Henry VII QUEENS—English

Henry IV, King of England KINGS—English

Henry V, King of England KINGS—English

Henry VI, King of England KINGS—English

Richard III, King of England KINGS—English

Warwick, Richard Neville, Earl of SOLDIERS—English

England—16th century

Anne Boleyn, Consort of Henry VIII, King of England QUEENS—English

Askew, Anne MARTYRS—English

Burghley, William Cecil, 1st Baron STATESMEN—English

Catherine Howard, Consort of Henry VIII, King of England QUEENS—English

Catherine Parr, Consort of Henry VIII, King of England QUEENS—English

Dee, John ALCHEMISTS—English; MATHEMATICIANS—English

Drake, Sir Francis EXPLORERS—English; NAVAL OFFICERS AND OTHER SEAFARERS—English; YOUTHS—English

Edward VI, King of England KINGS—English

Elizabeth I, Queen of England QUEENS—English; YOUTHS—English

Grey, Lady Catherine RELATIVES OF FAMOUS WOMEN—English

Grey, Lady Jane QUEENS—English

Heming, John ACTORS—English

Henry VIII, King of England KINGS—English

Howard, Henry, Earl of Surrey POETS—English; SOLDIERS—English

Howard, Thomas, 4th Duke of Norfolk STATESMEN—English

Marlowe, Christopher PLAYWRIGHTS—English

Mary I, Queen of England QUEENS—English

Mary, Consort of Louis XII, King of France QUEENS—French

More, Sir Thomas, Saint AUTHORS—English; RELIGIOUS LEADERS—English; STATESMEN—English

Overbury, Sir Thomas VICTIMS OF MURDERERS—English

Raleigh, Sir Walter EXPLORERS—English

Shakespeare, William PLAYWRIGHTS—English

Southampton, Henry Wriothesley, 3rd Earl of SOLDIERS—English

Stuart, Lady Arbella RELATIVES OF FAMOUS MEN—English

Suffolk, Katharine (Willoughby) Brandon, Duchess of WIVES OF FAMOUS MEN—English

Tyndale, William RELIGIOUS LEADERS—English

Udall, Nicholas PLAYWRIGHTS—English

Wolsey, Thomas, Cardinal RELIGIOUS LEADERS—English; STATESMEN—English

England—17th century

Adams, William NAVAL OFFICERS AND OTHER SEAFARERS—English

Bacon, Francis, Viscount St. Albans AUTHORS — English; PHILOSOPHERS — English; STATESMEN—English

Boyle, Robert CHEMISTS—English; PHYSICISTS—English

Bull, Dixey CRIMINALS—English

Bunyan, John AUTHORS—English; RELIGIOUS LEADERS—English

Catherine of Braganza, Consort of Charles II, King of England QUEENS—English

Charles I, King of Great Britain KINGS—English

Charles II, King of Great Britain KINGS—English

Coke, Sir Edward LAWYERS—English

Congreve, William PLAYWRIGHTS—English

Crashaw, Richard POETS—English

Cromwell, Oliver STATESMEN—English

Donne, John POETS—English; RELIGIOUS LEADERS—English

Dryden, John POETS—English

Evelyn, John AUTHORS—English

Flood, James CRIMINALS—English

Fox, George RELIGIOUS LEADERS—English

Grenville, Sir Richard SOLDIERS—English

Harvey, William ANATOMISTS—English; PHYSICIANS—English

Heming, John ACTORS—English

Herbert, Edward PHILOSOPHERS—English

Herbert, George POETS—English; RELIGIOUS LEADERS—English

Herrick, Robert POETS—English

Hudson, Henry EXPLORERS—English

James II, King of Great Britain KINGS—English

Jones, Christopher NAVAL OFFICERS AND OTHER SEAFARERS—English

Jonson, Ben AUTHORS—English

Locke, John PHILOSOPHERS—English

Marlborough, John Churchill, 1st Duke of SOLDIERS—English; STATESMEN—English

Marlborough, Sara (Jennings) Churchill, Duchess of WIVES OF FAMOUS MEN—English

Mary II, Queen of Great Britain QUEENS—English

Milton, John POETS—English

Mordaunt, John Mordaunt, Viscount STATESMEN—English

Newton, Sir Isaac MATHEMATICIANS—English; PHYSICISTS—English

Penn, William COLONISTS—American; RELIGIOUS LEADERS—American; STATESMEN—American

Pepys, Samuel AUTHORS—English

Purcell, Henry COMPOSERS—English

Raleigh, Sir Walter EXPLORERS—English

Shakespeare, William PLAYWRIGHTS—English

Smith, John COLONISTS—American

Southampton, Henry Wriothesley, 3rd Earl of SOLDIERS—English

Strafford, Thomas Wentworth, 1st Earl of STATESMEN—English

Stuart, Lady Arbella RELATIVES OF FAMOUS MEN—English

Temple, Dorothy (Osborne) AUTHORS—English; WIVES OF FAMOUS MEN—English

Walton, Izaak AUTHORS—English

William III, King of Great Britain KINGS—English

Wren, Sir Christopher ARCHITECTS—English

England—18th century

Addington, Henry, 1st Viscount of Sidmouth STATESMEN—English

André, John SOLDIERS—English; SPIES—English

Anne, Queen of Great Britain QUEENS—English

Anson, George Anson, Baron NAVAL OFFICERS AND OTHER SEAFARERS—English

Banks, Sir Joseph NATURALISTS—English

Bentham, Jeremy LAWYERS—English; PHILOSOPHERS—English

Blake, William ENGRAVERS—English; PAINTERS—English; POETS—English

Bligh, William NAVAL OFFICERS AND OTHER SEAFARERS—English

Boswell, James AUTHORS—Scottish

Burney, Fanny NOVELISTS—English

Cavendish, Henry CHEMISTS — English; PHYSICISTS—English

Charles Edward, the Young Pretender PRINCES—English

Chesterfield, Philip Dormer Stanhope, 4th Earl of AUTHORS—English; STATESMEN—English

Chudleigh, Elizabeth, Countess of Bristol WIVES OF FAMOUS MEN—English

Cibber, Colley ACTORS—English; PLAYWRIGHTS—English

Clinton, Sir Henry SOLDIERS—English

Cook, James (Captain Cook) EXPLORERS—English

Cowper, William POETS—English

Dalton, John CHEMISTS—English; PHYSICISTS—English

Darwin, Erasmus BOTANISTS — English; PHYSICIANS—English

Devonshire, Elizabeth (Hervey) Cavendish, Duchess of WIVES OF FAMOUS MEN—English

Fielding, Henry NOVELISTS—English

Fitzherbert, Maria Anne (Smythe) WIVES OF FAMOUS MEN—English

Gainsborough, Thomas PAINTERS—English

Garrick, David ACTORS—English

George III, King of Great Britain KINGS—English

Gibbon, Edward HISTORIANS—English

Hamilton, Henry STATESMEN—English

Handel, Georg Friedrich COMPOSERS—English

Hearne, Samuel EXPLORERS—English

Hogarth, William ENGRAVERS — English; PAINTERS—English

Ireland, William Henry CRIMINALS—English

Jenner, Edward PHYSICIANS—English

Johnson, Samuel CRITICS—English; LEXICOGRAPHERS—English

England—18th century—*Continued*

Lamb, Charles ESSAYISTS—English

Marlborough, John Churchill, 1st Duke of SOLDIERS—English; STATESMEN—English

Marlborough, Sara (Jennings) Churchill, Duchess of WIVES OF FAMOUS MEN—English

Montagu, Lady Mary Wortley AUTHORS—English

Nelson, Horatio Nelson, Viscount NAVAL OFFICERS AND OTHER SEAFARERS—English

Newbery, John PUBLISHERS—English

Newton, Sir Isaac MATHEMATICIANS—English; PHYSICISTS—English

Oglethorpe, James Edward SOLDIERS—English

Paine, Thomas AUTHORS—American; POLITICAL SCIENTISTS—American

Pitt, William, the Younger STATESMEN—English

Pope, Alexander POETS—English

Price, James CHEMISTS—English

Priestley, Joseph CHEMISTS—English; RELIGIOUS LEADERS—English

Radcliffe, Charles STATESMEN—English

Rodney, George Brydges Rodney, Baron NAVAL OFFICERS AND OTHER SEAFARERS—English

Rumford, Sir Benjamin Thompson, Count PHYSICISTS—English

Seward, Anna POETS—English

Siddons, Sarah ACTORS—English

Steele, Sir Richard AUTHORS—English

Stobo, Robert SOLDIERS—English

Swift, Jonathan SATIRISTS—English

Teach, Edward ("Blackbeard") CRIMINALS—English

Walpole, Horace ART COLLECTORS—English; AUTHORS—English

Wedgwood, Josiah POTTERS—English

Wesley, John RELIGIOUS LEADERS—English

West, Benjamin PAINTERS—American

Wolfe, James SOLDIERS—English

England—19th century

Addington, Henry, 1st Viscount of Sidmouth STATESMEN—English

Allenby, Edmund Henry Hynman SOLDIERS—English

Anderson, Elizabeth Garrett PHYSICIANS—English

Arnold, Matthew POETS—English

Austen, Jane NOVELISTS—English

Baden-Powell, Robert Stephenson Smyth Baden-Powell, Baron SOLDIERS—English

Bearsted, Marcus Samuel, 1st Viscount FINANCIERS—English

Bentham, Jeremy LAWYERS—English; PHILOSOPHERS—English

Blake, William ENGRAVERS — English; PAINTERS—English; POETS—English

Booth, William RELIGIOUS LEADERS—English

Brontë, Branwell AUTHORS—English

Brontë, Charlotte NOVELISTS — English; YOUTHS—English

Brontë, Emily NOVELISTS—English

Browning, Elizabeth (Barrett) POETS—English

Browning, Robert POETS—English

Burney, Fanny NOVELISTS—English

Burton, Sir Richard Francis AUTHORS—English; EXPLORERS—English

Butler, Samuel NOVELISTS—English; SATIRISTS—English

Byron, Anne Isabella (Milbanke) WIVES OF FAMOUS MEN—English

Byron, George Gordon Noël Byron, 6th Baron POETS—English

Campbell, Mrs. Patrick ACTORS—English

Cardigan, James Thomas Brudenell, 7th Earl of SOLDIERS—English

Cayley, Sir George, Bart. AVIATORS—English; INVENTORS—English

Churchill, Lord Randolph Henry Spencer STATESMEN—English

Churchill, Sir Winston Leonard Spencer YOUTHS—English

Cockerell, Sydney Carlyle MUSEUM DIRECTORS—English

Collins, Wilkie NOVELISTS—English

Constable, John PAINTERS—English

Curzon, George Nathaniel Curzon, 1st Marquis STATESMEN—English

Dalton, John CHEMISTS—English; PHYSICISTS—English

Darwin, Charles Robert NATURALISTS—English

De La Ramee, Marie Louise NOVELISTS—English

Delius, Frederick COMPOSERS—English

De Quincey, Thomas AUTHORS—English

Dickens, Charles NOVELISTS—English

Disraeli, Benjamin NOVELISTS—English; STATESMEN—English

Disraeli, Mary Anne (Evans) WIVES OF FAMOUS MEN—English

Dodgson, Charles Lutwidge AUTHORS—English; MATHEMATICIANS—English

Douglas, Lord Alfred Bruce POETS—English

Dowson, Ernest Christopher POETS—English

Doyle, Sir Arthur Conan NOVELISTS—English

Edgeworth, Maria NOVELISTS—English

Edward VII, King of Great Britain KINGS—English

Eliot, George NOVELISTS—English

Eyre, Edward John STATESMEN—English

Faraday, Michael CHEMISTS—English; PHYSICISTS—English

Fisher, John Arbuthnot NAVAL OFFICERS AND OTHER SEAFARERS—English

FitzGerald, Edward AUTHORS—English

Fitzherbert, Maria Anne (Smythe) WIVES OF FAMOUS MEN—English

Franklin, Sir John EXPLORERS—English

Gaskell, Elizabeth Cleghorn (Stevenson) NOVELISTS—English

George III, King of Great Britain KINGS—English

England—19th century—*Continued*

George, 2nd Duke of Cambridge SOLDIERS—English

Gilbert, Sir William Schwenck PLAYWRIGHTS—English

Gissing, George Robert NOVELISTS—English

Gladstone, William Ewart STATESMEN—English

Gordon, Charles George SOLDIERS—English

Green, Thomas Hill PHILOSOPHERS—English

Grenfell, Sir Wilfred Thomason PHYSICIANS—English; RELIGIOUS LEADERS—English

Greville, Charles Cavendish Fulke AUTHORS—English

Haggard, Sir Henry Rider NOVELISTS—English

Hardy, Thomas AUTHORS—English

Hearn, Lafcadio AUTHORS—American

Hopkins, Gerard Manley POETS—English

Housman, Alfred Edward POETS—English

Hudson, William Henry AUTHORS—English; NATURALISTS—English; YOUTHS—English

Hunt, Leigh POETS—English

Huxley, Thomas Henry BIOLOGISTS—English

Irving, Henry ACTORS—English

Jebb, Caroline Lane (Reynolds) Slemmer, Lady WIVES OF FAMOUS MEN—English

Jex-Blake, Sophia Louisa PHYSICIANS—English

Kean, Edmund ACTORS—English

Keats, John POETS—English

Kemble, Frances Anne ("Fanny") ACTORS—English

Kingsley, Mary Henrietta EXPLORERS—English

Kipling, Rudyard AUTHORS—English

Lamb, Charles ESSAYISTS—English

Layard, Sir Austen Henry ARCHEOLOGISTS—English

Leverson, Ada AUTHORS—English

Lister, Joseph, 1st Baron Lister of Lyme Regis SURGEONS—English

Luard, John SOLDIERS—English

Lucan, George Charles Bingham, 3rd Earl of SOLDIERS—English

Malthus, Thomas Robert ECONOMISTS—English

Marshall, Alfred ECONOMISTS—English

Martineau, Harriet AUTHORS—English

Maskelyne, John Nevil MAGICIANS—English

Maxim, Sir Hiram Stevens INVENTORS—English

Melbourne, William Lamb, 2nd Viscount STATESMEN—English

Mill, John Stuart ECONOMISTS—English; PHILOSOPHERS—English

Mitford, Mary Russell AUTHORS—English

Morrell, Lady Ottoline Violet Anne (Cavendish-Bentinck) AUTHORS—English

Morris, William ARCHITECTS—English; POETS—English

Nelson, Horatio Nelson, Viscount NAVAL OFFICERS AND OTHER SEAFARERS—English

Newman, John Henry, Cardinal RELIGIOUS LEADERS—English

Nightingale, Florence NURSES—English

Nuttall, Thomas BOTANISTS—American

Parry, Sir William Edward EXPLORERS—English

Pater, Walter Horatio CRITICS—English; ESSAYISTS—English; NOVELISTS—English

Peace, Charles Frederick CRIMINALS—English

Poltoratzky, Ellen Sarah (Southee) UNCLASSIFIED—Russian

Pope-Hennessy, Sir John STATESMEN—English

Raglan, Fitzroy James Henry Somerset, Baron SOLDIERS—English

Raverat, Gwendolen Mary (Darwin) YOUTHS—English

Rhodes, Cecil John FINANCIERS—English

Ricardo, David ECONOMISTS—English

Richardson, James EXPLORERS—English

Rosebery, Archibald Philip Primrose, 5th Earl of STATESMEN—English

Rossetti, Christina Georgina POETS—English

Rumford, Sarah Thompson, Countess DAUGHTERS OF FAMOUS MEN—English

Shaftesbury, Anthony Ashley Cooper, 7th Earl of REFORMERS—English; STATESMEN—English

Shaw, Charlotte Frances Payne-Townshend WIVES OF FAMOUS MEN—English

Shelley, Mary Wollstonecraft (Godwin) NOVELISTS—English; WIVES OF FAMOUS MEN—English

Shelley, Percy Bysshe POETS—English; YOUTHS—English

Smith, Emma YOUTHS—English

Smithson, James CHEMISTS—American

Sophia, Princess of Great Britain PRINCESSES—English

Stuck, Hudson IMMIGRANTS TO UNITED STATES

Sullivan, Sir Arthur Seymour COMPOSERS—English

Symonds, John Addington AUTHORS—English

Taylor, James Hudson RELIGIOUS LEADERS—English

Tennyson, Alfred Tennyson, Baron POETS—English

Terry, Dame Ellen ACTORS—English

Thackeray, William Makepeace NOVELISTS—English

Thomson, Sir Joseph John PHYSICISTS—English

Thornton, Marianne RELATIVES OF FAMOUS MEN—English

Tree, Beerbohm ACTORS—English; THEATRICAL PRODUCERS—English

Trollope, Anthony NOVELISTS—English

Turner, Joseph Mallord William PAINTERS—English

Victoria, Queen of Great Britain QUEENS—English

Wallace, Alfred Russel NATURALISTS—English

England—19th century—*Continued*

Wallace, Sir Richard ART COLLECTORS—English

Webb, Beatrice (Potter) SOCIOLOGISTS—English

Wellington, Arthur Wellesley, 1st Duke of SOLDIERS—English; STATESMEN—English

Wells, Herbert George NOVELISTS—English

Wiseman, Nicholas Patrick Stephen, Cardinal RELIGIOUS LEADERS—English

Wolseley, Garnet Joseph Wolseley, Viscount SOLDIERS—English

Woolf, Leonard Sidney YOUTHS—English

Wordsworth, Dorothy RELATIVES OF FAMOUS MEN—English

Wordsworth, William POETS—English

Zangwill, Israel NOVELISTS—English; PLAYWRIGHTS—English

England—20th century

Alexander, Harold Rupert Leofric George Alexander, 1st Earl of SOLDIERS—English

Allenby, Edmund Henry Hynman SOLDIERS—English

Amis, Kingsley NOVELISTS—English

Anderson, Elizabeth Garrett PHYSICIANS—English

Asquith, Herbert Henry, 1st Earl of Oxford and Asquith STATESMEN—English

Asquith, Margot, Countess of Oxford and Asquith WIVES OF FAMOUS MEN—English

Astor, Nancy Witcher (Langhorne) Viscountess STATESMEN—English

Attlee, Clement Richard, 1st Earl LABOR LEADERS—English; STATESMEN—English

Auchinleck, Sir Claude John Eyre SOLDIERS—English

Auden, Wystan Hugh POETS—English

Austing, Ronald PHOTOGRAPHERS—English

Aylward, Gladys RELIGIOUS LEADERS—English

Baden-Powell, Robert Stephenson Smyth Baden-Powell, Baron BOY SCOUT WORKERS—English

Bader, Douglas AVIATORS—English; PHYSICALLY HANDICAPPED—English

Bagster, Hubert PHYSICIANS—English

Bannister, Roger TRACK AND FIELD ATHLETES—English

Barbellion, W. N. P. BIOLOGISTS—English; PHYSICALLY HANDICAPPED—English

Bearsted, Marcus Samuel, 1st Viscount FINANCIERS—English

Beecham, Sir Thomas CONDUCTORS—English

Beerbohm, Sir Max AUTHORS—English

Bell, Julian PACIFISTS—English; POETS—English

Belloc, Hilaire AUTHORS—English

Bennett, Arnold NOVELISTS—English

Bentley, Phyllis Eleanor NOVELISTS—English

Bevin, Ernest STATESMEN—English

Bingham, Madeleine YOUTHS—English

Birkett, Norman Birkett, Baron LAWYERS—English

Bland, Edith (Nesbit) AUTHORS—English

Bone, Edith PHYSICIANS—Hungarian; SPIES—Hungarian

Bottome, Phyllis NOVELISTS—English

Braithwaite, Eustace Ricardo EDUCATORS—Guyanian

Bream, Julian GUITARISTS—English

Brenan, Gerald AUTHORS—English; JOURNALISTS—English

Brittain, Vera Mary AUTHORS—English

Britten, Benjamin COMPOSERS—English

Brooke, Rupert POETS—English

Bryher, Winifred AUTHORS—English

Campbell, Donald AUTOMOBILE RACERS—English

Campbell, Sir Malcolm AUTOMOBILE RACERS—English

Cary, Joyce AUTHORS—English

Catling, Patrick Skene JOURNALISTS—English

Cavell, Edith Louisa NURSES—English

Chamberlain, Neville STATESMEN—English

Chandos, Oliver Lyttelton, 1st Viscount BUSINESSMEN—English; STATESMEN—English

Chaplin, Charles ACTORS—English

Cherwell, Frederick Alexander Lindemann, Viscount PHYSICISTS—English

Chesterton, Gilbert Keith AUTHORS—English; JOURNALISTS—English

Chichester, Sir Francis Charles AVIATORS—English; NAVAL OFFICERS AND OTHER SEAFARERS—English

Christiansen, Arthur JOURNALISTS—English

Christie, John Reginald Halliday CRIMINALS—English

Church, Richard AUTHORS—English

Churchill, Clementine Ogilvy (Hozier) Spencer, Lady WIVES OF FAMOUS MEN—English

Churchill, John Spencer PAINTERS—English

Churchill, Randolph Frederick Edward Spencer JOURNALISTS—English

Churchill, Victor Alexander Spencer, 2nd Viscount YOUTHS—English

Churchill, Sir Winston Leonard Spencer HISTORIANS—English; STATESMEN—English

Cobb, John AUTOMOBILE RACERS—English

Cockburn, Claud JOURNALISTS—English

Cockerell, Sydney Carlyle MUSEUM DIRECTORS—English

Collier, Richard JOURNALISTS—English; YOUTHS—English

Compton-Burnett, Ivy NOVELISTS—English

Conrad, Joseph NOVELISTS—English

Cooper, Diana (Manners), Viscountess Norwich ACTORS—English

Cornford, John POETS—English

Coward, Noel Pierce ACTORS—English; PLAYWRIGHTS—English

Crabb, Lionel Philip Kenneth NAVAL OFFICERS AND OTHER SEAFARERS—English

Cunningham, Sir Alan Gordon SOLDIERS—English

Curtis, Margaret SINGERS—English

Curzon, George Nathaniel Curzon, 1st Marquis STATESMEN—English

Davies, William Henry POETS—English

England—20th century—*Continued*

Day-Lewis, Cecil POETS—English

Delius, Frederick COMPOSERS—English

De Valois, Dame Ninette DANCERS—English

Douglas, Lord Alfred Bruce POETS—English

Draper, Christopher AVIATORS—English

Drawbell, James Wedgwood JOURNALISTS —English

Durrell, Lawrence George NOVELISTS—English

Duveen, Joseph Duveen, 1st Baron ART DEALERS—English

Eden, Sir Anthony STATESMEN—English

Edward VII, King of Great Britain KINGS— English

Edward VIII, King of Great Britain KINGS— English

Eliot, Thomas Stearns POETS—English

Elizabeth II, Queen of Great Britain QUEENS —English

Elizabeth, Consort of George VI QUEENS— English

Ellis, Havelock SCIENTISTS—English

Epstein, Jacob SCULPTORS—English

Evans, Sir Arthur John ARCHEOLOGISTS— English

Evans, Timothy John CRIMINALS—English

Fairbrother, Nan AUTHORS – English; YOUTHS—English

Farjeon, Eleanor AUTHORS—English

Fields, Gracie SINGERS—English

Fisher, John Arbuthnot NAVAL OFFICERS AND OTHER SEAFARERS—English

Ford, Ford Madox AUTHORS—English

Forster, Edward Morgan NOVELISTS—English

Frankau, Pamela NOVELISTS—English

Frischauer, Willi JOURNALISTS—English

Fuchs, Klaus Emil Julius PHYSICISTS—English; SPIES—English; TRAITORS—English

Furse, Judith ACTORS—English

Garnett, David NOVELISTS—English

George VI, King of Great Britain KINGS— English

Gill, Eric ENGRAVERS—English; SCULP-TORS—English

Gillmore, Margalo ACTORS—English

Godden, Rumer AUTHORS – English; YOUTHS—English

Golding, William Gerald AUTHORS—English

Gollancz, Victor CRITICS—English; PUB-LISHERS—English

Graham, Sheilah JOURNALISTS—English

Grattidge, Harry NAVAL OFFICERS AND OTHER SEAFARERS—English

Graves, Robert POETS—English

Green, Henry NOVELISTS—English

Greene, Graham AUTHORS—English

Grenfell, Sir Wilfred Thomason PHYSICIANS —English; RELIGIOUS LEADERS—English

Grey, Beryl DANCERS—English

Guthrie, Sir Tyrone THEATRICAL PRO-DUCERS—English

Haggard, Sir Henry Rider NOVELISTS—English

Haig, Douglas Haig, 1st Earl SOLDIERS— English

Halifax, Edward Frederick Lindley Wood, 1st Earl of STATESMEN—English

Hammond-Innes, Ralph AUTHORS—English

Hardwicke, Sir Cedric ACTORS—English

Hardy, Thomas AUTHORS—English

Hartley, Leslie Poles NOVELISTS—English

Hathaway, Sibyl (Collings) Dame of Sark

Henrey, Madeleine (Gal) AUTHORS—French; YOUTHS—French

Hepburn, Audrey ACTORS—English

Hillary, Sir Edmund MOUNTAINEERS—English

Hitchcock, Alfred Joseph MOTION PICTURE PRODUCERS—English

Hollard, Michel Louis SPIES—French

Home, Alexander Frederick Douglas-Home, 14th Earl of STATESMEN—English

Houselander, Frances Caryll AUTHORS— English

Housman, Alfred Edward POETS—English

Howard, Leslie ACTORS—English

Hudson, William Henry AUTHORS—English; NATURALISTS—English

Hulme, Thomas Ernest POETS—English

Hunt, Sir John MOUNTAINEERS—English

Huxley, Aldous Leonard AUTHORS—English

Huxley, Elspeth Josceline (Grant) AUTHORS —English; YOUTHS—English

Ionides, Constantine John Philip HERPE-TOLOGISTS—English

Ismay, Hastings Lionel Ismay, Baron SOL-DIERS—English

Jebb, Caroline Lane (Reynolds) Slemmer, Lady WIVES OF FAMOUS MEN—English

Jellicoe, John Rushworth Jellicoe, 1st Earl NAVAL OFFICERS AND OTHER SEA-FARERS—English

Joyce, William ("Lord Haw-Haw") TRAITORS —English

Keynes, John Maynard ECONOMISTS—English

Kipling, Rudyard AUTHORS—English

Knox, Ronald Arbuthnott RELIGIOUS LEAD-ERS—English

Kokoschka, Oskar PAINTERS—Austrian

Kops, Bernard PLAYWRIGHTS—English

Korda, Sir Alexander MOTION PICTURE PRODUCERS—English

Laver, James AUTHORS—English; CRITICS —English

Lawrence, David Herbert NOVELISTS—English

Lawrence, Thomas Edward ARCHEOLO-GISTS—English; SOLDIERS—English

Lee, Laurie POETS—English; YOUTHS—English

Leigh, Vivien ACTORS—English

Lessing, Doris May AUTHORS—English

Leverson, Ada AUTHORS—English

Lewis, Clive Staples AUTHORS—English

Lewis, Rosa (Ovendon) HOTEL OWNERS AND MANAGERS—English

Lewis, Wyndham AUTHORS – English; PAINTERS—English

England—20th century—*Continued*

Liddell Hart, Sir Basil Henry HISTORIANS —English

Lightwood, Teresa NURSES—English; RELIGIOUS LEADERS—English

Lloyd George, David Lloyd George, 1st Earl STATESMEN—English

Lowry, Malcolm NOVELISTS—English

Lowther, Hugh Cecil, 5th Earl of Lonsdale SPORTSMEN—English

Macaulay, Dame Rose NOVELISTS—English

Mannock, Edward AVIATORS—English

Marshall, Alfred ECONOMISTS—English

Marshall, Peter VICTIMS OF POLIO—English

Mary, Consort of George V, King of Great Britain QUEENS—English

Masefield, John AUTHORS—English

Maugham, William Somerset AUTHORS—English

Maxwell, Gavin AUTHORS—English; YOUTHS —English

May, Allan Nunn TRAITORS—English; PHYSICISTS—English

Mendelsohn, Eric ARCHITECTS—German

Mitford, Jessica AUTHORS—English

Moffat, Gwen MOUNTAINEERS—English

Montgomery, Bernard Law Montgomery, 1st Viscount SOLDIERS—English

Moore, Gerald PIANISTS—English

Moore, Henry Spencer SCULPTORS—English

Morrell, Lady Ottoline Violet Anne (Cavendish-Bentinck) AUTHORS—English

Mortlock, Bill LAWYERS—English

Moseley, Henry Gwyn-Jeffreys PHYSICISTS— English

Moss, Stirling AUTOMOBILE RACERS—English

Moyne, Walter Edward Guinness, Baron STATESMEN—English

Murry, John Middleton AUTHORS—English

Newman, Ernest CRITICS—English

Nicolson, Sir Harold George STATESMEN— English

Noyes, Alfred POETS—English

O'Connor, Sir Richard Nugent SOLDIERS— English

Olivier, Sir Laurence Kerr ACTORS—English

Orwell, George AUTHORS—English

Parkinson, Cyril Northcote POLITICAL SCIENTISTS—English

Pearson, Hesketh AUTHORS—English

Philip, Consort of Elizabeth II PRINCES— English

Pontecorvo, Bruno TRAITORS—English; PHYSICISTS—English

Potter, Beatrix AUTHORS—English; ILLUSTRATORS—English

Powell, Anthony NOVELISTS—English

Priestley, John Boynton NOVELISTS—English

Quant, Mary COSTUME DESIGNERS—English

Quennell, Peter AUTHORS—English

Quinn, Edel Mary RELIGIOUS LEADERS— English

Rackham, Arthur ILLUSTRATORS—English

Ramsey, Arthur Michael, Archbishop of Canterbury RELIGIOUS LEADERS—English

Raphael, Chaim AUTHORS—English

Raverat, Gwendolen Mary (Darwin) ILLUSTRATORS—English

Ritchie, Sir Neil Methuen SOLDIERS—English

Rolls, Charles Stewart AUTOMOBILE INDUSTRY WORKERS—English; AVIATORS —English

Rosebery, Archibald Philip Primrose, 5th Earl of STATESMEN—English

Ross, Sir Ronald PHYSICIANS—English

Rothenstein, Sir John Knewstub Maurice CRITICS—English; MUSEUM DIRECTORS— English

Russell, Bertrand Arthur William Russell, 3rd Earl MATHEMATICIANS—English; PHILOSOPHERS—English

Sandes, Flora SOLDIERS—English

Scott, Peter Markham ORNITHOLOGISTS— English; PAINTERS—English

Scott, Robert Falcon EXPLORERS—English

Shaw, Charlotte Frances Payne-Townshend WIVES OF FAMOUS MEN—English

Shepard, Ernest Howard ILLUSTRATORS— English

Shute, Nevil AUTHORS—English; ENGINEERS, AERONAUTICAL—English

Sillitoe, Alan NOVELISTS—English

Sitwell, Dame Edith POETS—English

Sitwell, Sir Osbert, Bart. AUTHORS—English

Smith, Sir Sydney Alfred CRIMINOLOGISTS —English; PHYSICIANS—English

Snow, Charles Percy, Baron Snow of Leicester NOVELISTS—English

Spanier, Ginette COSTUME DESIGNERS— French

Spender, Stephen POETS—English

Spilsbury, Sir Bernard PATHOLOGISTS— English

Stanford, Doreen ENGINEERS, MINING— English

Stark, Freya Madeline AUTHORS—English

Stopes, Marie Charlotte Carmichael AUTHORS—English; PALEONTOLOGISTS— English

Strachey, Lytton AUTHORS—English

Streatfeild, Noel AUTHORS — English; YOUTHS—English

Swinnerton, Frank Arthur AUTHORS—English

Terry, Dame Ellen ACTORS—English

Thomson, Sir Joseph John PHYSICISTS—English

Toynbee, Arnold Joseph HISTORIANS—English

Tree, Beerbohm ACTORS—English; THEATRICAL PRODUCERS—English

Trenchard, Hugh Montague Trenchard, Baron AVIATORS—English

Turner, Reginald AUTHORS—English

Unwin, Sir Stanley PUBLISHERS—English

Vansittart, Robert Gilbert Vansittart, Baron STATESMEN—English

Vaughan Williams, Ralph COMPOSERS—English

Wain, John NOVELISTS—English

Walpole, Hugh NOVELISTS—English

England—20th century—*Continued*

Ward, Maisie AUTHORS—English; PUBLISH-ERS—English
Waterfield, Lina (Duff-Gordon) JOURNALISTS—English
Waugh, Alec AUTHORS—English
Waugh, Evelyn AUTHORS—English
Wavell, Archibald Percival Wavell, 1st Earl SOLDIERS—English
Wells, Herbert George NOVELISTS—English
Whitby, Jonathan PHYSICIANS—English
Whitehead, Alfred North PHILOSOPHERS—American
Whitehouse, Arthur George Joseph AVIATORS—English
Whyte, Lancelot Law PHILOSOPHERS—English
Williams, James Howard SOLDIERS—English
Wilson, Angus NOVELISTS—English
Wilson, Harold STATESMEN—English
Wingate, Orde Charles SOLDIERS—English
Wodehouse, Pelham Grenville HUMORISTS—English
Woolf, Leonard Sidney AUTHORS—English
Woolf, Virginia (Stephen) AUTHORS—English
Young, Desmond JOURNALISTS—English
Zangwill, Israel NOVELISTS—English; PLAYWRIGHTS—English
Zweig, Stefan AUTHORS—Austrian

Ethiopia—8th century B.C.

Piankhi, King of Ethiopia KINGS—Ethiopian

Ethiopia—20th century

Haile Selassie I, Emperor of Ethiopia EMPERORS—Ethiopian

Finland—20th century

Aalto, Alvar ARCHITECTS—Finnish
Nurmi, Paavo TRACK AND FIELD ATHLETES—Finnish
Saarinen, Eero ARCHITECTS—American; IMMIGRANTS TO UNITED STATES
Sibelius, Jean Julius Christian COMPOSERS—Finnish

Flanders—See Belgium

Formosa—20th century

Dickson, Lillian RELIGIOUS LEADERS—American

France—4th century

Martin of Tours, Saint RELIGIOUS LEADERS—French

France—6th century

Columban, Saint RELIGIOUS LEADERS—Irish

France—7th century

Columban, Saint RELIGIOUS LEADERS—Irish
Hubert, Saint RELIGIOUS LEADERS—French

France—8th century

Charlemagne EMPERORS—Roman; KINGS—French

France—9th century

Judith, Countess of Flanders PRINCESSES—French

France—12th century

Bernard of Clairvaux, Saint RELIGIOUS LEADERS—French
Eleanor of Aquitaine QUEENS—English; QUEENS—French

France—14th century

Flamel, Nicholas ALCHEMISTS—French
Froissart, Jean HISTORIANS—French
Philip II, The Bold, Duke of Burgundy STATESMEN—French

France—15th century

Cœur, Jacques BUSINESSMEN—French
Joan of Arc, Saint SOLDIERS—French
John the Fearless STATESMEN—French
Villon, François POETS—French

France—16th century

Bellay, Joachim du POETS—French
Calvin, John RELIGIOUS LEADERS—French
Cartier, Jacques EXPLORERS—French
Catherine de Médici, Consort of Henry II, King of France QUEENS—French
Chateillon, Sébastien RELIGIOUS LEADERS—French
Duprat, Antoine, Cardinal RELIGIOUS LEADERS—French; STATESMEN—French
Estrées, Gabrielle d' MISTRESSES OF FAMOUS MEN—French
Francis I, King of France KINGS—French
Henry IV, King of France KINGS—French
Mary, Consort of Louis XII, King of France QUEENS—French
Montaigne, Michel Eyquem de ESSAYISTS—French
Paré, Ambroise SURGEONS—French

France—17th century

Bossuet, Jacques Bénigne, Bishop of Meaux RELIGIOUS LEADERS—French
Champlain, Samuel de EXPLORERS—French
Descartes, René MATHEMATICIANS—French; PHILOSOPHERS—French
Fénelon, François de Salignac de la Mothe-, Archbishop RELIGIOUS LEADERS—French
Groseilliers, Médart Chouart, Sieur de EXPLORERS—French
Henry IV, King of France KINGS—French
Jogues, Isaac, Saint RELIGIOUS LEADERS—French
Joseph, Father RELIGIOUS LEADERS—French; STATESMEN—French
La Salle, Robert Cavelier, Sieur de EXPLORERS—French
Louis XIV, King of France KINGS—French
Marquette, Jacques EXPLORERS—French; RELIGIOUS LEADERS—French

France—17th century—*Continued*

Martin, Mère Marie (Guyard) RELIGIOUS LEADERS—Canadian

Molière, Jean Baptiste Poquelin PLAYWRIGHTS—French

Montespan, Françoise Athénaïs (de Rochechouart) de Pardaillan de Gondrin, Marquise de MISTRESSES OF FAMOUS MEN—French

Pascal, Blaise MATHEMATICIANS—French; PHILOSOPHERS—French

Radisson, Pierre Esprit EXPLORERS—French

Richelieu, Armand Jean du Plessis, Cardinal, Duc de RELIGIOUS LEADERS—French; STATESMEN—French

Sévigné, Marie (de Rabutin Chantal), Marquise de AUTHORS—French

Vincent de Paul, Saint RELIGIOUS LEADERS—French

France—18th century

Aïssé, Charlotte Élisabeth AUTHORS—French; SOCIETY LEADERS—French

Beaumarchais, Pierre Augustin Caron de PLAYWRIGHTS—French

Chardin, Jean Baptiste Simeon PAINTERS—French

Clairon, Claire Josèphe Hippolyte Legris de Latude ACTORS—French

David, Jacques Louis PAINTERS—French

Du Barry, Jeanne Bécu, Comtesse MISTRESSES OF FAMOUS MEN—French

Fénelon, François de Salignac de la Mothe-, Archbishop RELIGIOUS LEADERS—French

Lafayette, Marie Adrienne Françoise (de Noailles), Marquise de WIVES OF FAMOUS MEN—French

Lafayette, Marie Joseph Paul Yves Roch Gilbert du Motier, Marquis de SOLDIERS—French; YOUTHS—French

Lavoisier, Antoine Laurent CHEMISTS—French

Lebrun, Marie Louise Élisabeth (Vigée) PAINTERS—French

Lespinasse, Julie Jeanne Éléonore de AUTHORS—French

Louis XIV, King of France KINGS—French

Louis XVII, King of France KINGS—French

Marat, Jean Paul STATESMEN—French

Marie Antoinette, Consort of Louis XVI, King of France QUEENS—French

Michaux, André BOTANISTS—French

Montcalm, Louis Joseph de, Marquis de Saint Véran SOLDIERS—French

Orléans, Philippe II, Duc d' SOLDIERS—French

Pompadour, Jeanne Antoinette (Poisson), Marquise de MISTRESSES OF FAMOUS MEN—French

Prévost d'Exiles, Antoine François NOVELISTS—French

Richelieu, Louis François Armand de Vignerot, Duc de STATESMEN—French

Robespierre, Maximilien Marie Isidore de STATESMEN—French

Rochambeau, Jean Baptiste Donatien de Vimeur, Comte de SOLDIERS—French

Rousseau, Jean Jacques AUTHORS—French; PHILOSOPHERS—French

Saint-Simon, Louis de Rouvroy, Duc de AUTHORS—French

Saxe, Maurice, Comte de SOLDIERS—French

Staal de Launay, Marguerite Jeanne (Cordier), Baronne de AUTHORS—French

Staël-Holstein, Anne Louise Germaine (Necker), Baronne de AUTHORS—French

Talleyrand-Périgord, Charles Maurice de STATESMEN—French

Tencin, Claudine Alexandrine Guérin de AUTHORS—French; SOCIETY LEADERS—French

Voltaire, François Marie Arouet de AUTHORS—French; HISTORIANS—French; PHILOSOPHERS—French

Watteau, Jean Antoine PAINTERS—French

France—19th century

Augustin Marie du Très Saint Sacrement, Father RELIGIOUS LEADERS—German

Balzac, Honoré de NOVELISTS—French

Bartholdi, Frédéric Auguste SCULPTORS—French

Baudelaire, Charles Pierre POETS—French

Berlioz, Louis Hector COMPOSERS—French

Bernhardt, Sarah ACTORS—French

Beyle, Marie Henri AUTHORS—French

Bizet, Georges COMPOSERS—French

Bonaparte, Caroline, Countess of Lipona RELATIVES OF FAMOUS MEN—French

Bonaparte, Elisa, Grand Duchess of Tuscany RELATIVES OF FAMOUS MEN—French

Bonaparte, Elizabeth (Patterson) WIVES OF FAMOUS MEN—French

Bonaparte, Pauline, Duchess of Guastalla RELATIVES OF FAMOUS MEN—French

Braille, Louis BLIND—French; EDUCATORS—French; ORGANISTS—French; YOUTHS—French

Brazza, Pierre Paul François Camille Savorgnan de EXPLORERS—French

Cézanne, Paul PAINTERS—French

Charcot, Jean Martin NEUROLOGISTS—French

Chateaubriand, François Auguste René, Vicomte de STATESMEN—French

Clotilde de Savoie, Consort of Prince Napoleon Joseph Charles Paul Bonaparte RELIGIOUS LEADERS—Italian

Corot, Jean Baptiste Camille PAINTERS—French

Courbet, Gustave PAINTERS—French

Daumier, Honoré Victorin CARICATURISTS—French; PAINTERS—French

David, Jacques Louis PAINTERS—French

Debussy, Claude COMPOSERS—French

Degas, Hilaire Germain Edgar PAINTERS—French

Delacroix, Eugène PAINTERS—French

Désirée, Bernardine Eugénie, Consort of Charles XIV John, King of Sweden and Norway QUEENS—Swedish

Dreyfus, Alfred SOLDIERS—French

France—19th century—*Continued*

Dumas, Alexandre, Père NOVELISTS—French

Eugénie, Consort of Napoleon III, Emperor of the French EMPRESSES—French

Flaubert, Gustave NOVELISTS—French

Foucauld, Charles Eugène, Vicomte de RELIGIOUS LEADERS—French; SOLDIERS —French

Franck, César Auguste COMPOSERS—French

Gauguin, Paul PAINTERS—French

Gay-Lussac, Joseph Louis CHEMISTS— French; PHYSICISTS—French

Gide, André Paul Guillaume AUTHORS— French

Goncourt, Edmond Louis Antoine Huot de NOVELISTS—French

Hortense, Consort of Louis, King of Holland QUEENS—Dutch

Hugo, Victor Marie AUTHORS—French

Ingres, Jean Auguste Dominique PAINTERS —French

Josephine, Consort of Napoleon I EMPRESSES—French

Jullien, Louis Antoine CONDUCTORS— French

Laennec, René Théophile Hyacinthe PHYSICIANS—French

Lafitte, Jean CRIMINALS—American

Lasalle, Antoine Charles Louis, Comte de SOLDIERS—French

Lesseps, Ferdinand Marie, Vicomte de ENGINEERS, CIVIL—French; STATESMEN— French

Libermann, Francis Mary Paul RELIGIOUS LEADERS—French

Manet, Édouard PAINTERS—French

Maupassant, Guy de AUTHORS—French

Monet, Claude PAINTERS—French

Napoleon I, Emperor of the French EMPERORS—French; SOLDIERS—French

Napoleon II, King of Rome KINGS—Roman

Napoleon III, Emperor of the French EMPERORS—French

Ozanam, Antoine Frédéric HISTORIANS— French; RELIGIOUS LEADERS—French

Pasteur, Louis BACTERIOLOGISTS—French; CHEMISTS—French

Péguy, Charles Pierre AUTHORS—French

Pissarro, Camille PAINTERS—French

Redon, Odilon PAINTERS—French

Renard, Jules AUTHORS—French

Renoir, Auguste PAINTERS—French

Rimbaud, Jean Nicolas Arthur POETS—French

Robert-Houdin, Jean Eugène MAGICIANS— French

Rodin, Auguste SCULPTORS—French

Rousseau, Henri Julien Félix PAINTERS— French

Sainte-Beuve, Charles Augustin CRITICS— French

Sand, George NOVELISTS—French

Schweitzer, Albert YOUTHS—French

Seurat, Georges Pierre PAINTERS—French

Staël-Holstein, Anne Louise Germaine (Necker), Baronne de AUTHORS—French

Talleyrand-Périgord, Charles Maurice de STATESMEN—French

Talleyrand-Périgord, Dorothée (von Biron), Duchesse de RELATIVES OF FAMOUS MEN—French

Thérèse, Saint RELIGIOUS LEADERS— French

Tocqueville, Alexis Charles Henri Maurice Clérel de AUTHORS—French

Toulouse-Lautrec, Henri Marie Raymond de PAINTERS—French

Verne, Jules NOVELISTS—French

Vianney, Jean Baptiste Marie, Saint RELIGIOUS LEADERS—French

Walras, Léon ECONOMISTS—French

Zola, Émile NOVELISTS—French

France—20th century

Anouilh, Jean PLAYWRIGHTS—French

Apollinaire, Guillaume POETS—French

Balmain, Pierre COSTUME DESIGNERS— French

Beaudéan, Raoul de NAVAL OFFICERS AND OTHER SEAFARERS—French

Beauvoir, Simone de AUTHORS—French; YOUTHS—French

Bernhardt, Sarah ACTORS—French

Besnard, Marie (Davillaud) PRISONERS— French

Blum, Léon STATESMEN—French

Bonnard, Pierre PAINTERS—French

Braque, Georges PAINTERS—French

Bresson, Robert MOTION PICTURE PRODUCERS—French

Breuil, Henri ARCHEOLOGISTS—French

Bruckberger, Raymond Léopold RELIGIOUS LEADERS—French

Callaghan, Morley AUTHORS—Canadian

Camus, Albert AUTHORS—French

Chevalier, Maurice ACTORS—French; SINGERS—French

Colette, Sidonie Gabrielle AUTHORS—French; VICTIMS OF ARTHRITIS—French

Cousteau, Jacques Yves DIVERS—French; EXPLORERS—French; NAVAL OFFICERS AND OTHER SEAFARERS—French

Curie, Marie (Sklodowska) CHEMISTS—Polish

Darlan, François NAVAL OFFICERS AND OTHER SEAFARERS—French

Debussy, Claude COMPOSERS—French

Degas, Hilaire Germain Edgar PAINTERS— French

Derain, André PAINTERS—French

Dufy, Raoul PAINTERS—French

Fulda, Edeltraud PHYSICALLY HANDICAPPED—Austrian

Gary, Romain AUTHORS—French

Gaulle, Charles de PRESIDENTS—French; SOLDIERS—French

Genet, Jean PLAYWRIGHTS—French

Gide, André Paul Guillaume AUTHORS— French

Gilson, Etienne Henry PHILOSOPHERS— French

Green, Julian NOVELISTS—French

Gurdjieff, Georges Ivanovitch EDUCATORS —Russian

Hawkins, Eric JOURNALISTS—English

France—20th century—*Continued*

Henrey, Madeleine (Gal) AUTHORS—French; YOUTHS—French
Herzog, Maurice EXPLORERS — French; MOUNTAINEERS—French
Hollard, Michel Louis SPIES—French
Honegger, Arthur COMPOSERS—French
Jacques, Father RELIGIOUS LEADERS—French
Joliot, Frédéric PHYSICISTS—French
Joliot-Curie, Irène PHYSICISTS—French
Kessel, Joseph NOVELISTS—French
Landru, Henri Desire CRIMINALS—French
Laxalt, Dominique FARMERS—French; IMMIGRANTS TO THE UNITED STATES
Lecomte du Nouy, Pierre SCIENTISTS—French
Léger, Fernand PAINTERS—French
Lipchitz, Jacques SCULPTORS—French
Loewy, Raymond Fernand IMMIGRANTS TO UNITED STATES; INDUSTRIAL DESIGNERS—American
Lusseyran, Jacques BLIND—French
Malraux, André NOVELISTS—French
Maritain, Jacques PHILOSOPHERS—French
Maritain, Raïssa (Oumansoff) WIVES OF FAMOUS MEN—French
Mata Hari SPIES—Dutch
Matisse, Henri PAINTERS—French
Mauriac, François AUTHORS—French
Mendès-France, Pierre STATESMEN—French
Milhaud, Darius COMPOSERS—French
Monet, Claude PAINTERS—French
Monteux, Pierre CONDUCTORS—French
Munch, Charles CONDUCTORS—French
Nungesser, Charles AVIATORS—French
O'Brady, Frédéric ACTORS—French
Pagnol, Marcel PLAYWRIGHTS—French; YOUTHS—French
Péguy, Charles Pierre AUTHORS—French
Perrin, Henri RELIGIOUS LEADERS—French
Pétain, Henri Philippe SOLDIERS—French; STATESMEN—French
Proust, Marcel NOVELISTS—French
Ravel, Maurice Joseph COMPOSERS—French
Renard, Jules AUTHORS—French
Rouault, Georges PAINTERS—French
Saint-Exupéry, Antoine de AUTHORS—French; AVIATORS—French
Santos-Dumont, Alberto AVIATORS—Brazilian
Sartre, Jean Paul AUTHORS—French; PHILOSOPHERS—French
Schuman, Robert STATESMEN—French
Schweitzer, Albert ORGANISTS—French; PHILOSOPHERS—French; PHYSICIANS—French; RELIGIOUS LEADERS—French
Spanier, Ginette COSTUME DESIGNERS—French
Stein, Gertrude AUTHORS—American
Teilhard de Chardin, Pierre ANTHROPOLOGISTS—French; GEOLOGISTS—French; PALEONTOLOGISTS—French; RELIGIOUS LEADERS—French
Terray, Lionel MOUNTAINEERS—French
Valéry, Paul Ambroise AUTHORS—French
Vlaminck, Maurice de PAINTERS—French

Weil, Simone PHILOSOPHERS—French
Wildenstein, Georges ART COLLECTORS—French

Germany—5th century

Attila KINGS—German; SOLDIERS—German

Germany—13th century

Albert The Great, Saint CHEMISTS—German

Germany—15th century

Nicholas of Cusa PHILOSOPHERS—German; RELIGIOUS LEADERS—German

Germany—16th century

Cranach, Lucas PAINTERS—German
Dürer, Albrecht ENGRAVERS—German; PAINTERS—German
Luther, Martin RELIGIOUS LEADERS—German

Germany—17th century

Bach, Johann Sebastian YOUTHS—German
Guericke, Otto von PHYSICISTS—German
Kepler, Johann ASTRONOMERS—German
Schall, John Adam RELIGIOUS LEADERS—German

Germany—18th century

Bach, Johann Sebastian COMPOSERS—German
Frederick II, the Great, King of Prussia KINGS—German
Goethe, Johann Wolfgang von POETS—German
Handel, Georg Friedrich COMPOSERS—English
Kant, Immanuel PHILOSOPHERS—German
Riedesel, Friederike Charlotte Luise (von Massow) Freifrau von WIVES OF FAMOUS MEN—German
Riedesel, Friedrich Adolf, Freiherr von SOLDIERS—German
Steller, Georg Wilhelm NATURALISTS—German
Steuben, Friedrich Wilhelm von IMMIGRANTS TO UNITED STATES; SOLDIERS—American
Winckelmann, Johann Joachim ARCHEOLOGISTS—German

Germany—19th century

Andreas-Salomé, Lou PSYCHIATRISTS—Russian
Augustin Marie du Très Saint Sacrement, Father RELIGIOUS LEADERS—German
Barth, Heinrich EXPLORERS—German
Beethoven, Ludwig van COMPOSERS—German
Bismarck, Otto, Fürst von STATESMEN—German
Brahms, Johannes COMPOSERS—German; YOUTHS—German
Diesel, Rudolf INVENTORS—German
Ehrlich, Paul BACTERIOLOGISTS—German
Gauss, Carl Friedrich MATHEMATICIANS—German

Germany—19th century—*Continued*

Goethe, Johann Wolfgang von POETS—German

Groddeck, Georg Walther PSYCHIATRISTS—German

Gruber, Franz Xaver COMPOSERS—German

Hegel, Georg Wilhelm Friedrich PHILOSOPHERS—German

Humboldt, Alexander, Freiherr von EXPLORERS—German; NATURALISTS—German

Koch, Robert BACTERIOLOGISTS—German; PHYSICIANS—German

Marx, Karl ECONOMISTS—German; POLITICAL SCIENTISTS—German

Mendelssohn-Bartholdy, Felix COMPOSERS—German

Mergenthaler, Ottmar IMMIGRANTS TO UNITED STATES; INVENTORS—American

Nietzsche, Friedrich Wilhelm PHILOSOPHERS—German

Roebling, John Augustus ENGINEERS, CIVIL—American; IMMIGRANTS TO UNITED STATES; INDUSTRIALISTS—American

Roentgen, Wilhelm Conrad PHYSICISTS—German

Rothschild, Meyer Amschel FINANCIERS—German

Schliemann, Heinrich ARCHEOLOGISTS—German

Schumann, Clara Josephine (Wieck) PIANISTS—German; WIVES OF FAMOUS MEN—German

Schumann, Robert Alexander COMPOSERS—German

Schurz, Carl IMMIGRANTS TO UNITED STATES; JOURNALISTS—American; SOLDIERS—American; STATESMEN—American

Steinmetz, Charles Proteus IMMIGRANTS TO UNITED STATES

Sutro, Adolph Heinrich Joseph ENGINEERS, MINING—American

Sutter, John Augustus FRONTIERSMEN—American

Wagner, Richard COMPOSERS—German

Waldersee, Marie Esther (Lee) Grafin von MISTRESSES OF FAMOUS MEN—German

Germany—20th century

Adenauer, Konrad STATESMEN—German

Beckmann, Max PAINTERS—German

Binder, Theodor PHYSICIANS—German

Bodenheimer, Max Isidor LAWYERS—German

Brandt, Willy STATESMEN—German

Caracciola, Rudolf AUTOMOBILE RACERS—German

Ehrlich, Paul BACTERIOLOGISTS—German

Eichmann, Adolf CRIMINALS—German

Einstein, Albert IMMIGRANTS TO UNITED STATES; PHYSICISTS—American;

Furtwaengler, Wilhelm CONDUCTORS—German

Goebbels, Joseph STATESMEN—German

Göring, Hermann AVIATORS—German; STATESMEN—German

Groddeck, Georg Walther PSYCHIATRISTS—German

Gropius, Walter ARCHITECTS—German

Hess, Rudolf STATESMEN—German

Heusinger, Adolf Ernst SOLDIERS—German

Heydrich, Reinhard SOLDIERS—German

Himmler, Heinrich CRIMINALS—German

Hitler, Adolf STATESMEN—German

Huzel, Dieter K SCIENTISTS—German

Immelmann, Max AVIATORS—German

Jellinek-Mercédès, Emil AUTOMOBILE INDUSTRY WORKERS—German

Kästner, Erich AUTHORS—German; YOUTHS—German

Keitel, Wilhelm SOLDIERS—German

Kersten, Felix PHYSIOTHERAPISTS—Finnish

Kuehn, Ruth SPIES—German

Lehmann, Lotte SINGERS—American

Ludendorff, Erich Friedrich Wilhelm SOLDIERS—German

Mann, Thomas AUTHORS—German; IMMIGRANTS TO UNITED STATES

Mendelsohn, Eric ARCHITECTS—German

Moltke, Helmuth von SOLDIERS—German

Niemöller, Martin RELIGIOUS LEADERS—German

Oberth, Hermann ENGINEERS, AERONAUTICAL—German; PHYSICISTS—German

Planck, Max Karl Ernst Ludwig PHYSICISTS—German

Regler, Gustav AUTHORS—German

Richthofen, Baron Manfred von AVIATORS—German

Roentgen, Wilhelm Conrad PHYSICISTS—German

Rommel, Erwin SOLDIERS—German

Sauerbruch, Ferdinand SURGEONS—German

Schrader, Herbert Ludwig PHYSICIANS—German

Senger Und Etterlin, Fridolin von SOLDIERS—German

Sorge, Richard JOURNALISTS—German; SPIES—German

Strauss, Richard COMPOSERS—German

Tillich, Paul Johannes RELIGIOUS LEADERS—German

Ulbricht, Walter STATESMEN—German

Von Braun, Wernher ENGINEERS, AERONAUTICAL—American; IMMIGRANTS TO UNITED STATES; SCIENTISTS—American; YOUTHS—German

Vrba, Rudolf SCIENTISTS—Czech

Waldersee, Marie Esther (Lee) Grafin von MISTRESSES OF FAMOUS MEN—German

Walter, Bruno CONDUCTORS—German

Warburg, James Paul FINANCIERS—American; IMMIGRANTS TO UNITED STATES

Weber, Max SOCIOLOGISTS—German

William II, Emperor of Germany EMPERORS—German

Ghana—20th century

Nkrumah, Kwame PRESIDENTS—Ghanaian

Great Britain

See England; Ireland; Scotland; Wales

Greece—9th century B.C.

Homer POETS—Greek

Greece—6th century B.C.

Anaximander ASTRONOMERS—Greek; PHILOSOPHERS—Greek

Greece—5th century B.C.

Aeschylus PLAYWRIGHTS—Greek
Alcibiades SOLDIERS—Greek; STATESMEN—Greek
Aristophanes PLAYWRIGHTS—Greek
Euripides PLAYWRIGHTS—Greek
Heraclitus PHILOSOPHERS—Greek
Hippocrates PHYSICIANS—Greek
Parmenides PHILOSOPHERS—Greek
Pericles STATESMEN—Greek
Socrates EDUCATORS—Greek; PHILOSOPHERS—Greek
Themistocles STATESMEN—Greek
Thucydides HISTORIANS—Greek

Greece—4th century B.C.

Aristotle PHILOSOPHERS—Greek; SCIENTISTS—Greek
Demosthenes STATESMEN—Greek
Plato PHILOSOPHERS—Greek
Xenophon HISTORIANS—Greek

Greece—3rd century B.C.

Archimedes INVENTORS—Greek; MATHEMATICIANS—Greek
Bolos Democritos ALCHEMISTS—Greek

Greece—1st century

Plutarch AUTHORS—Greek; HISTORIANS—Greek

Greece—3rd century

Christopher, Saint RELIGIOUS LEADERS—Greek

Greece—4th century

Athanasius, Saint RELIGIOUS LEADERS—Greek

Greece—7th century

Giles, Saint RELIGIOUS LEADERS—Greek

Greece—19th century

Loues, Spiridon TRACK AND FIELD ATHLETES—Greek

Greece—20th century

Kazantzakēs, Nikos AUTHORS—Greek
Mitropoulos, Dimitri CONDUCTORS—Greek
Skouras, Spyros Panagiotes IMMIGRANTS TO UNITED STATES; MOTION PICTURE PRODUCERS—American

Greenland—20th century

Rasmussen, Knud Johan Victor EXPLORERS—Danish

Guatemala—16th century

Díaz del Castillo, Bernal HISTORIANS—Spanish; SOLDIERS—Spanish

Guinea—20th century

Touré, Sékou PRESIDENTS—Guinean

Guyana—20th century

Braithwaite, Eustace Ricardo EDUCATORS—Guyanian·

Haiti—18th century

Toussaint Louverture, Pierre Dominique STATESMEN—Haitian

Haiti—19th century

Christophe, Henri, King of Haiti KINGS—Haitian

Haiti—20th century

Mellon, William Larimer PHYSICIANS—American

Hawaii—18th century

Kamehameha I, the Great, King of the Hawaiian Islands KINGS—Hawaiian

Hawaii—19th century

Clemens, Samuel Langhorne HUMORISTS—American; YOUTHS—American
Damien de Veuster, Joseph RELIGIOUS LEADERS—Belgian
Kauhumanu, Consort of Kamehameha I, the Great, King of the Hawaiian Islands QUEENS—Hawaiian
Kaiulani, Princess of Hawaii PRINCESSES—Hawaiian
Kamehameha I, the Great, King of the Hawaiian Islands KINGS—Hawaiian
Liliuokalani, Queen of the Hawaiian Islands QUEENS—Hawaiian

Holland

See Netherlands

Holy Roman Empire

See Rome—8th century

Hungary—19th century

Liszt, Franz COMPOSERS—Hungarian; PIANISTS—Hungarian
Pulitzer, Joseph IMMIGRANTS TO UNITED STATES; JOURNALISTS—American
Semmelweiss, Ignaz Philipp PHYSICIANS—Hungarian

Hungary—20th century

Bang-Jensen, Paul STATESMEN—Danish
Bartók, Béla COMPOSERS—Hungarian
Bone, Edith PHYSICIANS—Hungarian; SPIES—Hungarian
Kádár, János STATESMEN—Hungarian
Kármán, Theodor von ENGINEERS, AERONAUTICAL—Hungarian; IMMIGRANTS TO UNITED STATES

Hungary—20th century—*Continued*

Koestler, Arthur   AUTHORS—Hungarian
Korda, Sir Alexander   MOTION PICTURE PRODUCERS—English
Mindszenty, Joseph, Cardinal   RELIGIOUS LEADERS—Hungarian
Reiner, Fritz   CONDUCTORS—Hungarian
Schick, Béla   IMMIGRANTS TO UNITED STATES; PHYSICIANS—American
Szigeti, Joseph   VIOLINISTS—Hungarian

India—6th century B.C.

Buddha   RELIGIOUS LEADERS—Indian

India—2nd century

Nagarjuna   RELIGIOUS LEADERS—Indian

India—16th century

Akbar, Emperor of Hindustan   EMPERORS—Hindustani
Babar, Emperor of Hindustan   EMPERORS—Hindustani

India—17th century

Jahānārā, Begam, Daughter of Shāhjāhan   POETS—Indian
Shāhjāhan, Emperor of India   EMPERORS—Indian

India—19th century

Gokhale, Gopal Krishna   STATESMEN—Indian
Ramakrishna   RELIGIOUS LEADERS—Indian
Tilak, Bal Gangadhar   STATESMEN—Indian

India—20th century

Chavan, Yashwantrao Balwantrao   STATESMEN—Indian
Corbett, Jim   EXPLORERS—English
Desai, Morarji   STATESMEN—Indian
Eldridge, Nigel   YOUTHS—English
Elwin, Verrier   ANTHROPOLOGISTS—English
Gandhi, Indira (Nehru)   STATESMEN—Indian
Gandhi, Mohandas Karamchand   RELIGIOUS LEADERS—Indian; STATESMEN—Indian
Gokhale, Gopal Krishna   STATESMEN—Indian
Jinnah, Mohammed Ali   LAWYERS—Indian; STATESMEN—Pakistani
Kaul, Brij Mohan   SOLDIERS—Indian
Krishna Menon, Vengalil Krishnan   STATESMEN—Indian
Mehta, Ved Parkash   AUTHORS—Indian; BLIND—Indian
Mukerji, Dhan Gopal   AUTHORS—Indian; YOUTHS—Indian
Narayan, Jayaprakash   STATESMEN—Indian
Nehru, Jawaharlal   STATESMEN—Indian
Nehru, Motilal   STATESMEN—Indian
Pandit, Vijaya Lakshmi (Nehru)   RELATIVES OF FAMOUS MEN—Indian; STATESMEN—Indian
Patil, Sadashiv Kamoji   STATESMEN—Indian
Rama Rau, Santha   AUTHORS—Indian
Sahgal, Nayantara (Pandit)   DAUGHTERS OF FAMOUS WOMEN—Indian

Saund, Dalip Singh   IMMIGRANTS TO UNITED STATES; STATESMEN—American
Scudder, Ida   PHYSICIANS—American; RELIGIOUS LEADERS—American
Shastri, Lal Bahadur   STATESMEN—Indian
Tagore, Rabindranath   POETS—Indian
Thimayya, Kodendera Subayya   SOLDIERS—Indian
Tilak, Bal Gangadhar   STATESMEN—Indian
Verghese, Mary   PHYSICALLY HANDICAPPED—Indian; PHYSICIANS—Indian

Indonesia—20th century

Sukarno   PRESIDENTS—Indonesian
Tantri, K'tut   AUTHORS—American

Iran—20th century

Gulbenkian, Nubar Sarkis   FINANCIERS—Iranian; PETROLEUM INDUSTRY WORKERS—Iranian
Najafi, Najmeh   SOCIAL WORKERS—Iranian

Ireland—5th century

Bridget, Saint   RELIGIOUS LEADERS—Irish
Patrick, Saint   RELIGIOUS LEADERS—Irish

Ireland—6th century

Columba, Saint   RELIGIOUS LEADERS—Irish
Columban, Saint   RELIGIOUS LEADERS—Irish

Ireland—16th century

O'Malley, Grace   SOLDIERS—Irish

Ireland—18th century

Sheridan, Richard Brinsley   PLAYWRIGHTS—Irish

Ireland—19th century

Gregory, Lady Augusta (Persse)   PLAYWRIGHTS—Irish
Kelvin, William Thomson, Baron   MATHEMATICIANS—Irish; PHYSICISTS—Irish
McClure, Samuel Sidney   IMMIGRANTS TO UNITED STATES
Moore, George   NOVELISTS—Irish
Palliser, John   EXPLORERS—Canadian
Parnell, Charles Stewart   STATESMEN—Irish
Shaw, George Bernard   CRITICS—Irish; PLAYWRIGHTS—Irish
Wilde, Oscar   AUTHORS—Irish

Ireland—20th century

Bowen, Elizabeth   NOVELISTS—Irish
Brown, Christy   VICTIMS OF CEREBRAL PALSY—Irish
Casement, Sir Roger David   STATESMEN—Irish
De Valera, Eamon   STATESMEN—Irish
De Valois, Dame Ninette   DANCERS—English
Gogarty, Oliver St. John   AUTHORS—Irish; PHYSICIANS—Irish
Gregory, Lady Augusta (Persse)   PLAYWRIGHTS—Irish
Griffith, Arthur   PRESIDENTS—Irish
Joyce, James   AUTHORS—Irish

Italy—19th century—*Continued*

D'Annunzio, Gabriele AUTHORS—Italian; SOLDIERS—Italian

Donizetti, Gaetano COMPOSERS—Italian

Duse, Eleonora ACTORS—Italian

Garibaldi, Giuseppe SOLDIERS—Italian; STATESMEN—Italian

Leo XIII, Pope RELIGIOUS LEADERS—Italian

Paganini, Nicolò VIOLINISTS—Italian

Pius VII, Pope RELIGIOUS LEADERS—Italian

Toscanini, Arturo YOUTHS—Italian

Verdi, Giuseppe COMPOSERS—Italian; YOUTHS—Italian

Volta, Alessandro Giuseppe Antonio Anastasio, Conte ENGINEERS, ELECTRICAL—Italian; PHYSICISTS—Italian

Italy—20th century

Alexander, Harold Rupert Leofric George Alexander, 1st Earl of SOLDIERS—English

Antonioni, Michelangelo MOTION PICTURE PRODUCERS—Italian

Benedict XV, Pope RELIGIOUS LEADERS—Italian

Caruso, Enrico SINGERS—Italian

Castellani, Sir Aldo PHYSICIANS—Italian

Ciano, Galeazzo, Conte STATESMEN—Italian

Creatore, Giuseppe BANDMASTERS—Italian

Cristiani Family CIRCUS PERFORMERS—Italian

Cunningham, James F. RELIGIOUS LEADERS—American

D'Annunzio, Gabriele AUTHORS—Italian; SOLDIERS—Italian

Dolci, Danilo AUTHORS—Italian; SOCIAL WORKERS—Italian

Duse, Eleonora ACTORS—Italian

Fellini, Federico MOTION PICTURE PRODUCERS—Italian

Fermi, Enrico PHYSICISTS—Italian

John XXIII, Pope RELIGIOUS LEADERS—Italian

Marconi, Guglielmo, Marchese ENGINEERS, RADIO AND TELEVISION—Italian; INVENTORS—Italian

Menotti, Gian-Carlo COMPOSERS—Italian; IMMIGRANTS TO UNITED STATES

Modigliani, Amedeo PAINTERS—Italian

Munthe, Axel Martin Fredrik PHYSICIANS—Swedish

Mussolini, Benito STATESMEN—Italian

Nervi, Pier Luigi ARCHITECTS—Italian

Pareto, Vilfredo ECONOMISTS—Italian; SOCIOLOGISTS—Italian

Paul VI, Pope RELIGIOUS LEADERS—Italian

Pius X, Pope RELIGIOUS LEADERS—Italian

Pius XI, Pope RELIGIOUS LEADERS—Italian

Pius XII, Pope RELIGIOUS LEADERS—Italian

Pontecorvo, Bruno PHYSICISTS—English; TRAITORS—English

Rosso, Medardo SCULPTORS—Italian

Sacco, Nicola ANARCHISTS—American; CRIMINALS—American; IMMIGRANTS TO UNITED STATES

Serenelli, Alessandro CRIMINALS—Italian

Tebaldi, Renata SINGERS—Italian

Toscanini, Arturo CONDUCTORS—Italian

Vanzetti, Bartolomeo ANARCHISTS—American; CRIMINALS—American; IMMIGRANTS TO UNITED STATES

Waterfield, Lina (Duff-Gordon) JOURNALISTS—English

Ivory Coast—20th century

Houphouet-Boigny, Félix STATESMEN—Ivory Coast

Jamaica—19th century

Eyre, Edward John STATESMEN—English

Jamaica—20th century

McKenley, Herbert TRACK AND FIELD ATHLETES—Jamaican

Japan—17th century

Adams, William NAVAL OFFICERS AND OTHER SEAFARERS—English

Japan—19th century

Boyer, Samuel Pellman PHYSICIANS—American

Harris, Townsend STATESMEN—American

Hearn, Lafcadio AUTHORS—American

Perry, Matthew Calbraith NAVAL OFFICERS AND OTHER SEAFARERS—American

Togo, Heihachiro NAVAL OFFICERS AND OTHER SEAFARERS—Japanese

Japan—20th century

Akihito, Crown Prince of Japan PRINCES—Japanese

Caulfield, Genevieve BLIND—American

Hatano, Isoko YOUTHS—Japanese

Hatsumi, Reiko YOUTHS—Japanese

Hirohito, Emperor of Japan EMPERORS—Japanese

Kagawa, Toyohiko AUTHORS—Japanese; RELIGIOUS LEADERS—Japanese

Matsuoka, Yōko YOUTHS—Japanese

Ozaki, Hatsumi POLITICAL SCIENTISTS—Japanese; SPIES—Japanese

Tange, Kenzo ARCHITECTS—Japanese

Togo, Heihachiro NAVAL OFFICERS AND OTHER SEAFARERS—Japanese

Watanabe, Kiyoshi RELIGIOUS LEADERS—Japanese

Yamamoto, Isoroku NAVAL OFFICERS AND OTHER SEAFARERS—Japanese

Jordan—20th century

Hussein, King of Jordan KINGS—Jordanian

Jugoslavia
See Yugoslavia

Kenya—20th century

Gatheru, Reuel Mugo YOUTHS—Kenyan

Huxley, Elspeth Josceline (Grant) AUTHORS—English; YOUTHS—English

Kenya—20th century—_Continued_
Kenyatta, Jomo STATESMEN—Kenyan
Mboya, Thomas Joseph STATESMEN—Kenyan

Korea—20th century
Anthony, Joseph YOUTHS—Korean
Koh, Taiwon (Kim) IMMIGRANTS TO
UNITED STATES; YOUTHS—Korean
Pak, Induk EDUCATORS—Korean
Pak, Jong Yong YOUTHS—Korean

Labrador—19th century
Grenfell, Sir Wilfred Thomason PHYSICIANS
—English; RELIGIOUS LEADERS—English

Labrador—20th century
Grenfell, Sir Wilfred Thomason PHYSICIANS
—English; RELIGIOUS LEADERS—English

Laos—20th century
Dooley, Thomas Anthony AUTHORS—American; PHYSICIANS—American

Liberia—20th century
Bowne, Elizabeth AUTHORS—American
Tubman, William Vacanarat Shadrach PRESIDENTS—Liberian

Lydia—6th century B.C.
Croesus, King of Lydia KINGS—Lydian

Macedonia—3rd century B.C.
Demetrius Poliorcetes, King of Macedonia
KINGS—Macedonian

Macedonia—4th century B.C.
Alexander the Great KINGS—Macedonian;
SOLDIERS—Macedonian

Malawi—20th century
Kayira, Legson YOUTHS—Malawi

Mexico—15th century
Montezuma I, Emperor of Mexico EMPERORS—Mexican

Mexico—16th century
Cortés, Hernando EXPLORERS—Spanish
López, Martín EXPLORERS—Spanish

Mexico—17th century
Catarina de San Juan UNCLASSIFIED—
Mexican

Mexico—19th century
Díaz, Porfirio STATESMEN—Mexican
Juárez, Benito Pablo PRESIDENTS—Mexican
Maximilian, Emperor of Mexico EMPERORS
—Mexican
Morelos y Pavón, José María Teclo STATESMEN—Mexican

Mexico—20th century
Buñuel, Luis MOTION PICTURE PRODUCERS—Mexican

Chávez, Carlos COMPOSERS—Mexican
Lee, Harper Baylor BULLFIGHTERS—American
Orozco, José Clemente PAINTERS—Mexican
Rivera, Diego PAINTERS—Mexican
Treviño, Elizabeth (Borton) AUTHORS—American
Vasconcelos, José PHILOSOPHERS—Mexican;
STATESMEN—Mexican

Monaco—20th century
Grace Patricia, Consort of Rainier III, Prince
of Monaco ACTORS—American

Mongolia—13th century
Genghis Khan SOLDIERS—Mongolian
Kublai Khan SOLDIERS—Mongolian

Mongolia—14th century
Tamerlane SOLDIERS—Mongolian

Nepal—20th century
Tenzing, Norgay MOUNTAINEERS—Nepalese

Netherlands—15th century
Bosch, Hieronymus van Aken PAINTERS—
Dutch

Netherlands—16th century
Erasmus, Desiderius EDUCATORS—Dutch
Joris, David RELIGIOUS LEADERS—Dutch
Linschoten, Jan Huyghen van EXPLORERS
—Dutch
Margaretha of Austria, Regent of The Netherlands REGENTS—Dutch
William I (William The Silent) STADHOLDERS—Dutch

Netherlands—17th century
Leeuwenhoek, Anthony van MICROBIOLOGISTS—Dutch; NATURALISTS—Dutch
Rembrandt Harmenszoon van Rijn PAINTERS
—Dutch
Spinoza, Benedict PHILOSOPHERS—Dutch
Stuyvesant, Peter COLONISTS—American
Vermeer, Johannes PAINTERS—Dutch
William III, King of Great Britain KINGS—
English

Netherlands—18th century
Boswell, James AUTHORS—Scottish
Leeuwenhoek, Anthony van MICROBIOLOGISTS—Dutch; NATURALISTS—Dutch

Netherlands—19th century
Gogh, Vincent van PAINTERS—Dutch
Hortense, Consort of Louis, King of Holland
QUEENS—Dutch

Netherlands—20th century
Frank, Anne YOUTHS—Dutch
Mata Hari SPIES—Dutch
Stikker, Dirk Uipko STATESMEN—Dutch
Wilhelmina, Queen of The Netherlands
QUEENS—Dutch

New Guinea—20th century

Harrer, Heinrich MOUNTAINEERS—Austrian

New Zealand—20th century

Davis, Thomas Robert Alexander Harries AN-THROPOLOGISTS—New Zealand; PHYSI-CIANS—New Zealand

McIndoe, Sir Archibald Hector SURGEONS—New Zealand

Mansfield, Katherine AUTHORS—New Zealand

Marsh, Ngaio AUTHORS—New Zealand

Opie, June VICTIMS OF POLIO—New Zealand

Rutherford, Ernest Rutherford, Baron PHYS-ICISTS—English

Smith, Sir Sydney Alfred CRIMINOLOGISTS—English; PHYSICIANS—English

Upham, Charles Hazlitt SOLDIERS—New Zealand

Nicaragua—19th century

Walker, William PRESIDENTS—Nicaraguan; SOLDIERS—American

Nigeria—19th century

Slessor, Mary Mitchell RELIGIOUS LEAD-ERS—Scottish

Nigeria—20th century

Balewa, Sir Abubakar Tafawa STATESMEN—Nigerian

Norway—10th century

Bjarni EXPLORERS—Norwegian

Norway—11th century

Ericson, Leif EXPLORERS—Norwegian

Norway—19th century

Grieg, Edvard Hagerup COMPOSERS—Norwegian

Ibsen, Henrik PLAYWRIGHTS—Norwegian

Nansen, Fridtjof EXPLORERS—Norwegian

Rockne, Knute Kenneth IMMIGRANTS TO UNITED STATES

Norway—20th century

Amundsen, Roald Engelbregt Gravning EX-PLORERS—Norwegian

Balchen, Bernt AVIATORS—American; IM-MIGRANTS TO UNITED STATES

Brandt, Willy STATESMEN—German

Flagstad, Kirsten SINGERS—Norwegian

Henie, Sonja SKATERS—American

Munch, Edvard PAINTERS—Norwegian

Nansen, Fridtjof EXPLORERS—Norwegian; STATESMEN—Norwegian

Nansen, Odd SOLDIERS—Norwegian

Sønsteby, Gunnar Fridtjof Thurmann SOL-DIERS—Norwegian

Pakistan—20th century

Ata-Ullah, Mohammad MOUNTAINEERS—Pakistani; PHYSICIANS—Pakistani

Jinnah, Mohammed Ali LAWYERS—Indian; STATESMEN—Pakistani

Palestine

See also Israel

Palestine—1st century

Akiba Ben Joseph RELIGIOUS LEADERS—Palestinian

Josephus, Flavius HISTORIANS—Palestinian

Palestine—4th century

Dorothea, Saint RELIGIOUS LEADERS—Palestinian

Palestine—20th century

Husseini, Haj Amin, Grand Mufti of Palestine STATESMEN—Palestinian

Persia

See also Iran

Persia—6th century B.C.

Cyrus The Great, King of Persia KINGS—Persian

Darius I, King of Persia KINGS—Persian

Persia—5th century B.C.

Cyrus, the Younger PRINCES—Persian

Xerxes I, King of Persia BIBLICAL FIGURES—Old Testament; KINGS—Persian

Peru—16th century

Pizarro, Francisco, Marqués EXPLORERS—Spanish

Porres, Martín de, Saint RELIGIOUS LEAD-ERS—Peruvian

Peru—17th century

Rose of Lima, Saint RELIGIOUS LEADERS—Peruvian

Peru—20th century

Binder, Theodor PHYSICIANS—German

Odría, Manuel Arturo PRESIDENTS—Peruvian

Tariri RELIGIOUS LEADERS—Peruvian

Philippines—20th century

Macapagal, Diosdado PRESIDENTS—Philippine

Magsaysay, Ramón R. PRESIDENTS—Philippine

Marcos, Ferdinand Edralin STATESMEN—Philippine

Romulo, Carlos Pena STATESMEN—Philippine

Poland—14th century

Jadwiga, Consort of Vladislaus II Jagiello, King of Poland QUEENS—Polish

Poland—16th century

Copernicus, Nicolaus ASTRONOMERS—Polish

Poland—18th century

Salomon, Haym FINANCIERS—American

Poland—19th century

Chopin, Frédéric François COMPOSERS—
Polish; YOUTHS—Polish
Gurowski, Adam ABOLITIONISTS—American
Paderewski, Ignacy Jan PIANISTS—Polish

Poland—20th century

Conrad, Joseph NOVELISTS—English
David, Janina YOUTHS—Polish
Gomulka, Wladyslaw STATESMEN—Polish
Kolbe, Maximilian RELIGIOUS LEADERS—
Polish
Landowska, Wanda PIANISTS—Polish
Monat, Pawel SPIES—Polish
Paderewski, Ignacy Jan PIANISTS—Polish;
STATESMEN—Polish
Rubinstein, Artur PIANISTS—American
Rubinstein, Helena BUSINESSMEN—Ameri-
can; COSMETICIANS—American; IMMI-
GRANTS TO UNITED STATES

Portugal—15th century

Gama, Vasco da EXPLORERS—Portuguese
Henry the Navigator, Prince of Portugal
PRINCES—Portuguese

Portugal—16th century

Gama, Vasco da EXPLORERS—Portuguese
Magellan, Ferdinand EXPLORERS—Portuguese

Portugal—20th century

Salazar, Antonio de Oliveira STATESMEN—
Portuguese

Prussia

See Germany

Puerto Rico—16th century

Ponce de Léon, Juan EXPLORERS—Spanish

Roman Empire

See Rome

Rome—6th century B.C.

Tarquinius Superbus, Lucius, King of Rome
KINGS—Roman

Rome—3rd century B.C.

Fabius, Quintus Maximus Verrucosus SOL-
DIERS—Roman; STATESMEN—Roman
Plautus, Titus Maccius PLAYWRIGHTS—
Roman

Rome—2nd century B.C.

Cato, Marcus Porcius STATESMEN—Roman
Ennius, Quintus POETS—Roman
Terence PLAYWRIGHTS—Roman

Rome—1st century B.C.

Antonius, Marcus STATESMEN—Roman
Augustus, Emperor of Rome EMPERORS—
Roman
Caesar, Caius Julius SOLDIERS—Roman;
STATESMEN—Roman
Catullus, Gaius Valerius POETS—Roman
Cicero, Marcus Tullius STATESMEN—Roman
Horace (Quintus Horatius Flaccus) POETS—
Roman
Julia, Daughter of the Emperor Augustus
DAUGHTERS OF FAMOUS MEN—Roman
Lucretius Carus, Titus POETS—Roman
Ovid POETS—Roman
Propertius, Sextus POETS—Roman
Spartacus GLADIATORS—Roman
Tibullus, Albius POETS—Roman
Virgil POETS—Roman

Rome—1st century

Agricola, Gnaeus Julius SOLDIERS—Roman
Berenice MISTRESSES OF FAMOUS MEN
—Roman
Caligula, Emperor of Rome EMPERORS—
Roman
Claudius I, Emperor of Rome EMPERORS—
Roman
Juvenal, Decimus Junius SATIRISTS—Roman
Nero, Emperor of Rome EMPORERS—Roman

Rome—2nd century

Aurelius Antoninus, Marcus, Emperor of Rome
EMPERORS—Roman
Hadrian, Emperor of Rome EMPERORS—
Roman
Ignatius Theophorus, Saint RELIGIOUS
LEADERS—Roman
Justin, Saint RELIGIOUS LEADERS—Roman
Juvenal, Decimus Junius SATIRISTS—Roman

Rome—3rd century

Aurelian, Emperor of Rome EMPERORS—
Roman
Heliogabalus, Emperor of Rome EMPERORS
—Roman
Plotinus PHILOSOPHERS—Roman

Rome—4th century

Julian, Emperor of Rome EMPERORS—Roman

Rome—6th century

Belisarius SOLDIERS—Roman
Benedict, Saint RELIGIOUS LEADERS—
Roman
Gregory I, the Great, Saint, Pope RELIGIOUS
LEADERS—Italian

Rome—8th century

Charlemagne EMPERORS—Roman; KINGS—
French

Russia—4th century

Nicholas, Saint, Bishop of Myra RELIGIOUS
LEADERS—Russian

Russia—15th century

Ivan III, the Great, Emperor of Russia EMPERORS—Russian

Russia—16th century

Ivan IV, the Terrible, Czar of Russia CZARS—Russian

Russia—18th century

Catherine II, Empress of Russia ART COLLECTORS—Russian; EMPRESSES—Russian
Peter I, The Great, Emperor of Russia EMPERORS—Russian
Potemkin, Grigori Aleksandrovich STATESMEN—Russian
Suvorov, Aleksandr Vasilievich SOLDIERS—Russian

Russia—18th century

Andreas-Salomé, Lou PSYCHIATRISTS—Russian
Antin, Mary AUTHORS—American; IMMIGRANTS TO UNITED STATES
Chekhov, Anton Pavlovich AUTHORS—Russian
Dostoevsky, Fedor Mikhaïlovich NOVELISTS—Russian
Gogol', Nikolaï Vasil'evich AUTHORS—Russian
Kshesinskaïa, Matil'da Feliksovna DANCERS—Russian
Maria Fedorovna, Empress of Russia EMPRESSES—Russian
Marshak, Samuil IAkovlevich YOUTHS—Russian
Mendeleyev, Dimitri Ivanovich CHEMISTS—Russian
Mussorgsky, Modest Petrovich COMPOSERS—Russian
Plekhanov, Georgi Valentinovich POLITICAL SCIENTISTS—Russian
Poltoratzky, Ellen Sarah (Southee) UNCLASSIFIED—Russian
Rubinstein, Anton COMPOSERS—Russian; PIANISTS—Russian
Sterne, Maurice IMMIGRANTS TO UNITED STATES
Tchaikovsky, Peter Ilyich COMPOSERS—Russian
Tolstoi, Lev Nikolaevich NOVELISTS—Russian
Tolstoi, Sofia Andreevna (Behrs) WIVES OF FAMOUS MEN—Russian
Turgenev, Ivan Sergeevich NOVELISTS—Russian
Uxkull, Boris SOLDIERS—Russian

Russia—20th century

Abel, Rudolf Ivanovich SPIES—Russian
Anastasía Grand Duchess of Russia DAUGHTERS OF FAMOUS MEN—Russian
Babel', Isaak Emmanuilovich AUTHORS—Russian
Balanchine, George DANCERS—American
Berdiaev, Nikolai Aleksandrovich PHILOSOPHERS—Russian

Blok, Aleksandr Aleksandrovich POETS—Russian
Chagall, Marc PAINTERS—Russian
Ciszek, Walter J. RELIGIOUS LEADERS—American
Daniel, IUlii Markovich AUTHORS—Russian
Ehrenburg, Il'ia Grigor'evich AUTHORS—Russian
Evtushenko, Eugenii Aleksandrovich POETS—Russian
Feodorov, Leonid Ivanovich, Exarch RELIGIOUS LEADERS—Russian
Gilels, Emil Grigor'evich PIANISTS—Russian
Gorbatov, Aleksandr Vassil'evich SOLDIERS—Russian
Gorky, Maxim AUTHORS—Russian; PACIFISTS—Russian
Gurdjieff, Georges Ivanovitch EDUCATORS—Russian
Horowitz, Vladimir PIANISTS—American
Kandinsky, Wassily PAINTERS—Russian
Karsavina, Tamara DANCERS—Russian
Kerensky, Alexander Fedorovich STATESMEN—Russian
Khrushchev, Nikita Sergeevich STATESMEN—Russian
Koussevitzky, Serge CONDUCTORS—Russian
Kshesinskaïa, Matil'da Feliksovna DANCERS—Russian
Landau, Lev Davidovich PHYSICISTS—Russian
Lenin, Vladimir Il'ich STATESMEN—Russian
Leonov, Leonid Maksimovich NOVELISTS—Russian
Lissanevitch, Boris HOTEL OWNERS AND MANAGERS—Russian
Mal'ko, Nikolai Andreevich CONDUCTORS—Russian
Maria Fedorovna, Empress of Russia EMPRESSES—Russian
Marshak, Samuil IAkovlevich AUTHORS—Russian
Mayakovski, Vladimir Vladimirovich POETS—Russian
Nicholas II, Emperor of Russia EMPERORS—Russian
Olga Alexandrovna RELATIVES OF FAMOUS MEN—Russian
Papashvily, George IMMIGRANTS TO UNITED STATES
Pasternak, Boris Leonidovich AUTHORS—Russian
Pavlova, Anna DANCERS—Russian
Piatigorsky, Gregor CELLISTS—Russian
Plekhanov, Georgi Valentinovich POLITICAL SCIENTISTS—Russian
Prokofiev, Sergei Sergeevich COMPOSERS—Russian
Rachmaninoff, Sergei COMPOSERS—Russian
Rand, Ayn NOVELISTS—American
Rasputin, Grigorii Efimovich RELIGIOUS LEADERS—Russian
Sarnoff, David ENGINEERS, RADIO AND TELEVISION—American; IMMIGRANTS TO UNITED STATES; INDUSTRIALISTS—American

Russia—20th century—Continued

Sholokhov, Mikhail Aleksandrovich AUTHORS—Russian

Sikorsky, Igor Ivan ENGINEERS, AERONAUTICAL—American; IMMIGRANTS TO UNITED STATES

Siniavskiĭ, Andreĭ Donat'evich AUTHORS—Russian

Stalin, Joseph STATESMEN—Russian

Stanislavski, Constantin ACTORS—Russian; THEATRICAL PRODUCERS—Russian

Stravinsky, Igor Fedorovich COMPOSERS—Russian; IMMIGRANTS TO UNITED STATES

Titov, German Stepanovich ASTRONAUTS—Russian

Trotsky, Lev STATESMEN—Russian

Ulanova, Galina Sergeevna DANCERS—Russian

Vigdorova, F. EDUCATORS—Russian

Vishinsky, Andrei STATESMEN—Russian

Waksman, Selman Abraham BACTERIOLOGISTS — American; IMMIGRANTS TO UNITED STATES

Woytinsky, Wladimir Savelievich ECONOMISTS—American; IMMIGRANTS TO UNITED STATES

Samoa—20th century

Calkins, Fay G. AUTHORS—American

Scotland—11th century

Malcolm III, King of Scotland KINGS—Scottish

Scotland—13th century

Alexander III, King of Scotland KINGS—Scottish

Wallace, Sir William SOLDIERS—Scottish

Scotland—14th century

Bruce, Robert, King of Scotland KINGS—Scottish; SOLDIERS—Scottish

Scotland—15th century

James IV, King of Scotland KINGS—Scottish

Scotland—16th century

James IV, King of Scotland KINGS—Scottish

Mary Stuart, Queen of the Scots QUEENS—Scottish; YOUTHS—Scottish

Moray, James Stewart, 1st Earl of STATESMEN—Scottish

Seton, Alexander ALCHEMISTS—Scottish

Scotland—17th century

Baillie, Lady Grizel (Hume) POETS—Scottish

Kidd, William CRIMINALS—Scottish

Montrose, James Graham, 1st Marquis of SOLDIERS—Scottish

Scotland—18th century

Black, Joseph CHEMISTS—Scottish

Boswell, James AUTHORS—Scottish

Burns, Robert POETS—Scottish

Hunter, John ANATOMISTS—Scottish; SURGEONS—Scottish

MacDonald, Flora (MacDonald) UNCLASSIFIED—Scottish

Mackenzie, Alexander EXPLORERS—Scottish

Smith, Adam ECONOMISTS—Scottish

Smollett, Tobias George NOVELISTS—Scottish

Watt, James ENGINEERS, MECHANICAL—Scottish; INVENTORS—Scottish

Scotland—19th century

Anderson, John Henry MAGICIANS—Scottish

Carlyle, Jane Baillie (Welsh) AUTHORS—Scottish

Carlyle, Thomas ESSAYISTS—Scottish; HISTORIANS—Scottish

Douglas, David BOTANISTS—Scottish

Grahame, Kenneth AUTHORS—Scottish

Livingstone, David EXPLORERS—Scottish; RELIGIOUS LEADERS—Scottish

Lyell, Sir Charles, Bart. GEOLOGISTS—Scottish

Macdonald, George AUTHORS—Scottish

Maxwell, James Clerk PHYSICISTS—Scottish

Muir, John IMMIGRANTS TO UNITED STATES; NATURALISTS—American

Pinkerton, Allan DETECTIVES—American; IMMIGRANTS TO UNITED STATES

Scott, Sir Walter AUTHORS—Scottish

Slessor, Mary Mitchell RELIGIOUS LEADERS—Scottish

Stevenson, Robert Louis AUTHORS—Scottish

Stewart, Sir William George Drummond, Bart. FRONTIERSMEN—Scottish

Wilson, Alexander ORNITHOLOGISTS—American

Scotland—20th century

Buchan, John, 1st Baron Tweedsmuir NOVELISTS—Scottish; STATESMEN—Scottish

Clark, James AUTOMOBILE RACERS—Scottish

Cronin, Archibald Joseph NOVELISTS—Scottish; PHYSICIANS—Scottish

Daiches, David YOUTHS—Scottish

Fleming, Sir Alexander BACTERIOLOGISTS—Scottish

Grahame, Kenneth AUTHORS—Scottish

Mavor, Osborne Henry PLAYWRIGHTS—Scottish

Sanders, George ACTORS—Scottish

Spark, Muriel NOVELISTS—Scottish

Senegal—20th century

Senghor, Léopold Sédar PRESIDENTS—Senegalese

Siam—19th century

Bunker, Chang and Eng SIAMESE TWINS—Siamese

Leonowens, Anna Harriette (Crawford) EDUCATORS—Welsh

Mongkut, King of Siam KINGS—Siamese

Siberia—20th century

Stanford, Doreen ENGINEERS, MINING—English

South Africa—19th century

Rhodes, Cecil John FINANCIERS—English

South Africa—20th century

Abrahams, Peter POETS—South African
Hofmeyr, Jan Hendrik STATESMEN—South African
Jabavu, Noni JOURNALISTS—South African
Luthuli, Albert REFORMERS—South African; STATESMEN—South African
Modisane, Bloke JOURNALISTS—South African

South America—19th century

Bolívar, Simón SOLDIERS—South American; STATESMEN—South American
San Martín, José de SOLDIERS—South American; STATESMEN—South American
Sucre, Antonio José de PRESIDENTS—Bolivian; SOLDIERS—South American

Spain—8th century

'Abd al-Rahmān I, Caliph of Cordova SOLDIERS—Spanish

Spain—11th century

El Cid Campeador SOLDIERS—Spanish

Spain—12th century

Maimonides PHYSICIANS—Spanish; RELIGIOUS LEADERS—Spanish

Spain—15th century

Isabel I, Queen of Spain QUEENS—Spanish
Luna, Álvaro de STATESMEN—Spanish
Torquemada, Tomás de RELIGIOUS LEADERS—Spanish

Spain—16th century

Balboa, Vasco Núñez de EXPLORERS—Spanish
Cabeza de Vaca, Álvar Núñez EXPLORERS—Spanish
Cervantes Saavedra, Miguel de NOVELISTS Spanish
Coronado, Francisco Vásquez de EXPLORERS—Spanish
Cortés, Hernando EXPLORERS—Spanish
Díaz del Castillo, Bernal HISTORIANS—Spanish; SOLDIERS—Spanish
Greco, El PAINTERS—Spanish
John of the Cross, Saint RELIGIOUS LEADERS—Spanish
López, Martín EXPLORERS—Spanish
Loyola, Saint Ignatius RELIGIOUS LEADERS—Spanish
Orellana, Francisco de EXPLORERS—Spanish
Philip II, King of Spain KINGS—Spanish
Pizarro, Francisco, Marqués EXPLORERS—Spanish
Ponce de León, Juan EXPLORERS—Spanish
Servetus, Michael RELIGIOUS LEADERS—Spanish
Soto, Hernando de EXPLORERS—Spanish
Teresa, Saint RELIGIOUS LEADERS—Spanish

Spain—17th century

Pareja, Juan de PAINTERS—Spanish
Velázquez, Diego Rodríguez de Silva y PAINTERS—Spanish

Spain—18th century

Goya y Lucientes, Francisco José de PAINTERS—Spanish
Serra, Junípero RELIGIOUS LEADERS—Spanish

Spain—19th century

Borrow, George Henry AUTHORS—English
García, Manuel del Pópolo Vicente SINGERS—Spanish

Spain—20th century

Azaña, Manuel PRESIDENTS—Spanish
Bell, Julian PACIFISTS—English; POETS—English
Casals, Pablo CELLISTS—Spanish
Cornford, John POETS—English
Dalí, Salvador PAINTERS—Spanish
García Lorca, Federico PLAYWRIGHTS—Spanish; POETS—Spanish
Gaudí y Cornet, Antonio ARCHITECTS—Spanish
Jiménez, Juan Ramón POETS—Spanish
Machado y Ruiz, Antonio AUTHORS—Spanish
Martínez Alonso, Eduardo PHYSICIANS—Spanish
Miró, Joan PAINTERS—Spanish
Picasso, Pablo PAINTERS—Spanish
Santayana, George PHILOSOPHERS—American; POETS—American
Segovia, Andrés GUITARISTS—Spanish
Unamuno y Jugo, Miguel de AUTHORS—Spanish

Sweden—17th century

Christina, Queen of Sweden QUEENS—Swedish

Sweden—18th century

Linné, Carl von BOTANISTS—Swedish

Sweden—19th century

Andrée, Salomon August AVIATORS—Swedish
Bernardine Eugénie Désirée, Consort of Charles XIV John, King of Sweden and Norway QUEENS—Swedish
Hedin, Sven Anders EXPLORERS—Swedish
Lind, Jenny SINGERS—Swedish; YOUTHS—Swedish
Nobel, Alfred Bernhard CHEMISTS—Swedish; INVENTORS—Swedish; PHILANTHROPISTS—Swedish
Strindberg, August AUTHORS—Swedish

Sweden—20th century

Bergman, Ingmar MOTION PICTURE PRODUCERS—Swedish
Bergman, Ingrid ACTORS—Swedish
Bjorn, Thyra (Ferré) AUTHORS—American; IMMIGRANTS TO UNITED STATES
Hammarskjöld, Dag STATESMEN—Swedish; UNITED NATIONS OFFICIALS—Swedish

Sweden—20th century—*Continued*

Hedin, Sven Anders EXPLORERS—Swedish
Kreuger, Ivar FINANCIERS—Swedish; IN-
DUSTRIALISTS—Swedish
Munthe, Axel Martin Fredrik PHYSICIANS
—Swedish
Wennerström, Stig SPIES—Swedish

Switzerland—14th century

Tell, William ARCHERS—Swiss; STATES-
MEN—Swiss

Switzerland—16th century

Paracelsus, Philippus Aureolus ALCHEMISTS
—Swiss; PHYSICIANS—Swiss

Switzerland—19th century

Agassiz, Alexander OCEANOGRAPHERS—
American; ZOOLOGISTS—American
Agassiz, Louis NATURALISTS—Swiss
Bodmer, Karl PAINTERS—Swiss

Switzerland—20th century

Barth, Karl RELIGIOUS LEADERS—Swiss
Honegger, Arthur COMPOSERS—French
Jung, Carl Gustav PSYCHIATRISTS—Swiss
Klee, Paul PAINTERS—Swiss
Le Corbusier (Charles Edouard Jeanneret-Gris)
ARCHITECTS—Swiss
Piccard, Auguste AVIATORS—Swiss; PHYS-
ICISTS—Swiss

Syria—5th century

Simeon Stylites, Saint RELIGIOUS LEAD-
ERS—Syrian

Tanganyika—20th century

Ionides, Constantine John Philip HERPE-
TOLOGISTS—English
Nyerere, Julius Kambarage PRESIDENTS—
Tanganyikan

Thailand—20th century

Caulfield, Genevieve BLIND—American

Tibet—20th century

Dalai Lama XIV RELIGIOUS LEADERS—
Tibetan; STATESMEN—Tibetan
Thubten Jigme Norbu RELIGIOUS LEAD-
ERS—Tibetan

Tunisia—20th century

Bourguiba, Habib ben Ali PRESIDENTS—
Tunisian

Turkey—16th century

Sulaiman I, the Magnificent SULTANS—Turkish

Turkey—20th century

Atatürk, Kamâl PRESIDENTS—Turkish; SOL-
DIERS—Turkish

United States

See also Alaska; America; Hawaii

United States—18th century

Adair, James FRONTIERSMEN—American
Adams, Abigail (Smith) MOTHERS OF FA-
MOUS MEN—American; WIVES OF FA-
MOUS MEN—American
Adams, John LAWYERS—American; PRESI-
DENTS—American
Adams, John Quincy STATESMEN—American
Adams, Samuel STATESMEN—American
Allen, Ethan SOLDIERS—American
Allen, Richard RELIGIOUS LEADERS—
American
Arnold, Benedict SOLDIERS—American; TRAI-
TORS—American
Attucks, Crispus SOLDIERS—American
Banneker, Benjamin MATHEMATICIANS—
American
Barlow, Joel STATESMEN—American
Bartram, John BOTANISTS—American
Boone, Daniel FRONTIERSMEN—American
Bowles, William Augustus INDIAN LEADERS
—American
Burr, Aaron STATESMEN—American
Bushnell, David INVENTORS—American
Byrd, William COLONISTS—American
Callaway, Jemima (Boone) DAUGHTERS OF
FAMOUS MEN—American
Carroll, John RELIGIOUS LEADERS—Amer-
ican
Clark, George Rogers FRONTIERSMEN—
American; SOLDIERS—American
Clinton, Sir Henry SOLDIERS—English
Colden, Jane BOTANISTS—American
Copley, John Singleton PAINTERS—American
Darragh, Lydia (Barrington) SPIES—American
Dexter, Timothy BUSINESSMEN—American
Franklin, Benjamin AUTHORS—American;
PHILOSOPHERS — American; PRINTERS —
American; SCIENTISTS—American; STATES-
MEN—American
Fulton, Robert ENGINEERS, MECHANICAL
—American; INVENTORS—American
Gallatin, Albert STATESMEN—American
Glover, John SOLDIERS—American
Greene, Nathanael SOLDIERS—American
Hale, Nathan SOLDIERS—American; SPIES—
American
Hamilton, Alexander STATESMEN—American
Hamilton, Andrew LAWYERS—American
Hamilton, Henry STATESMEN—English
Hancock, John STATESMEN—American
Henderson, Richard FRONTIERSMEN—Amer-
ican
Henry, Patrick STATESMEN—American
Honeyman, John SPIES—American
Ingles, Mary FRONTIERSMEN—American
Jay, Sarah (Livingston) WIVES OF FAMOUS
MEN—American
Jefferson, Thomas STATESMEN—American;
YOUTHS—American
Jemison, Mary INDIAN LEADERS—American
Jones, John Paul NAVAL OFFICERS AND
OTHER SEAFARERS—American
Kenton, Simon FRONTIERSMEN—American
Lafayette, Marie Joseph Paul Yves Roch Gil-
bert du Motier, Marquis de SOLDIERS—
French; YOUTHS—French

United States—18th century—*Continued*

Lee, Henry ("Light-Horse Harry") SOLDIERS —American; STATESMEN—American

Lisa, Manuel FRONTIERSMEN—American

Littlepage, Lewis STATESMEN—American

Lopez, Aaron BUSINESSMEN—American

Madison, James STATESMEN—American

Marion, Francis SOLDIERS—American

Martin, Joseph Plumb SOLDIERS—American

Mason, George STATESMEN—American

Mecom, Jane (Franklin) RELATIVES OF FAMOUS MEN—American

Monroe, James STATESMEN—American

Morgan, Daniel SOLDIERS—American

Morris, Gouverneur STATESMEN—American

Oglethorpe, James Edward SOLDIERS—English

O'Hara, James SOLDIERS—American

Otis, James STATESMEN—American

Paine, Thomas AUTHORS—American; POLITICAL SCIENTISTS—American

Peale, Charles Willson PAINTERS—American

Pontiac, Ottawa Chief INDIAN LEADERS—American

Putnam, Israel SOLDIERS—American

Randolph, Edmund Jennings STATESMEN—American

Randolph, Martha (Jefferson) DAUGHTERS OF FAMOUS MEN—American

Revere, Paul SILVERSMITHS—American; STATESMEN—American

Riedesel, Friederike Charlotte Luise (von Massow) Freifrau von WIVES OF FAMOUS MEN—German

Rittenhouse, David ASTRONOMERS—American; STATESMEN—American

Rochambeau, Jean Baptiste Donatien de Vimeur, Comte de SOLDIERS—French

Rogers, Robert SOLDIERS—American

Rowson, Susanna (Haswell) NOVELISTS—American

Rumford, Sir Benjamin Thompson, Count PHYSICISTS—English

Rush, Benjamin PHYSICIANS—American; STATESMEN—American

Salomon, Haym FINANCIERS—American

Schneider, Martin FRONTIERSMEN—American

Sequoya, Cherokee Indian INDIAN LEADERS—American

Serra, Junípero RELIGIOUS LEADERS—Spanish

Sewall, Samuel COLONISTS—American; LAWYERS—American

Smith, James FRONTIERSMEN—American

Steuben, Friedrich Wilhelm von IMMIGRANTS TO UNITED STATES; SOLDIERS —American

Stobo, Robert SOLDIERS—English

Stuart, Gilbert PAINTERS—American

Sumter, Thomas SOLDIERS—American

Washington, George PRESIDENTS—American; RELIGIOUS LEADERS—American; SOLDIERS—American

Washington, Martha (Dandridge) Custis WIVES OF FAMOUS MEN—American

Washington, Mary (Ball) MOTHERS OF FAMOUS MEN—American

Webster, Noah LEXICOGRAPHERS—American

West, Benjamin PAINTERS—American

Wheatley, Phillis POETS—American

Wheelwright, Esther RELIGIOUS LEADERS —Canadian

Whitney, Eli INVENTORS—American

Wiggan, Eleazar FRONTIERSMEN—American

Wilson, James STATESMEN—American

Woolman, John ABOLITIONISTS—American; RELIGIOUS LEADERS—American

Zenger, John Peter IMMIGRANTS TO UNITED STATES; JOURNALISTS—American

United States—19th century

Adair, Bethenia Angelina (Owens) FRONTIERSMEN—American; PHYSICIANS—American

Adams, Andy COWBOYS—American

Adams, Brooks HISTORIANS—American

Adams, Charles Francis, 1807-1886 STATESMEN—American

Adams, Charles Francis, 1835-1915 HISTORIANS—American; LAWYERS—American

Adams, Henry Brooks HISTORIANS—American

Adams, John Capen FRONTIERSMEN—American

Adams, John Quincy PRESIDENTS—American

Adams, Louisa Catherine (Johnson) WIVES OF FAMOUS MEN—American

Agassiz, Alexander OCEANOGRAPHERS—American; ZOOLOGISTS—American

Agassiz, Louis NATURALISTS—Swiss

Alcott, Louisa May AUTHORS—American

Aldrich, Thomas Bailey AUTHORS—American

Alexander, Edward Porter SOLDIERS—American

Alger, Horatio AUTHORS—American

Allen, James Lane AUTHORS—American

Allen, Richard RELIGIOUS LEADERS—American

Alston, Theodosia (Burr) DAUGHTERS OF FAMOUS MEN—American

Altgeld, John Peter IMMIGRANTS TO UNITED STATES; LAWYERS—American; STATESMEN—American

Anthony, Susan Brownell ABOLITIONISTS —American; FEMINISTS—American

Armour, Philip Danforth INDUSTRIALISTS —American

Ashby, Turner SOLDIERS—American

Ashmun, Jehudi ABOLITIONISTS—American

Astor, John Jacob FINANCIERS—American; FRONTIERSMEN — American; IMMIGRANTS TO UNITED STATES

Audubon, John James ORNITHOLOGISTS—American; PAINTERS—American

Ayer, Harriet (Hubbard) BUSINESSMEN—American; COSMETICIANS—American

Babcock, Stephen Moulton CHEMISTS—American

Baca, Elfego FRONTIERSMEN—American; LAWYERS—American; SHERIFFS—American

Bacon, Delia Salter AUTHORS—American

United States—19th century—*Continued*

Bainbridge, William NAVAL OFFICERS AND OTHER SEAFARERS—American

Baldwin, Mary FRONTIERSMEN—American

Banvard, John PAINTERS—American

Barnum, Phineas Taylor CIRCUS MANAGERS—American

Barton, Clara Harlowe NURSES—American; RED CROSS WORKERS—American

Beaumont, William SURGEONS—American

Beauregard, Pierre Gustave Toutant SOLDIERS—American

Beckwourth, James Pierson FRONTIERSMEN—American

Beecher, Catharine Esther EDUCATORS—American

Beecher, Lyman RELIGIOUS LEADERS—American

Bell, Alexander Graham IMMIGRANTS TO UNITED STATES; INVENTORS—American

Bellamy, Edward AUTHORS—American

Benjamin, Judah Philip LAWYERS—American; STATESMEN—American

Bennett, James Gordon JOURNALISTS—American

Benton, Thomas Hart STATESMEN—American

Berlin, Irving IMMIGRANTS TO UNITED STATES

Bidwell, John FRONTIERSMEN—American

Bierce, Ambrose AUTHORS—American

Bingham, George Caleb PAINTERS—American

Black Hawk, Sauk Chief INDIAN LEADERS—American

Blackwell, Antoinette Louisa (Brown) RELIGIOUS LEADERS—American

Blackwell, Elizabeth PHYSICIANS—American

Bonaparte, Elizabeth (Patterson) WIVES OF FAMOUS MEN—French

Bonney, William Harrison ("Billy the Kid") CRIMINALS—American; FRONTIERSMEN—American

Booth, Edwin Thomas ACTORS—American

Booth, John Wilkes ACTORS—American; CRIMINALS—American

Borden, Lizzie Andrew CRIMINALS—American

Bowditch, Nathaniel ASTRONOMERS—American; MATHEMATICIANS—American

Bowie, James FRONTIERSMEN—American; SOLDIERS—American

Boyer, Samuel Pellman PHYSICIANS—American

Bradley, Milton BUSINESSMEN—American

Brady, Mathew PHOTOGRAPHERS—American

Bridger, James EXPLORERS—American; SCOUTS—American

Bridgman, Laura Dewey BLIND—American; DEAF—American

Brooks, Phillips RELIGIOUS LEADERS—American

Brown, John ABOLITIONISTS—American

Brown, Tabitha (Moffatt) FRONTIERSMEN—American

Browne, Charles Farrar HUMORISTS—American

Browne, John Ross AUTHORS—American

Browning, John Moses GUNMAKERS—American; INVENTORS—American

Bryan, William Jennings LAWYERS—American; STATESMEN—American

Bryant, William Cullen POETS—American

Buchanan, Franklin NAVAL OFFICERS AND OTHER SEAFARERS—American

Buchanan, James PRESIDENTS—American

Burbank, Luther HORTICULTURISTS—American

Burnett, Frances Hodgson AUTHORS—American

Burr, Aaron STATESMEN—American

Burroughs, John AUTHORS—American; NATURALISTS—American

Butler, Benjamin Franklin SOLDIERS—American

Butler, Matthew Calbraith SOLDIERS—American

Butterfield, John POSTAL OFFICIALS—American

Cable, George Washington NOVELISTS—American

Cabrini, Frances Xavier, Saint IMMIGRANTS TO UNITED STATES; RELIGIOUS LEADERS—American

Calhoun, John Caldwell LAWYERS—American; STATESMEN—American

Cannon, Joseph Gurney ("Uncle Joe") STATESMEN—American

Carnegie, Andrew INDUSTRIALISTS—American; PHILANTHROPISTS—American

Carson, Christopher SCOUTS—American

Cassatt, Mary PAINTERS—American

Cather, Willa Sibert YOUTHS—American

Catlin, George ETHNOLOGISTS—American; PAINTERS—American

Cavarly, John Mansfield NAVAL OFFICERS AND OTHER SEAFARERS—American

Chapman, John FRONTIERSMEN—American

Chase, Mary Ellen YOUTHS—American

Chase, Salmon Portland LAWYERS—American; STATESMEN—American

Child, Lydia Maria (Francis) ABOLITIONISTS—American

Chivington, John Milton SOLDIERS—American

Clark, William EXPLORERS—American

Clark, William Andrews FINANCIERS—American; STATESMEN—American

Clay, Henry STATESMEN—American

Cleburne, Patrick Ronayne SOLDIERS—American

Clemens, Jane (Lampton) MOTHERS OF FAMOUS MEN—American

Clemens, Olivia (Langdon) WIVES OF FAMOUS MEN—American

Clemens, Samuel Langhorne HUMORISTS—American; YOUTHS—American

Cleveland, Grover PRESIDENTS—American

Cochise, Apache Chief INDIAN LEADERS—American

United States—19th century—*Continued*

Cody, William Frederick ("Buffalo Bill") SCOUTS—American

Cohen, Morris Raphael IMMIGRANTS TO UNITED STATES

Colt, Samuel INVENTORS—American; YOUTHS—American

Colter, John FRONTIERSMEN—American

Cook, Frederick Albert EXPLORERS—American; PHYSICIANS—American

Cooper, James Fenimore NOVELISTS—American

Cooper, Peter BUSINESSMEN—American; PHILANTHROPISTS—American

Cope, Edward Drinker PALEONTOLOGISTS—American

Cowles, Anna (Roosevelt) RELATIVES OF FAMOUS MEN—American

Crandall, Prudence EDUCATORS—American

Crane, Cora WIVES OF FAMOUS MEN—American

Crane, Stephen AUTHORS—American

Crazy Horse, Sioux Chief INDIAN LEADERS—American

Crocker, Charles RAILROAD OFFICIALS—American

Crockett, David FRONTIERSMEN—American

Cushman, Charlotte Saunders ACTORS—American

Custer, Elizabeth (Bacon) WIVES OF FAMOUS MEN—American

Custer, George Armstrong FRONTIERSMEN—American; SOLDIERS—American

Daly, Marcus IMMIGRANTS TO UNITED STATES; INDUSTRIALISTS—American

Damrosch, Frank Heino CONDUCTORS—American

Damrosch, Walter IMMIGRANTS TO UNITED STATES

Dana, Ethel Nathalie (Smith) YOUTHS—American

Dana, John Cotton LIBRARIANS—American

Dana, Richard Henry AUTHORS—American; NAVAL OFFICERS AND OTHER SEAFARERS—American

Daniels, Josephus JOURNALISTS—American

Davenport, Thomas INVENTORS—American

Davis, Jefferson PRESIDENTS—American Confederate

Davis, Richard Harding JOURNALISTS—American

Davis, Varina (Howell) WIVES OF FAMOUS MEN—American

Debs, Eugene Victor LABOR LEADERS—American

Decatur, Stephen NAVAL OFFICERS AND OTHER SEAFARERS—American

Dewey, George NAVAL OFFICERS AND OTHER SEAFARERS—American

Dewey, John EDUCATORS—American; PHILOSOPHERS—American

Dewey, Melvil LIBRARIANS—American

Dewey, Nelson STATESMEN—American

Dickinson, Emily POETS—American

Dix, Dorothea Lynde NURSES—American; PHILANTHROPISTS—American

Douglas, David BOTANISTS—Scottish

Douglas, Stephen Arnold STATESMEN—American

Douglass, Frederick ABOLITIONISTS—American; AUTHORS—American

Drake, Edwin Laurentine PETROLEUM INDUSTRY WORKERS—American

Duke, James Buchanan INDUSTRIALISTS—American

Dunbar, Paul Laurence POETS—American

Duniway, Abigail Jane (Scott) FEMINISTS—American; FRONTIERSMEN—American

Dunne, Finley Peter HUMORISTS—American

Du Pont, Éleuthère Irénée INDUSTRIALISTS—American

Eakins, Thomas EDUCATORS—American; PAINTERS—American

Earp, Wyatt Berry Stapp SHERIFFS—American

Eddy, Mary (Baker) RELIGIOUS LEADERS—American

Edison, Thomas Alva YOUTHS—American

Edmundson, Sarah Emma SOLDIERS—American

Elliott, Maxine ACTORS—American

Ellsworth, Ephraim Elmer SOLDIERS—American

Emerson, Ralph Waldo AUTHORS—American; PHILOSOPHERS—American

Ericsson, John ENGINEERS, MECHANICAL—American; IMMIGRANTS TO UNITED STATES; INVENTORS—American

Evans, Augusta Jane NOVELISTS—American

Evans, Charles LIBRARIANS—American

Farragut, David Glasgow NAVAL OFFICERS AND OTHER SEAFARERS—American

Ferris, George Washington Gale ENGINEERS, MECHANICAL—American

Field, Cyrus West FINANCIERS—American

Field, Eugene POETS—American

Fields, James Thomas AUTHORS—American; PUBLISHERS—American

Fiske, Minnie Maddern ACTORS—American

Fitzgerald, John Francis STATESMEN—American

Follen, Charles Theodore Christian ABOLITIONISTS—American; IMMIGRANTS TO UNITED STATES

Forrest, Edwin ACTORS—American

Forrest, Nathan Bedford SOLDIERS—American

Fortune, Amos UNCLASSIFIED—American

Foster, Stephen Collins COMPOSERS—American

Frankfurter, Felix IMMIGRANTS TO UNITED STATES

Frémont, Jessie (Benton) DAUGHTERS OF FAMOUS MEN—American; WIVES OF FAMOUS MEN—American

Frémont, John Charles EXPLORERS—American; SOLDIERS—American

Frick, Henry Clay INDUSTRIALISTS—American

Fulton, Robert ENGINEERS, MECHANICAL—American; INVENTORS—American

United States—19th century—*Continued*

Johnson, Andrew PRESIDENTS—American

Johnson, Reverdy LAWYERS—American; STATESMEN—American

Johnston, Joseph Eggleston SOLDIERS—American

Jolson, Al IMMIGRANTS TO UNITED STATES

Joseph, Nez Percé Chief INDIAN LEADERS —American

Jumel, Eliza (Bowen) WIVES OF FAMOUS MEN—American

Juneau, Solomon Laurent FRONTIERSMEN —American; STATESMEN—American

Kahn, Otto Hermann IMMIGRANTS TO UNITED STATES

Kane, Elisha Kent EXPLORERS—American

Keogh, Myles Walter SOLDIERS—American

Key, Francis Scott LAWYERS—American; POETS—American

Keyes, Frances Parkinson (Wheeler) YOUTHS —American

Klah, Hosteen INDIAN LEADERS—American

Kreuger, Ivar IMMIGRANTS TO UNITED STATES

Lafitte, Jean CRIMINALS—American

Lathrop, Rose (Hawthorne) RELIGIOUS LEADERS—American

Lazarus, Emma POETS—American

Lee, Robert Edward EDUCATORS—American; SOLDIERS—American

Leslie, Miriam Florence (Folline) Squier PUBLISHERS—American

Levy, Uriah Phillips NAVAL OFFICERS AND OTHER SEAFARERS—American

Lewis, Meriwether EXPLORERS—American

Libbey, Laura Jean NOVELISTS—American

Lincoln, Abraham LAWYERS—American; PRESIDENTS—American; YOUTHS—American

Lincoln, Mary (Todd) WIVES OF FAMOUS MEN—American

Lisa, Manuel FRONTIERSMEN—American

Lockwood, Belva Ann (Bennett) FEMINISTS —American; LAWYERS—American

Long, Crawford Williamson SURGEONS—American

Longfellow, Henry Wadsworth POETS—American

Lovejoy, Elijah Parish ABOLITIONISTS—American

Lowe, Thaddeus Sobieski Coulincourt AVIATORS—American; INVENTORS—American

Lowell, James Russell POETS—American

Lyon, Mary EDUCATORS—American

McClellan, George Brinton SOLDIERS—American

McClure, Samuel Sidney IMMIGRANTS TO UNITED STATES

McCormick, Cyrus Hall INDUSTRIALISTS —American; INVENTORS—American

MacDonough, Thomas NAVAL OFFICERS AND OTHER SEAFARERS—American

MacDowell, Edward Alexander COMPOSERS —American; PIANISTS—American

McDowell, Ephraim SURGEONS—American

McGillycuddy, Valentine Trant O'Connell FRONTIERSMEN—American

McKinley, William PRESIDENTS—American

Madison, Dorothy (Payne) Todd WIVES OF FAMOUS MEN—American

Madison, James PRESIDENTS—American

Mahone, William SOLDIERS—American

Mangas Colorados, Apache Chief INDIAN LEADERS—American

Mann, Horace EDUCATORS—American

Mann, William D'Alton CRIMINALS—American; JOURNALISTS—American

Marsh, Othniel Charles PALEONTOLOGISTS —American

Marshall, John LAWYERS—American

Maury, Matthew Fontaine NAVAL OFFICERS AND OTHER SEAFARERS — American; OCEANOGRAPHERS—American

Maxim, Sir Hiram Stevens INVENTORS—English

Mayo, William James PHYSICIANS—American

Meek, Joseph Lafayette FRONTIERSMEN—American

Melville, Herman NOVELISTS—American

Menken, Adah Isaacs ACTORS—American

Mercer, Asa Shinn FRONTIERSMEN—American

Mergenthaler, Ottmar IMMIGRANTS TO UNITED STATES; INVENTORS—American

Michelson, Albert Abraham PHYSICISTS—American

Miles, Nelson Appleton SOLDIERS—American

Miller, Alfred Jacob PAINTERS—American

Mitchell, Maria ASTRONOMERS—American

Monroe, James PRESIDENTS—American

Moran, Thomas PAINTERS—American

Morgan, John Hunt SOLDIERS—American

Morgan, John Pierpont ART COLLECTORS—American; FINANCIERS—American

Morison, Samuel Eliot YOUTHS—American

Morphy, Paul Charles CHESS PLAYERS—American

Morris, Gouverneur STATESMEN—American

Morse, Samuel Finley Breese ARTISTS—American; INVENTORS—American

Morton, William Thomas Green ANESTHETISTS—American; DENTISTS—American

Mosby, John Singleton SOLDIERS—American

Moses, Sinkiuse-Columbia Chief INDIAN LEADERS—American

Mott, Lucretia (Coffin) ABOLITIONISTS—American; FEMINISTS—American

Mudd, Samuel Alexander PHYSICIANS—American

Muir, John IMMIGRANTS TO UNITED STATES; NATURALISTS—American

Nast, Thomas CARTOONISTS—American; IMMIGRANTS TO UNITED STATES

Nordica, Lillian SINGERS—American

Norris, Frank NOVELISTS—American

Northrop, Lucius Bellinger SOLDIERS—American

United States—19th century—*Continued*

Sieber, Albert SCOUTS—American

Sigourney, Lydia Howard (Huntley) AUTHORS—American

Silliman, Benjamin CHEMISTS—American

Sitting Bull, Dakota Chief INDIAN LEADERS—American

Slocum, Joshua NAVAL OFFICERS AND OTHER SEAFARERS—American

Smalls, Robert STATESMEN—American

Smet, Pierre-Jean de RELIGIOUS LEADERS—Belgian

Smith, Jedediah Strong FRONTIERSMEN—American

Smith, John ("Raccoon") RELIGIOUS LEADERS—American

Smith, Joseph RELIGIOUS LEADERS—American

Smithson, James CHEMISTS—American

Sousa, John Philip BANDMASTERS—American; COMPOSERS—American

Southworth, Emma Dorothy Eliza (Nevitte) NOVELISTS—American

Sprague, Catherine Jane (Chase) DAUGHTERS OF FAMOUS MEN—American

Stanford, Leland RAILROAD OFFICIALS—American

Stanley-Brown, Mary (Garfield) DAUGHTERS OF FAMOUS MEN—American

Stanton, Edwin McMasters LAWYERS—American; STATESMEN—American

Stanton, Elizabeth (Cady) FEMINISTS—American

Steffens, Lincoln JOURNALISTS—American; YOUTHS—American

Steinmetz, Charles Proteus IMMIGRANTS TO UNITED STATES

Sterne, Maurice IMMIGRANTS TO UNITED STATES

Stewart, Sir William George Drummond, Bart. FRONTIERSMEN—Scottish

Stieglitz, Alfred PHOTOGRAPHERS—American

Stone, Lucy ABOLITIONISTS—American; FEMINISTS—American

Story, Nelson COWBOYS—American

Stowe, Harriet Elizabeth (Beecher) ABOLITIONISTS—American; NOVELISTS—American

Stratton, Charles Sherwood CIRCUS PERFORMERS—American

Stuart, Gilbert PAINTERS—American

Stuart, James Ewell Brown SOLDIERS—American

Stuck, Hudson IMMIGRANTS TO UNITED STATES

Sullivan, Louis Henry ARCHITECTS—American

Sumner, Charles ABOLITIONISTS—American; STATESMEN—American

Surratt, John Harrison CRIMINALS—American

Sutro, Adolph Heinrich Joseph ENGINEERS, MINING—American

Sutter, John Augustus FRONTIERSMEN—American

Swain, Clara A. PHYSICIANS—American

Taft, William Howard LAWYERS—American

Taney, Roger Brooke LAWYERS—American

Tanner, John INDIAN LEADERS—American

Taussig, Frank William ECONOMISTS—American

Taylor, Richard SOLDIERS—American

Taylor, Zachary PRESIDENTS—American; SOLDIERS—American

Tecumseh, Shawnee Chief INDIAN LEADERS—American

Thomas, Henry Andrew SHERIFFS—American

Thoreau, Henry David AUTHORS—American; NATURALISTS—American

Tiffany, Louis Comfort PAINTERS—American

Trudeau, Edward Livingston PHYSICIANS—American

Truth, Sojourner ABOLITIONISTS—American

Tubman, Harriet (Ross) ABOLITIONISTS—American

Tweed, William Marcy CRIMINALS—American

Tyler, John PRESIDENTS—American

Van Buren, Martin PRESIDENTS—American

Vanderbilt, Cornelius FINANCIERS—American

Vath, Sister Mary Loyola FRONTIERSMEN—American

Villard, Oswald Garrison JOURNALISTS—American; PACIFISTS—American

Wakeman, Edgar NAVAL OFFICERS AND OTHER SEAFARERS—American

Walker, William PRESIDENTS—Nicaraguan; SOLDIERS—American

Wallace, William Alexander Anderson POLICE—American

Ward, Samuel LOBBYISTS—American

Warner, Susan Bogert NOVELISTS—American

Washakie, Shoshone Chief INDIAN LEADERS—American

Washington, Booker Taliaferro EDUCATORS—American

Webster, Daniel LAWYERS—American; STATESMEN—American

Webster, Noah LEXICOGRAPHERS—American

Welch, William Henry PHYSICIANS—American

West, Ellsworth Luce NAVAL OFFICERS AND OTHER SEAFARERS—American

Westinghouse, George INDUSTRIALISTS—American; INVENTORS—American

Wheeler, Joseph SOLDIERS—American

Whistler, James Abbott McNeill ETCHERS—American; PAINTERS—American

Whitman, Marcus FRONTIERSMEN—American; RELIGIOUS LEADERS—American

Whitman, Narcissa (Prentiss) RELIGIOUS LEADERS—American; WIVES OF FAMOUS MEN—American

Whitman, Walt POETS—American

Whitney, Eli INVENTORS—American

Whittier, John Greenleaf POETS—American

Wiggin, Kate Douglas (Smith) AUTHORS—American

United States—19th century—Continued

Willard, Emma (Hart) EDUCATORS—American

Willard, Frances Elizabeth Caroline EDUCATORS—American; REFORMERS—American

Williams, William Sherley FRONTIERSMEN—American

Wilson, Alexander ORNITHOLOGISTS—American

Wilson, Samuel ("Uncle Sam") BUSINESSMEN—American

Wood, Ida Ellen (Walsh) RECLUSES—American

Woolson, Constance Fenimore AUTHORS—American

Woolworth, Frank Winfield BUSINESSMEN—American

Young, Ann Eliza (Webb) WIVES OF FAMOUS MEN—American

Young, Brigham RELIGIOUS LEADERS—American

Young, Ella (Flagg) EDUCATORS—American

Zakrzewska, Marie Elizabeth PHYSICIANS—American

United States—20th century

Aaron, Henry Louis BASEBALL PLAYERS—American

Abbott, George PLAYWRIGHTS—American; THEATRICAL PRODUCERS—American

Abelson, Philip Hauge PHYSICISTS—American

Acheson, Dean Gooderham STATESMEN—American

Adair, Bethenia Angelina (Owens) PHYSICIANS—American

Adams, Ansel Easton PHOTOGRAPHERS—American

Adams, Brooks HISTORIANS—American

Adams, Maude ACTORS—American

Adams, Sherman STATESMEN—American

Addams, Jane PACIFISTS—American; SOCIAL WORKERS—American

Agee, James AUTHORS—American

Aiken, Conrad Potter POETS—American

Akeley, Carl Ethan EXPLORERS—American; NATURALISTS—American; TAXIDERMISTS—American

Alexander, Lloyd PIANISTS—American

Alexopoulos, Constantine John BOTANISTS—American

Alford, Ed ("Fat") COWBOYS—American

Algren, Nelson NOVELISTS—American

Allen, Florence Ellinwood LAWYERS—American

Allen, Fred ACTORS—American

Allen, Ross HERPETOLOGISTS—American

Allen, Steve ACTORS—American

Alston, Walter Emmons ("Smokey") BASEBALL MANAGERS—American

Anderson, Leila W. RELIGIOUS LEADERS—American

Anderson, Marian SINGERS—American

Anderson, Sherwood AUTHORS—American

Andrews, Roy Chapman EXPLORERS—American; NATURALISTS—American

Anthony, Edward PUBLISHERS—American

Antin, Mary AUTHORS—American; IMMIGRANTS TO UNITED STATES

Arfons, Art AUTOMOBILE RACERS—American

Arlen, Harold COMPOSERS—American

Armstrong, Hamilton Fish JOURNALISTS—American

Armstrong, Louis TRUMPETERS—American

Arnold, Henry Harley AVIATORS—American; SOLDIERS—American

Arnold, Thurman Wesley LAWYERS—American

Astaire, Fred ACTORS—American; DANCERS—American

Astor, Brooke (Russell) YOUTHS—American

Atkinson, Brooks CRITICS—American

Austin, Mary Hunter AUTHORS—American

Ayrault, Evelyn West PSYCHOLOGISTS—American; VICTIMS OF CEREBRAL PALSY—American

Bailey, Emma AUCTIONEERS—American

Baker, Louise (Maxwell) PHYSICALLY HANDICAPPED—American

Balanchine, George DANCERS—American

Balch, Emily Greene ECONOMISTS—American; PACIFISTS—American

Balchen, Bernt AVIATORS—American; IMMIGRANTS TO UNITED STATES

Ballard, Bettina (Hill) COSTUME DESIGNERS—American; JOURNALISTS—American

Balsan, Consuelo (Vanderbilt) SOCIETY LEADERS—English

Banks, Ernest BASEBALL PLAYERS—American

Barnes, Albert Coombs ART COLLECTORS—American; PHYSICIANS—American

Barnes, Henry A. ENGINEERS, TRAFFIC—American

Barringer, Emily (Dunning) SURGEONS—American

Barry, Arthur CRIMINALS—American

Barry, Philip PLAYWRIGHTS—American

Barrymore, Ethel ACTORS—American

Barrymore, John ACTORS—American

Barrymore, Lionel ACTORS—American

Bartholomew, Freddie ACTORS—American

Baruch, Bernard Mannes BUSINESSMEN—American; STATESMEN—American

Bates, Daisy Lee (Gatson) EDUCATORS—American

Baugh, Samuel Adrian FOOTBALL PLAYERS—American

Baughman, Urbanus Edmund DETECTIVES—American

Baumgartner, Leona PHYSICIANS—American

Beach, Edward Latimer NAVAL OFFICERS AND OTHER SEAFARERS—American

Beard, Charles Austin EDUCATORS—American; HISTORIANS—American

Beard, Daniel Carter BOY SCOUT WORKERS—American

Beardsley, Helen (Brandmeir) YOUTHS—American

United States—20th century—*Continued*

Bechet, Sidney CLARINETISTS—American

Bedell, Harriet M. INDIAN LEADERS—American; RELIGIOUS LEADERS—American

Beers, Clifford Whittingham MENTAL HYGIENISTS—American

Behrman, Samuel Nathaniel PLAYWRIGHTS—American

Beiderbecke, Leon Bismarck ("Bix") TRUMPETERS—American

Belafonte, Harold SINGERS—American

Bell, Alexander Graham INVENTORS—American

Bellow, Saul NOVELISTS—American

Bellows, George Wesley PAINTERS—American

Belmont, Eleanor (Robson) ACTORS—American

Benchley, Robert Charles HUMORISTS—American

Benedict, Ruth (Fulton) ANTHROPOLOGISTS—American

Benét, Stephen Vincent AUTHORS—American

Berenson, Bernard ART COLLECTORS—American; AUTHORS—American; CRITICS—American

Berg, Gertrude ACTORS—American

Berger, Meyer JOURNALISTS—American

Berlin, Irving COMPOSERS—American; IMMIGRANTS TO UNITED STATES

Bernays, Edward L. PUBLIC RELATIONS COUNSELS—American

Bernstein, Leonard COMPOSERS—American; CONDUCTORS—American

Berra, Yogi BASEBALL PLAYERS—American

Berry, Martha McChesney EDUCATORS—American

Berry, Raymond FOOTBALL PLAYERS—American

Bethune, Mary Jane (McLeod) EDUCATORS—American

Bevington, Helen (Smith) POETS—American

Biddle, Francis Beverley LAWYERS—American

Bjorn, Thyra (Ferré) AUTHORS—American; IMMIGRANTS TO UNITED STATES

Blackburn, Howard EXPLORERS—American

Blackstone, Harry MAGICIANS—American

Blake, Florence G. NURSES—American

Bogart, Humphrey ACTORS—American

Bong, Richard Ira AVIATORS—American

Bonthron, William TRACK AND FIELD ATHLETES—American

Borah, William Edgar STATESMEN—American

Borglum, Gutzon SCULPTORS—American

Borland, Hal Glen YOUTHS—American

Boswell, Charles Albert BLIND—American; GOLFERS—American

Bourke-White, Margaret PHOTOGRAPHERS—American

Bowen, Catherine (Drinker) AUTHORS—American

Bowers, Claude Gernade AUTHORS—American; JOURNALISTS—American; STATESMEN—American

Bowne, Elizabeth AUTHORS—American

Boyington, Gregory AVIATORS—American

Braddock, James J. BOXERS—American

Bradley, Omar Nelson SOLDIERS—American

Bradley, William Warren BASKETBALL PLAYERS—American

Brandeis, Louis Dembitz LAWYERS—American

Brando, Marlon ACTORS—American

Breasted, James Henry ARCHEOLOGISTS—American; HISTORIANS—American

Brent, Stuart BOOK COLLECTORS—American; BUSINESSMEN—American

Bridgeman, William Barton AVIATORS—American

Briggs, Ellis Ormsbee STATESMEN—American

Brinkley, John Romulus PHYSICIANS—American

Brodetsky, Julian EDUCATORS—Russian; VIOLINISTS—Russian

Bromfield, Louis NOVELISTS—American

Brooks, Gladys Rice (Billings) AUTHORS—American; WIVES OF FAMOUS MEN—American

Brooks, Van Wyck AUTHORS—American; CRITICS—American

Broun, Heywood Campbell JOURNALISTS—American

Broun, Heywood Hale ACTORS—American

Brown, Claude YOUTHS—American

Brown, Jimmy ACTORS—American; FOOTBALL PLAYERS—American

Browning, John Moses GUNMAKERS—American; INVENTORS—American

Bryan, William Jennings LAWYERS—American; STATESMEN—American

Bryson, James Gordon PHYSICIANS—American

Buchanan, Wiley Thomas STATESMEN—American

Buchwald, Art JOURNALISTS—American

Buck, Pearl (Sydenstricker) NOVELISTS—American

Bunche, Ralph Johnson STATESMEN—American

Bunning, James Paul David BASEBALL PLAYERS—American

Burbank, Luther HORTICULTURISTS—American

Burchfield, Charles Ephraim PAINTERS—American

Burgess, Thornton Waldo AUTHORS—American; NATURALISTS—American

Byrd, Richard Evelyn AVIATORS—American; EXPLORERS—American; NAVAL OFFICERS AND OTHER SEAFARERS—American

Cabell, James Branch AUTHORS—American

Cable, George Washington NOVELISTS—American

Cabrini, Frances Xavier, Saint RELIGIOUS LEADERS—American

Cacopardo, J. Jerry PRISONERS—American; RELIGIOUS LEADERS—American

Caldwell, Erskine AUTHORS—American

Calkins, Fay G. AUTHORS—American

United States—20th century—*Continued*

Cummings, Homer Stillé LAWYERS—American

Cunningham, Glenn TRACK AND FIELD ATHLETES—American

Cunningham, James F. RELIGIOUS LEADERS—American

Curtiss, Glenn AVIATORS—American

Cushing, Harvey Williams SURGEONS—American

Cushing, Richard James, Cardinal RELIGIOUS LEADERS—American

Dahl, Borghild Margarethe AUTHORS—American; BLIND—American

Dahlberg, Edward AUTHORS—American

Damrosch, Frank Heino CONDUCTORS—American

Damrosch, Walter CONDUCTORS—American

Dana, John Cotton LIBRARIANS—American

Daniels, Josephus JOURNALISTS—American; STATESMEN—American

Darrow, Clarence Seward LAWYERS—American

Davis, Elmer Holmes JOURNALISTS—American

Davis, Richard Harding JOURNALISTS—American

Davis, Sammy ACTORS—American

Day, James Edward POSTAL OFFICIALS—American

Dean, Jerome Herman ("Dizzy") BASEBALL PLAYERS—American

Dean, William Frische SOLDIERS—American

De Angelis, Anthony CRIMINALS—American; FINANCIERS—American

Debs, Eugene Victor LABOR LEADERS—American; STATESMEN—American

De Forest, Lee ENGINEERS, RADIO AND TELEVISION—American; INVENTORS—American

De Kruif, Paul Henry AUTHORS—American; BACTERIOLOGISTS—American

De Mille, Agnes George DANCERS—American

Dempsey, Jack BOXERS—American

Derleth, August William AUTHORS—American

De Seversky, Alexander Procofieff AVIATORS—American; ENGINEERS, AERONAUTICAL—American; IMMIGRANTS TO UNITED STATES

De Toledano, Ralph JOURNALISTS—American

De Voto, Bernard Augustine AUTHORS—American

Dewey, George NAVAL OFFICERS AND OTHER SEAFARERS—American

Dewey, John EDUCATORS—American; PHILOSOPHERS—American

Dewey, Melvil LIBRARIANS—American

Dewey, Thomas Edmund LAWYERS—American; STATESMEN—American

De Wolfe, Elsie (Lady Mendl) UNCLASSIFIED—American

Dick, George Frederick PHYSICIANS—American

Dick, Gladys Rowena (Henry) PHYSICIANS—American

Dickson, Lillian RELIGIOUS LEADERS—American

Dillinger, John CRIMINALS—American

Di Maggio, Joseph Paul BASEBALL PLAYERS—American

Ditmars, Raymond Lee NATURALISTS—American

Dixon, George JOURNALISTS—American

Dolson, Hildegarde AUTHORS—American

Donlon, Roger H. C. SOLDIERS—American

Donovan, William Joseph ("Wild Bill") INTELLIGENCE AGENTS—American; LAWYERS—American; SOLDIERS—American

Dooley, Thomas Anthony AUTHORS—American; PHYSICIANS—American

Doolittle, Hilda POETS—American

Doolittle, James Harold AVIATORS—American; SOLDIERS—American

Dorset, Marion CHEMISTS—American

Dos Passos, John Roderigo AUTHORS—American

Doss, Helen YOUTHS—American

Douglas, Lloyd Cassel NOVELISTS—American; RELIGIOUS LEADERS—American

Douglas, William Orville LAWYERS—American; NATURALISTS—American

Drake, Frank Donald ASTRONOMERS—American

Dreier, Katherine Sophie ART COLLECTORS—American; PAINTERS—American

Dreiser, Theodore NOVELISTS—American

Drew, Charles Richard SURGEONS—American

Drexel, Mother Katharine RELIGIOUS LEADERS—American

Drury, Samuel Smith EDUCATORS—American

Drysdale, Donald Scott BASEBALL PLAYERS—American

Dubinsky, David IMMIGRANTS TO UNITED STATES; LABOR LEADERS—American

Du Bois, William Edward Burghardt EDUCATORS—American

Duffus, Robert Luther JOURNALISTS—American

Duke, James Buchanan INDUSTRIALISTS—American

Dulles, Allen Welsh INTELLIGENCE AGENTS—American; LAWYERS—American

Dulles, John Foster LAWYERS—American; STATESMEN—American

Dunbar, Paul Laurence POETS—American

Duncan, David Douglas PHOTOGRAPHERS—American

Duncan, Isadora DANCERS—American

Dunne, Finley Peter HUMORISTS—American

Du Pont, Irénée INDUSTRIALISTS—American

Durante, Jimmy ACTORS—American

Durocher, Leo Ernest BASEBALL MANAGERS—American

Duveen, Joseph Duveen, 1st Baron ART DEALERS—English

Eakins, Thomas EDUCATORS—American; PAINTERS—American

Earhart, Amelia AVIATORS—American

United States—20th century—*Continued*

Earp, Wyatt Berry Stapp SHERIFFS—American

East, P. D. JOURNALISTS—American

Eastman, Max JOURNALISTS—American

Eaton, Cyrus Stephen FINANCIERS—American

Edgerton, Harold Eugene ENGINEERS, ELECTRICAL—American

Edison, Thomas Alva INVENTORS—American

Egan, Daniel Francis RELIGIOUS LEADERS—American

Ehmke, Howard John BASEBALL PLAYERS—American

Ehrlich, Jacob W. LAWYERS—American

Einstein, Albert IMMIGRANTS TO UNITED STATES; PHYSICISTS—American

Eisenhower, Dwight David PRESIDENTS—American; SOLDIERS—American

Eisenhower, Mamie (Doud) WIVES OF FAMOUS MEN—American

Eisenschiml, Otto HISTORIANS—American

Elliott, Maxine ACTORS—American

Ernst, Morris Leopold LAWYERS—American

Erskine, John AUTHORS—American; EDUCATORS—American

Evans, Charles LIBRARIANS—American

Everest, Frank K. AVIATORS—American

Fairchild, David Grandison BOTANISTS—American

Farmer, James CIVIL RIGHTS LEADERS—American

Farrell, James Thomas NOVELISTS—American

Farson, Negley AUTHORS—American

Fast, Howard Melvin AUTHORS—American

Faulkner, William NOVELISTS—American

Feininger, Lyonel Charles Adrian PAINTERS—American

Feller, Robert William Andrew BASEBALL PLAYERS—American

Ferber, Edna NOVELISTS—American

Ferguson, John Thacker PHYSICIANS—American

Fermi, Enrico PHYSICISTS—Italian

Field, Marshall, III BUSINESSMEN—American; JOURNALISTS—American

Field, Noel Haviland SOCIAL WORKERS—American

Fischer, Robert CHESS PLAYERS—American

Fisher, Dorothea Frances (Canfield) NOVELISTS—American

Fisher, Irving ECONOMISTS—American

Fitch, John AUTOMOBILE RACERS—American

Fitzgerald, Alice Louise Florence NURSES—American

Fitzgerald, Francis Scott Key NOVELISTS—American

Fitzgerald, John Francis STATESMEN—American

Fitzsimmons, James E. HORSE TRAINERS—American

Flaherty, Robert Joseph MOTION PICTURE DIRECTORS—American

Flanagan, Edward Joseph RELIGIOUS LEADERS—American

Flanders, Ralph Edward STATESMEN—American

Flexner, Abraham EDUCATORS—American

Floyd, Theodora A. NURSES—American

Fontanne, Lynn ACTORS—American

Ford, Edward Charles BASEBALL PLAYERS—American

Ford, Henry AUTOMOBILE INDUSTRY WORKERS—American; INDUSTRIALISTS—American

Forrestal, James Vincent STATESMEN—American

Fosdick, Harry Emerson RELIGIOUS LEADERS—American

Fosdick, Raymond Blaine LAWYERS—American

Fowler, Gene JOURNALISTS—American

Fox, Sidney Walter BIOLOGISTS—American

Francis, Edward BACTERIOLOGISTS—American

Frank, Morris S. BLIND—American

Franken, Rose D. NOVELISTS—American

Frankfurter, Felix LAWYERS—American

Freitag, Robert F. ENGINEERS, AERONAUTICAL—American

Friedman, Herbert PHYSICISTS—American

Frost, Robert POETS—American

Fuller, Alfred Carl BUSINESSMEN—American

Fuller, Richard Buckminster ENGINEERS, MECHANICAL—American

Gable, Clark ACTORS—American

Gallery, Daniel Vincent NAVAL OFFICERS AND OTHER SEAFARERS—American

Garden, Mary SINGERS—American

Garland, Hamlin AUTHORS—American

Garland, Judy ACTORS—American

Geddes, Norman Bel SCENIC DESIGNERS—American

Gehrig, Lou BASEBALL PLAYERS—American

Gentile, Don AVIATORS—American

Gershwin, George COMPOSERS—American

Gertz, Elmer LAWYERS—American

Getty, Jean Paul INDUSTRIALISTS—American; PETROLEUM INDUSTRY WORKERS—American

Gibbons, James, Cardinal RELIGIOUS LEADERS—American

Gibson, Althea TENNIS PLAYERS—American

Gideon, Clarence Earl PRISONERS—American

Giesler, Harold Lee LAWYERS—American

Gifford, Edward S. PHYSICIANS—American

Gifford, Frank FOOTBALL PLAYERS—American

Gilbreth, Frank Bunker ENGINEERS, EFFICIENCY—American

Gilbreth, Lillian Evelyn (Moller) ENGINEERS, EFFICIENCY—American

Gildersleeve, Virginia Crocheron EDUCATORS—American

Giles, Henry Earl SOLDIERS—American

Glackens, William PAINTERS—American

Glasgow, Ellen Anderson Gholson NOVELISTS—American

Glenn, John Herschel ASTRONAUTS—American

United States—20th century—*Continued*

Gluck, Gemma (La Guardia) RELATIVES OF FAMOUS MEN—American

Goddard, Robert Hutchings ENGINEERS, AERONAUTICAL—American; PHYSICISTS —American

Godfrey, Arthur RADIO AND TELEVISION PERFORMERS—American

Goethals, George Washington ENGINEERS, MILITARY—American

Goett, Harry Joseph ENGINEERS, AERO-NAUTICAL—American

Goldberger, Joseph PHYSICIANS—American

Golden, Harry Lewis JOURNALISTS—American; YOUTHS—American

Goldman, Emma ANARCHISTS—American

Goldwater, Barry Morris STATESMEN—American

Gompers, Samuel LABOR LEADERS—American

Goodpasture, Ernest William PHYSICIANS—American; VIROLOGISTS—American

Goodrich, Annie Warburton NURSES—American

Gordon, Max THEATRICAL PRODUCERS—American

Gorgas, William Crawford PHYSICIANS—American

Gowan, Sister Mary Olivia NURSES—American

Gowdy, Curtis RADIO AND TELEVISION PERFORMERS—American

Grace Patricia, Consort of Rainier III, Prince of Monaco ACTORS—American

Graham, Martha DANCERS—American

Graham, Otto Everett FOOTBALL PLAYERS —American

Green, Abel JOURNALISTS—American

Green, Hetty Howland (Robinson) FINAN-CIERS—American

Greenslet, Ferris AUTHORS—American

Gregory, Dick ACTORS—American

Grissom, Virgil Ivan ASTRONAUTS—American

Groza, Louis FOOTBALL PLAYERS—American

Guggenheim, Daniel FINANCIERS—American

Guggenheim, Marguerite ART COLLECTORS —American

Guggenheimer, Minnie (Schafer) PHILAN-THROPISTS—American

Guion, Connie Myers PHYSICIANS—American

Gunther, John, 1901- JOURNALISTS—American

Gunther, John, 1929-1947 PHYSICALLY HANDICAPPED — American; YOUTHS — American

Gusweller, James Alfred RELIGIOUS LEAD-ERS—American

Guthrie, Alfred Bertram AUTHORS—American

Haast, William E. HERPETOLOGISTS—American

Hackett, John FOOTBALL PLAYERS—American

Hagedorn, Hermann AUTHORS—American; IMMIGRANTS TO UNITED STATES

Hale, George Ellery ASTRONOMERS—American

Hale, Nancy YOUTHS—American

Haley, Andrew Gallagher LAWYERS—American

Hall, Edward Wheeler VICTIMS OF MUR-DERERS—American

Hall, James Norman AUTHORS—American

Halliburton, Richard AUTHORS—American; EXPLORERS—American

Hallinan, Vincent LAWYERS—American

Halsey, William Frederick NAVAL OFFI-CERS AND OTHER SEAFARERS—American

Halsted, William Stewart SURGEONS—American

Hamilton, Alice PHYSICIANS—American

Hammerstein, Oscar, 1847-1919 OPERA MAN-AGERS — American; THEATRICAL PRO-DUCERS—American

Hammerstein, Oscar, 1895-1960 PLAY-WRIGHTS—American

Handy, William Christopher COMPOSERS—American

Harding, Warren Gamaliel PRESIDENTS—American

Hardy, Oliver Norvell ACTORS—American

Harris, Julie ACTORS—American

Harris, Mark AUTHORS—American

Hart, Moss PLAYWRIGHTS—American

Hartmann, Sadakichi POETS—American

Hathaway, Katharine (Butler) PHYSICALLY HANDICAPPED—American

Hauptmann, Bruno Richard CRIMINALS—German

Hayden, Sterling ACTORS—American

Hayes, Helen ACTORS—American

Hayne, Donald RELIGIOUS LEADERS—American

Head, Edith COSTUME DESIGNERS—American

Hearst, William Randolph JOURNALISTS—American

Hecht, Ben AUTHORS—American

Heifetz, Jascha VIOLINISTS—American

Heiser, Victor George PHYSICIANS—American

Heisman, John William FOOTBALL PLAY-ERS—American

Helburn, Theresa THEATRICAL PRODUC-ERS—American

Hemingway, Ernest JOURNALISTS—American; NOVELISTS—American

Henderson, J. Y. CIRCUS PERFORMERS—American; VETERINARIANS—American

Henie, Sonja SKATERS—American

Henrichsen, Margaret (Kimball) RELIGIOUS LEADERS—American

Henry, James Paget PHYSICIANS—American

Herbert, Victor COMPOSERS—American

Hewitt, Arthur Wentworth RELIGIOUS LEADERS—American

Hicks, Granville AUTHORS—American

Higgins, Marguerite JOURNALISTS—American

United States—20th century—*Continued*

Hill, James Jerome RAILROAD OFFICIALS —American

Hilton, Conrad Nicholson HOTEL OWNERS AND MANAGERS—American

Hirsch, Elroy FOOTBALL PLAYERS—American

Hirschmann, Ira Arthur BUSINESSMEN— American

Hiss, Alger LAWYERS—American

Hobart, Alice Tisdale NOVELISTS—American

Hodges, Gilbert Ray BASEBALL PLAYERS —American

Hoffer, George Nissley SOIL SCIENTISTS— American

Hoffman, Malvina SCULPTORS—American

Holmes, John Haynes RELIGIOUS LEADERS—American

Holmes, Oliver Wendell LAWYERS—American

Homans, Abigail (Adams) AUTHORS—American

Hoover, Herbert Clark ENGINEERS, MINING —American; PRESIDENTS—American

Hopkins, Harry Lloyd STATESMEN—American

Horne, Lena SINGERS—American

Horney, Karen (Danielson) PSYCHIATRISTS —American

Horowitz, Vladimir PIANISTS—American

Houdini, Harry MAGICIANS—American

House, Edward Mandell ("Colonel") STATESMEN—American

Howard, Elston Gene BASEBALL PLAYERS —American

Howe, Mark Antony De Wolfe AUTHORS— American

Howells, William Dean AUTHORS—American

Hubbell, Carl Owen BASEBALL PLAYERS —American

Hughes, Charles Evans LAWYERS—American

Hughes, Howard Robard AVIATORS—American; INDUSTRIALISTS—American

Hughes, Langston AUTHORS—American

Hull, Cordell STATESMEN—American

Humphrey, Hubert Horatio STATESMEN— American

Hurst, Fannie NOVELISTS—American

Ickes, Harold Le Claire STATESMEN—American

Ingersoll, Ralph McAllister JOURNALISTS— American

Insull, Samuel CRIMINALS—American; FINANCIERS—American

Isbrandtsen, Hans IMMIGRANTS TO UNITED STATES; SHIPPING EXECUTIVES—American

Ishi INDIAN LEADERS—American

Jacobs, Paul JOURNALISTS—American

James, Henry NOVELISTS—American

James, Will AUTHORS—American; COWBOYS—American; ILLUSTRATORS—American

Jeffers, Robinson POETS—American

Jelliffe, Russell Wesley CIVIL RIGHTS LEADERS—American

Jerome, William Travers LAWYERS—American

Johnson, Alvin Saunders ECONOMISTS— American

Johnson, Charles FOOTBALL PLAYERS— American

Johnson, Claudia Alta ("Lady Bird") (Taylor) WIVES OF FAMOUS MEN—American

Johnson, James Weldon AUTHORS—American

Johnson, John Arthur BOXERS—American

Johnson, Lyndon Baines PRESIDENTS—American

Johnson, Martin Elmer PHOTOGRAPHERS —American

Johnson, Nunnally AUTHORS—American

Johnson, Philip Cortelyou ARCHITECTS— American

Johnson, Walter Perry BASEBALL PLAYERS —American

Jolson, Al ACTORS—American

Jones, Jesse Holman FINANCIERS—American

Jones, Robert Tyre GOLFERS—American

Jones, Rufus Matthew EDUCATORS—American; RELIGIOUS LEADERS—American

Jones, Weimar JOURNALISTS—American

Jordan, Sara (Murray) PHYSICIANS—American

Jordan-Smith, Paul AUTHORS—American

Josephson, Matthew AUTHORS—American

Kahn, Louis I. ARCHITECTS—American

Kahn, Otto Hermann FINANCIERS—American

Kaline, Albert William BASEBALL PLAYERS —American

Kaltenborn, Hans von JOURNALISTS—American

Kaminsky, Max TRUMPETERS—American

Kaye, Danny ACTORS—American

Kazin, Alfred CRITICS—American

Keaton, Buster ACTORS—American

Kellar, Harry MAGICIANS—American

Keller, Helen Adams AUTHORS—American; BLIND—American; DEAF—American

Kellogg, Frank Billings STATESMEN—American

Kelly, Emmett CIRCUS PERFORMERS— American

Kelly, Harold Osman PAINTERS—American

Kelly, Walt CARTOONISTS—American; YOUTHS—American

Kennedy, Edward Moore STATESMEN— American

Kennedy, John Fitzgerald NAVAL OFFICERS AND OTHER SEAFARERS—American; PRESIDENTS—American

Kennedy, Robert Francis STATESMEN— American

Kenney, George Churchill AVIATORS—American; SOLDIERS—American

Kennon, Bob COWBOYS—American

Kern, Jerome David COMPOSERS—American

Kerouac, Jack AUTHORS—American

United States—20th century—_Continued_

Kettering, Charles Franklin AUTOMOBILE INDUSTRY WORKERS—American; ENGINEERS, ELECTRICAL—American; INDUSTRIALISTS—American; INVENTORS—American

Keyes, Frances Parkinson (Wheeler) NOVELISTS—American

Kieran, John JOURNALISTS—American

Kimbrough, Emily AUTHORS—American

Kimmel, Husband Edward NAVAL OFFICERS AND OTHER SEAFARERS—American

Kincheloe, Iven Carl AVIATORS—American

King, Martin Luther RELIGIOUS LEADERS—American

Kinmont, Jill PHYSICALLY HANDICAPPED—American; SKIERS—American

Kittinger, Joseph W. AVIATORS—American

Klah, Hosteen INDIAN LEADERS—American

Koufax, Sanford BASEBALL PLAYERS—American

Koussevitzky, Serge CONDUCTORS—Russian

Kreisler, Fritz IMMIGRANTS TO UNITED STATES; VIOLINISTS—American

Krutch, Joseph Wood AUTHORS—American; CRITICS—American

Kryl, Bohumir BANDMASTERS—American

Kunstler, William Moses LAWYERS—American

La Farge, John RELIGIOUS LEADERS—American

LaFollette, Robert Marion STATESMEN—American

La Guardia, Fiorello Henry STATESMEN—American

Lake, Simon ENGINEERS, MECHANICAL—American

Lamb, Edward INDUSTRIALISTS—American; LAWYERS—American

Landsteiner, Karl PATHOLOGISTS—American

Langford, Ned VICTIMS OF LEPROSY—American

Lardner, Ring Wilmer HUMORISTS—American

Lasker, Albert Davis ADVERTISING EXECUTIVES—American

Latham, Harold Strong PUBLISHERS—American

Lathrop, Rose (Hawthorne) RELIGIOUS LEADERS—American

Laubach, Frank Charles EDUCATORS—American

Laurel, Stan ACTORS—American

Law, Burleigh A. RELIGIOUS LEADERS—American

LeBaron, Edward Wayne FOOTBALL PLAYERS—American

Le Brun, George Petit CORONERS—American

Lee, Mabel (Barbee) EDUCATORS—American

Le Gallienne, Eva ACTORS—American

Lehman, Herbert Henry FINANCIERS—American; STATESMEN—American

Lehmann, Lotte SINGERS—American

Le May, Curtis Emerson AVIATORS—American; SOLDIERS—American

Leopold, Nathan Freudenthal CRIMINALS—American

Levant, Oscar PIANISTS—American

Levenson, Samuel HUMORISTS—American

Le Vier, Anthony William AVIATORS—American

Lewis, John CIVIL RIGHTS LEADERS—American

Lewis, John Llewellyn LABOR LEADERS—American

Lewis, Sinclair NOVELISTS—American

Lilienthal, David Eli BUSINESSMEN—American

Lilly, John Cunningham BIOLOGISTS—American

Lindbergh, Charles Augustus AVIATORS—American

Lindsay, Howard PLAYWRIGHTS—American; YOUTHS—American

Lindsay, Vachel POETS—American

Lippmann, Walter JOURNALISTS—American

Little, Malcolm ("Malcolm X") RELIGIOUS LEADERS—American

Lloyd, Harold Clayton ACTORS—American

Loeb, William BUSINESSMEN—American

Loewy, Raymond Fernand IMMIGRANTS TO UNITED STATES; INDUSTRIAL DESIGNERS—American

Logan, Joshua Lockwood THEATRICAL PRODUCERS—American

Lomax, John Avery FOLKLORISTS—American

London, Jack NOVELISTS—American

Long, Earl Kemp STATESMEN—American

Long, Huey Pierce STATESMEN—American

Loos, Anita AUTHORS—American

Louis, Joe BOXERS—American

Love, Edmund G. AUTHORS—American; YOUTHS—American

Low, Juliette (Gordon) GIRL SCOUT WORKERS—American

Luckman, Sidney FOOTBALL PLAYERS—American

Lunt, Alfred ACTORS—American

Lustig, Victor CRIMINALS—American

MacArthur, Charles PLAYWRIGHTS—American

MacArthur, Douglas SOLDIERS—American

McBride, Mary Margaret RADIO AND TELEVISION PERFORMERS—American

McCarthy, Joseph Raymond STATESMEN—American

McCarthy, Mary Therese NOVELISTS—American

McClintic, Guthrie THEATRICAL PRODUCERS—American

McClure, Samuel Sidney JOURNALISTS—American

McCormack, John IMMIGRANTS TO UNITED STATES; SINGERS—American

McCormick, Robert Rutherford JOURNALISTS—American

McCoy, Marie (Bell) BLIND—American

McCullers, Carson (Smith) AUTHORS—American

MacDonald, Betty (Bard) AUTHORS—American; FARMERS—American

United States—20th century—*Continued*

McDonald, Thomas FOOTBALL PLAYERS —American

MacDowell, Edward Alexander COMPOSERS —American; PIANISTS—American

McGinley, Phyllis AUTHORS—American

MacLeish, Archibald POETS—American

MacMillan, Donald Baxter EXPLORERS— American

McNamara, Robert Strange STATESMEN— American

Macy, Anne (Sullivan) BLIND—American; ED-UCATORS—American

Maddy, Joseph Edgar EDUCATORS—American

Maglie, Salvatore Anthony BASEBALL PLAY-ERS—American

Magnuson, Paul Budd SURGEONS—American

Mailer, Norman NOVELISTS—American

Mann, Thomas AUTHORS—German; IMMI-GRANTS TO UNITED STATES

Mann, William D'Alton CRIMINALS—American; JOURNALISTS—American

Manry, Robert Neal AUTHORS—American; EXPLORERS—American

Mantle, Mickey Charles BASEBALL PLAY-ERS—American

Mardikian, George Magar IMMIGRANTS TO UNITED STATES; RESTAURATEURS— American

Marion, Martin Whiteford BASEBALL PLAY-ERS—American

Maris, Roger Eugene BASEBALL PLAYERS —American

Markham, Edwin POETS—American

Marlowe, Julia ACTORS—American

Marquand, John Phillips NOVELISTS—American

Marquis, Don HUMORISTS—American

Marshall, Catherine (Wood) WIVES OF FA-MOUS MEN—American

Marshall, George Catlett SOLDIERS—American; STATESMEN—American

Marshall, Peter RELIGIOUS LEADERS— American

Marshall, Thurgood LAWYERS—American

Martin, Betty VICTIMS OF LEPROSY— American

Martin, Glenn Luther AVIATORS—American; ENGINEERS, AERONAUTICAL—American

Martin John Leonard ("Pepper") BASEBALL PLAYERS—American

Martin, Joseph William STATESMEN—American

Marx, Harpo ACTORS—American

Maryanna, Sister RELIGIOUS LEADERS— American

Mathewson, Christopher BASEBALL PLAY-ERS—American

Mathias, Robert Bruce TRACK AND FIELD ATHLETES—American

Matthews, Thomas Stanley JOURNALISTS— American

Mauch, Gene Williams BASEBALL MAN-AGERS—American

Mayer, Louis Burt IMMIGRANTS TO UNIT-ED STATES; MOTION PICTURE PRO-DUCERS—American

Mayo, William James PHYSICIANS—American

Mays, Willie Howard BASEBALL PLAYERS —American

Mead, Margaret ANTHROPOLOGISTS—American

Medina, Harold Raymond LAWYERS—American

Mellon, Andrew William FINANCIERS— American

Mellon, William Larimer PHYSICIANS—American

Mencken, Henry Louis JOURNALISTS—American

Menninger, Charles Frederick PSYCHIA-TRISTS—American

Menotti, Gian-Carlo COMPOSERS — Italian; IMMIGRANTS TO UNITED STATES

Menuhin, Yehudi VIOLINISTS—American

Meredith, James Edward ("Ted") TRACK AND FIELD ATHLETES—American

Merrill, Robert SINGERS—American

Merton, Thomas RELIGIOUS LEADERS— American

Mesta, Perle (Skirvin) STATESMEN—American

Michelson, Albert Abraham PHYSICISTS— American

Michener, James Albert NOVELISTS—American

Miers, Earl Schenck AUTHORS—American; VICTIMS OF CEREBRAL PALSY—American

Mies van der Rohe, Ludwig ARCHITECTS— American

Millay, Edna St. Vincent POETS—American

Miller, Arthur PLAYWRIGHTS—American

Miller, Henry NOVELISTS—American

Miller, Stanley Lloyd CHEMISTS—American

Mills, Billy TRACK AND FIELD ATHLETES —American

Mills, Eleanor (Reinhardt) VICTIMS OF MURDERERS—American

Mitchell, Margaret NOVELISTS—American

Mitchell, Wesley Clair ECONOMISTS—American

Mitchell, William AVIATORS—American; SOL-DIERS—American

Mitropoulos, Dimitri CONDUCTORS—Greek

Mize, Robert Herbert RELIGIOUS LEADERS —American

Mohler, John Robbins PATHOLOGISTS— American

Monat, Pawel SPIES—Polish

Monroe, Marilyn ACTORS—American

Monteux, Pierre CONDUCTORS—French

Moody, Ralph AUTHORS—American; YOUTHS —American

Moody, William Vaughn AUTHORS—American

Moore, Anne Carroll LIBRARIANS—American

Moore, Archie BOXERS—American

Moore, Leonard FOOTBALL PLAYERS— American

Moore, Marianne POETS—American

United States—20th century—*Continued*

Moore, Robert Rex BLIND—American

Moran, Thomas PAINTERS—American

Morgan, Russell Hedley RADIOLOGISTS—American

Morgenthau, Henry STATESMEN—American

Morison, Samuel Eliot HISTORIANS—American

Morse, Wayne Lyman STATESMEN—American

Morton, Charles W. JOURNALISTS—American

Moses, Anna Mary (Robertson) PAINTERS—American

Mott, Charles Stewart INDUSTRIALISTS—American; PHILANTHROPISTS—American

Mott, Frank Luther JOURNALISTS—American

Mountain Wolf Woman INDIAN LEADERS—American

Mulzac, Hugh Nathaniel IMMIGRANTS TO UNITED STATES; NAVAL OFFICERS—AND OTHER SEAFARERS—American

Mumford, Geddes SOLDIERS—American; YOUTHS—American

Murie, Olaus Johan BIOLOGISTS—American; YOUTHS—American; ZOOLOGISTS—American

Murphy, Patricia RESTAURATEURS—American

Murphy, Robert Daniel STATESMEN—American

Musial, Stanley Frank BASEBALL PLAYERS—American

Musica, Philip CRIMINALS—American

Muste, Abraham John RELIGIOUS LEADERS—American

Mydans, Carl M. JOURNALISTS—American; PHOTOGRAPHERS—American

Nash, Alice (Morrison) EDUCATORS—American

Nation, Carry Amelia (Moore) TEMPERANCE WORKERS—American

Neutra, Richard Joseph ARCHITECTS—American; IMMIGRANTS TO UNITED STATES

Nevins, Allan HISTORIANS—American

Newcomb, Kate Pelham PHYSICIANS—American

Niebuhr, Reinhold RELIGIOUS LEADERS—American

Nixon, Richard Milhous STATESMEN—American

Nizer, Louis LAWYERS—American

Nordhoff, Charles Bernard AUTHORS—American

Nordica, Lillian SINGERS—American

Norris, Frank NOVELISTS—American

Norris, Frank Holten SWIMMERS—American

Norris, George William STATESMEN—American

Novak, Kim ACTORS—American

Nugent, Elliott ACTORS—American

Nutting, Mary Adelaide NURSES—American

Oakley, Annie MARKSMEN—American

O'Brien, John NAVAL OFFICERS AND OTHER SEAFARERS—American

Ochs, Adolph Simon JOURNALISTS—American

Odets, Clifford PLAYWRIGHTS—American

Offenberg, Bernice SOCIAL WORKERS—American

O'Hara, John Henry NOVELISTS—American

O'Hara, Mary NOVELISTS—American

Oldfield, Barney AUTOMOBILE RACERS—American

Onassis, Jacqueline Lee (Bouvier) Kennedy WIVES OF FAMOUS MEN—American

O'Neill, Eugene Gladstone PLAYWRIGHTS—American

Oppenheimer, J. Robert PHYSICISTS—American

Osborne, Estelle (Massey) NURSES—American

Oswald, Lee Harvey CRIMINALS—American

Oswald, Marguerite (Claverie) MOTHERS OF FAMOUS MEN—American

Ott, Melvin Thomas BASEBALL PLAYERS—American

Oursler, Fulton AUTHORS—American

Owens, Jesse TRACK AND FIELD ATHLETES—American

Owens, William A. FARMERS—American; YOUTHS—American

Paar, Jack ACTORS—American

Paige, LeRoy ("Satchel") BASEBALL PLAYERS—American

Palmer, Bertha (Honoré) WIVES OF FAMOUS MEN—American

Papashvily, George IMMIGRANTS TO UNITED STATES

Parks, Gordon PHOTOGRAPHERS—American

Parks, Robert J. ENGINEERS, AERONAUTICAL—American

Parks, Rosa Lee CIVIL RIGHTS LEADERS—American

Parsons, Louella (Oettinger) JOURNALISTS—American

Patten, Gilbert AUTHORS—American

Patterson, Eleanor Medill JOURNALISTS—American

Patterson, Floyd BOXERS—American

Patton, George Smith SOLDIERS—American

Pearce, Louise PHYSICIANS—American

Pearson, Haydn Sanborn NATURALISTS—American; YOUTHS—American

Peary, Robert Edwin EXPLORERS—American; NAVAL OFFICERS AND OTHER SEAFARERS—American

Peattie, Donald Culross BOTANISTS—American

Pellet, Elizabeth (Eyre) STATESMEN—American

Penney, James Cash BUSINESSMEN—American

Percy, William Alexander AUTHORS—American

Perkins, Faith VICTIMS OF ARTHRITIS—American

Perkins, Maxwell Evarts JOURNALISTS—American; PUBLISHERS—American

Pershing, John Joseph SOLDIERS—American

Peterson, Virgilia JOURNALISTS—American

Petry, Lucile NURSES—American

United States—20th century—*Continued*

Ross, Harold Wallace JOURNALISTS—American

Royce, Josiah PHILOSOPHERS—American

Ruark, Robert Chester AUTHORS—American

Rubinstein, Artur PIANISTS—American

Rubinstein, Helena BUSINESSMEN—American; COSMETICIANS—American; IMMIGRANTS TO UNITED STATES

Ruby, Jack CRIMINALS—American

Rudolph, Wilma TRACK AND FIELD ATHLETES—American

Ruef, Abraham STATESMEN—American

Ruggles, Ora OCCUPATIONAL THERAPISTS—American

Runyon, Damon AUTHORS—American; JOURNALISTS—American

Russell, Charles Marion PAINTERS—American

Russell, Robert BLIND—American

Russell, William Felton BASKETBALL PLAYERS—American

Ruth, George Herman ("Babe") BASEBALL PLAYERS—American

Ryan, Frank Beall FOOTBALL PLAYERS—American

Ryan, John Augustine RELIGIOUS LEADERS—American

Saarinen, Eero ARCHITECTS—American; IMMIGRANTS TO UNITED STATES

Sabin, Albert Bruce PHYSICIANS—American

Sabin, Florence Rena ANATOMISTS—American

Sacco, Nicola ANARCHISTS—American; CRIMINALS—American; IMMIGRANTS TO UNITED STATES

Sagan, Carl BIOLOGISTS—American

St. Denis, Ruth DANCERS—American

St. John, Robert JOURNALISTS—American

Salinger, Jerome David NOVELISTS—American

Salk, Jonas Edward VIROLOGISTS—American

Salsbury, Clarence Grant PHYSICIANS—American

Samuel, Maurice AUTHORS—American; IMMIGRANTS TO UNITED STATES

Sandburg, Carl AUTHORS—American; YOUTHS—American

Sanders, George ACTORS—Scottish

San Romani, Archie TRACK AND FIELD ATHLETES—American

Santayana, George PHILOSOPHERS—American; POETS—American

Sarnoff, David ENGINEERS, RADIO AND TELEVISION—American; IMMIGRANTS TO UNITED STATES; INDUSTRIALISTS—American

Saroyan, William AUTHORS—American

Sarton, May AUTHORS—American; IMMIGRANTS TO UNITED STATES

Saund, Dalip Singh IMMIGRANTS TO UNITED STATES; STATESMEN—American

Saunders, Albert Edward RELIGIOUS LEADERS—American

Saunders, Raymond ("Raymond the Great") MAGICIANS—American

Sawyer, Ruth AUTHORS—American

Scarne, John MAGICIANS—American

Scharff, Alvin Freidheim CUSTOMS OFFICIALS—American

Schary, Dore IMMIGRANTS TO UNITED STATES; MOTION PICTURE PRODUCERS—American; YOUTHS—American

Schick, Béla IMMIGRANTS TO UNITED STATES; PHYSICIANS—American

Schirra, Walter Marty ASTRONAUTS—American

Schlesinger, Arthur Meier, 1888-1965 EDUCATORS—American; HISTORIANS—American

Schoenberg, Arnold COMPOSERS—Austrian

Schoenstein, Ralph JOURNALISTS—American; YOUTHS—American

Scott, Robert Lee AVIATORS—American

Scovel, Myra RELIGIOUS LEADERS—American

Seabury, Samuel LAWYERS—American

Seagrave, Gordon Stifler PHYSICIANS—American

Seaman, Elizabeth (Cochrane) JOURNALISTS—American

Sedgwick, Ellery JOURNALISTS—American

Segal, Debra Jean VICTIMS OF CEREBRAL PALSY—American

Segal, Lore IMMIGRANTS TO UNITED STATES

Seligman, Jacques ART COLLECTORS—American

Seton, Ernest Thompson AUTHORS—American; ILLUSTRATORS—American; NATURALISTS—American

Sevareid, Arnold Eric JOURNALISTS—American

Shaw, Wilbur AUTOMOBILE RACERS—American

Shawn, Ted DANCERS—American

Shelby, Carroll Hall AUTOMOBILE RACERS—American

Sheldon, Edward PHYSICALLY HANDICAPPED—American; PLAYWRIGHTS—American

Shepard, Alan Bartlett ASTRONAUTS—American

Sheppard, Samuel H. PRISONERS—American

Sherman, Allie FOOTBALL PLAYERS—American

Sherrill, Henry Knox RELIGIOUS LEADERS—American

Sherwood, Robert Emmet PLAYWRIGHTS—American

Shotwell, James Thomson HISTORIANS—Canadian

Shriver, Robert Sargent STATESMEN—American

Shull, George Harrison BOTANISTS—American

Shuttlesworth, Fred CIVIL RIGHTS LEADERS—American

Sikorsky, Igor Ivan ENGINEERS, AERONAUTICAL—American; IMMIGRANTS TO UNITED STATES

United States—20th century—*Continued*

Sinclair, Upton Beall NOVELISTS—American

Skinner, Cornelia Otis ACTORS—American

Skouras, Spyros Panagiotes IMMIGRANTS TO UNITED STATES; MOTION PICTURE PRODUCERS—American

Slayden, Ellen (Maury) WIVES OF FAMOUS MEN—American

Slayton, Donald Kent ASTRONAUTS—American

Sloan, Alfred Pritchard AUTOMOBILE INDUSTRY WORKERS—American; INDUSTRIALISTS—American

Sloan, John PAINTERS—American

Sloop, Mary T. (Martin) PHYSICIANS—American

Smith, Alfred Emanuel STATESMEN—American

Smith, Bessie SINGERS—American

Smith, Dean C. AVIATORS—American

Smith, Frank Ellis STATESMEN—American

Smith, Frank Kingston AVIATORS—American

Smith, Harry Allen HUMORISTS—American

Smith, Joseph Lindon PAINTERS—American

Smith, Kate SINGERS—American

Smith, Lillian Eugenia AUTHORS—American; YOUTHS—American

Smith, Margaret (Chase) STATESMEN—American

Smith, Paul Clifford JOURNALISTS—American

Smith, Walter Wellesley ("Red") SPORTS-WRITERS—American

Smith, Willie PIANISTS—American

Snead, Samuel Jackson GOLFERS—American

Snider, Edwin Donald BASEBALL PLAYERS—American

Snow, Carmel (White) JOURNALISTS—American

Snow, Edgar Parks JOURNALISTS—American

Solman, Joseph PAINTERS—American

Sone, Monica (Itoi) YOUTHS—Japanese

Sousa, John Philip BANDMASTERS—American; COMPOSERS—American

Spahn, Warren Edward BASEBALL PLAYERS—American

Spellman, Francis Joseph, Cardinal RELIGIOUS LEADERS—American

Spence, William H. RELIGIOUS LEADERS—American

Spock, Benjamin McLane PHYSICIANS—American

Stafford, Jean NOVELISTS—American

Starr, Bart FOOTBALL PLAYERS—American

Starrett, Vincent AUTHORS—American; BOOK COLLECTORS—American

Steenbock, Harry BIOLOGISTS—American

Steffens, Lincoln JOURNALISTS—American

Steichen, Edward PHOTOGRAPHERS—American

Stein, Gertrude AUTHORS—American

Stein, Michael ART COLLECTORS—American

Steinbeck, John NOVELISTS—American

Steinmetz, Charles Proteus ENGINEERS, ELECTRICAL—American

Steloff, Frances BOOK COLLECTORS—American; BUSINESSMEN—American

Stengel, Charles Dillon ("Casey") BASEBALL MANAGERS—American

Stern, Isaac VIOLINISTS—American

Stern, Julius David JOURNALISTS—American

Stern, Michael JOURNALISTS—American

Sterne, Maurice PAINTERS—American

Stevens, Wallace POETS—American

Stevenson, Adlai Ewing LAWYERS—American; STATESMEN—American

Stewart, Isabel Maitland NURSES—American

Stieglitz, Alfred PHOTOGRAPHERS—American

Stimson, Henry Lewis STATESMEN—American

Stone, Edward Durell ARCHITECTS—American

Stone, Harlan Fiske LAWYERS—American

Strainchamps, Ethel (Reed) EDUCATORS—American

Straughan, Robert P. L. ICHTHYOLOGISTS—American

Strauss, Joseph Baermann ENGINEERS, CIVIL—American

Strausz-Hupé, Robert IMMIGRANTS TO UNITED STATES; POLITICAL SCIENTISTS—Austrian

Stravinsky, Igor Fedorovich COMPOSERS—Russian; IMMIGRANTS TO UNITED STATES

Stuart, Jesse AUTHORS—American

Stuck, Hudson MOUNTAINEERS—American; RELIGIOUS LEADERS—American

Stuhldreher, Harry Augustus FOOTBALL PLAYERS—American

Styron, William NOVELISTS—American

Sullivan, Louis Henry ARCHITECTS—American

Sweezy, Carl INDIAN LEADERS—American

Swing, Raymond JOURNALISTS—American

Swope, Herbert Bayard JOURNALISTS—American

Symington, Stuart STATESMEN—American

Szigeti, Joseph VIOLINISTS—Hungarian

Szold, Henrietta ZIONIST LEADERS—American

Taft, Robert Alphonso LAWYERS—American; STATESMEN—American

Taft, William Howard LAWYERS—American; PRESIDENTS—American

Tallchief, Maria DANCERS—American

Tantri, K'tut AUTHORS—American

Tarbell, Ida Minerva AUTHORS—American

Tarkenton, Francis Asbury FOOTBALL PLAYERS—American

Tarry, Ellen EDUCATORS—American

Taussig, Frank William ECONOMISTS—American

Taylor, Elizabeth ACTORS—American

Taylor, Laurette (Cooney) ACTORS—American

Teale, Edwin Way NATURALISTS—American; YOUTHS—American

Teasdale, Sara POETS—American

United States—20th century—*Continued*

Terrell, Mary (Church) FEMINISTS—American

Tesla, Nikola ENGINEERS, ELECTRICAL—American; IMMIGRANTS TO UNITED STATES; INVENTORS—American

Thomas, Lowell Jackson AUTHORS—American; JOURNALISTS—American

Thomas, Norman Mattoon STATESMEN—American

Thompson, Dorothy JOURNALISTS—American

Thompson, Mickey AUTOMOBILE RACERS—American

Thompson, William Goodrich LAWYERS—American

Thomson, Virgil COMPOSERS—American; CRITICS—American

Thon, William PAINTERS—American

Thorne, Jim AUTHORS—American

Thorpe, James Francis ATHLETES—American; INDIAN LEADERS—American

Thurman, Howard RELIGIOUS LEADERS—American

Thurston, Howard MAGICIANS—American

Tiffany, Louis Comfort GLASS PAINTERS—American

Tittle, Yelberton Abraham FOOTBALL PLAYERS—American

Toscanini, Arturo CONDUCTORS—Italian

Trahey, Jane YOUTHS—American

Trapp, Maria Augusta IMMIGRANTS TO UNITED STATES; SINGERS—Austrian

Treviño, Elizabeth (Borton) AUTHORS—American

Truman, Harry S. PRESIDENTS—American

Tugwell, Rexford Guy ECONOMISTS—American; EDUCATORS—American

Tumulty, Joe LAWYERS—American

Tunis, John Roberts AUTHORS—American; SPORTSWRITERS—American

Tunnell, Emlen FOOTBALL PLAYERS—American

Unitas, John FOOTBALL PLAYERS—American

Untermeyer, Jean (Starr) POETS—American

Untermeyer, Louis POETS—American

Updike, John AUTHORS—American; YOUTHS American

Urey, Harold Clayton CHEMISTS—American

Van Allen, James Alfred PHYSICISTS—American

Van Brocklin, Norman Mack FOOTBALL PLAYERS—American

Vandegrift, Alexander Archer SOLDIERS—American

Vandenberg, Arthur Hendrick STATESMEN—American

Van Doren, Dorothy (Graffe) AUTHORS—American; WIVES OF FAMOUS MEN—American

Van Doren, Mark AUTHORS—American

Van Waters, Miriam PENOLOGISTS—American; SOCIAL WORKERS—American

Vanzetti, Bartolomeo ANARCHISTS—American; CRIMINALS—American; IMMIGRANTS TO UNITED STATES

Veblen, Thorstein Bunde ECONOMISTS—American

Veeck, William BASEBALL MANAGERS—American

Villard, Oswald Garrison JOURNALISTS—American; PACIFISTS—American

Vine, Louis L. VETERINARIANS—American

Vishniac, Wolf BIOLOGISTS—American

Von Braun, Wernher ENGINEERS, AERONAUTICAL—American; IMMIGRANTS TO UNITED STATES; SCIENTISTS—American; YOUTHS—German

Von Sternberg, Josef MOTION PICTURE PRODUCERS—Austrian

Wagner, John Peter BASEBALL PLAYERS—American

Waksman, Selman Abraham BACTERIOLOGISTS—American; IMMIGRANTS TO UNITED STATES

Wald, Lillian NURSES—American; SOCIAL WORKERS—American

Walsh, James Edward, Bishop RELIGIOUS LEADERS—American

Walter, Bruno CONDUCTORS—German

Warburg, James Paul FINANCIERS—American; IMMIGRANTS TO UNITED STATES

Warner, Edith BUSINESSMEN—American

Warner, Glenn Scobey ("Pop") FOOTBALL PLAYERS—American

Warner, Jack Leonard MOTION PICTURE PRODUCERS—American

Warren, Earl LAWYERS—American; STATESMEN—American

Warren, Robert Penn AUTHORS—American

Washington, Booker Taliaferro EDUCATORS—American

Waterman, Sherry AIRLINE STEWARDESSES—American

Waters, Ethel ACTORS—American; POVERTY-STRICKEN—American

Watson, Thomas John INDUSTRIALISTS—American

Weissmuller, Johnny ACTORS—American; SWIMMERS—American

Welch, Joseph Nye LAWYERS—American

Welch, William Henry PHYSICIANS—American

Welsh, Edward Cristy ECONOMISTS—American

Welty, Eudora AUTHORS—American

Wescott, Glenway AUTHORS—American

West, Ellsworth Luce NAVAL OFFICERS AND OTHER SEAFARERS—American

West, Jessamyn AUTHORS—American

West, Nathanael NOVELISTS—American

Wharton, Edith Newbold (Jones) NOVELISTS—American

Wheeler, Burton Kendall STATESMEN—American

White, Paul Dudley PHYSICIANS—American

White, Walter AUTHORS—American

White, William Allen AUTHORS—American; JOURNALISTS—American

Whitehead, Alfred North PHILOSOPHERS—American

Whitehead, Gustave AVIATORS—American

United States—20th century—*Continued*

Widdemer, Margaret AUTHORS—American

Wiggin, Kate Douglas (Smith) AUTHORS—American

Wigoder, Devorah RELIGIOUS LEADERS—American

Wilder, Laura Ingalls AUTHORS—American

Wilder, Thornton Niven AUTHORS—American

Williams, Tennessee PLAYWRIGHTS—American

Williams, Theodore Samuel BASEBALL PLAYERS—American

Williams, William Carlos AUTHORS—American; PHYSICIANS—American

Willkie, Wendell Lewis LAWYERS—American; STATESMEN—American

Wills, Maurice Morning BASEBALL PLAYERS—American

Wilson, Arthur RELIGIOUS LEADERS—American

Wilson, Edith (Bolling) Galt WIVES OF FAMOUS MEN—American

Wilson, Frank John DETECTIVES—American

Wilson, Woodrow EDUCATORS—American; PRESIDENTS—American

Winant, John Gilbert STATESMEN—American

Winter, Ella JOURNALISTS—American

Wise, Stephen Samuel RELIGIOUS LEADERS—American

Wister, Owen NOVELISTS—American

Wolfe, Thomas NOVELISTS—American

Wong, Jade Snow POTTERS—American

Wood, Grant PAINTERS—American

Wood, Ida Ellen (Walsh) RECLUSES—American

Wood, James Horace LAWYERS—American

Wood, Peggy ACTORS—American

Wood, William Barry FOOTBALL PLAYERS—American

Woodward, Stanley SPORTSWRITERS—American

Woody, Regina Llewellyn (Jones) Dancers—American

Woolf, George Monroe JOCKEYS—American

Woolworth, Frank Winfield BUSINESSMEN—American

Woytinsky, Wladimir Savelievich ECONOMISTS—American; IMMIGRANTS TO UNITED STATES

Wright, Beatrice Ann (Posner) VICTIMS OF POLIO—American

Wright, Frank Lloyd ARCHITECTS—American

Wright, Richard NOVELISTS—American

Wright, Wilbur AVIATORS—American

Wylie, Elinor Morton (Hoyt) AUTHORS—American

Wylie, Janice DAUGHTERS OF FAMOUS MEN—American; VICTIMS OF MURDERERS—American

Wynn, Keenan ACTORS—American

Young, Ella (Flagg) EDUCATORS—American

Zaharias, Mildred (Didrikson) ATHLETES—American; GOLFERS—American; TRACK AND FIELD ATHLETES — American; YOUTHS—American

Ziegfeld, Patricia DAUGHTERS OF FAMOUS MEN—American; YOUTHS—American

Zimmerman, Isidore PRISONERS—American

Zinsser, Hans BACTERIOLOGISTS—American

Zinsser, William Knowlton JOURNALISTS—American; YOUTHS—American

Venezuela—19th century

Bolívar, Simón SOLDIERS—South American; STATESMEN—South American

Miranda, Francisco de SOLDIERS—Venezuelan

Venezuela—20th century

Aparicio, Luis Ernesto BASEBALL PLAYERS—American

Pérez Jiménez, Marcos PRESIDENTS—Venezuelan

Ybarra, Thomas Russell SOLDIERS—Venezuelan; YOUTHS—Venezuelan

Vietnam—20th century

Diem, Ngo-dinh PRESIDENTS—Vietnamese

Donlon, Roger H. C. SOLDIERS—American

Wales—13th century

Llewelyn ab Gruffydd PRINCES—Welsh

Wallace, Sir William SOLDIERS—Scottish

Wales—14th century

Glendower, Owen PRINCES—Welsh

Wales—17th century

Morgan, Sir Henry CRIMINALS—English; STATESMEN—English

Vaughan, Henry POETS—Welsh

Wales—18th century

Siddons, Sarah ACTORS—English

Wales—19th century

Leonowens, Anna Harriette (Crawford) EDUCATORS—Welsh

Siddons, Sarah ACTORS—English

Stanley, Sir Henry Morton EXPLORERS—Welsh; JOURNALISTS—Welsh

Wales—20th century

Bevan, Aneurin STATESMEN—Welsh

Lawrence, Thomas Edward ARCHEOLOGISTS—English; SOLDIERS—English

Thomas, Dylan POETS—Welsh

Varney, Joyce James YOUTHS—Welsh

Vaughan, Richard YOUTHS—Welsh

Williams, Emlyn ACTORS—Welsh; PLAYWRIGHTS—Welsh; YOUTHS—Welsh

Yugoslavia—19th century

Pupin, Michael Idvorsky IMMIGRANTS TO UNITED STATES

Yugoslavia—20th century

Djilas, Milovan COMMUNISTS—Yugoslav

Tito, Josip Broz PRESIDENTS—Yugoslav

AUTOBIOGRAPHIES, LETTERS, AND PERSONAL ACCOUNTS

The publisher, date of publication, and symbols for the lists recommending each title may be found in the main text under the subject heading or headings.

Abbott, George. "Mister Abbott." PLAY-WRIGHTS—American—20th century; THE-ATRICAL PRODUCERS — American — 20th century

Abrahams, Peter. Tell Freedom: Memories of Africa. POETS—South African—20th century

Acheson, Dean Gooderham. Morning and Noon. STATESMEN—American—20th century

Adams, Henry Brooks. Education of Henry Adams: An Autobiography. HISTORIANS—American—19th century

Adams, John. The Adams-Jefferson Letters; ed. by Lester J. Cappon. PRESIDENTS—American—18th century

—Diary and Autobiography; ed. by L. H. Butterfield. PRESIDENTS—American—18th century

—The John Adams Papers; ed. by Frank Donovan. PRESIDENTS—American—18th century

Adams, John Quincy. Diary of John Quincy Adams, 1794-1845. PRESIDENTS—American—19th century; STATESMEN—American—18th century

Addams, Jane. Twenty Years at Hull-House; with autobiographical notes. PACIFISTS — American — 19th century; PACIFISTS — American—20th century; SOCIAL WORKERS — American — 19th century; SOCIAL WORKERS—American—20th century

Adenauer, Konrad. Memoirs: v. 1, 1945-1953; tr. by Beate Ruhm von Oppen. STATESMEN—German—20th century

Agee, James. Letters of James Agee to Father Flye. AUTHORS—American—20th century

Alexander, Harold Rupert Leofric George Alexander, 1st Earl of. The Alexander Memoirs, 1940-1945; ed. by John North. SOLDIERS—English—20th century

Alexander, Lloyd. My Love Affair with Music. PIANISTS—American—20th century

Algren, Nelson and Donohue, H. E. F. Conversations with Nelson Algren. NOVELISTS—American—20th century

Allen, Fred. Letters; ed. by Joe McCarthy. ACTORS—American—20th century

—Much Ado About Me. ACTORS—American—20th century

Allen, Steve. Mark It and Strike It: An Autobiography. ACTORS—American—20th century

Alston, Walter Emmons ("Smokey"). Alston and the Dodgers. BASEBALL MANAGERS—American—20th century

Anastasia, Grand Duchess of Russia. The Autobiography of H.I.H. the Grand Duchess Anastasia Nicholaevna of Russia, volume 1. DAUGHTERS OF FAMOUS MEN—Russian—20th century

Anderson, Leila W. Pilgrim Circuit Rider. RELIGIOUS LEADERS—American—20th century

Anderson, Marian. My Lord, What a Morning: An Autobiography. SINGERS—American—20th century

Anthony, Edward. This Is Where I Came In: The Impromptu Confessions of Edward Anthony. PUBLISHERS—American—20th century

Anthony, Joseph. The Rascal and the Pilgrim. YOUTHS—Korean—20th century

Armstrong, Hamilton Fish. Those Days. JOURNALISTS—American—20th century

Arnold, Thurman Wesley. Fair Fights and Foul: A Dissenting Lawyer's Life. LAWYERS—American—20th century

Asquith, Margot. Autobiography. WIVES OF FAMOUS MEN—English—20th century

Astaire, Fred. Steps in Time. ACTORS—American—20th century; DANCERS—American—20th century

Astor, Brooke (Russell). Patchwork Child: Memoir of Mrs. Vincent Astor. YOUTHS—American—20th century

Ata-ullah, Mohammad. Citizen of Two Worlds. MOUNTAINEERS—Pakistani—20th century; PHYSICIANS—Pakistani—20th century

Attlee, Clement Richard Attlee, 1st Earl. As It Happened. LABOR LEADERS—English—20th century; STATESMEN—English—20th century

Audubon, John James. Audubon in the West. ORNITHOLOGISTS—American—19th century; PAINTERS—American—19th century

Augustine, Saint. Confessions. RELIGIOUS LEADERS—African—5th century

Austen, Jane. Jane Austen's Letters to Her Sister Cassandra and Others. NOVELISTS—English—19th century

Austing, Ronald. I Went to the Woods: The Autobiography of a Bird Photogrpher. PHOTOGRAPHERS—English—20th century

Ayrault, Evelyn West. Take One Step. PSYCHOLOGISTS — American — 20th century; VICTIMS OF CEREBRAL PALSY—American—20th century

Babel', Isaak Emmanuilovich. Isaac Babel: The Lonely Years, 1925-1939. AUTHORS—Russian—20th century

Bagster, Hubert. Doctor's Week-end. PHYSICIANS—English—20th century

Bailey, Emma. Sold to the Lady in the Green Hat. AUCTIONEERS—American—20th century

Balchen, Bernt. Come North with Me: An Autobiography. AVIATORS—American—20th century; IMMIGRANTS TO UNITED STATES—20th century

Ballard, Bettina (Hill). In My Fashion. COSTUME DESIGNERS—American—20th century; JOURNALISTS—American—20th century

Balmain, Pierre. My Years and Seasons. COSTUME DESIGNERS—French—20th century

Balsan, Consuelo (Vanderbilt). Glitter and the Gold. SOCIETY LEADERS—English—20th century

Bannister, Roger. The Four Minute Mile. TRACK AND FIELD ATHLETES—English—20th century

Barbellion, W. N. P. The Journal of a Disappointed Man. BIOLOGISTS—English—20th century; PHYSICALLY HANDICAPPED—English—20th century

Barnes, Henry A. The Man with the Red and Green Eyes: The Autobiography of the Traffic Commissioner, New York City. ENGINEERS, TRAFFIC—American—20th century

Barrymore, Ethel. Memories: An Autobiography. ACTORS—American—20th century

Barrymore, Lionel. We Barrymores. ACTORS—American—20th century

Baruch, Bernard Mannes. Baruch: My Own Story. BUSINESSMEN—American—20th century; STATESMEN—American—20th century

—Baruch: The Public Years. BUSINESSMEN—American—20th century; STATESMEN—American—20th century

Bates, Daisy Lee (Gatson). The Long Shadow of Little Rock: A Memoir. EDUCATORS—American—20th century

Baughman, Urbanus Edmund. Secret Service Chief. DETECTIVES—American—20th century

Baum, Vicki. It Was All Quite Different: The Memoirs of Vicki Baum. NOVELISTS—Austrian—20th century; IMMIGRANTS TO UNITED STATES—20th century

Beach, Edward Latimer. Around the World Submerged. NAVAL OFFICERS AND OTHER SEAFARERS—American—20th century

Beardsley, Helen (Brandmeir). Who Gets the Drumstick? The Story of the Beardsley Family. YOUTHS—American—20th century

Beauvoir, Simone de. Force of Circumstance. AUTHORS—French—20th century

—Memoirs of a Dutiful Daughter. YOUTHS—French—20th century

—The Prime of Life. AUTHORS—French—20th century

Bechet, Sidney. Treat It Gentle. CLARINETISTS—American—20th century

Beecher, Lyman. Autobiography. RELIGIOUS LEADERS—American—19th century

Beerbohm, Sir Max. Max Beerbohm's Letters to Reggie Turner. AUTHORS—English—20th century

Beers, Clifford Whittingham. Mind That Found Itself: An Autobiography. MENTAL HYGIENISTS—American—20th century

Beethoven, Ludwig van. The Letters of Beethoven. COMPOSERS—German—19th century

Behrman, Samuel Nathaniel. Worcester Account. PLAYWRIGHTS—American—20th century

Belmont, Eleanor (Robson). Fabric of Memory. ACTORS—American—20th century

Benedict, Ruth (Fulton). An Anthropologist at Work. ANTHROPOLOGISTS—American—20th century

Ben-Gurion, David. Ben Gurion Looks Back in Talks with Moshe Pearlman. STATESMEN—Israeli—20th century

Bennett, Arnold. The Truth About an Author. NOVELISTS—English—20th century

Bentley, Phyllis Eleanor. "O Dreams, O Destinations": An Autobiography. NOVELISTS—English—20th century

Berczeller, Richard. Displaced Doctor. IMMIGRANTS TO UNITED STATES—20th century; PHYSICIANS—Austrian—20th century

Berenson, Bernard. The Bernard Berenson Treasury. AUTHORS—American—20th century; CRITICS—American—20th century

—Conversations with Berenson. AUTHORS—American—20th century; CRITICS—American—20th century

—One Year's Reading for Fun. AUTHORS—American—20th century; CRITICS—American—20th century

—The Passionate Sightseer: From the Diaries, 1947 to 1956. AUTHORS—American—20th century; CRITICS—American—20th century

—Rumor and Reflection. AUTHORS—American—20th century; CRITICS—American—20th century

—Selected Letters. ART COLLECTORS—American—20th century; AUTHORS—American—20th century; CRITICS—American—20th century

—Sunset and Twilight: From the Diaries of 1947-1958. AUTHORS—American—20th century; CRITICS—American—20th century

Berg, Gertrude. Molly and Me. ACTORS—American—20th century

Bernays, Edward L. Biography of an Idea: Memoirs of Public Relations Counsel Edward L. Bernays. PUBLIC RELATIONS COUNSELS—American—20th century

Besnard, Marie (Davillaud). The Trial of Marie Besnard. PRISONERS—French—20th century

Bevington, Helen (Smith). Charley Smith's Girl: A Memoir. POETS—American—20th century

Biddle, Francis Beverley. A Casual Past. LAWYERS—American—20th century

—In Brief Authority. LAWYERS—American—20th century

Bingham, Madeleine. Cheapest in the End. YOUTHS—English—20th century

Bjorn, Thyra (Ferré). This Is My Life. AUTHORS — American — 20th century; IMMIGRANTS TO UNITED STATES—20th century

Blackhall, David Scott. This House Had Windows. BLIND—Canadian—20th century; POETS—Canadian—20th century

Bland, Edith (Nesbit). Long Ago When I Was Young. AUTHORS—English—20th century

Bodenheimer, Max Isidor. Prelude to Israel: The Memoirs of Max Bodenheimer. LAWYERS—German—20th century

Borrow, George Henry. Romany Rye. AUTHORS—English—19th century

Boswell, James. Boswell for the Defence, 1769-1774. AUTHORS—Scottish—18th century

—Boswell in Holland, 1763-1764. AUTHORS —Scottish—18th century

—Boswell in Search of a Wife, 1766-1769. AUTHORS—Scottish—18th century

—Boswell on the Grand Tour: Italy, Corsica, and France, 1765-1766. AUTHORS—Scottish—18th century

—Boswell: The Ominous Years, 1774-1776. AUTHORS—Scottish—18th century

—Boswell's London Journal, 1762-1763. AUTHORS—Scottish—18th century

—Journal of a Tour to the Hebrides with Samuel Johnson, LL.D., 1773. AUTHORS—Scottish—18th century

Bottome, Phyllis. The Goal. NOVELISTS—English—20th century

Bourke-White, Margaret. Portrait of Myself. PHOTOGRAPHERS—American—20th century

Bowen, Catherine (Drinker). Adventures of a Biographer. AUTHORS — American — 20th century

Bowen, Elizabeth. Seven Winters: Memories of a Dublin Childhood & Afterthoughts, Pieces on Writing. NOVELISTS—Irish—20th century

Bowers, Claude Gernade. My Life: The Memoirs of Claude Bowers. AUTHORS—American—20th century; JOURNALISTS—American—20th century; STATESMEN—American—20th century

Bowne, Elizabeth. Gift from the African Heart. AUTHORS—American—20th century

Boyer, Samuel Pellman. Blockading the South, 1862-1866. PHYSICIANS—American—19th century

—Revolt in Japan, 1868-1869. PHYSICIANS —American—19th century

Boyington, Gregory. Baa Baa Black Sheep. AVIATORS—American—20th century

Boyle, Harry J. Homebrew and Patches. AUTHORS—Canadian—20th century

—With a Pinch of Sin. AUTHORS—Canadian—20th century

Bradley, Omar Nelson. Soldier's Story. SOLDIERS—American—20th century

Braithwaite, Eustace Ricardo. To Sir, with Love. EDUCATORS—Guyanian—20th century

Brandt, Willy. My Road to Berlin. STATESMEN—German—20th century

Brant, Alice (Dayrell). Diary of "Helena Morley." AUTHORS—Brazilian—19th century

Brenan, Gerald. A Life of One's Own: Childhood and Youth. AUTHORS—English—20th century; JOURNALISTS—English—20th century

Brent, Stuart. The Seven Stairs. BOOK COLLECTORS—American—20th century; BUSINESSMEN—American—20th century

Bridgeman, William Barton. The Lonely Sky. AVIATORS—American—20th century

Briggs, Ellis Ormsbee. Farewell to Foggy Bottom: The Recollections of a Career Diplomat. STATESMEN—American—20th century

Brittain, Vera Mary. Testament of Experience: An Autobiographical Story of the Years 1925-50. AUTHORS—English—20th century

Brooks, Gladys Rice (Billings). Boston and Return. AUTHORS—American—20th century; WIVES OF FAMOUS MEN—American—20th century

Brooks, Van Wyck. An Autobiography. AUTHORS—American—20th century; CRITICS —American—20th century

—Days of the Phoenix: The Nineteen-Twenties I Remember. AUTHORS—American—20th century; CRITICS—American—20th century

—From the Shadow of the Mountain: My Post-Meridian Years. AUTHORS—American—20th century; CRITICS—American—20th century

—Scenes and Portraits: Memories of Childhood and Youth. AUTHORS — American — 20th century; CRITICS—American—20th century

Broun, Heywood Hale. A Studied Madness. ACTORS—American—20th century

Brown, Christy. My Left Foot. VICTIMS OF CEREBRAL PALSY—Irish—20th century

Brown, Claude. Manchild in the Promised Land. YOUTHS—American—20th century

Brown, Jimmy. Off My Chest. ACTORS—American—20th century; FOOTBALL PLAYERS—American—20th century

Browning, Robert. Browning to His American Friends: Letters Between the Brownings, the Storys and James Russell Lowell, 1841-1890. POETS—English—19th century

Bruckberger, Raymond Léopold. One Sky to Share: The French and American Journals. RELIGIOUS LEADERS—French—20th century

Bryher, Winifred. The Heart to Artemis. AUTHORS—English—20th century

Bryson, James Gordon. One Hundred Dollars & a Horse: The Reminiscences of a Country Doctor. PHYSICIANS—American—20th century

Buchan, John. Pilgrim's Way: An Essay in Recollection. NOVELISTS—Scottish—20th century; STATESMEN—Scottish—20th century

Buchanan, Wiley Thomas. Red Carpet at the White House: Four Years as Chief of Protocol in the Eisenhower Administration. STATESMEN—American—20th century

Buck, Pearl (Sydenstricker). A Bridge for Passing. NOVELISTS—American—20th century
—My Several Worlds: A Personal Record. NOVELISTS—American—20th century
—My Several Worlds Abridged for Younger Readers. NOVELISTS—American—20th century

Bunning, James Paul David. The Story of Jim Bunning. BASEBALL PLAYERS—American—20th century

Burgess, Thornton Waldo. Now I Remember: The Autobiography of an Amateur Naturalist. AUTHORS—American—20th century; NATURALISTS—American—20th century

Burney, Fanny. Diary of Fanny Burney. NOVELISTS—English—18th century; NOVELISTS—English—19th century

Burns, Robert. Letters. POETS—Scottish—18th century

Byrd, Richard Evelyn. Alone. AVIATORS—American—20th century; EXPLORERS—American—20th century; NAVAL OFFICERS AND OTHER SEAFARERS—American—20th century
—Little America. AVIATORS—American—20th century; NAVAL OFFICERS AND OTHER SEAFARERS—American—20th century
—Skyward. AVIATORS—American—20th century; NAVAL OFFICERS AND OTHER SEAFARERS—American—20th century

Byrd, William. The Secret Diary of William Byrd of Westover, 1709-12. COLONISTS—American—18th century

Cabell, James Branch. Between Friends: Letters. AUTHORS—American—20th century

Cabeza de Vaca, Álvar Núñez. The Journey of Nunez Cabeza de Vaca. EXPLORERS—Spanish—16th century

Cacopardo, J. Jerry. Show Me a Miracle: The True Story of a Man Who Went from Prison to Pulpit. PRISONERS—American—20th century; RELIGIOUS LEADERS—American—20th century

Calkins, Fay G. My Samoan Chief. AUTHORS—American—20th century

Callaghan, Morley. That Summer in Paris: Memories of Tangled Friendships with Hemingway, Fitzgerald, and Some Others. AUTHORS—Canadian—20th century

Campanella, Roy. It's Good to Be Alive. BASEBALL PLAYERS—American—20th century

Campbell, Litta Belle (Hibben). Here I Raise Mine Ebenezer. LAWYERS—American—20th century

Campbell, Mrs. Patrick. Bernard Shaw and Mrs. Patrick Campbell: Their Correspondence. ACTORS—English—19th century

Camuti, Louis J. Park Avenue Vet. VETERINARIANS—American—20th century

Caracciola, Rudolf. A Racing Car Driver's World. AUTOMOBILE RACERS—German—20th century

Carlson, Gerald F. Two on the Rocks. EDUCATORS—American—20th century

Carlyle, Thomas. The Correspondence of Ralph Waldo Emerson and Thomas Carlyle. ESSAYISTS—Scottish—19th century; HISTORIANS—Scottish—19th century

Carmichael, Hoagy. Sometimes I Wonder: The Story of Hoagy Carmichael. COMPOSERS—American—20th century

Carnegie, Andrew. Autobiography. INDUSTRIALISTS—American—19th century; PHILANTHROPISTS—American—19th century

Carroll, Gladys (Hasty). Only Fifty Years Ago. NOVELISTS—American—20th century
—To Remember Forever: The Journal of a College Girl, 1922-1923. NOVELISTS—American—20th century

Carter, Hodding. First Person Rural. JOURNALISTS—American—20th century

Castellani, Sir Aldo. A Doctor in Many Lands: An Autobiography. PHYSICIANS—Italian—20th century

Catling, Patrick Skene. Better Than Working. JOURNALISTS—English—20th century

Caulfield, Genevieve. The Kingdom Within. BLIND—American—20th century

Cavanaugh, Arthur. My Own Back Yard. PLAYWRIGHTS—American—20th century

Cayton, Horace Roscoe. Long Old Road. SOCIOLOGISTS—American—20th century

Cellini, Benvenuto. Autobiography. GOLDSMITHS—Italian—16th century; SCULPTORS—Italian—16th century

Chambers, Whittaker. Cold Friday. AUTHORS—American—20th century
—Witness. AUTHORS—American—20th century

Chandos, Oliver Lyttelton, 1st Viscount. Memoirs: An Unexpected View from the Summit. BUSINESSMEN — English — 20th century; STATESMEN—English—20th century

Chapelle, Dickey. What's a Woman Doing Here? A Reporter's Report on Herself. JOURNALISTS — American — 20th century; PHOTOGRAPHERS—American—20th century

Chaplin, Charles. My Autobiography. ACTORS—English—20th century

Chase, Ilka. The Carthaginian Rose. ACTORS—American—20th century; JOURNALISTS—American—20th century

Chase, Mary Ellen. Goodly Fellowship. EDU-CATORS—American—20th century; NOVEL-ISTS—American—20th century

—A Goodly Heritage. EDUCATORS—American—20th century; YOUTHS—American—19th century

—White Gate: Adventures in the Imagination of a Child. EDUCATORS—American—20th century; YOUTHS—American—19th century

Chateaubriand, François Auguste René, Vicomte de. Memoirs. STATESMEN—French—19th century

Chesterton, Gilbert Keith. Autobiography. AUTHORS—English—20th century; JOURNAL-ISTS—English—20th century

Chevalier, Maurice. With Love. ACTORS—French—20th century; SINGERS—French—20th century

Chevigny, Hector. My Eyes Have a Cold Nose. BLIND—American—20th century

Chichester, Sir Francis Charles. The Lonely Sea and the Sky. AVIATORS—English—20th century; NAVAL OFFICERS AND OTHER SEAFARERS—English—20th century

Chotzinoff, Samuel. Day's at the Morn. PIA-NISTS—American—20th century

Christiansen, Arthur. Headlines All My Life. JOURNALISTS—English—20th century

Chrysler, Walter Percy. Life of an American Workman. ART COLLECTORS—American—20th century; INDUSTRIALISTS—American—20th century

Church, Richard. Golden Sovereign: A Conclusion to Over the Bridge. AUTHORS—English—20th century

Churchill, John Spencer. A Churchill Canvas. PAINTERS—English—20th century

Churchill, Randolph Frederick Edward Spencer. Twenty-one Years. JOURNALISTS—English—20th century

Churchill, Victor Alexander Spencer, 2nd Viscount. Be All My Sins Remembered. YOUTHS—English—20th century

Churchill, Sir Winston Leonard Spencer. Amid These Storms: Thoughts and Adventures. STATESMEN—English—20th century

—Churchill Reader: The Wit and Wisdom of Sir Winston Churchill. STATESMEN—English—20th century

—Great Destiny: Sixty Years of the Memorable Events in the Life of the Man of the Century Recounted in His Own Incomparable Words. STATESMEN—English—20th century

—A Roving Commission: My Early Life. STATESMEN—English—20th century

—Winston S. Churchill's Maxims and Reflections. STATESMEN—English—20th century

Ciano, Galeazzo, Conte. Ciano's Hidden Diary, 1937-1938. STATESMEN—Italian—20th century

Cibber, Colley. An Apology for the Life of Colley Cibber. ACTORS—English—18th century; PLAYWRIGHTS — English — 18th century

Ciszek, Walter J. With God in Russia. RELI-GIOUS LEADERS—American—20th century

Clapper, Olive (Ewing). One Lucky Woman. AUTHORS—American—20th century

Clark, Eugenie. Lady with a Spear. ICHTHY-OLOGISTS—American—20th century

Clark, James. Jim Clark at the Wheel: The World Motor Racing Champion's Own Story. AUTOMOBILE RACERS — Scottish — 20th century

Clark, Maurine (Doran). Captain's Bride, General's Lady. WIVES OF FAMOUS MEN—American—20th century

Clark, Septima (Poinsette). Echo in My Soul. EDUCATORS—American—20th century

Clemens, Samuel Langhorne. Autobiography of Mark Twain. HUMORISTS—American—19th century

—Letters from the Earth. HUMORISTS—American—19th century

—Letters to Mary. HUMORISTS—American—19th century

—Mark Twain-Howells Letters: The Correspondence, 1872-1910. HUMORISTS—American—19th century

—Mark Twain's Letters from Hawaii. HU-MORISTS—American—19th century

Cobb, Tyrus Raymond. My Life in Baseball: The True Record. BASEBALL PLAYERS—American—20th century

Cochran, Jacqueline. Stars at Noon. AVIA-TORS—American—20th century; BUSINESS-MEN—American—20th century; COSMETI-CIANS—American—20th century

Cochran, Louis. FBI Man: A Personal History. DETECTIVES—American—20th century

Cockburn, Claud. Crossing the Line, Being the Second Volume of Autobiography. JOUR-NALISTS—English—20th century

—View from the West, Being the Third Volume of Autobiography. JOURNALISTS—English—20th century

Cody, William Frederick. Autobiography of Buffalo Bill. SCOUTS—American—19th century

—Buffalo Bill's Life Story (Colonel W. F. Cody). SCOUTS—American—19th century

Coffin, Robert Peter Tristram. Lost Paradise: A Boyhood on a Maine Coast Farm. POETS—American—20th century

Colette, Sidonie Gabrielle. The Blue Lantern. AUTHORS — French — 20th century; VIC-TIMS OF ARTHRITIS—French—20th century

—Earthly Paradise: An Autobiography. AU-THORS—French—20th century

Collier, Richard. A House Called Memory. JOURNALISTS — English — 20th century; YOUTHS—English—20th century

Collinson, Frank. Life in the Saddle. COW-BOYS—American—20th century

Congreve, William. Letters & Documents. PLAYWRIGHTS—English—17th century

Cooper, Diana (Manners), Viscountess Norwich. Trumpets from the Steep. ACTORS—English—20th century

Corum, Bill. Off and Running. JOURNALISTS—American—20th century

Cousy, Robert. Basketball Is My Life. BASKETBALL PLAYERS—American—20th century

—The Last Loud Roar. BASKETBALL PLAYERS—American—20th century

Coward, Noel Pierce. Future Indefinite. ACTORS — English — 20th century; PLAYWRIGHTS—English—20th century

Cox, Wallace. My Life as a Small Boy. ACTORS—American—20th century; YOUTHS—American—20th century

Crockett, David. Autobiography. FRONTIERSMEN—American—19th century

Cronin, Archibald Joseph. Adventures in Two Worlds. NOVELISTS—Scottish—20th century; PHYSICIANS—Scottish—20th century

Crosby, Bing. Call Me Lucky. ACTORS—American—20th century; SINGERS—American—20th century

Cross, Wilbur Lucius. Connecticut Yankee: An Autobiography. EDUCATORS—American—20th century; STATESMEN — American — 20th century

Crossfield, Alfred Scott. Always Another Dawn. AVIATORS—American—20th century

Cullman, Marguerite (Wagner). Occupation: Angel. THEATRICAL PRODUCERS—American—20th century

Cunningham, James F. American Pastor in Rome. RELIGIOUS LEADERS—American—20th century

Curtis, Margaret. Planter's Punch. SINGERS—English—20th century

Dahl, Borghild Margarethe. Finding My Way. AUTHORS—American—20th century; BLIND—American—20th century

—I Wanted to See. AUTHORS—American—20th century; BLIND—American—20th century

Dahlberg, Edward. Because I Was Flesh: The Autobiography. AUTHORS—American—20th century

Daiches, David. Two Worlds: An Edinburgh Jewish Childhood. YOUTHS—Scottish—20th century

Dalai Lama XIV. My Land and My People. RELIGIOUS LEADERS—Tibetan—20th century; STATESMEN—Tibetan—20th century

Dalí, Salvador. Diary of a Genius. PAINTERS—Spanish—20th century

Dana, Ethel Nathalie (Smith). Young in New York: A Memoir of a Victorian Girlhood. YOUTHS—American—19th century

Dana, Richard Henry. Two Years Before the Mast. AUTHORS—American—19th century; NAVAL OFFICERS AND OTHER SEAFARERS—American—19th century

Daniels, Josephus. Shirt-Sleeve Diplomat. JOURNALISTS — American — 19th century; JOURNALISTS — American — 20th century; STATESMEN—American—20th century

—Tar Heel Editor. JOURNALISTS—American—19th century; JOURNALISTS—American—20th century; STATESMEN—American—20th century

Dante Alighieri. New Life (La Vita Nuova). POETS—Italian—14th century

Darwin, Charles Robert. Autobiography of Charles Darwin. NATURALISTS—English—19th century

—The Voyage of the Beagle. NATURALISTS—English—19th century

David, Janina. A Square of Sky: Recollection of My Childhood. YOUTHS—Polish—20th century

Davis, Sammy. Yes I Can. ACTORS—American—20th century

Davis, Thomas Robert Alexander Harries. Doctor to the Islands. ANTHROPOLOGISTS—New Zealand—20th century; PHYSICIANS—New Zealand—20th century

Day, James Edward. My Appointed Round: 929 Days as Postmaster General. POSTAL OFFICIALS—American—20th century

Day-Lewis, Cecil. The Buried Day. POETS—English—20th century

Dean, William Frische. General Dean's Story. SOLDIERS—American—20th century

De Kruif, Paul Henry. Life Among the Doctors. AUTHORS—American—20th century; BACTERIOLOGISTS—American—20th century

—The Sweeping Wind: A Memoir. AUTHORS—American—20th century; BACTERIOLOGISTS—American—20th century

De la Roche, Mazo. Ringing the Changes: An Autobiography. NOVELISTS—Canadian—20th century

De Mille, Agnes George. And Promenade Home. DANCERS—American—20th century

—Dance to the Piper. DANCERS—American—20th century

Dempsey, Jack. Dempsey, by the Man Himself. BOXERS—American—20th century

Denis, Armand. On Safari. PHOTOGRAPHERS—Belgian—20th century

De Quincey, Thomas. Confessions of an English Opium Eater. AUTHORS—English—19th century

Derleth, August William. Countryman's Journal. AUTHORS—American—20th century

—Walden West. AUTHORS—American—20th century

De Toledano, Ralph. Lament for a Generation. JOURNALISTS—American—20th century

De Valois, Dame Ninette. Come Dance with Me: A Memoir 1898-1956. DANCERS—English—20th century

Dickens, Charles. Selected Letters. NOVELISTS—English—19th century

Dickinson, Emily. Letters. POETS—American—19th century

Dickson, Lovat. The Ante-room. AUTHORS—Canadian—20th century; PUBLISHERS—Canadian—20th century

—The House of Words. AUTHORS—Canadian—20th century; PUBLISHERS—Canadian—20th century

Di Maggio, Joseph Paul. Lucky to Be a Yankee. BASEBALL PLAYERS—American—20th century

Dixon, George. Leaning on a Column. JOURNALISTS—American—20th century

Djilas, Milovan. Land Without Justice. COMMUNISTS—Yugoslav—20th century

Donlon, Roger H. C. Outpost of Freedom. SOLDIERS—American—20th century

Dooley, Thomas Anthony. Deliver Us from Evil: The Story of Viet Nam's Flight to Freedom. AUTHORS—American—20th century; PHYSICIANS—American—20th century

—Dr. Tom Dooley: My Story. AUTHORS—American—20th century; PHYSICIANS—American—20th century

—Dr. Tom Dooley's Three Great Books: Deliver Us from Evil, The Edge of Tomorrow, The Night They Burned the Mountain. AUTHORS—American—20th century; PHYSICIANS—American—20th century

—Edge of Tomorrow. AUTHORS—American—20th century; PHYSICIANS—American—20th century

—The Night They Burned the Mountain. AUTHORS—American—20th century; PHYSICIANS—American—20th century

Doss, Helen. The Family Nobody Wanted. YOUTHS—American—20th century

Douglas, Lloyd Cassel. Time to Remember. NOVELISTS—American—20th century; RELIGIOUS LEADERS—American—20th century

Douglas, William Orville. Of Men and Mountains. LAWYERS—American—20th century; NATURALISTS—American—20th century

Douglass, Frederick. Life and Times of Frederick Douglass; adapted by Barbara Ritchie. AUTHORS—American—19th century; ABOLITIONISTS—American—19th century

Draper, Christopher. The Mad Major. AVIATORS—English—20th century

Drawbell, James Wedgwood. James Drawbell: An Autobiography. JOURNALISTS—English—20th century

Duffus, Robert Luther. The Tower of Jewels: Memories of San Francisco. JOURNALISTS—American—20th century

Dufresne, Frank. My Way Was North: An Alaskan Autobiography. AUTHORS—American—20th century

Duncan, David Douglas. Yankee Nomad: A Photographic Odyssey. PHOTOGRAPHERS—American—20th century

Dunne, Finley Peter. Mr. Dooley Remembers. HUMORISTS—American—19th century; HUMORISTS—American—20th century

Durrell, Lawrence George. Lawrence Durrell [and] Henry Miller: A Private Correspondence. NOVELISTS—English—20th century

East, P. D. The Magnolia Jungle: The Life, Times, and Education of a Southern Editor. JOURNALISTS—American—20th century

Eastman, Max. Love and Revolution: My Journey Through an Epoch. JOURNALISTS—American—20th century

Eden, Sir Anthony. Facing the Dictators: The Memoirs of Anthony Eden, Earl of Avon. STATESMEN—English—20th century

—Full Circle. STATESMEN—English—20th century

—The Reckoning: The Memoirs of Anthony Eden, Earl of Avon. STATESMEN—English—20th century

Edison, Thomas Alva. Diary and Sundry Observations. INVENTORS—American—20th century

Edward VIII. A King's Story: The Memoirs of the Duke of Windsor. KINGS—English—20th century

—Windsor Revisited. KINGS—English—20th century

Ehrenburg, Il'ia Grigor'evich. Memoirs: 1921-1941. AUTHORS—Russian—20th century

—People and Life, 1801-1921. AUTHORS—Russian—20th century

Ehrlich, Jacob W. A Life in My Hands. LAWYERS—American—20th century

—A Reasonable Doubt. LAWYERS—American—20th century

Eisenhower, Dwight David. The White House Years: v. 1, Mandate for Change, 1953-1956. PRESIDENTS—American—20th century

—The White House Years: v. 2, Waging Peace, 1956-1961. PRESIDENTS—American—20th century

Eisenschiml, Otto. O. E.: Historian Without an Armchair. HISTORIANS—American—20th century

Eldridge, Nigel. The Colonel's Son. YOUTHS—English—20th century

Emerson, Ralph Waldo. The Correspondence of Ralph Waldo Emerson and Thomas Carlyle. AUTHORS—American—19th century

—Heart of Emerson's Journals. AUTHORS—American—19th century

Epstein, Jacob. Epstein: An Autobiography. SCULPTORS—English—20th century

Ernst, Morris Leopold. Untitled: The Diary of My 72nd Year. LAWYERS—American—20th century

Erskine, John. My Life in Music. AUTHORS—American—20th century; EDUCATORS—American—20th century

Evelyn, John. Diary of John Evelyn. AUTHORS—English—17th century

Everest, Frank K. The Fastest Man Alive: A Test Pilot Tells His Story. AVIATORS—American—20th century

Evtushenko, Eugenii Aleksandrovich. A Precocious Autobiography. POETS—Russian—20th century

Fairbrother, Nan. The Cheerful Day. YOUTHS —English—20th century

—The House in the Country. AUTHORS—English—20th century

Fairchild, David Grandison. World Was My Garden: Travel of a Plant Explorer. BOTANISTS—American—20th century

Farson, Negley. Mirror for Narcissus. AUTHORS—American—20th century

Fast, Howard Melvin. Naked God: The Writer and the Communist Party. AUTHORS—American—20th century

Faulkner, William. The Faulkner-Cowley File: Letters and Memories, 1944-1962. NOVELISTS—American—20th century

Fénelon, François de Salignac de La Mothe-, Archbishop. Letters of Love and Counsel. RELIGIOUS LEADERS—French—17th century; RELIGIOUS LEADERS—French—18th century

Ferber, Edna. A Kind of Magic. NOVELISTS—American—20th century

—A Peculiar Treasure. NOVELISTS—American—20th century

Fields, Gracie. Sing as We Go: The Autobiography of Gracie Fields. SINGERS—English—20th century

Fisher, Welthy (Honsinger). To Light a Candle. RELIGIOUS LEADERS—American—20th century

Fitch, John. Adventure on Wheels: The Autobiography of a Road Racing Champion. AUTOMOBILE RACERS—American—20th century

Fitzgerald, Francis Scott Key. The Letters of F. Scott Fitzgerald. NOVELISTS—American—20th century

—Scott Fitzgerald: Letters to His Daughter. NOVELISTS—American—20th century

Flagstad, Kirsten. The Flagstad Manuscript. SINGERS—Norwegian—20th century

Flanders, Ralph Edward. Senator from Vermont. STATESMEN—American—20th century

Flexner, Abraham. Abraham Flexner: An Autobiography. EDUCATORS—American—20th century

Ford, Ford Madox. Letters. AUTHORS—English—20th century

Forrestal, James. Forrestal Diaries. STATESMEN—American—20th century

Forster, Edward Morgan. Hill of Devi. NOVELISTS—English—20th century

Fosdick, Harry Emerson. Living of These Days: An Autobiography. RELIGIOUS LEADERS—American—20th century

Fosdick, Raymond Blaine. Chronicle of a Generation: An Autobiography. LAWYERS—American—20th century

Fowler, Gene. Skyline: A Reporter's Reminiscence of the 1920's. JOURNALISTS—American—20th century

Fox, George. Journal. RELIGIOUS LEADERS —English—17th century

Frank, Anne. Diary of a Young Girl. YOUTHS —Dutch—20th century

—The Works of Anne Frank. YOUTHS—Dutch —20th century

Frank, Morris S. First Lady of the Seeing Eye. BLIND—American—20th century

Frankau, Pamela. Pen to Paper: A Novelist's Notebook. NOVELISTS—English—20th century

Franken, Rose. When All Is Said and Done. An Autobiography. NOVELISTS—American —20th century

Frankfurter, Felix. Felix Frankfurter Reminisces. IMMIGRANTS TO UNITED STATES—19th century; LAWYERS—American—20th century

Franklin, Benjamin. Autobiographical Writings. AUTHORS—American—18th century; PHILOSOPHERS—American—18th century; SCIENTISTS—American—18th century; STATESMEN—American—18th century

—Autobiography. PHILOSOPHERS—American —18th century; SCIENTISTS—American—18th century; STATESMEN — American — 18th century

—The Benjamin Franklin Papers. PHILOSOPHERS—American—18th century; SCIENTISTS—American—18th century; STATESMEN—American—18th century

Frémont, John Charles. Narratives of Exploration and Adventure. EXPLORERS—American—19th century; SOLDIERS—American—19th century

Freuchen, Peter. Vagrant Viking: My Life and Adventures. EXPLORERS—Danish—20th century

Freud, Sigmund. Letters. NEUROLOGISTS—Austrian—20th century; PSYCHIATRISTS—Austrian—20th century

Frischauer, Willi. European Commuter. JOURNALISTS—English—20th century

Frost, Robert. Interviews with Robert Frost; ed. by Edward Connery Lathem. POETS—American—20th century

—The Letters of Robert Frost to Louis Untermeyer. POETS—American—20th century

—Selected Letters. POETS—American—20th century

Fulda, Edeltraud. And I Shall Be Healed: The Autobiography of a Woman Miraculously Cured at Lourdes. PHYSICALLY HANDICAPPED—Austrian—20th century

Fuller, Alfred Carl. A Foot in the Door: The Life Appraisal of the Original Fuller Brush Man. BUSINESSMEN—American—20th century

Gallery, Daniel Vincent. Eight Bells, and All's Well. NAVAL OFFICERS AND OTHER SEAFARERS—American—20th century

Gandhi, Mohandas Karamchand. All Men Are Brothers. RELIGIOUS LEADERS—Indian—20th century; STATESMEN—Indian—20th century

—The Essential Gandhi: An Anthology. RELIGIOUS LEADERS—Indian—20th century; STATESMEN—Indian—20th century

—Gandhi's Autobiography: The Story of My Experiments with Truth. RELIGIOUS LEADERS—Indian—20th century; STATESMEN—Indian—20th century

Garfield, James Abram. The Wild Life of the Army: Civil War Letters. PRESIDENTS—American—19th century

Garland, Hamlin. A Son of the Middle Border. AUTHORS—American—19th century; AUTHORS—American—20th century

Garnett, David. The Golden Echo: v. 3, The Familiar Faces. NOVELISTS—English—20th century

Garrick, David. Letters. ACTORS—English—18th century

Gary, Romain. Promise at Dawn. AUTHORS—French—20th century

Gatheru, Reuel Mugo. Child of Two Worlds: A Kikuyu's Story. YOUTHS—Kenyan—20th century

Gaulle, Charles de. War Memoirs: v. 1, The Call to Honour, 1940-1942. PRESIDENTS—French—20th century; SOLDIERS—French—20th century;

—War Memoirs: v. 2, Unity, 1942-1944. PRESIDENTS—French—20th century; SOLDIERS—French—20th century

—War Memoirs: v. 3, Salvation, 1944-1946. PRESIDENTS—French—20th century; SOLDIERS—French—20th century

Geddes, Norman Bel. Miracle in the Evening. SCENIC DESIGNERS—American—20th century

Gertz, Elmer. A Handful of Clients. LAWYERS—American—20th century

Getty, Jean Paul. My Life and Fortunes. INDUSTRIALISTS — American — 20th century; PETROLEUM INDUSTRY WORKERS—American—20th century

Gibbon, Edward. Autobiography. HISTORIANS—English—18th century

Gibson, Althea. I Always Wanted to Be Somebody. TENNIS PLAYERS—American—20th century

Gide, André Paul Guillaume. Journals of André Gide. AUTHORS—French—19th century; AUTHORS—French—20th century

—Self-portraits: The Gide/Valéry Letters, 1890-1942. AUTHORS—French—19th century; AUTHORS—French—20th century

Giesler, Harold Lee. The Jerry Giesler Story. LAWYERS—American—20th century

Giles, Henry E. The G. I. Journal of Sergeant Giles. SOLDIERS—American—20th century

Gillmore, Margalo. Four Flights Up. ACTORS—English—20th century

Gilson, Etienne Henry. The Philosopher and Theology. PHILOSOPHERS—French—20th century

Gissing, George Robert. George Gissing and H. G. Wells: Their Friendship and Correspondence. NOVELISTS—English—19th century

Glasgow, Ellen Anderson Gholson. The Woman Within. NOVELISTS—American—20th century

Gluck, Gemma (La Guardia). My Story. RELATIVES OF FAMOUS MEN—American—20th century

Godden, Rumer. Two Under the Indian Sun. AUTHORS—English—20th century; YOUTHS—English—20th century

Goethe, Johann Wolfgang von. Autobiography: Poetry and Truth from My Own Life. POETS—German—18th century; POETS—German—19th century

—Goethe: The Story of a Man, Being the Life of Goethe, as Told in His Own Words. POETS—German—18th century; POETS—German—19th century

Gogh, Vincent van. Complete Letters, with Reproductions of All the Drawings in the Correspondence. PAINTERS—Dutch—19th century

—Dear Theo, the Autobiography. PAINTERS—Dutch—19th century

—Van Gogh: A Self-Portrait: Letters Revealing His Life as a Painter. PAINTERS—Dutch—19th century

Gollancz, Victor. Journey Towards Music: A Memoir. CRITICS—English—20th century; PUBLISHERS—English—20th century

Gompers, Samuel. Seventy Years of Life and Labor: An Autobiography. LABOR LEADERS — American — 19th century; LABOR LEADERS—American—20th century

Goncourt, Edmond Louis Antoine Huot de. Pages from the Goncourt Journal. NOVELISTS—French—19th century

Gorbatov, Aleksandr Vassil'evich. Years off My Life: The Memoirs of General of the Soviet Army. SOLDIERS—Russian—20th century

Gordon, Charles George. Khartoum Journal. SOLDIERS—English—19th century

Gowdy, Curtis. Cowboy at the Mike. RADIO AND TELEVISION PERFORMERS—American—20th century

Graham, Sheilah. Beloved Infidel: The Education of a Woman. JOURNALISTS—English—20th century

—The Rest of the Story. JOURNALISTS—English—20th century

Grattidge, Harry. Captain of the Queens: The Autobiography of Captain Harry Grattidge, Former Commodore of the Cunard Line. NAVAL OFFICERS AND OTHER SEAFARERS—English—20th century

Green, Julian. Diary 1928-1957. NOVELISTS—French—20th century

Greenslet, Ferris. Under the Bridge: An Autobiography. AUTHORS—American—20th century

Gregory, Dick. Nigger: An Autobiography. ACTORS—American—20th century

Grenfell, Sir Wilfred Thomason. Adrift on an Ice-Pan. PHYSICIANS—English—19th century; PHYSICIANS—English—20th century; RELIGIOUS LEADERS—English—19th century; RELIGIOUS LEADERS—English—20th century

—Forty Years for Labrador. PHYSICIANS—English—19th century; PHYSICIANS—English—20th century; RELIGIOUS LEADERS—English—19th century; RELIGIOUS LEADERS—English—20th century

Greville, Charles Cavendish Fulke. The Great World: Portraits and Scenes from Greville's Memoirs, 1814-1860. AUTHORS—English—19th century

Grey, Beryl. Through the Bamboo Curtain. DANCERS—English—20th century

Gulbenkian, Nubar Sarkis. Portrait in Oil: The Autobiography of Nubar Gulbenkian. FINANCIERS—Iranian—20th century; PETROLEUM INDUSTRY WORKERS—Iranian—20th century

Gunther, John. A Fragment of Autobiography. JOURNALISTS—American—20th century

Guthrie, Alfred Bertram. The Blue Hen's Chick. AUTHORS—American—20th century

Guthrie, Sir Tyrone. A Life in the Theatre. THEATRICAL PRODUCERS—English—20th century

Halifax, Edward Frederick Lindley Wood, 1st Earl of. Fullness of Days. STATESMEN—English—20th century

Hall, James Norman. My Island Home: An Autobiography. AUTHORS—American—20th century

Hallinan, Vincent. A Lion in Court. LAWYERS—American—20th century

Hamilton, Alexander. Mind of Alexander Hamilton. STATESMEN—American—18th century

Hammarskjöld, Dag. Markings. STATESMEN—Swedish—20th century; UNITED NATIONS OFFICIALS—Swedish—20th century

Hammond-Innes, Ralph. Harvest of Journeys. AUTHORS—English—20th century

Han, Suyin. Many-Splendored Thing. AUTHORS—Chinese—20th century

—A Mortal Flower—China: Autobiography, History. AUTHORS—Chinese—20th century

Handy, William Christopher. Father of the Blues: An Autobiography. COMPOSERS—American—20th century

Harris, Mark. Twentyone Twice: A Journal. AUTHORS—American—20th century

Hatano, Isoko. Mother and Son: The Wartime Correspondence of Isoko and Ichiro Hatano. YOUTHS—Japanese—20th century

Hathaway, Katharine (Butler). Little Locksmith. PHYSICALLY HANDICAPPED—American—20th century

Hathaway, Sibyl (Collings). Dame of Sark: An Autobiography. DAME OF SARK—20th century

Hatsumi, Reiko. Rain and the Feast of the Stars. YOUTHS—Japanese—20th century

Hawkins, Eric. Hawkins of the Paris Herald. JOURNALISTS—English—20th century

Hayden, Sterling. Wanderer. ACTORS—American—20th century

Hayes, Helen. A Gift of Joy. ACTORS—American—20th century

Hayes, Rutherford Birchard. Hayes: The Diary of a President 1875-1881. PRESIDENTS—American—19th century

Hayne, Donald. Batter My Heart. RELIGIOUS LEADERS—American—20th century

Hecht, Ben. Child of the Century. AUTHORS—American—20th century

—Letters from Bohemia. AUTHORS—American—20th century

Heiser, Victor George. An American Doctor's Odyssey: Adventures in Forty-five Countries. PHYSICIANS—American—20th century

Helburn, Theresa. A Wayward Quest: The Autobiography of Theresa Helburn. THEATRICAL PRODUCERS — American — 20th century

Hemingway, Ernest. A Moveable Feast. JOURNALISTS—American—20th century; NOVELISTS—American—20th century

Henderson, J. Y. Circus Doctor. CIRCUS PERFORMERS — American — 20th century; VETERINARIANS—American—20th century

Henrey, Madeleine (Gal). Little Madeleine: The Autobiography of a Young Girl in Montmartre. YOUTHS—French—20th century

—Madeleine Grown Up: The Autobiography of a French Girl. AUTHORS—French—20th century

—Madeleine, Young Wife: The Autobiography of a French Girl. AUTHORS—French—20th century

Henrichsen, Margaret (Kimball). Seven Steeples. RELIGIOUS LEADERS—American—20th century

Herbert, Edward. Autobiography of Edward, Lord Herbert of Cherbury. PHILOSOPHERS—English—17th century

Hewitt, Arthur Wentworth. The Old Brick Manse. RELIGIOUS LEADERS—American—20th century

Hicks, Granville. Part of the Truth. AUTHORS—American—20th century

Hillary, Sir Edmund. High Adventure. MOUNTAINEERS—English—20th century

—High in the Thin Cold Air. MOUNTAINEERS—English—20th century

Hilton, Conrad Nicholson. Be My Guest. HOTEL OWNERS AND MANAGERS—American—20th century

Hirschmann, Ira Arthur. Caution to the Winds. BUSINESSMEN—American—20th century

Hiss, Alger. In the Court of Public Opinion. LAWYERS—American—20th century

Hitler, Adolf. Mein Kampf. STATESMEN—German—20th century

Hobart, Alice Tisdale. Gusty's Child. NOVELISTS—American—20th century

Hoffman, Malvina. Yesterday Is Tomorrow: A Personal History. SCULPTORS—American—20th century

Holmes, Oliver Wendell. The Holmes-Einstein Letters: Correspondence, 1903-1935. LAWYERS—American—20th century

—Holmes-Laski Letters: The Correspondence of Mr. Justice Holmes and Harold J. Laski, 1916-1935. LAWYERS—American—20th century

Homans, Abigail (Adams). Education by Uncles. AUTHORS—American—20th century

Honegger, Arthur. I Am a Composer. COMPOSERS—French—20th century

Hoover, Herbert Clark. Memoirs. ENGINEERS, MINING—American—20th century; PRESIDENTS—American—20th century

Horne, Lena. Lena. SINGERS—American—20th century

Howells, William Dean. Mark Twain-Howells Letters: The Correspondence, 1872-1910. AUTHORS—American—19th century; AUTHORS—American—20th century

Hudson, William Henry. Far Away and Long Ago: A History of My Early Life. AUTHORS—English—19th century; NATURALISTS—English—19th century; YOUTHS—English—19th century

Hughes, Langston. I Wonder as I Wander: An Autobiographical Journey. AUTHORS—American—20th century

Hull, Cordell. Memoirs of Cordell Hull. STATESMEN—American—20th century

Hunt, Sir John. The Conquest of Everest. MOUNTAINEERS—English—20th century

Hunt, Leigh. Autobiography. POETS—English—19th century

Hurst, Fannie. Anatomy of Me: A Wonderer in Search of Herself. NOVELISTS—American—20th century

Hussein. Uneasy Lies the Head: The Autobiography of His Majesty King Hussein I of the Hashemite Kingdom of Jordan. KINGS—Jordanian—20th century

Huxley, Elspeth Josceline (Grant). Flame Trees of Thika: Memories of an African Childhood. AUTHORS—English—20th century; YOUTHS—English—20th century

—On the Edge of the Rift. AUTHORS—English—20th century; YOUTHS—English—20th century

Huzel, Dieter K. Peenemunde to Canaveral. SCIENTISTS—German—20th century

Ibsen, Henrik. Letters and Speeches. PLAYWRIGHTS—Norwegian—19th century

Ickes, Harold Le Claire. Secret Diary. STATESMEN—American—20th century

Ingersoll, Ralph McAllister. Point of Departure: An Adventure in Autobiography. JOURNALISTS—American—20th century

Ionides, Constantine John Philip. Mambas and Man-Eaters. HERPETOLOGISTS—English—20th century

Ismay, Hastings Lionel Ismay, Baron. Memoirs. SOLDIERS—English—20th century

Jabavu, Noni. The Ochre People: Scenes from a South African Life. JOURNALISTS—South African—20th century

Jacobs, Paul. Is Curly Jewish? A Political Self-Portrait Illuminating Three Turbulent Decades of Social Revolt, 1935-1965. JOURNALISTS—American—20th century

James II. The Memoirs of James II: His Campaigns as Duke of York, 1652-1660. KINGS—English—17th century

James, Henry. Henry James: Autobiography. NOVELISTS — American — 19th century; NOVELISTS—American—20th century

James, Will. Lone Cowboy: My Life Story. AUTHORS—American—20th century; COWBOYS—American—20th century; ILLUSTRATORS—American—20th century

James, William. Selected Letters. PHILOSOPHERS — American — 19th century; PSYCHOLOGISTS—American—19th century

Jebb, Caroline Lane (Reynolds) Slemmer, Lady. With Dearest Love to All: The Life and Letters of Lady Jebb. WIVES OF FAMOUS MEN—English—19th century; WIVES OF FAMOUS MEN—English—20th century

Jefferson, Thomas. The Adams-Jefferson Letters. PRESIDENTS—American—19th century

—The Thomas Jefferson Papers. PRESIDENTS—American—19th century

—To the Girls and Boys, Being the Delightful Little-Known Letters of Thomas Jefferson to and from His Children and Grandchildren. PRESIDENTS—American—19th century

Jesus, Carolina Maria de. Child of the Dark: The Diary of Carolina Jesus. POVERTY STRICKEN—Brazilian—20th century

John XXIII. Wit and Wisdom of Good Pope John. RELIGIOUS LEADERS—Italian—20th century

Johnson, Alvin Saunders. Pioneer's Progress: An Autobiography. ECONOMISTS—American—20th century

Johnson, Samuel. Dr. Johnson: His Life in Letters. CRITICS—English—18th century; LEXICOGRAPHERS—English—18th century

Jones, Jesse Holman. Fifty Billion Dollars: My Thirteen Years with RFC (1932-1945). FINANCIERS—American—20th century

Jones, Robert Tyre. Golf Is My Game. GOLFERS—American—20th century

Jones, Weimar. My Affair with a Weekly. JOURNALISTS—American—20th century

Jordan-Smith, Paul. The Road I Came: Some Recollections and Reflections Concerning Changes in American Life and Manners since 1890. AUTHORS—American—20th century

Josephson, Matthew. Life Among the Surrealists: A Memoir. AUTHORS—American—20th century

Joyce, James. Letters of James Joyce. AUTHORS—Irish—20th century

Jung, Carl Gustav. Memories, Dreams, Reflections. PSYCHIATRISTS—Swiss—20th century

Kafka, Franz. Diaries, 1910-1923. NOVELISTS—Czech—20th century

Kaltenborn, Hans von. Fifty Fabulous Years, 1900-1950: A Personal Review. JOURNALISTS—American—20th century

Kaminsky, Max. My Life in Jazz. TRUMPETERS—American—20th century

Karsavina, Tamara. Theatre Street: The Reminiscences of Tamara Karsavina. DANCERS—Russian—20th century

Kästner, Erich. When I Was a Boy. AUTHORS—German—20th century; YOUTHS—German—20th century

Kayira, Legson. I Will Try. YOUTHS—Malawi—20th century

Kazantzakēs, Nikos. Report to Greco. AUTHORS—Greek—20th century

Kazin, Alfred. Starting Out in the Thirties. CRITICS—American—20th century

Keaton, Buster. My Wonderful World of Slapstick. ACTORS—American—20th century

Keitel, Wilhelm. The Memoirs of Field-Marshal Keitel. SOLDIERS—German—20th century

Keller, Helen Adams. Story of My Life. AUTHORS—American—20th century; BLIND—American—20th century; DEAF—American—20th century

Kelly, Emmett. Clown. CIRCUS PERFORMERS—American—20th century

Kennedy, John Fitzgerald. The First Book Edition of John F. Kennedy's Inaugural Address. PRESIDENTS—American—20th century

—Kennedy and the Press: The News Conferences. PRESIDENTS—American—20th century

Kennon, Bob. From the Pecos to the Powder: A Cowboy's Autobiography. COWBOYS—American—20th century

Kenny, Elizabeth. And They Shall Walk: The Life Story of Sister Elizabeth Kenny. NURSES—Australian—20th century

Kerensky, Alexander Fedorovich. Russia and History's Turning Point. STATESMEN—Russian—20th century

Kerouac, Jack. Lonesome Traveler. AUTHORS—American—20th century

Kessel, Joseph. They Weren't All Angels. NOVELISTS—French—20th century

Keyes, Frances Parkinson (Wheeler). Roses in December. NOVELISTS—American—20th century; YOUTHS—American—19th century

Kieran, John. Not Under Oath: Recollections and Reflections. JOURNALISTS—American—20th century

Kierkegaard, Søren Aabye. The Last Years: Journals, 1853-1855. PHILOSOPHERS—Danish—19th century

Kimbrough, Emily. Innocents from Indiana. AUTHORS—American—20th century

Kimmel, Husband Edward. Admiral Kimmel's Story. NAVAL OFFICERS AND OTHER SEAFARERS—American—20th century

Kittinger, Joseph W. The Long, Lonely Leap. AVIATORS—American—20th century

Klee, Paul. The Diaries of Paul Klee. PAINTERS—Swiss—20th century

Koestler, Arthur. Arrow in the Blue: An Autobiography. AUTHORS—Hungarian—20th century

—Invisible Writing . . . An Autobiography. AUTHORS—Hungarian—20th century

Koh, Taiwon (Kim). The Bitter Fruit of Kom-Pawi. IMMIGRANTS TO UNITED STATES—20th century; YOUTHS—Korean—20th century

Kops, Bernard. The World Is a Wedding. PLAYWRIGHTS—English—20th century

Koufax, Sanford. Koufax. BASEBALL PLAYERS—American—20th century

Krutch, Joseph Wood. More Lives than One. AUTHORS—American—20th century; CRITICS—American—20th century

Kshesinskaîa, Matil'da Feliksovna. Dancing in Petersburg: The Memoirs of Kschessinska, H. S. H. the Princess Romanovsky-Krassinsky. DANCERS—Russian—19th century; DANCERS—Russian—20th century

Kunstler, William Moses. Deep in My Heart. LAWYERS—American—20th century

La Farge, John. The Manner Is Ordinary. RELIGIOUS LEADERS—American—20th century

Lamb, Charles. Letters. ESSAYISTS—English—18th century; ESSAYISTS—English—19th century

—Selected Letters. ESSAYISTS—English—18th century; ESSAYISTS—English—19th century

Lamb, Edward. No Lamb for Slaughter: An Autobiography. INDUSTRIALISTS—American—20th century; LAWYERS—American—20th century

Latham, Harold Strong. My Life in Publishing. PUBLISHERS—American—20th century

Laubach, Frank Charles. Thirty Years with the Silent Billion: Adventuring in Literacy. EDUCATORS—American—20th century

Laver, James. Museum Piece; or, The Education of an Iconographer. AUTHORS—English—20th century; CRITICS—English—20th century

Lawrence, David Herbert. Collected Letters. NOVELISTS—English—20th century

—Selected Letters. NOVELISTS—English—20th century

Lawrence, Marjorie. Interrupted Melody: The Story of My Life. SINGERS—Australian—20th century; VICTIMS OF POLIO—Australian—20th century

Le Brun, George Petit. It's Time to Tell. CORONERS—American—20th century

Lee, Laurie. The Edge of Day: A Boyhood in the West of England. POETS—English—20th century; YOUTHS—English—20th century

Lee, Mabel (Barbee). And Suddenly It's Evening: A Fragment of Life. EDUCATORS—American—20th century

—The Rainbow Years: A Happy Interlude. EDUCATORS—American—20th century

Le Gallienne, Eva. At 33. ACTORS—American—20th century

—With a Quiet Heart: An Autobiography. ACTORS—American—20th century

Lehmann, Lotte. Five Operas and Richard Strauss. SINGERS—American—20th century

Leising, William A. Arctic Wings. RELIGIOUS LEADERS—American—20th century

LeMay, Curtis Emerson. Mission with LeMay: My Story. AVIATORS—American—20th century; SOLDIERS—American—20th century

Leopold, Nathan Freudenthal. Life Plus 99 Years. CRIMINALS—American—20th century

Levant, Oscar. The Memoirs of an Amnesiac. PIANISTS—American—20th century

Levenson, Samuel. Everything but Money. HUMORISTS—American—20th century

Le Vier, Anthony William. Pilot. AVIATORS—American—20th century

Lewis, Clive Staples. Surprised by Joy: The Shape of My Early Life. AUTHORS—English—20th century

Lewis, Meriwether. The Journals of Lewis and Clark. EXPLORERS—American—19th century

Lewis, Wyndham. Letters. AUTHORS—English—20th century; PAINTERS—English—20th century

Li, Shu-fan. Hong Kong Surgeon. SURGEONS—Chinese—20th century

Liddell Hart, Sir Basil Henry. The Liddell Hart Memoirs: v. 1, 1895-1938. HISTORIANS—English—20th century

—The Liddell Hart Memoirs: v. 2, The Later Years. HISTORIANS—English—20th century

Lightwood, Teresa. My Three Lives. NURSES — English — 20th century; RELIGIOUS LEADERS—English—20th century

Lilienthal, David Eli. The Journals of David E. Lilienthal. BUSINESSMEN—American—20th century

Lincoln, Abraham. Conversations with Lincoln. PRESIDENTS—American—19th century

—The First Book Edition of the Gettysburg Address and the Second Inaugural. PRESIDENTS—American—19th century

Lindbergh, Charles Augustus. Spirit of St. Louis. AVIATORS—American—20th century

—"We." AVIATORS—American—20th century

Little, Malcolm ("Malcolm X"). The Autobiography of Malcolm X. RELIGIOUS LEADERS—American—20th century

—Malcolm X Speaks: Selected Speeches and Statements. RELIGIOUS LEADERS—American—20th century

Loewy, Raymond Fernand. Never Leave Well Enough Alone. IMMIGRANTS TO UNITED STATES—20th century; INDUSTRIAL DESIGNERS—American—20th century

Lomax, John Avery. Adventures of a Ballad Hunter. FOLKLORISTS — American — 20th century

London, Jack. Cruise of the Snark. NOVELISTS—American—20th century

—Letters from Jack London, Containing an Unpublished Correspondence Between London and Sinclair Lewis. NOVELISTS—American—20th century

Loos, Anita. A Girl Like I. AUTHORS—American—20th century

Love, Edmund G. The Situation in Flushing. AUTHORS — American — 20th century; YOUTHS—American—20th century

Lowry, Malcolm. Selected Letters. NOVELISTS—English—20th century

Lusseyran, Jacques. And There Was Light. BLIND—French—20th century

Luthuli, Albert. Let My People Go. STATESMEN—South African—20th century

Lynch, Patricia. A Storyteller's Childhood. YOUTHS—Irish—20th century

MacArthur, Douglas. Courage Was the Rule: General Douglas MacArthur's Own Story. SOLDIERS—American—20th century

—Duty, Honor, Country: A Pictorial Autobiography. SOLDIERS—American—20th century

—Reminiscences. SOLDIERS—American—20th century

Macaulay, Dame Rose. Last Letters to a Friend, 1952-1958. NOVELISTS—English—20th century

—Letters to a Friend, 1950-1952. NOVELISTS—English—20th century

—Letters to a Sister. NOVELISTS—English—20th century

McBride, Mary Margaret. Out of the Air. RADIO AND TELEVISION PERFORMERS—American—20th century

McClintic, Guthrie. Me and Kit. THEATRICAL PRODUCERS—American—20th century

McCoy, Marie (Bell). Journey Out of Darkness. BLIND—American—20th century

MacDonald, Betty (Bard). The Egg and I. AUTHORS—American—20th century; FARMERS—American—20th century

McGinley, Phyllis. Sixpence in Her Shoe. AUTHORS—American—20th century

Madison, James. The Papers of James Madison. PRESIDENTS — American — 19th century; STATESMEN—American—18th century

Magnuson, Paul Budd. Ring the Night Bell: The Autobiography of a Surgeon. SURGEONS—American—20th century

Mal'ko, Nikolai Andreevich. A Certain Art. CONDUCTORS—Russian—20th century

Manet, Édouard. Portrait of Manet, by Himself and His Contemporaries. PAINTERS—French—19th century

Mann, Thomas. A Sketch of My Life. AUTHORS – German – 20th century; IMMIGRANTS TO UNITED STATES–20th century

–The Story of a Novel: The Genesis of Doctor Faustus. AUTHORS–German–20th century; IMMIGRANTS TO UNITED STATES–20th century

Manry, Robert Neal. Tinkerbelle. AUTHORS–American–20th century; EXPLORERS–American–20th century

Mardikian, George Magar. Song of America. IMMIGRANTS TO UNITED STATES–20th century; RESTAURATEURS–American–20th century

Maris, Roger Eugene. Roger Maris at Bat. BASEBALL PLAYERS–American–20th century

Maritain, Raïssa (Oumansoff). We Have Been Friends Together: Memoirs. WIVES OF FAMOUS MEN–French–20th century

Marsh, Ngaio. Black Beech and Honeydew: An Autobiography. AUTHORS–New Zealand–20th century

Marshak, Samuil IAkovlevich. At Life's Beginning: Some Pages of Reminiscence. AUTHORS–Russian–20th century; YOUTHS–Russian–19th century

Marshall, Alan John ("Jock"). I Can Jump Puddles. PHYSICALLY HANDICAPPED–Australian–20th century; YOUTHS–Australian–20th century

Marshall, Catherine (Wood). To Live Again. WIVES OF FAMOUS MEN–American–20th century

Marshall, Peter. Two Lives. VICTIMS OF POLIO–English–20th century

Martin, Betty. Miracle at Carville. VICTIMS OF LEPROSY–American–20th century

Martin, Joseph Plumb. Yankee Doodle Boy. SOLDIERS–American–18th century

Martin, Joseph William. My First Fifty Years in Politics. STATESMEN–American–20th century

Martínez Alonso, Eduardo. Memoirs of a Medico. PHYSICIANS–Spanish–20th century

Marx, Harpo. Harpo Speaks! ACTORS–American–20th century

Maryanna, Sister. With Love and Laughter: Reflections of a Dominican Nun. RELIGIOUS LEADERS–American–20th century

Masefield, John. So Long to Learn. AUTHORS–English–20th century

Massey, Vincent. What's Past Is Prologue: The Memoirs of the Right Honourable Vincent Massey, C. H. STATESMEN–Canadian–20th century

Matsuoka, Yōko. Daughter of the Pacific. YOUTHS–Japanese–20th century

Matthews, Thomas Stanley. Name and Address: An Autobiography. JOURNALISTS–American–20th century

Maugham, William Somerset. The Summing Up. AUTHORS–English–20th century

Mautner, Herman Eric. Doctor in Bolivia. PHYSICIANS–Austrian–20th century

Maxwell, Gavin. The House of Elrig. AUTHORS–English–20th century; YOUTHS–English–20th century

Mays, Willie Howard. Born to Play Ball: Willie Mays' Own Story. BASEBALL PLAYERS–American–20th century

–Willie Mays: My Life In and Out of Baseball. BASEBALL PLAYERS–American–20th century

Mehta, Ved Parkash. Face to Face: An Autobiography. AUTHORS–Indian–20th century; BLIND–Indian–20th century

Mencken, Henry Louis. Days of H. L. Mencken. JOURNALISTS–American–20th century

–Heathen Days, 1890-1936. JOURNALISTS–American–20th century

–Letters. JOURNALISTS–American–20th century

Mendelssohn-Bartholdy, Felix. Letters. COMPOSERS–German–19th century

Merrill, Robert. Once More from the Beginning. SINGERS–American–20th century

Merton, Thomas. Seven Storey Mountain. RELIGIOUS LEADERS–American–20th century

–Sign of Jonas. RELIGIOUS LEADERS–American–20th century

–Waters of Siloe. RELIGIOUS LEADERS–American–20th century

Mesta, Perle (Skirvin). Perle: My Story. STATESMEN–American–20th century

Michelangelo Buonarroti. I, Michelangelo, Sculptor: An Autobiography Through Letters. ARCHITECTS – Italian – 16th century; PAINTERS–Italian–16th century; SCULPTORS–Italian–16th century

–Michelangelo: Paintings, Sculptures, Architecture. ARCHITECTS–Italian–16th century; PAINTERS – Italian – 16th century; SCULPTORS–Italian–16th century

Miers, Earl Schenck. The Trouble Bush. AUTHORS–American–20th century; VICTIMS OF CEREBRAL PALSY–American–20th century

Milhaud, Darius. Notes Without Music. COMPOSERS–French–20th century

Mill, John Stuart. Autobiography. ECONOMISTS–English–19th century; PHILOSOPHERS–English–19th century

Millay, Edna St. Vincent. Letters. POETS–American–20th century

Miller, Henry. Lawrence Durrell [and] Henry Miller: A Private Correspondence. NOVELISTS–American–20th century

Mitford, Jessica. Daughters and Rebels: The Autobiography of Jessica Mitford. AUTHORS–English–20th century

Modisane, Bloke. Blame Me on History. JOURNALISTS–South African–20th century

Modupe, Prince. I Was a Savage. YOUTHS–African–20th century

Moffat, Gwen. Space Below My Feet. MOUNTAINEERS–English–20th century

Monat, Pawel. Spy in the U. S. SPIES—Polish
—20th century

Montgomery, Bernard Law Montgomery, 1st
Viscount. Memoirs of Field-Marshal the
Viscount Montgomery of Alamein. SOL-
DIERS—English—20th century

Moody, Joseph Palmer. Arctic Doctor. PHY-
SICIANS—Canadian—20th century

Moody, Ralph. The Dry Divide. AUTHORS
—American—20th century

—The Fields of Home. YOUTHS—American—
20th century

—The Home Ranch. YOUTHS—American—
20th century

—Little Britches: Father and I Were Ranchers.
YOUTHS—American—20th century

—Man of the Family. YOUTHS—American—
20th century

—Mary Emma & Company. YOUTHS—American—20th century

—Shaking the Nickel Bush. AUTHORS—American — 20th century; YOUTHS — American—
20th century

Moore, Archie. The Archie Moore Story. BOX-
ERS—American—20th century

Moore, George. Hail and Farewell. NOVEL-
ISTS — Irish — 19th century; NOVELISTS —
Irish—20th century

Moore, Gerald. Am I Too Loud? A Musical
Autobiography. PIANISTS—English—20th
century

Morison, Samuel Eliot. One Boy's Boston,
1887-1901. HISTORIANS—American—20th
century; YOUTHS—American—19th century

Morrell, Lady Ottoline Violet Anne (Cavendish-Bentinck). Memoirs: A Study in Friendship, 1873-1915. AUTHORS—English—19th
century; AUTHORS—English—20th century

Mortlock, Bill. Lawyer, Heal Thyself! LAW-
YERS—English—20th century

Morton, Charles W. It Has Its Charms . . . .
JOURNALISTS—American—20th century

Moses, Anna Mary (Robertson). Grandma
Moses: My Life's History. PAINTERS—
American—20th century

Moss, Stirling. All But My Life. AUTOMO-
BILE RACERS—English—20th century

Mott, Frank Luther. Time Enough: Essays in
Autobiography. JOURNALISTS—American
—20th century

Mountain Wolf Woman. Mountain Wolf Woman, Sister of Crashing Thunder: The Autobiography of a Winnebago Indian. INDIAN
LEADERS—American—20th century

Muir, John. Story of My Boyhood and Youth.
IMMIGRANTS TO UNITED STATES—
19th century; NATURALISTS—American—
19th century

Mukerji, Dhan Gopal. Caste and Outcast. AU-
THORS—Indian—20th century; YOUTHS—
Indian—20th century

Mulzac, Hugh Nathaniel. A Star to Steer By.
IMMIGRANTS TO UNITED STATES—
20th century; NAVAL OFFICERS AND
OTHER SEAFARERS—American—20th century

Munch, Charles. I Am a Conductor. CON-
DUCTORS—French—20th century

Munthe, Axel Martin Fredrik. Story of San
Michele. PHYSICIANS—Swedish—20th century

Murie, Olaus Johan. Wapiti Wilderness. BI-
OLOGISTS—American—20th century; ZO-
OLOGISTS—American—20th century

Murphy, Patricia. Glow of Candlelight: The
Story of Patricia Murphy. RESTAURA-
TEURS—American—20th century

Murphy, Robert Daniel. Diplomat Among Warriors. STATESMEN—American—20th century

Musial, Stanley Frank. Stan Musial: "The
Man's" Own Story. BASEBALL PLAYERS
—American—20th century

Mydans, Carl M. More Than Meets the Eye.
JOURNALISTS — American — 20th century;
PHOTOGRAPHERS—American—20th century

Najafi, Najmeh. Persia Is My Heart. SOCIAL
WORKERS—Iranian—20th century

—Reveille for a Persian Village. SOCIAL
WORKERS—Iranian—20th century

Nansen, Odd. From Day to Day. SOLDIERS
—Norwegian—20th century

Nehru, Jawaharlal. Toward Fredom. STATES-
MEN—Indian—20th century

Neutra, Richard Joseph. Life and Shape.
ARCHITECTS—American—20th century; IM-
MIGRANTS TO UNITED STATES—20th
century

Newman, John Henry. Apologia pro Vita Sua.
RELIGIOUS LEADERS—English—19th century

Nicolson, Sir Harold George. Diaries and Letters: v. 1, 1930-1939. STATESMEN—English—20th century

Nixon, Richard Milhous. Six Crises. STATES-
MEN—American—20th century

Nizer, Louis. My Life in Court. LAWYERS—
American—20th century

Nkrumah, Kwame. Ghana: The Autobiography of Kwame Nkrumah. PRESIDENTS—
Ghanian—20th century

Noyes, Alfred. Two Worlds for Memory. PO-
ETS—English—20th century

Nugent, Elliott. Events Leading Up to the
Comedy: An Autobiography. ACTORS—
American—20th century

O'Brady, Frédéric. All Told. ACTORS—French
—20th century

O'Casey, Sean. Drums Under the Windows.
PLAYWRIGHTS—Irish—20th century

—I Knock at the Door: Swift Glances Back to
Things That Made Me. PLAYWRIGHTS—
Irish—20th century

—Inishfallen, Fare Thee Well. PLAY-
WRIGHTS—Irish—20th century

—Mirror in My House: The Autobiographies
of Sean O'Casey. PLAYWRIGHTS—Irish—
20th century

O'Casey, Sean—*Continued*
—Pictures in the Hallway. PLAYWRIGHTS—Irish—20th century
—Rose and Crown. PLAYWRIGHTS—Irish—20th century
—Sunset and Evening Star. PLAYWRIGHTS—Irish—20th century
O'Connor, Frank. An Only Child. YOUTHS—Irish—20th century
O'Donoghue, John. In a Quiet Land. AUTHORS—Irish—20th century
—In Kerry Long Ago. AUTHORS—Irish—20th century
O'Faoláin, Sean. Vive Moi! AUTHORS—Irish—20th century
Offenberg, Bernice. The Angel of Hell's Kitchen. SOCIAL WORKERS—American—20th century
O'Hara, Mary. A Musical in the Making. NOVELISTS—American—20th century
Opie, June. Over My Dead Body. VICTIMS OF POLIO—New Zealand—20th century
Orozco, José Clemente. An Autobiography. PAINTERS—Mexican—20th century
Oursler, Fulton. Behold This Dreamer! An Autobiography. AUTHORS—American—20th century
Owens, William A. This Stubborn Soil. FARMERS—American—20th century; YOUTHS—American—20th century

Paar, Jack. I Kid You Not. ACTORS—American—20th century
Pagnol, Marcel. The Days Were Too Short. PLAYWRIGHTS — French — 20th century; YOUTHS—French—20th century
—The Time of Secrets. PLAYWRIGHTS—French—20th century; YOUTHS—French—20th century
Paige, Leroy ("Satchel"). Maybe I'll Pitch Forever. BASEBALL PLAYERS—American—20th century
Pak, Induk. The Hour of the Tiger. EDUCATORS—Korean—20th century
Pak, Jong Yong. Korean Boy. YOUTHS—Korean—20th century
Papashvily, George. Anything Can Happen. IMMIGRANTS TO UNITED STATES—20th century
Parks, Gordon. A Choice of Weapons. PHOTOGRAPHERS—American—20th century
Parsons, Louella (Oettinger). Tell It to Louella. JOURNALISTS—American—20th century
Pasternak, Boris Leonidovich. I Remember: Sketch for an Autobiography. AUTHORS—Russian—20th century
—Safe Conduct. AUTHORS—Russian—20th century
Patten, Gilbert. Frank Merriwell's "Father": An Autobiography by "Burt L. Standish." AUTHORS—American—20th century
Patterson, Floyd. Victory Over Myself. BOXERS—American—20th century
Patton, George Smith. War as I Knew It. SOLDIERS—American—20th century

Pearson, Grant H. My Life of High Adventure. CONSERVATIONISTS—American—20th century; MOUNTAINEERS—American—20th century
Pearson, Haydn Sanborn. New England Flavor: Memories of a Country Boyhood. NATURALISTS—American—20th century; YOUTHS—American—20th century
—The New England Year. NATURALISTS—American—20th century; YOUTHS—American—20th century
Pearson, Hesketh. Hesketh Pearson, by Himself. AUTHORS—English—20th century
Peattie, Donald Culross. Road of a Naturalist. BOTANISTS—American—20th century
Pellet, Elizabeth (Eyre). "That Pellet Woman!" STATESMEN—American—20th century
Penney, James Cash. View from the Ninth Decade: Jottings from a Merchant's Day-Book. BUSINESSMEN—American—20th century
Pepys, Samuel. Diary. AUTHORS—English—17th century
—Everybody's Pepys: The Diary of Samuel Pepys, 1660-1669, abridged from the complete copyright text. AUTHORS—English—17th century
—Passages from the Diary of Samuel Pepys. AUTHORS—English—17th century
Percy, William Alexander. Lanterns on the Levee: Recollections of a Planter's Son. AUTHORS—American—20th century
Perkins, Faith. My Fight with Arthritis. VICTIMS OF ARTHRITIS—American—20th century
Perkins, Maxwell Evarts. Editor to Author: The Letters of Maxwell E. Perkins. JOURNALISTS—American—20th century; PUBLISHERS—American—20th century
Perrin, Henri. Priest and Worker: The Autobiography. RELIGIOUS LEADERS—French—20th century
Pershing, John Joseph. My Experiences in the World War. SOLDIERS—American—20th century
Peterson, Virgilia. A Matter of Life and Death. JOURNALISTS—American—20th century
Pettit, Robert. Bob Pettit: The Drive Within Me. BASKETBALL PLAYERS—American—20th century
Piatigorsky, Gregor. Cellist. CELLISTS—Russian—20th century
Picon, Molly. So Laugh a Little. ACTORS—American—20th century
Piersall, James Anthony. Fear Strikes Out: The Jim Piersall Story. BASEBALL PLAYERS—American—20th century
Podhajsky, Alois. My Dancing White Horses. HORSE TRAINERS—Austrian—20th century
Polo, Marco. The Travels of Marco Polo. EXPLORERS—Italian—13th century
Porter, Cole. The Cole Porter Story. COMPOSERS—American—20th century

Potter, Beatrix. Art of Beatrix Potter. AU-THORS—English—20th century; ILLUSTRA-TORS—English—20th century
—The Journal of Beatrix Potter from 1881 to 1897. AUTHORS—English—20th century; ILLUSTRATORS—English—20th century
Pound, Ezra Loomis. Letters of Ezra Pound, 1907-1941. POETS—American—20th century
Powdermaker, Hortense. Stranger and Friend: The Way of an Anthropologist. ANTHRO-POLOGISTS—American—20th century
Prescott, Orville. Five-Dollar Gold Piece: The Development of a Point of View. CRITICS—American—20th century
Priestley, John Boynton. Margin Released: A Writer's Reminiscences and Reflections. NOVELISTS—English—20th century
—Midnight on the Desert: Being an Excursion into Autobiography During a Winter in America, 1935-36. NOVELISTS—English—20th century
Prouty, Olive (Higgins). Pencil Shavings: Memoirs. NOVELISTS—American—20th century
Pupin, Michael Idvorsky. From Immigrant to Inventor. IMMIGRANTS TO UNITED STATES — 19th century; INVENTORS — American — 20th century; PHYSICISTS — American—20th century
Putnam, Peter. "Keep Your Head Up, Mr. Putnam!" BLIND—American—20th century
Quant, Mary. Quant by Quant. COSTUME DESIGNERS—English—20th century
Quennell, Peter. The Sign of the Fish. AU-THORS—English—20th century
Rama Rau, Santha. Gifts of Passage. AU-THORS—Indian—20th century
Randall, Clarence Belden. Adventures in Friendship. BUSINESSMEN — American — 20th century
—Sixty-five Plus: The Joy and Challenge of the Years of Retirement. BUSINESSMEN—American—20th century
Rankin, William H. The Man Who Rode the Thunder. AVIATORS—American—20th century
Raphael, Chaim. Memoirs of a Special Case. AUTHORS—English—20th century
Raverat, Gwendolen Mary (Darwin). Period Piece. ILLUSTRATORS—English—20th century; YOUTHS—English—19th century
Rawlings, Marjorie (Kinnan). Cross Creek. NOVELISTS—American—20th century
Reeder, Russell Potter. Born at Reveille. AU-THORS — American — 20th century; SOL-DIERS—American—20th century
Regler, Gustav. The Owl of Minerva: The Au-tobiography of Gustav Regler; tr. from the German by Norman Denny. AUTHORS—German—20th century
Reis, Claire (Raphael). Composers, Conductors and Critics. COMPOSERS—American—20th century
Renard, Jules. Journal; ed. and tr. by Louise Bogan and Elizabeth Roget. AUTHORS—French—19th century; AUTHORS—French—20th century

Rexroth, Kenneth. An Autobiographical Novel. POETS—American—20th century
Reynolds, Quentin James. By Quentin Rey-nolds. JOURNALISTS—American—20th century
Rice, Elmer L. Minority Report: An Autobiog-raphy. PLAYWRIGHTS — American — 20th century
Rice, Grantland. The Tumult and the Shouting: My Life in Sport. JOURNALISTS—American—20th century; SPORTSWRITERS—Ameri-can—20th century
Ridgway, Matthew Bunker. Soldier: The Mem-oirs of Matthew B. Ridgway as Told to H. H. Martin. SOLDIERS—American—20th century
Riedesel, Friederike Charlotte Luise (von Mas-sow) Freifrau von. Baroness von Riedesel and the American Revolution; tr. by Marvin L. Brown, Jr. WIVES OF FAMOUS MEN—German—18th century
Riis, Jacob August. Making of an American. IMMIGRANTS TO UNITED STATES—19th century; JOURNALISTS—American—19th century; JOURNALISTS—American—20th century
Rinehart, Mary (Roberts). My Story. NOVEL-ISTS—American—20th century
Ritchie, Jean. Singing Family of the Cumber-lands. SINGERS—American—20th century
Rivett-Carnac, Charles. Pursuit in the Wilder-ness. POLICE—Canadian—20th century
Rizk, Salom. Syrian Yankee. IMMIGRANTS TO UNITED STATES—20th century
Roberts, Kenneth Lewis. I Wanted to Write. NOVELISTS—American—20th century
Robinson, John Roosevelt. Breakthrough to the Big League: The Story of Jackie Robinson. BASEBALL PLAYERS—American—20th century
—Wait Till Next Year. BASEBALL PLAYERS—American—20th century
Rockefeller, John William. The Poor Rocke-fellers. BUSINESSMEN—American—20th century
Rockwell, Norman. Norman Rockwell. IL-LUSTRATORS — American — 20th century; PAINTERS—American—20th century
Rogers, Will. Autobiography; ed. by Donald Day. HUMORISTS—American—20th century
Romulo, Carlos Pena. I Walked with Heroes. STATESMEN—Philippine—20th century
Roosevelt, Eleanor Butler (Alexander). Day be-fore Yesterday: The Reminiscences of Mrs. Theodore Roosevelt, Jr. WIVES OF FA-MOUS MEN—American—20th century
Roosevelt, Eleanor (Roosevelt). The Autobiog-raphy of Eleanor Roosevelt. AUTHORS—American—20th century; WIVES OF FA-MOUS MEN—American—20th century
—On My Own. AUTHORS—American—20th century; WIVES OF FAMOUS MEN—American—20th century

Roosevelt, Eleanor (Roosevelt)—*Continued*
—This I Remember.   AUTHORS—American—
    20th century; WIVES OF FAMOUS MEN
    —American—20th century
—This Is My Story.   AUTHORS—American—
    20th century; WIVES OF FAMOUS MEN
    —American—20th century
—Your Teens and Mine.   AUTHORS—Ameri-
    can—20th century; WIVES OF FAMOUS
    MEN—American—20th century
Roosevelt, Franklin Delano.   F. D. R.: His
    Personal Letters; ed. by Elliott Roosevelt.
    PRESIDENTS—American—20th century
Roosevelt, Theodore.   Autobiography of Theo-
    dore Roosevelt, Condensed from the Original
    Edition; ed. by Wayne Andrews.   PRESI-
    DENTS — American — 20th century; SOL-
    DIERS—American—19th century
—Theodore Roosevelt Treasury: A Self-Portrait
    from His Writings; comp. by Hermann
    Hagedorn.   PRESIDENTS—American—20th
    century; SOLDIERS—American—19th centu-
    ry
—Theodore Roosevelt's Letters to His Chil-
    dren; ed. by J. B. Bishop.   PRESIDENTS—
    American—20th century; SOLDIERS—Amer-
    ican—19th century
Rose, Anna Perrott.   Room for One More.
    YOUTHS—American—20th century
Rothenstein, Sir John Knewstub Maurice.
    Summer's Lease: Autobiography, 1901-1938.
    CRITICS—English—20th century; MUSEUM
    DIRECTORS—English—20th century
Rousseau, Jean Jacques.   Confessions.   AU-
    THORS—French—18th century; PHILOSO-
    PHERS—French—18th century
Ruark, Robert Chester.   Old Man and the Boy.
    AUTHORS—American—20th century
—The Old Man's Boy Grows Older.   AUTHORS
    —American—20th century
Rubinstein, Helena.   My Life for Beauty.
    BUSINESSMEN — American — 20th century;
    COSMETICIANS—American—20th century;
    IMMIGRANTS TO UNITED STATES—20th
    century
Ruggles, Ora.   The Healing Heart.   OCCUPA-
    TIONAL THERAPISTS — American — 20th
    century
Russell, Robert.   To Catch an Angel: Adven-
    tures in the World I Cannot See.   BLIND
    —American—20th century
Russell, William Felton.   Go Up for Glory.
    BASKETBALL   PLAYERS—American—20th
    century
Ruth, George Herman.   Babe Ruth Story.
    BASEBALL PLAYERS—American—20th cen-
    tury
Saarinen, Eero.   Eero Saarinen on His Work:
    A Selection of Buildings with Statements by
    the Architect; ed. by Aline B. Saarinen.
    ARCHITECTS—American—20th century; IM-
    MIGRANTS TO UNITED STATES—20th
    century

Sahgal, Nayantara (Pandit).   From Fear Set Free.
    DAUGHTERS OF FAMOUS WOMEN—In-
    dian—20th century
Saint Exupéry, Antoine de.   Airman's Odyssey.
    AUTHORS—French—20th century; AVIA-
    TORS—French—20th century
St.   John, Robert.   Foreign   Correspondent.
    JOURNALISTS—American—20th century
—This Was My World.   JOURNALISTS—Amer-
    ican—20th century
Saint-Simon, Louis de Rouvroy, Duc de.   The
    Age of Magnificence: The Memoirs of Saint-
    Simon; ed. and tr. by Sanche de Gramont.
    AUTHORS—French—18th century
Samuel, Maurice.   Little Did I Know.   AU-
    THORS—American—20th century; IMMI-
    GRANTS TO UNITED STATES—20th cen-
    tury
Sandburg, Carl.   Always the Young Strangers.
    AUTHORS—American—20th century
—Prairie-Town Boy: Taken from "Always the
    Young Strangers."   AUTHORS—American—
    20th century
Sanders, George.   Memoirs of a Professional
    Cad.   ACTORS—Scottish—20th century
Santayana, George.   Persons and Places.   PHI-
    LOSOPHERS—American—20th century; PO-
    ETS—American—20th century
Saroyan, William.   Here Comes, There Goes,
    You Know Who.   AUTHORS—American—
    20th century
—Not Dying.   AUTHORS—American—20th cen-
    tury
Sarton, May.   I Knew a Phoenix: Sketches for
    an Autobiography.   AUTHORS—American—
    20th century
Sartre, Jean Paul.   The Words; tr. from the
    French by Bernard Frechtman.   AUTHORS
    —French—20th century; PHILOSOPHERS—
    French—20th century
Saund, Dalip Singh.   Congressman from India.
    IMMIGRANTS TO UNITED STATES—
    20th century; STATESMEN—American—20th
    century
Scarne, John.   The Odds Against Me: An Auto-
    biography.   MAGICIANS—American—20th
    century
Schary, Dore.   For Special Occasions.   IMMI-
    GRANTS TO UNITED STATES—20th cen-
    tury; MOTION PICTURE PRODUCERS—
    American—20th century; YOUTHS—Ameri-
    can—20th century
Schlesinger, Arthur Meier, 1888-1965.   In Retro-
    spect: The History of a Historian.   EDUCA-
    TORS—American—20th century; HISTORI-
    ANS—American—20th century
Schnabel, Artur.   My Life and Music.   PIA-
    NISTS—Austrian—20th century
Schoenberg, Arnold.   Letters; ed. by Erwin
    Stein; tr. from the German by Eithne Wil-
    kins and Ernst Kaiser.   COMPOSERS—Aus-
    trian—20th century
Schoenstein, Ralph.   The Block.   JOURNAL-
    ISTS—American—20th century; YOUTHS—
    American—20th century

Schrader, Herbert Ludwig. No Other Way: The Story of a Doctor from East Germany; tr. from the German by E. Osers. PHYSICIANS—German—20th century

Schurz, Carl. Autobiography; an abridgment in one volume by Wayne Andrews. IMMIGRANTS TO UNITED STATES—19th century; JOURNALISTS—American—19th century; SOLDIERS—American—19th century; STATESMEN—American—19th century

Schweitzer, Albert. Memoirs of Childhood and Youth. ORGANISTS—French—20th century; PHILOSOPHERS — French — 20th century; PHYSICIANS — French — 20th century; YOUTHS—French—19th century

—On the Edge of the Primeval Forest & More from the Primeval Forest: Experiences and Observations of a Doctor in Equatorial Africa. PHYSICIANS—French—20th century

—Out of My Life and Thought: An Autobiography; tr. by C. T. Campion. ORGANISTS—French—20th century; PHILOSOPHERS—French—20th century; PHYSICIANS—French—20th century

Scott, Peter. The Eye of the Wind. ORNITHOLOGISTS — English — 20th century; PAINTERS—English—20th century

Scott, Robert Falcon. Scott's Last Expedition, from the Personal Journals of Robert Scott. EXPLORERS—English—20th century

Scott, Robert Lee. Boring a Hole in the Sky: Six Million Miles with a Fighter Pilot. AVIATORS—American—20th century

Scovel, Myra. The Chinese Ginger Jars. RELIGIOUS LEADERS—American—20th century

Seagrave, Gordon Stifler. The Life of a Burma Surgeon. PHYSICIANS—American—20th century

—My Hospital in the Hills. PHYSICIANS—American—20th century

Sedgwick, Ellery. Happy Profession. JOURNALISTS—American—20th century

Segal, Lore. Other People's Houses. IMMIGRANTS TO UNITED STATES—20th century

Senger und Etterlin, Fridolin von. Neither Fear nor Hope; tr. from the German by George Malcolm. SOLDIERS—German—20th century

Seton, Ernest Thompson. Trail of an Artist-Naturalist: The Autobiography of Ernest Thompson Seton. AUTHORS—American—19th century; AUTHORS—American—20th century; ILLUSTRATORS—American—19th century; ILLUSTRATORS—American—20th century; NATURALISTS—American—19th century; NATURALISTS—American—20th century

Sevareid, Arnold Eric. Not So Wild a Dream. JOURNALISTS—American—20th century

Sévigné, Marie (de Rabutin Chantal). Letters of Madame de Sévigné to Her Daughter and Her Friends; comp. by Richard Aldington. AUTHORS—French—17th century

Shaw, George Bernard. Bernard Shaw and Mrs. Patrick Campbell: Their Correspondence. CRITICS—Irish—20th century; PLAYWRIGHTS—Irish—20th century

—Collected Letters: v. 1, 1874-1897; ed. by Dan H. Laurence. CRITICS—Irish—19th century; PLAYWRIGHTS—Irish—19th century

—Sixteen Self Sketches. CRITICS—Irish—20th century; PLAYWRIGHTS—Irish—20th century

Shaw, Wilbur. Gentlemen, Start Your Engines. AUTOMOBILE RACERS—American—20th century

Shawn, Ted. One Thousand and One Night Stands. DANCERS—American—20th century

Shelby, Carroll Hall. The Cobra Story. AUTOMOBILE RACERS—American—20th century

Shelley, Mary Wollstonecraft (Godwin). Letters; ed. by F. L. Jones. NOVELISTS—English—19th century; WIVES OF FAMOUS MEN—English—19th century

—Mary Shelley's Journal; ed. by F. L. Jones. NOVELISTS—English—19th century; WIVES OF FAMOUS MEN—English—19th century

Shepard, Ernest Howard. Drawn from Life. ILLUSTRATORS—English—20th century

Sherman, William Tecumseh. Memoirs of General William T. Sherman, by Himself. SOLDIERS—American—19th century

Sherrill, Henry Knox, Bp. Among Friends. RELIGIOUS LEADERS—American—20th century

Short, Wayne. The Cheechakoes. EXPLORERS—American—20th century

Shotwell, James Thomson. Autobiography. HISTORIANS—Canadian—20th century

Shute, Nevil. Slide Rule: The Autobiography of an Engineer. AUTHORS—English—20th century; ENGINEERS, AERONAUTICAL—English—20th century

Sinclair, Upton Beall. Autobiography. NOVELISTS—American—20th century

Siniavskiĭ, Andreĭ Donat'evich. On Trial: The Soviet State versus "Abram Tertz" and "Nikolai Arzhak"; tr. by Max Hayward. AUTHORS—Russian—20th century

Sitwell, Dame Edith. Taken Care Of: The Autobiography of Edith Sitwell. POETS—English—20th century

Sitwell, Sir Osbert. Great Morning! AUTHORS—English—20th century

—Laughter in the Next Room. AUTHORS—English—20th century

—Left Hand, Right Hand! AUTHORS—English—20th century

—Noble Essences: A Book of Characters. AUTHORS—English—20th century

—Tales My Father Taught Me: An Evocation of Extravagant Episodes. AUTHORS—English—20th century

Skinner, Cornelia Otis. Family Circle. ACTORS—American—20th century

Slayden, Ellen (Maury). Washington Wife: Journal of Ellen Slayden from 1897-1919. WIVES OF FAMOUS MEN—American—20th century

Sloan, Alfred Pritchard. My Years with General Motors; ed. by John McDonald and Catharine Stevens. INDUSTRIALISTS—American—20th century

Sloan, John. New York Scene: From Diaries, Notes and Correspondence, 1906-1913; ed. by Bruce St. John. PAINTERS—American—20th century

Sloop, Mary T. (Martin). Miracle in the Hills. PHYSICIANS—American—20th century

Smith, Dean C. By the Seat of My Pants. AVIATORS—American—20th century

Smith, Emma. Cornish Waif's Story: An Autobiography. YOUTHS—English—19th century

Smith, Frank Ellis. Congressman from Mississippi. STATESMEN—American—20th century

Smith, Frank Kingston. Flights of Fancy. AVIATORS—American—20th century

Smith, Harry Allen. To Hell in a Handbasket. HUMORISTS—American—20th century

Smith, Kate. Upon My Lips a Song. SINGERS—American—20th century

Smith, Lillian Eugenia. The Journey. AUTHORS—American—20th century

—Memory of a Large Christmas. AUTHORS—American—20th century; YOUTHS—American—20th century

Smith, Paul Clifford. Personal File. JOURNALISTS—American—20th century

Smith, Sir Sydney Alfred. Mostly Murder. CRIMINOLOGISTS—English—20th century; PHYSICIANS—English—20th century

Smith, Willie. Music on My Mind: The Memoirs of an American Pianist. PIANISTS—American—20th century

Snead, Samuel Jackson. The Education of a Golfer. GOLFERS—American—20th century

Snow, Carmel (White). The World of Carmel Snow. JOURNALISTS—American—20th century

Snow, Edgar. Journey to the Beginning. JOURNALISTS—American—20th century

Sone, Monica (Itoi). Nisei Daughter. YOUTHS—Japanese—20th century

Sønsteby, Gunnar Fridtjof Thurmann. Report from No. 24; ed. by Maurice Michael. SOLDIERS—Norwegian—20th century

Soo, Chin-yee. Eighth Moon: The True Story of a Young Girl's Life in Communist China. YOUTHS—Chinese—20th century

Sousa, John Philip. Marching Along: Recollections of Men, Women and Music. BANDMASTERS—American—19th century; BANDMASTERS—American—20th century; COMPOSERS—American—19th century; COMPOSERS—American—20th century

Spanier, Ginette. It Isn't All Mink. COSTUME DESIGNERS—French—20th century

Stanford, Doreen. Siberian Odyssey. ENGINEERS, MINING—English—20th century

Stanislavski, Constantin. My Life in Art. ACTORS—Russian—20th century; THEATRICAL PRODUCERS—Russian—20th century

Stanley, Sir Henry Morton. The Exploration Diaries; ed. by Richard Stanley and Alan Neame. EXPLORERS—Welsh—19th century; JOURNALISTS—Welsh—19th century

Stark, Freya Madeline. Dust in the Lion's Paw: Autobiography, 1939-1946. AUTHORS—English—20th century

Starkie, Walter Fitzwilliam. Scholars and Gypsies: An Autobiography. VIOLINISTS—Irish—20th century

Starrett, Vincent. Born in a Bookshop: Chapters from the Chicago Renascence. AUTHORS—American—20th century; BOOK COLLECTORS—American—20th century

Stefánsson, Vilhjálmur. Discovery: The Autobiography of Vilhjálmur Stefánsson. EXPLORERS—Canadian—20th century

—Friendly Arctic: The Story of Five Years in Polar Regions. EXPLORERS—Canadian—20th century

Steffens, Lincoln. The Autobiography of Lincoln Steffens. JOURNALISTS—American—19th century; JOURNALISTS—American—20th century

—Boy on Horseback; reprinted from "The Autobiography of Lincoln Steffens." JOURNALISTS—American—19th century; YOUTHS—American—19th century

Steichen, Edward. A Life in Photography. PHOTOGRAPHERS—American—20th century

Stengel, Charles Dillon ("Casey"). Casey at the Bat: The Story of My Life in Baseball. BASEBALL MANAGERS—American—20th century

Stern, Julius David. Memoirs of a Maverick Publisher. JOURNALISTS—American—20th century

Stern, Michael. An American in Rome. JOURNALISTS—American—20th century

Sterne, Maurice. Shadow and Light: The Life, Friends and Opinions of Maurice Sterne; ed. by Charlotte Leon Mayerson. IMMIGRANTS TO UNITED STATES—19th century; PAINTERS—American—20th century

Stikker, Dirk Uipko. Men of Responsibility: A Memoir. STATESMEN—Dutch—20th century

Stone, Edward Durell. The Evolution of an Architect. ARCHITECTS—American—20th century

Strainchamps, Ethel (Reed). Don't Never Say Cain't. EDUCATORS—American—20th century

Straughan, Robert P. L. Sharks, Morays, and Treasure. ICHTHYOLOGISTS—American—20th century

Strauss, Richard. A Working Friendship: The Correspondence Between Richard Strauss and Hugo Hofmannsthal; tr. by Hanns Hammelmann and Ewald Osers. COMPOSERS—German—20th century

Strausz-Hupé, Robert. In My Time. IMMI-GRANTS TO UNITED STATES—20th century; POLITICAL SCIENTISTS—Austrian—20th century

Stravinsky, Igor. An Autobiography. IMMI-GRANTS TO UNITED STATES—20th century; COMPOSERS—Russian—20th century

—Dialogues and a Diary. IMMIGRANTS TO UNITED STATES—20th century; COM-POSERS—Russian—20th century

—Expositions and Developments. IMMI-GRANTS TO UNITED STATES—20th century; COMPOSERS—Russian—20th century

—Memories and Commentaries. IMMIGRANTS TO UNITED STATES—20th century; COM-POSERS—Russian—20th century

—Themes and Episodes. IMMIGRANTS TO UNITED STATES—20th century; COMPOS-ERS—Russian—20th century

Streatfeild, Noel. A Vicarage Family: An Au-tobiographical Story. AUTHORS—English—20th century; YOUTHS—English—20th century

Stuart, Jesse. Thread That Runs So True. AU-THORS—American—20th century

Sweezy, Carl. The Arapaho Way: A Memoir of an Indian Boyhood, by Althea Bass. IN-DIAN LEADERS—American—20th century

Swing, Raymond. "Good Evening!" JOUR-NALISTS—American—20th century

Swinnerton, Frank Arthur. Figures in the Fore-ground: Literary Reminiscences, 1917-1940. AUTHORS—English—20th century

Szigeti, Joseph. With Strings Attached: Rem-iniscences and Reflections. VIOLINISTS—Hungarian—20th century

Tantri, K'tut. Revolt in Paradise. AUTHORS—American—20th century

Tariri. My Story: From Jungle Killer to Chris-tian Missionary. RELIGIOUS LEADERS—Peruvian—20th century

Tarry, Ellen. The Third Door: The Autobiog-raphy of an American Negro Woman. EDU-CATORS—American—20th century

Taylor, Sir Patrick Gordon. The Sky Beyond. AVIATORS—Australian—20th century

Teale, Edwin Way. Dune Boy: The Early Years of a Naturalist. NATURALISTS—American—20th century; YOUTHS—Ameri-can—20th century

Teilhard de Chardin, Pierre. The Making of a Mind: Letters from a Soldier-Priest, 1914-1919; tr. from the French by René Hague. ANTHROPOLOGISTS—French—20th centu-ry; GEOLOGISTS—French—20th century; PALEONTOLOGISTS—French—20th centu-ry; RELIGIOUS LEADERS—French—20th century

Tenzing, Norgay. Tiger of the Snows: The Au-tobiography of Tenzing of Everest. MOUN-TAINEERS—Nepalese—20th century

Teresa, Saint. Life. RELIGIOUS LEADERS—Spanish—16th century

Terray, Lionel. The Borders of the Impossible: From the Alps to Annapurna; tr. by Geof-frey Sutton. MOUNTAINEERS—French—20th century

Terry, Dame Ellen. Ellen Terry's Memoirs. ACTORS—English—19th century; ACTORS—English—20th century

Thompson, Mickey. Challenger: Mickey Thompson's Own Story of His Life of Speed. AUTOMOBILE RACERS—American—20th century

Thomson, Virgil. Virgil Thomson. COMPOS-ERS—American—20th century; CRITICS—American—20th century

Thoreau, Henry David. Consciousness in Con-cord: The Text of Thoreau's Hitherto "Lost Journal," (1840-1841); ed. by Perry Miller. AUTHORS—American—19th century; NATU-RALISTS—American—19th century

Thorne, Jim. Occupation: Adventure. AU-THORS—American—20th century

Thubten, Jigme Norbu. Tibet Is My Country; tr. from the German by Edward Fitzgerald. RELIGIOUS LEADERS—Tibetan—20th cen-tury

Titov, German Stepanovich. I Am Eagle! ASTRONAUTS—Russian—20th century

Tittle, Yelberton Abraham. I Pass: My Story as Told to Don Smith. FOOTBALL PLAY-ERS—American—20th century

Trahey, Jane. Life with Mother Superior. YOUTHS—American—20th century

Trapp, Maria Augusta. A Family on Wheels: Further Adventures of the Trapp Family Singers. IMMIGRANTS TO UNITED STATES—20th century; SINGERS—Austrian—20th century

—Story of the Trapp Family Singers. IMMI-GRANTS TO UNITED STATES—20th century; SINGERS—Austrian—20th century

Treviño, Elizabeth (Borton). My Heart Lies South: The Story of My Mexican Marriage. AUTHORS—American—20th century

—Where the Heart Is. AUTHORS—American—20th century

Trollope, Anthony. An Autobiography. NOV-ELISTS—English—19th century

Truman, Harry S. Memoirs: v. 1, Year of De-cisions. PRESIDENTS—American—20th century

—Memoirs: v. 2, Years of Trial and Hope. PRESIDENTS—American—20th century

—Mr. Citizen. PRESIDENTS—American—20th century

Tugwell, Rexford Guy. The Light of Other Days. ECONOMISTS—American—20th centu-ry; EDUCATORS—American—20th century

Tunis, John Roberts. A Measure of Indepen-dence. AUTHORS—American—20th century; SPORTSWRITERS—American—20th century

Tunnell, Emlen. Footsteps of a Giant. FOOT-BALL PLAYERS—American—20th century

Unitas, Johnny. Pro Quarterback: My Own Story. FOOTBALL PLAYERS—American—20th century

Untermeyer, Jean (Starr). Private Collection. POETS—American—20th century

Untermeyer, Louis. Bygones: The Recollections of Louis Untermeyer. POETS—American—20th century

Unwin, Sir Stanley. The Truth About a Publisher: An Autobiographical Record. PUBLISHERS—English—20th century

Uxkull, Boris. Arms and the Woman: The Intimate Journal of a Baltic Nobleman in the Napoleonic Wars; tr. by Joel Carmichael. SOLDIERS—Russian—19th century

Vandegrift, Alexander Archer. Once a Marine: The Memoirs of General A. A. Vandegrift, United States Marine Corps. SOLDIERS—American—20th century

Van Doren, Dorothy (Graffe). The Professor and I. AUTHORS—American—20th century; WIVES OF FAMOUS MEN—American—20th century

Van Doren, Mark. Autobiography of Mark Van Doren. AUTHORS—American—20th century

Varney, Joyce James. A Welsh Story. YOUTHS—Welsh—20th century

Vasconcelos, José. A Mexican Ulysses: An Autobiography; tr. by W. Rex Crawford. PHILOSOPHERS—Mexican—20th century; STATESMEN—Mexican—20th century

Vaughan, Richard. There Is a River. YOUTHS—Welsh—20th century

Veeck, Bill. Veeck—As in Wreck: The Autobiography of Bill Veeck. BASEBALL MANAGERS—American—20th century

Victoria. Dearest Child: Letters Between Queen Victoria and the Princess Royal, 1858-1861; ed. by Roger Fulford. QUEENS—English—19th century
—Leaves from a Journal. QUEENS—English—19th century

Vigdorova, F. Diary of a Russian Schoolteacher; tr. from the Russian by Rose Prokofieva. EDUCATORS—Russian—20th century

Villiers, Alan John. Set of the Sails: The Story of a Cape Horn Seaman. AUTHORS—Australian—20th century

Vinci, Leonardo da. Leonardo da Vinci: Life and Work, Paintings and Drawings. PAINTERS—Italian—15th century; PAINTERS—Italian—16th century; SCULPTORS—Italian—15th century; SCULPTORS—Italian—16th century

Vine, Louis L. Dogs in My Life. VETERINARIANS—American—20th century

Von Sternberg, Josef. Fun in a Chinese Laundry. MOTION PICTURE PRODUCERS—Austrian—20th century

Vrba, Rudolf. I Cannot Forgive. SCIENTISTS—Czech—20th century

Wain, John. Sprightly Running: Part of an Autobiography. NOVELISTS—English—20th century

Walpole, Horace. Selected Letters of Horace Walpole. ART COLLECTORS—English—18th century; AUTHORS—English—18th century

Walter, Bruno. Of Music and Music-Making; tr. by Paul Hamburger. CONDUCTORS—German—20th century
—Theme and Variations: An Autobiography; tr. by J. A. Galston. CONDUCTORS—German—20th century

Walton, Izaak. Compleat Angler. AUTHORS—English—17th century

Warburg, James Paul. The Long Road Home: The Autobiography of a Maverick. FINANCIERS — American — 20th century; IMMIGRANTS TO UNITED STATES—20th century

Ward, Maisie. Unfinished Business. AUTHORS—English—20th century; PUBLISHERS—English—20th century

Warner, Jack Leonard. My First Hundred Years in Hollywood. MOTION PICTURE PRODUCERS—American—20th century

Washington, Booker Taliaferro. Up from Slavery: An Autobiography. EDUCATORS—American—19th century; EDUCATORS—American—20th century

Washington, George. The George Washington Papers; ed. by Frank Donovan. PRESIDENTS—American—18th century

Waterfield, Lina (Duff-Gordon). Castle in Italy: An Autobiography. JOURNALISTS—English—20th century

Waterman, Sherry. From Another Island. AIRLINE STEWARDESSES — American — 20th century

Waters, Ethel. His Eye Is on the Sparrow: An Autobiography. ACTORS—American—20th century; POVERTY STRICKEN—American—20th century

Waugh, Alec. The Early Years of Alec Waugh. AUTHORS—English—20th century

Waugh, Evelyn. A Little Learning: An Autobiography: v. 1, The Early Years. AUTHORS—English—20th century

Webb, Beatrice (Potter). American Diary, 1898; ed. by David A. Shannon. SOCIOLOGISTS—English—19th century

Weizmann, Chaim. Trial and Error: The Autobiography of Chaim Weizmann; ed. by B. Horovitz. CHEMISTS—Israeli—20th century; PRESIDENTS—Israeli—20th century

Wells, Herbert George. George Gissing and H. G. Wells: Their Friendship and Correspondence; ed. by Royal A. Gettmann. NOVELISTS—English—19th century

West, Ellsworth Luce. Captain's Papers: A Log of Whaling and Other Sea Experiences. NAVAL OFFICERS AND OTHER SEAFARERS—American—19th century; NAVAL OFFICERS AND OTHER SEAFARERS—American—20th century

West, Jessamyn. To See the Dream. AUTHORS—American—20th century

Wheeler, Burton Kendall. Yankee from the West: The Candid, Turbulent Life Story of the Yankee-Born U. S. Senator from Montana. STATESMEN—American—20th century

Whitby, Jonathan. Bundu Doctor. PHYSI-CIANS—English—20th century

White, William Allen. Autobiography. AU-THORS—American—20th century; JOUR-NALISTS—American—20th century

Whitehouse, Arthur George Joseph. The Fledgling: An Autobiography. AVIATORS—English—20th century

Whyte, Lancelot Law. Focus and Diversions. PHILOSOPHERS—English—20th century

Widdemer, Margaret. Golden Friends I Had. AUTHORS—American—20th century

Wigoder, Devorah. Hope Is My House. RE-LIGIOUS LEADERS—American—20th century

Wilde, Oscar. The Letters of Oscar Wilde; ed. by Rupert Hart-Davis. AUTHORS—Irish—19th century

Wilder, Laura Ingalls. On the Way Home: The Diary of a Trip from South Dakota to Mansfield, Missouri, in 1894. AUTHORS—American—20th century

Wilhelmina. Lonely But Not Alone; tr. from the Dutch by John Peereboom. QUEENS—Dutch—20th century

Williams, Emlyn. George: An Early Autobiography. ACTORS—Welsh—20th century; PLAYWRIGHTS — Welsh — 20th century; YOUTHS—Welsh—20th century

Williams, William Carlos. Autobiography. AU-THORS—American—20th century; PHYSI-CIANS—American—20th century

Wilson, Arthur. Thy Will Be Done: The Autobiography of an Episcopal Minister. RE-LIGIOUS LEADERS—American—20th century

Wilson, Frank John. Special Agent: A Quarter Century with the Treasury Department and the Secret Service. DETECTIVES—American—20th century

Wilson, Woodrow. A Day of Dedication: The Essential Writings & Speeches of Woodrow Wilson; ed. by Albert Fried. EDUCATORS—American—20th century; PRESIDENTS—American—20th century

—The Priceless Gift: The Love Letters of Woodrow Wilson and Ellen Louise Axson Wilson; ed. by Eleanor Wilson McAdoo. EDUCATORS — American — 20th century; PRESIDENTS—American—20th century

Winant, John Gilbert. Letter from Grosvenor Square: An Account of a Stewardship. STATESMEN—American—20th century

Winter, Ella. And Not to Yield: An Autobiography. JOURNALISTS—American—20th century

Wise, Stephen Samuel. Challenging Years: The Autobiography of Stephen Wise. RELI-GIOUS LEADERS—American—20th century

Wister, Owen. Owen Wister Out West: His Journals and Letters; ed. by F. K. Wister. NOVELISTS—American—20th century

Wodehouse, Pelham Grenville. Author! Author! HUMORISTS—English—20th century

Wolfe, Thomas. Letters of Thomas Wolfe; ed. by Elizabeth Nowell. NOVELISTS—American—20th century

—Thomas Wolfe's Letters to His Mother Julia Elizabeth Wolfe; ed. by J. S. Terry. NOV-ELISTS—American—20th century

Wong, Jade Snow. Fifth Chinese Daughter. POTTERS—American—20th century

Wood, James Horace. Nothing But the Truth. LAWYERS—American—20th century

Wood, Peggy. Arts and Flowers. ACTORS—American—20th century

Woodward, Stanley. Paper Tiger. SPORTS-WRITERS—American—20th century

Woody, Regina Llewellyn (Jones). Dancing for Joy. DANCERS—American—20th century

Woolf, Leonard Sidney. Beginning Again: An Autobiography of the Years 1911 to 1918. AUTHORS—English—20th century

—Sowing: An Autobiography of the Years 1880 to 1904. AUTHORS—English—20th century

Woolf, Virginia (Stephen). Writer's Diary, Being Extracts from the Diary of Virginia Woolf; ed. by Leonard Woolf. NOVEL-ISTS—English—20th century

Woolman, John. Journal; ed. by Janet Whitney. ABOLITIONISTS—American—18th century; RELIGIOUS LEADERS — American — 18th century

Wordsworth, Dorothy. Journals; ed. by E. de Selincourt. RELATIVES OF FAMOUS MEN—English—19th century

Woytinsky, Wladimir Savelievich. Stormy Passage: A Personal History Through Two Russian Revolutions to Democracy and Freedom, 1905-1960. ECONOMISTS—American—20th century; IMMIGRANTS TO UNITED STATES—20th century

Wright, Frank Lloyd. Frank Lloyd Wright: An Autobiography. ARCHITECTS—American—20th century

—A Testament. ARCHITECTS—American—20th century

Wright, Richard. Black Boy: A Record of Childhood and Youth. NOVELISTS—American—20th century; YOUTHS—American—20th century

Wright, Wilbur and Wright, Orville. How We Invented the Airplane; ed. by Fred C. Kelly. AVIATORS—American—20th century

—Miracle at Kitty Hawk: The Letters of Wilbur and Orville Wright; ed. by F. C. Kelly. AVIATORS—American—20th century

Wynn, Keenan. Ed Wynn's Son. ACTORS—American—20th century

Ybarra, Thomas Russell. Young Man of Caracas. SOLDIERS—Venezuelan—20th century; YOUTHS—Venezuelan—20th century

Yeats, William Butler. Autobiography, Consisting of Reveries over Childhood and Youth, The Trembling of the Veil, and Dramatis Personae. AUTHORS—Irish—20th century

Young, Desmond. All the Best Years. JOUR-
NALISTS—English—20th century

Zaharias, Mildred (Didrikson). This Life I've
Led: My Autobiography. ATHLETES—American—20th century; GOLFERS—American—
20th century

Ziegfeld, Patricia. The Ziegfelds' Girl: Confessions of an Abnormally Happy Childhood.
DAUGHTERS OF FAMOUS MEN—Ameri-
can — 20th century; YOUTHS — American —
20th century

Zimmerman, Isidore. Punishment Without
Crime: The True Story of a Man Who Spent
Twenty-four Years in Prison for a Crime He
Did Not Commit. PRISONERS—American
—20th century

Zinsser, Hans. As I Remember Him: The Biography of R. S. BACTERIOLOGISTS—
American—20th century

Zweig, Stefan. World of Yesterday: An Autobiography. AUTHORS—Austrian—20th century

INDEX

DIRECTORY OF PUBLISHERS
AND DISTRIBUTORS

A.L.A. American Library Association, 50 E Huron St, Chicago, Ill. 60611

Abelard-Schuman. Abelard-Schuman, Ltd, 6 W 57th St, New York, N.Y. 10019

Abingdon. Abingdon Press, 201 8th Av S, Nashville, Tenn. 37203

Abrams. Harry N. Abrams, Inc. 6 W 57th St, New York, N.Y. 10019

Aero. Aero Pubs, Inc, 329 Aviation Rd, Fallbrook, Calif. 92028

Am. Bk. American Book Company, 55 5th Av, New York, N.Y. 10003

Am. Federation of Arts. Am. Federation of Arts, 41 E 65th St, New York, N.Y. 10021

Am. Heritage. American Heritage Publishing Company, Inc. 551 5th Av, New York, N.Y. 10017

Am. Medical Assn. American Medical Association, 535 N Dearborn St, Chicago, Ill. 60610

Antioch Press. Antioch Press, Yellow Springs, Ohio 45387

Appleton. Appleton-Century-Crofts, 440 Park Av S, New York, N.Y. 10016

Arco. Arco Publishing Company, Inc. 219 Park Av S, New York, N.Y. 10003

Ariel Bks. See Farrar

Arnold. Edward Arnold (Publishers) Ltd, 41 Maddox St, P.O. Box 482, London, W.1, England

Assn. Press. Association Press (Nat. Council of Y.M.C.A.'s), 291 Broadway, New York, N.Y. 10007

Associated Booksellers. Associated Booksellers, 1582 Post Rd, Westport, Conn. 06880

Associated Press. See Golden Press

Associated Pubs. Associated Publishers, Inc. 1538 9th St, N.W. Washington, D.C. 20001

Atheneum. Atheneum Publishers, 122 E 42d St, New York, N.Y. 10017

Bantam. Bantam Books, Inc. 271 Madison Av, New York, N.Y. 10016

Barnes. A. S. Barnes & Company, Inc, Forsgate Dr, Cranbury, N.J. 08512

Barnes & Noble. Barnes & Noble, Inc, 105 5th Av, New York, N.Y. 10003

Barre. Barre Publishers, South St, Barre, Mass. 01005

Basic Bks. Basic Books, Inc. Publishers, 404 Park Av S, New York, N.Y. 10016

Beacon Press. Beacon Press, 25 Beacon St, Boston, Mass. 02108

Beechhurst Press. See Barnes

Biblo & Tannen. Biblo & Tannen Booksellers & Publishers, Inc, 63 4th Av, New York, N.Y. 10003

Black. Adam & Charles Black, Ltd, 4-6 Soho Sq, London, W.1, England

Blair. John F. Blair, Publisher, 404 North Carolina National Bank Bldg, Winston-Salem, N.C. 27101

Bobbs. Bobbs-Merrill Company, Inc, 4300 W 62d St, Indianapolis, Ind. 46206

Bond Wheelwright. The Bond Wheelwright Company, Porter's Landing, Freeport, Me. 04032

Bookman Associates. See Twayne

Bowker. R. R. Bowker Co. 1180 Av of the Americas, New York, N.Y. 10036

Braziller. George Braziller, Inc, 1 Park Av, New York, N.Y. 10016

British Bk Centre. The British Book Centre, Inc, 122 E 55th St, New York, N.Y. 10022

Bro-Dart Foundation. 56 Earl St, Newark, N.J. 07114

Bruce. Bruce Publishing Company, 400 N. Broadway, Milwaukee, Wis. 53201

Cambridge. Cambridge University Press, 32 E 57th St, New York, N.Y. 10022

Cape. Jonathan Cape, Ltd, 30 Bedford Sq, London, W.C.1, England

Cassell. Cassell & Company, Ltd, 35 Red Lion Sq, London, W.C.1, England

Cattell. The Jacques Cattell Press, Box 5001, Tempe, Ariz. 85281

Caxton. Caxton Printers, Ltd, Caldwell, Idaho 83605

Century House. Century House, Inc, Watkins Glen, N.Y. 14891

Channel. Channel Press, 250 Park Av, New York, N.Y. 10017

Childrens Press. Childrens Press, 1224 W Van Buren St, Chicago, Ill. 60607

Chilmark. Chilmark Press, Inc, 80 Irving Pl, New York, N.Y. 10003

Chilton. Chilton Company, Trade Book Division, 401 Walnut St, Philadelphia, Pa. 19106

Christian Science Pub. Christian Science Publishing Society, 1 Norway St, Boston, Mass. 02115

Citadel. Citadel Press, Inc, 222 Park Av. S, New York, N.Y. 10003

Clarke & Way. Clarke & Way, October House, Inc, 55 W 13th St, New York, N.Y. 10011

Clonmore. Clonmore & Reynolds, Ltd, 29 Kildare St, Dublin, Ireland

Coleridge Press. See Taplinger

Collier Bks. Collier Books. See Macmillan

Collins. William Collins Sons & Co., Ltd, 215 Park Av S, New York, N.Y. 10003

Columbia Univ. Columbia University Press, 440 W 110th St, New York, N.Y. 10025

Concordia. Concordia Publishing House, 3558 S Jefferson Av, St. Louis, Mo. 63118

Constable. Constable & Co, Ltd, 10-12 Orange St, London, W.C.2, England

Cooper Sq. Cooper Square Publishers, Inc, 59 4th Av, New York, N.Y. 10003

Cornell Univ. Cornell University Press, 124 Roberts Pl, Ithaca, N.Y. 14850

Coward-McCann. Coward-McCann, Inc, 200 Madison Av, New York, N.Y. 10016

Criterion Bks. Criterion Books, Inc, 6 W 57th St, New York, N.Y. 10019

Crowell. Thomas Y. Crowell Company, 201 Park Av S, New York, N.Y. 10003

Crown. Crown Publishers, Inc, 419 Park Av S, New York, N.Y. 10016

Day. The John Day Company, 62 W 45th St, New York, N.Y. 10036

Delacorte. See Dial

Denison. T. S. Denison & Company, Inc, 5100 W 82d St, Minneapolis, Minn. 55431

Devin-Adair. The Devin-Adair Company, 23 E 26th St, New York, N.Y. 10010

Dial. The Dial Press, Inc, 750 3d Av, New York, N.Y. 10017

Dietz. Dietz Press, Inc, 109 E Cary St, Richmond, Va. 23219

Dodd. Dodd, Mead & Company, 79 Madison Av, New York, N.Y. 10016

Doubleday. Doubleday & Company, Inc, 277 Park Av, New York, N.Y. 10017

Dover. Dover Publications, Inc, 180 Varick St, New York, N.Y. 10014

Duell. Duell, Sloan & Pearce, 250 Park Av, New York, N.Y. 10017

Dufour. Dufour Editions, Inc, Chester Springs, Pa. 19425

Duke Univ. Duke University Press, Box 6697, College Station, Durham, N.C. 27708

Dutton. E. P. Dutton & Company, Inc, 201 Park Av S, New York, N.Y. 10003

Encyc. Britannica. Encyclopaedia Britannica, Inc, 425 N Michigan Av, Chicago, Ill. 60611

Eriksson. Paul S. Eriksson, Inc, 119 W 57th St, New York, N.Y. 10019

Essential Bks. Essential Books, Inc. See Oxford

Evans. M. Evans & Company, Inc, 216 E 49th St, New York, N.Y. 10017

Farrar. Farrar, Straus & Giroux, Inc, 19 Union Sq W, New York, N.Y. 10003

Faxon. F. W. Faxon Company, 515-25 Hyde Park Av, Boston, Mass. 02131

Fell. Frederick Fell, Inc, 386 Park Av. S, New York, N.Y. 10016

Ferguson. J. G. Ferguson Publishing Company, 6 N Michigan Av, Chicago, Ill. 60602

Fleet. Fleet Press Corporation, 156 5th Av, New York, N.Y. 10010

Follett. Follett Publishing Company, 1010 W Washington Blvd, Chicago, Ill. 60607

Fortress Press. Fortress Press, 2900 Queen Lane, Philadelphia, Pa. 19129

Four Winds Press. Four Winds Press, 50 W 44th St, New York, N.Y. 10036

Franciscan Herald. Franciscan Herald Press, 1434 W 51st St, Chicago, Ill. 60609

Free Press. The Free Press, 866 3d Av, New York, N.Y. 10022

French. Samuel French, Inc, 25 W 45th St, New York, N.Y. 10036

Friendship Press. Friendship Press, 475 Riverside Drive, New York, N.Y. 10027

Funk. Funk & Wagnalls, 380 Madison Av, New York, N.Y. 10017

Gale Res. Gale Research Company, 1400 Book Tower, Detroit, Mich. 48226

Garden City. Garden City Books. See Doubleday

Garrard. Garrard Publishing Company, 1607 N Market St, Champaign, Ill. 61820

Geis. Bernard Geis Associates, 128 E 56th St, New York, N.Y. 10022

Ginn. Ginn & Company, Statler Bldg, Back Bay P.O. 191, Boston, Mass. 02117

Golden Press. Golden Press, 850 3d Av, New York, N.Y. 10022

Grosset. Grosset & Dunlap, Inc, 51 Madison Av, New York, N.Y. 10010

Grossman. Grossman Publishers, 125A E 19th St, New York, N.Y. 10003

Grove. Grove Press, Inc, 80 University Pl, New York, N.Y. 10003

Hale. E. M. Hale & Company, 1201 S Hastings Way, Eau Claire, Wis. 54701

Hamilton. Hamish Hamilton, Ltd, 90 Great Russell St, London, W.C.1, England

Hammond. Hammond Incorporated, Maplewood, N.J. 07040

Hanover House. See Doubleday

Harcourt. Harcourt, Brace & World, Inc, 757 3d Av, New York, N.Y. 10017

Harper. Harper & Row, Publishers, 49 E 33d St, New York, N.Y. 10016

Harvard Univ. Harvard University Press, 79 Garden St, Cambridge, Mass. 02138

Harvey. Harvey House, Inc., Publishers, Irvington-on-Hudson, N.Y. 10533

Hastings House. Hastings House, Publishers, Inc, 10 E 40th St, New York, N.Y. 10016

Hawthorn. Hawthorn Books, Inc, 70 5th Av, New York, N.Y. 10011

Heineman. James H. Heineman, Inc, 60 E 42d St, New York, N.Y. 10017

Helicon Press. Helicon Press, Inc, 1120 N Calvert St, Baltimore, Md. 21202

Hendricks House. Hendricks House, Inc, Publishers, 103 Park Av, New York, N.Y. 10007

Herder. Herder & Herder, Inc, 232 Madison Av, New York, N.Y. 10016

Hill & Wang. Hill & Wang, Inc, 141 5th Av, New York, N.Y. 10010

Holiday. Holiday House, 18 E 56th St, New York, N.Y. 10022

Holt. Holt, Rinehart & Winston, Inc, 383 Madison Av, New York, N.Y. 10017

Horizon. Horizon Press, 156 5th Av, New York, N.Y. 10010

Horn Bk. Horn Book, Inc, 585 Boylston St, Boston, Mass. 02116

Houghton. Houghton Mifflin Company, 2 Park St, Boston, Mass. 02107

Howell-North. Howell-North Press, 1050 Parker St, Berkeley, California 94710

Hyperion. Hyperion Press, Ltd, 52-53 Jermyn St, London, S.W.1, England

Ind. Univ. Indiana University Press, 10th & Morton Sts, Bloomington, Ind. 47401

Int. Pubs. International Publishers Company, Inc, 381 Park Av S, New York, N.Y. 10016

Johns Hopkins. Johns Hopkins Press, Baltimore, Md. 21218

Johnson Pub. Johnson Publishing Company—Book Division, Inc, 1820 S Michigan Av, Chicago, Ill. 60616

Kenedy. P. J. Kenedy & Sons, Publishers, 12 Barclay St, New York, N.Y. 10007

Kennikat. Kennikat Press, Inc, Box 270, Port Washington, N.Y. 11050

Kinsey. See Putnam

Knopf. Alfred A. Knopf, Inc, 501 Madison Av, New York, N.Y. 10022

La. State Univ. Louisiana State University Press, Baton Rouge, La. 70803

Las Américas Pub. Las Américas Publishing Company, 152 E 23d St, New York, N.Y. 10010

Lerner Publications. Lerner Publications Company, 241 1st Av N, Minneapolis, Minn. 55401

Lippincott. J. B. Lippincott Company, E Washington Sq, Philadelphia, Pa. 19105

Little. Little, Brown & Company, 34 Beacon St, Boston, Mass. 02106

Liveright. Liveright Publishing Corporation, 386 Park Av S, New York, N.Y. 10016

Living Books. Living Books, Ltd, 11 W 42d St, New York, N.Y. 10036

Longmans. See McKay

Lothrop. Lothrop, Lee & Shepard Company, Inc, 381 Park Av S, New York, N.Y. 10016

Luce. Robert B. Luce, Inc, 1244 N St N.W., Washington, D.C. 20036

McGraw. McGraw-Hill Book Company, Inc, 330 W 42d St, New York, N.Y. 10036

McKay. David McKay Company, Inc., 750 3d Av, New York, N.Y. 10017

Macmillan. The Macmillan Company, 866 3d Av, New York, N.Y. 10022

Macrae. Macrae Smith Company, 225 S 15th St, Philadelphia, Pa. 19102

Magi Books. Magi Books, Inc, 33 Buckingham Drive, Albany, N.Y. 12208

Marquis. Marquis-Who's Who, The A. N. Marquis Company, Inc, 200 E Ohio St, Chicago, Ill. 60611

Marzani & Munsell. Marzani & Munsell, Inc. Publishers, 100 W 23d St, New York, N.Y. 10011

Mass. Inst. of Technology. The M.I.T. Press, 50 Ames St, Rm 741, Cambridge, Mass. 02142

Meridian. See World

Merit Publishers. Merit Publishers, 873 Broadway, New York, N.Y. 10003

Merlin. Merlin Press, Inc. Current address unknown

Messner. See Simon & Schuster

Methuen. Methuen & Company, Ltd, 11 New Fetter Lane, London, E.C.4, England

Mich. State Univ. The Michigan State University Press, Box 550 East Lansing, Mich. 48823

Military Service. See Stackpole Books

Modern Lib. Modern Library, Inc, 457 Madison Av, New York, N.Y. 10022

Monthly Review. Monthly Review Press, 116 W 14th St, New York, N.Y. 10011

Morrow. William Morrow & Company, Inc, 425 Park Av S, New York, N.Y. 10016

Mus. of Modern Art. The Museum of Modern Art, 11 W 53d St, New York, N.Y. 10019

N.Y. Graphic. New York Graphic Society, Ltd., 140 Greenwich Av, Greenwich, Conn. 06830

N.Y. Univ. New York University Press, 62 5th Av, New York, N.Y. 10011

Nat. Gallery of Art. National Gallery of Art, 6th & Constitution Av. N.W, Washington, D.C. 20560

National Association of Independent Schools. 4 Liberty Sq, Boston, Mass. 02109.

National Council of Teachers of English. 508 S 6th St, Champaign, Ill. 61820

Natural Hist. Press. Natural History Press, American Museum of Natural History, Central Park W at 79th St, New York, N.Y. 10024

Nelson. Thomas Nelson & Sons, Copewood & Davis Sts, Camden, N.J. 08103

New Am. Lib. The New American Library, Inc, 1301 Av. of the Americas, New York, N.Y. 10019

New Directions. See Lippincott

Northwestern Univ. Northwestern University Press, 1735 Benson Av, Evanston, Ill. 60201

Norton. W. W. Norton & Company, Inc., 55 5th Av, New York, N.Y. 10003

Obolensky. Ivan Obolensky, Inc. Astor-Honor, Inc, 26 E 42nd St, New York, N.Y. 10017

Oceana. Oceana Publications, Inc, Dobbs Ferry, N.Y. 10522

Odyssey. Odyssey Press, 55 5th Av, New York, N.Y. 10003

Ohio State Univ. The Ohio State University Press, Hitchcock Hall, Rm 316, 2070 Neil Av, Columbus, Ohio 43210

Orion. Orion Press, Inc. See Grossman

Oxford. Oxford University Press, Inc, 200 Madison Av, New York, N.Y. 10016

Pa. State Univ. The Pennsylvania State University Press, University Press Building, University Park, Pa. 16802

Page. L. C. Page & Company, Inc. See Farrar

Pageant. Pageant Press, 101 5th Av, New York, N.Y. 10003

Pantheon. Pantheon Books, Inc., 437 Madison Av, New York, N.Y. 10022

Parnassus Press. Parnassus Press, 2422 Ashby Av, Berkeley, Calif. 94705

Pellegrini & Cudahy. See Farrar

Penguin. Penguin Books, Inc, 7110 Ambassador Rd, Baltimore, Md. 21207

Phaidon. See N. Y. Graphic

Philosophical Lib. Philosophical Library, Inc, 15 E 40th St, New York, N.Y. 10016

Piedmont Press. Piedmont Press. Current address unknown

Pitman. Pitman Publishing Corporation, 20 E 46th St, New York, N.Y. 10017

Platt. Platt & Munk Company, Inc, 201 5th Av, New York, N.Y. 10010

Potter. Clarkson N. Potter, Inc, Publisher, 419 Park Av S, New York, N.Y. 10016

Praeger. Frederick A. Praeger, Inc, 111 4th Av, New York, N.Y. 10003

Prentice-Hall. Prentice-Hall, Inc, Englewood Cliffs, N.J. 07632

Princeton Univ. Princeton University Press, Princeton, N.J. 08540

Public Affairs Press. Public Affairs Press, 419 New Jersey Av S.E, Washington, D.C. 20003

Putnam. G. P. Putnam's Sons, 200 Madison Av, New York, N.Y. 10016

Quadrangle. Quadrangle Books, Inc, 12 E Delaware Pl, Chicago, Ill. 60611

Rand McNally. Rand McNally & Company, Box 7600, Chicago, Ill. 60680

Random House. Random House, Inc, 457 Madison Av, New York, N.Y. 10022

Regnery. Henry Regnery Company, 114 W Illinois St, Chicago, Ill. 60610

Reilly & Lee. The Reilly & Lee Company, 114 W Illinois St, Chicago, Ill. 60610

Reinhold. Reinhold Publishing Corporation, 430 Park Av, New York, N.Y. 10022

Revell. Fleming H. Revell Company, Westwood, N.J. 07675

Reynal. Reynal & Company, Inc. See Morrow

Rinehart. See Holt

Rio Grande. The Rio Grande Press, Inc, La Casa Escuela, Glorieta, N.Mex. 87535

Riverside Press. See Houghton

Ronald. The Ronald Press Company, 79 Madison Av, New York, N.Y. 10016

Row. See Harper

Roy. Roy Publishers, Inc, 30 E 74th St, New York, N.Y. 10021

Russell & Russell. Russell & Russell Publishers, 122 E 42d St, New York, N.Y. 10017

Rutgers Univ. Rutgers University Press, 30 College Av, New Brunswick, N.J. 08903

Sage. Sage Books, The Swallow Press, Inc, 1139 Wabash Av, Chicago, Ill., 60605

Scarecrow. Scarecrow Press, Inc, 52 Liberty St, Metuchen, N.J. 08840

Schirmer. G. Schirmer, Inc, 4 E 49th St, New York, N.Y. 10017

Schocken. Schocken Books, Inc, 67 Park Av, New York, N.Y. 10016

Scholastic. Scholastic Book Services, 50 W 44th St, New York, N.Y. 10036

Schulte. Schulte Publishing Company, 80 4th Av, New York, N.Y. 10003

Schuman. Henry Schuman, Inc, Publishers. See Abelard-Schuman

Science Press. Science Press, 30 W Chestnut St, Ephrata, Pa. 17522

Scott. Scott Foresman & Company, 1900 E Lake Av, Glenview, Ill. 60025

Scribner. Charles Scribner's Sons, 597 5th Av, New York, N.Y. 10017

Seabury. The Seabury Press, Inc, 815 2d Av, New York, N.Y. 10017

Sheed. Sheed & Ward, Inc, 64 University Pl, New York, N.Y. 10003

Sherbourne Press. Sherbourne Press, 1640 S La Cienega Blvd, Los Angeles, Calif. 90035

Shoe String. The Shoe String Press, Inc, 60 Connolly Parkway, Hamden, Conn. 06514

Shorewood Pubs. Shorewood Publishers, Inc, 724 5th Av, New York, N.Y. 10019

Sierra Club. Sierra Club Books, Mills Tower, San Francisco, Calif. 94104

Signet. See New Am. Lib.

Silvermine Publishers. Silvermine Publishers, Inc, Comstock Hill, Norwalk, Conn. 06850

Simon & Schuster. Simon and Schuster, Inc, Publishers, 630 5th Av, New York, N.Y. 10020

Skira. Skira International Corporation, 381 Park Av S, New York, N.Y. 10016

Sloane. William Sloane Associates, Inc, 425 Park Av S, New York, N.Y. 10016

Smith, P. Peter Smith, 6 Lexington Av, Gloucester, Mass. 01932

Southern Ill. Univ. Southern Illinois University Press, Carbondale, Ill. 62903

Southern Methodist Univ. Southern Methodist University Press, Dallas, Tex. 75222

Speller. Robert Speller & Sons, Publishers, Inc, 10 E 23d St, New York, N.Y. 10010

Sportshelf. Sportshelf. Soccer Associates, Box 634, New Rochelle, N.Y. 10802

St Martins. St Martin's Press, Inc, 175 5th Av, New York, N.Y. 10010

Stackpole. Stackpole Books, Cameron & Kelker Sts, Harrisburg, Pa. 17105

Stanford Univ. Stanford University Press, Stanford, Calif. 94305

Stein & Day. Stein & Day, Publishers, 7 E 48th St, New York, N.Y. 10017

Stephen Greene. Stephen Greene Press, 120 Main St, Brattleboro, Vt. 05301

Sterling. Sterling Publishing Company, Inc, 419 Park Av S, New York, N.Y. 10016

Stuart. Lyle Stuart, Inc, 239 Park Av S, New York, N.Y. 10003

Studio. The Studio Books. See Viking

Superior Pub. Superior Publishing Company, 708 6th Av, N, Seattle, Wash. 98111

Syracuse Univ. Syracuse University Press, Box 8, University Station, Syracuse, N.Y. 13210

Tambimuttu & Mass. Tambimuttu & Mass. Current address unknown

Taplinger. Taplinger Publishing Company, Inc, 29 E 10th St, New York, N.Y. 10003

Theatre Arts. Theatre Arts Books, 333 Av of the Americas, New York, N.Y. 10014

Trident Press, 630 5th Av, New York, N.Y. 10020

Tudor. Tudor Publishing Company, 221 Park Av S, New York, N.Y. 10003

Tuttle. Charles E. Tuttle Company, Inc, 28-30 Main St, Rutland, Vt. 05701

Twayne. Twayne Publishers, Inc, 31 Union Sq W, New York, N.Y. 10003

Twentieth Cent. Fund. The Twentieth Century Fund, 41 E 70th St, New York, N.Y. 10021

U.S. Govt. Printing Office. United States Government Printing Office, Washington, D.C. 20402

U.S. Naval Inst. United States Naval Institute, Annapolis, Md. 21402

Ungar. Frederick Ungar Publishing Company, Inc, 250 Park Av S, New York, N.Y. 10003

Univ. Bks. University Books, Inc, 1615 Hillside Av, New Hyde Park, N.Y. 11041

Univ. of Ala. University of Alabama Press, Drawer 2877, University, Ala. 35486

Univ. of Ariz. The University of Arizona Press, Box 3398, College Station, Tucson, Ariz. 85700

Univ. of Calif. University of California Press, Berkeley, Calif. 94720

Univ. of Chicago. The University of Chicago Press, 5750 Ellis Av, Chicago, Ill. 60637

Univ. of Ga. University of Georgia Press, Athens, Ga. 30601

Univ. of Ill. University of Illinois Press, Urbana, Ill. 61801

Univ. of Ky. University of Kentucky Press, Lafferty Hall, University of Kentucky, Lexington, Ky. 40506

Univ. of Mich. University of Michigan Press, Ann Arbor, Mich. 48106

Univ. of Minn. University of Minnesota Press, 2037 University Av S E, Minneapolis, Minn. 55455

Univ. of Neb. University of Nebraska Press, Lincoln, Neb. 68508

Univ. of N. Mex. University of New Mexico Press, Albuquerque, N.M. 87106

Univ. of N.C. University of North Carolina Press, Chapel Hill, N.C. 27515

Univ. of Okla. University of Oklahoma Press, Norman, Okla. 73069

Univ. of Pa. University of Pennsylvania Press, 3933 Walnut St, Philadelphia, Pa. 19104

Univ. of Pittsburgh. University of Pittsburgh Press, 3309 Cathedral of Learning, Pittsburgh, Pa. 15213

Univ. of Southern Calif. University of Southern California Bookstore, Los Angeles, Calif. 90007

Univ. of Tex. University of Texas Press, Box 7819, Austin, Tex. 78712

Univ. of Wash. University of Washington Press, Seattle, Wash. 98105

Univ. of Wis. The University of Wisconsin Press, Box 1379, Madison, Wis. 53701

Univ. Press of Washington. The University Press of Washington, D.C. 927 15th St N W, Washington, D.C. 20005

Vanguard. The Vanguard Press, Inc, 424 Madison Av, New York, N.Y. 10017

Van Nostrand. D. Van Nostrand Company, Inc, 120 Alexander St, Princeton, N.J. 08540

Viking. The Viking Press, Inc, 625 Madison Av, New York, N.Y. 10022

Walck. Henry Z. Walck, Inc, Publishers, 19 Union Sq W, New York, N.Y. 10003

Walker & Co. Walker & Company, 720 5th Av, New York, N.Y. 10019

Warne. Frederick Warne & Company, Inc, 101 5th Av, New York, N.Y. 10003

Washburn. Ives Washburn, Inc, 750 3d Av, New York, N.Y. 10017

Washington Square Press. See Simon & Schuster

Watson-Guptill. Watson-Guptill Publications, 165 W 46th St, New York, N.Y. 10036

Watts. Franklin Watts, Inc, 575 Lexington Av, New York, N.Y. 10022

Wayne State Univ. Wayne State University Press, 5980 Cass, Detroit, Mich. 48202

Wayside. The Wayside Press, Inc, Wayside Publishing Division, 1501 Washington Rd, Mendota, Ill. 61342

Wesleyan Univ. Wesleyan University Press, 100 Riverview Center, Middletown, Conn. 06457

Westminster. Westminster Press, Witherspoon Bldg, Philadelphia, Pa. 19107

Whitman. Albert Whitman & Company, 560 W Lake St, Chicago, Ill. 60606

Who's Who in Am. Educ. Who's Who in American Education, Inc, 110 7th Av N, Nashville, Tenn. 37203

Wilson. The H. W. Wilson Company, 950 University Av, Bronx, N.Y. 10452

Winston. See Holt

World. The World Publishing Company, 2231 W 110th St, Cleveland, Ohio 44102

Wyn. A. A. Wyn, Inc. Ace Books, Inc, 1120 Av of the Americas, New York, N.Y. 10036

Yale Univ. Yale University Press, 149 York St, New Haven, Conn. 06511

Yoseloff. Thomas Yoseloff Publishers. See Barnes

Ziff-Davis. Ziff-Davis Publishing Company, 1 Park Av, New York, N.Y. 10016